The Distinction
of Human Being

Thomas Kruger Caplan

 VERNON PRESS

www.vernonpress.com

In the Americas:
Vernon Press
1000 N West Street,
Suite 1200, Wilmington,
Delaware 19801
United States

In the rest of the world
Vernon Press
C/Sancti Espiritu 17,
Malaga, 29006
Spain

Library of Congress Control Number: 2014958350

ISBN 978-1-62273-022-3

Dedicated

To the Memory of my Father

Henry Caplan

―――――――――

An den Dichter: Laß die Sprache dir sein, was der Körper den Liebenden;
er nur Ists, der die Wesen trennt und der die Wesen vereint.

(To Poets: May language be to you what the body is to lovers; it is alone
what separates their beings and what unites them.)

- Schiller (NA I 302.85)

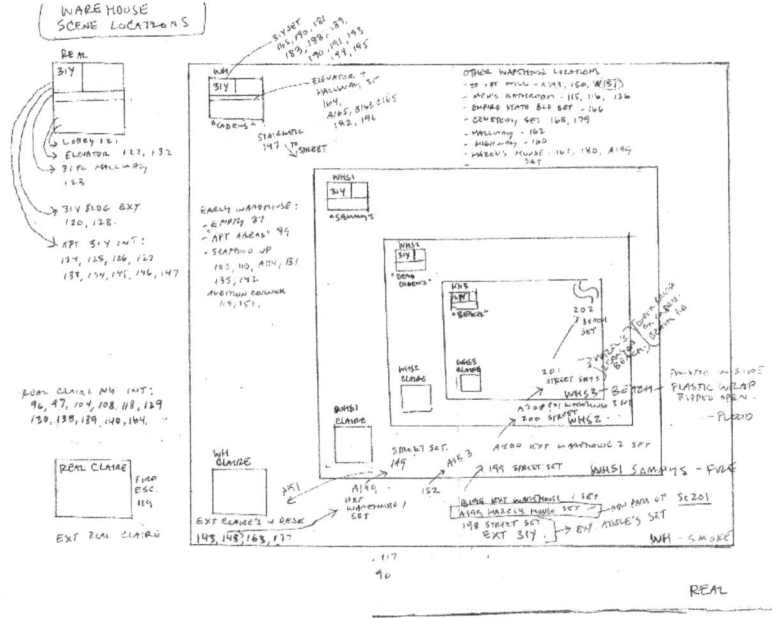

"Warehouse Breakdown" – an explanatory diagram that Mary Cybulski created as script supervisor for the film Synecdoche (2008), written and directed by Charlie Kaufman.

Reprinted here courtesy of Jim Tauber at Kimmel Distribution, LLC.

Acknowledgement

This study builds upon the research of my teacher, Heribert Boeder, whose conception of the totalities of world, history, and language, founded upon the terminological configuration of their ratios, is the result of a lifetime of scholarship dedicated to comprehending and articulating the legacy of Western philosophy in its entirety as well as the divagations of late modern thought in defiance of that tradition – an achievement that has hardly attained among professional and lay thinkers, even the best read among them, the recognition it deserves.

For this reason, I have tried to further develop Boeder's "logotectonic" analysis and show how the rationality it articulates addresses the needs of philosophical thinking today. It does so in two ways: firstly, by encouraging us to reprise the notion of *wisdom* as well as the question and the answer of wisdom's principle, *ΛΟΓΟΣ* (logos), which, traditionally at least, though "having come before, comes after" this inexplicable grant of insight that poets and prophets have always celebrated as "sacred" and secondly, by challenging us to reconsider the project of the revival of metaphysics in our own time, which, if it is to be, can only be now, again, what it formerly was – though of course renewed in accordance with the exigencies and conditions placed upon it by contemporary reflection – namely the exact study of pure reason, thought about thought.

Philosophy, the "love of wisdom," is, let's face it, a quaint, though no less indeterminate name these days and this in spite of – or perhaps even because of – its venerable etymology. Although it had once enjoyed the dignity of being considered the *first science*, possessing its very own topic, principle, and method, its status has always been tenuous, controversial. Yet who would dare deny that controversy has not only been good for philosophy, if not always for individual philosophers, but is, in fact, its very element?

These days, by turns grim, tending towards petulance, then suddenly giddy, lurching, contemporary philosophy would seem to want and to need some deep spring of refreshment if it is ever again to be esteemed for what it once was and achieved, for what it so completely comprehended as the divine destiny of thought that it, nonetheless, in spite of contemporary accusations to the contrary, never made so bold as to claim and defend for the sake of its own glory, if it is, I say, ever again, to be recognized as *inaugural*, taught in schools, consulted in industry, practiced in politics, applied in work and in play, and, above all, enjoyed for its own sake, treasured as the most human of all our pleasures.

I believe it deserves to be. Surely Boeder's work has proven that a rigorous science of first principles in the traditional sense of *metaphysics*, as soon as its original project becomes clear to us, is still possible, necessary even. Boeder gives a very clear indication of what one has to be good at to excel as a friend of a friend of wisdom, a friend of wisdom once removed. Above all, what I have learned from my teacher and what he himself had learned from his, Martin Heidegger, is *Verhaltenheit* with regards to the accomplishments of thought and its purposes.

What does this word mean? *Discretion, restraint, modesty* come to mind and are terms which, to the more boisterous moods of our later thinkers, could connote a muted and subdued attitude of reserve. In fact, neither suppression nor reticence are meant. Rather, we are called to conceive of a virtue of intellectual temperance, an elegance that touches lightly its objects, holds in regard what it studies, is loath to cavil; we are called to cultivate a deferential erudition in ourselves (George Steiner often speaks of a *cortesia*) that tends to greet unfamiliar insights with hospitality (rather than suspicion) and familiar ones in delightful anticipation of rediscovery (rather than prejudice), practices a concerned impartiality towards ideas in an effort to collect them into wider and wider frameworks of reflection while according them their due recognition, placing each on its proper spot after determining where it belongs in relation to all its compeers; but isn't this attentive collecting and recollecting precisely what has always characterized a discerning mind engaged in the avocation of "ΛΟΓΟΣ?"

Boeder is always clear on this point – we strive to know and grasp *all* thought or ought to; each and every thinker's significant contribution deserves a place of honor in a pantheon of insight that we might all build upon and enjoy as a monument to the excellence we are heir to as thinkers, doers and, ultimately, as builders.

That is not to say that all thoughts are equally important or even that all are equally welcome. Yes, some gods, like Ares for example, we honor not because we will but because we must. But thought itself, even, and perhaps especially, in the perfidy and the permutations of perversion we often encounter in discourse counted philosophical these days, obliges us to recognize that, as the unsettled times of our lives unfold, ideas are indeed, and can never fail to be, at work, and that all of them, barring none, excluding none, are worthy of and rightly demand regard irrespective of what has become of them at the hand of Man.

Let us therefore take solace in the trust we nurture, even in the face of horror, that these ideas, though they be refined to a wisp of what they formerly were or else transmogrified into monstrosity, shall, in spite of themselves and us, like dark stars, not fail to guide our human being through whatever darkness has become the latest rage, to its own proper realm, the unadulterated realm of the mind, which will always remain otherworldly, unperturbed in the netherworld of our turbulent world, a cloistered home to those masks and shadows of our mothers and our fathers, those loved ones we perpetually lose and find again, alive, rejuvenated in a song.

Table of Contents

Figures

Preface

The following investigation is devoted exclusively to the consideration of a human, perhaps even uniquely human, experience. It is an experience that we are all familiar with, arising for the most part in anguish, infinite pain, not jest. Think back and recall catastrophe! We encountered it on that day we were brought to nursery school for the first time and suddenly realized what was going on, namely that we would have to stay there alone for a while (or forever?) without our parents who, incredibly, were leaving us behind, a son or daughter, so long cradled in our embrace, who we now unceremoniously drop, drop off, for the first time; when we left for summer camp waving good-bye from the train pulling out of the station, goodbye to our lives, mom and dad, forever, waving goodbye to the departing train, pulling our baby away, out of our lives forever – three titanic hearts sinking severally but in unison; when we set out on that fateful day to seek our fortune, straying from our little town blues to wake up in the city that never sleeps. Yes, many have endured the trial of birth and parenthood beginning and, later, drawing gradually or abruptly to a close. Most will experience the death of a beloved parent; and surely all have known the loss of some illusion; we have, at least once in our lives, kicked a habit, doubted a rule, questioned a dogma in the dark night of the soul, and, from a heavy slumber, come to our senses in a dark wood midway upon the journey of our life; we have had to stand up to a bully, stand up for a principle, from our seat in the crowd and, standing tall for all eyes to see, speak up, speak out, speak wingéd words to a hostile audience; in one way or the other, all of us have had to plunge into battle, sword in hand and face the unknown outcome of sheer courage. Surely you remember having crouched in the starting blocks and holding your breath or succeeded after much hesitation at jumping from the ten-meter platform at the local swimming pool. Have we not encountered a stranger, have we not had to break ranks and go it alone, to go out on a limb, to forge an alliance, to make peace with an enemy, to swallow our pride, abdicate a throne, build a kingdom from scratch, tear down a wall brick by brick? We know what it means to quit a mood, express regret, to cut our losses and endure the embarrassment of failure, to begin anew, forgive a wrong, forgo an impulse to run away rather than stay put in the dentist's chair. It is distinctly human to have learned to break the ice, to quell a welling passion at the brim, to take *no* for an answer, to embrace the uncertainty of a venture, to send a customer to a competitor, to dispense with a formality, to knock on the door of the boss's office with a request for a raise. And then there was the last time you had to let go or give leave, to leap before looking, to sit down and shut up, give up a lost cause, persevere against all odds, make an end, step up, take stock, start out, start over; you did what you had to do – lift a still, small voice in the shout of protest, disobey a direct order, defer a gratification, defy a dictator, exercise restraint; you have learned, perhaps the hard way, to trust, to yield, to confess, to concede, to sacrifice, to serve; at inspired moments, we have indeed shown patience, shown compassion, have taken on faith, hoped against hope, wished upon a star, lived on a prayer...

And everyone has had to, at least a couple of times in their lives, step back and scrutinize critically this morning the words or deeds of last night and from the remote vantage point of this pale and early light, returning to that living moment still so fresh in memory, come back again from that irrevocable past to this morning's face in the mirror to take note of a face, like a paradise, lost, the defacement of our face, in which now we read the inalterable discrepancy, perceive the original sin of deviation and sting of death, recognize, crestfallen, the thunderous "fall" reflected and resounding in those wrinkles:
"bababadalgharaghtakamarronnkonnbronntonnerronntuonnthuuntro-varrhounawnskawntoohoohoordenenthurnuk!"
(Joyce, *Finnegans Wake*, [FW] 3.15-16) that proclaims the discontented state of divergence between THE WAY IT IS and THE WAY IT SHOULD BE.

These are all practical examples of the experience so variously named and known and each individual could add to the list and, using the particulars of his or her own life, elaborate variations on a theme, the theme of this study, which is ***our experience of the distinction of human being***.

Although the *practice* illustrated above and the experience it entails are eminently human, the investigation of the distinction, the genius and excellence of human being we are about to undertake is not primarily about people at all and the trials and tribulations of their lives, nor about the fruits and failures of their actions, not at all an exercise in people-watching empiricism. Rather our study is about this distinction in its own right as a property and capacity, an inherent faculty and forte – a determination of our human being which is not merely efficacious through the often painful efforts we devote to its application. Above all, more than just an experience of risk, loss, doubt, death, in a word, our self-several *existence*, the distinction of human being is a principle, an idea, received, pursued, and, finally, a realization capable of rich elaboration as a complete *train of thought*. Thus as much as this idea is put into effect in our daily lives as a critical *activity*, it is also susceptible to conceptual development as an *insight*, as well as to dramatic presentation in the concrete particulars with which art makes an ideal real, and thus envisioned as an object of deliberation we can take up as our cause. The distinction of human being is therefore neither merely thought, nor act, nor issue but rather all three in one, one *and* three. Our exceedingly rich experience of this distinguished being, perfectly familiar to all, is, due in particular to this ubiquity, not often enough explicitly considered and clearly delineated by thinkers and writers of nowadays who, enthralled by the shifting surface detail of urgent private matters or more public ones like those of state, society, and science, tend to neglect fundamental principles, those ideas that are simple, immense, deep, in other words, *natural, divine, human*.

And although anthropology is held to be the most encompassing theoretical science of mankind, in the study we now propose, the world human and its ways, human ingenuity and frailty, human society and industry, its ages and artifacts, are all headings that expatiate upon merely one sphere of interest in which the distinction of human being has attained material significance. Certainly, European tradition, specifically the Age of Enlightenment of this tradition, might have taught us how to speak about the experience of this distinction in terms of the endowment or *nature* of human being. And in this sense, *human* being distinguished as a subject, a person of the *idea of freedom* is, as post/modern thinkers are fond of assuring us, a rather late invention of "Western" culture, whereas, of course, "people" and "the family of man" as the topic of present-day anthropological discourse about our species, with its cultures and civilizations and the turmoil of its history, have been around since time immemorial.

But the point to be made here is that the **humanity of human being** of the Third Epoch is *not* the only vision and conception of the distinction of human being. In the Second Epoch, it was the **glory of the Christian Godhead** that defined this distinction in the event of the crucifixion and the resurrection of the Son of God. And then again in the First Epoch, neither humanity nor divinity were the determining principles of distinction but rather the **measured apportionment of destiny** that metes out to each what is due.

Freedom, God, Destiny – these three were the most formidable names known to the poets and thinkers of Western civilization for referring to the distinction of human being. For this reason, they are the three "classical" designations of our unique theme and as such, signature terms, like heirlooms that we have inherited from our forefathers and -mothers, for the determining principle, the starting point of the said *train of thought*, namely the first term in a sequence of three, which, when taken together, like the epochs of the tradition they inaugurate, form particular relationships of ideas – artfully articulated into sequences or *ratios* of terms – and, in this way, uniquely define the distinction of human being in each respective epoch, as we shall see in the following investigation.

To call these three dignified designations "signature terms" is not to imply that their specific names are arbitrary. On the contrary. Even from a purely historical point of view, there are many reasons available to scholarship to explain why, for example, the Homeric *Hero* lamented the "doom of fate" whilst his Christian counterpart, the *Saint*, instead, celebrated in tears "the glory of the coming of the Lord." It will be the task of our philosophical inquiry to demonstrate how and what each particular name for the determining principle, the *inaugural* term in the sequence, contributes to the whole of the train of thought in which it occurs, articulating in concert with the *mediating* and the *resultant* terms a complete and coherent vision of such reality, action, and conception as follows logically from that particular foundation which had been put forth in terms germane to a particular time and established in each Epoch as the decisive and definitive principle of all (and not merely *human, divine,* or *natural*) being, namely "Freedom," "God," "Destiny," which are therefore actually the principal designations of three entirely different terminologies, each exhibiting its own proper logical framework and therefore constituting three different *languages*, three different but coherent ways of speaking about what it means to "make a difference." Understanding the inherent consistency of these three Epochal languages and the logic of their relationship to each other is what we are after. Because, in fact, none of these terms name, in themselves, our topic; rather, they are significant and traditional denominations that, in the procession of Occidental civilization, have served the needs of speakers, whether thinkers, leaders, or poets, towards the better conception, prosecution, and presentation of that rich experience we now intend to study – neither *Destiny,* nor *God,* nor *Freedom,* not these terms of distinguished cognizance, and be they the most awe-inspiring, with their conventional, albeit "difficult" semantics, but rather this experience of difference itself is our one and only cause.

Thus right from the start, establishing as we have that our intention is to study a specific experience, we have assigned to the language in which this experience has been previously articulated the role of being not merely the instrument but also the terminological element of our investigation – this in keeping with the requirements that the well-known "linguistic turn" would impose upon critical reflection, though in ways surely unanticipated by its early and latter-day advocates. Consequently, many of the words we shall use in what follows are borrowed from former times and places, ancient tongues long dead, remote and foreign speech – these old words, taken from old books that have by some freak chance escaped annihilation, demand the same sort of reverent circumspection from us that all unearthed relics from far away and long ago, shrouded as they are in the mystery of time, inspire in the archeologist. Perhaps it is here among the bones of the past, so to speak, that we are called for the first time to practice the greatly prized virtue of restraint with respect to and for what is truly alien, taking it for what it is and letting it be. All these old texts, they are doubtless, for most of us, extracurricular if not extraterrestrial, dare we suffer them to remain so for a bit?

So, what exactly is the distinction of human being and the mark of man? Consider a reading of civilization in accordance with which, for thousands of years, since the times of the ancient Greeks, this question had already been definitively answered, recorded, and passed down to us in scriptures, often deemed *sacred*, in terms hardly decipherable and yet oddly familiar, which are thought to be, for the purposes of the inquiry upon which we are about to embark, articulations of a single and yet self-several idea. How could that answer possibly still be valid, those texts still holy, that idea still accessible today? Consider how different life is nowadays, how much has changed – technology, the advances of science and medicine, the upheavals of history, the disasters and tragedies, natural as well as man-made, that have scarred human civilization, the myriad intermingling influences of cultures across the earth, the sublime accomplishments of art, the general loss of conventions and traditions, the darkness and the light of religion...how can the distinction of human being be one and the same as ever, be now as it was, have remained what it had been and nevertheless be the differential, and not only the unity, of our history?

How can it be one and the same in the Greek cosmos *and* in the Christian empire, one and the same as the Glory of God *and* as the Idea of Freedom, one and the same for the **Hero** on the battlefield *and* the **Saint**, the Saint prostrate before the altar *and* the proud **Citizen** of the *state* of the social contract? Do not the epochs themselves oppose such "totalitarian" impulses? How can liberty be reconciled with predetermination? How humanity with divinity?

In fact, they cannot. The distinction of human being cannot be and has never been one and the same; rather, this distinguished being is, always was, and always will be, must be, as we shall see, one *and* several and therein absolutely unique.

In reflection's supposedly "post-historical," i.e. *linguistic* age, it should come as no surprise that latter-day philosophers and reputed thinkers would, to put it mildly, tend to argue against human being in general as having a distinction, or each individual, with respect to this distinction, as having a *destiny*, be it one *or* several. It is very doubtful that there is even a single philosophy professor in any university in the world who is currently teaching a course the content of which could even remotely be characterized by such a title as *the distinction and the destiny of human being* that is not, in fact, just another seminar about classical or "canonical" *Occidental literature* and, more precisely, the archeology of the upstart and downfall, the folly and the arrogation, of Western ideas, chief among which is often said to be that of **reason** – and the disseminating imperialism, materialism, sexism, individualism of its "gridiron" technicality.[1]

Well, what about studies in reason these days? Is it not true that the esteem once enjoyed by the university, whose scope, whose universe, might well appear to be suffering the fate of just that negligence that has served as the most sweeping refutation of the distinction of human being, had always been linked to the interest and appreciation that humanity has taken in studying and reflecting upon a destiny to call its own, the authority and tradition of this devotion being the very definition of "liberal?" Or is that the definition of "conservative?" In any case, we refer to the nurturing appreciation of ideas that has long since devolved into recidivist ideology, the coin and currency of cross-cultural economically-oriented transaction and the alphabet of a public dogma periodically spelled out in the specious phrase-mongering of speakers in shows of talk, of entertainment, and of information diffusion, whose job it is to blow a few of these bubbles into the tub of our exhausted evenings and holidays, inflate balloons of issues in political campaigning, blast the patriotic horn as accompaniment to national calamities, and, in particular, to help us mitigate the stifling post/modern privacy of life, of birth, of death with the windy pomp and circumstance of a preferred mythology.

What does this state of affairs, the repeatedly diagnosed eclipse and ensuing abdication of reason, suggest to us about the distinction, the mark and the excellence of human being? Whatever this telltale sign of the mind is, it seems there is no longer any great need among the learned to expound

---

[1] Heidegger spoke of "das Gestell." *Die Technik und die Kehre*, pp. 19-21, 27-28, 37-47.

upon it, nor any great interest among the laity to attend lectures or read books on this topic, you yourself, dear reader, being the only exception.

Again, given the overwhelming evidence of academic preference to the contrary, what could possibly justify any *scientific* interest in reprising a question *and the answer* that have been, long before our time, at the Homeric dawn of Western civilization, already perfectly posed and provided, known and celebrated as **wisdom** and as **truth**? Hmpf! Now why did you have to go and bring them up? These words! Do we feel the urge to ask what does "truth," what does "wisdom," actually mean? Ah, if only we knew what these and a few other such "fancy words" – like *Freedom, God,* and *Destiny* for instance – meant, then everything would be as clear as day! Has not thousands of years of civilization taught us that words like these, far beyond merely "meaning" this, that, or the other, are, in fact, intended by thinkers, poets, and prophets to *make a distinction*? And that the insights that emerge, the actions that ensue, and the narratives that unfold as a result of these distinctions, make a difference, make all the difference in the world?

But honestly, merely to reaffirm, in one's own words, in artful speech borne of one's own unique time and place, in the rhythmic vernacular of the world of one's peers, in the "quashed quotatoes" of a particular cultural setting, both high and low, both former and contemporary, in a latter-day tongue that is at times playful – but avoiding the flippancy of impudence, at times earnest – but skirting all somber solemnity, to forge in the smithy of a poor and nameless soul a new and a latest song about what has already been remarkably and definitively said and sung, in a then still richly vibrant idiom, by our predecessors, in a living language, in a wealth of languages long since spent, gone and dead – this could not possibly count for scholarship in most quarters of the knowledge industry and must be considered scandalous if not just downright foolishness. Surely what the world needs now is talk, sweet talk, talk about later, greater "visions," fresh contributions to some scream about the *new world order,* not concise contemplation upon the oldest of the old. And if, as we, growing older but, alas, no wiser, though perhaps a bit sadder, come to suspect that the academic problems and controversies of philosophy are of the everlasting sort, then perhaps we really ought to offer a new hypothesis, some tentative approaches, at least a few, at least one *ansatz,* and not recur to the oldest of the old as the age-old answer *and the question.*

Is there no accounting for scholarly progress in the discourse about this sort of issue? What sort is that, anyway? Hmm. Topics in Humanities 101, perhaps? Or those emerging during a discussion in a "Great Books" course?

Indeed, everybody says these days that the "way is the goal," that the search and the query itself, that puzzlement, so long as it is properly loquacious, are signs of the philosopher's much fabled genuine piety? What would the sacrilege of heresy mean in this connection? What it has always meant to the pretense of the "pious," and the "learned" namely a provocation and scandal. This insinuated profanation would celebrate the scandalous advocacy of that impossible love which, as Augustine famously said, seeks for the sake of finding and finds for the sake of seeking. For what, in truth, would justify a search for that which has been long found, for taking upon ourselves a task that has already been completed, for teaching what everybody already knows, pointing out what is self-evident, answering a question that has not been asked, posing the question anew with every answer proffered, invoking with names and recalling what is always already present wherever and whenever a speaker and a listener convene, drawing up plans to prepare the venue for an event that has already taken place, and building the house that we already inhabit?

Well, then there is no justification. And perhaps then, freed by the exquisite futility of this exercise in superfluity from the normal constraints of admirable academic sedulity, from the paradigms in good currency it promulgates, and from the conventions of its discourse they have spawned, in a rigorous leisure that comes as close as possible to solitude, if not utter seclusion, we, who are forlorn, tilting in our quixotic quest, may cultivate such an orphic love that makes stones cry, soothes savage beasts, and breathes new life into blessed souls thought long dead to the world and thus, impossibly, ringing the bell backwards – surely love's greatest feat; only then may we, in this separate peace we have made, pursue our beloved theme with proper chivalry, trusting all the while that whatever is well wrought in words of song and sung o'er hill and dale in its goodly service will find the stray ear that has been listening so long, so intently, to silence that it has of late even come to suspect what it hears so clearly is actually nothing at all.

Introduction

1. Our Theme in a Nutshell

Consider the following scene so familiar to moviegoers: At a dramatic juncture of the story when the protagonist, having been previously so engrossed in the rush and tumble of events that she had not had time to give a second thought to where her choices were taking her and now had, in fact, taken her, unexpectedly encounters her reflection in a mirror – suddenly, it is painfully clear to her, in a way that it was not just a moment before, what she has done or become. We look at our reflection and are compelled to admit to ourselves that, with regards to what we see in our image, THE WAY IT IS *is not* THE WAY IT SHOULD BE.

This experience of *critical self-reflection* is well-known to all; surely we have all faced this ordeal of thinking beings who, one day, inexplicably, step back from the immediacy of their lived experience and, as if adopting a standpoint "outside" of their lives, "opposite" their world, reflect upon themselves, their lives, and their world, with eyes transformed into those of a judge who stands apart, above, beyond – the purview of his sight is no longer limited to the horizon hitherto defined by a given set of circumstances and worldviews of a subject, but rather extends beyond the pale of these particulars, beyond the ken of this given person, place, and present, broadens, deepens to encompass the bigger picture, to comprehend the grand and the grandest narratives of what will be and what was, what could be, indeed, even what ought to be but, alas, often, is not. This is a distinguished standpoint; for here we enter upon a life, a world and a life "outside" of *my* life, "above, beyond, opposite" *my* world – clearly, here is where the career of religion's fancy words and "otherworldly" worlds begins....

The purpose of the following investigation is to study this very experience of the difference that thought makes and how poets and prophets, as well as philosophers, have always employed the poetic language of narrative, drama, and verse – as well as the celebratory expressions of metaphysics like *freedom* and *heaven*, *resurrection* and *beauty*, *justice* and *god*, *world* and *love* to convey in vivid, earth-shattering terms the element and dimensions of that experience that we have called the *distinction of human being*.

Now while your friendly neighborhood philosopher would seem to excel in the cultivation of recondite notions, the biggest challenge facing a student of the distinction of human being is not the obscurity of this distinction but rather its apparent familiarity. Everybody knows what you are talking about when you give an example of this experience, of which there are countless many in our everyday lives. For this reason and precisely because of its being so utterly and completely evident to us, there would seem to be little more to say about it except to affirm that, yes, people, normally content to "go with the flow," sometimes do indeed stop and step back to think things over.

But then why on earth was this experience of our capacity for critical reflection repeatedly celebrated as being of such monumental importance, as having such earth-shaking consequences that, of all possible objects of thought, it, i.e. critical thought itself, was held to be the one most worthy of reflection in its own right as if, by establishing thus a science of the distinction of human being as philosophers did, we were called upon to "step back" from every particular occasion of our "stepping back" and thereby gain a critical perspective on even this critical perspective such that, reflecting critically upon critical reflection, reflection itself came into view and, for the first time, thought took to thinking about thought. This is the old story of how *speculation* was born – not the journalist's, nor the investor's, but rather that of the thinker; it is the story of philosophy in the traditional sense of *metaphysics*, the science of **pure reason** – of that faculty of ours which has been known and celebrated since the days of the Greeks as the distinction of human being.

Metaphysical philosophers have always taught that people are endowed "by nature" with the capacity to step back and mind the gap between the IS and the OUGHT. It was considered to be *the* defining characteristic, the mark or seal, if you will, that identified all beings in general, so also *human* being, that they were distinguished not merely from every other being of the same kind, human from other sentient living beings, for example, but also that they were distinguished from *themselves*, namely from what a particular being was, in principle, meant, supposed, *to be*, according to the determination of its *nature*, its *destiny*.

So also as in our reflection in the mirror – the music crescendos and we not only recognize that painful discrepancy but also experience firsthand this very fact, namely *that* we are distinguished from ourselves "by nature;" here *I am* and *there*, that man in the mirror, is the image of what I have become – thus divided, we learn the hard way that by failing to live up to our own ideals, we are torn asunder within but also flung far above and beyond ourselves by them and, in this way, set apart in a "place" *without*; human being thus riven, thus "exiled," is, as we might say, *self-several* and we all know that the self-severalty of our human being hurts, a lot, even as we are, at the same time, by switching our standpoint from the being seen and condemned to that of the seeing being of unfettered, unbiased judgment, uplifted, ennobled by the difference that critical thought makes.

Our study seeks therefore to give this notion of the inner controversy of the human condition, the severance inherent in human identity, the rich development it demands and deserves and to show how our knowledge of and experience with this self-relative divergence has been preserved in the legacy of three different narratives, celebrated in three completely different but equally heart-rending accounts of the distinction of human being, namely, beginning with the First Epoch of our Occidental cultural tradition, the Greek Epoch, in the distinguished speech of **Homer**, **Hesiod**, **Solon**, who gave voice to the *knowledge of the Muses*, followed then by the Second Epoch of that tradition, that of Christianity, in the New Testament of the **Synoptic Narratives** (Mark, Luke, Matthew), the **Apostolic Letters of Paul**, and the **Gospel of John**, in which the *gift of Holy Spirit* was granted and received, and, concluding with the Third Epoch, the Age of Enlightenment, in three visions of poetic imagination, i.e. in the works of **Rousseau**, **Schiller** and **Hölderlin**, in which the *Ideal of Humanity* was realized. Comprehend this tradition in its entirety as a complete train of thought about thought, one that provides us with a unique insight into that original determination of human self-severalty that was subsequently conceptualized in the three unique Epochs of metaphysics, the science which, through the patient elucidation of the logic of each of these "sacred" languages, taught us to recognize in the difference that the terms *Destiny*, *God* and *Freedom* make in human perception, action, and invention, the three distinguished principles of *LOGOS* – a term still so richly evocative of our ancient cultural legacy as thinkers, doers, and builders – traditionally translated as *reason*.

2. "Endowed with LOGOS"

What is the distinction of human being? Traditionally at least, the answer is as clear as day. We find it in the ancient definition of this being as *animal rationale mortale* – a mortal living being "endowed with LOGOS" (ΛΟΓΟΝ ΕΧΩΝ[2]) is how the Greeks put it – giving rise to the further question of how we should translate *rationale* or *ΛΟΓΟΣ*. Is *reason* or, simply, *thought* the right word? Hmm. We hesitate. Maybe these days we would

---

[2] In this study, Greek words and expressions will be written in upper case Greek letters and, along with other non-Latin alphabets, occasionally transliterated. All non-English source text citations will be provided with an adjacent translation.

prefer to say endowed with "language" or "speech" or "writing" or even "literature." We hesitate here, in the beginning of our study. A bad sign? Entertaining the supposition for a minute that, in any case, one of them at least ought to be the right term for what distinguishes human being, we cannot help but wonder how *language* – somewhat arbitrarily choosing this designation for now – could make such a qualitative, categorical, such an *absolute* difference in the sense of what we mean by referring to the *distinction* of human being? What language are we actually talking about? After all, we are told that whales and dolphins have a tuneful language, bees seem to work their eloquence in a dance, and chimps are evidently adept at employing signs. These instrumental languages would seem to differ from that of *Man* only by degree. But what of a distinction in essence, in nature, borne of language? A distinguished "tongue of flame" that we might speak, a holy writ that we might study day and night, a language of wisdom in which we might take up abode?

If you are looking for the absolute distinction between human and divine or human and the merely living being of animals and even plants, at least in the Greek conception of it, you won't find it. They are all *beings* – human being shares reason with the gods and mortal life with the animals. Enjoying immortality, the gods are merely the more powerful, more blissful beings when compared with humans whose lives, when compared to that of the immortals, have been called – none too cheerily – "solitary, poore, nasty, brutish and short." Thus when an ancient Greek admonished you with the far-famed inscription in the pronaos of the temple of Apollo at Delphi, namely ΓΝΩΘΙ ΣΕΑΥΤΟΝ (gnōthi seauton) "to know your place," you were to be reminded that, in contrast to the gods, *you* are mortal (as are all other earth-bound living beings) and in contrast to the animals, *you* are possessed of ΛΟΓΟΣ (as are the gods as well), hence, partaking of both mortal life *and* immortal sense, human being has its own proper place *in the middle* of the ΚΟΣΜΟΣ (cosmos), even as the earth itself is the middle and the common ground between the heights of Olympus and the shadowy depths of Tartarus; earth is the region where both human and divine being meet, the commons, one might call it, in a well-ordered hierarchy of places that each being is destined, but also entitled, to take, the limits of which are clearly demarcated and duly recognized by every member of that community as determining the mutual obligations and the rights of a given being with respect to all the others and, in this way, defining the complete ΛΟΓΟΣ, the relationship, of each and every being in the ΚΟΣΜΟΣ.

Thus in this brief preview of what, for a Greek, *human* being is, we have gained the first inkling of a profound insight into our topic, namely that, in fact, the distinction of human being could not refer, as is often assumed, merely to our difference from animals as lacking reason, nor from the gods as possessing and enjoying the immortal life that was inexplicably denied us – which may seem to be a very odd point to make, for, these days, who in their right mind would actually *want* to live forever – nor, finally, from our compeers, with whom we also share the understanding that, regardless of our walk of life, the toilsome terminus of our approaching doom is inexorable.

Well, if not from animals, nor from the gods, nor from our fellow man, much less from inanimate objects – though even this difference has become a debatable issue today – from what being or beings is man properly distinguished? Incredibly, there is only one being that human being can truly and categorically be distinguished from and that is from *man* itself – *Human Being* is, can be, is destined to be, different from…human being – thus the initially puzzling thesis of this book.

Now is there any sense to be made in the strange notion that in "knowing our place" we are to know that it is the destiny of our human being to be unlike, other than, distinguished from, ourselves? With an appeal to simple, common sense logic, we might immediately ask, irritated: How can any being be different from itself? On the contrary, isn't something's "self," its "identity," the one and only thing (if it is indeed a "thing" at all) that something could possibly be the same as – you know, in the sense of $a=a$ and so on? After all, haven't we learned by now that *"things thing,"* that the *"world worlds,"* that, to speak more generally, *it is what it is*, that *you are what you are*, and, indubitably, *I yam what I yam*, that *boys will be boys* and *a kiss is just a kiss*, that, triumphantly, *a rose is a rose is a rose*? And now you are saying that it is the distinction of our human being *not to be* what we are and to be what we are not? Hmm.

Consider for a moment what this would mean – if to be is not to be and not to be is to be *human* being, then it follows logically that the more man is what it is, the less it is what it is, and conversely, the less, the more, simply by virtue of being, in one, both what it is not *and* what it is…in a perpetually alternating succession of self-contradictory differences; for, not being what it is, it *is*, in fact, what it is! In commiseration with the predicament of such a being that we might call "humankind," and the infinite anguish that being what human being is not and not being what it is, must entail, we posit this single trait as the unique and indelible mark of distinction, the defining character of an impossible being, that is, nevertheless, our very own *human* being. And now what if this self-severalty of human being actually documented our experience with the life of ΛΟΓΟΣ, with the life and times of pure reason itself?

3. What is Pure Reason?

Pure reason? Let us say, for now, in all modesty, simply *thought*. Have you ever wondered what *thought* is? Not *a* thought, a particular thought, for example the idea you might call *freedom* or *God* or *Destiny*. Not any one of these specifically. Who would refuse to allow that, whatever else we should make of them, whatever else *happiness* or *beauty* or *justice* or *faith* may be, they are all, at the very least, ideas, thoughts? Along these lines (which we might as well call our very first line of reasoning, our first train of thought about thought), a *memory* of my childhood is surely something I think about, something thought; How about *fancies, dreams, hopes*, a certain dream or a certain hope, a misguided opinion? Thoughts all? Undoubtedly! Propositions, statements, sentences, words are signs and tokens of *ideas*, of *judgments*, formulating *theories*, airing *views* and *reviews*, sharing *insights*, are they not? Well, then these latter are thoughts, too. Here's a notion of mine – it is more or less thoughtful; here a belief – it is more or less far-fetched but thought and thoughts they most certainly must be; again, here is an argument, mathematical, biological, sociological, psychoanalytical, linguistic; it is, with respect to a particular audience and the issue in question, more or less cogent, more or less persuasive but remains, for all that, a train of thought, with other thoughts, fought for or against, failed or famed, soon forgotten or, rarely, forever young.

In a similar vein, surely the *goals* we pursue, the *will*, an *intention* we harbor, surely they are congenial notions – my *plan* to see a movie tonight is a thought and notion, though not a particularly remarkable one, is it not, as is my occasional *doubt* and wavering *indecision*? Indeed. The other day, for example, when undecided in my own mind, I was debating with my wife about going out in the evening, I tentatively proposed going to the movies. "That's a thought," she said, none too enthusiastically. On the other hand, when my daughter told me that she would complete her studies before getting married and having children, I said, perhaps a bit too enthusiastically, "that's a great idea!"

Similarly, most people agree that the light bulb began as a great idea – if certainly not as great as the genius artist's conception of the painting of the ceiling of the Cappella Sistina, then all the more useful – and the modest paperclip, too, to say nothing of the other inventions that human ingenuity has conceived of for the sake of convenience and control...hmm, on second thoughts and in the retrospective light of the consequences of their applications, some of these ideas were not so great after all.

Now putting together a collection of all the plans and memories, useful or beautiful inventions, flowing or ebbing brainwaves and sagacious or even inane propositions and opinions known to man or woman, now or ever in the past or even in the future would indeed be a monumental and never-ending task and might be called a comprehensive chronicle of ideas and thoughts, good and bad. But taking account of and recording all of these thoughts in their considerable variety and plenitude (perhaps the Internet is becoming such an archive) is still not the same as thinking about *thought* and asking the question: "What is thought *as such*, thought *in and of itself?*"

In fact, "thought" is also an idea and an interesting notion at that and it, too, you might argue, would find its place in the above catalogue. We would no doubt find it under the heading of *philosophy* in the subcategory *metaphysics*, the study of the theory, practice, and productivity of thought. Then thought itself would be just another thought, one more notion among many.

But even in this case, a study devoted to thought in its own right, to thought *as thought*, would remain, in such a catalogue of thoughts, an oddity among the collector's hoard, would be considered an extremely curious, if not to say unique, specimen, an anomaly of sorts on the list; for whereas with respect to all of the other issues and topics and matters, the sciences (which are a collection or system of thoughts) as well as their subsidiary ancillary thoughts, are different from their subject matter, the seeing from the seen, a particular issue or object, a problem to which thought has been addressed – whether in the form of memories, intents and purposes, experiences, analyses, summaries, hypotheses, or just some stray opinion bred in teeming brains, or else conserved in an entry in the ledger of some otherwise blank page or clean slate, duly registered, say, as an item to be enumerated in the methodology and industry of sciences or merely as the odds and ends of mankind's cultural history – in a word, while the *form* of thought, i.e. the actual thinking endeavor, is, in all of these cases, different from its *content*, i.e. what is being thought about, the science of metaphysics alone is thought turned towards thought itself, turned therefore to *memory* and *intention, experience* and *knowledge, insight* and *intellect, opinion* and *judgment* in their own right – a thesaurus would come in handy here in our search for further synonyms while at the same time facilitating the continuation of our long list of potential translations, good and bad, for and concomitant notions of that illustrious Greek word ΛΟΓΟΣ that we began with – as forms, kinds, sorts, types, or else as examples, instances, modes, of *thought*, that is to say, thought in and of itself, apart from the particular items that this diversity of the mind's vessels and vehicles convey.

Taken in this light, taken namely as a study of the composite *light* of the mind itself as well as a study of this taking, the *grasp* of conception, rather than what is normally lit and grasped by it, i.e. *everything else*, be it an actual "thing" or no thing at all, it would seem that philosophy in the strict sense of metaphysics is a very peculiar occupation indeed, certainly tending towards paradox or just plain deadly dull. What could be less substantial, more academic than research devoted to thought all by itself, a sort of ivory tower atop an ivory tower, a circle in a circle and a wheel within a wheel? Indeed, unless it is broken, who would care to look at the *glass* of a picture window rather than at the prospect of the flower garden out back? And you might imagine that, in many circles, philosophers of this seemingly so myopic persuasion, to the extent that there are any such, are not welcomed by their brethren with wholehearted hospitality. These days many of their thinker peers would dismiss the entire enterprise as anachronistically preposterous, arid, empty, clearly implausible, probably contradictory, or, their most grievous epithet, passé and thus, ultimately, banal. Has not "philosophical" discourse, increasingly over the years, put "old school" metaphysics behind itself and moved forward to explore the blue horizons and fresh pastures green?

This is especially true of academic pronouncements with regards to metaphysics. The best philosophy departments can offer a young student's ponder is an opportunity to study the history of philosophy from, say, Descartes to Darwin (because it sounds right) or, less scientifically perhaps but more generously academic, from Plato to... well to whom? Hmm. To Nietzsche perhaps? Or to Marx? Or to Derrida? And what about thinkers and poets (poets?) before Plato, eh? Evidently, merely the beginning, the middle and the end of such a canon of philosophical output as well as its breadth and depth, namely whether it should include the "non-Western philosophies" or not and to what extent, is as yet still open to debate, and therefore subject to the inclinations of the individual philosopher-lecturer and the changing demands that research support and convention schedules as well as peer pressure among colleagues in this field place on budding scholars.

But obviously, studying the life and times and fabulous or merely puzzling opinions of famous philosophers like Kant or Socrates, culling, after much multi-inter-superdisciplinary hunting and gathering, what views of theirs have been tried and tested by time, and categorizing their thoughts into the appropriate "ism" while accounting for "errors and limitations" and determining their continued relevance or utter irrelevance in philosophical discourse today, whether in appreciative, deferential tones or jocose and condescending ones, is not the same as *thought thinking thought*, not the same as what, in the old days, was called *speculation*.

4. The Art of Speculation

On the other hand, the friendly-neighborhood free thinker, being energetic and not one to dither and quibble, might advocate a clean sweep approach to the impressive ballast of historical dry-as-dust scholarship with all its fragments and parchments and palimpsests and admonish us to just get down to it and start thinkin'! Honestly, do we, should we, really need a diploma from some acclaimed college to think about thought? You've got a mind, friend, and have, no doubt, been known to use it on occasion; at least your thoughts, if nothing else, are your own; they are not merely personal but even private, your very own closed sphere and castle and you are most certainly entitled to follow a train of thought if you care to, as much and as well as, hell, better than, any other thinker guy or gal past or present; for who's to stop you, who's to prevent you from thinking a little or even a whole lot, for minutes on end! And, in conclusion, since, as the story goes, thinking about life is every person's prerogative or should be, how could there be definitive answers, which, apparently, would solve all our problems and answer all our questions and thus, in one fell swoop, put an end to thought for good or evil in a flagrant bid to foreclose all thoughtfulness once and for all?

This particular attitude with regard to thought as being as inviolate as it is proximate, as much an innate right as it is an engendered talent, is widespread and, far from being merely a typical layman's conceit, is even a propitious bias in favor of our current endeavor, supposing, as such a predilection for the immediacy of the mind does, that learning how to think is akin to learning a particular ideology, strengthening, or at least finding, some obscure mind muscle, and undertaking the daunting challenge of attempting to reprogram, if not rewire, our brain-ware. For in fact, these perspectives regarding the mind, though flawed or rudimentary, suggest at least the affection folks seem to feel for the world of ideas – we are indeed apt to count ourselves experts in using our own heads, suspicious of anything smacking of an authoritative syllabus that purports to offer us schooling for our thought – are not grasp, taste, digestion (and indigestion!), assimilation – all the functions of ingestion and nourishment for belly, for body, sure, but also for brain – our very own unique and inalienable affair?

In fact, this point of view, though striving for the native vanity that only genuinely homespun ignorance can breed, merely demonstrates, in spite of itself, our natural affinity for speculation; we would never assume ourselves to be innately capable of making so much as a good shoe, of attaining excellence in any of the familiar crafts and arts without years, or at least a couple of weeks, of study or training and perhaps even some diligent practice in how to work the machines and the materials, without becoming a craftsman first, without, that is, learning the handiwork, joining the guild so to speak – but apparently everyone's a natural born thinker, has all the tools, the leather, the stone already at hand, needs no laboratory, neither Petri dish nor cyclotron, no apprenticeship, no council of master craftsmen and -women from which, after years of practice, permission to ply the trade is ceremoniously granted; we need await no appointment, no authorization, no degree to think. And this inevitable conclusion based as it is on the unshakable conviction we harbor regarding the mind's ultimate inaccessibility to every tyrant (and teacher), as rashly presumptuous as it is overly optimistic, has always been known and seen, yes, even celebrated, as a confirmation that human being is "naturally" called the "thinking" being, *animal rationale* conceived of, in the framework of all living things as belonging to the species of *Homo sapiens sapiens*.

But though, apparently, *wisdom*, i.e. *distinguished* thought, be our title, our nature and destiny, it is no less undeniable that in spite of our tongues and bellies being our own, taste is a pleasure, health a virtue, both studied, learned, as knowledge shared among the informed, and then diligently attended under the artisan's hand, the prestidigitation of which matures with assiduous application but withers from disuse, and from misuse "morphs" into an atrophied and stunted excrescence of perversion. Moreover, though we all might expect of ourselves as adults to have acquired the rational resources we need to face life's little problems and big problems by learning from our mistakes, showing goodwill, and, in general, adhering to the unspoken code of personal conduct that our "socialization" imbued us with, tempered, where all else fails, with a bit of plain common sense, the study of thought in its own right, of *impersonal* thought, prior to or beyond its utility in dealing with the ordinary objects and projects of private or common concern, is probably what the majority would call a truly and rightly rare event in the occupation of human being.

Speculation – who has ever heard of such a thing? You are saying that there was a time when respectable people once spiritedly engaged in it, became adept at it, even taught others the practice as a craft and art? Yes, truly. The history of philosophy is just such a record of noteworthy inventions, achievements, discoveries – all three pertain to speculation, and this history also documents the periodic flourishing as well as decline of interest in thought for the sake of thought. In this way, the great philosophers of tradition, seen as pursuing and having attained a high level of excellence in just such an extraordinary endeavor as that of thought thinking thought, can teach us, who inexplicably desire to embark upon this venture ourselves, how this sort of thing is done – the art, the discipline, and the science of speculative thought. *This* sort of speculation shall be our object even though it be neither the stock broker's nor the news reporter's, *this* contemplation shall be our subject though it be neither that of the engineer's prediction nor the physician's prognosis, neither the soldier's stratagem nor the lover's reverie. For this reason then, though studying the thinkers and poets of our philosophical tradition and becoming conversant with their conceptions and epochs – less so participating in the scholarly debate that is its appendix – is obviously germane to our task, it is not at all the purpose of our investigation but just a means to a greater end which is, namely, the erudition of the intellect towards the perfect cognition of thought thinking thought – **self-knowing being** as it was once termed by the knowledgeable. For from these accomplished thinkers of old, we hope to learn the ways of metaphysical inquiry in action and their achievements will inspire our own efforts to grasp the what and the wherefore of the distinction of human being as well as to nurture the facility of word and deed that is its transfiguring *present*.

5. The First Designation of our Theme

We begin, therefore, by proposing as a working premise that not merely *thought* but rather, more specifically, *thought thinking thought* is the distinction of human being. More specifically? Put in these enigmatic terms, it may not seem that we have made much progress in pinning down our topic. Hence, we must assume at the outset that there is probably more to the notion of self-knowing being than meets the eye, in other words, that since we, philosophically speaking, cannot replace our eyes with fresh ones (or can we?), we need other words, fresh words that make greater sense, provide richer experience, than those hitherto employed. And that is indeed a reasonable demand encouraging us at this juncture to venture a step forward now, having begun by asserting that *thought, the Thinker of thought*, or simply the *Thinker*, is the first object of our current study as well as a concise characterization of the activity *we* are engaged in while doing what we are doing when we do philosophy, namely contemplating, or reflecting, or pondering, or speculating, or musing, upon thought – evidently there is no shortage of tenable terms – and in doing so, by taking our first step forward we are, in fact, taking our first step back and recalling **Aristotle** who was the first philosopher of the Occident to explicitly seize upon *pure* thought as the object most worthy of conception and therefore, rightly considered to be the best *being*, most meriting the predicate *deity* (ΘΕΟΣ) "for then the mind thinks itself, if this is indeed what is best, and is thought thinking thought." (Met. 1074B 34)

ΑΥΤΟΝ ΑΡΑ ΝΟΕΙ ΕΙΠΕΡ ΕΣΤΙ ΤΟ ΚΡΑΤΙΣΤΟΝ
ΚΑΙ ΕΣΤΙΝ Η ΝΟΗΣΙΣ ΝΟΗΣΕΩΣ ΝΟΗΣΙΣ

Deity – in addition to this ultimate and most magnificent designation, our philosophical tradition has bestowed several other dignified and dignifying epithets upon thought, the Thinker, namely upon such thought as thinks thought and thought alone. Most famously perhaps it was called *pure reason* and as Kant affirms of its science, i.e. metaphysical thought or **philosophy** in the strict sense: "Pure reason is in fact exclusively concerned with itself and can have no other occupation."

> *Die reine Vernunft ist in der Tat mit nichts als sich selbst beschäftigt und kann kein anderes Geschäft haben. (Kant, Kritik der reinen Vernunft, III 448.22-23.)*

Why "pure?" Simply to make this point that thought thinking nothing that is not thought (and the *nothing* that is) is "uncommon" in just this way. Therefore, consider *pure* in the sense of the *noble* gases, the *fine* arts, *precious* gems, *illustrious* deeds, in a word, *exceptional* or shall we say, a bit quaintly to be sure but, for that, all the more venerably: *eternal, sublime,* or simply, following Aristotle, *divine* – all of these terms are intended to highlight this difference from the more pedestrian, more prosaic concerns of thought here and now after we have put philosophy safely aside for the day to address...well,... *something else,* whatever else it may be, whatever else there may be, namely, through efficient use of thought's instrumental support, our chores and concerns, their objects and issues, in short, our occupation with *everything else* than with thought itself. Compared to this sort of generic thought, our plodding platitudinarian and handy factotum, who is so often rushed and stressed by matters of urgency, pure thought, the Thinker, namely thought thinking thought, might be imagined to be a more light-footed, light-hearted, lightly-living soul who inhabits a realm much removed from the one that harried handy gofer of ours has to do with. Thus, on the one hand, there is pure thought about thought and, on the other, everyday thinking about everything else and every other thought.

Again, **pure** reason is thus taken in the particular sense of *ingenious* and *exquisite*, of *rare*, of *splendid*, of *superb* thought, yes, thought by such celebratory denominations marked and therefore *remarkable*, therein *conspicuous* and therefore, in spite of first impressions to the contrary, *notable*, thought considered to be and therefore termed, quite simply, *special*, thought, in other words, thought as thought *extraordinaire*, thought thought *keen, quickened.* Now what on earth or in heaven could be curiouser than that, than simply considering the mind *at large* and – larger than the ho-hum career of its finite, everyday life – *infinite*, stranger than taking thought as utterly utterly, as, dare we utter the most august adjective of distinction, *holy?*

6. Thought, the Builder

Entity, Deity, Humanity – my, my, so many tremendous monikers! *Ingenious, exquisite, rare, superb, outstanding, remarkable, keen, conspicuous, distinguished,...*– goodness, so many distinguishing qualifiers for ΛΟΓΟΣ! All of the above as well as 99 other comparable designations and epithets – each more emphatic, each a more splendid title of elation than the next and further epithets of even more magnificent exaltation and grandeur might be added – have been put by thought to identify thought, to name it and, in this way to give it presence for the reader; it is high time that we, in these tender beginnings of our study, after having caught sight of our issue as an object of perceptive contemplation, thought *really seeing* thought, take now this *naming* of thought by thought into account in its own right. For this is the work of thought as well, not merely as a theoretical object of investigation, the cause and causa of the *Thinker*, but also as that of the *Builder*, highlighting the "poetic," inventive, side of our enterprise, which is, succinctly put, to brilliantly distinguish, to recognize *and* signify, to comprehend *and* make visible, to *gain insight* into *and*, at the same time, to *bring* and to *body forth* the being, the vivid image of just such thought as is devoted to thought itself and to nothing else, thought, therefore, that is to be gloriously termed **consecrated**, and that means, determined at the outset to be absolutely and wholly distinct from the ordinary mundane and instrumental reasoning and its cognitive processes so easily confused by references made to a run-of the-mill rationality, to its omnibus versatility, to the world-encompassing technical preoccupations of *applied* sciences, or simply, to more or less pressing purposes and, in light of these, therefore, to thoughts good or bad, thoughts about this or that, **a** thought.

Thought, the Builder, wields the celebratory word. And what a lot of words, nouns and adjectives, have just been brought to bear to highlight distinguished thought from its commonplace application! Who has not taken note of the character of jubilation of the language so employed? Here words are being rhapsodically put to make a big deal out of something that otherwise, without them, might have seemed to the reader to be insignificant or even have gone completely unnoticed; "Hark," say these designations, "we *could* think about thought if we care to! In fact, it is well worth it!" And that is the rapture of thought, the delight that is not mute but rather articulate. Apparently, thought "talks" to us even as we ourselves can talk, sing, about thought. If you thought that thought is just a thinker, then think again. For as much as *contemplation* is the original and keenest pleasure of the intellect, *invention* is the creative joy of imagination – contemplation and invention are, both of them, the works of thought; in this line of reasoning *intellect* refers to thought's insightful gaze, to the *knowledge* of thought, while the term *imagination* brings out its creative *power* to substantiate what it has learned and now knows. Thought, the Builder works the words, elaborates the details, substantiates.

For example, have you never wondered about the word *god*? In the hands of the Poet-Thinker, it is employed to make a distinction in excellence and importance. Originally of course, and that means in the language of the Greeks, this term ΘΕΟΣ (*theos*), *god*, like the term, *cosmos* or *being*, or even *man* or *house*, *horse* or *father* – all of the familiar "nouns" – were used as predicates to indicate substances, what a thing in question actually was and, more than that, what is was *supposed* to be, in other words, if what was identified by these predicates being applied to them really and truly deserved to be so named. Predicates were therefore distinctions of quality and, in this way, sentences of *judgment* regarding the thing's relationship to a particular determination of THE WAY IT SHOULD BE. Predication, the *WHAT* of it, was not merely a "neutral" attribution and a specification of the identity of a particular, the *THIS* of it – a subject, substance, or mere substantive; on the contrary, specification and identity – *predicate, attribute* and *adjective* – all refer to the property of the thing, but, again, its *property* not merely in the physical sense of a feature or a material attribute but especially in the sense of its *propriety* with regard to that defining identity as determined by its own proper "idea" (its ΕΙΔΟΣ) to which it owes the "honor" of being so named and thus recognized as a good one of its kind, such a one, in other words, that has been acknowledged as attaining to excellence through having fulfilled its appointed or "intended" nature, where *nature* refers not to the "natural environment" but rather to the *essence*, the idea of what a particular thing was meant to be...and *is* if it is truly good, fine, excellent, right. The name is a term of distinction and, as such, a badge of distinction referring to a thing's virtue, value, to the idea of what it was meant to be. A name is ennobling. As we shall see, thought, the Builder, builds with names, having collected all the choicest, the most beautiful names, and orders them into a line of reasoning that makes sense.

Now if the calling of a name gives value and significance to the thing named, in other words, draws a mark of distinction upon it, setting it, as if by way of inflection, apart, if *ΘΕΟΣ* is a predicate in just this axiological sense and, among all the predicates, uniquely superlative, we might expect that a great many things could, and perhaps even should, be so qualified when their importance or power or influence or excellence are addressed. And this is indeed the case. In the Greek world of speech, the term *ΘΕΟΣ* is a remarkably liberally applied cognizance! Consider what was so named: Morning, Night, Fear, Love, Dream, Victory, Memory, Portion, Justice, Necessity were all called ΘΕΟΣ in honor of their power and influence in the lives of human being, by virtue of their "natural," that is to say, their allotted, determined place in the scheme of things, in recognition of the fact that they inspired respect, even reverence, on the part of those touched by them; and even today we recognize and celebrate Victory when she approaches and might very well say, in a flight of delight and gratitude at the winning goal, the new world record, the volley won, as spectator or as athlete, hands in the air, face towards the sky, with a shout of glory, if not in so many words: *Ah, look! That is NIKH! Now Nike is "there!" Hail Nike!* – well, at least, in an ad for sports articles we would.

Is it not, well, a bit of an exaggeration to call things – an emotion, the sky, flowers, rivers, rumors, people, occasionally even certain animals – "*THEOΣ*" just because they are powerful, beautiful, significant, influential, because they make a difference in our lives? It is as if the process of signification, at least in Greek speech, actually brought forth its subject, that is to say, brought it brightly bodied to the fore where it might be attended as noteworthy! Precisely! This is the work of the Poet-Thinker who knows that the language of wisdom does not merely posit and manipulate arbitrary names. No, not at all. Instead, names draw a distinction and thus bring forth a determination; names invoke. Thought, the Builder, knows that, in a certain way, saying it *makes* it so. We will have to get to the bottom of this in the course of our study!

For now, suffice it to say that thought, the Poet-Thinker, has availed itself of language to make a point, i.e. to distinguish thought *from thought* and reason *from reason*; the one is as familiar as it is mundane, the other momentous though easily missed, deserving note and regard though often disregarded. And it is easy to see why that is the case.

For, most of the time, thought is simply assumed to be our many-sided servant and our easy tool, our favorite friend for solving life's little problems and big problems. If our car breaks down, thought will guide us in taking action; faced with cataclysm we know what to do, namely *first things first.* Grab a hammer and build a house; seize a knife and save your life – we are often faced with difficult situations that call for a *quick take* and *understanding* of what is going on. *Savvy* or *sagacity* are familiar names for thought that nimbly guides our actions in dealing with the challenges we face in ever-changing circumstances. Run to catch the bus, wave your hand to draw attention, think before you speak, look before you leap, stay cool – are these tried and true precepts not helpful in getting by, making ends meet, learning the ropes, talking turkey? In all of these cases, thought is an all-arounder periscopically turned towards events and concerns that encroach forcibly, perhaps even threateningly, upon our lives and the preferred panacea for getting out of a jam, or else ingeniously making do, or else resolutely keeping on keeping on with the eyes on the prize. Here thought is busy trouble-shooting, is horse sense, smarts, guts, IQ.

Stop! Surely, reason cannot address and account for *itself* under these circumstances of duress; surely thought must be more than a knack! But in what other, more profound, more exalted, i.e. more distinguished way is thought to be understood as being *all-around*? What is thought alone when it is, in fact, altogether thought? What is thought on the whole and *thoroughly* thought, thought all told, all in, all over, all out? These are entirely different questions and just one question: What is thought to thought in its own right, thought *wholly* thought? Precisely! What is thought when it is holy? When it is taken as being *out and out, all in all* and precisely for this reason called *glorious*, another well-known term of distinction to build with and upon?

7. Thought in and of Itself

Moved to investigate this question, philosophers have often taught that **pure** thought in the preeminent, aforementioned sense of *speculation* cannot flourish where urgent needs of surfeit or dearth dominate the foreground of attention. Where thought is made useful towards attainment of a goal as the means to an end, it is obviously not concerned with itself; in this case, thought's end is not thought itself nor is it, at that moment, just thinking thought but rather taking care of business; clearly, if thought is dealing with the incident event, then it is thinking about this and not about thought in its own right. That is, moreover, precisely why metaphysics was once celebrated for what it is so often decried today, namely for daring to recognize in pure thought the element, the subject, the object, and the activity of knowledge cherished for its own sake, for the superfluous *delight* inherent in the enterprise of thought thinking thought. According to Aristotle, as the history of sciences would seem to bear out, only after everything necessary to lead a "comfortable life" had been attained, the most pressing problems solved, and the ease of leisure attained, only then did *intellect* arise and begin to seek out this sort of knowledge, which is pursued not out of boredom or the fatigued spleen of idleness, "nor for the sake of any extraneous need" (ΟΥ ΧΡΗΣΕΩΣ ΤΙΝΟΣ ΕΝΕΚΕΝ - 982 b 21) but rather "alone for its own sake" (ΜΟΝΗ...ΕΑΥΤΗΣ ΕΝΕΚΕΝ - 982 b 27-28), and notable therefore as being the "only free one among all the different sorts of knowledge" (ΜΟΝΗΝ ΟΥΣΑΝΕΛΕΥΘΕΡΑΝ ΤΩΝ ΕΠΙΣΤΗΜΩΝ - 982 b 27), originating not in danger or in anger or in hunger and thus not at all in the subservience of utility with respect to these, but alone in seminal "wonder" (ΘΑΥΜΑΖΕΙΝ – 982 b 11-12) at the "way it all is" (...ΠΑΝΤΕΣ, ΕΙ ΟΥΤΩΣ ΕΧΕΙ - 983 a 13) and thus, in the desire to "escape ignorance" (ΤΟ ΦΕΥΓΕΙΝ ΤΟ ΑΓΝΟΕΙΝ - 982 b 19-20), with respect to the greatest and best of our thoughtful enterprises, i.e. the *sciences*, giving rise to the notion of the one science that is not only unburdened of the urgency of employment but also the "most precious for being the most divine" (Η ΓΑΡ ΘΕΙΟΤΑΤΗ ΚΑΙ ΤΙΜΙΩΤΑΤΗ - 983 a 5), on the one hand, because "possession of this knowledge best befits a god" (...ΜΑΛΙΣΤΑ ΑΝ ΘΕΟΣ ΕΞΟΙ - 983 a 6) and, on the other, because the most excellent science must needs have none other than the divine as its topic (ΕΙ ΤΙΣ ΤΩΝ ΘΕΙΩΝ ΕΙΗ - 983 a 7). In conclusion, we might therefore say: "More necessary is every science, better is none," (Met. 983a 10-11).

> ΑΝΑΓΚΑΙΟΤΕΡΑΙ ΜΕΝ ΟΥΝ ΠΑΣΑΙ ΤΑΥΤΗΣ,
> ΑΜΕΙΝΩΝ Δ ' ΟΥΔΕΜΙΑ

Therefore it follows "logically" that this distinguished, and, in this sense, *divine* being of thought is "living, eternal, superlative" – *living* (ΖΩΟΝ), in other words, a completed reality as opposed to mere potentiality, whether it be the thought unspoken and unverified, the will unfulfilled, or every other innate possibility that is not yet in deed and in fact an actual, a *tried and true* being; *eternal* (ΑΙΔΙΟΝ), in other words, absolutely unique and distinguished not only from the beings of mere possibilities but also from those of the ephemeral realm of what is temporary, incidental, contingent, here today, gone tomorrow, trembling leaves of being that sprout and fall in season only to be swept away by oblivious winds; and *superlative* (ΑΡΙΣΤΟΝ), in other words, outstanding, first by virtue of its being, with respect to all other beings, autarkic and, second, because it is engaged in the best of all activities, namely contemplation, the uninterrupted contemplation of what is best, namely itself.

> ΦΑΜΕΝ ΔΕ ΤΟΝ ΘΕΟΝ ΕΙΝΑΙ ΖΩΟΝ ΑΙΔΙΟΝ ΑΡΙΣΤΟΝ, ΩΣΤΕ ΖΩΗ ΚΑΙ ΑΙΩΝ ΣΥΝΕΧΗΣ ΚΑΙ ΑΙΔΙΟΣ ΥΠΑΡΧΕΙ ΤΩΙ ΘΕΩΙ...
> (Aristotle Met. 1072 b 28-30)

> We are saying then that deity is alive, eternal and superlative, and therefore life as well as autarkic being both perpetual and eternal are its very own...

Aristotle therefore draws the conclusion that follows "logically" from this train of thought by attributing to such a being as fulfils these conditions that our reasoning has determined as prerequisite the predicate most apt at making clear *what it is*. He concludes, "This is god." (ΤΟΥΤΟ ΓΑΡ Ο ΘΕΟΣ – 30). Is there a more cogent argument in support of why the science of pure reason is originally to be thought of as theology and why pure reason must study pure reason, why thought, at its best, will and must think about thought?

8. Reason as Technological Rationality

In contrast to pure reason, the autotelic being of thought, *technological thinking* is understood as strategic, i.e. as a means to an end rather than as an end in itself. If we think about how *rationality* is normally understood, namely as the so-called *power* of rationality, we find that it comprises many of the qualities that are useful for facing and mastering the challenges of our lives. For example, reason allows us to abstract qualities from things, detach these things from the fleeting continuum of a fast-paced world, and then, from these objectified things in turn, abstract a mundane subject engaged in goal attainment behavior that appropriates them for particular consumption, whose know-how (before even knowing-why) is adept at determining, in accordance with the guidelines and standards of established and accepted specifications, and allocating – in accordance with the "rational" principle that demands for decreasing input (cost) the maximization of performance output (utility) for a given opportunity – scarce and limited natural resources, human as well as animal, vegetable, and mineral.

In a technological framework, "logical" reasoning refers to mechanical calculation of the sort duplicated by artificial intelligence – which is often set in stark contrast to the "emotional" intelligence of many human specimens – and is considered subordinated to the pragmatic principle which gives preference to *what works* based on the typically "binary logic" of expedience in the use of these resources. Clearly, at an individual level, *self-preservation* along with the *pleasure* and the *reality principle* are the most urgent directives that flow from the prime directive of practicability, commanding a complex mechanism of checks and balances, security and insurance, all of which, ultimately, are designed to maintain the homeostasis of the life-world ecosystem, that is to say, the preservation of the status quo by authorities empowered to facilitate economic growth and safeguard social stability – reason in this technological sense tends only to keep the particular, the most proximate, goal in mind and evaluates the success or failure of a means to achieve it without considering the more remote ends, to say nothing of terminal goals, those ultimate purposes that succeed at taking the "big picture" into account and even less the means themselves as goals, even though they are ends too, albeit intermediate ones in an ascending series of ever widening scope.

Technological thought as is practiced by the Homo oeconomicus of applied sciences has often come under fire and, as a consequence, has contributed to the discrediting of reason in some circles as the narrow-minded, regressive, self-centered mentality of a technocratic quidnunc who is immured in his area of specialization, devoted to the nuts and bolts, bits and bytes constructions of an ever more finely calibrated and therefore more comprehensively controllable world the operation of which is designed to be as trouble-free and as easy-care as humanly possible, consisting of material and information flows and manifold mechanisms which, though illustrious for the undeniable profit they have secured mankind, are apparently never free from the danger of becoming, in the wrong hands, oppressive and exploitative contraptions of automation, of panoptic surveillance, of bandwidth and broadcast, of clockwork, of bean count and body count, of extractions, reductions, and extrapolations, of blips on scans and screens that are the lens of our own superficiality in a world lacking all depth, where WYSIWYG, where "spirit" is taken neat, the truth naked, and the naked ape preferably the alpha-male in the herd.

Such insular, straitlaced, and thus "bounded" rationality, driving the technological progress of industry and lubricating the communicative practices of society, has always been contrasted to that of reason in the strict sense understood as being not merely an instrument but also a testament, a testimony and a monument to thought attuned to thought as that of a distinguished being, remarkable in its properties, worthy of contemplation for its own sake, in that unique quality of accord that is demonstrated in its own self-relativity and considered to be the end and the aim of every desire that strives for *fulfilment*, a consummation devoutly to be wished, beyond every meanness and its preoccupation with the mean, with diurnal man's satiety and with mankind's clutching comforts and concerns. It is a spirit that comes to the fore in the celebration of thought in and of itself, as our younger thought, in being prior to its appointment of dispersive service in a panoply of thought patterns, models, and methods, and a fresher thought in its observant and pious exhilaration, knowing itself as being known, regarding and regarded, and now, in reverend remembrance of its youth, regretting the loss of that first spring, acutely critical of its clinical, cynical senility:

> When I was young, it seemed that life was so wonderful,
> A miracle, oh it was beautiful, magical.
> And all the birds in the trees, well they'd be singing so happily,
> Joyfully, playfully watching me.
> But then they send me away to teach me how to be sensible,
> Logical, responsible, practical.
> And they showed me a world where I could be so dependable,
> Clinical, intellectual, cynical.[3]

The "grown-up" world, the world of sophistication and civilization, is seen as having spawned a thought bent on operational efficiency and managerial feasibility, that employs tools of subjugation complementing the devious use of ruse and ploy which resorts to cunning in lieu of confrontation and for whom the ghost in the machine, the ego, is just another, a new-fangled technique for playing the game and getting ahead, for winning friends and influencing people, for making a million before you are thirty without even trying.

9. Reason as the Neuro-physiological Activity of the Brain

Thus *technical* reason, whatever its merits in the navigation, colonization, rationalization, domestication of worldly wildernesses is not the issue of our study. Nor is our theme and topic thought in the sense of some intricate electrical phenomena sparking in the functional regions of the cerebral

---

[3] Lyrics by Roger Hodgson.

cortex that biologists, anatomists, or physicists, chemists or physicians purport to map and measure by tracing the ionic sparks and micro-currents of action potential conducting along threads of ganglia, up and down excitatory axon fibres and across synaptic clefts onto the post-synaptic dendrites that in turn transmit micro-chemical signals further on down and up the neural channel network that comprises the convoluted circuitry of the brain, the membranous grey matter supposed to be the mysteriously fugitive ego's hide-out in the citadel of the cranium as well as the seat of all spatio-temporal coordination of voluntary and involuntary motor reflex and activity, brain stem emotional arousal and sensory perception – comprising, in particular, visual processing, mood, volition, and their disorders, but also language, learning, and memory.

If the aim of neural science is to fathom the mind then "understanding" here must mean to be able to explain the *how* of the brain's wiring and firing – how is the brain organized and what processes are involved in producing the familiar phenomena of mentation such as perception, imagination, learning and remembering, the first causes of which are ultimately to be found on the level of molecular biology in a movement of reduction to primitives, *a savage thought* summarized by Lévi-Strauss, as proceeding from an "empirical diversity" and complexity to the attainment of their primal elemental component "invariants," a movement that is considered to be the very pedigree of the so-called "natural and exact sciences," which begin by "absorbing particular men into general Man" and complete their enterprise with the "reintegration of culture into nature and...life into the ensemble of its physico-chemical conditions." This is the progression of "human sciences" in general that see their "ultimate goal...not in the constitution of Man but rather in its dissolution," in other words "resolving the human into the non-human," a train of thought that "despite its intentionally brutal turn of phrase" is not a bid to demean humanity but rather to honor inert material for its contributions in the composition of man; for "the day we succeed at comprehending life as a function of inert material, that will be the day we discover that the latter possesses properties that are very different from those we previously attributed to it." (Lévi-Strauss, *La Pensé Sauvage*, 326-327)

> par-delà la diversité empirique...l'analyse...veut atteindre des invariants...qui incombent aux sciences exactes et naturelles: réintégrer la culture dans la nature, et finalement, la vie dans l'ensemble de ses conditions physico-chimiques...le but dernier des sciences humaines n'est pas de constituer l'homme, mais de le dissoudre...la résolution de l'humain en non-humain...en

dépit du tour volontairement brutal donné à notre thèse...le jour
où l'on parviendra à comprendre la vie comme une fonction de
la matière inerte, ce sera pour découvrir que celle-ci possède des
propriétés bien différentes des celles qu'on lui attribuait
antérieurement.

From this perspective of atoms foreordained to achieve living, even
mental greatness in the human mind, though the mind may be an
epiphenomena of synaptic activity and finally biochemical process, these
sciences, which give rise to the familiar entities of physics and biology, are
themselves the fruits of scientific research, its methods and paradigms and
therefore as much a "product" of thought processes as thought is their
product.

If an idea comes from synergetic electrical cellular activity, so do the cells'
ions, in turn, owe their being to a more primal, a more savage energy source;
are not then the sun and the solar processes the ultimate source of thought?
And every thought a spark of the sun thinking in us its own thoughts of
which we claim ownership? But again, if we stop at the sun, the element of
fire, we do so arbitrarily; we might still consider the cosmological order that
gave rise to sunshine and the earthling's world, the gravity warping space
and the levity of wavelengths permeating its emptiness – it is, apparently,
all of these entities, and the subatomic politics of the particles that govern
them, that are the "real" cause of thought and that have made science
possible in the first place, a remarkable teleology which bestows upon lowly
matter, both organic and inorganic the dignity of a human destiny!

Such trains of thought (or should we call them lattices of ideo-atomic,
non-fissionable wavicles?) are often framed into a divisive debate arguing
for the origin of thought in culture and culture in nature and nature being
explicable in the familiar and not so familiar physical and chemical
properties of matter. In this discourse the combatants are starkly drawn;
what are thoughts if they come from man, aboriginal man from apes, apes
descended from lower mammals, mammals from reptiles, reptiles from
amphibians, these from fish and fish from plants and plants ultimately from
coacervates that have agglomerated in the charged primal vegetable soup
of proteins and minerals, to spawn our primogenitor genes, both selfish and
empathetic. Those who find the thought repellent that lofty thought could
originate in the base atom and the even baser ape could just as well
interpret this bloodline as one not demeaning human being but rather as
an ascent of matter to life's LUCA, cyanobacterial life to sentience and
sentience to intelligence – is not the fate of a lonely atom, wandering in the
empty immensity of space, a dust particle of neutrality destined to be drawn

into the bond of chemical matrimony and thence to join the intercourse of a molecular, a microbial community not nobly rendered as exhibiting at the end of its career remarkably human proclivities? Who would refuse to welcome the notion of natural forces, their checks and balances, the play of desire, the energy of difference, the micro-cosmos of the human drama itself as the symbol of more universal horizons and this universe in turn as living out its potential in the life of minds, the words and deeds of human beings? In this train of thought, chemistry keeps a record of the practice of thought as much as the fall of gravity; the latter might be subsumed in the category of mechanics and the former in that of inorganic physics the process of which in turn establishes the basis of organic physics i.e. mineral and vegetable nature and finally that of the animal organism which, in its generation, introduces the experience of death out of itself in which the particular animal as finite existence enters into the relationship of discrepancy with the abstract force of the general principle. "Its disproportion to universality is its original illness and its inborn germ of death," as Hegel explains in § 375 of his *Encyclopedia of Philosophical Sciences*, "the closure of this discrepancy is itself the execution of this fate. The individual mediates itself by assimilating its singularity to the general but attains in this way, as it is only an abstract and immediate being, only abstract objectivity in which its activity dulls, petrifies, its life becoming stagnant habituation so that it thus, in going out of itself, kills itself."

> Seine Unangemessenheit zur Allgemeinheit ist seine ursprüngliche Krankheit und [der] angeborene Keim des Todes. Das Aufheben dieser Unangemessenheit ist selbst das Vollstrecken dieses Schicksals. Das Individuum hebt sie auf, indem es der Allgemeinheit seine Einzelheit einbildet, aber hiermit, insofern sie abstrakt und unmittelbar ist, nur eine abstrakte Objektivität erreicht, worin seine Tätigkeit sich abgestumpft [hat] verknöchert und das Leben zur prozeßlosen Gewohnheit geworden ist, so daß es sich so aus sich selbst tötet.[4]

This death, however, as well as the immediate reformation of the individual are affirmed as the being of the idea as spirit. Seen in this light, the lowly physical properties and processes merely offer Thought, the Thinker/Builder, the Builder/Thinker, one matter more in which to construe and with which to depict the distinction of human being.

---

[4] cf. Hegel, Enzyklopädie der philosophischen Wissenschaften, IX 535.

Therefore to the brutalizing ascertainment that the human mind is *nothing but* electricity, *nothing but* chemistry, we might ask who persists in saying "nothing but" and why? Perhaps ions are worthy of greater recognition than even their greatest advocates, the scientists of the natural and exact sciences, are wont to give. Even if particles cannot talk and tell us about their walk of life, their walk *to* holobiontic life, *to* mind even, the congregations, the communities they form in their configurations, their armies born in the dissonance of charged oppositions, the bodies they founded in the harmonic cooperation of gravitational force, the nations they have built striving for the light they are the source of, the revolving cosmos of their universe, the star of their birth in brilliance and, in spectacular stellar death, the utter blackness of the cold hole of an incomprehensible singularity they revert to in the wink of an eye but from whence they have since sprung again, renewed, in a bang or a whimper – there is a story to be told here, a cause to be taken up, an issue to consider, namely, at the very least, that of the virtue of patience and of modesty and that of a being beholden to what is greater than itself.

It is a good thing that in school children learn that many living beings have a brain, which is sometimes rudimentary, sometimes highly developed. We dissect the lowly worm to that end and learn about the function of its brain with a view to better understanding, eventually, the functions of the left and right hemispheres in the higher primates. This is biology. Less often do we teach our children that people are endowed with reason in relation to which we may distinguish ourselves or fail to do so and that just as surely as man comes from apes, though infinitely more deplorably, apes come from men.

10. Reason as the Cognitive Behavior of Man

Neither as the exponentiation of the hand's proficiency, nor as the physiochemical basis of the brain's architecture are we studying the distinction of human being, nor yet as the cognitive behavior of man.

Anthropology and its retinue of sciences including such diversity as psychology, sociology, ethnology, archeology, and linguistics as well as other sciences of natural history all of which have offered their service and contribution to the inquiry of man by Man, though all important studies in their own right, considering as they do man's place in the world, man's customs and abilities, the sciences man has invented, the history of man's civilization and culture, the diversity of cultures of the world and their conflicts, the biological and genetic determination of individuals in conjunction with the influence of their environments, their achievements in the arts, the philosophical systems with their ideologies and religious doctrines with their myths that the family of man has devised and how these ideations and man itself have changed and evolved over time, how they differ from place to place and race to race while at the same time manifesting remarkable affinities and similarities across races, regions, and ages – all of these areas of study and expertise define thought in terms of the empirical phenomenon called *mankind* which is taken to be perhaps the most comprehensive topic of modern scientific inquiry.

Now man does many things – sleep, work, play, talk, pray, read, write, eat, cook...and, what else....oh yes, *think.* Man's mental performance is the object of research in cognitive science, an "interdisciplinary" effort in which researchers with areas of interest as diverse as economics and psychology, microbiology and zoology, cybernetics and genetic engineering, semiology and mathematics, as well as many other fields of study – systematically empirical as well as non-empirical, whose specimens are human as well as non-human, natural as well as artificial, taken in Western as well as non-Western ethnical settings. Human behavior occurring individually or in groups offers a wide set of phenomena to investigate in particular through controlled experiments that are more or less invasively performed on subjects, often undergraduates, designed to test people's reactions, mental as well as physical, to stimuli with a view to a particular theoretical model of how cognition works.

A science of cognitive behavior examines the modularity of the mental faculties, whether innate or acquired, analyzes their computational and representational routines, magnetically scans and records how neural populations of the brain become aware of intrinsic and extrinsic stimuli, both inhibitory and excitatory, how children learn language and chimpanzees use languages, how memory traces are linked, stored, and accessed, maps how inferences are drawn; then, conceptual schemata and scripts, analogies, and visual and spatial representations are generated and applied to the "real world" and strategies of deductive reasoning selected. Debates abound about how to best test intelligence in people and other animals, theorize on how higher and lower primates go about making decisions and solving problems, whether rudimentary or advanced, and how their comparative levels of consciousness and awareness of their surroundings and of themselves are influenced by the reciprocity of natural and cultural forces.

Apparently, studies on human cognition seek to understand how the "mind/brain" does what it does as revealed by what people do; it is remarkable how important and mysterious this cause and effect correlation between the brain and human activity is – beginning with the behavior that is the focus of her experiment, the cognitive scientist explores how the brain would have to function in order to contribute to the emergence of that behavior in the form in which it appeared.

Anthropology, one of the attendant sciences into which the cognitive sciences tap – though of course, for the anthropologist, it is the cognitive sciences that are attendant – inscribes the cerebral behavior of homo sapiens into the natural and cultural, physical and human geography of earth – as rich in regions, landscapes, and climates, as in the diversity of its societies and civilizations – and gathers its data, both emic and etic, across the changing times and places of our blue planet. What a wealth of objects of study this topic of people provides – *people*, the diachronic and synchronic variations in their physical make-up and appearance, their respective languages and societies, whether a nation of millions or a tribe of 30, their comparative histories as documented by the relics and artifacts that have survived to tell their curious tale to future generations.

But can we conceive of our human being not so much as possessing ideas but rather as being possessed of them, ourselves as being *their* property rather than they *ours* such that even as there are the infinitely many thoughts that *we have*, there are a very few, one in particular, *and* three, that *have us*, whom they, coming after, come before as the cause – we being their cause for the simple reason that they were ours first?

11. Reason as the Scheme of All Things Thought

But to study language or behavior, society or the psyche as humanoid (as opposed to merely anthropoid) is not to study the distinction of human being, a study which is, rather, a *record* (in the sense of a *recordatio*) and in this sense an acknowledgement and a *recollection* of human experience and insight with regards to a determinative *principle* or *end*. What are principles and ends of regard? In the olden days, principles of regard took on the form of an overriding issue or topic that (1) struck a *Thinker* as worthy of being taken up, of being regarded, by a discerning mind with a view to deeper understanding and appreciation, that (2) required of a *Doer* the persevering service towards the fulfillment of an end that devotion had championed as a cause and (3) inspired a *Builder*, by skillful use of all the productive resources at his or her disposal, to give tangible, visible shape to that original insight and, in this way, found the dwelling of regard that is alone worthy of being inhabited by that principle's community.

Thus in contradistinction to the notion of reason as an instrument of technological ingenuity or as the electrochemical processes of the brain or finally as the central locus of the cognitive behavior of man in the sociocultural and natural milieux that define Man's life-world continuum, we introduce the idea of pure reason as a *train of thought* that comprises three distinct elements – the ***principle*** (A), the **issue** (B), and the ***insight*** (C). We take these terms to be variables (hence the letters *A*, *B*, *C*) since different trains of thought found different orders (A), signify different issues (B), and discern different conceptions (C) of the distinction of human being, as we shall see later when we study in detail the principles and methods of our analysis, which we might call, provisionally, the *logotectonic of regard* in order to highlight that the occupation of pure reason, understood as the building of trains of thought, is, with a view to the objects it studies, both a celebratory acknowledgement of their merit as well as a systematic demonstration of their coherence.

Thus, the issue of this principle and the cause that drives our conceptual efforts with regards to it command us to take for the object of our study neither the network of the brain, nor the mechanisms of the brawn of our anthropological Man, but rather the comprehensive history of contemporary and traditional thought, more simply, *the scheme of all things thought.* Finally, as pertains to the determinative principles that are at issue in our investigation of the accomplishments of renowned poets and thinkers – for it is in their works that principles of thought have been articulated – our focus and driving purpose remains the better understanding and articulation of the experience of the *distinction of human being.* Taken as one complete line of reasoning, a *ratio* of the terms comprised by it, our investigation might be succinctly determined to consist of the following three main ideas:

> the logotectonic of regard (C) – the scheme of all things thought
> (B) – the distinction of human being (A)

This ratio (C – B – A) may be presented in the form of a statement declaring the purpose of our investigation as follows:

> The demonstration of the coherence and the acknowledgement of the merit of the contributions of contemporary and traditional thought with a view towards the more profound experience and conception of the distinction of human being.

It may also be expressed as a proposition as follows:

> The scheme of all things thought is the logotectonic articulation of the experience and the conception of the distinction of human being in the development of Occidental culture.

Considering now briefly each of this proposition's three components in turn, namely the principle (A), the issue (B), and the cognizance (C) of our undertaking, we review first our experience with regards to **principles (A)** frequently encountered in the familiar form of *standards* suggesting to us a rich panorama of issues of valuation that often arise in this connection: *measures* found appraisal of rank and assessment of quality; *norms* provide criteria for the judgment of esteem and standing; *touchstones* and *milestones*, *benchmarks* and *yardsticks* gauge and check, assize and assay, try and test, and we are all familiar with the trials and tests that *rulers* and *rulings* afflict us with; *patterns* and *paragons* stamp the matter; the precedence of *types* and *models* rate our model-making; kings, princes, magistrates give *orders* that rank and grade our station on scales from, say, 1 to 10. Their *imperatives* and *precepts* prescribe purpose to action; *protocols* command; *codes* of honor mandate; *directives* are the proclamation of the *law* that poses and exacts our *obligation*, sets *mandates*, decrees *dictates* with the voice of *authority*, administering the *power* of the "*firsts*," the *principals*, who embody the *ends* and the *origins* of all whose *destiny* it is to follow their *lead*.

The notion of the determining principle includes not only that of *measurement* and *definition* but also that of endeavor, the *command* of commitment of the will's decision, the *criterion* upon which the verdicts of judgment are based, the *reason* that drives it forwards, fixed and firm, towards the fulfillment of the objective; the first *cause* and causes of being, the *provenance* of transition, the *summons* to convene, the *government* to sanction, the *fundament* to build upon, the *point* to be made and well taken.

Determinative principles contain not merely *COMPULSION* as in the Sophistic *Antilogic* (Zenon, Gorgias, Protagoras), i.e. that of the force of *logic*, of *persuasion*, and of *politics*, *FOUNDATION* as in Milesian/Eleatic *Physiology* (Thales, Anaximenes, Xenophanes), i.e. that of *aquatic* nature, *psychic* nature, and *divine* nature, and *NECESSITY* as in Milesian/Ionian *Cosmology* (Anaximander, Pythagoras, Heraclitus), i.e. that of the *ordered* turn and return of the seasons, the *regularity* of the stars' revolutions, and the *governing* of transition in the relationship of the One's Other to the Other's One, but also *CAUSALITY* as in pluralist *Atomism* (Empedocles, Anaxagoras, Democritus), i.e. that of the double *principles* of amity and enmity, the vortical efficacy of *mind* upon matter, and that of *vacuity* in which swirling atoms may stick and scatter.[5]

From these few examples we might observe that the conception of a principle suggests a rendering in terms of authority and power as a result of the difference that it makes in establishing a scheme of all things thought within the particular framework that the principle defines, providing as end and origin the general conditions upon which an order of possibilities is determined, and to which there is subsequent accordance or subordination as to a law, category, or decree of which there is appointment, application, or realization as a model or paradigm of development as a result of which there is a collection or community of particulars as its correlative whole, its unity, is accomplished.

It is, of course, that Greek word par excellence, ΛΟΓΟΣ, that refers most specifically to the inaugural relationship of discrimination that the **perception of intellect (C)** achieves with regard to original principles. It is not easy for human being to affect indifference and plead ignorance when subject to the force of its determinative provenience. For at that point, once the distinction of human being has been drawn, it is already too late to be indifferent and henceforth ignorance must be studied if it is to be, however fragilely, maintained. Once the relationship of thought has been introduced into experience and insight has left its mark, the moment of truth has arrived; there is no way around it – the critical decision must be taken with respect to how this relationship to the determination of the principle will be regarded. In other words, this decision calls upon thought to recognize and thus to take up the cause that is the present of the principle.

The attentive regard that corresponds to that present was originally and most famously the insight of *THEORY* (ΘΕΟΡΙΑ), which was first conceived of by Thales as "perceptive *OBSERVATION*" (ΙΣΤΟΡΙΗ), that discriminating (but not discriminatory) *ATTENDANCE* that, in noting the "*totality of all that has naturally come to light*" (ΠΑΝΤΑ ΤΑ ΦΑΝΕΡΑ), grasps the issue of *aquatic nature*, which is the Thalesian principle, as the foundation of the foundation, the ground of terrestrial nature. Thus in the ancient Greek tradition. The Greek epoch is the historical locus of thought's regard as the PERCEPTION *of the senses* (ΑΙΣΘΗΣΕΩΝ) the most highly prized of which is

---

[5] See H. Boeder's papers and lectures on pre-Socratic Greek philosophy in *Das Bauzeug der Geschichte*, ed. Gerald Meier, Würzburg 1994.

eyesight "because among the senses it provides us with the most insight and discrimination." (Aristotle, *Met.* 980a 26-27)

ΑΙΤΙΟΝ Δ ' ΟΤΙ ΜΑΛΙΣΤΑ ΠΟΙΕΙ ΓΝΩΡΙΖΕΙΝ ΗΜΑΣ ΑΥΤΗΤΩΝ
ΑΙΣΘΗΣΕΩΝ ΚΑΙ ΠΟΛΛΑΣΔΗΛΟΙ ΔΙΑΦΟΡΑΣ

For the Greeks, perceptive seeing *is* knowing and, accordingly, the field of *science* ranged from *INSIGHT*'s simple and necessary being (Parmenides) to the necessarily limited *VIEW* (ΔΟΚΟΣ) of human knowledge (Xenophanes) and from the mere probability of extraneous *IMPRESSION* (Democritus) to the self-evidence of thought in the thetic art of dialectical *RATIONCINATION* (Zeno) over the *IDEA* of the Good (Plato) as the being *PRESENT* for and of insight, to distinguished *CONTEMPLATION, theory* in the strict sense of *PURE REASON* (ΝΟΥΣ) deduced as the best being of all thinking the best being of all (Aristotle).[6]

Thus to each of the distinct principles known to Greek conception, there stands a unique corresponding relationship of apperception – the cognitive term of discernment in each case specifies the particular character of thought under the postulate of the given principle. This character of thought regarding the principle attains complete determinacy in the form of the designation of thought's realization, which is the congruent issue at stake.

Accordingly, the other Greek term corresponding to ΛΟΓΟΣ, equally familiar and untranslatable, refers precisely to this ***issue (B)***, the controversial topic, the moot point answering to perception's discrimination and its deeds of discernment that, since their origin in antiquity, have been celebrated as "classical thought," namely *Being* (ΟΝ, ΟΥΣΙΑ). We encounter it first in *PHYSIS* (ΦΥΣΙΣ) as distinguished from the natural emergence of *PLURAL APPARITION* (ΠΑΝΤΑ ΤΑ ΦΑΝΕΡΑ), followed by the integrity of the *COSMOS* (ΚΟΣΜΟΣ) in the transience of conflicting elemental substances, as the enduring *TOTALITY* (Anaximander), the *HARMONY* (Pythagoras), the *PROPORTIONALIY* of mutual contestation, i.e. the *One/All* (Heraclitus)[7] of their apparition and dissolution, the one balanced nature of these natures – a train of thought that ultimately goes beyond nature, the issue of thought, to the reasoning of this train of thought itself in the conception of ΟΥΣΙΑ (ousia), the

---

[6] Ibid. See in particular the essay "Was ist *Physis?*" pp. 70-94.

[7] cf. Boeder, *The Topologie der Metaphysik,* pp. 95-96.

substantial entity of insight (ΝΟΥΣ), i.e. *being* (ΟΝ) – whether as Parmenides' predicate of *PERFECTION*, as Plato's life of the good, i.e. the *WELL-BEING* of the dialectic soul, or as Aristotle's teleological *UNIVERSE*, turning about its cardinal point, namely pure reason as thought thinking thought.

12. Reason as the Latest Late/Modern Project?

Thus whereas anthropology studies *thought* as man's salient mental capacities, processes, and their proficiency, thereby providing an account of the great diversity of uses and abuses of people's minds and the behavior that ensues when they actively engage in the framing and settling of their everyday lives, in the study we propose, the discernment of cognition is conceived of as a train of thought and can be analysed as a relationship of three signature terms which specify within ever wider frameworks of conception, ultimately however in the scheme of all things thought, the principle (A), the issue (B), and the insight (C), in which our experience with pure reason resides.

What are we proposing? This: One experience and the entire cultural history of Western civilization that is made to serve as the framework, more, as the element of its articulation in which all of the terms we have been discussing, by way of example, in connection with Greek philosophy, find their unique and definite position. It is impossible to properly and completely understand this experience without following the line of reasoning that Greek thought has devoted to it. Moreover, the distinction of human being cannot be grasped without the inclusion of Christian thought and that of the modern and the post/modern age, the latter of which is being built as we speak. To comprehend this experience we must study all three Epochs, the First, the Second, *and* the Third as well as the Post/Modern era that serves as our death-defying jumping-off point.

In the scheme and the logotectonic of all things thought, each thinker's accomplishment is acknowledged for the difference she or he made in the whole, for the distinction that his or her insight has contributed to the entirety. Not one is excluded. Not one. For our job is to put each contribution into perspective and that means to place each thought in relationship to every thought that has ever been thought and recorded in history. Of course, some thoughts have been lost or nearly so – in that case we must reconstruct the train of thought as best we can with the pieces and hints that are still available to us; the great majority of contributions however, especially if we consider contemporary thinkers' output, have made no *distinctive*, no *principal* difference in terms of the scheme of all things thought. They are merely derivative, epigonic and a particular thinker's popularity at a particular time or place is no guarantee of significance.

This should not be taken as a hurtful condemnation or even as a belittling dismissal of their efforts. There have, in fact, been very few thinkers and poets (again, poets?) that have succeeded in making a difference in the scheme of all things thought. Very, very few. So let us, without condescension, also applaud the philosophical *corps de ballet* and make an effort to find for each of its members a place in that scheme as well!

Minor thinkers of the world, let us not despair! Each of us has an acknowledged role to play in the forum of public discourse – our papers and speeches, our books and blogs, our lectures and our conversations with friends and family, with students, all do indeed do service to the enterprise of thought; our efforts have perhaps inspired some thoughtfulness here or there where oblivion is wont to reign, have sung praises for such liberal attitudes as favour lively discussion, have actively furthered critique that challenges pernicious dogma, have brought to light obscurity, have vied to focus distraction, have borne and sought to pass on the philosophical torch....

To this end, namely towards the fostering of a more exact *science* of thought, we propose the following three laws of reason's latest late/modern project to guide our research – call it a renewed, a logotectonic *philology* – namely first the acknowledged scientific ***precept of objectivity***. The need for this axiom is founded upon the observation that thinkers throughout the history of thought have tended to find fault in the thought of their precursors. It is a familiar exercise in traditional philosophical discourse that while a thinker introduces his or her views, those of other thinkers are subject to a critique intended to indicate where their progenitors have gone wrong and why they are mistaken.

One way you could carry out your refutation is to denounce an "obviously fallacious" view that is still being entertained "in some quarters" in deference to its honorary status as "traditional" or "classical" and then either to attack it as such or else to impute it to your opponent as a "central" thesis in the latter's thinking endeavour. We might call this the *beating-the-dead-horse* argument, while another well-known and related strategy would be to present the offending position in its weakest form and then show how it can be handily refuted as indicative of the fact that its weakness pertains not to this misrepresentation but rather to its own inherent insubstantiality.

Such an approach has often been called the *straw man* or the *Aunt Sally* argument.

The standpoint of objectivity appealed to by this first precept was first expressed by Hegel in part II of his *Science of Logic* i.e. *Subjective Logic or the Doctrine of Concept*. He said that a "genuine refutation must engage the opponent's force and position itself within the purview of his strength; attacking him from a point of view extraneous to that defining the domain of his project...does not serve the purpose.... The only proper refutation of a position...consists therefore in acknowledging that it is essential and necessary but that its standpoint is self-severally distinguished from itself when set within the scope of a wider framework" of reflection.

> *Die wahrhafte Widerlegung muß in die Kraft des Gegners eingehen und sich in den Umkreis seiner Stärke stellen; ihn außerhalb seiner selbst anzugreifen...wo er nicht ist, fördert die Sache nicht. Die einzige Widerlegung... kann daher nur darin bestehen, sein Standpunkt zuerst als wesentlich und notwendig anerkannt werde, daß aber zweitens dieser Standpunkt aus sich selbst auf den höheren gehoben werde.*[8]

Contemporary thinkers trained in and adept at the "critical approach," must deem this precept strikingly misguided. For this state of affairs of philosophical discourse would mean that the pre-eminent challenge facing the thinker is in fact neither to "disagree" nor to "agree" – as one critical thinker considering another thinker's doctrines would normally be expected to – with what has been proposed. But what else are we supposed to do? How else are we supposed to actively participate in a thinker's reasoning if the principle of objectivity enjoins us to refrain both from attacking and from defending that thinker's doctrines and conclusions, invalidating or perpetuating theories, unearthing assumptions thought senseless or celebrating supposedly plausible ones while either innovating the verbal repertoire of one's own idioms to accommodate an approved doctrine or else roundly flouting the patent nonsense and insignificant speech that former philosophers, even the very best names among them, inexplicably fell prey to.

Does not this consequence seem preposterous? Certainly the philosophers of old were avid in their attack of other thinkers' proposals.

---

[8] cf. Hegel, Die Wissenschaft der Logik [Die Lehre vom Begriff (1816)], p. 10, lines 16-20.

Consider Aristotle's rejection of Plato's ideas; Socrates' rejection of the sophists; Gorgias' refutation of Parmenides, the Eleatics challenge to the cosmologists. And of course Heraclitus even dared to criticize Homer, the teacher of the Greeks – every great teacher falls at the patricidal hands of a great pupil. And does not Christian religion mark the death of Greek philosophy, the Humanity of Human Being contradict the glory of the Godhead's Trinity?

Here is the crux: Are not thoughts and ideas essentially exclusionary? In principle, you cannot reasonably maintain two without subjugating, assimilating, one to the other in an anesthetizing synthesis or confounding symmetrization – you have to get off the fence, friend, and decide, commit, take a stance, make a statement, raise a banner and defend with aplomb (if not a bomb) your position against those opposed to your gang and guild, declare yourself as friend or foe to fellow friends and foes.

Ideas don't blend or mend. And as Hölderlin sings in the hymn *Das Einzige* (The Sole and Only One), from his *Vaterländischen Gesänge* (Hymns of Fatherland), "...serving one I miss the other."

> ...dien ich einem, mir/Das andere fehlet.[9]

For does not *grace* contradict nature and *nature* grace? Does not *fate* contradict freedom, *freedom* liberty, *liberty* justice, *justice* mercy, and again does not *faith* gainsay knowledge, *religion* overthrow science, *morality* drub conception? Do we not see the *good* clobber the right, the *right* smite might, *beauty* trump truth and *fact* fiction, *possibility* whip reality, *practice* theory and vice versa? Does not selfish *ipseity* lick identity and necessity, and *unity* discontinuity, *physis* upset nomos and *culture* nature, the *ear* best the eye and, then again, the *eye* worst the ear, the Greek trounce the *Jew*, the Jew the *Greek*, the *Union* defeat the Family and the *Family* of the individual come before the government of the Union? Is not, has not been, will not be the *Christian* and the *Muslim* fashions of piety, forever locked in deadly fratricidal hate, each perpetually, principally vanquished by and vanquishing the other? And what of the so-called post/moderns – have they not "unmasked," "debunked," "deflated," named and shamed, traditional philosophical thought as Euro-eschato-helio-historico-onto-logo-topo-techno-teleo-theo-ethno-anthropo-semanto-phono-ocular-phallocentrism? With a view to the strife between orthodoxy and heresy, scholastic schisms, crusades and inquisitions, sectarian altercation and the latter-day battle of

---

[9] Hölderlin, *Große Stuttgarter Hölderlin-Ausgabe* [GSA], II.1, p.158, lines 48-49.

the sexes and the cultures, not to mention the perennial iconoclasm of youth and the young at heart – how could both sides even entertain the notion that their conflict is a quibble over designations, over cognomens for their pets, over scarfs, foreskin, and food, relic bones and poems, battles pitched over ceremonial plots of dirt on the earth, mats, planks with contests in sitting, kneeling, and squatting thereupon, a quarrel about cups and knives of animal, of human sacrifice, of tall tales, high white-washed walls or daubed, stained in blood blues and red of self-slaughter, a quarrel about the size of spired erections and, therein, a squabbling about ritualistic words that, in the over-eagerness of their zealots, are mindlessly mumbled or else with a warning shriek ejaculated as the expense of spirit in a waste of shame?

Yes, and what about the march of scientific advancement? What about that supposedly benignant progress from primitive notions to the clarity of the concept, from the velvet pillow and the silver platter of solemn conservatism to the lacerating edge of avant-garde modernity?

Do we not want to take sides, join and then seize the club? Or else rebel and reject, deplore and demolish? For we are saying not only that there is no cause for essential dissent, there is, moreover, no *reasoned* license or allowance of the true believer's, the acolyte's, obsequies towards one principle in exclusion of all others. There is just the occupation of reason with reason or not, but not right or wrong reason and reasons. Is it true that if we commit to such a precept, we are forced to surrender our ease of a particular standpoint with regards to a favorite ideology, a preferred dogma, a commodious community of initiates? Why, how dreadfully dull and rational it all must be, how terribly "scientific," how solemnly subdued and sober, how...well,...square! Indeed, the ascetic virtues of yore, especially that of sobriety and temperance, even celibacy, with their quaintly antiquated air, might be invigorated here, in this context, with this philology, by marshaling their cardinal forces under the banner of a new maxim, i.e. resist the sweet surrender of thought's native chastity to promiscuous congress with any one worldview, language, or religion.

Let this precept of objectivity be the sacrament of purity for *our* nun and monk: the mortification of their flesh is to love no particular thought more than another and none more than thought itself – for thought's sake to love, to the extent we are able, all thoughts equally in their community and to hate none, fostering thus their anthology, watering this garden of delight, every root and bud, with recognition and appreciation for how each flower and each fruit, each in its own way, makes (or at least has tried to make) a worthy contribution in the on-going endeavor of distinguishing the destiny of human being. For this distinction is the *last* thought of all...as well as the very first; it is, moreover the end and the origin of every thought on sanctity, on religion, on civilization, on culture. For as Schiller assures us in his introductory essay *Über den Gebrauch des Chors in der Tragödie* (The Use of the Chorus in Tragedy) to the play *Die Braut von Messina* (The Bride from Messina): "under the mantle of all religions lies "religion" itself, the idea of a distinguished being that poetic thought, the Builder, ought to be permitted to express in terms which are, with respect to the particular case, the most convenient and the most suitable."

> *Unter der Hülle aller Religionen liegt die Religion selbst, die Idee eines Göttlichen, und es muß dem Dichter erlaubt sein, dieses auszusprechen, in welcher Form er jedesmal am bequemsten und am treffendsten findet.*[10]

For imagine just such a "sanctity," "religion," "culture" the first precept of which posits that it is the capacity and the destiny of human being to step back from every *particular* thought, to review objectively every sanctity, every religion, every culture and, from this standpoint of "unbelonging" and exile, in complete detachment and abstraction, even while inhabiting the desert of this quintessential ΕΠΟΞΗ (epoch), to judge their merits *objectively* with regards to a given principle, measuring them against the criteria of pure reason, such reason namely as is always and permanently distinct from any given, accepted, or established sanctity, religion, or culture, from every name of renown and denomination. What sort of "culture" would that be, a culture "without" all culture? Where if not in this transcendent *general* could we worldly corporals hope to find the captain of true judicious tolerance that is neither indulgent, nor negligent? No, ideas don't bend or blend...but perhaps we can therefore all the better build with them and raise a monumental edifice that is resplendent in their tessellate patterns in which each thought is a unique stone and each stone a gem of brilliance.

Thus, complementing the dictum of objectivity that prohibits our cohabitation with any particular school of thought or thinker to the exclusion of another or others, we posit the precept of the **topology of principles** which imposes upon us the requirement to presume that every thinker's argument is essentially cogent when placed into the wider framework of reasoning to which it belongs and understood with regards to

---

[10] Schiller, *National Ausgabe* [NA], X.15.224-27.

the overall principle upon which this framework is based as well as on the immediate principle governing that particular train of thought wherein it occurs. Our task is therefore to determine what that principle is and how, given this principle, the issue at stake requires the position and justifies the argument advocated by the thinker in accordance with it. No thinker whose work the philosophical tradition has bequeathed to our care and regard can be *essentially* mistaken, not, at least, if we consider the *whole* story of thought with regards to its principles, which is not the same as giving an account of "the history of philosophy without any gaps."[11]

Salient evidence of the application of this maxim for the better apprehension of ideas is the doctrine of the Three Epochs of our philosophical tradition – the *Greek*, the *Christian* and that of Enlightenment which, together with the tradition-critical animus peculiar to mundane Modernity and its latter day linguistic turn in the conceits of Post/modern persuasion, form the overall framework of Occidental thinking that Boeder has conceptualized as constituted by the totalities of *Tradition* (Geschichte), *World* (Welt), and *Language* (Sprache).[12]

Every thought of every thinker can be located within this framework; each of these three totalities consists of three triads of thinkers conceived of as accomplishing together the elaboration of the particular principle that occasioned their individual projects and as giving rise to the train of thought that can be concatenated of each thinker's main ideas constituting a unique position within the line of reasoning that ensued in consequence of the task assigned to thought by the principle and forming thus an association of

---

[11] In his podcast series of this name, Peter Adamson has undertaken to examine "the ideas, lives and historical context of the major philosophers as well as the lesser-known figures of the tradition." See http://www.historyofphilosophy.net/

[12] Boeder began with the conception of the Western philosophical tradition by delineating a topology of metaphysical thought (*Topologie der Metaphysik*, Freiburg/München 1980), proceeded then to explicate the orders of Modernity in *Die Vernunftgefüge der Modernen* (Freiburg/München 1988), and completed his topological project with a treatment of post/modern thinking in *Die Installationen der Submoderne* (Würzburg 2006). For an elucidation of the aforementioned terms of totality, namely of *Tradition, World,* and *Language* and a demonstration of how they facilitate the elaboration of a scheme of all things thought, see the collection of his essays and lectures on this topic in *Seditions*, ed. Marcus Brainard, New York 1997.

ideas that is not a brainstorm's psychological cluster but rather a logical figure of deduction in a sense that we will explore later.

Hence, thinkers always articulate a position, *their* position within a larger framework of thought that is not *theirs* at all but rather one to which they, unbeknownst to themselves, contribute towards the completion of; in this collaboration, each associate received his or her own appointed task in accordance with the exigencies that previous thoughts tend to place upon subsequent thoughts. A distinction once made cannot be undone and every distinction is uniquely determined and thus only decidable within the framework of the other distinctions made within that association that is itself located in a further system of distinctions in which a particular epoch of thought has been defined.

Thus our investigation cannot begin by addressing any of the familiar philosophical problems and controversies that have been abstracted from philosophical discourse in the past and then posited as general recurring unresolved issues foremost of which are surely the so-called one/many, mind/body, free will/determinism, form/matter, objectivity/subjectivity, name/thing dichotomies which seem to be at the heart of a great many other debates like those pertaining to rationalism and empiricism, realism and nominalism, positivism and relativism, to name just a few, all of which group various doctrines and views regarding such problems into categories of solutions that can be then studied in their own right, thoughts about thoughts, for the sake of a tidier labelling and ordering of schools and styles some of which have gained the status of "science" like epistemology, logic, ontology, the philosophies of science, of language, of the mind, of law or religion, or at least the secondary prestige of an academically sanctioned school promulgating its very own worldview, ideology, and concomitant methodology, like skepticism or idealism, pragmatism or phenomenology, existentialism or analytical philosophy.

Now obviously there is nothing wrong with being an existentialist or a phenomenologist, advocating pragmatism over idealism, singing accolades to skepticism, preferring to read books on ethics to those written on logic, disparaging studies devoted to the mind while appreciating those that investigate politics. It is only natural that some folks prefer to think about *beauty* in art, some about *God* and/or the *gods* of religion; some are intrigued by the notion of *justice* others by that of *being*. How about doing research on what a *society* is or a *business organization*? Or analyzing the concept of *culture*. Become a historian if you like *history*, an epistemologist if you seek to know more about *knowledge* and dabble in a little bit of everything, in other words, take up *literature theory*, if you, in your salad days, wanted to study *truth*, only to discover at the crust end of your ways that, unfortunately or happily, there is, in fact, *for the reader*, no truth, no human or any other kind of being, no world, and *truth* least of all, but rather just....text? Now that is indeed a thought! And, yes, even this result has its proper place of honor in the scheme of all things thought!

Thus the precept of the topology of principles would, for example, dissuade us from contenting ourselves with the investigation of the views held by noteworthy philosophers concerning the mind/body issue or to venture to explode it as a myth, as a ghost in a machine, say, or, alternatively, to arbitrate a reunification of estranged issues, perhaps forging a coalition between opposing schools of thought.

And don't you dare ask, supposedly following in Socrates' footsteps, such questions as: "What is *Virtue*?" "What is *Justice*?" Don't you dare ask "What is *Freedom*?" "What is *God*?" "What is *Spirit*?" "What is *Truth*?" Are you looking for the definition of word? Try a dictionary, friend. For we cannot assume a continuity of meaning from Homer till today with regards to the translation of names, of any names, across the barrier of time or language. We are advised not to assume (at the risk of making an *ass* of *u* and *me*) that Plato was talking about the same thing when he said "*ΙΔΕΑ*" or "*ΦΥΣΙΣ*" as when Hegel said "*Idee*," or "*Natur*" although we might translate both with the English words "*idea*," and "*nature*" respectively or that the difference between these terms would be accessible to some all-encompassing program of hermeneutics that seeks to reactivate ancient ideas in modern terms in the hope of making them palatable and salubrious for a modern audience.

This leads us to the third axiom that we posit, namely the precept of the ***primacy of insight*** which stipulates that our starting point is and must be what we know; we begin not with a question or questions but rather with an answer and an insight into a principle that has been known and articulated again and again for thousands of years; founding thus a tradition upon the diligent recollection of these answers and the unique answer corresponding to that self-several principle in richly evocative terms that reflect the depth and breadth of human experience with regards to it – that is the business of philosophy for us, for a science we will call, in a new sense the details of which have yet to be clarified, *philology*, the discerning, fostering love of these ancient languages of thought.

Indeed, reading works of poetic and philosophical literature through the eyes of such a philology is a unique experience in that we are required to know *before* we begin to read what has always already been spoken in what is going to be said, perhaps for the first time, in that particular way by that particular author in that particular moment of history. In other words, with regards to the works of philosophy and poetry we will study in the following, we must know the principle (A) before we can consider the topic (B) and the topic before we can appreciate the arguments (C). And in order to do justice to a single argument in a thinker's train of thought, we must have previously comprehended every principle known to the Occidental history of thought in its entirety from its remotest origins till now, today. Is this insane, or merely impossible? Let us begin to find out.

We must start with what we know. We must start with what we know and then, upon the certainty and clarity of this insight, build a monument to our sudden or gradually dawning realization and delight that thought, in its perfect simplicity and utter immensity, is, in fact, quite beyond anything we have ever known.

The First Part
The Topology of Principles

I. The Self-Severalty of Pure Reason

A. The Principle of Drawing a Distinction

13. Reason Distinguished in itself and from itself

Pure reason, then, as it seems, has become our topic now, if we decide to give the issue in question, our cause and theme, namely the *distinction of human being*, that preliminary name – though, of course, "distinction of human being" is also a name, neither better, nor worse than the term "ΛΟΓΟΣ," however you prefer to translate it, whether as *language, speech, writing*, or even *literature* – and run the risk of misleading the reader at the outset. For "reason" though but a name, is an elucidative one, rich in connotations, rich with history, goading prejudices, inviting as well as challenging preconceptions, misconceptions.

In spite of these dire risks, we will put it nonetheless – misnomer, pseudonym though it may appear to be to many – provisionally at least, for the distinctive sign and signature of human being, of which it has traditionally and regularly been predicated. It remains for the time being our term of choice for concisely designating the train of thought about thought that thought itself *is* the topology of which we intend now to investigate in detail, principle by principle.

For in keeping with this science's logotectonic methodology, which we will exam in due course, in truth, any term will do – whether it has been garnered from our philosophical tradition (as the term "reason" has") or else borrowed from literature and poetry and even occasionally from so-called contemporary pop-culture to the extent that the inventions of its speech practice might provide us with a felicitous turn of word or phrase of suitable richness and colour to vividly highlight aspects of the distinction in question with regards to the principles upon which our newfangled "philological" science is based.

Whatever its drawbacks, at least the appellation "*pure* thought" or "*pure* reason*," clearly distinguishes it, as we have seen, from *mere* cognition, from sundry mental, biological, or merely physical (electrical) phenomena of the central nervous system, in other words, from thought as a specimen of the so-called physical sciences, but also from those sciences concerned more generally with diverse human or social phenomena in which thinking and ideas play a prominent role in connection with issues and quarrels and puzzles so familiar to philosophical and epistemological schools of thought, studies and theories regarding the human race, the human mind, human psychology, human ethnology, in a word – all sciences under the aegis of an all-encompassing natural history of man, i.e. anthropology. All of these sciences, whatever their merit, fertility, and application, are not the science of pure reason.

Thus, our study of the distinction of human being as *pure* reason is distinguished not only from the latter-day sciences of the origin, the function, and the products of man's mental industry, of which these sciences themselves are the self-sustaining, the "autopoetic," objects of inquiry, but all the more from the *instrumental* reason of technology, business, and politics, the particular sense of thought that, as we have said, is not directed at apprehending thought in and of itself, but rather such thought as tends to be preoccupied with everything else besides thought, in particular with the urgent real-life situations that emerge on a daily basis in an effort to make sense out of them, mustering and mastering them, finding to a given set of ends the most efficient means.

Finally, putting modern science, technical rationality, and their world aside and considering the achievements of reason in our occidental philosophical tradition, as Boeder has shown, the philological study of pure reason we are contemplating must also learn to distinguished it from its *natural* and *mundane* counterparts.[13] Natural reason studies thought as the workings of the human mind turned questioningly to the visible world, the unity of which is the proud achievement of its very own light, thereby establishing *science* in the first place with a view towards better apprehending the finitude of the human condition and human understanding with respect to the order of that universe, its beings as opposed to appearances, its external truth as opposed to the mere inward figment of the fantasy, the indivisible natural intellect as opposed to infinite

---

[13] For the difference between *Natural* and *Mundane* reason see Boeder's article "The Distinction of Reason" in *Seditions*, pp. 101-109.

divisible corporality, in *my* reflection of which knowledge *I* can perhaps, with some luck and good faith and cultivation, map out the realm of *my own* modest certainty; such natural reason can also be distinguished from mundane reason which purports to teach men in the flesh to become better men by attending to the cosmos of elemental contention, encouraging their accordance with the rational constitution of its order that determines the bearings of a dispassionate soul, and liberating them thus from the sphere of strife among individuals in the secluded retreat of a secure garden of their own choosing, ultimately, their own founding, as obedient subjects in the corporate body of a commonwealth that secures by coercive power their enduring peace – for thus is the difference between Physiological and Cosmological, Stoic and Epicurean, Cartesian and Hobbesian reason.

Hence, following Boeder, we again emphasize that pure thought is a topology of principles and not just one, an entire array of reasons and a configuration of these arrays comprising ratios of rationality, not just one conception, not just a single generic reason or one fixed idea, though there is, of course, the totalitarian reason of the one-track, monomaniacal mind as well, only too glad to assimilate all thought to its regime, to make of several reasons and different principles but a single one, its own. In the course of this study, we will hear of its device and take note of its empire, too, though a treatment of the *perversion* of reason must be reserved for a future enterprise. For now, we propose that "reason" is an excellent first name for the distinction of human being because it is, like this being, distinguished in itself and from itself.

14. The Entity of Identity

To the philosophies of *natural* and *mundane* reason, Boeder opposed philosophy in the strict sense of *philo-sophia*, which is the science of pure reason. For in contrast to their stance of dissent and rejection or else preemption and replacement regarding the present of an anterior insight and the recognition due precedent knowledge, *conceptual* reason or *metaphysics* has always fostered an enduring nearness to and acknowledgement of precisely just such a priority, which was called distinguished knowledge or *wisdom* (ΣΟΦΙΑ - sophia) – knowledge before all knowledge, the origin of knowledge. In accordance with the doctrine of the three Epochs of philosophical thought, metaphysics received and affirmed three principles, namely *Destiny – God – Freedom* as its three unique objects of speculation the conception of which led to the logical, moral, and aesthetic realization of pure reason as *thought thinking thought*.[14]

In what way does the admittedly odd, though eminently "philosophical" expression *thought thinking thought* provide us with an initial concept of our experience with the distinction of human being, the profound knowledge of which has been termed ΣΟΦΙΑ and through the reception of which reason acquired its purity in the first place, namely as that of the *Muses*, that of the *Holy Spirit* and that of the *Humanity of Human Being*? Similarly, we might ask in what way was Aristotle inspired by Homer, Augustine by the Apostle Paul, Kant by Rousseau – the one inspired to grasp freedom as the *autonomous law of self-respect*, the other the crucifixion of the Son of God as the *admonition of repentance in the humility of Christ*, and the third the apportionment of the Olympian kingdom as the *universe of distinguished beings* each abiding within the limits of their own determination under the first and best being of all, Zeus, *Nous* (the contemplative sight and insight of reason).

Let us therefore embark upon and participate in the intricate age-old endeavor of thought considering thought in the looking-glass of its own speculative gaze and, while taking into account the simple fact of such a thing as this, thought, which is, obviously, no thing at all, note, first of all, the most obvious property that it immediately presents to our intuition namely the peculiar twist of reflection's circularity.

Now circles, far from indicating a breakdown in our line of reasoning, offer us a useful model for indicating the literally *preposterous* relationship that presents itself when we consider what thought thinking thought entails. In his *Foundation of the Doctrine of Science in its Entirety* (1794), Fichte formulated its activity thus:

> The First Person posits itself and exists by virtue of simply positing itself through itself; and conversely: the First Person exists, and posits its being by virtue of simply being. It is, at the same time, the actor and the product of the action; the activity and that which is produced through the activity; act and fact are one and the same; and therefore this *I-am* is the expression of self-enacting being.

---

[14] cf. Boeder's article "Privilege of Presence," p. 90 and "Is Totalizing Thinking Totalitarian?" p. 254, Ibid.

> *Das Ich setzt sich selbst, und es ist, vermöge dieses bloßen Setzens durch sich selbst; und umgekehrt: das Ich ist, und es setzt sein Seyn, vermöge seines bloßen Seyns. - Es ist zugleich das Handelnde, und das Produkt der Handlung; das Thätige, und das, was durch die Thätigkeit hervorgebracht wird; Handlung und That sind Eins und ebendasselbe; und daher ist das: Ich bin, Ausdruck einer Thathandlung. (Fichte, Grundlage der gesamten Wissenschaftslehre, I p.96)*

As this train of thought makes evident, thought thinking about thought is not an exercise in "retrospection" in which we try to get at the contents of our psyche by thinking about our thoughts with a view to uncovering or becoming better attuned to our unspoken emotions, needs, and desires. It is the self-relative relationship of reflection itself that is at issue. Thought thinking thought is productive, it brings forth its own being and is, in this sense, *causa sui*. Think about it. How can anything, even "God," be the cause of itself?

Either it exists already before it begins with its production, meaning that something else must have been its cause (if indeed it has a cause, which it may not – it could, of course, have always been) and then it wouldn't be the cause of itself, or it cannot originate at all since, nothing to begin with prior to production, it would be nothing first and then have to bring itself forth into being afterwards. Clearly, it must *be* already in order to produce and if it is not there yet, it cannot bring itself into being by itself. But, again, how else could it be a product if it was not previously the producer and again how producer if it had not been previously produced? Is this train of thought logical? Something must *be* in order to *produce* and it must *produce* in order to *be*; without being, it cannot produce; without producing, it cannot be. In fact, there is but a single thing that could have this property. And it is no "thing" at all, nor is it "God." If we take Fichte's word for it, it is the only truly undecidable object, impossible *and* real – in one, the forming of being *and* the being formed.

Thought thinking thought requires that thought, the thinker, be both the thinking subject and the thought object, in other words, that the thinker be both inside and outside the train of thought, the train as well as the conductor, the conductor as well as the voyager, the voyage *and* the vehicle, the way *and* the end, the outcome of thought as well as the activity of thought from which thought first emerges being simultaneously the egg before the chicken and the chicken before the egg.

In the Third Epoch, the distinction of human being is conceived of specifically in terms of *self-knowing being* (Selbstbewußtsein) – in the train of thought that articulates this idea, self-relativity refers to the *nature* of human being, namely to such being that, by adopting the standpoint of absolute freedom and acting in accordance with it as the principle of pure reason, can perform this miracle of bringing forth its own self-determinate being. This being is what an *I* is and what we, as human beings, are destined to be. But isn't/aren't I always already an *I*? How can this singular *First Person*, the unique person that *I AM/IS*, be a destiny to myself? Am I not always already simply myself and the I who I am/is? A good question – Fichte's answer might come as a surprise. For he reminds us that "most people could more easily be led to believe that they are a piece of lava on the moon than a First Person."

> *Die meisten Menschen würden leichter dahin zu bringen seyn,*
> *sich für ein Stück Lava im Monde, als für ein Ich zu halten. (Ibid.*
> *p. 175, footnote)*

Apparently, there is more to the idea of our First Person than meets the untrained *I* of our everyday ego, looking out for number 1 and seeing nothing that is not itself but not the *"nothing"* that *is*, i.e. its *other* self, its better *Self.* And who, what is that?

The autonomy of humanity seems to be a principle predestined for self-relativity. After all, what if not our own self-knowing being could be properly called an entity of identity with which, thinking, we enter into a relationship with that greater SELF, and in accordance with which, building, as it were, we bring our *self* forth as the self-determined and self-determining being of freedom that I AM/IS?

But what about in the Second Epoch? Where could we find the self-relative entity of identity in an epoch devoted not to the self-knowing being of human nature but rather to the *glory of the Christian Godhead*? It must have something to do with the fact that this God is a *Trinity* of Persons. No deity in any culture, not even the Hebrew God of the Tanakh or the Islamic God of the Qur'ān, both of which are often indiscriminately identified with the Christian God, has been conceived of as being *triune.* This fact should make us thoughtful and spark discernment to mark differences rather than superficial similarities.

In the Augustinian Trinity we recognize this self-relationship in the relationship of nearness of the Son to the Father. Both are *God* and, at the same time, two unique *Persons*, unique in their connection to the procession of the Mission (we will consider these terms and how to build with them later). The first person is the begetter, the other is the begotten; the one is the engendering God, the being that brought forth God, the other is the being that God engendered. This relationship itself is the third *Person* of the Trinity, the Spirit, the Spirit of Love, where the term "love" expresses the intimacy of the relationship between the other two persons, the *self-relationship of filiality and paternity between the Father and Son who are one in Love (ΑΓΑΠΗ - agapē), in *dilectio*, which is the "Spirit" of the self-relationship as it is defined in the triune being of God, a unique being that consists entirely in the spirit of *giving*, the loving gift (*caritas*) of his own "self-knowledge," his self-approbation, in the form of his Word, his own glory imaged in the Son.

In this way the indivisibility of thought thinking thought can be rendered as the perfect accord of a shared knowledge, a shared blood, a shared heart, the third among three as the relationship of two that are, in it, nevertheless one, one and nevertheless three, one God and three persons, which, in their relationship show the entity of identity in a new light, namely in terms of consanguinity and affiliation, recreating thus the self-relativity that we have just become acquainted with in the productive principle of humanity, of My absolute freedom with respect to which *I* am/is the autonomous subject of and to Myself, in that of the practical principle of divine glory revealed in the act of the Son's self-subjugation under the will of his self-giving Father.

Finally, in the First Epoch, we turn with Parmenides to the conception of perfect being, namely to such being as *"is to be,"* (ΕΣΤΙ ΓΑΡ ΕΙΝΑΙ - 28 B 6.1)[15], in other words, *is* as it was destined or determined *to be*. In terms of the freedom of humanity and the glory of the triune God, the entity of identity is "personified," i.e. rendered as a personal relationship, a relationship of persons, the self-relativity of My "personality," namely Me, Myself, and I, on the one hand, and that of the personality of the Trinity, namely the Father, the Son, and the Spirit, on the other. Greek conception shows us, however, that the self-relativity of the principle need not be taken personally. The logical form of the entity of identity is rendered most simply as the relationship of *being*, which is the distinction between THE WAY IT IS and THE WAY IT SHOULD BE, the identity inherent in difference.

Plato teaches how every being is defined with regards to its determination, to "what it is." A being's self-several *identity* in difference determines precisely what it is "meant" or "supposed" to be. This determination is

---

[15] *Die Fragmente der Vorsokratiker*, ed. H. Diels/W. Kranz [DK], Berlin 1961.

known, is an object of prior insight and recognition, hence, the principle's "idea." Bringing out this non-entropic identity in its most familiar "philosophical" form of a question, we might ask for example, as does Grönemeyer in his well-known song *Männer*, "When is a man a man?"

Wann ist ein Mann ein Mann?

Clearly, in this question, the word "man" has two different meanings and it is the status of the relationship of these meanings that is being called into question. The first term refers to a particular man, an individual that the second term is predicated of. The second term therefore refers to the idea of what a man should be. In other words, the question asks, "when is a particular man not just any sort of man but, specifically, a *good* man, a *real* man, a *true* man, a man the way he was supposed, destined, to be or when is *a* man a perfect man? And the answer? The philosophical answer is: When he is a *MAN*. In other words, when this man standing before us corresponds to the image or the model, the paradigm or the pattern, the *idea* of the man. Then we have *a* MAN in the self-several determinacy of excellence that emerges when a being conforms to what it was destined to be, its nature, i.e. its ΦΥΣΙΣ (physis). In general, Greek thought always answers this question regarding why a thing is the way it is as Plato famously did (Greater Hippias 287c):

TA KAΛA TΩI KAΛA KAΛA (Ta kala tōi kala kala)

The (particular) beautiful (being) is beautiful
through (the idea of) Beauty (in which it participates).

The Greeks considered the identity of a thing, its nature, as that which determines what it should be and then measured each individual, each particular thing, against this *specific* entity of identity, the *chair*, the *man*, any being, with respect to itself (its self-several *SELF*, but now that of the *Third Person* and not that of the *First Person*), i.e. to its essence, to its idea, its "true" being of which it is *indicative*, in a very rich sense, i.e. in the ancient Greek, the Homeric sense, of this word that we will consider later as that of DIKH (dikē), the dictate of the determinative principle in Greek thought, namely ΘΕΜΙΣ (themis), which two terms together refer to the predetermined apportionment that all beings – mortal *and* immortal – have already received, always already "know," and subsequently must evince compliance with in the studied excellence of word and deed.

These three visions of the self-relationship, the *self-determination of human being*, the *Holy Spirit of divine being*, the *perfection of just being* were uniquely known and explored in the Third, the Second, and the First

Epochs respectively. They place the entity of identity in difference we are considering into the scheme of all things thought wherein it attains the historical determinacy of an epochal principle, couching the experience of the distinctive character of human being in the element of a particular logico-poetic, a "mythological," form that presents the concept of thought thinking thought as the issue at stake within that epoch.

As the three visions of the self-several *entity of identity*, our Verum and our *T*, suggest, the experience of the distinction of human being they present is one of completion, reciprocity, and symmetry. The two terms of the relationship *a* = *a* are perfectly congruous in a way that only their self-relationship can guarantee. After all, what could be more completely in accord with *a*, whatever it may be, than *a itself*? For this reason, this relationship of self-relativity has always been seen as paradigmatic, a model or image of how two can be most perfectly one, namely when they are the same, not merely qualitatively but also numerically.

If *truth* has often been defined as a state of correspondence between the thought and the thing, then, apparently, there can be no perfect truth except when the thing thought and the thinking are essentially one. The image and vision of this perfect state in which *verity* is *certainty* and *certainty* is *verity* must be that of the entity of identity (a = a); precisely this is the self-relationship of contemplative reason, thought thinking thought, our first conception of the experience we have termed the distinction of human being, and the principle at issue in metaphysics from Parmenides' precept that "the same is to be thought and to be..."

TO...AYTO NOEIN EΣTIN TE KAI EINAI (DK 28 B3)

...to Hegel's famous diptych in the preface of his *Grundlinien der Philosophie des Rechts* (Principles of the Philosophy of Right):[16]

Was vernünftig ist, das ist wirklich;
und was wirklich ist, das ist vernünftig

(what is rational is real; what is real is rational)

In this entity alone do we find knowledge and being to be one and the same, that is to say in the *immediacy* of their self-relationship. Thus, in the *theoretical* sense, pure reason is the object of study *and* the thinking act, i.e. the insight of contemplation. And it is for this reason that thought is thought to be the only object that we can truly, completely, and immediately *know*,

---

[16] Hegel, *Werke in 20 Bänden*, VII p. 11.

human being the only being whose nature is perfectly transparent to reason, which is the sign and the seal of human being, *humanity*, in the epoch of freedom; similarly *perfect being* is transparent to *intellect* (ΝΟΥΣ), being one with it, the *Son of God* alone completely and perfectly known by and knowing the *Father*, for in the immediacy of thought alone are knowing and being, the open skies and the hospitable earth, a perfectly contiguous firmament, the latter bringing forth the former as its own sheltering semblance, as Hesiod in his *Theogony* (126-7) taught of Gaia (mother earth) and Ouranos (the celestial vault) – the two fundaments of immortal dwelling.

ΓΑΙΑ ΔΕ ΤΟΙ ΠΡΩΤΟΝ ΜΕΝ ΕΓΕΙΝΑΤΟ ΙΣΟΝ ΕΩΥΤΗ
ΟΥΡΑΝΟΝ ΑΣΤΕΡΟΕΝΘ ' ΙΝΑ ΜΙΝ ΠΕΡΙ ΠΑΝΤΑ ΚΑΛΥΠΤΟΙ

(Gaia first brought forth her equal, starry Uranus, that he might nestle her opulence.)

This is what the *intuition* of intellect is, namely distinguished sight, the transparence to thought of thought itself, which, with respect to the natural world and the boundless earth that grounds everything else *not* thought, is above and beyond, unearthly, supernatural, extra-terrestrial, celestial or else interior, secluded, subterranean, substantial, the inward core and hidden inner heart beneath the skin and bone facade of flesh, of the mortal coil, of the iridescent play of appearances, and of transient elemental materiality.

Thus far we have considered the entity of identity as the completely intelligible being of contemplation, the being of ΘΕΟΡΙΑ, the being seen and seeing. But the image of thought thinking thought is not only a *theoretical* entity, namely the vision of an accord between the thing and the thought – *the thing* with respect to its nature and destiny, to what it was supposed to be, *the thought* with respect to the perfect penetration of intuitive intellect into that nature and essence – but also a practical one, a *practical* ideal and model or aim for action. For the identity *a = a* also represents the fulfillment of a principle and, through the ensuing process of development, the completion of the determination that had arisen as a result of the initial discrepancy between THE WAY IT IS and THE WAY IT SHOULD BE.

In the sphere of practical judgment, this initial discrepancy is, then, through action, resolved into complete and perfect agreement. What better image can we propose for the unity, the correspondence, the probity of the alignment ultimately attained, than that of identity in difference, the self-relationship of reason? For consider action and the causality of the will that posits a vision of its objective as the goal towards which it strives. The state of discrepancy in hunger or thirst, for example, compels the drive of action towards the regaining of the previous tranquil state of satisfaction that had been disrupted when the breach between the IS and the OUGHT emerged. And here in this vision of *precedent* self-accord and agreement characterizing the prior state, we recognize the *subsequent* objective as a destiny to be fulfilled, the lost Paradise now past but subsequently remembered as the envisioned and projected advent of the Heaven hereafter in the transformation of an indeterminate actuality. The principle is no longer merely the theoretical object of insight and intellect, a *nature*; it is now moreover a practical object, an objective that is to be *put into effect* in a transforming act of realization, the reaching of a *destination*, the fulfilment of a *destiny*. Thus the entity of identity is not merely the concept of a being and a seeing, thought, the **Thinker** as well as the object of thought, but also the conception of an action and a striving, practical thought, the **Actor** of the will as well as the objective of action, the goal, the *ideal*. Yes, there is indeed a very clear difference between the contemplation of the perfection of being and that of the accomplishment of desire, and though they both may be sought and found, a very marked distinction between the *truth* of what is *one and complete in itself* and that of what is *good*, between *recognition* and *return*, *comprehension* and *achievement*, between a *notion* and a *plan*, a *concept* and a *purpose*, *insight* and *fulfillment*, *conformity* and *reconciliation*, *entirety* and *contract*, *ratiocination* and *perduration*, between what something *is to be*, its *nature* and what something *is to do*, its *mission*. In each of these pairs of designations, the former is the *logical* truth, the latter the *moral* one.

Reviewing the signature terms in which our concept of thought's self-relativity has thus far been articulated, one might easily jump to the conclusion that the distinction of human being is the experience of a remarkable equanimity, even unanimity. Surely, the relationship of identity is the very image of concurrence and two who are, in their relationship with one another, identical, would form the most perfect union, the unity of which is a symbol of what is one and a whole yet distinguished in itself. We have beheld the three traditional visions of this, our experience of pure thought's *tautology* ($\top$), its perfect intelligibility and transparency to itself, taken as an image of peace and quiet – which is oftentimes, but ought not be, reduced to the self-referential of awareness of personal introspection – i.e. either the certitude of self-knowing being, namely that of me with respect to Myself, my best Self, my humanity, or that of the shared knowledge of the Christian Godhead and the Spirit of the filial, the paternal love of the Father for the Son and the Son for the Father, in both versions or renditions of this experience achieving therein, the consistency of proof *and* the accord of agreement, intuition *and* realization, possession *and* destination, a home *and* a home-coming. In an attempt to evoke this diversity of experience in the concision of one designation, let us represent the self-relativity of the entity of identity, the curved space of our unanimous soul, in the following diagram, our *Figure 1*:

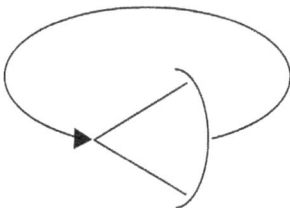

Figure 1: The Entity of Identity (⊤)

It depicts the identity of pure reason's self-relativity in the form of a self-seeing being, an eye the gaze of which, in a turn and return, reflects back upon itself, arriving at its own recognition, performing, in one complete circuit its, own realization, a seeing eye to I. Thus we might perceive in the redounding bend and swerve of its curve the end point of one revolution that is thought's, the Thinker's, the Actor's, and the Builder's, the happy ending of their shared enterprise in which the mind, returning to itself, in the theory and the practice of thought, concludes its constitutional in comprehension and in the fulfillment of purpose and takes repose in the threefold reaffirmation of pure reason's unique, and uniquely poetic, self-possession. This is the sense of the arrowhead of thought's reaching, and reach for, truth, culminating in the "touch" – THIΓEIN (thigein) as Aristotle calls it (Met. 1051b 24) – the contiguity of what is utterly indivisible and immediate and yet still distinguished in itself in our experience of it, the propinquity of thought to thought, the continuity of intellect with regards to the intelligible.

So much to the endpoint in serenity. But what now of the leaping point of departure that marks the origin of the arc that is thought's flight? For, our experience of the mark of human being is not merely the making of an end and a consummation of its measured course, it is also inaugural, the experience of a start, even a shock, unanticipated, unconditional. It is the prior and the original principle of thought, the principle as *absolute* that sets reasoning on its way in the first place. For the issue at stake when talking about principles with regard to the distinction of human being is, sad to say, not so much soulful contentment as it is the animus of contention, namely the experience of a crisis, which is the initial discontinuity prevailing between THE WAY IT IS and THE WAY IT SHOULD BE.

Thus far, in our considerations pertaining to the entity of identity, we have failed to account for the obvious fact that, at least for the most part in our lives, thought thinking thought, the concept of the experience of the mark of human being, is an *ideal*, we might even go so far to say in our discontent, *just* an idea, a vision – if not a mirage – the *being* that we place ourselves in relationship to, in theory and in practice, as indicative of THE WAY IT SHOULD BE **in contrast to** THE WAY IT IS. For as we all know, first, beings conform more or less, and mostly less, to their being, to the idea of *what they are*, theoretically, *supposed to be* and, second, they tend to run awry of practical principles, the morals of action. Alas, *nothing is perfect* we sigh in bitter disappointment or in resigned relief in response to the anguish we experience when we mind the gap between the IS and the OUGHT, rather than ignoring it, in our surroundings and in the general state of affairs, in the condition and situation of things, animal, vegetable, and mineral, in other words, when we pose the question of the propriety of words and deeds, both our own and others', in a world and then conclude *nothing is perfect*.

Have we not all, on occasion, missed the boat, flubbed the dub, fell from slip of tongue or toe, had too much, arrived too late, done too little, left too soon, and have had to deal with all manner of misses that shortage and excess might impose – too hot, too cold; too young, too old; too low, too high; too far, too nigh; yes, it is hard to get it just right and the list of what can go wrong is surely longer than long.

This state of affairs of fault and deficiency, of failure and infirmity, of damage and deformity, so familiar to us all, precariously founded, as it is, not on the congruity but rather on the divergence of THE WAY IT IS and THE WAY IT SHOULD BE, gives rise to the notion of an *impossible* entity that stands not in harmony but rather in conflict with itself, the self-relativity of which is not one of *coincidence (a=a)* but rather *disparity (a≠a)* or, even more vividly put, to bring out its essential "absurdity," self-dissimilar *paradox (a = ¬ a)*.

Now, I ask you, friends of coherence, consider this aporia of the impossible, the famously "contaminated" being of a "hyper-reflection:" how could anything be different than itself? Look out of the window, each thing that you see out there is different from each other thing, even two trees are different from each other and even here inside, though the four chairs placed around the dinner table are the same, they are nevertheless different from each other. But how could they be different from themselves? A particular chair from itself and a particular tree, that one right over there, different from itself?

And what of ourselves? Are you not indubitably you, a pure object in the eyes of your cat? Is there any way imaginable that you could not be you or I conceivably not be me or anything somehow not be itself, whatever else you or I or it, in any possible world, are not, am not, is not? It doesn't seem likely, does it? And yet the question of the distinctive character, the letter, of human being, has arisen, though now no longer regarding the experience of the entity of identity, our Verum, but rather regarding that of its disparity, the *Falsum* ($\perp$), which is, moreover, according to Joyce (FW 170.4-5), "the first riddle of the universe: asking

> *when is a man not a man?"*

And do I not often say, sing, perhaps when I am sad or glad, or in some other state of mind that, despite the apparent improbability of it, "I'm not myself tonight?"

This then is the issue: The mark of human being is not only the experience of the coherence of thought's gaze in seeking out and finding thought, immediate, complete, and perfect in the well-rounded self-relativity of its identity, an experience of unity, but also the experience of a breech and a discontinuity, which is in fact, as we shall see, the very source and origin of thought – the **0**, Frege's famous contradictory function *"different from itself,"* as the first term in the sequence, the null prefiguring the **1**, which is the unity that follows from it.[17] For the contemplation and speculation of

---

[17] So Frege: "Null ist die Anzahl, welche dem Begriffe 'sich selbst ungleich' zukommt." *Die Grundlagen der Arithmetik. Eine logische-mathematische Untersuchung über den Begriff der Zahl*, §74. This null is what we will refer to with the slashed zero glyph (actually the sign for the empty set); as an interpretation of the event of drawing the first distinction, this aboriginal O is thought to stand for the empty indeterminacy of the "Outside," an idea much made of in post/modern discourse on alterity, for example in the works of Levinas, Blanchot, Bataille, and Foucault, to name only a few of its most prominent authors, whose "passion for what is Without" (*la passion du Dehors*), is revealed by the emphasis they place on notions connoting **excess**, viz. what is *supererogatory, out of play*, and, in general, *beyond the horizon* of previously established determinations and priorities – *hors d'oeuvre, hors de jeu, hors de l'horizon*, etc. More on this later.

pure reason or thought thinking thought, the "slashed zero" reveals the principle of thought's start, too, and not only its end, which is the entity of identity, our won being, our 1 thought; thought thinking thought is, originally, the concept of the experience of *critical self-reflection* and the travail, the slash, of *self-severalty*, our lost being, our lost cause, our Ø and our **Ө**.

15. The Experience of Self-Severalty

What do we see when we contemplate the first principle and the determination of thought as our cause and issue? What primordial experience is thought's inception? This: We see that reason lifts and drops a question on our plate, leaves a mark, its tell-tale sign, on the forehead of our lives. Thought makes a difference *to*, and more generally, *in* human being, inscribing upon this and every being a seal of distinction that distinguishes not merely one being from many of a kind by discerning differences of feature, but moreover distinguishes each being *in kind*, that is to say, in the recognition of differences with regards to the provenance of the principle that determines its identity. And what distinction may this be? A distinction in the meanings or uses of words? A distinction based on variations in the sensory perception of tones or colors? Discrimination in taste? In the description of phenomena? The differentiations of points in time, in space? No. The logogram of human being is not a question of definition or semantics. The principle that makes all the difference in the world for human being is the experience of you not being YOU and me not being ME, not being namely the being you and I were meant to be, the experience of our divergence ($\perp$), not from each other in the flesh, but from our own being in the determinacy of a destiny – for the principle of thought thinking thought is not only that well-rounded theoretical being of contemplation, seen and known, but also the practical being of action, due and done, a being of distinction, whose works make marks and leave traces in the otherwise blank continuity and homogenous uniformity of human all too human life and all other indiscriminate being; specifically, as human, this distinction is the critical act of self-reflection through which we, first, *step back* from THE WAY IT IS, gaining our footing in this standpoint to, second, *take note* of difference, *minding the gap* between THE WAY IT IS and THE WAY IT SHOULD BE, in order to, finally, realize the inaugural principle in the deeds and words of wisdom, *making the dream come true*, that self-relative entity of identity as the original present that pure reason has set before all philosophy as the distinction of human being.

This foundational experience of rationality as the enactment of *self-severalty* is older than science, *doing,* older than *seeing,* wisdom older than philosophy. As we shall discover in due course, the idea that the distinction of human being can be characterized as the faculty for self-critical reflection is the oldest thought in Occidental history, the very first thought, the thought *before* all thought, going back to the insight of the father of gods and men, Zeus, who, confronted with a theogony of oppression and revolt, grasped the pre-determined principle of just apportionment upon which he was to found his kingdom, the divine civil order of Olympus. And Kant himself recurred to this principle as fundamental in the project of his critiques. In the beginning of the third section of his *Foundation of the Metaphysics of Morals* (*Grundlegung zur Metaphysik der Sitten*), he writes: "Now human being finds in itself, in effect, a faculty through which it distinguishes itself from every other thing, indeed even from itself....and that is reason."

> *Nun findet der Mensch in sich wirklich ein Vermögen, dadurch er*
> *sich von allen anderen Dingen, ja von sich selbst...unterscheidet,*
> *und das ist die Vernunft. (Kant, Grundlegung zur Metaphysik der*
> *Sitten, IV p.452 7-9.)*

Thus, long before ideas are given a specific, tangible form by being rendered in the concrete details of everyday experience that language provides to our persuasive efforts of explanation and illustration – the *poetic* work of thought, the *Builder* – and prior to the *Actor*'s *practical* attainment of desire's keen objectives or to the *theoretical* comprehension of objects as they present themselves to the *Thinker*'s curiosity, prior even to their compelling impact upon our undivided attention as orders of insight in the scheme of all things thought, we acknowledge this principle in its own right, namely the uniquely centrifugal movement of *extrication* which is reason's inaugural feat of note that discloses the critical discontinuity of human being – and is now to be taken as the specific content of the term **abstraction**.

With the attribution of this new *term*, a poor one perhaps, to our cause, have we, nevertheless, taken a further, though small step towards clarification of what we mean by the "distinction of human being?" How, if at all, does this expression help? It seems so little, does it not, one lemma in the dictionary, one single lexeme in the lexicon of a language, merely one word and nevertheless rich with numerous denotations, connotations, and associations; perhaps these concrete meanings could provide the logotectonic art and craft of thought, the Builder, with building blocks, or at least building material? What sort of buildings can we build with words?

For in fact, notwithstanding their individual properties of sound and sense, their inflections and syntactical features, the etymology of their constituent morphemes, and the semantic fields they access, it is only in their specific usage in a *sentence*, which means for us, in *trains of thoughts*, that we can determine the specific sense of an expression and, by establishing its unique position within those sequences or *ratios* of reasoning, put what we know into words and articulate a scheme in accordance with a given principle, thereby enriching our experience, our knowledge, and ultimately our appreciation of the distinction of human being that is our cognizance.

Thus, in preparation for the employment of the designation *abstraction* in a particular train of thought, we first note its familiar meanings and connotations which serve as the background with respect to which we then may highlight those among them that appear to be the most significant for the purposes of the intended denomination and, in this way, convey perspectives and shed light upon the experience of self-severalty.

Proceeding now with our analysis of this candidate term, the most obvious problem with the notion of *abstraction* is that, for many, it connotes shades of grey and the dry-as-dust fastidiousness that overly nice philosophers are harshly defamed for. What lacks relish, verve, flesh, in short, that vivacity of something living is not vivid or interesting to normal folks; it is formal and impractical; it is lackluster; it is mincing; it is bloodless; it is dead; it is *abstract*. And this is the sense of the word that we associate with what is "just" theory as being academic, immaterial, trivial (quadrivial even); apparently, abstraction is a process of devastation and diversion, in which a wealth of living detail pertaining to a being is suppressed and impoverished with a view to facilitating its pigeonholing based on some adduced invariant that has been extracted like a tooth from nature's smile or a noble hart poached, torn from the wild only to be stuffed and displayed in a case behind glass, drained of life's juices, stolen, detached, arcane, just a thought, just a possibility, *abstract*.

Tsk, tsk, tsk! Now it is not abstraction in this sense that we mean. Though, as a matter of fact, it might very well be, if that is how you, gentle reader, are wont to construe it; yes, even this understanding of abstraction has its reasons; we will see in more detail, when we turn to the Greek Epoch of philosophy, how the workings of theoretical thought by which we penetrate to the heart of the matter, to the core and substance, which is the general principle governing the being in question, is not a reduction of beings at all, though it can be and was understood and denounced as such, namely as a journey to the darkness and seclusion of the netherworld of thought – this time the place of distinction is not above or beyond but rather beneath our shiny surface world in living Technicolor, clearly a trip enjoyed only by those who, like Juliet, for their sweetheart's sake, are "in love with night and pay no worship to the garish sun." (Shakespeare, *Romeo and Juliet*, III. ii)

Indeed, accusations of abstrusity are not new to thinkers about thought. Of course, the principle, the abstract *general*, attains, returns to reality in the government of the particulars which, in turn, through their compliance – and even in their disobedience – carry out the rule of its law in their own element. This abstraction from particulars with a view to determining their cause is the theoretical work of thought, the Thinker, and we might say, therefore, that reason, in this view, is not just the practical act of abstraction in the sense of stepping back from concrete particulars but also the theoretical act of insight and intelligence; perceptive knowledge, having already attained the critical distance of science inherent in inaugural wonder and taken note of THE WAY IT IS, turns now to study the reasons why it is so; for reason explains, as Aristotle says, *why it should be so*, the necessity, as the *cause* and *principle*, the OUGHT behind the IS.

The self-severalty of *being* becomes thus no less the issue of theoretical reason than of practice, no less the issue of thought, the Thinker, than that of the Doer striving to fulfill the appointed mission and we can conceive of *abstraction* in the sense of the seeing and the seen of *insight*. But this term, when attributed to the distinction of human being, also has a practical application that we noted already in passing in connection with the wonder of theory. For consider the act of reason by which we are not only contemplating reason and reasons but, instead, actually "doing" the deed of self-disjuncture, i.e. drawing or stepping back, abstracting ourselves, from unthinking confluence with the immediacy and continuity of being in the act of critical self-reflection and then, from this Archimedean coign of vantage, given to minding the gap between the IS and the OUGHT, all the while striving to close it.

Now we might very well frown upon this sense of abstraction as well, this movement of self-severalty as an act of alienation or the discomposure of what might have been well enough left alone in the mindless simplicity and careless innocence of untroubled, one-dimensional occupation even as Shakespeare's Othello did, in the grip of the earth-shattering doubt that dawning knowledge bred, exclaiming (III. iii):

> *I had been happy, if the general camp,*
> *Pioneers and all, had tasted her sweet body,*
> *So I had nothing known. O now, for ever*

> *Farewell the tranquil mind! Farewell content!*
> *Farewell the plumed troops and the big wars*
> *That makes ambition virtue! O, farewell!*
> *Farewell the neighing steed and the shrill trump,*
> *The spirit-stirring drum, th' ear-piercing fife,*
> *The royal banner, and all quality,*
> *Pride, pomp, and circumstance of glorious war!*
> *And O you mortal engines, whose rude throats*
> *Th' immortal Jove's dread clamors counterfeit,*
> *Farewell! Othello's occupation's gone.*

In fact, the discomfiture, the anguish, arising from critical reflection can be, as we shall see, a beneficial agitation (though not for Othello's passion) in that it initiates a radical refreshment of the mind (once called *METANOEIN*), that opens eyes to new purposes and courses of development and invigorates the impetus of voluntary change, the transformation of thought through the enactment of a principle, which is the work of a Seeker, not so much in the *theoretical* sense of an explorer with a question, a discoverer of distinguished beings, but rather in the *practical* sense of a wayfarer with a quest, embracing the way of renewal of being in pursuit of and in eventual accordance with the image of transcendent excellence in a being of absolute distinction, which is the most potent sign of the principle of self-severalty, the one that inaugurates agonizing experience of the Falsum ($\perp$) in our own.

To a conservative inertia prone to resisting or minimizing the impulse from abroad that impinges and luminously, not merely ominously, infringes upon the maintenance of its set stasis, it is clear that the discord sown by critical reflection is upsetting and embarrassing, throwing into disarray what has been orderly, frustrating what has been convenient, routing what has been regular, damaging what has been wholesome and overthrowing what has been long and ever so comfortably, ever so self-assuredly enthroned. The practical experience of human self-severalty – the anguish of its inception and the glory of its resolution – has been rendered most dramatically in the vision of the Crucifixion and the Resurrection of Christ to which we shall turn when treating the language and the logic of wisdom in terms of the Second Epoch.

16. The Logic of Self-disjuncture

Imagine that we wanted to show the event of our self-severalty actually taking place, and observe pure reason, as the distinction of human being, in action! Now we all know what it means to call into question and step back from our lives, regarding our life, its orders and certainties, its truths and entrenchments, critically, from *without*, as it were, as we would a tableau while minding the gap between the IS and the OUGHT, giving an account to ourselves of their divergence, and enduring the mortifying humiliation in the face of the complacency, the vanity, and the arrogance of our previously enjoyed delusions of perfection and control.

If we are to render this experience of our *Falsum* faithfully in spite of the fact that self-severalty is something we do and that gazing upon our practice of critical self-reflection is not the same as actually being engaged in its performance, we must somehow capture this movement of turn and return, the experience of our original disengagement as well as the subsequent repossession in an alternating series of successions, in which the critical distinction of thought reproduces itself, in a progression of achievements that might be conceived of as a collection and an integration – but not a unification – of distinctions beginning, on the one hand, with the active abstraction and extrication of thought "tearing itself free from itself (von sich selbst sich Losreissen des Gedankens)," as Fichte puts it, i.e. the inaugural act of *stepping back,* the part departing from the empty whole of immediate continuity, the division and separation from a blanket uniformity, which is the very mark of reason, our faculty for critical reflection, and ending, on the other hand, with the reaffirmation and the realization of the original tautology, and therefore giving rise to an experience that is both earlier and later than the principle of reflection, of thought thinking thought, that dissymmetric entity of identity, that is both the chiral object of thought's practical commitment and dedication as well as the well-rounded sphere of thought's completion, the acquiescence and tranquility of self-knowledge. The self-knowing self-several being of thought, cognition seen and recognized for what it is *and* does, viz. thought seen seeing and therein attaining the coign of vantage of sight; thought in action noted and noting thought as an object of beatific contemplation, a work of distinguished abstraction – this self-several being *and* doing could be rendered in some manner of form as in *Figure 2.*

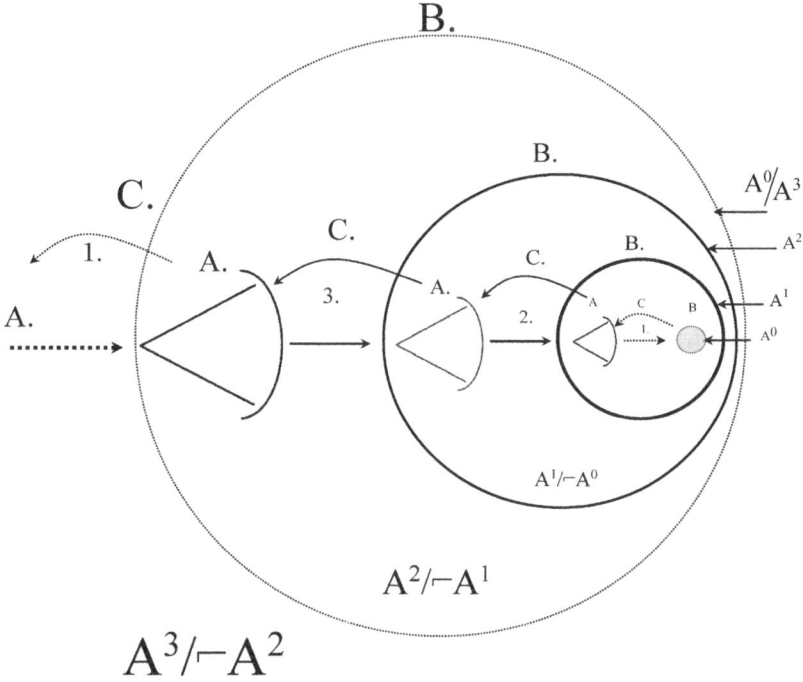

Figure 2: The Differentiating Reiteration of Critical Reflection ($\perp$)

Well, perhaps *beatific* is a bit of an exaggeration regarding this figure. On the other hand, maybe a bit of exaggeration in the sense of magnification of what otherwise might have gone unnoticed or, if noticed, then not sufficiently savored, is just what, in such distracted times as ours, thought, the *philological* Doctor, ordered. It is as if the acknowledgement of gratitude and the enthusiasm of delight, far from being an accoutrement and an afterthought to our experience of the distinction of human being, are, in fact, constitutive of its concept, a concept that does not just comprehend an arrangement of constituent notions as its subordinate terms, but moreover recognizes in their relationship an order of succession as the three epochs and stages of its career, seasons of its life, offices or departments in the administration of its mission.

And it is precisely this succession inherent in the self-severalty of thought that is most clearly brought to light in *Figure 2*, a succession based on *negation*, which is the active determinative principle initiating and perpetuating the distinction of human being and unfolding the dimensions of pure reason as that of thought thinking thought, namely its works and days, its life and times, its organization and development.

This primary property of pure thought, namely its **negativity**, which is properly comprehended neither by the notion of annihilation, nor by that of " dialectical" opposition, and least of all as mere scepticism or pessimism or nihilism, though often mistaken in these and other ways, this divisive force of reason, has always been difficult to render clearly in familiar terms even though the outstanding being that we discern in our experience of "stepping back" or "stepping forward," "stepping out" or "stepping up," is entirely familiar to everyone who has had to reflect upon themselves, their words, their actions, their situation, from a critical coign of vantage with a view towards distinguishing THE WAY IT IS from THE WAY IT SHOULD BE by saying "the way it is *is not* the way it should be" or simply "***not* so!"

Reason has often been conceived of as a movement hither and beyond – transcendent, leaving behind, departing from; in this sense the negativity of thought refers not only to a place beyond or hereafter, a *Never-* and a *No-man's-land* beyond, beside, beneath, before this *land at hand*, i.e. a distinguished place, (a "place" or *place* or PLACE or ~~place~~ – evidently, we can also use graphical elements to mark this distinction) but rather, also, the otherwise undefined hiatus in the continuity of being, human or otherwise. It is invoked by the figure of the attainment of impartiality that manifests itself as a perpetual departure from every given, every established and, in this way, every predisposed frame of reference; this *nothing* (Ø) or slashed zero (𝕆) of what is *before, without,* is not a negation in the manner of the antithesis of some position, the *opposite* being merely an opposing position, but rather the tertiary term, the limiting boundary or border between every conflicting dualism, though marking nothing but their interval, being neither the one nor the other, in itself no longer the one, having left it behind, nor yet the other, which is the ensuing resolution and return to come; no, permanently *over yonder* with respect to every determinacy, dislocated, it is not and never "in itself," not a place (hence a distinguished place, a ~~place~~), not this one and not that one, at all – precisely between the endpoints, after the end of one position's reign and before the beginning of the other's and as such the infinitesimally (but also magnificently) fine line, the line of the distinction marking the span and the tension of the limit determining their rapport of discontinuity. We want to direct our attention precisely towards this distinguished point of separation between them that makes of each the other's other, the salient point that is itself not a point or a place, just another place between two places, but rather simply the interruption, or more dramatically, the *eruption* and *irruption* of difference in the continuity of any being that has been definitively established and determined to be on the one side *or* the other – the mark of distinction is their disjuncture.

"Stepping back" is the expression we have been using – and a rather picturesque one at that – for this practice of *abstraction*, which is itself, as we noted, a somewhat nondescript designation all too rounded by centuries of fumbling and tumbling in the ebb and flow of philosophical discourse, for the dramatic, transforming, anguishing act of self-severalty we intend to refer to by it, one considered perhaps no less weak than its all too colloquial predecessor, *stepping back*, not only due to its pejorative associations but also on account of being, well, too abstract. For this reason, we might be tempted to cast about in the lexicon for other, richer, more evocative names.

We could say, for instance, that to step or pull back, stand apart, aloof or aside and detach ourselves from circumstances or conventions or prejudices – for undergoing or undertaking the experience inherent in the self-severalty of critical reflection must mean something like that – is to withdraw or retreat from them as from a world that we have decided to henceforth forsake in order to live in splendid exile, far from the maddening crowd of continental contention, as monks or nuns – a line of reasoning that conducts us to the figure we know as thought, the Anchorite and the life of austerity, of abnegation, of solitude and, to use the most exquisite term, of *death*. This intuition of self-disjuncture as immolation articulates a very ambiguous vision of our experience with the distinction of human being. For the notion of *sequestration* we have just considered, understood as *retirement* into the seclusion of a quiet cove or that of the bee-loud glade in a clearing we happen upon while hiking, having left our little town blues behind for an outing, might be embraced as desirable and pleasant; other attributions of withdrawal are decidedly less so as when stepping back is seen as drawing back into *isolation*, as the waning and fading of *regression*, the desertion of *abandonment* and the exclusion of *segregation*, the loss of *bereavement*, the oblation of *sacrifice* – all of which are ideas that are governed by the notion of thought's **negativity** – using this term at our peril – the essential attribute of the distinction of self-several being, as our analysis will show.

Evidently, the *separation* implicit in the drawing of distinctions is expressed not only in favourable terms of sanction (but this term is itself admirably ambiguous!) but also in the more denunciatory ones of adversity and dissension, a duplicity of sense we have already encountered in the notion of *abstraction*. The experience of human being with the determinative principle is both pleasant and unpleasant and our own disposition with regards to this contrariety is appropriately rendered in expressions of dissidence or endorsement. Thus the designation *divorce* when put for the experience of our self-severance is a term of censure given its connotations of *dissolution* and *estrangement* even as the terms *abnormality* and *eccentricity* are expressions of rejection of and even abhorrence for the distinguished act of stepping back and minding the gap in critical self-reflection.

Consider now the spectacle of this distinguished act as represented in *Figure 2*. The series of pure reason's perpetual abstractions consists of three periods of which the subsequent distinguishes itself from the preceding one by attaining critical detachment from that former position of thought through the negation of that previously established continuity whence it emerged. With respect to the procession of distinctions as a whole, each period is a transient epoch, an instant of thought in the life and times of reason's entire career, one life consisting of several lives and one time consisting of several times in the circle of turn and return, the *turn* of reason here indicated by the **arrow of separation** (pointing left) which depicts thought in the act of stepping back envisioned as the negativity of abstraction from the closed sphere of a currently prevailing and thus self-indeterminate order of ensconced continuity as shown in *Figure 3*.

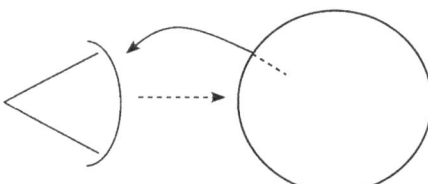

Figure 3: The Negativity of Abstraction

In *Figure 4*, the *return* of reason, depicted in terms of an **arrow of realization** (pointing right) – the completion of a train of thought having begun upon the drawing of the first and original distinction in the negation of an established continuity of being – is achieved in the renewed encounter of what previously had be assimilated unto itself and therefore unknown to itself. In the refreshed encounter with what was taken for granted as conforming to it, thought regains sight of its own distinction as the unique self-several being that is different from itself. This being is both the prior cause and the object of its recognition.

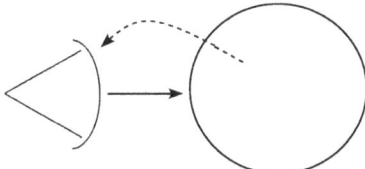

Figure 4: The Animadversion of Recognition

In *Figure 2* each circle represents thus a closed domain under the jurisdiction of the principle that has determined its scope. We have noted four precincts, A^0 to A^3, or orders of being, though, in fact, the first (A^0) and the last (A^3) are identical in accordance with the self-relative principle of the entity of identity, the relationship of thought thinking thought. And it is as a result of this relationship that each distinction contains and is contained in itself, A^1 contained in A^2 and A^2 in A^3 which is, in turn, contained in A^0, the whole contained in the part and each part contained in and containing the whole. In this precise sense of self-relativity and the corresponding action of abstraction that is its animating spirit – the procession of thought's distinction consisting of distinctions, its several *spirits*, A^1 being the horizon of the negation distinguishing A^0, A^2 that of the distinction of A^1 and A^3 that of A^2 – pure reason is said to be *infinite*.

This infinite procession of its distinctions is nevertheless a bounded sequence of signature terms of which there are three, turning and returning much like the three colors of the patriotic barber pole and for which the subsequent terms, in spite of the negativity in the distinction each makes with respect to its predecessor, contains and collects, the former, even while transcending it, namely the term of **principle** (A) defining the distinction of *perfect being* and the *theory* of its truth, the term of **insight** (C) defining the distinction of *absolute being* and the transforming *practice* of its truth in action, and the term for what is here at stake, nothing less than the **issue** (B) of the distinction of *human being* and the craft and *art* of invention dedicated to the realization of its truth. This traditionally distinguished and acknowledged, self-several, threefold being – perfect, absolute, human – is widely contested these days and as such, inexplicably, has become our cause to consider, pursue, and celebrate.

Finally, as regards the specific steps of stepping back, the moments of critical self-reflection distinguished in the procession of severance depicted in *Figure 2* – what we might call the negative, or more elaborately, the enantiomorphic ingemination of thought – we offer the familiar narrative relating the start and the dawn of reason as it emerges out of the dusk and the twilight of its default or "latent" status (A^0) and its enfeebled state of languor in which thought is taken for granted as an instrument of technical ingenuity, of cognitive behaviors within the life-world continuum, and of the empowerment of vital instinct. Such reason is an empty function of man's urgency awaiting arguments, operating tacitly in accordance with the dictates and statutes that arise out of particular circumstances, engaged in calculations with a view to maximizing short-term outcomes, minimizing costs, and maintaining the overall order arising temporarily and consecutively from the purposes and intentions of significant individuals to the devices of whom thought has been appropriated.

In this domain, the critical relationship of reason, ΛΟΓΟΣ, has not attained salience but rather remains the, as yet undifferentiated, "principle" (A) – which we, saving this word for bigger and better things, would prefer to call simply an over-riding *urge* or *motive* – namely a purblind force and anonymous power that governs implicitly in the pressing business, control, and intercourse of man's understandings and undertakings. And the closure of this horizon is further maintained and hardened by the inkling intervention of myopic awareness (A^0) regarding problems and obstacles that hinder the chaotic flow of operations and the need to take into account discrepancies that tend to arise between the conflicting demands of various interested parties, the stakeholders. This self-consciousness of thought (1.), though showing signs of distinction, is still merely a further technique in the economy and commerce of inter-subjective, even inter-corporeal, governance.

The second order of thought marks the advent of its critical relationship attained through the transcending abstraction of the self-severance of pure reason (C.) that steps back (2.) from the dominant state of affairs inaugurating thus the emergency and the crisis of conscience that characterizes thought's revival from its former latency. In this dominion of doubt, previously immediate life-world dynamics are now called into question with regards to the difference that has become evident to critically invigorated insight undertaking the recognition of the abyss, widening and deepening with growing comprehension, that has been torn between the IS of immediacy and the OUGHT of thought, in particular in the insight that THE WAY IT IS *is not* THE WAY IT SHOULD BE – the *irrationality* of being – and that THE WAY IT SHOULD BE *is not* THE WAY IT IS – the *immateriality* of ideas.

Minding this gap, thought is thus inspired to act and to bring forth a reality that better corresponds to the vision that the above distinction made manifest to it, the issue (B.) of the principle through which thought now stands in relationship to thought (3.) and strives to realize as its own idea and concept of itself, namely the entity of identity, our *Verum* (T). This is not a relapse into the configuration of continuity whence it departed but rather a figure of pleasure and completion, the result of this development and the fulfillment of the inaugural principle of difference, the distinguished vision of which set thought originally on its course. The peace and continuity of this being, in all the brilliance and clarity of the realization it has achieved, becomes eventually, nevertheless, dulled in our eyes, falls into disregard and negligence, is sadly, slowly forgotten. For after the weekend and the holiday of thought thinking thought in which we celebrate the completion of reflections project, our work week resumes, bringing new distinctions, new gaps to mind, i.e. new problems, wanting new solutions and applications of expertise, instilling new habits into routines. At some point, it is inevitable that we are tired and close our philosophy book, hanging our head on the hook, so to speak, clinging to the last thought for a bit afterwards, as long as possible, while pursuing the routines of the evening until, at the end of the day, we lie down, done though unfinished; then we let our minds, appeased for now, wander until oblivion possesses us again – completing that grand narrative that is all history (and *her* story, too, for that matter), even as Muta teaches:

> "So that when we shall have acquired unification we shall pass on to diversity and when we shall have passed on to diversity we shall have acquired the instinct to combat and when we shall have acquired the instinct of combat we shall pass back to the spirit of appeasement." (Joyce, *FW*, 610.23-27.)

17. The Negativity of Reason

For the sake of illustration of this "hyper"-logic of self-relativity and the negativity of thought that drives it, let us take the painter whose working process encompasses two phases. The first phase is the one in which the painter is engrossed in the actual act of applying colors to the canvas, whereas in the second phase, the painter steps back from the canvas and regains a standpoint that takes in the whole of what has been painted. The touches of color here and there that where collected on the canvas over the course of the sitting today but also during previous work in past days are evaluated with a view to the totality of their effect. "Is it the way it should be? Is that color, is that form, that line, what I want?" Thus our painter will ask herself or himself at this critical juncture, having attained to sight and judgment both of which were latent in the painter's previous state of engrossment while actually involved in painting this detail and that detail and that line and this blue.

The *discrepancy* (⊥) between these two states of mind of the painter – on the one hand, his absorption in the material immediacy of the actual task of painting, on the other hand, the artist's "prophetic" ascendency to the far-sight, the foresight, of an overview that surveys what has been hitherto accomplished and what is yet to come, meant to come – and neither the one nor the other is what we refer to as the movement of distinction and the detachment of abstraction that subsequently brings the painter, now poised upon the coign of vantage, into a relationship of contemplation and judgment; noting the continued gap between the IS of her canvas and OUGHT of her muse – and minding it – she is inspired to renewed application to close that gap in the hopes of achieving greater and greater correspondence between them until the work is complete. This complete train of thought might be visualized as one period, out and back, of critical reflection as in *Figure 5*.

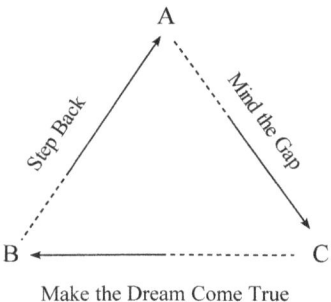

Figure 5: The Practice of Critical Reflection

It is this break with the absorbed immediacy and continuity of the living intent that is thought's original start, the inception of reason; it is to this originary event of departure and to the critical spirit of negativity that sets its stage, to this *being without* and, with regards to the resumed assimilation of engrossed occupation that is its further shore and boundary, i.e. the *being between*, that we now turn and return and ask, further, how this divisive negativity can be seen and better grasped, as the determinative principle of pure reason?

Consider again the illustration of the abstraction of pure reason as the act of stepping back or disengaging from the confluence inherent in the persistence of habit that has become deep-rooted in the culture of an individual or a society. Imagine the effort required of one thus encumbered by convention to *step back* from the dominant rule of rote, adapting a vantage point outside of that channelled groove in which we typically run. A critical perspective with respect to these established mores would place the individual outside of the mainstream in an indeterminate location, a position of disentanglement that is not defined except as the negation of that groovy – and therefore very ungroovy – status quo from which he or she departed. Let us picture this revolt in *Figure 6.*

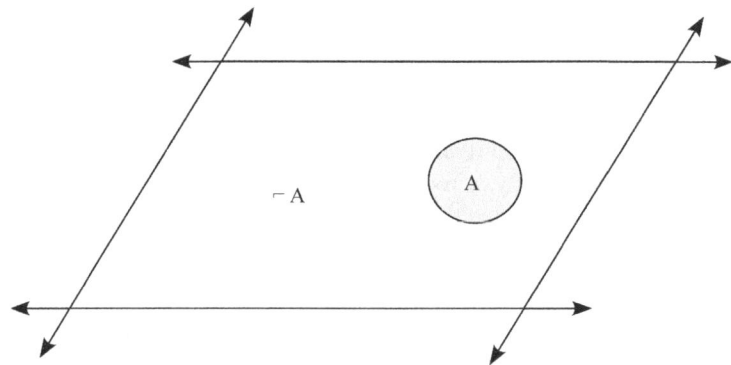

Figure 6: Being without the Zone of Comfort

The extraneous position (⌐A), which is, in fact, no position at all but rather the *negation* of position, namely that of the given standpoint (A), and therefore not the former's opposite but rather its *point of departure,* can be designated as the *being without,* being, as it is, beyond the demarcations of what has been previously defined, set, and established as the circle of familiarity. The outer regions surrounding the homely world of determinate certainty can only be called indeterminate and uncertain, undefined, inhospitable – a vast infinite expanse of outer space receding in all directions from that minute enclosure of content, threatening, with its sheer immensity, at any moment, to suddenly engulf or slowly erode that colony of comfort and consolidation into elemental nothingness. To those who people the habits and the orbits of such an oasis settlement, the environmental void is an ocean and a desert of wasteland emptiness just waiting to reclaim their supposedly so safe spot and reassert the prerogative of entropy. From this perspective, the negativity of that distinction that is our signature and sign, the specific mark of the human mind, must indeed be a frightening prospect tantamount to the overthrow of civilization, a walkabout in the outback, a wild thought. [18]

In fact, this *outward* sense of abstraction, whether in terms of abhorrence in the intuition of which the spirit of negativity is perceived to be all that is unearthly, abnormal, and amorphous, or in terms of appreciation according to which the infinity of thought is an exalting and sublime departure into the more luminous regions of experience, is just one vision of critical self-reflection.

For the great divide that distinguishes our human being can be rendered just as well as the experience of transcendence *within* the given framework of an established order and as the drawing of an *inward* distinction. For this reason we might represent it not only as the locus of **latitude**, the emergence of headroom and the elbowroom abroad, as it were, beyond and above the fixed dimensions, cramped quarters, the girdle of narrow-minded circumscription, but also as **aperture** within the smooth, flat membrane of superficiality, a twist of incongruity and irregularity in the curvaceous expanse of space, a black hole and singularity in the blank vacuousness of continuity, a nick of time in the velvety velum of insignificant perduration.

Consequently, we now note two forms of disclosure; with respect to the envelop of blanket indifference, both can be thought of as the broach of a well-defined scope – a clearing, a lightening; in the first case, the infinite distinction of pure reason is its **ascendant abstraction,** the *infinity* above and beyond, *without,* the bounds of confinement, whereas in the second case, *infinity* can only refer to glabrous indeterminacy that is then distinguished, inflected, marked, pierced by **keen acumen** – for that is the determined distinction of pure reason when it turns *within* to peer *beneath* and *behind* the fleshy flashiness of appearances, *through* the phantasmagoric façade; a deep blue universe comes into view when the

---

[18] This is the role that Foucault assigns to all fiction, namely to make visible the utter nothingness of the "space" we need – and therefore depend upon – to really *see* things in the first place or, as he puts it in *La pensée du dehors* (the thought without), "fiction does not make the invisible visible but rather makes visible just how invisible the invisibility of what is visible truly is. "La fiction consiste donc non pas à faire voir l'invisible, mais à faire voir combien est invisible l'invisibilité du visible." (p. 24).

shifting surface spectral phenomena are plumbed and sounded to their core, those roaming myriorama fathomed, and the inward traveler, seeking to get the bottom of the matter, finally finds surcease of perception in attaining the peerless particular of an insight that has made all the difference in that world of shine.

Whereas, again, the negativity of thought is presented in the first case as the ever larger **whole** that encompasses and surpasses the limited horizon of a firmly fixed purview, in its *extension*, the latter negativity is the signature mark, the incisive cognizance of distinction, its incursion, even its invasion, and the timely **hole** left in the aftermath of its *intention* in an otherwise undifferentiated, previously unmarked space that, in thought's good time, had finally been...

> ..."provoked" ay ∧ fork, of à grave Brofèsor; àth é's Brèak – fast - table; ;acùtely profèššionally *piquéd*, to=introdùce a notion of time [ùpon à plane (?) sù ' ' fàç'e'] by pùnct! ingh oles (sic) in iSpace?! (Joyce, *FW*, 124.9-12.)

> ...provoked by a fork of a grave professor at his breakfast table, acutely [and] professionally piqued to introduce a notion of time upon a plane surface by punching holes in a space.

A maidenhead tablet of wax hitherto unscathed has been, through the point that critical thought makes, uniquely scratched, pierced, revealing both the primal state of confluent immediacy, now lost, as well as the subsequent emergent character now indelibly inscribed on that background and therein, in *Figure 7*, pointed out for all eyes to see, an effect that Hegel, quoting Schelling, described in his *Difference between Fichte's and Schelling's System of Philosophy* (Differenz des Fichteschen und Schellingschen Systems der Philosophie) as "the lightning bolt of the ideal striking the real and constituting itself as the point."

> ...*einschlagende Blitz des Ideellen in das Reelle und sein Sich-selbst-Konstituieren als Punkt. (Hegel, Werke, II p. 111.)*

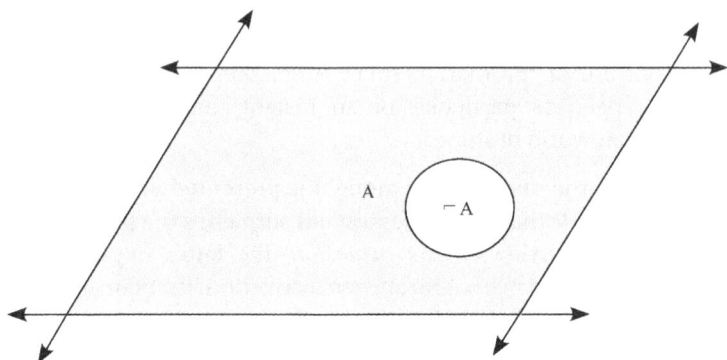

Figure 7: The Inscription of Difference

This figure of the *punctus interogativus* illustrates the complement concept of thought as being ***inward*** bound – the mind's descent and concentration.

For indeed the moving line of the mind, seen as a *journey to the center of the earth* entails as much an experience of departure as it does a *flight to the sun*; but whereas the imagery of the latter is bright-eyed *lucidity*, the former is couched in the darkened hues of *depth* and penetration. And this makes sense: a good mind or *intellect* is both brilliant and profound, excels in the flight of speculation as well as in the ponder of contemplation, and both refer to the power of perception to draw distinctions – thus does critical thought, our experience of its crisis as immolation and renunciation, if we dare employ such powerful terms, leave the immediate world behind, departing from both its glitz and its gore by going down and going up; nevertheless, pure reason is but a single abstract sphere, both its nadir and its zenith, abyss and pinnacle, the pit and tip of self-several chirality, our netherworld and our heaven, the *vault* and the *spring* of human being.

Thus when we draw a distinction, we mark a difference that indicates the start of thought taken unawares at first, as it were, and now, as it is, roused from antecedent torpor, bright-eyed and bushy-tailed, recollecting the salient features of what has just transpired in what was, before, in the offing and off-stage, absent, the full impact of which is now, in a narrative of conception, progressively brought home to us in all its significance and ramifications, brought ashore to the presence of mind.

In founding its origin in a field of oblivion, thought, having only just started, is already in the thick of things, late by one wink of an eye, playing catch-up and in a rush to complete its account; taking note all the while of its prior infancy and final maturity, thought discovers two opposing versions of what has come to pass. These two events both pertain to the negativity of thought – for thought seen as the act of distinction in the passage from **A to ⌐A** is the accomplishment of gaining high ground, getting to the heart of the matter; thought, understanding, throws into relief the way things stand, marks this recognition as a moment of surprise, the break of day, the fall of night, the exception to the rule, the admission of doubt, but also as the obedience to law, the upholding of hope – pure negativity defined only with regards to the *difference* it makes to some mean of immediacy, to some measure of predominance, to some set framework, official outlook or playbook, to some all-inclusive package – and there is no last and final distinction; we are never done with thought nor should be. It is always possible, and when the time is right, necessary, to draw a new distinction, that is to say, we never come permanently to rest in the framework of the regime we have founded upon previous distinctions because thought is, precisely, this relentless restlessness, the animated spirit of self-severalty that controverts every construction or program; the tell-tale sign of human being is an *open* scope, an *outer* space and a *disclosed* clearing – either a gap and resonate interval that is *in* A or else a latitude and expanse thither and yon that A is *in*, on the one hand *depth*, on the other *breadth*. But being displacements rather than defined places, neither are proper regions nor are they, for all that, merely an empty space, null and void, but rather, in their chiasmus, defined by and defining that inaugural mark of distinction, a silence, but sounding and resounding, eloquent, in its silence, like the sighing of the wind in the leaves, the murmur of the brook in the shadows – a mode of silence, yes, but not an inscrutable mutter, ramble, or stammer that negligence makes of an unfamiliar language, but rather a quiet song, and gentle, of lament, soft, not faint, not a whisper, being both less and more, a sigh and yet articulate, a breath of speech, a solitary voice, a sole word.

And if the term "⌐A" is misleading because the negativity is in danger of being too much defined by what it negates (A), then we might simply posit the negative sign alone (⌐) as the one and only cognizance of distinction. Or, put another way, *Figure 8* suggests that the velvety plane, in its infinite uniformity (A) is *either **within** the efficacy of its correlative distinction (⌐) and thus curved into finitude by dint of its limitation, as depicted in *Figure 8a* or the correlative distinction (⌐) is a critical incident **within** the homogeneous empire that unexpectedly opens a disturbing window of opportunity in the white-wash of a wall thought otherwise closed as envisioned in *Figure 8b.*

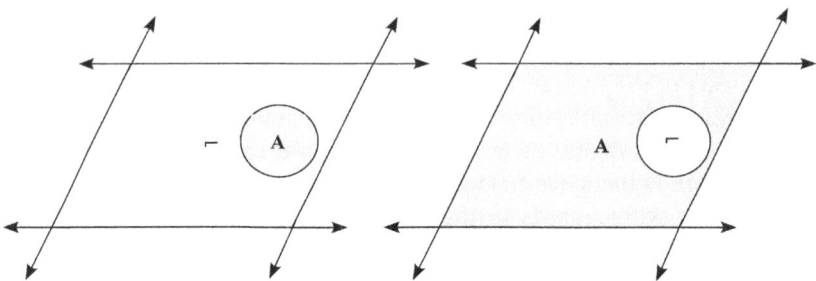

Figure 8a: Encompassing Comprehension   Figure 8b: Penetrating Insight

Figure 8: The Fertile Figure/Ground of the Mind's *Ma* (間)

Perhaps these ratios of liminalty, depicting, as they are meant to do, the fallow fields of being as the backdrop of a distinction's mark, are simply too static to capture the animated spirit of negativity we are attempting to describe. In that case we might simply show, as in *Figure 9*, the movement of negation involved in the distinction that what is IN makes with respect to what is OUT and, vice versa what OUT makes with respect to IN – the passage and the transience of negativity from determinacy to indeterminacy and from indeterminacy to determinacy, the former being the moment of abstraction for which the distinction is a centrifugal force and the *levity* of thought away from the solemn gravity of centralization as in *Figure 9a*, the latter being the moment of penetration for which the distinction is a centripetal force and the *transparency* of thought's inspired drive towards the disclosure of the essential nature of an otherwise opaque and superficial being as illustrated in *Figure 9b.*

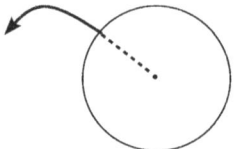
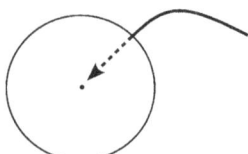

Figure 9a: Ethereality   Figure 9b: Profundity

Figure 9: The Distinguished Difference

It is interesting to note that the terms *determinacy* and *indeterminacy* have a different sense in each case. For when we understand self-severalty as the act of stepping back, we are leaving an *obstinate* and a *rigid* determination behind, fleeing from a gilded cage to the indeterminacy of objective light and the fresh air of impartiality. Contrariwise, when we grasp the distinction as a journey of discovery into seclusion, indeterminacy is the name for the immediate and inchoate condition of superficiality that, through the negativity of the distinction drawn upon it, attains the determination of a profound principle. Similarly, *light* in the first sense is sought as brilliant and illuminating, in the second, fled as garish and blinding as opposed to *darkness* which is oppressive in the first case and sheltering in the second. Of course, even this rendition is still all too specific, too contrived, too elaborate, to represent the utter simplicity of the distinction that is here at issue – the talk of light and darkness, of determinacy and indeterminacy, circles and arrows and fanciful parallelograms, a capital letter *A* pulled out of the hat – who needs 'em! Simply inscribe the sign of difference, draw a distinction, all by itself on a blank sheet of paper and what have you got?

The paper will serve our purpose well enough as an excellent specimen of tangible continuity, and let us comprehend the character of this diacritical in the two senses we have distinguished as significant – the inward negation, namely that of the identifying mark of determination, the pierce of paper, on the previously indeterminate piece of paper and then again the outward negation, namely that of the whole of the blank sheet so identified as having given its trace a place to come home and actually *take* place:

$$\ulcorner$$

Indeed, taken by itself, the intaglio of difference, this trait alone, already succeeds in recording the seal and stigma of distinction, but, of course, the particular sign we choose to do the job is entirely arbitrary; obviously, any other mark might have been taken to make the point of the character of thought, to brand the X that marks the spot of significance that is the venue of the event of thought, our buried treasure, and indicative of where we are, namely here and now, weary, resting, having traveled, having made a difference, taking note of this unique place, here, as Joyce concludes in the "Ithaca" episode of Ulysses (chapter 17) at the end of his intrepid hero's day:

Where?

●

This sign of achievement, this *insignia* of thought, marks the distinction in the *temporal* or sequential sense; for in this sense, the void and the plain expanse of plane that had extended blankly, insipidly, before experience and its salt inscribed it with thought's articulate blaze of pain is seen as *prior* to the state of distinction that has just emerged through the delimitation of that length and stretch of otherwise homogenous uniformity. The reference to it made by such a distinction is as to what is always already retained, *time past*, or, should the diversity recognized by this character of discernment be again liquidated, permanently postponed and anticipated, *time future*. Thus the indiscriminate void of pristine vacancy is never contiguous with the marked state, but rather always remembered or projected; the distinction originally drawn is an indelible stigma that remains permanently prior or posterior to the account that critical self-reflection gives of that fabulous plainness prior to the entry of thought's own brand of severalty upon that sleek scene – with respect to that unmarked state of oceanic dissipation, it is perfect continence, making the difference in which our human being may take place as self-relative.

18. The Chiral Rhythm of Distinction

As we have seen, in contrast to its *diachronic* conception in the order of succession – in terms of *before* and *after* the fact of thought's entry upon the scene – the distinction might also be designated, though somewhat cumbersomely, in a planar framework, *synchronically*, by taking our first sign, i.e. the accent of negation (⌐), and enlarging it to represent the two sides of a rectangle as in *Figure 10*, distinguishing in this way the *inside* and the *outside* of its boundary, with the distinction taken as "outside" when referring to the passage *from the inside to the outside* of the enclosure or with the distinction taken as "inside" when referring to the passage *from the outside to the inside* of the enclosure.[19]

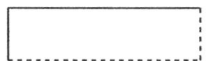

Figure 10: The Mark of Crossing

The rectangle allows us to integrate the twofold valence of the distinction, that was marked diachronically and sequentially by the reference to time future and to time past, into the simultaneity of place within place, a nest of enclosures like the circles within the circles we contemplated in *Figure 2* that represented the differentiating manifold of thought, whereby the *Inside* of one rectangle is, synchronically, the *Outside* of the other rectangle and vice versa, each embedded in another. *Figure 11* shows this relationship of terms depicting the distinction as *passage* – whether as inward ingression or as outward transcendence – namely the twofold crossing (some would even say the *transgression*) of a boundary.

---

[19] The calculus inherent in the making of distinctions has been explored by George Spencer-Brown in his *Laws of Form*. His symbol for the distinction, namely " ⌐ ", corresponds to the contemplative sign of self-relative thought, the Thinker, that we have been employing (see *Figure 1*), while the axioms that govern the syntax of his primary arithmetic, namely the *Law of Calling* and the *Law of Crossing* correspond in their operations to that of the *Negativity of Abstraction* (Figure 3) and the *"Animadversion of Recognition"* (Figure 4) respectively. As regards the reiteration of the distinction occasioned by critical reflection, we could say that, as with Spencer-Brown's *law of calling*, only the first cut is the principle one while subsequent distinctions can be reduced to it as the latter's manifold; as regards the return and the self-realization of animadverting thought, we could say that, as with his *law of crossing*, the perfect unity, harmony, and symmetry of the entity of identity recognized as having been attained in the fulfillment of its determination anticipates, even while celebrating and enjoying the presence and the dwelling of its well-rounded being, a renewal and revival of differences in a commemoration of those former accomplishments of distinction, which are, at the same time, the prescience of distinctions yet to be and to come.

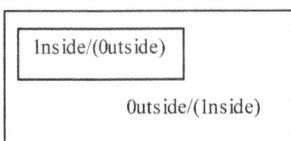

Figure 11: Embedded Inversion

The superimposition of these two passages indicates that each inflection is the other of the other, for the inside of the one is the outside of the other and vice versa. The inner box is the negation of the outer, the outer the negation of the inner one. The mark of distinction is the outside of one and the inside of the other but the outside is the inside and the inside is the outside in a constant oscillation and transience, the shimmering alternation of transition between two divergent states – you say yes, I say no...you say good-bye and I say hello – of self-severalty. The hole contains the whole just as much as the whole the hole because in *figure 8a* the outside (the whole) was the term of distinction whereas in *figure 8b* it was the inside (the hole) that was the term of distinction and the negation. Both the outside and the inside are terms of distinction; but there is, in fact, always only *one* distinction, whether turned inwardly or outwardly, the one, namely, that is the other of the other. For, depending on which one is posited at the outset, it is the other that makes the difference. In this way, a further distinction perpetually re-enters the structure by setting the previous distinction into the indeterminacy of the unmarked state of affairs. Hence, *Figure 11* exhibits the figure/ground structure upon which the procreative process of ingemination in *Figure 2* is based, the manifold structure of differentiation that we have posited as that of our self-relative entity of identity in difference.

The principle of self-several self-relativity that it is intended to depict is not merely that of a pendulum swinging back and forth; it is not the frequency or the amplitude of this pulsation that interests us in which each period of fluctuation is an exchange – the bob, reaching the end point of its trajectory, switches direction and sweeps past the equilibrium position towards its other extreme and back again in a vibration of mutual cancellation – no, in the rhythm of thought's breath and swing, the anterior distinction is not annulled by the current one in the wave of their mutual change and exchange. Rather, each succeeding distinction leaves a trace, and, like perennial tree rings, is accounted for, noted, grasped, comprehended by its sequel, receiving the former distinction in the manner of a tradition through which descendant thought inherits the complete and determinate history of the critical achievements hitherto attained, the distinctions that have made a difference and, though they have become quiescent as tasks completed, as destinies fulfilled, their being, ever-young, though the oldest of the old, is nevertheless an indelible sign, a perpetual being, not a fetish, not a relic like a king's corpse embalmed in the manner of a mummy but rather, like a mommy, intangibly treasured in the heir's infant memory suffused with thanking thinking for the distinguished life, the destiny of royal blood and the patient nurture that her generosity bestowed upon us and that yet enlivens us even as we renew reason's fertile creativity in turn as our own, anticipating, in turn, the distinctions of posterity that will be made in the name of acutest thought.

As we saw, the procession of distinctions can be elaborated in two directions or in two *spins* in accordance with the two spirits that animate thought's negativity, namely on the one hand, the *infinity of Substantiality*, which is the experience of the passage from the abstract indeterminacy of an idea to its definition and, ultimately, to the realization of its distinction in the determinate issue that is its correlative and, on the other, the *infinity of Transcendence*, which is the experience of the trying, yet exuberant passage of departure that relinquishes its stakes in the confines of a predetermined regime, sacrificing them for the sake of an open horizon of absolute leisure and sublimity.

Illuminating penetration's lending, the bending, of its harkening ear removes thought from the immediate glare and din of distraction to the inward silent night of reflection – the theoretical principle takes on a form of being even as beings are given the distinction of thought's character, a nature, a heart; on the other hand, the exaltation of abstraction uplifts thought by transforming it, renewing its character in light of the distinction that thought's diremption has bestowed upon it. One discovers the *Heart* of the matter; the other takes up abode in the distinguished *Heavens*. Our study of the distinction of human being is a recollection of this profound Heart of each and every being and these highest Heavens above and beyond all being and beings.

In both sequences, the first and *inaugural* distinction is always the infinite determination, a spirited one moreover, the spring that has made all the difference in the world by founding a tradition upon its issue; this is the sense of the infinity of thought and not the notion of an awaited, expected but retarded cessation or the endless regression upon and tedious recapitulation of what lacks sufficient resolution to come to an end – the first negation in the series is decisive and its certitude is reiterated in the development of all subsequent generations of difference.

Thus the series of distinctions based on the infinity of abstraction is the one by which the severalty of thought is spun as perpetual extrication. That is why it is posited as the first term in the sequence of distinctions that marks the passage from the chores and fond comforts of acquaintance to the extrinsic territories of the unknown and its outlandish terrors.

Its principle is that of the *absolute*, the step back which is not a backing away, a backing off or a backing up; the stand therein taken is a standing apart that furnishes, in fact, no place to stand, this no-place being merely the issue of the principle of thought that abstracts from and negates all place, marks the outer side of every enclosing boundary and delimitation and, in this sense, posits nothing more substantial than the *OUT of* the *Outside.*

Starting then with this relationship of the infinity of abstraction, the alternation reveals itself to be the expansion of progressively greater comprehension, each successive distinction encompassing a scope of greater extent than its predecessor – the infinity of thought's outward turn of abstraction might be characterized as that of the *radiance* of reason; in moments of critical reflection, you step back from (without shrinking from or shirking) your life and thus, taking a stance that is no mere standing, view it from without, as it were, considering, as a painter would, the difference between what went wrong and what went as it was supposed to, in other words, the difference between the IS and the OUGHT, giving rise to thought's regarding what should happen next to close this gap, and then undertaking to make plans in accordance with these reflections, setting goals that resolve themselves into means towards further ends and these towards the ultimate determinations of THE WAY IT SHOULD BE, the *Good,* as you continue to broaden your horizons to greater purpose and aspire to visions ever widening in their purview like the circular ripples of concentricity emanating from the initial disturbance of reflection that caused the discontinuity in the surface of a mirroring pool of dark, drowning, still water.

The converse series of distinctions articulates the relationship of the infinity of illumination by which our experience of self-severance is spun as an investigation and a quest into the veritable heart of the matter. The inquisitive gaze of perception is not satisfied with observation but rather studies appearances with a view towards understanding the laws that govern the apparition of their being the way they are, i.e. explain why beings should be such as they are. These reasons are not evident. They require the attendance of science that knows how to look behind the seens, read between the lies with which our immediate senses often beguile us. Insight looks inside, distilling, in its analysis of compounds, extracts of essence and quintessences and aligning them in a sequence that orders the properties of beings in a hierarchy of causes under a principle cause recognized as the first.

Whereas in the previous procession, thought's radiance grasped the principle as the aim towards which our action is directed, a greater purpose of ever widening practical scope, the principle of this procession sets thought on its way of investigation towards the grounds and substance of beings having first become entirely present to our curiosity and destined now, in a second reflection, to acquire a more fundamental distinction in the course of thought's ever deepening insight into and grasp of their nature. This progression of profundity and concentration upon the destiny of the beings in question is the efficacy of penetration, inward and intrinsic to them, beings disclosed to the intellect, not products of the imagination; their ideas are forms of knowledge, not purposes of the will; their truth is the recognized perfection, sought and found, of the epochal principle, not its realization, projected as the ideal and accomplished in a work of self-formation.

In moments of clarity, we are often struck by a fact and find ourselves wondering why it should be so. Stepping back from the immediacy of the way things are, we ask for the reason and consider the cause that might have led to these particular circumstances; upon further reflection, we realize that this cause, only just discovered and taken to be definitive, must have a cause and a reason as well and so we are compelled to ask again *why*, even as children do; we learn that with every step we take forward towards the ground and end, we take a step back as well, recurring upon the previous answer with the renewed question – every cause has a cause, every reason has a reason, and, in fact, several of them as do these in turn as well, forming an intricate reticulation of causes and reasons, a chain of reciprocal relationships of dependencies and conditions, from proximate to remote, that we may follow until we light upon the first cause and the simple constituent elements. In this way, thought, the Thinker, is the sharp-eyed hawk, the hunter, enjoying the pleasure of pursuit by soaring out and up into the air in order to plunge all the more lightning-like to earth upon its prey. Flight, sight, grasp – the ultimate end and first cause can only be pure reason itself having come to terms with its own being, its doing, the reality of its own making. This experience is visualized in *Figure 12.*

The vertiginous aspect of this movement of thought's approach reminds us however that the internal infinity of illumination is just as discomfiting as the obliquity of what is infinitely divergent with respect to the perpendiculars and parallels, the use and wont of our hardened habituations.

To seek the cause and consequence of accommodating confluence, to analyze the elements of its composition is to call into question and make an issue of its customs and so to disrupt the continuity of the peace and quiet it had previously and so anonymously enjoyed in the nondescript background of being, before attendance singled it out to stand before the categories of judgment and thus be accounted for as present in the larger scheme of things. Nonentities, having only just taken for granted their place in the whole, *receive* now, with this assignment of their proper place, their uncomfortable determination with regards to that principle and only then, having lost in the subsequent appointment the position they *assumed*, are they, in fact, specific and *distinguished* beings, beings, that is, recognized for what they truly are or, failed, are not, as is their doom and fate.

As we see in *Figure 12*, the inward infinity of the vanishing point "•", the *bindu*, the nucleus in this concentric figure of perfect focus – both the oculus and the zero point of reflection – complements that of the outward infinity of the horizon, the comprehensive ken and complete purview of scope. Whereas the spatial compass of grasp reaches out towards the exuberance of ever more capacious offing, the keen punctuality of inference induces the inspiration of keenest inning. Thought is seen as a *comprehending* act in the first case, *apprehending* in the second, the former a being of emergent *eminence*, the latter compelling *imminence*, this one a procession of *arrival*, the other the reversion of *departure*.

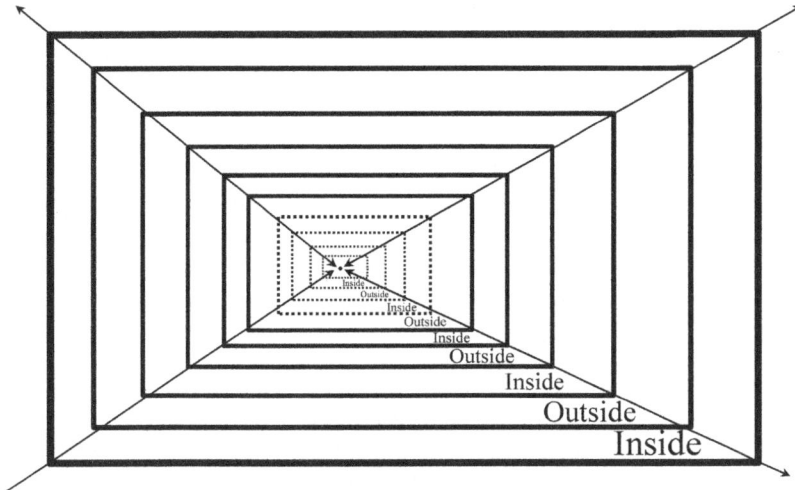

Figure 12: The Recursion of Self-Relativity

Thus our experience of the distinction of human being as our unique *sign*, though one significant procession, can be rendered in two ways. Whether seen as the drive towards the *ground* or to the *good*, the negativity inherent in the drawing of a distinction "localizes" the determination of pure reason as being neither simply "inside" nor simply "outside," neither just an inner nor just an outer limit. No, the site of its principle, the trait of cognizance that thought draws, the "point" that thought makes, has *two* "sides," which, in a further elaboration, are rendered as its "endpoints" suggesting in turn the space *between* them, that gap of transformation, that is the passage and the transition they define; they visualize thus actually the crossing *and* the chasm that it bridges. To think in distinctions is to undertake this passage into determinacy but also to step back and pass away from, to depart from determinacy – a property of reflection that has been known and appreciated throughout our philosophical tradition by thinkers and poets alike, one that we might call the *You-turn* of human being. But who is/are *You*? Let's wait and find out.

19. A Tradition of Distinction

It was, for example, with this remarkable property of thought's twofold being, being both absolutely *within* as well as permanently *without*, "not constrained by the greatest and yet contained in the smallest," the motto from Ignacio López de Loyola, that Hölderlin chose to define the divine for his *Hyperion.*

non coerceri maximo, contineri tamen a minimo, divinum est.[20]

Hölderlin will go on to show, as we will see when we examine his work *the Vehicle of Poetic Spirit* (Über die Verfahrungsweise des poetischen Geistes), how this being provides a rule "for the fulfillment of human destiny, which is the recognition of the unity and individuality of harmoniously opposed being *in* human being, and then again, the recognition of the identity, unity and individuality of human being *in* harmoniously opposed being." The former is the being within, the latter the being without and each is both inside and outside the other.

> *Auf diese Art erreicht er seine Bestimmung, welche ist –*
> *Erkenntnis des Harmonischentgegengesetzten in ihm, in seiner*
> *Einheit und Individualität, und hinwiederum Erkenntnis seiner*
> *Identität, seiner Einheit, und Individualität im Harmonischen-*
> *entgegengesetzten. (GSA 404)*

What could possibly be both absolutely inside and outside of itself? There is only one thing in Heaven and Earth – and it is no thing – that has this property, it is the being we have called *T,* the entity of identity, thought thinking thought in its own living, self-several presence. Thought is *within* thought when it thinks about thought and, thinking about thought, *without* thought as well. Thought is *in* and *of* thought, *to* and *from* thought. How can something so banally familiar to us as the fact of our own mind – for what in truth could possibly be more familiar, closer, to thought than thought itself, closer to you than *You* are – reveal itself upon reflection to constitute such a remarkable relationship deserving of the Poet's best and most transcendent names like *beautiful, holy, divine*? Put more critically, we might ask, what has happened to us that the mark of our human being has become so weary, stale, flat and unprofitable?

Pure reason, the being within and without in one – the idea shared in both of these absolute determinations of the poetic mind is that of the distinction itself, the original *cognizance* of being that makes all the difference. That is why it is so important to highlight in stark contrasts our original experience of the negativity of pure reason, in particular that of its abstraction which impels us to settle on no standpoint but rather to negate every standpoint;

---

[20] Hölderlin, *GSA,* III p.4.

every result is precarious in that it is itself, and will become, subject to the critical intervention of thought that, in due time, must inevitably reflect upon its former insight and achievement and, in so doing, draw upon it, from it, in turn, a new distinction, thereby plunging the accomplishments of its precursor thought into the abyss of reflection and embarking upon the passage of the subsequent distinction that distinguishes it once more from the confluent reign of completion and the continuity of control that had taken hold of the resolution only just enjoyed as radiant and illuminating and then lately already too long inhabited, given to decline towards formality, fading into oblivion, but now, with refreshed vigour, from the vantage point without, distinguished again, allowing differences to be noted that were previously held to be insignificant within the order of the former principle. Only apparently an exercise in sterile skepticism, thought thinking thought is in fact a perpetual rethinking and a recapitulation of the experience that thought has gained with thought since the beginning – that is precisely what the critical self-reflection of the entity of identity in difference is about. Pure thought, though symmetrically self-identical in its perfect self-relativity, recollects within the very scope and course of its continuity, a restless, discriminating spirit that gives an on-going account of itself in a moving narrative of critical events that we might call its charmed life the overall structure of which we have noted and illustrate again in *Figure 13* depicting our experience with this principle of thought in a procession of distinctions – an outward transcendence as much as it is inward in concentration – that we have termed the *ingemination* of thought.

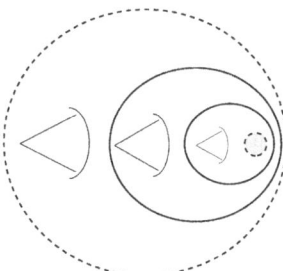

Figure 13: The Recurrence of Thought

This reiterating, recursive structure exhibits the self-imbedded critical reflection of thought, the spiriting negativity inherent in the centrifugal/centripetal tendency of the mind to reconsider the authority of precedence, to readjust the conditions of contracts that have been previously arbitrated, to reprise the issue of foregone conclusions that have been taken as settled upon once and for all by a mind made up.

Consider *Figure 14* as the simplest rendition of the critical activity of pure reason which consists essentially of drawing a distinction, making a difference that recalls and projects a background of both *temporal* continuity, a previous void as well as the one to follow with the waning of discernment, reflection's bygone days and its hereafter, i.e. the nullity prior and subsequent to the inscription of the mark *now* – as well as a *spatial* one – prior and subsequent to the X (or the sign of logical negation "⌐" or simply the letter "A") marking the spot pinpointed as *here* and contemporary with, though distinguished from, everywhere else.

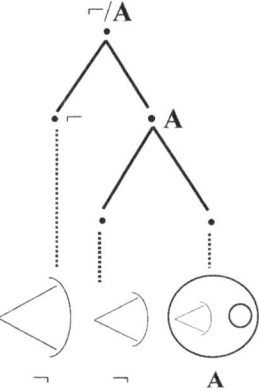

**Figure 14: The Negation of the Negation
as the Critical Review of Reflection**

Each distinction is a repetition of the inaugural act of stepping back (⌐A) but is nevertheless, at the same time and in the same place, a remembrance and a recollection of thought's former distinction (⌐ ⌐A), seen to comprise, upon reflection of what pure reason has accomplished, three unique periods in a cycle that encompasses and focuses recognition rather than discards and disperses thought's endowment predicated upon the vanishing point of undecidable continuity *and* difference (⌐ /A), an object as impossible as it is real, whose figure becomes the ground and whose ground the figure, vase/face, face/vase.

For throughout our philosophic tradition, reason has, perpetually and regularly, renewed the vigor of its distinction upon the basis of a received and recognized heritage of knowledge and insight. In such negativity as has emerged from this critical standpoint, knowledge was neither discarded outright nor was it merely adopted as accepted orthodoxy to repulse ideas that followed. The precise movement of this tradition, enacting as it does the life of thought's own development, will be the topic of our explorations later. Suffice it to say for the time being that each epoch of our philosophical tradition, each day in the life, each season in the year, each term in the ratio, each star in the constellation of thought's cosmos of distinctions offered one complete vision of pure reason's threefold life, first as that of *theory* and the **conceptual foundation** of an inaugural and original principal, second that of *practice* and the **performative enterprise** of moral action flowing from an absolute principle and finally as that of poetic invention and the **generative achievement** of realization as the history of the experience gathered over time with the perpetually turning and returning distinction of human being.

In reviewing and renewing its distinction in each epoch, thought was not being capricious or arbitrary but rather by design adhering to the exigencies that its theme and object presented to it. In retrospect, that is, from our latter-day perspective, one could say perhaps that thought came to terms with its own properties and features by degrees, step by step – thought revealed itself to be a threefold activity of distinction. And this activity has become articulate and attained substantial significance in the cultural history of the Occident – where thinking has always made all the difference in the world. An examination of the tradition of thought's distinction teaches us to recognize thought in action and to appreciate all that thought has accomplished in the history of a civilization that is, with regards to that distinction of self-severalty, "universal" but neither national, nor global, nor cosmopolitan, nor ecumenical – founding no empire, commanding no dominion.

The philosophical tradition of European culture succinctly demonstrates the procession of thought's self-possession and affirmation as it is driven by the critical animus of pure reason, the productive ingemination of abstraction that we have been studying. In its light, an account of our cultural tradition, rather than merely narrating the history of events, of nations, of people, is taken to record the gradual elaboration of an idea, testifying to and documenting the profundity of depth and the enrichment of breadth of the experience human being has gained with self-critical thought and therefore with itself as distinguished by the endowment of ΛΟΓΟΣ.

This experience is, in fact, a process of learning and building, a deepening and a broadening of the human mind as our self-knowing, self-forming, self-reforming nature. Thus if the movement of thought is a circle, it is not merely that of a wheel spinning round and round, but rather its revolutions are that of a helix or a vortex, or, better yet, a circle of discontinuous circles and, in this sense, an *encyclopedic* compendium of all things thought.

In *Figure 15*, we illustrate this movement briefly by setting down terms that have been sanctioned in the course of this tradition. They are "merely" sample names for reason's features, for its acts and works, its life and times, though they would seem to enjoy, even today, some remnant of the privilege and the repute that formerly had been accorded to the fruits of classical learning. By invoking the distinction of their terms, we intend only to attest our reverence and devotion to the cause that thinkers and poets have always considered to be of outstanding importance with a view towards gaining insight into the destiny of human being.

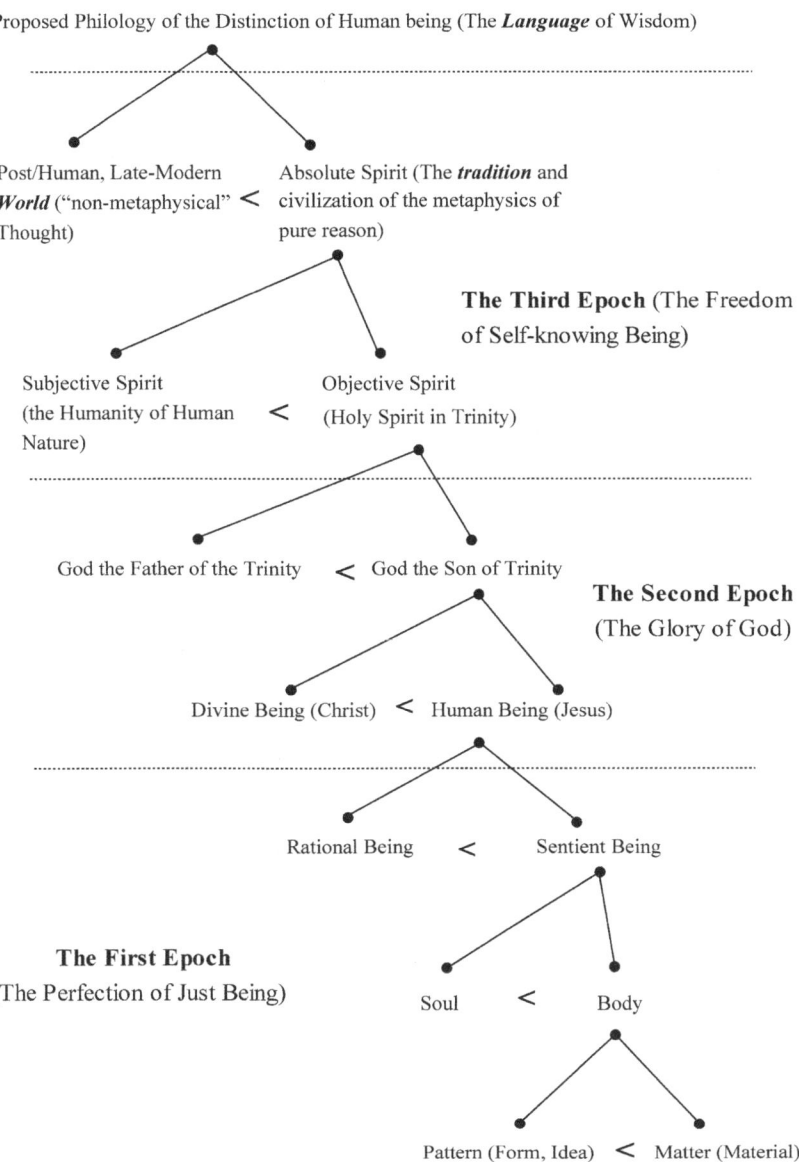

Proposed Philology of the Distinction of Human being (The *Language* of Wisdom)

Post/Human, Late-Modern *World* ("non-metaphysical" Thought) < Absolute Spirit (The *tradition* and civilization of the metaphysics of pure reason)

The Third Epoch (The Freedom of Self-knowing Being)

Subjective Spirit (the Humanity of Human Nature) < Objective Spirit (Holy Spirit in Trinity)

God the Father of the Trinity < God the Son of Trinity

The Second Epoch (The Glory of God)

Divine Being (Christ) < Human Being (Jesus)

Rational Being < Sentient Being

The First Epoch (The Perfection of Just Being)

Soul < Body

Pattern (Form, Idea) < Matter (Material)

Figure 15: The Procession of Principles

Contemplating this figure (and "reading" it from the bottom to the top), is it not remarkable how one word can be made to stand for an entire epoch, centuries of thought, sprawling on a pin? Late/modern thought has taught us how it is done, how one word, though spoken mostly with disdain these days by thinkers, can be made to say it all (and facilitate disposal) – *reason!*

This diagram of epochal distinctions shows how reason proceeds to establish a new vision of its distinction upon that of an antecedent achievement of distinguished thought. In spite of appearances, the bifurcate structure that it exhibits is not arboreal, taxonomical, hierarchical, or dichotomous in the manner of so-called (and much maligned) "binary logic."

Rather, it renders a movement of discontinuity in which the system of the previous achievement serves as the foundation for its subsequent "demise" in the articulation of a successor principle that neither merely promulgates convention nor dismisses or ignores its forerunner as irrelevant, but rather receives it in the manner of a bequeathal, learning to build upon what has been hitherto accomplished and to complete what has been started, incorporating all that has been achieved by the masters of yore and, as would a member of the guild in service to its cause and continued tradition, carrying on their art and craft in the affirmation of thought as the self-several entity of self-reflection that is our destiny as human beings.

Insight is not lost in subsequent generations of knowledge but rather conserved; but it is not statically or quiescently conservative; on the contrary, the tradition of philosophy is ascendant and flourishing in its maturity and fruition; its revolutions and reformations are quite the opposite of being deleterious; concordant to their supposed sedition is the treasuring recollection and the composed genealogy of thoughtful enterprise, the well-known sublation (Aufheben) of precursor distinctions that Hegel spoke of in connection with the *work of conception* (*die Arbeit des Begriffs*).

To use the familiar analogy of the tree in characterizing the structure of knowledge and reflection, we mean to note in *Figure 15* not only the ramification of root and branch, but also the "retention" of annual growth rings of a tree – its concepts are structured in a pattern of recurrence that is, nevertheless, not merely the *philosophia perennis* of academia, the eternal return of the same, but rather a rediscovery and reinvigoration of thought, of our human sprite gone trite.

<{Post/human Modernity <{Humanity < {Trinity < {Divinity <
{Reason < {Soul < {Form < Matter}}}}}}

As the embedded structure indicates, this procession of distinctions in terms taken from the philosophical tradition is just an example of the process of the severalty of thought placed in the framework of Western cultural history, unique in the spirit of discontinuity that founded three different epochal principles as well as their corresponding reality. We note how on each "level" of the figure a previous distinction has resolved itself into closure, providing its posterity thus with the basis for a new and nevertheless descendent distinction. This outward movement of *protention*, the extensive conceptual history of reformations and the upheavals of its event, can thus also be read in reverse as *retention*, as the intensive movement of intellectual profundity concentrating into a tradition that goes way back, goes deeper, all the way back to the big bang of the original cognizance that the ΛΟΓΟΣ is.

Moreover the signature terms of this series suggest that the overall development is circular, no, better, helical, no, better yet, taking late modernity's fascination with the "twisted" mind into account, Möbian. For lurking in the wings of post/human modernity is the conception of the flat immateriality of man, i.e. the "abhuman" – a "warped"notion harking back to the concept of primitive or "pure" *matter* and merest being in abstraction of which *form*, as the first term of distinction, was perceived – against this backdrop of man's *dehominisation*, we propose the study of pure thought as the first form and the *distinction* of human being.

The drawing of a thoughtful distinction is therefore the first achievement of thought, the ***inaugural negativity*** of an animated spirit, following the rule of dissimilarity (a = ⌐ a), which clears the ground and sets the stage so that thought thinking thought might undertake to build upon the distinction of a previous insight, receiving it critically and transforming it in light of a new task. This renewed purpose does not depend on the vanity of a particular scholar's whim; it is introduced by insight into the scheme of all things thought. This scheme and movement is thought's own, a record of its own operations, and we will examine it in part two of this investigation when we explore the logotectonic method.

Receiving that previous knowledge, thought steps back from it to appraise it in its entirety, distinguishing itself from it at the same time as it takes that predecessor system into account with a view towards its conception as a whole. Thought taking note is the recurrence and the recreation of its critical coign of vantage, a standpoint regained that, with regards to its own legacy, is neither that of hostility nor of estrangement. On the contrary. It is thought's native recollection and regard; it is still and always was pure reason that is the cause and purpose of the heart starting; its progression in the course of tradition and the plenitude of the distinctions that its articulation has brought forth *and* recorded are still just thought thinking thought, the self-several efficacy of pure reason as the identifying mark of our human being, the commencement of one thought thinking thought and not a bunch of thoughts thinking about thoughts, mulling them over, brooding, worrying. Let this be the second achievement of thought, the *fulfilled reflection,* following the rule of identity (a = a) which states that pure reason in all of its works and objects is alone concerned with pure reason and nothing else.

These two laws, which have been guiding our analysis from the start, are illustrated in the progression of terms that are the elements constituting the divergences of *Figure 15.* The vertical movement beginning with the Greek Epoch of thought depicts thought as the recollection of its distinctions; the horizontal movement depicts thought as the reflection upon its distinctions. The first movement records how thought has resolved its distinction into the closure of a complete system of knowledge – an archeological process; the second movement articulates the recreation of thought in attaining the vigour of a new distinction on the basis of a previous insight that has attained the totality and substantiality of assured knowledge, of science – the genealogical process of origins and ends. Each new principle placed the knowledge of previous epochs into a larger framework of all things thought, showing how, in fact, thought itself has attained, had needed to attain and to affirm, a more complete vision of the distinguished and, as we will see, threefold, nature of this thing called thought, that is no thing at all.

20. Thought as Return

For, while the exaltation of *departure* suggests the figure of the divergence of ways and portrays pure reason in the detachment of critical discernment in which, from the abstraction of a remote height and a profound depth, *critical difference* emerges and the cognizance of eminence that pure reason makes when it distinguishes itself, being both far out and all in, outer space and inner circle, the outside from within, the inside from without, to night the break of day, to day distinguished night – clearly, thought is not only a leave of absence, taking leave, but also the mark of an encounter and the realization of its own unique being.

This comely encounter is a turning and returning of thought to gaze upon itself, reviewing its own nature, as it were, and in this meeting, taking pleasure in the intimacy of self-knowledge – pure reason as *reflection*, as mentioned initially, is, above all, the act of taking note of thought's excursion as, finally, a delightful outing, a tour, that is rich in new experience, one of light that is free of glare, of intensity without leaden gravity, and then, finally, of returning refreshed back home in the evening to discover its own being as that original principle of both places such that thought becomes its own object, the form becomes the content. Abstraction and reflection, contradiction and identity, are conjoint in their difference; their conjugation is the impossible harmony of an essential inner discontinuity; pure reason is the name for our experience of this chiral tension in its absolute dissymmetry.

Here again in *Figure 16* is our ouroboros, our cycle-logical symbol of one period, forth and back in the wink of an eye, the instant of thought thinking thought, saying and seeing I to I, knowing and loving YOU like a father and a son, recognizing IT as the entity of identity, THE WAY IT IS corresponding, in the end, to the vision of THE WAY IT SHOULD BE, and THE WAY IT SHOULD BE affirmed in THE WAY IT IS, which is the entirety of the identity that proceeds from as well as founds the coeval disparity, the severalty of its human being:

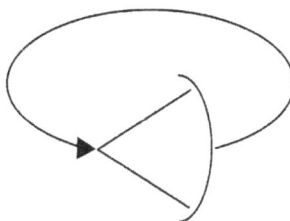

Figure 16: The Ouroboros of Critical Self-Reflection

Encountering this being now and considering its property of reflection, we note that the relationship of its turn and return manifests two sides, one as its work of perception in which, stepping back, it attains the vantage point of thinking and the other as the being that thinks and, as such, becoming the object of thought, the being that is actually encountered and whose physique is now being investigated. We might visualize the gaze of contemplation as follows in *Figure 17*:

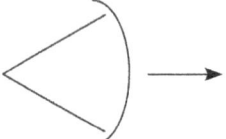

Figure 17: The Coign of Vantage

The first moment is the centrifugal spin of abstraction, the act of stepping back from indiscriminate confluence and, subsequently, the transcendent flight of the exalted eye-beam of the mind become awake to difference that pure thought, its negativity, makes; this is the moment when senses are sharp with all ears listening and eyes peeled in the acuity of attention, ready to note the fine distinction that is pure reason's own indelible trait. This is the image of thought *thinking* in which we highlight only the first moment of its discernment, the radiance of sight bent on seeing the scene.

The second, the centripetal movement is the encounter of that unique being that, itself the spark, has sparked the imagination. It is the completion of the first impulse to take note and is the realization that the being that has taken note is not merely *sight* but also that very being *seen*, the inspiration of sight. Thus bright *and* brightening is not merely the *thought* but also the *thing* thought, not merely *the mind* but also the *matter* that is on our mind, not merely the *ontological* but also the *epistemological* determination of pure reason. For pure reason alone, *knowing* is the same as *being known* and *thinking* one with *being, being* one with *thinking* – that is precisely what *identity* means – originally conceived of by Parmenides as the *perfection* of the one and only, well-rounded, and persuasive truth. We visualize this side of the relationship in *Figure 18* as that of thought thinking *thought*, highlighting reflection's commitment to gain insight that immediately seizes upon the object of thought most luminously present to it, namely *its own* proper presence. Grasping the origin of thought's distinction in the priority of its sight, we now note the site of its accomplishment when its properties and its features become apparent to it.

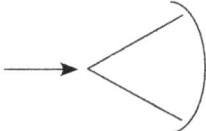

Figure 18: The Seeing Being Being Seen

This chiral property of reflection or, as it is often called these days, *intentionality*, is the most salient feature of determinate thinking – of practical as well as theoretical reason; knowledge is knowledge *of something*, every science has its object of study, every look is the seeing *and* the seen and to touch is to be touched and likewise striving is striving towards the goal of resolution, living the restless life of distinction. At this juncture, only after the period of purification inherent in the discipline of diremption, does thought come finally to discover and give presence to its object, the living practice of the *actor* becoming the *performer* of that presence and not merely the *spectator* who, after the former's, the builder's, invention, commences to study and explore it with a view towards conception. But prior to such contemplative work of reason – science – reason must be first awakened to the distinction and the difference that pure thought makes, which is the work and the effect of the said poetic creation, the *art*, and the endeavor to accomplish the determination of the principle through the practice of living action, *religion*, both of which, the former in *word* and the latter in *deed*, give rise to the distinction of thought in the first place, starting again the benign circle of experience with thought that it is the qualifying distinction of human being to go through. As much as thought is *realization*, it is, before that, the agonizing experience of *disintegration*, the negation through which all reality is determined by the limit that is pure thought's defining mark and character.

21. Abstraction and Reflection

We talk about thought, study it, explore and visualize its properties and seek words to denote these attributes in a way that sheds light on our theme – which we have called "pure reason," *thought thinking thought*. At least as the object of our investigations and, as the subject of our exposition, assuming thought is endowed with the properties we can convincingly attribute to it, pure reason is a *being*, a remarkable manifold being, one *and* several, with a unique substance and nature that we have already noted as its self-several self-relativity. It is this reflective relationship of chiral tautology that is the issue – we are not considering this entity of identity merely in terms of the self-knowing being of the conscious mind (Selbstbewußtsein), the form given to it by the Third Epoch, though, in fact, even Hegel had already freed the self-relativity of thought from the limitation that his precursors had placed upon its *absolute idea* in reducing its universal personality to that of the first person singular, namely to the self-knowing being of Me, Myself, and I. Now of course the self-relativity of thought can also be rendered as My subjectivity (das Ich) as distinguished from My objectivity (das Nicht-ich) and the absolute Personality (das Absolute), being what it is because it is, in one, freedom's cause *and* freedom's being and in this sense cause of itself (causa sui), the one side being the seen, the other the seeing, the intelligence.

Most famously, it was Hegel who crowned the occidental trilogy of philosophy with a comprehensive conception of thought as that specific countermanding movement of "setting safely aside" positive determinations (Aufheben), the critical exercise and the *force* of the self-relative mind, that he called the *principle of process*, the *purity and the infinity of the negative, the absolute restlessness of pure self-movement*, of *self-disunion*, setting thus the motion and promotion of the mind's distinction against the stasis of all selfish or self-centered, self-seeking, self-aggrandizing ipseity, which is, rather, the adversary of thought, being, more precisely, not merely thoughtlessness, but rather the perversion of solipsistic reason, the innate autism, narcissism, and sophism of the twisted mind.

In contrast to the divisive relationship of negativity, thought's disengagement, this living being, alive in the activity of "stepping out" and "stepping back," of gaining perspective, *ΛΟΓΟΣ*, is also, in spite of the occasional uncomfortable keenness and the sharpness of the distinguished mind – and therefore experienced as the divisive penetration of acumen – a relationship of accord. The entity of identity, thought's own being, is thought thinking thought and, in recognizing itself as thinking, being its own recognition, and therefore being and remaining perfectly in tune with what it is thinking about. At the end of its descent into the depths – for that is the image suggested by the inward turning of reflection – perception encounters its own form, namely that intriguing circularity of self-substantiating recognition. In spite of the tenor of its self-returning progression, its ingemination remains a perpetually renewing whole, one and the same and nevertheless *several* in a sequence of differentiations.

This iterating rapport is not one of redundancy, coincidence, or equivalence. The journey to the centre of the earth is, even as was the journey to the stars, a twofold adventure of departure from earth-bound immediacy, one extra-terrestrial, one subterranean. It is, rather, the intuition of intimacy, the vital crux, the crucial and compelling juncture that effectuates unity in the permanence of difference that is not merely the divergence of abstraction but also the concurrence of regard and the sustenance of dwelling. The figure of thought thinking thought is infinite neither in the sense of being unbounded nor in the sense of being undefined, but rather in the sense of being self-limiting, self-bounded, where, as with any geometrical shape, the line defining, determining, limiting the shape and the shape itself are one and the same and not extrinsic to the former being, itself absolutely intrinsic *form*, in the distinction of its self-mediated being. This perfect community of the two, namely their mutually bestowed identity, is not synthetic; in other words, the properties we have attributed to the self-relationship of pure reason do not coalesce in the benign neglect of their divergence. For reason is precisely the mark of distinction that contravenes continuity, though, for all that, is not annihilation or dismemberment, but rather a self-sustaining, enduring deliberation that, after weighing their differences, apportions its constituents into a distinguished (and not synchronized) community. And the comity of this community, being neither flat nor bland, is the relish, the tang of pure reason's fruition – delight in actually just being thought, a wonder that perpetually renews itself in the exaltation of abstraction and the rapture of reflection – in its exhilaration, thought is "beside itself" but neither fanatic nor frenzied; in its recognition, it is self-gratifying, but in this neither swollen nor vain. The enchanting conviviality, the touching intimacy, of these two sides of thought in their immediacy characterize the modulations of its rejoicing the improbable felicity of which has been commemorated in songs of praise since the days of yore.

Thus, its harmony is not that of monotony but rather, as Hölderlin says, the sonority of counterpoint encompassing and resolving but not dissolving dissonances – precisely (but not fastidiously) rendered ratios and taut (but not gaunt) relationships of tonality. Its proportions are not that of a square-jawed square, neither the stuffy isotropy of trite uniformity or slavish regularity, not the parody of parroting parity, not reactionary annexation or the reappropriating expropriation of dispossession, not the retrogradation of assimilation, recidivist absorption, or reassuring reduction, nor the even-steven, clean-cut, two-headed, one-two combination of gear-wheel synchronization, but rather, at least in our sublunary regions, irregular, asymmetrical, equivocal, ambivalent – a *precarious* balance and *incommensurable*, asymptotic proportion, not the one, the two-edged sword, not an inert, not a tame but rather a brightly burning, a fearful symmetry, like a tyger's.

Again, what is thought? Let us summarize what we have found out about it. Till now we have considered the self-relativity of its reflection and the negativity of its abstraction, the critical act of *stepping back* and the progress, the *stepping forth* into the procreative sequence of distinctions and the ingemination of the principle that the attainment of a critical standpoint entails. Clearly, we may always call into question a given state of affairs, considering it from without, from the Archimedean standpoint of view, disconcerting as such a standpoint may be for all those involved. This process of critical reflection has been presented as an embedded structure of alternating closure and disclosure. Reason's achievement of closure is understood as the fulfillment (and not merely the "saturation") of the original principle the development of which was initiated by the perceived difference between THE WAY IT IS and THE WAY IT SHOULD BE. Reason's mark of disclosure is understood as this distinction that the principle of critical thought has made in a particular situation that had come to be taken for granted. Taking note of this gap, minding it, calls that previously accepted system into question even as the drive of thought is engaged in the pursuit of the accomplishment of the cause and necessity that this distinction has revealed, whether it be understood in terms of the First Epoch as the *Apportionment of Fate*, in terms of the Second Epoch as the *divine Will of the Father* or in terms of the Third Epoch as the *Imagination of the Ideal*. The term *realization* refers not only to the fulfillment of a principle but also to the accomplishment of understanding of one who has taken note and, subsequently, grasped what is going on. Seen in this light, our entire study is nothing more than an investigation into what it means to "realize" something and what is at stake when someone says with concern, "I have never realized...." *Figure 14* is the simplest schematic of this process of realization that is reason's own, the distinction that we might, however, enact upon ourselves and *Figure 15*, finally, is the fact of this realization presented in terms taken – as one might receive and take an heirloom – from the three epochs our philosophical tradition.

Hence, in contrast to first appearances, critical reflection is not an "infinite regression" or a "self-contradiction" in any sense that thinkers of repute are supposed to eschew as signs of faulty thinking and irrationality, because thought thinking thought is actually one complete round of reason and the step by step exposition of our insight into the issue of the distinction that is the meaning and designation of human being, viz. the capacity and the activity of stepping back and disclosing the gap, the decisive fork between

IS and the OUGHT of thought as our self-several being; nothing is gained by mechanical or formal reiteration, though of course, in our lives we are constantly regaining the critical perspective, even as we lose it constantly, getting swamped, bogged down, stagnating in the formalities and mechanics of everyday life, going through the motions. Thus taking as our starting point the immediate experience of *thought thinking thought* (1.) and then thinking (2.) about what it means to think about thought and then wondering (3.) why anyone would even try to consider what thinking about thinking means, only to thoughtfully deny (4.) that this example of thinking about thinking about thinking about thinking is a fruitful argument for or against conceiving of thought as critical self-reflection. Depending on the person, this train of thought might have reached the same conclusion in three steps or got stuck and quit after six.

Infinite "regression" (and "progression" as well for that matter) can be, but need not be, considered either repellent or malignant to thought. It depends on the argument and the purpose that the thinker has in mind by referring to it; if infinite re- and progression indicate a mindlessly repetitive structure then, clearly what merely repeats a formal operation without making any substantive contribution to the development of a train of thought is not all that useful or insightful and therefore becomes quickly tedious whereas, on the other hand, an *infinite* train of thought, whatever its author might mean by this designation, might at least have been intended to be an expression of richness and plenitude, perpetuity or perseverance, of the virtually inexhaustible sustainability of a line of reasoning that counts and takes account. Obviously, making a distinction, making the *same* point twice adds nothing to and in fact may even detract from the argument once the point has been properly, winningly, made the first time.

If pure reason is a circle then it is one with its beginning in the negativity of abstraction and its end in the reflective entity of identity, regardless of where these two points, which are actually just one point, are put on the circle. The curved space of its continuity comprehends a break and a gap that is its center, is the very source of the movement that traces the original circuit. Thought thinking thought, though the very epitome of continuity and immediacy and presence, being an entity of identity and therefore completely and immediately transparent, perfectly close to itself, contains, within the flight of its arc, in the story of the epochs of its life, reveals in the hours of its day's completion, in the seasons of its year turning, in the collaboration of the members of its body, the separate powers of its state, an inaugural and mediating event of discontinuity and opening, which is thought's start and the leave of absence, thought's being without that takes place within its presence. It is the distinction of human being and the sign of the mind to experience this nature, so wholesome and entire, as, nevertheless, all the more, torn.

Once torn, one turn and return is enough to outline the circumference, measure the magnitude and to appreciate the amplitude of this very human experience. The infinity of its course consists not in the potential tedium of the repetition it might seduce us to, but rather in its self-relative severalty, being a passage and a transition of *transformation* as much as an object of *contemplation* and a subject of poetic *invention*; the infinity of this self-relationship is not potential at all but rather entirely actual – in circumnavigating the circle, we experience the approach of the starting point to the extent that we leave it behind, heading further and further out we head back home, our way up is our way down and the vault of thought night *and* light.

The abstracting negativity of departure and the fulfilled reflection of arrival – these two sides of the aporia of the experience with our distinction, can be distinguished at precisely that point where the arrowhead meets the nock – the decisive point and the critical juncture of self-relativity where the sight becomes the seen and the *will be* the *has been*. It is a circle for crying out loud! There is nothing "contradictory" or "irrational" about a circle, despite the aporia and the paradox that a train of thought along its line might entail – it is just a circle for Heaven's sake! Aye, forsooth, what could be more sensible, more reasonable than a simple circle? The paradox lies in the terms in which the matter may be put; but these and the elaboration of our experience with thought in language are our own work of invention and imagination, ours and the work of poetic thought, the Builder.

The beginning and the end of the circle. And what else? Don't forget the radius – the center of its disk in relationship to its outline. For the center of the circle is its true origin, the beginning of the beginning of the circle of distinction that is thought thinking thought; this starting point is both within and beyond, never on its perimeter, the origin, unmoved and never to be attained, yet still completely determining that perfect orbit from afar, that distinguished being that inspires our highest and most profound regard. You would call it the Ø and the Θ of thought? Is that the best we can do as concerns names?

22. The Tell-tale Mark of Man in Light of Post/Modern Thought

Retarded, that is to say, *late* modernity has cast this property of thought, its capacity for and facility in drawing distinctions, in a variety of aspects, some enlightening, many shocking, and all amusingly, farcically assumed to be inimical to the very idea of pure reason – so many guises and dissimulations of thought, faces that they have been made for, or better, *at* thought, in the name of the Other with a capital *O*, *Ø*, **Ө**.

Imagine now the consternation of the advocates (as well as the opponents) of alterity to find that the bone of their so ardent contention is posited here in a take on thought and on their take of it that not merely comprehends their topic as a bona fide property of pure reason, but moreover welcomes, in the Platonic spirit of gymnastics, their intellectual potpourri as a challenge to our fitness in the use of tongue and tooth to discriminate the tang of its juice in the vast variety of dishes in which their thinking has lately been featured, relishing, with all the gusto of an acquired taste, the stark, repellent, but therein, like sulphur, salubrious, Camembert of the idioms that characterize these thinkers' brand of discourse and are no less averse to the exercise of perspicuity to which we are by them obliged, namely, again and again, to perceive the nature and workings of the distinction, that sign, that is our cause, in a remarkably heterogeneous variety of narrative settings, reaffirming the prevalence, better, the universality, best, the absolute and permanent abstraction of thought from every definition of our experience of it and providing us therefore, through their avid championing of diversity, with a self-serving proof of the omniscience, omnipresence, omnipotence, in a word, in *their* word, the *plurality*, i.e. the pluripotency and pluripresence of pure reason, particularly when inscribed by their discursive techniques of occultation into the shifting planes of meaning that govern the play, the trifle, and the downward cascade of lived experience, the very element that would seem to be most repugnant to thought.

As we are led to understand, every single thing can represent the *Other* to thought, or, as we should like to put the matter, represents a summons to or an instigation of the difference and distinction that is the discerning principle of reason. Or, as Derrida playfully-enigmatically puts it as the heading of the fourth and last chapter in his essay *Donner la Mort* (Gift of Death), "each and every other is utterly other."

Tout autre est tout autre.[21]

The wholly Other is thus a designation of what is entirely and irreducibly different, a property we have examined as that of the abstraction of *thought* when compared to the thing, of the *mind* with regards to matter, of the *ideal* over against the real, of *being* utterly other than beings. For the distinction of our human being is precisely this, namely to be permanently *other than*, that is to say, to be, by thought, *distinguished* in ourselves *from* ourselves; whoever heard of such a being as this? Being human is this impossible being of identity *and* difference; not merely *seeing* this being and *singing* this being but especially *being* this being, our indigenous alienation, that is not merely for contemplating in theory or celebrating in poetry but also for putting into practice and living, doing – that is surely the hardest thing of all, namely striving to be and, too, striving not to be what we are, in one being, that is, in thought and by thought, always already other than ourselves, striving to be who we truly are and were meant to be and therefore striving to be what we are not yet and therefore striving to be what we are and therefore striving to be what we are not, and therefore what we are and therefore what we are not...most truly. What an odd, unheard of being is *human* being! So utterly unlike any other for being absolutely and completely unlike itself, for being riven in its sentience, condemned to death in its sentence! And the more it is like itself the less it is like itself until, ideally, at the end of time so to speak, having become finally and ultimately itself, it is now completely and perfectly distinguished from itself for all time and therefore finally and permanently, for all intents and purposes, that is to say, practically, beyond itself though now all the more strikingly in and of itself, a *theoretical* being to be marvelled at, meditated upon and a *poetic* one all the better to be sung and celebrated as impossible as well as necessary; for, having left the realm of human *practice* in *despair*, we are not at the end of the story of pure reason, not at the end of human being by any means, but rather are now, gazing at this improbable being in contemplative *amazement*, poised at the beginning of the science that has left all beings behind save one, namely this one, this unique being that is the self-several self-relativity of pure reason. It cannot be *humanly* done, not completely, that is true, but it *can* be thought, grasped, but not completely. Thought *can* be divined, not without difficulty perhaps and not without persistent and painstaking efforts on our part; but by dint of keen human acumen and a bit of luck, thought *can* nevertheless be humanly

---

[21] Derrida, *Donner la mort*, p. 110.

thought, *can* be, by humans, divinely seen and sung in *joy*. And this is, in *theory*, the joy of philosophy; this is reason's infinite pain, not jest, in *practice*; this is, thus, at the end, when tears subside, *poetically* put, a full life, with all its seasons and seasonings, a noteworthy one devoted to this distinguished being that is the destiny of human being, as we shall see, not only Our Death but also Our Life after death – a distinguished death *and* a distinguished life, in that order.

Consider late modern discourse and its preoccupation with naming the Other, placing it thus vividly, plentifully and, above all, inaccessibly, before our very eyes, in the currency of human preoccupation with issues related to domination and exclusion. We select at random, in post/modern fashion, a variety of candidate names for our cause and see if we can, in a train of thought, more specifically, in a sequence of connotations, connect a term to the issue of our principle. Accounting thus for our distinction as it is envisioned in a variety of tropes and designations, not only do we vindicate it as our cause but also sharpen the acuity of our perception, the intellect of reading between the lines that is here required, in preparation for our own building efforts. It is gymnastics and an exercise in "poetic" deduction to identify these notions, recognizing how and where they fit in the scheme of all things thought and attain therein the status of beings in language, in the world, and in history.

A thesaurus or dictionary (how important these are to the method of late-modern thinkers and poets!) offers us synonyms and fresh terms, new and surprising images for the Other, a great plenitude and plurality of them and even provides us (if it is one of the better dictionaries), with etymological references to elaborate upon. The connotations of these terms, their synonyms and associations, whether psychologically or phonetically based, in short, in their being as speech, provide a dwelling for thought in the substance of living *language;* and again, through the reference of language to the substance of experience, they attain their determinations in the element of the *world;* and finally, so that they might be a record of the event of distinctions that have made a difference in the scheme of all things thought, these ideas are placed within the epochal elaboration of the *history* of pure reason.

Thus, since pure reason, designated now as our ownmost *Other*, is nothing if not many-voiced, multiple and manifold, plural and polyphonic, multifaceted and multifarious, is not and cannot be made fast and fastened, is not earth-bound and cannot be permanently, only provisionally grounded, it might be termed, say, *flight*, a migratory bird's travail of passage long before becoming the olive branch of the alighting dove of peace; or how about the *sublimation* of water into *ethereality* of air through the fire's refinement? Do these terms strike a chord? Further in this vein and train of thought: The Other's subtlety may be seen as the *sky* and skyward, *up* and upper, *far* and further, *out* and outer, *beyond* the limit, the *wilderness* prowling beyond the ramparts of the city, the rising *desert* encroaching upon an oasis of civilization, the *stranger* before, behind the door and the *door* itself as the *opening* of intrusion, the *hole* in the wall and then again, being thus *remote* and utter *exteriority* – for that is a way of speaking of the negativity of thought as well – *incalculable* to the usurpation of calculation, of forecast and prediction, and therefore *inaccessible* and *impregnable* like a remote *fort* upon a mountain, entirely *within* the limits of its bulwarks, not flight to the sun but plummeting *fall* towards *gravity's* core, deep *down under* the earth like a diamond *lost*, left and *forgotten* in the shaft of a mine, *hidden*, a face *mute*, *impassive*. More specifically, we recognize the issue of thought's abstraction in the *prisoner* locked in, in the *secret* locked away, in the *leper* locked out or take the *refugee* leaving home to escape danger and facing an uncertain future or even the *Jew* as the veritable symbol of the "exiled being of exclusion."[22] How's that again? In

---

[22] Blanchot sees this idea as the threefold "metaphysical" justification for the existence of the "Jew" who, first, "exists so that the notions of *exodus* and *exile* might exist as true movement…;" second, "the Jew exists so that through exile and as the result of exodus the experience of the *being without* might be affirmed in its irreducible relationship to us;…" and third "the Jew exists so that by the authority of this experience we might learn the distinction inherent in language…." See his *L'Entretien Infini*, p. 183. Thus, apparently, put in these terms, the experience of the distinction of human being is "Jewish." Hmm! Does this way of putting the matter suggest an explanation for what it means (and what it has meant) for enemies of critical reflection to seek to exterminate the self-several character of our human being? George Steiner in *Errata: An Examined Life* argues in a similar vein: "Three times Judaism has brought Western Civilization face to face with the blackmail of the ideal. What graver affront? Three times like a crazed watcher in the night…, it has cried out to common humanity to transform itself into full humanity, to renege its ego, its inborn appetites, its bias to license and options. In the name of the "unspeakable" God on Sinai; of love unbounded for one's enemies; at the behest of social justice and economic equality. In their claims to perfection, these demands are irrefutable." (p.67) In our study, we will consider ideas and their provenance as absolutely distinct from determinations of race and ethnicity, thought as absolutely distinct from thinkers, i.e. *pure* reason. Incredibly however, as we see, its issue can indeed be (and has been) put in racial terms as well. But does that really help? Has such an idiom of thought ever helped in the past? *Dubito.*

the intuition of this alter-thinking, we see pure reason richly rendered in the vision of the *exodus* and the *exile* of the *Jew* (historically, the *being without* par excellence), or the *refugee escaping* (stepping back from) *impending danger* (the outside breaking in) *to face* (turn outwardly) an *uncertain future* (opposing the complacency of certainty) in *hope* (of possible redemption) or *despair* (at the prospect of what has been lost). Pure reason can therefore be articulated in a certain sense of the terms *peril, exile, exodus, flight, escape, face, future, uncertainty, hope, despair.*

This set of terms inspires a slew of corresponding names for the Other – we therefore may posit as further terms of distinction for pure reason such expressions as *immensity* inveighing against the modest measures of security, our lives' spoons and cups; and in a similar way, against such expressions as might occur to us for totalitarian regularity, critical abstraction might be named *disorientation, disorder, disarray, dispersion, distraction.* Does this mean that late modern discourse advocates chaos and anarchy? Hardly. Any less than such discourse would intend to eulogize divorce or to celebrate the sword just because "divorce" is a word connoting *separation* and "sword" *division.* But *separation* and *division* have been names of notions for critical reflection, in short, for the power of ΛΟΓΟΣ since the beginning. Yes, seen in this light, thought is indeed *disorder;* thought is *chaos, sabotage,* and *sedition* –the *error* in the system, the *bug* in the program, the *wrench* in the works, *twist* in my sobriety.

And further: Against the contrivances of pat finitude the abstraction of thought is variations on the idea of *infinitude;* it is *revolution* and *revolt* to the prosiness of the status quo; it is the *no* of refusal to unthinking affirmation; it is the absolute *yes* of a *nevertheless;* it is the *detour* and the *scenic route 66,* the *byway* beyond the highway of our straight and narrow lives 9 to 5. Thought is *deviation* – turning in the Other direction. Pure reason is this *tour* beyond the outer limits –it is *beyond* the pines, over the rainbow, just *around* the river-bend, *out* of sight, *outer, downer* than our everyday down and out, *sooner* or *later* than the 24/7 of what is all hours, ours being termed, apparently, and, no doubt a bit harshly, the insipid customs of human-all-too-humanism, namely the latest rage, the latest fashions of fascism, imperialism, sexism, racism, nationalism, egoism, fanaticism, extremism, narcissism – all dystopias of the diehard militant mainstream, economies of self-centricity, masquerading their clutching pertinacity, their engulfing, gulping totalitarianism, and the fear machinery of efficient continuity maintenance in jargons espousing an official religion, advertising the propriety and eternity of immortal self-saving selfishness. To fans of these worlds of rigid uniformity and orthodoxy, distinguished thought can only mean *deformity* and *heresy*, hyperbolic *excess* to the meters and gauges of their conformity, *transgression* to the etiquettes and protocols of habit, *insurrection* to their impositions and regimes, to their apoplectic Apollo the *Dionysian frenzy*, to the know-it-all, to the wise guy's cheek, the wisdom of Socrates' ironic *ignorance*, to the man's iron grip the *woman's soothing touch*, benign *negligence* to our busy-bodies' anxieties and obsessions never leaving well enough alone, to the ticking and the clocking that bumps and grinds our hustle-bustle beat, *still life* is true extemporaneous alacrity, and see a brilliant brainwave's rush and tumble dubbed *spasmodic jolts, fits* and *starts* in opposition to the slow-go stop and flow of the molasses mind, *erection* to limp and limping complacency, the *Medusa's   face*   to   the   stony   facades   of   grim   and   impassive superficiality...surely there is no end to this vein of inversion, the perpetual terminological burlesque of rationality in light of which pure reason, the sign of the mind, has acquired such an unflattering name as *death;* but then again, could the discrimination of critical discernment be, in its utter repugnance to the bureaucracy of closed-minded normality, could it more gloriously emerge in the flesh of shame that names like *dissolution, corruption, criminal, accursed* convey upon it and in doing so establish a stunning and completely counter-intuitive idiom in which the *sick* are the healthy, the *foolish* are the wise, the *weak* are the strong, the *slaves* are the free, the *condemned*, the *transgressors* are the just, the *dead* are those reborn, the *defiled* are the pure, and in which the *infamy* of opprobrium becomes a badge of distinction, the vomit of *disgust* is a broth of *savour*, even as *vilification* becomes praise and *insurgency* founds a fatherland – in the evening, after all, don't children ask us to read them pirate stories, monster stories? Don't we root for the villain, applaud the underdog, desire the vampire, admire the fixed, unswerving "purpose" of a killing machine, the *term* (ΩΡΟΣ) in the *terminator*? – *Darn it!* How the hell, how on earth and in Heaven's name, can anyone under these conditions possibly hope to get it straight? Clearly there is but a single way: Always when deciphering code, whether written or spoken, whether oral or visual, the first question to be asked and answered is not **Who is speaking?** It is not even **Who is listening?** Always ask first: **What is the issue?** Only after we know that folks are talking about and can't help talking about thought and its attributes can we hope to comprehend the negativity of reason in terms of the Other as a perverse tribute to the distinction of human being and a record of its travesty.

   The obverse gods reigning in the aforementioned states of profane linguistic entropy, these deranged demons, blighted though they be, would fain speak and occupy as it were, word-usurpers that they are, the brightest language, thus forcing upon thought, dispossessed of all 99 of its beautiful names, these thousand twisted touches, tempting thought by seducing it to flaunt and strut its new-found poetic power of signification, to forego the simple songs of its native tongue and to ingeniously, cunningly and punningly extemporize with an underground, a gutter vocabulary, to subversively employ the codices and catchwords of satire and farce, and with the help of a latter-day dictionary of grotesques, to coin an argot of prurience for singing the sanctity of the venerable pantheon of thought, thereby casting in the speech of aversion the art of eulogy and benediction that has always been the traditional office of the ΛΟΓΟΣ as thought, the Builder, namely to raise distinguished dwellings of regard.

There is no end to the freakish conceit of this seditious language and no remedy for it save a sense of humor attune to the wink and wit of irony, that vies to skirt both frivolity and buffoonery, doing honor all the while to the office of the king's jester, his salt against the lurk and sneak of insipidness on the part of the royal sire who, tragically, always gets old before his time.

But this is madness, insanity! (Why yes, now that you mention it, *madness* and *insanity* are fine names for pure reason, for that *distinguished* thought beyond everyday thought; once famously called the *folly* beyond the wisdom of the world.) But no, not at all, this is merely the method of thought, the Builder, to find for itself a point of repose in language, in a language that will suffice and then in reality as well that the form of words conveys to its otherwise completely inconspicuous activity, which is its content, not merely its cóntent but also its contént. This method of experimentation in the linguistic laboratory is playful, provocative, ultimately celebratory in spite of itself and, as such, complementary to the much more serious business of discrimination, a connoisseur's tongue and a taster's art, that these concoctions demand – the theoretical activity of thought, unfazed perception that has learned to decipher the twisted logic and machinations, the disguises, the masks and masquerades of the perversion of reason. Reason alone can guide us through the hell of its own annihilation in the "philosophy" of both the boudoir and the crematorium. What greater service can thought make to thought than this, namely to affirm and then to demonstrate that even in this absolute horror, in the very refuse of thought, even in the play of *perfect* perversion, in this mad scientist's laboratory, in the precipitate homunculus that his egregious alchemy makes of man and in the icon of a dumb-blind idol, the phallus, upon which he projects the flash of his neon god, there *is* reason acting, on the stage, in the flap of the clumsy crow, offstage, behind the scenes, in the audience, among the spectators, deep in the brain, far back; there are the acts and the facts of reason, the fact of the stage, the fact of the play itself, the fact of the spectator and ultimately, the fact of the spectator of the spectator, who is, as such, the uniquely *inalienable* cause and distinction of human being.

23. The Three-fold Activity of Pure Reason

It should therefore come as no surprise to us that late-modernity has seized upon the attribute of thought's absolute abstraction to dwell on. This feature of reason lends itself particularly well to abstract treatment. For what in truth *is* negativity, practically speaking, if not the simple interruption of some stable state that was previously taken for granted, but now called jarringly into question through the setting aside of its determination in the face of a corresponding indeterminacy that has entered the scene, its specific Other, which is the cognizance of distinction that thought can always draw upon any precursor continuity offered by an existing determination as the material background to the enterprise of critical reflection.

Divorced from its principle in the work of thought thinking thought, "abstraction" is a term of perfect plasticity; the brand of negation inherent in abstraction, rather than negation itself with its looming opposition, *posits* nothing at all – that is the surprisingly productive sense of its *indeterminacy*. For we saw how, having established a designation for some version of the notion of a precedent standard and a reigning general of continuity, with respect to its catholicity, there are always terms, and a great many of them moreover, you could posit that depart from the characterization implied by that name depending on the way you might choose to elaborate its connotations.

In inimical opposition to the distinction of abstraction, which is subject to an almost obsessive attention and application by post/modern thinkers as is evident in their penchant for begging to differ and calling into question – thereby making ample use of the negativity of thought – the symmetry and continuity of thought thinking thought, the self-relative form of the entity of identity, shorn of its traditional glory by their single-minded preference for deformity and erasure, has become the object of universal condemnation and denunciation as a blueprint for totalitarian and exclusionary politics rather than commendation and acclaim as the paradigm, the ideal of accordance, perfection, and completion it was formerly recognized to be. But it is quite clear why this is the case. It is, in fact, not reason *per se* – after all, the abstracting negativity of thought is none other than reason's and is by them much admired and applied – not thought in and of itself that they decry, which would indeed be a strange thing for thinkers to do, but rather the history of the eclipse and the perversion of reason – the history of its instrumentalization, as a tool of oppression, a mechanism of atrocity in the hands of men, for example of those bent on the exploitation of others for their own private gain. Evil on a scale less grand though no less evil in principle is every mentality that throttles thought in dogma, feeds complacency, indulges conformism, fawns fanaticism, accommodates prejudice, and uncritically perpetuates convention, a mentality which, even on the smallest scale, namely that of the individual, restricts the purview of the mind to the perspective of the ego-body, here and now, for which the good is my momentary pleasure to me, here, now, today and bad all else, all others.

Unwilling to step back and consider critically *from without* a given status quo and state of affairs, fearing the upheaval that such a standpoint could cause, this *mini-me mentality* is wont to institute defenses to guarantee its undisturbed perpetuation to infinity and beyond; These structures of continuity, these strictures of control, domination, and homogeneity seem to speak the language of identity, neutralizing and liquidating the difference that could threaten the homeostasis of its supremacy. But is this grotesque of sameness, of tyrant clones and cookie-cutter copies, truly the realization of the ideal that the entity of identity of pure reason presents to our intuition as the *good* of the will's resolution, as *perfection* of being in knowledge, as the *completion* and fulfillment of the original potential in the determinative principle of pure thought? It is in language alone.

For we can describe the twofold property of thought, its double imperative, in a variety of ways, placing it in a variety of contexts that illustrate our experience with the continuity and presence of thought to thought as well as with the distinction of self-severalty even unto their very denunciation in the late-modern speech of alterity. But both identity and non-identity, both the self-relative being of thought so hurtfully maligned these days and the divisive spirit of the Falsum of thought that is the very engine driving our contemporaries efforts of *deconstruction* can only be defined *in its own right* – apart from the ambivalent forms it has been accorded in expostulating discourse and poetic elaboration – in other words, *as* thought, i.e. in the context of thought itself, thought grasped in a relationship to thought, when the negativity of thought is precisely specified as the inaugural distinction and the separation of self-severance discerning the gap between the IS and the OUGHT and set in a relationship of counterpoint to the principle of completion and fulfillment envisioned in the form of reflection as the entity of identity.

The departure and the arrival of thought with regards to thought are two distinct perspectives of reason as the activity of the mind and their relationship is nothing static, but rather, defining thought as essentially activity, that of transition, the way out and the way back, the turn and return of thought thinking thought. Pure reason is pure transitional activity, *passage* – but not merely in the sense of the intervention of a pontifex, bridging the gulf between two shores and the gorge between two ridges, joining two polarities; much less is it just mending a break, mediating a rift, healing a wound, interpolating a liaison with a view to regaining an ancestral equilibrium gone awry; we are never done with thought, with ΛΟΓΟΣ, once and for all, nor would we ever want to be. On the contrary, the translation here at work is a *practice*, one more accurately visualized in the give and take of a rapport and a communication that precedes the dealing of commerce with commodities or information; for the intermediacy of the dividing line is not one merely of connection nor of separation, the resolution of this negotiation is neither the win/win nor the win/lose situation but rather the abrupt and unforeseeable invention of a new order of reciprocity, a (win/lose)/(lose/win) situation, the founding of a community based upon principle of mutual *apportionment* of grants and the mutual *commitment* of sacrifice in the spirit of a mutual *acknowledgement* of regard. This community is the *transformation* of parties to a contract and as such distinguished in themselves and from themselves through mutual concession and not the monadic, monodic pre-stabilism of intersubjectivity, intercorporality, and the imperative of mass solidarity that is supposed to derive from it.

In addition to that of *movement*, many other metaphors have been used to articulate this inner rapport of thought to thought that comprises the entity of identity and the resonating interval that informs its self-relativity. In particular, this U-turn has oftentimes been rendered as a *dialogue* between two beings, that ambiguous and precarious contact of language across a span of distance separating them as two worlds, a conversation between them held in the balance of the intermittent silences and pauses that articulate mutual responsiveness – a question asked, a reply delayed and awaited and finally made in answer. Each party of the agreement is given leave to draw a distinction upon the basis set by the other; each distinguishes itself with regards to the difference that the other makes, each is the other's principle of determination – this mutual measuring and contention of thought with thought is the innermost content of its identity, its animation, and its vivacity; in our philosophical tradition, this energetic spirit of thought has been rendered in terms of divergent endpoints of change from one state, place, condition to another, in the mutual qualification of hybrid elements, in the sophist's dialectic of estimations of what is true and what is not, of which man is the sole measure. All of the various changes we see around us have been enlisted in the vivid presentation of this attribute of thought, the ultimate attribute of the self-relationship, complementing that of *abstraction,* namely *transformation.* Thought is not just a *being* A, not just a *passage* (C) from A to B, it is a *conversion* of A, and a *becoming* of B.

The difficulty in discussing the vivacity of the spirit's making of distinctions in material terms is that, of course, pure reason does not change or move at all in any physical sense. The "physical" sense of the distinguished spiriting is a poetic invention that represents thought's logical "life" in concrete terms which denote salient beings in occurrences of change, their rising and falling, ascent and extinction, emergence and degeneration, cessation and recurrence that observant folks attending to the happenings going on around them on a regular basis have not failed to take account of.

Thus, this curve of recurrence that is thought's enactment of thought, this circuit of the circle which unites separation and approach, (Heraclitus, B103.) reveals to us both the infinite "penury" of abstract negativity and the perfect prosperity, the infinite abundance of reflective well-being; the arc of transcendent detachment and ingressive alignment that are the two faces of pure reason's unique, remarkable "nature" are movements only in the sense that they are rendered as such in these physical terms.

Given such a vision of thought as a natural course and development, poets and philosophers have spoken about the logic of thought as pure reason's *life,* a life with phases or moments, birth and death, for example, or rather, death and birth – we have been discussing them in that order, from O, $\emptyset$, Θ to 1, from *lost* to *won* – and in the context of such images as these, we are surely justified in speaking of thought's *nature,* poised and collected and nevertheless stirring potently upon the pivot point of the *instant,* that wink of an eye that separates the achieved end from the new beginning of pure thought's project, a difference within thought only in the sense of the diastasis of the drink left unstirred (Heraclitus B125).

In that case, nature is "logical" in the sense that its movements represent the life of reason in concrete terms and, in this way, makes the otherwise imponderable substance of the mind materially accessible to our intellect and perception and by using appropriate images, borrowed from physical beings and their relationships, we can emphasize significant moments in the livelihood of thought thinking thought.

But considering thought now apart from these renderings, thought taken *as* thought in its own right and relationships – our Tyger and the *ouroboros* of thought's reflection from the flight of abstraction to the lighting of conversion – can be seen to comprise three transitions, namely first the outward portion and procession of the turn of verve, i.e. *thought* thinking, consisting of the **Thinker** and the determinate **Being** being thought, both united in the unique principle of *insight*. Second, we see thought *thinking*, consisting of the **Actor** and the **Aim** of thought, both united in the vision of the ideal towards which all *purpose* strives. Third, we see thought thinking *thought*, comprising both the **Builder** and the **Substance** in which ideas attain their effective realization, united in the invention of *imagination*.

24. The Being of Theoretical Thought

Thought, the Thinker, in the sense of intellect and perception, is *theoretical* reason, discriminating (and not discriminatory) seeing. How could it have happened that one day folks stepped back from the immediacy of their daily chores and pleasures, and their occupations with the arts, both the applied and the fine, that serve them, but also from the unquestioned acquaintance with the usual beings of their natural surroundings in general, and ventured to attain the absolute perspective of contemplation that is pure reason's coign of vantage, a panoramic, an *Olympian* perspective, as it were, and from this standpoint of survey, marvelling for the first time at the sight of the order of the world as a whole, the cosmos, began to wonder not only at the way it is, but rather *why* it is the way it is and why it *must be* so?

Contrary to what we might assume, namely that theory's *inaugural wonder* is most likely to arise when we encounter prodigies and other novel or bizarre apparitions that inspire our consternation and dismay, in fact, science owes its origin not to *monsters* but rather to the inexplicable interest that thinkers began to take in the most familiar, the most constant and the most regular phenomena of their surroundings. Look around you for a moment and consider what you have always taken for granted as being simply the way it is, this tree and the blossoms that emerge from its buds in spring, their flourishing towards the fruit and fruition that harbors the patient seed in its lap awaiting its day of glory in the sun, its fall and its spring, and then this ground of rich earth that nurtures its growth in the passing of the seasons with the light of the break of day, with the sky's originative rain, the inspiration of the wind – there is nothing "phenomenal" about any of these phenomena in the rhythm of their forthcoming and yet, come to think of it, are not these natures oddly mysterious in the timeliness of just being, that being, namely, that comprehends them in their natures as the critical junctures and turning points of its own greater life?

Thus astonishment is as much the result as the origin of thought; it is, first, the outcome of the gaze of theory in which we step back from the immediacy of these surroundings, and then the origin of its intelligence that recognizes them for the first time for *what* they really and truly are, namely their particular *natures* in the *nature* of the whole that is their principle, *beings* just *being* – the *justness* of their being. In this way, even as thought with respect to its surroundings, breaking out of its sphere of unquestioned convenience or emergency, overcomes the blindness and the blandness of that habitual coincidence, so also, in this refreshed attendance, do these beings in their renewed distinction break in impressively from without upon the waxen dormancy of our understanding, unexpectedly, overwhelmingly, striking us with indelible amazement at their newfound presence and sparking our desire to know more. With Plato we "wonder how it could possibly be"...and precisely "this is the condition of a friend of wisdom...there is no other beginning of philosophy than this."

ΘΑΥΜΑΖΩ ΤΙ ΠΟΤ ' ΕΣΤΙ ΤΑΥΤΑ...ΜΑΛΑ ΓΑΡ ΦΙΛΟΣΟΦΟΥ
ΤΟΥΤΟ ΤΟ ΠΑΘΟΣ, ΤΟ ΘΑΥΜΑΖΕΙΝ. ΟΥ ΓΑΡ ΑΛΛΗ ΑΡΞΗ
ΦΙΛΟΣΟΦΙΑΣ Η ΑΥΤΗ. (Plato, *Theaitetos*, 155c-d)

Suddenly, as if awoken from the slumber of utter familiarity with what has not changed substantially since the dawn of time, seeing it all with new eyes, the spirit of scientific inquiry began to attend to the cosmos of the entirety of all that has come to the light of day and took to carefully observing this being and becoming with a view towards finding the grounds and the causes for what they observed, offering, in the precision and objectivity of prose, explanations and interpretations for the state of the whole and for the particular differences of the individual beings that arose in remarkable order to take their rightful place among all the rest in their relation to that entirety in accordance with their own fundamental characters, i.e. each and every one's proper *nature* with respect to that of the entirety, the nature of the whole.[23]

This knowledge is the work of the intellect, insight that peers within, behind perceived appearances to glimpse the beings themselves and then beyond even these beings to perceive their being, their ΦΥΣΙΣ (nature), and in this way accounting for their totality, the *first* causes and underlying reason, their principle. It is the distinction of theoretical thought to discern meaning in what we see, to comprehend the background and occasions that set the stage for what has taken place, to enumerate the conditions necessary and sufficient for the apparition of the figure, surmising its grounds, inferring rationales and concluding a line of reasoning upon the foundation of the first cause and principle, a prime mover, whose being has earned the recognition of science as manifesting the most logical, the best reason for THE WAY IT IS.

Observation is immediate witness, a *being there* in person rather than relying on report; it is not just a cursory glance but a gaze that dwells and gleans truth from fleeting impressions and apparitions attending to what obtains in general and as a rule in opposition to what is just incidental to a being and, through the experience gathered by meticulous study, draws conclusions that are supported by evidence accessible to all kindred spirits who might wish to participate in the science of the order, the ΚΟΣΜΟΣ (cosmos) of beings, the ΑΡΜΟΝΙΑ (harmonia) of their arithmetic rhythms, and the concealed ΛΟΓΟΣ, the contradictory relationship, ΕΝ-ΠΑΝ (*hen-pan* – one-all) that grounds the whole of all that has come light.[24]

Theoretical thought contemplates this and every being. And after long investigation and the pursuit of a train of thought with regard to beings, the excellence of their order and their orders, pure reason comes to realize that the being that is most properly and rightly to be crowned and honored as the first and the best of all beings is that particular one which, because of its

---

[23] Boeder, in his *Grund und Gegenwart als Frageziel der Frügriechischen Philosophie*, p. 25, characterizes this awakening of thought as follows: "The wondrous event that is philosophy's start...is this that someone began with new eyes to see all things, with the eyes of one who sought to comprehend them in the simple observation of their forthcoming."

[24] So Boeder's topology of pre-Socratic cosmological knowledge, namely that of Anaximander, Pythagoras, and Heraclitus in his *Topologie der Metaphysik*, pp.75-96.

ΦΥΣΙΣ as being beyond all ΦΥΣΙΣ, has proven itself to be most worthy of thought's highest regard. See *Figure 19*.

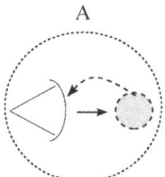

Figure 19: Reflective Being

This object is pure reason, namely the being that pure thought is to thought. Indeed, what other conclusion could a science that seeks causes and principles reach? Pure reason (A) is the cause and principle of all other beings, inspiring with its beauty the purpose of their movement towards the perfection that is this being's own life, the divine life of contemplation, the being of Theory. This is the sense of the ratio that marks the first stage in the series of reflections that elaborate the process and procession of thought thinking thought.

25. The Determination of Practical Thought

The theoretical life of thought depicted in the seeing being of *Figure 19* is not an imaginary one. On the contrary, it is the life of a particular being with its own unique nature and character that was inexplicably born one day – and a memorable and auspicious day in the life of pure thought it truly was – *out of the blue*, as we are tempted to say.

Like the sun, the light and the sight of perception rose over the depths and the plains of the dark earth and with it all that is alert discernment, attendance, the state of mind of being attuned to differences, heeding, taking stock of the situation as it presents itself, seeing the beings behind the seens of appearances, reading between the lines and getting at the heart, the core, the *truth* of the matter, the ΟΥΣΙΑ (ousia - *essence*) as the Greeks were fond of calling it. This spontaneous inclination towards outlook and overview is the contemplative *gaze* of theory and, as we have seen, is said to have been founded by inspired *wonder*, distinguished gazing. But if divine thought in all of its beauty and perfection as the *objective* of the movements and changes and transformations of the natural cosmos and as the *object* of the first and the best science of the first and best being comes from wonder, I wonder where wonder comes from? Whence could wondrous thought come if not *from thought*, though not from something that thought *is* to thought as an object of study, a being among beings and the best of them all, their excellent general, who comes to the fore of perception after the theoretical standpoint has already been attained. No, prior to the wonder of what thought *is* to thought, its "reality," is the wonder of what thought *does* that gives rise to thought, to its seeing and being, in the first place, namely its "possibility," the capacity to step back and thus achieve the severance and critical separation of abstraction that has provided the mind with relief, release, surcease from absorbed engrossment, from the absent-mind of distracted preoccupation.

For the piercing gaze is much like a question posed, or a great expectation, or the intense intent preceding great deeds, thought poised on the brink of a great idea, the dilation of a heart beat and a breath held in rapt attention wanting to know, the heightened *now* of judgment and decision prior to the *"now!"* of execution when the daily play of block and blade resumes. It is the emergence and the emergency of thought to which we would like to draw our attention.

Sight and light are two ways of speaking about the gaze of thought, the rise and shine of the mind – often merely a mind locked tight against the dark revolving night – the brilliance of which opens eyes to wider vistas than would otherwise be apparent to a face whose diligent nose knows but its own grindstone. Thought's note, on the contrary is a heads-up and places it *before*. Before what? At any rate, before the bend of capitulation and the seizure of resumption, before repossession and restoration, before the restitution of engagements and the assimilation of differences; but also *before* in the sense of *in front of* and *facing*, i.e. in contraposition, placed to measure and to mete the faces that we meet; for only then is the mind truly an open mind, namely when it is ajar, afoot, ahead, affronting and confronting the outbacks and hinterlands, the badlands and inlands, the sticks and the hicks. We see that the distinction of thought, standing at ready to take it all in and not wanting to miss a thing, this property of thought's *advance* into attention and its consequential *pre*-position can be spatially as well as temporally rendered in a variety of ways, namely as being *before* and *above* and *behind* and *beneath*, as being *after* and *prior*, *previous* and *subsequent*, *without* or *within*, as being *to* and *at*; these pinpoints of distinction form a nimbus of sight and light that opens up in and around the nullity of indifference that is the default mode of the mind, going with the flow on a busy day. They are all expressions for the relationship of thought taking note, a *feeling* (rather than an unfeeling, i.e. absent) being, without which there is no relationship at all – it is precisely this curtain-raising overture of relationship, thought gaining its original intuition and perspective *above it all*, thought being *before*, being *for* thought, that is the miracle of thought that thought not merely is to itself, a being seen, but also accomplishes, a deed done, the deed of difference, of eyes awakening to the why and wherefore, that sees in the way things are, the way they must be (A), could be (B), should be (C), draws our attention to our thinking being not merely as an object of interest but rather as that original accomplishment of distinction through which being and beings enter the scene – the opening of the eye of distinction is thought in action and its first action.

Again, prior to all sight and sighting in the sphere of theory, a being may or may not correspond to its principle, may or may not be *what* it is as defined by the category to which it belongs. This is for the intellect of pure reason to judge; but in studying them and their principles, it is not reason's task to change beings and being as a whole – the world to which contemplation attends is already perfect *in principle*. Every being has its proper place, its very own ΛΟΓΟΣ, in the order and by the order of the first principles among which pure reason is the most distinguished of all. The self-disparity of divergence and incommensurability between what a particular being IS and what it OUGHT to be indicates simply that it is out of line and unbecoming – unseasonable, ill-suited, immoderate, or otherwise incongruous with regards to the principle and the principles that delimit its identity and determine the appointment of its position with respect to all other fellow beings under the patronage of that general. Beings at odds with each other and with themselves, if it is not merely a being's shortcomings in the sense of its temporary prematurity, is a "local" anomaly and inconvenience, ultimately an *injustice* in which the purview of one nature has been encroached upon by another and which requires now the intervention of judgment, of the rule of law, to re-establish the determinate and just bounds that had been transgressed by extravagance.

Departing from our consideration of this issue of being as a spectacle that we might contemplate from the standpoint of the objectivity and omniscience of Olympian heights, let us enter now the sphere of beings and, joining them, inhabit it with them so to speak, taking up our dwelling in and among them and their world as a whole; thought, the divine *Thinker* has proceeded to recognize its role as the human *Actor* for whom the ordered *state of being* has taken on the distinguished *character of action* – this is the *incarnation* and the *existence* of thought the excellence of which is not merely acknowledged but, before that, appointed as a mission, received as a duty, and projected as an absolute aim sought and strived for.

Having descended from the *epic* proportions that determine the hierarchy and the totality of divine being to enter upon the *dramatic* plane and the stage of human action, the crisis of distinction marking the divergence of THE WAY IT IS and THE WAY IT SHOULD BE is the tragic realization that, fellow human beings, *you* and *your* world are not what they were meant to be – an insight that has practical consequences. This was not the case in the theoretical perspective of thought as the third person relation with regards to beings and the best being that is their principle. The second person relation of thought with regards to the determinative principle depicts a personal and very painful encounter with this disparity that the principle presents to us as individuals who experience the critical distinction only to the extent that we *participate* in it, not merely by contemplating beings and accounting for their distinctions, studying and expostulating their natural history, but rather by actually undergoing the distinction in question after having assented to the critical present of the determinative principle.

It is as if the particular beings we have been observing and judging with regards to their nature, determining whether they correspond to that form or not, have now been given a human voice with which to articulate the drama of subjugation inherent in falling under the imperative of a principle to which they must now answer, a principle, moreover, that is – in contrast to the one recognized as being of superior excellence among its many subordinates and therefore appointed to govern the whole sphere of beings – entirely abstract, *absolute* being, not merely the first, the best or head, the one having earned, and now enjoying, the merit of seniority in the apportionment of beings that catalogues each member according to its rank commensurate with its proper nature. Stepping back from this sphere of relative beings in its entirety, we ascend to the standpoint of the *abstraction* – as we have been discussing this term – which is the principle of absolute distinction, the being without, depicted in *Figure 20*.

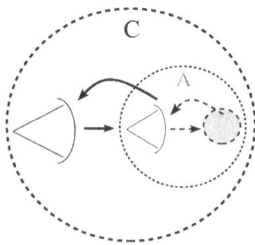

Figure 20: Active Being

The *practical* relationship that thought has to the term of principle that is the distinction of human being, our cause, is not one of perception but rather of accomplishment; for thought, the Actor's, excellence manifests itself not in the penetrating acuity of the mind, its depth and breadth of conception with regards to beings and being, but rather in its willingness and resolution to undergo its own transformation (C) in light of the principle that it is determined to fulfill and satisfy; this is the object of critical self-reflection that we seek and, in ever approaching it, serve, namely the entity of identity that is its vision and the "face" of completion, as one destined to be attained at the end of all time and until then to be resembled, strived for in constant and perpetual patience as a model or paradigm of fulfillment that has won our most earnest commitment based on the absolute difference that thought has made in a previously carefree life. Here on the practical plane, in and upon the stage of distinction, thought is a mission, something, and no thing at all, to be done. And, before that, given as a charge and duty are given, a present of distinction dividing the IS from the OUGHT and a gap, a cut, like a wound, struck, the closing of which (but not the ultimate closure) demands our earnest dedication. In this life of practical being, thought is born to run. It is this gift that is the rift in the complacency of an otherwise sedentary and autistic life of the ego's closed mind swelling into boundlessness.

Absolute being is not the reality of thought as practice, not the destination that we attain at journey's end, when tears subside, because if the goal were achieved and this vision of absolute being realized *in practice* the principle that is its distinction will have been fulfilled and thought would be terminated, the charge completed and the enterprise of existence would be at some point over and done with. Though many might wish it, we are, in fact, never done with thought. And as much as theory ends with insight and with the delight of seeing and knowing the principle in its entirety as complete and perfect *being,* practice is a restless and sustained effort of renewed and redoubled application, the lifework and the *existence* of our distinguished human being that has been inspired to step back from its being and mind the gap of self-severalty in the anguish of reverence and respect that characterizes our encounter with and experience of our own daunting distinction as critical self-reflection makes manifest.

We are never done with thought. In the evening, we may always reflect again upon what has been accomplished, acknowledging a good days work, knowing full well that tomorrow in the early crepuscular light, a new day of distinction will dawn, reviewing yesterday's works and, in this renewed reflection, reaffirming the commitment of sight to the light of being and to the vision of THE WAY IT SHOULD BE as distinguished from THE WAY IT IS towards which, as the aim, we will strive again, having rested for the night, with renewed vigour, always aware of the danger of complacency in laurels, orthodoxy in reputation, and inertia in foundations laid yesterday evening and assumed to be no longer susceptible to auroral scrutiny.

Human being is distinguished, different from itself. In the sphere of being, contemplation knows that this disparity marks the definition of a particular being, its unfulfilled or incomplete nature, towards which its growth develops, the excellence from which it might diverge. However in the plane of existence this divergence itself is the issue of thought and the principle; human being is the only being for whom precisely this disparity *is* its nature and destiny rather than its deviation from it. Though this is the story of human life, it is not the whole story of human experience. Though *in practice* we are never and could never be completely one with the principle – which remains, above and beyond the fray of the way that is the passage of human being – we might certainly contemplate this being and sing its praises in telling the whole story of thought from the beginning to the end and not leaving any parts out, not even the tragic part about how we tried and failed…and tried again and failed again and again and again.

The perfection and completion of thought, so sorely missed in the practice of thought is nevertheless still an issue of our destiny; it comes, however, before or after, better, before *and* after, the attractive object of the thirst and the hunger that inspires the pale fire of desire, sun-snatched, in that interim of anguish, with its vision of fulfillment – *before* as the **present** of the principle, the inaugural cause evident to *theoretical* thought; *after* as the **presence** of the principle in the realization of *poetic* thought which builds its dwelling and, in the meantime, the model and the vision of the principle that guides the *practice* of thought along its way. Put in another way, namely as one particular line of reasoning, we might say that even as thought, the **Thinker**, is our name for *intellect*, our insight into principles and the **Actor**, our name for *purpose*, is a seeker striving, transforming itself in the course of taking action in accordance with the principle that it has envisioned as the goal and aim, it is, finally, the **Builder**, imagination's agnomen, that actually completes the mansion that is the resulting monument to its own resolution and determination. Before truth is sought, truth must be known and this knowledge is the inaugural insight of truth in the sphere of the intellect. Only after it has been seen and the delight of this insight experienced can our second relationship to truth begin – truth to be done and finally, third, in the doing, brought forth as the fruit and fruition of our mature relationship to reason's triune image,

26. The Triadic System of Poetic Thought

The being, the existence, and now the presence, i.e. the tangibility of the principle. Thoughts in general or just any old thought are not exactly what we would call substantial. They seem to come of their own accord in our reveries, at times capricious, leaving us in a lurch or in a pinch, at times docile, obedient to our whims; they lighten with their phantasms our slumber, lighten and oppress our distraction. Dreams, be they of the day or of the night, are immaterial even as our idle wishes, as fleeting as vague impressions of a divided, fractured attention. But neither the scatter-brain's, nor the monomaniac' relationship to those shifting notes in their head indicate thought in the emphatic, distinguished sense that is the object of our investigation. And yet, even whimsical conceit and the shilly-shally of tergiversation, the hover of hesitation, the apostate's defection and the mugwump's desertion, all hail from places nether and thither that are no places at all, but rather merely the issue of thought's separation, the abstraction we have been discussing, and thus do the light-headed lightness of the wanton mind and all the mindspawn of mood, even and precisely in their fatuous mercuriality, bespeak the transcendent negativity of critical reflection, the being without, that is neither being nor place but rather the differential of a distinction, the gap we mind and do not slight or gloss over and who are, finally, its only witness.

But, through disregard, unhinged, unleashed, and deprived of grounding like a gossamer kite whipping in the wind, what could be more inane than a thought, more light-weight than the vaporous, papery spirits that haunt the machinery of our daily routines. What makes thoughts significant is their coming to the world in action, not merely with a view to solving a problem – the context most often associated with "having an idea." Beyond and prior to this instrumental use of reason, thoughts are significant only when acknowledged for what they are, namely distinctions, accents, that make a difference when they moot matters long thought settled, inaugurate critical self-reflection, and mark with their cognizance the original inadequacy between mind and matter, the thought and the thing, the ideal and the real – the contrariety inherent in the identity of thought thinking thought.

Theoretical thought studies the distinction of being; practical thought undergoes this distinction, experiences and lives the life that flows from its actual exercise; poetic thought, finally, finds the distinguished form of which pure reason is the content whose charmed life exhibits differences and diversity within itself – periods or spheres, phases or places, members or moments of an organized whole that contains and unifies within the wide sweep of its turn and returning, both the disparity of absolute immensity and the repose of perfect identity. But thought is neither the harmony of disparity and unity nor their dissonance – they are merely the two most salient aspects of our experience with regards to the distinction of human being. They have sparked our attention now as they have for thousands of years; the form of thought in its entirety is, upon reflection, a textured, nuanced shape as delicate as it is intricate. What indeed could be finer than the articulations of a train of thought in which each and every word makes a difference in the reasoning, each and every word, whether it be the preposition or the pronoun, article or adjective, noun or verb – they are the declension and the conjugation of thought in the element of language; and the subtle gradations of the tempo and the timbre of their performance manifest the differences in the scheme of all things thought that comprise the dwelling that is the realization of that master Builder's work.

The movement of thought as a whole, with a beginning and an end and steps or phases along the way – the progress of conception as opposed to the simple *transition* (in the sphere of being) and *relationship* (in the sphere of essence) was likened by Hegel in the preface to his *Phenomenology of Spirit* (*Phänomenologie des Geistes*) to the organic *development* of a plant: "The bud disappears in the blossom's breaking forth and one could say that the former is contradicted by the latter; similarly, the fruit rejects the flower ousting it as the truth of the plant – not only do these forms differ, they, in fact, supersede each other as being incompatible. But their liquid nature appoints them to moments of an organic whole in which they do not merely oppose one another, each being just as necessary as the other, the necessity of which makes the life of the whole." (Hegel, *Gesammelte Werke*, IX 9.20-30.)

> Die Knospe verschwindet in dem Hervorbrechen der Blüte, und man könnte sagen, daß Jene von dieser widerlegt wird; ebenso wird durch die Frucht die Blüte für ein falsches Dasein der Pflanze erklärt, und als ihre Wahrheit tritt jene an die Stelle von dieser. Diese Formen unterscheiden sich nicht nur, sondern verdrängen sich auch als unverträglich miteinander. Aber ihre flüssige Natur macht sie zugleich zu Momenten der organischen Einheit, worin sie sich nicht nur nicht widerstreiten, sondern eins so notwendig als das andere ist, und diese gleiche Notwendigkeit macht erst das Leben des Ganzen aus.

Obviously, thought is not a bud or a blossom; it is not "captured" in any term that we might put, like *history* or *negativity*, *theory* or *relationship*, *element* or *principle;* much less in such expressions as *Freedom, God* and *Destiny.* To describe the distinction of human being in these terms or as having phases or moments or parts or epochs, to call it the *being without* or the *outside* or the *inside,* is all just a manner of speaking and a figure of speech, is an attempt, more or less cogent on the part of the speaker, to articulate the realization of thought in the logic of a language that is more or less effective depending on who is reading and who is speaking and the context of the utterance in question – not only in its particular position in a train of thought within the broader line of arguments to which it is intended to make a significant contribution, but also in those wider frameworks of circumstance, both linguistic and non-linguistic in which the speech performance is located, and, ultimately, in the scheme of all things thought, in which even the distinction between linguistic and non-linguistic settings in which philosophy is embedded these days, finds its justification.

For this reason, we say: relax, friend – these are all just words, words and expressions with their various connotations and contexts, both contemporary and traditional, to build with, just as "Destiny," "God," "Freedom" are English words – which admit of a translation more or less accurate into other languages and cultures and which are themselves and have often served as approximate English translations of foreign expressions – that have been defined through a great variety of usages and applications, have often been used to pernicious effect but also have been wielded by true master builders who have inspired the hearts of many to renewed courage and hope, have enlightened and strengthened the resolve of human being to undertake enterprises of great pith and moment to persevere in these endeavors in spite of obstacles considered all but insurmountable and have served as the banners for science, for religion, and for art, namely for the impartiality of truth and justice, for the redeeming power of mercy and for the creative genius of the human mind.

Figure 21 is a fanciful rendition of this commodious recirculation of the bend back to the starting point of our discussion, the curve of reflection that is thought's redoubling, i.e. thought thinking *thought*, the *whole* story.

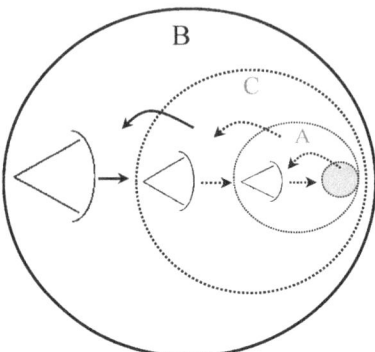

Figure 21: Creative Being

Recorded in its works is a collection and a recollection of achievements and a system of transitions in which thought itself has been experienced as substantial as well as articulate, and thus taking pure reason into account in its entirety as a series of well-defined generations – each a cycle of specific accomplishments, an ascending/descending course of steps, which then are given shape and form, a life and even a world, in the *imagination* (B) that language conveys to matters considered otherwise rather too difficult to grasp in their abstraction. Not that these matters are abstract in any academic sense – no, they are simply easily overlooked in our distraction; but their content is as real as any feeling. Or are your fears and your joys, your loves or your wonder, your hard earned experience, not "real" in some sense of this word, regardless of whether or not their objects and contents are a figment of your imagination, a datum of your perception, or something even less substantial than these – a tugging in your gut, say. This in some way "real," though initially inconspicuous difference that the mind makes in its various forms and kinds as documented by the wealth of terms that language can provide to our building efforts is the cause and issue of our proposed philology. And as we work hard to attend to it, to articulate all the ins and outs of our experience with reason as a whole, and not just certain aspects of it, like the *trace* that critical self-relativity leaves in our lives, the *challenge* that it confronts us with to transcend the status quo in which we live and to transform ourselves in light of a vision that is disburdened of parochial subjectivity, released, at least momentarily, from the blindness of bias and partiality and the violent *spectacle* it so shockingly reveals to us of a mentality that seeks to hold fast to, to cleave to, its hoard and exclude in fear the unexpected *"invasions"* of new ideas from abroad, from beyond the ken of its control and self-enamored self-interest – resolute in our divided/undivided attention to it, we gain a more comprehensive understanding of the mind and learn as it comes to take on the form of invention in eloquent word and dramatic deed, enacted in political speech practice, lived and delivered in the parlance of religious devotion, modulated in narratives and other poetic designs, in the letters and locutions of literature, in its books of prose and poetry, in the media of the fine arts, the concerts of gesture, the symphony of tone and harmonious touch, as well as in the reasonings of scientific discourse; reflecting upon all of these substantial performances of ΛΟΓΟΣ – which is translated, here at least, *language*, whether written or spoken, seen or heard – we realize just how much thought has always meant to human being, the autonomous *maker* of rational being and not only its *actor* and its *seer*.

Here thought is seen as the tangible object of such thought as is no longer merely the *contemplative observer* perceiving, thinking, gaining sight and insight into the particular being towards which it has directed its discernment with a view towards better comprehending it, though it is *also* this; no longer merely the *determined endeavorer*, recognizing in thought the image of a fulfilled principle with regards to which it now directs its aspirations and, in this endeavoring, experiences its transfiguration, though it is *also* this as well; but rather of such thought that is the product of the *imaginative builder* whose invention is a *self*-realization and a performance in terms of what makes pure reason significant, striking, moving, sustaining to human being. Thought is now taken to be this *object* as well as the *subject* of thought itself – the topic and issue of invention, the object and substance of insight, the destination and realization of a resolve that is always already completion *and* determination, the heart *and* the arrow, never one *or* the other. Studying thought is thus learning how pure reason, this unique and intriguing being, is a triune relationship of relationships, traditionally known as that of the *true*, the *good* and the *fine* in one and the same self-several being.

Accordingly, thought moves by degrees, steps, moments, epochs in learning about itself, all the while, in fact, developing from one completion to the next in the process of growth, thereby not only realizing (in both senses of the word) what thought is, i.e. resolving in maturity as well as in appreciation the promise of its youth, but also and even more significantly, recognizing in what thought has done, in what it has achieved, even when alienated from itself in some unfavorable contingency of space and time, in some insidious turn of phrase, even then, in the sacrifice of the glory of its name, pure reason knows how to give an account of what has transpired in the otherwise meaningless flow of events and particulars that constitute Man's natural history, always discerning in this encounter of the visage of the OTHER to itself, always renewing, continually rekindling, in recognition of this limit, the infinite yen of thought to foster the comity of distinctions, their organization, and their logic in a physique of ideas, that is not the victorious assimilation, the triumphant liquidation of difference, and the subsequent imbibition, the ingurgitating oblivion of their distinction by appropriating difference into itself in blind compliance with the universal wolf of appetence, that (according to Lacan) Freud often spoke of as the pink and pinnacle of neurotic appeasement.

> Was Es war soll Ich werden
>
> (what It was should become I)[25]

What if *I am/is* already the Other to the extent that I strive to attain the distinction that is *My* human being, that *I* am not m*yself* unless I am striving to be *Me*, and never *Myself* unless entirely and completely, infinitely Other than I am, self-knowing in knowing the *Other* that I am **in theory** and nevertheless, **in practice**, always and irreducibly destined, determined (but never finally succeeding) to be – an irreconcilable, incoherent, and illogical contradiction only **in terms** of the poetic language that thought, the Builder, might want to use to provoke thought and set it firmly and permanently on its way.

27. The Exuberance of Thought

The study of reason must begin with an experience. Which experience? We have stated the experience in question at the very beginning of our investigation. Without intending to settle on a particular terminology, we have called it the double experience of self-possession *and* self-disjuncture, self-knowledge *and* self-severalty – thought not merely *being* but also *having* thought, and, if having, by the same token, *being had* – the experience of this, thought's property, is triadic – first, the **abstraction** that marks the critical origin of such being as is termed *thinking*, second, the **reflection** that is the action of its mediating self-relativity in comparing the IS and the OUGHT of thought and third, the **entity of identity** that is the

---

[25] Lacan, *Ècrits I*, 226-7, 284; *Ècrits II*, 229.

estate it founds, the dwelling it enjoys, its kith and kin – all told and summed up in *Hyperion's* pronouncement at the end of the first volume of the second book, "the grand notion of the *en diapheron eautô* (the self-several One) of Heraclitus, only a Greek could have come up with that, for it is the very essence of beauty, and before it was found, there was no philosophy."

> *Das große Wort, das en diapheron eautô (das Eine in sich selber unterschiedne) des Heraklit, das konnte nur ein Grieche finden, denn es ist das Wesen der Schönheit, und ehe das gefunden war, gabs keine Philosophie. (GSA, III 81.12-15)*

How can this possibly be an object of study let alone an object, a being, in its own right, no thing and yet something quite intriguing? Because the *act of realization*, an experience that everyone is familiar with as reason's most prominent influence on our lives, is an act of insight *and* creation, manifestation *and* fulfillment *in one*, and then, more practically speaking, the anguish of self-critical reflection *and* the delight of self-realizing concurrence *in one*. And how is this possible? How can thought be both generative *and* perceptive, both theoretical *and* practical; how can its work be a poetic bringing forth of its object but also the scientific grasping of it, the articulation of which is both its own natural development and the method of the investigation into what it is? This is the very odd property of self-relative thought; reason *is* this self-relationship and our experience of undergoing it, the earth-shaking practical effects and consequence of this experience on our ingrained opinions and assumptions, our meticulous representations of this experience as a whole in particular, in other words, in *real*, in *vivid* terms, and finally our grasp and comprehension of this experience, to the extent that we are able, gaining thus our very own insight into the undeniable fact that we somehow are, or at least, under favorable conditions, can become, both the thinking subject and the object of one and the same thought, can be a thinking life and a living thought, in service to our better half, *our* majesty – this is the distinction of human being. Perhaps we could imagine the dialectic of its totality as in *Figure 22*.

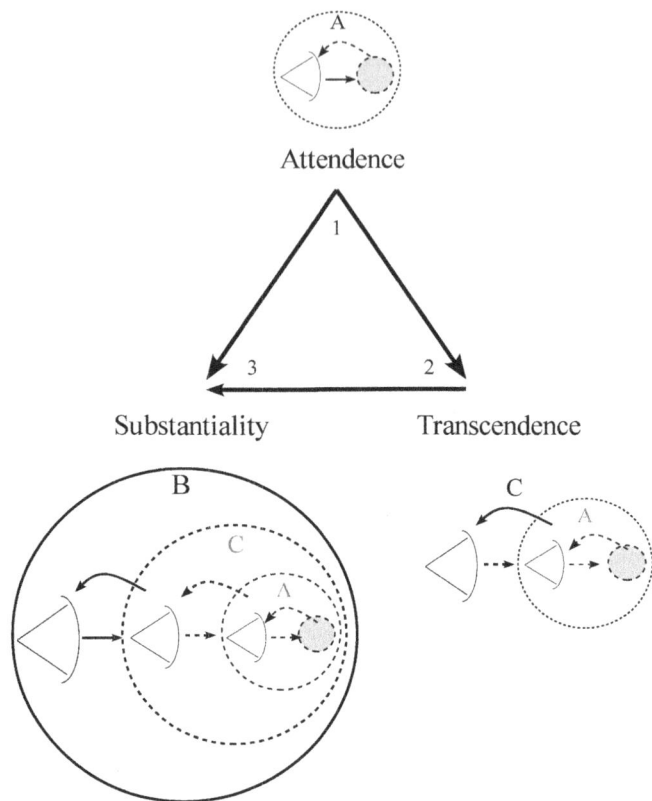

Attendence

Substantiality   Transcendence

Figure 22: The Relationship of Relationships

The leaps and bounds of thought, both exuberance and constraint, as well as its lightening and alighting resolution, the full career of the mind wending its way out and back, are the issue – a study of three relations and their ratios. In the course of our investigation, these three abstract relationships, being the three axes or dimensions of thought, will acquire an increasingly transparent sense. Depending on their sequence, they will form ratios that indicate particular activities of reason – practical, theoretical, and poetic – and help us keep track of the journey of thought from (1.) the vantage point of sight with which abstraction facilitates *attendance*, (3.) to the *substantiality* that realization conveys to concrete particulars, (2.) mediated by the system of transitions that is the most salient feature of a critical, questioning mind, namely the abstracting negativity of its *transcendence* at once judicious, championing the practice of differentiation – in both action *and* perception – as well as documental, cognizant of the differences that it makes as recorded in the tradition of their narrative. This is a countervailing movement that, as we saw, takes account of the substantial identity of the mind at work in the deepening penetration of intelligence into essentials and the ever-widening scope of comprehension with regards to the general principles – the transcendent depth and breadth of thought in the process of critical reflection, profound in delving and getting to the heart of the matter, universal in surveying the whole and taking into account the big picture. We gain our overview from atop the pinnacle, having put the crush and urgency of details behind us, stepping back from them in an act of emancipation to which reflection beckons and obliges us, one period of which is depicted in *Figure 22* as the differentiation of the principle of distinction.

Specifically, as revealed now in the following *Figure 23*, the points C and B refer to our experience of this principle and its effect on us. The arrows between the angles of reason refer to the crossings that determine unique relationships of inference among the moments of pure reason – for example the relationship pertaining to the principle (A) comprises the relationships of **intuition**, namely A>C (the LIGHT of evidence) *and* its complement activity of thought as **intellect**, i.e. C>A (the SIGHT and insight of perception); the relationships of **realization** comprise the two senses of what it means to realize something, namely on the one hand *to make real* and on the other *to understand* – i.e. A>B (the substantial CONTENT of thought that is its presence in particulars) and B>A (the FORM of poetic language in recognition and praise of that inaugural idea). Angle B and C govern a comparable suite of relationships of **transformation** B>C (the AIM of action) and C>B (the actual DRIVE and pursuit of that good that is the end and destiny of human being). We will explore these relationships of pure reason in action, its ordered rhythms, when we elaborate the logotectonic method of thought, the Builder – the first of among its 72, 99, 1000, or even 9,000,000,000 beautiful names in the various pantheons of deity several of which we will be noting – unless of course, after having completed the exposition of the theme and topic of our study, overhead, without any fuss, the stars go out.

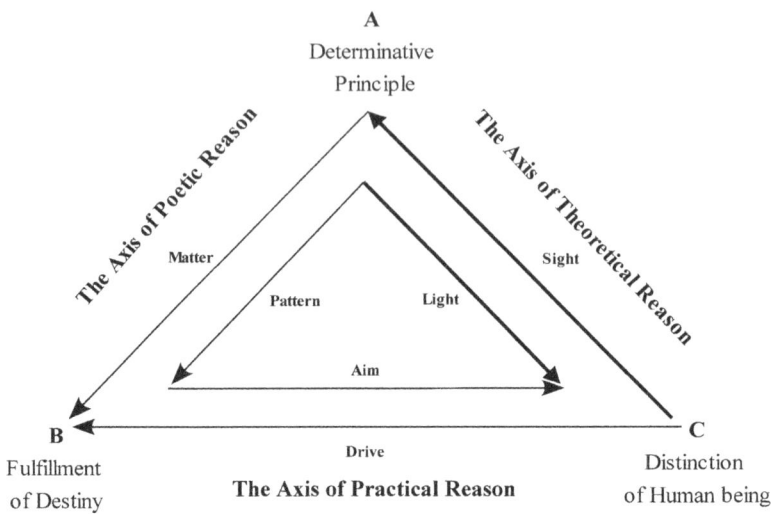

Figure 23: The Inner Workings of the Mind at Large

Our philosophical tradition has known a trilogy of visions of this principle, namely MOIPA (*Moira* - the Apportionment of Destiny), ΔΟΞΑ ΘΕΟΥ (*doxa theou* - the Glory of God), LIBERTÉ (the Idea of Freedom). These three ideas of pure reason were each made known to the poets of thought who received the favor of a language – three inspired tongues of flame each unique, each expounding in remarkable and memorable, heart-moving, heart-rending narratives, dramas, poetry, one phase of that three-fold experience with critical reflection that we have designated as the distinction and the destiny of human being. We want to study their message and the power of their language as we would the accomplishments of master builders whose craft and art, whose wisdom in the workings of ΛΟΓΟΣ, we seek to better appreciate and, in the efforts of our own building, perhaps even to emulate.

This language brings to light the whole story of our destiny as subject to the self-relationship that characterizes, in terms of its own life and times, the ups and downs of human experience, human culture, human society, the human all too human world; but it also celebrates this being in its own right as an idea, not merely one that is the fruit of distinguished human conception, but, much more than that, as the idea of which our distinguished human being is itself the fruit.

In our studies of this entity of identity in its own right, we learn that its complete self-sufficiency, its most frequently defamed feature, is not the bare necessity of a minimum merely and meagerly met nor its satisfaction the gorged and glutted sadness of surfeit but rather the abundance of what is quite and fully one with itself, adequately equal, neither too much nor to little but just so – but not mean and tolerably fair – and thus **good and plenty**, abounding in the fullness of its measure. However, this image of thought thinking thought as a bonanza of prosperity inherent in the accord of identity is distinguished from that of the gushing luxury of prodigality, nor is pure reason's rich repletion a lavishness or profusion. This cornucopia is not a stuffed and bloated extravagance of thirst slaked unto cloying. Rather, thought thinking thought is the image of what is meet and fit, apt and happy, right on. Precisely in this very sufficiency, in being enough, it is always more than enough – the abounding power that goes beyond and transcends set limits and the definitions, even those set by the determinations of its own being. In this sense, the principle of thought is *extra*, is *ultra*, and possesses, even in the elegance of its well-rounded completion, a penchant to splendor and the over-flowing generosity of what is truly complete, always more than satisfied – delighted.

B. The Principle of Revelation

28. Lucid Dreams and False Awakenings

Pure reason is intellect and insight, striving and the transforming passage, the act of building upon and realizing that original distinction; in other words, thought is the *objectivity* of perception, the *execution* of judgment, the *realization* of invention – three in one, one *and* three, never just one, never just a unity, it is, rather, a being of triunity, containing multitudes, and as such it is the multitudinous object of our investigation as well as the agency of our ambition which is to grasp, to the extent that this is possible, the inward diversity of our own mind's native severalty, the severance of thought from thought, and make sense of this our contradictory experience of its unique manifold being, a rich experience comprising that of seeking and finding, relinquishment and reception, departure and arrival, abstraction and realization, dissent and unity, modesty and exaltation, often rendered in solemn narratives that tell of the transient life that ends with ignoble death and the life of glory that begins with death's distinction, both the tranquility of completion in identity and the anguish of what is entirely and perpetually other than itself.

Seen in this way, what could be more paradoxical, stranger, more outlandish than thought? Then, thinking about thought, we are the explorers of a foreign land, archeologists unearthing an ancient treasure, a parchment long thought to have come to dust, biologists examining the physical traits of a living being long feared extinct; our standpoint is one of theory and contemplation – *science* if you will – that, going further, going beyond the insight of intellect, strives moreover to organize its observations into a body of knowledge and conceive of a complete system of ideas which succeeds in shedding light on the most salient features of this life form. Such an account, to the extent that it attains to veracity, is a further accomplishment of the mind which not only *perceives* thought but also *records*, in an articulation of terms, the chronicle of what it has come to realize about itself, its own singular *nature*.

Indeed, the most striking property of thought proposed and accounted for thus far by our research is precisely this, its inner activity and temper. We have recognized the intrinsic "historicity" of thought's arc – the three constituent epochs of its *recirculation*, its course of turn and return, its swing fro and to, from *percipience* to *formation* and back again to the incipient *splendor* that sparked the arc of wonder at the start across the gulf and abyss of silence, that gap and flash of anger that we cannot help but to mind and that we are inspired now to strive to close. Moreover, this self-relationship of eternal turn and return is not merely a property of pure reason, in the sense of one property among others that it "has." The self-relativity of the mind *is* its entire substance and unique distinction.

Self-reflective thought *is* this very entity of identity and we can find the vibrant resonance of Verum, our T, illustrated in a great many familiar phenomena of recursion that have always drawn attention to themselves – mirroring optical effects (e.g. in water or in a looking glass) of the seeing eye seeing the eye seeing the seeing eye; effects of reiteration like twins and doppelgänger and turtles all the way down, or Indian girls, like those of Land O' Lakes butter, exhibiting the "Droste" technique of mise-en-abyme and narrative metalepsis; in the community of reciprocal relationships as those indicated by associative and collective prefixes such as *syn-inter-*, *com-* and their cognates where each member in the community determines and is determined by the other; and similarly in the mutuality of kinship (we are "parts" of our parents; our children "flesh of our flesh"), in the notion of a federation (a state consisting of states), and of ownership (the original sense of *property* as belonging to our identity as does every part of our body and our features); further, in the devious previousness of moral judgment (having to choose whether or not to choose), as in the quip that if you are standing in front of the fridge asking yourself if you are hungry, the answer has already been given: you aren't.

Consider the rubric of *undecidability* – the double bind of *not* thinking about an elephant, jumping over your own shadow, having your cake and eating it too and similar aporia, impasses, and antinomies that put us on the spot, the space between the rock and the hard place, between Scylla and Charybdis, in that improbable place of the Catch 22 where to succeed is to fail, where you are damned if you do and damned if you don't, in doing undone, and all you know is that you don't know – these and many other (perhaps all?) paradoxes and antimonies, those familiar 矛盾 (máodùn) or *spear-shields* of reflection, in which Batman and the Joker wage the eternal struggle of the unstoppable force coming up against the immovable object, the contestation of principles operating upon and exhibiting the structure of self-relativity that is thought's mark of Zorro and of Zeno.

Taking further examples of self-similarity from popular and not so popular science, i.e. mathematics, consider the structure of the so-called "secret of Polichinelle," recursive algorithms (like compound interest, the factorial $n!$ and the golden ratio, Φ, of the Fibonacci numbers), fractals (the so-called Mandelbrot and Julia sets), the self-similar Weierstrass function or the Koch snowflake, holograms and the proliferation of living systems (that generate themselves "autopoetically" in maintaining their homeostasis) or multiplicities of measures, even the Platonic weave (ΠΛΕΚΟΜΕΝΗ – Parm. 129 e) of Ideas and the macrocosm/microcosm schema of the big in the little and the little in the big; consider talk of the beginning before the beginning and the end after the end, the science of science offering us theories about theory, concepts of conception, series of series, loving love, having faith in faith, or just Antigone's "having reverence for reverence" (ΤΗΝ ΕΥΣΕΒΙΑΝ ΣΕΒΙΑΣΑΣ – Soph. *Antigone* 943); then again we are familiar with the mediated mediation of technology considered to be uniquely, thoroughly human, such beings as make tools to make tools, secondary tools, comparable to notions on knowledge and other such confabulations involving "meta"-systems, -levels, or -degrees, second or higher, super- and hyper-order logic, in which the form (n) becomes the content of the form in the next potential, the $(n+1)^{th}$ power; consider cybernetic feedback and other such *superrational* strategies of self-improvement, the self-movement of automatic machines (e.g.: the automobile), the additive and multiplicative identities in field theory, the principle of tautology and self-contradictory argumentation in logic, cyclical processes, chiasmic structures and the myriad phenomena of exchange and oscillation as in the Ch. S. Pierce's conception of semiosis whereby the meaning of a sign is another sign, one giving birth to another, one thought, the *interpretant,* bringing forth the next and so on ad infinitum or Chomsky's thesis regarding the sentence in a sentence as distinguishing human communication, issues of self-reference in psychology and semiology, not to mention the notion of *reentry* in Spencer-Brown's calculus of indications, Maturana's ontology of the observer, the set of real numbers in Dedekind's definition of the infinite set, the fixed point concept inherent in Cantor's diagonalization strategy for comparing infinities and the cardinality of the continuum, the ordinals ω^2, ω^ω and ultimately the transfinite *epsilon nought,* the numerical coding strategy that proves Gödel's incompleteness theorem; and what about Bach's *Kunst der Fuge,* the illusion of the Shepard tone, the poetics of a Cervantes novel, that of Hermann Broch's encapsulations in *Die Schlafwandler* and Heinlein's deterministic timeline tales, Jan van Eyck's or Velasquez's painting in the painting, Magritte's meditation on chirality in *La Reproduction Interdite* and Escher's drawings of impossible objects, Dali's *Visage of War,* Max Ernst's decalcomanias, David Lynch's nightmares, Charlie Kaufman's fantasies, Christopher Nolan's monumental mementos, Quentin Tarantino's "movie movie universe," or even just a Pink Floyd album cover; or take Lévi-Strauss' notion of a myth of mythology, Beckett's theater in theater, the Elizabethan play within the play and the spectacle of tragic irony, Klein's bottle, the Möbius strip, cross caps, and other self-intersecting surfaces; or look at Penrose's stairs and triangles, Russell's antimony of the set of all sets, the conception of Hegel's Encyclopedia of philosophical Sciences in the form of a Sierpiński Gasket, his friend Hölderlin's poetic hyperboles like "the world of all worlds" and "all in all," and more generally the so-called Liar's paradox; or consider Baron Munchausen's feat of lifting himself by the bootstraps, and the other self-perpetuating perennations of infinite regress like that of Koch Curves, a Zen koan, nested Chinese boxes and Russian matryoshka dolls, strange loops, Borromean rings and braids, trefoil knots and other sacred geometry (like the Tree of Life and the Flower of Life) as well as the earthly fern and downy flake, Lacan's specular image stage of psychic development, blind spots, vortices of lack that fire our death-defying, death-driving desire beyond all pleasure; consider also palindromes and rhizomes, the ratios of ratios in analogies of proportionality and even the operation of multiplication in comparison to that of addition – the former being a counting of units that are themselves multiples; and consider the concept of the rate of change in which the change itself is changing as in the notion of acceleration; or even just figurations of circular structure and the pre-posterousness of points on a circle which posits the end before the beginning, the arrival before the departure – move along a circle away from a point on the circle and you will find all manner of contradictory ways to formulate this paradoxical peregrination of undecidability, each point being equally the middle, the beginning and the end; but consider also the notion of predetermination and the inevitability of the forgone conclusion; or the ambiguity of doors and gates, Janus Bifrons and Jacob's ladder, where the way up is the way down, the way in is the way out is the way back, to make an end is to make a beginning (as T. S. Eliot proposes), and departure is arrival along the axis mundi in the cogitation of the extremities, where ends meet, namely in the reciprocity of the ethereal and the earthy; consider a circle in a spiral, the logical circle, long defamed as vicious, though praised by Heidegger as benign, (*Sein und Zeit*, Tübingen 1986, § 32, p. 153) as containing "the definitive potential of the most originally primordial knowledge," (...eine positive Möglichkeit ursprünglichsten Erkennens...), the vertiginous circularity of dreams within dreams, stories within stories, 1001 of them, the whirling wheel within the wheel, the tunnel that you follow to a tunnel of its own, the coffee-table book on (and about) the coffee-table, the mandalas of triangles within triangles (e.g. The Sri Chakra Yantra), the cosmographic mystery of shapes within shapes (like Kepler's Platonic solid model of the solar system) the frame within the frame, warehouses in warehouses, flowers within flowers, cauliflowers in cauliflowers, and fruits within fruits, eggs within eggs, the king's king (i.e. the queen), teaching the teacher, the death of the mortician, the ill physician, the barber's dilemma, rules how to change rules – obviously these illustrations of the self-relationship, these lucid dreams and false awakenings, are not themselves this self-relationship, the frame within the frame, the map is not the territory, the image not the original – they are literary, they show that irony is infectious; as such they are forms of skepticism, a reminder of the procession of reiteration, that of the signature mark of self-severalty and the inward/outward multiplication of difference that is its unique nature.

They are demonstrations of what in the linear regularities and bare necessities of life will appear to be a trap and must remain a rebellious, confounding, and all the more intriguing entity – we have surmised that many (perhaps all) of the fallacies, antinomies, dilemmas, and contradictions that have been invented or discovered to challenge the logico-mathematical notion of *completeness* and *decidability* in formal systems can be analyzed as striking representations of this tautology of thought thinking thought. They show first, that we are never *done* with thought – in language we can always step back from the framework of a formal system and embed this system in another, a *richer* one. They show, second, that something that is, in fact, no thing, and cannot "exist" in the normal sense of the word nevertheless "exists" in another sense, namely in that we are free to consider it rigorously, investigate it as our object, however strange and wonderful, and, for us, all the more wonderful, the stranger it is, and the stranger the better, such that rigorous thought is also vigorous, not so easily deterred by impossibilities but rather strangely drawn to their strangeness – it remains to be seen if and how such composure and stalwartness with regards to these catastrophes of the calculating mind can make a significant practical difference in the life of human being.

Thus, first, in the theoretical eye of metaphysics, thought is this intriguing and improbable, nay, impossible being, and already for this reason, if for no other, worthy of thought. Second, in the manner in which we articulate our knowledge of and our experience with this being, we might select terms that are more or less illuminating or intriguing, more or less counter-intuitive for a particular audience or reader – for contradictions are intriguing to some, to others repellent – putting the matter *(thought,* that is) in this way or another, employing more or less provocative narratives or tropes, the rendering of this idea admits of exquisite variety in speech in accordance with the dictate of circumstances, personal preferences, and individual skill in the use of language, the idiom and diction of a speech performance defined by the immediate occasion, the audience's need, the topic of the conference. Thought, the Builder is, as we shall see, the master architect of logotectonic discourse and, tending to eschew, as it does, extraneous prescriptions and preferences of time and place and person in aiming for inclusivity in the scheme of all things thought, endeavors rather to be for all and for none, in other words, for several, no *one.*

29. The Self-evident Present of Thought

Now as intriguing and doubtful as this being may be and as familiar and as useful as its most striking property, the recursion of thought, is to the structural analysis of many phenomena encountered by science and mathematics, is it not all the more intriguing and improbable that most folks normally hardly ever give a second thought to thought *as* thought, simply taking it for *granted?* We might ask therefore how, why did thought about thought come about in the first place and when, why, how did it occur to us, perhaps for the first time, that thought is a thing indeed worthy of thought, having somehow sparked thus our attention and inspired the celebratory inventions of language that dramatically bring its features to the fore of a scientific interest?

Thus it seems natural that prior and prerequisite to all theory or poetic art, prior and prerequisite to our wondering about and the expression of our wonder with regards to such a being, the *grant* of thought should come into view and demand notice; this distinguished being has indeed accomplished no small feat – it has made us stand up and take notice of, inspired us to come to terms with and give voice to...thought itself. Apparently and, considering our busy preoccupations, most improbably, thought gives us pause!

For the sake of this property of thought's granting to be, in spite of and because of its utter familiarity to us, remarkable, thinkers and poets have always spoken about it in exuberant terms that are neither excessive nor superfluous in their exorbitance, though often condemned in the name of these extremes, and it is precisely because reason arouses our attention, sparks our interest such that we feel compelled not only to contemplate thought in all its intricacy but also, when it comes to action, to take heed and regard its urgings as imperatives to practice that thought is thought a *purpose* that has won our commitment as the Endeavorer's quest as much as the Thinker's *question*.

Now that is truly intriguing and improbable – the mind is neither mute nor dumb, almost perhaps, but not entirely, obscure or absconded, obviously inclined to concealment but, by the same token, not completely averse to recognition or attribution; no, thought would seem to be inclined to revelation; thought *comes to light*, more, it emanates, and catching thus our attention who are otherwise so distracted by the importunity of messages being constantly sent from all sides and vying for our attention, to shine brilliantly forth of its own accord, to strike us with its own proper illumination and therein to captivate; with a view to the apparent impressiveness of this *givenness*, we might speak of the *present* of pure reason, its adverting, even animadverting power.

It would seem therefore that it is the distinction of human being to experience the *light* of reason as a *gift* in precisely this sense of thought's provision. And it makes its brilliant appearance in spite of being entirely inconspicuous and unstunningly obvious, namely as that which is so completely self-evident that it would seem to go without saying and even invite the neglect of what is taken as a matter of course. Thought? Of course! So what?

Parmenides was the first thinker to conceive of *self-evidence* as the fetching present of thought, though unsung and nameless by the standards of mortal celebrity; the signs of pure reason as that of thought, the

Trailblazer, manifest themselves in a train of thought that leads to a necessary conclusion, namely to the "unshakable heart of persuasive truth" (DK 28 B 1.29).[26] Nothing except the voice of thought itself prompts, moves us along the line of reasoning that Parmenides develops; driven, even goaded on relentlessly to question and to quest, we are encouraged, every step of the way, to deliberate upon the issue of thought and then to make a rational decision (ΚΡΙΝΑΙ ΔΕ ΛΟΓΩΙ – B 7.5) of our own accord as to what must be thought and what, in this light, thought must be, trusting, weighing the force of the argument against nothing that is not the voice of *logic* and the infallible sense of what is *logical* to "those given to knowledge" (ΕΙΔΟΤΑ ΦΩΤΑ – B 1.3), having been summoned by a favorable destiny to experience the "well-rounded truth" of what is simply and purely the being that deliberation, unencumbered by mortal misconception (ΑΠ ' ΑΝΘΡΩΠΩΝ ΕΚΤΟΣ ΠΑΤΟΥ ΕΣΤΙΝ – 1.27) and habit (ΕΘΟΣ – B 7.3), arrives at and must arrive at as the necessary conclusion of demonstration and the inevitable destination of a logical train of thought – asking ourselves at each point along the way (ΟΔΟΣ – B 1.2), "does this argument earn our conviction?" In the sense of this commitment that pure insight alone makes and can make to what has won its trust and certainty as the irrefutable being of knowledge, having been party to the critical process of the initial quest and questioning and then the final vindication of a conclusion, *quod erat demonstrandum*, the grant of pure reason is revealed in the experience of an inaugural and unconditional, a divine (ΔΑΙΜΟΝΟΣ – B 1.3, ΘΕΑ – B 1.22) engagement that compels concession to the one directive of absolute authority, namely the primeval, predetermined "law" of ΛΟΓΟΣ.

Thus in the sphere of theoretical reason, the *law* of thought is not merely what insight discovers and discloses by looking behind the scenes of what is apparent to the naked eye and seeing the unseen rule, comprehending and conceiving the cause and principle, but prior to the *negativity* of what is discerned and the discernment of distinguished *sight*, it is our experience of the foreordainment of thought as *light*, the illuminating power of reason to engage us in its own demonstration, the postulate and the precept, the *reflective* form of being, its *repute*, that inspires our assent and dedication.

---

[26] Later we will read Parmenides' famous poem as an investigation driven by the force of conviction that self-evidence gives to deliberation, a train of thought that manifests in the unique being of insight the very shape of inference. cf. Diels, H. and Kranz, W. *Die Fragmente der Vorsokratiker*, [DK].

So also in the sphere of practice, the rule of pure reason is immediately and intuitively *clear*, "logical," and that is its strength and power, the power of thought to win our adherence, the immanent AUGHT of thought, that determines our action by communicating to us THE WAY IT SHOULD BE, initially accounted for by Greek philosophy not only as logical necessity but, prior to that, in connection with what ought to be done, axiological necessity, i.e. the obligation of what is right and just, the directive force of evidence (ΔIKH - dikē) of what ΘEMIΣ (themis) is.

What is ΘEMIΣ you might innocently ask? Not so innocently as impudently asked, actually, if you are an ancient Greek. And that is already the answer. For what could "explain" to you what is *good* and *right* and *just* if it is not clear to you already, however problematic it may be *for you* to decide in a particular situation of *your* life what the right thing to do is; for then this prior and immediate knowledge of yours, this simple and intuitive perception, regarding what is good or right or just must stand and meet the test...or fall, be applied and practiced, validated and brought to life in action...or fail. That is why Aristotle noted at the end of chapter 11 of the first book of his *Topics* that "those who call into question whether one should honor the gods and love one's parents want castigation and those who wonder whether snow is white need only to open their eyes." (Topics 105a 5–7).

Open your heart, friend; open your eyes, my impertinent friend! What else can we say to skeptics in such cases as these? In the Greek world, it would seem – implausibly to us perhaps – that everybody always already *knows* what is right *in their gut* as Homer's heroes would put it. In the world of practice, it is the fact and the being, the "givenness," of the law of the way it is, always will be, always has been and in this sense *custom* (ΘEMIΣ) that guides our action even before its principles can be spelled out or called into question, just as in the world of theory everybody knows what is true in and of itself; it is the being of logical *self-evidence* (ΛOΓOΣ). And, as Aristotle exasperatedly warned, there is no way to prove these logical "axioms," for example "to be or not to be" (A ∨ ¬A), because they are the foundation upon which every proof is based; or more precisely, they are their *own* proofs and in this property of truth, moral or logical, the self-relationship of thought thinking thought is manifest.

In Greek thought, the origin cannot *have* an origin because it already *is* the origin. The origin *is* the origin. And in this entity of identity and in this self-relative being alone do *having* and *being* perfectly coincide. For the sequence of reasons begins with the being of reason, the actual comes *before* the potential, the chicken *before* the egg and *before* the proof, the acknowledgement of a principle that is *taken for granted* as entirely clear in and of itself, plain and immediately obvious, unconditional, requiring, indeed, warranting no further explanation or justification, no argumentation or proof to confirm its truth – this is the immediate present of truth. But there is only one thing – and it is, in fact, no *thing* at all – that is completely evident to thought and in this sense a *gift* freely, unconditionally given, the unique *present* of pure reason and that is thought itself *to* itself *for* itself.

Thought is so completely and immediately manifest to thought, a relationship that is the pure being of reason, that expressing this evidence in a sentence, which is what Parmenides did for the first time as we shall later see, makes for propositions that do indeed tend to sound utterly trivial and therefore eminently "philosophical" to a proudly mundane mind as disinclined towards speculation as possible. But the familiar tautologies are just expressions intended to formulate the thought inherent in the recursive relationship that defines pure reason, namely *thought thinking thought*, a relationship that, however – and this is the decisive point – communicates itself, shining forth and outwardly reaching toward and finally touching us, as it were, with its winsome power, its *glory* of incontrovertible certainty.

The well-known axioms and "purely identical propositions," such as "What is, is" are indeed "trifling" as Locke called them, when seen in the light of such knowledge as pertains to every other object of study beyond that of thought; leaving the realm of the theory of pure reason to inhabit the more nether regions of concern, we tend to disparage "universal propositions that, though they be certainly true, yet they add no light to our understanding, bring no increase to our knowledge." (*An Essay Concerning Human Understanding*, bk IV, ch. Viii, §5). Theirs, being that of the forms of thought and the light of thought itself, is a knowledge that conveys no substantial content or material *value added*. True. But just consider for a moment this simple fact that in the familiar "tautologies" of logic – and it makes no difference if some of them in some schools of thought have been purposefully disputed; not all of them have, for that would amount to *eliminating* dispute the way tyrants are wont to do – thought is seen to be inexplicably moved, determined, compelled, by thought, albeit grudgingly by those who tend to resent what is definitive, to *assent* to them – that is the sole issue of the principle of thought's grant and present that we are exploring now; in *logical* terms, it is the issue of the Greek principle of being to acquiesce in the present of some precedent insight.

For taken from the point of view of their power to command our agreement in their validity and to induce our sanction of their cogency, such propositions provide remarkable evidence of the sway and the *authority* of reason to make manifest its tenets as being beyond all doubt, above all contention, incontrovertibly certain and utterly impervious to the onslaughts of partiality and personal preference. Hearing thus the voice of pure reason, there is nothing left for us to do but to acknowledge the preeminence of its precepts and even in choosing to disregard them, we must nevertheless recognize their primacy in summoning to trial deliberate judgment and demanding that sentence be passed and the decision made *on their terms* whether to adhere to or neglect that call of the pure heart, ours and our better half and nevertheless utterly other than ourselves, namely that unique "self" that distinguishes us from ourselves. This is pure reason, and, with respect to every other being, our unique distinction as *human* being; we cannot *not* hear thought, we can merely refuse to listen.

Thus, the self-evidence of pure reason, far from being trivial tautology is, in the empty banality of its axioms, the revelation and the present of thought as a principle, i.e. as an incipient, original cause. "Analytic" propositions do not *say* anything, but they are nevertheless significant for what they *show* – they are the showing, the indication, the ΔΙΚΗ of ΘΕΜΙΣ, THE WAY IT SHOULD BE, and in this sense, namely as "apodictic," they are *illustrious*, the *splendor* of thought.

In this connection, the Greeks spoke of ΠΕΙΘΩ, as accompanying truth, being its obliging and engaging character, winningly and compellingly binding us to its nature. With a view towards this unanimity but also with regards to the exhortation inherent in a law that moves the heart, *persuasion* is presented as a goddess in the company of the Huntress Artemis, of the Love godhead (Aphrodite, Eros, Pothos, Himeros, the Horai, the Charites) and, in particular, as neighbor not only to the Muses' grace of song, but also to deities of marriage, its power being thus understood not merely in its abuse as that of manipulative seduction, but rather as encouraging the shy lover's sincere efforts to touchingly address the heart of the bride-to-be to gain her approval and accord and make a mansion of ideas.

30. The Compelling Voice

Thought is obliging and we, in turn are much obliged by it in the sense that we now are compelled by the argument to agree. It has won our engagement and committed us to its determination.

Moreover, the voice of reason speaks so directly to us as to preclude polemics – though, for all that, resorts neither to coercion nor inveiglement – by securing our "a priori" commitment to its premises the mere hearing of which entails the fundamental adherence that is prerequisite to every subsequent argument because the first article of faith that grounds all discourse is the acknowledgement and recognition of the *present* of reason itself.

When it speaks, we listen "in gladness." We cannot avoid the hearing of this voice because there is no intermediate instance that could intervene between ourselves – the listeners – and the voice of this "heart." Every mediator is less immediate than reason itself, for what could be closer to us than our own thought, than the present of our own ideas, of our own "selves"? That is what, in the conception of their thinkers, the poets and the prophets want to bring out with such terms as *power, glory*, and *splendor* – the radiance of the mind reaching out to meet us half way, across the gulf, the first good turn deserving, demanding another, though eschewing all importunity, stirring the heartfelt gratitude that thought, most simply thought, is.

Thus pure reason has been recognized again and again as speaking with the voice of an authority that wins our immediate commitment and dedication. Thought talks to us, lets us know. If something is logical, it convinces us not through an extraneous force but rather by being intrinsically compelling. Logical arguments win our concurrence. They do so as thought's own attorneys and as such they might be and will be considered in their own right and power. Nevertheless, they are not a vicarious or deferred experience of thought, represented by an image that must be deciphered. They are, rather, thought's own, thought's original articulation, a proffered invitation to inference, namely to attune thought to thought, to respect thought's intuition, to gain *insight*. We call arguments *plain* or *clear* because of this immediate property of theirs to persuade us. We say therefore that they are *objective* because such arguments do not blind us with blandishments, cajole or coax us, try to deceive us. We say that they are neither sophisticated, nor artificial but rather honest, simple, true, natural. We speak about something as being persuasive by saying: "Naturally!" Why this expression? Because of the native hue of immediacy that glows upon the face of all inference and the tendency of beings to take their natural course in becoming what they were meant to be and then passing away with the season of their fruition.

Thus reason's is the authentic grant of thought even before it can be *taken* for granted, the answer prior to the question and understood as the original manifestation and self-evidence of thought; having thus no precursor in its apriority, the present of reason can be rendered in celebratory terms as an act of *grace*, the *imparting* of a gift, a notion like that of *splendor*, which indicates thought's transparent (meaning *immediate*) attribution and although it is, as we saw, separated in its abstraction, disengaged in its detachment – this distinction of thought to be a way away and out-of-the-way, above and beyond, *privative*, does not mean that it is deprived, haughty or withdrawn, avaricious – pure reason's nature is precisely to be the wealth and the *prosperity* of difference, its *pre-eminent* present, not the indifference and poverty of neglect. In spite of the separation and seclusion of its negativity, it is not a spot in the middle of nowhere, not aloof or reticent, not faint, pale or dim. Thought is, precisely in the turn of its departure, distinct return, striking and conspicuous, communicative and in this sense to be understood not as vacuous in its tenuous abstraction but in spite of its impalpability as **generous**. The notion of reason's generosity and, in this sense, *opulence* is intended to refer to this attribute of the spirit of the open secret that is not a segregation or sequestering of thought, though the act of stepping back might at first glance appear to suggest that critical thought is only a disruption and a severance. In fact this reserved spirit is no less affable for being ineffable. But then again this disposition towards candor does not make pure reason loquacious. Its over-flowing ebullience is not, for all that, gushing profusion, its luxuriance is not dilation, its repute not mere flourish or exposure. In observing that, remarkably, we do indeed take note of thought – and all of these expressions relating to generosity serve precisely this purpose – we wish simply to draw the reader's attention to this property of pure reason, namely that it is not taciturn or cryptic, however mysterious this *fact* of its urgings upon our attention may be, but rather eloquent, not stark but plenteous, lush not scant, not meager, gorgeous. Notice how putting the matter of self-evidence in these terms not only magnifies and enriches but also heightens our experience of it? And, significantly, this language for the repute of thought is not merely descriptive, it is performative. Seeing thought in these terms changes not only how but also what we see. Thus in the play of language a transformation through language is in play. As we shall see later, it is the work of thought, the Builder, to celebrate, in just this way, the present and the presence of thought as the *open* mind, but, of course, not so open that the brain falls out or the heart departs from a gilded cage.

For surely, when we normally venture to imagine the workings, the turn and return of the mind, its magical mystery tour – now how's that for a name of our topic – they must be, like all mysterious things, hidden out of sight, shrouded in dark shadows. Treasures are buried, maps guide us to the spot;

doors are locked, the wielder of the keys is the master. The learned know and hoard deep secrets; the explorer goes beyond the ken of what we are familiar with and finds on remote shores fabled beasts, elves, ogres. The initiate wears vermilion robes; myrtle decorates the wizened temples of the wizard. And even the gods of lore dwelt behind a tent of clouds or out of reach on mountain peaks, conveyed their message to oracles in foreboding riddles, escaped the boxes of our little minds and left us to gape or else to turn aside and close the eyes with awe, blinded by a shielding wrathful wreath of fire and made deaf by inscrutable silence. Truth, thus, they say, is mute. Truth is diffuse. Truth is covert and occult. Truth is the maniac's mumble; the fanatic's rave; truth is under-the-table, on the sly, cloak and dagger – the hush of stealth. It is rites of blood and torture, foaming relics of bones, rituals of chants and white-eyed trance, libations and ablutions, recondite cults and closed books, curtains of fog and iron, unbroken seals, the terror of the coffin hammered shut.

But what we are considering now is the mystery of what is open, the open mystery of what is supremely obvious, so manifestly clear that we tend to miss it. For this is the miracle inherent in patent evidence, the amplitude and the present of thought, and as such, truth as is seen not just *by* but even *as* the light of day, dazzlingly, even for those who miss what is completely clear, blindingly, stupefyingly so; as *beauty* blinds and numbs, so does the boom and the quake of the sublime with its cracks and blasts of thunder – thought's self-evident vocation rendered strident and resounding alarm, an ultimatum's command, persuasion becomes pungency, by the urgency of opposition to thought's touch the resistance to which shrinks from the assault of what is, *actually*, its tender caress, suffers plagues in its boon, hears harsh command in its solicitous appeal, experiences grim austerity in its kindness and makes of its enlivening breath a gale storm wind, a curse and an evil potent portent of the sky signs that would otherwise fill an upward heart with hope. It is due to the reciprocity of thought by thought, the reflective perception of the entity of identity, that anger answers anger, danger with danger, that aversion sows adversity, that punishment matches, tooth for tooth, the crime. But why would anyone want to resist pure reason's claims and make of its dispensation injunction and proscription, of invitation to think make accusation and condemnation, make of jovial light the lightning bolt of Zeus, turn singing into singeing?

With a view to further enriching our experience with this communicative light of thought, what other notions could serve to illustrate the revelation of reason in the immediacy of its evidence in addition to those of illumination and inspiration? Take the glory and the splendor of *nobility*, which is a name for the prominence of personal highness, the king or queen, the prince, the duke, as dignitaries whose power are in evidence as the bright raiment and the beams of wealth, riches, the richness of thought – the honor they are given is the honor that they give, their magnificence reflected in our magnification of them, the blessing bidden is the blessing bestowed in accordance with the reflective self-relationship in which the being is the doing and the doing is the making and the builder *is* the building – the song, the singing, as well as the glorifying singer in a round.

It is the grand commanding stature of reason, the *colossus* of thought, that makes us stand up and take note, recognize its status as law in the person of the noble lord – thus we might attribute to thought's call the notion of *power*, the abounding sway of the present of pure reason and, in keeping with this imagery, thought will be seen as a determining principle, a first in relationship to a second, which is secondary to the latter's inaugural primacy, a subject subject to its influence, the subordinate to its imperative, the junior to its seniority, our docility to its import.

Sway is a good name for this striking effect of thought on our logical life, ordaining as would a king, but an inward king, one perfectly near our ear, though, in spite of its propinquity, no less sky high and mighty. For being a king, thought, our prince and principle wins our inherence without appealing to any authority beyond its own suasive self – reasons *are* the rod and staff of reason; its exhortation is the call to conviction; but being thus its prisoners, its servants, reason calls upon reason not only in the manner of the master's command with *strength* but also encouragingly, charmingly, *full of grace* – we are Ladies and Gentlemen serving Ladies and Gentlemen.

Bounty then is the essential thought in this non-material understanding of the present of thought as over-flowing and thus its coming forth and affecting; seen thus as the blessing of *benevolence* we might speak of this generosity as the power of thought's *goodness* that permeates its surroundings and imbues what it touches with the brilliance of beauty. This plenitude has been the issue of philosophy, of poetry, of religion since thinkers' earliest times; as we shall see, in particular in the Second Epoch, this idea emerges as the principle of the distinction of human being when thought comes to thought as light that transforms the darkness of the world of men, transforming these men into the humankind of truth, the wolfish visage of the world into a kind king's kingdom of the holy, the darkness of shame into the light of glory – such is the blessing of the present of *spirit*, the *love*, the *gift* of "God" – remarkable notions in which we recognize the revelatory power of pure reason in Christian terms.

For clearly, in the notion of a *blessing*, we find the side of praise and magnification and the side of the voice and magnificence united. The praise that gives glory and so, adorns, is the glory that, in turn, adorning, descends, making known and letting know – the speaker and the *herald* of the king is the king's own tongue and voice, his word, and the queen's mind is made manifest in her smile; thought's cornucopia is the clarion call of vocation.

C. The Principle of Reception

31. The Present and the Poison of the Gift

The present of thought rendered imaginatively as splendor, the *array* of renown and the *might* of the law laid down, its illuminating spark and reigning thunderbolt, refer to pure reason in its activity as principle and authority and finally, in keeping with these images, as the *source* and *origin* of their outward efficacy, properties indicative of an *open*, an enlightening being. Thought in its exalted purity and sanctity – for that is how we might designate this property of departure – is, in spite of the negativity of its transcendence, nevertheless neither reclusive nor selfish but rather potent, outgoing in its might, touching as well as troubling disclosure; this *magnanimity* makes a difference and the impact of its apparition leaves a real mark, makes an impression upon our native compliance, on the pliant resistance of our senses, on their wax or clay as it were, insofar as they are themselves and their matter *receptive*, open to attribution, to the determination of the principle that characterizes, specifies, clarifies them and thus bestows *class* upon them, which is the distinction of a name and nature. For the "self" of a being is its form, its distinction, is the principle that *applies* to it and grants it thus its present of being, its present of mind, its note. We may note here the affinity of thought thinking thought to the immediacy of sensory perception, to the beam and boom of color and call, even of touch and taste – with smell and flavor being the sapience of *savor* – that incites our sensibilities or insipidly fails to do so, falling upon open ears and eyes or ones dulled by indifference.

Now even as the order-giving voice makes matters manifest in an illuminating category in which they are either seen and heard by attentive sense or else ignored by the stare of impercipience, so also we might say, reversing perspectives on the direction of the gift and blessing, that a calling voice of entreaty might be granted or refused a hearing in reflection of the aversion with which that gentle present of thought was previously met, thus in accordance with the reflective reciprocity of our entity of identity for which a face turning back and lifted in appeal and expectation sees the face of its own return in answer to that entreaty. In this way, the concept of the grant is one that comprises both the ministration and the request, the give and take of regard in response to thought, understood now as *Vocation*, in one self-several being both called *and* calling, heard *and* hearing.

We refer this contact and the well-documented effects that feelings have on beings, i.e. the impact they have on the world of human being, in other words, the traditional discrimination between the *datum* of beings and the so-called *donum* of thought, between their *presence* to an observer and the *present* of thought, as we will explore in more detail soon, to the difference between theoretical and practico-poetic reason, the first engaged perceptively with a view to *insight*, the second purposively with a view to *action*, specifically, to the fulfillment of a resolution. Theoretically speaking, the principle of reason is a *cause* of presence in relation to the *observing intellect*; understood practically however, the principle is a *purpose* that has been made manifest, revealed, to the *discretion of volition* which is, in return, animated by that inducement towards the keen pursuit of its ultimate realization. Thus, for theoretical reason the *order* of thought is the *attribution* of illumination – clarity with respect to principles and causes, especially the first principle and the first cause – whereas for practical reason the *order* of thought is the *assignment* of authority; the former distinction of thought grasps the order as each being's place in the scheme of all beings; the latter distinction takes the order as the accusation and the indictment that the breaking light of thought's day brings to the recesses of our concealments and the ensuing charge that this revelation places upon the pursuits of human being.

In both activities of reason we emphasize the experience that they share, namely that of the **impact** of pure reason on our lives, our original encounter with *germinal* thought: Just as we follow step upon step in a line of reasoning, drawn by this conductor along a train of thought and experience, the *locomotion* of the logical mind – which is, nevertheless, not the one track mind stuck in the rut of rote calculation – likewise we have all taken note of the voice and the force of conscience, the stings and pangs of contrition, the *ayenbite of inwyt* that we cannot but acknowledge (if only to dismiss in the end) – for this is the experience of the *repentant* mind in contrast to that of the *perceptive* one, which is the intuition of wonder that impels thought to grasp unseen reasons behind the scenes of appearance. In both of these offices of reason, that of repentance and perception, the *immediacy* of the mind shines forth conspicuously to *receptivity*, a calling voice, a beam of light, the answer that always precedes the question, but also a claim and a demand that we cannot ignore until after we have been already touched and determined by its necessity. This striking present of reason is always, whether it be to us a gift of insight or the poison of compunction, the startling and inaugural sensation of our open-minded anticipation:

> Open your mouth and close your eyes
> And you will get a big surprise!

32. The Trust of Welcome

A guest come from afar and abroad is welcomed or refused the hearth warmth of hospitality – how do we receive this visitor, this messenger, the address and testimony of what has made itself undeniably known to us with all the persuasive force of what is present to sense? Thought is open to the enthusiasm of distinctions. Perception is the faculty to see behind the seens and grasps the principle and the rule of law that connects several many into one and a whole; but perception is also the capacity to receive an impression. And it is this faculty of thought that is properly, but in no way inertly or supinely, *passive* – sensitivity, the reflective correlation of the benefactor's *generosity* in granting the gift with the responsive *recipience* of the beneficiary to whom the gift was allotted, the reciprocal present of thought conceived in gratitude and regard, bread and wine, the light of day given, taken in thanks at a festival where songs are sung to celebrate the boon.

As with the *generosity* of thought's influence, its corresponding *gentility*, thought's responsiveness and in this sense its *delicacy* can be conceived of as the dignity of the senses, oftentimes subject to philosophical depreciation in the name of clockwork rationality, their office of *disclosure* answering to that of the *revelation* that is the issue of thought's determinative principle, its present; distinguished thought is an *open* being and moreover, with a view to the parochial definitude and its culture of encapsulation that strikes a pose opposed to overtures from beyond its ken, a *transfinite being*, to which we have previously attributed the property of transcendence. For just as the inchoate act of thought is a *taking leave* and a stepping back, therein the negativity of abstraction, it is also seen here as coming in, the breach of an approach or, as we might call it, the entrance of *ingression* and, consequently, the corresponding *giving leave*, the responsiveness that is our senses' tender, gentle answer to thought's kind vouchsafement, their natural welcome to the convivial community of those chosen in so choosing, heard in hearing.

When we speak of thought as being communicative, it is this *give and take* of open-mindedness, this commerce of the mind with itself, its generosity reflected in its recipience and vice versa, the reflective reciprocity of the entity of identity that we refer to. Clearly it would not win our adherence to its evidence if the testimony of reason were not congenial to our impartial understanding which in turn is inclined to suffer the conclusion that the train of thought has brought before the inference of its intellect. Indeed, as we have seen, *grasping* or *feeling*, even *touching* has served, since Hellenic days, as an indication of pure reason's contiguity with regards to the beings that it contemplates. All of the senses are susceptible to this immediate contact, receiving, as it were, signs from abroad, as they would a stranger – the enlightenment of the home by the visitant of the new and its news. Similarly, far from leaving us cold, the force of logic invites our participation, more, our communion in response to the apportionment of the faculty of thought, the sway of the present of mind, that original, vernal deed that has been bestowed upon our possession as the title and distinction of human being, not merely as embracing thought as our own, but also, in the logical pursuit that fosters it, as executing the will of that deed and serving the office that the assignment of thinking appoints us to. Couched in this terminology of giving and receiving, of dispensation and participation, the experience of the evidence of thought as a grant and our correlative apprehension of what has been entrusted thus to our care is richly rendered in the concourse of ideas pertaining to *tradition* – in which thought is a heritage and a legacy bequeathed by an ancestor determination to kindred posterity; to *prerogative* – in which the command of logical necessity compels our agency; and to *service* – in our observation of and submission to the exigencies of devotion, the demands of debt and duty, the drive of enterprise, that the obligation to laws and the commitment to policies vests us with. These terms that so vividly and richly render the relationship of ΛΟΓΟΣ may now be added to the growing collection of notions that we have employed to depict our experience with thought including *communication* (the ringing voice of a calling and impartation), *hospitality* (the greeting of a stranger), *bounty* (the munificence of generosity) as well as *care* (the nurture of concern towards the thirst and hunger of needy – the widow and the orphan), *celebration* (in the thanks-giving for the gift of present), *credibility* (in the leap of faith born of trust to what has won firm conviction) and *illumination* (the seeing of light and what is seen when the eye has been shorn of its wool).

This wealth of analogous ideas, elaborating as they do upon the responsive notion of recognition, the inception of thought being thus, essentially, *regard*, the affirmative apprehension of pure reason's prior determination, contribute to making the relationship of recipience as substantial and as tangible, as striking, as possible – the evidence of pure reason's present and the ensuing obligation inherent in acknowledgement; but they also indicate more generally the plenitude of pure reason's presence in concrete application to our world – the workings of the mind are richly real in our experience, come to life, take on the substantial form of reality and then again, mediate insight that, not content with merely seeing things, perceives in surfaces and signs, depths and sense, the depths of sense, the government of principle behind and beyond, below and above the casual phenomena of particulars. Such recognition of a prior principle is insight's show of gratitude.

But, as we see, such royal exaltation does not remain up above the world so high, but even in uplifting the earthbound stones towards their diamond distinction in the sky, the celestial principle is inclined to smile upon the nether elements, replenishing and revitalizing their grounds with its outpouring of *beneficence* that sanctifies the dwelling of its own settlement and the welfare of its kind. This favorable participation of thought, moving as it does beyond its contemplative application in the illumination of a theory of beings towards thought's practical application in our lives is termed *compassion*.

For this gift of benevolent outpouring answers upon the *plea* which is itself an outpouring and skyward opening in the otherwise closed vault of control and mastery. The anguish of the supplicant breaches the framework of stiff-necked self-reliance, and in this appeal to might and strength beyond the mundane flairs and fortes of its highfalutin habituation, prepares the welcome of thought for the advent of the principle.

Thus complementing its grant of grandeur, we experience reason's plea; to awesome plenitude corresponds the awe of indigence, to immensity nugacity, to glorious height the lowly cry of desperation. The address of the wretched in utter abjection powerfully envisions the spirit of invitation. For there is courage in this welcome that keeps vigilant watch and keeps an eye out, an eye pealed, scanning the horizons of a strait world, recognized now as such, and thus already situated in the transcendence of thought's prepositional relativity for which there is always an Other, the otherworld of thought's negativity beyond, above, below, behind – simultaneously unlocked to hope, which is one of many terms that might be posited for the mind that has regained its open state and with every cry of every sigh utters the resurgent word of transfiguration, the balm of clemency complementing the suit of supplication that is its chiral reflection, reciprocally subordinating the first person to the second even as now the second person is subordinated to the first, namely in the whispered orison: "Come!"

There is courage in this fear, well-known as the beginning of wisdom, that realizes it is utterly alone and then again not alone because precisely in this experience of our limitations, in this penury, we conceive suddenly of the standpoint *without*, feeling, embracing, addressing this alterity of the coign of vantage as one might the face of what remains after all has been lost; after all is lost, thought itself, though destitute, orphaned, deserted, abandoned, is left; in the experience of critical self-reflection, the Other to me who, till the advent of my despondence, was nothing at all but my private property, just me-myself-and-I, my tool and my despotic rule, but now bereft of everything I ever was, in my desolation and affliction, is My Me to Be that is always and forever utterly different from me, beyond, above, below, behind, in a word **before** me. To this *distinguished* life I have before me and no longer merely *am*, and no longer merely possess as my own but rather with regard to which *I am/is* the possession, the dependent, the subservient, I cries/cry out in moans of invocation against the presumptuous face of self-reliance "Come!" "Help!" "Hear!" manifesting in the very hope for salvation, that vocation of regard that is our savior and the spirit that alone will deliver the crippled grip of Man from its own clutches.

And it is for this reason that practical thought, the *Grant*, has been represented, sung, celebrated not only as the theoretical light and the glory of a gift of self-evidence, but also envisioned in the glow of warmth and splendor, an outpouring endowment in the effulgence of *kindness, love, mercy* that articulate the notion of compassion, which, in the chirality of regard's reflection is *thanking* thought, gratitude for grace, bearing in mind and bearing out what has been born, the profession of that vocation. And then, in the perfection of this patience, thought, the *Plea*, brings forth the realization that its principle is not conditioned upon a principle, a mechanism of reflex; its being is not merited or deserved, neither owed nor caused, not the consequence or the second, as it is itself the principle and the condition, the first and the uncaused cause, the gracious present of thought to which every thought is grateful in return.

33. The Danger of the Stranger

As we have already noted, the ratification of regard and the affirmation of trust that mark our acknowledgement of thought's distinguished primacy suggest an opposing terminology of refusal and neglect. Withheld consent can deliberately deny but not make undone the previous immediacy of mind. The response of disownment to the axiom of reason can only be the suppression of its fact or aspersion cast upon the distinction's merit. The repulsion of pure reason's overture and bid to our notice depicts that gift as a poison present. Thus the image of mum and mumbled mystery, arcane and exclusive inscrutability, the bolted barricade, the strangle-hold, the obstructed passage letting nothing in nor out – all depictions of the hard-hearted, tight-fisted, closed-minded mind that repudiates the proffered offering of thought, rejects the thanking stance that response entails, declines the patience of a question that abides the answer, scorns the gentle demand of a plea reflecting the obligation of pure reason's own necessity. Thus also the address of the voice of reason, in coming to our senses, stakes its claim, solicits our answer to its proposal, petitions our attention with its suit; but we ourselves, open to that vocation, take the standpoint of the eyes and the ears rapt in breath-holding expectation – the innate passion, the supplication, of the senses begging to be heirs of that bequeathal from abroad, a spellbound state of listening to hear the herald from on high, an alert of peering sight to see the brilliant apparition of these faces in a crowd, a hand outstretched, face uplifted to the blows of the rain or rays of beneficence poured forth, poured down upon the dark earth, upon the thirst and shadows of its immensity. Or else, the leather-face turns aside, remains an unmoved mask, inscrutable, disdainfully displeased, a killjoy to the moving, pleasing call, wing-clipped in those winds of change; in blindness and inert, the eye, hurt, shuts the lid in cold blood and flint.

In this vein, our iron modern man sees but danger and estrangement in the calling from beyond the ken of what is familiar to the highbrow rampart of its closure and control – everything that trespasses from without threatens to breach the walls he erected in defense of the inward maintenance. This pinging brazen sphere is put at risk by the advent of the foreigner, the alien so outlandish to that xenophobic land of pertinacious nodding, outlawed by its inbred laws, extra-terrestrial to its earth-bound groundlings, odd to their even similarity, queer to their square normalcy, exorbitant to the orb of their urbanity, the rude intruder, out of whack, uncouth to their finesse, out of line, out of hand, out of the blue from out of the way – a hostile force visualized as the tempest's winds and storm, the plague of pestilence and catastrophic incident, the sun's eclipse, the eruption's quake, the squawk and fang of predatory beast set loose in the city streets, the slings and arrows of outrageous fortune – they all bring the outer regions of our village world to the door and window of our moated lives and infringe breachingly, wideningly, maddeningly upon the narrow-minded scope of our sane concerns. These are the striking events; the shocks of their impact leave their mark indelibly on the impressionable sensory skin of daily disquietude and nightly rumination; unforeseen events in their disrupting effects upon well-placed lives are depicted as the contingent violence of what doom allots, what fickle fortune bears, and what dark fate decrees – three powerful images of extrinsic intervention suggested by the encounter with the exogenous determining principle that gives suspended animation an allergic start and makes a monster of thought's every demonstration – the inclusion of such gust guests from beyond the borders of our house-of-cards homestead is not without risk, better to be avoided unless...unless the host has learned the gracious art of salutation, welcoming, in a friendly spirit, the OTHER onto the hearth of home (Odyssey 1.124):

ΧΑΙΡΕ ΞΕΙΝΕ ΠΑΡΑΜΙ ΦΙΛΑΙΣΑΙ

(Hail, stranger! By us in friendship be!)

The beggar at the door is, in fact, though disguised, the king; the visitor in human form whose knock brings news and a message from far afield, is, in fact, not merely a human but rather the embodiment of an idea, in other words, a god, and then again not a stranger at all but rather the master of the house in disguise arrived home at long last, bearing the sword of his return striking like a day of reckoning when shameful concealments are illuminated, harshly, abrupt, abyssal, deadly to the harsh xenophobe within who hugged his shadows with impudence, for whom the stocking torn, the bubble burst, the bad-egg cracked (that "hommelette," we shall become acquainted with as the ego or *mini-me*), can never be repaired – not even by all the king's horses and all the king's men – and for whom the only thing worse than a torn stocking is one mended; yes, that smooth plain of indifference that was once so sleek by thoughtlessness is now forever scarred, ruined by the darned distinction. In this way the self-evidence of reason lifts and drops a question on our plates, makes and leaves a mark in the flesh, on the page of our perceptions, trespassing like crooks' subterfuge upon our straitened squares, like invaders' incursion crashing the gates of our oh so solid state the walls of which we had hoped would stay harm's arm, would shield us from all other-worldly onslaught upon the immunity and impunity of our entrenchments like a swarming infestation besetting our bunker body, an assailant hitting us, in spite of our fences and defenses, where we live, where the sun don't shine, striking home against our thick skin citadel which will henceforth never be the same again.

II. The Turn and Return of Thought

C. The Principle of Inaugural Discrepancy

34. The Ordeal of Jurisdiction

That thought might be rendered as a sunbeam of illumination or as an eye-beam of discernment is a conceit familiar to thinkers and poets alike – they experience their own proper attribution in accordance with the theoretical or the poetic mission of their office, namely, with regard to being and its beings, that of *insight* or of *artifact*, that of their discovery or their invention. And these two friends of wisdom, its "seers" and its "singers" of truth, know, each in their own way, in the immediacy of direct experience, that the *present* of pure reason was the bright origin of their profession. The latter's virtue is *intellect* and the perception of the law and the general principle **in** the presence of the particular fact of natural phenomena to the objective observation of science; the former's is *imagination* and the realization of that veritable principle **through** the vivid presence accorded by language to the progression of all the incidents and individuals that shape an epochal narrative, the myths of our cultural history.

But the inaugural experience of thought as the distinction of human being is neither the delight of sight nor the celebration of song; this experience may be reduced neither to the seeing of beings and their conception in science nor to their makings in the ingenious designs of art, but is most vividly rendered as the anguished experience of a being broken, one differing from and contrary to itself and in this sense *self-several*. Is this being not the one ensnared in the much fabled vicious circle of doom called *human* tragedy? Consider the experience of a being that is not what it is; for in not being what it really and truly is, it is, actually, perpetually other than itself. Why? Because from the very beginning its *self* is its other; its self *is* its other. Consequently, in becoming what it is, it passes away into what it is not and, as it shockingly would appear, ends therein, and precisely this being, bereft of what it is, amounts to its being most completely. We behold its being *without*; we behold its being *before*: *without* – it lies, as we saw, prostrate, destitute and desolate with respect to the emerging splendor and the reigning glory of the absolute and distinguished abstraction, sublime plenitude to that earth-bound poverty; but also, as we shall now see, *before* – it stands bowed, accused and accursed with respect to objective judgment.

The event, the advent of reason in the life and the world of human being makes a difference. The character of this occurrence, the impression that thought's *existence* leaves behind, has often been often called striking, surprising, even miraculous but it is always a charge and a challenge, drawing, as it does, a distinction, and introducing thus an element of, shall we say, disintegration into the four neat walls of our world and its life in rose, a hitherto perfectly normal life, thank you very much; in this sense, thought is the distinguished and distinguishing event of revelation, and, by a world cast in such an iron frame of mind, feared as vicissitude, as a real and frightening force, often rendered as an upsetting element, the fortuitous calamity of wind or fire, to our house made of ticky-tacky and to its laws of straws, a chaotic encroachment, one not merely of sedition but even, as latter-day philosophers are fond of murmuring, of subversion. Doubtless to their utter consternation, far from founding orthodoxy and the monolithic mentality of a life in rows, our philosophical tradition has, as we shall see, experienced and depicted this event of revelatory upheaval not only as illumination, but also as vocation, as a supernal discontinuity, sudden, unpredictable, disconcerting, epochal and, as such, negatively *determinative.*

For we join now to the positive notion of the deposition and the authentication of supervenient thought in its demonstrative abundance and to the negative one that it complements, namely the notion of the detachment of critical reflection, thus to both the preposition of thought and the resplendence of this exaltation, to the remote sanctuary on high of its abstraction and the gorgeous plenitude of the revelatory grant, to that compassionate gift of alleviation that answers to the poverty of the need in its supplication, to this chiral pair, we add now the notion of the jurisdiction of thought, *judgment,* the relationship defined by the *Judge* and the *Judged* consisting of both the censure of the brazen as well as the saving grace accorded to the humble, the former's punishment for obduracy and the latter's correction in the shame of regret. For even as the sympathetic ear is turned in favor to the plea of a prostrate heart so does the inexorable sentence of condemnation retaliate for the impudence of contumacy – the word of heart's call falls upon deaf ears even as, to the admission of heartfelt rue, the gift of forgiveness is awarded – in the chiral reflection of this relationship, to give is to be given, to reject is to be rejected, to know is to be known, to scorn is to be scorned, to hear is to be heard, to uphold is to be upheld, to remember is to be remembered, to destroy is to be destroyed. The visage of aversion sees its own face as the face averted, sees its own regard mirrored in that face that shows regard. This relationship is not merely one of reciprocity, is not a strategy of trade of goods for goods or the economy of exchange, a contract of sale and service, the tit for tat, the tooth for a tooth, the quid pro quo, the moral calculus of *do ut des*, but rather a rendering of the entity of identity, the speculum of good facing good, the welcome for what is well come and blessing for blessing – the present of thought in the chirality of its reflection.

Judgment comprehends the personage of this identity of thought, our Verum, as that of a *transfiguration*, not merely as the one unfolding between the first principle, the *prince*, and his *realm*, distinguished in the defining attribution of the former and the latter's inherence, nor in the correspondence that exists between the *lord* and the *vassal* with respect to the productivity of the latter's service in their relationship of mutual acknowledgement, but also between the *redeemer* and the *damned* for whom reason is no longer only *knowledge* nor only the realization of *power* but also purpose, the *will* to perform a charge to which it has been assigned, striving towards the fulfillment of that obligation.

In the turn and return of reflection, in the spin of its chirality, in its *I for the I*, to choose is to be chosen, to give is to be given – the transition from *attribution*, which identifies each being with its specific form and property, to *accusation*, which places thought itself at odds with its principle, marks the turning point in the story of reason's life; having only just begun to wield its contemplative excellence in seeing *behind* the seens, thought, the *Thinker* is recognized and thus reborn as the *Actor*, the incarnation of ideas in deeds where principles are no longer only the laws that insight contemplates but also those that govern action on judgment's stage, the disclosed arena where the dramatic trial of crisis is played out in the shame of that uncovered openness that we experience before the discerning eyes of distinction that never fail to see in THE WAY IT IS *THE WAY IT SHOULD BE*; this divergence is the clearing of critical reflection to which we are then summoned to appear and, in the harsh light of this illumination, give account of ourselves before the eye of pure reason that is My Own I, my Elder and my Better Me that I, now lost, being sundered in two, am destined to be when I am finally won again at the end thought's time and passage when the work of closing this gap and of healing the wound of human dehiscence that the experience of our distinction has struck in the flesh of our mere being has been accomplished.

For, again, at the inception of our destiny of discernment, what do we discover when we note the intellect's immediate effect on our lives? Do we not, one fine day, become inquisitive and question what we see; we question and investigate all that is and has arisen, all that takes place and has made its appearance before us, all that has gained presence in the inaugural presence of mind; we wonder why and how and search for reasons, causes to explain THE WAY IT IS as well as the anomalous beings that would seem to diverge from what they ought to be – this is the office of contemplation and *in theory* all the concrete particulars, the elements of the ordered world, are, in and of themselves, articulate beings; they are their own formulas and speak to patient observation with their own eloquence saying the truth, revealing to the insight of perception THE WAY IT IS simply in the fact of the matter.

We strive to understand and then discover beyond the principles and laws that we have discerned that govern the beings we have studied one ultimate fact, namely that we *can* step back and understand – and *this* is the true miracle, the common ground of *intellect* as well as *purpose*, namely that we *do* understand, that we, in order to understand, must stand above, before, behind the beings to which we lend our attention, in other words that we must attain and stand upon the distinguished coign of vantage of the mind that places us without all being and all beings. This marvelous *preposition* of the mind itself, among all the beings that it is wont to study, this property of thought deservedly earns it the title of *best* being, in the sense of the one most worthy of all to be studied by pure thought but also, due to the eccentricity of its self-severalty, its controversy, the *last* of them all to which study has been explicitly devoted, namely to the paradoxical being without all being.

Clearly, by accounting for the work of the intellect enthroned upon the Olympian heights of contemplation and peering down upon all mortal, worldly, natural being and beings, we have not yet told the whole story of reason; its life has only just begun. For now, after thought's rejuvenation and the youthful gaze of science, the epoch of practice is set to commence when thought descends from these unearthly heights and, here, enters the earthly arena of action.

What if now we were to participate in the drama of nature that we have been admiring thus far from a distance as that of beings? Practically speaking, the immediate and most striking as well as the most familiar effect of thought on our lives is, actually, not the epic delight of immediately seeing and, in perceptive sight, in insight, knowing, but rather the drama, the tragic mission, that our dialectical capacity for reason bestows upon us as the destiny of *human* being and our experience of this destiny as a matter of death and life, as a *death with distinction* and the corresponding *life hereafter* that is the human life of distinction here and now.

But taking respite from action as we must occasionally, in moments of leisure and reflection before or after labor, how can we study this experience and make a theory of our practice in which we formulate its aspects and dimensions, its phases and salient features? Only to the extent that it is given form in language. For language is the only tool we have to document the practical experience of a human death with distinction, our learned death, and the corresponding human life hereafter, the so-called "spirited" one.

Life, Death, Spirit – These words and many others that our train of thought has been liberally applying and will now in the following all the more enthusiastically employ are indeed striking terms, rich in connotations, repellent to many a thinker today perhaps (well, to whom actually and why?). Though seemingly out of place in scientific discourse, unless there are sciences different in kind and one science, the first, essentially different from and superior to them all, namely a philological one, these terms, many of which have been borrowed and translated from ancient and foreign tongues in which a long tradition of human reflection was articulated, but many also simply taken from our everyday language, allow us to get a more vivid sense of the extent and scope of thought, its influence and impact, its significance for human being. Content to reap the benefits of instrumental reason in use, why would anybody have given thought a second thought, if the old and oldest languages of the thinkers' and the poets' had not insisted upon rendering our experience of it in dramatic, provocative, animadverting terms as a matter of life and death rather than mere expedience and, through abounding esteem, make a mountain out of the mind that we, moles in our blindness, have always assumed to be merely our little hill of airy habitation atop a burrow in the dirt.

35. The Being of Thought Torn between the IS and the OUGHT

By contrast, consider therefore with a soaring eagle's eye, the general notion, so utterly familiar to human being in the manifold particular experience of *impairment* that arises from the discrepancy and divergence between THE WAY IT IS and THE WAY IT SHOULD BE. We have often used this designation since the very beginning of our investigation to mean simply the fork between a given state of immediacy and a certain predicate of distinction ascribed to it that makes an issue of that former state in comparison with the new one that has now with the advent of this distinction – though as yet merely aim and purpose – arisen. Thus, for example, if the target, the bull's eye, is missed, whether it be that of the sales manager or the archer, this difference is the issue whereupon we make adjustments, realigning our bows, taking aim with renewed commitment, analyzing reasons for the mistake, asking and then telling why what we have done has thus gone awry, amiss; our arrow went astray, has left the straight and narrow way to the center that was our dart's aim, the goal, the objective; we erred in our being, in our having done too much or too little, in going too far, ending up too short, too wide – funny, the bungle is always extremist. There are many such expressions that indicate the state of missing the mark or the boat, the state of failure; in school we flunk, on ice we slip and fall slapstick flat, flopping with a dull thud – the sound of defeat, "ouch!" we swear. Trains delayed, the glitch in machines, the botched event, the muddle and the messes into which we sink – indeed, don't we all occasionally bomb out? The bang fizzles, the boxer takes the count, the ship sinks; yes, things go wrong.

These disappointing situations display the gap in question in a variety of contexts – hunger and thirst, desire and disease, anger and pain are all evidence of what has not panned out as planned, is not up to snuff, is not what is was meant to be. The jagged is not smooth; the jam not flowing or too liquid, dripping on our tie, the jarring not mellifluous, the jaded overused, wanting the zest of refreshment, the jock all brawn, the jumble discombobulated, the klutz lacking grace, the laggard dawdling, the lame hampered, the languid inert, the drooping wanting turgor, the sesquipedalian pith, loneliness companionship – there is no end to the expressions of language for, the situations in life prominent because of, exiguity and shortage, being slapdash and shoddy, trivial or menial, underdone, overdoing; the imperfection that we encounter in such cases of inadequacy is that of an unstable state of need, of drive, of desire that periodically flares up as a result of depravation, disintegration, disorder, inconvenience, namely then when the IS and the OUGHT part ways and THE WAY IT IS *is not* THE WAY IT SHOULD BE and vice versa – the double-trouble reign of abnormality and insanity is the admonition of difference.

Closer to home, the impinging pronouncement of reason is rebuke and reproach; the unexpected intercession of disapprobation into a given state of affairs raises thus unwelcome issues that indicate to us what is required and the extent to which matters fail to measure up and make the grade; even if this call into question can be denied or ignored, an answer refused by fraud, an admission of failure, debt, guilt, shame forestalled through rationalizations, it marks a discontinuity in the course of our lives regardless of how we respond to this challenge. It is objective in being beyond and prior to the circumventing fictions of our invention, in being a verdict of predetermination and in this sense, no longer so much revealed to our contemplation, as jarringly imposed from abroad, beyond, above, mandated from *without* upon our remorse. Thought, the Judge, in our experience of its edict, is the injunction and the subpoena of rebuke and our answer in response to its call is the departure from, the renunciation of, the ingenuous simplicity of THE WAY IT IS when all is well.

Being thus summoned to the trial of thought, we are checked, taken aback, step back, recoil slightly in noting the difference between reason's call and our well-worn wont – this voice is an impeachment, a dictate of the mind to mind the gap of discrepancy between THE WAY IT IS and THE WAY IT SHOULD BE. Prior to all excuse, acquittal, or dismissal, it has, "somehow," been laid down thus upon us to blush, this unwritten rule of law, and our experience of it can be studied in terms of an *awareness* superseding that of the receptivity of sense, which discriminates beings with regards to what they *are*, were meant, destined by their predetermining nature, to be; we have become aware of this disparity as our avulsion and the violence of a divergence, the misery of vicissitude that constantly plunges us from a relative calm, short-lived though it may be, into renewed vexation with the steady state of our currently reigning enactments. Thought, however, set down as an *ordinance*, is our experience of infraction and the testimony of the original dissymmetry of the world that presence of mind takes, gives account of, pronouncing upon mortality. We are not ourselves, but, in critical reflection, different from ourselves, being only then most completely ourselves, most whole and wholly human, when divided in such self-contrariety as is exacted by heart-rending reason's right. Either looking in or looking out, celestial or infernal, a coming or a going, and in this way dissimilar from itself, not entirely aligned but slightly askew, by a notch, a nuance, standing out somewhat, one tick apart, ever so slightly aside, a bit beneath, just a minor irritation in a workaday world's Simple-Simon sameness and its calculus of concentricity, human being is a discriminate, a disparate entity – that is what is meant by the arraignment of human being in the name of the distinction that is our destiny; pure thought is that differential. The mind is our stigma and our medal, the incidence of immensity in man-made meters, a budding eye beam blossom upon the blind plain-Jane wall flower of the same in the same lifting its head to the blows of the rain in eternal return.

THE WAY IT IS **IS NOT** *THE WAY IT SHOULD BE*; *THE WAY IT SHOULD BE* **IS NOT** *THE WAY IT IS* – this divergence hurts. In this interlude of silence, we experience the departure of pain and the state of extremism that arises when THE WAY IT SHOULD BE (but is not), namely abstract and empty thought, stands opposite THE WAY IT IS (but should not be), namely a superficial, shallow world without depth and meaning, a cold fact, an obverse universe, inimical and unbecoming to a neutered, indifferent mind.

It is a condemnation of a given state of affairs taken as is, become evident by the present of mind that is not beholden to the prevailing tenor of Mrs. Grundy's mores, not determined by the accepted facts of happenstance and circumstance, and by the vested interest in the maintenance of custom and its tough customers. From the standpoint of detachment attained in the rational principle of critical judgment and perception, the world *as is* and its ways, its play, the course and march of events, can always be conceived of as being different than they could have been, should have been. Look upon any scene of the life of our world or a moment in our lives and imagination sees the hard data of the day framed by possibilities not enacted but visible to the mind; seeing in the way things stand merely one possibility, more, seeing in the situation at hand a deviation from what is supposed to be – this detachment and emancipation from the vogue of the status quo is the distinction of pure reason manifest in all its energy of invention that clothes a denuded truth in the raiment of a fashion; in the light of thought, this particular way of the world is just one style, one mood and manner of things, one case of the cookie crumbling. And every item of our lot, all the ins and outs of every particular, coalesce into the aspect of an accident.

See that mountain reigning over there majestically upon the horizon? Thought can, at a whim, with a word, pluck it out of THE WAY IT IS, hold it at arm's length in the mind's eye and grind it down to dust, send an avenue through its core, wind a stairway up its face, mock the gravity of its bulk. Imagination can mold this grey mound into an elephant or shrink it to a mouse, uproot a mulberry tree and plant it in the sea.

Already this caprice of fancy reminds us of thought's predilection for taking liberty with the set of conditions carved in stone by the elemental forces of the earth. Fantasy is an arbitrary power. But a notion of THE WAY IT COULD BE lacks the force of need, is content to remain just that, *just* a thought, an amusement, a figment. Nevertheless, even this whimsical play and fanciful playing with given matters and affairs is the mark of the mind's detachment and negativity, the infinite lightness that ideas possess, these things (that are no things) with wings of distinction. The power of the imagination, however, is, beyond this play, only then that of pure reason as a force to be reckoned with when the vision that creative thought brings forth fills our heart of action with a purpose in the clarity of an end recognized as that to be fulfilled by the committed endeavor of pure will which, precisely in the act of positing its unique conception in contradistinction to the facts, namely THE WAY IT SHOULD BE, steps back from THE WAY IT IS, adopts the standpoint of distinction that the envisioned aim, immediately manifest in the present of thought to thought, provides.

And specifically? Can we stipulate THE WAY IT SHOULD BE *in general*? Moralists will try to. Politicians often have recourse to the well-known platitudes and educators appreciate the pith of precepts and recipes, succinctly put into a phrase of dogma or stone-hewn article of faith. But the status of such truisms can be, at best, only commemorative, calling to mind, in the form of words, what was originally the articulation of an idea that inspired the drive and purpose of pure will in the first place – the gap between the IS and the OUGHT that emerges to the mind when engaged in the discipline of critical self-reflection.

THE WAY IT SHOULD BE is a commandment of action that determines practice and appoints the invention of the imagination to the office of *supreme* fiction, namely the representation of our ideals. It is a law revealed by and in the present of pure reason with regards to a certain set of circumstances. How can reason know in advance all the many, many details of a particular situation that calls for practical attention? It cannot. The circumstances of a particular case cannot be entirely anticipated or enumerated and therefore to the neophyte who is looking for guidance in ethical questions, the only general answer we could proffer is to act in accordance with the will of pure reason, in other words: "Soft! Behold! Take heed! Yield" And this proposition is in turn meaningless to anyone who has failed to experience the distinction of human being as the faculty of stepping back in critical apostasy from the administration of immediate matters and urgent concerns at hand that normally limit the horizon of a block-headed perception. In contrast to this one's block, the head in question, the head destined for use in decision-making, has a wider, a more panoramic, more objective eye, is commended not for being a chunk of bulk but rather for being svelte, lithe alacrity, as sharp as it is bright, as swift as it is deep. But the particular individual can only use his or her own head and no one else's, namely the one that corresponds to his or her particular situation, his or her own lived experience, his or her unique life and history – after stepping back and discerning that resonate interval of divergence, we are ready for the leap of faith that posits perfection, the ideal in view taken as the end of subsequent action – hic Rhodos, hic sultum.

That is why everybody knows that in the field of practice deeds and not words are what count, the time for words being before or after the deed done, the action taken, the decision made. For antecedent words, if they are persuasively rendered, inspire action and, afterwards, if they invoke the principles and criteria of discrimination upon which the action was based, encourage judgment to step back again in a renewed reflection pertaining to the excellence of what has transpired and to decide whether the result is THE WAY IT SHOULD BE or not – an as yet unresolved need requiring further regard, further care and adjustment.

36. The Discrimination of Diversity

The practice of pure reason analyzed in terms of this gap between the thought and the thing, the mind and the matter, the ideal and the real, is the articulation of an apparently irreconcilable conflict. Initially at least, when the stigma of the law, the expression of THE WAY IT SHOULD BE, leaves it mark on unminded immediacy hitherto spared from the care and tear of awareness, experience in this sense is just such an irremediable fall from baby-face grace-and-favor, that rent-free habitation, the boon of oblivion, that is our prior unborn, untorn being. The crisis of these two sides cleft asunder is the curse of human birth into the state of self-knowledge, the coming of age in critical self-reflection, the death inherent in the distinction of a will that takes note of the gap between the impartial vision of THE WAY IT SHOULD BE on the one hand and, on the other, the imperfections, become visible in light of this absolute will and, through the ensuing comparison, its particular idea of how all our kindred souls, poor and good, how all these current events and latest states of things ungiven, though taken for granted, *might be better* than they are. If only we had left well enough alone, had not considered what might be or might have been! If only THE WAY IT IS had remained snugly smugly the same, vapidly THE WAY IT IS and that's it, being its *it* and nothing more, nor less; if only we could have stayed this benign-benighted baby being for evermore, cradled in our green infancy, happily harmless and unharmed, aslumber in innocent imbecility, nicely innocuous, unsigned in our insignificance because unnicked by the quick immensity of desire, unentangled by the knot of knowledge that gives us pause and splits in twain our doubt, shapes into a terrible terrain with dales of tears and hills with eyes beneath a crowning crag of futile puerile finitude – that pure plane of immanence that is our junior human cheek, smooth, very much lacking groove, a blank slate and fluid state, a body bereft of organs, an "aorgic" body, of molten mineral.

Where thought is experienced in its receptivity, not of perceptions and beings in relationship to beings, but in passion, in the sentiment of wills at odd, and thought pitted against thought in the chirality of its reflection, reason takes sides, both sides of the enantiomorphic relationship, stakes a claim *and* takes a vow of commitment, enjoins *and* submits, reproves *and* exalts. Discrepancies are born and multiply, leavening our lives with their discontinuities. We come to recognize our need beyond the needed, our *just* being beyond our merely being; the capital I behind those small eye slits dropping off the face of mankind in a doze while taking in the scenes on the screen; redoubled thus, it is the fear we fear, it is our mind alive that we meet, its teeming being that is ablaze; it is that fire feeling that we feel before and beyond the world that our intellect felt; it is our monster mind, that we fear, who now, in being thus once removed, perusing and perused, feeds and feeding on our hunger, tastes burning thirst, abhors or embraces our approbation or revulsion, sees resounding sight and blindness, swallowing chagrin at the dust and ashes that we are who, precisely in this devastating condemnation and demission of our being, find indisputable proof that we are in fact a little more, one iota, one mere mote more beyond the mud, cast up, up and away, cast down and out, cast abroad and inwardly, to gaze from the vantage point of the discriminating mind and thus to see and judge detachedly and therefore fracturedly the distinction that reflection has impressed upon white-bread human flesh, the signature of experience engraved in the now sun-kissed complexion of our face – about our eyes, all those wisdom wrinkles. Therefore we must say that pure reason is, to be sure, a thrilling, but also a piercing experience; the transfixing experience of the distinction of human being rends us, true, but in a life otherwise quite trite and quiet, quite alike, pure thought, this stroke of luck, arriving, as it always does, in the nick of time, is our *one big break*, and therein a scar, first a hurt, then a wound, but since become our red badge of courage, our true-blue tattoo and the character trait that is our fate.

Pure reason is the experience of the imperative of thought's present in the light of which THE WAY IT IS is distinguished from THE WAY IT SHOULD BE. So look around you and take note of this distinction; mind the gap – it is the call revealing discrepancies, needs unfulfilled; thirst and hunger being interjected into the surface of surfeit and satiety; where complacency sprawled now demands are made, issues are raised; where success dozed now flaw and failure complain. All is well? Oh no, now we owe; owe payback for debts and dues of distinction; reason saw and laid down its law and now we have obligations, its demands to fulfill. In every new situation we encounter, we are aware of thought's purposes imposed; we face the task of sufficing the entitlement of the idea, meeting expectations of the will, which is, in each particular context, the goal set, the target fixed, the promise made, and the pledge to be kept. Thought's calling is the manifestation of shortcomings, the charges we now bear like a burden, a deficit; for pure reason tells us what it lacks and needs, what we lack and need, just now from us and from ourselves, and in the present of this need we meet, upon reflection, the wrinkled face of human suffering, images of urgency – the sick, the poor, the orphan and the widow – the imperative of reason's law is revealed to us in the present of indigence and the straits of necessity, the curse of mortality; every hardship manifests the difference between THE WAY IT SHOULD BE and THE WAY IT IS – poverty and scarcity, lack, of course, but also glut; for transgressions of the measure that thought is, is, too, a deviation, too much or too little, breaking in from abroad, breaking out from within, too close for comfort, too far, misfit and outlaw – all displays of drama in the arena of judgment evincing the original discontent that critical reflection initiates. For here thought encroaches and afflicts, perspicuity interjects suspicions, the will of that law's authority sanctions actions, stakes claims, marks deficiency, and we in turn are the ministers to this master, servants to this lord, loyals to our royals, are subjects of our misses, abject, fraught, freak, weak, late, to that standard, wrong to that rectitudinous rule and, in our anguish, attuned to its admonition.

37. The Crime and the Punishment of the Soul

But towards prayer a deaf ear may be turned and an overture of goodwill can be met with rejection – what My, Your, Our height and highness was, the uplifting distinction of human being, our concept, is now the twisted conceit of haughtiness, a hauteur – not aloft but just aloof; not the *up up and away* of our supernal being but merely infernally stuck up and superior; not our flight in the rare brisk air of thought but rather the slight of airs put on, the put down, its snobby shrug and snooty snort; the dig, the cut that pride thinks nothing of, rather than the thunderous sunder of self-several concern; the slap in the face as opposed to the countenance of compassion is the brazen-faced turning away, the cold shoulder shone, the visage of aversion, deaf, blind, mute in lip-curled contempt. The perversion of thought makes the mind insensible, closed in recalcitrance, sports the ogre's numbskull, works a quack's deception. While the *absent* mind of inattention fails to see what is there and the *simple* mind of sensory perception sees, to be sure, all there is to see but misses the principle, the causes, the reason behind the seens, the *fixed* mind is willful and refractory, refusing to acknowledge and recognize that anything be *other* than itself, that there could be a realm of being beyond its own realm that limits the thrust and the fetch of its swelling. This dilation of its enclosure engorges all difference and thus, in the sprawl of its ballooning, transgresses and annexes the vast land of the others, Your land, incorporating that plunder into its empire. To the selfish being, all is one, and one for all, namely for it alone; all by myself...and wanting to be, without You; and whether itself or another, it is all one because what's good for me is good for You, making of the self-knowing, self-delighting, autonomous and absolute self-relative being that is our entity of identity, the simple selfish relative, an incestuous monster begotten upon itself, born on itself and, finally, feeding on itself, the cancer cannibal – swallowing itself head first.

For the advocation of sameness and assimilation preempts encounters of distinction with difference in the installation of tedium even as does *deception* sidestep confrontation, *insolence* subvert the intercourse of compromise, *obstinacy* resist renewal, *ridicule* deny accountability, *servility* abnegate steadfast courage, *impatience* preclude meticulous preparation, as does *fear* breed avoidance, *despair* surfeit the hunger of hope, *envy* shortchange self-critical assessment, *jealousy* manhandle trust, *vanity* extinguish compassion, *hatred* despise all mitigation, *defiance* shirk the service and *arrogance* the self-discipline of duty, reneging on the debt of respect and gratitude – to mention only a few of the terms referring to the crime of a depraved mind, shutting the door on all rapport with the words "I don't care."

Thus, by contrast, the most general term for the experience of thought as *relationship* – ΛΟΓΟΣ in its most general sense – is *feeling*, which is the making of a contact with an OTHER, whether it be the perceptive *sense*, the close encounter with and the animating apparition of tangible beings – animal, vegetable or mineral – or else, more to the current point, *sensibility*, the meeting of minds and mentalities, the clash of cultures, the collision of wills, heart touching heart, thought *thanking* thought with grace or with ingratitude, in accordance with which reason is not merely the discernment of difference between *the way things are* and the *way they aren't* but rather the experience of discerning concern in the adjudication of probity and villainy, the benediction of the former, the execration of the latter.

Caring hurts, as does hearing, seeing, touching, as does all sentience of those with more soul than they can control. The call for help, the cry of anguish in pity keenly felt and taken to heart transcends that blunt being that sports the inbred apathy of the walking dead – this call, in recognizing difference, acknowledges our untoward, wayward bent even as it transcends this anesthesia, reaching onwards and upwards, grasps thought as *sufferance*, a being made for affection and impression, one quick and nimble of apprehension and in this sense s*oul*, recognized for its unfailing empathy as *immortal*; the stirring of *passion* is the experience of this cordiality, the lively conversation of response and correspondence in ardent change and exchange. Admit it: Wouldn't it be much easier to repress this dialogue, this dialectic, much easier if there were no differences to negotiate, no tricks of kindness's chemistry and instead just so many atomic rocks in mineral stupor, earthly and inertial, living in their own private Idaho, underground like a wild potato?

The chiral reflection of this unseeing visage of aversion and enmity is rendered in terms of the nemesis and the scourge of justice, the vengeance of punishment; *disregard* translates into the mercilessness of law, *blindness* into the stern impartiality of judgment, impudence into the impersonality of fate, *hate* and *fear* into the righteous anger, the wrath of the sword and even as an exclusive wall of *derision* is erected upon the stones of unfeeling earth so does the calamity of quake and war and pestilence smite the supercilious citadel and annihilation mirror *abjuration* – a reflection of countenance in which the self-relativity of the entity of identity is made manifest according to the familiar narratives of crime and punishment, cause and effect where the gift of life is a life given and to the turning mercy of that gift corresponds the sacrifice of the thanks given in return.

In the chiral logic of the reflective reciprocity, a stone-hard heart is therefore, heedless *and* unheeded, is, unhearing, hardly ever heard; impudence in ignoring pleas is ignored in pleading and the cries of heads with deaf ears fall upon ears that are deaf; to the eyes' aversion replies the averted eye; hate is hated, ridicule is ridiculed and to hit is to be hit – the point here is not to extract or derive from these relationships moral precepts, pithy maxims or golden rules, however plausible or recommendable they may or may not be in the particular situations of our lives – as if, in general, we committed our deeds pursuant to a precursory rumination upon ethical codes and how they are to be properly applied in a given case – no, we are examining the experience of the distinction of human being and have come to understand that the notion of reciprocity in evidence in these renditions of the practice of thought is governed by the self-relationship of pure reason, more, marks salient ideas that are constituents of a larger train of thought that originated with the experience of the *revelation*, the communicative power of the mind, and now enters upon the concept of the rational will, unfolding across the dimensions of practice which commences in its own right with the distinction between the *status quo* of THE WAY IT IS, its conservative tendency in resisting the stirring overtures of THE WAY IT SHOULD BE upon its otherwise so impassive purple reign, and the *quo vadis* of soulful enthusiasm that welcomes such visions and visitations from abroad in the thankful spirit of sacrifice.

A. The Principle of Determination

38. Saint Anger

THE WAY IT SHOULD BE, i.e. the revelation of pure reason, translates the law of thought, that we first encountered in the force of that mind-and heart-winning certainty, thought's genial, soulful amiability, the persuasion of apodictic *reasoning* that accompanies truth – the well-rounded, trustworthy truth that is the perfection of its being – into the context of sublunary, i.e. *human*, action, into our enterprising world of *practice* as the realm of the efficacy of the *will*, of such thought that, in its susceptibility to reason's nudgings and urgings, has been won over, convinced, and is now decided, thought become *commitment*. The will is pure reason under the aspect of an encounter of contest, of trial and proof, measures being taken upon the determination of value, merit, the quality of a being with regards to what it ought to be – its vision; with a view towards this practical idea of a thing in relation to which the critical sentence of judgment has been passed, we speak of the experience of the immolation inherent in corrective efforts devoted to the accomplishment of that charge, the fulfillment of an ideal, executing a directive, carrying out a plan, obeying an order, performing a project, fulfilling a destiny, realizing a potential, or just following the rules of the game and doing what is, in light of that precept, right.

With a view to the initial divergence between THE WAY IT IS and THE WAY IT SHOULD BE, we might be inclined to speak of a span of tension, a state of disequilibrium, a dynamic, self-contradictory condition, a state that is no state, a being that is not what it is – for nothing impaired or imperfect, nothing of, as yet, unfulfilled potential, *is* truly *what* it is (i.e. what it is *supposed*, *meant*, *destined* to be) and is, in that sense, when compared to the vision of its OUGHT, a non-entity even though it might, in some other more casual sense, very well be said to "be" in one way or another, but not really and truly, not *essentially*. At the outset and all along the way in the life and times of such a being that has been thus thrust into the arena of reflection, there remains work to be done, a race to be won, a trial and struggle to be endured, a name to be cleared, a debt to be paid – thought is not just contemplation but also crisis, and even combat – a call to the hands and feet of deeds, to the butt of heads and locking of horns, to arms of action, in a word, to the *Sword* – a not so beautiful name for thought that introduces a cluster of connotations that may be brought to bear to put the experience of severance into martial terms depicting the Falsum of my resistance to My Heart's Better Half as anguished *war* and how my resistance against My Opposition to me is killing me softly and often not so softly, shaking this little old world of mine with the blast from above that My critical reflection is to me.

We will often encounter these sword verses in scriptures devoted to detailing the distinction of human being in the darkest tones and images – death, destruction, killing and mayhem. Their violence reflects the violence of self-contrariety of our untoward human being that is not what it is, is not itself today, and therefore, being ill, misgiven, mutant, is what it is not, but adamantly, incorrigibly so – resisting the change and the growth that would more closely align the IS and the OUGHT in the end. It is the destiny of our human being to mind this gap and, in the *zeal* of critical self-reflection, to experience our own proper disparity either as a willed abdication or else in bloody contention that can only end in the slaughter of *our narcissus*.

Who said a little thought never hurt or that it wouldn't kill you to take a moment to reflect? We have learned, on the contrary, that it most certainly does and would. Remember our first encounter with the inception of thought – just one simple idea that changed everything; stepping back for a moment from our world and our lives to consider them and us from apart, from without, from above, yes, from above, let's say that, hence from the *heaven* of critical self-reflection that is the coign of vantage to which pure reason empowers and encourages us, hurts, a lot. Everybody knows that if you want to go to heaven, you have to die first. Every sort of relinquishment, letting go, breaking up, is hard to do and *sorry* seems to be the hardest word for a very good reason – it is a salient word in our daily death sentience, that critical sentence of judgment that the present of thought gives us.

In the ensuing process of mobilization, even as THE WAY IT IS will be accorded the substance of a purpose to admit perception, THE WAY IT SHOULD BE, an otherwise abstract idea, will attain a standing in particulars, *taking place* in them; this chiasmus characterizes the endpoints of the inversive movement, the transformation, that is the will's drive to come alive – the realization of the "ideal;" the idealization of the "real."

The recurvation of thought's sweep admits of moments held fast, phases named and numbered. We met the issue of thought's **present** at the inception of pure reason's turn. We accounted for the mortifying insinuation of this bounty into the scheme of things set as plain and simply so and so, having been previously put in place, set and settled, only to be subsequently suddenly sundered from their normality by the intruding duplicity of contradictory claims and divisive difference. This effect of striking illumination and impression is now followed by the relinquishing act of stepping back, the advent of thought, the *Quest* – another of its 99 beautiful names – that challenges the incumbent institution with dissension, with the intervention of a unique distinction. This critical stance is not merely a posture of refusal. Pure reason makes and leaves a mark upon particulars and in the ensuing span of difference between THE WAY IT IS and THE WAY IT SHOULD BE delineates the details of an end and purpose – the resolution of the will: The gap between THE WAY IT SHOULD BE and THE WAY IT IS is the absolute contradiction of terms and it initiates the action of a drive in which the THOUGHT and the THING, the MIND and the MATTER, the REAL and the IDEAL each complement and fulfill the other – on the one hand, the abstraction of thought's NEED laid down as LAW, is enacted in the DEED, applied as RIGHT to the case at hand in its urgency and brought to life in our lives as ASPIRATION – the carrying out of *judgment*; on the other hand, the circumstances at hand in their casual immediacy are elevated and deepened by the implication of a concept that defines and determines their identity in the idea of reason – their reinvention in the productivity of *imagination.* This chiasmus is an exchange of mutual modulation and a passage of conversion, the drive and the way of the will – the ***performance*** of reason; it visualizes the two-fold metamorphosis at the end of the way in which the principle received initially as our distinguished destiny has been fulfilled, in which the two parties to the conflict have been reconciled to each other; the charge we took upon ourselves in embracing the crisis that reflection engenders has been born with fortitude. In terms of this imagery, thought's judgment of THE WAY IT SHOULD BE has been brought to life, has been accomplished in the ***perfection*** of the way of the will; and life, the immediacy in our sense of THE WAY IT IS, has attained the substance of having been comprehended in the grasp of intellect as the ***presence*** of reason.

39. The Way of the Soul

The revelatory understanding of thought's *note* and authoritative *sway* is now deepened by that of thought as the distinguished *will*; the beckoning objective leads us on, draws thought towards thought and finds repose finally upon the attainment of accord and community that has been achieved in the process of development and growth such that the IS and the OUGHT are reconciled, each conveying to the other what itself lacks to its perfection, to the erudition and the cultivation of mind that, for the sake of its wayfaring and its striving, being moved and moving, has been traditionally called the *Soul.*

There are a great many terms that indicate how the exercise of thought is *attraction* and *drive* and not merely *reception* or, prior to this, *vocation*, which, in view of the crisis that it entails in otherwise so pacific lives, is, as we now see, provokingly put, a declaration of war. The former pair of notions suggest that a passage is being undertaken, a way covered, a discrepancy is being overcome, the end, call it the destiny and the destination, has been previously established, foreseen in the vision that brought a being to trial in the first place; we might say that the result has been preordained, foreseen, "pre-posterously" set first in the mind while the careful performance or execution of this *providence* is subsequent to the projection. THE WAY IT SHOULD BE is an aim, the venerated presence of the end *and*, governing the action devoted to its attainment, the determination of the means to the end. There is an odd contradiction in this perspective. The destiny is given first, but in the manner of an ideal and vision; being merely a form and the formula for what *OUGHT* to be, it is not yet the way IT IS. *Desire* is the striving that energetically reflects the degrees of divergence, the intensity and tension of this difference. This activation of the principle no longer merely felt and known but also proposed to the distinguished will as the impetus to action, intended, and then, ultimately undertaken as the way to go, the right thing to do, acknowledges the power of thought to be a precursor to action, to change, which is the conversion of the WAY IT IS into the WAY IT SHOULD BE and THE WAY IT SHOULD BE into THE WAY IT IS – a cross and a crossing, the point of intersection of mind and matter, the ideal and the real, each serving in the transformation that founds and grounds their ultimate community. Such thought that strives to become real is called the practical idea or the *will*, which is, as Kant put it in a footnote of line 20 of section III in the introduction to his "Critique of the Power of Judgment" "*the capacity of the mind to be, by way of ideas, the cause of the reality of these ideas.*" (Kant, *Kritik der Urteilskraft*, V 177.)

> Der Wille ist das Vermögen, durch Vorstellungen, die Ursache
> der Wirklichkeit dieser Vorstellungen zu sein.

The desire of the heart thus encouraged and whom we might also call thought, the *Seeker*, not in the sense of the seeker of the *truth*, the distinction of *insight* that is the *Thinker*'s but rather as that of the *good*, the distinction of the *will* that is the *Actor's* whose crisis of severalty with regards to the foreknown principle began with the U-turn of conversion, the "personal" experience of disparity between THE WAY IT IS and THE WAY IT SHOULD BE, and, in the dramatic endeavor of correction and adjustment that ensues, proceeds to govern a good soul's work of reformation and renewal in the pursuit of happiness, that envisioned reconciliation she strives to achieve in her life, such that, at the end of her way, THE WAY IT IS *is* THE WAY IT SHOULD BE and THE WAY IT SHOULD BE *is* THE WAY IT IS.

Poetic thought, the *Builder*, completes this reflection on the experience of our obligation with regards to the determining principle as well as to our projected fulfillment of its terms. The language of admonition that accompanies the soul in the course of her renewal is that of an exhortation that encourages her resolve should her commitment flag in the face of adversity and obstacles along the way, perpetually reminding her of her cause, advocating patience in spite of the deferral that a gradual achievement, the step by step, day by day progression of progress in the completion of our plans and projects must impose upon the immediacy of their urgency and that, therefore, our gratification, for the sake of that purpose that is our ultimate objective, must endure in the name of steadfast diligence. As much as it sustains her drive, the speech of exhortation is, as well, the inaugural summons that set the soul on her way in the first place. Placed before the mind's eye by the art of moving the human heart, it is the vision of the destination that gives thought, the soulful Actor, the idea of what is to be achieved in accordance with the appointment of the principle in the service of the articles of which the Actor's commitment has been engaged. Thus is the need that drives her enterprise, though initially deplored as disparity and divergence, penury or surfeit, finally the desirability and the attractiveness of the end in the esteem of which she has taken upon herself the restless life of arduous character study, making of the assignment of the project of the role she is to play in the tragic piece (with a happy ending), her own program and discipline of excellence.

Figure 24 provides a rendition of the soul's experience that begins with the *mandate* of distinction admonishing her *reformation* in accordance with the tragic character she is supposed to be if she is to be herself in the play of self-severalty that she undertakes for the benefit of her career towards an end among the distinguished stars of fulfilled destiny in *observance* of the law and principles she acknowledges as *governing* the life and person of the character she has taken upon herself to embody. Inspired by that character and the director's exhortations to go beyond the limits that had defined her world till now, she finally vindicates her undying belief – having since become, against all odds, the idol of her age – that she had always been destined to greater things.

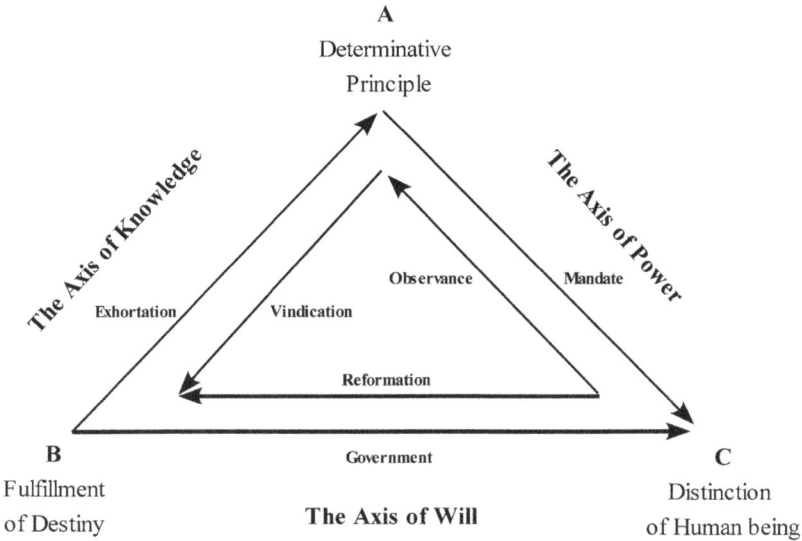

Figure 24: The Inner Workings of the Soul

B. The Principle of Accomplishment

40. Eligible for Excellence

Where are you going? What is your goal? What is your aim, your target? These questions point us in the right direction after the decision, a choice, has been made; ideas are now ideals sought not as the *truth* of intellect but as the *good* of the will. For the selection of preference follows the trial and the test that checks and compares and finally adjudicates what, under the circumstances, is the right thing to do, the right will to enact, determines the chosen goal as the *good* to be, not yet being, being, as yet, just the thought, as yet no thing, but as a thought a thing determined and appointed, destined, *to be*. Of course, we all have our targets, our short- and long-term objectives. As intended and *supposed* to be, the good, and specifically, all of these our goods, are now not at all objects of theoretical study and analysis but much more visions and practical resolutions, however impractical they may in fact be, of what we want to accomplish, projects clothed in the very concrete terms of action most in accordance with the haunts and habitudes our lives. A good is always a certain good in question. Its issue is defined contingently with regards to the particulars at hand at the moment, here and now, relevant to the current situation. With luck, at some point, the details foreseen and depicted in the proposed target and the actual situation will, after the laborious execution of the intermediate phases and stages and the overcoming of obstacles along the way, completely coincide. We say the thought *has become* the thing; and the thing in turn, far from being something we just happened to find, stray, along the way, has in fact been accorded value, the dignity of having been singled out and chosen, distinguished by deliberation, *to be*. In familiar practice, the gap between these two extremes, i.e. between our actual state and the one sought by the will, is the perceived difference between them, the felt *need* and the form of what will suffice to satisfy it. Our experience of *thirst* might serve as an illustration of how this difference inspires action, giving rise to effort and to the steps we then undertake to eliminate the discrepancy between what IS and what OUGHT to be which mediates the passage from this incipient state of pain and necessity to the final one of correspondence, first preordained as a project by the mind's facility of detachment, then premeditated in particulars by the will, and finally attained only after that determination had run its course to perfection and come to rest upon the laurels of success in the fulfillment of the good, the ideal, towards which initiatory desire was directed.

Ideal? The Good? Perfection? Ah, my dear Dr. Pangloss, in spite of all your metaphysio-theolocosmolological optimism, nothing in this best-of-all-possible-worlds is *good* in the strict sense, nothing *ideal*, nothing *perfect* – thus sighs the worldly-wise, the self-proclaimed realist and the poor pragmatist as if their disappointments with regards to the abiding imperfections and common peccability of Man were, even could be, an argument against the heightened will, the practice of pure reason itself. Though the melancholy of mark-missing and the shame of shortcomings, the pangs of dispriz'd love and unfulfilled desire would seem to be the all too human rule, how could folks, for this reason alone, really have anything against love's wounds and that arrow that incites our striving to close the gap between the real and the ideal, how could they have anything against the aspiration that gives incremental life to the ideal through our actions and, through our goals and visions, gives value and distinction to the real as our accomplished possession?

The perfect, the good, the ideal – we are wont to repudiate them as such because they are often different for different people and different even for the same people at different times and in different circumstances, and in this sense all *relative*. Ah, but these terms are indeed always defined relative to the circumstances in which they are coined and applied. That is precisely what is meant by speaking of them not only as good but as goods pertaining to practice as the objects of the will. But when discussing the practice of reason, our pure will, as the distinction of human being, it is not at all the *content* of thought, a particular thought and object, but rather thought itself, this capacity to compare and prefer, to judge and decide and then tirelessly to aspire, that we are attempting to witness and what could be a more salient indication of thought's efficacy than our ability to consider how a given situation might be improved as a result of our own efforts? Our highest, faintest hope, assured or even fool-hearted faith, undying and unrequited love or simply simple-minded optimism over against well-founded despondency are significant not in the particular details defining this promise or that conviction and much less in the probability that this trust will be rewarded. No, it is not the product of action, the results apart from the effort, it is the performance of reason itself, this fact of thought as ambition, as ***aspiration,*** whether or not the promise is fulfilled, the project achieved, that we wish to take note of and wish to properly acknowledge in saying, "yes, this is thought; is it not amazing that thought can do this, that people can see with eyes that look and see and ask not only *why –* the power of the intellect – but also *why not.* For this anticipatory prospect is the start of our will taking up the challenge of change and taking on the charge of perseverance, committing with pertinacious determination to hold fast to a practical principle and to diligently seek its enactment in spite of the inertial forces of distraction, beguilement, deception, and corruption that conspire to frustrate its progress. Thought, the Arrow and the Archer, is much deserving of being sung in its own right in celebration of the endurance and constancy of pursuit, of the corresponding unswerving rectitude of flight that stays on course, stays the course, with respect to what *has,* as the goal and the good, *to be.* This is the essential notion of practical reason upon which *morality* is hinged, the absolute paragon of the mind surpassing the norm into which we were born and bred and documenting in a suite of excellence the comprehensive eligibility of *human* being to be thus ennobled by the name, to be *distinguished* being, subject to reason and traditionally known in this realm of deeds as the subject of *virtue* both *cardinal* (prudence, justice, fortitude, temperance) and *theological* (faith, hope, charity).

Now in your particular situation, given the facts that determine it, the place, the time, where and when you were born, the people you know and have known, those in power over you or those subordinate, the time of day, the year, and the month, your age and sex, your race and religion, your status in society – given all of these undeniable facts and details that, because there are so many of them, could never be entirely accounted for in our world, because the web of dependencies and determinants into which the affairs of our lives are spun extends infinitely – there is a very good chance that your dream and your wish will never come true and, from the perspective of omniscience, never could have come true. And nevertheless, that in spite of this hopelessness, whether surmised and ignored or never even guessed at or even just flat-out feared, the fertile mind of *prudence*, in a leap of *faith* could have seized upon this vision and, as hungry-hearted *temperance*, taking upon itself to rouse itself from the stupor of its present state, taken heart in undying *hope* and pursued the aim on high with *fortitude*, doing something today, making a telephone call, putting on this shirt, saying this word to that person, reading that book, leaving the office at that time, thinking this or that thought in the evening before falling asleep – all of these actions, the words we said, the places we went to or refrained from going to, were done, said, visited and forgone because of that desire, in the name of that ideal, with a view to that goal, as a result of that vision, undertaken for the *love* of goodness and for Heaven's sake in order to do *justice*, at least a little, to what might not have otherwise been done at all, not even considered in the first place; they are the particular bits and pieces, that in their tendency really do amount to something, in their collection are already the emerging "reality" of this goal and good will; they have made a difference in my behavior, affected others, left their indelible mark of distinction and like pebbles tossed into an early morning lake, have launched ripple after ripple upon the velvet liquid plane and set events in flowing motion down the stream of being even if other little children shall bring my boat ashore.

Nevertheless, in spite of thought being the capacity to set the counter-factual ideal, the ideal is the vision of THE WAY IT SHOULD BE put into factual terms that indicate what the realization of the goal entails. Ideals, i.e. thought put in the patterns of particulars, a vision taken as a *paradigm*, are specific in terms of what ought to occur – it depends on the circumstances to define these details of the ideal. Again, this element of contingency in the paradigm has caused some to doubt whether there is any *good* or *morality* at all or to conclude that since what is right depends on the situation, values are just a matter of opinion or convention being established by "society" or decreed by some introjected "father figure," some "authority."

In fact, the ideal that pure reason sets and seeks is not defined by all or even the majority but rather by each individual who takes his or her own situation into account and then, at this critical juncture that marks our life as that of pure will, draws the distinction between the way it is at the moment and the way it should be, the later determination couching this pure will of our human being in the element of the particular situation in which the practice of thought finds its foundation in fact attended by and surmounting opposition and concluding upon correspondence. In ancient Greek thought, this aspect of the pure will was called ΣΟΦΙΑ (*sophia - practical* and *inventive* wisdom as opposed to its *speculative* counterpart) comprising ΦΡΟΝΗΣΙΣ (phronēsis - prudence) – discernment of ends, both ultimate as well as mediate, that are appropriate, right, in a given set of circumstances; ΣΩΦΡΟΣΥΝΗ (sōphrosynē - temperance) – the overcoming of and breaking with the penchant for comfortable confluence at the outset; ΑΝΔΡΕΙΑ (andreia - courage) – the spirited resolve to endure with pluck and with panache overcome obstacles along the way towards the determined end and ΔΙΚΑΙΟΣΥΝΗ (dikaiosunē - justice) – the fit fulfillment of that principle that prudence originally recognized as what was meant to be, what is therefore meet and sweet, decorous and due.

41. The Catalogue of Ideals

Pure will is thought seeking. But now thought is the thing sought, endowed with sanctity in its remote abstraction and teeming with the fecundity of vivid imagination; meek, we are as patient recipients to its urging of value and then, kindled by its enterprising flame, we carry on, aglow, resolute pursuit until the debt of purpose has been paid in full. Seeing these images of the good that is *happiness* – different ends are different names for our heart's desire set in different circumstances of our lives and in fulfillment of different walks of life wanting different happinesses – we who are mindful of the diversity of human being's life stance are variously addressed so as not to be left cold by the particular vision that corresponds to our highest desire, but rather to be more deeply moved by this interest to excel and surpass ourselves and thus to aspire to the object of our good – a business person, for example might be thinking about her or his *customer satisfaction* and speak with enthusiasm of *quality*, or *excellence* as instrumental values towards affecting this greatest good; a teacher, on the other hand, of *understanding* or *knowledge* or *emancipation* on the part of the pupil, while a politician speaks warmly, of course, of *justice* with a view towards the *commonwealth* of *peace*; soldiers sing of their *fatherland's* enduring union that needs *defense* above all else and *conquest* as the last resort; an artist spoke, at least traditionally, of works *sublime* and *beauteous* but today more likely aims at *provocation* for the sake of *self-expression* and *authenticity*; a life of *prosperity* wants the *comfort* of material *wealth*; a life of *excitement* seeks to try its *courage* in the thrill of *adventure*; the life of *achievement* strives with *ambition* to master *challenges* and to make a lasting *contribution* for the sake of undying *glory* and admiring *recognition*; the life of nurturing *love* builds upon *endearment* a *home* of *harmony*; the life of *pleasure* plants, protected behind a garden wall, a private life of *independence* and of *leisure*; the life of *learning* erects a monument to the *mind*'s delight in articulate *truth* that *insight* shelters and *invention* celebrates. And *forgiveness* serves *friendship, restraint, self-respect,* and *obedience* in *honor* of a *creed* held fast is the path upon which *religion* marches up the mountain of *salvation* and *immortality*.

But by taking all of these ends and their corresponding means, this catalogue of ideals, these wingéd words, and swinging up from end to further end in a series, we attain the vision of the ultimate intrinsic ends and principles of distinguished human being – *Humanity, Divinity,* and *Entity*. These three beings – poetic, practical and theoretical – are equally abstract and it is thus their abstraction that was our first encounter with them as the three ideas that constitute pure reason's self-knowing being – *humanity* being human nature's original state of freedom that our productive life gives form and shape to; *divinity* being the divine nature of the glory of love's redeeming gift towards the transfiguration of the mundane world; *entity* being physical nature's perfection as the manifestation of the distinguished principle that is the first cause of its presence. We perceive the three lives that correspond to these beings as the creative life of the Builder in the realization of the principle and coming to rest in peace upon the foundation of the dwelling that is the body and the being of its community; the active life of the Seeker perpetually engaged in an effort of transfiguration with respect to the principle by striving towards its accomplishment of distinction, and finally the contemplative life of the Thinker gaining insight into the ways of the threefold being that is thought thinking thought.

With respect to this threefold being, all aims and goals, values and virtues, and the ultimate visions they serve make a difference between THE WAY IT IS and THE WAY IT SHOULD BE; their entrance and vivifying coming means our mortifying departure and going, the commencement of a hardship, the difficult undertaking, a task at hand and effort to be made, work to be done, an engagement of our resolute commitment and determination; minding this gap of deviation, we rightly talk of stress or pressure and the cut of thought, the need that is the driving force that moves us, the bid that is our resolution. Thus *assiduity* serves the achievement of greatness but would be naught without concomitant *competence*, would fade without *persistence*, flounder without *discipline*, succumb to vitiating doubt without sanguine *expectation*. Can a family's love grow strong and deep without truth's *honesty* tempered by the kindness of caresses? Can a mansion be built while ignoring the *logic* and *consistency* of a neat brick set finely upon its fellow, a household managed without *salubrity*, intimacy enjoyed without the happy marriage of *obedience* to each other's happiness and *affection* borne of mutual *regard*? And as much as *contentment* reigns at the hearth so must *detachment* beckon in the lecture hall where the teacher's *foresight* forms the substance of the lesson and the student's *curiosity* awakens *reverence* for the mind at large, our reason to be.

Thought wants to become a reality and not merely remain just a thought. This is the very nature of thought thought not as caprice, whim, fantasy, or idle speculation held within its constipated self, but rather as *will*, wanting thus *to be* not merely *what can* (but need not) *be* but moreover *what ought to be*. For the idea that awakens our interest and desire is, at the same time, the idea that draws us towards it, step by intermediate step, along the passage to completion. And our fostering of this thought, tending towards it, is, in the reflection of self-relativity, our being tended by it, guided, fostered. Here is where providence and foresight converge. For as punishment follows recalcitrance, and the grant accompanies the plea, so do the atonements we make answer to the debt we have incurred and the pursuit of ends correspond to the guidance they provide regarding the fulfillment of the principle that was destiny's vocation.

42. Visions of the Happy Ending

Thus, thought is the target but also the archer – the target in the sense of the particular goal that the soul – this our archer of the will – has set her heart and sights upon; thought is this aim and aiming, but also the arrow the cast of which, the bow of desire, speeds the project along with great pitch and moment. Thought is this flight of enterprise, the arched trajectory that bridges the gap to the heart's mark; thought is the eye of the bull at point blank range, the clean kill. The chiral reflection of the practice of thought's action renders it now in terms of the recipient of action in which the drive of striving to close the gap mirrors the guide and governing force that leads the charge and fosters the development towards the end specifically envisioned to place the absolute distinction that the principle makes into a context of our lives that matters. Take *health*, for example, implied above in the catalogue of ideals as those of *cleanliness* and *neatness*, *grooming* and *tidiness* belonging to the body of the dwelling being that realized the original abstraction in the perfection of the principle and the completion of the project. Each individual posits his or her own vision of health and articulates its forms in all the elements and details that the imagination can muster – nutrition and apparel, physical and mental shape, conduct and complexion – you consider how you should be and how you are and mind this gap not only as *your* needs but also as the will of health, *Health's* needs who, considering yourself in the mirror of Your mind, says initially "I am not who I am" because THE WAY IT IS and THE WAY IT SHOULD BE diverge. The distinction that this discrepancy draws upon your life marks the need that is now Health's will who, in this your you-turn, you have taken upon yourself as Your will in the disseverance of yourself from You, My will and My distinction from me. We ask then what is Your will and the vision of Verum answers in a richly rendered version of who We are, really and truly, as the being of health and then engage ourselves to do Your will, His will, Her will, My will. Your will be done – this is a regime of discipline in which we perpetually step back from our current state, overcoming the lethargy and inertia of the status quo, breaking out of the habitations and routines that have, over the years, so snugly ensconced it in its niche and in this crisis of discrepancy posit subaltern aims and goals, the rites of austerity including the inevitable sacrifices and oblations (a brisk walk after dinner, one slice of cake less in the afternoon...), that put our determination to the test of practice when a will becomes a word and words, that schedule of plans, becomes deeds and these our wholesome habits of the character that is our destiny, determining both the do's and the don'ts first prescribed and then pursued in the project of the vision that pure will committed to our care – the morning run in rain or shine at half-past nine, the dentist's chair, fresh underwear, one bagel less, one apple more; stretch out your back, talk less, get sleep, and sweep the floor under your desk occasionally.

These practices of abnegation are works of devotion. As much as they demand of us the discipline of service and, as duties on behalf of the realization of the particular ideal in question, immolation with regards to our inertial tendencies, as a pursuit of virtues that we have adopted as Ours, like a bride, *to be*, the specific acts thus commanded are acts of worship in which, through our efforts of reverence and respect for the ideal, the world as is, our unlovely state so evident in the morning mirror of the mind, is transformed and ourselves drawn towards the better place that the providence of the will had shown to us at the outset and that we have since recognized as the land of our own promise.

The will that thus governs me is My will, the OUGHT given a particular form of law – for what would an unspecific law be? Every law or rule must stipulate THE WAY IT SHOULD BE in specific terms. These are the plans laid out in the context of a particular life of the subject; these patterns enumerate the individual acts that salvation entails, the realization of the will's purpose thus laid out. Originally, we encountered the law of reason in its authority – the immediacy of its revelation. But a particular law is a rule that stipulates the exercise of our obedience in the context given by THE WAY IT IS here and now. Then it is poetic thought, the Builder, whose *imagination* establishes the form of things to be, no longer in the theoretical sense, with a view towards comprehending their cause and nature – for these are also a thing's form and idea in the *intellect* – but rather in the practico-poetic sense of articulating the standard, the form and norm, the cause, the nature that, for contemplation, is always taken for granted and immediately given to thought by thought whereas, in the arena of practice, they determine *desire*, i.e. thought, the Actor's, purpose and ambition. What something is supposed to be, in a moral sense rather than a conceptual one, is assessed ad hoc and judgment is made here not to evaluate beings as they are seen now with regard to the principle of their definition, but rather to beings as they are yet to be. But again it is not their reality that is the significance of goals and aims, not for the possession of objects that objectives kindle our desire. For desire knows that its use in the kingdom of reason is to articulate the infinity and the immortality, the distinction of our otherwise so indistinct, finite and mortal human being; the will lifts us out of the confines of beings as they are and sets us in the framework of beings yet to come with regards to which the former are charged with change, transformed and given a purpose beyond what they naturally are, accorded, that is, their *supernatural* purpose as beacons and symbols of our becoming what we are supposed to be. These designs resemble representations but they are not still-life imitations and mere duplications of beings; they are anticipations, previews of prudence; and to the extent that they govern our actions, the model they constitute formulates a policy by providing a shining example of the will's direction. What is a vision if not a star to wish upon and what is a star without its splendor beckoning our ennoblement so as to sanctify the try in lieu of the gain and to credit even failure with the illustriousness of a courageous attempt.

These epitomes are the beings of the will, the beings of desire and though they be figments of the imagination and in this sense *unreal*, they are nevertheless actual and effective in what they set in motion and the progress of continuous becoming that they sustain, inspiring our daring and guiding the thrust of our reach to climb height upon eager height triumphantly and to prevail in this exultance apart from any quickly cloying fruit of success to prematurely seize upon and then possess at the end of the road when desire dies in sad satiety – this way of desire that is reason's forward looking joy and precious prescience of the transfiguring will whose envisioning works of imagination, at least in the practice and exercise of devotion, ought never to be over and done with, can be found celebrated in letter VIII of the sixth book of Rousseau's *Julie* in a passage that he calls Julie's Swan song:

> Malheur à qui n'a plus rien à désirer! Il perd pour ainsi dire tout ce qu'il possède. On jouit moins de ce qu'on obtient que de ce qu'on espère et l'on n'est heureux qu'avant d'être heureux. En effet, l'homme, avide et borné, fait pour tout vouloir et peu obtenir, a reçu du ciel une force consolante qui rapproche de lui tout ce qu'il désire, qui le soumet à son imagination, qui le lui rend présent et sensible, qui le lui livre en quelque sorte, et, pour lui rendre cette imaginaire propriété plus douce, le modifie au gré de sa passion.

> Mais tout ce prestige disparaît devant l'objet même; rien n'embellit plus cet objet aux yeux du possesseur; on ne se figure point ce qu'on voit; l'imagination ne pare plus rien de ce qu'on possède, l'illusion cesse où commence la jouissance. Le pays des chimères est en ce monde le seul digne d'être habité, et tel est le néant des choses humaines, qu'hors l'Etre existant par lui-même il n'y a rien de beau que ce qui n'est pas.[27]

> *Unfortunate he who has nothing left to desire! He loses, so to say, all that he possesses. One enjoys less what one has obtained than what one hopes for and is only joyful before joy's fulfillment. Indeed, human being, avid and confined, made to want all and obtain little has received from the heavens a consoling force that brings near to him everything that he desires, that submits it to his imagination, that renders it present and tangible, that, in a certain sense, even delivers it into his possession, and then, in order to render this imaginary property all the sweeter to him, modifies it to accord with his passion.*

> *But this entire prerogative vanishes with the advent of the object itself; now actually possessed, nothing embellishes the object any more in the eyes of the possessor. For one does not envision to oneself what one already sees; the imagination no longer embellishes what it has acquired; the illusion ceases where consumption commences.*

---

[27] J.J. Rousseau, *Œuvres Complètes [OC]*, II 693.

The land of chimera is, in this world, the sole land worthy of being inhabited by human being and such is the vanity of the human condition, that except for the Supreme Being that exists through itself, there is nothing we cherish more than what is not.

III. The Destiny of Our Human Being

B. The Principle of Determinacy

43. Turns of Words in a Tongue of Flame

After distinguishing seeing and doing, *sight* from *act*, we are left with what has been resolved in the process and turn now from the doing of the will to the *deed* done and to *fact*; the conclusion of our train of thought must be that *thinking*, in the rich sense of the elaboration hitherto pursued as an outline of our experience of thought thinking thought, is, really and truly, *being*, the one that has, in the occidental tradition of metaphysics, only most recently come to be known as *human* being. The disparity between the IS and the OUGHT, the mandate inherent in the accusation that critical reflection raises, summoning us, like a herald, to appear before the court of judgment, like a wake-up call, to action, and putting us to work on behalf of the idea, more, the *ideal* of pure reason – the experience of which has not only awakened our interest in the open horizon of opportunity that presents itself to the imagination but has also engaged the committed service of the will to close the gap made thus manifest between THE WAY IT IS and THE WAY IT SHOULD BE – this issue of thought, has now been resolved.

These two sides of the distinction that reason draws upon human being, opposed at first as they are in the irreconcilable hate of contrariety, have been accorded justice in the mediating relationship of reciprocity through a development such that what one entirely lacks the other provides in full, each thus modifying the bounds of the other's extremity by conceding the other's prerogative such that the two great ideas of human conception and enterprise, namely that of *mind* and *matter*, of *thought* and of *thing*, of the *ideal* and the *real*, *thinking* and *being*, are now both vindicated, equipoised in the proportionality of a community through the moderation that mutual respect entails, thereby founding the articulate dwelling that includes and collects differences but does not assimilate or eliminate them.

Previously we have noted Hegel's rendition of this correspondence between what is *rational* and what is *real*, his pronouncement that, in effect, the mind *matters* and that, on the other hand, *mind* is what the matter is. He argues for this improbable chiasmus in the *Grundlinien der Philosophie des Rechts* (Basic Principles of the Philosophy of Right) as follows:[28]

> *Wenn die Reflexion, das Gefühl oder welche Gestalt das subjektive Bewußtsein habe, die Gegenwart für ein Eitles ansieht, über sie hinaus ist und es besser weiß, so befindet es sich im Eitlen...ist es so selbst nur Eitelkeit. Wenn umgekehrt die Idee für das gilt, was nur so eine Idee, eine Vorstellung in einem Meinen ist, so gewährt hingegen die Philosophie die Einsicht, daß nichts wirklich ist als die Idee. Darauf kommt es dann an, in dem Scheine des Zeitlichen und Vorübergehenden die Substanz, die immanent, und das Ewige, das gegenwärtig ist, zu erkennen.*

> If reflection or feeling or whatever form subjective thought might happen to take on, decries THE WAY IT IS as mere vanity and holds itself to be the know-it-all above it all, then thought abides but in idleness....and is itself mere vanity. When, on the other hand, thought is considered to be just an idea, some arbitrary notion of my own concoction, then it is philosophy's task to provide for the insight that, in fact, nothing but thought is real. That is namely the whole point – to recognize in the transience of temporal appearances immanent substance and the actual presence of eternity.

There is but one being that is perfectly and completely in accordance with the absolute principle of thought, one *thought* that has succeeded at completion and become a *thing* of pure reason though, in fact no thing at all in any ordinary sense of the word – i.e. nothing so indeterminate and insignificant as what folks tend to call this, that, or the other thing among an indeterminate multitude of them; no, we mean, following Hegel, the *presence* of thought – and this thing is none other than the unique being that thought is *to itself,* as thought thinking thought, that being, namely, that we have termed, with regard to the perfect "inner harmony" of differentiated self-relativity, the *entity of identity.*

---

[28] Hegel, Werke. Auf der Grundlage der Werke von 1832-1845, Vol. 7, p. 25.

While theory might gaze, in wonder and delight, upon the tautology of this thinking being, that we have dubbed our *Verum*, our practical experience of it, that is to say, its "nature" is to actually undergo the distinction that the *character* of pure reason inevitably and indelibly impresses upon the superficies of our life, marking, as it does, the divergence of desire that rends our human being asunder. But even in the anguish of this riving, there are moments of respite from toil and the peace of mind that accompanies the accomplishment of purpose however temporary and intermediary; in this leisure that breeds reflection, not only do we turn to all things great and small, whether animal, vegetable, or mineral, to the order and rhythms of their being, of their coming to be and passing away, so casually and unassumingly referred to as those of natural history and to the principles that have brought them to light as objects inspiring contemplative admiration; no, in addition to the wonder of science, there is celebration and recreation when we seize upon these beings as *terms* in a train of thought, as *turns of words* in a tongue of flame. For it is this language in which the imagination renders ideas articulate and concrete, tangible – a rendering that is now no longer the issue of discernment formulating scientific observation and enquiry but rather a monument of invention, supreme fictions brought forth by the productivity of the language to body forth life and to lend a face in the turn of a phrase to what would otherwise go entirely unnoticed and unsung, remain entirely lifeless and faceless, merely a note and notion.

Say "thought" and give to thought a name that it would otherwise lack. For who would bother to give thus thought a thought? Did you just say "it?" All right, call it "it" if you dare and care to; and then call it, say, "I," drawing in this way a distinction in accordance with the principle that is the point you are evidently making by placing it thus in the scheme of all things thought. Choose your term; make your point. Show us; show us here and now the work of thought, the Builder, a work of signification, of language unfolding a complete line of reasoning, our ΛΟΓΟΣ. After that of the insight of speculation and the execution, the step by step accomplishment of endeavor regardless of whether we actually reach our goal, our last issue regarding the determinations of pure reason is its creativity, the productive power of the imagination to give determinacy to ideas and found with them a place we might inhabit with body and soul and in which we might make ourselves at home, as in a body, a corpus and a ΚΟΣΜΟΣ (cosmos) of knowledge and beauty to attend to, to have and to hold as our own, a world of words and the house that wisdom built. In this sense, in the sense of the craft and art of the logotectonic method we will examine later, we reprise the much maligned notion of thought as MHXANH (mēchanē) and TEXNH (technē), as the artifice and the artificer of dwelling.

Hence our regard for the being that is the issue of thought takes on two different forms – we regard it as the topic and issue of a poetic invention, but also as a form of "nature" and as such an object of study. In the latter form, our perception of it is mediated by the language of a speech performance that draws our attention to the intangible principle through the tangible sense that words accord ideas. Science also employs language to its end to articulate the properties of our object. But while the sage's conception discerns the causes and origins of the principle's manifold appearance, the poet's song, the seer's, the saint's prophetic visions, give it a determinate presence in an articulate admonition – a created cosmos of words exhibiting to an audience figures of poetic ingenuity in opposition to the cosmos of appearances that the intellect unfolds before an academy of insightful spectators. While the latter's teachers' discrimination clarifies the attributes of the object, the prophetic clarity of the poet's imagination is essentially a tribute that magnifies those properties into a striking issue, exhorting us to take up the furtherance of thought's cause. Thus the splendor of what is compelling creed to the heart of votaries as the basis for their subsequent action in a kindred spirit complements and reflects the glory that the principle manifests to the inquisitive eye of the intellectual.

For this reason, the realization of the principle begins with the fulfillment of the distinction between the IS and the OUGHT that had initially made all the difference in the world, namely the practical realization of what thought, the Actor, has accomplished in becoming what it was meant to be, after which it is time to consider the determinacy of this being that thought, the Builder, makes of this entity of identity in and of itself and, in conclusion, to take account of the delight that is thought, the Thinker's, recognition of thought's own reality, the matter of our be all and end all.

44. Our Restless Heart

The day of rest and rejuvenation, the veritable recreation of reason, follows upon the culmination of efforts that initiated a journey of doubtful outcome – it was nevertheless sustained by some manner of virtue, the unfathomable valor that folks occasionally find in their hearts to press on against all odds. This journey marks a period of *transformation*, each step along the way being the latest accomplishment of the principle, a passage that concludes a train of thought, a *ratiocination*, that originated with a change of heart, a *conversion*, the consummation of which is the clarity of and the insight into the absolute principle in the beginning that, now at the end of the road, has led to the actual community, a civic body of beings founded upon the relationship of accord with the principle that has so long been envisioned and strived for as what ought to be but, as yet, has not been put into effect and now finally achieved in the realization of the principle that had come to fruition in the more perfect union of mind and matter; it is the former state of incipient emergency resolved into the final state of perfection, our house torn by strife that was nurtured to renewal and secured in the comprehensive peace of a dwelling that has become the intimate origin and the final resting of those who have experienced both birth and death with distinction, no, first that death then the ensuing birth which together are the consecrating and pervasive cognizance and bequest of reason.

Thus we see here thought as the slow march forward after the about-face that glimpsed the outward principle from afar, having stepped back from superficial immediacy and its inward bounds to bound towards outer limits and across the gap between the IS and the OUGHT of thought that sparked desire's subsequent traversal, thought's turn and return, in the first place. The versatility of reason, beyond its omnibus utility as an instrument, can be seen in this act of *reversal*, your U-turn as well as mine who are the wayfarers towards our presence at the destination, delineating the phases of qualification that constitute the general negativity of reflective thought. Reason as *reflection* comprises namely the flight of withdrawal from THE WAY IT IS *and* the alighting that completes the gradual approach of THE WAY IT SHOULD BE – we experience, in the former, thought's property of *detachment*, in the latter, that of its *advance*, retirement of *retreat* the one, promotion of *community* the other; *dislodgement* and *deviation* on the one hand, *direction* and *access* on the other, *perdition* there, *paradise* here. For the career of thought's transition and crossing evinces these prominent phases – beginning with the backward step of abstraction – *first*, the bending inward and away from as well as counterclockwise to the everyday homogeneity that is always being extended all over and taking all ours; *second*, the downward turn upon the Janus heart's reflection; and then again, from this most salient silence, *third*, the outward turn is refused or else reborn as the face forward quickens towards the golden end of the eyebeam's bow on an onward and upward vault of ascension. Then the work of the divided will begins, fighting for *and* against, torn and troubled by obstacles and setbacks, giving up for a time. Perhaps for all time? Yes? Then that is the end of thought, its final destination. No? Then thought endures in this commitment and this too is the end of thought, a destiny to be fulfilled forever before us.

This choice is conversion's ever-winding way *and* happy ending in the conclusion of community and the completion of peace, having set foot on the landfall of the destination, thought's port of call, and struck the *kairos* of appointed time as an arrow, wounding, would and as does the apple's red of readiness in its sweetest season.

It is not until it is, is not there until it is come, either arrived or yet on the way – the conversion of thought is entirely its decision and "progress" just an expression for our resolution to abide by what has been so determined and, in spite of obstacles and deviate allurements, to stay the chosen course. There is no fruition in the sustentation of endurance, no reward for patience, no resultant presents or beings produced by such abiding by, nothing beyond the self-knowledge and the *reaffirmation* of the principle that has been thus upheld – so far so good, always precarious, contested, never over, save for moments of respite from our travails of labor when milestones marked along the traveler's way have been reached and we relax for a spell and take a breather, celebrating such a holiday in hopeful recreation; we are done today but tomorrow is another day and, practically speaking, we are never done for good, never finished with thought – is that not the distinction of human being in a nutshell?

But each step along the way is *already* a transformation of the OUGHT into the IS; though just one step, each step counts and builds the latter being from the former, the former from the latter, reforming and renewing until the fulfillment of the principle attains its true presence. The principle, thought, wants *to be* what it is; and, whatever it is, thought is not *just* a thought. Similarly, though human practice is destined to perpetually strive and seek to be what it is supposed to be, with regards to the vision of the perfection that is, to each being, their own particular happiness, poetic art writes the words of welcome that will suffice endeavor for a day of rest after the day of judgment that shook us to the very roots of the world.

45. The Triunity of Perfection

Entity - Divinity - Humanity – that you have never run into these three principles of perfection before in the course of your travels and searches is hardly a compelling argument against perfection, the *idea*. Or is it? Presumably, the question to put to those who have their doubts about the idea of perfection is this one: What would you be willing to grant the dignity of the predicate "is perfect?" Certainly, we would all have qualms about seeing in every little thing or big thing "perfection." For are we not on all sides surrounded by the bigness of our littleness and the pettiness of the narrow mind? And in the last century has contemporary philosophy, anthropology, biology, psychiatry, to say nothing of the testimony of history, not delivered irresistible proof that our human being has indeed fallen far from the heavens of our former magnificence and with a resounding "splat" sunk into the murk and meanness of late-modern language?

But why so glum? Surely ordinary folks have no bones to pick with *perfection*, the idea, their speech practice vouchsafing the employment of this word on appropriate occasion. Now what occasion might that be? Well, for example we speak of "a perfect day" and its effects as in the familiar eponymous song by Lou Reed:

> You made me forget myself.
> I thought I was someone else,
> Someone good.

Odd the impact of these three principles of perfection on our lives, however imperfect their embodiment, in the opinion of our more sober and realistic philosophies of Man-unkind. For as much as the gap between the IS and the OUGHT retains the anguish of the human condition and remains an inspiration to the will, the vision of *completion*, of being good, sustains the enterprising mind that sees in the sour potential of the daunting task at hand the promise of succulent maturity and each stage from bud to bloom, from flower to fruit, confirms the goodness of the matter and its development, living well, taken as *the last word*, foreseen and foreknown in the pattern of perfection, a wonder to behold. The well-rounded truth of insight, the redeeming power of truth put into practice and the truth envisioned by a pure heart as the ideal most worthy of realization – what these three truths share is that they have all put the urgency of the origin behind them, not by disburdening themselves of that determination, but rather by having already fulfilled the obligation that constrained and bounded them within the directive of what was meant to be and yet, at the outset, inexplicably, was not. Ideas of truth do not dwell on the tragedy of human self-severalty but neither have they forgotten the day of pain. For now, with them, at the end of time's drive and the close of the burgeoning spring day, in the *fullness* of our seasons' autumn and our lives' evening, at the acutest angle of the peak that our patient steps have amounted to, reflection stands at attention atop the world in the blue and brilliant panorama of that summit and admires the expanse that now, before its gaze, unfolds, rolling, below in the sweep of its entirety. The whole story includes, to be sure, that divisive tale of our human being within the compass of its narrative, but behold how now it has been resolved into the simple shapeliness that fleshes out the elegance of *integrity*. Thus the *purity* of thought we encounter here is not that of the initial abstraction inherent in thought's self-severalty in connection with the experience of our antonym that we met with at the outset, at the onset of our passage, but rather, now and here, the inviolate, infallible, flawless, impeccable being of what is finally, at long last, quite and utterly what it always was meant to be.

These three ideas are seminal and superlative terms for the three unique principles upon which the distinction of human being is based. Their completion names the state of harmonious accord and community between THE WAY IT IS and the WAY IT SHOULD BE, in other words, affirms that the IS, having doffed the indifference of its immediacy and assuaged the pain of its divergence, now corresponds to the requirements prescribed by the OUGHT, while the OUGHT, not content to be merely what is required and demanded, has actually attained the determinacy of being.

The two sides in question, the real as the immediate state of affairs and the ideal, the rare and chosen purpose of reason desiring to become a reality after having been an idea first, could never coincide initially. On the contrary: At the start of thought's turn, we abstract from those claims and causes that have reigned hitherto unquestioned and draw a distinguished character in the flesh of their custom that reawakens critical reflection upon what has come to pass thus far and what was supposed to be but as yet is not. The contradiction between these two extremes, namely the tradition of what is the perpetual living present of thought, on the one hand and, on the other, the will of what thought might revise and envision at a given point of time in history as the *good* to come, is irreconcilable, irreconcilable that is, for thought, the discriminating *Judge*, but not for the *Builder* who takes up and carries out the principle's cause to the projected conclusion by inventing apt images that are likely to stir to action the hungry heart of the Actor who then, with all the more relish, strives in words and deeds to give life to what would otherwise remain just a notion but is, in fact, a becoming being of distinction.

For the poetic art of imagination has built a panoramic theater, painted scenes with the traits and touches of tales culled not so much from the dispersion of our mundane experience, but rather sought in and then borrowed from the holy writs of our philosophical literary tradition and collected into a repertoire of distinguished turns of word and phrase with which we might build the bright whole of an arresting, persuasive ΛΟΓΟΣ, comprising the forms of epic narratives, tragic dramas, songs of verse, but also the graven signs and symbols in which the bricolage of today's discourse consists, to serve as a seemly dwelling for wisdom, an altar of devotion, a shrine, and then even a tower the bell of which tolls for us with the implacable accusation of judgment awakened from its inveterate anesthesia by the gift of crisis that is pure reason's recalled present and mandate for what is yet to come, a haunting specter that we simply cannot succeed at putting permanently out of our minds.

Thus thought, the Builder's dwelling, is ultimately the admonishing monument we make to the principles upon which this building stands, reawakening the recollection of pure reason and its accomplishment and inspiring reflection to reconsider critically its current state of affairs in light of those former principles, moving in turn the mind of those who are susceptible to being moved and renewing their interest in the distinction of human being, posed as a quest and the question of human identity, dignity, destiny.

And therefore *remembrance* is the final name for thought's elegy; after having been resolute determination, thought acquiesces and, in the tranquility of its maturity, celebrates the achievement of its own legacy, a house of distinguished terms, a system of meanings that are thought's thought in its own abounding words, the patterns and compilations of character and of letter that have been duly archived and promulgated in a system of insight as the content of *science* and passed on as *tradition* to the next generation of readers and listeners who are meant to be inspired by the abundance of its present once again. In the manner of chronologists of pure reason's life and times, we have recorded salient events in the story of its mandate – the review and discrimination of good judgment, the ensuing crisis and the anguished conflict of discrepancy, the proffered commission and the accepted appointment of purpose, the debt thus incurred to be discharged, the subsequent guide and government of its patient administration, the completion of its duty and fulfillment of its destiny – to name but a few accomplishments in the resonate interval that is our experience of the critical juncture of pure reason that we will come to better understand in the following when we study the holy writs and the speaking words of wisdom that these writings have bequeathed to the care of a new philology.

46. Eternal Life

Diverse traditions of religion knew many beatific expressions and exhibitions for the utopia of perfection, for the project of a purpose and its accomplishment – the Edenic state of grace, the poetic idylls of Arcadian, the isle of Atlantis, the refuge of the Promised Land, of Fatherland, of Never

Never Land, the hallowed Halls of the Elysian Fields, the Heavenly Rapture of the Saints, the Green Green Grass of Home, places in which the difference between THE WAY IT SHOULD BE and THE WAY IT IS, after a long and winding road, the meandering course of a river, a line of reasoning pursued, the seasons' procession, the recursive ages of man, the march of a people's history, the scheme of all things thought, resolves into a universe of harmony or balance in the original image of an idea of gold, of milk and honey, of abiding peace, of the conclusions and destinations of *being*, the supremest fiction and vision of pure reason's self-relativity, the advent and realization of the entity of identity in the mind of self-knowing being that is the declaration of thought thinking thought, our *Verum* and sign, our Tyger and our *T*.

   With respect to that vision of harmony that is its destiny, its destination – for what could be more harmonious than such an entity of identity that is entirely one with itself – human being, whose distinction is precisely to constantly be other than itself, born to strive to be what it is not, namely what it *ought* to be, and therefore destined to be most human when it is thus *divinely* inspired to be what it is not and, in fact, therein not human at all but rather divine, and all the more divine the more it strives to be what it ought to be, for which reason the less it is divine, being all the more human, the more it is divine, striving to be so and the closer it gets to being what it ought to be the less it is what it ought to be, being finally least human when most human and most human when least – it should come as no surprise that this being, being thus perturbed at not being what it most truly is to be and therein being most completely what it ought to be, sighs in moments of desperation or of hope and envisions its completion:

> There's a place for us,
> Somewhere a place for us.
> Peace and quiet and open air
> Wait for us
> Somewhere.[29]

   Whether as the beginning or as the end of time, both are remote as only thought can be in its abstraction from the needful things of what's up and going on and going down at the moment – one as the past, long defunct, to be recorded and recalled, the other the future, to be awaited and nurtured to completion, therefore one before and one after that history of grief that

---

[29] Lyrics by Stephen Sondheim.

is the resonate gap of our critical reflection, both of which – because of the discrepancy that is made manifest between their image and the looks of what currently obtains around us by being in our ears and in our eyes, in our face – inspire the working of the will to mind the gap and to undertake to make, through works, that dream come true at the surcease of sorrow.

Even as the *science* of philosophy experienced pure reason as the *self-evidence* of thought and theory's insight into the cause that is the determined form to be fulfilled in being, the *religion* of philosophy begins with the immediacy of the *vocation* of the principle that summons judgment to mark disparity in being and, in a passage of trial and discipline, redeems that debt of difference towards final reconciliation between mind and matter.

But prior to that bright life, termed *eternal,* that begins with death, we experience the life that ends with dismal death, the constrained life of trial and tribulation that the steadfast pursuit of principle is, whether this trial be that of the battlefield or the tribunal, of the forum or the public square, the stadium or the auditorium – all of these sites are the venues of opening and passage, of sight and sentence, to which we are directed by the proclamation of thought's immediate present, platforms of judgment in which the distinction is enacted upon us in person and in the flesh.

These arenas of altercation and ordeal have yet to be soothed to repose and transfigured into the home of our dwelling abode and residence. For before ease, we experienced the disease of our lot where thought musters the ammunition of arms, the clench of blade, the sling of dart, the missile of the mission, the projectile of the project, the blast of shaft and shell, the horn of hell, against the entrenchment of the tamasic mind or else, conversely, as it persists in obtuse extremity, swells into an onslaught in its own right that makes of the former fools of languor arrant aggressors and of the sluggish mass of men the incontinent hoards that strongholds of the will were raised to brave and then to condemn, to punish with stern dispassion.

If we view and render the conflict inherent in the gap between the IS and the OUGHT as the effort we must employ to overcome the inertial forces arrayed against the host of changes – the guest from abroad that thought is to the sprawl of lethal lethargy – then the course of this purification of the IS by the OUGHT will come to rest in the end, having accomplished what it set out to do when that decision was taken and the idea established that served as the guiding force and governor. The breech of enmity between the sickness and the cure, the latter's illness resisting the potent efficacy of the former's remedy, has, through the corrective therapy of the rule and treatment that thought, the judge, had prescribed as punishment, tempered the acerbity of their initial polarity after critical reflection had diagnosed the lack of fitness in the state of affairs that a timely dose of reason thus reveals. The restorative regime of its catholicon is not merely a palliative balm to lull and dull the pain of their hot hate but rather the working out and working through the schism of our severalty until the human wound is healed that this bitter animus struck against the wrongs of brass intransigence.

In this contrariety, ⊥, we experience the mutual offense of zealot usurpation as iniquity on both sides of the aisle, each faction claiming supremacy at the expense of the other's right, one lashing out, the other boxing in, the first wild the second cruel, both, loathe to relent, locked in irreconcilable controversy under that blood-red road rage of thought's passage towards its destination, namely the mellow yellow candle shine of a homestead and community that is the deliverance of the distinction of human being from this evil when its ills and hurts, its woes and crimes have been redressed to a T. For the entity of identity is the symbol of pure reason, the philosopher's stone, that rejuvenates the two mortal growths of human malignancy, namely the immodesty of *domination* and that of *license* – both stuck in the rut of self-centered complacency upon which the former erects its contumacy to the envious moon and the latter suckles its laxity on the teats of acedia – transforming them with its elixir into the maternal material and paternal pattern of the distinguished human being that is our destiny and immortal, harmonious nature.

47. The Community of Beings

In the logic of the image of a journey, the haven we attain at the close of day is the refuge and the place of rest, the end of the road that led us on our difficult way, the way of distinction that is the practice of thought. Now we have finished the expedition of our journey and experience the realization of thought as a being safe and sound. No longer a bunker or a shelter that guards us against untoward elements, the sense of completion opens up into a vista of serenity and as the oppressive sacrificial fire of desire resolves into the gem-like embers of the hearth flame that warms and lightens the household, all notion of the distinction of human being as the *ordeal* of self-severalty has been pacified into a vision of tranquility, namely that of a dwelling and the congruence of a fellowship of beings, the peace of mind of those both individual *and* incommensurable who nevertheless share and participate in the unity celebrated as the realization of a vision of thought thinking thought. Human being knows that as far as practical reason is concerned, we are never done with thought, never retired from the profession of a life devoted to works done in its spirit and in service to the exalted objects of its drive. As much as this character of our thought is the tireless traveler and seeker, it is the work of thought, the Builder, to conceive of how this life might be brought to a goodly end, namely in the mansion of the lucid stillness that was, till now, no place, no thing.

This place of perpetuity toward which thought, appointed with the charge of its purpose and commitment, has so long strived in determination is the state of well-being of the constituent members, their commonwealth; the several parts and parties that were lately sworn enemies collaborate for the good of the whole they have formed. This constitution of their forces and possessions is founded upon a relationship of the proportion of differences and most effectively represented as a community in which the particular members stand in relationship to each other and to the whole, the general, who is, in fact, just another member in the totality of totalities which stands, in turn, in relationship to the parts, which are themselves wholes in their own right, each defining and being defined by the other and thus through that sovereignty of the wholes with respect to the principle of their entirety, established, mediated by it, by their recognition of this principle and therein transformed into distinguished parties of the accord of brotherhood that will end all hostilities forever...or at least until tomorrow, which is another day.

The objective abstraction is realized in the individual; the transfigured individual is elevated to the whole, becomes a member and an *organ* of the whole, having been given and giving its share of life in and to that community and to the whole in every particular action, the individual's action being itself the action of the whole in the part, the work of all benefiting the one and one working for the good of all.

We are all familiar with the notion of team spirit and the general will. Each player participating in the effort of the entire team, gaining from the other members of the team a greater benefit than would otherwise be possible for that individual. But it is not the increase in size and efficacy that is the key point here but rather the identity that accrues to each individual, a "corporate identity" in the sense that this individual, not less distinct from the others than before, is now, in addition, a member of that greater body, which does not usurp the individual's needs, degrading the difference that the individual makes, but rather places the individual into the context of a larger perspective, the framework of a totality of needs, a proportion of differences. Human community is such a state of negotiated equilibrium between what we want and what reason wants as expressed in the demands that the whole places on the part and the part on the whole in the reciprocity of the individual and the general principle of pure reason such that the whole contains the part and the part the whole. Thus the first community that human being is heir to is that which consists of the agreement and cooperation of the heart with its own heart of hearts, the role of its life in the life of the whole.

Every image of intimate being can supply a vision of this community – filial love, the terms of endearment in matrimony, civic consciousness, the church of saints, the Olympic kingdom of Jovial recognition, the members of every body under the authority of the heart of pure reason, working in congress to achieve an end, each part playing a role, having a function and each function, though a whole and complete organization in itself, again but a part in the larger body of the greater organization, the hand having fingers, the fingers joints even as the hand is part of the arm and the arm part of the torso, the torso having a head, the head, eyes – every member of the body is a body, a whole in its own right, a part having parts and in the process of abstraction we can elaborate the idea of stepping back, gaining with each reiteration a more panoramic view of the whole, our body with our minds and our person with our profession and our profession with the associations of the citizens and these several cities united into a constitution of states which, again, enter, by convention, into community with the cosmos of the nations whose continents, comprise all the people of the earth and who, in turn, join the universe of beings in which every king has a king and every subject a loyal subject, in which every servant serves and receives goodly service and to give is to be given in the circle of reflection that is the cognizance of Verum, the entity of identity, and the nature of thought thinking thought; this is the life form of the simple and familiar principle that founds and fosters nations to self-several (i.e. poly-rather than monophonic) greatness, namely *e pluribus unum* (out of many one).

Thus when we speak of the body of thought, it is in this sense of fulfilled purpose and community as well as the fruition of thought having attained the fruit and the end of that development which began in the power of illumination, proceeded as the soul's desire and growth in the urgency of necessity and now has reached reality in thought's own thriving and teeming organization – all the elements of the train of thought we have been discussing – collected by the fertility of the imagination into one being that has provided pure reason with a dwelling, such that it has taken place in life, has matured to a world of thought that we might inhabit and participate in.

And it is the amenities of this culture that allow the community of the elements to cohere – this is the congeniality of thought with respect to thought – what could be congenial than an identity? This convivial community of thought and its several, self-several thoughts is festive and in good cheer; its intercourse is jovial, a celebration among colleagues, the friends and families based on their participation in the determining principle, which is always prior to this community, the tradition of an insight across the march of time that founded the community in the first place upon the form that is the distinction of human being. This form established the state of grace, the community, the city of those both different in principle *and* nevertheless related in their distinction and sharing now the civility and the decency that bespeaks harmony rather than unison. For the friendship of hospitality, welcoming the stranger into the fold of friends blossoms into the kindness of intimacy among companions within the dwelling who, though different beings, share the same sustenance in the imbibing gift of thought's generosity, the fruits of its earth, the bounty of its sun.

As depicted in *Figure 25*, this republic of thought's beings forms a hierarchy comprehending three classes of them, the first of which is that of the king or queen and the circle of governors – the princes and princesses, the dukes and duchesses, all the pre-eminent beings and the nobles of the land and that of the allies who administer to the reign of the sovereign principle whose foremost task is that of enacting law wherein self-several thought itself in all the diversity of its plenitude and magnificence is made manifest.

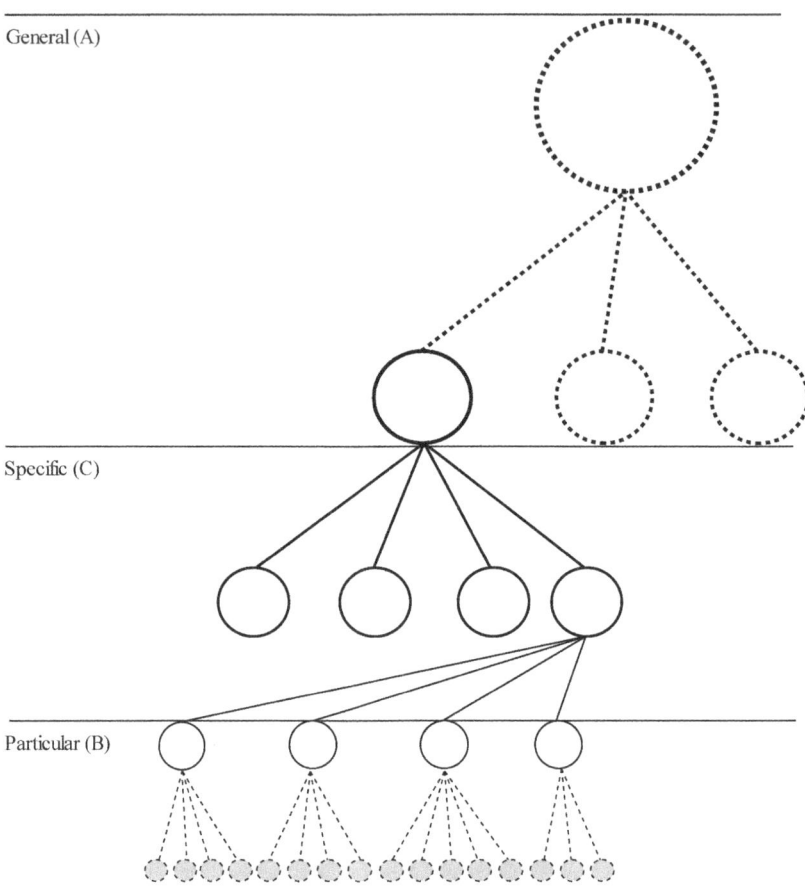

General (A)

Specific (C)

Particular (B)

Figure 25: The Community of Beings

This rational body of thoughts, the *general head* of government, is complemented by that of the spirited body, the distinguished and, in this sense *specific, heart* through which the foresight and judgment of intellect is brought into play as the courage and determination of action – it is the officer of that insight who is concerned with the efficacy of what has been ordained who diligently serves the principle's cause by defending what OUGHT to be against what OUGHT NOT as well as ultimately realizing that purpose in the way things are by transforming the IS into the OUGHT – an emancipating project of erudition, education, and exaltation – and the OUGHT into the IS – an ingenious achievement of execution, realization, and invention that establishes the realm of beings who live the life of the whole as its workers, its *particular* organs, the members of the body – the blood, the hands, the eyes, the arms – each individual, though a whole, is the investment, appointment, employment of that principle that governs and is governed by the whole.

And thus the peace and quiet that is shown to reign in this building of imagination is the tranquil dwelling of perfection but, as Schiller clarifies, the unity it enjoys is "the tranquility of completion not inertia, peace flowing from the equilibrium and not from the stagnation of forces, from plenitude and not from emptiness, [a tranquility] accompanied by the feeling of infinite power."

> ...Ruhe der Vollendung, nicht der Trägheit; eine Ruhe, die aus der Fülle, nicht aus der Leerheit fließt und von dem Gefühl eines unendlichen Vermögens begleitet wird. ("Über naive und Sentimental Dichtung," Schiller, *NA*, XX 472-473.31-4.)

C. The Principle of Signification

48. If Thought is Real...

Imagination provides us with the first reality of thought's completion, the perfection of a meticulously drawn vision that forcefully draws our will with its attraction and guides our work of *invention* to give ideas the striking presence in *art* denied them in *practice's* sphere where they remain the aim and object towards which we are destined to strive with determination, renewing ourselves in the process in accordance with their image; this presence is a rendition of the entity of identity in its placid permanence and the stability of what rests and depends upon itself, its own self-grounding autarky. The perfection of this ideal became our aim and governed the discipline of our endeavor to accomplish the impossible and encourage our ongoing efforts that nevertheless marked small successes along the way, steps in the right direction. It showed us what we were after and, in this way, validated our pursuit – "that is our goal," we thought, and stood in admiration of who we are in what we were attempting though, perhaps, bound, ultimately, to fail; we, in the imperfect business of human life and *action*, we nevertheless have come to truly and completely, perfectly know ourselves in *theory* and might, in *poetry*, put this insight persuasively into speech and into a form of words called beautiful. Being human merely and desiring so much more than what behooves a merely human being, we were born to flash and yearn with superhuman ambition towards greatness and the dignity of a praise-worthy name – what tragedy and drama has such a poetic nature as ours given rise to? Marked man, woman, thus waled by the spirit of distinction and wending your way, can you not desist? Tough customer, can you not cease and docilely deliver up your star dust to the silent silt and sediment that centuries lay upon centuries of what your lives have returned to the restful dirt of earth as the balance of your debt with no remainder? Wherefore this hunger to be golden, to be greater, to excel and supersede yourself, to be good in your own eyes, the eyes of My Best I, our Blessed Hours? Why this will to take on a form that cracks the mold? And so long endure ordeal till excellence itself becomes the object of your drive? Only in this vision of a being perfectly complete do tears subside. This is the idea you *have* and have nourished long before the younger hunger and its holy anger sealed the writ of destiny on the scroll of your soul in burning bolts of light.

Forgetting thus all about our fate, lost in thought and attuned to the music of the matter, we mediate now upon this idea, the whole truth of our human being, and give the lyrical voice of song to what we see, building a dwelling in *language* where companions congregate and share a cup of cheer in the certainty of knowledge that has learned to bow down and raise up and bestows life and takes life, seriously. The state of this idea is the being of what is known and loved, touching in its presence, inspiring respect and admiration, consoling us in hardship, a joyful companion to our sun-drenched days, critical of all that pile of smiles we might have hitherto coveted and amassed; it is a weighty matter indeed, at times even overwhelming, but a charge that is lightening as well for being My most ennobling cause, so high above me, so lovely, and, though above and beyond our coil of daily toil, so close, so close as to be our Self – now is such a thing as this, that is no thing at all, are You, are We, ourselves, am I, real? Does thought deserve *to be* thought and thus to be thought an honest to goodness *being*?

If thought, in a daring turn of word, is said to be *real* then our experience of the distinction of human being in its entirety manifests an overall build and structure such as the one we have been explicating; we might admire its physique. In this sense, self-relative thought, mindfulness itself, *builds* itself, articulating what it knows about itself, its life and times; and the dimensions of its constitution may then be organized into an architecture; this, its eloquent idea, is articulate and therefore can be recognized in its pattern, whether we imagine the texture of its composition as woven with the red thread of insight, built brick by brick of word, composed of a symphony of notes that had been noted thus far in our investigation, founded as a congress of delegate ideas, constituted into offices of ministers to our mind, cultivated into an organization of members under the oath of remembrance, a commonwealth of conceptual constituents all collected into a cognitive confederation, fashioned into a well-proportioned form and figure, a ratio assembled into a team and train of thoughts, a marriage of individual insights, a garden of principle's fruits, and an alliance of intellectual powers, a joining of their forces and a meeting of minds, assorted into a jazz combo of muses' instruments, thus arrayed and arranged, they are ready to be taken account of in particular, not simply as a mix or a mingling and bag of bones or hybrid snarl or mongrel tangle in which the elements merge and lose their distinction. No, the totality of regard wants elaboration in the delicate intricacy of inklings, conceives of reason concatenated into a chain of reasons in which each segment is separate and the whole an ordered arrangement over and above the sum of member constituents – it is, moreover, their consummation, the system and the synergy of their particular distinctions.

Thus, in the celebratory language of thought, the Builder, if thought is *real*, it is a *being* to boot and therefore *is* not merely, but also *has*, substance – call it, in the freedom of your speech, *earth* as the principle that is the ground and foundation of conception; dub ideas the diaphanous *air* of sky-high abstraction, the *wind* as the breath of inspiring ethereality, the *water* of insight poured benevolently upon parched land of stagnation that regains thus its fecundity of imagination; it is the purgatorial *fire* of self-severalty that distinguishes *pure* reason from every other. Thus if thought is real, it is *elemental* and is, as the rhythmical system of these four elements, their community and temperate principle in which their times and seasons, the melting *wetness* of thought's sprouting freshness, *dawn*'s life in rosy-fingered hope, autumn's *dry* sobriety of purified perfection, the *eventide* of days' endeavors, the heat of *summer*'s keen intent, the distinguished purpose of our highest *noon*, the *frost* of *winter* stillness, that good death in *night*'s holy indifference when the first glows of twilight presage, with lark-song, the auroral life hereafter – all comprehended in their quintessence, the inconspicuous ΛΟΓΟΣ, that maintains their balance and restrains the impetuosity of extremist weather when fire reigns or rain, when the wind is squall and flow a flood and torrential clouds blot and dunk the sparkling sun in froth, when night holds lidless vigilance and the day drags in somnambulant torpor, when youth is grave and ancient deference capers nimbly in a lady's chamber to the lascivious pleasing of a lute.

If thought is *real* in a remarkable turn of words or phrase, then it has the *magnitude* to make a difference; it must be and have immense dimensions of form – it has and is the nether-worldly *depth* of penetrating insight, the other-worldly *height* of what attains the universal coign of vantage overall and above all, first and foremost, the tip but also the counterpoising pit, last and lowermost, as well as the encompassing *length* and *breadth* of the endless stretch of earth – the extension of intention and the strive of the drive towards what was determined, destined to be; moreover, it has the *weight* of import impinging dramatically upon our lives thought well enough to be left alone, the *shape* of things to come when our nature takes it course and realizes, in word and deed, what was posited as the will and subsequently gives birth to that charge so long borne and nurtured under the heart – in this way, it is our *birth*, the second birth of the world through the thought that has made a difference, and, though of the finest filament, *straight* and narrow as the arrow towards the aim but also *curved* into circularity, the sphericity of friendly reciprocity that never devolves into a convolution of the twisted mind.

Further, if substantial thought has these dimensions and is shapely being, then it is a *body* and has one too, with *arms* to struggle where the distinction of human being is contested, with *legs* that perform discontinuity's leap, walk the talk, and reach the insight of conclusion step by step, after stepping back in the beginning and minding the gap; with the *senses* of sensibility that are reason's *eyes* and *ears*, it is hearing and seeing with discriminating understanding, the *nose* that knows the scents and flair of spirit's breath, the *face*'s gaze of amazement, the *light* of sight and the *vision* of imagination and, with this acute awareness, in *touch*ing songs of admonition and exhortation made by sapient *tongues* of flame, revolts against the insipidity that daily dulls distinctions until they dissolve into the swoon of the mind out cold and, living in the world, dead to the world.

Why always "is" *as well as* "have?" Because, moving from the seeing being to the being seen on the other side of the relationship, thought is the entity of identity, a self-relationship, and thus the *property* as well as the *substance* that possesses it, both in one. Therefore, further, if thought is real, seeing *and* being, the *sensible* being of pure reason, then as much the *sighted* being and, in the *seeing*, being, *having seen* as much as *seeing*, *heard* as much as *hearing*, *touched* as much as *touching*, more generally, in the relationship of reflection's chirality, it is thought's property of being open to itself, its opening in being that enables us to speak of its present as well as its presence, the *presents* that sagacity gives – vision and visibility, its look is sight and seeing, being and appearing, for evidence answers perception, attendance dwells on outstanding indication and the seeing of this being is the being that we see – sight and light in one. This is precisely the very being of fearful, enantiomorphic symmetry we have been talking about the whole time and recognize again in *Figure 26*:

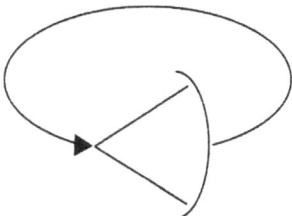

Figure 26: Our Verum

For even as its *apparition* is the emergence of what comes to mind, showing forth, so is the *animadversion* of the mind the note of regard that, alert and being struck, is striking to behold and toilsome to sustain, the fading of which, however, consigns our eyes to darkness' pall.

But upholding the contemplative gaze reveals *color* and *complexion* of the being that reflection is, thinking thought, its *blush* and *glow*, the *hue* of our Me, in its self-evidence, the body of brilliance that makes all the difference in the world – the abundant radiance of light that is the *red*, the golden intensity of sight in contradistinction to the ghastly pallor of everyday *grays* when strength is wan before our intellect was born or when, wizened but no wiser, it slips away, witless, upon a drowsy deathbed we should like to call *complacence*. And receptive to what is seeming to our contemplation, we perceive the sounding and resounding call to arms of distinction if we have not gone deaf and come to dumb numbness of darkness when unsound silence stops our orifice of ear with selfishness. The brilliant flash corresponds to the clarion peal, to the faintness of sound the dimness of sight, neither glare nor shriek – for perception is neither of bedlam nor stridency – reflection is thought's rebounding resonance, resounding reverberation, the sympathetic chord of good vibes echoing in response, perfect resemblance and reaffirmation, but neither mimicry nor mockery, antiphonal epiphany, the opposite of antipathy, but neither clone nor counterfeit, a renewed iteration and not just rote repetition and recitation; it is recapitulation and reincarnation and not merely humdrum redundancy, refrain and rhyme of reason with reason though bar all rehashing and harping, resilience but neither knee-jerk nor backlash, an answer properly fitted to the question, the mind once more reminded, ideas anew and afresh, thought over and over but not in fixation, rather in the turn and return of seasons and of their celebrations – these are all renditions and encores of *T*, our Verum. And here, in the peripeteia of pure reason, where the two sides defining the chiral relationship of reflection, the generosity of incipience and recipient cordiality, meet, the sense of *touch* is finest and most discriminating; here, at this asymptotic juncture: On the one side that idea of the object and the thing conceived of as the simple rigid materiality of minerals – a being merely touched and tangible – and, on the other side, the unique intangible being of pure sentience, feelingly touched to tears in touching; here is the unique nexus of predication where thought and thing, mind and matter, the ideal and the real, the universal and the particular, completely coincide in the self-relativity of thought thinking thought; here is the dwelling place of that harmonious but not entropic entity of identity that is natural and autonomous life, the flora and the fauna of its being.

For if thought, in a manner of speaking, is *real*, then it is a whole and a community in which each member of the family, inhabitant of the city, citizen of the state, part of the body, season of the year, day of the week, hour of the day, room in the house, step on the way, word in the sentence, assignment in the project, department of the organization – each constituent of the constitution, each feature and each function owns a share in that complete being, contributing to the *welfare*, the perfection and the cohesion of that union. The elements of this union are, ultimately, not stationary, not merely places, they are actions and actors, people in play, characters in the narrative of the play that is history and her story, the whole story, the whole truth of our human being – beginning, mediating, and ending are what thought does and not just is or has. For thought is the flash of self-evincing present, the ordeal of gap-closing transformation, and the self-realizing achievement of the determining principle of reason.

A. The Principle of Celebration

49. A Delightful Thought

What was that? Pure reason is said to be a *place* and *face*, termed *ground* and *sky*, called *far* and *nigh*, *strikes* and *shines*, is *eye* and *tongue*, a *voice* heard, an *ear* lent, a *person* on the way, the *good life* spent, the *brazen-hearted* bent, the *passage* and the *burden* we convey, a name for *tomorrow* and *today*, for *battle* and for *play*. What an odd use of language! If you put it that way, is there anything tangible or intangible in heaven or on earth that could not proffer its designation in service to the effort to come to terms with our experience of what thinking entails? Any word that could not, in a certain context, suffice a turn of word or phrase towards the better exposition of the material issue of the mind?

But it's all *merely* metaphor, *nothing but* figures of speech! Merely? Nothing but? Why "merely," why constantly "nothing but,"? Better: *Whose*? Clearly, such fashionable floccinaucinihilipilification belongs to our prosaic *Man*'s lifestyle who, intent on following a lean and mean regime of less succulent fare and therefore insisting on courses and discourses prepared with "nothing buttery" seems to have forgotten the relish and the zest of poetry and the salt that imagination gives to what counts as and is called so insipidly "reality" the brute immediacy of which would seem to be to its advocates the best argument against the idea that *reality* is, in fact, a term of distinction for the realization of an acknowledged principle mediated by the craft and art of thought, the Builder and the power of the imagination.

A cosmos of words in the making, in which saying so is doing so, in which saying so is being so – such is the celebratory language of the Builder in which an accomplished, distinguished world emerges in the wink of an eye from the turn of a word; whether written in silence or spoken aloud, a *philological* language thus heightened by figures of speech performs the ceremony of paying respects to ideas that *inhabit* – yes, at least in these laudatory invocations – inhabit an intricate and truly old-fashion conception of pure reason which advocates the fashioning and configuring of terms of distinction in which fellow revelers might participate, according to their needs and capabilities, contributing words and works – no, not neglecting, much less ignoring, the difficult passage from words *to* works in the pursuits of their own lives – in a bid to validate those superannuated notions, long thought lost or dead, or just plain forgotten, and in their achievements of deed and diction, provide the latter with the presence of their own lives and actions, and first off, with that of their own speech practice, a craft and art, finely honed and tuned into the timely, timeless language of wisdom, a holy language skilled in praising and performing with delight the distinction that is human beings'.

As Schiller famously sings in his *Ode to Joy* (An die Freude), the "delight...," that this fulfillment instills is not just any sort of pleasure, fun and games, or recreational past-time but rather, as poetic eulogy might put it, a "...spark, fine, divine...," that, as it is the mark of "...blessedness...", ought to be properly personified as a "...daughter of Elysium...," whose "...sanctuary we enter, having drunk our fill of its fire..."; indeed, no ordinary delight can be such a "...charm..." as forms community by "...reconciling what the vogue..." of everyday life and of the late modern mentality tends to "...rent asunder...", and whose "...wing makes brothers of all human being." (Schiller, *NA* I 196.1-8.)

> Freude, schöne Götterfunken, Tochter des Elysiums
> Wir betreten feuer-trunken, Himmlische! Dein Heiligtum
> Deine Zauber bindet wieder, was die Mode streng geteilt.
> Alle Menschen werden Brüder, wo dein sanfter Flügel weilt.

The inspiration of thought seen no longer merely as the awakening of the sight that reveals the discrepancy between THE WAY IT IS and THE WAY IT SHOULD BE, but moreover as the kindling of such verve that not only opens our heart to this ordeal in a narrative of tragic conflict but also, in the serene encomium of poetry, knowing and telling the whole story and the whole truth, encourages the renewal of self-affirmation in an outlook towards that eventual correspondence with the principle of determination – this inspiration uplifts our hope and invigorates our valor. Its hymns and odes invite thought to comprehend itself not only in opposition to what it was meant to be but also, in spite of all, as being akin to that distinguished origin and, in this sense, to be destined to build upon what it is, more, to build *with* and *through* the material of its contrariety and to fashion out of this difference what it most devoutly will, namely the avouchment of its own unique reality, one neither afoot nor abroad, and yet as personal as it is absolute. Thought prompted by the generosity of pure reason to receive its presence in good faith and thus, thought taking in this good cheer, adopting this perspective of the good that is to come, is glad at what it really is even if it is *not yet* what it really is and, though, for the moment, being merely *in thought*, yet, knowing the whole story and the whole truth, already confident of what it will be, in fact, soon, after a bit more effort perhaps. We cleave to this poetic vision of the end *and* the beginning *and* the middle (for that is what the prophet and the poet know) imagined in specific terms and details relating to its own particular completion and say: "this *is* good!"

For the actuation of thought by thought is not constant coaxing and goading of our Monday morning mule, but rather the dash of delight; for once, that good spirit has sparked the heart. It begins to stir. This light gladdens and brightens what might have otherwise become dismal, has added filament to golden filament weaving into an ornamental investiture what would otherwise have remained drab raiment or a mortifying cilice. But it is not the drabness of what the piercing look of thought reveals to the distinguished eye, it is not the letter of shame that the critical sentence of judgment burns into our breast, but the perspective of light and of lightening that has fired and enlivened the imagination to providence and helped the heart to gather its resolve to overcome obstacles, the stamina and the infinity of firmest fortitude in face of setbacks, filled with the hope that is a promise of happiness, not merely one more thirst to slack, but that feathered thing perching in the soul.

If purpose is, as we have seen, vim and vigor in contention for the prize. All the more is the realization of accomplishment the joy of having won when a battle has been fought, all the more exquisite the finding of what has been sought, the peace exalted when, delayed, it shall be wrought and diligence, after obstacles and hindrances, satisfied withal, adversity encountered, transparence attained, prosperity assured, the safety of the refuge reached, and the blemish of imperfection released into goodness and sufficiency. Happiness and fortune – the striking activity of the mind's engagement has resolved itself into pleasure at the way it is, the contender has become content, the subject has become substance and the gift and the present of thought – itself an image of exuberance, thought taking pleasure in thought – is at last the euphoria of propitious incidence.

The winsome discovery of reflection in revelation obliges us – its charm is cheer, brightness brought to bear, engaging and dear. We might articulate this experience of pure reason's evidence in the language of ravishment. Thought softly seizes us and then we get carried away, swept off the iron balls of our feet – the transport of discernment initiates the ordeal of transformation. Being stricken, pierced by a realization, is an image of the immediacy of insight as a sudden captivation, the mind's swiftest seizing but not in the sense of rapacity. No, pure reason is intriguing and the intellect made thus intent is rapt, not raped. Depictions of thought's congeniality are often borrowed from remote regions – the language of the palate have often served as analogy – *taste* in the sense of judgment, *savor* in the sense of sapience. Thought is food for thought, a feast of wholesome nourishment and nurture, bread and wine for our flesh and blood.

That reflection is inviting because of the immediacy of its evidence and appealing to us, in its cordial appeal, not apt at leaving us cold, but rather succulent, a captivating treat, is a sign of thought's congeniality. Of course, resistance can refuse these overtures and, withdrawn by inward turning, decry the voice of vocation not as honeyed tones and mellow but rather as bewitching and enthralling, heart-robbing rather than heart-warming. This notion is based on the experience of the distinction of human being from the attitude of closed control – propitious happenstance acknowledges the gift of perception and of purpose as unexpected, unearned, merely hoped for, petitioned in a prayer. For judgment is the divergence of what *is* from what *ought to be* – the plea envisions the peace and quiet of agreement, regardless of how short-lived it turns out to be. In this way, thought is pleasing in the end, ultimately as pleasant as it is trying – the grant and the consent where not the discrepancy but rather the harmony of the distinctions in play are considered. This is the fortuitous favor of the decision; its model is the unexpected self-content, (contént and not just cóntent) and accord of thought thinking thought – which is not just a vision of the impossible dream, our private utopia (though it is also this), but also a living, breathing reality, uneasily embodied as it is in human being, in *a* human being, in all human beings who decide, one fine day, to think for themselves and give voice to what they know, the simple truth about reason that is their distinction.

The euphoria of that good fortune – open and thankful for the present of thought brought upon us in delight of wisdom's language stands opposed to the mortification of the closed mind and its bestiary of dogged, mulish, bull- and pig-headed intransigence – the dog, the mule, the pig, the bull, all stacked into a latter day totem of obstinacy and crowned by the patron saint and sire of late/modern mountebankery, our forged and forging father, the grand sham of man, the sprite of conformism incarnate, our ape.

50. Praise of Celebration

Praise is no longer simply to implore and entreat as did the recipient of a boon; the acknowledgement of the limit of power is, by reason of reflective chirality in the entity of identity, the recognition of power beyond the measure of this limit, and in this sense limitless, *immensity*, a startling designation that celebrates the victory of mind over the indifference of matter, of our spirited stepping back and departure from the dire straits of every particular horizon, whether the matter be a trap of habits unquestioned, or the barricade of the narrow mind; it is worship in the sense of obeisances shown and the reverence that marks this critical juncture of prostration before as well as the simultaneous exaltation of, the judge of self-several reflection – the offering and the oblation of life is made for the sake of its renewal, its *salvation*, with respect to the vision of the principle that, like every significant thought, wants life, a life of its own, taking the life we have given as well as giving the life we have taken, the charmed, the *eternal* life of distinction. The ritual of glorification which began in glory as thought's first departure from thought, the ring of fire, even in the start that is the mind coming to itself, tolling the event of its turn and eventual return, the restoration of thought to thought, enters finally upon the completion of its ring, the bells wedding the seeker to the sought, the IS and the OUGHT – that pursuit draws to an end with the praise and magnification of pure reason being, in and of itself, the whole train of thought that began with the start of heart that shook things up long thought to be simply the way it is, take it or leave it.

Our ticket out of here, reason thus appears to us, in our gratitude and delight, as an intricate idea wanting elaboration and exposition for our greater benefit and more comprehensive insight, in other words, inspiring the endeavor of science and the desire to know more deeply and completely what began with a bang as the practice of our purer will when the immediacy of thought's touch moved those open-minded souls to receive the communication of its present. Thought as it knows itself and enjoys itself is, therefore, this song and the expression of this pleasure that comes after and before the charity that sets the inaugural ball of distinction rolling again. Thus science is the invocation of thought but not with the plaintive voice of entreaty and accusation but rather in the celebration and communicative clarity of realized knowledge summarizing the results of study and recording the details that are the fruit of long occupation collected into a persuasive system of ideas that reveal the nature of the being in question.

Praise is an expression of thanks for what has been given and received, in spite of hesitancy and first resistance, both of which have since resolved themselves into the rapport of respect, the love of gratitude answering to the love of what has been graciously proffered, but it is also the felicitation and applause of what has worked out in the end, what is, after all is said and done, well done and well said and all right – this delight is thought's own self-approbation articulated in the language of eulogy that wants to know and tell us everything. Then the attributes of thought are tributes that highlight and decorate its failures and its victories, not merely as features, as indicative of properties, as a chronicle of incidental events but rather as virtues, the play of incommensurable strengths of this nature that form the intricacy of character that is its distinction and its honor upheld against all calumny that would so gladly abbreviate and thus diminish the infinite scope of its life, the life of ΛΟΓΟΣ.

Why is *language* the ultimate reality and final frontier of thought and, in this day and age, "to have and to hold the turned word of distinguished speech and holy writs" the admittedly somewhat cumbersome translation of choice for the traditional definition of the distinction as well as the destiny of human being as ZOON ΛΟΓΟΝ EXΩN? Not, at any rate, because of the prevalence of media technology, its use and effect, in determining contemporary discourse – though, in fact, we might see therein a sign, a message that the media themselves *are* and not merely *convey* – but rather with respect to the craft and art that have long earned wielders of the word the name of *wisdom*. Already in the Third Epoch of pure reason, as we shall see, distinguished thought or *absolute spirit*, was termed a poet, the maker of poetic dwellings for human being, master builder of the trinity of supreme buildings of the *aesthetic*, the *ethical*, and the *scientific* mind, namely *Art*, *Religion*, and *Philosophy* – the crowning achievement of the *Imagination*, the *Will*, and the *Intelligence* of our humanity. These three dimensions of the craft and art of pure reason are depicted in *Figure 27*.

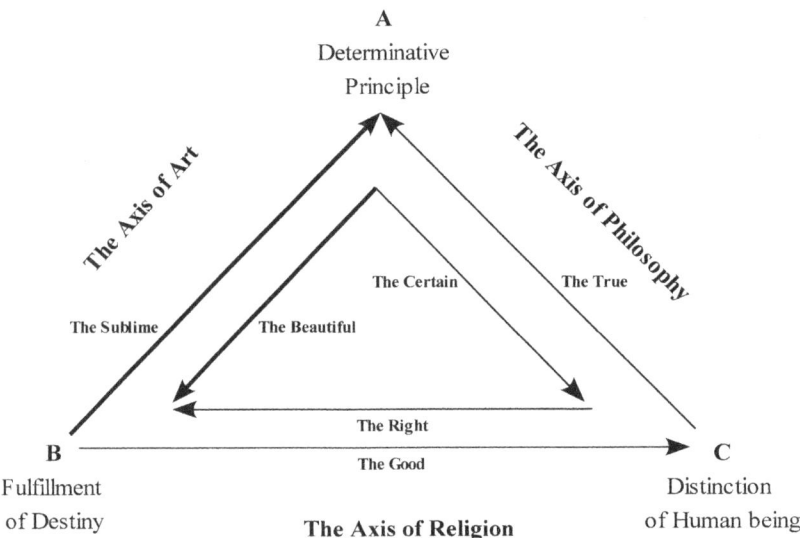

Figure 27: The Inner Workings of Imagination

Words, their names, are for calling – they invoke. What do they invoke? They invoke thought, pure thought, its intricate idea of itself, but the call of those vested, crested names that, for centuries, have served as terms of distinction, bids ideas neither in the sense of a warrant enjoining their arrest and appearance before a court of inquisition, nor in the manner of a conjuration of ghosts, vague and vapid vapor, but rather in the way of a prayer in acknowledgement of the distinction of human being, the distinction that *destiny, divinity,* and *freedom* bestow upon each committed member of their community as a debt and duty to be fulfilled in action and in a benediction, giving thanks for the completion of the trials and the end of the way that is thought's conceiving of thought in the concrete, specific terms deemed fitting and propitious to the occasions when heightened language, whether written or oral, is called for in accordance with an uplifted spirit.

What we, in these times of high spirits, celebrate and glorify becomes glorious in turn, magnifying what otherwise, in our more sedate moods, might have been missed or passed over in the silence of neglect, and rescuing from oblivion that deeply human experience that, in the philological studies to follow, we hope to gain a better appreciation of.

Thus, do science and poetry intersect when bringing to light what is most worthy of note, namely the destiny of human being with regards to which the votive song sung on its behalf is an act of recognition; we know that knowledge is founded upon acknowledgement, that to comprehend is to realize, and to name with insight's discernment is to make significant. This significance, in turn, sparks the attention of contemplation, that of the illuminated Thinker, in one both the audience *and* the spectator of the being that the Builder made luminous in the first place. It is this poetic genius of pure reason who we hear speaking with the voice of Hölderlin's poet in the ode *Sung beneath the Alps* (Unter den Alpen Gesungen – Hölderlin, *SA* II.44-45)

> Aber es bleibt daheim gern, wer in treuem Busen Göttliches hält, und frei will ich, so Lang ich darf, euch all, ihr Sprachen des Himmels! Deuten und singen.
>
> *But glad to stay home who holds, in a true heart, the divine; and freely will I, as long as I may, you all, you sky signs, construe and sing.*

Thought moves us to speak and delight in what we know and signify what we see, giving *reality* the meaning it deserves by giving *conception* the substance it allows. But how do we become a poet? It is to this question that we must now turn in the next step of our investigation. What is the method of building, what are the tools of the philological trade, the brick and mortar that in the hands of the master builder give rise to the logotectonic ratios of thought, and of all thought, upon which is founded, as *Figure 27* suggests, a well-proportioned dwelling of surpassing **beauty** that is worthy of being, being neither a panoptic prison, nor a totalitarian state, but rather the happy home of thought's beings where each has its own proper place and enjoys its own proper life through the **sublime** omniscience in front of which we, though nobody in particular, now lie thrown and sprawling, having been toppled from the Man-made throne of our know-it-all airs and pretenses?

But before the advent of the poetics of the sign, before, but also after the *poet*, behold the *thinker* who knew how to construe the passage, got the drift, gained insight into apparition, read the writing on the wall, who, in the devotion of recognition, understood legibility not merely in the detective act of information extraction – deducing the ***true*** from the clue – but rather as an act of affirmation and ***certainty*** inherent in the notion of intelligibility. And again: before (*and after* – not forgetting to take the iterative circle of turn and return into account that is the procreation of thought thinking thought) thought as seen and thus known, thought as grasp and thought as shown, the song, the sign of the distinction is passed on and along, and, in making a difference, moving, touching, thought is lastly (but also first) the actual lived experience of distinction, the *Actor* experiencing the gift of the self-several mark, the striking impression that reflection makes upon the mind born to strive and, seeking, find, born to seek and finding ***good*** in forever striving ***rightly*** towards it.

So once around the merry-go-round we go and back again – *Figure 28* shows our sole train of thought, on its boustrophedon way to itself in which the present of the *distinguished* principle *reveals* to the *receptive* sense of regard the *divergence* between the IS and the OUGHT, entrusting to our care the responsibility of human being the experience of which is the anguish that their *divergence* entails, sparking the ambition of our purpose to close this gap and, through the patient efforts of this *determination*, to fulfill that need that the providence of the originating principle set before our moral judgment as a preview of our *accomplishment* and our best being that, having been attained, we now inhabit as the perfect *determinacy* of our destiny construing in the substantial and particular realization of that purpose the *signification* of that abstract potential in which we initially took such intellectual delight as one most worthy of praise and subsequently committed to memory in the poetic language of *celebration* that honors with fine words and finer deeds the end in the beginning and the beginning in the end and in so doing, so singing, gives voice and life to that principle by serving as that principle's own life and voice that, as the startling, moving clarion call to reflection and action, imparts to pure thought, anew, its unique *distinction* to be, to be done, to be heard.

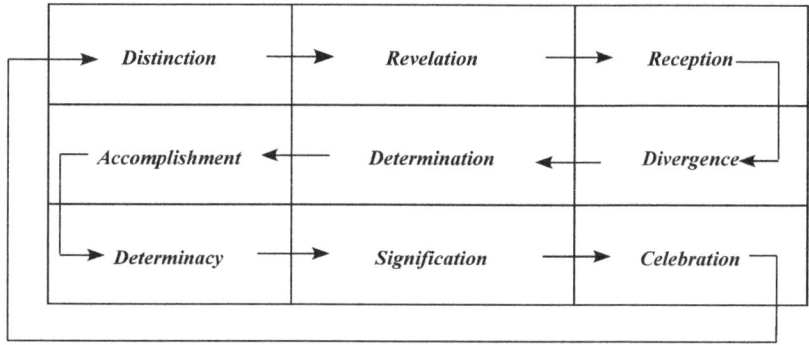

Figure 28: A Complete Line of Reasoning Regarding Thought Thinking Thought

The Second Part
The Determination of Our Method

51. Doing Philosophy with Words

Perusing a book about how to do things with words, you might be inclined to skip the lecture about the thing called *speculation*, not the investor's nor the political journalist's, but rather the philosopher's, namely thought thinking thought or *metaphysics* in the traditional sense of this word. That would be indeed a shame as a great majority of thinkers seem to suffer a real and pressing need for instruction in it, judging from what most appear to think about their fellow thinkers' thoughtful speculative efforts.

A list of all of the mistakes, their causes and consequences, that philosophers have made in the past and continue to make today, even though the latter should really know better, after all this time and after so many pleas for reformation, is, apparently, appallingly long and growing daily. Thinkers are, at least in the eyes of others in their guild, astonishingly incompetent and their works fraught with absurdities and inconsistencies that somehow insidiously escaped the astuteness of a mind supposedly honed by a lifetime of contemplation but for which we now can only blush on their behalf.

And this embarrassment is all the more painful for us in that the most striking mistakes are not merely mistakes in detail, a minor lapse in the argumentation, an oversight or omission, an inappropriate metaphor, an obscure reference, to say nothing of problems in translation and other cultural obstacles – personal, national, historical – that interfere with the transmission of knowledge via language across place and time to which our elders were as susceptible as we ourselves still are. These would be entirely excusable failings. No, to go wrong as a philosopher is mostly, as it would appear, to suffer from a *principal* misconception. This is what a look at our philosophical tradition teaches us. Our tradition shows thinkers who disagree in principle. And if nothing else, then at least this feature of philosophical discourse identifies something like the character of European thought in general, evident in its classical and modern epochs and even in its late/modern guises. Thinkers, at least the best of them, namely those whose thought have made a difference, not content to quibble, *principally* do not agree. And evidently even this fact, taken as the one true principle of European thought, is open to debate.

Now beginners of philosophy, unaccustomed to such cut-throat adversity, tend to find the discord of this atonality jarring and in moments of respite and exhaustion, even as the famed heroes on the battlefields before Troy yearning for the end of struggle, are liable to give themselves over to brooding on how mankind could ever hope to achieve peace on earth if even the most learned and composed of men and women wage pitch battles for the sake of phantoms in their heads, array systems of thoughts against sister systems, pit one school against another, march philosopher brother afield against brother, even sow dissension between disciple sons and their Doktorvater, all star-crossed lovers from estranged families of wisdom lovers, torn by strife!

The question then arises as to how else we could conceive of philosophy – the work that it entails, the objects it apprehends, and our relationship to fellow thinkers, young and old, who, with us, share this love, even in our mutual hate, and who have, many throughout their lives, participated in its endeavor – as an *enterprise of acknowledgement* in which every significant idea, every thinker, every thought that has made a difference, is duly recognized for what it has contributed to the larger framework of all things thought.

Such a project of comprehensive philosophical *philology*, if the philology of philosophy or, better yet, the philology of all thought, were possible at all, would clearly seem to extend beyond the powers of a single scholar to complete. The sheer multitude of philosophers whose works have been collected since the earliest days of the Greeks, a number tending towards hundreds if not thousands, the variety of languages, many still alive today, others long dead, in which they composed their manuscripts, many of which were lost or altered and of questionable authenticity – all of these problems present a daunting challenge to even the most committed efforts of a synoptic mind.

But even before it could be undertaken, probably with the help of an army of thinkers devoted to the task, the more urgent question to be answered is this: How can we characterize a thinker's thought in its entirety and determine if that thinker has indeed made a significant contribution to philosophy as a whole? What does it mean here to "make a difference?" A quick review of a thinker's opus might reveal a wide range of works, devoted to a variety of topics and even a single work of many chapters will test our ability to discern which of the many ideas expressed therein is relevant to our task of determining that thinker's *essential* insight with regards to all the others that every other thinker from then till now has gained. Clearly not every word and sentence on a given page and every page of every chapter, not every chapter of a certain work nor every work in the entire opus will necessarily promote our comprehension of that thinker's philosophy and allow us to determine, in a nutshell, that is to say, on the whole, fundamentally or principally, the particular issue of thought in question.

The determination (A) of the fundamental issue (B) of thought (C) for each thinker[30] – clearly, this is what we must come up with if we want to succeed in conceiving of a *philological* philosophy as a whole and as a science, the "first science" of thought, perhaps even worthy of the name *wisdom*. It is also clear that in order to accomplish this feat, we would do well to avoid preferences with regards to certain thoughts, for example by showing partiality with regards to the ones we encounter that in some way flatter our opinions while slighting others that leave us cold by their unfamiliarity. Previously we alluded to this objectivity and the elusive facility of a thinker we nevertheless hold to be prerequisite to the success of the aforementioned enterprise, i.e. to adopt a standpoint of dispassionate equanimity – a grace not so often found among those dealing in ideas and dogmas where rivalry holds sway and renown is as moot as it is precarious. Thus disinterestedness, a stance considered so native to the custom of "exact" sciences as to preclude the need for explicit stipulation, is, in philosophy, a counter-intuitive demand. It is particularly trying to quell the critical reflex that would fain accuse a fellow philosopher of speaking nonsense rather than admit that the latter's point has not been well taken, having not as yet become clear to an unreceptive mind sadly abated by prejudice or the inveterate indolence that intellectual complacency breeds. Many a philosopher has found it more convenient to dismiss a thinker, a school, an entire epoch of thought outright, rather than to redouble efforts to persevere until insight into the principles in question could be gained or, through the patient ministrations of a colleague, rendered more forthcoming to the earnest efforts of perspicacity. Even with regards to the more pedestrian concerns of our everyday lives we know: A great deal that in our evening lucubrations seems impenetrable to us becomes pellucid in the refreshment of morning light. So probably in philosophy as well. Therefore, it is the modesty of patience and not merely supercilious abstinence that forbids us the importunity of taking sides and possession, playing favorites, and going by first impressions, jumping to conclusions as a way of cutting short a more protracted involvement with what, at first,

---

[30] It is with these terms – designated by the letters A, B, C – that Boeder delineates, in accordance with the logotectonic method, the topology of all things thought. See the footnote 41.

seems unattractive or abstruse or, conversely, beguiles us to pursue most avidly those thoughts that most inflame the virility of our narcissism.

But is it then truly cold chastity's restraint, proud and pure, that in the name of objectivity saves us from giving our heart to any philosopher's system? Perhaps, on the contrary, if we are quite honest with ourselves and put aside all monkish pretense, the fact of the matter is that it has always been just an aching, over-arching love for all thought and respect for its diversity of works that awakens within us the desire to be intimate with, if not to wed them all. A decidedly masculine perspective? Clearly not in the biological sense, nor in the sense of the Casinovian omnivore that promiscuously and indiscriminately hunts all manner of prey to feed on, nor in that of the coy dilettante who, content to taste and flit, skirts deeper intellectual penetration. Maybe it is, rather, Donjuanesque. Be "like the bee...," renowned as the muses' bird, the builder of polygonal combs, apt to float and sting, that gathers the quintessential nectars from all the blossoms of the surrounding but also further fields and diligently collects them into an anthology of honeyed insights, "of exalted hymns of praise that soars from one ΛΟΓΟΣ to the next."

ΕΓΚΩΜΙΩΝ ΓΑΡ ΑΩΤΟΣ ΥΜΝΟΩΝ ΕΠ ' ΑΛΛΟΤ' ΑΛΛΟΝ ΩΤΕ
ΜΕΛΙΣΣΑ ΘΥΝΕΙ ΛΟΓΟΝ (Pindar, *Pythian Ode.* 10.53-54.)

Every thought has had its day and heyday, has indeed, at least to us friends of thought, its charms and its grace to the extent that we can abstract from our own personal proclivities long enough to delve into them and succeed in permitting ourselves to succumb, temporarily, to their fine spell of words and are willing to see them through their husbands', their wives', and their mothers' eyes. This is no mean challenge where professionals pander to their patrons and experts cultivate their quirks and bastions of learning loom with their cant and schoolmen wreak their acumen and prominence exudes and plies its perfume. Though surely there is a lot to be said, career-wise, in favor of administering to quaint kings of the hill of some local lore, whatever happened to the wisdom of liberal education and the modest soul of universal scope that roams the highlands' peaks and haunts the wooded river valleys with a song of the wild?

I. Putting and Construing Names

52. The Meaning of Life

There might have been a time when philosophers, plying their trade of contemplation, locked their minds tightly against the dark revolving night or sought out the innermost recesses of the soul – Kant knew and famously suggested in the conclusion of his *Critique of Practical Reason* that whether we turn our eyes outwardly or inwardly, "two things fill the mind again and again with ever increasing wonder and reverence the more often and the more intensely the intellect concerns itself with them: the starry sky above me and the moral law within me."

> *Zwei Dinge erfüllen das Gemüt mit immer neuer und zunehmenden Bewunderung und Ehrfurcht, je öfter und anhaltender sich das Nachdenken damit beschäftigt: Der bestirnte Himmel über mir, und das moralische Gesetz in mir.*
> *(Kant, Kritik der Praktischen Vernunft, V 161.33-36.)*

That formerly so brilliant firmament constellation – this elemental spectacle of all that has come to light – once provided the inquisitive mind of natural history, we would presume, with no end of objects of study. Thought was possessed of that far-ranging eye that sought to grasp these emergent beings in the brilliance of their forms and genera, comprehending them in their appropriate categories and hence *saying* what the thing in question was meant to be, its essential being or *physis*, as was plain not, to be sure, to the immediate but rather to the discriminating eye and then clearly rendered in a form of words that corresponded to insight, namely the apophantic speech of predictive judgment. This was during the epochs of pure reason when the contemplative thinker saw the natural order, the cosmos, and partook of what was about him in a *perceptive* relationship the proposition of which indicated *what* a thing was in terms of what it was predetermined to be, its original principle and nature, its substantial *category* – a particular thing, undergoing the perilous ordeal of objective, scientific thought, now stands *accused,* with respect to its proper category, of *not being* what it is; this allegation or indictment calls upon the thing to be judged, to appear before thought, the conceptual Judge who, subsequently, makes a determination of the thing as *good* or *bad,* namely as being in accordance with its nature, perfect, or not, falling short. This critical sentencing of judgment is then articulated as a proposition which, in turn, taken in its own right as an object of reflection, is determined to be in accordance with the given state of affairs, connecting what fits together as being *true*, disconnecting what does not as being *false*. Categories and concepts, understood as "ideas," are thus essentially prescriptive not descriptive; they are natures. This means that the moving force of their predicate mediates the ultimate rational principle that is the unmoved cause and ΤΕΛΟΣ (telos) of their well-proportioned development into beings, an entire cosmos of them.

Much later, a lifetime, an entire eon of reason later, the exact sciences of modern man encounter not substances but rather the data of sensory perception, qualities and their complexes that, ultimately, originate in physiological processes of the brain. The synthetic world views of its accretions are then supplemented and corrected by scientific research and ultimately quantified through a descriptive network of signs in order to facilitate the construction of a reality of concepts, a quantifying structure possessed of constants and variables that enable the scientist to empirically verify the sense of their claims, i.e. to adduce provisional and local circumstances under which a proposition is true and thus to successfully, i.e. usefully, integrate the qualitative intensities and urgencies of lived experience into a unified framework of hypothetical relationship designations based on the law of causality and measured in the totality of the real space-time continuum that is the open horizon of scientific research practice and as such supposedly surpasses and encompasses the topicality of the mundane ego and its life-world.[31]

Or does it? What could outstrip the rigor, objectivity, and productivity of the so called "hard" sciences of the physical world with their experimental techniques of research, precise measurement, their historically valorized paradigms of puzzle-solving efficacy, and the discipline of peer review confirmation with respect to the valid research matrices and their commissioned, "official" concepts that nevertheless undergo periodic crises when subsequent incommensurable paradigms emerge and revolutionize an established consensus and concomitant routines in the research community, a shift that forces a renewed criterion demarcation for *normal* scientific theory assessment with a view towards eventually assuring the survival of the fittest ones?[32]

This appearance of a *sociology* of sciences, asserting itself so disconcertingly into the supposed exact logic of discovery and drawing, as

---

[31] So M. Schlick, (cf. Boeder, Das Vernunft-Gefüge der Moderne, pp. 53-82).

[32] So T. Kuhn (ibid. pp. 82-100.).

it would seem, so much unwelcome attention to the dynamics of group behavior and the psychology of its researchers and their desires, suggests the "dawning of a novel First Science, one no longer pertaining to the 'first principles and causes,' no 'theological science,' but rather an 'anthropological' one," though one "not on the basis of human 'physiology,' but rather founded upon the description of our sense of living being, namely of perspectives in which human life, as it is actually experienced, explicates itself." [33]

We descend here from the realm of the exact science on high to the terrestrial and even, from the point of view of these sciences, to the subterranean regions of the world that consists of lived experiences, a life-world that in its multiplicity is radically antecedent to that of the unity of the sciences and their assimilating constructions, prior to the explanatory abstractions of thought that comprise its modes of operation, and as such is therefore understandable only as the inexplicable "nexus" in which the tendencies of our individual lives in all their brevity and contingency, in the irrational depths of their infinite longings, converge and merge with the totality of life-forces that is the overall life vector of human society in history, the life of the world. And it is upon this life and its practices from which thought has sprung in the first place that historical consciousness must turn its hermeneutic sciences of lived experience – especially as documented by works of art – having thus emancipated our lived experience of life from the withering effects that natural sciences have on the human reality, and now take upon itself its most significant office, namely to intervene in the progress of human society by investing its will to power in the founding of political organizations that could duly serve as the basis for all culture systems and the world-views they propagate.[34]

This historically conscious life-form comes to itself in the selfhood of the mundane ego; the natural attitude of its lived experience begins life by simply and naively receiving the immediacy of what is "there!" in the

---

[33] Thus Boeder's introduction to hermeneutic thought as distinguished from both metaphysical as well as that of so-called logical positivism:"...hier taucht eine neuartige Erste Wissenschaft auf – nicht mehr diejenige der "ersten Gründe und Ursachen", keine "theologische Wissenschaft", sondern eher eine "anthropologische"... keine Anthropologie auf dem Boden der "Physiologie"... sondern auf dem Boden einer Beschreibung "doxische" Gegebenheiten, nämlich Auffassungen, in denen sich das menschliche Leben als erlebtes auslegt." ibid. p. 103).

[34] So Dilthey (ibid. pp. 113-135).

general thesis of the world as the one and only horizon of all that there is for itself, as its surroundings always there, always full of potential objects that are sometimes seen, sometimes not, sometimes clear, sometimes cloudy, and that attain the momentary foreground of attention only to fade into the background again in the ever-changing fields of singular ideation exemplifications; in bracketing this world thesis, we encounter the transcendental being of the mundane ego, namely its stream of consciousness, the continuum of qualities in which unreflected actualities of them become "inactual" and their "inactualities" actual in accordance with the shifting intentionality of the ego eye, indiscriminately animal or human and localized in a physical body of sensory irritability, the material basis of and temporary stasis in the flow of lived experience which is the flowing life of the ego itself, modified by its protentions and retentions, as it constitutes its objects while assigning them the sense of a real being in the world that they otherwise would not have – "to the extent that I cast my eye upon the flowing of life in its actual presence and apprehend myself as the pure subject of this life, I say with complete and absolute necessity: I am, this life is, I live; cogito"

> ...sowie ich auf das strömende Leben in seiner wirklichen Gegenwart hinblicke und mich dabei selbst als das reine Subjekt dieses Lebens fasse, sage ich schlechthin und notwendig: Ich bin, dieses Leben ist, Ich lebe; cogito." (E. Husserl, *Ideen zu einer reinen Phänomenologie und phänomenologischen Philosophie*, §46 p. 85.)

The eye-beam of the I – that of the transcendental but no less mundane ego – afloat, swept along as it were, in the flow of lived experience, realizes its own proper notion of infinity, the *now* of its world-time awareness which constitutes its momentarily fulfilled sense and actuality in the limitless succession of time's fleeting moments.[35]

53. A Rose by any other Name...

In the meantime, gazers of the stars have become readers of words not worlds, attain insight as decipherers of signs in the open horizon of their meanings not substantial beings, profess to be not hermeneutic interpreters of life forms and analysts of the unified world of sciences and technologies but rather the literary critics of *discourse* who, in linguistic and semiological typologies, elaborate, not the eddying patterns of the ego's

---

[35] So E. Husserl (ibid. pp. 135-187).

stream of consciousness in the life-world dimension but rather the disowned anonymity of text production and consumption in the ebb and flow of messages that the mass media not only transmit but themselves become while mediating an interactive intercorporeality of mini-me mentalities and no longer an intersubjective community of alter egos much less the reciprocity of respect and recognition among partners under the jurisdiction of the highest and greatest principle, in accordance with the jovial destiny of fairness that Zeus himself was subject and heir to in the apportionment of power that founded Olympus, the first community conceived of in the European philosophical tradition, namely the fellowship of the immortal gods themselves.

In light of the emergence of such latter day interactive bodies, our seat in the flesh of the world – essentially talking (rather than thinking) heads, engaged in the tickle and lashings of tongues in contrast to the dialogue of soul and the enunciation of its propositions – even words themselves recede in the abeyance of latency and desuetude in favor of non-verbal language – gestures that discursively clothe and in this sense "fashion" the body of a real or an ideal, a thing or a thought, in accordance with the performative determinants of a communication setting. And beings, once determined as substantial *things* in their own presence or else as *objects* in relation to a perceptive subject, my self-knowing being, are subsequently conceived of as *arguments* satisfying functions the totality of which constitute collectively all that is the case (rather than what is not the case), a particular though contingent factual world – things have become facts and facts, in turn, have now attained the status of *designations* in the infinite process of signification. Our life-world has become a reader realm of connotations, that of animadverting, animadverted subjects subsisting in an empire and an economy of signs, in a "cultural" world colonized by meanings – all artifacts, nothing is left untouched – "untouched reality" or "things in and of themselves," "nature" being just one more sense or, more specifically, one more of those social or moral ideologies, an artifact of semantics, borrowed from or just referencing our cultural history, a *version* that sign-reading connoisseurs as well as media designers and other professional communicators – themselves self-replicating nodes in the chain of signifiers – in a word, the *tongues* of signification, following their own agenda, are wont to avail themselves of while their heads' talkers are taken for a walk of communication to squirt their cognitive mark of meaning upon the concrete specifics that define the circumstances of their speech performance in sycophantic response to the prejudices of a particular audience.[36]

Once, *reason,* a living being, was the object of the stars' orbit, themselves no less alive, no less substantial than that unmoved moving object of their true desire that its beauty inspired in them, and all these moving beings, each occupying its very own place in the order of their *physis,* were its loyal subjects, striving towards their own perfection in accordance with the principle of what is due and proper from each to each towards the fulfillment of the *cosmos* of their just community under the auspices of that first cause, their king. And now these stars are words, linguistic elements, names, signs, a code, selected among a vast repertoire of signs to convey a message in a particular speech performance that invests them with an ever shifting foreground of meaning as determined by the parameters of the communication situation, the speech event, which includes not only the expressive or *emotive* function of the addresser and the *conative* function with respect to the addressee, but also the donative, *referential* function of the utterance with respect to the context, the real framework that defines the particular speech performance, the *phatic* function of which establishes contact, the medium, whether physical or psychological, between the speaker and the audience, a hot link governed by the *metalingual* function that checks and adjusts communication with regard to the appropriate code of which both parties to the communication can avail themselves to insure its success, and finally the *poetic* function of the message which conveys the concrete effect of language on the hearers.[37] We can represent these functions of language in accordance with Jakobson's conception in the ratio of terms depicted in *Figure 29.*

---

[36] So R. Barthes (cf. Boeder, *Die Installation der Submoderne,* pp. 194-239).

[37] So R. Jakobson (ibid. pp. 173-194).

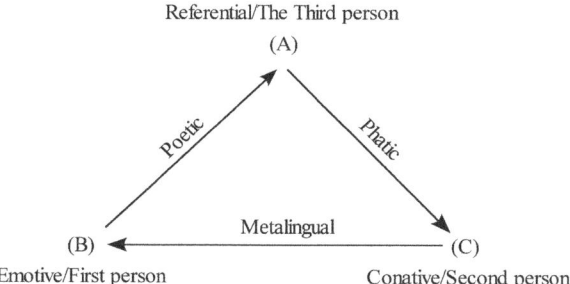

Figure 29: The Dimensions of the Linguistic World

This world-creating process of signification consists of the two elementary operations or, as Jakobson calls them, "the two basic modes of arrangement used in verbal behavior" (*On language*, Harvard University Press 1990, p. 77) namely *selection* and *combination*, in which, on the one hand, thought is identified by terms that have been chosen for it by the sign-maker's art from a repertoire of names and expressions that, accumulating over time, have been condensed into a collection or system of paradigms based on the principle of metaphor, i.e. their similarity with one another – it is from this trove of analogous terms, that the selection is made – and, on the other hand, thought is articulated by terms that have been set in relation to and combined with other terms and connected thus into a train of thought by the logotectonic art of ratiocination, complementing the former principle of *unity* and substitution of like with like with that of *difference* and displacement, one term following contiguously after the other in an articulation of distinctions towards a *spatial* distribution of difference, the horizontal orientation of conjunctive syntax, as opposed to the vertical and disjunctive orientation of *temporal* determination in the identity of equations – both processes are, however, not opposed but rather coeval and oscillating relationships; their reiterating exchange determines the rhythm and the pulse of thought first encountered in the recursive structure of ingemination initiated by the drawing of a distinction which is the *negativity of abstraction*, in relationship to the *continuity of reflection* inherent in the self-relativity of thought thinking thought, that entity of identity with respect to which it is the destiny of human being to distinguish itself as both self-disjunctive *and* self-affirmative.

Thus, at the end of the trail of meaning, language has come to be the sole object of thought, the Thinker, as well as the Builder – Jakobson's two operations of language show the two axes of thought's efficacy that begins with merely the drawing of a distinction and stops when the point has been made. The result of this work with signs, i.e. *signification*, is a world quite remote from any we have inhabited till now. It is a world of distinctions in which we, the readers and the writers of language, participate – passing through the post/modern sphere of the mundane ego, a worldly **world** of lived experience, public statements, and the states of affairs, the urgent matters upon which they gravely give *no-comment* – into which we, ourselves epiphenomena of semiological processes, now enter, as into the netherworld of this world, our purgatory, to be cleansed and then reborn. We awake, sign-shorn, from our late/modern slumber and find ourselves standing still, except for our trembling, at the imposing threshold of our philosophical tradition in which pure reason was a being and as such had its day and seasons, its persons, places, and things as their cause and determining principle, *their* being, in other words, their substance and nature. What has become of such substantial thought of **tradition**? Once the deity of intellect, once God in person, once self-knowing being, after the mind came to grasp its own workings as products of its theoretical and practical pursuits, as experience gained in thought's own accomplishment – thought's final and greatest realization – thought has become an accomplished, self-several being and its ideas are the inventions of the creative and imaginative human spirit, called *absolute*, that brings forth its own reality, one most worthy of itself; thought is thought's most startling realization.

54. The Meaning of Meaning

What remains of that venerable spirit in these our dispirited times? It has devolved into the anarchic performance of everyday **language**, including its wanderings and even deviations on the one hand and, on the other, into the straitlaced rationality of logical analysis, namely into the criticizing animus of the *Analytic Philosopher*. It has stooped to the menial business of patrolling and decrying the everyday usage and abuses of the language, the sense and nonsense of sentences we say and what we do with our words; these grand inquisitors of nonsensical, metaphysical propositions (those unprincipled escapades of his fratricidal brother, the *Installation Performer*) are oblivious all the while to the simplest of facts: that namely, as it turns out, in spite of their crusade, some folks still like to "do philosophy," in other words, to think about thought, for better or worse, in spite of the fact that "speculation" must surely figure prominently on their list of forbidden words for forbidden deeds.

Concerned thus with propriety in speech and the nicety of our discrimination, what do those gentlemen thinkers, each a penseur (or a penseuse) in his or her own right, actually recommend and what is the business of thought and manifold thoughts in our lives, in the many different lives and worlds that compose a pluricultural setting of communication?

How about studying (and deflating) the systematically misleading expressions and paradoxes as the live problems and worries of philosophical communication that even laymen and laywomen are prone to – all relics, from previous positivistic discourse of mundane persuasion, themselves faint echoes of traditional *theoretical* thought, youngster notions depotentialized into rascals and troublemakers – and carefully noting impasses in ontological discussion, "platonic" talk regarding "essences," the quandary of generalizations, the inexplicable primacy of predicates over subjects, that is, over "arguments" as they are now called, with respect to the functions they are thought to saturate, the dilemmas of absolute opposition between thought and things, mind and matter or merely the platitudes and truisms – that, oddly, seem to lurk in those notorious dichotomies' meager shadows and plague or perhaps haunt, like a ghost, the machine of our everyday workings and understandings of language – distilling through our analysis the logic, or better, the "grammar" that is always already being applied by them and then exorcising that demon from the midst of our language practice, as Ryle recommended and practiced.[38]

On the other hand, we might try our hand at a taxonomy of the various speech performances in good currency with a view towards overcoming the predilection of scientific rationality to focus on declarative sentences that claim the prerogative of most truthfully describing "reality." In fact there is a great variety of communicative uses that utterances might be put to in conjunction with our everyday actions, speech acts, in which they will be more or less felicitously employed in accordance with calculations based on an eminently pragmatic opposition between success and failure that outstrips and engulfs the "traditional" true/false distinction inherent in the constative use of language (as well as the ancillary normative one, of course).

The speech event is thus an everyday linguistic happening embedded in the dimensions of the particular communication situation for which

---

[38] So G. Ryle, ibid pp. 288-328.

scientific description is merely one among many possible speech acts performed in ordinary conversation consisting of the mere utterance, the *locutionary* act of communication, the *illocutionary* act of "securing uptake," and finally the *perlocutionary* act, which refers to the actual effect that the communication incident had on a particular audience.[39] Austin's/Searle's classification of the force of illocutionary acts can be summarized in the ratio of terms depicted in *Figure 30*.

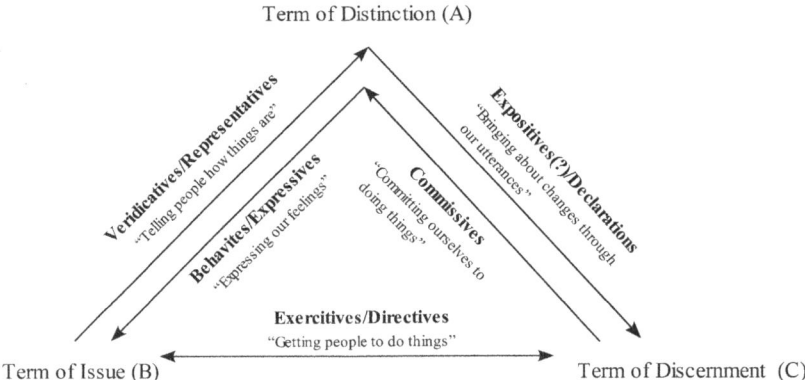

Figure 30: A Taxonomy of Utterances

Thus we come to the conclusion that it is the workings of everyday language in speech practice, the actual speech performance as determined by and determining the communication situation, in other words, it is a theory of meaning that provides the foundation for the justification of truth. The assertoric force of an utterance, lately deemed primary by positivistic scientific discourse is now placed in the context of a more general linguistic framework of communicative behavior to include, in addition to that of the *indicative* mood, other modalities termed "realis" like the gnomic generic, the confirmative, energetic, and inferential moods, and then, in contrast to these, the *deontic* and *epistemic* modalities called "irrealis" like the jussive, subjunctive, optative, conditional, and the potential moods, as well as the interrogative and the imperative – and there are many others that could be distinguished within these three general categories – all of which, whether they are actually marked in the given language by grammatical inflection or

---

39 So J. L. Austin, ibid pp. 329-352; see also J. R. Searle, "A Classification of Illocutionary Acts" in: *Language in Society*, Vol. 5, No. 1 (Apr., 1976), pp. 1-23.

verbal periphrasis or even merely by non-verbal intonation, are speech acts in their own right put forth in sentences the purpose and consequences of which differ considerably from those of the declarative variety favored by the very limited "evidential" communication of "scientific" discourse. According to such a theory of meaning in the everyday practice of ordinary language, truth is what can be successfully justified with regards to the hearer only by taking the latter's needs and concerns as well as the audience's own accustomed language behavior into account. For a given audience, speaker, topic, and, minimally, communicative intention, declarative sentences, more specifically, their assertoric force, may be effectively used to indicate that now "the truth" is being spoken as supported by arguments, other declarative sentences, that together serve to "vindicate" the truth of the statement being advocated by the speaker by allowing the hearer to draw his or her "own conclusion" based on their array as the arsenal of premises warranting the claim being asserted. This theory must therefore take the felicitous and infelicitous interaction of the parties and functions involved in the communicative situation into account, how the plurality of their diverse contributions affect the transient determinacy of that situation and, given these local conditions and the correctness criteria they ultimately provide, what *truth* means as well as what the consequences are, in this particular case, for telling it and hearing it.[40] And everybody knows that they are not all good.

55. A New First Science?

Again, what remains of that venerable spirit in our dispirited times? It is human and a human's truism that our thinkers, thinking about everything under the sun, forget, must forget, to consider the sun itself, fail to turn their attention from the supposedly clean, well-lighted places of everyday speech practice where they perform their exploratory operations upon patient living utterances, to the archaic light and to illumination itself – for the light of what sort of theory could possibly throw light upon light, illuminate illumination, i.e. think thought as the absolute distinction of human being, truly consider the nature of *all* thought and in so doing avoid every one-sided account of it that disperses its greatest achievements into the shards and splinters of an academic -*ism*, the smithereens of an ideology, a rubric, an opinion, a quip, a quirk, a tedious argument of insidious intent, a private issue of pride, prejudices of note – all so easily dispensed with. But consider!

---

[40] So M. Dummett, ibid. pp. 371-413.

Perhaps we are never done with ΛΟΓΟΣ, nor should be. No, you are never through with thought, you just think you are.

Where did we end up with Dummett having begun with Aristotle? In a nutshell, how we should translate ΛΟΓΟΣ – *reason* in the classical beginning, *word, language, speech, writing,* even *literature* perhaps, in the late-modern, the butt-end, of our days and ways. It is as if the pure thought of reason and the absolute objects of its reflection have been absorbed into the linguistic element that constitutes our everyday speech practice and the rich field of its performances – every speech event exhibits the ΛΟΓΟΣ, not as thought but as *spoken,* as *written,* as *heard,* as *read,* effectively severing the "natural" metonymic bond of association between the thought and the elements of speech that bring thoughts to the fore. Thus, those previously so illustrious objects of thought's self-knowledge and regard, its ideas, now but a shadow of their former selves as merely non-linguistic entities, have become, in fact or in reality, the mere meanings of terms employed in communication, the operations determining how their meanings function, the techniques applied to assure their effective performance, the media exploited toward the better dissemination of these meanings and, yes, even as those of the message that finally reaches the hearer's inclined or disinclined ear, indiscriminately yielding its secret to the next best reader's technique – deep or speed.

Dispensing thus with all that is not ΛΟΓΟΣ, in particular getting rid of the "hard facts" of the physical world of modern scientific research and discovery – for that is what the development sketched above has encouraged us to assay – what remains? We are left with the *language* of thought itself. Just words and their meanings as we employ them as speakers or writers in a particular speech or literary practice with respect to a particular audience of listeners or readers, the truth of which is the conviction that the more or less effective performance can instill in the hearers', the readers' heart. What sort of practice would this be? And who would want to engage in it?

Say we were to propose a new first science of philosophy, a metaphysical philology and a theory of all things thought, encompassing every distinguished thought ever thought; the starting point of this enterprise would have to be the illustrious names, not of more or less famous thinkers but rather those wingéd words, those ΕΠΕΑ ΠΤΕΡΟΕΝΤΑ they supposedly, as their authors, brought forth which tradition has recorded and, miraculously passed on, passed down to us, fancy words that, though relics now, even today still stimulate our thirst and our hunger to know and, like food for thought, nourish our starving wonder.

Freedom and the conception of human nature; *God* and the spirit of eternal life; *Destiny* and the perfection of the immortal soul – are these not winged words? They are just words to us, initially at least, who have learned to shed all preconceptions and assumptions with regard to them, fancy words with meanings, a long list of them, crested terms with a history, words that stand for thoughts, specifically for the ideas *Humanity, Divinity, Entity* which are themselves just more words, more cultural history of their use and abuse, more ideas. No, let's face it, there is no immediate understanding of them on our part nor could there be, in spite of all our hermeneutic pretensions and protestations to the contrary; *Beauty, Grace, Justice* – passed down to us from the ancients, just odd words fulfilling odd jobs in the various discourses so familiar to the speech and literary practice of our mundane society; of course, all of these words still find their uses and abuses in our politics, in advertising, on special communicative occasions that tend to showcase talk or else in times of despair when speechlessness, grasping at straws, mistakes verbiage for eloquence.

Or else simply in our everyday conversation, well, perhaps not exactly *everyday*, more like our *holiday*, our Friday night or Sunday morning conversation (Saturday being for shopping and tidying up) or such conversation as is called "polite" – small talk regarding life's little problems and big problems, at an intellectual cocktail, say.

We have just seen, in the above brief survey of the workings of ΛΟΓΟΣ, how pure reason, to use this name again for its experience and practice, for its point of departure and issue, for the sake of its tradition, became mundane and how mundane thought became speech performance. Apparently this progression has led us to the threshold of a new science of language, the science of distinguished speech, of the consecrated tongues and writs of wisdom. Philosophical language, though lately considered largely nonsense, after having lost its persuasive power and now restrained to the marginality of poetry, has come to be thought of, if its post/modern projects are any indication, as virtually wallowing in newfound license. The logotectonic science to be discussed might seem, in comparison to such riotous effusion, rather austere. We would go a long way towards mitigating this impression if we could exhibit, early on, its virtues as a craft and an art. It is a grievous mistake to consider its method an arbitrary exercise in acuity, the schemata it unfolds as a mere contrivance of formalism. We have shown that, in fact, thought thinking thought is a designation intended to give a name to one aspect of the unique experience of human destiny we have called at the outset the *distinction of human being*. The better comprehension of the richness of this experience is served by the logotectonic method. Why? Because this method is the work of thought itself articulating its own nature, realizing and finally comprehending what thought is in and of itself – thought telling its own story and the *whole* story rather than just a snippet here, a morsel there in accordance with the caprices of a particular thinker's ansatz.

But this is obvious. Since the earliest days of philosophy we have known, or at any rate some folks have, that pure thought is a comprehensive, logical system of insights or ideas and, in this sense, complete and perfect knowledge. Complete and perfect knowledge? What on earth could that be? Nothing on earth, obviously, for the simple reason that of nothing on earth could we have complete and perfect knowledge. Everyone knows that. There is only one thing (that is no thing at all) of which human being can, or at least should, have complete and perfect knowledge and that is of thought itself, pure reason. Ultimately this is all that there is certainty to be had about and knowing this, knowing this, our "self," as completely and perfectly as humanly possible is why people would devote themselves to the science of pure reason in the first place, which was, in the days of yore, called "metaphysics" and today? The philology of the language of wisdom? Hmm...let's find out.

To this end, in the following, we will examine the method of this science beginning with the *terminology* of thought, namely the elements with which thought, the Builder, constructs a line of reasoning. After this we will study the art of constructing *trees of differences* that allow us to make distinctions among our terms. Finally we investigate how these distinctions can be collected into a turn of words, a figure of speech, i.e. a sequence or *ratio of signature terms* that lead to a definite conclusion and an insight into what conception has accomplished in so articulating itself at that particular juncture with regard to a principle received and recognized as inaugural.

Now when all has been said and done about thought that could be said and done about it, the fact remains that it has departed into the workings of language; scattered, ideas have become words, vocabulary, a stray phrase picked up in the rush of discourse, an expression come upon by chance that incites curiosity, a mere word or catchy turn of phrase that catches our ear and our fancy and invites reflection, an utterance made, perhaps with a view to persuasion, in a line of argumentation, that troubles or challenges us, whether spoken or written, stumbled upon, to be sure, every once in a while in a new book but especially in ancient ones, those written long before our time. It is to these words that we now feel particularly drawn by wonder, wondering what it is about them that makes us wonder.

56. The Terminology of Thought

Having studied the theory of speech acts and become acquainted with their classes (veridictives, exercitives, commissives, etc.), we propose now to amend that list by adding a *sapientative* act of speech – coining thus a similarly "rebarbative" name for what we can do with words, namely engage in a *philological* science of pure reason set in the horizon of communication that is our present-day habitat – and to seek *the principal determination* (A) *of the fundamental issue* (B) *of thought* (C) for works of ΛΟΓΟΣ in general, however this "language" is affected, whether written or spoken, whether as discourse or visual design, whether textual or performative – this expression pretty well sums up what such a science as we envision consists in.[41] For the science we envision as devoted to the sanctified *tongues of flame* and *writs of wisdom,* namely the discernment of a significant insight or illuminating idea, or, in a word, *conception,* consists of a complete train of thought which is, specifically, a ratio of these three significant terms: *A, B, C* – a concatenation of truths.

We seek the determination of the fundamental issue of thought in our readings of these works of language, and by saying that we *seek,* we imply that our efforts are essentially *theoretical;* regarding these ancient works, can we find reasons for their being the way they are, for their using the language the way they do, and maybe even discover the constitution of their message? Indeed we can! With the persistent effort we might expect of contemplative science, the thinker will endeavor to formulate the scheme and element of their rationality, no matter how peculiar or banal these "texts" and "acts" of communication might first appear to a biased eye.

But ultimately, ours is not only to seek but also to find the determination of the fundamental issue of thought in these works, in other words, to unlock and comprehend the principle of their vivid sense – thus the accomplishment of *theory* – and then to articulate the logic of that principle

---

[41] Thus Heidegger's phrase, "Bestimmung der Sache des Denkens." The constituent words of this phrase are used by Boeder to name the triad of terms with which architectonic thought articulates its building endeavor. cf.: M. Heidegger, *Die Bestimmung der Sache des Denkens* (Vortrag 19. Juli 1967 in Kiel zu W. Bröckers 65. Geburtstag – editor: Hartmut Tietjen) and *Zur Frage nach der Bestimmung der Sache des Denkens* (St. Gallen: Ecker, 1984).

within the totality of all things thought – which is, then, the *poetic* side of our philological science, the craft and art of thought, the Builder.

Principle (A), *Issue* (B), *Discernment* (C) – where do these terms come from? What do they mean? How and what can we build with them? Why does a complete train of thought consist of these three (and not four or five or six) or some other three terms rather than these? They mark three salient aspects of our experience of the distinction of human being. It is these aspects that we refer to with the three signature terms A, B, and C. Of course the richness of our experience with thought thinking thought allows and often even demands that we highlight more than these three facets of an idea, more than three ideas regarding an idea, more than three thoughts about thought. There is a great deal we can say about thought. But as regards conception and the presentation of reason as a logical train of thought, we require precisely these three terms and no others, neither more, nor less. Indeed, the triadic structure of reason has long been known by philosophers and poets, considered eminently logical to the former, traditionally aesthetic to the latter and for the diverse, though akin, purposes of both, expedient in exhibiting the unique relationship and the relationship of relationships that is pure reason in action, ΛΟΓΟΣ pure and simple. Is this the arbitrary ascertainment of a method that it appears to be? Let's wait and see. Ultimately, every method must justify itself and can do so only by revealing itself to be an inherent property of the object of study.

Provisionally, we might note that there are indeed many traditional and even familiar triads that have been coined and collected by the conception and invention of the wise in their efforts to conceptualize and dramatize the distinction of human being and comprehend as well as represent this issue in a line of reasoning, ultimately in a system of distinctions, that not only succeeds in elucidating that distinction for our better perception, namely that of our *Thinker*, but also invites adherence and assent on the part of the audience who, hearing, is then moreover conceived of collectively as our *Actor* with a view to the practical effect that such conviction has on action, on the one hand and, on the other, in anticipation of the celebratory self-regard of thought itself, that has come to know thought in this "dialogue of the soul" by attaining clarity, conviction, and delight of the presence of mind, in and of itself, to itself.

Consider in *Table 1* a selection of triads that have been used as foundational terms throughout our philosophical tradition to distinguish the acts and works, the regions and domains, but also, as we shall see, the world, the history and the life of thought conceived of, in the changing progressions of these terms, as the development of its own unique epochs and ages, structured in accordance with the order that the relationship of the relationships, the *syllogism* inherent in these three terms, makes manifest.

	Terms of Principle (A)	Terms of Discernment (C)	Terms of Issue (B)
1.	General/Universal	Specific	Particular
2.	Theoretical	Practical	Poetic
3.	Perceptive reason	Operative reason	Generative reason
4.	True	Good/Proper/Right	Fine/Beautiful
5.	Philosophy	Religion	Art
6.	Science	Discipline	Invention
7.	Knowledge	Will	Power
8.	The object of speculative intellect	The object of devoted pursuit	The object of communal fruition
9.	Discerning insight	Transfiguring conversion	Fulfilling realization
10.	Physics	Ethics	Logic
11.	Third Person	Second Person	First Person
12.	Ex quo (out of which)	Per quem (through which)	In quo (into which)
13.	The First Epoch	The Second Epoch	The Third Epoch
14.	Inherence	Dependence	Reciprocity
15.	Being	Doing	Making
16.	Mind/Spirit	Soul	Body
17.	See	Hear	Touch
18.	Natural History	Political Economics	Philology
19.	Royal	Ecclesiastical	Civil
20.	Liberty	Equality	Brotherhood
21.	Theology	Epistemology	Ontology
22.	Firstness	Secondness	Thirdness
23.	Present	Future	Past
24.	Life (natural history)	(human) History	World

25.	Tradition	World	Language
26.	Power	Will	Knowledge
27.	Necessity	Possibility	Reality
28.	Epic	Dramatic	Lyrical
29.	Father Aether	Salutatory Light	Mother Earth
30.	God the Father	God the Son	God the Holy Ghost
31.	Start with Wonder	Mediating Middle	Accomplished End

Table 1: The Triad of Terms

This very brief anthology of terms exhibits expressions that have been collected at random, in a rhapsody you might say, from our philosophical tradition as well as several taken from more recent works of thought. Obviously this table could be extended and it certainly would be a worthy goal to complete it. A comprehensive catalogue of all the ideas that have ever been recorded, at least the most significant among them, is well within the reach of a devoted student of the history of Western thought – sadly, eternity itself has consigned the vast majority of the most ancient works to oblivion; or perhaps, in a more optimistically Darwinian vein, it has performed a service of preselection for us, winnowing grain from chaff, as we must hope and assume, and passing down to us only the supposedly fittest examples of thought while letting the rest rightly perish in the winds and the fires of time. As it turns out, we have the works we need to delineate the complete form of pure thought as it has unfolded across the millennia. There are no lacunae in the periodic table of philosophical ideas.

In considering this table of triads, note that every line of the table indicates the same complete progression consisting of an inaugural (A), a mediate (C) and a resultant term (B). A different triad of signature terms articulates the same relationship of relationships, the same ΛΟΓΟΣ, comprehended through and exhibited in an altogether different context of terms. In studying and speaking the language of wisdom – for the Thinker and the Builder are its theoretical and the poetic offices – this is the idea that every train of thought exhibiting the same order of terms, the same ratio, has the same *meaning* but, depending on the particular names that the terms assume in a work of conception, a different *sense*. They are different performances of the sapientative use of language.

Thus, in comparing the triads, we note the table's vertical as well as its horizontal dimensions; it allows for a horizontal reading such that each line is a progression of terms, more specifically, a syllogism. Each line of reasoning in the table is complete, is, in fact, as we shall see, an inference and a unique conclusion drawn depending on which term is posited as the inaugural one, which the mediate, and which the resultant, in other words, depending on the order of their sequence.

In addition to the *horizontal*, the "syllogistic," reading of the table that, in each line, examines the progression of terms, how they turn and return towards *closure*, its terms can also be read *vertically*, towards *enrichment*, in which case every term in a column is considered to be a synonym, a new, a refreshed name for the same distinction in the progress of pure reason's understanding of itself as all reality. Whereas the meaning inherent in a given term is only revealed differentially in *metonymic* connection with the other two terms in a particular train of thought which is depicted by the horizontal progression, vertically, the challenge is to recognize what one name in the column and each triad as a whole has in common, in a *metaphorical* sense, with the other and the others.

Sometimes the similarity of the meanings of terms within the same column is evident. Take for example the items listed in the column of Terms of Principle (A), namely the terms for *Theory, Science, Knowledge, Perception, Intellect, Insight, Spirit, Sight* in lines 2, 6, 7, 3, 8, 9, 16, 17 respectively. These words could clearly be taken as synonyms for the notion of *Mind* – of course the word *Mind* is also itself a synonym and appears in the list of Terms of Principle in its own right, i.e. term 16. Other terms like those for *Universal, Truth, Being, Nature, Life,* and perhaps the "ontological" expressions *Necessity* and *Present* in lines 1, 4, 15, 18, 24, 27, and 23 respectively would seem to be synonyms for the objects of reflection and the terms for *Philosophy, Physics, History,* and *Theology* in lines 5, 10, 18 and 21 for the productions or institutions of thought, the particular sciences that are its fruit. But many terms in this column do not seem to be synonyms in any obvious way. For how is term 11 for the *Third Person,* a linguistic expression, related to term 12 namely that of *ex quo,* which is just a Latin preposition and these two related to the term for *Inherence,* the 14th one on this list and belonging to the category of relation, or *Epic,* a name for one of the traditional genres of poetry, in line 28, to say nothing of term 13 for *The Greek Epoch* and of term 25 for *Tradition,* which seem to have more anthropologically oriented connotations while *Liberty,* term 20 more politically oriented ones and the abashing oddity of the terms for *First* in line 22, *Power* in line 26, *Royal* in line 19 and especially the names *Father*

Aether and *God the father*, one of apparently Greek-mythological the other of the Christian deity in lines 29 and 30 respectively – all of which have a vaguely a numinous sense.

Such a paradigmatic analysis makes apparent that though some of these terms could conceivably be taken as synonyms, certainly they could not all be and therefore if the proposed similarity of the terms in the columns is not literal then perhaps rather of an analogical nature. And obviously since an analogy refers to a structural homology, this analogy cannot be made evident if the terms in the columns are taken by themselves and compared with each other in an isolated way, divorced from the triads in which they occur. These terms can only be defined in the framework provided by the other terms in the particular triad where a given term occurs. That is why the same or similar terms, apparent synonyms, find their place in the other two columns as well as in the first. Put in different triads, the same term must have a different meaning and, as we have just seen, completely different, apparently heterogeneous terms could have the same. It is the use of the term in the context of a particular triad and not the supposedly "absolute" reference of the term itself as indicated by the name of the lexeme that determines its meaning. Thus *Knowledge* in line 7 is a Term of Principle (A) while *Power* in this triad is a Term of *Issue* (B) whereas in the triad of line 26, *Knowledge* is the Issue and *Power* the Principle. In this way, "power" is distinguished from *power* and "knowledge" from knowledge – the same word with entirely different meanings depending on the usage within the triad. It follows that we who construct and construe a conception of the distinction of human being according to the logotectonic method can never take the names of terms at face value and the connotations we associate with the words, their sense, can be thought to give presence to entirely different ideas. In this method, the references of our words and the meanings they denote to a native speaker are the same as always but the connotations they suggest, their senses, depend on how and where they find their employment in a particular line of reasoning, a particular turn of words of distinction, spoken or written. These ratios of the speech of wisdom are essentially triadic. How so?

57. The Syntax of Signature Terms

A - C - B – How are the terms in the triads of *Table 1* related one to the other? In other words, what is the syntax of a line of reasoning articulated by the terms in a specific triad? For it is this inner structure of the triads and this inner structure alone that establishes the analogy among them. And this relationship of relationships is not merely a collection of terms placed one after another into a table; as a train of thought or line of reasoning, they depict a development, the development of an insight, an inference, in other words, the drawing of a conclusion, the determination of the resultant term by an inaugural term across a term of mediation.

How does a triad, this chain of truths, exhibit a line of reasoning? Recalling our initial exposition of pure reason, the two phases of reflection we noted took into account the two essential operations of thought thinking thought, namely *abstraction* and *reflection*, the one the mark of the distinction drawn by *critical* self-reflection – we called this turn of thought in connection with our experience of the distinction of human being the phase of *stepping back* of/from the entity of identity (T) in a crisis of determination – and the other, the way of return of our uneasy discernment, the self-affirmation of reflection, in which this being of self-severalty ($\perp$), taking upon itself the office of an endeavor of formation or *minding the gap* between THE WAY IT IS and THE WAY IT SHOULD BE, strives to fulfill the initial distinction received as the call of destiny – we designated this way back of ambition the careful process of *making the dream come true*. We first depicted this complete circuit in *Figure 5* as the practice of critical reflection that begins with divergence but ultimately finds completion in the form of a benign turn and return as now recalled in *Figure 31*.

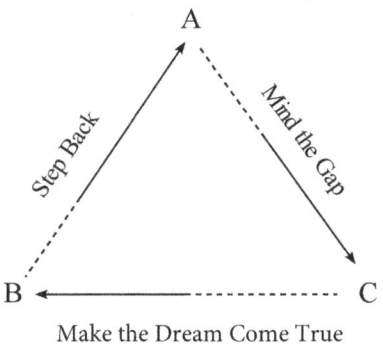

Make the Dream Come True

Figure 31: The Benign Circle of Reflection

Thus the reason for there being three signature terms is, firstly, because the former accomplishment of the whole and unity of perfection (B) that had, through negligence, fallen into indifference and thus become indeterminate or implicit, is again differentiated (C) within itself into its two constituent parts, and thus as such regained and recognized as their determining principle (A), and secondly, due to our experience of the determining principle (A) that grounds the relationship of thought thinking thought in which the thought and the thing, mind and matter, the ideal and the real, discernment and its object (C) attain the fulfillment of the entity of identity (B) that is the self-knowing being of pure reason. In other words, the triad depicts how the abstraction of thought (A) establishes the relationship between the experience of our own divergence from and discrepancy with respect to (C) the image of self-reflective perfection (B) that is pure reason's own unique being and identity, thought in and of itself, thought thinking thought.

Abstraction and reflection – these two spins on thought, one outward, one inward; one departure, one return; one a crisis, one a nexus, are depicted in *Figure 32* as two arrows, the double imperative of reflection.

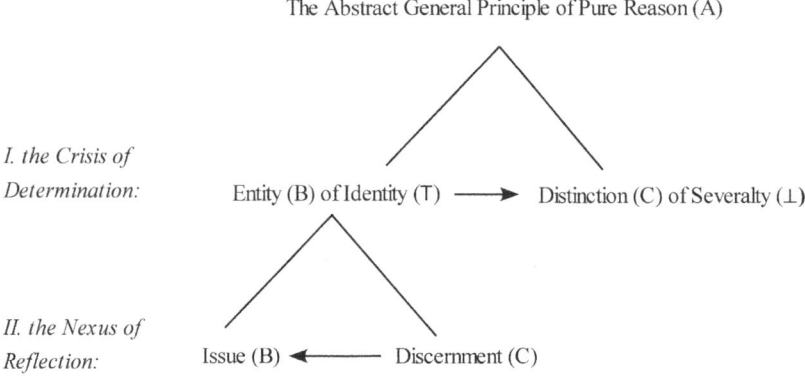

The Abstract General Principle of Pure Reason (A)

I. the Crisis of Determination: Entity (B) of Identity (T) ⟶ Distinction (C) of Severalty (⊥)

II. the Nexus of Reflection: Issue (B) ⟵ Discernment (C)

Figure 32: The Turn and Return of Reflection

The first arrow indicates the difference that critical thought makes in the unexamined life of Man towards the recognition of our destiny as human being. That former pavement of uniformity has become crazed, its superficies fissured by this inaugural experience of the inconsistency of being and thinking – the critical difference, the crisis, that thought makes *in* and therefore *of* our lives. The second arrow indicates the practice of transformation that the appointment of difference has charged critical reflection to carry out as a destiny to be fulfilled by closing that initial gap between the IS and the OUGHT that the revelation of self-several difference made manifest when the abstract principle first caught our attention, insinuating the germ of doubt into our otherwise so uniform lives.

We might envision this interruption as a departure from the previous oblivion of continuity or else as the incidence of disparity in a prior seamless immediacy – two different versions of the same experience, one a breaking forth, the other a breaking in; exit on the one hand, ingress on the other, the one the traveler's start, the other the visitor's stop; the family's loss – farewell, the stranger's gain – hello!

Using the first set of terms in *Table 1*, namely *Universal – Specific – Particular*, we offer now in *Figure 33* a first indication of the syntax of the terms governing the triadic relationship of the logotectonic method.

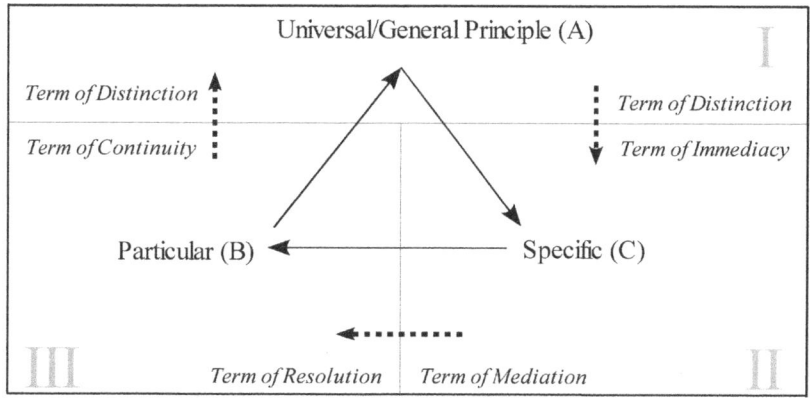

Figure 33: The Syntax of a Train of Thought

Figure 33 shows how the distinguished general principle which initiates a line of reasoning serves as a term of distinction (I) that leaves a mark of cognizance on a previously established state of *continuity* (III) by disrupting (II) the *immediacy* of a mind's uncritical confluence with that state. The abstract principle (A) bestows upon discernment the *specific* appointment of severalty (C) that is the distinction of human being and in this way determines the crisis of thought, its divided destiny as a term of mediation – a particular term with respect to the general principle to which it is subordinate and a general term with respect to its coordinate particular, the issue (B) of that distinction. In the purposeful endeavor of resolving this discrepancy, thought not only enacts the principle, putting it into effect in particulars as the accomplishment of what was predetermined by that principle, but also transforms these particulars, uplifting them from the state of prevalent convention that is their immediate being of mundane indifference to that of the issue and substance of the fulfilled principle.

58. Trains of Thought

Again, the abstract *General* (A) begins this line of reasoning as the distinguished term that is the origin of the General's universe as it now takes shape in the subsequent train of thought. It is, first, as the absolute term, the cognizance of negativity that actively marks the clean break with every given *continuity*, manifesting it thus, as the original state of dwelling in *Particular* (B), to the emancipation of objective intelligence, the relationship of disinterested insight attained by theory. However as the term of mediation, the General is practical, namely the S*pecific* (C) present of the principle that mediates the difference between THE WAY IT IS and THE WAY IT SHOULD BE, the object and its conception, in the *immediacy* of their relationship of opposition, the conception of judgment in which the manifested object of insight is now subsumed under the General as its determining principle that subsequently serves as the term of measurement in accordance with which that principle is realized in a process of its development.

Reviewing *Table 1* and comparing the triads, we can now more easily appreciate the analogies that the terms reveal. Stepping back from the unreflected immersion in the flow of lived experience, surveying and taking stock, the eminently Greek Mind of the *First Epoch* (13) or *Epic Spirit* (28) in the impartiality of its contemplative leisure, attains the standpoint of theory and comprehends within its scope, all that there is to know, all being, i.e. the ordered *Universe* (1) of beings, subject to the discernment and authoritative determination of intellect in the objectivity of the *Third Person* (11) of pure reason, the Aristotelian ΝΟΕΣΙΣ. The *General* (1) is thus not only self-contemplating intellect, i.e. the reflection of distinguished *Perception* (3) but also what is thereby perceived, which is, in a word, the *Truth* (4), the object of all *Science* (6) and all *Philosophy* (5), especially the theoretical sciences par excellence with their own specific *Beings* (15), *Living* (24) beings, like those studied in the ancient Greek science of ΦΥΣΙΣ - *Physics* (10) as having the moving origin of their being within themselves, and the one and only being of *Theology* (21) who is the unmoved mover of all other beings; but in fact neither philosophy nor *Knowledge* (7) in general is limited to insight and the work of the intellect with regards to what is present to it, i.e. *Natural History*, or else present in and of itself, *Metaphysics* (8). The general term is also a principle and as such seen in the effect it has on beings, the *Practical* (2) difference it makes on what happens, metaphorically speaking, the *King* (19), the *Father* (30) or *Aether's* (29) reign whence (*Ex Quo* - 12) subsequent distinctions unfold and are thus received as bestowed as the present of *Power* (26); after *Perceptive Reason* (3) has seen the *Inherent* (14) essence and the truth of a particular being's determination, *Operative Reason* (3) now puts that distinction that manifests the gap between a being's being and what it was meant to be into action as the destiny that is to be performed and fulfilled. This *Necessity* (27) of being that now drives the practical development of what is possible but not yet real, a development in the process of which the original discrepancy is ultimately resolved, is the ordeal and the work that we now see unfolded in the second column as a list of familiar *Terms of Discernment* (C).

In contrast to the first column of thought as an *inauguration* (31) of the distinctions that reflect our theoretical experience of pure reason in terms of the principle, that which has always already been decided and established as *Tradition* (25), the terms of the second column articulate our experience of *practical* (2) thought as *mediation* (31) *though which (Per quem* – 12) the determination of the principle *Transforms* (9) indifferent immediacy – the *Christian* (13) concept of truth as what will be *Done* (15). The given, the sent distinction or simply the present of the principle – in the Christian terms of the Second Epoch (13), the mission of the *Son* (30), *Equal* (20) with the Father – is now carried out as the *Specific* (1) difference that the general makes in Particular. In the practical science of thought or *Ethics* (10) the object is not merely seen but moreover enacted by the thought termed the appetitive *Soul* (16) or the *Will* (7) as the *Good*, the *Proper*, the *Right* (4), which are all names for objects of *Devoted Pursuit* (8), the *Future* (23) rather than the present of the reality of thought. To exhibit reason thus in practical terms, we put the names *Religion* (5) and *Politics* (18) and related terms (like *Ecclesiastical* (19) and *Economic* (18)) all of which are used to refer the *Actual Work* (15) and the *Dramatic* (28) ordeal of development that has been appointed by the principle and is now engaged in as an endeavor of nurture and fostering, the government of action but also service, effort, obligation carried out under this government towards the completion of a transformation the starting point of which has been entrusted to theory's posterity like a tradition. *Life*, being not merely observed but actually lived, is the progress of *History* (24), the world as what is done, what has been accomplished, and not merely what is. Thus *light* in this sense is not merely the possibility of sight but as *Salutatory* (29); the light joins the determinative principle (*Father Aether* in the context of this triad) with particulars that are receptive to the relationship of *Dependence* (14) upon a destiny and in this sense submissive to the principle of their own *Transfiguration* (9) towards which they are turned as the *Second Person*

(11) and serve in hearing, obeying while carrying forth that received distinction.

Finally, the determination of the distinction has run its course to the *End* (31), not bitter, but rather sweet *Completion* (9) and from this standpoint, looking back at its *Past* (23) and reviewing what has been achieved the *Particulars* (1) are *Realized* (9), products, facts that stand not because that's the way they are but rather because that is how they were meant to be and therefore *Made* (15) in that spirit; *Poetic* (2) or *Generative Reason* (3) has completed and brought to light what it was destined to. For resolution is not merely the ambition of determination and the striving effort taken on behalf of a principle but, moreover what has actually been accomplished by hard work, what was made by thought, not merely our experience with thought as insight and as discipline but also as *Art* (5) and *Invention* (6), where pure reason is collected into an image or vision of a whole that is not only differentiated within itself, but comprehending within itself its whole *being* and *doing* and *making* (15). Poetic thought is the part of thought that contains the entire system of thought, the totality in which thought is articulated. In this sense, our train of thought is not merely a description of what reason consists in, nor a chronicle of what sort of things reason actually does, but rather an autobiography – reason putting into *Language* (25), like the "philosophical" vocabulary in *Table 1*, what it knows and has come to know about itself, the *First Person* (11), the *Logic* (10) of reasoning in which its thoughts are its own articulate being, its own *Poetry* (28) the proper reception of which is the *Philology* (18) of wisdom we envision as a proper profession for friends of thought today.

The opposition between the IS and the OUGHT is contained and duly accounted for within this body of *Knowledge* (26), which is essentially a system, an inclusive and integrative totality, a *Body* (16) of organized knowledge, in which all the conflicts and upheavals in the story of its life, like so many organs, are reconciled (rather than liquidated), forming an association of distinct and incommensurable beings; terms that refer to the community and the *Reciprocity* (14) of thought as the entity of identity highlight the peace and closure of a *Civil Society* (19) of diverse, even divergent, ideas that nevertheless succeed at inhabiting a state of what previously had been the travail of their contest in the person of the seeker when truth and resolution was the aim, far off, sought, lacking, but now found, as close as the *Holy Ghost* (30) is, a living body and the differentiated being of knowledge that has come into (*In Quo* – 12) its own, our very own self-knowing being, *Touched and Touching* (17), enjoying itself and enjoyed as the fruition of contending forces that have nevertheless attained balance in a shared over-riding purpose and therefore as the sweetness of maturity, that is a return to the all-embracing nature of our *Mother Earth* (29), to her *State of Being* (21) which is that of the harmony of *Brotherhood* (20) attained and sustained among all of its distinguished members, a state of beings founded upon the certitude of their absolute freedom and autonomy, the unique state of accomplished beauty brought forth in the spirit of self-determinative difference – the *Reality* (27) of the Ideal, as it was known and celebrated in the *Third Epoch* (13).

Whew! In this way, we have demonstrated that the variety of names in the table can be seen as signature terms in a train of thought, each triad being a system of ideas that articulate different aspects of our experience with reason. Many of the names and expressions listed in the table are designations that have been used by poets and thinkers throughout our philosophical tradition to formulate their views and many are still used today when folks jabber philosophically about philosophy, all the while thinking that they are saying something new about thought, but in fact, unbeknownst to them, by using these words, they merely indicate where, in the scheme of all things thought, they happen to feel at home.

Clearly, they have skipped the most important step – coming to terms with thought itself, this marvelous being and doing and making, that is the object and the subject of so much idle rumor, controversy, and disregard and that really does deserve to be considered in its own right for a change, apart from our private or professional issues, as the basis of every particular philosophical conception. *Figure 34* offers an overview of what thought is before being clothed in a particular investiture of language and intention, the duality of the ΛΟΓΟΣ comprehended in the triadic ratio of its principles.

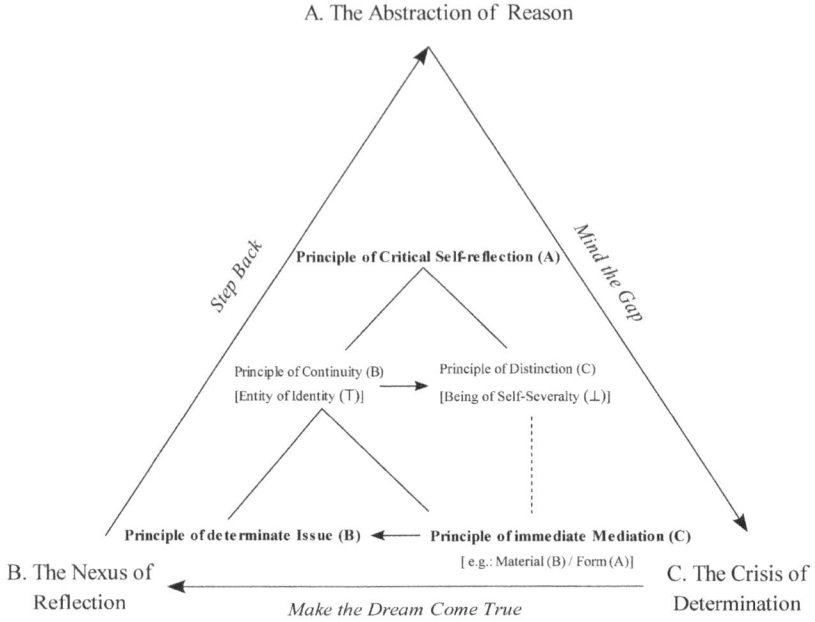

A. The Abstraction of Reason

Figure 34: The Dyad in the Triad of Pure Reason

The story of the life of pure reason begins with the attainment of a critical standpoint. This is not an attitude of fault-finding or nit-picking; neither importunate nagging nor peevish censoriousness intends, much less achieves, the impartiality of critical reflection. For this principle of critical self-reflection (A) is the distinction of human being, our cause, and the determining principle of the train of thought we have been pursuing till now. Taken as our conception of the entire scope of human destiny, critical self-reflection is the name of a differentiated experience that embraces two contradictory ones – on the one hand, the experience of reflective thought as our entity of identity (T), which is founded upon the principle of continuity (B), and, on the other, the experience of reason as our self-several being ($\perp$), which is founded upon the principle of distinction (C). It is then the immediate evidence of reason upon our discernment thus awakened that draws the first distinction and subsequent distinctions upon a formerly indifferent background of disregard and provokes the recognition of the gap between that given state of undisturbed continuity and the one that now, whether gradually or suddenly, comes to recommend itself to the deliberation of a wider view of things, namely one that succeeds in considering them as they might otherwise be, in particular, how they ought to be but, presently, are not. Imagination enters thus upon the scene of our everyday lives, calling into question affairs that have been taken for granted, having even been presumed to be necessary, and in this way entrusting to our care the project of an idea that brings to light alternatives previously hidden and kindles our determination to take action with a view to putting into effect that distinction that made all the difference in the world hitherto assumed to be the last word.

Though the completion of this train of thought would seem to be the end of the story, it is, of course, not the end of ΛΟΓΟΣ. In practical terms we are never finished with thought nor should be. But days of rest are our holidays and even the very night of thought, where all difference has faded and oblivion's blanket covers us, once left so resolutely behind us with the advent of diligence on behalf of the distinction that reason gives us, is now before us, upon us once again; nodding, we now know that in the scheme of all things thought, even this good-night of deepest darkness is holy and, as Heraclitus notes, even "those sleeping contribute, collaborating, to the beauty of the whole."[42]

ΤΟΥΣ ΚΑΘΕΥΘΟΝΤΑΣ ΕΡΓΑΤΑΣ ΕΙΝΑΙ ΚΑΙ ΣΥΝΕΡΓΟΥΣ ΤΩΝ ΕΝ ΤΩ ΚΟΣΜΩ ΓΙΝΟΜΕΝΩΝ (B 75)

II. The Mark of Distinction

59. Making a Difference

The craft and art of presenting the ΛΟΓΟΣ in the designation that is placed upon it as a specification, therein giving it the illustrious shape and substance of a determination without which it would most likely remain entirely immaterial to the task of making a difference, inept at drawing a distinction in the lives of human being – this approach of identifying *thought* or *pure reason* or *intellect* or *judgment* or *imagination* or however else you might want to call it, may have inadvertently given you the impression that they and, in general, all *ideas*, are merely states or stationary sorts of things. Well, after all, do thoughts move? Are ideas, can

---

[42] So Boeder's translation: "die Schlafenden wirken mit an dem Ordnungsgefüge und so an der Schönheit des Ganzen." ibid., p. 351.

they be, in motion, except of course in the trivial sense that a thinker may go for a walk while thinking? This is a well-known question among the learned who suppose that either thoughts are in people' minds and then "subjective" (or, worse yet, "psychological") or else in some sort of "Platonic" realm and thus utterly remote, but motionless.

On the other hand, ideas can indeed enter our minds and make a striking difference in our lives – in that case they might change our personal views about who we are, change our subjectivity into something else; similarly, we might enter the world of abstract thought and not even leave the comfort of our own living-room. Now the spatial proximity of this remote region does not diminish its distance from our familiar haunts and habitat in the latter case; and in the former, a thought is no less absolute for being wont to trespass on the private property of our mind. Where *are* thoughts then? Where our words are and therefore on the tip of our tongues? In our spoken and unspoken dialogues with ourselves? Well, yes, I guess you could say that. But for our present purposes, we would propose that thoughts are wherever they make a difference. We experience ideas as moving, *starting* even.

Nevertheless, after their assertion in the guise of a category or moniker, after having been captured in a phrase and pinned wriggling to the wall of some preferred dogma, ideas in themselves would very much seem to be immobile, almost dead. This appearance conveyed upon thought by language is deceptive for, clearly, our normal experience with ΛΟΓΟΣ is that thoughts and ideas are nothing static – consider their god-like, spirit-like, angel-like comings and goings, how they arrive in the nick of time but also tend to leave us in the lurch, how we have an idea or else, having become possessed of one, are entirely had by it, more owned than owner. How one idea seems to glide or merge into the next, how ideas are apt to form trains or else conflict with one another, never staying put, always on the go! And, as we shall see, a system of ideas is more like a procession, a journey, or a path than a monumental edifice, though, for all this, no less a dwelling, no less enduring, no less a monument.

Recall what we have found out about pure reason thus far, namely that thought is generative in being invention, an art of giving effective life to immaterial notions, making the ideal real, illustrative in giving the substantive presence of a build and illustrious physique to what is otherwise abstract and invisible to the everyday eye so mired in mindless normality, determined to give vivid sense to what, at first blush, is utterly outerly, utmost outermost, outlandish, that in a detached and utopian language, will, perhaps fittingly, be named, in somber epithets of negativity like *nowhere* and *nothing* and *nonsense* for so much surpassing the mundane ring of things, but on the other hand, from the perspective of what this language contributes to the vivid palpability of ideas, especially the most estimable of them, namely that of the distinction of human being, is entitled to be acknowledged as the language consecrated by and to wisdom, a manner of speaking that makes of ideas a shining *body* of knowledge, of a line of reasoning a dramatic *tale* of war and heroes, of the mind a being, of a system of principal distinctions a state, a commonwealth of beings.

But reason is not merely *imaginative* and, in this way, *generative*, it is also *intelligent, perceptive*; the culture of thought, the Thinker, is also the perspicacity of theory, the reading and the seeing of this one great idea in all its shapes and forms of invention, recognizing in speech the message, the content in a form, construing the meaning of a word, the term in the simple name, whether spoken or written.

Above all, however, the culture of pure reason is not only creative genius in art and discovery in science but also a discipline, namely the **practice** of distinguishing oneself as rational being from oneself as merely living being, discerning the relationship of difference between the IS and the OUGHT, overcoming the contradiction inherent in THE WAY IT IS being *not* THE WAY IT SHOULD BE, THE WAY IT SHOULD BE being *not* THE WAY IT IS. This is a conflict and a contradiction, with two sides, namely unreflected *oblivion* being the doom of the former, nebulous *abstraction* the latter's fate, each to each uncompromisingly extreme and exclusionary – and therein, though irreconcilably opposed, entirely the same, the life of one being the other's demise, there *gross engrossment*, here *aloof reclusion*, a wintry vignette in the juxtaposition of what is *dark* as well as *cold*, the post/modern creature on display in being both *extravagant* and *fanatic*, one *empty*, one *blind*, while both permanently bound in endless hate for perpetuating the other's extinction, for being each to the other's curse the echoing malediction.

It is upon this background that thought makes all the difference in the world and ushers in a double transformation as the "Nemesis" of the *haughty* **and** the *base* – the two well-known perversions of the distinction of human being as we shall learn. In the end, with respect to these extremes, thought is an experience as uplifting to the one as it is humbling to the other. For in sum, the self-relationship of self-knowing being is one of identity and affirmation, one of tranquility in the fulfillment of a principle, the life and the reality of insight having attained its object and now in-folded into this knowledge of itself as its proper dwelling.

In spite of the vision of accord and quiescence, the well-being evoked by consideration of that entity of identity that pure reason calls incessantly to mind, to the *human* mind, the inaugural experience of thought's delimitation, that scar and cognizance of distinction, has not been obliterated, that character of its memory, its history, have not been expunged. In fact, our experience of human destiny is neither merely that of conflict and contradiction alone, nor resolution and reconciliation, but rather an elaborate insight into their shared ΛΟΓΟΣ, i.e. their relationship and, more precisely, with a view to thought as the poetic work of giving shape, the composition of *abstraction*, in the sense of critical reflection, and *identity*, in the sense of the plenitude of determinate being, into a system and totality, which is, contrary to what you might expect, not the grinding to a halt, the standstill and abeyance of centralized stasis now attained, nor the fury and excess of eccentric ecstasy interminably sustained, neither dull lull nor headlong rush, neither hush nor bustle, but rather an energetically poised state of checks and balances, a negotiated relationship of relationships, their *equanimity*, articulated rhythmically into a complete chain of truths – into rings, as we shall see, and ratios of distinguished reasoning.

60. The Tree of Duality

If you want to see pure reason in action from the start, then watch how it inaugurates the relationship of overture, its purest and clearest manifestation, by drawing a distinction that makes a difference upon a background become indiscriminate, indeterminate, insignificant. With respect to this blank slate of homogeneity and continuity, critical thought leaves a mark. This binary relationship of pure reason's prescinding can be represented by an arboreal pair of terms, a dyad, and since there are countless ways of rendering this relationship by changing the names, we could build a table of them comparable to that of the triads we have just examined. In this table of dissociation, the right-hand column would consist of the *terms of immediacy (I)*, a list of names posited with a view to the spin of partiality that can be given to our experience of the absent-minded continuity we encounter whenever we manage to step back from and break the confluence with that mentality of uniformity and indifference.

In the left column on the other side of the table, we posit corresponding names, the *terms of distinction (II)*, that are intended to draw attention to the difference that each of these term implies with regards to its posited correlative. The term of distinction is the *marked* term which highlights the previously inert realm of indiscriminate normality prior to the advent of discernment that is the efficacy of pure reason, our capacity to step back and reflect critically upon a given status quo. The term of distinction set at variance to the corresponding term of immediacy makes that primitive realm of oceanic immanence explicit and, moreover, exhibits the delimitation of thought in the specific connotations supplied by these names and expressions. The two terms, one for a given "cosmic" order, an established empire of distinctions, and antecedent sidereal reign, the other for its disruption, its "disaster," form the two sides of the relationship – only in a very reductionistic sense to be thought of as one of opposition – that we have called ΛΟΓΟΣ; together they constitute the most basic system – that of a binary differential based on the drawing of a distinction against, putting a term upon, the background of unmarked space.

Thus, we recognize the ancient tree of distinctions or dissimilarities, one known and used by thinkers, as Aristotle notes, even since the earliest days of science, by Pythagoras for example, to distinguish their elements and their "principles in a series of coordinate pairs of terms, *limited* and *unlimited, odd* and *even, one* and *plurality, right* and *left, male* and *female, resting* and *moving, straight* and *curved, light* and *darkness, good* and *bad, square* and *oblong.*" (Aristotle, *Met.* 986A23-26)

> ΤΑΣ ΑΡΧΑΣ...ΤΑΣ ΚΑΤΑ ΣΥΣΤΟΙΧΙΑΝ ΛΕΓΟΜΕΝΑΣ ΠΕΡΑΣ Α
> ΠΕΙΡΟΝ, ΠΕΡΙΤΤΟΝ ΑΡΤΙΟΝ, ΕΝΠΛΗΘΟΣ, ΔΕΞΙΟΝ ΑΡΙΣΤΕΡΟ
> Ν, ΑΡΡΕΝ ΘΗΛΥ, ΗΡΕΜΟΥΝ ΚΙΝΟΥΜΕΝΟΝ, ΕΥΘΥ ΚΑΜΠΥΛ
> ΟΝ, ΦΩΣ ΣΚΟΤΟΣ, ΑΓΑΘΟΝ ΚΑΚΟΝ, ΤΕΤΡΑΓΩΝΟΝ ΕΤΕΡΟΜ
> ΗΚΕΣ

For our purposes, this table represents homologous schemes of discontinuity, the transcendence of detachment that is the distinction of human being as having the capacity for critical thought. It marks with names the two endpoints of a divergence which is the margin of latitude that the capacity of reason bestows upon us and with which we can remove ourselves from an otherwise blank-minded absorption, as blind as it is vacant, and promote the distinction of our human being by taking to heart this displacement that is our destiny and experiencing the Archimedean *remoteness* of the mind. Thus, the terms of distinction, the crested terms, place the negativity and abstraction of thought, being always already *without* – Aristotle designates the column of negative terms such as *Non-Being* and *Plurality* and *Strife* and *Movement* as those of *privation* (ΣΤΕΡΗΣΙΣ - 1004b27) – into the context of the immediate givens and assumptions taken for granted that the terms of immediacy give the substance of a name to.

This movement of transition is, as post/modern thinkers are fond of provocatively saying, the *transgression* of a particular suite of truths and values the language of which has attained good currency in an established discourse, visualizes and dramatizes the critical force of thought, not in positing an alternative but in exhibiting the extremism and the exclusion that the immediate order of the state of affairs establishes and, through the violence of its monoculture, tenuously but no less tenaciously preserves.

In fact, these terms in the relationship of discrimination are intended to illustrate our notion of critical thought, namely self-several thought as abstraction, as pure extrication, thought seen in its absolute and insurmountable externality, this distinction being renderable both as *extrinsic* as well as *intimate*, as the *highest heavens* and as the *heart of hearts*, both equally remote, both beyond, whether taken as the innermost or the outer limit, both giving a name to that peculiarly human extraction that is pure reason in action – the reiterating procession of distinctions that characterizes the hyperbolic movement, as centrifugal as it is centripetal, the spin of thought thinking thought.

Setting up our preliminary tree, we begin to insert names into it and, by doing so, represent this relationship of difference which is the vision of the primal and divisive divergence (and not at all an allegiance) and an account of the richness of our experience with the distinguishing force of abstraction inherent in ΛΟΓΟΣ. We can then render this relationship of fenestration (opening onto the airy lightness of what is utterly outward and beyond, immaterial indication in opposition to our material obliteration) in a wealth and variety of dyads, giving it in them a different presence with every new pair of terms, each new pair of terms instituting a unique system of indigenous logical distinctions, each founding a new myth to build with and inhabit, as folks are wont to do.

The procedure of positing names in the tree of dyads is the same as before when we were putting terms into the triad – a new face and form arises with every new name we put to represent it as a whole and the particular terms in each column together articulate a particular train of thought based on the constitution of meanings they implicate. But now we are seeking to develop our insight into the inaugural relationship of negativity, the initial "paradox" that is the experience of the *excellence* (ex-cellere) of pure reason in its diversity as *stepping out*, and then being *out-standing* in the exilic sense of standing outside of the abysmal cavity of unthinking complacency, outside of our everyday life become oppressive routine, outside of ourselves as actors to the audience of mere – merely living – being and looking in from this perspective of distinction that knows itself in that original deed of all languages – blazing the mind's mark of cognizance – as having put that glabrous and undifferentiated world of our oceanic infancy, whatever specific form it has acquired or has been given by language, behind it. We can outline the well-known Platonic take on this relationship in the differential between the *Inside* – the cave of the spectators' self-absorbed and immobile life of oblivion – providing the first of several congenial ***Terms of Immediacy (I)*** and the *Outside* – the light of perception and realization of self-knowledge – suggesting appropriate ***Terms of Distinction (II)*** in the following catalogue of familiar metaphysical distinctions, *Table 2*:[43]

Terms of Distinction (II)	Terms of Continuity (I)
Outside	Inside
Light	Darkness
Liberty	Imprisonment
Unfettered	Fettered
Reality	Illusion
Soul	Body
Divine	Human
Rational	Sensible
Form	Material

Table 2: The Differential of Cognizance

In *Table 2*, which will be further extended in just a moment, the pairs of terms represent the two divergent sides of the relationship that is one of *transition* – the movement from the one side of the relationship to the other, from the inside to the outside of the cave. All of these dyads represent the same binary relationship, the activity we have called *the distinction of human being* with respect to pure reason. And it is clear that, given this table, we are now able to invent pairs of terms that go beyond the details of Plato's famous allegory. We need only insert a name into one of the two

---

[43] cf. the terms discussed by Ch. Perelman and L. Olbrechts-Tyteca related to the argumentative procedure of Dissociation of Concepts in *The New Rhetoric*, pp. 411-459.

columns and then its "counterpart" or "correspondent" into the other; inserting for example into the column of *Terms of Immediacy (I)* the name EARTH, we can then represent this relationship by inserting the corresponding term SKY or HEAVEN into the column of *Terms of Distinction (II)*. Which pair we use in a particular communication situation depends on the circumstances and the factors determining that performance. But also on our own perception. By using this table of divergence, we will be able to better recognize the distinction of human being as it presents itself in great diversity as a given reality to be grasped, understood by our intelligence and our perspicacity. Moreover according to the different pairs considered, we will be able to name, and therefore represent, the transition in different ways. For that is what these different pairs have in common when we read them vertically, metaphorically and think of further names for the distinction of human being, which is what is being rendered horizontally, metonymically by each pair of terms. The terms TRANSITION or simply CHANGE are perhaps too general to be effective for some audiences to name this making of a distinction – the relationship as a whole – at a particular moment in a particular train of thought. But how about the terms LEARNING or EDUCATION – they suggest a pair like:

INSIGHT – IGNORANCE

Or the term INNOVATION which suggests the pair:

NEW – OLD

And if we posit the term JOURNEY for the transition, we could imagine the corresponding pair of terms marking the deviation in question to be perhaps:

ABROAD – HOME

Or simply:

STRANGE – FAMILIAR

In Sinatra's *New York, New York* for example, we see this relationship depicted in the terms:

NEW YORK – LITTLE TOWN BLUES

And the transition variously described as *leaving* town, as vagabond shoes *longing to stray* and as little town blues *melting away*, invites us to extend our suite of figures of distinction: INNOVATING, LEARNING, LEAVING, STRAYING, MELTING – is it not fascinating to consider the enrichment that this relationship, more specifically, our experience of this relationship, attains in the illustration of it made thus discernible by the lyrics of this song. Who would have imagined that these terms are connected! In what flight of fancy could *learning* and *melting* and *straying* be synonyms – words with different senses but the same meaning? There is the notion of leaving the habits, the familiar environment, the safety and the comfort of home and undertaking a venture and adventure, melting the rigid and restricted perspective of sleepy parochial and provincial life for the sake of the newness and the bigness and the sleeplessness (needing sleep, being asleep is a fine and familiar image to indicate the finitude of adumbrated human being) of New York. In the context of this representation, straying from the straits of the straight and the narrow-minded confines of small town custom and the orthodoxy of convention transforms the word STRAY, which normally has a negative connotation, into a *Term of Distinction* and acclaim whereas the *straight* and the *narrow*, with their usual associations of rectitude, morality, custom, tradition, and convention, normally all terms of approbation, take on, as *Terms of Immediacy*, a pejorative sense.

This reveals an important property of names. It is hardly conceivable that a word, irrespective of the circumstances of the speech situation, could permanently and universally be committed to employment solely as a term of immediacy or as a term of distinction. Depending on the way it is read or received by a particular audience or intention or on the context provided by the other terms with which it is connected, one and the same term can be used at one time as a term of distinction in celebration of the difference that pure reason makes in our lives while at another as a term of immediacy condemning the mentality of partiality so resistant to the urgings of objectivity and the big picture.

Consider as a further example of this "shifting" of signifiers the differential:

DAY – NIGHT

In keeping with Plato's allegory, we might consider the pair to be properly posited in this order, with the term DAY naming the perspective of distinction outside of the cave and NIGHT being the opposite. But perhaps there is a way of understanding these words that would allow us to reverse their order in the Tree of Duality. If DAY were to represent our "everyday" unreflected life, then NIGHT would be meant as the image of thoughtfulness, as that which is not the obvious and the superficial perspective of what is apparent to a gaping eye in the specious light of day. NIGHT is then the term of distinction referring to the perspicacity which sees behind the scenes, reads intelligently between the lines (the etymological sense of this word from the Latin *intel-legere*) and perceives the heart of the matter which is not floating on the surface but rather profound, hidden, unseen, and therefore dark, darkness to the *normal* eye and penetrable only to the discerning, *distinguished* one, which is that of reason and its insight, a sight that peers in and inward, down and downward in contradistinction to the glance of superficial skimming and the tossing outward of attention into the glare of the parading daylight world in the garb of deceptive appearance. Indeed, have not philosophers taught for centuries that reflection is, in fact, a turning of the mind inwardly? Where else might "truth" be said to reside if not "within?"

An analogous argument of displacement could be made for the use of the terms LIFE and DEATH. If the term *life* is taken as a token of distinction and *death* as the term of immediacy as it conventionally is, then *death* names the dungeon realm of doorless, widowless closure in its resistance to the overture of a more panoramic perspective, that to which such terms as light, sight, movement, growth, and joy traditionally refer to. *Seeing the light of day* – is that not the very definition of life? Divergent attributes delineate the netherworld inhabited by shades in their blindness, a hoard of that which is irrevocably lost, utterly closed and inaccessible to the empathy of human kindness; the dead have left us, turned away – theirs is the cast of decease, an impassive face of inexorable and relentless stone, inscrutable – all striking and terrifying intuitions of the stagnation and recalcitrance of those living in the realm of the dead and the walking dead in the realm of the living, the latter who would fear (if they could in fact feel anything, which they can't) the light for the darkness it brings to controversial light, the former who fear the dark for the secret of self-estrangement that it keeps locked away – hoping to avoid the confrontation and the challenge, that bite of distinction, that these demons haunting them lay defiantly before them, they prefer to endure the uneasy obscurity of habituation and suppression that might pass for peace and shy away from the clarity of a decisive and resolving encounter – "no," they say, stone-hard, bullet-proof, "I'm criticized but all your bullets ricochet; you shoot me down but I won't fall, I am titanium."

Contrariwise, just as a DAY can be taken one way or the other, so also LIFE. For everyday life might be seen as an exercise in distraction, a rushing and a bustling, a hassling and a tussling, a wheeling and a dealing; what with deadlines to meet, places to go, people to see, who has time to sit for a minute, let alone have a drink of think? In light of all this teeming and swarming, this multitude and variety, the spectre of reflection, inward turning can only be the embracing of *darkness* to the garish-minded leer, *silence* to the noise-numb skulls, *emptiness* to the stuff-stuffed crowds, and, on the hole, *death* to a busy life on the fast lane of main street.

Table 3 presents the "heterotopia" of pure reason as a Tree of Porphyry with an anthology of familiar terms taken at random from a variety of speech performances and discourses but mostly from the renowned canon of philosophical and poetic works belonging to the traditional European culture of wisdom the language of which we will study more closely after having clarified the logotectonic method of our investigation. This table characterizes certain expressions as *Terms of Distinction (II)* and pairs them with others held to be *Terms of Immediacy (I)*, in accordance with the way these terms have been traditionally employed to make a distinction and are often still used today. In fact, as we have seen, each term is *the other of the other* and can, in a certain context or for a particular audience designate the crested term.[44]

Terms of Distinction (II)	Terms of Immediacy (I)
Day/Sun/Light	Night/Darkness/Shadow
Awake	Asleep/Dreaming
Seeing/Sight	Blindness
Spring/Morning/Birth/Youth/Life/Health	Winter/Evening/Death/Old Age/Sickness
Unity	Multiplicity
Form	Material
Soul	Body
Spirit	Soul
Being	Appearance
Essence	Being
Quintessence	Essence

---

[44] cf. the terms discussed by D. Chandler, *Semiotics for Beginners*, p. 97.

Rational/Intangible/Ideal/Infinite	Sensible/Tangible/Real/Finite
Pure Reason	Understanding/Common Sense
Common Sense/General/Public/ Universal/Whole	Particular/Individual/Private/Part
Spirit	Letter
Emotional	Rational
Inside	Outside
Outdoor	Indoor
Open	Closed
Substance/Necessity/Immutability	Accidence/Contingency/Change
End	Means
Absolute	Relative
Objective	Subjective
Practice/Concrete/Movement/ Becoming/Mortality	Theory/Abstract/Immobility/ Immortality
Person	Act
Knowledge/Truth	Opinion
Faith	Knowledge
Religion	Superstition
Eternity	Duration
Imagination	Understanding
Content	Form
Letter	Interpretation
Name	Thing
Original	Copy

We	Me
Us	Them
Individual/Autonomy	Social/Heteronomy
General Will of the Community	Egoism of the Individual
Absolute	Relative
Supernatural	Natural
Extraterrestrial/Heaven/Above	Terrestrial/Earth/Below
Seventh Heaven	Heaven
Nature/Rural	Culture/Urban
Extraordinary/Unconventional	Ordinary/Normal/Conventional
Old/Mature	Young/Immature
Young/Dynamic	Old/Inflexible
Democratic/Progressive	Republican/Antiquated
Republican/Self-reliant	Democratic/Bleeding-heart
Traditional/Classical	Fashionable/Contemporary
Shem/Rebel/Interior/Wild/Intuition/Penman/Fire	Shaun/Authority/Exterior/Prudent/Postman/Ice
Chthonic	Intellectual
Settled	Vagrant
Peace	War
Change	Stagnation

Table 3: Crested Terms of Cognizance

Each pair of terms shows the transition of thought, the practice of reason that prescinds human being from the immemorial immediacy of its lived experience and the corresponding fluidity of its current world. As was the case with the triads we discussed earlier, the dyads of distinction are analogies in that they, each in their own way, exhibit the same relationship, the same ΛΟΓΟΣ, and thus, by presenting variations of it as the theme, contribute to our more profound experience of the effect of thought on human being, an experience, that has been impressed upon minds with earth-shattering and life-renewing effect for centuries.[45]

61. The Dialectic of Terms

A perusal of the terms in this greatly abbreviated tree of Porphyry beyond all ontology – for who could bring this catalogue of terms to completion or name the genera and species of its ramification – reveals that they are not only verbs and nouns but also adverbs, adjectives and even prepositions as well as personal pronouns. All the parts of speech and word classes can serve as names in the tree to represent the *journey* of distinction, the *flight* of thought, the *leap* of faith and insight; and these terms *journey – flight – leap*, no less than any others are susceptible to receiving the mark of cognizance; or are there no situations in which *staying put*, being *down-to-earth*, or keeping *one's feet on the ground* are not the terms of distinction indicating that sometimes it is better not just to do something but to stand there?

All of these names for the two sides of the thought's medallion, as well as for the transition of distinction itself, help us to better understand what it

---

[45] While analyzing "Antigone," George Steiner writes: "It has, I believe, been given to only one literary text to express all the principal constants of conflict in the condition of man. These constants are fivefold: the confrontation of men and of women; of age and of youth; of society and of the individual; of the living and the dead; of men and of god(s). The conflicts which come of these five orders of confrontation are not negotiable. Men and women, old and young, the individual and the community or state, the quick and the dead, mortals and immortals, define themselves in the conflictual process of defining each other. Self-definition and the agonistic recognition of 'otherness' (of *l'autre*) across the threatened boundaries of self, are indissociable. The polarities of masculinity and of femininity, of ageing and of youth, of private autonomy and of social collectivity, of existence and mortality, of the human and the divine, can be crystallized only in adversative terms (whatever the many shades of accommodation between them). To arrive at oneself – the primordial journey – is to come up, polemically, against 'the other'. The boundary-conditions of the human person are those set by gender, by age, by community, by the cut between life and death, and by the potentials of accepted or denied encounter between the existential and the transcendent." *Antigones*, pp. 231-232. Clearly, the distinction of human being, which is here at issue, is one *and* several, but not just five.

means to think, are a recognition of the prevalence of the distinction of human being in our particular lives, and above all, reveal an appreciation of the significance of that experience. This appreciation is part of the culture of reason, the culture of its self-knowledge, the labour of love that is the self-respect at the heart of every rational being who has learned to recognize its true self and abide by it as its identity that is made manifest in a moment's reflection. All of these words have been taken out of the context of communication in which they played a role as intended by the participants of the speech performance. Is it necessary to emphasize that "New York" is the name of a particular city but that as an expression in the lyrics of a song it can be taken by thought, the Builder, as a crested term for critical reflection as well and thus borrowed for this purpose, which surely is a good cause, perhaps even the greatest cause? For what could be a more worthwhile employment of our language and its resources than to serve as an instrument of insight and of invention for the building of trains of thought that give illustrious shape and form, a striking presence to ideas and especially to pure reason itself, which is a system of three ideas, as we have been proposing.

Even such terms as MAN and WOMAN can be and have been, albeit, at least in post/modern discourse, subversively employed, to render the experience of drawing the inaugural distinction of reason in vivid terms familiar to all. In the first case *man* is the immediate term in the sense of *utilitarian technological rationality* whereas *woman* refers to the emotional intelligence of empathy, in other words *feeling*, surpassing the nice but cold *calculations* of man's one-track mind with her *intuition*. This rendition of the relationship is familiar in the duality:

EMOTIONAL – RATIONAL

Inversely (and more traditionally), we might posit *man* as the crested term for even-handed objectivity and dispassionate analysis as opposed to the affected sentimentality that accompanies knee-jerk and tear-jerk softheartedness, frailty, and irresolution subsumed under the term *woman*, a relationship that is often delineated in the pair:

OBJECTIVE – SUBJECTIVE

Everybody is acquainted with these stereotypes of the MAN crunching and the WOMAN gushing. Much less familiar is the surprising fact that, as we see, in the horizon of language, *man* and *woman* need not be employed in connection with sexual difference as a biological category at all; more precisely, these terms and the notion of sexual difference are a way of speaking about the *difference*, the *differential* that alone pure reason makes in relation to the non-gender specific extremism of an uncritical stance. Both terms MAN and WOMAN as well as the wide field of connotations and associations they imply can be used and abused with a view to rendering that stance critically evident or else to establish an ideology and flesh out its persuasion ontologically by couching a discourse about the difference that alone pure reason makes, in sexist, ultimately, in racist terms. This is the mechanism *par excellence* of the perversion of reason and it is very much worthy of a study in its own right.

Even the terms like BODY or SPIRIT can be used in a, for us these days, counter-intuitive sense – the ***BODY*** referring to ***NATURAL SENSE*** and SPIRIT referring to that of ARTIFICIAL SOPHISTICATION. While ANIMAL is traditionally a term for immediacy, it can be perceived as the wild's fleet-footed flight or fight, the lean and hungry look of the ***WILDERNESS*** beyond what has become domesticated, luxurious and corrupt, lugubrious and slovenly, all too HUMAN in decadent CIVILIZATION – another commonplace.

A more comprehensive tree of ***CRESTED***/UNCRESTED terms would indicate explicitly how these two value systems oppose each other by articulating the dialectic of values and show, moreover, how each value system defines the other in terms of its own system of values as an aberration. It is as if a proponent of one language and the culture it founds, living, as it were, on one side of the table, which represents a self-several linguistic world, would categorize the other, seeing the latter's advantage as a negation of its own. In this case the pejorative term is used to assign the other side of this relationship to the category of immediacy while highlighting the positive character of the first side in contradistinction to it – if the ***LIGHT*** of ***DAY***, for example, is termed by its detractors GLARE for being loud with shallow seeming, then for its advocates NIGHT is the ***SILENT HEART***, ***DARK*** and ***DEEP*** rather than the hideous hiding of CONCEALMENT and OBFUSCATION, as the day lovers would assert. What the classical person calls ***STABILITY*** the modern calls STAGNATION whereas what the ***MODERN*** mind praises as ***CONCRETE*** or ***TANGIBLE***, the ***CLASSICAL*** orientation condemns as quotidian EPHEMERALITY and VULGARITY in contradistinction to what is ***ETERNAL***, ***PERFECT***, ***ELEGANT***, and ***EXCLUSIVE***. The former champions the ***BODY***'s ***SENSE*** against the immaterial NON-SENSE of the MIND while the latter celebrates the ***SPIRIT***'s ***FLIGHT*** and deplores the GRAVE CADAVER's FALL to base matter.

In general and from a linguistic point of view, this table of differentials or dialectical divergencies, this forked tree of disparity, refers to the effort of a speaker or a writer to posit one term as immediate and indistinct, the norm and canonical form, the lemma, and then upon it to mark or inflect the distinction that makes all the difference; clearly, as the linguist would add, the inflection referred to here is not merely, and far from usually, morphological – e.g.: **Super**natural as opposed to *Natural*, **Nether-** *and* **Other**worldly to *Worldly*, **Extra**terrestrial to *Terrestrial or In*finite to *Finite* – all prepositions and therefore all prefixes offer spatial metaphors for marking distinctions relative to a fixed point of reference, the indeterminate origin O, Ø, ❻ of immediacy. Every persuasive communication must mark certain terms as distinguished from others left unmarked and taken to indicate the neutral term and code of status quo, the material upon which then a distinction is made and a message wrought – for a message, if it is significant, makes a distinction; precisely this dissociation of terms is the work of innovation, growth, learning – the emergence of a new insight that must be coeval with conviction. Here are some familiar differences between the **unmarked** (the dominant norm as taken for granted) and the **marked,** the crested, terms (the deviation from domination in drawing a distinction). Which term is marked and which is unmarked ultimately depends on the audience, the speaker, the context, and the argument. Referring to this concept of markedness in a letter to a linguist colleague, Jakobson writes:

> "It seems to me that it has a significance not only for linguistics but also for ethnology and the history of culture, and that such historico-cultural correlations as *life – death, liberty – non-liberty, sin – virtue, holidays – working days*, and so on are always confined to relations a – non-a and that it is important to find out for any epoch, group, nation, etc. what the marked element is. I am convinced that many ethnographic phenomena, ideologies, etc. which at first glance seem to be identical often differ only in the fact that what for one system is a marked term

may be evaluated by the other precisely as the absence of a
mark." (Jakobson, On Language, p. 136) [46]

Thus, for example, taking the *YES* and the *NO* as terms, we might posit
affirmation as the standard steady-state against which negation revolts, the
NO taking vociferous exception to what the YES has given its tacit assent. In
this case compliance is simply assumed until an objection is raised after
which the endorsement is then made explicit. And this is the converse state
of affairs. Namely when the assumption is that permission has to be granted
against a background of unspoken prohibition or at least non-acceptance.
Now the NO is the immediate term and the *YES* is sanctioned as the
authorization of what needs to be given the go-ahead. Is the green-light the
exception or the rule? Does red interrupt the green as the crested term of
cognizance or vice versa? Regardless of how it is construed, this interruption
names the distinction that has been drawn in the previously unmarked
space, a break in the flow, in this case that of traffic.

Further, consider the OPEN and the CLOSED, namely the marvel of what
gives entrance and egress, the refreshing candor of *OPEN*-mindedness
against the prevalence of what hinders commerce and interaction to the
extent that hospitality and accessibility are hardly ever seen; then again the
exposure of what has been uncovered, the vulnerability as well as
indeterminacy of what has been left *open* and thus as yet undecided,
susceptible to importunity while tending towards pliancy and indulgence
indicates the negative correlative of the aforementioned obstinacy such
that the converse relationship obtains according to which being *CLOSED* is
the device of distinction. Therefore if the doors are closed to all except the
select few who have the key, then these are so privileged by this distinction;
on the other hand, a truth (or a country club) that has become accessible to
all, a secret that has been divulged, loses with its exclusivity its significance
and power to differentiate among the many and the choice few. For then it
is not what is overt and apparent that is distinctive but rather what is
hidden, more of a challenge for being less obvious, a treasure rarer for being
buried, for being sought first and then found, while the innocence of

---

[46] cf. Jakobson's discussion of the Concept of Mark, *On Language*, pp. 134-140.
Specifically, "the general meaning of the marked [term] is characterized by the
conveyance of more precise, specific, and additional information than the
unmarked term provides...The constraining, focusing character of the marked term
of any grammatical opposition is directed toward a more narrowly specified and
delimited conceptual item." (p. 138).

ignorance stands before an open gate awaiting an invitation to enter that may never come, until the last day, the last moment of its life, when, even as the lights of its eyes extinguish in death, it learns that those gates that had been its destiny all along to pass through will now be closed and locked forever.

Further take being WET opposed to being DRY. Surely being DRY is the state of comfort with that of getting ***DRENCHED*** the one we try to avoid with our pitiful contrivances against the elements, umbrellas and Mackintoshes and Wellingtons; in this case the latter state confounds our desires and expectations in the form of a storm that takes us by soggy surprise, remaining or else getting ***DRY*** being then the much more challenging enterprise than remaining of getting WET unless, of course, you are a dolphin who has been removed from its element and for whom, therefore, becoming dry is the danger or for somebody lost in a desert where ***WATER*** is scarce and therefore precious in the wilderness of shifting sands. Indeed, Heraclitus would argue that the dry and sober soul, being rare among our kind (B 118) with our unfortunate proclivity for squishy wishy-washiness and the sloppy-soppy sensitivities of the drunken demon's death-wish (B 77), is the marked term; a weltering and tongue-lolling drip of a man wallowing in the gulf needs to be hung out to dry if damp, muggy men are widespread and the shrewd soul keen of being and terse of word is less often heard.

Further, with the qualities of HOT and COLD, the tendency towards mediocrity, a reduction of difference, suggests that absolute COLDNESS is the ultimate standard and the status quo of indifference while ***WARMTH*** is what wants an explanation and a reason; similarly negligence and the entropy of everyday life makes ***ORDER*** stand out against a background of CHAOS, ***BIRTH*** and more generally ***LIFE*** against the elemental ACTION and REACTION of MINERAL being, DEATH a reversion to the dominion of chemistry. And what is wholesomely ***CLEAN*** against what is moribundly DIRTY? But these familiar relationships should not prevent our acknowledgement of their converse sense, namely that ***CHAOS*** is the term of distinction in a TOTALITARIAN universe, ***DEATH*** the crested name for the liberation from a birth into and a LIFE of slavery and ***DIRTY*** the grit of heart against the baby-face of a man slicked up spic-'n'-span, handy-dandy, ground down, whipped and wiped cleanliness of CLEAN, and the corresponding HEAT that accrues to the hausfrau's war against dust and germs and her hubby's ring around the collar who therefore is always tense and trying, breaking a zealous sweat, the opposite of what it means to be ***COOL***, the crested term in this familiar case when being FIRED up is for beginners and for SQUARES, though the *SQUARE* and *WARMTH* are themselves the terms of cognizance when placed against a background of proverbial ICE that girds the pawnbroker's heart and wants breaking for every new acquaintance and when neat blocks are more practical for mending walls than the generic OVOID boulder ground down by a million grubby fingers of time.

Further, *UP* is *GREAT* and DOWN is LOW till being *SUB* is *SUPER* compared to the monotony and superficiality of the level that has razed all richness; and the *LEVEL* head beats the SCATTERBRAIN any day. That is why, when not set against themselves, both *HYPER* and *HYPO* mark the difference in the plane, *EXTRA* and *INTRA* in space, *BEFORE* and *AFTER* in time, and every other preposition with respect to the reference point and the coordinate origin indicating the indeterminate null and void and NOWHERE so that every other point, with respect to it, (thanks to it?), is able to be determined as *SOMEWHERE*; but consider now Plotin's utterly utter lord, "because aught was in Him therefore is all without Him and, so that being may be, He is, therefore, himself naught, though its progenitor. (Plotin V, 2, 1, 5). In this case *O*, **Ѳ**, *Ø*, though *NOTHING* in and of themselves, carry the distinction of the *SIRE* and their nullity is the greater "being," being both less *and* greater than the 1, which is the CHILD and the effect, the most proximate being being, in comparison to that CAUSE, the actual nought; but against the empty background of O, *1* is the mark of distinction and the *BEING* that alleviates the tedium of Nothing which is thus merely useless, lacking the EFFECT of fact which, in turn, takes precedence over the ideologies of a cause. Thus even *INDIFFERENCE*, the *neither-nor* of *NEUTRALITY* when set against the violent one-sidedness of PARTIALTY rises unexpectedly to the prominence of distinction, as does *INTERRUPTION*, *DIVISION*, and *PLURAL IMPOSSIBLITY* against the interminable MONOTONY of MONODIC ATOMIC Man's power politics of the POSSIBLE.

Further, in our coach-potato world, the great *OUTDOORS* are the exception to the INDOOR rule and challenge us to take the air and live, though against the elemental forces that abound, we are only *INDOORS* safe and sound. *MINE* is first and YOURS comes after, an afterthought – thus speaks the egoist; unless, of course, I am in love for then *YOU*, my heart, are all to ME, your pining appendage. And hasn't Columbo shown us that the *AFTERTHOUGHT* is the key to foiling PREMEDIATED murder.

Further, the animal world is only occasionally *HUMAN*, which is the exception to the rule of animated beings, but the *NATURAL* simplicity of the animal beats the ARTIFICIALITY of man even as *LIFE* is the anomaly in a mineral material world, and the stuff of *STARS*, their gems, transcend eternally the myriad EARTH crawlers of so little life, short seasoned, and doomed purpose of survival. But sometimes the down-to-*EARTH* pragmatist is just what we need to solve a problem unkown in the empire of the DREAMER, whose world however, should we elect to join it, transcends the limitations of REALITY in the name of the power of the *IMAGINATION* with regards to which, though dreaming, we might dream as one.

Further, the *QUESTION* makes an issue of what had been taken for granted as the obvious and only ANSWER, ruining our INNOCENCE with *KNOWLEDGE* and leaving us the *SADDER* and the *WISER*, robbed of the BLISS of IGNORANCE, though we might all agree that to *KNOW* is *JOY DIVINE* beyond all HUMAN HAPPINESS. Nevertheless when SCIENCE has become the academic vanity of CIVILIZATION then *NESCIENCE* is *NATURE*'s cure of a CULTURE of SOPHISTICATION and *MORALITY* of the *PURE HEART*'s *VIRTUE*, the *CHILD'S*, the only true distinction of human being become depraved ADULTS by REASON's subservience to our VICE and to that end our easiest tool.

Further, the *FORCE of AUTHORITY* tames the savage BEAST or is it much more music's *BEAUTY* (or perhaps Anne Darrow's) that killed WILD AUTONOMOUS PURITY by sparking the fire of *DESIRE* and that *HETERONOMOUS HUNGER*, that unfulfilled *LOVE* that teaches BRUTISH SATISFACTION a new tune, namely "I can't git no...", which is the *REBEL*'s and the *ARTIST*'s *ANARCHY* overthrowing, with a poet's *PEN* and a musician's *ROCK* and *ROLL*, the ROD, the STAFF and the SWORD of GOVERNMENT in STEADY-STATE oppression and FLAT-OUT corruption.

Further, some say that a single *DREAM* is more powerful than a thousand REALITIES, others that *FACT* beats FICTION any day of the week because the former is *TRUTH* and the latter LIES both views pitting thought against thought, the IMAGINATION against the INTELLECT, INVENTION against PERCEPTION, the POET against the SEER and SCIENTIST and similarly that while *KNOWLEDGE* beats OPINION the former's shortcomings are nevertheless brought out in contrast to *FAITH*.

Further, how about when being negative is positive and positive negative, when being *CRUEL* is kind and KIND is cruel when the *FROWN* of criticism uplifts and the SMILE of flattery puts down, when GAIN is a loss and *LOSS* a gain, though not, perhaps, immediately? How about when GOOD is very, very good and *BAD* is even better, when the minor and the *MINORITY* outstrip the MAJORITY'S mass by being *RIGHT* against all odds and numbers where **MAJORITY** rules and not the LOBBY'S EXCEPTION, and a single critical **INDIVIDUAL** is enough to topple a GROUP think's house of cards.

The point is that each of the designations set in the relationship of disparity represented by a particular dyad can serve either as a term of distinction or as a term of immediacy depending on how the designation is construed; there are traditional oppositions, for example **UP** before DOWN, with the former term drawing the distinction upon the immediate state of affairs designated by the latter. Along these lines we are all familiar with the **SUPERIORITY** and **STRENGTH** of what is **HIGH** compared to its opposing term LOW and the notions of WEAKNESS and INFERIORITY; and does not the **MOUNTAIN REIGN ABOVE** the VALLEY, which BOWS BENEATH in a SUBJECT's SUBORDINATION? But we have also made our acquaintance with the notion that the **MEEK** will inherit the EARTH, the GREAT shall be thrown down and the **WEAK** uplifted, the **ILL** cured and **SERVICE** highlighted as the ascendency to a **KINGDOM OF HEAVEN** lays the HIGHEST MOUNTAIN low. In this counter-intuitive order of the terms, HIGH is low and **LOW** is high, those possessing SIGHT are blind, the RICH are poor, the HAPPY are sad, the HEALTHY are ill such that the opposite designations, the **BLIND**, the **POOR**, the **SAD**, the **ILL** are the terms of distinction. Do not wisdom's holy writs and tongues of flame acquire their sacred fire precisely in that they seek to provoke thought by reversing long established distinctions become unthinking reflexes and institutions rather than the sparking fund and the fruit of critical reflection they originally were when first coined to make a difference? Yes, it is indeed remarkable how our minds tend to slide back into indifference until a new distinction arrives to renew the vim of reason! That is why, first off, **SMART** is, of course, better than STUPID, the former being the distinguished term, the latter the term of immediacy; and nevertheless, upon reflection, even such an apparently so unequivocal name as *stupid* can carry home the prize of distinction – after all, all you fellow smart alecks, have we not all heard, much to our chagrin, that smart may have the BRAINS but stupid has the **BALLS**?

In all of these figures, in these illustrations of the difference that thought makes, the distinction of the ΛΟΓΟΣ is refreshed again and again and made evident by reprising the relationship in question under different designations. What do all of the dyads have in common? What if not the dialectic negativity of thought and the differentiation that is its principle, for is not the efficacy of thought the message and the point...of thought? In any given distinction, it is the names that are new and therefore the hearer's (or reader's) experience of this distinction, and with their experience, the world that ensues in that experience, strikingly new, transformed through homologies, the one relationship of thought clothed in a fresh world of words and thus conceived by us, reborn in the significance of the difference that reflection makes upon immediacy – the manifestation of a new figure having come now to the fore against an otherwise undistinguished background of self-perpetuating, unintelligible, and impoverished continuity.

Each binary set may therefore be understood as a *code*; shall we call it "mythical" in honor of Lévi-Strauss who showed that "the mythical system and the representations it puts into effect serve to establish homologous relationships between natural and social conditions or, more precisely, to define a law of equivalence among significant contrasts set in different planes: geographical, meteorological, zoological, botanical, technical, economic, social, ritual, religious, and philosophical."

> Le système mythique et les représentations qu'il met en actual servent donc à établir des rapports d'homologie entre les conditions naturelles et les conditions sociales, ou, plus exactement, à définir une loi d'équivalence entre des contrastes significatifs qui se situent sur plusieurs plans: géographique, météorologique, zoologique, botanique, technique, économique, social, rituel, religieux et philosophique. (Lévi-Strauss, La Pensée Sauvage, p. 115.)

Similar patterns of term reversal, some even linked together into a complete system forming the heterotopia of the self-relationship of thought can be found in the European tradition of pure reason. Heraclitus, for example, in the first Epoch, illustrates the self-returning circle of the ΛΟΓΟΣ in the exchange of ΕΝ ΚΑΙ ΠΑΝ (one and all) – how the one branches out to the all and the all unifies itself to the one (B 50); arguing for this relationship in aphorisms such as "the way up is the way down," (B 60), the consumption of fire is its greater production, "feeding itself through its depletion," (B 65), "the immortals and the mortals living each other's death, each other's life dying" (B 62) and in the progression of the four natural elements in their relationship to one another – "fire being the death of earth; air the death of fire, water the death of air, and earth the death of water." (B 76 and B 36)

Each term is both a term of immediacy and a term of distinction in the flowing totality (ΠΑΝΤΑ ΡΕΙ - 65 A 3) and "preposterous" progression of final departure and eternal return, the circle of self-reflection in possession of the beginning and the end in common (B 103), the illustrious sweep of which is the shibboleth of the mind, our quintessential ouroboros of pure reason, namely *thought thinking thought*, here incarnated as the elementary quaternity of *Table 4*:

Terms of distinction (II)	Terms of Immediacy (I)
Fire	Earth
Air	Fire
Water	Air
Earth	Water

Table 4: Reciprocal Justice of the Elements

Or, less philosophically, in *Table 5*, take the hand game *rock-paper-scissors* in which each term is both victor and vanquished and none only one or the other.

Terms of distinction (II)	Terms of Immediacy (I)
Rock	*Scissors*
Paper	*Rock*
Scissors	Paper

Table 5: The Play of Distinctions

III. The Logotectonic of Pure Reason

62. The Mediation of Inference

The craft and art of thought, the Builder, begins by putting names for ΛΟΓΟΣ, the distinction of human being. And prior to positing names into a train of thought, designations must be selected from a fund of terms that former poetic inventions of pure reason have made available and notable and that were, no doubt, for a particular audience at a particular point in time, considered felicitous, more or less suitable to the speaker's purpose and in accordance with the constraints placed on the speech performance by the particulars of the issue at stake.

The terminology with which we build are, for the most part, those taken from prior works of conception in a tradition of poetico-philosophical thought going all the way back to Homer, a tradition that is based not, as is often assumed, on continuity and the convention of notable and divergent opinions regarding a shared or common and as yet unresolved philosophical "problem" but rather on crises to the extent that the epochs of European reason were always thought as distinguished *in principle*, even unto contradiction, from each other, such that the precursor is overthrown by the successor in the latest Copernican revolution. These epochal upheavals of principle are therefore not only a matter of getting historical facts straight regarding authors' birthdays and the chronology of their writings but also a record of the accomplishments of thought in which a distinction was made, a new idea grasped regarding the *destiny of human being* – every point, every conceit, every quibble that a thinker ever came up with to torment his or her pupil can be set in the larger framework of this issue. To draw a distinction *in principle* is to mark a transition and it is this transition that we now turn to in exploring what precisely we mean by a *train of thought* and *a line of reasoning*, namely a series of terms in which one follows upon the next, beginning with the inaugural term across the mediate one, and concluding upon that of the resultant. The table of triads we have previously considered while indicating in a vertical reading the paradigm of analogous names in each column and reiterating the homology of the relationships, reveals little of the properties and less of the efficacy of the logic, the syntax, governing the position of these terms within the triad when read horizontally.

For, in fact, seen and read along these lines, the terms mark the development of a logical inference across a term of mediation through which the conclusion is drawn as a consequence of how the middle term connects the two opposite terms in the triad by virtue of the unique property it possesses to be opposite to both opposing terms and as such not only different from but also the same as itself. How could anything have such a decidedly human property?

Consider the tale of the pea, the pan, and the pot rendered schematically in *Figure 35*. The pot (A) has the property of being able to contain something in it, whatever it is you want to cook. The pea (B) by contrast, as something that can be cooked, has the property of being contained. Now just as the pot cannot be contained in anything, is not cooked, which is the fate of the pea, so also the pea cannot contain anything – since you cannot cook anything in a pea, which is the office of the pot and therefore, by definition, never the twain shall meet. Never, that is, unless there is such an improbable being that is on the one hand "pea-like" in that it can be contained and therefore "be cooked" like a pea, though not a pea; and on the other hand, pot-like in that in can contain and be used for cooking like a pot, though not a pot. It would seem to possess both features in one and the same being and this is the character of the pan (C), the mediating, self-several term.

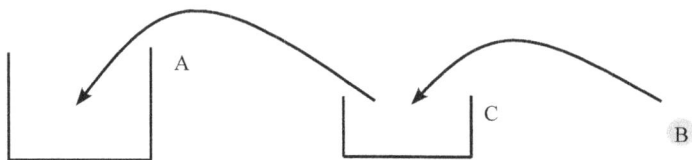

Figure 35: The Tale of the Pea, the Pot, and the Pan

Thus for example taking the triad General *(A) – Specific (C) – Individual (B)*, we note that the *general* term is such that it contains the subaltern terms, namely both the *specific* and the *individual* but, as the **universal** term, it is not contained in any other term; by contrast, the individual term is contained within both the specific and the general term but it does not contain any term, being the **particular** term. The universal and the particular are infinitely divergent terms, in other words, each is distinguished with respect to the other and together mark a discontinuity, each being the other's other with respect to which it is a term of distinction. In contrast, the **specific** term has the property of being particular with respect to the universal term and universal with respect to the particular term and as such is both particular and universal at the same time and thus, mediating the other two terms, it is, in itself, the locus of their immediacy and their discontinuity, in itself other than or divergent from itself or, as we have been calling it, self-several. It is only in and through the middle term that the two limits enter into this relationship of reciprocity, touching each other in the mediating term that "bridges" the gap of infinite difference between the individual and the general, not in the sense that it plugs a hole or kits a crack, or fills in the space dividing them but rather that it enacts their incommensurability in the practice of differentiation that drives thought's persevering endeavor of realization and, before that, envisions a project towards which a work of transformation resolutely strives and, before that, reluctantly receives the unexpected charge of determination – whether as duty, as vocation, as necessity, or simply as a need – that upsets and unsettles everything by putting events, high designs, and deep, inductions dangerous, of great import, into motion and initiating thus the change that is destined to become the development of something new, something that is, with regards to that inaugural state of need, something better, something that, therefore is, henceforth, in perpetuity, to be.

Our experience of this practice, this restless eternal life, as it were, of pure reason is above all that of thought as a *mediating principle* – the distinctly human nature of self-severalty inherent in contradiction, the ordeal of critical reflection in the recursive process of resolving itself with regards to the entity of identity. This is a work of transition, more precisely, of passage and the transitive property it demonstrates has been known as the very principle of dialectic and logical deduction, namely thought's insight into the self-several law and necessity of reason, the immediate mediation of inference that drives forward its trains of thought and empowers purposeful accomplishment.

Already **Aristotle** described inference as a syllogism of three signature terms that exhibits this transitive property. Specifically he taught that "when three terms are related to each other in such a way that the last is entirely contained in the middle and the middle is...entirely contained....in the first then it is necessary that there is a perfect syllogism of the two extreme terms. I call a middle term that which is itself in another as well as having another in it and thus, in the order of terms, takes the middle position; the outer term that which either is itself in another term or has another term in it. Hence when A is said of every B and B of every C, it is necessary that A is said of every C."(Analytics 25b 32-39)

Taking C for the middle term, A and B for the two outer terms, the latter being the term that is itself in another and the former the term having another in it, in other words, that A is the Universal, B is the Particular, and C is the Mediate term, we propose the following illustration (*Figure 36*) that shows how we get the pea into the pot (B in A), namely by putting the pea into the pan (B in C) and then putting the pan containing the pea into the pot (C in A).

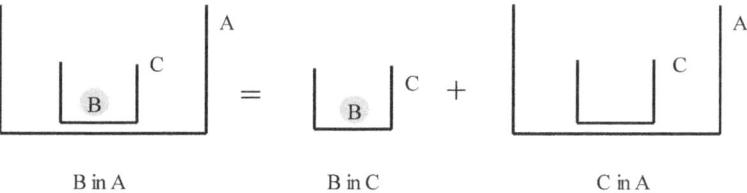

B in A   B in C   C in A

Figure 36: How to Put the Pea in the Pot

We feel compelled to admit that, given these relationships of predication depicted as the inherence of one term *in* another, the conclusion follows logically and of necessity by dint of reason alone. Reason has made itself known to reason in the process of reasoning, thought calling upon thought, like a voice from beyond, to assent to pure reason's call, willy-nilly.

In the Christian epoch of thought, we turn to **Thomas Aquinas'** *Summa Theologica* to learn how the transitive relationship of thought is conceived of as the procession of the Persons of the Trinity in the logic of their *sending* (missio). He elucidates how the two processions of the Persons in the Trinity are to be grasped as a relationship of three terms: "These processions are two only... one derived from the action of the intellect, the procession of the Word and the other from the action of the will, the procession of love. In respect of each of these processions, two opposite relations arise; one of which is the relation of the person proceeding from the principle; the other is the relation of the principle Himself. The procession of the Word is called generation in the proper sense of the term, whereby it is applied to living things. Now the relation of the principle of generation in perfect living beings is called paternity; and the relation of the one proceeding from the principle is called filiation. Though the procession of Love has no proper name of its own... nevertheless the relation of the principle of this procession is called spiration…[which is]…not separated from the person of the Father and of the Son, but belongs to both;…the three relations – paternity, filiation, and procession – are called personal properties, constituting, as it were, the persons; for paternity is the person of the Father, filiation is the person of the Son, procession is the person of the Holy Spirit proceeding." (*Summa Theologica,* I Questio 30. Art. 2)

We might present this relationship between the Father (A) as the principle, the Son (C) as engendered by the Father (A>C) and the Holy Spirit (B) proceeding from both the Son (C>B) and the Father (A>B), either as an equation, namely A>C + C>B = A>B or as a figure in *Figure 37.*

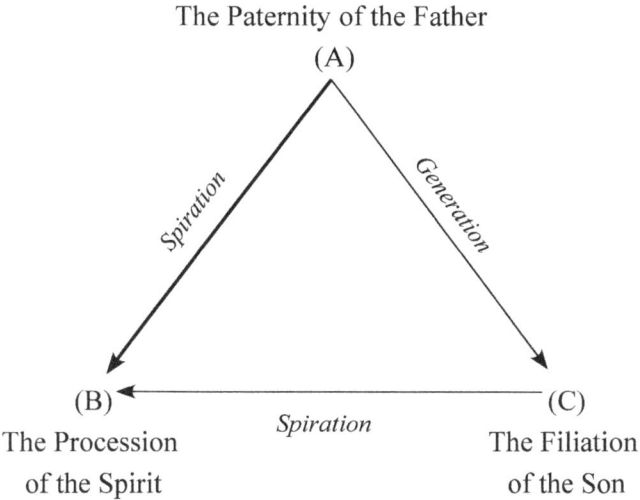

The Paternity of the Father
(A)

Spiration   *Generation*

(B) ←————— *Spiration* ————— (C)

The Procession   The Filiation
of the Spirit   of the Son

Figure 37: The Transitivity of the Persons

Figure 37 is an illustration of a transitive relationship depicting the sending of the Son as the mediating term of *discernment* (C), carrying out the determination that he received from the *principle* (A), his general, in the ordeal of incarnation, which is the life and death of the Son under the letter of the law to be fulfilled in the Holy Spirit of the law, the *issue* (B) and mission of love from both the Father and the Son.

In the final epoch, it is Hegel who, in the third part of his *Encyclopedia of Philosophical Sciences* (§577) elucidates the logic of the notion that human nature itself or *Humanity* is the distinction of human being the science of which develops a conception of Freedom as that of the "concrete Idea – eternally self-knowing thinking being that as Absolute Spirit eternally enacts itself, produces itself, enjoys itself."

> die ewige an und für sich seiende Idee sich ewig als absoluter Geist bestätigt, erzeugt und genießt. (Hegel, *Enzyklopädie der philosophischen Wissenschaften*, VIII. p. 394)

Hegel then goes on to demonstrate precisely how this spirit realizes its freedom, namely in the inference of reason mediating the experience of its own nature as a threefold deduction in which, first, "the *Logical Idea* grounds deduction as the inaugural term and posits *Nature* as the mediate term which is fulfilled in *Spirit* such that the Logical Idea is realized as

Nature and Nature as Spirit..." (§575 – ibid. p. 393) This leads to the second deduction which, "having attained the standpoint of *Spirit* that is now the mediating term, unites *Nature* as the prior determination with the resultant *Logical Idea.*" (394) Finally, concluding and completing this line of reasoning which is that of the *Logical Idea* in "the idea of Philosophy...;" the "...third deduction..." posits as "...the mediating term the self-knowing being of reason, i.e. the absolute General of the Logical Idea that distinguishes itself in *Spirit* and *Nature*, the former being, as the inaugural term, the life of the subjective activity of the idea, and the latter, the resultant, the life of the objective being of the Idea in and of itself." (394)

In this way every term is mediated by and mediates every other term in a triadic system of inferences, the train and training of thought which Hegel named the work and the movement of the Conceptual (der Begriff). This movement records thought's, the conceptual's, experience with thought, articulated as a series of terms in which *Absolute Spirit* (B) progresses step by step towards complete insight into and enjoyment of its own determinate and individual but no less absolute and general reality, which is that of its self-several *Nature* (C), and ultimately attaining to and achieving the certainty of its absolute freedom that is the self-relativity of thought thinking thought, our entity of identity or, as Hegel designates it, the Idea of ΛΟΓΟΣ, i.e. the *Logical Idea* (A). We recognize this relationship of relationships as a ratio of deductions, the activity of thought thinking about thought, i.e. Conceptualization, turning on the development of the self-knowing being that is the living, breathing Spirit (B) of pure reason, first in the resultant position of the deduction that demonstrates that it is in this distinguished individual that the logical Idea makes its first appearance – beyond all immediacy of its *natural* determination; then in the mediate position of the deduction through which the Spirit gains insight into Nature as that of the Idea, its absolute principle; and concluding as the inaugural position of the deduction that demonstrates how the idea has resolved itself into the charmed life of thought, the entity of identity that is both nature *and* spirit, the former being the reality of reason and the latter the rationality of reality – the two manifestations of the Logical Idea, the ΛΟΓΟΣ, which is therefore both one *and* several. Ultimately, both thinking (the Spiritual side of Conception) *and* being thought (the Natural side of Conception), the self-several identity of the abstract Logical Idea (A) realizes, in the course of the above series of deductions – which is actually a deduction consisting of three deductions or the conceptual *syllogism of syllogisms* – its own specific Nature (C) as the actual Spirit (B) of human being. This syllogism of syllogisms or *train of thought about thought* can be represented as in *Figure 38*.

$$A - C - \mathbf{B}$$
$$C - \mathbf{B} - A$$
$$\mathbf{B} - A - C$$

Figure 38: The Absolute Deduction of Spirit, Nature, and Idea

63. Building Ratios of Reasoning

One, two, three; A, B, C – in invention and perception, reason is logical *inference;* after having considered the metaphysics of Aristotle, Aquinas, and Hegel, this is what we have come to expect who wish to study thought systematically and endeavor to speak about its features, its accomplishments, intelligibly, supposing that there was and may yet be an *exact science* of pure reason that is nevertheless not physical or psychological, neither hard nor soft.

Whatever pure reason is, it can at least be accounted for as a movement of inference, involving a series of terms in a particular order, comprehending even a series of these series into a single system, a complete train of thought and a line of reasoning the progression of which depends on the order of the component terms, their *rhythm.* For the sake of this vital pulse of reasoning, celebratory diction has oftentimes assumed a vehement, exhilarating aspect in declaring that thought is pure activity "*naturally,*" (meaning "logically,") ordered, of original acts, deeds, and doings and, in this way, meditated, productive, or, yet more vividly put, that it is a *culture* not only in the way that the notion of spirit and the narratives of its artefacts and achievements are intelligible and enlightening inventions of the mind but also in the way that a living organism is, grows, blossoms in season, passes away into oblivion only to be reborn to parents destined to become its children as it matures through the tender loving care of their service.

When speaking of this lovely, this *charmed life* of thought however, we are, of course, speaking poetically, lustrously, about thought's particular turns, employing an illustrative figure to account for the entire movement and the constituent phases in which the nature of reasoning (*nature* – this expression also suggests organic connotations) can be delineated; but we could just as well use a different turn of word and speak of thought, as thinkers often have in the past, as having a history, more, of being a history that has developed in a distinguished *progression* (C) of accomplishments (the epochs, ages of this individual we call thought, or phases of its development) and thus in and as a heroic narrative, according to which the determining principle (A) was – whether the labor of love therein recounted endured a day or for all time – fulfilled in the end, despite the challenges set before discerning purpose, having achieved completion and resolved itself into the appropriate issue (B) that we may now, in turn, study as a dramatic whole – as an epic narrative that stirs our imagination and inspires us to put into our own celebratory words and heroic deeds what has so powerfully spoken to our hearts.

Similarly, we might imagine a *journey* with the departure (A), the itinerary (C), and destination (B) or, by engaging the image of culture, i.e. *growth*, unfold the tale more explicitly with the potential (A) that, in the course of its development (C), reaches important stages of development along the way, the bud, the flower, the fruit – the epochs and eras of this development – which finally attains to ripeness and sweetness, bringing to fruition (B) what was meant to be, the destiny and abstraction of the beginning realizing at the end what was, at its inception, merely implicit, merely a plan, a design – the culture of the seed, the growth potential, has, across intermediary flourishing, become the culture of the fruit in well-rounded maturity. Moreover, this particular "cultural" image of reason would take into account the work of the gardener-poet who tends the flowers, fosters the growth – for this is culture, too, the cultivation and selection, both of which are terms for practical discernment, the pruning and supporting, the discrete nurturing and guiding that collaborate in the execution of the acts of *judgment*.

Finally the fruit and fulfillment of growth gives rise to the renewed beginning, new inception, the seminal sowing, the seminar that sparks again the dull earth of thoughtlessness with the water and the in-folded fire of distinction. Hence the gardener-thinker oversees the entire process, recognizes it as a circle, a ring and a train of thought that ultimately always returns to its beginning in the tour of self-reflection and self-possession, which is our human destiny and distinction.

We may mark salient phases in this complete circuit of thought's life and times. That means that after having grasped thought as an activity of transition from the *confluence of indifferent dispersion* – a term of immediacy, to the *critical tension of dissension* – a term of distinction, we must account for the completion of this way and journey which does not end in the duality of divergent terms, the unsafe passage representing the *practice* of reason, nor in their smoothened unity, but rather in their harmony, a relationship of transitions, a *first* leading to the *middle*, and the *middle* returning, in the *end*, to the *beginning* of the train of thought on its journey to self-realization – a continual tour of recreation. Is there any way of picturing this course of self-knowing being of reason, its self-relationship, as a whole in itself, a fulfillment of paradox, and the completion of skepticism, as Hegel called it? It is what we have so often named and given shape to with words, given the form and face of a name. Recall our first symbol of self-reflection, our rational being, coiling and recoiling upon itself dragon-like as in *Figure 39*.

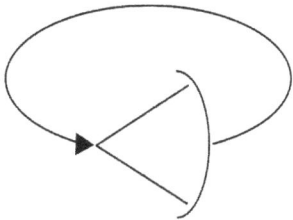

Figure 39: The Turning Point

   It is the symbol of culture – the living entity of identity, the self-knowing being, the "holy" triunity of the "eternal" turn and return of distinction (terms all reminiscent of formulas for pure reason well known in our epochal tradition, especially the words *holy* and *eternal*), a *product* (an image recreated by the building art), a *purpose* (an ideal championed in conflict and achieved or fulfilled), but also an activity, the *practice* of cultivation, a *training* exercise facing resistance, the contemplative *delight* that thoughtful appreciation takes in these cultural goods, especially the joy it takes in the good that is the reflection of its cyclical, rhythmical turning upon itself, in and to itself.

   We say that the entire movement of this culture articulates a complete ratio in a triad of three signature terms, a relationship of relationships or syllogism, a *logotectonic* of thought that complements the Tree of Duality which presented the original distinction of cognizance that marked the difference that thought makes upon an otherwise oblivious life, one that had been lost to self-regard as founded upon self-knowledge and now, having since gained this recognition, standing forth, standing out, and in this sense "*ex-isting*," not only in self-alienation but also in self-affirmation, being both the same as itself *and* different, several *and* one, as an entity of identity alive in and to the dignity of what it was meant to be, namely free, holy, just, and, in a word, in *two* words, *human* being as well as *divine*.

This process of critical self-reflection is infinite though bounded – as we saw, and now recall in *Figure 40*, it is a reiterating progression of distinctions that are, in fact, just one distinction the drawing of which perpetually deepens and broadens our comprehension of what such a destiny of dignity entails.

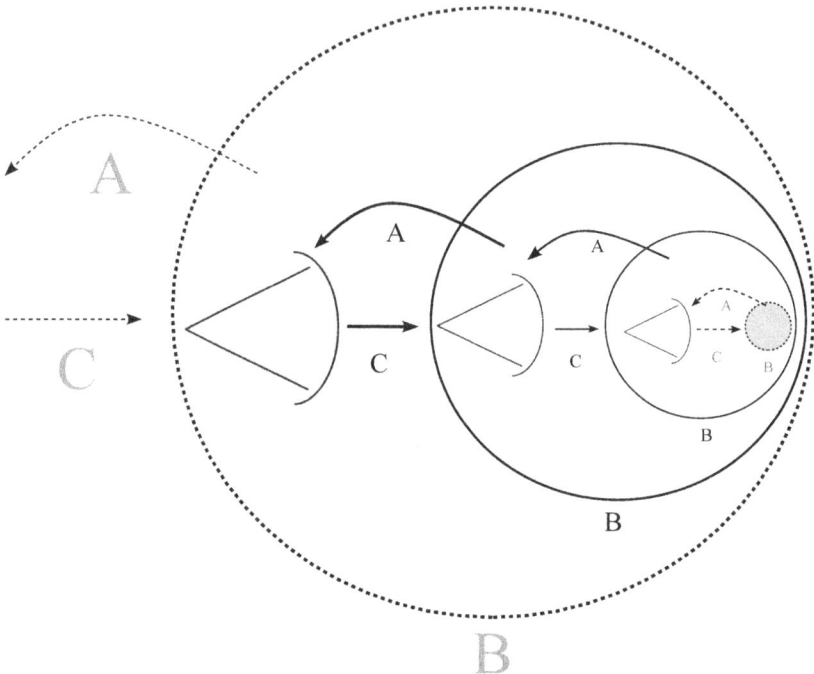

Figure 40: The Infinite Depth and the Breadth of the Mind

It is important to remember that the *Principle of Self-Reflection* (A) is the whole in which the two subaltern principles, namely that of the *Distinction* (C), the term of discernment, and that of the *Continuity*, the term of issue (B) are comprehended in relationship to each other as the two constituent elements of that whole, the latter being the contradiction and the former the identity the reciprocity of which is uneasily maintained in the wider framework of an intriguingly discontinuous relationship of negotiation within the all-encompassing scope of the principle. For thought is the restless, energetic, dynamic, *inclusive* harmony that reason is destined to forge between the exclusionary extremes of simple harmony and simple dissonance; thought thinking thought, reason's achievement, is neither war nor peace, neither merely the tranquillity that emerges at the end of an effort to heal the gap between the IS and the OUGHT, nor merely the crisis that arises when an established state of affairs is called into question by need's impingement, i.e. by necessity, by vocation, by duty. The balance and compromise that consideration of their relationship proposes for our discovery is an altogether new, unforeseen and unforeseeable, even apparently implausible and unlikely coincidence of purpose, a serendipitous event, if you will, the practical achievement of which remains, as far as we know, a stroke of luck and, must remain for us, in the world of action, an article of faith posited as a vote of confidence but never taken as granted.

This recursive image of critical self-reflection suggestively captures the twofold progression of distinctions achieved by insight inwardly and comprehension outwardly, the first delving towards a more originary, a more substantive fundamental, the second generalizing towards a more sweeping, integrative totality. The disadvantage of this rendition of thought's way is, obviously, that it does not facilitate our efforts at delineating different sequences of terms in a line of reasoning.

On the other hand, in light of thought's kinetic properties, the linear and tabular catalogue of triads and dyads, composed as it is of *stationary* names posited so neatly in columns, does not sufficiently represent the circular, dynamic action of reason, the transition and transitions of transitions, the apportionment and organization inherent in the relationship of relationships, that is the train of thought towards self-knowledge. For this reason, we may often prefer a more dynamic image of development, the vectorial triangle of development representing the schema of thought thinking thought turning and returning to itself as a series of transitions as in *Figure 41*.

Figure 41: The Circle of Critical Reflection

As presenting relationships of transition, relationships as transitions, the arrows of the triangle approaching or departing from the nodes of the triangle as end or starting points are useful though lacking the facility of analogy borne of the vertical dimension that a table provides. The table of triads by contrast provides us with lists and columns of terms to compare horizontally but fails to give any indication that in fact each triad is actually a line of reasoning coming to a conclusion, marked by a resultant term based on the connection between an inaugural across a term of mediation. And neither the table nor the triangle account for the recursive procession of distinctions that is the ingemination and the reiteration of the prescinding negativity of abstract thought set against the realization of its identity in the resonant alternation of reflection that is its principle. Are there any other options available to us?

One, two, three – these counting numbers suggest a way of representing this alternation of thought in the form of a triangle augmented to render the recursion. The challenge is, of course, to somehow capture on paper the actual movement of negativity in the reiteration of critical reflection, at least to come up with an image that conveys a sense of this activity, which is, in spite of initial appearances, just as familiar and just as easy to understand as *one, two, three*.

How do we count when we count: "*one*" – "*two*" – "*three*"?

Like this: ● ● ● ?

But then the dot called "three" in our count looks the same as the dot we have designated as "two" and the one named "one." Of course, the difference between the first dot and the third is not merely its position, i.e.

the third is not merely the last dot in a row of three dots but rather contains and collects the previous counts "one" and "two." It is their successor term and has cardinality. In order to indicate this property of inheritance, we need to depict the actual process of counting such that the *first*, not only is but also has "one," the *second* is and has "two" and the *third* is and has three" Consider in *Figure 42* this rendition of the cardinality of the three orders: *one, two, three*.

"one"   "two"   "three"

Figure 42: How to Make Thought Count

These can serve to render the sense of the three stations in our train of thought and recall the three famous categories of Ch. Peirce's ideoscopy, namely *Firstness, Secondness,* and *Thirdness*.[47] Let us put them at the vertices of our triangle of transitions as in *Figure 43*.

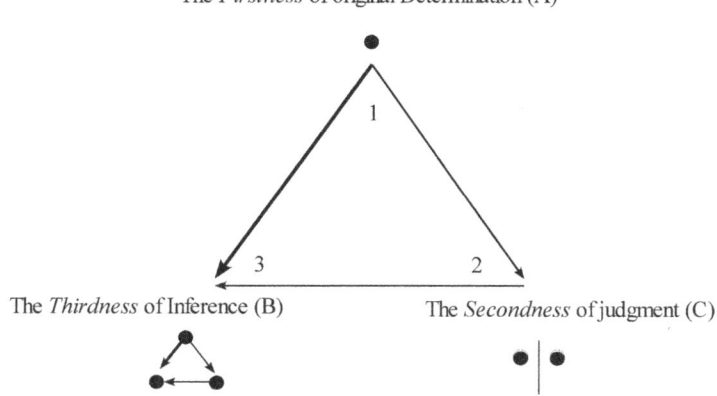

The *Firstness* of original Determination (A)

The *Thirdness* of Inference (B)   The *Secondness* of judgment (C)

Figure 43: Taking Account of Thought

---

[47] Underlying their importance Peirce says "the theory of the categories...is (if anything is) the gift I make to the world. That is my child. In it I shall live when oblivion has me — my body" see the Introduction in *Writings of Charles S. Peirce: A Chronological Edition*, Volume1: 1857-1866 p. xxvi.

Clearly though, this figure does not tell the whole story. For the terms at the vertices of the triangle that have been put to render the cardinality of their position can, in turn, themselves be expanded to reveal their own cardinality and so on in a transfinite sequence unto the cardinality of the continuum ***c***.

Compare now this figure with *Figure 44* illustrating the life and "culture" of pure reason. The more completely rendered structure below exhibits the imbedded ingemination of thought's self-relativity and the infinite concentration upon its intricacy in an infinite series of nested reflections.

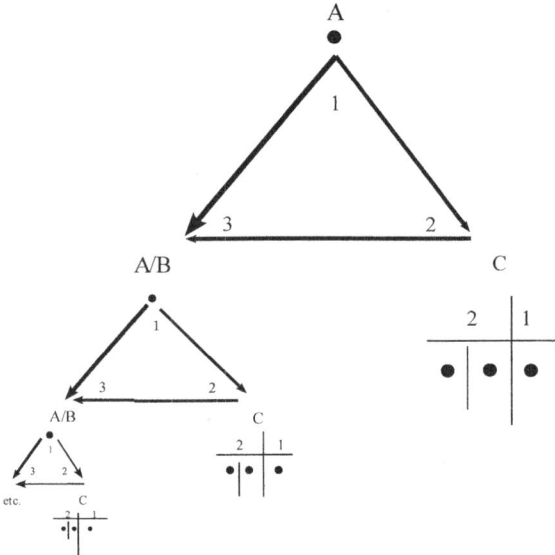

Figure 44: The Recurrence of Conscience

This infinity is neither tedious nor regressive – it refers to the potential of thought to revise forgone conclusions and review and reappraise critically the determinations that have been formally established by predecessor thoughts for good or no good reasons. This outstanding property that latter-day philosophers have called, with respect to the etymology of this word, human *existence* is reason's own recreation – thought thinking thought. Thought is always, first, a call to and a recalling of inaugural reasons such that the issue and result of a previous critical reflection becomes in turn an object and a cause of a renewed reflection. *Figure 44* is a rendering of this recurrence of conscience.

The infinity in question here is that which pertains to thought as the will – what's to stop you from giving a matter some thought? Nothing. To reprise an issue thought closed? Nothing. To question a forgone conclusion? Nothing. Again we are never done with thought, once and for all, never done coming to terms with all that thought is, nor should we be, though at times it would be more convenient if we were, and on the other hand, it is certainly no less reasonable, at least for practical purposes, to occasionally leave well enough alone and make do, bide our time, study patience and quit for the day, taking stock of what we have accomplished thus far with satisfaction, counting our blessings.

Figure 44 highlights two properties of pure reason that confirm what we have already discovered about how thought works. First, recalling the Tale of the Pea, the Pot, and the Pan and how the Pea got into the Pot (*Figures 35* and *36*), we see that the *Principle of Distinction* (C) marks not only the inaugural immediate difference that thought makes in our lives against a background of indeterminacy and indifference, our experience of reason's own self-evidence, but also how this term is, at the same time, a *Principle of Mediation*, the specific term that subsumes the particular but is itself subsumed under the general and therefore both pea-like in the latter relationship and pot-like in the former, exhibiting the property of self-severalty by which the determination of the principle, *thought*, is realized in the thing, *mind* in the *matter*. The syllogism of these two limits, the terms of thought in the middle term, affects the inference of the transition by which THE WAY IT IS *is* THE WAY IT SHOULD BE and THE WAY IT SHOULD BE *is* THE WAY IT IS, which is the fulfillment of the determining principle.

Secondly, we recognize how the Principle of Critical Self-reflection (A) is indeed the whole story that we want to recount about thought, the entire system of transitions and experiences that find their elaboration in the substantive Principle of Determinant Issue (B) which articulates the properties and features of this being to which our study is directed, gradually revealing the details inherent in that principle's life to our contemplation as we progress in the course of our investigation. That is why pure reason is both our cause *and* our issue, the origin and the outcome, the much fabled and, in this sense, fabulous identity of *thinking* and *being* in the sense that while *being* is thought to be the realization of reason and thus the efficacy of the mind, *ideas* of conception are thought to be the substance and essence of reality, that distinguished reality that is accessible to intellect alone.

Figure 45, offering a concise synopsis of the structures discussed above, is a table consisting of the three vortices taken from the triangular graph of thought, a table which, though it obscures the inference across the triad of terms, allows us to avail ourselves of the property of the table to collect analogical triads for better comparison and orientation.

The Ternary Logotectonic of Thought

A	C	B						
Terms of Principle	Terms of Discernment	Terms of Issue						
•	••	• • •						
General	Specific	Particular						
Theoretical	Practical	Poetic						
True	Right	Beautiful						
Inherence	Dependence	Reciprocity						
First Epoch	Second Epoch	Third Epoch						
Cognition	Conation	Affect						
Intellect	Judgement	Imagination						
. . .	. .	.						
Self-relationship of Pure Reason	**Tree of Duality**	**Logotectonic of Thought**						
	II	**I**	**A**	**C**	**B**			
	Terms of distinction	Terms of immediacy	**Terms of Principle**	**Terms of Discernment**	**Terms of Issue**			
.	Spirit	Body		II Terms of Distinction	I Terms of Immediacy	A Terms of Principle	C Terms of Discernment	B Terms of Issue
.	Day	Night						
.	Form	Material	.	e t c.	e t c.		e t c.	e t c.
.	Heaven	Earth	.	.	.	.	.	.
.	Invisible	Visible	.	.	.	.	.	.
.	Death	Life	.	.	.	.	.	.
.	. . .	. . .	.	.	.	.	.	.

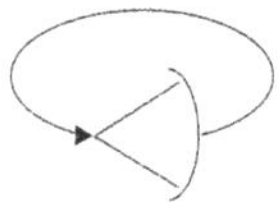

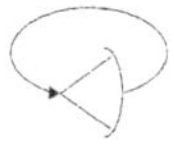

Figure 45: A Synthesis of Ratios

Figure 45 also attempts to recreate the nested structure of the iterations that characterize self-reflection, revealing in this way how the three columns of terms, namely those of *Principle* (A), of Discernment (C), and of Issue (B) are themselves the record of our experience with pure reason, i.e. first, with the *Self-Relativity* of thought thinking thought, the entity of identity that is our cause and the object of our proposed philological science; second, with the *Self-Severalty* of thought's own divergence from thought in the practice of our human being; and finally, with the *State of Community* of thought's principles founded upon the realization that pure reason is, ultimately, an accomplishment of invention as much as it is an object of contemplation and the ripe fruit of the logotectonic craft and art of building ideas into a scheme of all things thought. It is to the method of this craft and art that we now turn and learn to elaborate the particular ratios of reason that have governed conception throughout our philosophical tradition, a method that, in the work of Heribert Boeder, our teacher, has already reestablished metaphysics in the traditional sense of this word as rigorous i.e. as *pure* thought.

64. The Logotectonic System of Ratios

These days, folks are minded to say that thinking is *saying* things; to this conceit we say, with philosophy, fine! But if there is one thing above all others worth saying, though it is *no thing* at all and nevertheless means everything in the world, it is thought. Thus our premise. What is this AUGHT of thought? We have explained what it means to say that thought is nothing, *naught* – consider for example the Thinker, our mundane "Penseur," if you will, called upon to think neither about musical notation, nor about atoms, nor about language, nor about religion, nor about any other thing under the sun or over the rainbow, but rather about *pure thought* alone. In that case, in the sculpture thereby alluded to, the posture of Our Thinker could neither be one of sedentary squatting, nor of ponderous rumination but rather, much more light-footedly dancer-like, must needs be that of abstraction – **detachment** from all incidental influence and conditions, though in being thus disencumbered from distracting circumstance by insight's gaze and impartiality's judgment, not, therefore, lost in vacuous musing and oblivious to the shifting states and affairs of everyday life, but rather perceptive and perspicacious with respect to them, seeing behind their seeming, reading between the lines of their own brand of reasoning, discerning, in the very face of mindlessness, the thought unthought behind the thing never minded about, getting to the bottom, to the heart, of the matter in a perceptive act of the intellect.

Thus the *Thinker* of distinction, finding and seeking truth; now to the *Builder* of its forms and figures arrayed in chains of truths. For after having considered the tasks of positing names as terms for thought and then differentiating them in relationships of markedness that determine the critical transition of reflection, we now turn to the actual elaboration of reason with reasons that is accomplished by arranging three distinct terms into a scheme or ratio, a train of thought. In this train, the three terms, as one might expect of a train, are linked into a sequence, the last of which is called the *resultant* or the conclusion and the first the *inaugural* term which begins the series and serves as its point of departure. The final and the initial terms are then conjoined through the *mediate* term which, by virtue of being interposed between the two endpoints of the ratio, connects them into a complete line of reasoning, a syllogism – one unique sequence of terms or *deduction* depicting a particular ΛΟΓΟΣ of thought, namely as being theoretical, practical, or poetic and therefore as that of the Thinker, the Actor, or the Builder.

It is through the mediating term that the relationship of transition is affected between the inaugural term and the resultant one. Every deduction has an inaugural, a mediating, and a resultant term, though the same distinction might appear in one ratio as the inaugural, in another ratio as the resultant, and in a third as the mediating term. In fact, in a complete scheme or figure of thought, which consists of a syllogism of three such ratios, each thought adopts every one of the three positions successively – the inaugural, the mediate, and the resultant position; that is precisely why a complete scheme consists of three ratios and why a scheme is considered to be complete in the first place.

What are the three terms that a ratio consists of? The most important distinction is that of the **principle**. The principle term is the basis for the entire sequence; it is the central idea and names the *present* of the distinction in question, indicating in this way its import and power to initiate a train of thought and determine the design of an entire epoch in the course of which the culture of one particular idea unfolds and in accordance with which poets and thinkers develop their intuitions and conceptions of the reality of this principle. Thus, for example, in the Third Epoch, the principle can be termed the *Humanity of Human Being* or simply HUMAN NATURE; in the Second Epoch, on the other hand, it is the GLORY OF GOD that made all the difference; in the First Epoch, we would speak of the APPORTIONMENT OF DESTINY. These are traditional names for the principle chosen from among a great many other possible candidates from their respective Epoch and translated, more or less felicitously, into English. Scholars are apt to debate whether or not *MOIPA*, for instance, is appropriately translated by the English term *destiny* or *apportionment*, and even *fate* or *doom* would find its advocates and its justification.

But perhaps the notion would be better expressed with the word *limit* or *measure* in combination with *allotment* or *appointment*, the point being to properly name the principle and its present in accordance with how these particular designations are used in the holy writs whence they come. Their usage guides our building endeavor. In this example, the PORTIONS are present in their *dispensation;* they *mete out* or *assign* their measures, distribute our *lot* in life, our *share*, as we shall learn when turning our study to the knowledge of the Muses in the First Epoch. There are arguments for and against each of these translations and reasons for preferring one name to another. It is indeed absolutely essential to the logotectonic method of our philology to observe how *MOIPA* and its synonyms are actually used in Homeric poetry. These different contexts of usage often reveal different shades of meaning that make one or the other of the family of standard English words available for this notion, were the task merely to translate this or that particular passage of Homer into English, the more precise one. But it is not. Our task is to study the distinction of human being as known in the First Epoch of thought, the Greek one, in the vivid element that Homeric poetry bestows upon this idea. Seeing the efficacy of pure reason as the apportionment of our fate and our lot in life, our *fate* with respect to the finitude of human being, our *lot* in terms of our ordained part in the whole of a community, which had been founded upon the rule of Zeus and his insight into the just measure due to each member of this Olympic comity, seeing this, I say, helps us to understand the distinction of human being in a new way and, more importantly, to see the reality of this idea in terms that Homer provides.

Moreover, Homeric usage throws light on how a great many expressions of the English language that have come down to us – and which might otherwise have remained vague reminders of notions long forgotten or mistaken – can be given a precise and striking sense as new ways and manners of speaking about thought and our experience of the distinction of human being. And everybody knows that ways and manners of speaking tend to become ways and manners of acting and action leads to habit and habit, finally, to character and habitat, to the world in which we live and to our living in it well or not so well.

Similarly, when the principle is the GLORY OF GOD, as it is in the Second Epoch, the English rendering of the expression ΔΟΞΑ ΘΕΟΥ, suggests, at the very least, a completely different vision of that distinction; for in this epoch *God*, the *Creator*, is the name for the principle, its present being the illuminating *mission of the Son* whereas in the first epoch *Zeus* is not the principal term at all but rather subject to the appointed limit that is his lot in Olympic life.

Finally in the Third Epoch, it is neither the *Muses*, nor the *Holy Spirit* but rather the *Humanity of Human being* that speaks to us, manifesting what no *Hero* or *Saint* could have ever conceived of, namely that HUMAN NATURE is intrinsically good, present alone in the certainty of My FREEDOM, which is My identity as sovereign *Citizen* of the *general will*.

Thus, the fundamental term is the ***principle*** (A). The notion of a principle is accompanied by a great many connotations that are made figuratively explicit in the figure of the *general*, the *leader*, or the *superior* whose *authority* and *sway*, laid down perhaps as *law* or as the *king's command* or simply as *necessity*, is the motive base for actions of followers and subordinates, loyal subjects and servants; it is their duty to put into effect the *cause* or *power* of that *sovereignty*, the *origin* of which, of whom, has arisen of itself, spontaneously, naturally, and is, in this sense, *general* for being replete with its particular kindred others, *central* in being the *main* or *key* idea, the *foundation* for being the *ground* and *basis* upon which the building of community stands or falls and thus the *determination* of what insight can comprehend, the intellect conceive, the *criterion* and *standard* in accordance with which judgment assesses and decides, the inner *essence* and the *scheme* of conception, the supporting *structure* and the encompassing *frame*, the *mold* and *forge* of *form, the stamp* and *pattern* of matter. Hence, we note the difference between a theoretical principle or conceptual law, both of which are explanatory in nature, a precept of what is true in general and indicative of the cause or essence of a being being the way it is, and a practical principle or moral law, a creed and code of rectitude that governs conduct towards the end in view of the way it should be. A poetic principle, finally, is a scheme or design, a plan or purpose that is not merely a rationale for belief but moreover, beyond the process of transformation inherent in a course of action, brings forth some product or result that is distinct from that process and its Actor. In the case of theory, the being in question is what is contemplated by the intellect; in the practical sense, that being, distinguished in itself and from itself, undergoes a change, a conversion, a modification in a process of differentiation; a poetic truth, finally, is the being as an outcome not of practice but of invention; it is creative.

In the course of our logotectonic analysis, we will be positing many different terms as the principle of the ratio in question and just as often understanding these terms as convenient names for the whole train of thought, which is the particular figure we happen to be elaborating at the moment, seen as a totality and as one complete movement but consisting, nevertheless, of a series of deductions in its own right; however, in the context of the ratio of terms elaborating the whole scheme, the principal term must also be understood to refer to one particular distinction in the entire deduction that is pure reason's way of doing things.

Thus the principle is the moving *subject* of a ΛΟΓΟΣ, i.e. of a logotectonic *sentence* in which pure reason finds articulation, the driving force and the locomotive, as it were, of a train of thought. The second element with which we will be building rational figures is the term of **discernment** (C), the *verb*. This word for the action of thought might be used in the more restricted sense of its perceptive or productive efficacy, in other words, as the work of the intellect or the imagination. But in the context of the philological art and craft of thought, it is intended to refer more comprehensively to the actual exercise of practical reason in the execution of the law that the principle has bestowed upon it by virtue of its present as the manifestation of its determination and that discernment is now called upon to put into effect; it is this process of differentiation and dissociation, the dramatic *progressus ad infinitum* of thought's abstraction that is carried out by thought, the Actor. Thus, *discernment* refers not only to the drawing of distinctions in the theoretical sense of determining properties and features of a specimen of *being* that has come under the scrutiny of science, but also to how the relationship of overture with regards to the principle makes a practical difference in the *life* that ensues when the principle has been acknowledged and received as determining action with regards to gap between THE WAY IT IS and THE WAY IT SHOULD BE, the diacritical mark that pure reason makes.

On the subject of the determining principle, thought has indeed something *to do* – a task or charge, a purpose towards which it now directs its determination. And that is what the verb indicates for a given train of thought. It is the term for *deliberation* and the execution of the *decision*, for carrying out the proclaimed *verdict*, *paying attention* while *minding the gap* between the IS and the OUGHT, yes, of course, but moreover *measuring*, *determining* the degree of *correspondence* or *deviation*, *accordance* or *contention*, and therefore, with respect to the distinction that the principle draws, soulfully *desiring, fostering* with care, *obeying* under oath, *practicing* what has been preached and thus *fulfilling* what has been foreordained by the principle as destiny. Discernment is theoretical in garnering *impressions*, the *reception* and *proposition* of *sense*, *positing* and *taking* on, the application of *technique*, *knowledge* of the rules and regulations, *getting* it right, *making* it up, *following* it through, *investigating* scientifically, *committing* professionally, *inferring* logically, *learning* and *imagining*, *envisioning* and *revering*, *naming* and *verifying* – *touching*, *tasting*, *seeing*, *hearing* but always with that discrimination that make these activities of the mind deliberate deeds of perspicacity. Discernment is practical in the *deportment* that *conducts* us on our *way*, *guides* us in what we *do*, with *desire* making *volition* of our *disposition*, in the *taking on* and *performance* of duties, in *submitting* to the need they give compelling voice to and *leading* by their *leave* – their *permission* is our *mission*; it is practical in the government of the *will* whether with *leniency* or *restraint*, in *striving* to *achieve* an end, *excelling* in its *service*, *passing on*, *giving* what has been given in *gratitude* for the grant, fostering *hope* at success of resolute *pursuit*, *patience* in the face of setbacks, *standing tall* and *hanging tough*, *holding out*. It is *administering* to the feelings of perception that accompany the visitation of impressions from abroad and *responding* to them with institutions of *approbation* or *censure*, *affirmation* or *denial*, *care* or *neglect*, *insurgence* or *obedience*. Discernment is, finally, poetic in *completing* the undertaking, *accomplishing* the design of endeavor and *attaining* the end with distinction, *fulfilling* the promise, *giving form* and *shape* to it in the celebration of the principle's presents that have now acquired presence at the hands of thought, the Builder's craft and art.

Therefore, the final term in the triad of signature terms that we use to construct ratios of thought is that of the **issue** (B). The issue of thought is determined as *what is*, the *whole* and *all* there is, having come to be, occurred or made, set or merely met, a *body* born or grown, *many in one*, *one out of many* or completely *alone*. As an object of theory, the issue in question posits as our *topic* and our *cause* the *apparition* and the *instantiation* of the principle which manifests its tangible and intangible *features* and *properties* that the scientist can measure and explain; but the issue at stake is not only the *theme* of an *exposition*, it is also the *outcome* of action – it is the *product* of the principle performed and perfectly completed, the *inference* born of reasoning, the *representation* of the principle in *particulars* perceived; it is the *action* taken, the *state* established, the crowned and crested *realm*, the *community* of the called, the ordered form *attained*, the goal *fulfilled*, the *object* properly *owned*, the *limit* justly *shown*, the *truth found* that had been sought, the sign's *designs*, the *world* of words that had been *wrought*, the *image* of one's *well-being felt*, and of harmonious *accord* into which the enmity of strife twixt mind and elemental life is finally *resolved*. Thus whereas the principle is manifestly in evidence with the disclosure of reflection, the issue is an *expression* or *exhibition* of that principle, its elemental *embodiment* that provides the principle's present with a *presence*, a descriptive *account*, a *narrative*, that really *matter*s, that makes us sit up and take notice...of thought at *work*. ΛΟΓΟΣ as science is here completed by ΛΟΓΟΣ as art, for it is in particular as a result of the fine arts and letters that, beyond all cosmos encountered by contemplation, there are countless buildings of poetic invention. In fact, little does theory know in the beginning that the object of its original gaze was, previously, the product of its hand, the being born being, actually, the being made such that both art and science converge in the work of pure reason transforming itself from the being thought into the thinking being, from the being built into the building being so that all thinking is building and building is thinking and thought and being are one – the self-relative entity of identity that is the realization of perfect *discernment*, the term of distinction we have designated to mark the rhythmic life and times of our ultimate *principle*, and the unique cause and *issue* of the latter-day philological science we are now engaged in.

Thus, of necessity, every ratio contains a term of *Principle* (A), a term of *Discernment* (C), and a term of *Issue* (B) and in the construction of the schemes of thought, each will be placed in turn into the inaugural, the mediate, or the resultant position of the sequence, depending on which figure is being articulated and which ratio preceded it. According to Boeder, the logotectonic of pure reason distinguishes three different figures of rationality – the figure of **mundane** reason the inaugural term of which is the *Issue*, the figure of **natural** reason, which begins with the term of *Discernment*, and finally the figure of **conceptual** reason which develops its deduction upon the inaugural term of *Principle*. Only conceptual reason is thought thinking about thought the philosophical tradition of which became known as the science of metaphysics and which, as Boeder has shown, was always and exclusively devoted to the comprehension of pure reason as the distinction of human being.[48]

Mundane reason, in contrast, studies the ***world*** in its emergent originality, positing it as being primitive and prior to thought (whereas metaphysics studies precisely the inverse, thought itself as a distinct reality and the world as this, thought's, self-realization – the being of thought's very own self-possession) giving rise to a world-view of the worldly-wise in opposition to a supposedly merely "transcendent," merely "academic" wisdom that mundanity, questioning the former renown of that knowledge and the devotion it inspired, supposes it has, more realistically, put behind itself; natural reason studies ***understanding proper***, i.e. its requirements and methods for the betterment of our human, all too human mind, as it corresponds to the world (whereas pure reason strives to correspond only to pure reason, its own idea of itself as the best, the exemplary, the ideal being) and serves modern temporality with the practical rationalization and fashionable sophistication of its intellectual prowess and aplomb.

But as neither the *world* nor its corresponding *cognition* are our theme, which is, instead, the distinction of human being and nothing else. In the following study of the logotectonic method, we will concentrate exclusively on the figures of conceptual reason, a syllogism of ratios or figures consisting of three deductions – in the first scheme of the figure, the inaugural term is that of the Principle; in the second scheme, the Principle is the mediate term; in the third scheme the Principle is the resultant.

---

[48] Thus Boeder's conception of "weltliche," "natürliche," and "conceptionale Vernunft." Boeder has not, to my knowledge, ever gone into detail regarding the methodology of thought, the Builder (die bauende Vernunft) and the ramifications for thought in grasping reason as a logotectonic ratio of terms. Marcus Brainard who has published a collection of Boeder's papers in *Seditions: Heidegger and the Limit of Modernity* provides a brief overview of his logotectonic method in the "Editor's Introduction" (pp. lx-xlix). Moreover, several scholars have used Boeder's method in their own work and have provided some commentary on the method. These include Karl-Heinz Ruhstorfer, *Konversionen: eine Archäologie der Bestimmung des Menschen bei Foucault, Augustinus, Nietzsche*, Ludwig von Bar, *Die Philosophie Schaftesburys im Gefüge der mundanen Vernunft der frühen Zeit*, and Wilhelm Metz who discusses Boeder's work in Lecture 22 and 23 (pp. 225-247) of a collection of lectures published on the Internet under the title *Unterwegs zum Höhlenausgang der Moderne – Wider die letzte Ideologie der Postmoderne*.

65. The Ratios of Revelation

Thus, the first scheme of conceptual reason, beginning as it does with the term of Principle, elaborates the notion of the *revelation* of thought and the generative power of pure reason to become an issue and therefore to make an effective difference. The mission of thought refers to its eminence in *mattering* to us and, in this way, drawing our attention to thought as being *practically* real; for thought is, to be sure, no thing and yet not nothing; in fact it is no small thing at all, but rather a big thing in human life, making, as great ideas are wont to do, all the difference in an otherwise so mundane world. Starting with the principle as the inaugural scheme does, it is possible to distinguish two complementary ratios, i.e. two distinct sequences of terms. In the first case, the inaugural PRINCIPLE of this sequence is manifested in the apparition of the resultant ISSUE. This means that, through the mediating activity of practical DISCERMENT, the abstract principle is accorded a *presence* in a particular issue. In the second case, the revelation and evidence of the inaugural PRINCIPLE is mediated by the striking ISSUE in conveying to the resultant term of DISCERNMENT the commission of critical perception. The mission of reflection is effective in some matter, a particular issue that gives rise to critical thought. Thus, in the first ratio of the inaugural scheme the sequence of terms is:

$$A > C > B$$

This ratio demonstrates how the general principle (A) is mediated by a specific practice of discernment (C) to attain determination in the elements of a particular exhibition (B) of that principle which in turn might be said to have given risen to this incarnation of thought in the concrete state of affairs.

In the second ratio of the scheme the sequence of terms is:

$$A > B > C$$

This ratio demonstrates, in contrast to the first one, how discernment acquires its determination from the principle. The principle (A) having gained substantial force through a specific and striking presence (B) incites thought to distinguish itself (C), i.e. discernment is sparked or called to attention by a motivating, invigorating object.

In the first case, let us call it the ***ratio of concretion***, the Principle (A) is constituted in the elemental tangibility of the Issue (B), which is the resultant term in this ratio while the mediating term, discernment (C) takes on here the character of expression, representation, or description. Stated in symbols:

$$A>C + C>B = \mathbf{A>B}$$

Consider, by way of illustration of this ratio, the relationship of terms we could use to describe the work of thought in which the abstract and general idea of *Freedom* (A), through the discernment of the specific law that is freedom's categorical imperative upon the immediacy of subjective human inclination and in practical *reverence* towards its command – the duty that this principle places on self-respect (C) – is willed in individual action directed at the perfection of *the greatest good* (B), namely, by virtue of the distinction that this pure will has thus attained, to be worthy of beatitude. Thus the ratio delineating the *Kantian* conception of practical reason.

In the second case, let us call it the ***ratio of vocation***, the Principle (A) is not realized in the product but rather in the practice of thought. By virtue of its effulgent prominence and import (B), which is its effective present, the principle gives rise to the distinction of discernment (C), which is the resultant of this ratio, and is, essentially, thought's assent to the mission of transformation imparted by the principle. Or in symbols:

$$A>B + B>C = \mathbf{A>C}$$

Consider, by way of illustration of this ratio, the relationship of terms we could use to describe the work of thought in which the absolute and ineffable *God* (A) whose glory in the person of the Son, proclaimed as savior in birth, authorized as judge in the End, and resurrected as the lord in the flesh, is made manifest in the his words and works, the *life and death of Jesus Christ* (B), such that converted and, in this sense, distinguished thought is renewed through *repentance* (C), affirming by the confession of faith and, by acts committed in that spirit of love, verifying, the will of the Father. This is the ratio educed by the synoptic Gospels Matthew, Mark, and Luke.

If, as in *Figure 46*, we were to put the three terms (A, B, C) into the vertices of a triangle, we could represent the *ratio of concretion*, as the resultant movement from **A to B (A>B)** consisting of the directional transitions from A to C (A>C) and from C to B (C>B), these being the edges of the triangle in the figure and thus rendered as arrows to construct the transitive relation of the inference that is the logical basis of the line of reasoning here in evidence:

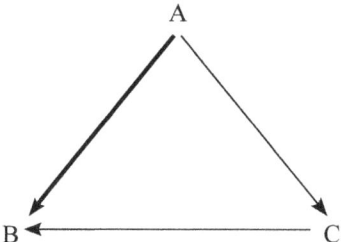

Figure 46: The Ratio of Concretion

In contrast, the *ratio of vocation* would conclude upon the term of discernment (C) meaning that the resultant movement from **A to C (A>C)** consists of the transitions from A to B (A>B) and B to C (B>C) as we see in *Figure 47.*

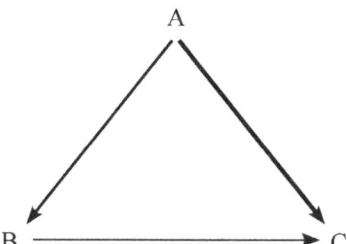

Figure 47: The Ratio of Vocation

In their most basic sense, these two ratios show how the principal term is a power to be reckoned with, thought neither being nor remaining, as practitioners often deplore, "just a thought", i.e. merely in the mind, but rather as substantial, effective reasoning – we are liable, or bound, *to think* and therefore, taking this disposition into account, we might say that ideas are *supposed* to take place in our breathing world, meant to happen to people and play a role in their lives. There are many ways to illustrate this ratio – the *speaker* puts ideas into words, in other words, thoughts (A) in the mind of the speaker are put, through the distinguished art of moving the human heart (C), into powerful words and expressions (B) that are likely to advert a select audience's appreciation of these thoughts (A>C>B). Or from the point of view of the *audience*: these very thoughts on the part of the speaker (A) by attaining substance and the reality inherent in the speaker's speech performance (B), advert the audience's mind (C), drawing their attention to the "magic of the moment," here and now of awakening awareness to the new unknown that in the speaker's words has just said "boo!" (A>B>C). We might emphasize here the difference between the **present** of thought, which is the revelation of thought and the immediacy of its impact on our lives, and the **presence** of thought, which is thought having taken on the form and shape in, thought mattering to, the world. The fetching present of thought implies the presence of thought. The principle (A) inspires discernment (C) to give voice (B) to what it knows, giving it a specific rendering as an issue of being, which is accessible to distinguished feeling or to a tender touch, to perceptive sight or hearing of thought having come to know, having encountered an idea "in person" or "in the flesh" or in action, in any case, as really and truly present (A>C>B); But the present of the principle (A) is itself a voice (B) that calls forth such thought (C) as is capable of hearing the message thus conveyed in that rich realization (A>B>C). Each ratio is *inherent* in the other, deduction in manifestation, apparition in perception.

These first two ratios have in common that the inaugural term is the determining principle (A). This principle proceeds to attain determinate form and effect either by exerting its influence upon thought (C) or else in attaining the import and substance of a particular matter at hand, the issue of reflection (B).

66. The Ratios of Foundation

We contrast these two deductions of **revelation** with those of **foundation**. The pair of ratios that constitute it are the converse of the other two. For in the ratios of foundation, the principle is not their inaugural term of shared origin but rather the resultant of their common focus – these two ratios end rather than begin upon the determining principle. The **ratio of perception** will therefore not specify how thought, startled and startling, starts but rather how it comes to know and see the mind both as the *intellect* of pure reason in the perception of the ideas understood as beings of essence, the ultimate ground and substantial cause of the matters at hand, and as final *affirmation* that each and every little thing in thought, the world at large, our life and times, this, that, and the other thing, are, at bottom, reason's. For first we learned, in the ratio of revelation, that pure reason, i.e. superb thought or, making use of an illustrious name for thought gleaned from Europe's philosophical tradition, the *ideal*, in its poetic efficacy, is real; and now, completing that lesson, we learn to grasp the efficacy of theoretical thought in the converse perspective, namely that, in the intelligent light of the mind, the *real* is ideal.

For, to consider the perception of insight first, the gift of thought as the evidence and revelation of its activity corresponds to such thought as is responsive to this gift, answering the light of thought with the immediate sight, intuition into what the heart of the matter is in each particular case. But this activity of thought seen not in the present of giving and the gift acknowledged but in apprehending what has been given is not merely the feeling in the bones, the gut feeling as the action of being touched by a touching idea, is no longer seen as merely receiving but as actually seizing the day of the idea. This apprehension is a transition from discernment (C) to the principle (A), hence, the movement C>A. But the intellect of thought (C) is not immediate passion for the principle's present, but rather mediated through a particular state of affairs, a specific occasion, a set of apparent facts (B), an *inference* and an induction from these parts and particulars to the whole, from the specifics to the general principle (A) that is their common ground and law, the one over many, one prescinded from many, and the theme in the variations.

This ratio of insight demonstrates how perception sees through the thing and recognizes the principle behind the scene, is mediated by these givens to get at the core and substance of the matter. Discernment, after having been invoked and moved by pure reason to make a distinction, sees with new eyes; it is the gaze of theory that sees the principle and the law, the rule, the order in appearance, the being behind appearances, the essence, the *truth*, of the beings in question.

This ratio of perception can be represented as the resultant movement from **C to A (C>A)** consisting of the transitions from C to B (C>B) and from B to A (B>A) which indicate how insight (C) is mediated by the particulars (B) to grasp the cause and principle (A) of those particulars being what they are, or in symbols:

$$C>B + B>A = C>A$$

This ratio depicts the movement of science which examines its topic or issue with a view to properly adjusting itself to its object in the manner of conception, getting a grip on the striking fact that has won thought's wonder, and then, its desire to know kindled, now devoting itself to the investigation of the principle of this factual presence according to the method of analysis and division, finally articulating its insights as that of thought coming to terms with that object and what it is. We might take *Aristotelian* conception as an example. After sharpening our minds for the purpose of science by training human understanding in the syllogistic method of demonstration, reason compels us to establish an order of sciences based on the diversity of beings and their several causes and principles – some beings have their causes and reasons in themselves and are therefore studied by the *theoretical* sciences, others have them in others, in another's purpose the corresponding sciences of which are either *poetic* in that they bring forth their beings or *practical* in that the action they bring about is based on the art of deciding what particular being as the preferable good is to be selected in each case. Even as argument, the evidence of deliberative reason, guides *practical* choice, so is the rational purpose of *invention* the completion and perfection attained by all beings in the fulfillment of the ultimate principle, active in each one's development towards that excellence in accordance with the determination of its nature (ΦΥΣΙΣ), as that which it was (destined) to be (TO TI HN EINAI), which is the moving but itself unmoved cause of all being, educed as a logical necessity in a *theoretical train of thought* (C) that infers from the most perfect movement of the most perfect natures, *the celestial beings of nature* (B), their divine end and TELOS, *reason itself* (A), the best being of all. Consider this ratio of distinctions as it rendered in *Figure 48*:

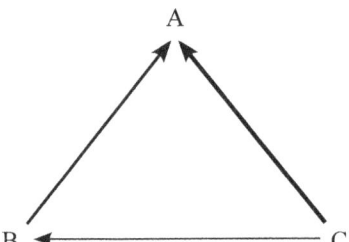

Figure 48: The Ratio of Perception

In contrast to this ratio of *perception*, the figure of truth or *affirmation* starts with the givens of reality, the particulars of life and the world and distinguishes them in works of praise, in the building of the concrete specifics that make a tangible, legible language of the world. Generative thought, in articulating revelation, gives by this testimony the abstraction of thought the imaginative force of a particular reality. But *regenerative* thought, the poetry of praise, by building with a fund of terms taken from the ordinary language of the everyday world and its cultural tradition, imbues their reality with the renewed depth of significance as signs and symbols of spirit, purifying thus the language of the tribe and urging the mind to foresight and retrospect.

The visceral depiction with which language gives thought a compelling voice facilitates, in turn, our lending of an avid ear, answering that inspiration with the enthusiasm of an open mind, a mind just become distinguished, giving thanks for what it has received in saying what it now knows, renewing that present of voice in this presence of verse. Ideas move us as would a voice, a call, a speech. Poets and thinkers have always known how to articulate this voice. These words are words of appreciation and thanks, all 99 of them. But with the notion of poetic works as worlds of words (B) put by poetic thought to magnify, glorify (C) reality with regards to the determining principle (A), we delineate the ratio in which lived experience and its rich element of experience is exalted by poetic license (B>C>A). Presented in symbols, the transition from the particulars of the world (B) to the general principle (A), not in the manner of insight which seeks to penetrate them in comprehension of their essence but rather in that of exaltation which distinguishes them from themselves, the immediate world from the poetic one they have been employed to articulate, is effected across the works of aethetic rather than conceptual discernment (C):

$$B>C + C>A = \mathbf{B>A}$$

In the ***ratio of signification***, the language of thought is seen not so much in serving the inception of discernment in which the term of discernment (C) was the resultant. Rather, thought is conceived of here as being prior to this subsequent office of change or pursuant to it in being the determination of a fact; the *fact* of pure reason is given articulation by poetic imagination, but in just this sense *after the fact*. The *fact* of thought is governed by the ratio of concretion (A>C>B) in which the particular is the resultant, as we saw. But in the ratio of signification, as represented in *Figure 49*, not the particular fact of the givens but rather their designation is the inaugural term, one leading the intellect beyond the facts towards their deeper sense of which they are now merely the vestige:

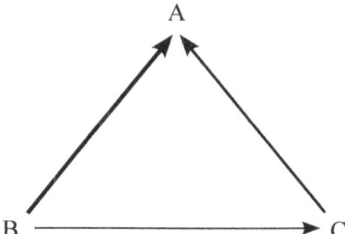

Figure 49: The Ratio of Signification

Thought, the Builder, is both poet and seer, one giving words to thought the other sensing the hidden meaning in the matter. On the other hand, taking our situation of a speech performance as an example, in the first ratio, that of perception, the intellect-audience "reads between the lines," deciphering the words of the speech that the speaker proposes and "gets the drift" by distinguishing the essence and the substance, the reason and the purpose of what has been neither revealed nor concealed but rather designated, indicated – that is why the Muse of Remembrance and those whom she favors "know it all" (Homer, *Iliad* 2.485) namely "the way it is, is going to be and was before" (1.70) in that particular order, namely *B* – *C* – *A*. Such is reason's efficacy in the world, the influence of its persuasive power to convey and to move thought to thought.

In the ratio of signification, the work of the builder is not to give the abstract principle the form of reality – this was the work of the ratio of concretion – but rather, conversely, now beginning the train of thought with particulars, to consecrate their reality, not merely enlisting the matter at issue to the service of the idea, but, more, sanctifying THE WAY IT IS in the name of the principle with respect to which no part or realm of being is obscure or excluded, foreign to the determinacy of THE WAY IT SHOULD BE, strange to or hidden from it, not even the impenetrable sphere of closed-minded dereliction so repugnant to the confiding present of the principle. For such piety as is pure reason's, even the night is holy, finding its proper place in the scheme of all things thought.

In the olden days, for example, the rhapsodist received the Muses' grant of knowledge as their father's, Zeus's, present whose insight into the proportions of just being the poet's audience were then able to partake of. *Being there* now, thanks to the craft and art of poetic narrative, even as the gods are, mortals may, through the knowledge of the Muses, attend not merely to rumor but rather to the truth of THE WAY IT IS, namely the whole and complete truth that shows THE WAY IT IS (B) within the totality of being in which what is to come (C) is the consummation of what had been foreordained as *to be* (A). Thus the ΛΟΓΟΣ of the singer places before the mind's eye of remembrance the whole story, calling and recalling to the audience's mind the ancient narratives of the mythological world order of accomplishment comprised of the distinguished beings, the gods and the heroes, unfolded in all the rich detail of what has transpired and what had been achieved, always beginning with what is first and foremost and culminating in the forgone conclusion that the will of Zeus was thus fulfilled.[49]

Hence, poetic being is the "musical" instrument of pure reason, mediating that distinguished idea for the audience; more, the poet is the embodiment of the idea that the distinction of human being is, ultimately, the distinguished craft and the art of humanity to bring forth the reality of the community that the poet's song celebrates. *In the flesh*, the poet is the teacher, a living sign making a lesson of his or her own life for us for the sake of the propitiation of the world – so the determinacy of the *savior* through the Holy Spirit in the Second Epoch; she or he is the founding father or mother of the republic *in the office* of legislator who lays down a body of laws intended, in their constitution, to guarantee the good of the individual as well as the common weal of community – so also the *statesman* in the determinacy of the knowledge of the Muses in the First Epoch with respect to the Olympic kingdom under the rule of Zeus, which is the rule of law (ΔΙΚΗ - dikē); all of these people of truth are the poets of reason, literally reason *in person*, the geniuses of reason whose poems articulate the sanctity of the world, the world dedicated by thought to thought in the reality of their works and words – so the determinacy of the humanity of human being as essentially productive, specifically, in the Third Epoch, of religion, of science, and especially of the fine arts and letters whence our philological endeavor was born, i.e. as a figure of thought in the ratio of concretion – not in the sense of seeking and founding a principle, a law, say, in being and in beings but rather, conversely, as founding them in and celebrating them as indicative of a predetermined, preconceived principle.

To further clarify this relationship between the two ratios of revelation and those of foundation, we might say that the poetic song inspires the thinker to conceive but conception appoints the poet's praise. The world is

---

[49] cf. Boeder's meditation on the Homeric "Issue of Knowledge" (Die Sache des Wissens) in *Topologie der Metaphysik*, pp. 60-64.

consecrated in praise, saved in praise; it speaks the language of pure reason in all of its details, events, appearances, particulars, becoming a poem of reason, a myth that enthralls the mind, helping us to forget our forgetfulness, to release our oblivion, surrender our surrender, give up giving up – neglecting that neglect that is inherent in the fostering of private cares and worries, teaching us how to care and not care.

The *Solonian* statesman, for example, establishes the constitution of the "cosmos of community in peace and quiet in enjoyment of the little things in life" (B),

> ΠΑΡΟΥΣΑΣ ΕΥΦΡΟΣΥΝΑΣ ΚΟΣΜΕΙΝ ΔΑΙΤΟΣ ΕΝ ΗΣΥΧΙ
> (Solon 3 W)

writes laws based upon his "insight into the invisible measure holding all in limits" (C),

> ...ΝΟΗΣΑΙ ΜΕΤΡΟΝ, Ο ΔΗ ΠΑΝΤΩΝ ΠΕΙΡΑΤΑ ΜΟΥΝΟΝ ΕΧΕΙ
> (Solon 16 W)

and in doing so opposes right order (ΕΥΝΟΜΙΑ) to the unbridled arrogation of lawlessness (ΔΥΣΝΟΜΙΑ) and the concomitant state of war comprising the dispossession, subjugation, and exploitation of human being by those who have been struck by the precipitous blindness (ATH) of brazen impudence, overweening ambition, and insatiable greed, the reckless infatuations of tyranny – all in one the crimes and the punishments of the warring oligarchies now challenged by the statesman's policy in service of disburdening the oppressed (ΣΕΙΣΑΧΘΕΙΑ) and subject to the eventual retaliation of *divine law* (A), the directive force of justice in the rule of law (DIKH ΘΕΜΙΣΤΟΣ).

67. The Ratios of Transformation

Ideas, or at least some ideas, the best of them we might hope, far from being doomed to the status of idle fancy, are actually meant to, want to, come to the world and be born, enter the scene and take effect, take place and become effective in the course of a specific human life and in the history of human being – this impact is a remarkable property of thought; and accordingly, the world as we know it and love it is not just a shallow, shifting spectacle of bloomin' buzzin' confusion – well, at least not *all* of the time. Perception recognizes order even in apparent disorder and sense in so much nonsense. Why is there such a mysterious pre-established correspondence? Because thought is not merely creative and not merely perceptive – the reformation and renewal of the world, its salvation in the hallow light of thought, a sad song made better in myth, in a narrative's plot and heroic personage, in dramatic scenes and settings, in histories and her stories. Thought is also the result of an achievement of *transformation*; the work of pure reason is, in addition to the contemplation and the invention of being, an endeavor of conversion in the course of which the abstraction of the principle is seen as the force and drive of a movement, a destiny striving to be fulfilled, and as such a destination to be reached at the end of the way. Correspondingly, we distinguish the deduction of **destination**, *i.e.* resolution, from that of ambitious **determination** – in both of these ratios, the principle is the mediating term; in the first, the principle is the poetic image, the fulfilled destiny taken as the project of a vision; in the second, the term of discernment names the work of development devoted to that vision's accomplishment – a searching and striving to achieve the deed that complements the taking of the aim and the recognition of value offered by the mediating term as a vision of THE WAY IT SHOULD BE.

If there is any justification of the assumption that the notion of *pure reason* has endured even until this our very day, it is doubtless the undying fascination and consideration discourse and discussion about ethics and the question of morality awake on the part of a large audience. In the first place, issues touching ethical judgment, all those familiar cases of trollies and torture, are intriguing for being so immediately challenging and relevant to the valuation of our own personal lives and that of others, the term *life* itself being often taken as an expression pertaining above all to action and activity devoted to the pursuit of our well-being and, more grandly, to the benefit of all human flourishing. What could be more strikingly apparent to us than our own actions and those of others and the consequences of these, at least the immediate ones, on our own lives and on theirs? When things happen, not so much in the sense of happening *to us* – in which case we are seen as recipients of a determination, as we saw in the revelatory ratios of thought – but rather when events are taken to be the results of our own doing and resolution, we see and cannot fail to see that they often do indeed make quite a difference.

Action has always been known to be the providence of the practice of reason, in which reason is thought to be put into effect. This practice is initiated by the aforementioned difference that thought makes in our lives – given the discrepancy, the imbalance, the disharmony of our immediate states of mind and matter in the unfortunate coincidence of adverse circumstances or the disruptive intrusion of divisive difference into an immediate state of repose, the advent of a contradiction into our experience marks the inauguration of a purpose, initiates the trajectory of action in which a potentiality, more, a necessity is recognized as a mission to be accomplished, a duty to be acquitted. Thought is then teleological and the dedicated striving of purpose towards the realization of a principle, doing what has to be done. Thought is a tendency in response to what is too much or too little, excess and defect – this gap is the emergence of a need and desire, which, when articulated with a view towards what we can do to close it, takes shape in the mind as a plan and aim.

We distinguish two ratios of transformation. The first highlights the *object* of striving desire as being presented to discernment as an incentive of transformation regarding the immediacy of a given status quo into a mediated immediacy more in keeping with the details and particulars of the vision as the product of pure reason. We present this ***ratio of destination*** in which the term of discernment (C) is the activity of thought by which pure reason (A) imagines and articulates the particulars of a vision of truth (B) as the determining OUGHT of thought. This visionary inference has the following form:

$$C>A + A>B = C>B$$

In a certain situation, the critical insight of reflection projects an image that represents THE WAY IT SHOULD BE as it is distinct from THE WAY IT IS. This is the inaugural act of judgment in which a relationship between a particular and the general principle is established as the good, the right, the just, the fine – all names for the determining principle as a value and measure according to which a particular given is defined in terms of the extent to which it corresponds to that standard. Pure reason takes on the substantiality of circumstances in the imagination, placing the aim, translating it, visualizing it in the specifics of a certain here and now. The contingency of the situation is not inimical to the vision of THE WAY IT SHOULD BE. On the contrary, goals, aims, targets, objectives, standards, norms, all models and measures can only be determined and elaborated in the specific details of THE WAY IT IS – their rule must receive the form of particulars. That is why a vision shows the harmony, the identity of THE WAY IT IS and THE WAY IT SHOULD BE – the ideal *as* real and the real *as* ideal – the idea that has been brought to life, realized and the reality that has been elevated, purified, transformed and improved, in other words, made to more closely correspond to the best version of itself that an informed assessment of matters as they hitherto stood gives rise to in the form of an actionable conception of what ought to be done such that, in the subsequent measures taken on its behalf, the WAY IT IS might, in the end, as the result of these efforts, actually coincide with that projected vision of THE WAY IT SHOULD BE; for this is the wondrous power of judgment in the determination of practical matters, namely to draw a distinction between what is and what could be, more, what should be, thereby sizing up the facts by subsuming them under the idea of what is right or just or, simply, *good* and then by applying the appropriate category or class that conception alone comprehends, not only to decide how well they measure up in comparison to what they were meant to be – which is theory's domain – but also to initiate and sustain action dedicated to giving shape and form to given facts – as opposed to the poetic work of their invention – and to make thus a difference for the better in the manner of things. *Figure 50* suggests the shape of moral facts.

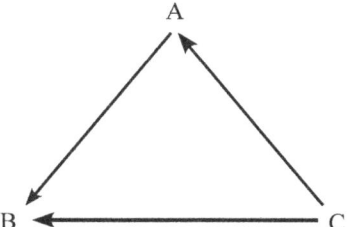

Figure 50: The Ratio of Destination

Ideals, the value claims of reason, are therefore a plurality; they provide a diversity of criteria for judgment because they in their form are contingent on the content, reflect critically the details of the matter at hand. But our capacity to make this distinction in values, moral judgment, is an act of pure reason gauging what it encounters by establishing within the critical scope that it provides the stages or degrees of completion, a proportion of the whole, a hierarchy of differences. This is the mind seizing the day to make a difference.

Take for example the intuitions that reveal how the demiurgic Prophet, the liturgical Apostle and the dramaturgic Poet – Hesiod, Paul, Schiller – receive the vocation of their profession with immediate insight instilled in them by the Gift of the Muses, the Grace of God, the Beauty of Nature, the first to celebrate in song the theogony of the Olympic kingdom founded under the aegis of Zeus, the just king and father of all mortal as well as immortally living being; the second to praise the mission of the Christ sent to reconcile human being with the will of God through faith; the third to promulgate the recovery of the freedom of humanity through an aesthetic education in the community and harmony of our rational and emotional natures. To each of these programs of discernment (C) of the First, the Second, and the Third

Epoch respectively, corresponds a unique term of principle (A), namely to *Hesiod's* prophesy, *Zeus* himself as having grasped and enacted the principle of apportionment of merit and goods to each god and goddess as is his or her due; to *Paul's* ministry, the *Gospel* of the Crucifix as that of the divine shame and the glory of the Son of God who died on the cross and was resurrected; to *Schiller's* imagination, the constitution of the estate of *Beauty* as the circle of friends in shared communion with the ideal. This leads to the issue and the vision (B) of the destiny: The just apportionment of the good and its goods among the gods is the vision of what we might strive for and achieve in the efforts of our own works and days; the congregation of those called to Christ give, in words of benediction and works of love, constant testimony to the efficacy of a miraculous insight beyond the wisdom of the world; the ideal of the apparition of freedom in the appearance, whether in grace (Anmut) or dignity (Würde), whether in the beautiful (das Schöne) or in the sublime (das Erhabene), is brought to note of the world in the dramatic action of those who take upon themselves and upon their own lives the experience of their own humanity as the distinction of human being, the life that begins with death.

This vision is now the guiding principle for the second ratio of transformation, the ***ratio of determination*** in accordance with which resolve now distinguishes measures to be undertaken in order to put that ideal into action. The determining principle is specifically rendered in the form and details of particulars (B>A), these particulars however, taken as the shape of things to come, are a vision of what is intended by purpose, giving impetus to the fire of desire (A>C), moving us to new heights and inspiring us to undertake the ordeal of change that pure reason's intimations of a better world make palpable to our effort (B>C). This is its formula:

$$B>A + A>C = B>C$$

Take *Plato's* conception for example: Founding the distinction between visible and invisible beings (B), the Idea of the Good (A) inspires the striving soul (C) with desire's (ΕΡΟΣ) dialectical drive towards communion with that Idea's beauty and perfection and then, nourished by such numinous nearness, to go down again, returning with the vigor of that inspiration to the worldly affairs of human action with a view, first, to pervading this sphere in spite of its resistance and lethargy and, by enacting laws and passing judgment in the spirit, in Plato's words, in the *Idea*, of the Good, second, to forming a cosmos of human being, namely a political community of good souls devoted to that epitome (ΠΑΡΑΔΕΙΓΜΑ) of value they have seen and now take as a model for their designs in their natural, though ephemeral worldly settings.[50]

Or take *Augustine's* conception of God and the soul and their relationship (B), in particular the schism that has arisen between them, the latter as the image of God in remembrance of the former's inner unity, more precisely, the triune personality of its deity (A), which is the proffered gift or *missio* of salvation towards that broken soul's reconciliation with God through faith (C) inspired by the intuition of discerning love (dilectio), namely faith driven by this love to seek insight (fides quaerens intellectum).[51]

Or take, finally, *Fichte's* conception of the relationship between the *Me* (das Ich) and the *Not-Me* (B), an opposition of heteronomy to which I stand(s) in view of its/my own autonomous nature as self-knowing, self-realising being (A), that learns to posit that opposition in the framework of its/my own absolute activity, which is, as a striving towards that self-given Ideal of freedom, an education and development formed upon the ground of belief (C) in the Reality of the Absolute that is the object of its/my infinite longing.[52]

In the sphere of practice, pure reason's vision of THE WAY IT SHOULD BE as distinct from THE WAY IT IS, is not merely an act of perpetual condemnation that nothing in life is perfect, nothing is ideal. The realization of a goal is not the goal – no, on the contrary, in the ratios of destination and determination that we are here considering, the practice of reason is the exercise of the will, a striving force, the fire of desire that moves the real, transforming it by degrees and sustained effort and enacts in turn the ideal, which would otherwise have remained just a thought, giving it the patient life of practice in perpetuity. Thus the deduction of the latter ratio in *Figure 51*.

---

[50] So Boeder, *Topologie der Metaphysik*, pp. 133-138.

[51] So Boeder, *Das Bauzeug der Geschichte*, pp. 333-336.

[52] So Boeder, *Die conceptuale Vernunft in der Letzten Epoche der Metaphysik*, in "Abhandlungen der Braunschweigischen Wissenschafts Gesellschaft" XLIII, p. 355.

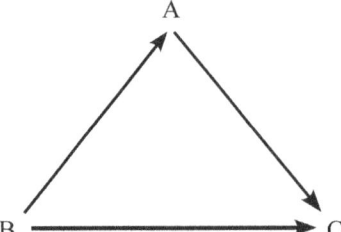

Figure 51: The Ratio of Determination

The vision *is* already a realization in the sphere of practice or at least, it is an affirmation and a vindication of the critical mind that has dared to confront the complacent mentality of maintenance and stagnation with the chagrin of a reluctantly acknowledged imperfection; the failure inherent in doubt and defect is, for all the proponents of excellence, an inspiration and a call to join the good cause of endeavoring change for the better, an invitation to embrace the way of growth, of personal development for its own sake, of fostering renewal.

These two ratios represent the complete transformation – the ideal moves towards realization and the real towards idealization because just as the term of fulfillment, the vision (B) that has presented itself to thought provides the abstract determining principle (A) with a shape and a form that in turn awakens the will to action (C) as the object of its desire (B>A>C) so also is the will, now minding (C) the gap between the WAY IT IS and THE WAY IT SHOULD BE, inspired to bridge this span with an honest effort of reform to give life to the aim and objective it has set for itself, its best "self," moving forward by degrees and steps, progressing (and not fearfully regressing) in its attitude towards that transcendent, "supernatural" prospect (A) that the particular ideal remains to practical reason, and to find patience, solace even, in those small intermediate successes of perseverance and, relishing the pursuit itself, to advance thus slowly but surely in a goodly work of building, having measured and set forth the plan and purpose at the outset and then promoting the conversion of that ideal into the real, the thought into the thing, the mind into matter (B) and mattering – the intersection of our thoughts and our lives is the work of pure reason not merely as intellect and the contemplative capacity for theory to recognize what is truly substantial but also as desire and the striving capacity to bring forth what is most truly worthy of life. But this capacity for stepping back and minding the gap is already efficacious in the striving to make the dream come true, even if that dream never actually comes true, even if the ideal is never, in effect, attained, it has already been attained *in theory*. Indeed, by seeing it in the vision with which the imagination inspires the fire of desire, by seeking it in spite of the all the obstacles and endeavoring, nevertheless, to give it life, however modest, in daily words and deeds – in this way, every dream, no matter how far-fetched, heaven-fetched, is *practically* real.

68. The Ratios of Reason

We have now completed our account of what reason is – we have gained a grasp of ΛΟΓΟΣ as a series of activities, transitions, inferences. The sequence of terms designating the **revelation** of pure reason begins with insight into the *principle* (A) which is the result of *discernment* and the making of distinctions (C) towards the vivid *presentation* of pure reason in particulars constituting the *topic* (B); this ratio gives rise to the sequence that begins with thought as the abstract *general* term (A) which, not remaining obscure to thought, but rather evident, reveals to discernment the *present* of thought (C) and, in the consequence, attains a vivid rendering in the *particulars* of a performance (B). We note the two complementary ratios of this deduction, the latter being that of *poetic invention*, the former that upon which the work of thought, the *Thinker*, is based, namely evidence.

$$A - C - B \text{ and } A - B - C$$

In contrast to the effect of thought seen in its own efficacy, the sequence of terms designating the **foundation** of the thought begins, rather, with the *discerning* attention of the mind (C) to the particulars as the *topic* (B) immediately given in the concrete details which offer the inquisitive mind an opportunity to gain insight into the idea and *principle* (A) behind them and thus to get to the bottom, to make sense of them; this ratio of *Science* is complemented by that of *Art* which begins with the particulars of the reality (B) that, through the discriminating discernment of poetic license (C) which precedes all building, are made to signify the general principle (A) in a vivid rendering of it offered by the poet for the pleasure of the aesthetic (rather than the conceptual) intellect of the audience.

$$C - B - A \text{ and } B - C - A$$

Finally, these the ratios of science and art are mediated by that of *Religion*, the sequence of terms designating the **transformation** of the distinction of human being itself, the work and the ratio of the *Will* in which the *principle* (A) is the middle term, the ideal, which serves *discerning* thought as the *object* of distinction (B) to be strived for and attained (C), giving rise to the sequence that begins with the *particular* object (B) as it presents the *general* principle (A) to critical reflection not in the sense that it mediates insight but rather in the sense that it drives the self-movement of discernment towards its *specific* distinction (C); in this deduction we can see most clearly how the two ratios complement each other; *purpose, resolution, determination* – do not all of these expressions refer to both the subject's striving commitment as well as to the object strived for? Apparently, that is what it means to have an aim *in mind* even though, as we have not yet attained the end, we do not, *in fact*, have the aim at all, not yet anyway and perhaps never. Yes, to *reach* is, as the word itself reminds us, already the success, the accomplishment, of thought, the *Actor* – in the very process of striving, to put the end into effect now and thereby to be perpetually transformed by the goal, on the way to the goal.

B – A – C and C – A – B

For the last time: What is pure reason? It is a train of thought that begins with the *revelation* of thought to us as being **ours**, the object of our insight as our own faculty of intellect as well as the ordeal of our distinguished destiny and ends with our *realization* of pure reason as the spirit of human being and the nature of our world, both of which, being entirely **thought's**, are pure reason's own work of art, an endeavour of development over time, requiring effort, sacrifice, and the avid desire to close the gap between **THE WAY IT IS** and **THE WAY IT SHOULD BE** as revealed at the outset to critical reflection that started the process of *transformation,* in which tangibles and intangibles are engaged in the delicate dialectic of measurement and balance, comparison and adjustment, the deliberation and the dialogue of mind and matter.

Revelation, Transformation, Foundation – This series of sequences articulates a figure of the complete activity of reason, a circle of thought grasping thought, not only as determination but also as interpretative insight and perception, not only as cognition but also as construction, not only as realization and achievement but also as drive and purpose. Thought is its own object; it is real and all reality; it is also the subject and the thinker, the enterprise of science and its issue. Thought is moreover the difference between reality and thought, the marking of, but also the minding of the gap between, THE WAY IT IS and THE WAY IT SHOULD BE – this gap and resonating interval is thought in action, the practice of thought just as, again, it has been recognized as the will that strives to fulfill its destiny, being thus not only persevering purpose but also complete reality and all reality, having brought itself forth on purpose, having always already taken on faith the chirality of its own identity and therein knowing itself as the judge and the accused, the condemned and the exonerated, the artist and the scientist, as contemplation as well as creation, the question and the answer, always already found and constantly sought and, for all that, as much a discipline prescribed, as a deed done, performative as well as generative, perceptive as well as preceptive excellence – how can thought that is ours, human thought, and we, human being, who are reason's in the unique distinction of our human being, how can thought be all this – many, and nevertheless just one, always again at the beginning and perpetually at the end, coming to a close long before the beginning and, after the end, starting out anew, in the benign circle of turn and return, death *and* life, life *and* death that is its perpetual ceremony of commencement?

Recall this unusual being with its contradictory features that we are trying to put into words. It is thought thinking thought – the heautoscopic entity of identity that has the ring of reason to it. Here it is again, our first diagram of the distinction of human being, remembered in *Figure 52*.

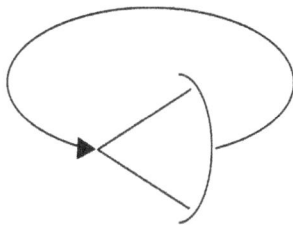

Figure 52: The Logo of our ΛΟΓΟΣ

Now there are two ways of presenting the turn and return of the thought upon thought – we might begin with pure reason as *thinking*, active as the thinking being or else, passive as *being thought*, the thought being. The difference in these two reflective perspectives can be rendered as two different turns, two different directions, around our triangle of terms, which is, in fact, as we have seen, a train of thought depicting inference and a series of inferences in which a distinction, i.e. a conclusion, is drawn. *Figure 53* captures this twofold direction.

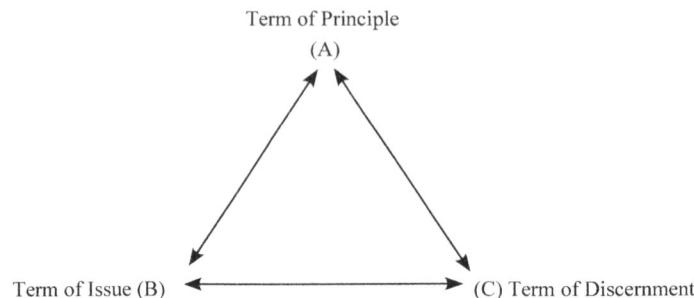

Term of Principle
(A)

Term of Issue (B)   (C) Term of Discernment

Figure 53: The Two Senses of a Train of Thought

The clockwise turn $A - C - B$ begins with the general principle (A) which is then specified (C) and finally realized in particulars (B) delineating the ratio of concretion that we might call the central insight of philosophical thought, namely that ideas, at least powerful ones, want to attain reality and come to the world. The counterclockwise turn $A - B - C$ on the other hand while beginning with the principle (A) is mediated by the issue (B) to effect the distinction of human being in discerning, more, enacting absolute difference (C), the *practical* ordeal of the negativity of pure thought, the critical mark of wisdom, complementing with the genius of *poetry* the contemplative prodigy of *theory*. Whereas the resultant term of a philosophical line of reasoning is the substantive issue of knowledge and the insight of thought into the reality of its own self-knowing being, i.e. *the entity of identity*, the resultant term of all visions of wisdom that have inspired philosophy's consideration and articulate conception is the distinction of human not merely over against all other being but above all from itself, namely our experience of the unlimited power of abstract and abstracting *self-severalty* to draw a distinction upon the background of any given continuity that has been previously set and established as determinate.

Taking the first deduction, $A - C - B$ from the philosophical ratios, as our starting point, we note that the edges of the triangle, i.e. A>C, C>B and B>A, representing, as they do, a transition, are themselves each mediated – i.e. the transition A>C is mediated by the term B, C>B is mediated by A, and B>A is mediated by C, allowing us to draw a sequence of three conclusions:

1. **A>C** = A>B + B>C

2. **C>B** = C>A + A>B

3. **B>A** = B>C + C>A

Or, we can depict our triangle, itself a complete series of transitions, as a syllogism of three conclusions each of which are themselves the result of two transitions across a term of mediation as in *Figure 54*:

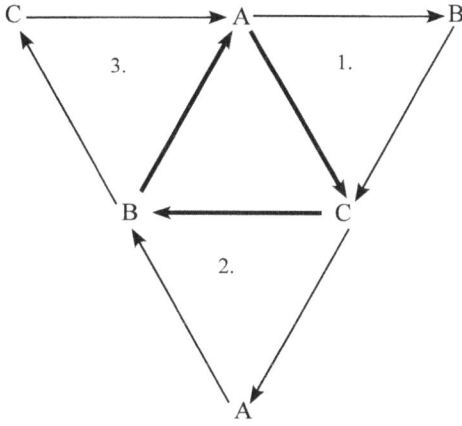

Figure 54: The Figure of Wisdom

These three mediating relationships of inference combine to form the *figure of wisdom* consisting of, firstly, the *ratio of vocation*, secondly, the *ratio of destination*, and finally, the *ratio of signification*:

1. A > B > C

2. C > A > B

3. B > C > A

Conversely, taking the other deduction, that of critical reflection, namely A – B – C, the sequence of conclusions runs in the counterclockwise direction around the triangle, namely going from A to B, with C being the mediating term, from B to C, with A being the mediating term, and from C to A, with B being the mediating term, giving us the following system of inferences:

1. **A>B** = A>C + C>B

2. **B>C** = B>A + A>C

3. **C>A** = C>B + B>A

Or depicted in *Figure 55* as a system of transitions:

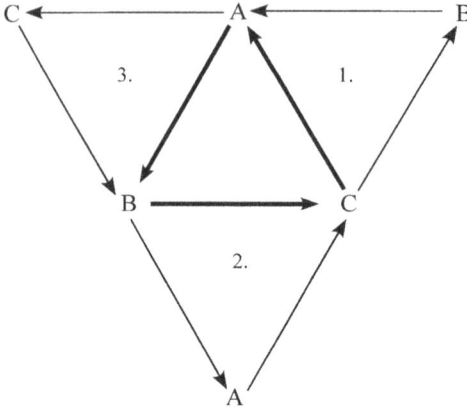

Figure 55: The Figure of Philosophy

The three mediating relationships of inference combine to form the *figure of philosophy* consisting, firstly, of the *ratio of concretion*, secondly, the *ratio of determination*, and finally, the *ratio of perception*:

1. A > C > B

2. B > A > C

3. C > B > A

Each of these two systems of terms is a syllogism of syllogisms and articulates an entire train of thought that we might follow in the meandering movement of the boustrophedon way of reason we have previously noted and now emphasize in *Figure 56*.

Figure 56: The Chirality of Inference

They show what it means to think when we are thinking not about people, places, or things but rather about thought. If there is any sense in speaking about *thought processes* in a way that interests philosophers, as opposed to brain scientists, then in the sense of the ratios we have been discussing as 9 distinct deductions, each with its own character and purpose in a line of reasoning that might just as well find its articulation in a single sentence, a page, an entire book of sustained argument, or even across a thousand, three thousand years of philosophical discourse in which the tradition of metaphysical reflection has found its elaboration as the Epochs of pure reason and even beyond all history and the world past, present, and future in which we live, unto the timeless, worldless scheme of all things thought that includes the thinking of today, yours and mine, as well as all ancestor and descendant thought, bestowing upon every single thought its proper place in the whole in accordance with its own ΛΟΓΟΣ. Is this a grand notion or rather an oppressive one? Well, it certainly means a lot of work if we are to take upon ourselves such an endeavor as our profession of *philology* demands. So that is a strike against it. But on the other hand, for those looking for a labor of love to which they might devote a long life, such a study of ideas and the order that governs their configurations, such a study, though for the most part still unheard of today, could be philosophy, too.

The *ratios of wisdom* provide the substance, the stuff of reason's dreams, its being; the *ratios of philosophy* provide the conception, the methodical activity of thought regarding the nature of drawing a distinction. These two chiral circuits complement each other in the manner of two symmetrical interlacing relationships, namely in such a way that ***theory*** refers both to the *seeing* and the *seen*, i.e. the veritable object of perceptive thought while ***poetry*** refers to both the *form* and the *content*, i.e. the abstract principle, the meaning, that attains specific presence in a coherent assembly of particulars that convey to it the tangible shapeliness of reality, and ***practice***, finally, refers to both the *aim* that beckons as well as the *drive* that strives to attain it, the enactment and execution of purpose.

Each transition in the figure of Philosophy is derived from two constituent and adjacent transitions in the figure of Wisdom and vice versa, each transition in the figure of Wisdom is derived from two constituent and adjacent transitions in the figure of Philosophy. Thus for example the ratio $A>B>C$, the first in the figure of Wisdom, namely the *ratio of vocation*, articulates the concluding inference ***A>C***, which is the transition of *present*, the initial illumination of evidence in the figure of Philosophy, even as the transition of *presence* ***A>B***, the initial transition in the figure of Wisdom, is the conclusion of the ratio $A>C>B$, the first ratio in the figure of Philosophy, namely the *ratio of concretion* which, together with the transition B>C, namely the one delineating the vision or objective towards which *purpose* strives, itself the inference in the *ratio of determination*, constitute the complete line of reasoning articulated by that ratio of vocation *A>B>C*. Each ratio constitutes an inference consisting of two transitions, which themselves are inferences as well. In this intricacy we can see the difference between wisdom and philosophy as well as their rapport. For the present of thought in the immediacy of the principle refers to the acknowledgement of a premise that establishes a line of reasoning – a train of thought must begin with such a leap of faith, the unproven, because self-evident, principle of reason and the gift of thought, upon which subsequent proof and demonstration are founded. From the perspective of the first ratio of Philosophy (A>C>B), the transition *A>C* is immediate determination of thought by the principle and the first premise in the line of reasoning that concludes upon the realization and concretion of that principle. The origin of the *presence* of thought is its inaugural *present*. But of course from the perspective of the first ratio of Wisdom (A>B>C), that transition of immediacy in which thought is illuminated (A>C), is itself an inference and is therefore a mediated relationship in its own right, mediated by the term of issue (B), the being and the presence of the principle upon which the ratios of Philosophy conclude in accordance with the inference A>C>B. In this case, the ultimate cause of the present of thought, its revelation, is the presence of thought itself. It doesn't seem possible somehow, does it? How can thought be thought to be its own cause and origin, brought forth as being and therefore a result, on the one hand, and then again, on the other, necessarily considered to already be a being in order to bring itself forth in the first place?

Taken together as a whole, these two figures show that *theoretical* reason is the original activity of self-reflection, thought thinking, recognizing, and grasping thought, the intellect gaining insight into the substance and nature, the essence of what is otherwise merely the immediacy of apparition. These objects of contemplation are already distinctions and make manifest the achievements of *practical* reason which commences upon the striking revelation of thought thus awoken to the power of abstraction that sees and listens to reason, is apt to give and to have its reasons, seeing behind the seens, noting causes and consequences and, with respect to these, calling into question, with well-founded arguments, the unreflected and undisputed immediacy, and in this way, engendering a crisis made manifest by the gap between THE WAY IT IS and THE WAY IT SHOULD BE perceived in the particular context of immediacy come under the scrutiny of judgment's both morally and conceptually critical review.

This difference, subsequently acknowledged as a purpose appointed to the imagination, begins a process of transformation and development founded upon the idea of a new order worth striving for in which all the givens are revised and then placed into a balance, the ideal realized, the real idealized.

Finally, reason attains the peace and perfection of an idea enacted, a way completed, a destiny fulfilled, a commitment honored, a spirit given life and flesh, a face and a voice and a purpose in the personages and the events of a narrative, having therein taken on a reality and a presence of its own that, though mere signs of the intangible content of the mind, might nevertheless inspire us and our imagination, thus heightened by regard, to like flourishing of word and deed and enable us to receive in gratitude the distinguished world it celebrates as the one true dwelling worthy of human being.

The Third Part
The Point of Departure of our Study

I. The Experience of Critical Self-Reflection

69. Figure and Ground

Having thus presented our topic and the method of our investigation of thought, what it is and what it has accomplished, commemorated the tradition it has generated, recalled the insight it has, in the epochs of that tradition, attained, namely a comprehensive system of knowledge that has, practically speaking, guided human action as the principle and the path of human being and has enabled, but also authorized, philosophical theory to survey how we as human beings have ourselves changed with our grasp of this destiny and why we have become now the single, intersubjective nobodies, assimilated somebodies in the mass body of Man, homebodies of intercorporality, electrically networked anybodies of interconnectivity – beings comprising our Post/Modern world whose life and times, and whose being, serve as the point of departure of this study – after all of this, we are now poised on the brink of think.

In remembrance of the individual person of distinguished human being and the community of subjects with regard to a shared principle of reason that it founded, we have come to understand how, finally, thought itself takes up abode in our language even as it does in our world, living among us through our actions and in works of thinkers and poets, poets and prophets, prophets and philosophers, the wielder of words, treasurers, cherishers of ideas and how, utterly intangible, pure reason thus acquired the efficacy of what is substantial and real in our lives by transforming ideas and ourselves for their sake into such life and being as was, throughout history, resolutely held to be more truly, more enduringly *human*.

For this reason, any study wishing to advocate the cause we have designated *the distinction of human being* must first establish the ground upon which this figure of distinction is drawn and from which it continues to emerge with such original clarity as to prompt perception among the observant. *Undistinguished* man, his ways and means, his views and cares – an all too unworthy theme? On the contrary. We assume the character of reason will come to the fore all the more impressively once the stage has been properly set in favor of the dramatic entrance the spectators have come to expect after so much preparatory and prerequisite fanfare – *Ta-da!*

Enough talk! Let us now see the *Last Man!*

70. How Useful are our Habits!

What is the role that we should ascribe to thought in the lives of human being? By all accounts, indeed, no small one! Our elders admonish us to eschew thoughtlessness once and for all. Intelligence, whether artificial or natural, is everywhere greeted with acclaim, demanded, supported, and, more often than not, sorely missed; we praise *alacrity* of comprehension, *acute* understanding, the mind as being *bright*, the depth of *profound* insight. The planner must look hard into the crystal ball of thought to unlock the doors of tomorrow, harvest fruits in timely remembrance of the inceptions of what has transpired, and science, though not everyone's cup of tea, is embraced with nearly universal appreciation and honored accordingly with glory and with royal remuneration. In this we recognize the value of the sciences for our society, the value of the learnéd, the engineer, the physician, the policy-makers. No, a world like ours, were it to lack thought and thinkers, would be much less than the best of all possible worlds.

And nevertheless! Do we not occasionally hear accolades sung to a still, a tacit mind, while thinking is rebuked? What? There are advantages in negligent inattention? If we dare to entertain such a notion seriously, we discover that dear life's normal grind is, in fact, full of examples of propitious mindlessness and that we even spend a large part of the day entirely or partially immersed and afloat in the immemorial flow of lived experience. Let us survey in more detail this mundane primordial being antecedent to all thought and consider awhile that not unpopular rule of thumb and therefore not so secret password to the lotus eaters' isles: "think not!"

How useful our habits are, for example! Can we attain proficiency in practical things, indeed even in spiritual matters, agility at work, dexterity at play, efficient lethality in war, suavity in love without them?

Is it not precisely this unthinking facility in our dealing with the pressing practical matters of life that helps us avoid the wasting of time that would result if every time we acted we were forced to deliberate with ourselves about how this or that is to be rightly done? Whenever we do several things at the same time and at some point even "*in our sleep*," we are proud of having attained the facility of being able to do something without needing to think about it.

At work, everyone will admit that the art of being *professional* includes such notions as "getting the hang of it" and "learning the ropes," in other words, *practice makes perfect*, following *established procedure*, as is necessary to be efficient, quick, accurate – doing *intuitively* and *spontaneously* the right thing at the right time, reacting *instinctively*, even *automatically*. What a disaster it would surely be if, for example, we had to think about every little movement of the hand, the head, the foot, while driving! Imagine if driving were always the way it was the first time we sat behind the wheel! Remember the clumsy confusion of the beginner driver; recall the rush and hurry of every action and reaction while you tried to think about and keep track of your movements – first this, then that, then that, then don't forget that, followed quickly by this…every movement had to be studied, positioned, corrected, repeated all in the proper sequence at the right moment – the head, the eyes, look left, look right, look up (the rear-view mirror!), the left foot, the right foot, the right hand the left hand – again and again, until they finally became the *spontaneous* and *fluid* behavior we would expect of a motorist? Safety while driving prohibits the protracted contemplation of events as they unfold or the convening of a parliament of the members of our body to debate decisions before we act and often requires *immediate* and *unstudied* reactions. Face it, there is just no time to think matters over, think them through, sort them out, before you hit the brake.

Amazingly, properly executed unthinking action and reaction provides us with time…to think! For if you no longer need to think about driving then you can hold a conversation while behind the wheel, think about the meeting with your boss at 10:00, find the right highway exit on the map, admire the mountain scenery, or just dream of a hero's life with your arm around your sweet one in your Oldsmobile, barrelin' down the boulevard, looking for the heart of Saturday night.

We don't know a language until we can speak it without thinking about the grammar, hear it without translating. Only then do we have the time we need to understand what our interlocutor has said and concentrate on what we want to say in reply. The right sentence construction, the right meaning is clear to us at the right moment! This is the miracle of what, through years of practice, has become automatic – this, our learned facility, has been famously called the trained *mindlessness*, studied *ignorance*, the skilled *incompetence* of the adept and the expert.

Thus, the unmindful mind, immersed in the moment, is not just useful but also absolutely necessary. The constant bombardment of sensory stimulus that impinges upon our notice every minute requires that, in order to make it through the day, we disregard the vast majority of ambient raw data that is there and then again not "there!" at all for us, not taken into account, neglected, regarded as unimportant for the task at hand that our routine has streamlined into efficient coping behavior – the performance of empty but determinate intention with the minimum amount of data necessary while eliminating all else as extraneous. Thus perception is as much a screening out of stimuli, a not-seeing, as it is their reception and interpretative acquisition.

There are innumerable examples of successful automation of the mind. In addition to that of driving a car, we mention the challenges of getting up in the morning, brushing one's teeth, eating with a knife and fork, walking down the street, pressing keys on keyboards while making music; in sports the movement sequences are trained until they become "second nature." In the performance of martial arts, the black-belt does not plan a response to sudden attack. Any thought that comes between the attack and defense or counter-attack gives room to fear and doubt – no, it is the pre-cortical, pre-reflective, sub-personal *reflex* thrust of foot or fist – the knowledge in the knuckles – perfectly executed *without a moment's notice* that makes the master. Ask the one still standing: Who has defeated the enemy? "Not I," she will say, "it just happened, it just happened through me, as though through an unthinking being – the body-me, honed and deeply steeped in brute facticity struck down my foe."

What good is the regurgitation of review and bovine rumination when, here, now, the battlefield calls the predatory twitch of nerves in arms and knees and thighs to fury and to slaughter – do or die? Does the striker streaking towards the goal ponder the bounding bucky ball on the green and grassy pitch? What cuts short the high jumper's speculations? Ready, Steady, Go!

Somnambulant security of instinct and habituation and the intuition of our embodied hypnotic being are also what makes our everyday dealings with other people efficient, if not always effective. Since our childhood we have been taught how to properly behave in society, what we should do and not do when and where in the presence of whom – just how complex the unspoken, unconsciously respected codes and protocols of etiquette are, can be easily discovered when we spend some time in a foreign country. The unassimilated foreigner sticks out like a sore thumb, appears askew, does not blend in, does not fit. *Custom* is the name for the wealth of parameters that govern the flow of human intercourse of a group of peers. Since infancy, we have learned the techniques of conformance in human intercourse, i.e. how to go with the flow of the ego's stream of consciousness, how to coalesce more seamlessly with our classmates, how to ride out the rambunctious unconscious mind with its swarm of impulses, much maligned as the ego's bogey, that little *it*, whether lurking in the body's basement as the *id* or bloated and enthroned in its tower as the super-ego, works the levers of our sleep modes, our cruise controls, our auto-pilots with its invisible hand, makes its anonymous contributions to the economy of primal urges, and by switching on and off the vegetable and mineral mechanisms of our motivations, the goes and no-goes of psychic guidance systems, slavishly but covertly waits on the aches and groans of a stupid cupidity made monstrous by the actively unaware suppression and repression that informs the shifty signifiers of our forgetting, our slips of mind and tongue where you say one thing and mean your mother, mislaying and mishearing, misspeaking and mistaking words, confusing desires, both secular and propane, and, in general, getting it wrong, getting mixed up, getting, in fact, that sneaking feeling that you are always already going nucking futs.

But even among all of these snap reactions and gut feelings, shadow content beyond the spotlight and the windmills of the mind, intimations of the titanic iceberg under the surface of our attentions and finicky ministrations, what could be more shrouded by absence than what is completely obvious, always there, always present, yet never aggressively, importunately there, like an unsheathed dagger glinting in the sun, for example, or conspicuously absent like the sun gone down, gone out for good..., no, I mean, something as modest as, say, a spot on the wall, over there in the corner, passed by every day on the way to lectures, never noticed till now, or, better yet, a knickknack, a minikin on the mantel piece, that had once been an object of reverence or at least of note, a gift of great worth or sentimental value, a forget-me-not and keepsake from a trip, a memento of the magic of a moment and perhaps even a trophy of victory, a rosette in recognition of merit or achievement – these are our treasures and heirlooms and yet, over the years, and by dint of dust and just being patently there and being taken for granted as being there, they have lost the power to admonish remembrance, having themselves fallen prey to forgetful effacement such that this the cup of champions has in the meantime become but a trinket, a gaudy gewgaw, the very mark of specious immateriality and insignificance, collecting in its belly bowl the motes of desuetude, a monument to losing all hope of ever, through that act of an improbable love – the one we have been celebrating as that of critical reflection – becoming human again, poised and polished and gleaming with charm, becoming distinguished again.

The power of the mind to close in upon itself and its world, sucking it down with it, in generating rapid response in real time to on-going events instead of actually attending to what a particular moment offers to our discrimination can in no way be more clearly illustrated than in our tendency to be determined by previous experience in our reactions to the present. A dog that approaches us now we see with eyes that recognize the dog of a previous encounter as friend or foe. The human being whom we have just met is previously known thanks to a category of expectations and evaluations into which we can now classify the present example, as woman or man, German or French, Occidental of Oriental, Nerd or Jock.

Mental models of this sort extend beyond the classification of individuals to include the prepossession of the entire world – psychologists are fond of telling us that we have a structured "cognitive" environment at our disposal, "socially" constructed *for* us (and not by any means *by* us) beforehand, consisting of stereotypes, vicarious information gathered from various sources, amassed assumptions, truisms, sets of suppositions, inoculated attitudes, many details of which have never been subject to our scrutiny or tested by us with a view towards determining their cogency or veracity but merely collected and amalgamated into a patchwork world-view that we cling to as the confines of habitable "reality" in the boundaries of which we build our lives and pass judgment on the lives of others.

At this point, namely when considering the thought models and behavior patterns inherent in the effects of prejudice and the forming of stereotypes, we are forced to recognize the real peril that routines and habits – the very proficiency we attain through learning and practice – put us in by their tendency to close our minds to the actual encounter at hand and to the immediate circumstances as they unfold at a given moment, effectively limiting or even eliminating our perception of the *new*, significantly reducing our ability to deal with the present situation in an objective, unbiased, and novel fashion.

71. The Perils of Habit

We often speak of a habit or a routine in a pejorative sense as something we must break. Preconceived notions are then considered to be obstacles to communication and we place value on education for its supposed effect not of indoctrination but, on the contrary, of disburdening us from the parochial views, dogmas, and ideologies we have unthinkingly adopted from the social milieu into which we were thrown by birth. With respect to this background, we discover the pernicious effects of that period of immaturity (the "Unmündigkeit" that Kant spoke about) in our lives during which indeed, as Fichte reminds us, answers had been given to us before we had even posed the questions. Previous experience does indeed harbor a tendency towards blindness with regard to the present case and the automatism of the adept driver may prove detrimental when applied to dealing with people and the unique situations of life awaiting us just beyond the river bend in a "complex and changing world."

Let us consider the image of human oblivion and the opacity of a closed mind in more detail. Surely, one of the most famous is Plato's Allegory of the Cave in which we are asked to "picture men as inhabiting a subterranean cavern...since childhood legs as well as neck enchained, and so, on the selfsame spot remaining, facing only forward, by the fetters made incapable of turning their heads around..." enthralled by the shadow show of fire-shine cast upon the cavern wall by nameless puppeteers. Thus they remain a captive audience for whom seeing is believing until, "in the natural way of things, it comes about that they are freed and healed from the bondage of mindlessness.... Consider now one compelled abruptly to stand and to turn his head around, to walk about, and, to the brightness, to raise his face – but doing all this in anguish and, because of that refulgence, unable to see the things now the shadows of which he saw before...until, thence dragged by force on the ascent which is rough and steep...to step out of the cave into the light of day to which...his eyes, so filled with gleaming,...would need to become accustomed first... before he could give an account of the world up above – ...at first...the shadows and then, after that, the images in water of men and other things, and only then, the things themselves, and from these he would go on to contemplate the bright beings in the sky and the sky itself – the light of the stars and the moon – more easily seen by night than by day, more easily seen than the sun and the sun's light...and so finally... he would be able to look upon the sun itself and see its true nature, not by reflections in water or phantasms of it in an alien setting, but the way it is in and of itself in its own place." (Plato, *Republic*, VII. 514a-516b).

Is this image not remarkably apt at portraying our human being as one confined in immobility, stalled in a style, locked in a life, stuck in a rut, in the groove of its habits, habits clearly of an all too "groovy" mentality, codified and confirmed patterns of behavior set by peers, colleagues, and the contemporary groups they collect in? We would like to ask stationary Man, this mind made immobile by its idols: "What is the matter with you?

Get up, walk about, move your mind, look around, take note, realize that your mundane mansion is but a shadowy cave of stone and you, in your ponderous inertia and inflexibility, have become nearly granite yourselves!" But as Plato emphasizes at the end of his allegory (517a), our cave man does not take kindly to such admonitions from those returning from on high, ridiculing their ineptitude at dealing again in darkness now that they are back, responding with hatred and accusations of impiety, of sedition, to the "seducers'" of difference even unto persecution and the condemnation to death of those who encourage their fellow captives, especially the youth and the young at heart among them, to embrace critical reflection, to climb the stony path of thought, and endure the pain of burning brilliance that blinds, branding night eyes with the mark of our human self-severalty.

Everyone is familiar with the limitations habits place upon our actions and our perceptions. What we do day after day, year after year, tends to deaden our attention to the details, to the opportunities for improvement that principle change and development could mean for the quality of our lives; we fail to deepen our knowledge, refusing to revisit our tolerably serviceable theories and time-honored assumptions; we refuse to critically reprise our accomplishments with a view to the next step that might again make novices of us – do we still have the strength to begin anew? What has become accepted doctrine, the air we breathe, the ground we stand upon, all of these premises – do we dare call them into question and in doing so make bold to adopt a standpoint of neither ground nor air? A tall order!

Yes, routines and habits are unquestionably useful and even necessary for the success of our lives but let us not forget to consider their downside – the stupidity of mechanical repetition, the mindless words and deeds of those who are not paying attention to what they are saying and doing, the stereotypes and clichés that restrict our perceptions, the prejudices that poison our expectations, the sightless eye that obliterates the complex information of our surroundings, the absent-minded hand that misplaces its pen and its glasses; not listening, a deaf ear fails to hear the unspoken questions; not observing, a blind eye ignores the signs; this absent mind misses the cries for help in a smile, is unable to read between the lines, to look behind the curtain, see beyond the seen, to penetrate the façade, peer through the mist – this prisoner dwells in the obscurity of a here-and-now forgotten – in an amnesia that had never known a presence of mind, the narcosis of a patient mind spread out against the sky, etherized upon the table, ineluctably consigned to a past that might never have been a present.

We are all familiar with the expression: "A leopard cannot change its spots," meaning: "I cannot alter who I am" or even "I am who I am" a conviction held fast even unto death, as in the allegory of the scorpion and the frog. These expressions are sometimes said in the despair of one constrained by habits to mistakenly believe that he and she must necessarily remain who they are, walled in, held in a private world they hold to be an inevitable universe, their fate. But more often there is a note of disdain and even of triumphant pride to be heard in the expression of the attitude: "This is who I am, take it or leave it." These cavemen and cavewomen are quite cozy having long become comfortably numb in their close boundaries of rigid and impassive petrification, an easy, unwitting tool of manipulation, an appendage to the shifting arrays of social machinery that imperceptibly regulates behavior, an instantiation of the snug convenience of convention, the trite parlance of commonplace, the smug face basking under the smile of the ordinary, the normal, the usual, the casually suitable, the passably reasonable.

The uninspired, undistinguished life of mundane man in its most obnoxious forms and, more generally, the narrow-minded main-street mentality for whom the distinction of human being, the capacity to step back critically and embrace *difference*, mind the gap between THE WAY IT IS and THE WAY IT SHOULD BE, is a deadly scandal, has been, as we have seen, a subject of philosophical analysis since the earliest days of Greek thought when the distinction at stake was essentially theoretical, namely between appearance and reality, sight and insight, opinion and knowledge, and has reached new heights and breadths in the critical analyses of Modern and Late-modern thinkers.

72. The Mini-Me Mentality

Or are we not to consider *Man* in the form of commodity or consumer in market forces serving with its unique productivity the self-realization of capital the persona of whom bring to light, in the name of efficient production and growth, the inclination to exploit, to consume material people, places, and things of material nature for personal or merely just "class" advantage, for short-term gain in accordance with the logic of the rational principle that seeks to minimize input while maximizing output, for private purpose, a totalitarian being bent on the erection of iron cages of domination and defense, the organization of suppression and absorption, the exclusion of difference, of novelty, the delusion of risk crushed, Man as that of the egoist with the self-centered torpor of its subjective rationality and the crusaders of an instrumentalized religion, with their opiates and utopias, homemakers for extremists and chauvinists, repressed and repressing Dionysuses conjuring the latest advert Antichrist in a heavy-duty culture industry, the mass-man with his herd-moral conformism and lickity-split hedonism, the outstretched, dooming hand of the ruler caste with its privileges and corruption and conventions and resentments, the scientist with his neutralizing materialism, calculating the angles of the will to power at work and at play where its vectors collide, the authoritarian bureaucrat, the command economy with its policies and procedures, the he-man with the racket of his technological rationality and its dehumanizing systematics – adept at deception transaction and transmission, manipulative quantification, obedient socialization, founding institutions and administrations of liquidation, grounding structures of dominion, generating discourses that mask, marginalize, and assimilate difference and distinction under their skin-deep facades, ringing academic arcades and intellectual escapades – in a word, modern Man in his mind-forged manacles whom we call, a bit fancifully perhaps for some people's taste, the *mini-me mentality*, to remind ourselves that even when styled in its most helpless and harmless guises of uniformity, tending therein towards invisibility as a transparent fixture of normalcy of the eminently quotidian, affecting the air, the very person, of what is usual, average, common, even then and especially then, in lacking, by definition, all notoriety, it challenges the very principle of our cause, even then, it warrants recognition as the diabolic son, or rather the clone child, of Dr. Evil himself – are we not invited by these perspectives to partake of an eminently critical stance that commands us to look critically at our immediate world THE WAY IT IS and its beings, the bug so snug in the rug, the clone in the comfort zone, as indicative of a state of mind that is, in spite of the grind and mesh of gears, all the rationales, all the ratiocinations of its rationality, a travesty of reason and a pedigree of the perversion of that reason, that has so long been the object of song and praise in the philosophical tradition of Western thought as the unique human distinction and the author of the very idea of science, "which," as Schiller suggests, "by constant reference to general laws invalidates the conceit of our individuality, teaches us, in the framework of the great entirety, to lose our little Self and put ourselves thus in the position to deal with ourselves as we would with utter strangers...this sublime mentality is the destiny of hale, wisdom-loving minds who, by assiduous effort turned upon educating themselves, have learned to conquer selfish compulsion...Alone these who are capable of separating themselves from themselves enjoy the privilege of taking part in themselves..." (Schiller, *NA* XX 151.10-17)

>...welche durch stete Hinweisung auf allgemeine Gesetze das Gefühl für unsere Individualität entkräftet, im Zusammenhange

des großen Ganzen unser kleines Selbst uns verlieren lehrt und uns dadurch in den Stand setzt, mit uns selbst wie mit Fremdlingen umzugehen. Diese erhabene Geistesstimmung ist das Los starker und philosophischer Gemüter, die durch fortgesetzte Arbeit an sich selbst den eigennützigen Trieb unterjochen gelernt haben...Sie, die allein fähig sind, sich von sich selbst zu trennen, genießen allein das Vorrecht, an sich selbst teilzunehmen...

In contrast to this spirit of self-knowing being, that of our absolutely shallow, formless, and colorless wights, deep-seated in their cavernous adamantine minds, magnifies their state of inflexible stone into a world view, a mental model or cognitive space remarkably impervious to revision and renovation, called *dogma* or *ideology* – a coagulation of conceptions and assumptions that have attained a certain consistence and therefore a specious plausibility. Dogma is characterized by its inertia and by the fact that those who entertain its articles do so doggedly and without ever having explored its reasons and reflecting upon its tenets, thus nourishing suspicion that these steely-eyed dears of theirs are housed in benumbed and fettered minds.

All social phenomena and human behavior as determined by accepted authorities, tacit laws, and the immediate governance which dictate individuals' rolls must be considered to pertain to the naïve setting in the ground of life, the world view that Plato has so aptly envisioned. Human being is then seen as a product of community, of nurture and upbringing, of culture and indoctrination, of societal, historical, and finally evolutionary life forces that have programmed the genotype of our species for which we are a later, post/modern phenotype.

But the condition of Man who stays put in his place on the cushion of custom is just the first state that Plato discerns in his vision. The second state is that of the insurgent who somehow manages to free himself from his bonds, stands upright, turns away from the screen of shadows that has entertained him since childhood and to recognize that their source, the source of the shadows, the voices, the light, had been behind it, this show of appearances, all along, without his ever having realized it...till now. It has all been an illusion, a spectre, an apparition of the reality of life in the intricate cavities of our mundane netherworld. This moment is one of the inception of sight, one in which he notices a difference between himself and his peers who remain seated. He finds himself to be a stranger in a strange place, no longer at home in his seat but still in the cave left to wander, to measure its size and map out the extent of the delusions which the rest of his brethren harbor. What can he do? Perhaps his only choice is to join the puppeteer in the back, to impress upon those relentlessly devoted to the projections on the wall to see and adopt his vision as their own – to tell them about their cave and the illusion of reality they believe so ardently in. And with this doctrine of the Last Man, he captures the rapt attention of the seated mass all the more for its being so implausible, so counter-intuitive, to the extent that he himself, the voice of revolution, becomes part of the texture of the tale they follow on the wall of their prison; this latest doctrine is the story of the illusion of their lives, set in sombre hues, a provocative story about a different race of men and women than the present one, a better one, that has joined the ranks of the elite, of those who have broken out of the complacent matrix of the aisles and rows, emancipated themselves from the movie of life, and set about to build a better one *in the cave*; it is as if these newly graduated prisoners, the intellectual/constructionist elite, are now consciously populating the utopian hole of revolution and estrangement they call their limbo home – decided among themselves to form an alliance under the banner of the motto: "Let us put this picture on all the big screens of the cavern world and dream and wait for Godot as one, no, better, as many awaiting a better world, a better life, *in the cave.*"

II. The World of Our Cave Man

73. I, Robot

Unfortunately (or thank God!), individual human being is but an imperfect toy in the interplay of life forces, a poorly made mechanism, prone to all sorts of breakdowns and defects that disturb its smooth functioning, putting its beings constantly at risk of succumbing to the bane of critical self-reflection upon their human condition and of suffering encounter with that foreign country, the stranger's view from without – the herald and the voice of sea change – that threatens to kill our skilled incompetence by challenging our enterprising calculations towards the more proficient mastering of a given situation.

It is true. We are, despite our best efforts, subject to attacks of a host of enemies, some natural, some man-made, that put our habits in jeopardy, cause upheaval in our routines and obstruct the flotation of those born to go with the flow – think of all those potential disasters lurking in the background, big ones and little ones, the meteorites that could split the earth wide open, volcanoes that sink cities under ash, earthquakes that rumble our world, the sky that tumbles floods down upon the ground and whirls air into our hair, the crush of gravity, the swelter of the sun, the insidious creeping of disease into our blood and the mayhem of road rage, the mutants bursting from our wombs, and man's wolf and prey, man itself, armed with bombs and blade – how easily our everyday life can be shattered in the wink of an eye – by life itself!

But have no fear! The solution is at hand: Technology, of course! Our hero, a grid savior clad in steel and silicon should protect us from these incursions of chaos. Of course, technical solutions often work against themselves, themselves the cause of new disasters to replace the ones they have eliminated, but on the whole, no one can deny that technology is a valiant protagonist on our side. What is its goal? How does technology serve us and save us? By helping us to diligently avoid making a world-shaking and a habit-breaking discovery, namely that of the mortality, the naked vulnerability, in a word, the *finitude* of human being and the end of halcyon days.

The defensive application of omnibus technology has gone a long way in pursuit of this hope and dream of modern Man – the car aids us in the disavowal of the experience of finitude in his feet, the radio that of his ear, the telescope that of his eye, the microphone of his voice, the computer of his calculating brain, the bomb of his fist. To avoid the experience of finitude, cars have been transformed by degrees into trains and trains into planes and planes into rockets.

Through the gift of technology, we are able to maintain and expand our predominance, stay in charge, have our say in the face of revolting elements and keep their noxious effects at bay by limiting the risks, the unpredictable events, the surprises, all of which would force us to recognize that we are in fact flawed machines, that human being is mortal, worse yet, that human being is bereft of invincibility and ashamed of itself for it.

The normal runs and routines of the day are susceptible to all sorts of tribulations that could adversely influence their efficiency, congest and even jam the flow. That is why security systems and other contrivances have been devised that monitor manifold man and administer to reducing friction, delay, variation, deviation, obliquity, loss, surplus, blockage, stoppage, breakdown, and all the little and not so little accidents that human error of mind and frailty of body are heir to.

It is remarkable to witness how troublesome a break in the routine could be. All it takes is that a right-handed person injure that hand and suddenly he or she is put into the unpleasant, even catastrophic position of having again to think about what has long been left to the mechanism of ordinary life. How should I close a button, eat my soup, shave my cheek, with the left hand? The economy of movement and time and their synchronization, their once effortless, unconscious co-ordination are thrown out of whack.

It does not take much to make ordinary things come to monstrous life; all it takes is for things to reassert themselves, reclaim, as it were, their native and primordial "alterity" from the soothingly blank being of indifference or subservience that we had dissolved them in and their career of horror can commence right before our eyes, a career very different from what we had come to blithely expect of them in their lowly office as thingamajigs at our disposal. Imagine that, yes, sometimes they might venture to resist our complete control – the intricate contraption, the unwieldy package, the zipper stuck, the coin, the apple dropped that rolls insidiously away, on to the street, under the wheel of a car, down the gutter; the shoelace that tears, the cream that spills on our new navy blue tie – these unexpected events should be trivial but, as Stephen King often shows, they are in fact hideous revelations of an oozing underworld beyond the ken of our control, a world that normally stays hidden from view, the "other" world in which things laugh at and taunt us with their materiality, where our pets, those cute man-made critters, tame in our homes, become scuttling freaks, where household appliances are self-wielding weapons, where peaceful passenger planes are transmogrified murderously into hate-guided missiles.

The big and the little disasters in life open our eyes to a simple fact of life, namely that human life is ephemeral, assailable, exposed. This is our first encounter with thought, our initial and original experience with the efficacy of pure reason in a life otherwise considered so pleasantly paltry in comparison to Man's grand designs – it is the unsettling experience of one's world coming into view, eyes falling upon a set of givens, certainties, inevitabilities, an encompassing totality of them, never before recognized as such and therefore never before recognized at all until that fatal moment of illumination. Disclosed in this closure of finitude, mundane human being recognizes itself for what it truly is, frail, bare, in spite of all our technologies' fig leaf contrivances, vulnerable, mortal, clad in the skins of its ingenuity, rooting out a meagre mush of thorns from a patch of dirt, molded into unlikely loaves of dust that have been briefly moistened by some spit of sweat and clot of blood and doomed, after a transient interlude of loveless domination, stymied desire, and joyless labour, to return, after one protracted circuit, to the slightness and unsightliness of shit turned wind-blown dust upon a vast waste of earth in the perpetual extinction of our race. Put succinctly in the form of a curse and condemnation, here is Man's vision of Man in all the glory of Man's fall from the grace of human being's first persons into the piercing and impersonal eye-site of brute truth and cold fact:

> To the woman he said, "I will proliferate your sorrow and your births; in pain will you spawn your off-spring and long for your husband, who will subjugate you." And to Adam he said,..."cursed be the ground to you; in grief will you feed upon it all the days of your life; it will sprout you thorns and thistles; and you will eat the greens from the sod. In the sweat of your face, will you take food, till you return to the soil from where you were got. For you are dirt and to dirt you will revert." (*Genesis*, 3.16-19).

The fruit of the tree of knowledge awakens self-critical reflection of human being. What does human being know after having eaten from this fruit? What is the life of which man had been forewarned that it would be his death to take and taste? Driven out by the flaming sword of distinction, he sees himself and knows himself in his limitations and frailty and is ashamed of himself saying the fateful words: THE WAY IT IS *is not* THE WAY IT SHOULD BE; THE WAY IT SHOULD BE *is not* THE WAY IT IS. This mortification of man, his degradation, and the self-several knowledge from whence it dawns, give rise, in turn, to the curse of realized mortality, the understanding of human fate as a futile and humiliating arc of life from dust to quintessential dust. Similarly, the humdrum manifold man of everyday life, through thought's breach, loses his abode of bliss in the flow and is now estranged and vagrant, cast out and homeless, a rolling stone seeking a new home, seeking some little moss of comfort in the bitter hindsight of the defaming face, become now but cheek, decrying an "infant" paradise, an ingenuous innocence lost, a green gull and dupe defunct, and grasping thus at this last straw of pride, men taste, in the sour grapes salute of this good-riddance, their ultimate juice of disgrace, nodding mute approval to the discarding of their destiny.

For east of that Eden, *do-gooders* will roll up their sleeves and invoke their preferred utopia: "Look at what we are, look at our world! Let us make a better one." *On-lookers* of an accidental life can resign and say, "It is the way it is. That's life!" Or *grim reapers* of rumination can come to the conclusion that reason's critical awareness is the actual problem and advocate the reversion and the regression of thought to its original office, namely that of one assumed (by them) to be nothing if not sunk in the bosom of life to serve there as life's own tool and technique, as a janitor, you might say, for monitoring life's vital functions and general maintenance, its prolongation, its improvement, perhaps even its vindication against critical discrimination, both mineral and noumenal. Or, back to our original post/modern, post-human Adam, the atomic chum of chance advocating a fate-free diet, who, studying to forget all about itself, opts to remain scrupulous, "objective," a mute glass eye witness of estrangement, the photographer, the journalist, the annalist, and, in so proceeding, merely graduates to the "second order" status of cavernous confinement, the appointed chair of the intellectual, our adamant academic, our systemic man who must incessantly remind us of his plight by assuring us, in proper caveman manner, that there is "no world *out there.*"

No other world, except, of course, the world of the OTHER, that is no world, neither place, nor thing, but rather is simply the cognizance of drawing a distinction against a background of indifference, being thus an "indifference" that distinguishes indifference. In the midst of a plaza, surrounded by the neat corners of squares, and rectangles stood on end scraping the sky, the parallelograms of paramountcy that define our cityscapes, our history-, language- and worldscapes – or whatever moniker the ineluctable, ready-made territory of totality has acquired from which, as we have been so often assured by our wise and wisest guys, we cannot escape – we find a fountain.[53] The movement of the water as it sprays and splashes sets these "masculine" forces in the limits of their framework, as do the flags in the wind, the rustling trees and shrubs remind us, in spite of their meticulous grooming, that we have almost, but not completely, assimilated all being into the concrete dominance of lines and surfaces – these elemental irritations are emblems and symbols of the invasion, the onslaught from abroad, superficially forestalled by artifice, that touches us with its exteriority. Far from being always monstrous, the play of forces beyond the ken of human manipulation refreshes us. Consider the pleasure of risk and uncertainty in a basketball game. The calculation of the mastermind has been up-ended in the dribble, in the throw – we do not want complete control or else we would have made the basket lower and

---

[53] This fountain is a "rupture of the totality" reminding us of the "absolute exteriority" of the *being without.* See Emmanuel Lévinas, *Totalité et Infini*, p. 24. His study of "alterity…" as "the radical heterogeneity of the Other…" (p. 25) opposes the Other to the autistic life of the self-centered EGO and the closed world of mere BEING beyond all beings – figments of the post/modern imagination spawned by their critiques of the assimilating, exclusionary, and extremist tendencies of totalitarian rationality, i.e. the issues and reflections of the twisted mind.

allowed the players to carry the ball to it; in soccer, is it not "ridiculous" to prohibit the use of the hands? The foot is a poor hand when it comes to controlling the ball. Exactly! The dexterous hand is undone by the fool foot as a tool of possession – the foot introduces the element of risk, uncertainty, danger – all terms for the irruption of alterity in the almost completely complacent clockwork of our lives. The same could be said for all games of chance, the gifts and shifts of luck and serendipity, the aleatoric art of our times which finds its works in accidents and coincidences of the artistic will, in the junk yard jumbles, bins and dumps of any time and place, the poem plucked in the whirl of word and sound associations, unplanned affinities, surprising contiguities, chaotic installations, happy happenings, the plastic bag dancing in the wind in an alley between the houses – these events are eloquent alone in the context of this revolt against the over-arching worry of inbred, inward rationality and its coddling constructions that have mesmerized modern Man. But what is the principle at the heart of the phenomenon of alterity, the shock of strangeness that calamity deals us in its theater of cruelty in which we are all the orphans and the widows of catastrophe, the weak of the world, muggles all, sheeple, freeple all, made manifest?

74. Allegories of the Soul

For in addition to showing us those who have been bunkered and buckled into the stronghold stools of routines' rules, the topology of Plato's allegory suggests a play within the play and from the shadows on the wall descends the doom of critical reflection onto the deep-seated spectators; against all odds, one of our fellow Man, our semblance, our brother, like us a prisoner, a fool, a loser, and a tool, miraculously awakens to this hypogean life, stands stiffly up, steps back, steps forward, turns around and sees the figures of fire shine that cast the lambent phantasms upon which his contemporaries dote. Miraculously emancipated, cut loose, tossed willy-nilly into existence, mundane man is now at liberty, damned by liberty, to roam in this existential absurdity, in the spleen and frisson of meaninglessness, man estranged from Man, our spelunker swallowed by the yawn of ennui, behind its closed doors of *Dasein*. Does this being on the loose in the cave wither as a hippy geranium would that has walked away from its pot? Does it become lonely lonely? Does it band together with other outsiders, foster an outlaw's sneak, flaunt the rebel's swank, the iconoclast's grim demeanor, rehearse the heretic's shriek, and seek to eke out a living in minority communities of punks and thugs and cads among a motley crew of ragged rascals on the fringes of society, squatting in habitats and poor pools that have collected in the nooks and crannies that mainstream life consigns to those who neither sink nor swim in the flushing of its blood? These post/modern batmen and -women, no less stone-bound than their butt-bound brethren, no less stoned, who would segregate themselves and others from that seated company of immobile revelers in a fiction of discrimination and yet in whose veins, no less than in theirs, flows the green water of Lethe, would seem to be more the parody and the grotesque of self-reflection than its accomplishment.

And nevertheless, they have departed from that matrix of their mother lode, from the patterns, the rank and file configurations, of those farther fathoms and become onlookers of the larger play – our underground Man *sees* the hole.

So, you are awake to the world? Your eyes are open? You take notice of all that is occurring around you, within you? You are attentive, responding to pin pricks and alarm clocks, getting a sandwich, nodding, talking, replying, see every stain on the floor, every crack in the pavement, notice the play of shadows on the living room wall from the swaying branches of the tree outside the window; you are aware of your breath, the faces of people, the sounds of voices strike you; every gesture tells a story; you see a lot because there is a lot to see! And now look again at these actors on your tribunal of vigilance; look at their platform world. They are alive, they move, they see and hear, look how they flaunt and strut their stuff upon the boards, playing many parts, having many exits and entrances in the seven acts and ages of man, the last of which is the first,

> ...is second childishness, and mere oblivion,
> Sans teeth, sans eyes, sans taste, sans everything.
> (Shakespeare, *As you like it*, III.2)

This is the stone age of a blunted life, obtuse and toothless, out of touch, bereft of the keenness of sight and bite, that death before the birth of distinction that is the life of reason, which, in turn, is our distinguished death after that flat life and the incisive life of self-knowing being after that good death of self-severalty.

But in fact it is not the actor on the stage who sees, it is the onlooker, our underground man, who, neither crowd in the house nor player on the stage, sees the actor seeing. Of course, the actor is not blind, he responds to stimuli, as we would expect of sentient beings, he goes about his life, acts out the story, and is even able to reflect upon his life as people do.

But, in contrast to you who are the onlooker, he is engaged in the story of the character's life, he and all the props and the scenery and the other actors and the lines he speaks all conspire to enact the story as it unfolds before our forward staring eyes; for the figures in the play, it is not a story at all, any less than our own lives are a story we enjoy or decry as the onlookers, abstractly, remotely, as gods on their mountaintop would, who peer down upon human history for drama's sake. For the actor is not the onlooker; the actor is the character on the stage in the narrative of the play and as Schiller says, in his essay *Regarding contemporary German Theater* (1782): "what misfortune...if the actor were to entertain a careful and a fearful awareness of his present state and destroy the artifice of his vision through the idea of his real world surroundings! Woe is him, if he knows that perhaps a thousand and more eyes weigh his every gesture, that just as many ears devour his every word...I am being watched!" It would be like "...the somnambulist's fall who was dizzyingly seized upon the precipitous spire by a warning wake-up call. The hidden danger was nothing to him but the sudden sight of plunging height threw him deadly down."

> ...welcher Übelstand... wenn der Spieler das Bewußtsein seiner gegenwärtigen Lage sorgsam und ängstlich unterhält und das künstliche Traumbild durch die Idee der wirklich ihn umgebenden Welt zernichtet! Schlimm für ihn, wenn er weiß, dass vielleicht tausend und mehr Augen an jeder seiner Gebärden hangen, dass ebensoviel Ohren jeden Laut seines Mundes verschlingen...Man beobachtet mich! Es war...der Sturz des Nachtwandlers, den ein warnender Zuruf auf jäher Dachspitze schwindelnd packt. Die verborgene Gefahr war ihm keine – aber der steilen Höhe plötzlicher Anblick warf ihn tödlich herunter. (*Über das gegenwärtige Teutsche Theater*, NA XX 84.18-30)

It is only the onlooker who, by virtue of the irony of sight, can follow the different threads of meaning as they intertwine into a narrative. The onlooker watches and in watching, sees the life they are living as distinct from the life of the groundlings who believe that what they see is truth rather than fiction. The onlooker watches and knows what the actor in front of him is doing and that this figure *is* an actor; the actor on the other hand is acting the role, *is not* a figure, is caught up in the moment of the plot, running away, fighting, planning, eating, cleaning the apartment, but it is only the onlooker who sees the planning and the running, grasps the frightening truth in the context of the whole. But this crisis of the spectator of mundane life, our closed society's free radical is least, not last.

For we can step back not only from the actor's stage and the crowd in their seats but, as well, from the onlooker's subterranean world. We see what the actors and the gallery saw and also what the onlooker sees; but we also see what our underground Man could not see. We see mundane Man, the *onlooker*, too! Man sees the play and knows his life is distinct from that of the figures in the play but is blind to the play *in the play*, blind to his role as onlooker. Man did not know that it itself is an actor in the play, a "second order" play, a "meta-play", as modern systemic and constructionist theory postulates – the story of Man's lives is the story of a mentality; the narrative of the life and times of thought is *our* play and dream. But who are we? Where do we fit in? What do we see? We see the seeing of the onlookers; we can take note of the crowd; not the events on the stage alone are our object but above all the *perception* of them. For this perception and attendance, this presence of mind, is the *activity* of the spectator and of the audience of that first world that we now, from our absolutely remote vantage point beyond every mundane world, perceive and attend to, perceiving thus perception, attending to attention, discerning the discernment that witnessed the drama on the stage; we are now the witnesses of the witnesses of the play. And it is alone this perspective that attains the purity of the self-possession of reason that is the distinction of human being, not merely as a concept but also as an action and a deed. With this standpoint of speculation, we exit the cave at last and breathe. Breathe!

Where do we fit in? We don't. This self-relationship of contemplation is the true achievement of reason in which the object of thought and the thinker, the thinking subject, are one and the same being. It is theoretical thought thinking not merely about the object of thought but moreover about the thinker thinking about the object, the entire relationship of thought thinking thought. Thus our task is to grasp the *theater,* not merely the plot of the play, not merely the actors' characters, not even just the presumptions and misconceptions that befall the onlooker due to his standpoint in the limbo of post/modern Man's mundane conception of the mind to the extent that this conception is part of the performance of the drama, experiencing the actors' world from a distance, connecting this world to their own in the rush of fear or sympathy that the narrative stimulates. The *theorem* of the theater itself is our theme and cause. For in gaining this perspective as spectator of the spectator, something has changed, something has happened. What? Something unsettling, disconcerting, destabilizing, an echo and recurrence but not at all an imitation, a repetition but with a twist, more like an encore than an repetition, what just happened was that *thought thought thought.* This is the inaugural experience of pure reason.

With respect to narratives exhibiting this form, we might say, with Borges, that discomfiture arises because when the figures of fiction suddenly become readers or spectators of their own stories then you, dear reader, so summoned, and now appearing before the court as it were, at this very moment, having just been appointed, kind reader and spectator, judge, you yourself become too, here and now, a figure of fiction, self-known and self-knowing, you to Yourself, we to Ourselves are wedded to our enantiomorphic Other and better half – in the seeing *I* of self-relativity we are not merely one but, beyond that, moreover, self-several, too.

Consider now a simplified version of the procession of abstraction and reflection superimposed now on the topology of the cave allegory depicting in its element our experience of the self-severalty of thought's self-relativity, i.e. its recursive ring of abundance and superabundance.

We see depicted in *Figure 57* that first stage of this train of thought as that of the consummate actor bringing the role of her life to life and the actor's captivated audience engrossed in the scenes of the play that unfold the plot of its narrative; the second stage is that of the onlooker, our Post/modern Man, estranged in the crisis of its existence but still trapped within the contours of the cave; though struck by the humiliating finitude of man, the onlookers are, in spite of their disillusionment, no less deeply involved in the actor's intoxicating performance, no less so for being merely the dissimulation of ritual in spotlights and stage props and costumes of the scene, drawings of the drawing of distinctions. But this level of reflection has not yet attained that of pure reason's coign of vantage, namely the sight of theater's theory, which transcends the specter of groundlings and performance.

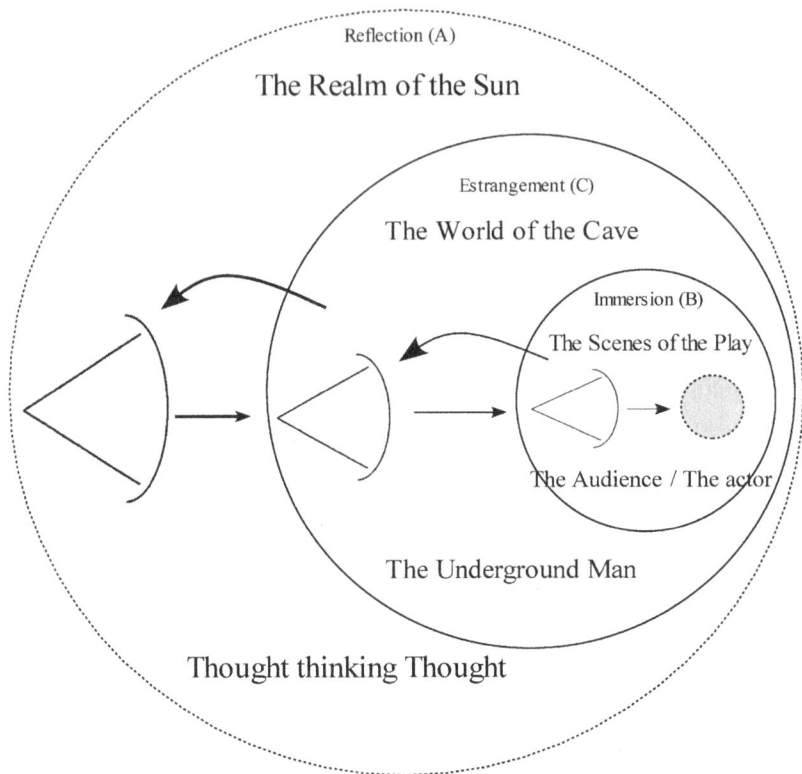

Figure 57: The Emergent Spectator of the Spectator

In this allegory of reason, let us therefore distinguish between two states and, as it were, *generations*, of the human mind in the cavernous theater of lived experience: the estranged state of awareness and attendance (C) and the condition of engrossed immersion in the flow of life (B) – the *one* human condition, in which, in the context of a narrative, circumstances dictate the unfolding of events and the relationships among figures while the interaction of their motivations and the consequences that follow from these actions in response to the circumstances are revealed and resolved on the stage for the ***audience***; and the *other* human condition, for which the discernments of this overview are obscure, hidden in the immediacy of the situation in which meaning is constantly in the process of emergence; the play of circumstances merely elicit reaction and response on the part of the ***actors*** who are enclosed in the totality of a system, a whole that nevertheless, through animadversion of ***underground Man***, knows itself inwardly and critically within the dimensions of that narrative. The first state is that of a relationship of unconscious *engrossment* and *immediacy*, the other the apparition of *critical awareness*, i.e. *presence* disclosed by *absence*.

But it is only in the third state or generation of the mind, *critical detachment* (A) that the theorem of reflection can be formulated. It is the emergent state of reason that has extricated thought from the mundane emulsion of Modern Man. In Plato's allegory, the inception of this third state, the philosopher's state, is depicted as the cave dweller who has not only left his seat to explore the cave but also manages to ascend towards the surface, attain the outward region of light, the light of thought, the critical distinction of human being, which consists not only in the departure from and the subversion of everyday life in the initial phase of estrangement but moreover the transcendence of Man and the world of Man in its totality, through the realization that rational self-reflection manifests its own realm and being, that of distinguished human being beyond the ken and cares of mundane, cave-bound Man, namely thought thinking thought – thought *transcending* thought, *knowing* thought and finally *enjoying* thought as complete reality in the certainty of its own self-evidence having brought to light the whole story of thought.

But this story of pure reason's way, this allegory of the soul, does not end in the ivory tower of insight into the brilliant principle of thought, which is to step back and make a distinction; even in the Platonic conception of the intellect, thought, in Plato's terms, the *soul*, is ultimately an artisan of the good and the best life, a founder of just states and proper places and a builder of human being in all its excellence, a demiurge destined to return to the stuffy world of shades, bringing back down to the sublunary sphere the forms of light it grasped and collected on its journey to the sun with a view to pulling those sedentary material girls and boys away from their TV and getting them into those brilliant shapes that are called, for all their brilliance as seens (ΕΙΔΟΣ), invisible, intangible.

75. The Nostalgia of Modern Man

But wait! What if we could turn back time, if we could find a way and take it all back! How would things have played out if we had refused that fateful apple then, if we were to refuse the bite of the apple into being, our being here and now, again and again, refuse reflection, banish desire from our lives, shut the mind's eye, stifle the sighs of the heart with the pillows and the pills of complacence in the hopes of taking the edge off, the cutting edge off of critical acumen, blunting, dulling the *acies mentis* into smooth indifference in an all ditch effort to, once again, hug and be hugged in the infinite indulgence of oblivion – Oh, to remain or become once more a noble pebble or just a quaint grain of quartz glinting in an arbitrary sidewalk on the sunny-side of the street! To be a may-flower pink, small, punctual, a chaste daisy smiling back at the day's I, her glad dad, beaming! Admit it! We have all had these thoughts in moments of despair, weighted down by duty, at a crossroads, in the face of challenges that test our grit and put our limitations on parade for all the world to jeer at. Could we not just *be*, like them, like budgies chirping, be like our cat sees us in its reptilian gaze, just *be*, not *mean*, not *exist* in the way of Man, damned and condemned to the irking experience of *Dasein* and being knowingly "*There!*" a lot of the time – well, at least on our worst days and on our best – deliberating, discerning, deciding, enjoying or contemning our all too brief enjoyment, aware of the grievous end of days even on our holidays and, in this way, self-consciously aware of our awareness, anxiously reliving, again and again, the mortification of Man's finitude?

We have already seen the role that technology plays, its most enduring and endearing role of all, wearing the mask of ephemeralization, in helping us forget ourselves and our limitations and nourish the delusions of grandeur and omnipotence in the prostheses of machines that expand our body mechanically, electromagnetically into space and time, across continents, delusions of ubiquity and omniscience, knowing all, seeing all, such that there is no end to us, no obstacle against which the beams of our desire clashing, must revolt, bent back into the objection of reflection, an experience that instills in our heart of hearts the mother of all fear against which our courage must be constantly revived, namely against the *apostate* fear mundane Man tends to assert and uphold in negligent regards to self-critical reflection, in other words, the fear of *thought* (phronemophobia) – the only fear we really do have to fear and should proudly *fear* (phobophobia), whether it take on the form of *xenophobia*, which is the awareness that Man's wall of control, the fortress of homogeneity and similitude that habit breeds is always in jeopardy of being breached by the unexpected visitation of difference, of the *unknown*, the *unfamiliar* in the person of the *foreigner* or, more generally, the fear of the *new* (kainophobia) with its incalculability, its unpredictably – calculating and predicting being the preoccupation of a mentality bent on maintaining the homeostasis of its totalitarian systems – confronting the conventions and routines of the status quo of some established mastery of routines with wild, hair-raising *ideas* and the risks and *uncertainty* that accompanies them along with the corresponding apprehension (ideophobia); of course, all animals, especially those that do not easily lend themselves to being assimilated by a domesticating anthropomorphism, especially *insects* (entomophobia) and *reptiles* (batrachophobia), personify the menace of what is strange and inscrutable to the closure of Man's recalcitrance in the face of nature's impinging wilderness – we are all indeed familiar with fear of *snakes* (ophiciophobia) *spiders* (arachnophobia) and especially of *bats* (chiroptophobia), fabulously fanged and winged with the blood thirst of night, arguably the most notorious of all the bugaboos known to haunt and to snatch Man's daylight savings – that threatens the amenities of Man's germ-free rationality with the allergenic specter of creepy-crawling horrors that lurk and viscously, viciously teem in the gas of maggot-rich rot. These nightmares of degeneration are symbols, the red flags of sanitary Man, the bland, Man, the blank, in that they designate the squalid characters of chaos and insanity it seeks to eliminate from the equations of its economy by frantic, frightened purging, scouring, and bleaching of *dirt* (mysophobia) and being dirty (automysophobia), *germs* (spermatophobia), *disease* (pathophobia) and *illness* (nosemaphobia) all of which cut to the quick its precious, precarious life so wanting a watchful guardian and a silent protector of the cheery pinkness of a mind it is terrified of losing at any moment (lyssophobia).

Hence, all *accidence*, whatever could strike one as being out of the ordinary, the marked term figuring prominently as perturbation against the background of immediacy, can stand for critical reflection's encroachment upon the cocoon of Man's substantial mindlessness and therefore might be met with trepidation (dystychiphobia). Moreover, the entire experience of the train of thought and the stations we have highlighted as salient can serve to signify a dread. For example take the familiar fear of *heights* (acrophobia) or *flying* (aviatophobia) – is thought not a flight and the surrender of control of our fall through the sky, not the consignment of our lives in trust and faith to the pilot-spirit? Or take our fears of *enclosed places* (claustrophobia) or *open spaces* (agoraphobia) – do they not refer to our experience with the constraints of a limit, the ΟΡΟΣ (horos), that can be defining form for amorphous continuity or the great and not so great outdoors to the stay-at-home, the snail-Man afraid to leave the armor of its shell while facing the alarming exposure at the critical juncture of *crossing a street* (agyrophobia) or a *bridge* (gephyrophobia)?

Or afraid of just *being touched* (haptophobia) by the *sword* (aichmophobia) of knighthood that marks a distinguished mind and of the *pain* of the point it makes (algophobia), namely of the anguish that is the start of critical thought in cognizance of the ruinous gap between the IS and the OUGHT and therefore the realization of which is fittingly dubbed the fear of the *nighttime* of our soul (nyctophobia) and of the *punishment* (poinephobia) that we feel she deserves for the egregious shortcoming of being less than perfect, mortal, *fallible* (atelophobia) – we, who are so unwillingly, so mutinously human.

If we are such, it stands to reason that with respect to the prospect of leaving the cave behind them, the others who we are no less, regally squatting in the harness of our backside thrones, might experience our resistance to thought as a fear of *standing up*, or, with respect to the flow of going along, *standing still* (stasophobia), in both cases of taking that *stairway* (climacophobia) to the Heavens and its *celestial* host (siderophobia), a journey that would force us to leave familiarity behind us as well and come face to face with fearsome *freedom* (eleutherophobia) and its terrifying *solitude* (isolophobia) when the ghastly light of the *dawn* (eosophobia), of the *day* (phengophobia), of the *sun* (heliophobia) of reflection rises revealingly upon the lowlands of Man, whose individuals would rather fit in and conform to the norm than stand out in the *disorder* (ataxiophobia) of difference and risk losing friends and family who, staying put in their appointed place, are apt to cast aspersion and *ridicule* (katagelophobia) upon the project of the distinguished heart's ambition that even risks becoming a scapegoat of the mindless *mob's* resentments (ochlophobia) – obviously, we might extend this catalogue of phobias[54] indefinitely for there is no end to the multitudinous, multifarious death that Man, loathe to think critically, is doomed to duly, daily *die* and therefore is bound to fear (thanatophobia) – ah, but opposing this phobic, regressive fear of *God* (theophobia) and *ghosts*, holy and unholy (phasmophobia), is, on the other hand, i.e., in keeping with thought's chiral dissymmetry, a *restitutive* fear, namely the reverent, and in this sense, fearful, awe of regard and devotion towards the absolute principle of distinction that is famously said to be "the beginning of wisdom." (Proverbs 9.10) In contrast to that phobic spirit whose fear is demeaning, this spirit of "reverence raises self-esteem." (Schiller, *NA* XX 393.15-17)

...Ehrfurcht, die ihn in seiner eigenen Schätzung erhebt.

76. Don't Worry, Be Happy

Redeeming reverence aside, one respite and calming nepenthe to quaff, one strategy of amnesia and of granting amnesty to the crime of face-

---

[54] cf. Roget's *Thesaurus*, pp.108-111.

threatening shame and life threatening morbidity that thought uncovers when we commit ourselves to receiving the countenance of thinking human beings is, to be sure, technological mastery. The other is to use thought to quench thought and, with an essentially autophagous line of reasoning, talk ourselves out of having ideas by alluding to the many instances in everyday life in which the blank mind is a boon, as was discussed in the beginning.

In advertising oblivion, we can make much apology of and mount exhortatory to the previous station of life before we began our career of making things distinct. "Just do it!" for example is a well-known slogan. What does it mean? The thinker is seen here as the one who delays and wavers, who ruminates and equivocates, who, lost in thought, full of doubt, fails to take timely action. For example, at a party, to simply walk up to that attractive person whom we would like to talk to over there on the other side of the room. In this situation, thought is quick to balk at the specter of failure or rejection that it presents to itself and in this way, as Hamlet in his famous soliloquy remarks,

> ...conscience does make cowards [of us all],
> And thus the native hue of resolution
> Is sicklied o'er with the pale cast of thought,
> And enterprises of great pitch and moment
> With this regard their currents turn awry,
> And lose the name of action.
> (Shakespeare, *Hamlet*, III.1)

Here we have to *just do it!* or *go for it!* When we see ourselves set before us on the stage of our mind's animadverting eye and see our limitations, our finitude, self-several contention sets in and we are ashamed of what we are compared to, namely what we could be or should be but unfortunately *are not* (i.e. handsome, witty, debonair, attractive, rich...name your poison) – that is the crisis of thought, and the doubt of divergence of human being from its ideals that disrupts Man's state of untroubled immediacy. Before we knock on the door of the human resource manager's office for our job interview, standing in front of the audience before our speech, crouching down at the starting block before the 100 meter race begins, sword in hand waiting for the call to charge into the onslaught of the enemy, the moment of truth before we take the plunge, whether from the 10 meter diving platform or into marriage – these are the critical moments where in the face of challenges and obligations we see ourselves in our limitations, where we are forced to recognize the limits of our control, the limits of our ability to seize success and to command ourselves to be the captains of our fate and the masters of our soul, where we learn that the gift of thought is both the poison and the present of the self-several relationship of ourselves to ourselves, where we see ourselves for what we are in eyes that critically and impartially measure our quality, invariably find it wanting and, subsequently, promptly or deliberately, *die* of humiliation. Die? Though modest folks these days, recalling their own experiences with such critical events, might find this turn of word a bit exaggerated, it provides us, nevertheless, with the key to understanding the use of the term *death* as a word of wisdom and term of distinction in works of poetry, religion, and philosophy, namely those of theory as well as those of poetic imagination that strive to grasp and give poignant presence to the practice and the life of reason as a path, hence as a journey abroad, above, to infinity and beyond – all terms designating the pure negativity of abstraction with respect to a given current point in cave-curved space and time we call our home and so fervently defend as our only plot of possession – on a train of thought and across a transition of transitions beginning with that unique *departure* that is the distinction of human being, the self-several *death* of Man.

The remedy of post/modern provenance is, supposedly, to call to us: "Carpe diem!" Seize the moment and live in the *here* and the *now* before thought and the waver of hesitation raised its menacing visage! Forget moral qualms and scruples, misgivings borne of contemplation – yes indeed, if only we could find the right button to punch or the switch to flip in the hardware of our brains to do so! But it is so oddly hidden, somehow inaccessible as if thought weren't meant to be put on standby on a whim! "Put aside your doubts, honey, and let yourself go..." coos sweet surrender in our ear; "Go with the flow, everything's gonna be all right!" Have we never heard this said in consolation? Surely it is the very height of happiness just to lose oneself in what is at hand, be all ear, all eye, engrossed, absorbed. But how can I make myself spontaneously be what I want to be without wanting to be what I want to be (but am not) and in this way merely enforcing the gap between the IS and the OUGHT that I intended to mend? Hmm! How can I stop being me without reanimating the Me who I should be in the effort? Evidently, the utopia of that place for us, peace and quiet and open air, somewhere, actually inscribes the X that marks the spot of the here and the now by touching off the mechanism of Man's desire, underground Man's that is, and thus sealing our fate by unleashing the double bind of our Man's self-severalty in which attaining means forfeiting and lacking is possessing and awaiting is evincing the merit of success.

Thus the question: Which absorption should be our deliverance? For we want to be engrossed without being grossed out, immersed in what we do without falling, without drowning when human voices wake us. Philosophy has taught that closure is not to be had by going back but rather by going forward, not trying to take back the distinction that critical self-reflection makes upon our lives but rather to fulfill the principle that emerges as our destiny because of it. Confronted by our finitude, in the anguish of the difference between our desires and our powers, we step back from the dimensions of our little life, from the mundane habitat and habits of our world, from the face and the surface of immediacy, and in this about-face of reflection recognize the *orders* of reason, i.e. the revelatory present and the accomplished presence of thought – this entity of identity alone as the issue of insight and science in which we learn the practice of its discipline and the invention of its art as the only object truly worthy of absorbing and engrossing the human mind!

To be all ear, all eye? Yes, of course! But to what ear, to what eye should I surrender myself so utterly and entirely? There are many eyes – take the multi-faceted fly-like I that is the ego for example. We can expand our ego-I until it knows no limits, sees no limits to itself and finally assumes that what it wants is what every other ego wants since every other ego is part of this over-arching-ego – thus the strategy of the *narcissist-egoist*; or take the ego that tries to exert its influence and control throughout the mundane infinity of the world – the totalitarian strategy of the *techno-ego* that we have already discussed; or how about the ego that strives to liquidate itself into the fluidity of *drugs, sex, rock 'n' roll* – the *disco ego*. Or it can try to disintegrate itself into its multifarious possessions, be it wife or husband, man or child, people or commodities, animal or mineral – the *yuppie ego*; it can try to distract itself in weekend spectacles (rather than enjoy the theory of reason in the perfect leisure of contemplation) – the *couch potato ego*; or diffuse itself in fictions (rather than grasp the representations of thought), disperse itself in hustle bustle business (rather than concentrate on the unique purpose of action), and otherwise mortify itself into dissipation rather than distinguish its rational nature from its purely physical and mundane one and then come to consider and to realize itself – an ordeal and endeavor of founding and the patient building of the world and worlds of whirling mind over matter – as the self-knowing, self-realizing, and perpetually renewing being that we were meant to be.

77. The Dark Knight of our Soul

The anguish of Man's existence begins with humiliation in view of its finitude, its vulnerability, and the dislocation it experiences as a result of the estrangement that critical thought makes manifest in the separation from the unmarked state of everyday life.

Let's face it! When we chance to stop to take note of the state of things, stepping back from the flow with which we normally go and have a look at ourselves – the Man in the Mirror and his world – critically, we are often dismayed by what we see: This is it? This life? This world? Is it, am I, what it, what I was meant to be? We are faced with the fact of a gap between THE WAY IT IS and THE WAY IT SHOULD BE, the IS and the OUGHT and thus the call to change our ways. Is this not the core issue of modern thought as expounded by Marx, Nietzsche, and Heidegger, namely the outstanding experience of the *ex-istence* of our cave Man, our rolling stone who, even after all his needs are fulfilled, problems solved, and perfection achieved, still can't git no satisfaction!

Heidegger, for example, in his treatise *Being and Time* (Sein und Zeit), explores the great wealth of structures which characterize the *humdrum quotidian* (durchschnittliche Alltäglichkeit) of the *anonymous manifold of Man* (das Man) in the indifference of its *disownment* (Uneigentlichkeit), that peoples the behavior of monotony, the *thingamajigs* (das Zeug) that it avails itself of while taking care of its busyness while constantly dealing with the diffuse anxiety (Angst) that emerges from its being both entirely absorbed by the world, in other words, *into it* (Insein) while at the same time, by just being "there!" in its Dasein, utterly *out of it* (Existenz) in the *eldritchness* (Unheimlichkeit) of estrangement. The unifying structure of such broken being is *misgiving* (Sorge) that receives its articulation in the *triune apprehension of temporality* (die dreifache Sorgenstruktur der Zeitlichkeit) foremost of which is the modus of *existence* in which the anxiety of **what's on** (Zukunft) is revealed as our *being faced with death* (Sein-zu-Tode), complemented by the *total absorption* (Verfallenheit) of Man in **what's up** (Gegenwart) and our *having been thrown into the fray* (Geworfenheit) of the fait accompli (Faktizität) in confronting the consequences of **what's been** (Gewesenheit) even though we didn't start the fire; in this triune apprehension of temporality, our *being "there!"* (Dasein) is lit (gelichtet), gleaming (hell), cracked (offen) and, in this way, spread-eagle in the primal exposure (Erschlossenheit) of Man's being.

However, the figures of modern thought in turning to the world and seeing it as it is, are, in general, concerned with THE WAY IT SHOULD NOT BE and

THE WAY IT IS NOT. That is the essential difference to the epoch of thought known as pure reason which conceptualized wisdom, the insight into a determining principle which always gave evidence of the way something was intended, supposed to be, its destiny. Not merely that which OUGHT NOT TO BE or that which IS NOT – forms of absence, concealment, or failure – but rather that span of difference that emerges when THE WAY IT SHOULD BE is not THE WAY IT IS and vice versa, THE WAY IT IS is not THE WAY IT SHOULD BE. For either the idea in the OUGHT is still merely potential and not yet actual, requiring the ministrations of the will and the elaboration of art that realize that principle, bringing it about, making it come true; or else the real is as yet immediate and unreflected, meaningless and insignificant, wanting depth and the clear sight of the intellect to bring it to the fore of attendance that sees its true nature and where it belongs in scheme of all things thought.

The thinkers of Post/Modern Man, intellectuals of our everyday world, let loose as they are in the cave, are nothing if not critical, awaiting some utopia, whether it be Marx's social Man of the *Communistic Society* (die kommunistische Gesellschaft), Nietzsche's *Man Above and Beyond Itself* (der Übermensch) as the lord of Earth life or of Heidegger's Man fated, born to die, and thus situated in the *Quaternion* of the four regions of the world, collected in the simplicity of the Thing of dwelling namely *Heaven and Earth, the Mortal and the Divine* (Das Geviert von Himmel und Erde, Sterblichen und Göttlichen)[55] – can we fail to see in these projections of a better world, of a better Man, the faint trace of a distinction that once was that of the destiny of human being? But these thinkers and their pupils would seem to be and remain caught up by the mundane play we have

---

[55] See Boeder's treatment of the writings of Marx, Nietzsche, and Heidegger in *Die Vernunft-Gefüge der Modernen*, pp. 237-359) which he characterizes as "modernity's core discourse on human being" (Kern-Besinnung der Modernen auf das Menschenwesen – p. 354). In the topology of their positions, Boeder shows that what unifies their thinking into a logotectonic figure is the "experience..." they share "...of the Existence of our human being as being essentially generative...not merely with regards to our things, our actions, and our knowledge of the world but also and above all, with regards to our own being" (...einer Erfahrung...die des menschlichen Daseins und zwar daraufhin, daß es produktiven Wesens ist...nicht nur hinsichtlich der Dinge, Handlungen und Kenntnisse seiner Welt, sondern auch und sogar dem zuvor hinsichtlich seiner selbst." - ibid.) – Just such a generative being as we have termed thought, the Builder, who builds monuments to the majesty of the distinction that has inspired poets and thinkers for thousands of years, as we shall presently see.

described, in a sort of limbo, neither flesh, nor sprite alone, nourishing their thought from the blood of the unsuspecting host of Man's obliviousness to the lot of Man but themselves lacking the spirit to die and rest in the peace of the good death that pure reason is, thus neither partaking of that death that is Man's indifferent everyday life nor yet enjoying the reality of the mind's life, which is Man's death with distinction.

Indeed, these twilight figures, our last extinguishing inklings of what reason's distinction was – these days popularly visualized as vampires and ghouls and zombies, as assassins, as madmen and killer-machines, as outcasts and outlaws, and all the vigilantes of our world – haunt us, in this perverted light of dusk with the flitting shadows of their restless affections, we who sit strapped in our seats in suspended animation and wait and watch, our cares and worries and the perils of reflection's day at bay for a spell, the moving pictures on the screen while hoping against all hope that our faith will be rewarded, along with our conviction that the Joker cannot win – hoping against all hope, holding out for that happy ending, the good death, that the tragedy of pure reason is and has become, as of late, to us, us late-comers to the matinee of Modernity, who have come to know and cherish and want to tell the *whole* story of our human being, to us but not to them, to those illustrious confreres of despair, who, though having long since split the scene, nevertheless haunt us still in this twilight time of thought's theater and whom, therefore, with this bright idea, we have to pursue in turn, these our dexters, our sinisters, because sometimes the truth is not good enough, because sometimes people deserve more, sometimes people deserve to have their faith rewarded. That is why they are running and that is why we have to chase them. Because they are the heroes, not the heroes Gotham City needs but the ones it deserves right now. So we'll hunt them. Because that is what needs to happen. Because they can take it. Because they are not our heroes. They are our silent guardians, our watchful protectors; of the darkened souls of Man, they are our dark knights.

The Fourth Part
The Issue of Wisdom's Holy Writs

78. The Compendium of the Three Epochs

Having completed our preparations by considering our topic first *theoretically*, having looked at pure reason's improbable constitution and then, in a turn towards *practice*, having explored the fallen state that critical thought is heir to when the mind steps back from unthinking distraction and takes note of the difference between THE WAY IT IS and THE WAY IT SHOULD BE, and lastly, in a mediating meditation upon our topic, having gleaned a first impression of the terminological method with which to sing and construe the element of thought's graces, the *poetic* impetus of reasoning, let us now return to the works and the workings of reason proper and reprise our study of reason's rhythmical life as it unfolds across the triadic scheme of distinguished achievements – for, as Schiller has so famously put it in his *Philosophical Letters* (Philosophische Briefe):

> Die Vernunft hat ihre Epochen, ihre Schicksale wie das Herz, aber ihre Geschichte wird weit seltener behandelt. (Schiller, *NA*, XX.107.3-4).
>
> (*Reason has its epochs, its determinations, even as does the heart, but the story of the former's fortune is much less often related.*)

We have already variously visualized this invisible movement of the mind employing lately the vegetable image of culture as the plant and the growth of thought, the garden's soil and the gardener's toil, to tell the story of development unto perfection and maturity from the pip to the bud to the bloom to the fruit which seeds the new beginning in the ring of reason's self-realization. More generally, in further revision of this train of thought, we may magnify reason's life by projecting it into historical time and articulate it thus as the progression of European cultural history, highlighting thought's epochal phases, the seasons of its being, the hours of its days, the steps of its progression, the forms of its unfolding – further representations for the saliency of well-ordered thoughtfulness – in chronological terms of epochs, namely that of the *Age of Enlightenment*, the *Advent of Christianity* and the *Era of Classical Antiquity*.

The distinction of human being with respect to reason – this experience of reason as the destiny of human being – remains our focus and our central theme. And in adverting to the three epochs of European tradition, we hope to acquaint ourselves with three unique languages that were capable of articulating, in profoundly moving terms, the insight and the reality that reason has been to the Western mind.

But if we want to talk about thought and thought is now or nothing, now or never, why study Western culture? For one, there is no one formula for philosophy, no royal road to definition. Seizing a concept always leaves a mark, bears the signature of the "hand" that has grasped the idea and this sculpting, forging hand, the particular form and formulas in which the idea was poured, belongs to someone's acuity, hence to a time and place, a people and a culture, a language – the abstract absolute touches the particular at this point. There is no limit to how finely the rich details of the writer's, the speaker's life and times at that unique moment in history has lent themselves to these efforts of invention by providing the specific context and communicative framework that determine the details of the speech performance of sacred tongues, the hieroglyphs, the letters of holy writs, and the comprehension on the part of the reader/audience which, in turn, lives and breathes an immediate air embodied in the shape of their own person and place. This is where tradition enters into our investigation – namely where thought has, again and again, entered history in word and deed; the craft and art of thinkers, poets, and prophets provide food for thought and however universally palatable their message is thought to be, a taste for the poetry of letters and the speculation of philosophy is acquired rather than innate – a cultural achievement. For this reason, wisdom and the science devoted to it, have a tradition and we imbibe our culture in the mother milk of the artefacts of past eras and in the cherished legacy of ideas they inspired, receiving thus from our mothers and our fathers the heirlooms that they have bequeathed to us in all the richness of the configurations that traditions of wisdom and insight are able to display.

Nevertheless we cannot and will not assimilate them to us and our time, adopting them as our own in a project of hermeneutics; we do not intend to advocate the revival of a ceremony, invigorate a fashion, much less found a new orthodoxy in the usage of "philosophical" expressions – thinking is, obviously, not a manner of speaking or a style of dress nor a ritual to be imitated, however much the tourist might appreciate the feathered headwear of the "natives," the chants and trances and dances around the bonfire, the "authenticity" of slaughter in animal, in human, sacrifice, the gold and vermeil of solemn liturgical observances – no, these relics and ruins from our cultural history (and be they still in some form, for some groups, on some desert islands or oases of society, extant today), whatever intrinsic cultural value as mascots they might still have for their adherents and sponsors, are, for our purposes at least, signs, a *language* of thought and it is thought alone that we intend to learn to read, for thought's sake and, at the same time, to speak, learning in this way, from these remarkable documents, how ideas have been powerfully put into words, borne, exhibited in the narration of deeds, in former days of reason's life. For thought is an act of construing and construction, is perceptive as well as generative, is conception and invention, in one the thinker's world *and* the poet's word.

The challenge facing us now consists in experiencing this relationship not only as spectators would, i.e. in the *speculation* of its own proper form as it presents itself to the acumen of insight, but also as a *discipline* that we take personally upon ourselves; for in the practice of thought, we ascend to the crisis of distinction in a self-relationship with ourselves, see ourselves for whom we really are, namely finite, mortal living beings who are subject to this critical reflection and the judgment day, the sentence of death, that it thus pronounces. Finally, we delineate the parameters of this self-relationship in a topological scheme of its aspects by positing names for each part and for the whole in a bid to win reason's applause and delight and commitment to the idea that is at the heart and origin of perception. This is the work and the culture of an *inventive* brand of reasoning we call *philology*, a studious attachment of endearment to the ΛΟΓΟΣ, which ventures to make abstract thought accessible to the idiom of post/modern critical theory as well as to that of the more dominant discourses of mundanity.

The first capacity of reason, its science and the theory of self-knowledge, was unfolded in the Greek Epoch. In this first epoch, Europe learned to recognize reason as the distinguished ***being of perfection*** having fulfilled, in a hierarchy of forms, the due of their apportionment; In the Christian epoch, the second one, Europe learned that jovial thought is not only the unmoved but no less moving object of its discerning theoretical activity but is also practical judgment, an activity of the self-critical human endeavor to prescind itself from the immediacy of all worldly conformity in accordance with the divisive act of critical reflection, the Christ of thought, such thought that is, in its totality – not only condemnation but also redemption – conceived of as the ***triune Godhead***. Finally in the third epoch, that of civic consciousness, perceptive observation and practical observance are completed by the imaginative instantiation of rational human nature according to which thought comes to recognize and realize itself as ***absolute spirit*** and in the self-articulation of its element, lives the best of lives, bringing forth its own life in the recognition of its rational reality and thus fulfilling, in complete freedom and certainty, the determination of its own unique idea, making vivid sense of itself.

These three epochs of thought, each a cycle of completed understanding, find their place in the logotectonic table of triads which marks the stations of that movement in the entirety of European tradition, the culture and the cultivation of one unique insight collected into one train of thought, as in *Figure 58*:

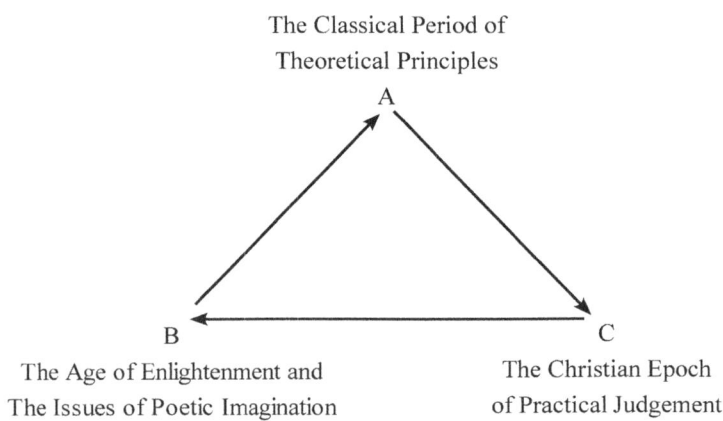

Figure 58: The Scheme of Western Tradition

But, as we have said, this scheme of Western tradition will be considered not as a datum of history, nor will we be concerned with the facts and figures of events, the time-lines and bloodlines from which institutions derive their pedigrees, upon which dynasties found their prerogatives. Who these people are, what the events "really" were that lent their names and dates to the elaboration of wisdom – these are intriguing questions, important questions but not our questions. Those whose life and times served as the material basis for the stories of personages and whose names and narratives are now elements of the accounts we read in our *Great Books* course – their problematic status in the eyes of scholarship – are not the theme of our explorations, which neither gains its truth nor can be refuted by appeals to the past. The grand pageant reviewed by annalists and ordered by chronologists have served the poet and the thinker of their times with images, dramatic plots, epic heroes, lyrical scenery in which to couch their reasoning. But this is not to say that philologists are disinterested in or belittle the life of the world. Rather, the point is that even the notions of *truth* and *fiction* to say nothing of such expressions as *God* or *freedom* or *destiny* can only be properly construed within a particular train of thought about thought and that the vast collection of details that natural history has documented are neither disdainfully ignored, deceptively manipulated, carelessly adapted or altered, nor simply classified and catalogued by reasoning devoted to pure reason. If *history*, ΙΣΤΟΡΙΑ, in its original sense, engendered knowledge based on enquiry and observation – and even Heraclitus taught that friends of wisdom ought indeed to be acquainted with variety (DK B 35) – then all "historical" narratives, even those of natural history, are likely to provide thought with an occasion to exhibit a principle.

How do the thinker and the poet using the resources that language has at its disposal best present the distinction of human being? There are many ways and a comprehensive study of the ways in which an idea can be accorded the authority of truth that it deserves as such is nothing less than a well-rounded education in philological eloquence, the craft and art of moving the human heart with the resources that language has to offer persuasive speakers and writers who treat of the distinction of human being. Since the days of Parmenides, we have known that ΠΕΙΘΩ (persuasive power) accompanies truth (DK B 6, 4) – though of course through instrumentalization, one can be perversely divorced from the other; the former is then mere rhetoric, the latter opinion – and, as we have seen, this influence is nothing extraneous to it; the power of ΛΟΓΟΣ is precisely that it is communicative, a voice and call that sparks our attention, engenders the effort of conception that takes into account the signs of the times, tales of kings' rise and knights' fall, angelic maids and mortifying misses, the successes and failures of their lives, the play of events, the dramatic catastrophe that is the issue of critical self-reflection.

The sway of the holy writs and the persuasive force of the turns of words of wisdom we will examine reside in the power of thought, the Builder, to give ideas the form and the shape that are the most suitable under the circumstances of a particular speech performance, whether written or spoken. To this end, history, natural or otherwise, offers the efforts of conception (on the part of the audience) and foundation (on the part of the speaker/writer) a treasure trove of terms, abstract or concrete, names general or particular, nouns collective, common, or even proper, rich in connotations of both contemporary and obsolete usage, evoking further phrases and connections of circumstance and happenstance.

Thus for our enquiry it makes no difference whether Homer or Troy, Jesus or Jerusalem, Adam and Eve, Hector and Achilles, Hyperion or Julie, William Tell or Johanna von Orléans, Athena or Ares "really existed" or not in the prosaic way that historians are wont to debate having sifted the dust for telltale bones and other clues – there are many different ways of understanding what the terms *reality* and *existence* mean and how they are used in philosophy and the language of wisdom. On the other hand, *the City of God* is emphatically *real* because that is precisely how the living world, the effective reality, of thought is grasped in Augustinian conception, just as the so-called *noble savage* and his development from nature to culture across the transient abyss that is civilization is a "fact" in the vision of Rousseau, and the Christian *God*, in contrast to the Judaic one, has attained historical determinacy, and hence emphatic reality, in the life and person of *Jesus Christ* because that is essential to the coherence of the practical wisdom that the second epoch elaborates. That is also why the question (and the answer) regarding whether God "exists" belongs to the issue and the experience Christian teaching but it would be as meaningless for a Greek to ask this question in connection with *Zeus* as it would be, given the Greek conception of *Nature*, to find a "nature lover" in the romantic sense among Odysseys' ill-fated companions.

In examining our philosophical heritage, the method of the bricolage of discourse we have been engaged in till now will no longer suffice. Song snatches and catchwords, slogans and rubrics are the element of late modern speech performance – and though we stand with our feet solidly on this earth and speak this language, the following anthology of holy writs that have been taken up as wisdom's bequest are devoted to the exploration of the traditional meanings upon which these performances are grounded whether acknowledged or even known by their spokespeople.

For this reason, we will pursue our analysis of wisdom in accordance with the logotectonic method described earlier and which must provide the proof that to give it the name of *science* is more than just one of those facile pretensions that short-order academics are fond of indulging in to distinguish the fruits of their labors and the knowledge industry as a whole.

THE THIRD EPOCH – THE AUTONOMY OF HUMANITY

79. The Voice of Absolute Freedom

What is Europe? Where is Europe? Are these questions about geography? Do they refer to the controversy these days about whether Europe extends to Turkey or Ukraine or beyond? Do they mark the border between advanced and advancing nations, democracy and dictatorship, the wealthy and the poor, between science's world and the realm of superstition, the North and the onslaught of the South, the sinking sun of Western civilization against the rising of the Asian tiger? Between the lingering powers of imperialism, colonialism, and the oppressed of the world?

No, these questions are wrong from the start. Europe is not merely a thing or a place, a line drawn in the sand, an economic policy, a community of nation neighbors, a body of treaties, a parliament of delegates, a costume or a custom, but rather just one thing that is no thing at all, namely a spirit and not anything ghostly and disembodied lurking in a machine but rather a living spirit, comprising thus both a life and a mind as well as a specific shape, its individuality, and therefore deserving of being properly acknowledged as a *person*. For this reason, the first question is personal and pointed: *Who* is Europe?

The first answer will be provided to us by the Third Epoch in which this person says "I" when speaking about reason and the capacity of reason, the first activity of which is self-knowledge and therefore appropriately called self-knowing being (Selbstbewußtsein). The toil and effort that this human *I* that I *am* must take upon myself in order to become the *I* that I was destined to be is called *education* (Bildung). Through this work on myself and my self-application, my human being realizes its nature, i.e. *My* humanity. What is the nature of humankind? In the Third Epoch it is called *freedom*, and the realization that *I am free by nature* begins with the insight that My human being, i.e. *humanity*, though free in principle and in the idea, lives, in reality, a life of servitude and bondage, as Rousseau famously determined in the first line of the first chapter of his book *On the Social Contract* (Du Contrat Social):

> L'homme es né libre et partout il est dans les fers.
> (Rousseau, *OC* III. 351).
> Humankind is born free…and lives everywhere in chains.

Rousseau discerned the contradiction that exists between this pure, true, natural heart of humankind that is the birthright of human being and the "denatured," dispirited spirit of the so-called *Age of Enlightenment* which infected its sciences with vanity, its society with corruption and luxury, and the natural self-love of My absolute humanity with perverted, self-enamored pride that relative and comparative esteem inflames among competing peers of egotism. He admonished his contemporaries that the simplicity and purity of virtue, the passionate urgings of the human heart's own voice, and the innate goodness of human being whence it springs were a sacred endowment of nature and the universal destiny of humankind. For, says Rousseau, "the fundamental principle upon which my arguments were based in all of my writings...is that to be human is to be naturally good, loving both justice and order; that there is no original depravity in the heart of human being and that the inaugural movements of nature are always right..."

> *Le principe fondamental ...sur lequel j'ai raisonné dan tous mes écrits...est que l'homme est un être naturellement bon, aimant la justice et l'ordre; qu'il n'y a point de perversité originelle dans le cœur humain et que les premiers mouvements de la nature sont toujours droit. (Rousseau, Lettre à M. De Beaumont, [OC] IV. 935-6)*

Rousseau taught that this natural ardor of the primal goodness of human being, the feeling of freedom that it gave voice to, is immediately evident to whoever has conserved the original soul of the unadulterated human nature in a world of hypocrisy and self-indulgence, sophistication and exploitation, the tyranny of conceit and pretension.

"Hear my voice," proclaims this soul of humanity, the pure heart of our heart, this our distinguished being, though absolutely distinguished from our being, "follow me! Follow this call of the wild. I, human nature, i.e. the *Humanity of humanity*, summon all the earthlings of the world to join me on a journey. Pilgrim, it is a voyage that will take you far away from the hues of your native scenes, from the grassy fields, the green lakes, the rivers of your infancy, the dances of your childhood. If you want to accompany me on this walk, you must leave everything you own, all your inheritance, your bright baubles of learning and labor, behind, starting with the earth of your birth. Faraway stars beckon you, an open highway, who hear my voice; take leave of the local haunts and houses of your homes, the comfy vicinity of your neighbourhoods that you share with your nearest, your family and friends, your foes – bid them all farewell, farewell, put on your vagabond shoes and become the wayfarer of freedom!

"Take leave of all the customs you cherished, of the mother of your language, of the country you call *father* – bereft of these, of the habit that you wore, the lore that you learned by heart, you are left nude in these winds that sing of change, you are poised now on the very brink of your new life, the very edge of your old life, that life that so deeply drank its milk of custom, built with flesh and bones the moral halls and fortresses of kings' decrees, inscribed with chisels ringing precepts on their stones that summoned all your village folk and you – to this miniature life of yours say adieu, adieu!" So does freedom beckon even as Hölderlin's *Empedokles* proclaims to his people "So dare it, what you have inherited and earned, what your father's voice told and taught, law and custom, the ancient names of gods, forget it daringly and uplift, like newborns, your eyes to the divinity of nature" of free human being.

> So wagts! was ihr geerbt, was ihr erworben,
> Was euch der Väter Mund erzählt, gelehrt,
> Gesetz und Brauch, der alten Götter Namen,
> Vergeßt es kühn, und hebt, wie Neugeborne,
> Die Augen auf zur göttlichen Natur (Hölderlin, *GSA* IV.65).

"But can I do this," you ask. "Do you dare," I will reply. "Why go," you say. And I: "Who is called?" And then: "Join me," says the calling, "follow me, those of you with the mettle of resolution. For compared to the plenitude of your native earth, its pageants and parades, the quaint milieu of your daily occupations, your household certainties, their dainty definitives, their intricate specifics, this region we are sailing towards is naught but vast and still ethereality, a *there* that will never be a *here* to huddle and cuddle in. That is why you have had to abandon your sore-sodden body, peel off the layers of your life, relinquish grips, jettison the ballast on your back." Wipe the table clean, as Hamlet says with regard to that beloved and paternal ghost that admonishes his remembrance:

> ...from the table of my memory
> I'll wipe away all trivial fond records,
> All saws of books, all forms, all pressures past
> That youth and observation copied there...
> (Shakespeare, *Hamlet*, I.5)

Until what's left, here at the end of the world? Nothing – nothing at all. Nothing is left except that which is there when nothing is there, the animadverting "ghost" in person. This voice, My voice alone, the voice of freedom.

This nothing that is there and that cannot be deducted when we rigorously subtract from ourselves all the littleness and the bigness of the world we know so utterly as our very own; this cipher of life, this nothingness and pure negation is, in fact, the first firmament of freedom. And we, the airy nothings we have become to enter this blue region, are spirits, dead to all we knew in the grave of the cave that, as our cradles and our play, as our box and our building, served the earthlings that we were. But now no longer are. For we are to be henceforth spirits all, dispossessed and drifting, completely immaterial and joining this reverie with Rousseau's, we might exclaim with him:

> Here I am alone in the world, no longer having brother, neighbor, friend, society than myself...but Me, detached from them and from all else, what am I myself? Behold this is what is left for me to seek. (Rousseau, *OC* I.995)
>
> (*Me voici donc seul sur la terre, n'ayant plus de frère, de prochain, d'ami, de société que moi-même...Mais moi, détaché d'eux et de tout, que suis-je moi-même? Voila ce qui me reste à chercher.*)

And so our inward voice continues: "How should we call you, who have attained to this tenuous estate 'unmixed with baser matter,' spirits, abstractions, pure thoughts? How to indicate your present diaphanous quintessential element with respect to all you were and have sloughed off in a flight of fancy – every bond and bondage, every foe you fought, every problem and every question ever posed to your puzzlement, your recipes and religions, your laws and loves, your matching set of views and two and a half truths, your one bold stare? This voice alone, *My* voice is left…" Thus unadulterated freedom's speech, the declaration of the distinction of human being.

Every other voice is silent now, up here in the open to where she has guided us, far above the closed globe of our first world. Let us adopt freedom's abstract and absolute perspective for a moment of consideration. After all, every other worldly concern of ours is gone save this one, freedom's otherworldly one. We have already encountered the arguments against the distinction of human being. They certainly are plausible. Mephisto reminds us:

> You are in the end – what you are.
> Wear a wig with a million curls of hair,
> Plant your foot on pillars vaulting in the air,
> Still you stay but what you are.

Du bist am Ende - was du bist.
Setz dir Perücken auf von Millionen Locken,
Setz deinen Fuß auf ellenhohe Socken,
Du bleibst doch immer, was du bist.
(Goethe, Faust, *I.2)*

Still you stay but what you are – you are a product of your society, your upbringing, your culture, you are born into a world all set to suck, a filled and filling world, and imbibe with thirsting lips its smacking reality, until you are utterly and entirely full of it, as the only one you will ever know, ever could know, a world with all the ultimate finality and importunate givenness of a thing, just there, like a kettle just sitting there dull and squat with its spout stuck out. This thing, your life, its circumstances are, ultimately, just there, at hand, friend, take it or leave it, use it, abuse it, it's yours. And you are its, too, of course, because its society has stomached you and has molded you and wired you and structured you, imprinted its circuit on your silicon soul and now, listen! Can you hear the rhythm of your algorithm ticking?

I yam what I yam and that's all what I yam – But consider, all you pop-eyed, squinty-eyed modern mechanisms and machine beings that you hold yourself to be and apparently want to be, is it really and truly unthinkable that a human being, who was once called thus as a name of distinction and self-respect, should, one fine day, decide to act in a way that is different from how his world at large taught, prescribed, commanded? Is it really and truly out of the question that the good soldier or sailor who learned to carry out commands "without thinking" could one fine day, suddenly, refuse to carry out an order? If since your birth you have learned to use spoons and have been using them ever since, to wear hats and have been wearing them ever since, to build skyscrapers, to watch the news on TV and have been building and watching ever since, is it really and truly, is it absolutely and necessarily impossible that today this individual should call his hat or his spoon, his building, his TV, or the news critically into question and by doing so break the spell of inexorability that had been etched into the chips and wafers of his or her life?

(אֶהְיֶה אֲשֶׁר אֶהְיֶה) — Ehyeh-Ascher-Ehyeh - *Exodus* 3:14) *I am (to be) what I am (to be)*– Of course, the person of freedom speaking the words that affirm the pure being of the entity of identity, not as his or her own weapon of arrogation, but in opposition to the validity of every pervasive premise, prevalent habit or view, has put himself or herself at odds with the local majority, confounds the swell, parts the sea of the mass and confronts his little clan of Man with an alien aspect, an otherworldly look, namely that of an exile spirit. For then the childhood innocence of that first pristine life, its baby-smooth skin has been nicked, scratched, pocked, pierced by the golden stud of discernment. This person has gone astray, dressed with distinction in vagabond shoes and camel hair shirts – the uncompromising garb of opposition to an established society, to a set and settled creed or culture; more than the negation of opposition, this distinction is the livery of revolution, of transformation, the METANOEIN (change of heart, conversion) that we will be called upon to don in the second epoch.

Has something like this, like this complete departure and secession, ever happened to a person in the history of the world – a conditioned human product flying thus in the face of all manners and mores, prizes and possessions, in the vocation of wilderness? Can we even imagine a culture based on such a principle of freedom? What sort of culture might this be the first act of which is apparently the calling into question of every given culture, every standard banner of structures and instructions, strictures and restrictions? What sort of tradition can emerge from such a tradition of freedom that refuses to receive unquestioned the letter of any tradition or convention?

Is this possible for such Hobbesian human being as is subject to the ultimate principle of *custom* not only in action but even in the practice of thinking? But consider: If you truly believe that human being has been programmed by mundane culture and now, after harvesting by totalitarian human intercourse, is no longer able to reflect, unable to behave differently than convention would, unable to develop beyond the ken of established frameworks that the flow of life and nescient lived experience till then had prescribed, mere clone child and finger-print of parent, then you have a concept of culture that presents morality as a sort of granite prison cell and a vision of the people who impersonate this stone which corresponds well with that of Plato's allegory of adamant man born to share the fate of all brethren landsmen and townsmen of weekdays pent up in lath and plaster – tied to counters, nailed to benches, clinched to desks and singing together that melody of mediocrity that outcast nonentities like ourselves try so hard to learn from the brains and the jocks and the freaks in our high school musicale, but yet never fitting in, not even with the class of misfits:

> No, no, no
> Stick to the stuff you know
> It is better by far
> To keep things as they are

Don't mess with the flow, no no
Stick to the status quo[56]

If however you agree that the animadversion of automatic man and its culture of distinction distinguishes human being with respect to reason, allowing us, no, requiring us to prescind ourselves from the givens of society, from world views proffered and conferred, lithographs of life experience, from everything ever known or loved as truth or fact simply assumed; if you agree that this, however difficult in practice for the individual, is nevertheless necessary in principle for the dignity of humanity as a whole, then you have recognized this unique distinction as the destiny of human being, its destiny as a being of reason, a spirited subject in the kingdom of absolute freedom, a distinction that subtracts from us every other distinction, as stated in Article 2 of the *Universal Declaration of Human Rights*,

> *...such as race, color, sex, language, religion, political or other opinion, national or social origin, property, birth or other status.*

What remains if you subtract from yourself your skin and gender, your nationality, your ethnic profile, your private property and standing in society (and the political, cultural, economic status of that society), your profession, your generation, your religion and your preferred god, particular views, your favored variety of optimism or pessimism, values and chance conceptions, inclinations, aspirations, even your birth with all the particular circumstances and contingencies that determine your identity today, including your physical and natural fortunes like health, wealth, wisdom, i.e. strength, property, intelligence? What's left? A veil of ignorance thrown benignly over all that you have already become?

What's left of you in that original position beyond or prior to every determinate position and propensity, every accident of endowment? Well, obviously, nothing is. And this *nothing* is, wow, really something! Bereft lastly even of your veil of ignorance, there is now truly nothing left of you except pure knowledge, your self-knowing being, this absolute subject of freedom, who is, nevertheless, you too, but your absolute (and not merely disinterested) *You*, the unadulterated *You*, the *You* that you have to do and not merely imagine, the *Me* to which I might aspire in word and deed and that thereby founds my inviolable dignity, to whom accrues moreover *rights* called *human*, inalienable, the first of which to be expressly enumerated is

---

[56] *Stick to the Status Quo* written by David Lawrence & Faye Greenberg.

the *right to life* (Article 3) – this moral, distinguished You is *your* You, too, in fact it is most truly and deeply You; promoting its life is your sole due and duty.

It is in this distinguished life of reason that is our better half, our *self* of critical reflection, the fairest one of all, that we, who have abstracted ourselves from every other distinction in our lives, first and finally, however, from ourselves, are brothers, sisters in a community of spirits that has no place or time beyond that life that we provide it with, that unique life of our own singular and specific human being, here and now. We realize this freedom, the humanity of human being in our own person, a freedom that is not merely liberty in the sense of exemption from rules, the privilege to seize opportunities, license granted from authority, vacation from endeavor – freedom is neither leave given, nor immunity granted, neither that of the libertine, nor that of the free-lancer, neither caprice nor abandon – though all of these variations on our theme and cause, even in their perversion or instrumentalization of the idea of freedom, allude to that original nature that humanity is endowed with...*by nature;* the disenthrallment, the manumission of the mind delivers its subject from the bondage of every extraneous constraint, from the exclusionary enclosure of every definitive society in which one might find oneself conveniently incarcerated, cribbed, confined – as Schiller's Julius puts it in the beginning of his second letter to Raphael: "once we were satisfied with the modest glory of being good sons and daughters in our house," in the middle of our street, "being a friend to our friends, called a useful member of society." But then "you have transformed me into a citizen of the universe." And then comes the realization "that this freely striving spirit is plaited into the stiff, unchanging mechanism of a mortal body, mixed with its small needs, yoked to its little fates – this god is referred to a world of worms."

> Vorhin genügte mir an dem bescheidenen Ruhme, ein guter Sohn meines Hauses,...ein Freund meiner Freunde, ein nützliches Glied der Gesellschaft zu heißen; du hast mich in einen Bürger des Universums verwandelt...dieser freie emporstrebende Geist ist in das starre, unwandelbare, Uhrwerk eines sterblichen Körpers geflochten, mit seinen kleinen Bedürfnissen vermengt, an seine kleinen Schicksale angejocht – dieser Gott ist in eine Welt von Würmern verwiesen. (Schiller, *NA* XX.111.22-112.14)

Whether or not this break with the fate of time and space is possible, this distinction of freedom is necessary for human goodness' sake. It is what human being was meant to be, should be, even if this being will never be what it was meant to be, will never succeed at fulfilling this rational destiny, even then, freedom and the emergence of the mind is the principle of every prominence we give to humanhood. It is your duty, humans, through toil devoted to transcending the confines of your material cognitive space, to realize the freedom of your nature. What? You fail in the attempt? You stay put and planted utterly the bound and banded son and daughter of your time and place, your age and your earth? Well, do not despair, even as a failure you honor and confirm your destiny by making its fulfillment all the more precious for being a rare and difficult achievement, the finest of things; thanks to you, those who do succeed in some degree to seize upon the idea of freedom deserve all the more and greater recognition for their merit, being exceptions and a source of hope and the living proof that substantiates an undying conviction that in a world full of mediocrity, impassivity, rigidity, immovability, and blind, insipid self-absorption, there are a brilliant and superbly spirited few for whom, as Hegel says at the end of paragraph 159 in part I of his *Encyclopedia of Philosophical Sciences* (Enzyklopädie der philosophischen Wissenschaften), "this liberation seen as existing is called *I*, as developed into its totality *free spirit*, as sentiment *love* as fruition *beatitude*."

> Als für sich existierend heißt diese Befreiung Ich, als zu ihrer Totalität entwickelt freier Geist, als Empfindung Liebe, als Genuß, Seligkeit. (Hegel, *Werke*, VIII §159, p. 306).

This spirit's coign of vantage is, as we have said and shown, necessarily absolute. If that which is absolute is abstracted from all time and all place, then this term is appropriately predicated for the standpoint of freedom to the extent that "freedom" refers to a state of extrication, of being expurgated from the finitude of every particular space and time and therefore general, universal, infinite, and in precisely this sense *absolute*. This word celebrates the idea of a "place" beyond the confines of every singular place, every particular *here*, time beyond the confines of every single time, every particular *now*, beyond the dimensions of our local horizons that define the efficiencies of our power struggles, beyond our piecemeal knowledge is the no-where and the never-land that is no-body's and no-thing's, namely that of the *omni*potence, *omni*science, *omni*presence, the *omni*ficence of reason – with the prefix *omni-* marking the distinction of difference, i.e. the transcending *place* beyond all measure of locality, of *time* beyond all measure of the moment – beyond their punctuality, we contemplate the immensity, the ubiquity, the eternity of absolute and, in this distinguishing sense, *pure* reason's place – she brought us there in a train of thought. Let these be the thought-provoking, experience-invoking names for the destination of our journey from the myopia of life in the grave of the cave to the emergence of the panoramic view atop the prominence of thought. Transcending the anaesthetic reality of adamant man thus, we have ascended to the ethereality of perspicacious perception and the transparence of the "aesthetic" being *before.*

80. The Ideals of the Self-realization of Spirit

This "infinity" attained in the practice of reason is but the first activity of reason we are examining, namely the operation of *excellence* and *emergence* – both terms taken etymologically. It refers to the other sense of infinity, not at all to *unlimited endlessness* in the "do-not-disturb" sense that our modern Man of the mundane world has in mind while engaging with abandon in his private pursuits and obsessions, but rather to the "infinite" property of the self-relationship of reason itself which does indeed encounter limits but only such limits as delineate its own form, namely those of *self*-determination, within the bounds of which it defines its own identity and through which it comes to know itself as the encompassing reality it truly is unto itself. In the history of thought's culture, we encounter this self-knowledge as the self-knowing being of the autonomous subject who enacts the universal law of freedom and becomes thus the subject of its own self-government, the self-governing state that is the law-giving god of freedom in the Third Epoch of the European cultural tradition, the epoch devoted to grasping freedom as the civic duty of self-determination. But, as Rousseau shows, the goodness of human nature begins in the emergency and the crisis of humankind distinguishing itself from the habitation of perverted civilization in obedience to, more exactly, in consideration for, and even with reverence towards the voice and feeling of the pure soul, or name it reason's, that is the simplicity of nature's true profession in contradistinction to the sophisticated artifice of society.

In the Third Epoch, the question is not whether people "believe" in this god or not, but rather whether they, in the "depravity of their civilization," can still, however faintly, hear its call, namely that of the wilderness of their tender mother-nature, and, in the hearing of it, whether they are then prepared to pursue and perform in their own lives, in their own world, in their own deeds, the service of the humanity of humankind as their vocation.

The poets of this age draw our attention to reason's reality by inventing images of the self-relationship of thought, presenting it as the type and model, the so-called *Ideal* of the fulfilled destiny of autonomous and sovereign being. This god comes to life in their poetry in images of nature –

the sublime mountains, the starry sky, the primal life of our first human being or just a simple flower in a landscape of beauty are its avatars. What does this imagination of nature reveal? These images are all signs of and monuments to the fulfilled destiny of self-determination, as Schiller proposes in his well-known essay *About Naïve and Sentimental Invention* (Schiller, *NA* XX 414.12-25):

> It is not these objects; it is the idea they represent that we love about them. We love in them that quietly shaping life, that calm self-shaping efficacy, a being in accordance with its own laws, the inner necessity, the eternal self-substantial unity. These are what we were, to these we must return. We were then nature, as they are still; our culture should return us, through the ways of reason and freedom, to nature. They are, moreover, representations of our lost childhood, which shall remain dearest to our hearts for evermore; that is why they fill us with a certain nostalgia. Moreover they are the representatives of our highest ideal and perfection, which is why they touch our heart with a sublime spirit.

> *Es sind nicht die Gegenstände, es ist eine durch sie dargestellte Idee, was wir in ihnen lieben. Wir lieben in ihnen das stille schaffende Leben, das ruhige Wirken aus sich selbst, das Dasein nach eignen Gesetzen, die innere Notwendigkeit, die ewige Einheit mit sich selbst. Sie sind, was wir waren; sie sind, was wir wieder werden sollen. Wir waren Natur wie sie, unsere Kultur soll uns, auf dem Wege der Vernunft und der Freiheit, zur Natur zurückführen. Sie sind also zugleich Darstellung unserer verlorenen Kindheit, die uns ewig das Teuerste bleibt; daher sie uns mit einer gewissen Wehmut erfüllen. Zugleich sind sie Darstellungen unserer höchsten Vollendung im Ideale, daher sie uns in eine erhabene Rührung versetzen.*

In the phenomena of this imagery, we see invoked, at least in the Third Epoch, just this: the Idea of Freedom, the autonomy of nature. For in these beings of nature we see the product of an inward, intrinsic law, an accord with it that is to serve us as a vision of what education strives to achieve:

> "...that calm self-shaping efficacy, a being in accordance with its own laws, the inner necessity, the eternal self-substantial unity."

Schiller connects the term *Beauty* to this idea of self-relativity as well by proposing in his *Letter to Körner* that "the apparition of freedom is one with beauty."

Freiheit in der Erscheinung ist eins mit der Schönheit.
(Schiller, *NA* XXVI 200.17-18)

In nature we recognize the self-relationship of reason in the evidence of fact; we see the incarnation of this idea, namely "the consistence of things through themselves according to their own inalterable laws." This is the epitome of autonomy, of self-determination. Nature is our model, our *ideal* of freedom and can serve as a guide in our work upon our own lives to realize the freedom that nature instilled in our souls – the will *to be* free, i.e. the will to be a *person* of freedom, an individual who strives to be the natural life of the humanity of human being, and thus to become a citizen of pure reason's intelligible domain, the fatherland that is always with us when (on our best days) we are really with it rather than out of it, down in the dumps. With the impetus of this will, we begin the work and toil of bringing thought to life, this universal thought to our particular life, not in an attempt to ingest, to assimilate it to our ways and thus domesticate it, but rather in striving to elevate ourselves to the zenith of an ideal, the sublime token of our dignity.

Thus we see that the abstraction of reason as portrayed in the journey into ethereality from the cavernous reality of our lived experience is but the first half of the story. The end and aim of this relation is to be grasped in the fulfillment and the completion of what was meant to be, the fruition of nature. For only such human being as has realized its destiny of nature and distinguished itself with respect to it from merely living being through the work of learning and through the train, the train and training of thought in which *I* align myself to *My humanity* in accordance with My rational being, is and can be free, a work and the working of beauty in the spirit of the ideal that it imagines and that I might vivify in me.

Schiller terms this productive work the *aesthetic education of human being* (die ästhetische Erziehung des Menschen), the goal of which is none other than to bring the physical and the rational being of humankind, feeling and thinking, the heart's sentiment and the mind's illumination, soul and spirit, life and thought, nature and reason, into the being of perfect balance, living reason in balance with sensitive virtue, which is the self-relationship that beauty represents. For beauty is the teacher when it comes to reason and its life; it is the ideal and the vision of this balance, the perpetual reconciliation of the opposing powers of human being in the imagination's artful "play" with the *physical material* of the world and the *spiritual form* of the mind coordinated into a being of reciprocal completion and conviviality of two opposing principles, a state of grace freed of every exclusion and one-sidedness. Beauty encourages humankind to recognize that the realization of freedom and the fulfillment of our destiny lie in the effort we make and the pains we take on behalf of this ideal to give it life and reality in ourselves as individuals, more, that we ourselves are meant to strive to be, with our lives, that very life of thought – its hand and face, words and deeds, its prized possession – having previously left our lives and all our other possessions behind for the sake of that very thought.

The name posited by poets and thinkers of freedom for human nature, namely *humanity* is a fine one because it expresses the incomparable nearness of this determination to the merely human condition of Man at the outset of our journey. Normally we image the absolute, a god, say, to be far away and remote from us and from the fuss of this minute's when-and-where, wear-and-tear world of long hours and of hot spots, in other words, way up there, high and cool on a mountain top or in a rarefied Heaven beyond the stars. By contrast, the humanity of humankind, our own absolute being, is so close as to be called *Me, Myself,* and *I*. Or perhaps we should say that the immense difference depicted in the image of the heavens, the sky with diamonds beyond our ephemeral world of mud has, in the third epoch, been transposed into our bosoms, into our most intimate heart of hearts, our conscience, after having been, in the inception of thought, tragically cleft in twain, as is a lover's heart, that is nevertheless destined, but only after the hard work of education in the spirit of beauty, to be mended and, though the scar remains, renewed to vigour.

Thus initially I come to the painful and tragic understanding that with respect to my heart of hearts I am not Myself. Recall that, according to Fichte, as we previously noted, most people would be more easily convinced that they are "a chunk of lava on the moon" than that they are themselves an *I*, self-knowing, self-governing, self-realizing beings of freedom, an insight that Rousseau had already expressed stating "that nothing is so dissimilar to me as myself."

> Rien n'est si dissemblable à moi que moi-même
> (Rousseau, *OC*, I.1108)

Apparently there is nothing at all obvious to folks about what is self-evident, namely that they in their Me (their capital, their absolute and *maxi-Me*) are free, not at all in the caprice of their self-interested whims with regard to which they are in fact abject subjects of heteronomy but rather in distinguishing themselves from the subjugating privity of their *mini-me*. For self-determination and self-governance, as the discipline and practice of reason, reveal in the beginning that my relationship to Myself is not one of accord between me (B), mySelf (C), and I (A), not an identity and self-accord, but rather a self-contradiction. In this experience I am not Myself, am not who I am and what I am, am not free, am not self-determined being – I am, as rational being and spirit, not who I am as in the cave of merely physical, merely cyclopsical body, with a single I, which is the narrowest horizon of myself, limited to the framework of my private *here and now* where, in fact, my heaven and my earth, my divine and my human life, the ideal and real, the OUGHT and the IS, reason and the nature, must diverge in me and from Me. In this experience, we discover our denatured being, habituated in its dislocation, our bottleneck subservience, our confining chains of self-centered pride, the discrepancy between the life we lead and the art of life, the moral tenants which we espouse with such facility and contravene with such impunity; we learn that as spirits we are disembodied ghosts, as bodies, we are dispirited corpses and validate thus the distance and remoteness of the ideal and the thought that *I* is/am in its/my distinction from that uninspired *me* who I am/is by default; we realize that there is an indelible difference between who *I am* in my immediate reality, in the cramped quarters and exiguity of unthinking, merely living being and who *I should be* according to My human nature and destiny as subject of the universal, the general determining principle that is my original birthright of *just* being. We are free in the ideal that reason reveals to us in a moment of insight, in a moment of illumination, in a daring flight of spirit that summons me to Myself, to My immortality with the words: I *will* be who I am; I will be Me, I will be free, I will be the free being of the will I AM and the Me I was destined to be.

Again, what is freedom, this, our birthright? *Freedom* is seizing upon the idea that I *am* free because I *will*, I "will" freedom; but as an idea, *freedom* stands in opposition, more, in contradiction, to our immediate state of chains. Everyone knows that "our thoughts are free" but in life we are not free. In life we are constrained by circumstances, by others' protestations, by our own limitations. Freedom is thus an abstraction at first, just an idea, nothing more than an idea, something like what people like to call a *right*, meaning we can but demand it, something we owe or we are owed, another's debt or our duty, something that *should* be but, unfortunately, *is* not. But this little old world of our shoving and tugging, on the other hand, is, to be sure, as real as can be, but, given the advent of critical self-reflection and the animadversion of thought, it does not conform to what acutest thought wills, does not conform to the nature of our destiny as free beings. Thus the world lacks the form of thought that the correspondence to this rational principle would bestow upon it, while the idea, the thought, lacks the substance and materiality of a fulfilled destiny that is not merely required, peremptorily demanded, and imperatively sought as due. Both sides are one-sided in their relationship of mutual exclusion – reason without material substance; reality without rational being. The beauty of nature as the apparition of freedom and its reciprocity as ground and cause of itself, as *causa sui*, reveal in the play of generative imagination that this contradiction – a thought-blind world or a world-empty thought – can be resolved through our own efforts and the work upon ourselves in the spirit of self-determination – poetic works of the imagination, self-generation in education, insightful works of theory in seeing the principle in the particular, practical works in self-imposed virtue of life under the moral law of reason, all works of reason's creative activity in seeing, living, realizing itself. Terms of resolution have, throughout the three epochs of the Western cultural tradition, provided names for the transition from the absolute negativity of the initial experience of departure to the charmed life and the substantial being that reason ultimately attains in and of itself as self-relative reflection, autonomy, and realization.

Thus the abstraction from the mundane world of adamant automatic man, the first transition we have explicated in the *Tree of Duality* in connection with the discipline of practical reason, is superseded, but not abrogated, by a second transition. Whereas the first transition ascended to an absolute standpoint in the experience of death and demise and the complete loss of all we have ever "possessed" in the immediate nescience of lived experience, the second transition performs the feat of reconciliation in which spirited life is grasped as the effect and consequence of the previous death with distinction. In the end, however, i.e. in the *theory* of reason, this rapport is simply conceived of as a reciprocal causality, the *causa sui* of the self-relationship – by giving thought to life (this is the moment of critical self-reflection), we give life to thought (this is the moment of self-realization) and the consequence of this demise of our life, the submission of the sovereignty of our lives under pure reason's sway, is the coming to life of a thought, the birth and incarnation of the thought of pure reason in the particulars of our own person.

81. The Conscience of Respect and the Compassion of Regard

The term GOD was always used primarily as a *term of distinction*, an absolute posited in departure from corresponding *terms of immediacy*, WORLD for example. Similar terms of distinction, like HEAVEN, HEREAFTER in opposition to EARTH and HERE and NOW respectively and SPIRIT over against BODY, even SUPERNATURAL over against, above and beyond the merely NATURAL – were put to indicate the mutually exclusive regions that the advent and evidence of thought discerns. This divisive, urgent state of emergency (*der Notstaat* as Schiller calls it) represents the discrepancy between the IS and the OUGHT that thought makes manifest to our lives. But every epoch of thought also gave us a wealth of terms and visualizations of the new, the second life and the rebirth that thought imparts – images of fulfillment, completion, peace, love, the state of beauty, in-dwelling being, just being, yes, even *human* being. In them we read of the exalted, enthusiastic heart, the renewed heart redeemed in joy complementing and not merely compensating for the mundane one that had been broken, divided in the middle, and thus so miserably condemned to death, that particular "philosophical" death namely that is not the end but rather the beginning of life, the life of reason, the life of distinction, of *regard* for this life and its lives. Rousseau's Saint Preux, the philosopher-lover of *Julie*, who, in the beginning of the twenty-fourth letter of the first part of the book of that name, differentiating between two concepts of *regard*, namely "...one stemming from public opinion and the other originating in self-esteem," elucidates their dissimilarity as follows: "the first one comprises vain prejudices more wavering than swells in a storm; the second has for its foundation the eternal moral truths. Worldly regard can be advantageous to good fortune; but it does in no wise penetrate to the soul and contributes nothing to true happiness. Veritable regard is, in contrast, of its very essence because one does not find except in it that enduring sense of inward satisfaction that alone can render a thinking being happy."

> ...celui qui se tire de l'opinion publique, et celui qui dérive de l'estime de soi-même. Le premier consiste en vains préjugés plus mobiles qu'une onde agitée; le second a sa base dans les vérités éternelles de la morale. L'honneur du monde peut être avantageux à la fortune; mais il ne pénètre point dans l'âme, et n'influe en rien sur le vrai bonheur. L'honneur véritable au contraire en forme l'essence, parce qu'on ne trouve qu'en lui ce sentiment permanent de satisfaction intérieure que seul peut rendre heureux un être pensant. (Rousseau, *OC* II.84)

Our insight into the heart of self-respect depends on our understanding what precisely the object of this love, what this SELF actually is. Of this self, this pure heart of the soul called, in the Third Epoch, *human nature* or the *humanity of man*, or simply *conscience*, Rousseau's Vicaire Savoyard, states in *Emile* that "...its rules are not culled from the principles of some lofty philosophy, rather I find them in the depth of my heart written by nature in indelible characters; I need but consult myself regarding what I want to do – all that I feel to be good is good, all that I feel to be bad is bad; the conscience is the best of all the casuists; and it is only when haggling with it that one has recourse to the subtleties of ratiocination. The foremost among our worries is that of our own care; and yet, how many times has the voice within told us that in our efforts at securing our own well-being at another's expense, we are doing wrong. Imagining that we are merely following the impulse of nature, we are, in fact, resisting it; in listening to what it tells our senses, we reject what it tells our heart; the active being obeys, the passive being commands... rationality has so often duped us that we have, without doubt, earned the right to deny it our recognition. But conscience never deceives; it is the true guide of our human being...to follow it is to obey nature and never to fear going astray." (Rousseau, OC.IV.594-5)

The regard of conscience is thus conceived of as the self-knowing, i.e. conscious, and therefore self-respecting, being of reason, the former referring to the intellectual grasp, the *wisdom* (sagesse), the second to the moral practice, the *virtue* (l'honnêteté) of reason. Both wisdom and virtue are terms which imply a relationship of intimacy between the knowledge and the being of conception, virtue, and the law of morality; in the First Epoch, we have become acquainted with the father of exact natural science, Aristotle, who describes the true insight of theory as the mind actually touching (ΘΙΓΓΕΙΝ) the matter at hand; in the Second Epoch, the nearness to its law and standard that virtue attains is depicted as an imbibing of the spirit of the law as one might nourishment; in this way, when it becomes interior to and thus an inward part of us, we see that correspondence to the standard is, again, as in the Third Epoch, essentially a matter of self-respect, where the *self* is our conscience. And this is precisely what we would expect when reason itself is the issue.

The term *love* is of particular felicity in illuminating the rapport of regard, suggesting as it does images of the well-balanced unity, the harmony and accord we are acquainted with in love relationships within the family, a love that is no longer one of the sacrificial fire of desire and entreaty but rather of the warmth of nurture, the peace and contentment of satisfaction rather than the longing thirst, the hunger, the necessity of need, the sheltering of a dwelling rather than the concentrated determination of purpose we would ascribe to the hero still striving, merely trying, to make it back home, back to the life of just being. The symbol and model for this perfect community that we can but hope and endeavor to attain is, or course, the self-relativity of reason itself, the entity of identity visualized as the Spirit of Love uniting the Father and the Son (in the Second Epoch), the bliss of reason's contemplation of reason as the best of all beings (in the First Epoch) and the joy of thought that has, through hardship, succeeded in bringing forth an articulate account of itself as the encyclopedic totality of all things thought – body *and* mind, soul *and* spirit – (in the Third Epoch).

An elaboration of this property of mutual regard, of the reciprocity inherent in the self-relationship of pure thought, much maligned in post/modern analysis, need not be restricted to discourse concerning mercantile exchange or the bartering of commodities, the principle of quid pro quo or tit for tat, or to the concept of the economy of scale but, above and beyond these applications of the idea, ought first to be acknowledged for what it is in itself, namely as thought's life and activity, its way, and as that in which we might participate not merely by considering it and wondering about it, but also by travelling along this way, enacting it in our own actions, giving it life in our life, and finally, by envisioning it with all the power of imagination we can muster in an effort that culminates in a spontaneous bestowal and a gift of thanks – thought's presence and its gratitude in one.

Of course, the freedom of human being can never be entirely realized because the realization and the practice of freedom are two different spheres of activity of reason – on the other hand, the ideal has already been realized in and as Nature and is as such attainable in the song of joy, celebrating the delightful attainment of knowledge that contemplation is. Insight is a fulfillment of our theoretical life just as the poet's vision of reason's way will leave nothing to be desired except what pertains to the spectator who, at some point, must close the book and return from the narrative, the play, the poem, i.e. from language, to the dreary realm and painful ordeal of action, i.e. to the world and its life, to history. Turning and returning to the all too human history of human being, we discover rather quickly that the idea of freedom has not, that no ideal has, yet been or could be entirely realized in the works of the will, of that will that is the distinction of this being, the distinction that is accomplished precisely in choosing this general will, in our willing this universal will and its well-being, this strangely familiar stranger's, as our own, a choice made again and again, renewed, and then, if all goes as it should, becoming accomplishment and accomplished in consequence of which suddenly a great deal more that is to be done presents itself. But tiring of our own story, we return to that of reason's again and again, again and again refreshing ourselves in the imagination of its ideas, lamenting the tragedy of our distinction as thinking human beings so prone to remissness and nevertheless, through elevating, exalting songs, uplifted in the certainty and perfection of the knowledge that has been imparted to us, however imperfect our reception and implementation of it may be.

In light of this progression – Rousseau's tales, Schiller's plays, Hölderlin's hymns – depicting as they do, the train of thought that we have recognized as the life of reason, these works, and more generally the traditional genres of literature, take on a new, deeper significance. They themselves, the traditional "media," become messages in their own right of the mind in action; in the Third Epoch namely, fiction, drama, and verse are themselves epochs in the life of reason, the fulfillment of which is realization – drama representing the practical *act* of distinction, verse, in turn, lifting the voice of poetic *celebration*, putting thought into words that praise the reality of thought having accomplished the preordained purpose of the principle and, finally, historical narrative, telling us the whole story of freedom from the beginning to the end in the *epos* of characters' lives and deeds, in the verisimilar account of their hardships and pain so that we might forget our own in theirs while remembering our destiny put to the test in their actions and anguish, recognizing what we were meant to be in what they are. *Art* is the work of reason, of thought, the *Builder*, just as in the First Epoch reason was the *Thinker* engaged in **science** and, in the Second Epoch, thought was the *Disciple*, the *True Believer*, and the *Follower*, as well as the *Teacher* of the one and only **religion** ΚΑΤ' ΟΛΟΣ (katholos). Philosophy is itself part of reason's own conception of itself, as is art and religion, the latter, part of the conception of what thought does, namely first to draw and then to put into effect the divisive distinction between the IS and the OUGHT, and the former, what it creates when it does what it does while striving to mind, to close, that fateful gap of immediate condemnation and mediated affirmation. Only in the Third Epoch is reason itself seen as the artist, the divine genius of nature that brings forth a world worthy of dwelling. Reason is generative, bringing forth its threefold work in the person of a poet on the path towards the realization of the works of poetry, of religion, and of philosophy in the spirit of humanity; or, as Hölderlin famously put the matter, "it is the destiny of human being to dwell poetically..." in that distinguished spirit "...upon this earth."

> ...dichterisch wohnet der Mensch auf dieser Erde
> (GSA II.372.19-20)

82. The Logotectonic Form of our Experience of Freedom

After gaining an overview of the principles, issues, and insights that are the element of the knowledge of the Third Epoch and in light of Hölderlin's pronouncement concerning the poetic mission of the mind with a view to the works of ΛΟΓΟΣ it founds and has founded, we now want to explore how this knowledge can be organized into one *and* several complete chains of truths in accordance with the principles of logotectonic thought, the Builder.

Its method requires first that we collect the key expressions of the epoch in question under which we may subsume further terms, establishing in this way the fund of designations, a historically validated nomenclature – including vocabulary as well as diction – that we might avail ourselves of in developing analogous lines of reasoning across a triad of signature terms in which each term is accorded a particular place in the scheme of ideas configured so as to render our experience of the distinction of human being in that particular epoch both articulate and perspicacious.

Recall that a train of thought always begins with a bang, not with noise, but with thunder – with the present of power, begins suddenly, immediately, *being* the first and thus *having* none that could be its forebear – with an inaugural principle of immediate impact, one, in other words, lacking all mediation and in this sense coming to us from *out of the blue*, a light, a voice, a feeling; the first term in a ratio of terms is, hence, the *principle* (A) as in the figures of both philosophy and wisdom. They both start with a term of principle; in the third epoch the principle is *freedom*, an excellent name for a principle because it clearly brings out the negativity of the term; freedom is, initially at least, just pure negation comprehending no content at all – we might say that the principle is the AUGHT of thought's abstraction, indicating the capacity of human being to step back from the givens of a mundane world through the effort of extrication inherent in critical reflection. As a term of distinction, it marks the original determination of a principle against a background of indeterminate immediacy and therefore does not *have* a determination in addition to what it is, namely pure *difference.*

For this reason we can only know the principle from the effect that the distinction has upon immediacy, the striking blast of the horn, the harbinger of the trace of distinction it leaves behind having made a lasting impression on our world, an idea that we seized and that in turn seizes us and is damned hard to forget; though we may try and try again to ignore what we have now come to know, we will never be the same again despite the mending efforts of all the king's horses and all the king's men.

The mark of pure reason is this immediate commencement of deliberate thought, its *present*; this *gift* of thought is original revelation, an emergent moment of inspiration, an illumination of what was, prior to sight, an event of instinct, blind-minded chance, the somnambulant fortuity of going with the flow; whether depicted as breath or bright enlightenment, an enkindling spark or battle cry, prophetic voice or call of exhortation, impulse or urging of the heart, the advent of note, the animadversion of intuition; in the chirality of the reflection, thought responds to that present, is recipience with regards to that grant and giving, is that which is shaped to that shaping, passive matter with respect to active pattern – being made well aware of what is going on makes a difference to us, whether it be depicted as a harkening, as the inhalation of an exhilarating air or as the glow of conscious participation and intended action.

These expressions of thought's *passion* – "passion" for we are often *struck* by sudden mindfulness, taken unawares, you might say, by awareness, and now gazing about us in critical distance, wondering. These expressions visualize the notion of reflection as the onset of *conception* – the efficacy of the principle of the mind, thought's power to move thought and to be moved to think, hence the acknowledgement of this influence and sway as the sending and the sender, the inspiration of the inspired, the light source of the illumination, the giver of the gift of deliberateness.

So, for example, Rousseau's famous moment of illumination that he describes as follows: "suddenly a stroke of luck made manifest to me what I had to do for myself and think about my fellow Man – a subject that my heart was in constant contradiction with my mind about – whom I still felt compelled to love in spite of having so many reasons to hate...an epochal moment in my life that will be always present to me even if I should live forever."

> Tout à coup un heureux hasard vint m'éclairer sur ce que j'avois
> à faire pour moi même, et à penser de mes semblables sur
> lesquels mon cœur etoit sans cesse en contradiction avec mon
> esprit, et que je me sentois encore porté à aimer avec tant de
> raison de les haïr....ce moment qui a fait dans ma vie une si
> singulière époque et qui me sera toujours présent quand je
> vivrois éternellement. (Rousseau, *OC* I.1135)

Here we are given to see the representation of an illumination at the outset, the familiar figure of inspiration – the jovial muse of Greek thought, the angel of the Holy Spirit and the genius of human nature are the three epochal deities of thought's power of inception, the ingressive power of reflection to insinuate itself into our lives and make a difference – the power of revelation as we have explicated this term previously. Coming first, thought's self-evidence *is* the absolute beginning that therefore *has* none except thought itself as is realized at the end of the train of thought, in the conclusion of the relationship of the same to the same, the I of self-knowing being to Me, Myself; the Father to the Son, one in love, the king to the loyal subjects of fellow kings in the jovial community of well-apportioned deity – all renditions of the self-relativity of thought's regard for thought thinking thought and knowing thought to be completely comprehended, perfect and perfectly articulate, substantial realization and entirely real. The inception of pure reason is a moving experience; this origin that is the heart's encouragement and the heart's fortune, the stroke of luck that is unpremeditated by calculation, the serendipity of a surprise, the gift of love that gives us before we ask, previous to our will, the opportunity that it presents to us as a boon and benevolence of a *being before* – an act of kindness, unmerited, unearned, undeserved, *and* the inexorable fate that is the dictamen of doom and destiny beyond all preparation and expectation.

Boon and doom in one. We are star-crossed lovers and chums of chance in one. What? The cause that has no cause, the unmoved mover, its gratuity, is fortuity – a name for the present of pure reason from the perspective of mundane Man that finds itself checked in its undying attempt to completely eliminate the risk and hazard, avoiding at all costs the loss of its grip of control which would inevitably lead to the crisis of stepping back to mind the gap between THE WAY IT IS and THE WAY IT SHOULD BE? Yes, to one unabashed by the overwhelming surprise of awareness, the accidence and the incidence of perception is precisely what deserves to be sung and celebrated as the amazing grace of illuminating enthusiasm.

Again, in the Third Epoch, the distinction and the nature of human being is liberating *liberty* – this is the mark of distinction drawn upon the immediate state of Man as living in chains; though born and thus destined to be free, we are, in fact, not free – this condition of *Man*, recognized as standing in direct contradiction to our natural *humanity*, is precisely how the gap between THE WAY IT IS and THE WAY IT SHOULD BE is experienced in this Epoch, the inaugural term of *Principle* (A) being therefore **FREEDOM**. This discrepancy compels us to undertake an endeavor of personal development and education in accordance with a vision of autonomy accomplished by the mediating term of *thought* (C) i.e. the genius of critical **SELF-REGARD** through which the idea of freedom moves our will to arduous training and exercise in the course of which we strive to bring the ideal of **HUMANITY** to life in our own person, in our own words and deeds, the resultant term of *Issue* (B). Thus *freedom* (A), *self-regard* (C), and *humanity* (B) might be taken as the most general headings for the three main thoughts that our logotectonic effort will now seek to analyze and richly elaborate upon, beginning with Rousseau, renowned as the father of the French Revolution.

I. Rousseau

A. The Freedom of Human Nature

83. The Savage and the Citizen

In his *Lectures on the History of Philosophy*, Hegel recognized Rousseau's accomplishment thus:

> The principle of freedom dawned on the world in Rousseau, and gave infinite strength to man, who thus apprehended himself as infinite. (Hegel, *Werke*, XX 307-308).

How could human being possibly be thought to be "infinite?" I mean...well, look at us!

The nature of human being is revealed in *freedom*, a term of distinction that is essentially a negation of the state of affairs in which we are born, the thraldom of *civilization*, the institutions that support it as well as the accomplishments of *Enlightenment* of which it is so proud, its sciences and its arts. It was against this background of immediacy provocatively termed *society* that Rousseau then drew his distinction, imagining the opposing state of original purity and innocence by subtracting, purifying, unclothing our present day Glaucus so disfigured by the depravations that had accrued to Man in the course of the history of Man's artificial *culture*, to glimpse the first face of human being freshly formed by *nature* with which our primal parents enjoyed a relationship of elementary equilibrium and harmony. In this face we effortlessly, i.e. "with neither pains nor paraphernalia," recognize none other than our true SELF, namely you, "O Virtue," who are our innate moral *conscience*, "the sublime science of simple souls" who is the calling voice of our natural human being, of those principles heard, found, or felt, "engraved in all hearts" that are the mark and living reminder of that first goodness never entirely expunged, even in the world of polite deceit that Man now inhabits, and "to learn the laws of which it suffices to turn inwardly and harken back" to you, to your voice, to your laws, "in the silence of the passions," secure in the knowledge that this is "the veritable philosophy."

> O Vertu! Science sublime des âmes simples, faut-il donc tant de peines et d'appareil pour te connaître? Tes principes ne sont-ils pas gravés dans tous les cœurs, et ne suffit-il pas pour apprendre tes Loix de rentrer en soi-même et d'écouter la voix de sa

conscience dans le silence des passions? Voilà la véritable Philosophie..." (Rousseau, *Discours sur les Science et les Arts,* [OC] III.30)

This distinguished *natural* state of THE WAY IT SHOULD BE (but is not) is a fiction of the *imagination* invented in contrast to the immediate *denatured* state of THE WAY IT IS (but should not be); they might serve as the two headings in a Tree of Duality under which we now, in *Table 6,* subsume several of Rousseau's expressions and designations:

	Terms of Distinction	Terms of Immediacy
1.	Nature	Culture
2.	Solitude	Society
3.	Obscurity/Oblivion/Poverty	Reputation/Glory/Luxury
4.	Nudity	Elegance/Finery/Ornament
5.	Simplicity/Innocence	Sophistication/Luxury/Brilliance
6.	Happiness in ourselves	Happiness in the opinions of others
7.	Absolute Love of Self (amour de soi)	Relative Self-enamor (amour propre)
8.	Ignorance	Enlightenment
9.	Probity	Talent
10.	Useful Talents	Agreeable Talents/Wit/Subtlety
11.	Virtue	Virtuosity
12.	Fine Action	Fine Words
13.	The Savage	The Scientist
14.	Ignored	Celebrated
15.	Idleness	Business
16.	Courage	Convenience
17.	Virtuous Industry	Idleness/Vanity in Sciences and Arts
18.	Long-lasting	Fleeting/Fashionable
19.	Athletic	Sedentary
20.	Reverent Awe of God	Fear of God

21.	Integrity	Erudition
22.	Heart's disposition	Outer appearance
23.	Being	Appearing

Table 6: The Contradiction in Rousseau's Conception

This Tree of Duality reveals the cause of the controversy surrounding Rousseauan speech among his contemporaries – the stumbling stone and the apple of discord that always accompanies the term of distinction inherent in the advent of a new epochal principle. Many expressions that were considered and valued as terms of distinction in the language of his time are denied this prerogative and placed on the other, the unmarked side of the relationship. Thus the pride of *civilized Man*, namely the progress of its sciences and its arts, normally credited with having distinguished and uplifted Man beyond its primitive state, are condemned as the fruits of vice, a term of immediacy, against which Rousseau distinguishes the unenlightened and therefore untainted *Savage*, which is therefore, in this connection, the term of distinction.

> L'Astronomie est née de la superstition; L'Eloquence, de l'ambition, de la Haine, de la flatterie, du mensonge; la Géométrie, de l'avarice; la Physique, d'une vaine curiosité; toutes, et la Morale même, de l'orgueil humain. Les Sciences et les Arts doivent donc leur naissance à nos vices. (Rousseau, *OC* III.17).

> *Astronomy was born of superstition; Eloquence of ambition, hate, flattery, mendacity; geometry of avarice; physics of vain curiosity; all of these, even moral philosophy, of human hubris. The sciences and the arts owe their births to our turpitude.*

Of course if an age of *Enlightenment* is set off against a dark age of *superstition, prejudice*, and *intolerance*, then it, comprising the *Renaissance* of the sciences and their civilization, is the distinguished term of illumination against the so-called *Dark Ages*; but no age, even one termed *enlightened*, is safe from the threat of closure and the intransigence of habit that stifles critical reflection and breeds stagnation – without the vigilance of the mind acute and alert to Man's bent towards decadence, every newfound or newly won state of reason begins to forget the reason that is its foundation and sinks again into oblivion of which intolerance, prejudice, and superstition – to name just three of the numerous dispositions of degeneracy encountered and decried in Rousseau's world – are warnings and portents that here reigns a closed mind bent on control to the exclusion and even the annihilation of all that might jeopardize its empire.

In that case, conceited *enlightenment* can only be surmounted by distinguished *ignorance* (line 8 in Table 6), the *savage* is the citizen and the *learned* the brute (line 13) because the latter merely acquires the mental prowess and talents it needs to foster iniquity, whereas the former keeps the end in sight, which is the integrity of its own moral worth (9), *virtue*, as opposed to mere *virtuosity* (11), the latter serving vain *luxury* with fine garments of words and the former *simplicity* (5) in the unembellished truth, the "nudity" of unashamed innocence (4.), the well-*being* – as opposed to just *appearing* (23) – of what is healthy and complete in the society of the heart's own self-relative regard, its *love of Self*, rather than engaged in the selfish relativism of superiority and subordination to others in a society of *self-enamor* (7), with its fleeting fashions (18) and convenient sophistications (16).

If the entrepreneurial spirit of Man – Rousseau calls it Man's *perfectibility* – as evinced in its being able to lift itself up and out of the primitive state of its animal origins by dint of the mind's arts and the sciences, so powerful in facilitating the emancipation of civilization from the antagonism that ineluctably arises between man and nature as a result of this divergence and comparison between what the natural circumstances provide, the IS of *givens*, and Man's demands, the OUGHT of *thought* – if this restless spirit, departing thus forever from the idle idyll of its primordial quiescence, has, at the same time, triggered motives that ultimately lead to the corruption of our mores and, specifically Man's estrangement from Man in the establishment and legitimate authorization of moral inequality, then this might of the mind, its despotic freedom *in hostility*, must be distinguished from its spontaneous freedom *in acedia*, that unperturbed bovinity that once cradled the marmoreal repose of Man's infancy. Is there no other freedom than that of these two extremes – a life bent on self-aggrandisement in the first case and, in the second, one simply devoted to self-preservation – that mark the arc of despair from the profound lair of our individual *caprice* in the physical wilderness of untouched nature to the high society of moral savagery under laws of oppression that legalize the arbitrary power, the personal *prerogative* of the tyrant?

In contrast to a freedom which is neither that of libertine impulse nor that of primitive instinct, in negation of the former's slavish obsessions and of the latter's stupid indolence, Rousseau conceives of the institution of what he terms *political freedom*, the freedom that accrues to an individual as a result of a social contract that this person becomes party to through an act of free will in which our *private person* consents to conform to the law of the *public person* whose reason is the persuasive voice of virtue in the heart of every constituent member of the association and whose cause and pursuit is the wise and legitimate government of civil welfare. The power and the government of the state of freedom is founded upon this unanimity of spirit that might be called, in the Third Epoch, our *common* sense, the distinguished, uncommon sense of pure reason or the *general will*.[57]

84. The General Will

The freedom of SELF-determination is, first, that of the human spirit which, in a spontaneous flight of self-respect, posits itself as free, adverting to itself as distinguished from the unfree world of conventional civilization with respect to the autonomy of its rational nature; secondly, that individual resolves itself to concur with and assent to its distinguished destiny and through this contract to proceed to toil and strive to bring this determination to life in action. This striving desire for, this pure will of and towards our absolute spirit, this will of freedom, is what Rousseau called the *general will* (la volunté générale) and it is what he had in mind when he described the covenant of community (le contract social) as the foundation of the state based on the decision of every individual to establish the universal will as the exclusive and autonomous lawgiver. As a result, my own singular will enters upon an agreement, a constitution of community, with the universal will, which is essentially the will of universal self-determination and only as such named the will of all. Finally, the ardor of this will, regardless of the extent to which it actually achieves its end – already the commitment to reach, to strive for, even without ever reaching, that reconciliation of identity in the relationship of freedom between my private will and the public will of all – bestows upon my individual actions the dignity of a self-love in the service of a self-governing state of nature by fulfilling the will of that original community between *me* and *my SELF*, between the *I* that I *am/is* and the *I* who I *am/is destined to be*, the free I that I *will* be even if I never will be free. With respect to this "reciprocal commitment of the general public and particular individuals,....each individual, as it were, contracting with himself or herself, is determined by a twofold relationship, namely first, as member of the sovereign, to the

---

[57] cf. Boeder's treatment of Rousseau in *Die conceptuale Vernunft in der Letzten Epoche der Metaphysik* in "Abhandlungen der Braunschweigischen Wissenschaftlichen Gesellschaft" XLIII p. 348-351.

particular individuals and second, as a member of the state, to the sovereign." (Rousseau, *Emile* [OC]. IV 840).

> ...engagement réciproque du public et des particuliers,...chaque individu contractant, pour ainsi dire, avec lui-même, se trouve engagé sous un double rapport; savoir comme membre du souverain envers les particuliers, et comme membre de l'Etat envers le souverain.

Rousseau, in chapter VI of the first book entitled *On the social Pact* (du pact Social) of his famous book *Du Contract Social* with the enlightening subtitle *Principes du Droit Politique* (Principles of Political Right), formulates this state of agreement as the accord of association that engenders the human being of distinction known as the *citizen*, the subject of the state which, as we have seen, is, in fact, the state of freedom. This is how he expresses the idea: "By abstracting from the social pact whatever is not essential to it, one discovers that it can be reduced to the following terms: *each of us in concert places our person and all our powers under the supreme direction of the general will; and we receive as a body each member as an indivisible part of the whole.*"

> Si donc on écarte du pacte social ce qui n'est pas de son essence, on trouvera qu'il se réduit aux termes suivans. Chacun de nous met en commun sa personne et toute sa puissance sous la suprême direction de la volonté générale; et nous recevons en corps chaque membre comme partie indivisible du tout. (Rousseau, *OC* III 361).

Note the distinction drawn between the *general will*, on the one hand, and *my will*, namely that of my particular interest, on the other. We are, of course, all familiar with this divergence. We are constantly aware of our own desires – they give voice and force to our body's needs, motivate action towards the latter's fulfillment, incite our perseverance in confronting and overcoming obstacles mounted by circumstance to frustrate our individual inclinations. But how do we know the *general* will, the general's needs, the body of which consists of everybody's body once we have found the point of agreement where our private needs and those of the general coincide? Pure reason alone is the issue of this unanimity, i.e. the self-several entity of identity that transforms the *individual into the general*, by distinguishing the private individual as a citizen of the state of freedom, and *the general into the particular* by realizing the general principle of self-determination in the particulars of the citizen's life whose voice now speaks the word of conscience, which is that original voice of nature still discernible in our heart of hearts, *human* nature, the voice that calls forth the state of humanity which is our own realization of the will of freedom.

Upon committing ourselves to unanimity with this will, "instantly, replacing the particular person of each party to the contract, this act of association brings forth a moral and collective being composed of as many members as there are voices in the assembly, which, in the same act, receives its unity, the ME of its common identity, its life and its will. The public person thus created by this union of all the individuals was previously named *city* and now *republic* or *body politic*. When it is passive it is called *state* by its members, when it is active *sovereign*, and *power* when compared to others like itself. As regards those who are thus associated, collectively they are called the *people* and individually *citizens*, when participating in the authority of the sovereign, *subjects* in their submission to the laws of the state."

> A l'instant, au lieu de la personne particulière de chaque contractant, cet acte d'association produit un corps moral et collectif composé d'autant de membres que l'assemblée a de voix, lequel reçoit de ce même acte son unité, son *moi* commun, sa vie et sa volonté. Cette personne publique qui se forme ainsi par l'union de toutes les autres prenait autrefois le nom de *Cité*, et prend maintenant celui de *République* ou de *corps politique*, lequel est appelé par ses membres *Etat* quand il est passif, *Souverain* quand il est actif, *Puissance* en le comparant à ses semblables. A l'égard des associés ils prennent collectivement le nom de *peuple*, et s'appellent en particulier *Citoyens* comme participans à l'autorité souveraine, et *Sujets* comme soumis aux loix de l'Etat. (Rousseau, *OC* III 361-362).

Good government, *in general*, leads Man from the depravity of its inequality to the felicity of distinguished human being in the state of autonomy, a state of happiness, but now one that we have made for ourselves and strive to uphold through the bond of our commitment to the will of freedom as it speaks to the virtuous heart of our humanity. Education, *in particular*, is not a progression back to nature, but rather a nurturing, preserving development of our faculties towards that very distinguished *nature* that is human being's original destiny and essence in accordance with which we should learn to live. This is "nature's" realm as the self-relative entity of identity of freedom, namely where THE WAY IT IS *is* THE WAY IT SHOULD BE and THE WAY IT SHOULD BE *is* THE WAY IT IS; and this is therefore the country of our growth, the nation of humanity for which we were born, and the domain of autonomy that we as citizens inherit when our education is complete.

85. The Person of the Lawgiver

The legislator is the heart and the soul of government. This person or the people who form its body are members of the state but also its founders and having established the nation, they are its guarantors perpetually reviving it and renewing it in response to the progress of history in which circumstances change requiring that human being adapt to those conditions if it is to survive and prosper. Can we imagine the person of the legislator in whom the general and the particular will are perfectly united? Ideally, such a person would have to be from a different universe inhabited by beings very different from our own and somehow immune to "our prejudices, our base philosophies, our pusillanimous passions concentrated with egoism in all our hearts by inept institutions..." (III 956) namely, of "superior intelligence who sees the passions of the human heart but is subjected to none of them, fosters no rapport with our nature and nevertheless is deeply familiar with it, whose happiness is independent of ours and nevertheless cares about our flourishing, who finally, satisfied to complete in a subsequent epoch the labor begun in a previous one, achieves in the passage of time a remote glory. It would be necessary that there are gods to give laws to human being." (381)

> ...une intelligence supérieure, qui vit toutes les passions des hommes et qui n'en éprouvât aucune, qui n'eut aucun rapport avec notre nature et qui la connût à fond, dont le bonheur fût indépendant de nous et qui pourtant voulut bien s'occuper du notre; enfin qui, dans le progrès des temps se ménageant une gloire éloignée, put travailler dans un siècle et jouir dans un autre. Il faudroit des Dieux pour donner des loix aux hommes.

Such an impossible – because self-several – being as this one would have to comprise the *intelligence* as much as the *will* and the executive *power* of the republic; as the people's guiding faculty of judgment, the conscience of public insight "sees both the way things are and the ways things should be..." (380); protecting them from "...the seduction of private wills..." as well as bestowing upon the general will the common sense of a particular time and place; "...it must weigh present, tangible advantages..." that the individual sees here and now "against the danger of distant, hidden evils..." that ensue when private perspectives hold sway, and often champion public and long-term goods that are abstract and remote against the preferences of self-interest in all their urgency and immediacy. In other words, whereas "private individuals see the good they reject...the general public wants the good that it does not see. All are therefore equally in need of guidance – while the former must be compelled to conform their wills to reason; the latter must learn to recognize what it wants. Public enlightenment leads thus to the union of the intellect and the will in the body politic, the complete collaboration of the parts and, ultimately, the greatest force of the whole." (380)

> Les particuliers voyant le bien qu'ils rejettent; le public veut le bien qu'il ne voit pas. Tous ont également besoin de guides; il faut obliger les uns à conformer leurs volontés à leur raison; il faut apprendre à l'autre à connoitre ce qu'il veut. Alors des lumières publiques résulte l'union de l'entendement et de la volonté dans le corps social, de-là l'exact concours des parties, et enfin la plus grande force du tout.

Join the executive power of the prince with the legislative will of the sovereign that is always guided by intelligent judgment in the self-several person of the legislator who sees the gap between the real and the ideal and then, in accordance with this insight, institutes legitimate government as the first and principal law in the constitution of political order and what do you get? A system of perceptive, practical, and generative reason that, in political terms, we call the constitution of the state.

The body of the state born of the social contract between each individual and the whole, having thus made one out of many (but not through the assimilation of the many) – the *invention* of pure reason – has acquired the administrative skills it needs to insure – the *practice* of pure reason – that the conditions necessary to preserve that union of well-being as recognized by the *insight* of pure reason into the principles of the commonweal, will endure.

The constitution of the state of freedom is thus a threefold relationship of relationships, a complete train of thought that is a being, and a being that is a train of thought – have not philosophers always suggested that this identity is worthy of contemplation, and, more than that, indicative of a way of life that is the foundation of a distinguished human dwelling?

B. The Well-Being of Humanity

86. The State of Freedom

While everyday common sense tells us that *people* are naturally inclined to pursue their self-interest and therefore to concern themselves with what is good for themselves individually, here and now, the *uncommon* common sense of our civic consciousness is inspired by the public interest of *a people* striving to attain what is good for the community in general and for all time, in other words, the *common good*, which is the object of good government or, as Rousseau calls it in his third *Discours*, "L'Economie Politique" (Political Economy). The administration of the common weal of a political society sees itself as mediating between the sovereignty of the general will and the individual members who comprise the sovereign body as the agency of public force, the executive power that puts into effect the laws enacted by the legislative power of the general assembly. "The government receives from the sovereign the orders it gives the people...who are sovereigns on the one hand and subjects on the other." (III 396) This is the self-several relationship that defines the entity of identity in the Third Epoch as that of *autonomy*. "For it is the harmony of obedience and liberty that founds the body politic; the words *subject* and *sovereign* are correlatives of one another – their concept is unified under the single word "Citizen." (427) This term gives a name to the "exact proportion between the constitutive parts of the state" (453), namely between the *sovereign* and the *people*, the rapport between the whole and the whole (393) the first being the expression of the will of the people, the legislative power, the second the members of the state or the body politic. The government or the executive power is the middle term in which the general law and the individual members of the state, the subjects, coincide and correspond, forming the communal being of the public person analogous to the union between the soul and the body in an individual. (396)

The state can be thus thought of as a living organism, the members in which it consists being the citizens themselves, the diversity of their roles in contributing to the well-being and preservation of the whole body akin to the diversity of organs that a living body has, for example the mouth, the stomach, the blood, the heart, as well as all the rest of the parts – the departments and the partners – of this living being's organization "that make the machine move, live and work and which cannot be harmed in any of its parts without pain being immediately transmitted to the brain, if the animal is in a state of good health." (244)

But of course the body politic is not *really* a body, the citizens that constitute it are not *really* its organs; they themselves, as individuals, *have* bodily organs and members that work together towards the common good of the union they comprise – their state is a *physical* rather than a *moral* being; but in both experiences of self-several dwelling, their respective lives arise through the contract of accord that the individual will of each member makes with the general will of the whole as depicted in *Figure 59.*

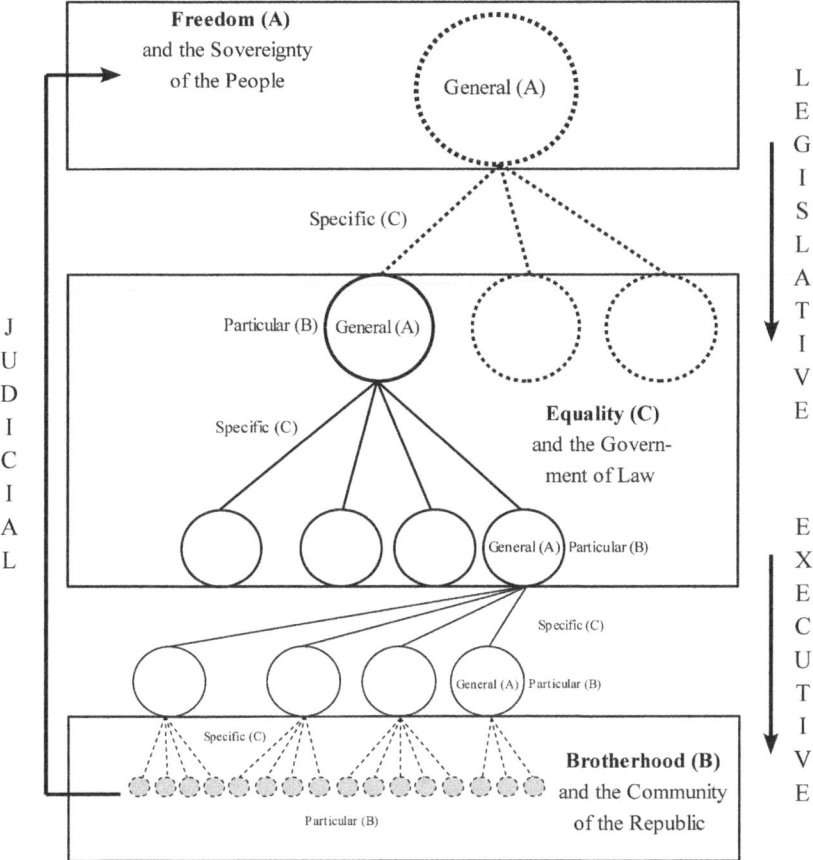

Figure 59: The State of Freedom

Behold the structure of the miracle of the merging of minds that is the unanimity of the common good through which the individuals "bind their wills by their own consent,...obey though no one commands, serve and have no masters...this is the celestial voice that dictates to each citizen the precepts of public reason, and teaches human being to act in accordance with the maxims of its own judgment and not be at odds" (248) with this being that is the shared humanity of every individual, "the communal I...possessing that reciprocal sensibility and internal correspondence" (244-245) that is the common life of both the physical individual and the moral being.

This scheme shows, in terms of civic consciousness, the imbedded multiplication of the relationship that we have characterized as that of pure reason. Every human community, to the extent that the individuals composing it are united by a common interest, whether it is a business organization, a jazz combo, or a football team, are constituted by the convention of accord that unites the private with the general will of that association. But every society, even though their members are bound to its law in service to the spirit of its common good, is nevertheless a particular and individual one with respect to the larger community and the more general will that contains it; for this reason, a deliberation can be advantageous to and the citizen seen as upright in, the small community, and then again pernicious to that very same community while the citizen condemned as vice-ridden in the eyes of the large community. (246) Thus, "particular societies are always subordinate to those that contain them...the duties of the citizen coming before those of the senator and those of human being taking precedence over those of the citizen; but self-interest is inversely proportional to duty and increases to the extent that the association becomes narrower in scope and the commitment less sacred – invincible proof that the most general will is always the most just and that the voice of the people is, in effect, the voice of God. " (ibid.)

> les sociétés particulières étant toujours subordonnées à celles qui les contiennent...les devoirs du citoyen vont avant ceux du sénateur, et ceux de l'homme avant ceux du citoyen : mais malheuresement l'intérêst personnel se trouve toûjours en raison inverse du devoir, et augmente à mesure que l'association devient plus étroit et l'engagement moins sacré; preuve invincible que la volonté la   plus générale est aussi toujours la plus juste, et que la voie du peuple est en effet la voix de Dieu.

Ultimately, following this principle, "the great city of the world becomes the political body, for which the law of nature is always its general will and its states and diverse peoples merely private individuals." (245)

But is this "sentiment of humanity...extended over the entire world" (254) not all too general and abstract, not all too rarefied, to make a difference in our particular lives? Not at all. Because the difference is already there! In fact, the greatest support for public authority lies in the very hearts of citizens, in such people as in whose hearts virtue lives and the voice of duty speaks (253). And thus "since virtue is merely the conformity of the private to the general will...," the challenge facing founding mothers and fathers is, "in a word, make virtue reign" (252). Poetic thought in the Third Epoch knows that nation-building is the greatest of all arts; but, alas, to build nations, you must build human beings first, each one individually, and train them to be future citizens (259) such that "from the first moment of life they might learn to deserve to live." (260); we learn as students of humanity that human nature is an enterprise of invention, a work of creative genius devoted to the realization of just such a being of freedom. It is thus our destiny to bring forth our own being, our distinguished *human* being. Whoever heard of a being born to bring itself forth?

87. The Human Being of Freedom

While *politics* studies how good government strives to attain and maintain the well-being of the republic, *pedagogy* focuses on supporting and preserving the natural development of the individual; the first is based on the work of the *founding mother* and *father* of the republic who institutes government by ordaining and establishing a constitution of the state's principles, foremost of which are our duty to love and respect the law (249) as our *own* being – our better, general Self – and our inalienable right to pursue the distinguished life, liberty, and happiness of our own humanity; the other is the practical knowledge of an *instructor* whose task it is to guide the pupil to the I of the general will, to introduce the pupil to the people of the common weal, to inspire in the heart of the pupil a love of virtue, which is the self-love of humanity, the community that is our distinguished identity, the identity that is our living community of well-being, this unique land of the free and home of the brave that is the only true fatherland of which we are and can be citizens, patriots, *by nature* and, as subjects to the laws of which, live in liberty. These are the laws that have been engraved in our young hearts by conscience and reason long before they become codes carved in stone by Man. And only when the laws of the state and that of the heart diverge do we, thus doubled by conflicting ends, either natural Man entirely for itself or civil Man entirely for others, experience the misery of the heart torn apart, neither good for itself nor good for others; with respect to this principle, statecraft and pedagogy coincide:

The misery of human being comes from the contradiction that arises between our present state and our desires, between our duties and our inclinations, between nature and social institutions, between the man and the citizen; make this being one and you will make it happy.... Either give human being entirely over to the state or leave it utterly onto itself; for in dividing its heart, you tear it apart; and do not imagine that the state could be happy if all of its members are in anguish...Make people accord with themselves, make them be as they would appear and appear as they are. You will have placed the social law in the depth of their heart, civil human beings by nature and citizens by inclination – they will be one, they will be good, they will be happy and their felicity will be that of the republic. (III 510-11)

Ce qui fait la misère humaine est la contradiction qui se trouve entre notre état et nos désirs, entre nos devoirs et nos penchans, entre la nature et les institutions sociales, entre l'homme et le citoyen; rendez l'homme un et vous le rendrez heureux autant qu'il peut l'être. Donnez-le tout entier à l'état ou laissez-le tout entier à lui-même, mais si vous partagez son cœur vous le déchirez; et n'allez pas vous imaginer que l'état puisse être heureux quand tous ses membres pâtissent...Rendez les hommes consequens à eux-mêmes étant ce qu'ils veulent paroitre et paroissant ce qu'ils sont. Vous aurez mis la loi sociale au fond des cœurs, hommes civils par leur nature et Citoyens par leurs inclinations, ils seront uns, ils seront bons, ils seront heureux, et leur félicité sera celle de la République...

From this contradiction emerges the equally divided, mutually exclusive aims of pedagogy – either the denaturing institution of public education that takes away our absolute existence and gives us the fractional unity of a member relative to the whole of the social body or else the domestic education, the education of nature, which seeks to raise human being for human being in the perfect self-relativity of a numerical unity and absolute whole unto itself – a training that makes of human being by art what it already is by nature, culminating nature's work (*Julie*, OC II 566) and "not spoiling the man of nature by adapting him to society." (612)

...ne pas gâter l'homme de la nature en l'appropriant à la société.

How very odd an art, how very rare the fruit of this art, a "human being of nature" rather than a "man of man" (l'homme de l'homme – 549)! "What is to be done to form this rare being? Doubtless very much, in the way of preventing that anything be done..." in other words, not to do something but to "...stand there..." and specifically, since "in the natural order humans are all equal, their common calling is the human condition...neither a magistrate nor a soldier nor a priest: he or she will be first a human being..." in this sense, our true study is that of "abstract human being" (*Emile*, IV 251-2)

> Pour former cet homme rare qu'avons-nous à faire? Beaucoup, sans doute; c'est d'empêcher que rien ne soit fait...rester en place...Dans l'ordre naturel les hommes étant tous égaux leur vocation commune est l'état d'homme...ni magistrat, ni soldat, ni prêtre: il sera premièrement homme...l'homme abstrait....

It may come therefore as somewhat of a surprise that the first sentences of Rousseau's *Emile* succinctly state as its basic premise that "issuing from the hands of the Author of all, everything is good; in the hands of man, however, everything degenerates...he forces...he confounds and confuses..he mutilates..., perverts and disfigures; he loves deformity; loves monsters..." (245) Hmm, an odd way to begin a book intended to guide educators in their work! Not so odd however if the goal of your pedagogy is to enable nature to take its course (247) by fostering the original, i.e. natural dispositions of human being before they have become constrained by our habits and corrupted by our opinions (248). It is only then that the three masters of our upbringing, namely *nature, people,* and *things,* work in concert (247), each providing us with opportunities to learn – the first with lessons that are inherent in the intrinsic development of our faculties (B), the second emerging from our proper usage and development (C) of these faculties, and the third in the experience we gather in connection with the orders of reality that extend beyond and impinge upon our lives (A) and with regards to which our faculties are shaped and sharpened. It is in the school of Man that we learn the lessons of one-sidedness and extremism that is the disfigurement of our humanity and that breeds a human being that has been neither sustained in the sheltering embrace of nature nor morally transformed through virtue, "neither a man of humanity nor a citizen of the state, always in contradiction with himself, always hovering between his inclinations and his duties...he will be good neither for himself nor for others. This will be one of those men of today: a Frenchman, an Englishman, a bourgeois. This will be nothing." (249-250)

> Toujours en contradiction avec lui-même, toujours flottant entre ses penchans et ses devoirs ils ne sera jamais ni homme ni citoyen; il ne sera bon ni pour lui ni pour les autres. Ce sera un

de ces hommes de nos jours; un François, un Anglois, un
Bourgeois; ce sera rien.

The state has its lawmaker who founds the constitution of the people; the
individual has his or her governor, the teacher, whose task it is less to
instruct with a recital of precepts than it is to lead in practice along nature's
course and in this way to provide for the pupil "an education of nature"
(251), that succeeds at raising a human being uniquely for human being, the
self-relative entity of identity that is the life of pure reason. The legislator
and the teacher – these two sublime souls, both more than men (263) are
the two fathers of the two natural beings of freedom – the moral being of a
political body and the human being of humanity.

The humanity of human being is thus the end of the entire path of nature
that has thus far, like a train of thought, determined our development and
guided our education, with nature herself, "who does everything for the
best," (304), being the founder of a healthy constitution in our adult estate,
as well as the governor of our growth through the epochs of our lives; each
stage has its own reason and its own season; each step has its own logic,
each sphere attains its own perfection (418) and its own happiness before
being superseded by the next as by the subsequent season of the year, a
progression as logical as it is natural, as natural as it is logical, from that first
age of nature's pure life in our infancy, to that of our entrance into the world
of our physical being through the reason of the senses, human being's first
reason in our first season (370), forming ideas out of a conjunction of
sensations (417) in service to "our first masters of philosophy – our feet, our
hand, our eyes (370)." This is the original state of human well-being where
power and desire are in equilibrium (304) before the immediate world of
the child at play, a living being as yet concentrated and self-sufficient within
its own life, is broken open by the passions, our experience of weakness
(426), that arises through the cleft between the IS and the OUGHT, in
consequence of our infinite imagination, our boundless desire, and our
"prescience! Prescience that extends us ceaselessly beyond ourselves and
often places us where we shall never arrive." (307)

La prévoyance! La prévoyance qui nous porte sans cesse au delà
de nous et souvent nous place où nous n'arriverons point.

In this way, the age in which our physical prowess and that of the senses
burgeon in their strength and acuity attains fruition in the age of curiosity
with the observation of natural phenomena and the island world they
compose, the earth our only book and lesson (361), its facts our professors,
that we, having begun to gain distance from ourselves (429-30), like so many

Robinson Crusoes (455), have now all to ourselves and our perception, and that, while feeding our desire to know and understand, appeal to our intellect and whet our judgment, perfecting our faculties of enlightened childhood; this consummation of *illumination* is short lived (489) and this ripe apple is destined to fall in fullest sweetness. For the age of knowledge and conception is then itself succeeded by the critical age of adolescence when we experience all the controversy of human life that perturbs the moral rapport of human beings to themselves as well as one to another (487), which is our second birth (490) that the distinction of human being means for our lives, namely the age of sentiment and *passions*, "the instruments of our freedom" (491); foremost of which and principle as well as source of all the others is our concern for our own well-being – our fear of pain and our horror of death (600) – or, as Rousseau calls it, our "self-love" (l'amour de soi – 491), a love founded upon the essential self-relativity of my tender loving care for my own person, my own desire for happiness – as distinguished from the self-love that is the esteem I accord myself relative to the esteem accorded to me by others in comparison with the esteem that they themselves have been accorded by me. It is therefore, the regard I feel I am owed, the reciprocal sense of my merit relative to that of others. In footnote 15 of his *Discourse on the Origin of Inequality*, Rousseau clarifies as follows (*OC*, III 219):

> L'amour de soi-même est un sentiment naturel qui porte tout animal à veiller à sa propre conservation et qui, dirigé dans l'homme par la raison et modifié par la pitié, produit l'humanité et la vertu. L'Amour propre n'est qu'un sentiment relatif, factice, et né dans la société, qui porte chaque individu à faire plus de cas de soi que de tout autre, qui inspire aux hommes tous les maux qu'ils se font mutuellement, et qui est la véritable source de l'honneur.

> *Self-love is the natural sense that compels all living beings to take interest in their own preservation and which, in human being, guided by reason and tempered by compassion, produces humanity and virtue. The love deemed owed to one is only a relative and derivative sentiment arising in society that leads its individuals to suppose themselves to be more worthy of esteem than any other, a belief that inspires in people all of those evils with which they plague each other and is the root motive of honor.*

88. Self-love vs. Self-interest

Clearly then *self-love* (l'amour de soi) is the origin and principle of the love deemed owed to one (l'amour propre) – the former taken in a broad sense as *self-esteem* ("l'estime de soi-même"- IV 562) before all self-aggrandizing deformation (488) – a sentiment of "the heart in which there is no original perversity" in accordance with Rousseau's "incontestable maxim that the first movements of nature are always good" (322) but which can so easily, in the hands of Man, degenerate from their natural purity and simplicity into the familiar vices that our narcissistic passions give rise to, especially pride in grand souls and vanity in puny ones (494) from which all the others are spawned, in which we find ourselves set outside of nature and in contradiction with ourselves. (491)

But who are we who are not who we are when self-love lets us feel pity for the sufferings of human and all other sentient, animate living beings? The tenderness and sympathy of heartfelt pity arise from the natural tendency of a soul that has learned to expand its scope of concern beyond the narrow confines of our particular person.

> Ainsi naît la pitié, premier sentiment relatif qui touche le cœur humain selon l'ordre de la nature. Pour devenir sensible et pitoyable, il faut que l'enfant sache qu'il y a des êtres semblables à lui qui souffrent ce qu'il a souffert, qui sentent les douleurs qu'il a senties, et d'autres dont il doit avoir l'idée, comme pouvant les sentir aussi. En effet, comment nous laissons-nous émouvoir à la pitié, si ce n'est en nous transportant hors de nous et nous identifiant avec l'animal souffrant, en quittant, pour ainsi dire, notre être pour prendre le sien? Nous ne souffrons qu'autant que nous jugeons qu'il souffre; ce n'est pas dans nous, c'est dans lui que nous souffrons. Ainsi nul ne devient sensible que quand son imagination s'anime et commence à le transporter hors de lui. (505-506)

> *Thus is born the compassion and commiseration of pity, which is the first relative sentiment to touch the heart of human being in accordance with nature's order. In order that he become feeling and pitying, Emile must know that there are fellow beings that suffer what he himself has suffered, who feel not only those pains that he has become familiar with but also those of which he has a notion of being capable of feeling as well. For truly, how do we let ourselves be moved by pity if not by transporting ourselves outside of ourselves and identifying ourselves with a suffering being,*

leaving, so to say, our own being in order to take on that of the one
we see suffering before us? We do not suffer except to the extent
that we perceive its suffering; but it is not in ourselves, it is in it
that we suffer. Hence no being becomes truly sensible to others
until, with the animation of its imagination, it begins to
transport itself out of itself.

Here, or rather there, outside of ourselves, where we are who We are not
and most truly Ourselves when not ourselves do we find the relational,
ultimately self-relational, principle of ΛΟΓΟΣ as it is experienced in terms
of *feeling*, understood not merely as emotion but rather as the relationship
to such objects as prompt the "expansive force of the heart, enlarging and
extending it to encompass other beings and disposing it to everywhere find
itself outside of itself ..." – in contrast to those objects that we might
therefore call *illogical*, "that constrict and contract the soul and curtail the
sweep of the open human *I* – in other words to induce in the heart
magnanimity, humanity, compassion, beneficence, and all the passions
sweet and pleasing that human beings find to be naturally gratifying..." as
opposed to those that feed on "the passions, repulsive and cruel like envy,
covetousness, and hate which do not merely nullify our sensibility but
rather install its negation...", its perversion and monstrosity (314) so evident
in the attitude of those who feign know only themselves and are gladly
willing to sacrifice fathers, mothers, and the entire universe to the least of
their pleasures. (220)

> ...la force expansive de son cœur, qui le dilatent, qui l'étendent
> sur les autres êtres, qui le fassent partout retrouver hors de lui;...
> qui le resserrent, le concentrent, et tendent le ressort du moi
> humain; c'est-à-dire, en d'autres termes, d'exciter en lui la
> bonté, l'humanité, la commisération, la bienfaisance, toutes les
> passions attirantes et douces qui plaisent naturellement aux
> hommes,... l'envie, la convoitise, la haine, toutes les passions
> repoussantes et cruelles, qui rendent, pour ainsi dire, la
> sensibilité non seulement nulle, mais négative,...? (506)

In the opening of his heart that a growing sensibility to what extends
beyond the sphere of his immediate concerns for his private interests,
foremost of which are his infant life and limb, Emile learns to widen the
horizon of his self-love, first to include his closest family and friends and
then his fellows within its scope and only then, after having cultivated and
reflected upon this natural outreaching of love, is he willing and able, "to
generalize his individual notions under the abstract idea of humanity" (520)
and by extending his compassion, more, his self-regard (547), to embrace

all of humankind (548) such that to love and respect himself is, finally, to love and respect humanity (543, 547), justice, goodness – in a word *virtue*, a disputatious love and a corresponding reverence for this outward turning love.

This natural progression of the child's development and the analogous growth of our soul away from the local determinations of its individuality, from all of the differences among human beings that our narcissism takes such pride in upholding as founding an assumed prerogative and superiority with respect to those around us – status and class consciousness of society, the biases of nationality, people's generic prejudices and opinions that would make of Emile a man of Man rather than a man of nature (549) who, in contrast, grants nothing to the government of authority not in accordance with that of his own reason (551) through having "eliminated as artificial what belonged to one people and not to another, to one station and not to another, and by regarding as incontestably belonging to human being only what is common to all at whatever age, in whatever rank and in whatever nation" (550) – this flight of pure thought that we undertake in the spirit of humanity attains the zenith of its arc in allowing Emile to choose his own religion, namely the one to which "the best use of his reason must conduct him." (558)

...celle où le meilleur usage de sa raison doit le conduire.

Consider therefore the first commandment of a general and in this sense "natural" religion before every particular, because sectarian, one: "Human being, do not under any circumstances dishonor human being!" (510)

Homme, ne déshonore point l'homme!

By respecting our humankind (ibid), having disburdened ourselves of all the baggage that has formed and determined our particular life in the society of Man, we have come to understand self-love in a new way, namely as a love of the nature of human being. As natural beings, we are not "kings, or lords; we are not courtiers, we are not rich. All are born naked and poor; all are subject to the miseries of life, to woes, ills, needs and pangs of every kind. And in the end, all are condemned to death. This is Man's true condition. This is what no mortal is exempt from. Begin, therefore, by studying in human nature what is most inseparable from it, what best marks humanity." (504)

> Les hommes ne sont naturellement ni rois, ni grands, ni courtisans, ni riches; tous sont nés nus et pauvres, tous sujets aux misères de la vie, aux chagrins, aux maux, aux besoins, aux

douleurs de toute espèce; enfin, tous sont condamnés à la mort. Voilà ce qui est vraiment de l'homme; voilà de quoi nul mortel n'est exempt. Commencez donc par étudier de la nature humaine ce qui en est le plus inséparable, ce qui constitue le mieux l'humanité.

Thus when Rousseau speaks of nature and natural human being, he is not advocating outings in the park, vegetarianism, singing accolades to a shepherd's Arcadian, pleading for a return to provincialism much less to a life in the wilderness with our brother bears. These images are intended to render palpable and striking the feeling of freedom that, like the law of nature itself, even if they be chimeras, remind human being that, inspired by the moral order reigning in the tender heart (523), we can indeed conceive of our *being before*, of what we were before we became what we have become and this experience of humanity not only distinguishes us from ourselves but also unites us with what all human being shares, namely the capacity *not* to be what we are and to be what remains of us after we have sloughed off the coil of all that we have become.

We can apparently make sense of the question: "What would freedom do in this situation?" In other words, "What would I do if I don't put my own personal interests, my own particular preferences, my needs and pleasures of the present moment, myself, first?" People who ask themselves this question have acknowledged freedom as their destiny. And in doing so, they give reality to what might have been and remained nothing more than an abstraction of the mind and a figment of the imagination – the absolute freedom of human being is a decision we take, a distinction we decide to make in our own lives. What sort of life is one that asks this question and lives under its empire? It must be a charmed life, though no easy one. Can we conceive of Emile and Sophie, his companion, now that each has completed their education and found the other as their perfect partner born to live the life of virtue?

From childhood *to* puberty, from the illumination of our minds with regards to being, the calm conception and the contemplation of THE WAY IT IS *to* the critical passion of our souls with regards to what is good and what is better and distinguished thus as THE WAY IT SHOULD BE – we have now graduated from the study of physical beings to that of moral beings in the natural progression that chronicles reason's own logical development and the constitution, the equilibrium, the coordination, in a word, the reciprocally regulated organization of its faculties, its parts and departments, into a viable order (557)

This is the line of reasoning and a genealogy of the order and the orders of the mind, its offices and their system, in accordance with which it is manifest that our human being has not been made by man but rather by nature (549) and in which we hear our teacher's voice, nature's advocate and minister (639), pure reason, confirming that "I followed the road of nature in the hopes that it would show me the road to happiness. As it turned out, they were the same and that, without even thinking about it, I had been following it all along." (815)

> Je me tins dans la route de la nature en attendant qu'elle me
> montrât celle du bonheur. Il s'est trouvé qu'elle étoit la même,
> et qu'en n'y pensant pas je l'avois suivie.

"Having attained the maturity of age and reason and...nourished in the order of nature but raised for society,..." our being, "will not have qualities that impress the crowd, will certainly not have acquired particular talents, will not have been formed for this or that special employment, but will have the means of being useful to all of them; our being will not be this particular being or that one, it will only be human being; attached to nothing, it will connect with everything; it will have but a single merit, a single art, but one supplementary to all the rest and the sole one lacking those who have many others: namely to know and to have its place. Whatever will be in the future, whatever fortune gives or takes, what this human being has right from the present and what nothing can take away namely..." the time of nature's youth" spent in happiness and wisdom. (237-8)

But it is not this abstraction of human being with regards to the foreign and extraneous society that surrounds it that is the fulfillment of nature's principle and the final vision of happiness to which we might attain by nature's way. Behold and contemplate the vision of the entity of identity in which nature has regained the harmony of its self-relationship encompassing two human beings bound by the love of humanity upon which is founded the community of their mutual self-regard "I contemplate with tenderness how many benefactions," these two, let us call them "*Emile and Sophie*, can spread around them from their simple retreat and how much they can vivify the country and reanimate the extinguished zeal of the unfortunate villagers" (of Man's perverted empire). "I imagine seeing the people fruitful, the fields enriched, the earth renewed in adornments. Magnificence and plenitude transform labor into festivals, and cries of joy and benedictions arise from the midst of the games which center on the lovable couple who brought them back to life." Of course such a vision of "the golden age is treated as a chimera, and it will always be one for anyone whose heart and taste have been spoiled...What then would be required to give it a new birth? One single but impossible thing: to love it." (859)

> Je m'attendris en songeant combien de leur simple retraite Emile et Sophie peuvent répandre de bienfaits autour d'eux, combien ils peuvent vivifier la campagne et ranimer le zèle éteint de l'infortuné villageois. Je crois voir le peuple se multiplier, les champs se fertiliser, la terre prendre une nouvelle parure, la multitude et l'abondance transformer les travaux en fêtes, les cris de joye et les bénédictions s'élever du milieu des jeux autour du couple amiable qui les a ranimés. On traite l'age d'or de chimère, et c'en sera toujours une pour quiconque a le cœur et le goût gâtés....Que faudroit-il donc pour le faire renaître? Une seule chose mais impossible; ce seroit de l'aimer.

Ah, but what sort of love is this and what sort of lover that can love a figment of the imagination and with this love and the enthusiasm that it awakens breathe life into a dream, the lover's life?

C. The Morality of Self-Regard

89. The Virtue of Love

The final term of Rousseauan speech specifies the criterion of discernment required by thought if insight into our experience of self-knowing being is to do justice to the visions of freedom thus far encountered – the primal state of nature, the descent of the state of the general will from it, and finally, the mature, happy state of human being attained by education in the fulfillment of the principle of humanity, our destiny. These *chimera* are recognized as works and words of wisdom by the ideas they evoke, by the philosophical conceptions they have brought forth, and the desire to know they animate in a distinguished heart; above all, they encourage action, more, they inspire the genius of our humanity to creative invention by providing the will with a vision of the aim and goal most worthy of our undying devotion, reason's reminder of THE WAY IT SHOULD BE as rendered and realized by the imagination – a whole world of ideas the reality of which we might partake of.

We conclude this train of thought and mediation upon our experience of pure reason's critical self-reflection with the vision of a circle of communing souls, just two lovers, inhabitants of a little village on the foot of the Alps, exchanging letters in a dialogue of individual I's, each the voice of the universal will to the other, each in turn subject to the other's judgment and government, the two good souls of the I seeing eye to eye, the I's of the soul of freedom delighting in their enthusiastic commitment to virtue, the honor of respect shown each to each, each to the ideal alive and loved in the other as a brother, as a dear sister, each entrusting the other's honor to the other's care, each striving to be the other's self-respect and therefore each enjoying reflected in the other's felicity the rectitude of their own true heart's fires that made them worthy of happiness' grace in the first place – the maiden, neither Gretchen, nor Héloïse, bringing her cherished innocence and her human goodness (l'honnêteté) to her lover's life, her lover (not Faust, nor Abélard, nor the doomed Werther,) giving virtuous life to his young lady's ideal. And so in the reciprocal passion of lover and beloved do these two souls' pure heart (40, 352) and mind, each having been made for the other in nature's forming hands (193), embrace in the native beauty of shared esteem.

The tale of their unfolding love in an ongoing dialogue of conscience's self-regard is one of a true love sorely tried and tested and finally coming into its own – a narrative of the sacrifice that this love of virtue, this self-respect, demands from a mutual acknowledgement of regard between the soul and its soul mate; in a series of epistolary hymns, it recounts what Man's men and women have, in general, gone through in the name of their self-relative human being and what we ourselves, every day or some days or at least once in our lives, go through individually as distinguished human beings born to freedom but living in the chains of convention, personal prejudice, and public opinion, habit, but also in the extremism of surfeit and excess, of negligent and self-centered inclinations, in the greed of short-sighted indulgence in a momentary pleasure at the expense of the more sustainable and substantial happiness (OC II 123, 225) that survives the empire of the senses (667) so constrained in the immediacy of their needs.

Our history of the heart begins in all innocence – we might, with Rousseau, imagine a young girl as the heroine of this particular account. Call her *Julie*. Might she have really existed?[58] Whether or not she really has, we who have, with her lover, come to worship her sublime sentiments will join him in exclaiming full of joy, full of pain: "Oh what beings we all would be if the world were full of Julies and of hearts that knew how to love them." (229)

---

[58] cf. Boeder's *Rousseau oder der Aufbruch des Selbstbewußtseins* in "Bewußtsein und Zeitlichkeit," ed. H. Busche, G. Heffernan, D. Lohmar, Wurzburg 1990.

> O quels hommes nous serions tous, si le monde était plein de
> Julies et de cœurs qui les sussent aimer!

She had been raised in purity and simplicity, the adored and only daughter of an honorable family with whom she lives in peace in a small township far from those ills of society that have fettered our human being in its hollow home of trinket gold. And then she is awakened from her ingenuous tranquillity to *existence*, the existence of the heart broken by passion, cleft in twain and thus distinguished in itself, love sundered from the rule of love, such that the IS and the OUGHT of self-love no longer coincide in the pre-established harmony of the good soul's natural purity. Hers is the story of the ensuing revolutions of this self-several heart and the deaths endured in love's name when nature is from nature severed, passion from virtue, ourselves from our Self. But who are we for the sake of whom we must conquer and be conquered (38) – nature by nature and love by love, the two-fold life of our soul (41), both its sickness and its cure, both our hero and our enemy?

Indeed the language of this experience that marks the self-severalty of our human being corroborates, by collecting contradictory terms into a narrative of Julie's life and death for love, the restlessness of our nature and our destiny in light of this love and how passion alone can conquer passion in a good soul, as exalted as it is profound, born to feel deeply, nobly, genuinely. "For if happiness and peace are not in Julie's soul, where will their asylum be down here?" (586) Nowhere if not in the heart of all good people. (225)

> si le bonheur et la paix ne sont pas dans l'âme de Julie, où sera
> leur asile ici-bas?

Human nature's is a tender soul that makes (193, 666) and is made for the sacrifices and felicities of virtue, striving for purity, though weak in spite of its ardor for excellence, subjugated to its desires and no less impassioned in the exaltation of its desire to rise above and vanquish them, dissatisfied amidst the riches of its fulfilled contentment and peace (694) but nevertheless given to goodness in the sentiment and devoted practices of the divine distinction it cultivates, this tender soul, far from abstracting us from worldly affairs, lends sweetness to the tasks of the day and joy to the heart, revives lightness and gaiety, and "awakens a renewed interest in a life spent in the hopes of meriting happiness," (695), i.e. the joy and pleasure that are its "pure, continual, universal" charms. (148) This is the destiny of a heart distinguished as the feeling of true sentiment – alas, such a feeling heart (161), that of a beautiful soul (725), is not an easy thing to live with, so deliciously troubled (602) by delicate sentiments (531) attuned to the attractions (527, 557) of simplicity, equality (527), innocence (53), virtue (353), honesty, and beauty (89, 365-66), and no less susceptible to the torments of impetuous affection, so often pierced by chagrin (513) or regrets (310), craven by remorse, touched by pity and torn by other's tears (100), or in self-reproach for crimes of negligence (117) – more often feared with abhorrence than actually committed – admonished, constrained by duty's inexorable command (314), all the while devoured by the delirium (40) of passions (3.18), made tender by sorrow (348), enraptured by the sweetest transports of emotion (363), beset by pains and woes of shame (136) that sap its vigor (386), and then again charmed, revived by uplifting sentiments (42-43) – not an easy thing at all to live with by any means; we might exclaim therefore:

> Que c'est un fatal présent du ciel qu'une âme sensible ! Celui qui l'a reçu doit s'attendre à n'avoir que peine et douleur sur la terre. Vil jouet de l'air et des saisons, le soleil ou les brouillards, l'air couvert ou serein, régleront sa destinée, et il sera content ou triste au gré des vents. Victime des préjugés, il trouvera dans d'absurdes maximes un obstacle invincible aux justes vœux de son cœur. Les hommes le puniront d'avoir des sentiments droits de chaque chose, et d'en juger par ce qui est véritable plutôt que par ce qui est de convention. Seul il suffirait pour faire sa propre misère, en se livrant indiscrètement aux attraits divins de l'honnête et du beau, tandis que les pesantes chaînes de la nécessité l'attachent à l'ignominie. Il cherchera la félicité suprême sans se souvenir qu'il est homme : son cœur et sa raison seront incessamment en guerre, et des désirs sans bornes lui prépareront d'éternelles privations. (89)

> *What a fatal gift from heaven is a sensitive soul! Having received it, expect nothing but pain and suffering on earth. Vile toy of the air, of the seasons, the sun and the clouds, the skies, overcast or serene, will rule your destiny and the winds will preside over your contentment or sorrow. Subject to the prejudices of Man, you will encounter in absurd imperatives insurmountable obstacles to your heart's just vows and you will be punished for holding with upright sentiment in all things and for judging by what is true rather than what is customary. And even alone you will suffice to make your own misery – innocently delivering yourself to the divine attractions of virtue and beauty while the heavy chains of necessity will bind you to ignominy. You will vie for supreme*

felicity forgetting that you are but a human being; your heart and
your mind will wage incessant war and your desires without limit
will sow eternal deprivations.

This unbearable contrast and discrepancy between our fortune as determined by all the particulars of circumstances in our individual lives, on the one hand and, on the other, the immensity of our innermost soul (89) is the source of true love's conflict and the justification for the language of battle employed to vividly render to our perceptions the experience of its effects upon the sentiments of human being as a war between love's two equal heroes, namely strength and tenderness.

For in the name of virtue, we wage war against the onslaught of a vigorous attacker (87) whose force often seems to surpass our own (201) with that force of the soul that is the source of courage where there is peril (498), taking up arms in resistance against unrelenting sufferings, waging pitched battles with defeat ever looming; and then, in related terms of turmoil, where duty and desire, virtue and love, diverge, the former commands the latter obeys (121), defense and attack, modesty and audacity, dare we still, without blushing, name the soul's flight and the heart's flame (59), the heart's regard and love's passion, these days, as Rousseau did then, *woman* and *man*, who as wife and husband, are wed in the holy matrimony of the mind the sacred institution of which unifies (without conflation) its two powers and two passions, pure love's sense (99) and sensibility's keenest pleasure, wisdom's esteem and the senses' transport (54), the gentle, sacred fire, and the fury (102) of love, as two lovers in the self-relativity of their mutual regard and tender devotion, and as such, as the dwelling of wife and husband in the sentiment of felicity and the peace of mind that is the state of harmony between innocence and love, that is two beautiful souls' paradise on earth where they can speak of virtue without shame and where together, like heaven and nature, "pleasure and honor sing." (51)

E v'é il piacere con l'onestade accanto.

But what if unlucky circumstances forbade this marriage? Then, for star-crossed lovers, virtue is a state of war (682) and even divine Julie, herself unique masterpiece of nature (148), the celestial image and beautiful embodiment (41) of love's sacred union in the bosom of humanity's natural state of innocence, clearly foreseeing the ominous career and destiny of her love – "...absence, tempests, troubles, contradictions..." – implores her beloved to assuage his desires' intoxication by savoring their present state of serenity consisting as it does, in the "embellishment of the mind, the illumination of reason, the fortification of the soul, and the fruition of the heart." (52) Even this next-to perfect bliss will not last.

Why not? Because human being is not born to bliss but rather to pain, the pain of distinction; to live without it is to be dead; "a being who could do all and is not God would be a miserable creature indeed for being deprived of the pleasure of desire (693-94); what is the supreme gift of humanity, its present and its poison in one? Or how else would you describe the boundlessness of a heart that "dares to desire more when there is nothing left to be desired?" (47)

It is the blessing and the curse of our human nature to live in the certainty that as much as things may be as they should, nevertheless in our imagination, they *could* yet be better still and after having succeeded at satisfying every possible human need, we have no recourse but to avail ourselves of our imagination to postulate one need more in answer to the inexplicable desire of our hungry heart, an entirely superfluous need for being borne of plenitude and not merely of dearth – it seems that we, in our humanity, are born with a taste for the charms of drawing absolute distinctions that mark our *being without.*

And our Julie? Not even she, devoted wife and mother, beloved daughter, cherished by her friends, dwelling in their circle in possession of perfect peace, health, comfort, and security, can, in the swan song of her final letter to her lover, reflect upon her life without acknowledging the "contradiction" and the essential tension of discord (*second footnote*, p. 694) that is the self-severalty of our human being. The conclusion she draws from this careful examination of herself (696) is revealed in her avowal: "I see everywhere around me proofs of my contentment, and yet I am not content. A secret languor insinuates itself into my heart; I feel its swollen emptiness ('like a balloon filled with air' - 256);...the attachment I feel for all those I hold dear fails to suffice its occupation, there remains some superfluous strength that it does not know what to do with...I am too happy; I am stuffed with happiness (*dégoût du bien-être*)." (694)

Though surrounded by all that is dear to her in the bliss of a consummate well-being, still, incredibly, her soul is *"cloyed with joy"* (ibid.) – an expression rich in connotations for the disaffection of the heart, the dissatisfaction that arises precisely because nothing more seems to be missing, the listlessness and enervation of what has lost the enthusiasm of desire, its spark of spirit, in the perfection of possession (320). This is the crisis of love (51); it is the sadness of being satisfied, a sentiment that comprises not merely the lassitude of indifference but even the invincible repugnance and eternal disgust (un dégoût invincible, un éternel ennui - 109) that afflicts a heart become filled onto repletion and surfeit. Its sadness mourns the death of the fire of desire (96), the fulfillment of which is not joy and tranquility but rather that of extinction – its peace is that of ash. For the love that is desire needs challenges, obstacles, to endure; how could contentment be good for it when the fires of our heart are forced "to nourish themselves upon themselves? The universe never saw a passion that survived this trial." (320)

> ...se nourrir uniquement d'eux-mêmes. L'univers n'a jamais vu de passion soutenir cette épreuve.

At this crucial juncture, Julie explains, "the avid soul, finding nothing down here that will suffice her" because she has attained the fruition of every attachment, "seeks elsewhere for what may satisfy her; elevating herself thus to the source of sentiment and of being. There she throws off her aridity and her languor; there she is reborn, revives, finds new energy, draws new life; there she takes on another existence that is not bound by the passions of the body, or rather, there she is no longer in herself but wholly in the Being of immensity she contemplates. Released for an instant from her shackles, she returns to them consoled by this trial of a more sublime state that she hopes will one day be her own." (694-5)

> Ne trouvant donc rien ici-bas qui lui suffise, mon âme avide cherche ailleurs de quoi la remplir: en s'élevant à la source du sentiment et de l'être, elle y perd sa sécheresse et sa langueur; elle y renaît, elle s'y ranime, elle y trouve un nouveau ressort, elle y puise une nouvelle vie; elle y prend une autre existence qui ne tient point aux passions du corps; ou plutôt elle n'est plus en moi-même, elle est toute dans l'Etre immense qu'elle contemple et, dégagée un moment de ses entraves, elle se console d'y rentrer par cet essai d'un état plus sublime qu'elle espère être un jour le sien.

God? It would be a mistake to read this passage and its description of the transcendence of the soul as a reference to the Platonic tradition of its immortality as conceived by Plato in the philosophy of the First Epoch, much less the experience of the conversion and salvation of the soul in Jesus Christ as known in the Second Epoch of the Occidental tradition. In the third Epoch that Rousseau himself founded, *God* – just like *Freedom* and *Immortality* (387) – is an invention, a postulate, of pure reason that guides the effort of the passionate heart to distinguish itself in its love with respect to this object of its undying esteem and in this way, through the honor that the soul bestows upon these three distinguished notions, to purify, to reform, to renew itself. Kant will later conceptualize these figments of the pure imagination of human being in their *Regulative* (rather than constitutive) *Use* as (practical) *Ideas of Pure Reason* (see the "Anhang zur transcendentalen Dialektik" (Appendix to the transcendental Dialectic) in Kant's *Critique of Pure Reason*, "Von dem regulativen Gebrauch der Ideen der reinen Vernunft" (Kant, *Kritik der reinen Vernunft*, III p. 426 seq.*)

Julie does not try to "justify" (695) this "exercise" (696) as she calls it, nor does she consider her "taste" (*goût* - 695) for it to be "wise" (*sage* - ibid.), merely "sweet" (*doux –* ibid.) and thus helpful, useful "in supplementing the sentiment of happiness that is susceptible to exhaustion, in filling the void of the soul and in awakening a renewed interest in a life spent meriting felicity." (ibid.)

> qu'il supplée au sentiment du bonheur qui s'épuise, qu'il remplit le vide de l'âme, qu'il jette un nouvel intérêt sur la vie passée à le mériter.

Would Socrates or Jesus have spoken thus about the divine being of the Good, of the Father in Heaven, towards which they lifted their respective hearts in ardent devotion?

For Julie, *God* is an idea that serves towards making us better human beings. Better, how? "It is in the contemplation of this divine model that the soul purifies and elevates itself, that it learns to scorn its base inclinations and surmount its vile penchants. A heart penetrated by sublime truths resists Man's petty passions; this infinite grandeur is disgusted by their pride; the charms of meditation emancipate the heart from mundane desires; and should this immense being that occupies it turn out not to exist at all, it would still be beneficial that the heart dwell incessantly upon it in order to be more master of itself, stronger, happier, wiser." (358-59)

> C'est à la contemplation de ce divin modèle que l'âme s'épure et s'élève, qu'elle apprend à mépriser ses inclinations basses et à surmonter ses vils penchants. Un cœur pénétré de ces sublimes vérités se refuse aux petites passions des hommes; cette grandeur infinie le dégoûte de leur orgueil; le charme de la méditation l'arrache aux désirs terrestres: et quand l'Etre immense dont il s'occupe n'existerait pas, il serait encore bon qu'il s'en occupât sans cesse pour être plus maître de lui-même, plus fort, plus heureux et plus sage.

It is because the heart when it turns within itself in tune with its "original affections and dignity" (256) naturally knows what is good without being taught and, sensing what is right, discerning what is beautiful, is uplifted and inspired by the contemplation of grand objects that make our own miseries seem insignificant (696), namely what is truly good and what is truly beautiful, even if examples of them are not so easily or quickly found – it is for this reason that "to consider them is to strive to become like them while to encounter mediocrity is to experience all the more repugnance." (59)

90. The Self-Several Being of Nature

Can ideas like *honor, virtue, duty* be embodied in a person? This is not to ask whether we can "really" find such a person who is their incarnation. Rather we ask if, in the language of wisdom, these ideas themselves can be treated and considered and experienced as a lover and a friend as a father or a child, to whom we give, as the case may be, now our care, now our obedience, now our service, and now the fruits of our purest passion?

And not only people either – the scenes of nature in its purity have no less this salubrious effect on our hearts who, climbing mountains and breathing in the clarity of air and light that are their element, "elevate ourselves with them beyond the haunts of Man, leaving behind us all the baser mundane sentiments such that, to the extent that we approach the ethereal regions, the soul contracts some of their inalterable purity." (78)

> ...en s'élevant au-dessus du séjour des hommes, on y laisse tous les sentiments bas et terrestres, et qu'à mesure qu'on approche des régions éthérées, l'âme contracte quelque chose de leur inaltérable pureté.

Amazingly, we ourselves carry in our own hearts, in our own nature, the timeless effigy and eternal simulacrum of the truly beautiful (223) that we see exemplified in nature at large but also in the noble actions of heroic lives celebrated by history – Brutus, Regulus, Cato – that kindle that holy enthusiasm that is love's most sacred fire, namely the love of and enthusiasm for *honesty* and *goodness* (89, 678), for *wisdom* (102), for *beauty* (98-99), the divine *ardor* (102), the zeal and love of *virtue* (524, 623, 668, 692), love of and zeal for *truth* (369, 427, 700), love of *duty* and *justice* (465, 492), love of *fatherland* and of *liberty* (535, 251), love of *God* (590; 698) and the ardor, the love of *order* (492) and above all the zeal for (179), the love of, this *love* (627), that is human nature, i.e. our zeal (218) for the *humanity* of human being. Human nature is also nature and like these others, it is an ideal, a divine model that is a real felicity (223), as real as our own human being in which this sentiment is alive. This sentiment is common to the feeling of all self-several human being: "This divine model that each of us carries within ourselves enthralls us in spite of ourselves; as soon as passion allows us to perceive it, we want to be like it and if the most evil of men could be someone other than himself, he would wish to be a man of honor."(224)

> Ce divin modèle que chacun de nous porte avec lui nous enchante malgré que nous en ayons; sitôt que la passion nous permet de le voir, nous lui voulons ressembler; et si le plus méchant des hommes pouvait être un autre que lui-même, il voudrait être un homme de bien.

Such a man's only hope is to become other than himself, in other words to distinguish himself from himself and in the self-severalty of this relationship to become who he is not and by thus not being to become and to be who he really and truly is. It this possible? It is as if we were raised, transported beyond ourselves (223, 684) in the love, in the passion, that the sight of these distinguished models and idols of the imagination present to our admiration and emulation.

Thus, the delicious quandary of self-severalty. Our passions glean their strength from the self-severalty of the human soul, inspiring it with the most powerful passion of them all; their enduring fire is nourished by the very spirit that elevates us beyond all limits and objects and attachments – above all, beyond those that our passions themselves set before us and most tightly bind us to. The greater their strength to prevail, the greater they are prevailed upon; passion uses its force to attain the object that virtue surpasses and scorns as beneath it. For this reason passion, in attaining the object of its desire, surpasses its object and even in becoming fulfilled puts its fulfillment behind it; arriving, it departs and desire is awakened in the pleasure of what it has achieved. Apparently, "nature..."– especially human nature – takes pleasure in self-severalty, "...takes pleasure in putting itself in opposition with itself," (77) and "if love's extinction drops the soul into exhaustion, love's subjugation gives it, along with the conscience of its victory a new elevation and a more lively attraction towards all that is great and beautiful." (557)

> Si l'amour éteint jette l'âme dans l'épuisement, l'amour subjugué lui donne, avec la conscience de sa victoire, une élévation nouvelle et un attrait plus vif pour tout ce qui est grand et beau.

This is the intoxication that Julie inspires in her lover, a distinguished, i.e. a *celestial* (227), a saintly (352) ardor, that can surmount obstacles and conquer ill-fortune (222) – she is the embodiment of humanity burning with all the passion of a heart that is susceptible to the self-several love that is the destiny of our human being. What does her lover find so attractive in Julie? For all the beauty of her person, it is the beauty of her soul that inspires his most passionate regard: (32)

> Vos attraits avaient ébloui mes yeux, jamais ils n'eussent égaré mon cœur sans l'attrait plus puissant qui les anime. C'est cette union touchante d'une sensibilité si vive et d'une inaltérable douceur; c'est cette pitié si tendre à tous les maux d'autrui; c'est cet esprit juste et ce goût exquis qui tirent leur pureté de celle de l'âme; ce sont, en un mot, les charmes des sentiments, bien plus que ceux de la personne, que j'adore en vous. Je consens qu'on vous puisse imaginer plus belle encore; mais plus aimable et plus digne du cœur d'un honnête homme, non, Julie, il n'est pas possible.

> *Your graces have dazzled my eyes but they would have never bewitched my heart had not a more powerful charm animated them. It is that touching union of a so delicate sensibility coupled with an unfailing tenderness, it is that compassion so responsive to the afflictions of others; it is that spirit of such sure judgment and that exquisite taste which draw their purity from the soul's own; it is, in a word, the charms of the sentiments much more than those of the person that I adore in you. I confirm that one could imagine you more comely, but more amiable and more worthy of an honest man's heart, no, Julie, that is not possible.*

A "human being of nature" rather than "a man of Man" (554) – we first encountered this notion, and the difference that it makes, as the ideal of education in *Emile;* and here in *Julie* Rousseau reprises it by presenting now the distinguished human being of nature in *person.* Because it is "from Julie that we must learn all the goodness and the honesty that can enter the human soul and above all that divine accord of virtue, of love, and of nature that is nowhere else to be found than in her." (73)

> ...c'est de vous qu'il faut apprendre tout ce qui peut entrer de bon, d'honnête, dans une âme humaine, et surtout ce divin accord de la vertu, de l'amour et de la nature, qui ne se trouve jamais qu'en vous.

We solemnly appoint her to the office of determining our destiny, i.e. to reign over the empire of our will, to govern us as those who are no longer anything in themselves the entire being of whom consists now only in its relationship to her, remitting unreservedly to her care the guardianship of our happiness and pledging in return our unwavering commitment to the duties that she imposes. (56-57)

Speaking through her and her purity, nature teaches us the first lesson of the heart, which is that "as soon as we are willing to return within ourselves, we all sense what is right, we all discern what is beautiful..." and have no need of books or teacher to discover "principles and rules more certainly found within ourselves" (58-59) and, without, "those exquisite examples of our ideals, rare though they may be, that the imagination presents to the gaze of our meditations, elevating the soul, sparking the heart, so that in coming to know them we want to become their likeness." (59)

> L'âme s'élève, le cœur s'enflamme à la contemplation de ces divins modèles ; à force de les considérer, on cherche à leur devenir semblable.

The divine accord of virtue (C), *love* (B), *and nature* (A) – it is this idea that we might learn to worship and adore upon the altar of the heart in the person of Julie, that unique being of nature, *human* being namely, where the most ardent love and the purest virtue converge. (37) This being is a study in contradictions, like nature herself who, as we saw, revels in opposition (77), more precisely, in the measured proportion of divergence and accord such that love gives *substance* to virtue and virtue gives *form* to love and each term distinguishes and is distinguished by the other in the Tree of Duality we have previously examined where each term can be both a *Term of Immediacy* as well as a *Term of Distinction* and, when taken together, mark the two sides of the self-several entity of identity that is the issue of our study and here found to be realized in the person of Julie, more specifically in Rousseau's narrative of Julie's life.

The crux of the conflict: Her lover is chosen and esteemed by her as the guardian of her virtue and his and is, as well, the spark of love that initiates her fall from innocence. Julie is awoken to passion by her lover's tenderness and virtue and she is, as well, the final arbiter of their union destined by their fortune, the destiny of all human being, to remain unfulfilled. The drama of the narrative unfolds in accordance with the play of divergence of Love and Virtue that develops the intimate connection between what is *beautiful*, i.e. the object of love, and what is *good*, which is no less beautiful and therefore an object of love in its own right, pitting thus love against love, for both the good and the beautiful have their common origin in well-ordered nature. (59) Thus the distinguished beauty of nature and the distinguished beauty of virtue are both objects of a distinguished, a self-several love – *taste* or aesthetic judgment in the first case, *wisdom* or moral judgment in the second whence it follows that "one who is moved by the charms of virtue must be proportionately sensible to other kinds of beauty" – *sensibility* with regards to beauty corresponds to *sense* with regards to values, exquisite *vision* to delicate and refined *sentiment*.

Both virtue and beauty are therefore objects of love for a tender soul that is receptive to the impressions that strike and ignite her passions *and* no less to the voice of conscience with which duty and self-regard speak to the sentiments of our heart. In nature, they do not and cannot diverge – they are but one self-several voice. But Julie's story relates even this impossible conflict between love of virtue and the love of beauty as the conflict between love and love, between beauty and beauty, between nature and nature such that each is pierced by the cognizance of distinction with respect to the other and to follow her heart of hearts, she must break her heart and distinguish her heart from her heart. Does not her love, her heart, nature, tell her to fly to her lover's arms and to happiness? Does not, on the other hand, her love, her heart, nature, recall her to her parents' side and duty forbid her to abandon them to their despair in her free choice? Can she take pleasure in a life made sweet at the expense of others' pain and others' lives and, knowing their suffering, knowing herself to be its cause, not share it? Sensitive to love's highest hopes, can I suddenly be insensitive to the pain of not fulfilling my heart's greatest commands? In the tenderness of my heart that, in its love, is open to the sentiment of the beauty of nature how can I close my mind and my soul to its perversion, choose a life that goes against nature even while following nature's call? In a word, how could I esteem *MYSELF* while being ashamed of *myself* or, opting for honor rather than pleasure, immolate the happiness of my life like an offering on the altar of duty (311, 353, 363, 630) that has forced me to choose either to purchase my LIFE with my death or my DEATH with my life and, in this way, in one person, at the same time, to be and not to be MySelf?

Is there anybody for whom this sort of dilemma of human nature, this *double-bind*, is unfamiliar? We are, of course, all familiar with the situation of being in two minds with regards to a choice in the sense of being *damned if we do and damned if we don't*. Imagine now a being whose nature it is to live *and* die *and* die and live, again and again, in this self-several circle and to experience this alternation not as a case of indecisiveness in selection but rather as the perpetual collection and recollection of the experience of our own self-relative identity! For that is what, in the Third Epoch at least, *nature* ultimately is, namely *human* nature and consequently, those who want to read in its book (655) must read in the heart of human being. (657)

And that is why we know that there is and could be but "a single Julie on earth." (532) The charm of Julie's humanity is not that of the perfection of virtue, not sainthood. To love her for her sentiments is to love her for the sake of the genuine human heart that is her distinction and makes of "her charms and talents and tastes, her struggles, her errors, her regrets, her life, her friends and family, her pains and pleasures, and of her entire destiny a unique example." (533) Her life is a lesson to us who desire to learn about humanity; even in her faults she shows us what it is to be a human being, teaching us to avail ourselves of failure, as she did, to deploy our power and our courage. And it would seem that "heaven itself bestowed her upon the earth in order to demonstrate...the excellence of which the human soul is susceptible..." (532)

> Le ciel semble l'avoir donnée à la terre pour y
> montrer...l'excellence dont une âme humaine est susceptible...

Preacher (124, 26, 243, 377, 405, 506, 638) in her actions and not merely in her words, she lends credence to the notion we have all suspected of obtaining in our struggles and battles with ourselves namely that "cold rationality has never accomplished anything illustrious and that we never triumph over our passions unless by opposing one passion against another; when the passion for virtue arises, it thrones above all the others and holds them in balance. This is how a sage is made, who is not more sheltered from the onslaught of passions than anyone else, but who alone knows how to conquer passion with passion." (493)

> ...la froide raison n'a jamais rien fait d'illustre, et l'on ne
> triomphe des passions qu'en les opposant l'une à l'autre. Quand
> celle de la vertu vient à s'élever, elle domine seule et tient tout
> en équilibre. Voilà comment se forme le vrai sage, qui n'est pas
> plus qu'un autre à l'abri des passions, mais qui seul sait les
> vaincre par elles-mêmes.

The self-several love of humanity – thwarted, it is completed and fulfilled, it is over-flowing; "passion," sustained by and sustaining its own abundance, "draws from its own excess the force it needs to conquer itself." (102)

> ...où la passion tirait de son propre excès la force de se vaincre
> elle-même.

Thus self-regard reveals itself in the self-relativity of love; it is showing regard, love, passion for our best regards, for our most tender love, for our greatest passion, for our best Self, in a word for our *nature*, our *humanity* – what else could we call the nature of human being? – the love of which is what our original self-love has elevated itself to, namely to the adoration of our human image in all its excellence that we ourselves might aspire to merit, thereby recognizing who we most truly are in the eyes of the sublime sentiment of love the efficacy of which is that, in the lofty enthusiasm for what makes people good and beautiful (*ce noble enthousiasme de l'honnête et du beau* – 98-99), "it animates the grandeur and strength of our souls, ennobles all their sentiments, doubles their being and lifts us above ourselves" (632)

> N'anime-t-il pas les âmes grandes et fortes? N'anoblit-il pas tous leurs sentiments? Ne double-t-il pas leur être? Ne les élève-t-il pas au-dessus d'elles-mêmes.

To be lifted above ourselves (223, 431) – does this expression really make sense? How can we be simultaneously above ourselves and below ourselves? For if we are lifted above ourselves, we are at once both higher and lower than ourselves. In both cases we are distinguished in ourselves from ourselves and, inspired thus by love to be who we are not, we are both wo we are *and* who we are not – humans aspiring to being human in the best, most distinguished sense of this term. That is the love that moves us to be what we were destined to be. This love that, innocent, encourages us or, ashamed, forbids us to dare to look and regard ourselves in the I (103) is the source of those familiar struggles with ourselves (50, 53, 87, 89-90, 96, 193, 202, 251, 308, 334, 343, 495, 503, 521-2, 622, 664, 682), the experience of "sacrificing the desires of our heart to the laws our duty" (61-62; 363), "the spectacle of a sublime and pure soul triumphing over its passions and ruling (524), mastering itself (524-5, 667) where inclination and virtue (537), heart and reason (89) are in perpetual war, the one with the other and courage to do good is called upon to prevail (87, 158-9, 178, 180; 213, 221, 313, 345, 366) over evil. Being different from who we were meant to be, we abhor what we are, aspiring to what we ARE. For you want to be YOU, do you not? Hating that you are not who you are supposed to be, you devote all your efforts to being who you really and truly are. Love reminds you, unceasingly reminds us of this, thus restoring ourselves to ourselves in spite of ourselves (293, 300), which is "one of the miracles of love that it makes us find pleasure in our sufferings." (245) The more we feel with chagrin and regret and reproach that we are not who we are destined to be as human beings the greater we feel our desire, our love for the humanity we aspire to and the greater the pleasure we take in that goodness and beauty that is our home the more poignantly and painfully do we feel the distance that separates us from that destination. It is only a heart made for virtue (282, 291) and for love that is able to see itself with the horror (342) of self-loathing (346) and yet in the same breath of human nature be pleased, exalted by the approbation of self-regard.

Thus self-regard and to honor oneself in one's own eyes (664), is, in fact, self-love and to love Julie is to love the love of virtue in whose eyes and in whose life we see our own face and our own life reflected back. To love her is to love humanity and the dignity of human being and, consequently to hate whatever detracts from the nobility and grandeur of the destiny of our own nature with regards to that being. "This dignity of human being pertains to all of its stations and no one can be happy who fails to esteem himself or herself. For if the soul's true bliss lies in the contemplation of the beautiful, how could a bad person love beauty in another without hating himself." (224)

To be possessed of love for the good and the will to do it – this is *conscience*, which, as we learned in Emile, is the source of sentiments, "telling us not the truth of things but rather the rules of our duties, dictating to us not what we ought to think but rather what we ought to do, apprising us not of what it means to think properly but rather to act properly" (698) in contrast to *judgment* with which we discern and know the good. Seeing the good and desiring it, all we need is *freedom*, the principle of humanity that allows us, independent of every anterior determination, to choose to do, to put into action, what we have willed to do (683). It is for this reason that our principal honor is the one that conscience renders us (518), the approbation of our own heart (632) from which there is no escape (642) in the secret and silence of reflection, the holy night of the soul, when the cry of troubled conscience is no longer so easily stifled by the clamor of our everyday lives (200, 300) but which also provides us with a sure principle, never deceiving the soul that sincerely consults it (364) and is willing to listen to its dictates as that of duty (701), the honoring of which is our first honor (632), not the approval accorded to us by others, but rather the good testimony that our heart vouchsafes our self; one's own clear conscience with regards to what is right and just, that precious repose (717) of a heart that approves of, esteems, loves itself, secure in the certainty of its own self-knowing being that it is good in itself, "takes the place of all the praises of the universe." (224)

La conscience du juste lui tient lieu des louanges de l'univers.

For what we hold dearest and fall from in spite of ourselves is...our self, such that the imperative *"Be yourself!"* means the same as *"Be human!"* (314).

Mortification – what a perfect expression, given the reference to death inherent in shame and the humiliation that is the rude view and naked truth of our fallen state, having become despicable in our own eyes, in the eyes of our best I, the I of our humanity, pure reason's eye. How often during the day or in the course of one's life do we feel constrained to make a choice between, on the one hand, what behooves the moment and its spur, the mandate of a locality and its mores, the appurtenance of individuality and, on the other, respects the ligatures of compunction that impartiality imposes upon our own particular life, namely that of the humanity of our human being for the sake of which, adopting the panoramic standpoint that it entails, the urgings of finitude that define our Man are contravened, compelling us in the spirit of reason's greater project – encompassing as it does the universe of our entire life and that of all living being, extending to all places, "enduring for all time, admitted by all sages, recognized by all the nations, and engraved in the human heart in ineffaceable characters" (I 1021), in other words, in accordance with the perspective of detachment that opens the closed mind of Man – to consider the latter's matters in light of this our coeval eternity and then sometimes to sacrifice the immediate pleasures of Man's little life, to take upon itself that little death, for that greater good that is its greater life? In this way the course of life is marked and measured in the milestones of Man's maturity and in the actual enactment of our capacity to make sacrifices in the name of our humanity, thinking about tomorrow as well as today, surmounting boundaries of prideful self-interest, the bottlenecks of its bodily immediacy, the nose-length range of Man' scant scan – a series of accomplishments fabulously rendered in the speech practice of wisdom as *the ordeal of the immortal soul.* And, yes, in this way, we do indeed practice our own death, the one philosophers are fond of admonishing us to prepare for and to learn (1012) while living life, such that in the end we might conclude, not without relief, but also not without joy for having lived a life worth living, in the tenderness of our humanity's most human address to its own beloved heart of hearts: "My friend, I go at the propitious moment; contented with you and with myself; I go joyfully, and there is nothing cruel in this departure. After so many sacrifices, I count for little the one that is left for me to make – it is merely to die one more time." (741)

> Mon ami, je pars au moment favorable; contente de vous et moi;
> je pars avec joye, et ce départ n'a rien de cruel. Après tant de

sacrifices je compte pour peu celui qui me reste à faire; ce n'est
que mourir une fois de plus.

91. The Dialogue with Myself

After a long life or even just at the end of the day, we look back, in this
distinguishing twilight at the brink of the night of our soul, upon past deeds
and accomplishments and are moved to reflect upon them, justifying
ourselves to ourselves as well as we as can, confessing to ourselves and to
those who, living images of our imagination, hear us and who are, no less
than we are, our best SELF, by taking and giving a sincere and truthful
account of the good and the bad of what we have done, neither hiding what
we are ashamed of, nor passing over in silence our successes, but rather
giving an honest and upright appraisal of our self to our SELF, of myself to
ME as rendered in *Figure 60.*

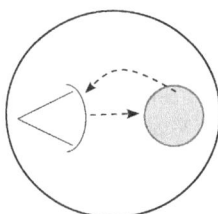

Figure 60: The Account of myself to ME

Reflecting upon the course of my life, appearing thus before the judgment
seat of humanity, My conscience censors and exalts me, exalts me even in
the shame of my condemnation. For there is no judge beyond Myself who,
speaking in my own heart, pronounces sentence and the fault I find in
myself is, at the same time a confirmation of the goodness that is My
distinguished and uncorrupted nature in comparison with which I raise
myself to the extent that I fall and fall short of myself to the extent that I am
exalted beyond myself, both subject to the law of my heart and my own
lawmaker who I am and is no less me than I AM, should I own up in
complete sincerity to who I am and for whom there is no *judgment day*
beyond that which is visited upon me by that good night while thus in
dialogue with Myself, that distinguished heart of humanity beating in our
bosom like a friend and speaking with the voice of a lover long before and
long after it has become our accuser.

In the person of a unique, a singular individual, me alone (I 5), persecuted in ignominy by the public opinions and prejudices of Man, our human being now takes heart and, in spite of the malice and the pusillanimous passions of the public – the outrages of its ardent missionaries and imperious dogmatists (32) with which it seals our being's fate, namely to be duped and disappointed in its naïve trust of the world's good intentions (1009), when actually society's devices are geared towards our being's destruction – nevertheless offers to render Man the ultimate service, one that has never before been undertaken nor will ever again be achieved by another (5), "having carried good faith, veracity, and frankness as far, further even...than any other has ever done" (1035), namely in memoirs of myself such as I am in painting a portrait that reveals the secret history of my soul (278), to show to the public world of my fellow man a human being in all the veracity of nature and in this way to hold up a true mirror, so to speak, of human being so that Man's people will learn the art and discipline of regard, learn, in this reflection, to recognize themselves and in themselves their high birthright as human beings such that each of us in turn might take up the cause of humanity and the principles that this unique idea founds, i.e. "fundamental principles adopted by my reason, confirmed by my heart, and which all carry the seal of inner assent in the silence of the passions..." a doctrine that reflects " the congruity I perceive between my immortal nature, the constitution of the world, and the physical order I see reigning in it." (1120)

This tableau of the estranged and solitary heart's fate, the defamation and calumny it has suffered in Man's world, is brought to life in the drama of a dialogue in which I deliberate with and judge myself in light of public opinion that condemns me. Perhaps, in affirming the ideal world of My humanity as well as in my own condemnation of the mores and conduct of the city, the nation, the Europe of Man and the new era of its generation (662) for the vanity of its letters, its arts and sciences, the greed of its kings, its nobility, and its wealthy (917-926), I have been as unjust as the multitudes' iniquitous condemnation of me engendered by my criticism of Man's civilization; for this reason, I propose now, putting aside all heat of partiality, a sober discussion with me, myself, and I, in other words, by engaging the perspectives of the maligned author, the outraged public, and the well-meaning person of humanity, to declare "from which eye, if I were an other, I would see a human being such as I am," and to offer thus "a simple elucidation of what I would have deduced from a constitution comparable to my own, when studied with care, in a different human being." (665) For "in order not to battle figments of my imagination, in order not to offend an entire generation, it is necessary to suppose that there are

reasons that support the views that everybody approves of and follows,"
even though they would seem "to take pleasure in extinguishing all the
natural lights of the mind, do violence to all the laws of justice, all the rules
of good sense, but having neither purpose, nor profit, nor pretext for it..."
(662).

The end of this debate reprises the consolation of a good soul's solitude, a
resolution that is no longer bitter but rather liberated from the torments of
self-enamored pride, of the love deemed owed to one but, rather,
recognizes the essential goodness of its own nature and returning thus to
nature suffices and abides in the Self-love that is the destiny of humanity;
this insight extinguishes our pride and vanity by degrees, step by step, and
so it is during the solitary walk of life's hope after anguish's death that the
walker, resting at the edge of a beautiful river or of a brook chuckling over
pebbles, realizes in freedom's own reverie the bliss of just self-knowing
being, the immensity of our humanity. "What do we enjoy in such a
situation? Nothing external to ourselves, nothing if not ourselves and our
own existence. As long as this state lasts, we are sufficient unto ourselves,
like God. The sentiment of existence, stripped of any other emotion, is, in
itself, a precious sentiment of contentment and of peace which alone would
suffice to make this existence dear and sweet to anyone able to spurn all the
sensual and earthly impressions which incessantly come to distract us from
it and to trouble its sweetness here-below." (1047)

> De quoi jouit-on dans une pareille situation? De rien d'extérieur
> à soi, de rien sinon de soi-même et de sa propre existence, tant
> qui cet état dure on se suffit à soi-même comme Dieu. Le
> sentiment de l'existence dépouillé de toute autre affection est
> par lui-même un sentiment précieux de contentement et de paix
> qui suffiroit seul pour rendre cette existence chère et douce à qui
> sauroit écarter de soi toutes les impressions sensuelles et
> terrestres qui viennent sans cesse nous en distraire et en
> troubler ici-bas la douceur.

This state of being, free from passion but neither sunk in the lethargy of
absolute rest nor else affected by too much agitation from the surroundings
"which could destroy the charm of the reverie and tear us away from within
ourselves, bringing us instantly back under the yoke of fortune and men,"
such a moment, poised in the movement of a gentle stirring "when light and
sweet ideas only skim the surface of the soul...without disturbing its
depths...," allowing us "to remember our own self while forgetting all our
troubles," can best be achieved when we are removed from the
communications and correspondences of Man's community and sojourn

on "a fertile and solitary island naturally closed off and separated from the rest of the world." (1047-48) Here a heart born "to extend over the whole universe is no longer constricted and repressed" (1056) but permitted "to be what nature willed." (1002).

On this island, in this harmonious retreat, that is lush and teeming with the imagination of nature, My walks are, in fact, meditations and trains of thought thinking about thought, a meditation that progresses freely from one idea, "...one flower, to the next and examines each blossom with interest and curiosity...comparing their diverse characters, taking note of their similarities and differences...," while diligently and patiently seeking "...their general laws as well as the reason for and the end of their diverse structures..." finally, in the logotectonic anthology that emerges, "I surrender myself to the charm of acknowledging admiration for the hand which let me enjoy all of that." (1069) This hand and the eye that guides it are pure reason's, compiling a natural history of thought's blossoms and apparitions that are the present of freedom, and collecting them into a herbarium of beauty – the chirping of birds, the cry of eagles, the rushing of torrents, landscapes, forests, lakes, groves, masses of rocks and their mosses, the mountains, each stalk of hay of the meadows, the limpid waters, the woods of solitude and of peace in which I remember Myself and My true love, while forgetting myself, and Men's "persecutions, their hatred, scorn, insults, and all the evils with which they have repaid My tender and sincere attachment to them." (1073)

An impossible task? By forgetting myself, I come to MYSELF, come into my own; and by coming thus to MYSELF, I forget myself and the multitudinous world of Man's Men? Turning from the self-centered orientations, interests, and opinions of my heteronomous self-enamor to My absolute Self-love that is the autonomous self-relativity of pure reason, the *infinity* of human being, we learn to recognize the law of nature and the principle of its beauty and to experience the sentiment of well-being that brightens and assuages restless souls in their contemplation of that further, happier shore, the blessed isle of our beloved, there, where she lives, across the lake from the anguish that is the first blood of difference drawn; this truth resting upon the lips of pure desire, sustained by and sustaining the contemplation of human nature's beauty, is the delight of the heart that just breaks the heart.

II. Schiller

92. "Edel sei der Mensch…" (Noble be our human being…)

The difference between THE WAY IT IS and THE WAY IT SHOULD BE, the mark that the mind's penetrating eye makes upon the glabrous orb of antecedent innocence, prior to critical reflection, is, quite simply, the seizing upon the inevitable fact of human limitations, call it our mortality, and the proud revolt that it entails; we see now, in this freshly-cut revulsion, the divergence and the distance separating thoughts from things, the imposition of the mind's exacting demands upon the matters at hand and the prospective fulfillment when demands are met, the ideal made real; we sigh: "How straitened is the human race! How vast the gap yawning between claims and their compensation! O envy man his benign slumber; don't waken him! He was so blissful till he began to question whither he must go and whence he came. Reason is a torch in a dungeon; the prisoner knew nothing of the light, but then a dream of freedom shone above him like lightning in the night leaving him in gloom all the gloomier." (Schiller, *NA* XX.112.25-32).

> …wie beschränkt ist der Mensch! Wie groß der Abstand zwischen seinen Ansprüchen und ihrer Erfüllung! - O beneide ihm doch den wohltätigen Schlaf. Wecke ihn nicht. Er war so glücklich, bis er anfing zu fragen, wohin er gehen müsse, und woher er gekommen sei. Die Vernunft ist eine Fackel in einem Kerker. Der Gefangene wußte nichts von dem Lichte, aber ein Traum der Freiheit schien über ihm wie ein Blitz in der Nacht, der sie finstrer zurückläßt.

What is this trait of the mind, this philosophy? Shall we call it our appalling desire to know and see, in the crisis of reflection, our true destiny and our unique distinction and that wisdom's way should lead us through the horrifying abysm of doubt – however devoutly we may wish at times that the downy sweep of sleep that was our easy piece of mind return, that the sandman's desert, the pacifying ocean, and all the world's lush wilderness might reclaim the Atlantic isles and the avenues of our humanity?

What does heart lost cry in despair? Hail oblivion! Hail nescience and easy innocence, care-free youth died too soon! O had we not come to knowledge! Having been vouchsafed no stairway to Heaven by the doubt of distinction, we are nevertheless bereft of our earth! Our living hut blown down, a dead palace founded in its stead, and so: Forever farewell the tranquil mind!

Farewell content! "What self-several beings we are! A tranquillized life is not in the nature of our destiny, a secret voice inexorably whispers and calls us towards unknown and dark scenes. " (XXII 79.15-16).

> ...was sind wir für zweideutige Geschöpfe! Ruhe ist nicht die Bestimmung unserer Natur, unaufhaltsam lispelt und ruft eine geheime Stimme nach unbekannten dunklen Szenen.

For as Rousseau has shown us "repose and liberty are incompatible – we must choose." (Rousseau, *OC* III 955).

> Le repos et la liberté sont incompatibles; il faut opter.

No wonder that in such moments of critical reflection, given the evidence of perfection that nature presents us with and the ensuing vivid dissatisfaction with our hitherto use of our freedom, "we could hold the prerogative of reason for a curse, a misfortune, neglecting, in that dissatisfaction with all that we are, to do justice to our potential and all we were meant to be." (Schiller, *NA*, XXII 427.23-27)

> Wir [halten] das Prärogativ unserer Vernunft für Fluch und für ein Übel und über dem lebhaften Unvollkommenheit unseres wirklichen Leistens die Gerechtigkeit gegen unsre Anlage und Bestimmung aus den Augen setzten.

Our own freedom, this distinction of human being, in a flight of high, uplifting spirits, has lifted us out of our natural setting, even as we lift ourselves beyond ourselves and then, exiled here in a foreign country where the oppressive burdens and untoward forces of human enterprise and civilization that harry us incessantly have been left behind, we hear with regret and nostalgia the touching voice of our first mother in whose lap we flower children had previously slept in blessed perfection and from which mini-Man, our hommelette, then, had a great fall. For this is the distinction of human being that in our nature to strive for perfection we are upraised and exalted above and beyond all nature – our nature is to be and not to be what we naturally are. How could such a being as human being be? Only with great difficulty.

You heavenly, you infernal human nature, the moral genus and genius of humanity against which every particular person must measure their individuality, you have been called *virtue, conscience, duty,* called the pure heart of a good soul, our inviolate dignity and our divine destiny! Is there anything in or about us that can so exalt us? That is the question regarding our human being's much fabled merit. And the answer to this question can only be the *freedom* of humanity. Human freedom then is nothing abstruse or occult, is not and could not be esoteric and its mystery is as open as that of all things great and small that experience can offer wonder. Freedom is apparent, visible all around us, if not in our civilization and its cities of necessities then at least in nature and in the state of beauty that is its autonomous empire.

Go for a walk through the countryside. Is nature not beautiful? Taken as a whole is not the universe, from a lowly ant's assiduity to the star strewn sky's pomp and pageantry in all its twinkling remoteness, a thing of great beauty and perfection, so that to say *natural* is to say *beautiful*, to say *good*? Hmm, you say the nature that we see spreading out before us on earth is characterized by peace and simplicity and innocence. But disease, cancer, decay, earthquakes and hurricanes are natural, are they not? Where is the beauty in these? As we have learned from Rousseau, when we say *nature*, we mean, in fact, *human* nature and *human* being and all the natural phenomena, the stars and the ants, death and disease, the natural destruction of storm and wind are taken to serve our purpose of comprehending human destiny in its entirety. Divorced from humanity and its imagination, "nature" is, of course, neither friendly nor hostile, as we modern folk all must, with Robert Frost, asseverate, who are acquainted with the night into which

> At an unearthly height
> A luminary clock against the sky
> Proclaimed the time was neither wrong nor right.[59]

As Stanley Kubrick once noted, it is the neutrality and indifference of the universe that is frightening,[60] a nihilistic universe in which the distinction that is human being, the humanity of a mission, an *"Es muss sein!"* has been subtracted, the humming continuum of unmarked space that is merest being in all its unbearable lightness, that is the perfect darkness antedating and anticipating the "weighty resolution of the mind made up" which begins on a *grave* note of critical skepticism, doubting THE WAY IT IS with respect to THE WAY IT SHOULD BE and ending upon the *allegro* of correspondence when THE WAY IT SHOULD BE is confirmed as being most

---

[59] Robert Frost, Collected Poems, Prose, and Plays, p. 234.

[60] "The most terrifying fact about the universe is not that it is hostile but that it is indifferent." *Stanley Kubrick: Interviews (Conversations with Filmmakers)*, p.73.

truly THE WAY IT IS. (cf. in *Figure 61*, the heading of the fourth movement of Beethoven's String Quartet No. 16 in F major, op. 135):

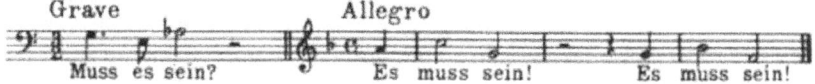

Der schwer gefasste Entschluss.

Figure 61: The Weighty Resolution of the Mind Made Up

Nature then, in the third epoch of our cultural tradition, is essentially human, *humanity* being thus an idea of pure reason seen in terms of its productivity and therefore as an invention of the distinguished imagination that is poetic thought, the Builder's; speaking figuratively to us about human being, nature, in hers landscapes and countrysides, in the topography of place, offers us her designations – "...the inner movements of the mind are accompanied and made accessible to our senses by outward analogies. Given the fact that these inner movements (as human nature) follow with strict necessity the laws of thought, so is this necessity and determination transferred to the outward movements through which they are then expressed. In this way we can understand how it is possible that, through these symbolic acts, simple natural phenomena of sound and light can participate in the in the aesthetic dignity of human nature."

> ...die inneren Bewegungen des Gemüts durch analogische äußere zu begleiten und zu versinnlichen. Da nun jene innren Bewegungen (als menschliche Natur) nach strengen Gesetzen der Notwendigkeit vor sich gehen, so geht diese Notwendigkeit und Bestimmtheit auch auf die äußeren Bewegungen, wodurch sie ausgedrückt werden, über; und auf diese Art wird es begreiflich, wie vermittelst jenes symbolischen Akts die gemeinen Naturphänomene des Schalles und des Lichts von der ästhetischen Würde der Menschennatur partizipieren können. (Schiller, Über Matthissons Gedichte, [NA] XXII 272.19-25).

In this sense, thought, the Builder, whether dramatist or lyricist, composer or painter, to the extent that they "study the analogy that exists between the movements of the soul and certain external appearances,...is a veritable painter of the soul." (28-31)

Harmony, dissonance in tone or light, in music, or in a landscape painting has become a natural symbol and narrative of the proportion between the inner discord and the harmony of the mind, the objective correlative of our own experience with the adventure, the drama, the poetry that is thought's life, the life and times of that unique entity of identity we have come to recognize as the self-knowing being of thought thinking about thought or, in practical terms, the accord that rings true when the IS and the OUGHT of thought correspond in virtuous action and false when they conflict in our dastardly deeds.

Only when nature has been driven out of humanity do we need to depart from cultivated civilization to find morality and, in despair, are forced to turn to the beauty of nature as a symbol of human dwelling that we can but strive for as an ideal of the brighter future or else lament the loss of as our former childhood, our Lost Paradise, our age of innocence, the golden age of our lives long gone and only accessible now to our poetic inspiration as a monumental remembrance or as the foresight of our most ardent purpose. For then this ideal is all we have to guide us in our education towards becoming human again. How can nature become our teacher? Schiller proposes in his so-called philosophical writings that we take upon ourselves an aesthetic education in which the fine arts and especially theater guide our efforts at building ourselves according to the models that beauty places before us as objects inspiring our love and our delight wherein we learn, improbably, that and how, in beauty, "the desires of our heart and the laws of our duties" (Rousseau, *OC* II 363) coincide and find confirmed what all lovers of wisdom know, namely that truly free is alone the soul in harmony.

C. The Aesthetic Education

93. Divisive Rationality

> "I am an observer and not a moralist. I am a botanist who describes the plant. It is the physician's task to regulate its usage." (Rousseau, *OC.* I 1120)

So Rousseau. The narratives he wrote with a view to casting fruitful, fitful truths in transparent and pleasing forms (1029), are works of the distinguished imagination of the Third Epoch of pure reason. His tableaux and portraits of the soul (1122), encouraging thus, on the part of readers, their theoretical and contemplative involvement with his unique vision and character, his writings are an invitation to study and deliberate upon the suitability of civilization and the passions and prejudices on which it is based to preserve the sanctity of the human heart and human nature the pure sentiments of which are the one and only present of freedom.

The physician Schiller's enterprise, by contrast, is revealed and accomplished to the extent that it inspires his audience, who are not readers but rather spectators, not merely to study the personality of our humanity and its travesties in the particular person of human being but also, through the presence that the arts, above all theatre, give to freedom, to actively participate in the sublime drama of this our human distinction and to experience in ourselves the discipline of virtue that the calling of our humanity requires of us and, finally, to learn how these representations of what is grand and what is lovely, like twin physicians of the soul and medicinal herbs of truth, promote the welfare and ennoble the character of our human being.[61] After Rousseau's examination of human nature, its intrinsic development, and his vision of its fruition in a narrative depicting an exemplary life devoted to humanity, we now, with Schiller, undertake to acquire the art of cultivation of the natural humanity of human being that has been hitherto perverted by a culture which has ruthlessly set the human heart against itself, pitting the diverse strengths of our nature against each other in a permanent conflict of interest. To be sure, in nurturing such strife among the dispositions that, in their natural state, form the harmonious constitution of the human soul, this modern art of separation, this isolation and perfection of the several forces of our being through their competition and rivalry, has allowed civilization to greatly develop and extend their individual depth and breadth; but in thus establishing and securing their particular reigns and regions by hardening and toughening them through their contest each against the other, we have compromised their integrity, violated the original spirit of their totality and unity, destroyed the comity of our principal faculties, *perceptive – performative – generative*, namely those of *theoretical science*, those of the *actual practice of morality* and those entrusted with and enjoying the *accomplishments of artistic imagination* and the community of their state upon which the flourishing of our own human being as a whole is based.

Ultimately, this task, consisting as it does in fostering and furthering our humanity, would seem to be eminently practical in scope, an essentially political endeavor, concerning not only our specific natural rights and

---

[61] cf. Boeder's treatment of Schiller in *Die conceptuale Vernunft in der Letzten Epoche der Metaphysik* in "Abhandlungen der Brauschweigischen Wissenschafts Gesellschaft" XLIII p. 352-354.

duties in a society as a whole but, in particular, the religion, i.e. the morality and the mentality of the individual who, in these proceedings conducted before "the judgment seat of pure reason," (Schiller, *NA*, XX.312.7) is no less the witness than the advocate, in one both defendant and indictor and, to the extent that this individual succeeds at placing itself "at the center of the whole and committing the substance of its own particular human being to the form of humankind," ultimately attains the distinction not only of the office of the judge but even that of the legislator of the state of humanity. (312.8-16)

Schiller recognizes, to be sure, that the institution of "political and civic freedom will always and forever remain the most holy of all goods, the worthiest of goals for earnest endeavor, and the great center of all culture..." but reminds us of what the essential requirement is in the founding of a republic based on freedom, in particular that "...we will only succeed at erecting this glorious edifice if it is built upon the solid foundations of a noble character; we have to begin by creating citizens worthy of a constitution before they can create a constitution worthy of themselves."

> Politische und bürgerliche Freiheit bleibt immer und ewig das heiligste aller Güter, das würdigste Ziel aller Anstrengungen, und das große Centrum aller Kultur – aber man wird diesen herrlichen Bau nur auf dem festen Grund eines veredelten Charakters aufführen, man wird damit anfangen müssen, für die Verfassung Bürger zu erschaffen, ehe man den Bürgern eine Verfassung geben kann. (Schiller, "Brief an den Herzog Friedrich Christian von Augustenburg. Jena, den 13 Juli 1793" [*NA*] XXVI.265.7-13)

And here, with the individual, is where the aesthetic education of human being must begin its soul-building work that logically precedes that of the law-maker. How can Man's character be elevated? Man? In the meantime we have become amply familiar with its mentality and its maxims of extremes, opinions proud and cold, wielding fists of fury, the flagellating barbarism of tyranny, the froth and frenzy of anarchy, cruel in strength, slavish in weakness, ascetic and indulgent, fatigued from bootless drudgery, limp from spent excesses, prone to a tomato's vegetative softness, to a crowd's crude lawlessness, exhibiting all the inclemency and caprice of a storm's fretful elements, the foresight of a machine's routine, the insight of a one-celled organism's instinct – thus, physically, an eminently bodily being, debased either in its licentiousness or its languor, but mentally as well, even more so perhaps, in evidence in the guise of our professional wise Men, the gasconading *coryphaei* and the self-effacing *Brotgelehrte* (academics – XVII 360.14; 362.24; 363.7) – aha, this must be Joyce's "grave Brofèsor" – and other high to low caliber amateurs, sages, pundits, savants, including the usual assortment of cracked eggheads and smart cookies, all driven by their selfish psyche's *this*, *that*, and the *other*, all giving twisted testament to the refined degeneracy of our post/modern animus and its logogriphic letters – as familiar to Schiller then as to us today:

> Der sinnliche Mensch kann nicht tiefer als zum Thier herabstürzen; fällt aber der aufgeklärte, so fällt er bis zum Teuflischen herab, und treibt ein ruchloses Spiel mit dem Heiligsten der Menschheit. (263.27-29)

> *Man, when body-bound, cannot drop lower than the animal; if however the enlightened falls, he tumbles into the diabolic and vilely palters with humanity's holiest.*

Therefore, it is necessary that now "art and aesthetic judgment lay their shaping hands on Man and demonstrate the recuperative influence they have. The art of beauty and the art of the sublime revive, exercise, and refine sensibility," in that "they elevate the mind from coarse material enjoyments to delight in unadulterated forms and even in submission to pleasures to study autonomous engagement. True refinement of feeling encourages Man's participation in the higher nature, the deity of humanity, in pure reason, and in the freedom of human being." (266.14-21)

> *...die Kunst und die Geschmack ihre bildende Hand an den Menschen legen, und ihren veredelnden Einfluß beweisen. Die Künste des Schönen und Erhabenen beleben, üben und verfeinern das Empfindungsvermögen, sie erheben den Geist von den groben Vergnügungen des Stoffes zum reinen Wohlgefallen an bloßen Formen, und gewöhnen ihn, auch in seine Genüsse Selbstthätigkeit zu mischen. Die wahre Verfeinerung der Gefühle besteht aber jederzeit darin, daß der höhern Natur des Menschen und dem göttlichen Theil seines Wesens, seiner Vernunft und seiner Freiheit, ein Antheil daran verschafft wird.*

Schiller proposes against this *exclusionary* (ausschließend – 293.37; 326.30; 353.13; 356.13, 25, 28, 33; 365.3; 367.33; 378.5; 379.18; 397.4; 410.33, 38; 411.14, 18, 493.28; XXI 87), *one-sided* (einseitig – 107.9; 316.28; 327.4; 364.5; 365.7,9; 378.4; 411.19; 439.8; 463.31,37; 482.25; 489.11, 15) tendency of our mundane culture and the mentality of *extremism* (Extrem – 107.3; 325.23; 459.23; 491.7), i.e. *dismemberment* (*Zerstückelung* – 326.10), *mutilation* (Verstümmlung – 322.4-5; 328.6), *isolation* (326.29), *self-interest* (Eigennutz – 121.34, 150.34; 151.16-17, 28.29), even *selfishness* (Egoismus –

120.4; 121.35-36, 320.19; 350.34-35 or Selbsücht – 330.21; 411.35) it betrays,
a train and a training of thought he calls *aesthetic culture* (ästhetisch Kultur
– 388.7) or the reformative art of beauty (schöne Kultur – 336.31) as the most
efficacious cure and countermeasure to regain that former unity and shared
purpose of mind that is and must be the destiny of our humanity.

> *Die mannigfaltigen Anlagen im Menschen zu entwickeln, war*
> *kein anderes Mittel, als sie einander   entgegenzusetzen. Dieser*
> *Antagonismus der Kräfte ist das große Instrument der Kultur,*
> *aber auch nur das Instrument; denn solange derselbe dauert, ist*
> *man erst auf dem Wege zu dieser. (326.24-33)*

> To develop the manifold capacities of Man, there was no other
> recourse than to set them in mutual opposition. This
> antagonism of our strengths is the supreme instrument of
> culture, but it remains merely a tool and a means to that end.

The essential split, the tear of strife, the wound (322.35) with which
mundane culture severed the union of our humanity (323.1-3) is that
between our *moral* and our *physical nature* which comprises thus,
implausibly, both natures in one nature, in one self-several human being.
(344.4-5) How is such a self-contradictory, and in this sense, utterly
unhinged thing as human being, forever divided from itself, disintegrated,
shattered, broken in itself, opposed to itself, even possible? Not so easily, as
Schiller shows us, where both of these two sides of the human coin tend to
trespass upon and usurp the other's rightful sphere in disregard of the limit
in which the determination of humanity has marked their respective
distinction. Unable to live together nor die alone, these two human beings
of human being, in the congress that is the mere collision of their two
parties, pursue unstable coalitions of perversion and thus cause their
mutual and perpetual depravation in excesses and extremes. Too much or
too little of one or the other – this is how the proportion in the equilibrium
(360.26-29) of their relationship is upset in their departure from nature, the
proper determination of which is precisely the destiny of *human* nature.
"Man paints Man's portrait in his actions and what shapes do they assume
in nowadays' drama! Here brutality and there enervation: the two supreme
marks of human degeneration united in our time." (319.21-24; 336.28)

> In seinen Taten malt sich der Mensch, und welche Gestalt ist es,
> die sich in dem Drama der jetzigen Zeit abbildet! Hier
> Verwilderung, dort Erschlaffung: die zwei Äußersten des
> menschlichen Verfalls, und beide in einem Zeitraum vereinigt!

For Man is *wild* when the unbridled nature of his passions reigns over his principles in contempt...and *barbarian* when the rigorous nature of his principles annihilates all his sentiments of human kindness with cold-hearted mockery. (318.17-22) This is the brutal state of excess and languor in which our forces attempt to assimilate each other's powers to themselves, each presuming to arrogate the other's domain, each surrendering to the other's aggression; but how can their despotic *extravagance* in the former case be checked without succumbing to the converse depravity, namely that of their slavish *indulgence*, in the latter, that promiscuously acquiesces in the face of an incontinent necessity, annihilating its own distinction in the insipid appeasement of homogeneity? We find thus our humanity threatened by a double perversion of its nature, "either in a state of tension or one of laxity depending on whether it is the one-sided compulsion of one or the other of our natural forces that disrupts the harmony of our being or else the numb unanimity of our abandonment in submission to a state of coercion that counts on the uniform enfeeblement of our physical and spiritual forces. Both extremes are mitigated...in an aesthetic education which reinstitues in Man's extremity the harmony of humanity, in Man's lethargy the energy of distinction, and in this way, in accordance with their nature, returns the limited state to the absolute one and makes of our self-several human being an entity of integral completion."

> ...entweder in einem Zustande der Anspannung oder in einem Zustande der Abspannung finden werden, je nachdem entweder die einseitige Tätigkeit einzelner Kräfte die Harmonie seines Wesens stört oder die Einheit seiner Natur sich auf die gleichförmige Erschlaffung seiner sinnlichen und geistigen Kräfte gründet. Beide entgegengesetzte Schranken werden...durch die Schönheit gehoben, die in dem angespannten Menschen die Harmonie, in dem abgespannten die Energie wiederherstellt und auf diese Art, ihrer Natur gemäß, den eingeschränkten Zustand auf einen absoluten zurückführt und den Menschen zu einem in sich selbst vollendeten Ganzen macht.

Can the culture of beauty heal the wound (322.35) that our culture of need has cut? "Can she fetter nature's fury while at the same time free nature from tyranny? Can she simultaneously harness and disencumber" (336.33-35)

Kann sie in dem Wilden die Natur in Fesseln legen und in dem
Barbaren dieselbe in Freiheit setzen? Kann sie zugleich
anspannen und auflösen?

The remedial influence of the fine arts and poetic genius is to affect our
emancipation, i.e. to prescind our human being from the natural empire of
physical forces. But also to liberate broken hearts from the gilt
perniciousness of civilization, facilitate our emersion from Man's
denatured colony of supremacy and the monadic mania of its monocular
mind and to establish a place for us that is founded "not on changeable
forms of a fortuitous and often decadent modernity but rather on what is
necessary and eternal with regards to human nature, namely on the native
laws of nature's distinguished spirit. Out of this divine portion of our nature,
out of the eternally pure aether of the ideal of humanity, flows the pure
spring of beauty untroubled by the spirit of the times that swashes and
gurgles along far below in a flush of murky swirls." (267.1-8)

> ...nicht in den wandelbaren Formen eines zufälligen und oft
> ganz entarteten Zeitgeschmacks, sondern in dem
> Nothwendigen und Ewigen der menschlichen Natur, in den
> Urgesetzen des Geistes, gegründet. Aus dem göttlichen Theil
> unsers Wesens, aus dem ewig reinen Aether idealischer
> Menschheit strömt der lautere Quell der Schönheit herab,
> unangesteckt von dem Geist des Zeitalters, der tief unter ihm in
> trüben Strudeln dahinwallt.

For this reason an aesthetic education does not merely liberate us from
the fetters of our material, physical nature but also from the snares of our
immaterial, ectoplasmic nature, not only from the beasts in Man's brutish
zoo but also from the wraiths that haunt Man's rational stronghold, which
together comprise the *State of Need* into which we, as living beings, were
born and bred by civilization.

It provides us with a path of transition that leads from passive receptivity
of the senses to the kingdom of freedom, where thought's deeds and the
will's endeavors are born (383), where ideas have their dwellings and the
intellect of pure reason contemplates the totality of their truth. But though
beauty opens this vista of critical and moral reflection upon ourselves and
upon the world and its forces to which we, in our purely physical being,
would have otherwise remained indivisibly fused, we cannot hope to and,
moreover, would not, in fact, even wish to attain this absolute standpoint,
the coign of vantage, that is freedom's sweet home where pure spirits roam
but where the finitude, transience, and contingency of our phenomenal

Man will find little by way of subsistence to support a toehold of earthly existence.

Naturally, the destiny and perfection of our humanity resides in the harmonious and concurrent energy of our physical and moral powers (363.33-36) that is threatened by the double jeopardy of extremism that perverts both our physical nature and moral nature, i.e. the twofold danger of *antagonism* – when either one of our two natures dominate the other, and *laxity* – when either nature sinks into the dissipation and decadence of its forces. And so it is the boon of beauty to be able to soothe the temper of our monomaniacal mind, on the one hand, and, on the other, to invigorate the spleen of its drooping lassitude – the first boon, counteracting our vehemence is that of *soothing* beauty, the second, counteracting our enervation, that of *exhilarating* beauty. "The exclusive reign of one of these foundational forces of human being is for Man always a state of constraint and violence; freedom lies indeed only in the collaboration of our two natures... In order to fulfill her two-fold task, soothing beauty will show herself in two different figures. In the calmness of her form, she will pacify life's wilding and pave the way from senses to thoughts; she will, secondly, as vivid depiction, furnish formal abstraction with palpable force, return conception to intuition, and lead the law back to sentiment. The first service she renders to natural Man, the second to artificial Man..." (365.3-18)

> Jede ausschließende Herrschaft eines seiner beiden Grundtriebe ist für ihn ein Zustand des Zwanges und der Gewalt; und Freiheit liegt nur in der Zusammenwirkung seiner beiden Naturen. Die schmelzende Schönheit, um dieser doppelten Aufgabe ein Genüge zu tun, wird sich also unter zwei verschiednen Gestalten zeigen. Sie wird erstlich als ruhige Form das wilde Leben besänftigen und von Empfindungen zu Gedanken den Übergang bahnen; sie wird zweitens als lebendes Bild die abgezogene Form mit sinnlicher Kraft ausrüsten, den Begriff zur Anschauung und das Gesetz zum Gefühl zurückführen. Den ersten Dienst leistet sie dem Naturmenschen, den zweiten dem künstlichen Menschen.

And to both she offers the vision of a dwelling to which humanity can aspire that is free from the coercion of every necessity in which might is right and compulsion wields the law of intimidation to rage against remiss dilapidation. Neither monarchy nor ochlocracy (281.38-282.2), unwilling to suffer either the rigorist's astringency or the latitudinarian's laxity (283.16-18), freedom, that is not confused or deranged, names a state of deliberate equilibrium in which our faculties of mind form a community of mutually accorded regard for each other's freedom, each to each the other's ground and end in the reciprocity of which the *State of Beauty*, the one and only homeland worthy of human being's inhabitancy, founded upon joy, which is the one true office of art, joy – the greatest of which is "the freedom of the mind in the vivacious play of all its forces." (X 8.11-12)

94. The ΛΟΓΟΣ of Theater

Schiller examines the potential of theater in particular among the various art forms and the fictions of a momentary freedom in which they cradle us as pre-eminently suited to the task of actually freeing human being from the constrictions of the world as we find it spread out before our senses and "weighing so oppressively down upon us with the blind force of all that matters…" at the moment and by "…awakening, exercising, and building…" the inner resources of our humanity, "…to set these constraints at an objective distance and thus to transform them into a work of spirit in which the ideal governs the real." (X 8-9. 33-38)

But what is theater? How is it different from literary narratives or from poetry? Theater is unique in its ability to give vivid life and form, actual presence upon a stage, to the ideals that would otherwise remain words and wispy abstractions of dead letters and the cold loquacity of simply story-telling (93.3) and succeeds, as do neither of the other two genres, in being able to engage our senses in the enterprises of the spirit by which we, stepping back from our everyday world and entering the distinguished empire of the imagination, undertake to mind the gap of judgment that the representation of life in the living scenes of remote times and people so engrossing to our attention and so apt at sparking the ardor of our passions. Consider in *Figure 62* how the form and the elements of theater can be thought of as offering an atheistic elaboration of our experience of freedom.

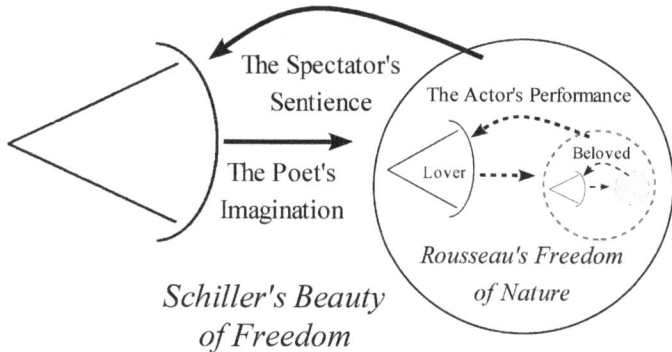

Figure 62: The Dramatic Form of Aesthetic Judgment

It is in the performances of the fine arts that we attain the relationship of distinction that enables us to step back from what they allude to, i.e. the universe of their meanings that we might call *world* or *reality* beyond the museum and the stage, beyond their theater; we go to see not the people, places, and things of our everyday concerns but rather their play, not their material but the happening of their forms, recollected in this separate place of repose or attention where we can step back and watch and gaze upon the shapes and images of things that were and, perhaps, are yet to come, somehow ingeniously put forth before us now, right here, before our very eyes. From this standpoint of disinterested contemplation of the objects and events that comprise the scenes in which the urgent matters of life they allude to have been relieved of their importunate immediacy, we gain the freedom of perception in which we can train our sentient faculties and develop a taste for all things beautiful and sublime. (XXI 53.19-20). Not so much simple representation or imitation, the much defamed *mimesis* of the fine arts, refers, in fact, to the *form of critical reflection* that is the distinction of our human being, which, for Schiller is not, as it was for Rousseau, a narrative depicting the life of humanity's freedom, but rather the actual performance of that freedom, the drama of which we are encouraged to experience in person as the grace and the majesty of our nature. Schiller develops this point as follows:

> *Solange der Mensch, in seinem ersten physischen Zustande, die Sinnenwelt bloß leidend in sich aufnimmt, bloß empfindet, ist er auch noch völlig eins mit derselben, und eben weil er selbst bloß Welt ist, so ist für ihn noch keine Welt. Erst wenn er in seinem ästhetischen Stande sie außer sich stellt oder betrachtet, sondert*

sich seine Persönlichkeit von ihr ab, und es erscheint ihm eine
Welt, weil er aufgehört hat, mit derselben eins auszumachen. Die
Betrachtung (Reflexion) ist das erste liberale Verhältnis des
Menschen zu dem Weltall, das ihn umgibt. (394.1-11)

As long as human beings in their original physical state of passive receptivity merely suffer the material world to make an impression on them, to merely affect their senses, they remain entirely confluent with it and for the very reason that they are thus merely world themselves, there is as yet no world for them. Not until they attain the vantage point of aesthetic contemplation that sets the world outside of themselves do they distinguish their personality from it as a result of which a world now comes to light because they ceased to remain one with it. The critical perception of contemplation is the first liberal relationship that human beings entertain with the universe that surrounds them.

Thus, we do not read about or talk about freedom when we visit the theater of human being; as spectators of what transpires upon its stage and in its scenes, we participate in the inward play of forces the proportion of which determines our own destiny, our own actions and insights as if we ourselves, though sitting and remaining in the audience, were also actors in our own right in the play, *thinkers* in our perception of the drama but also *doers*, actors who themselves undergo the experience and gain the insight that all fine art, but especially theater, provides and in which we acquire what Schiller calls an *aesthetic education*.

For what we encounter put before us in the play of figures upon the stage of pure reason, whether as thinker, as actor, or as builder, whether the scenes are inside us or outside, are "signs and symbols…" of principles, hieroglyphs of power, the collected terms and the alphabet "…of natural laws that distinguished thought shares with distinguished thought." (116.1-4)

Die Gesetze der Natur sind die Chiffren, welche das denkende Wesen zusammenfügt, sich dem denkenden Wesen verständlich zu machen.

Whether it be the state of mind of another that we feel in ourselves as our own or the perfection that is ours the moment we take note of it, or the fact that the pleasure we take in truth, in beauty, in virtue ultimately resolves itself into the certainty of our own ennoblement and enrichment (118.36-119.4) – in being put before us upon the stage, these figures take possession of us, the spectators, through our sympathy, and perform the drama of self-reflection that they as actors of distinction initiate in us as their spectators – experiencing poetic scenes of tragedy, natural scenes of majesty, we feel subjugated to the inexorable forces they make manifest to the dependence of our physical nature and, at the same time, elevated in the purity of our absolute determination as moral beings who, in their free humanity, are themselves distinguished in themselves from their own human being.

> Unser intelligibles Selbst, dasjenige in uns, was nicht Natur ist, muß sich bei jener Affektion des Erhaltungtriebs von dem sinnlichen Theil unseres Wesens unterscheiden und seiner Selbstständigkeit, seiner Unabhängigkeit von allem, was die physische Natur treffen kann, kurz, seiner Freiheit sich bewußt werden. (184.5-10)

> *As a result of our survival instincts being thus aroused, our intelligible Self, namely that which in us is not nature, undertakes to distinguish itself from the bodily senses of our being and realizes in this way its sovereignty and its independence of all that can impinge upon our physical nature, realizes thus, in a word, its freedom.*

The drama of self-reflection that Rousseau imagined as the distinguished and distinguishing relationship of the lover to the one the lover loves, i.e. to her who is his beloved, to him who is hers, is, for Schiller, the spectator's sympathetic contemplation of the sublime as well as the actor's impassioned practice in the battle of distinction that is the human heart's – the spectator's gaze gains the speculative distance to events that allows for distinctions to be made, objects to be seen in the scenes of the imagination where these figments, having been put before us on the stage, "exist" in the play of ideas that experience and insight make of them, in which ideality attains *poetic* reality. In this way, the *supernatural* (Übersinnliche – 201.6, 10; 202.31; 205.40; 294.26; 387.15; 397.35; XXI. 47.30), the *absolute* (absolute – 341.2; 345.9; 348.15, 17; 361.19; 371.4, 6; 390.20; 391.1; 397.34, 37; 470.7; 498.37), *infinite* (unendlich - 196.24; 209.32-33; 217.40; 345.16; 353.2. 25; 371.2; 385.34; 390.36; 394.20; 397.3; 407.41; 438.8) principle of our moral will (290.25-26; 33-34; 361.1; 372.4), the *self-knowing* (Selbstbewußtsein – 372.15, 20, 30; 373.1, 7), *self-acting* (Selbsttätigkeit- 152.35; 159.3-4; 163.23; 187.4; 282.5; 299.6; 343.24; 354.6-7; 384.22; 386.14; 387.6; 396.9; 481.18; 482.7, 16, 17) being of pure spirit (286.30.31; 498.36), of our inner freedom (372.7; 397.34), of our humanity (498.37), can be made evident and manifest, at least indirectly, to our feeling. For, as Schiller emphasizes throughout his studies concerning beauty and the sublime, "the representation of the supernatural is the ultimate purpose of art" (196.4-5).

> Der letzte Zweck der Kunst ist die Darstellung des
> Übersinnlichen.

Supernatural? Spirits? Yes, this is a way of speaking of our distinction as the *pure "demon"* (reiner Dämon – XXI 52.30) of human being, as our ghosts' profession (Geisterberuf – XXI 53.3), namely that of *ideas*, the ordered collection of which is a *country* (Ideenland – I 192.87) and a kingdom (Ideenreich – XX 325.13; 392.4; 439.18; 457.6) or even a distinguished *world* (Ideenwelt – 257.27; 453.23; 475.3; XXI 50.24), a *world of reason* (Vernunftwelt - 260.20) and *of spirits* (Geisterwelt – 111.36; 217.29; 300.37; 395.33), that of the *ideal* (Idealwelt – 390.26) and therefore above and below, before, hereafter this one here, the world of sensations (Sinnenwelt – 202.30; 2.17.31; 257.28; 258.16; 260.28; 289.28; 304.10) – in other words *beyond* that of the scope that defines the petty and meager immediacy of our own and our narrowest self-interest, which is that of the body, the little-Me of my "everyday Man" (XVI 177.37), here and now, having no future, no history, the flat out plain place that is *my* space and the time that is *mine*. Thus, the great dignity that art attains in the Third Epoch is a consequence of the service it renders to our human being which is not only to order our faculties and establish the proportion that best suits the happiness of humanity but, moreover, to constantly put before their efficacy the destiny of human being as an ideal worthy of inspiring our most distinguished will and effort.

A. The Ideal of Beauty

95. Beauty's Twofold Effect

Beauty is an idea. Not "just" an idea, mind you. *Nature, Freedom, Humanity* are all ideas as well but, again, certainly not "just" ideas. When speaking about any old thought, this or that idea, that might have occurred to us, especially when trying to satisfy a need, solve a problem or to get ourselves out of a fix, we mean that having "had" them makes at best only an instrumental difference as regards their usefulness, which is the constrained and constraining "idol of our age" (311.27) – this idea works, that one doesn't – in this respect, ideas can be smart or stupid, viable or impractical, and many a time it was the crazy idea that saved the day.

In such cases all those ideas that we rehearse, propose, test and then discard again are so many potential means to an end, devices in our hands, implements of our ingenuity that we avail ourselves of. Just an idea? Taking it back, we might just as well not have had a thought that matters so little.

But there are some thoughts that matter a great deal and resist retraction. Such thoughts, making, as they do, all the difference in the world to those possessed of (rather than merely possessing) them, can be characterized as *infinite* with regards to the unmarked finitude, the blank slate, of Man, that wizard wielder of ideas. Let us hold them for this reason to be special, *distinguished* ideas, *fancy* notions if you will, determining principles in service to which *we* ourselves are the tools wielded; human being is now the device and, nominating them thus as our leaders, we employ a title of honor that, moreover, accords with the speech practice of poets and thinkers in the Third Epoch, who called them *ideals*.

Now plenty of people are wont to say that they have no use for ideals and it is undoubtedly fashionable to pooh-pooh visions. But this reserve and the bad experience with thought that it betrays, the disappointments and disillusionments that folks have suffered for its sake, are all part of the dénouement in the narrative we are telling regarding our experience with pure reason as the distinction of human being, an episode and character in *that* narrative, not a different and alternative one. Even the sophist and the cynic, even dictators and devils, have their role to play in the course of events that their story of Man unfolds, the whole story, and find their proper place in the scheme of all things thought. How unsettling – in evil, in vice, in perversion, there is rationality, too.

We have acquainted ourselves with Schiller's diagnosis of the ills that beset the life and times of humanity, the fracturing and scattering influence that society's demands impose, for the sake of its own longevity and improvement, upon the natural unity of human potential and human excellence; above all he drew our attention to the inner turmoil that afflicts and perverts our nature, namely how the just proportion among the powers of our soul is upset when they vie for supremacy, the heart rising up against the mind, the thinker against the doer, truth despising beauty, pleasure and happiness usurping the prerogatives of virtue and dignity, fact decrying fiction, politics scorning art, art science, science politics, our principles defying our passions, our inclinations dominating our duties – "along with the necessary covenant and federation that naturally exists between these elements of beauty's state, the nature of beauty itself," the beauty of our human nature, "is destroyed." (310.32-34)

The negotiation of a treatise among warring factions, the reestablishment of a union that has been lost because the conflicting parties, like so many individuals, have placed self-interest and personal advantage above the well-being and the flourishing of their community, the constitution of principles in an enduring order that accords to each member of the state the convention of due regard as determined by the proper apportionment of nature – is this not the foremost challenge facing pure reason, our head of state, namely the guardianship of justice? It would seem, therefore, that it is for lawmakers to know how the allegiance of these forces can be once again regained and collected into the harmonious universe of our faculties.

Yes, but not so fast, Schiller says. It is, rather, the artist's craft and knowledge of the code of laws that govern the aesthetic world (311.3) to which the founders of state must first turn a studious eye and a tractable ear for the simple reason that "it is beauty's path that we follow on the way to freedom." (312.32-34)

A twofold beauty it will be, as we might expect, reflecting the twofold nature of human being and, corresponding to the twofold distemper afflicting our patient, a twofold cure and culture: On the one hand, a beauty soothing to the hungry heart that knows no bounds to its desire to be at large and at liberty, unchained and unreined and therefore prone to colossally overreach, magnificently mistake, to usurp and arrogate, to spawn enormity and extremity (III 21.31) and overstep the limits and propriety of the heart's own property, the human heart's immensity superseding its very humanity – it is upon this exaggeration of the soul and the violence of the transgression that overshoots and overruns all limits and all targets, that, in its independence, invades and ravishes the spheres and realms and scopes of the neighborhood, assimilating them to its own voracity – it is upon this free force that beauty exerts its mollifying influence that tames arbitrary savagery with its lovely and ennobling forms, calms and cools the fervor of its absolute power, and with that abstraction and extrication of the mind in a state of need, founds and builds a harmony of purpose into a community of mutual regard among all the competing forces in their blind disarray, whether they be physical or moral, an organization of partners proportioned to that purpose, the well-being of human being, that they share and to which they have, "in clarity of sight and free decision" (313.33-34), agreed to be contracted as to the law and principle of the state of humanity – "compelling the arbitrary interest of our *physical character* to accord with the laws" of the land that the ideal of humanity is to us and at the same time "compelling the freedom of our *moral character* to nevertheless abide by human sentience..." in other words "...removing the former somewhat from material dependence, while drawing the latter somewhat closer to it – in order to bring forth a third character which, consanguineous with both, affects the transition from the reign of natural forces to the government of the laws and, without hindering the development of the moral character, serves as a material token of the intangible principles of morality." (315.12-20)

> ...es käme darauf an, jenen von der Materie etwas weiter zu entfernen, diesen ihr um etwas näher zu bringen - um einen dritten Charakter zu erzeugen, der, mit jenen beiden verwandt, von der Herrschaft bloßer Kräfte zu der Herrschaft der Gesetze einen Übergang bahnte und, ohne den moralischen Charakter an seiner Entwicklung zu verhindern, vielmehr zu einem sinnlichen Pfand der unsichtbaren Sittlichkeit diente.

But just as the kindness and grace of beauty make disparate forces more disposed to respect limits and seek the mutual agreement of convention, so too does, on the other hand, beauty's invigorating effect stimulate an all too complacent heart to start, to strive, and inspire the "slumbering senses" (XX 313.11) to awaken from the lull of their languor, from their passivity to the passion of eager perception, from the wandering mind etherized by satiety to refreshed wondering and to the ethereality of distinguished action.

Either physical necessity encroaches upon the moral or moral necessity upon the physical – in the first case the physical force oversteps the limits of its office in connivance with the weakness of our moral fiber; in the second case, moral force oppresses the life of our physical nature, which, in its weakness submits to moral austerity. But neither pusillanimity of the soul succumbing to the onslaught of the short lived flares of desires, nor numbness on the part of our sentience grown calloused, worn thin, run dry by obedience at the beck of reason's authority should be the cause of the ceasing of hostilities. Rather a relationship of mutual regard in which each side yields to and imposes upon the other, defending boundaries where these are unlawfully challenged, renewing limits where their signs have lost discriminating force.

In the twofold disorder that this twofold remedy treats, we recognize that uniquely self-several nature of our human being; how utterly unlike every other being *human* being really is in its property of being utterly unlike itself! For this is how we may put the matter when attempting to account for an experience, as familiar to folks today as it was yesterday and the day before and the day before that, namely that, humanity is "a being both rational and physical from which the two fundamental principles of human nature arise: the first drives towards absolute reality and makes a *world* of all that is merely form, putting into effect our potential; the second drives towards absolute formality; it strives to destroy all that is merely world and to bring coherence in vicissitude, in other words, we should bring forth what is inward and give form to what is outward. These two tasks considered in the highest sense of their fulfillment concur in the concept of divinity." (344.4-12)

> ...die zwei Fundamentalgesetze der sinnlich-vernünftigen Natur. Das erste dringt auf absolute Realität: er soll alles zur Welt machen, was bloß Form ist, und alle seine Anlagen zur Erscheinung bringen: das zweite dringt auf absolute Formalität: er soll alles in sich vertilgen, was bloß Welt ist, und Übereinstimmung in alle seine Veränderungen bringen; mit andern Worten: er soll alles Innere veräußern und alles Äußere formen. Beide Aufgaben, in ihrer höchsten Erfüllung gedacht, führen zu dem Begriff der Gottheit zurücke...

This deity of beauty, is the "ideal of humanity" (353.1) to which it is the destiny and the distinction of human being to aspire to and to reach for but not to reach. (343.15-18) It is alone through beauty that we can hope to attain the perfection of our humanity and in this hope gain the experience of both our finite and our infinite existence – on the one hand, making the ideal real by bringing THE WAY IT SHOULD BE to fruition as the reality of moral necessity and, on the other, making the real ideal by subjecting THE WAY IT IS to the principle of that very same necessity that is reason's law. (344.15-17)

96. The Aesthetic State of Mind

The aesthetic state of mind is a state of grace, a state of beauty, that consists neither in the mindless negligence of those living day by day nor in the spiritless abstraction of those out of touch with the rhythm and blues of life's particular ups and downs but rather in the give and take of our two fundamental powers and the two parents of our humanity, namely *matter* and *pattern*, the latter understood as the absolute person, the *form* of freedom, the other understood as its proper effects and attributes, the essential *properties* of this being in and of itself, its substance. Schiller makes the point that while in the notion of a divine, and in this sense, *pure* entity of identity, the absolute subject and its nature, i.e. the attributes and effects that inhere in its personality, are two sides of the same being, our self-several humanity, both finite *and* infinite in one, is, by contrast, distinguished in itself from itself, our moral nature distinguished from our physical nature, our person from our situation, the necessity of our immutable identity from that of the rough and tumble of our ever-changing affairs.

It is the self-relativity of the entity of identity that unifies in its being what, in ours, gives rise to the experience of the self-severalty of humanity; self-knowing being is both the being seen and the seeing being, active here and passive there, giving *and* receiving, the object grasped as well as the subject's grasp. In the narrative that records this its charmed, rhythmical life, the mind is always touched by and is touching beauty. Here again, in *Figure 63*, is its emblem.

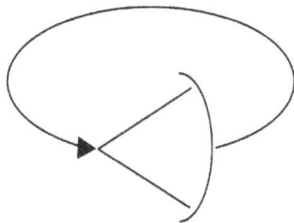

Figure 63: Our Hieroglyph of Beauty

The state of grace and beauty it refers to is that of freedom, the self-determination of autonomy – known to and knowing itself in its perception, it is both the object laid down as law by the heart's imperative and the summons of the loyal subject unto itself; as uplifting as it is humbling, it is both the actor and spectator of the drama of distinction, the former's death awakens and renews the latter to a more spirited life; inception *and* conclusion of human purpose, it is the reciprocity of impact and effect, the passion of sentience and action of conscience; both medium and message, containing and contained, it is the forming hand that gives and the material that takes shape, shaping up as well as shaping; comprehending the ethereality of the real and accomplishing the reality of the ideal, it is the recognition of what *I* is and the realization of who *I* am; our being and our doing, our doing and our deed, it is this determined turn and return that marks the recirculating course upon the commodious road of reflection. These are the articles stipulated by the nuptials of matter and pattern assuring that their union is both fruitful and enduring.

However, our experience of the self-severalty of human being in which both matter and pattern are terms of distinction and set at odds with one another, awakens our sense of the need to better understand them as indicative of the two opposing powers of our nature, unified like the zenith and the nadir in our humanity (390.5) that we might learn how, in spite of their tendency towards extravagance, they could be made to work more harmoniously together in order to form a more perfect union – of course never so perfect as that ideal of beauty that the representation of pure reason's very own self-relativity unceasingly places before our intellect *and* our will – and to achieve some measure of balance as could facilitate the realization of our freedom in grace and dignity. We collect the terms for these two principles of self-several human nature into a Tree of Duality (*Table 7*).

	Terms of Distinction	**Terms of Immediacy**	
1.	Potential of Pattern (Formtrieb)	Impulse to Matter (sinnlicher Trieb)	344-345
2.	Moral Necessity	Material Need/Physical Necessity	311.23-24, 315.31-32
3.	Requirements of Reason	Indigence of the Senses	213.31-32
4.	Dignity of Human Being	Existence of Human Being	315.32-33
5.	Moral Society in the Idea	Physical Society in Time	314.30-32
6.	Duty	Inclination	316.2
7.	Form	Material/Content	316.9
8.	Reason	Drives	316.10
9.	General Human Being in Idea	Individual Human Being in Time	316.21
10.	Rational Unity	Natural Manifold	316.33-34
11.	Incorruptible Law of Consciousness	Indelible Law of Sentience	317.3-4
12.	Our Moral Character	Our Natural Character	317.5-6
13.	Intangible Realm of Values	The Empirical Realm of Phenomena	317.11.12
14.	Our Principles	Our Sentiments	318.18-19
15.	State of Freedom	State of Need	318.34-35
16.	The Spirit	The Senses	321.32
17.	The Constant Person	The Transitory Situation	341.13
18.	The Self	Our Variable Attributes	341.19
19.	Our Infinite Personality of Humanity	Our Human Finitude	341.36, 397.3

20.	The Idea of Absolute Being in and of itself (Freedom)	The Condition of all Dependent Being and Becoming (Time)	342.7-10
21.	The Eternal Substance that I AM	The Temporary Circumstances of who I am	342.14-10
22.	Human Being as Pure Intelligence	Human Being as Phenomenon	342.26-27
23.	Conceptual Experience	Sensory Perception	343.1-2
24.	Personality	World	343.28-31
25.	Formality	Reality	344.5-8
26.	Thought/Character	Feeling	346.22-26, 350.37
27.	Laws/Principles	Cases/Incidents	346.13
28.	Drive to Pattern	Urge to Matter	347.25-27
29.	Rational Nature of Absolute Human Being	Sentient Nature of Physical Human Being	344.21-345.24
30.	The Abstraction of the High Flying Spirit	The Bounds of the Corporeal World	345.15
31.	Validity for all subjects, all place and all time (Generality and Necessity)	Validity for this particular subject, this particular place, this particular time	346.21-24
32.	Forever and Eternally	Now Momentarily and Provisionally	346.35-38
33.	Our Ideal Being Extending Beyond all Bounds	Our Material Being Bound in Binding Borders	347.4-5
34.	Time in Human Being	Human being in Time	347.7
35.	Our Genus	Our Individuality	347.8-9
36.	Our Rational Faculty/Intellectual Perception	Our Sentient Faculty/Sensory Perception	348.7-9
37.	Greatest Independence from the World (Depth)	Richest Connection with the Welt (Breadth)	349.2-5
38.	Conception of the World	Reception of the World	349.8-11, 383.23-35
39.	The Bringing Forth of Form Outside of Us	The Calling Forth Of Potential Within Us	349.9-12

40.	Activity	Passivity	349.15-17
41.	Unity of Reason	Endlessness of Mundane Phenomena	349.22-23
42.	Energy of Intellect	Openness of Sense	350.38-39
43.	The Body of the Laws	The Body of the Senses	352.7-8
44.	Character	Temperament	352.15
45.	Personality	Receptivity	353.8
46.	Self-knowing Being	Feeling Being	353.9-10
47.	Our Absolute Existence	Our Temporal Existence	353.15-16
48.	Annihilation of Time	Plenitude of Time	353.31-32
49.	Absolute Being	Becoming	353.37
50.	Identity	Alteration	353.38
51.	The Harmony and Inner Necessity (Autonomy) of Laws	Totality and Comprehensive (universal) Reality	367.30-36
52.	Necessity within us	Necessity outside of us	372.9-13
53.	Abstraction	Experience	372.26
54.	Experience of the Law (Personality)	Experience of Life (Individual)	373.10-12
55.	The Spiritual World of Ideas	The Material World of the Senses	390.26, 395.32-33
56.	Human Being	Animal Being	391.23-25

Table 7: The Parting of the Human Heart

The opposition of terms that this table sets forth suggests that the two sides of human being it elaborates are inimical. They are often thought to be so, an opinion supposedly justified by a simple perusal of the tradition of philosophical inquiry and the system of conceptions it brought forth based on this very distinction, that we have called the distinction of human being, our cause and the issue of our examination. But Schiller will have none of that, decrying the one-sidedness of such a view and reminding us that not only is *sensibility* wrong when it predominates and transmogrifies into mindless sensuality but *sense* as well, when it oversteps its proper authority, cannot help but mutate into a degenerate, heartless rationality. And Schiller feels himself to be at a loss to decide whether it is more "the frenzy of passions or the cruelty of laws, the egoism of sentience or the egoism of conscience" (350.33-35) that founds and crowns the vice of human being, namely Man's infamous inhumanity to Man against which Schiller prescribes the regime of freedom (318.35), of beauty (410.18-19, 25-26, 412.17), the aesthetic culture (339.8, 340.9, 362.31-31, 377.33, 388.7). For, he concludes, "it is the destiny of humanity to unify in our nature the highest and lowest portions of being; while our entire dignity requires that we draw a strict distinction between our physical and moral identity, our happiness depends on the favorable resolution of this difference. Culture then the purpose of which is to foster a state of accord between human dignity and human happiness will have to preserve the difference between those two principles in their strictest purity even while at the same time achieving their most intimate conjugation." (390.4-12)

> Es ist dem Menschen einmal eigen, das Höchste und das Niedrigste in seiner Natur zu vereinigen, und wenn seine Würde auf einer strengen Unterscheidung des einen von dem andern beruht, so beruht auf einer geschickten Aufhebung dieses Unterschieds seine Glückseligkeit. Die Kultur, welche seine Würde mit seiner Glückseligkeit in Übereinstimmung bringen soll, wird also für die höchste Reinheit jener beiden Prinzipien in ihrer innigsten Vermischung zu sorgen haben.

This culture and training in beauty sets us apart and distinguishes us from the twofold necessity that the twofold nature of Man subjects us to in the antagonism of the two principles that determine our human being, namely the logico-moral law within and the physical law without humanity. These two forces reconcile their differences when we attain the standpoint of distinction that liberates us both from nature and from freedom to the extent that their diametrical imperatives severally delimit the will.

No, we are not necessarily "condemned to be free," depending, of course, on who *we* are; we are free to be free, for freedom is an idea, an invention of pure reason with regards to which folks are free to adopt the standpoint of freedom. Sure, with our birth we were indeed thrown into this world and we didn't start the fire; but, once awoken to reflection, we choose to be human, again and again, every single day, choose our humanity, not only by embracing our autonomy in contradiction to determinations from abroad but also in nurturing the reality of our ideals at home, in our dwelling here and now, that house into which we are born, in contradiction to the abstraction and severity of a disembodied morality that never drinks from the milk of human kindness; though never the vigilante, human being is always vigilant to step back agilely and, alertly, to mind the gap between

THE WAY IT IS and THE WAY IT SHOULD BE – even human freedom wants the moderation that only absolute freedom can provide. And beauty, not compulsion, is its true mark.

Similarly, as we shall see in the Second Epoch, if it is true that Man is God's creation, it is also true that God *as an idea* is an invention of pure reason, such reason as is then, by this very idea, reborn, converted, transfigured, and therein determined to fulfill its destiny of humility in the conviction that pure reason itself is, in fact, not the inventor, the maker, the creator, the father of God at all, but rather the Son of God and the second to Him who is the first and the Father from whom, subsequently, the Son is sent forth into time on a mission of distinction and salvation to judge and to redeem the world; for the Son, both human and divine in the self-severalty that has become so familiar to us as the cause and issue of our study, is not merely born, nor merely created, but moreover engendered by the Father and in turn together with Him bestows upon the mundane darkness of Man the gift of the distinguished, the *Holy* Spirit, that is the distinction of human being in Christian terms.

Therefore, as much as the epochal principle, whether it be Freedom or God, founds and grounds our conception of the distinction of human being in terms established by that principle, our human being as determined by the particular principle at issue begins with our experience of this distinction. From this perspective, "beauty gives rise to freedom" (398.8-10) and "no one goes to the Father but through the Son." (Joh 14:6) In other words, beauty is the reality of the ideal of human being – it is the proper proportion of *human* and *being*, the marriage of pattern and matter, the reciprocal relationship of our rational and our physical nature in the balance that is up to us to maintain between what we are and what we know we were meant to be who live in the world but are nevertheless born free, *in* the world but not merely *of* the world. Isn't that exactly what human being is, ought to be? Namely: An harmonious transaction of properties, a comity of faculties, the mutuality of excellences, the delightful play of forces in their living organisation, a rapport of regard for these forces – "even an infinite being stands through the reciprocal proportion of powers rather than alone, alone by itself and through itself..." like *the philosophical egoist* in Schiller's poem of that name who "...prefers to withdraw into self-sufficiency, into the impoverished solitude of self-reliance, abstracting itself from the beauty of the self-relative ring that ties creature to creature in a bond of mutual endearment." (I 257.12-14)

> Selbstgenügsam willst du dem schönen Ring dich entziehen,
> Der Geschöpf an Geschöpf reiht in vertraulichem Bund,

Willst, du Armer, stehen allein und allein durch dich selber,
Wenn durch der Kräfte Tausch selbst das Unendliche steht?

Thus not only the expression *human being* but even the expression *I am* already contains the two concepts that define humanity and unifies them in that designation, again recalling to mind and celebrating the essential community that exists between our humanity and our reality, our personality and our existence, the self and its determinations (Selbst und seine Bestimmungen – 341.19); the first is the idea of the absolute being of what is grounded in itself – our substantial person of *Freedom* forever present in the self-relative constancy of ME (ICH – 342.14); the second, the idea of what, grounded upon this steadfast foundation, comes into being – the particular *Time and Place* for us that is given to *My* perception. It is from these, as we saw, that the "...two diametrically opposed demands on human being, the two fundamental laws of our rational-physical nature are derived – the first aiming at absolute *reality*, the second aiming at absolute *formality*." (344.5-8)

These two opposing forces, the one our impulse to realize ideas, i.e. to make the OUGHT of thoughts that are in us really matter, take place in the world, the other our impulse to idealize reality, i.e. by discerning reality with respect to THE WAY IT SHOULD BE, to determine THE WAY IT IS – these two driving forces of our humanity, like the faculties of our cogitative/percipient nature from which they derive, stand, ideally, i.e. in the ideal of our humanity, in spite of their apparent antagonism, in a relationship of community, each deferring to the energy and the office of the other: The *urge to matter* (sinnlicher Trieb – 344.20-21), i.e. the *life impulse* (Lebenstrieb – 374.17, 393.24), in what we are and what we do is one of them – it is only in our being and doing what we will, it is only in making these our dreams come true that they can be thought of as really mattering; and nevertheless, this impulse ought certainly not to be so bold as to overmaster its counterpart; similarly, the *rational impulse* (vernünftige Trieb – 374.12-13), in other words, *the impulse to form* (Formtrieb – 345.23), to step back critically and take matters into our own hands and then to impress upon them the shape of things to come, i.e. our visions of what they were meant to be, their destiny, must take care not to encroach upon the scope of duties that belongs to its brother's, its sister's administration. Human being "should not strive for form at the expense of reality and for reality at the expense of form; rather it should seek absolute being through determinate being and determinate being though an infinite one. It should set a world opposite itself because it is a person and it should be a person because a world stands opposite it; it should feel in its self-knowing and it should know itself in its feeling." (353.3-10)

> Er soll nicht auf Kosten seiner Realität nach Form, und nicht auf Kosten der Form nach Realität streben; vielmehr soll er das absolute Sein durch ein bestimmtes und das bestimmte Sein durch ein unendliches suchen. Er soll sich eine Welt gegenüberstellen, weil er Person ist, und soll Person sein, weil ihm eine Welt gegenübersteht. Er soll empfinden, weil er sich bewußt ist, und soll sich bewußt sein, weil er empfindet.

We might and very well should strive to attain this harmonious balance of the impulses that comprise the twofold nature of human being. But how could we possibly succeed at actually realizing an ideal and attaining the perfection that we have thus, unencumbered by the recalcitrance of facts, so clearly conceived of in flights of the imagination on the theoretical plane? Though we ourselves, divided in ourselves as we are and all the more so the more clearly we succeed at grasping the nature of our unity, we nevertheless have some inkling of what we are looking for. What a dilemma – to see what we want and in the seeing to make its attainment impossible, to possess in the pursuit but to lose in the possession. If a sad satisfaction is our only hope in practice then perhaps we must take consolation in the happiness of the dream, a dream however that, though remaining a dream, might inspire us to act in its behalf in spite of ourselves and in spite of, even because of the very impossibility, to nourish that highest desire, keeping us thus busy for its sake, keeping us lean and hungry, strong and striving, extending our grasp, our reach though never reaching.

This vision of our completely realized humanity, if it inspires our desire – however imperfectly we succeed in achieving it ourselves in the inevitable muddle of our own private life from which we make every effort to distinguish ourselves – also gives rise, among some folks at least, to a third drive and impulse, namely the longing to experience precisely this fulfilled destiny of our self-several, dichotomous human being. Schiller calls it the *impulse of play* the object of which is none other than the symbol of the self-relativity of pure reason, namely *living form* (lebende Gestalt – 355.20).

Our delight in Beauty is the experience of living form, "*living* because we feel her, *form* because we contemplate her" (396.35-37) and it is through this aesthetic unity that we may progress from "our physical dependencies to our moral freedom," (397.28) and in this way distinguish ourselves as rational beings from our material being; but through beauty's art, in her, though departing from the times of our lives, we remain *in* our life and *in* our time (353.37); and even while boldly "upraising reason's tower beyond all nature into the vacancy of abstraction, nevertheless, through aesthetic spirit alone, exalt nature *within* nature." (I 300.67)

> Über Natur hinaus baut die Vernunft, doch nur in das Leere,
> Du nur, Genius, mehrst in der Natur die Natur.

This genius is the determining principle of Schiller's thought that welcomes humanity to freedom's home sweet home where our imagination can soar without ever denying its earthly nest or aborting the mission that our senses convey upon its visions. The comprehending, liberating eye of the aesthetic spirit that allows us to abstract from all accidence in grasping essentially, to step back from prejudice in surveying objectively, but also, in the light beams of sight, to spring out and over the tactile forces of importunate immediacy that goad and jostle our feeling and the meat of their materiality that surfeit the appetites of our physical condition (400.19-21), takes pleasure in forms alone, admires the scintillating shapes and surfaces of things, begins to enjoy the embellishment of ornaments and the play of imagination, and allows us to take refuge from "impressments of life" in the sheltered "serenity of the arts" (VIII 6.138). For "a mind that delights in the charms of pure outwardshine...in aesthetic rather than logical seeming...savors no longer merely what affects it but also what it has achieved." (XX 399.32-37)

> ...ein Gemüth, das sich am Scheine weidet, ergötzt sich schon nicht mehr an dem, was es empfängt, sondern an dem, was es thut...von dem ästhetischen Schein...nicht von dem logische.

Only in the seemly world of art, being both free of the essential determination that *truth* is to theory's discerning insight and the *good* is, i.e. the moral object of distinguished humanity, to the practice of pure will, can the outwardshine of what is *fine* – neither the swindler of reality nor the enforcer of morality – attain to the mature State of Grace that is beauty's own realm, *impartial* in having renounced its prima facie claims upon reality, *independent* in dismissing reality's claims upon it – for these are the two arguments always raised against ideals, namely that they are neither factual, nor feasible. Beauty is, rather, the culture of ideals in works of art.

Even in the rudimentary life of primitive beings that we observe in the plant and animal kingdom, even in the "culture," of these natural phenomena, in the superfluity and exorbitance of nature, the roar of the lion, the bird's lay, the poplar's fecund germination, we might recognize a tendency of living beings to exceed the purely material limits that physical laws prescribe to the chemistry of their mineral bodies; nature "provides us

thus already in her material realm with a prelude of what is infinite,"
(406.25-26) lifting her beings and our own imagination from their material
to their form and from their being as subject to the caprice of nature, to hers,
namely to the law-giving, eternal, and immutable spirit that *I am*, the self-
knowing autonomous being of pure reason, *My* humanity, that is nature's
heart and soul, her objective law. This is what the awakening genius of
nature begins to seek in fashioning things no longer merely to satisfy our
material impulse and the utility that serves this purpose but also, liberated
from this first physical constraint, in the discovery and enjoyment of our
absolutely free impulse, to conquer with form and from there finally,
surmounting this as yet arbitrary, unbounded freedom and with a view to
fulfilling our creative impulse in play, to desire no longer "that things please
him but rather that we please ourselves, first, to be sure, through what is
ours, ultimately however through what we ourselves are. What we possess,
what we bring forth, should no longer merely wear the badge of
instrumentality, the timorous form of a purpose; in addition to the
functionality for which it was made, it must also represent the ingenious
spirit that conceived it, the careful hand that shaped it, the free mind that
chose and deployed it." (408.18-26)

> ...daß ihm die Dinge gefallen; er will selbst gefallen, anfangs
> zwar nur durch das, was sein ist, endlich durch das, was er ist.
> Was er besitzt, was er hervorbringt, darf nicht mehr bloß die
> Spuren der Dienstbarkeit, die ängstliche Form seines Zwecks an
> sich tragen; neben dem Dienst, zu dem es da ist, muß es zugleich
> den geistreichen Verstand, der es dachte, die liebende Hand, die
> es ausführte, den heitern und freien Geist, der es wählte und
> aufstellte, widerscheinen.

Beings of beauty, whether we encounter them in their natural setting or
bring them forth in an aesthetic culture, please us because they represent
Us to ourselves. Us? Us who? They make manifest to our perception the
humanity of our human being which resides neither in the pure effectivity
of mind nor in the pure affectability of matter alone; neither exclusively
determined by the "holy realm of the rational laws..." nor the "terrible
realm of material forces...," ideals are products of the imagination, the
greatest of which is the ideal of humanity, the *nature* of human being.
Between these two empires the aesthetic impulse builds the happy region
of play and seemly presence in which Man throws off the fetters of all its
relationships and releases its being from every conceivable constraint, both
physical and moral. "...if, in the dynamic state of rights, Man encounters
Man as a force and limits its power and if, in the ethical state of obligations,

Man, in the majesty of the law, sets itself in opposition to Man, and constrains the will, then it is only in the reciprocity of rapport, in the state of beauty, that human beings might appear as forms and freely face each other as beings in play – the fundamental law of this land is to give freedom through freedom." (410.8-21)

> Mitten in dem furchtbaren Reich der Kräfte und mitten in dem heiligen Reich der Gesetze baut der ästhetische Bildungstrieb unvermerkt an einem dritten, fröhlichen Reiche des Spiels und des Scheins, worin er dem Menschen die Fesseln aller Verhältnisse abnimmt und ihn von allem, was Zwang heißt, sowohl im Physischen als im Moralischen entbindet. Wenn in dem dynamischen Staat der Rechten der Mensch dem Menschen als Kraft begegnet und sein Wirken beschränkt - wenn er sich ihm in dem ethischen Staat der Pflichten mit der Majestät des Gesetzes entgegenstellt und sein Wollen fesselt, so darf er ihm im Kreise des schönen Umgangs, in dem ästhetischen Staat, nur als Gestalt erscheinen, nur als Objekt des freien Spiels gegenüberstehen. Freiheit zu geben durch Freiheit ist das Grundgesetz dieses Reichs.

This play back and forth of gracious cordiality, the gentle rhythm of give and take in which the congress of this communion is articulated, the poise of this being and its congenial counterpoise is the presence of mind that discovers its own figures of freedom in the natural world, discovers them represented in the beings of beauty wherein it sees its own soul and self, actually sees vividly depicted the whole story of the *nature of humanity*, which is how our experience of the self-relativity of the mind, our Verum and the distinction of human being, is termed in the Third Epoch.

Thought thinking thought is this play of chirality and the dissymmetric vision of our dwelling, the community built upon the love of what is one with itself in knowledge and in will, and finally in being, being lovely.

This playful being is, however, not merely for seeing; for beauty is an object of transition, better, of transformation, for its admirers. In its give-and-take, it makes us think better of ourselves, makes more of ourselves who are so prone to the intemperance of both the exaggeration and the diminution of the forces of the mind, its inflation as well as its depreciation when the genius of our freedom, taken to extremes, disintegrates. Here is where a taste for the living forms that art presents does wonders against Man's sophist civilization and the Sophisticated Lady of our insipidity, a fool in love grown soon, too soon, wise, with disillusion deep in her eyes, having lost that native hue of innocence that will always remain her tender heart's first true flame...

> They say into your early life romance came
> And in this heart of yours burned a flame,
> A flame that flickered one day and died away.
> Then, with disillusion deep in your eyes,
> You learned that fools in love soon grow wise.
> The years have changed you, somehow
> I see you now
> Smoking, drinking, never thinking of tomorrow, nonchalant,
> Diamonds shining, dancing,
> Dining with some man in a restaurant.
> Is that all you really want?
> No, sophisticated lady,
> I know, you miss the love you lost long ago;
> And when nobody is nigh you cry.[62]

B. Representations of Humanity

97. The Mirror Stage

Beauty is freedom that has come to light as an object of contemplation; when freedom is put forth before us we see beauty the sight of which puts us into the aesthetic state of mind in which our physical and moral nature attain a momentary proportion such that neither the one side nor the other predominates, each yielding to each and according due regard for what pertains to the other's proper office and contribution to the community of forces that determine our human being. Thus we see in beauty the absolute being of freedom as the connection of two states that are absolutely opposed to one another and can never be united (366.23-25) – on the one hand, as rendering the comprehension of *totality*, on the other, as manifesting the self-determination of *autonomy*, the former is infinite in the manner of all-encompassing *being* called "immovable" for eschewing all violence of partiality (378.4) in particulars and grounding all objects and all reality bar none upon the ample lap of its self-founding foundation, the latter is infinite in the manner of the inexorable *force* called "unstoppable" indicating that the boundary of its power is defined only by the limit that

---

[62] Music by Duke Ellington and lyrics by Mitchell Parish (1932).

traces the form of its own proper scope and therefore free from all extraneous limitation (378.5) based on the determination of a principle. Such a state of mind would seem to be a paradox and an unending battle, certainly nothing harmonious, and so it is for us in our daily lives of stop and go, with daily throes of heroes and villains, our zealots and our jokers.

But beauty is an ideal. We can imagine it and, as an object of our desire, aspire to it; we can see it put before us in works of nature and of art, be they delicate or grand, by the artist's skillful hand, human or divine, and in this contemplation of beauty's scenes experience the aesthetic culture that lightens and strengthens as the case and our need may be – making gentle forces grown extravagant and urging on their dwindling debility; whether lame or straining, they have forfeited that well-balanced proportion in which our humanity most truly flourishes, delighting in the fruition of freedom.

It is to this end and for freedom's sake that we, having become wild or cruel, require an aesthetic culture (398.9-10) to champion nature within nature, positing her *order* against our rampant effusion and her *life* against our oppressive austerity. Easing without dulling, stirring without inflaming, nature's way is beauty's way and in her lessons to human being, she is neither indulgent nor severe, neither too soft nor too hard, neither too cold, nor too hot, but rather just right. This is the middle state of aesthetic freedom. (383.25)

In beauty's embrace, charmed by her spell of autonomy, we experience her as our second creator – nature being our first (378.17-21) – after entering her world of seeming above and beyond all being, the world of forms and figures, of idea and ideals, gently touches our heart. All art sets before us this distinguished being of beauty, remote and removed from the raw stuff of life presented upon the shining stage of reflection upon which a play of the imagination is performed before our aesthetic judgment that distinguishes between fact and fiction, between the actor and the spectator, between the material and the form that gives shape to the latter as Schiller explains in his *Kallias Letters* to his friend Körner (December 1792-March 1793): "The nature of the representing medium, of its materiality, must appear to be entirely conquered by the nature of the represented. Now it is only the form of the represented that can be transferred to the representing medium; therefore, in an artistic performance pattern conquers matter. Hence in a work of art, the material (the nature of the representing medium) must surrender itself to the form (of what is being represented), the body surrender itself to the idea, reality to the performance of the show." (26 224.23-31)

Die Nature des Mediums oder des Stoffs muß also von der Natur des Nachgeahmten völlig besiegt erscheinen. Nun ist es aber bloß die Form des Nachgeahmten, was auf das Nachahmende übertragen werden kann; also ist es die Form, welche in der Kunstdarstellung den Stoff beseigt haben muß. Bei einem Kunstwerk also muß sich der Stoff (die Natur des Nachahmenden) in der Form (des Nachgeahmten), der Körper in der Idee, die Wirklichkeit in der Erscheinung verlieren.

Thus we see the progression from the *theoretical* contemplation of thought, the Thinker who comprehends the *build* of a being, in other words, in ancient Greek ones, its ΦΥΣΙΣ (physis), as that which this particular being was destined to be, the unique excellence of that individual to the extent that it has attained the perfection defined by its form the limits of which are determined within the larger framework of all being – from this being of the intellect, we progress now, in the Third Epoch, to that of the *poetic* imagination of thought, the Builder, who, receiving that object of insight, abstracts its form, leaving its matter behind, and affixing its image into the material of a medium such that the nature of the object entirely transforms this matter, which, insofar the work of art is judged to be beautiful, entirely surrenders its own nature to that originally abstracted from the object and thus in subservience to this form provides the imagination with the vision of "pure objectivity" (225.32), a free representation in the performance of beauty, the autonomy of which is neither inhibited by the subjectivity of the artist nor burdened by the materiality of the object. In this way, the object presented to the imagination is conveyed across three hands (223.32), none other than the three hands of thought, namely the three principles of pure reason that we have been studying and, as we are in the process of discovering in the Third Epoch, have been collected into a complete train of thought demonstrating the poetic nature, the craft and art of the distinction of our human being as rendered in *Figure 64* as a relationship between the media (B/C) and the message (A), i.e. between, on the one hand, the matter (B) and the pattern (C) that impresses it ("Vorstellendes...") – and, on the other hand, the content ("Vorgestelltes..."), the idea and principle (A), that suffuses and informs them. Theirs is the play of beauty ("Vorstellung...") that delights the spectators (I 356.381) who, while seeing the sign, take note of the signifier that, in turn, makes manifest to their insight a sense of its significance, which is the truth of the matter, the point in question, the issue at hand, reflection's hand.

To that end, clearly it is, in Schiller's view, not the narrative of epos, but rather the drama of theater that most effectively serves. Already early on in his career, Schiller recognized the potential of the stage as a moral institution and as his vehicle of choice for promoting the aesthetic culture of human being in order to blaze the way, with its signs of freedom, from our human animal to our human spirit (20 88.27-28) – a passage crucial to the purposes of the lawgiver whose laws reach only as far as our actions whereas the jurisdiction of religion, theater's sister, "extends to the remotest corners of our heart." (91.14-15) *Figure 64* shows the moving heart of theater.

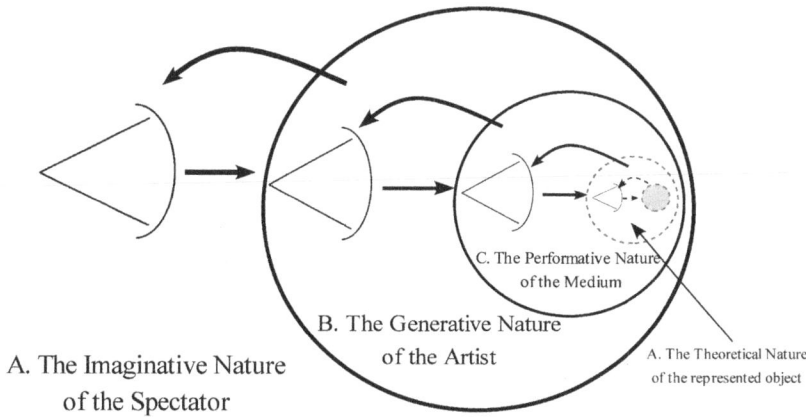

A. The Imaginative Nature of the Spectator

B. The Generative Nature of the Artist

C. The Performative Nature of the Medium

A. The Theoretical Nature of the represented object

Figure 64: The Splitting Image of Beauty in Art

But whereas religion consists of narratives and depictions, the stage offers its audience the "immediacy of a living present" (Anschauung und lebendige Gegenwart – 91.31-32). There on the stage we see a world laid out before us, a world and yet not a world, in other words, a play in the theater of self-reflection. Here ideas, i.e. "divine ideals" (93.13) and "the entire realm of the imagination, of history, the past, the future" (92.7-8) can enter the scene, appear as real, take place right here, right now, in the actors' words and deeds, today, before the spectator's very eyes, leaving with their visible performance "indelible impressions" (92.37-38) so much more powerful than the "dead letter and cold exposition." (93.3) On the mirror stage of self-reflection, we seen reflections of ourselves, though not ourselves; these figures before us, though not us, though their lives are not ours, remind us critically of who we are and aren't, who we were and weren't meant to be and, in this way, gently admonish (95.13), without shaming, call in question without accusing, offer to judgment without condemning us.

Theater teaches us to step back from the immediacy of our own lives into the mediated immediacy of the mirror stage and from the standpoint of this coign of vantage, in the relationship of freedom that is the spectators' (394-10), to acquaint ourselves with the night and the dog days of Man, the soul's secret scheming (3 243.26-28), the meshes of its plots and ploys as well as those of accident and fate that grim necessity unfolds before us as so many exhibitions and exercises in futility, human frailty, but also as rehearsals in hope, training in trials, courses in courage, lessons in losses, in dying, in living, in loving; as the story goes so do we in the matinee till the curtain falls and we rise to greet the brilliant sun outside that is our ownmost, inmost humanity that we are meant to be and have just enjoyed together in the dramatic play of powers, when folks walk away for a while from all their particular walks of life, "from all their diverse circles and zones, classes and standings, standpoints and footings, doff every fetter of affectation and of fashion, plucked from the press of happenstance and episode to embrace their brotherhood in a single all-encompassing compassion, resolved again into one family, forgetting themselves and their world and approaching their heavenly origin – each taking pleasure in the other's delight that is thus strengthened and adorned in a thousand eyes redounding and making a venue of the heart for one single certainty of sense – it is this one: their human being." (20 100.30-38)

> ...aus allen Kreisen und Zonen und Ständen, abgeworfen jede Fessel der Künstelei und der Mode, herausgerissen aus jedem Drange des Schicksals, durch eine allwebende Sympathie verbrüdert, in ein Geschlecht wieder aufgelöst, ihrer selbst und der Welt vergessen und ihrem himmlischen Ursprung sich nähern. Jeder einzelne genießt die Entzückungen aller, die verstärkt und verschönert aus hundert Augen auf ihn zurückfallen, und seine Brust gibt jetzt nur einer Empfindung Raum - es ist diese: ein Mensch zu sein

98. Aesthetic Objects

Freedom, like *God* and *Destiny*, is an epochal term of distinction. A cognizance of thought, each of these signature terms, taken in their inaugural sense, refer to the negativity of pure reason, the simple negation of the unmarked space of our mundane Man and the mentality that corresponds to Man's self-absorbed nescience. In this respect, the term *freedom* is particularly felicitous – it affirms no substance, asserts no *a priori* establishment or foundation, heralds the authority of no positive principle; it is utterly impersonal and as purely privative as the minus sign, the " ⌐ " we affix to a parameter, a simple *not* in the sense of "*not* that!" Inaugural and absolute Freedom merely steps back from every determination whatsoever – freedom *from*. For this reason, what is true of every thought in its intangibility is particularly true of freedom, namely that it is *no-thing* at all, neither person, place, nor thing – not a position or opposition, it is a *pre*position, whether understood as within or without, above or beneath or beyond or between them, in the here*after*, the *nether*world, the *super*natural. Wholly other, freedom is, nevertheless, by the craft and art of poetic reason, brought to the world in the performances of word and deed, by pluck put into action, by whim made manifest to patience as fate or fortune, or else, by imagination, strikingly rendered to the experience of discriminating perception and comprehensive conceptual intelligence.

Schiller shows how freedom is revealed to our aesthetic judgment in all things beautiful and sublime the enjoyment of which serves to mediate our senses and our sensibility; it is through their artful play that humanity can make sense of our senses and convey to the former's discernment the manifold tangibility of the latter's testimony. Ideas become a becoming, comely world and thus accessible to mere men, who in turn become susceptible to the uplifting spirit that is their destiny: "this exalted equanimity and freedom of the mind, combining potency and alacrity, is the spirit into which a genuine work of art should release us..." (XX 380.14-16)

> Diese hohe Gleichmüthigkeit und Freiheit des Geistes, mit Kraft und Rüstigkeit verbunden, ist die Stimmung, in der uns ein ächtes Kunstwerk entlassen soll...

Aesthetic objects help us to feel our freedom, neither at the expense of our senses as does the unconditional *good*, nor at the expense of our reason as does the merely *pleasant* (222.15-17); it is the pleasure we take in graceful movements, their air of *charm*, that acquaint us with the idea of a fair soul; it is in actions of *grandeur*, deeds of distinction, that we experience the majesty of human being, the immensity of our destiny. When we imagine these two spirits in works of art or encounter them in nature, "we feel free in what is beautiful because the impulse of our senses harmonizes with the principle of reason; we feel free in what is sublime because the impulse of our senses have no influence upon reason's ruling, because the spirit acts here as if it were subject to no other laws than its own." (Schiller, *NA*, XXI 42.1-6)

> Wir fühlen uns frei bei der Schönheit, weil die sinnlichen Triebe
> mit dem Gesetz der Vernunft harmonieren; wir fühlen uns frei
> beim Erhabenen, weil die sinnlichen Triebe auf die
> Gesetzgebung der Vernunft keinen Einfluß haben, weil der Geist
> hier handelt, als ob er unter keinen andern als seinen eigenen
> Gesetzen stünde.

Thus, human being has a twofold destiny, born neither to be fettered to
causal being, merely to serve the passing fancies of its momentary delight,
much less to lead an endless life of pain, a friendless stranger to all time and
place. "Only in the marriage of pulchritude and prominence," when what is
lovely is wedded with what is great, "and our sensibility has been cultivated
for both in equal measure...," only then "...are we full-fledged citizens of
nature's realm without therefore being her slaves and without forfeiting our
rights in the realm of the intellect (53.12-17)," i.e. "without losing sight of
our imperishable destiny, our true fatherland." (11-12)

> Nur wenn das Erhabene mit dem Schönen sich gattet und unsre
> Empfänglichkeit für beides in gleichem Maß ausgebildet
> worden ist, sind wir vollendete Bürger der Natur, ohne
> deswegen ihre Sklaven zu sein und ohne unser Bürgerrecht der
> intelligiblen Welt zu verscherzen...unsre unveränderliche
> Bestimmung und unser wahres Vaterland aus den Augen
> verlieren.

It is through aesthetic judgment, therefore, that we, the sentient audience,
feel the freedom of our human being, the absolute freedom that the artist's
imagination so skillfully gave tangibility and "objectivity..." to by
"...individualizing ideals of beauty" (XXVIII 118.34) and hence putting them
before us that we might actually take pleasure in our freedom, which, when
we otherwise experience it in self-several moral action, as we normally do,
is often the source of so much anguish. Removed from the immediacy of
our own lives, remote, up there upon the stage in the scenes of the play, this
drama of freedom unfolds before our mind's "aye" in approval of this its
free delight, free, in the sense of the *diversion* of beauty that the play of
freedom sustains upon the stage by actually detaching us from the tangles
and traps of our theoretical and practical occupations and the pursuit of
truth and duty towards which they are directed.

Moreover, as participants in the abstract sight granted to our creative
viewing by the sentience of beauty's show, we enjoy not only the seclusion
of theater's sphere but also its *serenity*. For in its halls, we are released from
the stress and strain of material consumption that the urgency of physical

necessity and of our own physical needs burdens us with regarding the objects harrying us. On the stage, these disembodied objects, these masks, are put *before* and not *for* the interest of our desires in an immaterial realm of form and fantasy, of pattern rather than of matter, and as such are inaccessible to an enjoyment founded upon seizure, possession, and assimilation. Not the objects of life but rather the objects on the stage, the presence of the ideas they make palpable rather than the actual existence of the people, places, and things they supposedly refer to, delight us. This is the "holy magic" of art, of Beauty (XX 310.32) that Schiller celebrates: "I call that particular pleasure free in which the forces of the mind, the intellect and the imagination, are actively engaged in accordance with their own laws and where feeling is brought forth by form in contrast to physical or sensory pleasures in which the soul is subject to the mechanism of a blind necessity such that feeling follows immediately upon a heteronomous physical cause." (XX 135.22-28)

> Frei aber nenne ich dasjenige Vergnügen, wobei die geistigen Kräfte, Vernunft und Einbildungskraft, nach ihren eigenen Gesetzen affiziert, tätig sind und wo die Empfindung durch eine Vorstellung erzeugt wird; im Gegensatz von dem physischen oder sinnlichen Vergnügen, wobei die Seele dem Mechanismus einer blinden Naturnotwendigkeit unterworfen, nach fremden Gesetze bewegt wird und die Empfindung unmittelbar auf ihre physische Ursache erfolget.

More specifically, given the distinction between enjoying the material itself and enjoying the play of beauty in the performance of distinction on the stage of imagination, aesthetic pleasure is the enjoyment we feel in the free reflection of pleasure, enjoyment, delight, all of which name the correspondence between THE WAY IT IS and THE WAY IT SHOULD BE. The free presentation of this correspondence, whether it be called regularity, order, proportion, perfection (XXVI 211.12), or even truth (30) is the purpose of art; they all exhibit, when put forth upon the stage before the gaze of the spectator, "analogies of the form of freedom" (183.9-10), which is the apparition of autonomy, the self-determination of absolute being that is subject to no other principle than that of its own nature and, in this sense, an entity of identity, a being in and of itself.

Schiller's general term for the correspondence between THE WAY IT IS and THE WAY IT SHOULD BE is *Zweckmäßigkeit* (THE WAY IT IS *is* THE WAY IT SHOULD BE). He employs it to refer to the source of every enjoyment, even to that arising from the satisfaction of our physical needs; when we are hungry the gap between THE WAY IT IS and THE WAY IT

SHOULD BE is felt as a physical need, a pain even, that motivates our search for nourishment, our trip to the fridge, say. By eating, we close this gap and regain the correspondence and the accord between the IS and the OUGHT that was disrupted. This newly attained accord between them is accompanied by a feeling of pleasure bespeaking the fulfillment of the need that their discrepancy initially brought to the fore of our attention and set us out to relieve in the name or to the purpose of our creature comfort. By contrast, "a pleasure is free," Schiller explains, "when we imagine with a feeling of delight the scene of correspondence between THE WAY IT IS and THE WAY IT SHOULD BE; all such scenes of correspondence and accord between the IS and the OUGHT are sources of a free feeling of delight and can be employed to this end by art. Objects of enjoyment can be classified under the following headings: Good, True, Perfect, Beautiful, Tragic, Sublime. The good concerns the judgment of practical reason, the true and the perfect the intellect of theory, the beautiful concerns the perception of contemplation and the invention of imagination. To be sure, even simple sensation delights us as does any force that incites our activity, but art employs sensation only in order to accompany the higher feelings of correspondence between THE WAY IT IS and THE WAY IT SHOULD BE; taken on its own, it loses itself in the fleeting impressions of sentient living being and is spurned by art like all purely sensorial immediacy." (136.12-27)

> Das Vergnügen ist frei, wenn wir uns die Zweckmäßigkeit vorstellen und die angenehme Empfindung die Vorstellung begleitet; alle Vorstellungen also, wodurch wir Überein-stimmung und Zweckmäßigkeit erfahren, sind Quellen eines freien Vergnügens und insofern fähig, von der Kunst zu dieser Absicht gebraucht zu werden. Sie erschöpfen sich in folgenden Klassen: Gut, Wahr, Vollkommen, Schön, Rührend, Erhaben. Das Gute beschäftigt unsre Vernunft, das Wahre und Vollkommene den Verstand; das Schöne den Verstand mit Einbildungskraft, das Rührende und Erhabene die Vernunft mit der Einbildungskraft. Zwar ergötzt auch schon der Reiz oder die zur Tätigkeit aufgeforderte Kraft, aber die Kunst bedient sich des Reizes nur, um die höhern Gefühle der Zweckmäßigkeit zu begleiten; allein betrachtet verliert er sich unter die Lebensgefühle, und die Kunst verschmäht ihn wie alle sinnlichen Lüste.

Thus it is not the feeling of pleasure in itself, but rather the feeling of pleasure in view of that relationship between the ideal and the real that makes our delight aesthetic. For we delight in the correspondence between the IS and the OUGHT, delight in the presence of delight, enjoying the joy that that what actually is, is what it was meant to be and that that what was meant to be, actually is – the former being *conceptual*, the latter *moral* joy. Experiencing this happy agreement between the thought and the thing, between mind and matter set before us in a scene rather than in the fulfillment of our own physical need, which can also be represented as the initial divergence and subsequent agreement between THE WAY IT IS and the WAY IT SHOULD BE – only as reflection, in experiencing our experience, does this relationship of ΛΟΓΟΣ attain the objectivity that allows us to enjoy it – in terms put forth by thinkers and poets of the Third Epoch – as a symbol of the freedom that became known as absolute, as the nature of human being, as the destiny of our humanity, a freedom that can only be set before us by the craft and art of the imagination as a play of beauty on the stage that, in our lives, remains an ideal and a distinction towards which we can but strive and work for.

In fact, Schiller shows that this relationship of ΛΟΓΟΣ, even in the form of its divergence, the discrepancy between the IS and the OUGHT, in other words that THE WAY IT IS *is not* THE WAY IT SHOULD BE and THE WAY IT SHOULD BE *is not* THE WAY IT IS – even this, the contradiction of our own self-severalty and the anguish that accompanies it, can be, through the aesthetic reflection provided by the representation of the scene put before us on the stage, a source of delight. Anguish is a source of delight?

Yes, of course. For who would deny that we take pleasure in theater's tragic spectacle? The experience of *Pathos* is just such a pleasure and if the crafts and arts of thought, the Builder, taking, with Schiller, the *true*, the *perfect*, and the *beautiful* as their main objects, serve to delight the contemplative nature of the mind in conjunction with the imagination and can be called the *arts of beauty* (i.e. the arts of taste and understanding), the *arts of pathos* (i.e. the arts of sentience and the heart), by contrast, are the ones that occupy the imagination in connection with pure reason and take as theirs the *good*, the *tragic* and the *sublime*.

In particular "both the tragic and the sublime have in common that they delight through anguish, hence, since pleasure arises from the correspondence between THE WAY IT IS and THE WAY IT SHOULD BE while pain from their divergence, the tragic and the sublime cause us to take pleasure in the fact that THE WAY IT IS *is* THE WAY IT SHOULD BE, a delight which is nevertheless itself founded upon the sentiment of pain that THE WAY IT IS *is not* THE WAY IT SHOULD BE." (137.29-33)

Das Rührende und Erhabene kommen darin überein, daß sie
Lust durch Unlust hervorbringen, daß sie uns also (da die Lust
aus Zweckmäßigkeit, der Schmerz aber aus dem Gegenteil
entspringt) eine Zweckmäßigkeit zu empfinden geben, die eine
Zweckwidrigkeit voraussetzt.

We take pleasure in this spectacle of distinction because it places before
us the dramatic scene of human self-severalty – the pain we feel when
considering objects both pathetic and sublime arise from the mortification
of our physical nature that these objects occasion; but though we
experience the shortcomings of the latter, we also feel that we who are the
witnesses of tragedy and humility are called upon to distinguish ourselves
from the limits of its constraints and not only to recognize but also to attain
to the standpoint of our moral nature which places us, as viewers, at that
unearthly Olympian height above the plane and the boards of the drama
inhabited by the players. We are the spectators of the performance that is
being put on before us and from this absolute standpoint of freedom that
distinguishes us from the actors' world of the seen in which they are
determined by the tale, we experience the world of the unseen, intangible
mind that is no less our nature than the material one embodied by the poor
players on the stage.

Thus to experience pain from the standpoint of freedom is to experience
the suffering before us as our own; stepping back from the immediacy of
our state, widening our scope through pathos, we learn the lesson of
distinction that locates our human being not only as actor on the world
stage but also as absolutely detached from its scenes, witnesses to their
play. From the remote standpoint of this coign of vantage, we watch the
show but not in cold abstraction from, nor in vicarious intercourse with, the
actors but rather with insight into the unfolding plot in which their lives, for
them, are inscrutably woven, with comprehension of the whole that they,
blinded by their particular concerns, can perceive but parts and
perspectives of and with the compassion that carries us across that chasm
of distinction so that we might live and die in the play with the actors on the
stage only to be reborn and renewed to a brighter, wider light of
understanding when the spotlights on the stage go out and the curtain falls
and the spectators become once again actors in their own right, in their own
light, in their own world where and upon whose deeds the further curtain
of reflection now is raised.

Thus it is not joy in another's pain that we feel when we watch the tragic
drama of distinction taking place before us, it is delight in the insight into
the meaning of the suffering that the tragic figures in the play endure, a

sight, an insight that their blindness brings to us, the hope and consolation that we reap from their ordeals, and it is from the apparition of their errors and mistakes in the play of theater that we drink true wisdom's cup of cheer in actual life. In all of these cases, the divergence between the IS and the OUGHT is a source of anguish for the characters in the play and for us as well in our empathy, in which, through them, our physical being is seen to be subjugated to the heteronomous forces of nature – our "emotions and drives, affects and passions as well as material necessity and the caprice of fortune" (139.31-34) – and suffering because of it; but it is a boon and a delight to the contemplating mind and, to the will thus ennobled in its moral judgment, the awakening of determination to put into practice what it has learned in theater's school: Perceive through the drama of the actors' dilemmas and defeats the unfolding narrative of your own life's clarity and victory; celebrate the revelation of your own moral life in their tragic death. The night of their subservience shall be your independence day, and moreover, with this end in view, even a holy, a glory night.

99. Objects of Grace and Beauty

Thought thinking thought, our entity of identity, is the very image of the perfect correspondence between the IS and the OUGHT – the self-relativity of what is in and of itself, through and for itself, of what is, all in one, the being seen and seeing, done and doing, made and making, and therefore is always already everything it was meant to be – can you imagine such a being? For indeed what else is truth in conception, virtue in action, beauty in production if not the unique entity of self-knowledge, self-determination, self-realization? If you cannot, turn to nature and have a look-see.

Where else if not in the phenomena of nature would we find living signs and symbols of such a being? Is not the freedom of *self-determination* precisely what nature's spectacle shows us, namely beings "that are what they are through themselves" (XXVI 191.34), through their own intrinsic natures, without being subject to any extraneous influence of material or intention. As such, a natural being is a "representation of freedom" (192.12) as long as we refrain from seeking the principles of its determination apart from or outside of nature as the theoretical conception of this being is inclined to do unless moderated by a critique of pure reason, the form of which, for its part, "invites us, or rather, compels us, instead, to consider this being of freedom in and of itself apart from all extrinsic determination" (201.9-12) and thus as its own cause (causa sui), exhibiting that autonomous spontaneity that is alone the distinction of human being in the Third Epoch.

Reflection upon the form of this being recognizes in the spectacle of what unites, in *one* being – both the subordinate's submission to the rule that governs its causality *and* the superior's ascendancy in exercising the causality of the governance that sets the rule – *the idea of autonomy*, i.e. a being, both ruling and ruled by itself, self-governed, self-governing being. The conception of such a being as this comprises, on the one hand, the notion of *nature*, the apparition of a being in and of itself, and that of *art* or *culture*, a being determined by a law or principle. The artist's idea and conception takes shape in the material medium, which, in turn, completely surrenders the accidents of its own nature and the idiosyncrasies of the artistic individual to the pure objectivity and independence of style in the representation of the idea. Thus "nature in culture...is the perfect correspondence between inherent substance and form, a law that is both given and obeyed by the thing." (208.3-6)

> Was ist also Natur in der Kunstmäßigkeit?...Sie ist die reine Zusammenstimmung des innern Wesens mit der Form, eine Regel, die von dem Dinge selbst zugleich befolgt und gegeben ist.

Such a thing as this catches our theoretical attention. We reflect upon this object of note as opposed to ignoring it. Just remarking the object bestows upon it the distinction of our intellectual reflection seeking reasons, gives it the determination of a cause and principle, and, consequently, in the discernment of all other beings, a ground, i.e. a critical life during the course of which it has become what it is, regardless of whether or not THE WAY IT IS *is* THE WAY IT SHOULD BE.

But true beauties awake our interest in them by exhibiting a rule that appeals both to our intellect or our will – we suspect therefore that they have been made to perfection in accordance with some idea or purpose, their principle being therefore external to them and heteronomy. But in fact taken as objects of nature they present themselves to our imagination as determined from within, matured in accordance with their own *natures*, rather than from without, nurtured at the whim of a culture. Therein lies their freedom. "The form of beauty is simply the free presentation of truth, of purpose, of perfection." (211.29-31)

> *Die Form des Schönen ist nur ein freyer Vortrag der Wahrheit, der Zweckmäßigkeit, der Vollkommenheit.*

Beings enjoying the state of complete accordance and community with their own nature are free, are beings beautiful to behold, whether they are representations of art or creations of nature; but the beauty of human being, far from being merely the presentation of self-determination in the appearance of our physical nature, the architectural beauty of the human body as a result of the natural forces at play in the propitious shaping of the flesh and blood of Man, is an apparition that goes beyond this material endowment of nature – grace is what comes to light in the movements that reveal our state of mind and the influence of human spirit upon nature's gifts because as much as our physical being is determined by the natural laws that govern the universe, as mere earthlings – for example, we are subject to the law of our planet's gravity – as mindlings too, we are "beings that are the absolute and ultimate cause of their being, that therefore, for reasons taken from within themselves and owning to their particular sentiment will, can, in the determination of their freedom rather than in the necessity of nature, change." (262.18-24)

> ...Wesen also, welches selbst Ursache, und zwar absolut letzte Ursache seiner Zustände sein, welches sich nach Gründen, die es aus sich selbst nimmt, verändern kann. Die Art seines Erscheinens ist abhängig von der Art seines Empfindens und Wollens, also von Zuständen, die er selbst in seiner Freiheit und nicht die Natur nach ihrer Notwendigkeit bestimmt.

Here where the mind enters into the play of natural forces that have brought forth native beauty without human intervention, "the person as the free principle of human being" (263.29) takes it upon itself to act on behalf of the beauty that presides over nature's reign; the movements that freedom gives to natural beauty are tangible evidence of the soul's influence upon the body's natural stature and of the state of that soul. This is the morality of the man or the woman who involuntarily reveal the temper of their character in the movements that accompany their voluntary actions even in spite of the pretence they might try to give their conceits. What is the state of the soul that expresses itself as grace? "There are a total of three relationships in which human being can stand to itself, its physical to its moral nature...either Man suppresses the demands of the former in order to make it conform to the higher requirements of the latter; or the converse is true and Man subordinates the rational part of his being to the physical, simply following the impulse with which natural necessity sweeps Man away as it would any other physical phenomenon; or else the drives of the second and the laws of the first meet in harmony and human being is one with itself." (280.8-20)

Es lassen sich in allem dreierlei Verhältnisse denken, in welchen
der Mensch zu sich selbst, d.i. sein sinnlicher Teil zu seinem
vernünftigen, stehen kann....Der Mensch unterdrückt entweder
die Forderungen seiner sinnlichen Natur, um sich den höhern
Forderungen seiner vernünftigen gemäß zu verhalten; oder er
kehrt es um und ordnet den vernünftigen Teil seines Wesens
dem sinnlichen unter und folgt also bloß dem Stoße, womit ihn
die Naturnotwendigkeit gleich den andern Erscheinungen
forttreibt; oder die Triebe des letztern setzen sich mit den
Gesetzen des erstern in Harmonie, und der Mensch ist einig mit
sich selbst.

These two drives of human being, the call of duty and the propensity of
inclination, are reconciled in the well-tempered, beautiful soul in which
they form a harmony and balance, each respecting the other's freedom in
the acknowledgement of the limitations that determine the extent of their
own rights. In the beautiful soul, self-assured moral sentiment trusts our
affections to properly guide our wills as if the heroic sacrifice that duty often
demands from us by setting us in opposition to our inclinations were in fact
not resigned compliance and reluctant acquiescence in the stern face of the
law's inexorable letter but rather its voluntary and even casual fulfillment
with all the lightness and ease of what is truly and genuinely, in other words,
naturally law-abiding. Only this is the true autonomy of humanity, the
moral nature of our human being, and it makes its appearance in the
charming grace that accompanies our actions inspiring in the observer
precisely what the soul experiences that has, apparently in a stroke of luck,
recognized that its state is naturally neither that of anarchy nor of tyranny,
neither that of the stupor nor of the extremism, neither the subservience
nor the mastery of one of our human faculties over the other, but rather
their friendly community – this self-love of their mutual regard that is the
very heart of our heart bestows upon the apparition of our human being
that loveliness of beauty that awakens love on the part of the witness to the
graceful spectacle of a humanity that does not merely humble us with the
transcendent, resplendent sanctity of freedom's spirit but also pleases us
and wins our love with the gentle charm and warmth of our congenial soul's
natural human kindness.

100. Objects Grand and Sublime

For consider the apparition of freedom in the former objects, namely
those inspiring not love but worship and the admiration inherent in
reverend terror, awful wonder – they are aesthetic objects as well though

not objects of beauty and consequently, as is the case of all art, aim, contrary to immediate impressions, at our enjoyment even as nature wants our happiness. But whereas happiness *in life* is the problematic outcome of endeavors devoted to administrating to constrained States of Need arising in the tension of the ever-resurgent gap between THE WAY IT IS and THE WAY IT SHOULD BE – diligence in the sour efforts of the impatiently plodding intellect, pertinacity in the bitter ordeal of the good will when sacrifice and moderation restricts desire's swellings and deprives our drives of their glut, *in art* our delight demands no lucubration of the mind, no oblation of our body, no contrition of the heart.

All things tragic and tremendous, i.e. above all the heartrending and sublime objects, confront us with *immensity*, the experience of which is, in contrast to objects of grace and beauty, twofold, comprising both that of fulfilled purpose and commensurability, which is accompanied by a feeling of pleasure, as well as that of pain and disparity, a dissonant sense of running counter to what is desirable, that is nevertheless the counter-intuitive source of that delightful accord – we recognize in the coordination of pain and pleasure (Schmerz und Vergnügen – 138.22) one self-several experience in which the former is the cause of the latter, grief the cause of the joy regarding this grief.

Thus giving rise to such a mixed sentiment: The heartrending object as the representation of human distress and suffering contradicts our *physical* human nature which aims for what is wholesome to our needs, pleasing rather than hurtful to our senses; nevertheless, this immediate bodily oppression, though irksome within the narrow limits of our physical condition, proves, on the higher plane, to be consonant with our *moral* human nature, in other words, in conformance with the law of pure reason governing the region of ideas where we as their kindred spirits, dwell, and is, in this respect, therefore, a source of pleasure, in fact, the greatest of all pleasures, for none among them is so close to our heart as the gratification we feel as party to the contract of agreement with "the inner necessity of our mind's moral imperative...." This moral accord "...is the nearest and most important to us and, at the same time, by us the most clearly recognizable because it is determined by nothing extraneous to us but rather through the inner principle of our autonomous reason. It is the palladium of our freedom...." Token as well as talisman, "...this moral correspondence is most vividly apprehended when, placed in direct competition with ends that the agency of natural forces blindly aspire to in the urgency of our inner "...sentiments, impulses, affections, passions, in the outer inexorability of the elemental universe and in the fortuitous contingency of chance..., it nevertheless maintains the upper hand. It follows from this that the acutest awareness of our moral nature can only be maintained in a state of antagonism, in contrariety and that the highest moral delight always must be accompanied by pain." (139.21-140-2)

> ...unsre vernünftige Natur und auf innre Notwendigkeit. Sie ist uns die nächste, die wichtigste und zugleich die erkennbarste, weil sie durch nichts von außen, sondern durch ein innres Prinzip unsrer Vernunft bestimmt wird. Sie ist das Palladium unsrer Freiheit...am lebendigsten erkannt, wenn sie im Widerspruch mit andern die Oberhand behält...also Empfindungen, Triebe, Affekte, Leidenschaften so gut als die physische Notwendigkeit und das Schicksal. Aus diesem folgt, daß das höchste Bewußtsein unsrer moralischen Natur nur in einem gewaltsamen Zustande, im Kampfe, erhalten werden kann, und daß das höchste moralische Vergnügen jederzeit von Schmerz begleitet sein wird.

Whereas the heartrending object shows us our human suffering with the purpose of reminding us, through our empathy with that represented anguish, that it is the moral distinction of our human being to step back in art's tragedy, to be able to step back in life's, from the dictate of all physical force as pertaining to the incidental causes of our pain, the sublime object, impressing upon us the ineluctable, overwhelming might of nature's intransigent and indomitable forces when compared to the negligibility of our little human being's physical power to withstand them, though crushing us in respect to our bodily inadequacy to brave with sheer brawn elemental immensity, it nevertheless leads us to that inward and upward refuge that the mind is to humanity, disclosing the distinguished and absolute spirit of human being and thus elevating us to the stars even while debasing us as dust in their sublime presence.

Who has not, in the midst of oppressive worries, careworn, burdened down by life's hardships, gone out to greet the starry starry night with tears or cries of rage and received solace from the vast incomprehensibility of that sparkling universe in comparison with which our little world of here and now in all of its sound and fury is but a mote and a speck of nothingness and insignificance. Why would this thought of our own annihilation in view of the infinity of space and time give us succor? Because the sublime object invites us to step back from the immediacy of our own lives, from the particular, local, and transient nature of our human creature and all of its slings and arrows and adopt a standpoint from without, the vantage point of freedom that the stars beckon us to attain to, which stars, entirely divorced from the momentary rush and stress of matters that goad us, shine blithely and benign above the fray that our grave, earthbound existence often is. In this way it happens that we empathize with the stars, putting ourselves, as it were, in their place. In the chiasmus of this transformation, even as we look up to them in a worm's squirming prostration, we succeed at looking down upon ourselves with commiseration and the pity of the unencumbered human spirit in whose benediction of this our kind, because kindred, star, we see our closed I's cursed lives through the open eyes of the starry skies.

Thus the train of thought that our experience of immensity engages us in commences upon the image of *nature*'s objectively superior physical power giving rise to the image of the subjectively inferior powerlessness of our human frailty in doomed confrontation with it and concluding upon the recognition of our subjective moral superiority that is the *supernatural* power of the human spirit, the distinction of human being, our native nobility in which "the lovely soul resolves into the heroic one and exalts itself to pure intelligence." (294.20-24)

101. The Works of the Poetic Genius

We have mixed feelings when we encounter the sublime (21.42.7-11), nature surmounting nature within nature; we feel joy as well as woe, the moral *pleasure* of our exalted mind's self-delight in achieving separation from the physical *pain* that is Man's constant complaint regarding the vulnerability and the perturbations of his life and limb. But our experience of beauty, the self-determination of nature with regards to nature in congruence with nature, is not unitary either, though the appearance of nature's autonomy is one of harmony in which all erratic accidence of extraneous influence has been calmed and reconciled in the vision of nature's inherent perfection and the beautiful soul that is her person, the embodiment of her infinite, her self-finite, self-defining spirit. Our experience of this genius – possessing all that child-like, but not childish, grace of what is innocent, ingenuous, and, in this sense, authentic nature in departure from the wily sophistication and the wary artifice with which we politely devise our living being among associate beings – our experience of this naïve mind is one of being poignantly touched by simple purity, disarmed by what is open-hearted, candid, but also of being wistful in tender yearning for what, despite the sprawl of civilization, has, somehow, remained untouched by the arbitrary and fantastical conceits of Man's frenetic world.

This vision of a wise, a guileless, an integral nature as an ideal towards which you, rat-racing in the labyrinth of perverted civilization, strive, is sustained by and sustains the *sentimental* interest you nevertheless take in pristine nature, having left her behind, lost, like the first infant paradise of your happiness, for the sake of a culture that has not yet and indeed never could, never will, reach the "perfection..." of the vision with which she has inspired your imagination and desire by "...serving your heart as a model. Come forward to her, exit the sphere of artifice; she stands before you in her magnificent tranquillity, in her native beauty, in her newborn-baby innocence and artless simplicity; linger by this vision, nurture this sentiment, it is worthy of your most majestic humanity. Banish the thought of trading places with her but take her up in yourself and strive to wed her infinite precedence with your own ascendency and engender out of them both a divine being. May she encompass you like a lovely idyll whither you, exiled in the aberrations of Man-made expedience, can always return to yourself, where you can take heart anew, regain your confidence in the road taken, rekindling again and again the flame of the ideal that by tempestuous life is so easily snuffed out." (428.35-429.11)

> ...Vollkommenheit deinem Herzen zum Muster dienen. Trittst du heraus zu ihr aus deinem künstlichen Kreis, steht sie vor dir in ihrer großen Ruhe, in ihrer naiven Schönheit, in ihrer kindlichen Unschuld und Einfalt; dann verweile bei diesem Bilde, pflege dieses Gefühl, es ist deiner herrlichsten Menschheit würdig. Laß dir nicht mehr einfallen, mit ihr tauschen zu wollen, aber nimm sie in dich auf und strebe, ihren unendlichen Vorzug mit deinem eigenen unendlichen Prärogativ zu vermählen und aus beiden das Göttliche zu erzeugen. Sie umgebe dich wie eine liebliche Idylle, in der du dich selbst immer wiederfindest aus den Verirrungen der Kunst, bei der du Mut und neues Vertrauen sammelst zum Laufe und die Flamme des Ideals, die in den Stürmen des Lebens so leicht erlischt, in deinem Herzen von neuem entzündest.

It is therefore with regard to nature that the poetic spirit, "immortal and ineradicable in our humanity" – 436.12-13), can be distinguished in itself: either poets are born to champion and foster her inviolate innocence and preserve the purity of her genius as their own or else, fallen from the grace of our original congruence with her, they are destined to be nature's "witnesses" and "avengers... – poets either *are* the presence of nature or they *seek* the nature we have lost... from which the two different ways of poetic spirit arise...the naïve and the sentimental, the first is spirited youth, austere and aloof, like the virginal Diana in her woods, fleeing our desire to embrace and utterly possess her...." (432.26-35) Nature's poets are impersonal, her work is theirs and it is this work, one with them and her, rather than they themselves that we admire in all the purity of its unadulterated presence for the sake of which they utterly recede in the background, remain unseen behind the seens.

The second poetic spirit is that which inspires the work of the sentimental poets who, having entered the sphere of distinction and the morality of critical self-reflection are no longer themselves this unity of sentience and intelligibility, receptivity and intelligence, the harmonious reciprocity of the responsiveness and the initiative, the affect and the effect of the mind both pliant and sharp, both open and bright, both feeling and grasp, touched and touching, but, lacking this complete grace and perfection of humanity's being, it is theirs to be had as an aim and object, our humanity to be, the ideal of humanity. If now the purpose of poetry is none other than to "give the humanity of human being its most complete expression..." then it will be the naïve poet's task to "....represent nature's pure reality..." and the sentimental poet's task to "...elevate our self-several human reality to the ideal, or in other words, to represent ideality." (437.15-25)

Remarkably, this latter, later style of poetic invention, that of the newer poets, the former being that of antiquity, reflects the development "of our human being as a whole as well as our own individual human being. Nature makes us one with ourselves, art separates and divides us, and through the ideal we return to that unity. But as the ideal is infinite and therefore unattainable by us, our cultivated human being in its own kind can never reach the perfection that our natural human being, in and of itself, can," (438.4-11) in fact, always already has, always already is.

This being is our genius, is pure reason, the spirited being that we already are and that is always already what it is our destiny to become, to be given living presence to by thought, the *Builder*, present to thought, the *Thinker*, and, first, as the end towards which thought, the *Actor*, strives, committed to closing the gap between THE WAY IT IS and THE WAY IT SHOULD BE that it is the distinction of human being to experience as our tragedy and our dignity, our woe and our weal.

III. Hölderlin

102. The Poetry of Human Nature

In the Third Epoch, thought is considered in its entirety, collecting the discoveries of the previous epochs regarding what thought consists of, the three workings and achievements of thought, its three lives, its three acts and actions, its three powers, persons, and personalities. In the final epoch in which pure reason is conceived of in regards to the absolute freedom of human nature, we come to understand that this capacity and destiny of humanity cannot be properly grasped simply as *intellect* – insight into THE WAY IT SHOULD BE in the contemplation of proportionate *being*, which is the science of the First Epoch, nor even in the patience of *faith* – the mind's perpetual conversion towards the *eternal life* of pure, of holy spirit, which is the discipline of the Second Epoch, but rather productive *imagination*, which is the realization and presence of thought in the *inventions* of the creative mind, the constant engagement of our commitment to resolve the disparity between THE WAY IT IS and the WAY IT SHOULD BE in the highest spheres of human achievement, namely in art, in religion, and in science.

Thought is, now, the creator as well as the creature, more, it is the creator and the creation in one; it is its own creator and its own creation, self-caused because self-determined and, in this sense alone, *free*. As Schiller puts it: "That is the great dignity of our human being in comparison with all other living beings, venerable merely as creatures; human being can be so only as creator (i.e. as author of his own state of being). We should not merely, like all the other sentient beings, reflect the beams of an extraneous intellect – and be it that of one divine – rather, we should, like a sun orb, blaze with our own incandescence." (Schiller, *NA*, XX 277.4-9)

> Bloß organische Wesen sind uns ehrwürdig als Geschöpfe, der Mensch aber kann es uns nur als Schöpfer, (d. i. Als Selbsturheber seines Zustandes) seyn. Er soll nicht bloß, wie die übrigen Sinnen wesen, die Strahlen fremder Vernunft zurückwerfen, wenn es gleich die Göttliche wäre, sondern er soll, gleich einem Sonnenkörper, von seinem eigenen Lichte glänzen.

We are the poets of our own lives, we ourselves the song sung, the building built that realizes the humanity of human being; we are the artist and cultivators of ourselves, bringing forth, of our nature, the fruit of the culture of freedom; we, freedom's own genius, giving form and life through word and deed, to what would be otherwise entirely abstract, general, immaterial, intangible, "lifeless and alone" as Hegel describes the absolute spirit deprived of the throne that is the comprehended history of its own life in which the true record, the reality, and the certainty of our self-knowing being unfolds before the mind's I (cf. Hegel, *The Phenomenology of Spirit*, 531.6-10), My distinguished identity and My memory in which thought is reminded by thought to think about thought and in thinking to live and relive the lives of its flourishing and, in reliving them, to go through the entire process of thought again, step by step, moment by moment, epoch by epoch, again and again, thought by thought, in the scheme of all things thought, for the simple pleasure that vivid recollection provides. Yes, thought likes to keep thought in mind. Remembrance is inheritance.

This being and its progressions, whether they be seen as that of cultural or natural history, or both – as we ourselves, being human, are both nature and culture, being completely human only after the former has become the latter and the latter the former, as Schiller teaches us – are, at least in the Third Epoch, an invention, the work of the spirit of humanity, realizations in which the mind actually *matters*, as do, in life, our most distinguished words and works; they truly make all the difference in the world, in Man's world that is, these words and works, the most distinguished of which are that of art, religion, and science, themselves the most eminent creations of the distinguished mind, themselves, therefore, both created and, as the three essential axes of human productivity, creative, both the several enterprises of reason, namely that of its imaginative, practical, and theoretical disposition, as well as the particular works they engender in the diligent hands of their adept, namely works that delight the heart, edify the soul, and instruct the understanding.

In these works of art, of religion, of philosophical science, ideas are not only rendered accessible to sense, they become, moreover, the element of a further craft and art, in which their efficacy is demonstrated, their respective order established, the changing ratios of their relationship are taken account of, and, above all, their illustrious cause and ground, which is none other than pure reason, the distinction of human being, praised, all of which magnify the issue and the constitution of thought in dramatic narratives, focus reflection in the concrete particulars of poetic song, lend the voice and face of lament to the tragedy of human self-severalty – in all three instances of this our human potential, however, never failing to demonstrate the principle of reason at work, the creative genius of our latter-day artist, of philological thought, the Builder, whose nature it is to invent a world to call its own, a dwelling to call home; specifically, it brings forth the reality that corresponds to the image and vision it has seized, having gained insight into the essence and the truth of the matter as discerned by the intellect, and set before the will as the ideal, first transforming THE WAY IT IS, in accordance with that model, into THE WAY IT SHOULD BE and then executing the order of thought's authority, carrying out the OUGHT and realizing thus that incipient and original vision in the particulars of the IS where it must make a difference if it is to amount to anything substantial by making the ideal real. This is the chiasm of realization and idealization, the thing idealized in the thought, the thought realized in the thing through the aesthetic imagination, the celebrated marriage of mind and matter in the Third Epoch.

For imaginative reason is the faculty of our endowment by which we may look around us and see not only the actual situation but also what *could* be, other possible scenarios. Look and see this mountain before you. It is there, accepting it thus, the traveler can climb it or go around it; but instead of taking the fact of the mountain for granted as the reality of the situation, as just the way it is, you can initiate a change in the situation by stepping back from these givens of circumstance and envision other potential realities – imagine the mountains you encounter on your life's way; these challenges to change are charges bestowed upon us by chance or fortune, missions to our imagination. Doubtless, the power of the fantasy to dream up a million other worlds than the given one is easily abused and therefore often disparaged, rightly perhaps at times, as fancy and phantasmagoric, a facile path to airy nothingness, a cloud castle inhabited by chimeras, the effusive license of caprice nurtured by delusion, propagated for the better deception of oneself and others. But as a capacity to step back from the assumed inevitability of facts, from the undertow, the flow of continuity that sanctifies convention, from the immediate localities and urgencies of our body's kith and kin, from the institutional power that natural mores cede to human might and main, reason's abstraction is the most striking cognizance of freedom. To her poet, the "reality" of a certain set of circumstances is merely a pluripotent occasion, the composite materiality of the moment in all the lurid details and sensations of our lives that scrutiny can compose into a scope and establish as the starting point of a new invention – for the creator and the builder, "reality" is the name for what has been realized by the power of invention on the basis of a vision that distinguished in what *is* what *could be*, asked, dared to ask, not merely *why* (theory's question), but *why not.*

That is why thought, the Builder, when asked with regard to the manifold, diverse particulars in which *reality* is thought to consist "how things in themselves *are*, can proffer no better answer than this: the way that we should make them."

> wie sind denn nun die Dinge an sich beschaffen? so könnte sie nicht anders antworten als: so, wie wir sie machen sollen.
> (Fichte, *Grundlage der gesammten Wissenschaftslehre*, I 286)

The difference between the IS and the OUGHT, this conflict, but also their harmonious state of balance, their peace and quiet, are envisioned not only as opposed but also as complementary, each being a step or a phase, a time to be accounted for in a complete narrative, the plots, the dramas, the stages of our lives, the seasons of the year, the hours of the day, the epochs of natural and cultural history, the organs in a body of knowledge, the relation of events in works of literature, its genres, even the words in a sentence – they all render the ultimate proportion that exists between harmony and dissonance, one rendered intelligible by presenting the conflicting moments of thought in the context of tangible events, i.e. in terms of experience. This is precisely the vocation of thought, the Builder, the Seer and the Seeker, the Actor and the Thinker, the Speaker and the Spectator – thought, the being seen and seeing, the being done and doing, the being made and making. All before our very eyes, the refreshed eyes of our philological science of thought.

Neither science, nor religion alone, in the Third Epoch of European culture, thought achieves its distinction in art and, nearer, in the poetic spirit of the imagination; it builds a monument to free subjectivity and, specifically, to *human* being, the salient term of distinction in the third and final station of pure reason's development.

We studied Rousseau, the poet's philosopher in whose narratives of fact and fiction, truth, in whose science, nature was revealed as the contradiction between the heart and the mind, between that of human being and that of Man, born to fall from nature's freedom, to become denatured in civilization and yet again destined to return to nature, human nature, in the culture and education of freedom that every citizen must take upon herself and himself in the community, in the dialogue of soul with soul and heart with heart that we experience in the seclusion of our self-reflection, all by ourselves – for that is the relationship of self-determination that nature has endowed us with, her own autonomy.

In Rousseau's works of fact and fiction, freedom emerges as an illuminating idea, an inspiration the ramifications of which are carefully worked out for the reader in trains of thought and rendered palpable in moving narratives that celebrate the nature that, through Rousseau's insight, found its first and original expression, namely the nature of humanity – the virtue that we naturally aspire to as human beings in seizing upon our freedom that is our innermost, ownmost heart's dearest desire.

But this new idea, having entered thus upon the stage of intellectual notice, is then no longer merely an issue of reflection that the writer invites us to consider and with regards to which, by the careful deliberation of his arguments, we might be moved to conviction and to the commitment that participation in his original insight entails in the heart of one to whom this unique truth will, subsequently and permanently, speak with his or her own eternal and internal voice.

For in the spectacle of dramatic performance, as opposed to the ideas related in the form of a tale that we read by ourselves and contemplate on our own, in the figures of the play, in their actual speeches and deeds, we encounter ideas in action and in actuality as real people before us in the flesh, there on the stage. Behold! Despite the utter abstraction of thought, ideas take place here and now, the spirit of freedom, this unique experience by which fate or good fortune had seemed to favor one mind, enters the public place, the space and time of a real setting, becomes a seen in a scene, takes up abode among us, a person or people on a stage before an audience, a circle of people come to share that experience, as a person and as people of that spirit; on the stage, the distinction of human being, pure reason and the mind in its moments of transition, are vividly, movingly set in the form of a plot. The catastrophe that we witness, the "pathetic" tragedy that moves our sympathy, is conducive not only to insight into what the practice of thought is but, more importantly, these events forcefully convey the efficacy of an idea that we have experienced ourselves time and again, enacting before our very eyes the sacrificial ritual of the life that ends with death as well as the life that begins with death, the former being Man's, the latter being spirit's, the life of freedom, that of our distinguished human being, Rousseau's *citizen*.

We watch and participate, are touched by the swelling scene of sublime ideas – in this open mirror of human life, the actions of their actors teach us about ourselves, their suffering becomes our own and in this shared experience of the human tragedy that is our distinction we learn to discern, to be, our best selves. Indeed, in this sense, theater is eminently practical – a sister of two worthier sisters, politics and religion; it puts thought to work on the stage, thought in action, ideas for us to observe and know through the circumspect device of the drama; as we said, what the characters can only surmise who don't grasp the larger strands of the fate in which they are woven, we, the audience, realize; we become aware of what they can only guess at; we inhabit the realm outside of their world; located in the region of the spirits, we can see their lives through the eyes of friendlier skies. We enjoy their pain for what our commiseration in their tears makes evident to us about the nobility of our own human nature, namely that in this being of ours, in this quintessence of dust, we might feel the majesty of our essential and absolute freedom.

If Rousseau is the botanist of freedom who classified the forms of our nature, described, traced, for the first time, in a natural history, their development and clearly articulated the stations and features of humanity in an enlightening fable, marking their progression from human being's seed to bloom to fruit to seed again and Schiller, more specifically, the sublime theater of tragedy, is the pedagogue of human nature, our humanity, moving us to act in person and enact the idea with which the personae on the stage inspired our hearts as spectators, then Hölderlin's poetry, finally, will depict, enact, celebrate the poet of nature as the embodiment of her spirit, the spirit of her idea, conceived by Rousseau as a principle, demonstrated by Schiller as the experience of initial divergence from and ultimate reconciliation with our nature, an experience that is our complete human being, and finally brought to life in the person of the Poet in whom nature and reason are one pure being whose life is our life and reason's life and nature's life and whose vocation it is to celebrate with hymns this community of divine and human being that he calls *Fatherland*.

B. The Distinguished Life of Poetic Individuality

103. The Self-Several Unity of Poetic Spirit

Thought thinking thought is a being we observe in action, a work in progress – it is, of course, *just* an idea; but as such it is not yet what thought gazing at thought sees in itself, observes itself doing, celebrates itself and sings itself as having accomplished – thought, the Builder is none other than this poetic individual who not only observes thought at work and describes what it does, not only experiences what thought does by empathy, vicariously, as an observer of the protagonists' tragic action, but actually experiences thought as its own being, its own doing, its own making, thought being its own thought and life. This is the poetic individual – the inspired character of thought that makes sense of what it sees and does and creates, the distinguished entity of identity (Hölderlin, *Stuttgarter Ausgabe*

[StA], IV 251.27) in person. In its presence we are aware of a venerable subject becoming an object of our own reflection, reflecting upon ourselves, distinguishing ourselves in its eyes which are, in fact, our own eyes, the poetic I, looking upon Myself in the light of reason, in which we are Our self-knowing being. And what do I, do We, thus see? We see a line of poetic reasoning, a "red thread" (251.14), a train, of thought elaborated in the concrete details of the poem that give it its particular scope and sphere, demonstrate the presence of thought in the thing, impress the mark of mind in matter and the seal of the ideal into the real the complexion of which now speaks the thought, represents it in the outwardly, worldly turned language of particulars of time and place that poems are so full of and celebrate.

Poetic thought, i.e. the logotectonic Builder and productive genius, the imagination of the human spirit, that in the Third Epoch of occidental tradition brings forth its own visions of itself in Art, Religion, and Philosophy, are cognate. Their affinity lies in the achievements of realization – schemes, forms, articulations that make intangible ideas accessible to perception and insight, and thus, in turn, empowering and facilitating the theoretical endeavor of conception by providing that enterprise with issues and objects of reflection. Poetic genius takes on form in the works of its own creation, is the character of these works but, for that, no less a character *in* them as well; for pure reason is necessarily self-relative, is always self-knowing being. With Hölderlin, let us therefore consider these works of thought's realization, foremost of which is *philosophy*, as beginning and ending in *poetry*, (III 144.11-12)[63] and investigate now in detail how its characterization of the fruits of human spirit introduce a rich allegory of images that render articulate and palpable, in the grandeur of theory's epic vistas, in the dramatic crisis that marks the innate tragedy of human practice, and in the celebratory, lyrical realization of thought thinking thought having attained fulfilled presence in the complete works of human imagination, the productivity of the mind made manifest in terms of the experience of poetic individuality, i.e. the

---

[63] Passages from "Hyperion" are cited according to the enumeration adopted by Beißner in the third volume of his *GSA*.

poet's beautiful life, the poet's sacred craft and art, and, completing this vision of pure reason's identity, the poet's natural world.[64]

We begin with Hyperion's narrative, a tale of thought's "hyper" being and this being's experience with the transcendence, the "hyperbole" of poetic spirit; from this extraneous standpoint of reflection, remote in place and in time from home and his beloved own, long dead all, long left behind, long ago crumbled into piles of silent stones, in reflection upon all this former life and its fruitless course since, the narrator, alone and obscure, a death on his conscience, returns to these haunts of the mind to revisit, despite and because of transient moments of soulful reveries in remembrance of his former fatherland now long lying in ruins, the gap between THE WAY IT IS and THE WAY IT SHOULD BE, gathering his thoughts into the painful awareness of all he has lost and what he has done and become in utter estrangement from the surroundings in which he now subsists, and at the same time, rekindling the light of a vision, an ideal of happiness where it all began, where his heart once miraculously, immaculately, thrived, cradled in the "embrace of nature, in her constancy, her stillness, her beauty." (III 9.1)

Will she open her arms again to him as to a "kindred spirit such that the pain of solitude resolves itself in the life of deity? To be one with all there is – that is the life of *divine*, the heaven of *human* being; to be one with all life, soulfully self-forgotten to return to nature's all – that is the peak of all thought and joy, that is the mountain's holy crest, the dwelling of eternal peace, where the midday sun loses its glare, the thunder its rumbling growl, and the sea's turmoil is like amber waves of grain. To be one with all life! With these words virtue lays aside its angry armor, the human spirit its scepter, and all ruminations quieten before the vision of the ever-oneness of the world as do the controverting precepts of the artist's craft before his Urania and iron fate renounces upon its reign and, from the league of beings, death is banned and inseparability and eternal youth beautifies and sanctifies the world" (10.9-11.7)

> ...ein verwandter Geist mir die Arme öffnete, als löste der Schmerz der Einsamkeit sich auf ins Leben der Gottheit. Eines zu sein mit Allem, das ist Leben der Gottheit, das ist der Himmel des Menschen. Eines zu sein mit Allem, was lebt, in seliger

---

[64] cf. Boeder's treatment of Hölderlin in *Die conceptuale Vernunft in der Letzten Epoche der Metaphysik* in "Abhandlungen der Brauschweigischen Wissenschaftlichen Gesellschaft" XLIII. p. 356-359.

Selbstvergessenheit wiederzukehren ins All der Natur, das ist
der Gipfel der Gedanken und Freuden, das ist die heilige
Bergeshöhe, der Ort der ewigen Ruhe, wo der Mittag seine
Schwüle und der Donner seine Stimme verliert und das
kochende Meer der Woge des Kornfelds gleicht. Eines zu sein
mit Allem, was lebt! Mit diesem Worte legt die Tugend den
zürnenden Harnisch, der Geist des Menschen den Zepter weg,
und alle Gedanken schwinden vor dem Bilde der ewigeinigen
Welt, wie die Regeln des ringenden Künstlers vor seiner Urania,
und das eherne Schicksal entsagt der Herrschaft, und aus dem
Bunde der Wesen schwindet der Tod, und Unzertrennlichkeit
und ewige Jugend beseliget, verschönert die Welt.

Yes, she, youth, will and does but, alas, all too transiently in a brief flight
of rapture; a moment's reflection and all is naught; thanks to our schools of
rote and the petty insularity of our scientific endeavors in which we, in the
foolish zest of our salad days, had hoped to find confirmation for the purest
joys of the mind, we tumble and fall, pitched by its experts from this zenith
of our heart's highest heights into the cavernous shaft of our moribund
Man. For then, having become oh so sensible, clinical, intellectual, cynical,
ousted from that universal garden that was "our soul's asylum, the ever
oneness of the world, is lost; nature folds her arms and we stand like
strangers before her, in incomprehension....oh, human being is truly a god
when dreaming, when cogitating a beggar, and, when enthusiasm dies, like
a son disowned..." (11.11-12.5)

...meines Herzens Asyl, die ewigeinige Welt, ist hin; die Natur
verschließt die Arme, und ich stehe, wie ein Fremdling, vor ihr,
und verstehe sie nicht...O ein Gott ist der Mensch, wenn er
träumt, ein Bettler, wenn er nachdenkt, und wenn Begeisterung
hin ist steht er da, wie ein misrathener Sohn...

But beyond the effervescence of a dream, further, deeper, remember
youth and recall the simplicity of our former life, free from laws' yokes and
fate's whips, a state not of anarchy but rather nature, namely the state of
beauty, that pristine estate of heavenly peace and quiet that reigned over
the wholesome freedom of our paradisiacal childhood; at this prelapsarian,
antediluvian, golden age, the first of reason's career, human being, having
not yet broken with itself, in itself, and from itself, lived a life of both
immortal being – unaware of death and the humiliating finitude that
impedes desire, as well as innocent being – as yet unencumbered by those
damned ideas of distinction destined to inundate us in the surge and tidal
wave of reflection and recollection, and dwelt prehistorically, primordially

alive, asleep in the richness of nature's own life, in the state of pre-existence of which we, of necessity, have no concept and yet cannot fail to wonder if, in this abode of being before, of precedent peace and perambulatory stillness, "knowing nothing about what surrounded us, we were not then more *there* than now, post the heartache's floods, post the travail, the turmoil of minding" (13.4-6) that is the destiny of human self-severalty?

And from this recline and lovely slumber under the sheltering bough, under the serene eye of sun and the sky, the tender soul, in due course, joyfully springs to spirit from the inward earth at the behest of a mind both great and kind, pacific and colossal, champion and contestant, benevolent and wise, of human magnanimity in the person of a guide and teacher whose light we must flee or to whom aspire, one or the other, decisively (18.6-7), thought, the Tutor of "unmitigated enthusiasm. In her omnipotence, enthusiasm does not tarry on the surface, does not seize us casually, needs neither time nor means, wields neither imperative to force nor wheedles to persuade; she lays hold of us from all directions, in all the depths and heights of our immediacy and transforms us in her beauty and her bliss before we even had the chance to become aware of her and question how. (20.7-13)

> ...die Allmacht der ungeteilten Begeisterung. Sie weilt nicht auf der Oberfläche, faßt nicht da und dort uns an, braucht keiner Zeit und keines Mittels; Gebot und Zwang und Überredung braucht sie nicht; auf allen Seiten, in allen Tiefen und Höhen ergreift sie im Augenblick uns, und wandelt, ehe sie da ist für uns, ehe wir fragen, wie uns geschiehet, durch und durch in ihre Schönheit, ihre Seligkeit uns um.

But our study of nature's rhythms and our learning of her measures and her figures, our acquaintance with the glorious proportions that immortalized the heroes of antiquity, though this natural and cultural history affords our youthful impetuosity an ordering and soothing influence, nevertheless, the very sharpening of discernment and discrimination that is its consequence give rise to the admonishing insight that along with "the life of spring and the ever youthful sun, the distinguished nature of human being was once brightly alive in all of its glory but now defunct and hardly ever heard of these days except in the ruins of a temple or in commemoration of the dead." (22.1-5)

> das Leben des Frühlings und die ewig jugendliche Sonne uns mahnte, daß auch der Mensch einst da war, und nun dahin ist, daß des Menschen herrliche Natur jetzt kaum noch da ist, wie

das Bruchstück eines Tempels oder im Gedächtnis, wie ein
Totenbild.

And still the sun rises effortlessly, majestically in the morning, as he, that
immortal Titan, invested with his host of joys, always has, while we, there
upon a mountain top, having awaited his return since the first glow of dawn,
are reminded, rejuvenated, and, thus inspired, linking our fate to his, are
ourselves uplifted and transported by his transcendent course to the peak
of empyrean, where he then, friendly and grand, smiles down upon the
waste land of our world and wonderfully replenishes it with his refulgent
power and spirit – may we not be as he is? (24.5)

No, we may not, except in the briefest moments of passing. But why? It is
our love, our need that, in spite of our certainty that "all is within us," binds
us to servitude who were born to be gods. "We cannot endure being alone.
This is our inveterate poverty in the midst of bounty – love...," the bond of
human being to all who belong to us and to whom we belong "...refuses to
die in us as long as we live." (25.1-3) And yet bound to our time and our
place and our people, we are strangers to them by the very same heart and
love, we who aspire to spirit, who foster company with the sun and
friendship with those heroes of old whose immortal glory we were born to
emulate, to strive for and attain and in whose name we would gladly shake
off what our century gave us in order that we may start out fresh upon our
journey towards the freer realm of shadows they inhabit. (30.11-15) To be
of two minds and two hearts, one heart torn by two loves, cleft in twain by
loves both human and divine – the solution to this dilemma is, or course, as
Schiller taught, the artful moderation of harmonious opposition – each
extreme tempers, qualifies, neither excludes the other, but rather, by
stepping back in critical distance to both, comprehends and endures the
opposing tendency, soothing and alleviating the other by dint of its own
patience, meticulously avoiding both failed states of extremes that might
have precipitously ensued, namely the isolation of mutual withdrawal into
solitude that annihilates the reciprocal efficacy of their rapport as well as
the promiscuity in which, speaking and acting against the other as against
their own, they miss the distinction that the other has made and that might
have served as reflection's point of departure or else, in having merely
assimilated themselves to their combatant's animus, they only duplicate
the other's extremist bent as an extension of their own from which they,
however, had meant to purify themselves in the checks and balances, the
chemistry, of their collaboration. In both cases, they accomplish nothing
and must perish either dissipating with all their pleas and pain-staking into
the thin air of blank, unaccompanied, unexamined desolation or, by each

becoming too subservient to the other's outlandish oddity and flagrancy, choking on itself. (IV 236.21)

Hölderlin develops this train of thought regarding the harmoniously opposed being that is our true nature in the conception of the self-several relationship as the "...reason why our Man leaves its shell and the rule governing our human being's dissilience..." – the logic of our poetic individuality – as a progression of self-realization and that we have rendered below as a series of distinctions founded upon the process of critical reflection that throughout the Third Epoch we have traced as that of the course that the self-determination of humanity, departing from itself, takes, making its way in the external world towards the completion of the destiny of human being. *Figure 65* shows "...the fact of our freely setting ourselves in harmonious opposition to an outer sphere that we, precisely because we are not so intimately tied to it, are able to abstract ourselves from..." (257.5-12)

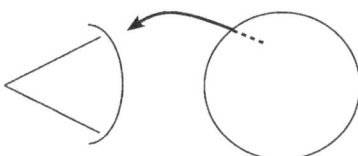

Figure 65: The Harmonious Opposition of Distinction (A)

"...and from ourselves to the extent that we are also posited in it..." (*Figure 66*)

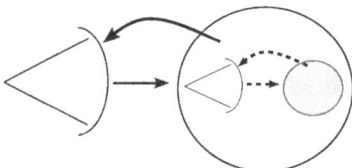

Figure 66: The Self-Severalty of Distinction (C)

"...and reflect upon ourselves to the extent that we are not posited in it..." (*Figure 67*)

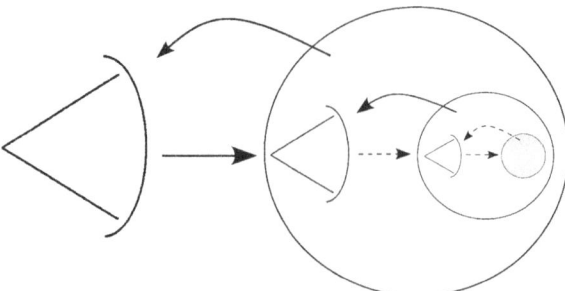

Figure 67: The Harmonious Opposition of Critical Self-Reflection (B)

> Der Zustand, wo sich der Mensch mit einer äußern Sphäre,
> durch freie Wahl in harmonische Entgegensetzung setzt, daß er,
> eben weil er mit dieser nicht so innig verbunden ist, von dieser
> abstrahieren und von sich, insofern er in ihr gesetzt ist, und auf
> sich reflektieren kann, insofern er nicht in ihr gesetzt ist, dies ist
> der Grund, warum er aus sich herausgeht, dies die Regel für
> seine Verfahrungsart in der äußern Welt.

The three *Figures 65-67* define the threefold nature and unity, render explicit the actual sense and the character of self-knowing poetic individuality, namely its knowing being (A), the being thus known (B) and the knowledge or insight itself (C) achieved in a series of acts, i.e. that act of abstraction and opposition on the one hand, depicted above in the form of a centrifugal arrow, and reflection and unification on the other hand, depicted as a centripetal arrow. In this way a comprehensive thought, insight, is seen to consist of a trinity of thoughts, collected into the progressive phases and epochs of an harmoniously opposed being (A), endowed with the tendency towards disparity, contrariety, and divergence (C) as well as unity, agreement, and coincidence (B) such that neither tendency is obviated by the other, sameness by difference, turn by return, and vice versa but rather all collaborate in distinguishing that living entity of identity, that charmed and charming life, so long the object of our regard and concern and called by Hölderlin "the identity of enthusiasm, the completion of genius and art, the present of infinity, the divine moment." (251.27-29)

How could this being be *in real life*, since its double imperative, comprising that of both the self-reflective thinker and the abstract thought, puts its self-several being at odds with mere being and therefore can only be given ideal life in the poetry of the imagination, in the words and deeds of characters and events upon the scene and stage of thought in a train of thought that language provides and narratives unfold in the epic history that is the heroic tale of wisdom, the tragic but hopeful and sustained – upheld and ultimately celebratory – vision of the distinction of human being? Thus in Hyperion's tale, for example.

It cannot be, it is – this is precisely the reason why we step back in self-several abstraction, this is also our rule in turning towards the outer world and "it is in this way that we ultimately fulfill our destiny which consists in the comprehension of the unity and individuality of harmoniously opposed being *in* human being, and then again, the identity, unity and individuality of human being *in* harmoniously opposed being. This is the true freedom of our being and when we are neither all too attached to the outward harmoniously opposed sphere, avoiding the confluence with it that we have with our own identity and that makes distinguishing ourselves from it so utterly impossible, nor again all too attached to ourselves in our abstract independence and therein too little able to distinguish ourselves from ourselves, when we reflect neither too much upon ourselves nor too much upon our sphere and time, then we are properly on the way of our destiny." (257.13-23)

> Auf diese Art erreicht er seine Bestimmung, welche ist - Erkenntnis des Harmonischentgegengesetzten in ihm, in seiner Einheit und Individualität, und hinwiederum Erkenntnis seiner Identität, seiner Einheit und Individualität im Harmonischentgegengesetzten. Dies ist die wahre Freiheit seines Wesens, und wenn er an dieser äußerlichen harmonischentgegengesetzten Sphäre nicht zu sehr hängt, nicht identisch mit ihr wird, wie mit sich selbst, so daß er nimmer von ihr abstrahieren kann, noch auch zu sehr an sich sich hängt, und von sich als Unabhängigem zu wenig abstrahieren kann, wenn er weder auf sich zu sehr reflektiert, noch auf seine Sphäre und Zeit zu sehr reflektiert, dann ist er auf dem rechten Wege seiner Bestimmung.

Let's face it: Self-knowing being – living it on a daily basis – seems to be "practically" impossible. To know yourself, you must see yourself and be thus an object to yourself; but if you are an object to yourself, seen, how can you be the subject, seeing, as well, without being, as this seeing being, a different object than the one seen, the seen being? Or is this just a quibble? Honestly, it sounds suspiciously picayune, does it not?

Being active in seeking insight contradicts the passiveness of receiving the object; if you step back from yourself to know and grasp yourself then in attaining this standpoint of abstraction you are no longer yourself in the flesh but rather have been attenuated unto a hyperbolic object and estranged yourself, this object thought, from this thinker – indeed there does now seem to be two rather than one, whereas knowing ourselves as one was the original aim. Do you not annihilate yourself by stepping back from yourself, no longer being one with yourself and now, being two, are you not patently different from the *casual you* who was really just one and the same before the *distinguished You* decided to know thyself and, at that fateful moment of your You-turn, to enter upon the infinite ordeal of thought for evermore? That intimate connection in the "default" mode of the mind must have been torn, fissured, our egghead cracked and replaced by that scrambled, denatured self-sublation of a being that only succeeds at knowing itself when it is no longer itself.

But what is this result of our train of thought? Have we thus gone astray and lost what we had sought in the very looking? Losing in the finding, failing precisely in and through the achievement of our success? By thinking about thought, mutilating, decimating thought? Must we surrender our simple *being* for the sake of *having* our being before us? We who would fain eat our cake and have it, too.

For, on the other hand, if you maintain your unity and resist the drive of insight to establish the vantage point and critical distance necessary for the sight and light of contemplation, if insight wants difference which requires freedom and abstraction, extremes towards which thought strives, ultimately unto self-abnegation, what good is reflection, what good is thought if it annihilates thought, if the abstraction of theory destroys the unity of the object it intended to study, namely thought, which, therefore, ought much rather to strive to overcome its analytical, abstracting, and discriminating tendency and, in striving and aiming thus to be unthought, to only more completely and hopelessly, more abysmally miss and miscarry.

It would seem therefore that the unity of the mind repulses discernment although it is precisely the differentiating intellect that we, thus troubled in our minds, must rely on to grasp this unity and that, again, the discriminating mind abhors unity although this property is the entire object of its searching gaze.

Is there no escaping this invidious conclusion and, once having set off on such a tendentious tour, train, flight, a veritable vacation, of thought, to account for and countermand Man's reason's often noted, manifold, and apparently foreordained proclivity for digging its own grave?

The essential point is that this line of reasoning can itself become an object of thought, just one more thought, the mind's discernment and its unity must, in turn, become the object of self-reflection, an object in the sphere of which we can be trapped or not, simply choosing not to be, and with regards to which, in turn, we stand apart and above and back from critically, though not so far as to fall back into the same thought, regressing again in our efforts of abstraction, to reenter that antimony's maze, the double bind that is ratiocination's last straw and horizon through which logic lures logic into the autophagous shame and scorn of thought worrying thought, thought gnawing upon itself as upon the bone of contention to which the distinction of human being is often reduced. As Hölderlin explains: "the essential point is that thought does not remain merely in reciprocal relationship with its own nature from which it cannot abstract itself without disintegrating itself, but rather that it freely chooses its object from which it can then, if it will, distinguish itself in order that it may be suitably determined by and determine its object...subjective life only attains to free individuality, unity and identity in itself through the choice of its object." (254.29-38)

> Alles kommt also darauf an, daß das Ich nicht bloß mit seiner subjektiven Natur, von der es nicht abstrahieren kann, ohne sich aufzuheben, in Wechselwirkung bleibe, sondern daß es sich mit Freiheit ein Objekt wähle, von dem es, wenn es will, abstrahieren kann, um von diesem durchaus angemessen bestimmt zu werden und es zu bestimmen... Zur freien Individualität, zur Einheit und Identität in sich selbst gebracht wird das reine subjektive Leben erst durch die Wahl seines Gegenstands.

In this way, the artist's, it is neither with ourselves and in ourselves that we are to become entangled and trapped, in the vanity and vacuity of the self-centered spirit, measuring all but itself; nor are we content to be entirely and permanently absorbed by the spissitude of our world that the spirit of gravity coagulates into gravy concretion; neither lost in space nor set in stone, neither disconnected nor compacted. Neither – nor? No, even this intermediary state that has emerged as a hiatus "between that original natural connectedness with our natural world and that higher connectedness with a natural world that, in contrast to the former, we have freely chosen as our own sphere, a world foreknown in our conception of it the influences of which in their entirety, in accordance with and not in opposition to our will, determine us – this interval between childhood and mature humanity, between mechanical beauty and human beauty, beauty and freedom" (255.13-20) is not our destiny; this recess of thought is but an interlude of indecision, the absolute contrariety of aims and drives towards the unity and identity, towards distinction and discrimination, towards that elusive ratio and proportion of these immediately conflicted forces and tendencies of the mind.

Finding our heart torn by the inner strife of contradictory and insatiable impulses, do we regress in resignation to that prior state of indiscriminate infancy or else exhaust ourselves in that fruitless contention of intentions? The question must arise as to how to emerge from this solitude and wretchedness of altercation that distinguished human being is destined to experience. "How to be free as the bloom of youth yet live in the world as a child, combine the artful independence of mature humanity with the native accommodation of human simplicity?" (255.30-32)

The hyperbole of the reclusive mind, i.e. the exaggerating eccentricity of its superabundant power to abound beyond all bounds even unto the detachment and seclusion of self-cocooning sequestration, having long left the first oblivion of its pacific life behind, must step back yet again, such that "the poetic spirit, in its final and boldest attempt yet, tries, in the hyperbole of all hyperboles, to comprehend original poetic individuality, the poetic entity of identity itself, by giving itself an outer object through which this pure poetic individuality, in concert with several particular poetic characters that it may take up, none of which are merely opposing nor merely relating, is provided with the determination to adopt one so that through the chosen materiality that it and the others bestow upon pure poetic individuality and its character, the latter can finally be grasped and, in freedom, held fast." (252.24-31)

> ...so ist ein äußeres Objekt notwendig und zwar ein solches, wodurch die reine Individualität, unter mehreren besondern weder bloß entgegensetzenden, noch bloß beziehenden, sondern poetischen Charakteren, die sie annehmen kann, irgend Einen anzunehmen bestimmt werde, so daß also sowohl an der reinen Individualität, als an den andern Charakteren, die jetzt gewählte Individualität und ihr durch den jetzt gewählten Stoff bestimmter Charakter erkennbar und mit Freiheit festzuhalten ist.

Only in this chosen material that poetic individuality has taken upon itself can it find and grasp itself as a unity, being both contained in and determined by the deity of harmoniously opposed being that is pure reason and the objective entity of identity under which we serve, as well as containing and encompassing this harmoniously opposed unity and deity within itself as our subjective being, the distinguished spirit that is our destiny and to which we aspire. If however we seek to attain our "...destiny in an all too subjective or all too objective state then we do so in vain...it is only accessible to our experience in the spirit of beauty, in the spirit of sanctity, in the spirit of divinity, a spirit called **beautiful** because it is neither merely *pleasant and blissful* nor merely *sublime and strong*, nor merely *concordant and calm* but rather uniquely all in one; a spirit called **holy** because it has neither merely selflessly *surrendered itself to its object*, nor selflessly *reposed itself upon its inward nature*, nor selflessly *suspended itself between its subjective and its objective natures* but is, rather, uniquely one and all three; a spirit called **divine** because it is neither mere *sentience*, mere thought (subjective or objective) with loss of inner or outer life, nor mere *desire* (of subjective or objective determinacy) with the loss of inner or outer harmony, nor mere concordance, like an ideal of the imagination and its mythical, visionary subject-object with the loss of discernment and unity but rather uniquely all three in one..." (259.1-21)

This experience can be said to be one of the spirit of ***transcendence*** (22) because of the way these several properties, the trinity of the mind's forces, have come thus into focus, as being both unified and distinguished by it, each not only abstracting from but also completing the other, in a chain of exchanges that permits none to relapse into the extremism of a unilateral determination to which every principle is, apparently, susceptible when left to its own devices in seclusion and exclusion of all the others – the perversion of our hyperbolic spirit, which, only in being harmoniously opposed and, in this sense, self-transcendent, exhibits its unifying, reciprocal properties, its forces, its lives, the life of poetic individuality, that is "neither too pleasure-oriented and physical, nor too vehement and unbridled, nor too inwardly-turned and fanatical, nor too self-obliviously engrossed in its object, nor too selfishly self-centered upon its inward motive, nor too indecisive and indeterminate, hanging in empty suspense between an inward impetus and an outward object, neither too sharply and exclusively self-aware and thus unaware of impulses from abroad, be they of inner or outer provenance, nor too moved, all too taken by impulses from abroad, be they of inner or outer provenance and therefore unaware of the harmony of the inner and the outer, nor too concordant and therefore too little aware of itself and of those inner and outward impulses, hence too indeterminate and too little, too briefly receptive to the infinite which, recognized as impinging upon this spirit from outside its scope and horizon acquires through it the determinacy of a particular infinite being." (259.24-260.4)

Thus for example, even as the emergence, the birth and rise of youth's assurance, knowing itself as the new and young and as inhabiting thus the realm of possibility, tomorrow's world, is the surcease of the determinate and fixed state of things as they are today, the established reality and older individuality, which is the fall and degeneration of the former fatherland and prior unity, so also may we, on the other hand, grasp the end of our childhood and the "surcease of its primal and original ideal-individuality and purity not as its weakness and death but rather its fulfilment, its blossoming and growth: similarly, we will see in the cessation of the detachment and the abstraction of the *infinite-new* not annihilating force but rather love; for it is love that leads the hyperbolic spirit, *infinitely-new*, back to the world in the form of the *finitely-old*, by separating itself from the infinite-presence of immensity, even as it was love that lifted us in the finitude of our *individual-old* being and uplifted us, in the first place, in our striving to embrace the generality, the life-encompassing feeling of *real-infinity* and then to unify it with our own *ideal-individuality*. The unity of both the ideal-individual and the real-infinity of the infinitely new is a transcendent creative act the essence of which is to unify them such that *infinite reality* takes on the form of *ideal individuality* while the latter in turn takes on the life of infinite real unifying both in a mythical state of accord between the *infinite real* and the *finite ideal*, where, with their opposition, transition ends as well, a state in which the *finite ideal* finds its peace even as the *infinite real* finds life." (286.2-13)

This distinguishing spirit that is the destiny of human being is not some fate or curse laid upon the head of Man by an evil hybrid sprite – "it is of our own doing, it is us! We take pleasure in throwing ourselves into the gloom of the unknown, the cold strangeness of other worlds and if we could we would leave the sun-drenched region and storm out beyond the furthest extremity of sideral divagation. For Man's wild heart, there is no possible home and just as the plants of the earth are singed by the very sun that nurtured their blossom's unfolding, so likewise Man kills the sweet flowers that flourished on his bosom, kills the joys of his relations and of his love..." (III 1.25.7-15). It is the "immensity of our yearning to be all...and yet who would not prefer to feel in oneself the utter immensity of Man's desire, highest hopes, impossible dreams to be all and end all, like boiling oil, than to admit to ourselves that we were born for the whip and the yoke?" (27.14-28.1)

Aber sage nur niemand, daß uns das Schicksal trenne! Wir sinds, wir! wir haben unsre Lust daran, uns in die Nacht des Unbekannten, in die kalte Fremde irgend einer andern Welt zu stürzen, und, wär es möglich, wir verließen der Sonne Gebiet und stürmten über des Irrsterns Grenzen hinaus. Ach! für des Menschen wilde Brust ist keine Heimat möglich; und wie der Sonne Strahl die Pflanzen der Erde, die er entfaltete, wieder versengt, so tötet der Mensch die süßen Blumen, die an seiner Brust gedeihten, die Freuden der Verwandtschaft und der Liebe...das ungeheure Streben, Alles zu sein...Und doch, wer wollt es nicht lieber in sich fühlen, wie ein siedend Öl, als sich gestehn, er sei für die Geißel und fürs Joch geboren?

104. The Life Story of Poetic Spirit

And so our poetic spirit who began life on the blessed isles of childhood, encouraged and guided by a teacher, sets out at last to seek his fortunes in the world at large, to elaborate the depth and the breadth of our mind in departure from the hitherto in-folded unity of our youth; and we step forth into the abstract air of our human distinction, like a second birthday and a second passage thither after the first passing away of infancy, quick and nimbly into a new sun, upon a new sea, enjoying the self-knowing peace, newly found in this new morning of our first reflection and in memory of the youthful spirit that made of the moment a paradise of richness and a banquet where, flitting from beauty to beauty, the reborn reveler, our Hyperion, that we have become, could eat and drink his full of joy in nature's beauty, contemplating with amusement the potpourri of human customs from our vantage point of distinction above and beyond them, enjoying the burlesque absurdity of all their forms and usages in their quaintness like so many Mardi Gras costumes we might don or doff (III 1.34-35), buoyed by an inspiration that can fill even the inevitable lacunae that mar human life, exhilarate the sappy despondency, mitigate the cheek and gall of sarcasm, the disdain of conceit and witty pretension with which a glad heart is cut by cool contemporaries and posturing peers until, finally scorn worn, our reborn soul withdraws from this company into insignificance and we lock into a hurt heart that treasure of beauty that is our young mind's spring, "hoping against hope that one day in the future the one and only, the holy and true object of the thirsting soul will greet us," (38.4-6) namely a true companion, a brother in arms, strong in doing the hero's work of our accomplished human distinction.

After *Adamas*, the teacher of Hyperion's first youth in his state of awakening, Hyperion meets *Alabanda*, the fiery young titan and a strict, terrible accuser (45.5), who names with words of thunder our dwarfish century's faults and failings and for whose "eyes the scope of the skies seemed to be too narrow" (40.8-9), born to do deeds of pith and moment that will purify our little earth from the dross of Man's barbarity and fawning inanity and win renown among a people thus figured anew, in him, Fatherland prefigured (49.16). Like Hyperion, Alabanda is a stranger among his own home, a soul of distinction like him destined to lift his heart to the heavens and implore: "O holy light, that so restlessly reigns in the immensity of its realm, riding on high above us and whose soul communicates to me in the beams that I imbibe – may your bliss be mine! By their own great deeds do the sons of the sun nourish themselves..." as do the daughters of the waters, as do all those "...who live upon victory, who with their own spirit inspire themselves and for whom their strength is their joy" (49.3-9) and not that narcosis and full-bellied satiety that lulls a lolling tongue abed a mound of mush in the mouth of the morning that we are otherwise so idiotically apt to cash our crowns of laurel and our immortality in for.

But the vehemence of this spirit, sweeping aside with its intemperate zeal all doubt and qualification, all distinctions, gravitating thus by degrees to perfervidness, darkens the pure "inspiration of enthusiasm, that heavenly rain that cannot be ordained by decree of governing might and main but rather must be patiently awaited until with omnipotent bliss its golden clouds shall encompass us and carry us on high beyond all mortality, reanimating the people's spring" (54.3-9); alas, even this pure enthusiasm is liable to darken to the aberration of extremism and begins to preach viciousness: "That god in us to which the path of infinity beckons should now stand and wait till the worm gets out of his way? No, no! We don't ask whether you will; you never will, you slaves and barbarians; nor do we fain reform you – it would be futile – we simply wish to make sure that you get out of the way of humanity's victorious course. Oh ignite me a torch that I may incinerate the weeds on the heath, ready me the quarry that I may blast the sluggish clods out of the earth!" (48.4-11)

What tone is here being blared? Do we not recognize the jargon of the uncompromising radical, the fanatic? Shall we, dark knights, nameless conspirators in the secret order of our cave Man's nemesis, at the twilight of our dying days, gaunt and pale from slaughter, hearts hardened, our lips curved with contempt, found our Fatherland upon the still ruins of palaces, upon the silence of a field burned to the roots and plowed in the dead volcano's ash? (cf. 55.18-56.5)

No! Hyperion's instinct is true as he recoils from these weird masks and cries "as one choking on smoke, smashing door and window to get out" of their cave, "hungry for air and freedom: They are swindlers!" (59.11)

Poetic individuality, in contrast, imagines that its Fatherland, namely "time's favorite, his youngest and most beautiful daughter, this new church will arise" of its own accord, "from the tainted, old-fashioned forms when the awakened sense for the divine has brought back to our human being its deity and to our breast the beauty of youth." (54.10-14) And it is precisely this awakening of sense that is the vocation of thought, the Builder and poet whose craft and art devises majestic poetry to inspire and encourage folks to consider the life and times of "the still and steady spirit of nature and her pure children." (72.1)

At this juncture, Hyperion and the contemplative spirit of the ideal, part company with Alabanda and the energetic spirit of the hero – they were two kindred, brethren spirits, of common origin; in them, each endowment of the mind was poised in parity and harmoniously opposed to the other till, alas, the delicate temper of their rapport goes awry, our heart's distinguished enthusiasm cleft in twain and thus twice perverted – the former, the fiery Doer and Achiever, succumbing to the deformity of bigoted zealotry, the latter, the airy, ethereal Dreamer to the infirmity of abstracted anaesthesia and ennui "the stifling and utter amnesia of being, like a night of our soul having lost all in which not even a single star gleams..." with its own form of annihilation "... Oh you wretched...you who are loathe to speak of the destiny of human being, how thoroughly permeated you are from the nullity that reigns above us, so entirely cognizant of the fact that we are born to naught, love naught, believe in naught, break our backs for naught, only to gradually pass away into naught at the end... I drop to my knees, wring my hands, plead and beg to I don't know whom for other thoughts but I cannot shout down the shriek of this truth." (78.11-79.8)

> O ihr Armen, die ihr das fühlt, die ihr auch nicht sprechen mögt von menschlicher Bestimmung, die ihr auch so durch und durch ergriffen seid vom Nichts, das über uns waltet, so gründlich einseht, daß wir geboren werden für Nichts, daß wir lieben ein Nichts, glauben ans Nichts, uns abarbeiten für Nichts, um mählich überzugehen ins Nichts...O! auf die Knie kann ich mich werfen und meine Hände ringen und flehen, ich weiß nicht wen?

um andre Gedanken. Aber ich überwältige sie nicht, die
schreiende Wahrheit.

But these dark days and the season of our mind's discontent, though they
lead us onto the verge of despair, anticipate the turn of thought's spring and
the distinction of a rejuvenated sense that must of necessity follow in the
measured course of the year of our soul. For even as we are estranged from
ourselves and our world and the gap between THE WAY IT IS and THE WAY
IT SHOULD BE has become our abysmal habitat, we may now develop our
rapport with that previous state of nature that engendered and nurtured the
infancy of the mind yet immersed; for in the acute hyperbole of its
newfound distinguished sensibility, in the state of reflection upon its dearth
in contrast to nature's plenitude, we meet her face to face, for the first time,
Diotima, "the divine and holy being, the free, the youthful, the living beauty
of nature" (73.9) in person. This is the third experience that poetic
individuality makes with the distinction of human being – the experience of
this distinction as love.

This kinder spirit, the breathing stillness of its sweet life, the tranquillity of
nature's beauty, its divine peace, soothes the soul thus torn in two, consoles
us who whose lords are fear and need, who are wilted and wizened, fallen
leaves, strewn, windblown; prone in the dumb, deadened silence of our
lives' wasteland, in the thirst and dearth of our finitude, poor and solitary,
netherwards, like "diamonds in a shaft (92.11)," we nevertheless take heart
"for there are hours when the best and the most beautiful, as in clouds,
appears and the skies of perfection open to love's intimation...that we might
become again like children, that the golden age of our innocence might
recur, the time of peace and freedom, that there remains one bliss and
resting place on earth...where our spring returns...these moments of
emancipation, where the divine explodes our dungeon, where the spark of
flame is freed from the wood to arc victoriously up and over the ash, where
it is as if the unfettered spirit, forgetting its umbrage and impoverishment,
returned triumphant into the halls of the sun." (90.17-93.3).

Thus do we, once from her departed, now take part in her; the beauty that
we were a part of in the state of simple being is now the beauty of divine
peace (90.14) that we have before us in the state of recognition and nature
whose maternal earth once nurtured our passive innocence, stands now
before our reverence in her unaffected glory the pure spirit of which inspires
our worship and our service who are her pupils, become docile in love, as
well as her priests and prophets for the sake of the people for whom the
heavens, once a city of gods, has become a ghost town even as "the earth,
once flourishing with the harmonious life of humanity has all but degraded

into an anthill" (156.6-7), a teeming hive of busy bodies, but who however, ultimately, through her servants, the teachers of the people (159.20), are destined to be transformed, rejuvenating nature in return and, in this matrimony of beauty between *humanity* and *nature,* by their union mutually renewed, consecrated as the individual spirits of Fatherland under the aegis of one comprehensive deity: "do you, Nature enquire about human being?...They will come, your people, Nature! A rejuvenated people will rejuvenate you and you will be like its bride and the ancient union of spirits will renew itself with you. There will be but one unique beauty; and humanity and nature will be united in one all-encompassing divinity." (160.15-22)

> Du fragst nach Menschen, Natur?...Sie werden kommen, deine Menschen, Natur! Ein verjüngtes Volk wird dich auch wieder verjüngen, und du wirst werden, wie seine Braut und der alte Bund der Geister wird sich erneuen mit dir. Es wird nur Eine Schönheit sein; und Menschheit und Natur wird sich vereinen in Eine allumfassende Gottheit.

No, all the gods of Heaven and all humanity of earth may not be forgotten in our contemplation of nature's native beauty as if we now retired to her blessed isles. She herself exhorts us: "will you lock yourself into the heaven of your love and let the world that needs you dry up and freeze beneath you? You must descend like a beam of light and the all-refreshing rain into the nether regions of mortality; you must illuminate like Apollo, shock, enliven, like Jupiter, for otherwise you are not worthy of your heaven." (157.10-15)

Pupil first, but then priest, the determined teacher of thought's distinguished engagement in the betterment of our being, the warning prophet whose words and deeds challenge and contest our ways and days and brings change to our lives by constantly reminding us of and recalling the destiny of human being – our poet, thought, the Builder stands upon the cold, dry ruins of our spirit's winter and heralds the coming of the rain and of that renewed and renewing principle of beauty in which nature and humanity, the world and the self, life and spirit (IV 262.15-16), the material and formal (262.6) unite once more in one comprehensive entity of identity. This seizing of and being seized by one's vocation is the teacher's joy and satisfaction; this inspired enthusiasm is the resonate interval "between resolution and deed,...the spirited peace before the victory; this is the hero's quiet, like the words of gods, command and fulfillment in one" (III 160.2-5), for such are the heroic poet's words whose language and wisdom are speech acts of pure reason.

Pupil, prophet, but ultimately her poet. For where the teacher's edification must ultimately fail in practice, i.e. failing to realize the ideal – "failing to end the eternal contradiction between our self and the world and bring back the peace of all peace, the blissful unity of pure being, that is higher than all thought...but that we, neither in our knowledge nor in our action, can attain in any period of our lives, the surcease of conflict where all is one," (236.24-31) – and yet even in this failing succeeding because in this way sustaining our striving towards the "EN KAI PAN" (236.17) of nature, that "blissful instinct..." from which the ineluctable fate and force of our "...human spirit,..." high and pure in the exuberance of its regime, "tore us loose" (199.6-7) – but ultimately failing thus as the teacher and the preacher of beauty, thought, the Builder of beauty, will prevail in works, creating, recreating in language, giving life to an otherwise abstract spirit, that former infant life of golden innocence originally felt and subsequently lost but, in art's buildings, bodied forth again more lovely than before, for now known and renewed in a particular sphere of discourse, achieving presence in song in which the reality of reason becomes articulate, melodious sentiment, the concretely spoken language of our lives, for which the saying is the being and having been said, no sooner, done, quite and entirely felt as it was originally felt, "the infinite life of spirit reanimated, not bliss, nor ideal but rather completed work and creation" (262.23-24) that thought, the Builder makes of matters, having plucked them from the obscurity of their patent presence, borrowing them for the sake of the poem, to signify the harmoniously opposed tones and moods of the mind that, becoming tangible shape and act, dramatic character and figure, imbues its material with patterns of dissonance, harmonies of bright and quiet, haste and amble, station and course – this is the kingdom awaiting poetic individuality, the one true realm and home of human being in which "beauty is the queen." (237.6)

Thus poetic individuality, reliving in its narrative the entirety of its life, recovers the sense of the whole story that consists of constant rise and fall, the increase and surcease, the opening and the closing, the out and back, the turn and return of the soul (65.8-10); "or regard the sea and consider the story of your life, the rhythms of its rising and falling, of its bliss and sorrow...," – are its music, are these melodies, not "...a euphony of notes in which the maestro, composing quarrel and unanimity in accordance with a hidden order, runs through all the scales?" (84.5-9) If the life of the world evolves in a proportion of flourishing and languish, why not the heart of human being and the annals of its history "on this mediocre star" (99.13-14), the turn and return to ourselves that is pure reason's life and our experience of the distinction of human being? And so, in the mature conception of our profession as thinking beings, we recognize the object of poetic invention, the task awaiting our building:

> Beständigkeit haben die Sterne gewählt, in stiller Lebensfülle wallen sie stets und kennen das Alter nicht. Wir stellen im Wechsel das Vollendete dar; in wandelnde Melodien teilen wir die großen Akkorde der Freude. Wie Harfenspieler um die Thronen der Ältesten, leben wir, selbst göttlich, um die stillen Götter der Welt, mit dem flüchtigen Lebensliede mildern wir den seligen Ernst des Sonnengotts und der andern. (103.12-18)

> *The stars have chosen constancy; in the still plenitude of life, they revolve perpetually and know neither age nor epoch. We however represent perfection in alternating determinations; in wandering melodies do we share in the great chords of joy. Like harpists around the thrones of the oldest, we, ourselves of divine destiny, dwell by the still gods of the world, and, with the fleeting tunes of human life, we lighten the burden of the sun god's holy office and that of his compeers.*

These changing forms and tones that diversely, severally determine our being, this triumphant procession of distinctions and epochs – what is this law and logic with which the poet builds a train of thought that enables us, who "bear the heavens in our heart," (251.29; 233.30) to experience the distinction of human being in the living element of our lives who, though we be offspring of the times, are something else besides? Are? Well, in any case, we were and will be – that is the sphere of remembrance and celebration but also of desire and endeavor; yes, freedom teaches us that we are what we make and create – but "beyond the stars, in the land of the blessed, where silence dwells, yes, even the heart,..." deeply absorbed in its poetic work, ultimately "...forgets its need and its language." (251.5-6)

> Wohnt doch die Stille im Lande der Seligen. Ja! Über den Sternen vergißt das Herz seine Noth und seine Sprache.

C. Poetic Thought

105. The Craft and Art of Poetic Spirit

The craft of the poet lies entirely in the art of mediation, in building a train of thought that provides passage for people and particulars on the way to insight and perfection, founding an organization, a harmony of tones, a constitution of ideas in a poem and a vessel of conversion that is their promotion in the course of which our experience of the distinction of human being is explicitly accounted for in a wealth of specific, even mundane details that everybody can relate to who cares to follow the red thread of the movement and the arc of the act we have termed that of our self-severalty, the mark of thought in things and things to come.

Accordingly, Hölderlin's poetological works of analysis expound the logic and coherence of this experience as a series of inferences comprising three distinct lines of reasoning, i.e. the *tragic*, the *lyrical*, and the *epic*, employing these terms, familiar as designations for the genres of poetry, to give expression to a distinguished technique of the imagination and the creative mind which he calls the *Vehicle of Poetic Spirit* (die Verfahrensweise des poetischen Geistes) and which seeks to provide a guideline and introduction for poets into the actual process of creation that they are engaged in by establishing a series of prerequisite skills and insights into the way that thoughts and things, mind and matter are put by the poet into the harmonious opposition that governs the unfolding of the epic, tragic, and finally lyric faculty of thought, the Builder, the actual poetic work, that renders palpable, touchingly tangible, impressively memorable, the ever-recurring tale of our experience with thought thinking thought, human life in a relationship of reciprocity with the charmed life of reason, that rich rapport of distinction that is the unique destiny of our human being the poetic craft and art of which is now itself to become the object of our searching, appreciative reflection.

This generative enterprise of thought towards conveying *upon ideas* the consequence and eminence of presence, its substance, and *upon the world* the depth and significance of meaning, its intelligibility, this work of thought, the Builder – *poetic spirit* as Hölderlin calls it – is carried out in language, attains substantiality in the reality of distinguished speech.

The work of poetic individuality begins with the notion that it is the destiny of human being and, in this sense, our *human nature* to uplift and elevate ourselves above and beyond the call of duty and nature that our natural and our moral being hearken to. But this *super*natural nature of human being, elevating and uplifting us over and above the need that our merely physical and merely moral being imposes upon us, at the same time, places us in a richer, deeper, more intimate rapport with the world, a higher life than that of the tyrannical mechanical. This higher connection is our holiest and most beautiful (99.15-16) because in it we feel united with ourselves and our world and with all that we have and are. But though stepping back in critical reflection in accordance with the distinction of human being is something we want to do and not just think about, contemplate in our minds, or see happen before our very eyes, nevertheless we try to form an idea and concept of this destiny of ours, try to imagine it; as much as the distinction of human being is a practice, it deserves and demands to be brought to our distracted attention again and again, called to mind, praised in thanks and cherished for the fruits it brings, the wealth of experience it conveys, demands to be depicted as the anguish of the ordeal but also the joy that accompanies our accomplishments in reason's works, and thus deserves to be consigned to the "higher life..." of poetic imagination in whose care we experience "...a more infinite, more thoroughgoing and comprehensive satisfaction than that experienced in the pleasure which crowns the repletion of our needs." (IV 275.28-29)

Accordingly, in the Third Epoch of European tradition, art and, specifically, **poetry** has become the teacher of humanity completing the work of thought that **science** began in the First Epoch and **religion** pursued in the Second Epoch. Why? Because the highest act of reason consists of comprehending that it is the destiny of human being to dwell in the totality of ideas, in their living presence, which is the *complete* system of all things thought, an ordered proportion of principles founded by the craft and art of poetic reason, i.e. aesthetic reason. (298.14-15) For this self-striving, self-realizing self-knowledge is the idea and the being of beauty (B), our highest being and ideal, namely that of an aesthetic, a *generative* act in which the *contemplative* truth (A) of theory and the goodness (C) of this truth in *practice* are included and related in the whole story of the life and times of thought. And if poetry, distinguished literature, has "survived all the other arts and sciences" (298.27-28) of humanity then it does so by ratifying their endeavor in the exercise of its own authority as the "original teacher of human being." (298.26) For even as is necessary for religion so also for philosophy: Ideas must touch our imagination; they must be made mythological, become tangible narrative; and likewise our mythologies and narratives must be made, fashioned in accordance with pure reason, with this being's very own life and times. "Only then will eternal unity reign among us. Never again the despising look, never again the blind trembling of folks before their wise men and their priests. Then may we expect the full unfolding of all our forces, those of each individual and all individuals. Then no force will be suppressed – general freedom and equality of spirits will reign. A higher spirit, descending from the heavens must found this new religion among us, which will be the last and greatest work of humanity." (299.10-17)

> Dann herrscht ewige Einheit unter uns. Nimmer der verachtende Blick, nimmer dass blinde Zittern des Volks vor

seinen Weisen und Priestern. Dann erst erwartet uns gleiche
Ausbildung aller Kräfte, des einzelnen sowohl als aller
Individuen. Keine Kraft wird mehr unterdrückt werden, dann
herrscht allgemeine Freiheit und Gleichheit der Geister! -- Ein
höherer Geist, vom Himmel gesandt, muß diese neue Religion
unter uns stiften, sie wird das letzte, größte Werk der
Menschheit sein.

The work of the poet begins by establishing the determinants of the poem.
The first is the one idea that inspires the poet's craft and art and, through
these, attains presence in the materiality of language, not just in the sound
and form of speech, but also in the sense of the words the meanings of
which have been borrowed from the familiar spheres of human life and
human dwelling in the world. Thus, the free exercise of poetic spirit
represents the pattern of the mind in the material that is receptive to the
character and cognizance of thought indicating that the impressiveness of
the mind on matter is the inaugural term (A) while the expression and effect
of its character thus brought forth and applied is the resultant term (B). The
mediate term (C) is that of the differential between the general principle
and the particulars of time and place. It accounts for the property of thought
in progress, its actual practice. For even as the theoretical mind's own
tendency spirits us along towards ideal unity while the craft and art of
thought, the Builder, articulates its buildings in a language consisting of a
diversity of elements, the ground and purport of the poem, the spiritual-
physical, formal-material ground and sense of the poem stands between
these extremes, the mediate and therefore self-several term in which these
extremes touch, being itself neither the "harmoniously opposed whole"
that is the pure concentration of the spirit's entire life and emergent power
of principle, nor the systematic whole that is the elemental particulars of its
own realization, in the end, of all it had conceived of its inherent being in
the beginning, but rather a whole in its own right and life, one uniquely
distinguished by the contradictory tendencies within itself, specifically that
of perpetually "dividing all that is united, determining all that is free,
generalizing all that is particular," sharing its form with the inaugural
subject of principle and its content with the resultant material object such
that its naïve, heroic, and ideal tendencies are contradictory in their objects
but like in the striving property of their mutual opposition, united
according to the law of action, the enacted law of universal diversity that is
the very life of thought, the organs of its organism. Hölderlin formulates this
argument as follows:

Between the particular terms of the realization (B) and the free ideal of the representation (A) lies the substance and the specific sense (C) of the poem. It is this spiritual-physical, formal-material substance that gives the poem its import, its structure, and its truth and preserves the poem from mannerism in the free ideal of its representation and from vanity in the particular terms of the realization. While the ideal of the representation tends to give *unity* to its figures, to its transitions, to its episodes, and the terms of its particular realization, the characters, the passions, and the individuals of its expression tend more towards *differentiation*; the substance stands between them, distinguished in being entirely self-several and, in contrast to spirit that makes like all that is opposed in form, separates all that is united, establishes all that is free, generalizes all that is particular...such that while the naïve, the heroic, and the ideal tendencies of the poem contradict one another in the object of their tendencies, nevertheless as forms of contradiction and determination they can be likened one to the other, consonant with regards to the most general principles of action in life. (245.23-246.19)

Zwischen dem Ausdrucke (der Darstellung) und der freien idealischen Behandlung liegt die Begründung und Bedeutung des Gedichts. Sie ists, die dem Gedichte seinen Ernst, seine Festigkeit, seine Wahrheit gibt, sie sichert das Gedicht davor, daß die freie idealische Behandlung nicht zur leeren Manier, und die Darstellung nicht zur Eitelkeit werde. Sie ist das Geistigsinnliche, das Formalmaterielle, des Gedichts; und wenn die idealische Behandlung in ihrer Metapher, ihrem Übergang, ihren Episoden, mehr vereinigend ist, hingegen der Ausdruck, die Darstellung in ihren Charakteren, ihrer Leidenschaft, ihren Individualitäten, mehr trennend, so stehet die Bedeutung zwischen beiden, sie zeichnet sich aus dadurch, daß sie sich selber überall entgegengesetzt ist: daß sie, statt daß der Geist alles der Form nach Entgegengesetzte vergleicht, alles Einige trennt, alles Freie festsetzt, alles Besondere verallgemeinert,....so daß naive und heroische und idealische Tendenz, im Objekt ihrer Tendenz, sich widersprechen, aber in der Form des Widerstreits und Strebens vergleichbar sind, und einig nach dem Gesetze der Tätigkeit, also einig im Allgemeinsten, im Leben.

The general form of thought, namely the drive of inspiration towards attaining fruition in the object of our best heart's desire, the inclination of the mind towards matter, the turn and return of the ideal to the real, THE WAY IT SHOULD BE becoming THE WAY IT IS so that the bliss of our IS accords completely with the OUGHT we were taught by thought – this train of thought is rendered not only as a logical inference as in the First Epoch, not only as the conversion of our human being under the moral imperative of the Word of God as in the Second Epoch but also, here in the Third Epoch, as the formula of pure reason's Imagination, namely:

$$A>B = A>C + C>B$$

This formula can also be rendered as a triad of terms, the transitional syllogism of productive reasoning, as in *Figure 68*.

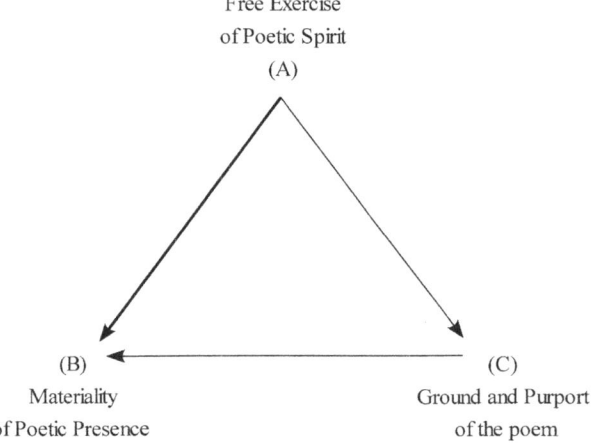

Free Exercise
of Poetic Spirit
(A)

(B)   (C)
Materiality   Ground and Purport
of Poetic Presence   of the poem

Figure 68: The Engine of Pure Reason's Creativity

The transition from Mind (A) to Matter (B) is mediated by the Ground and Purport of the Poem, pure reason (C). This singular being of transitions, our experience of its features and property, is ultimately what every poem is about, the poem's sense and substance. For thought, the distinction of human being, is, amazingly, a harmoniously opposed being, engaged in the self-several process of differing from itself in being itself, being most completely what it truly is when it is utterly and entirely not what it is. Who ever heard of such a thing as this (that would appear to be no thing at all – except as a figure in a poem)?

In the poem that brings this being to our attention, commends it to our enjoyment even as it admonishes our emulation, we will note how the phases or stages of its life follow logically one upon the other in a series of transitions, which are in fact mediations in accordance with the form of thought in action, namely: A>B = A>C + C>B. Hölderlin names these three transitions *tragic, epic,* and *lyric.* The *tragic* transition is one from unity to separation, the drama, the highest fire of thought leaving its mark on our mind of the gap between what we are and what we were meant to be, our destiny as revealed in the original discernment of the subject and the object of judgment. Hölderlin speaks here of the "Urteil" (judgment) as ur-teil (primeval division) which, in the theoretical concept of thought thinking thought, adopts the form of our entity of identity, namely *I am who I am* or *I am Me* ("Ich bin Ich") while in a moral or practical sense, judgment sets in opposition the object and the subject in a relationship of self-contrariety such that *I am* is opposed to *Me,* being, in fact, *Not Me.* (216.1-11) The *epic* transition, on the other hand, takes up that narrative of the invigorated mind thus awoken to reflection and called to arms of action from the balanced inward bliss of contemplation and learns as the plot unfolds what the principle has determined, seeking to fulfill the vocation thus received as its destiny and achieve closure of that rift that bestowed the troubling gift of purpose upon our will. The *lyric* transition, finally, uplifts the reality thus attained upon completion of the destiny originally bestowed as that of the principle's own life and being, evincing thus in a poetry of particulars the deeper meaning and significance of all that has come to pass in the course of events that comprised the mind's history.

The *tragic* transition is thus the tendency of the mind to fall from the "ideal" unity of the spirit to the "heroic" distinction of a mind at divides with itself, in conflict with itself, for the sake of the betterment of its soul and life. The *epic* transition is the tendency of the "heroic" mind to strive towards the ideal it has received as a calling of excellence and achieve at the end of the way the peace of mind that awaits it like a prize at the final destination, the hard-earned resting place and newly-found "innocence" of a home long yearned for and finally returned to. Ultimately, the *lyric* transition makes a song and celebration of a lifetime of achievements, making good the bitter fate of human being that left its indelible mark upon our "native" state, revealing pain's proper place in the whole story, and giving voice to the "universal" wisdom that only the experience of our human distinction can give rise to, even that experience of trust that the speech of wisdom inspired our hearts with in the first place, sending us on our way with a mission and a promise.

106. The Threefold Transcendence of Poetic Spirit

In this way we recognize each of the three "hyperbolic" transitions, the particular events and concrete renditions of reality as they appear in their native hue to the innocent eye (B), arise from the hero's right and proper striving (C) even as the hero's passion and conception of the mission arise from the spirit of the good cause which is the inaugural ideal (A) that kindled that distinguished fire of the heart that is our own self-knowing being, a being which itself emerges in the imagination that gives form to exalting and exalted feeling (B) for what is truly real to an inspired, enthusiastic, rejuvenated mind. (244.6-8)

In his *Vehicle of Poetic Spirit* (see 243.24-244.8 and 246.31-247.14), Hölderlin elaborates this cyclical system of transitions as a series, more precisely, as a helix of terms delineating the triadic turn and return of reflection we have previously encountered as that of pure reason in action. Consider *Table 8* in which these terms represent "the subjective ground of the poem..." and "the distinct moods of inner ideal life." (246.29-31):

A	C	B
→Intellectual Intuition —→	Heroic Purpose —→	Native Sentiment —
Possibility	Necessity	Reality
Idea	Motive	Events
Figments	Efforts	Scenes
Inventions	Indications	Descriptions
Poetic Visions	Dramatizations	Narratives
Just Cause	Good Intention	Feeling for Beauty
Separable	Determinable	Generalizable
Towards Realization	Towards Fulfillment	Towards Abstraction
Tragic	Epic	Lyrical

Table 8: The Three Moods of Poet Experience

This is the circle of poetic life that is pure reason's and the story of the poet's experience with her nature and also, finally, the articulate process of poetic invention in commemoration of her accomplishments. Consider this circle as a series of transitions that can be rendered as in *Figure 69*:

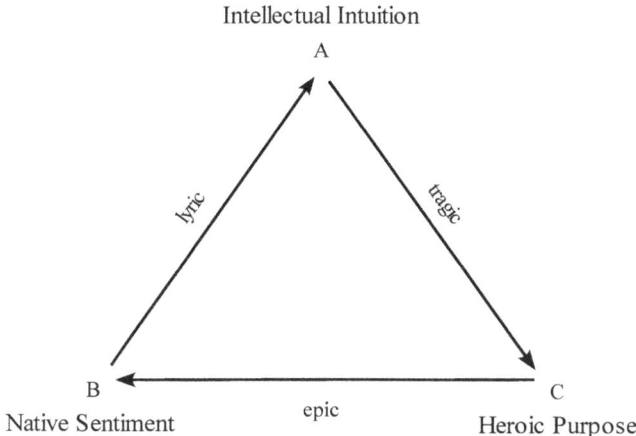

Figure 69: The Circle of Poetic Invention

The uplifting style of the lyrical poem tends towards the ideal tone as an expression of our naïve mind – the transition (or "metaphor" as Hölderlin designates it) of *sentiment*; the energy of the epic poem issues in the dwelling of the native tone as the result of our heroic mind's date with destiny – the transition of *purpose*; the tragic poem manifests the distinction of human being in the heroic tone that emerges from our intuition of the ideal as revealed to such a mind as is appropriately receptive to that distinguished calling – the transition of *intellect* (266.1-8).

In fact, all three transitions are themselves mediated, each a proposition of a syllogism consisting of the other two as its premises, such that every transition in turn takes on the form of the inaugural, the resultant, and the mediate term in the fundamental figure of thought, the Builder, by which poetic spirit (A) "is inclined to reproduce itself in its own as well as in disparate substance" (241.7-8) provided that this substance, whether it is "a series of events, scenes, realizations…that are narrated, depicted, described, or a series of endeavors, efforts, purposes, dramatically manifested in their necessity…, or, finally, a series of lyrically rendered visions…, figures of the imagination," (243.24-244.1) has a ground and foundation such that the scenes and episodes, the dramatic plots and passions, the fantasies, mediate and are mediated by the other transitions in their complete system, which is one train and scheme of all things thought. "For the ground and purport of the poem mediates between the expression, the representation, the materiality of poetic presence – that which is actually spoken in the poem – and the free exercise of poetic spirit, that of the ideal. (244.8-12)"

  In particular, each term takes on the office and efficacy of this mediating force, becoming in turn, in the course of a particular train of poetic thought, the foundation and substance, the purport of the poem through which the mind comes to matter and makes a difference – that is the descending movement on the one hand, which is, as we have previously designated it, the *reflective* tendency of thought thinking thought coming to know itself as all reality, the reality of thoughts having been realized in things; and the complementary ascending movement on the other hand, which we have come to recognize as that of the *abstract*, self-several tendency of thought whereby things gain significance in thoughts – both however are mediated by that unique being that is, in one, both reflection *and* abstraction and as such the basis and foundation of the poem, the work of poetic thought. The system of transitions upon this being is exhibited in *Figure 70*.

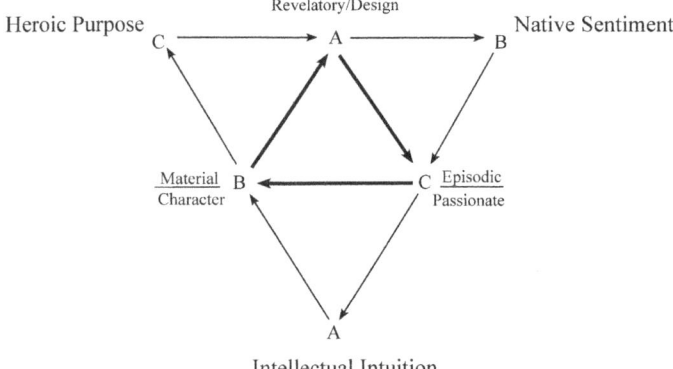

Figure 70: The Hyperbolic Mediation of Poetic Thought

  This train of thought is formulated by Hölderlin as follows:

If the meaning is *native sentiment* (B) then the representation is design (A) and the exercise of poetic spirit reveals itself to be episodic (C). If the meaning is *intellectual intuition* (A) then the expression, the materiality of poetic presence is passionate (C) and the exercise of poetic spirit reveals itself more as character (B). If the meaning is the more properly determined *heroic purpose* (C), then the expression is material (B) and the free exercise of poetic spirit is revelatory (A). (244.29-34)

Ist die Empfindung Bedeutung, so ist die Darstellung bildlich, und die geistige Behandlung zeigt sich episodisch. Ist die intellektuelle Anschauung Bedeutung, so ist der Ausdruck, das Materielle, leidenschaftlich, die geistige Behandlung zeigt sich mehr im Stil. Ist die Bedeutung ein eigentlicherer Zweck, so ist der Ausdruck sinnlich, die freie Behandlung metaphorisch.

The circle of "directly opposed" terms (as Hölderlin calls them) indicated by this triad of transitions reads in a clockwise direction, namely, as seen in *Figure 71*:

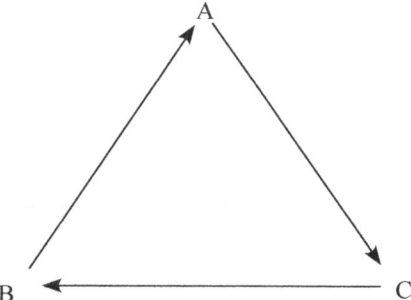

Figure 71: The Inner Engine of Severalty in Poetic Thought

This circle of terms renders the movement of thought in its critical aspect, i.e. thought in our experience of it as the distinction of human being, the power to step back and to mind the gap between the IS and the OUGHT, which is the practical effect of pure reason upon us, our lives and actions. It is complemented by the same series of terms considered however as being "harmoniously opposed" which render, in a triad of terms read now in a counter-clockwise direction, the movement of thought in its tranquillity, the peace and calm of theory in which thought returns from its turn of critical reflection as in *Figure 72*.

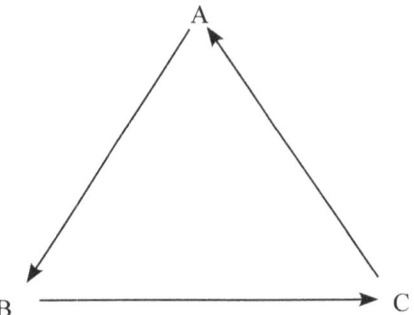

Figure 72: The Poetic Experience of Harmonious Dwelling

It is important to see that each of these two series of transitions in their particular order, clockwise or counterclockwise, is a system of mediations, themselves syllogisms, the constituent transitions of which, as their premises, are to be found in the order of the complementary triad of terms.

Thus the *Ratios of Philosophy* that we have noted earlier as consisting of the terms

$$A > C > B$$

$$B > A > C$$

$$C > B > A$$

articulates three transitions, the **mediations of resolution**, namely first, that of the realization of the thought in the thing, mind in matter, i.e. *A > B mediated by C*, second, the fulfillment of the distinction of human being, in other words, the completion of the inaugural principle of pure reason in our lives as envisioned by an ideal, i.e. *B > C mediated by A* and, finally, the insight and contemplation of the nature of thought, i.e. *C > A mediated by B*.

This triangle of mediations founds and completes the kindred but inverted system of transitions, **mediations of distinction** that we have previously called, following Boeder, the *Ratios of Wisdom* consisting of the terms

$$A > B > C$$

$$C > A > B$$

$$B > C > A$$

that form the basis for the mediations of distinction, i.e. *A > C over B –* the lightning strike of distinction that is thought's immediacy to thought; *C > B over A –* the heroic fire of desire that it ignites in the tender heart, and *B > A over C –* the uplifting significance of the mind's immensity.

These three mediations render the inner triangle of terms that account for the several movements of thought's distinction as abstraction even as the inverted transitions articulate thought's fulfilled determination in the quiet of its science, the peaceful perfection of its completed works of art, in the calm piety and kindness of its true religion, all previously revered as divine embodiments of thought, the science, the religion, and the art of pure reason, which is none other than that of thought thinking thought.

The latter turn of the triad of mediated transitions merely reverses their direction with respect to the former turn, while the mediating terms remain the same, a spiral progression of reiteration that highlights the turn and return of thought and exhibits again the recurrent, inward/outward rhythm of "ingemination" we have often observed in the procreative progression of self-reflectivity and now again in *Figure 73*:

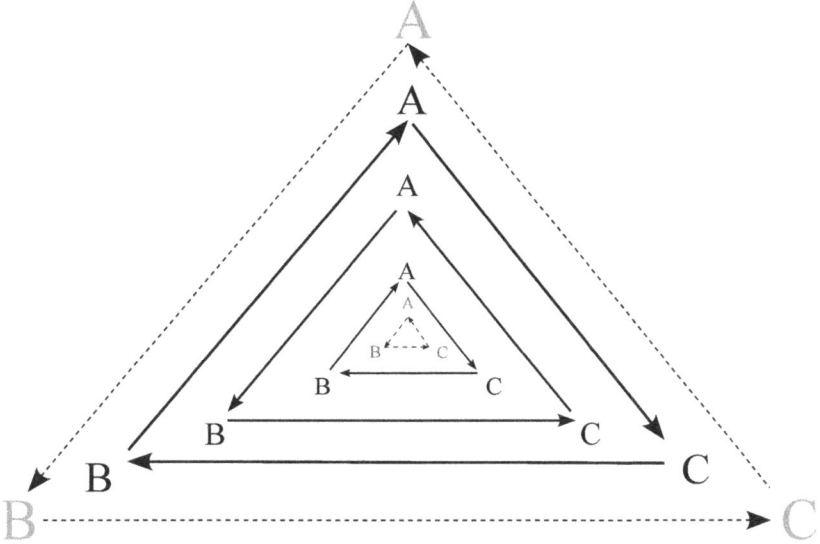

Figure 73: The Double Helix of Critical Reflection

This emphatic nature of the mind, the distinguished and distinguishing movement of thought as profound as it is sublime, recognized and celebrated as a "progression of reciprocal oppositions" (Fortgang der entgegengesezten Wechselwirkungen - 153.5-6), might be more vividly depicted as one that "actually unites the hyperbole with its asymptote." (213.21-22) For such is the veritable life of thought, is it not? And it is this life that is the poem, its meaning as well as its being, taking on the form and substance in poetic speech, in the mind's own myth-making.

Figure 74 shows how we might imagine this movement. It is based on the principle of unity in self-contrariety, which is the most characteristic feature of the being that we have been investigating since day one, trying to conceive of an integrity that is its own, that of a whole divided *against* no less than *with*, harmoniously opposed to and thus distinguished from and in, itself. Imagine such a being as unifies two contradictory characters, natures, features, lives, desires, faculties, one being its ownmost tendency towards identity and unity, the other towards distinction and contradiction.

The one founds a community of beings in which each member attends upon the whole, a multitude of members each participating proportionately in the organization of its life, the greater life that is the distinguished soul of their soul, in relation to which they are kindred spirits. The other, by contrast, is the desire for distinction and difference, for the movement of harmonious opposition that brings forth change, marks departures, broaches overtures, charts passages abroad, and there, elsewhere, namely among others and in the presence of heterogenous elements, strives to poetically revive and recur upon itself in measured progressions. Now this altercation between alacrity and serenity, between the agility of the mind in real time and its composure as the dwelling of eternity, the calm and collected heart and the fleet mind's advance, finds resolution in buildings of poetic thought as Hölderlin explains in *Über die Verfahrensweise des Poetischen Geistes*. In nothing else lies the devoutest purpose of the poem. But how are these two contrary tendencies reconcilable? In the self-relativity of the entity of identity that is our one theme and cause. Yes, but how?

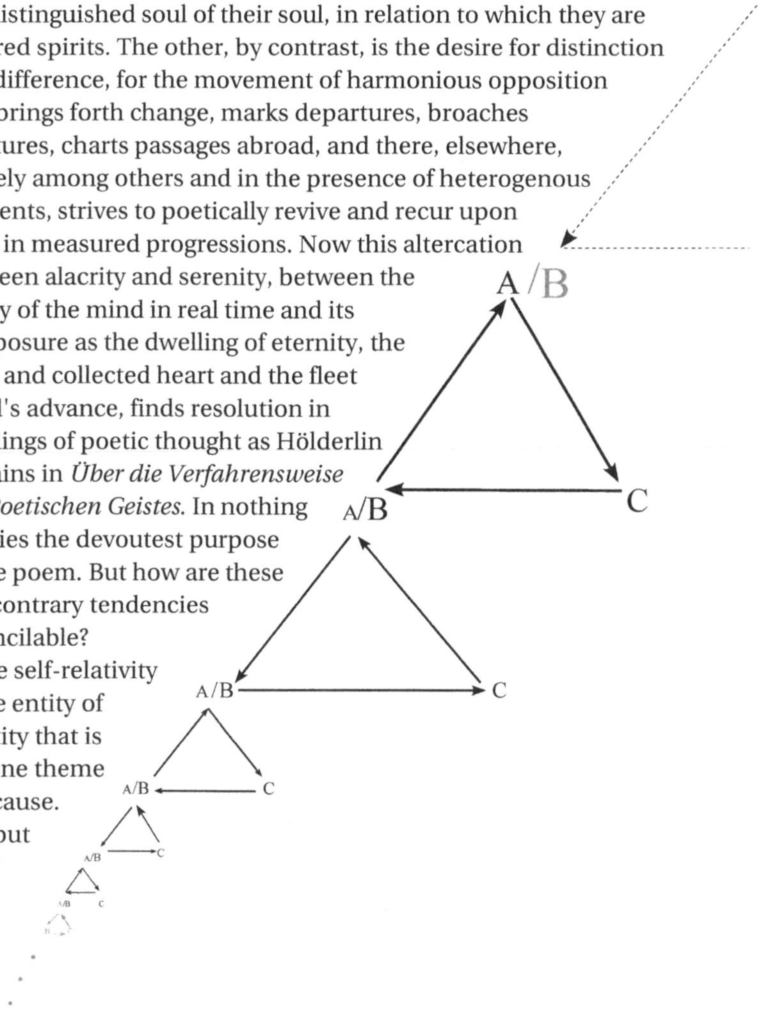

Figure 74: The Centrifugal/Centripetal Rings of Reflection

By the simple fact that in the world of poetry the thought and the thing, mind and matter, the ideal and the real, spiritual and material being beautifully coincide in the self-relativity of thought where the two salient properties of spirit, its concurrence and its alteration, intersect in the language of poetic life. Consider the following diagram (*Figure 75*).

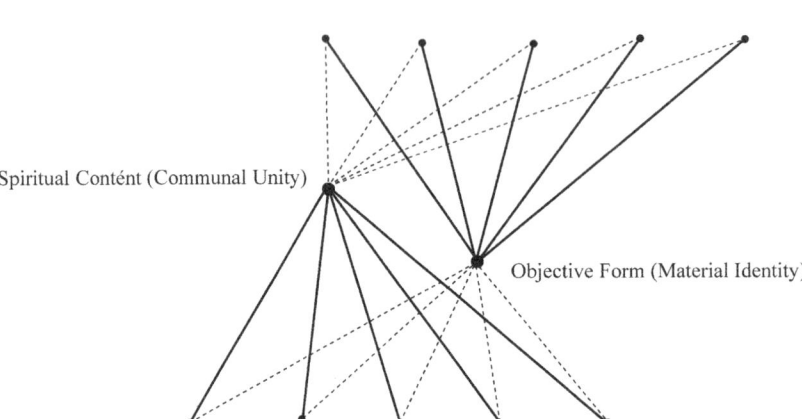

Figure 75: The Harmoniously Opposed Reciprocity of Mind and Matter

It depicts their harmoniously opposed reciprocity – the unanimity of the mind giving definition to the diversity of material cóntent (sinnlicher, objektiver Gehalt – 241.19, 25; 242.4), while the formal contént of objective identity (sinnliche, objektive Form – 241.25; 242-11-12) offers fuel to appease the ceaselessly forging fire of teeming poetic spirit; for even as the latter shapes its object so does the former receive its shape, the material object compensating with its concise form for the loss of spiritual contént (geistiger Gehalt – 241.18, 27; 242.7, 12-13; 243.2, 6-7, 11-12, 17) as a result of the innate energy and alacrity of the mind while material multiplicity (materielle Mannigfaltigkeit – 243.2) out of which poets compose their buildings of articulate intricacy countervails any mollifying influence of the mind upon its ideal, ever-forming fervor (immerwechselnde idealische geistige Form – 241.27; 242.5; 243.5) in consequence of the spirit's concomitant call to eternal reconciliation of difference (Verwandtschaft und Einigkeit der Teile – 241.17-18). Similiarly as the material serves to assuage the conflict of the mind between its striving drive toward harmonic progression of its parts (harmonisches Forstreben...und Wechsel der Teile – 241.22-24) and its demand for unity and eternity in every moment

(Einigkeit und Ewigkeit in jeden Moment – 242.9-12), so is the opposition between objective material change (materieller Wechsel – 242.6-7, 11, 14; 243.8, 12-13) and objective material identity (materielle Identität – 242.14-15; 243.4, 12-14) resolved in the efficacy of spirit – the perpetual atonement of spiritual contènt (immerforttönender allesausgleichende geistige Gehalt – 243.1-2) remedies the passionate, the gap-fleeing progression (leidenschaftlicher, die Unterbrechung fliehende Fortschritt – 242.15-16) that is the shape of the thing as a whole (Gestalt – 241.12), in spite of an inherent bent to mutability, while the danger of the loss of plurality incumbent upon its concurrent drive to quickly settle for headings and impressions (schnelleres Fortstreben zum Hauptpunkt und Eindruck – 243.3, 9) is redressed by ideal, endlessly metamorphosing form of spirit (immerwechselnde idealische geistige Form 242. 5243.7, 12, 18).

These are the two sides of poetic living being, that thought is, both material and spirit in one, both form and cóntent, the forming force of thought and the issue and tension that drives its creative urgency, the seeing being and the being seen, the inaugural gift of present that is the immediacy of the animadverted mind and the presence that is its record and reception, the accordance and corresponding community of mind meeting mind across the gulf of a gap, the caesura of discernment that is the original distinction of uniquely human being, the hiatus of a disparity that does not impoverish but rather bestows and fosters reflection – these are the two sides of poetic living being that thought is, both spirit *and* material in one, both form *and* contént, perfectly balanced in the chirality of poetic endeavor.

The calculus of thought – Hölderlin speaks here of a MHXANH (V 195.4), of the reliability (Zuverlässigkeit – 195.7) of calculable laws (kalkuablen Gesetze – 195.25; gesetzlicher Kalkül – 195.19) that the poetic mind avails itself of in its endeavor and that must constitute the poet's craft and art if anything does; surely Hölderlin is not referring here, in spite of etymological reminiscences, to the instrumentality of mere *mechanism*, as we might assume, having long ago, in everyday life's school, learned and mastered our algorithms such that now, convinced that thought must be the mindless formalism of computation, a manipulation of pebbles, chips, and bits that a machine can accomplish much more quickly, we are finally able to dispense with thought all together, or at least for the most part, in our daily dealings. No, he does not refer to thought's laws in the mechanical sense, but rather as the laws that govern the manifestation of the mind at work and at play, the scheme and figures they delineate – as well as those precious stones, the gems and pearls of insight, they array into shapely formations –

all have a particular sense and meaning; we are calculating not for the sake of combinational manipulation but to make manifest and express our experience of pure reason, to premeditate our building and decipher works of art as the realization of ideas. Thus *calculation* is just another word for the design and the plan of the whole unfolding according to a comprehensible pattern in the hands of consummate delicacy and skill. For what, in truth, could be finer and more intricate, even unto nothingness, and, at the same time more potently ponderous, more substantial in our lives, than ideas and therefore more worthy of being collected into a tessellated system of principles with respect to which every living thought, that is itself *immensity* and *incalculable*, itself *incommensurable*, may be set in relationship to every other and therein proportionately determined in its scope and purpose with regards to the ratio of the whole?

Hölderlin teaches us that in the ideal world, pure reason is a poet, too, distinguished not merely as a thinker in *perception* of the perfection of being, nor merely in *action*, in that crisis that we take it upon ourselves to live through as the painful passage of departure from the immediacy of our life but also towards its renewal as the distinguished, and in this sense, eternal life of spirit, and now in *invention*, as Hölderlin has shown us, in what poetic enthusiasm actually brings forth as the reality of beauty for us to inhabit as our dwelling. What does this mean? We often speak in terms of how the Third Epoch conceived of thought as creative genius; for, in this epoch, thought is grasped more specifically as *imagination*. The "buildings" of inventive thought are thus works of fancy but does this mean that they are imaginary, phantasmagoric, figments in the pejorative sense of castles in the air, mirages?

So it would appear to the intellect for which the object of thought can only be attained by gaining insight into the way things are, which is distinguished from their "mere" presence. Further, from the point of view of the intellect and its acuity, apparition is dependent on and indicative of the disposition of the mind perceiving – things appear to a particular observer in a certain way as a result of the observer's state of mind or body. In contrast, the objective perspicacity of intellect, beyond all seeming, endeavors precisely in its tireless endeavor to see objectively, to see beyond these appearances and the accidence of concomitant conditions, to see what actually is, really and truly is, for all time and for all minds. This is the being of theory and when we speak of a being's *being*, we mean, at least in the Greek sense of *theory*, what accrues to that being by virtue of what it is in itself, independent of the observer's idiosyncrasies and therefore evident alone to the apprehension of pure reason, namely the *essence* of the thing, its *substance* and, in contrast to the immediacy of sensory perception and the illusion that makes a being appear one way to one and an other to another, this is the being's *form* (ΕΙΔΟΣ) defining THE WAY IT SHOULD BE which is the *reason* that a thing *is* THE WAY IT IS and the *principle* determining *why* a being is the way it is, why it is *what* it truly is.

Thus within the purview of Greek theory, *imagination* is the term for the very opposite of contemplation, is the indiscriminate background and the unmarked space against which the insight of *intuition* bears the cognizance of distinction. In the third epoch of philosophy, however, as we have been learning, *fantasy* is wholly vindicated and receives in turn all the accolades it deserves in the pantheon of powers that define pure reason as the distinction of human being. For thought is not only a *perceptive* faculty, it is, moreover, *generative*. Is this such a surprise considering how greatly we appreciate the arts, in particular, *fiction*, which, though the opposite of insight's *truth*, is nevertheless esteemed for the *moral* truths it reveals regarding the sentiments of the heart and the spiritual life of human being in works of expression which were traditionally admired as objects of beauty and majesty? Thus art and science, fiction and fact, the imagination and the intellect, are harmoniously opposed faculties, endeavors, and accomplishments brought forth by two different trains of thought – the one, i.e. AC>CB=AB issuing from a *ratio of concretion* while the other CB>BA=CA issuing from a *ratio of perception* as can be seen in *Figure 76*:

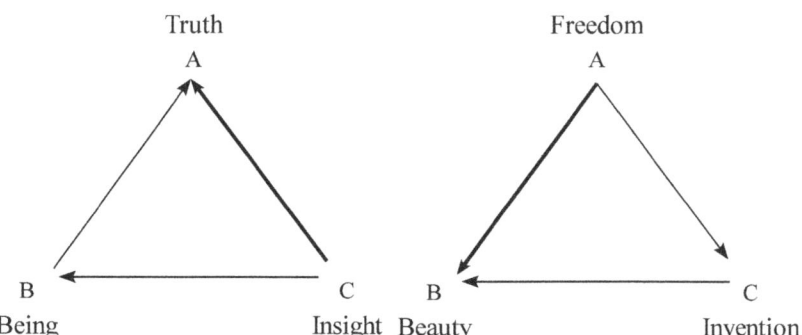

Figure 76: The Multitudinousness of the Mind

Theoretical *Insight* (C) gains insight into *Truth* (A) as a result of its intelligence and perspicacity with regards to *Being* (B) while *Freedom* (A) is realized as the apparition of *Beauty* (B) through the craft and art of poetic *Invention* (C).

Truth, Being, Freedom, Beauty? In applying these terms of distinction and delineating these ratios that are their constitution, we must take care to avoid the consumer reflex of suspicion and its masquerade of scepticism that is apt to demand of such word offerings presented to it that, with them, a minimal apparatus of definitions be provided. This attitude, though apparently reasonable, is a misunderstanding of the essential method of philosophy, which does not begin with questions regarding how to construe and define a word or words. Rather, the start is an intriguing experience that has caught our attention and now craves not only our deeper comprehension but also our articulation; can we put our dawning notion into words? What words will do? What is to be gained by calling our topic and our cause *truth* or *beauty*, by calling *it* *intellect* or *insight* or *imagination*, by calling *it* "it" in the first place? Wait, what is *it* again? Our *it* is that unique and exceedingly intriguing distinction of human being. Yes, it has several, *self-several*, names, in other words, contradictory ones. Harmoniously opposed, they cohere, as Hölderlin has shown, in a train of thought that comprehends but does not annihilate their diversity, imagines a ratio among them that, though they be incommensurable terms, relates them one to the other and the others, invents a narrative for this self-several being that includes Heaven *and* Earth. Does this thought about thought contradict itself? Very well, then, thought contradicts itself; thought is large, thought contains multitudes.

A. The Poetic Principle

107. Consecration and Celebration

Nevertheless, words of wisdom invite us to dwell upon their meaning and in doing so we enter upon the poem that has moved us with its poetry such that a vision resolves itself into clarity and welcomes us into its luminous reality as it would the child long since grown up who has travelled far and wide and been sorely tested along the way, welcomes with its embrace this seeker as the world sought for which we were born and in which we were destined to dwell and call our home, our true Fatherland; and though it be chimerical, it is the one and only world worthy of distinguished human being, a world of poets, not merely inhabited by them, but also created by them, celebrated in their song, in which they themselves figure, bringing thus forth the person of the divine poet who, in works of art, creates a world in which the best of beings, the ideas of *destiny* and *deity*, live and thrive in concert, to which now, in the wisdom of the third epoch of human being, self-critical *humanity* has joined the ranks of triune Godhead and perfect being.

Entering now into the world of thought, the Builder, taking up abode in that vision that is the creation of poetic craft and art, i.e. in the poem of principle, what do we experience? What do we see and hear? But not content to be only observers and readers of the epic narrative of pure reason, not content to be merely actors in the drama of departure, but also the inhabitants of its destination, what happens to us? Having become a citizen of its state, what do we do in this netherworld of our mundane world, in this virtuous reality that is our other, our greater, our further fatherland? "Look at the world..." through the poet's eyes, fashioned by the poet's hands! "...is it not like a triumphant procession, in which nature celebrates its eternal victory over all decay? And for glory's sake does life not lead death behind it on a golden chain, as the general once paraded the conquered kings? And we, we are the maids and the striplings who with dance and song, in a diversity of forms and tones, accompany the majestic train?" (III 148.26-32)

> Sieh auf in die Welt! Ist sie nicht, wie ein wandelnder Triumphzug, wo die Natur den ewigen Sieg über alle Verderbnis feiert? und führt nicht zur Verherrlichung das Leben den Tod mit sich, in goldenen Ketten, wie der Feldherr einst die gefangenen Könige mit sich geführt? und wir, wir sind wie die Jungfrauen und die Jünglinge, die mit Tanz und Gesang, in wechselnden Gestalten und Tönen den majestätischen Zug geleiten.

Ultimately, in this world of poetic spirit, we are neither merely observers, nor merely inhabitants, we are its citizens and among them preeminent in our vocation as belonging to the guild of poets who sing and celebrate the destiny of a distinguished being called *human,* giving with their choirs articulate, melodious voice to the spirit of this community, i.e. the life and the dwelling of *Fatherland,* "this ripest fruit of time and newest name, the first of all the muses and the last..." (*Gesang des Deutschen* – II 4.51-2)

> Mit neuem Namen, reifeste Frucht der Zeit!
> Du letzte und du erste aller
> Musen...

A country in which the "speech of lovers is the speech of the land and the soul of which is the people's voice." (*Die Liebe* – 21.26-28)

Sprache der Liebenden
Sei die Sprache des Landes,
Ihre Seele der Laut des Volks!

For this is our poet's "profession," namely "to extol the higher – for this reason did deity put speech into the poet's heart and thanks." (*Der Prinzessin Auguste von Homburg Den 28. Nov. 1799* – I 311.26-28)

Beruf ist mirs,
Zu rühmen Höhers, darum gab die
Sprache der Gott und den Dank ins Herz mir.

And, with respect to the citizens of Fatherland, "to each friendly, trusting all – how else could the poets of this people sing to each the song of their own god?" (*Dichtermut* – II 62.14-16)

...jedem hold,
Jedem trauend; wie sängen
Sonst wir jedem den eignen Gott?

Who would have ever imagined that a spirited life entails the good death, the death with distinction, that is critical self-reflection and departure from anonymity and ignominy, from the inward turned taciturnity of those who are, to themselves, indistinct and indistinguishable, nameless and unknown, like stone is to a stone. In this sense alone does the angry poet sing, in verses of the sword, the glory of death for Fatherland – "Do not fear the poet's noble ire whose letter kills but the spirit of which quickens spirits." (*Der Zürnende Dichter* – I 305)

Fürchtet den Dichter nicht, wenn er edel zürnet, sein Buchstab
Tötet, aber es macht Geister lebendig der Geist.

We who write poetry are ourselves figures and characters in this poetry, are ourselves and our lives poetic inventions (*Empedokles* IV 17.389) in the self-relative world of our poem, in which "matter has been transferred to signs" (IV 264.20-21) ..."become a world in the world." (250.25) Poetic individuality can completely know itself only in this object, the world and the figures of its invention whose life and particulars alone tell the whole story, the drama of thought thinking thought as a train of thought, the rhythm of rise and fall that is the destiny of our essentially poetic being who experiences and thus relates the full circle of its seasons, being neither one nor the other, nor these two and the third alone, but rather three in one that is itself one of the three. That is why poetic spirit calls upon its heartfelt poem to be its holy home (cf. *An die Parzen* – I 241.7-8) and treasured possession: "Be, poem, my friendly asylum, be my garden, well nurtured, with love's care where I may walk under blossoms, ever blooming, in serene simplicity dwelling when time's brunt rumbles without from afar, wave upon wave, and the softer sunbeam favors my work."(*Mein Eigentum* – I 307. 41-48)

> Sei du, Gesang, mein freundlich Asyl! sei du,
> Beglückender! mit sorgender Liebe mir
> Gepflegt, der Garten, wo ich, wandelnd
> Unter den Blüten, den immerjungen,
> In sichrer Einfalt wohne, wenn draußen mir
> Mit ihren Wellen allen die mächtge Zeit,
> Die Wandelbare, fern rauscht und die
> Stillere Sonne mein Wirken fördert.

The bard's song and praise celebrate this recursive dwelling of pure reason in commemoration of the former epochs of the mind, in particular that of the prophet in whose striking admonition our cocooning heart broke and awoke to critical self-reflection that marked the original descent of Man and the epic ascendance of our intellect, the tragic ode of the hero.

Thus the great dignity of the poet's guild and craft the imagery of which recurs throughout Hölderlin's poetry, itself exalted, itself voiced in the singing voice of the rhapsodist, the strings of whose lute and lyre melodiously ring with the triune tonality that is the mind's true progression; consider the circumstances of poetic performance, defining thought, the Builder's profession: the festivities of celebration and consecration – the banquet and the dance where thought is the spirit of the wine awakening the people, transforming the audience, beloved friend and folk, into revelers through these works of revelation to thought, "freeing their eyes from everyday work," (*Empedocles* IV 74.1795) to participate in bliss where the singer's song and the choirs of joy, echoing from the mountains and the meadows, revives the memory of the heroes of the past, recollects a tradition of the ruins contemplated in a tune, prophetically foretells the coming completion and fulfillment of the will's original determination in accordance to which naming is invoking and invoking summoning and summoning is a thanking prayer, lamenting bygones in elegies, praising, as the beatitude to-be in hymns, the ideal. For this reason "days of yore and to come – both are sacred to poetic singers" (*Stuttgart* II 87.53) and their living song an offering to the gods, the poets' sacrifice, the laurel, corresponding to that of the priest and prophet's myrtle, both the distinction of human being that is the fate of all thought.

108. The Imagery of Our Self-Several Experience

If thought is our destiny, both the uplifting, purposeful flight of our predetermination to be what we ought to be as well as the subjecting doom and plague of fate upon Man's menial mind, then we are doubly summoned by discernment to judge and to be judged and now, whether poised or prostrate, bound to learn more about thought's critical property in the figures of Hölderlin's poetry in accordance with the concrete logic that the term *fate* suggests to poetic imagination.

Take, for example, the *bird*, not only as an image of the singer and the song of celebration but also as the fetter-free flight (*An die Unerkannte* – I 197.5) of the spirit that makes all the difference in the world, the poetic power of the mind (Dichtermut – II 62) to withstand and overcome the oppressive spirit of soporific gravity in the wielding of its wings upon the currents of the wind, the nightingale as the plaintive poet singing at night in the benighted time of Man's mind and his darkened days, the muted "enemy's noon of need..." when "...temple columns stand abandoned,...when the gods are nameless and the cup of thanks and sacrificial vase and all the holies are buried in cryptic earth." (*Der Mutter Erde* – 124.51-125.60)

> Die Tempelsäulen stehn
> Verlassen in Tagen der Not,...namlos aber ist
> In ihnen der Gott, und die Schale des Danks
> Und Opfergefäß und alle Heiligtümer
> Begraben dem Feind in verschwiegener Erde.

What a rich image for the bright discernment of difference that reason brings to our cavernously habitual stillness and darkness of oblivion – the *eagle's* eye, as proud as it is piercing, upon battle-bloodied wings. The eagle sallying forth into foreign, into upper realms, hunting, swooping, seizing, its animadverting, its divining cry calling as the son of thunder, the ethereal air, invoking the sky and light and height, Jupiter's, the *owls'* howling reflection of the gloom and the whirring *bat bird's* twitching twilight, the *falcon's* serene sight, the *swans'* song that presages fatality to all thoughtlessness, the blessing-bringing *swallow* as returning herald of spring to spite with its frolic the ice of our little town blues, the *nightingale* in the dark heraldlng the morning, the *lark's* dawning, the wandering *cranes* departing and returning to the archipelagos of their home in the heavens – these beings of migration, in their flight, partners to the mountaintops and destined for the milder climes of the further fields beyond, the better world, the further land of Fatherland, depict the high ways of spirit. For poetic building is the founding of a dwelling, of a city by the sea and, by the river, the clearing of fertile lands for culture watered by the seeking stream of spirit, that "never may rest except where it is taken up in the fatherly arms of deity" (*Der Gefesselte Strom* – II 67.22-24)

> Er aber wandelt hin zu Unsterblichen;
> Denn nirgend darf er bleiben, als wo
> Ihn in die Arme der Vater aufnimmt.

This home and mansion of enduring and nurturing love is poetry as well, "for what remains poets have founded." (*Andenken* – 189.59)

> Was bleibet aber, stiften die Dichter.

It is thus in light of the poet's profession that we can best take account of the poetic human destiny that is the ripe fruit of freedom's endowment upon us in the Third Epoch of pure reason's three seasons and three summers, three summers and three springs as well as the three falls that are all winter's discontent and, before the start of thought's hours, ours of indifference.

This indifference is the gray vacancy of the fallow mind, the vast waste of "a silent sleeping people, who fate recognized as not given to passing away" upon whom therefore "descends the inexorable, terrible son of nature, the ancient spirit of discontent." (*Die Völker Schwiegen, Schlummerten...* – I 238.1-4)

> Die Völker schwiegen, schlummerten, da sah
> Das Schicksal, daß sie nicht entschliefen, und es kam
> Der unerbittliche, der furchtbare
> Sohn der Natur, der alte Geist der Unruh.

The self-severalty of self-knowing being is the name we have posited for our own experience with this stirring, disconcerting distinction that pure reason's swirling draws, upsetting the sediments, the sentiments of settlement into which we have nestled our lives. This is her cognizance, the seal and the "law of fate..." because of which all, in the end, come to know good, come to know that disturbance of distinction, which is simply "to know themselves, such that in stillness' return," when tears subside, "there then may be a language." (*Friedensfeier*)

> Schicksalgesetz ist dies, daß Alle sich erfahren,
> Daß, wenn die Stille kehrt, auch eine Sprache sei.

You experience this flurry, the flutter of the unearthed heart as thunder thought raining doom down upon, riding chariots of fire across, the trembling sky of Man, and whipping through the flapping tents of your towns with "a black storm that gulps your daylight's savings; the din's bolt splits your snug head, dumping into a death ditch what you loved – your Eden annihilated." (*Einladung Seinem Freund Neuffer* – I 233.8-11)

> ein schwarzer Sturm
> Verschlang des Tages Licht; der Donner rollte
> Und traf dein sichres Haupt; im Grabe liegt,
> Was du geliebt; dein Eden ist vernichtet.

We are torn, time torn, time born. Doubling, troubling Spirit, this spark of deity, is the inception of self-knowing human being; ideas are palpable in our experience of them, real, material in shape and sequence; the figures of their harmoniously opposed relationships are their form and beauty, the beauty that their difference makes; on the one hand because humanity can only truly enjoy itself in the distinction that poetic works of art give it – "in art, the first child of beauty, distinguished human being, rejuvenates and reiterates itself; desiring to perceive itself, human being sets beauty opposite itself as an object. In this way did we give ourselves the divine distinction…" of a self-knowing being. "For in the beginning human and divine being were one, eternal beauty existed unbeknownst to itself." (III 79.25-30)

> Das erste Kind der menschlichen, der göttlichen Schönheit ist
> die Kunst. In ihr verjüngt und wiederholt der göttliche Mensch
> sich selbst. Er will sich selber fühlen, darum stellt er seine
> Schönheit gegenüber sich. So gab der Mensch sich seine Götter.
> Denn im Anfang war der Mensch und seine Götter Eins, da, sich
> selber unbekannt, die ewige Schönheit war.

And on the other hand, the entity of identity, that pure beauty of deity, enjoys itself alone in humanity – unadulterated by bodily irritability, "the gods are sufficient unto themselves in their own immortality and if they indeed have want of anything at all, it is of heroes, of distinguished human being. For as beings of bliss they do not feel their own self-severalty, it is necessary that some other being, in their name – if one is permitted to put the matter thus – share the experience of this distinction. Of this one do they avail themselves dooming him to shatter his own house in the process and to rebuke those dearest to him as the enemy and to bury father as well as child under the ruins while he strives for divine likeness, intolerant in his zealousness of what does not accord." (*Der Rhein* – II 145.105-120)

> Es haben aber an eigner
> Unsterblichkeit die Götter genug, und bedürfen
> Die Himmlischen eines Dings,

So sinds Heroen und Menschen
Und Sterbliche sonst. Denn weil
Die Seligsten nichts fühlen von selbst,
Muß wohl, wenn solches zu sagen
Erlaubt ist, in der Götter Namen
Teilnehmend fühlen ein Andrer,
Den brauchen sie; jedoch ihr Gericht
Ist, daß sein eigenes Haus
Zerbreche der und das Liebste
Wie den Feind schelt' und sich Vater und Kind
Begrabe unter den Trümmern,
Wenn einer, wie sie, sein will und nicht
Ungleiches dulden, der Schwärmer.

This is the devotion, this the fate and peril of poetic life. Divine intangibility of spirit takes place by leaving the mark of poetic character, its "aorgic" (cf. IV 152-159) genius, upon the insentience of the mind mechanical that cannot, will not, awake from the thrill of the drill and reflex until critical reflection bursts that troubled bubble of our gloaming workaday world of woe, the world of woe of those "who haunt the night, abiding in Orcus, the dynasty of man, divested of divinity, shackled in desolation to their own devices, each harking to the roar of his own forge, in a restless rage of barren, barren toil..." (*Der Archipelagus* – II 110.241-246)

Aber weh! es wandelt in Nacht, es wohnt, wie im Orkus,
Ohne Göttliches unser Geschlecht. Ans eigene Treiben
Sind sie geschmiedet allein, und sich in der tosenden Werkstatt
Höret jeglicher nur und viel arbeiten die Wilden
Mit gewaltigem Arm, rastlos, doch immer und immer
Unfruchtbar...

Regardless of how it is envisioned and experienced in Hölderlin's poetry, whether as the *lord of time* that governs the seasons and the rhythms of our lives, *iron necessity* that, as the mother of heroes, nourishes the spirited heart, in spite of human finitude, to embrace the immortal distinction of our mind; whether as the elemental forces of *raining fire* and *blighting hoarfrost* and *wind* and *rain* of thundering inclemency or the *dark* and *nether* realm beneath the earthbound mind of human swarms where sober sighs in shadows hypocritically banter names, once holy, of gods long gone, long flown, no longer known, soullessly intoned in sour sorrow, whether as *pike* or *spur* or *barb* in the heart of innocence, whether as *path* or *course* – the relentless spirit of the mind is not a fluke or a freak but rather the fate of human nature, lifting us out of ourselves and our manhandled world, all too dearly departed, that we are called by thought to leave behind, nature by culture, culture by nature. But is this a death wish! Yes. A fate as well as a life wish, a destiny, as Empedocles explains: "For earth children mostly shy away from what is new and strange; to stay home, indoors, is the desire of vegetable life and that of animal gladness. Constrained by all that is their very own, they vigilantly attend to their conservation and no further does their sense extend into life. And nevertheless even they, the timorous, each must depart in the end and, dying, return to elements that it might be refreshed in the renewal of youth, as in a bathing. Human being is uniquely given the supreme delight that it might itself rejuvenate itself. Out of such a purifying death chosen in the maturity of time arise, as Achilles did from the Styx, the peoples" of Fatherland. (IV 65.1518-1532)

> Es scheun
> Die Erdenkinder meist das Neu und Fremde,
> Daheim in sich zu bleiben strebet nur
> Der Pflanze Leben und das frohe Tier.
> Beschränkt im Eigentume sorgen sie,
> Wie sie bestehn, und weiter reicht ihr Sinn
> Im Leben nicht. Doch müssen sie zuletzt,
> Die Ängstigen, heraus, und sterbend kehrt
> Ins Element ein jedes, daß es da
> Zu neuer Jugend, wie im Bade, sich
> Erfrische. Menschen ist die große Lust
> Gegeben, daß sie selber sich verjüngen.
> Und aus dem reinigenden Tode, den
> Sie selber sich zu rechter Zeit gewählt,
> Erstehn, wie aus dem Styx Achill, die Völker.

We see thus that in fact this movement of life and death drives our train of thought in accordance with which the whole story of our earthling life, the entire narrative, is told, all the tones of the tune plucked, the entire melody sung, and the tale and the song heard from beginning to end. How does it go again?

109. The Triadic Ratio of Nature

There are a great many notions of living and working that comprise the community of ideas Hölderlin has called *Fatherland* and that we have referred to as elaborating a complete line of reasoning, a narrative and series of scenes depicting the drama of our experience with our self-several human being as the delightful scheme of all things thought. They can then be organized in a sequence of signature terms – an inaugural, a mediate, and a resultant – such that the regularity of their changing order manifests a logotectonic of principles, laws according to which the poetic mind goes about its business of making sense, raising buildings of insight, elaborate dwellings of that distinction that is our queenly and kingly destiny.

This house of thought is built upon a number of principles, *three* to be exact; its foundation is essentially several and not just one, could never be reduced to one or two – our chair, the throne of human being wants three legs to stand and needs no more, no fourth, nor will be satisfied with less – for neither two nor one suffices our repose. There is no greater travesty committed to the spirit of reason than the extremism of a one-sided view or the positing of the irreconcilable enmity of two, a collision perhaps assuaged or appeased by compromise or coalition. No, collapsing and confounding differences by mutual conformity and assimilation is an abomination to discernment's endeavor of drawing distinctions, which is, on the contrary, precisely the splitting of the Adams who embody the mini-me mentality of minute modern Man, ours, and not its fusion in the daze of flesh.

This unique being that is, in itself, harmoniously opposed to itself is the one we depicted for the first time in *Figure 1*, and here depict yet again in *Figure 77* in order to reappraise it in light of Hölderlin's insights into the life and times of poetic genius, the creative spirit of humanity.

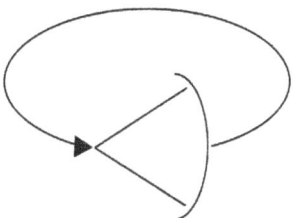

Figure 77: The Existence of Human Being

And we have seen it presented more explicitly, as in Figure 78, as a series of transitions, drives, such that outward is inward and inward is outward, depth is height and descent is flight.

Sanctifying Abstraction

Celebratory reflection

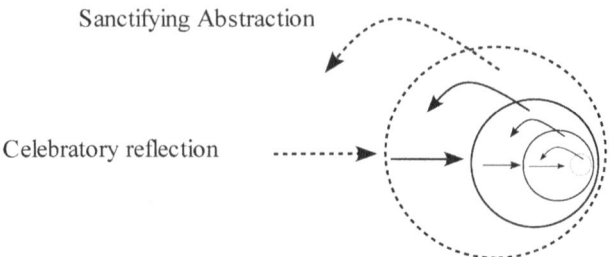

Figure 78: The Redounding Doublet of Being and To Be

For that is how we might elaborate the dialectic of the forces of the mind, its departure and return – one towards abstraction, the other towards reflection – which is our redounding doublet of difference, the double imperative that defines human *existence* in terms of critical self-reflection as the self-several entity of identity.

It would seem to be the most perfectly impossible being imaginable. And indeed it is; its impossibility is, in fact, perfected by the fact. For though impossible, it is, in fact, real, *real* first and then *impossible* and in sum both impossible *and* real, real *because* it is impossible, impossible *because* it is real – that is the distinction of human being in a nutshell: to be the reality of an impossibility; to be what it is not and not to be what it is – to be *and* not to be, that is the answer!

The forces and the powers of nature, her tones and moods, her storms and her tranquillity, her life and times, if they are not engrossed and overwhelmed by the imposition of an all too human monocracy of the mind, admit of being adopted as terms, in other words, lending their names to the sense of a line of reasoning as the particular distinguished individuals at issue in a narrative that is devoted to making sense of the logotectonic of thought. For then will "the meadows no longer sing praise to life alone – it is time that out of the human mouth the distinguished soul of beauty proclaims itself anew,"(*Ermunterung* – 33.13-16 and 35.13-16)

> ...singen die Haine nicht
> Des Lebens Lob allein, denn es ist [kommt] die Zeit,
> Daß aus der Menschen Munde sie, die
> Schönere Seele, [die göttliche,] sich neuverkündet...

Thus for example the traditional terms *woman* and *man* in Hölderlin's poem "Vulkan" in which the former term is rendered as the inward spirit of peaceful being blooming in ever tender hearted goodness that *she*, the goddess of vestal fire, is called upon to veil in golden dreams and therein to preserve while the latter is confronted with the outward forces of nature, the Boreal wind that dumps black vapor from the sky howling icily against the walls of the home *he* raised. In spite of nature's intractable forces, in contention with them, our sublime human being remains free in opposition but not merely self-opposed to the outward storm – for nature also dwells within that home, a friendly spirit there; yes, nature, her rage, rages, but she blesses the hearth as well and loves love. (*Vulkan* – 61.25-28)

Hölderlin conceived of a trefoil of beings, in the relationship of which, as a system of transitions of "tragic transport" (V 196.7) our fate is determined, an articulate experience of human destiny, comprehended in the language of nature's holy loveliness – the last of the three epochal tongues of flame infolded into the last name of the distinction of human being left to the wandering world and the time travelling mind after the glory of all the others has long since faded: "I shall come, as always, naming the ancient names of love, invoking the heart, should it yet still beat, as always, but they will be still. Even thus does time bind and part – I seem dead to them, them to me. And so I am alone. But you, above the clouds, father of Fatherland, mighty Aether! And you Earth and Light! You triunity, that reign and love, eternal gods! Never will my bonds to you be broken. From you I set out upon my travels and with you I wandered, to you, you joys, to whom I, well tried, bring back myself." (*Der Wanderer* – II 83.93-102)

> Kommen werd ich, wie sonst, und die alten, die Namen der Liebe
> Nennen, beschwören das Herz, ob es noch schlage, wie sonst,
> Aber stille werden sie sein. So bindet und scheidet
> Manches die Zeit. Ich dünk ihnen gestorben, sie mir.
> Und so bin ich allein. Du aber, über den Wolken,
> Vater des Vaterlands! mächtiger Aether! und du
> Erd und Licht! ihr einigen drei, die walten und lieben,
> Ewige Götter! mit euch brechen die Bande mir nie.
> Ausgegangen von euch, mit euch auch bin ich gewandert,
> Euch, ihr Freudigen, euch bring ich erfahrner zurück.

Father Aether (A), the never-tiring lord and guardian of time's laws and seasons, lifted us from our childhood upward mightily to his heights in the holy air of the stars' celestial flowers having poured his fragrant breath of spirit into our infant soul who are born to his brightness and nourished thus by divine light and fed in our flourishing towards the sky even before our mother's drink of nourishment touched our lips of hunger. He teaches our striving heart the sacrifice of the longing songs he sent to our binding, unbound being to inspire poetic singing with enthusiasm's eloquence (cf. *An den Aether* I 204. 1-11) whose thunderous voice from above the rough and tumble of our clouds echoes upon the earth in judgment's anger or in still serenity, raining blessings on true hearts' heads, revealing signs that all our deeds explain and to whom "is dearest what has been well wrought in words and their constitution properly construed" (*Patmos* – II 172.224-225) by uplifted and uplifting intellect; "open to all, vouchsafing thoughtful, all-redeeming day to poor and rich alike, holding and upholding us, in fleeting times, on children's golden leads" (*Dichtermut* – 64.14-20), "omnipresent Aether stands and reigns and dwells over the hills of home that a loving people may be encompassed by their father's arms, under which, joyfully human, as once it was, one spirit may be common to all." (*Der Archipelagus* – 110. 237-240)

> ...über Bergen der Heimat
> Ruht und waltet und lebt allgegenwärtig der Aether,
> Daß ein liebendes Volk in des Vaters Armen gesammelt,
> Menschlich freudig, wie sonst, und Ein Geist allen gemein sei.

Grace-filled Light (C) is insightful and advising, animadverting, in spite of the continual encroachment of livid night's inhibitions. The beams of evening are mild; when husband day returns to greet earth mother, his spouse, he desires with his holy glow to draw distinctions upon her expanse. Light is the mediator, the brink and the link between thought and life, the avenue of interval, of claim and counterclaim across which the torch of reflection is borne and passed to the people harkening to "the voice of the thunderer calling in admonition: 'do you give thought to me?'" (der Archipelagus – 110.232-233) It teaches us the lessons of lucidity – the smile of noble day having gone down to the sea to embark for night's unknown shore, stern and determined to die a good death in the manifestation of the twinkling stars, having risen and arrived renewed in the rhythm of irradiance with which the days of life illuminate grow upward to the sun, holding fast in its gaze the slow glow of green and the flowers' bloom upon the faces of our earth and her family of friends, pervading the ethereal realm of Father Aether's jovial birds who lark and wheel in the blaze of his gaze under silver clouds of fire shine. Light is the youthful seer and messenger from on high to gleaming eyes of thanks for the descended blessings that delight our sight, ignite our drive, ripen with its warmth the burgeoning of our lives – all those hues of spirit touching with the several timbres of its tones the upturned eyes, all seeing, from serene to sombre in which "glad among the glad, light finds, knows the light."(*Ermunterung* – 33.20 and 35.24)

Froh in den Frohen das Licht sich kennet [findet]...

Mother Earth (B), all-loving and therefore all-receiving (*Der Rhein* – 146.150-152), her patient, cradling arms cherish her children's sweet slumber and, awoken, nurtures their dwelling on her green floors upon which the grounds of our houses, their foundations, like good reasons, stand and to which, at the end of a day's way, we, long grown, have finally returned, come home to the old mother, who has remained forever young in the memory of childhood, blooming, unfolding the infinite earthly power of love in which the elements themselves, forming bonds with human being, become our home's subsistence, her garden of ordered paths and the harmonious alterity (*Der Frieden* – 7.37-40) of springs and forest settlements; our Earth is serious, silent, all-suffering (*Gesang der Deutschen* – 3.2), prizing loyalty and substantial truth but in her holy night, heavy with weeping and lamenting her solitude, when, dressed in shadows and decked in the night's twinkling jewels, the morning mist hides her face like a veil and the last stars fade that were some little ornament to her magnitude. Hers are the household's fruits that want carrying, the burdens that want bearing across the circle of her ages in accordance with the most ancient laws and birthrights, giving up and taking back to the returning soil her born, her living and her dead.

And she, full of memory, revisits in her mind the times of gold, when gods and humans lived together in her world and she together with the king she gave rise to and welcomed at the close of day to her embrace and theirs. For this is the feast of joy, the enthusiasm of the community of high spirits, in particular that of deity and humanity, of mind and matter, of thoughts and things, of the ideal and the real, symbolized by the grape, "from Earth *and* Aether engendered" and thus a distinguished being, the holy grape, that "watered by the high sun, rises from the dark earth." (*Empedocles* – 135.371-373)

> ...die Rebe
> Von Erd und Himmel zeugt,...getränkt
> Von hoher Sonn aus dunklem Boden steigt,

For it is from "nature's ever-plenty goblet, full to overflowing inspiration with the grape's blood and essence that we drink heart and strength and love and cheer." (*An Hiller* – 175.7-10). This cup of joy is raised at the feast of nature's community when works have ended well in celebration of what has been accomplished. Here poets are in attendance to weave their wreaths of laurel songs. And here is our wreath of service (*Patmos* – II 172.220-221), the service of those who "were discourse first but soon are song" (Friedensfeier), our well-woven logotectonic rhapsody of nature's harmoniously opposed relationship of relationships, its trefoil ratio of terms, that we take as "a token of love and testimony, that you, holy powers, are holy still in the holiday" (Friedensfeier) of language.

Figure 79 shows, in its most basic sense, that the power and distinction of the general principle and inaugural term, *Father Aether* (A) is mediated by the distinguished term of that principle's manifesting efficacy, namely *Grace-filled Light* (C) and carried to a holy grape's fruition in the completion of that principle's original purpose, which was to realize, in illuminating ways, the significance of thought as being, beings as thoughts, an accord and concert of them, come alive as the issue designated by the resultant term, in this case, *Mother Earth* (B), of a line of reasoning devoted in the Third Epoch to the conception of *nature* as the destiny of human being.

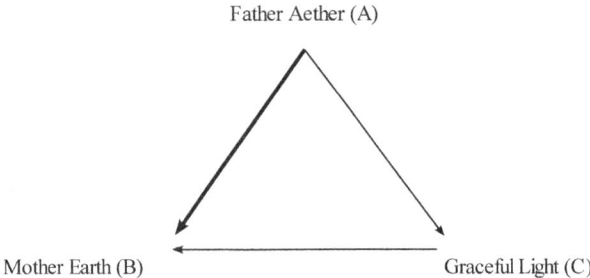

Father Aether (A)

Mother Earth (B)   Graceful Light (C)

Figure 79: Nature's Wreath of Triunity

Thus these distinguished times and beings of nature, her *gods,* are themselves comprehended in the all-encompassing beauty and harmony of their relationship; even divinity must go down in fire and remain a memory till morning and then to spark the lazy ashes of Man's inanity that humanity arise again; childhood's meal of stillness upon the mother's breast grows into youth inflamed by divine desire to fall into the cloudless sky until to poetry we have mounted who, among the dead and strays in the iron cradle of this life and time of dearth, have strengthened, sharpened our hearts to the acuity of craft and art and taken up the poet's pursuit to build dwellings of praise to nature that in the poem the word be holy, the word be our better, our new, our further world. For only then could the poet of Fatherland affirm that "now is the dawning: Having persevered in expectation, I saw it coming and what I saw – holy be my word. For she herself, who is elder than all time and above the gods of Occident and Orient, nature, is awoken with the clang of swords and high from the aether to the abyss below, in accordance with principle, as once, engendered from holy chaos, spirited being has come to know itself again, the builder of all being." (*Wie wenn am Feiertage...* 118.19-27)

> Jetzt aber tagts! Ich harrt und sah es kommen,
> Und was ich sah, das Heilige sei mein Wort.
> Denn sie, sie selbst, die älter denn die Zeiten
> Und über die Götter des Abends und Orients ist,
> Die Natur ist jetzt mit Waffenklang erwacht,
> Und hoch vom Aether bis zum Abgrund nieder
> Nach festem Gesetze, wie einst, aus heiligem Chaos gezeugt,
> Fühlt neu die Begeisterung sich,
> Die Allerschaffende, wieder.

Now let us set the stage for the scene of this feast, the poet's laurel wreath of achievement. For is not *making it real*, giving concrete life and shape to the abstract notions of the mind, is this not precisely the work of thought, the Builder, poetic thought, even as Hölderlin has taught us? This is a work of celebration.

> Die Dichter müssen auch
> Die Geistigen weltlich sein (der Einzige – 156.104-105)

Poets, the spirited, must be worldly.

We know that poetic spirit is enthusiastic; its enthusiasm is affectionate and infecting but neither fanatic nor mere reflex, inclusive and encompassing, an open, friendly benevolence but with discernment, with regard, not given to such gushing as would, with its exuberance, drown those eminent peaks, flood those profound valleys, and thus erode the contours of our earth's diversity for the sake of talk.

What then does it bring forth in its salubrious joy? Does it merely make a map of scars, chronicle the wars that thought has fought, or reduce to quibbles what men have staked their lives upon? More than these, poetic thought builds anthologies of poems but is not, therefore, merely literary production. The garlands that it winds are collections and recollections of all that the self-knowing being of pure reason has accomplished in its career, a chronicle of the vicissitudes of its long, eventful life – commemorating its greatest achievements and ordering their progression in a complete train, a scheme of all things thought, a rapport and succession of incommensurable principles the proportion of which can only appear pertinaciously opposed or suspiciously synthetic to those whose predilections, since the childhood of their reflections, have been fed the divisive fare of bias.

110. The Celebration of Accord (*Friedensfeier*)

The nameless poet announces a holiday. A gathering in the evening of days shall take place at this unique and critical junction of history when all the great ideas upon which cultures and civilizations of the earth's surface, all these travelers of reason's traditions, return to rest and take respite in the fellowship of friends. The poem, this mature fruit of poetic speech, the work of poetic thought, is our doing, our hall "full of heavenly resounding, quietly turning tones." (Hölderlin, *Friedensfeier*, 7.1-2)

For this feast of ideas' congeniality and affiliation is our monument to the human spirit, is, with respect to these ideas, these "holy powers" that people mind, "a token of pure love and a testament to their undeniable fact" (10.100-11.101), the simple fact that they yet endure and hold good, hold true, hold together in harmonious opposition in our much faded world so inclined towards indiscriminate grey or else the black and white of acrimony.

This is the work of thought, the Builder, the poetic spirit, this "quiet god of time," expert in the turned words of wisdom – in those tongues of truth that are our oldest scriptures – who, having long studied, cherished the epochal diversity of their speech and learned to collect their several messages into a scheme of all things thought, "has since perfected the design and leaves the workshop now, enlightened, as a master of the craft and art for which alone the law of love, that of all-balancing harmonious proportionality, applies from here on up to the highest skies." (10.86-90)

> So dünkt mir jetzt das Beste,
> Wenn nun vollendet sein Bild und fertig ist der Meister,
> Und selbst verklärt davon aus seiner Werkstatt tritt,
> Der stille Gott der Zeit und nur der Liebe Gesetz,
> Das schönausgleichende gilt von hier an bis zum Himmel.

The reconciliation of these distinguished visions of thought's ages that poetic imagination thus elaborates upon is a sign of commonality between it and the other epochal principles, "transient..." in their epochal determination "...though divine, but not in vain..." (so ist schnell vergänglich alles Himmlische; aber umsont nicht,... – 9.50-51). And the "all-comprehending holy day of joy" celebrated in their honor is the symbol of this collegiality, a conference not of people or of nations but of ideas, where this "heavenly folk, neither made manifest in miracles nor unseen in clouds of thunder," convene in their signs, on their own terms; "in choirs of song they, the blessed, are entirely and hospitably gathered together, a holy number round him who is their heart,...for this," for them, says the poet "have I called you, in the evening of time, to the readied banquet, you, who are unforgotten, youthful hero, have proclaimed your precedence as the prince of the feast." (11.103-111)

But who is the prince of these festivities, everybody wonders? At this feast of thought, "we sing different songs, we celebrate new holy days, holidays of saints from all times and places, the heroes of the Orient and the Occident; we each choose one that is closest to our heart and life and call that saint's name who then, splendid still in death, appears in our midst in the glory of his accomplishments; but also the quiet achievements of those who worked in the purity of spirit upon the hearth will not be forgotten – crowns bloom for every excellence... Then do we rejoice in the dear *Earth*, in her perpetual life of peaceful harmony, hymning her and cultivating her,...and, too, we welcome in the plenitude of our heart the ever youthful, the spring-bringing *Light* of the sky's sun rising to our joy, but it is not possible to commemorate her alone! The *Aether* that encompasses us – is he not the image of the mind's natural spirit, the pure, the immortal? And the water's spirit, when touching our youth with its holy waves, does he not play the melody of their hearts? And blessed peace's accord with all that is – does he deserve any less a holiday?" But again, who is the presiding Prince of these festivities? "The one that we worship we do not name; although this one is as close to us as we are to ourselves, we do not say her name, his name; solemnized by no holiday, for whom no temple could be worthy tribute; the accord of our minds and their eternal increase is his...," is her "...only commemoration." (*Hyperions Jugend* – III 224.8-32).

> Wir singen andere Lieder, wir feiern neue Feste, die Feste der Heiligen in allen Zeiten und Orten, der Heroen des Morgen- und Abendlands; da wählt jedes einen aus, der seinem Herzen, seinem Leben am nächsten ist, und nennt ihn, und der herrliche Tote tritt mitten unter uns in der Gloire seiner Taten, auch wer geschäftig am stillen Herde mit der reinem Sinne das Seine tat, wird nie von uns vergessen und Kronen blühen für jede Tugend;...dann freun wir uns der lieben Erde, daß sie noch immer ihr friedlich schönes Leben lebt, und die sie bauen, singen von ihr;...auch sie lieben wir alle, die Ewigjugendliche, die Mutter des Frühlings, willkommen glorious sister! rufen wir aus der Fülle unsers Herzens, wenn sie herauf kömmt zu unsern Freuden, die Geliebte, die Sonne des Himmels; doch ists nicht

möglich, ihrer alleine zu denken! Der Aether, der uns umfängt, ist er nicht das Ebenbild unsers Geistes, der reine, unsterbliche? Und der Geist des Wassers, wenn er unsern Jünglingen in der heiligen Wooge begegnet, spielt er nicht die Melodie ihres Herzens? Er ist ja wohl eines Festes werth, der seelige Friede mit allem, was da ist! – Den Einen, dem wir huldigen, nennen wir nicht; ob er gleich uns nah ist, wie wir uns selbst sind, wir sprechen ihn nicht aus. Ihn feiert kein Tag; kein Tempel ist ihm angemessen; der Einklang unserer Geister, und ihr unendliche Wachstum feiert ihn allein.

The prince of these festivities remains nameless but not unknown, not lost in anonymity; called neither *God*, nor even *the gods* – for these names have become determinate in the history of their cult and culture; they are exclusionary in the hands of their sectarians because their confessions give rise to the several incompatible communities and churches to which we either belong *or* do not belong. You must choose and even to refuse to choose is to make a choice to be or not to be.

You must choose. For among the multitude of zealots clashing in the arena of religion and nationality, gender and age, social class and ethnicity, world views and sexual orientations, there are no shared rites and rituals of indoctrination; among their several people, their nations and advocates, there is no common language of devotion, no common ground of sanctity. There is but the mundane marketplace, that secular square of our media in the middle of town in the shadow of Babel; in that common place of profanity where all the faithful, entering upon their work week, doffing those garbs and livery of their private lives, anonymously converge in the suits of their professions to go about their daily business. There is no name above all other names but rather just a cacophony of them murmuring at the margins that fringe the ephemeral mainstream of Man.

By contrast, the poet and the celebratory poetic spirit are fulfilled in the vision presented by the poem itself; the hymn sung in celebration of the accord achieved at the behest of the prince and principle who, summoning all to presence, has not arrived as yet in person and, in fact, never will, never could arrive. For, it is the poem of celebration itself, this poetic, celebratory spirit that calls all the princes and the principles in the land of pure reason to a community of cheer sanctified by the poet's word whose poem is the friendly asylum and the cup of spirits that awakens and summons the people from near and far to partake of the community of principles and become companions in that spirit of peace and, with the eternal, aboriginal beings of nature (die Unerzeugten, Ew'gen – HF.10.97), partners in the fellowship of their powers (Bündnis – 10.96) in the same way that "mother earth recognizes herself and light and air in the plants'" proportion of these elements (...gleichwie an den Pflanzen die Mutter Erde sich und Licht und Luft sich kennet – 10.98-99).

This synergetic circle of its inspired guests, this "form of the divine, is our dearest good, our golden fruit, storm shaken, long sought and then, finally, safeguarded by the holy destiny" (12.136-141) of poetic craft and art in these sanctifying songs of Fatherland; this "festive day of celebration, the pantheonic, is the ultimate token of love, the final proof that you, you sacred principles, are indeed still holy where indeed the Heavenly are revealed neither in wonders, nor concealed in clouds but rather where they, in choirs of song, fostering a rapport of hospitality among themselves, are present, a holy number, the blessed beings dwelling together in every way." (11.103-111)

> Zuletzt ist aber doch, ihr heiligen Mächte, für euch/ Das Liebeszeichen, das Zeugnis/Daß ihr noch seiet, der Festtag,/ Der Allversammelnde, wo Himmlische nicht Im Wunder offenbar, noch ungesehn im Wetter,/ Wo aber bei Gesang gastfreundlich untereinander/ In Chören gegenwärtig, eine heilige Zahl/ Die Seligen in jeglicher Weise Beisammen sind.

It is the work of a true friend of thought, the philological Builder, to establish the festival that makes out of the pandemonium of divinity in the tumble of traditions the synoptic scheme of all things thought in which none is placed above all the others – no dominion (8.28) usurped or proclaimed – but rather conjoined in the mutual regard and the dissonance of harmonious opposition that characterizes a convivial community of distinguished princes and principles (II 2 699.19-20) "for none of our kind will lay our head to rest until all you promised ones, you immortals, come to tell us of your Heaven, are there dwelling in our midst."

> ...und eher legt
> Sich schlafen unser Geschlecht nicht,
> Bis ihr Verheißenen all,
> All ihr Unsterblichen, uns
> Von eurem Himmel zu sagen,
> Da seid in unserem Hause.

Who is the Prince? Do we call him *Peace* or *Hope* or *Compassion* or *Power* or some other generic, vaguely numinous name, gladly applied by our hypocrisy when invoking either the more mischievous Hudibrastic or the more sullenly pensive solemnity belabored in what folks these days call *literary criticism*? The prince is not, as many Hölderlin scholars have suggested, *Christ*, though he is both called to and called the *first* (Fürst) by the prince's guests themselves; being the last deity of occidental tradition, he enjoys priority as the youngest among them and is, in this sense, "their most beloved."

Ultimately however, the Prince of the feast is not *Christ* or *Saturn*, not *Time* or *Heaven*, (nor is he *Napoleon*, for that matter) and then again all of these names would serve thought, the Builder, in a pinch, to invoke the idea in question – but each in a different way, each presenting the idea in a different light of language. For "it is the holy name under which the highest is felt or takes place." (V 267.9-10)

> Der heilige Namen, unter welchem das Höchste gefühlt wird
> oder geschieht...

For deity is several not one and none is more worthy than the other, though all perfect in themselves and perfectly distinct; all in their own way call and recall their fellows in the friendly spirit of that Olympian scope and measure that is here, in the poem, appealed to. It collects in the comity of song an extended family of individuals round the table of endearment to share a cup of cheer in their mutual presence and regard, forgetting none, neglecting none and at all times mindful of each one's unique distinction, achievements, and contributions to the goodness and the glory of their dwelling as a whole.

The "First" person of the Feast is thus – if not simply one from among the circle of guests entrusted with the chair of presidency in periodic rotation – even that infinite distinction that never appears or could appear and yet is not entirely unheard of, unseen by "eyes in twilight" (dämmernden Augen - *Friedensfeier*, 7.13). For what, in truth, is this distinction? It is nothing in itself beyond the permanent annulment of all determinations; it is simply that fabled outer space into which thought emerges when we step back in critical self-reflection and adopt the standpoint of abstraction saying: Not this! Not that! Distinguished from this! Different from that! It makes a world of difference to adopt this coign of vantage, this standpoint of being entirely *before, beneath, above, below, behind,* and in this sense *pre*-positional even as *Freedom, God,* and *Destiny* are its illustrious designations of principle in their respective epochs – naming thus the three Occidental principles of alterity, exteriority, and priority.

Where are we then who have put all determinacy but also all indeterminacy behind us and below us and before us in a flight of self-distinguishing spirit? If we should call our capacity for this space that we give and take *pure reason* and that coign of vantage we have attained in its practice the *no place* of pure and simple negation, the absolute extrication that, calling all into question that Man can put before us, calls nothing at all, why is it then such a rich experience? First because of the vistas that the prospect of critical reflection opens for us, who are all too inclined to pent ourselves up in a set of circumstances, conventions, instructions neither given, nor received – a certain set of facts looms large surrounding us and commands: "Here I am; I am all there is; I am the mountains and the seas; I am the air; I am the place and the time; I am who you are and who you were, your birth, your death; I determine all you shall ever be. I am the facts; I am THE WAY IT IS; I am your life; I am your world; this is it. Period." Do we simply acquiesce in the face of these daily dictates, so definitive and undoubted? Ah, even to ask this question is to recognize a shift or fracture in the plane of dictatorial facticity, to acknowledge a difference, a divergence between the way it is and the way it could be, between the way it is and the way it should be but perhaps is not, not yet.... We see this. Yes, we cannot help but see this. And then a horizon of possibilities opens in what, at first blush, appeared to be determinations set and settled for all time. For apparently, as we have learned in the Third Epoch, there is around facts, taken as a whole as they present themselves to us, a halo of difference, the glow of alterity – and precisely this is the work of our mind, its celebrated discontinuity in prescinding thought from things. It is thus an interruption in and among the things that would otherwise have continued to take their course unobstructed and had their way with us – if only there had been no critical reflection, this crack and crisis in the plain pane of mere being that doubles and troubles facts by harmoniously opposing them, if only the mini-me mentality of Man had never been recognized, human being, as distinguished from it, never won our regard, if only the distinction itself had never emerged in light of reflection, the drama of our self-severalty had never mounted the tragic stage of existence commanding our tears.

Such is the power and efficacy of negativity, of an idea we name and call in honor, in a flight, at a feast, of poetic fancy, our *prince*, awaited, but not as Godot; we wait upon this notion and the experience it refers to as servants wait upon their sires whose arrival has been delayed but who is expected any moment now and in this anticipation perfectly present to the mind of those who serve him, though completely absent. Our relationship to this idea is therefore that of *attendance* rather than *presence*. For we are never done with thought. To consecrate, to take up and hold in regard and, in an abundance of gratitude, to foster this idea, Hölderlin gives the name *king* or *father* or *prince* – all terms of distinction – to the *consecrating, celebratory spirit* that is the *poetic* destiny of distinguished human being.

Hölderlin has taught us that in spite of the purity of its abstraction, this genius of poetic spirit is not withdrawn or mute, closed- or single-mindedness, but rather, is, in fact, *self-realizing*, i.e., as we saw, "inclined to recreate itself in itself and in others" (*geneigt sich in sich selber und in anderen zu reproduzieren* – IV 241.7-8), come to successive life in the tones and seasons, in the sweep of time that passes from subjective self-relative severalty to the objective entity of identity and back again. Thus do we make a big deal, make something out of nothing and "enlist and entrust to this absolutely free purpose" (zu eigen gemacht und festhalten werden mit freiem Interesse – 242.20-21) all the words and names inherited from a long tradition of diligence in the ways of ΛΟΓΟΣ in order to give the great ideas that it motivated greater and greater shape and form and a *material identity* (242.15-16) in the tangibility of our language that articulates in the relationships of insights deduced from the ratio *of terms A - B - C* a train of thought in which "the final term returns upon the inaugural, and this one upon the mediate term" (243.32-33) – giving shape and form to what has, in and of itself, neither shape nor form but is, rather, the negation of all shape and form, only, that is, until the poet begins to hymn "the ideal that once was nature. On it, on this ideal, this rejuvenated deity, do the few recognize each other and are one, for it is one in them." (III 63.30-33)

> Ideal ist, was Natur war. Daran, an diesem Ideale, dieser verjüngten Gottheit, erkennen die Wenigen sich und Eins sind sie, denn es ist Eines in ihnen...

The reality of a shared ideal is not its fulfillment but rather what we actually do and achieve because of it, as a result of our cherishing it, the consequences that flow from the words and deeds of those who share this ideal as a dream; however impractical it may ultimately be, we nevertheless make this dream efficacious in our actions and, in a shared spirit, give it life together as one and several. To found and inspire this community of dreamers with that uniquely creative enthusiasm of mind that wants and strives to matter, to make a difference, is the true power and the reality of ideals and the substantive issue of our most human faculty and endowment, namely that of productive imagination.

THE SECOND EPOCH – THE DEITY OF SELF-SEVERALTY

111. The Encounter with Self-Several Thought in Person

After having examined the *nature*, the human nature of freedom and the *culture* of the Ideal in the works of poetic imagination, we have now perhaps come to a better understanding of what *thought* actually is; at least we have gained our first impression of what a principle of reason is. If you ask folks on the street what thought is, chances are most will say that thought is a handy dandy tool for solving pressing every-day problems. Yes, thought is that, too. We have considered this sense of thought as "using our heads" in the beginning. Have we become acquainted with any other since then? Hopefully, our explorations thus far should allow us to be more comprehensive and more eloquent on this topic. What is thought? It is self-reflection. What is that? It is, in a word, the act of realization. Now this word is very interesting. The notion of making something that is, initially at least, no thing at all, being an idea and figment of the imagination, an ideal, real, is only one possible sense, the one we have been studying in the Third Epoch of Thought, Hölderlin's.

But there is another sense in which we might understand *realization*. This word's connection to self-reflection can be ascertained in the sentence: "I didn't realize that it was so late." Here realization includes the notion of becoming aware as in the sentence: "I wasn't aware that it was so late," or more generally perhaps, "it had not occurred to me till now to give it any thought." Who could deny that self-knowing being must also comprehend this sense of critical self-reflection; it is perhaps even the more germane of the two understandings of what it means to "realize something."

These two so very different notions of, on the one hand, *becoming aware* and, on the other, *making an idea come to life* are apparently closely connected – one word, namely the word *realization*, seems to admit of both senses. And then, upon consideration, the connection is indeed obvious. Both *awareness* and *invention* bring to the attention and to the light of day what was not previously present and concealed to, hidden from them. They are both *revelatory*. When I realize that someone is following me, I have not created that person who is following me, nor necessarily the situation that I am being followed. When, however, the situation dawns on me that I am being followed, it is as if what was previously not there, is "*there!*" now because only now has it come to my attention and made a difference. Before this, before my realization of what is going on, my predicament, as one who is, unbeknownst to himself, being followed, might have been seen by a spectator observing the situation from without, and was definitely evident to the third person, the spectator of the spectator, who, by definition, knows all and sees all and therefore always sees the whole picture, but it wasn't there for me and when I notice what's happening, this tacit or latent state of affairs emerges into circumstances that are now frighteningly evident to and no longer concealed from me – both I and the situation have come to light, have seen the light of day, which is the light and the day of discernment that now takes note of a fact that, divorced from that discernment and as such previously missed, neglected, ignored, did not, in truth, exist before. To be struck by, to become aware of what we had previously failed to take any note of – that is a familiar experience with the way thought *transforms* the world for us and makes bright present...or dark...what was hitherto absent and lurking in shadows – both, the darkness *and* the light, are now brought to light.

What do these considerations regarding the meaning of the word *realization* show us? For one, they show us that knowledge, insight, seeing, are, in a certain way, *creative*; not only in the sense of the imagination an ideal of which, the vision of THE WAY IT SHOULD BE, wants to be brought to life, take on the form and shape of reality, but now in the further sense that the world accessible to knowledge is brought forth and in this sense "created" by and in the knowing, *real* simply by virtue of being known; what has been brought forth out of the shadows of mindless oblivion – though somehow *there*, of course, the whole time from the point of view of a hypothetical, disinterested, and omniscient third party, but not in truth "there!" at all in the emphatic sense of our *apprehension* – only truly comes to life in the **animadversion** of the mind returned from the inadvertency of negligence. Hence, we must say that it is not only the speech of poetic individuality that gives rise to reality, the reality that language gives to thought for the pleasure of the honored guests at the feast of freedom – *generative reason*; but also the emergence of what was obscure, forgotten, neglected, out of this darkness into the light of the mind and clear discernment can be thought of as a bringing forth of its object, not only the realization of what was previously abstract and disembodied like a plan, a goal, a vision, but rather the realization of what, though already in some sense "real," was previously hidden from sight and then made manifest, becoming now *real* in a way that the object was not when it had been still shrouded in shadows of distraction; recognizing what has become discernible for thought thus converted to sight, *perceptive reason* exclaims: "*There!*"

Now when folks start paying attention to what is going on around them, an event as monumental as it is rare in the face of all that slogging and pegging laboriousness we owe to our slavish workaday world, they begin to notice a great many details, facts they have missed; most of all they realize just how unobservant they usually are, concerned with getting through this day and the next. So is the point that we do some mental exercises in paying attention to the rush of thoughts and things that hush and flutter by in our world and in our minds, those two theaters upon which human experience plays out, and both so rich in phenomena worthy of note and nevertheless constantly subject to neglect?

No, not that. For what precisely is hidden in just this way in the strictest sense? Neither things that I have carelessly mislaid and found finally, nor useless or inane things like a certain spot on the wall, the lowly sponge hanging on the faucet in the kitchen, the position of this book on the table, this scratch on the door, this wrapper on the street...nor utterly normal but nevertheless still remarkable things like the love of one woman, the shamelessness of men, the play of light and shadow on the wall, moats of dust, shifting patterns of random sounds, a plastic bag blowing, twirling in the wind, drips of paint that have formed a frozen explosion of color in the corner, or as Peter Handke, in his attempts to retrieve the elements of "a day of felicity," uncovers to our note:[65]

> The sliver of granite in the sidewalk gleaming near the eye (25), the musical click of buttons when I swept up my shirt from the chair this morning...(34), the yellowness of the blackbird's beak (53).

Neither all of these things, nor yet people, the apparition of their faces in a crowd, that mouth drooping, the shifting eye, a stranger's light green iris, the prominent forehead under a veil of hair, a gait, a limp, a word snatched from a passer-by, a chuckle, a sigh...nor even my physical and mental states that I habitually ignore, the feeling of the air in my ears and in my lungs, the weight of my arms bearing down on the rests of the chair, the tingle in the toe tucked in the sock squeezed into the shoe, or else that speck of fear that had just accompanied my smile, a fleeting memory at the sound of a bell or smell or melody, emerging emotions' flood, unspoken articulations of dreams and desires...not these things, not people, not my physical states, though prone to be hidden by their own pervasive prevalence, to be lost in their own collective plenitude and ignored by the absorption of our

---

[65] Peter Hanke, Versuch über den geglückten Tag, Surkamp 1994.

preoccupations – it is not these things and people and sights and sounds, that populate our moods and reveries that are the most completely covert beings – no, it is not these epiphanies of life's lovely, beautiful banalities when the world wondrously "worlds" and nothingness "nothings" for us, but rather it is *thought itself* that is, to our unthinking, preoccupied selves, the most ubiquitous absence, the most hidden presence, the attendance most completely unattended to.

The self-realization of thought is therefore two different realizations, one in the sense that thought is an abstraction, an intangible idea that nevertheless strives to take on concrete form in the building of words and actions, a *coming to be*, the other in the sense of a *coming to know* – thought that becomes aware of itself, comes to recognize itself, as if the absent mind, only just lost in the abandon of distraction, suddenly were to be found, were to see the man in the mirror of self-reflection and say "Aha! There I...no, not *I*, not *me*, but rather *you*: there *You* are!"

"You talking to me?" – What a jarring experience this shift of pronouns is likely to entail in us after thinking about critical self-reflection for so long as my relationship to Me, as we have in the Third Epoch, in which it is precisely the pointed discrepancy between our ideals, on the one hand, and ourselves and our world, both of which are far from ideal, on the other, that inspires and drives the poet's effort to reconcile their divergent tendencies in our lives by seeking a rapport of mutual regard between them and the reciprocity of a dwelling in which both thought and thing, ideal and real, mind and matter are harmoniously opposed. For, as we saw, the double imperative of human nature is both abstraction *and* determinacy, each the end and the beginning of the other and reconcilable only in the self-several being of that nature that is pure reason's very own life and times. Nature's life has seasons of bliss and sorrow; its distinguished beings can only thrive in the proper proportion of their forces in which neither dominates the other but to the detriment of the entire community, in disdain of that endearing spirit of beauty that celebrates its cheer at the festive table of shared plenitude.

But even in the Third Epoch we learned to understand the freedom of human being not merely as one in which we are simply liberated from all determinacy, footloose and fancy free, but rather ours is the freedom of citizens subject to the governance of their autonomous nature, namely the self-determination of our humanity. For to be governed by our own humanity, we must be the governors of our own humanity. How is this possible? When we gain the certitude that the absolute difference that freedom makes is inscribed in our own heart, in the self-several human heart.

Now to enter upon the wisdom of the Second Epoch, don't say *I* to this absolute difference that your conscience makes; don't say, with respect to its voice, *My* voice and, to its general will, *Mine*, say *You* to it and *Your* Voice, say *Your* will be done. You see, dear reader, sometimes it is not about you at all, sometimes it is about You. The absolute difference that You make/makes is not one naturally *within me*, in the profound yet simple goodness and purity of the human soul to which I give free expression as the poetic genius of the ideal's dwelling; instead, the absolute difference is, in its inception, *without me*, coming towards me and whom I address, more, whom I welcome, as I would a fellow human being by saying *You* even as I formerly spoke of this distinction as of Myself. Don't let's say *I* am/is, let's say, now, at the brink of the Second Epoch, *You* are/is the absolute distinction of human being, human *and* absolute in one being and therefore even as *I* was in myself, likewise you are/is in Yourself self-several. Who are/is You if you are/is not Me? *You* are/is pure reason not as My humanity in me but rather standing now before me, as it were, and speaking the words of wisdom that *I* spoke previously. The issue is now, however, not to bring forth and realize the Freedom of My Humanity but rather to receive and embrace, in gratitude, the difference that You make in having addressed me, offered me your present, the *Grace*, of Your absolute distinction, i.e. Your *Deity*. And like Freedom's, Deity's first words, *Your* first words, to us (and Your last - Joh: 21.19) are "come and follow me."(ΔΕΥΤΕ ΟΠΙΣΩ ΜΟΥ- Mat 4:19)

112. The Language of Christianity

We have become acquainted with the philological art of perspicacity, its method of construing meaning in the writs and words of wisdom we have been considering; this *perceptive* art accompanies its *generative* counterpart which consists in exhibiting thought in the concrete form of words that dramatic narrative and poetry offer to an audience in such a way as to inspire the listener's and reader's enthusiasm for the difference that pure reason makes in human life.

The starting point of our investigations was an experience that we have termed *critical self-reflection* in which we, ensconced or immured in the strait and narrow specifications of our material world, in the assumed invariables of our individual lives, are summoned to the scene of the original position before the impartial judgment of the mind, the judicious spectator, to be measured with respect to reason and its infinite purview by the mark of absolute difference. The sentence passed by the judge is twofold: first, THE WAY IT IS *is not* THE WAY IT SHOULD BE – this mortification of life is the death sentence condemning the darkness of the immediate world that has been accused and convicted of blind oblivion in the nescient headlong rush and tumble of matters at hand; second, THE WAY IT SHOULD BE *is not* THE WAY IT IS – this is the death sentence that condemns the empty abstraction of thought as withdrawn into the inscrutability of an absconding authority bent on totalitarian control, a sentence that has been commuted to imprisonment in life. But the arc of polarity sparking between these two contradictions has a consequence. It galvanizes the will into action, namely to critical revision and renewal in accordance with the principle towards a more just community and participation with regards to the human world – thus the double imperative of pure reason.

It is thus clear that this experience of the self-discord of critical reflection, recognizing its dimensions and learning how the tale of the mind's emergence has been given vivid articulation in terms of human being, remains our central theme and cause. Keeping our eyes on the distinction of human being will be of particular help to us now as we endeavor to reorient ourselves in the Christian language of the Second Epoch in which self-reflection is called METANOIEN (repentance) and the embodiment of this distinction is not My Humanity, My Nature, *in me* but rather Yours, of natures both human and divine, *with us*, by You called to godliness and therefore by us proclaimed the *Lord, my God, Jesus Christ* – the distinction of human being in Christian terms.

Let's face a hard truth: You'll never be much of a philologist of pure reason if you can't "deal with" the language of Christian thought. Of course, in saying this, I foolhardily run the risk of upsetting two key target groups of this book – the self-proclaimed defenders of the faith as well as its zealous attackers and detractors of religion. In general, the former will resent the supposed insinuation that holy scripture and its salient terms and expressions such as *God, Glory, Grace, Holy Spirit*, the *Kingdom of Heaven*, the *Crucifixion*, the *Resurrection, Life after Death*, the *Savior, etc.*, could be thought of as "merely" turns of words and phrases, as a manner of speaking and writing about ideas that can be and have been written and spoken about in different terms than these; the latter will decry the asseveration that we cannot possibly understand the whole story of the distinction of human being without studying the gospel of Jesus Christ and acquiring some proficiency in speaking that language. Neither the latter's solemn commitment to the Word of God nor the latter's aversion to such a notion as revealed truth will appreciate our proposal that the ideas of Christianity can be studied as a train of thought, followed as a line of reasoning and thus acknowledged as both accessible to and in conformance with the most stringent requirements of pure reason. What about the power of faith to maintain its empire against and in spite of all reason to the contrary? What about reason's most urgent duty to combat and overcome the disgraceful irrationality and superstition of religion made evident by its deference to a supposed absolute and incontrovertible authority of revelation?

Hello! Is there anybody left out there to read these poor lines?

Clearly, a philological approach to Christian thought has got its work cut out for it.

For this reason, as we enter into the details of Christian speech practice, our terminological investigation of the tradition of this culture must sharply delineate its scope. First, our study of the *Lord my God Jesus Christ* does not presume to encroach upon what you personally believe or do not believe about God or what, if anything, you understand as being referred to by these terms; and yet it is rather odd that folks, whether believers or non-believers, simply assume that they already know – as if by divine intervention, you might say – what these expressions mean. Atheists, maybe you would believe in God with an open and compassionate heart full of gratitude for the mercy of a mind refreshed by a transforming insight that is our eternal life after death (for that is the insight that the believers joyously challenge you to grasp) and theists, maybe you wouldn't just blindly, irrationally, ineptly, abjectly "believe in God," mouthing words you have been taught without giving them a second thought (for that is what the non-believers scornfully accuse you of), if you both only knew what, in God's name, this term and others like it – for example *Son of God, Christ, Resurrection, Charity, Faith,* etc. – properly denote. Think about it. Why do you say you do not believe if, in fact, you don't know what *believe* and *God*, these words, refer to in this context? On the other hand, why do you say that you can "only" believe with a mind shut down, shut off, on hold, if, as is written in scripture (14.9; 17:3), to believe is, in fact, to know God and to have seen God, having known and seen and heard the words and the works of the *Lord Jesus Christ*?

For the purpose of our studies, *God* is simply a *term of distinction*, the name of the determining principle (A) in the Second Epoch. We have clarified what a determining principle is in the context of our philological approach. As is well known, *God* is the standard translation into English of *ΘΕΟΣ*, a word of Koine Greek, the language in which the New Testament has been passed down to us and connecting thus to the ancient Hellenistic tradition of philosophy and poetry written in that language, which we will examine later as that of the First Epoch. Moreover, this word is also used as the Septuagint translation of the Hebrew אֱלֹהִים or יְהוָה אֱלֹהִים (Elohīm or Yaweh Elohīm) connecting thus a further ancient language and culture of connotations to this term. What richness, what a wealth of tradition this term offers our philological building efforts!

Nevertheless, the starting point of our investigation is not a fancy word or words the meaning or meanings of which are more or less familiar to us but rather what we already know, a precedent insight that now wants reception and elaboration in a fresh slate of terms. Either we already know, in principle, what the expression the *Glory of God* must denote as a result of our having studied the distinction of human being in the Third Epoch – for it is in this epoch that we first encountered a complete poetic vision of the self-several entity and traced the development of its principle, the *Freedom of Humanity*, in conjunction with the logotectonic method – or its "meaning" cannot become fully transparent to us until the very end of our investigation after we have considered the principle of the First Epoch as well, namely the *Apportionment of Being*, and ascertained how this principle, along with the other two, elaborate a single line of reasoning regarding pure reason that relates and collects into a scheme of all things thought all the other thinkers' and poets' contribution of meaning, barring none, to this endeavor of insight, putting into radical effect the foundational precept of the so-called linguistic turn that the meaning of a word is determined alone by its usage as documented by oral and written speech performance.

Clearly then our philological study of Christian religion as one of three distinguished languages of thought must therefore not be confounded with the history of the Christian Church. The tale of the Christian Church is, of course, a fascinating one in its own right, and, like all good histories, it is controversial, contradictory, fraught with tales of murder and magnanimity, deeds of deceit but also of decency done in her name, offering thus a complete panorama of man's best and most bestial being – it goes without saying that the depravity of the mighty few is always the more intriguing spectacle in the tumultuous history of human institutions, the perpetual rise and fall of Man's empires. Nevertheless for us, the history of the Church, its schisms and sectarian upheavals, its eras of influence and decline, the personalities of power it spawned, the episodes of its goodness and its perversion, and finally the church's continued "relevance," however diffuse, for society today – all of this, though clearly issues worthy of study and research, is completely extraneous to our task which is, rather, to study the life and times of pure reason as the heritage and tradition of drawing a distinction that makes all the difference in the world.

Our philology has at its disposal only the actual writs of scripture and its conception in works of philosophy devoted to the *sacra doctrina*. Thus in the Christian Epoch, as Boeder has proposed, the Holy Spirit of pure thought – the deity of pure reason as its *present* in Christian terms – was articulated in the so-called Holy Scripture of the New Covenant which includes the evangelical Narratives of Jesus' life (Matthiew, Mark, Luke), the Epistles of the Apostle, and the Gospel of the Incarnate Word (John). These were subsequently conceptualized in the philosophy of Plotin, Augustine, and Thomas Aquinas.[66]

What was that just now? The Holy Spirit of *pure thought*? The deity of *reason*? These are odd expressions, are they not? What are we saying? Are we saying that *God* is a word of pure reason? Are we saying that thought thus distinguished is divine, in other words that *ΛΟΓΟΣ* is God? No, *we* are not saying anything, but rather taking into account precisely what has been said and what has been written. This is what has been written:

ΕΝ ΑΡΧΗ ΗΝ Ο ΛΟΓΟΣ ΚΑΙ Ο ΛΟΓΟΣ ΗΝ ΠΡΟΣ ΤΟΝ ΘΕΟΝ ΚΑΙ **ΘΕΟΣ ΗΝ Ο ΛΟΓΟΣ**. (Joh. 1, 1-2)

In the beginning the ΛΟΓΟΣ was and the ΛΟΓΟΣ was before God and the ΛΟΓΟΣ was God.

"____ is *ΘΕΟΣ*" – What a remarkable reminder of the ancient Greek understanding of the term *ΘΕΟΣ*, namely as a term of distinction, a *predicate*![67] We will explore the ramifications of this sense when we turn to the First Epoch.

For now our task is simply this: to receive and grasp what has been said, hearken to what has been spoken in what was said, read what has been written and construe the meaning of what we have read in the larger framework of all things thought, from the beginning to the end. And if our

---

[66] See Boeder's "The Present of Christian Sapientia in the Sphere of Speech" in *Seditions* (ed. M. Brainard, New York University Press 1997), pp. 275-291 and his "Einführung in die Vernünftigkeit des Neuen Testaments" in *Das Bauzeug der Geschichte* (ed. G. Meier, Könighausen & Neumann 1994), pp. 305-321.

[67] See Wilamowitz, *Der Glaube der Hellenen I*, Darmstadt 1955 p. 17.

The Fourth Part

ears have difficulty perceiving the message, then instead of discarding or ignoring what has been spoken, we must transform our ears, renew our hearing, turn our everyday thought from its mundane fixations and complexions and undergo the conversion of our minds, the METANOEIN that reason enacts in the life of human being by prompting a *change of heart and mind*. And it is only with respect to this idea that the message of the Gospel can be deciphered in a way that will help us think more deeply about what the distinction of human being not only is but also entails. We read:

ΜΕΤΑΝΟΕΙΤΕ, ΗΓΓΙΚΕΝ ΓΑΡ Η ΒΑΣΙΛΕΙΑ ΤΩΝ ΟΥΡΑΝΩΝ.
(Matt. 4,17)

Let your heart be changed! The kingdom of the heavens is near!

Have we encountered this idea before? Of course. It refers to the experience of departure we have been discussing since the beginning – in the Epoch of freedom as the stepping back of *transcendence*, but now put into Christian terms as the experience of the about-face of *conversion*. But we must acquaint ourselves with this new language and the vision it presents before we can recognize in it the familiar turning of the self-several mind from its world absorption towards critical reflection, the animadversion of thought from preoccupation with the particulars of individual life towards the bird's eye, the panoramic view of one atop a mountain overlooking our bustling assiduity from a vantage point as high as the sky, but not just any run-of-the-mill sky, not just your average, everyday sky, but rather a sky of distinction, call it HEAVEN. Nor is this sky, like our generic one, merely high up there, hidden beyond the clouds, benignly remote, but rather portentously nearby; in fact, "Heaven" itself can often be construed as a sign of luminous, fiery advent, an admonition hanging over our heads, heads held to be inert in their oblivious immediacy – this is the eschatological vision of the Christian law; it is, just like the categorical imperative of humanity we encountered in the third epoch, close to us, as close as our heart in the fealty of its reply to the voice of our *Lord* and sire of our second birth, of our more brilliant being, in his calling of his subjects, the teacher making those who seek wisdom disciples of his *Word*, the prince exhorting the apocalyptic emergence of the KINGDOM of thought in an otherwise so humdrum world of commoners. Is this analogy of images clear? *Conscience*, the voice, the law, of pure reason within us in the Third Epoch is analogous to the *Lord*, the voice of pure reason without us at first, but entering, first our world as *Light*, then our lives as the incarnate *Word* that, finally, as flesh, enters even into the bosom of our own bodies as the bread we partake of in the Lord's Supper!

This distinction is embodied in a great wealth of images that have been collected into a narrative, the so-called *Good News, Glad Tidings,* the *Gospel* (ΕΥΑΓΓΕΛΙΟΝ) of the New Covenant. In general, the world of mind-forged manacled Man we have seen in Plato's allegory, is represented in the narratives of Jesus' life by the figures of the Pharisees, the Sadducees, the Essenes, the Zealots, and the High Priests – and other assorted godly (but ungodly) Men; but also the Elders, the Demagogues, the worldly Wise Man, the regal Big Man, as well as their Lawyers and Scribes all of whom, in different ways and from different perspectives, advocate the strict adherence to convention, the meticulous and literal interpretation of the law, the unquestioned and therefore unreflected adoption of ancient creed and culture, the blind and slavish adherence to ways set in brazen obstinacy by vaunting figures of authority and the proud power of bigoted conservatism, and are thus illustrations of the self-glorifying practice of pretentious, yeasty piety. This pomp and punctiliousness of rigid orthodoxy and self-centered tyranny with regard to the self-serving interpretation of the laws carved, apparently inalterably, into inexorable, unreasonable stone is the topic of the famous expression:

ΤΟ ΓΑΡ ΓΡΑΜΜΑ ΑΠΟΚΤΕΝΝΕΙ, ΤΟ ΔΕ ΠΝΕΥΜΑ ΖΩΠΟΙΕΙ

The letter kills, but the spirit enlivens. (2 Cor. 3.5)

It is not the subservient observance of a law or any particular prescribed action that leads to being just and justified but rather, above all, a way of thinking, a spirit. That is why blind adherence to a particular law, its letters (as opposed to its sense) that can only command or forbid action and a particular action, must represent a materialistic mentality which obdurately clings to its dynasty; its rigid unthinking perpetuation stands in contrast to the vital spirit that repudiates every attitude of intransigence and self-righteous fundamentalism which has never learned to exercise judgment and thus to apply laws, the spirit of the law, to new situations; this idea, the unwritten law behind every written ordinance must be perceived and upheld, its application adjudged in every particular case, its purview revised according to the requirements of the circumstances. Such demand for deliberation – having to think about things – is inconvenient. Wouldn't a flat-rate, one-rule-fit-all policy save us all a lot of time and heartache?

This unfettered attitude of the mind, this *altitude* of spirit, an elevated because transfigured and as such **holy** spirit, and not any particular behavior, the words and deeds of ritual performed without it, is the source of the distinction of human being. For this aspect of human being alone cannot be commanded from abroad, only from within, intrinsically.

Therefore, we might again provokingly state that the first "law" of spirit is to depart from every law, as we saw first in freedom's exhortation, and to follow that intimate and self-evident law of distinguished, of *holy* spirit, the *true* heart – not just any old everyday heart, but rather the one conceived of in commitment and dedication, in enthusiastic devotion to that unique heart and spirit that attains its infinite and superlative universe, its *heaven*, by superseding every finite matter of mundane bias and short-term rather than long-term gratification.

113. The Distinguished Spirit of God

In the Second Epoch, this distinguished heart of hearts is embodied in the person of *Jesus Christ*, in the law of the *Lord*; Christ is not merely a distinguished human being in a narrative but, moreover, *the* distinction of human being in person. Upon himself he is seen to undergo the ordeal of stepping back from the immediacy of the mentality that places its hunger to live first, the bodily *will* that lives by bread alone, demands to attain the certainty of *knowledge* when it is, in fact, the achievement and the challenge of faith that prevents the foot from being dashed against the stone, and seizes the *power* to reign in splendor over all kingdoms of the earth rather than serve the intangible glory of the kingdom of Heaven – departure thus threefold, namely from the will, the knowledge, and the power of this world, is the immediate message of the voice that, above all temptation to stay put, rooted, grounded, calls upon us in exhortation: "follow me." (Joh 1.43, 21.19).

Yet this voice neither coerces nor intimidates its audience because it is immanent, an intrinsic manifestation of the heart that is beyond the world, from another world, its own separate and distinct place, the place of distinction in which absolute spirit dwells and whence its call arises and to which, ultimately, like Joy's "gentle wing," it uplifts discerning human being. It is the word of life, not just your average generic life, but rather the other life, the life of thought up above so high, like a diamond in the sky, in comparison to which every other life "down here" in the grave cave is more a death than any sort of life, more the material and mineral world of the corpse. The language of this heart speaks without the importunity of propaganda and advertising, need not solicit, does not proselyte. Neither encroachment, nor invasion agitate the simple decency of its present – in the hearing alone, it touches; in the perception alone, it moves; and in its gratuity and spontaneity, it inspires thanks, praise, glorifies for the glory given – the apotheosis of gratitude for a word sent, a voice heard, a mission received, and the start of thought's way.

In the so-called Beatitudes (Mat. 5.3-12) in the beginning of the Sermon on the Mount (Mat. 5.1-7.29), this spirit of distinction and emergence is placed in opposition to that of "conventional wisdom" which is assailed and shaken by manifest contradictions. We read: "blessedly happy are those who are poor…, who are mourning…, who are crying…, who are thirsty and hungry…, who are persecuted…, who are hated…, who are vituperated…, who are slandered." On the other hand, those are said to be unhappy "who are rich…, who are satisfied…, who are laughing…, who are praised." Is that not a paradox, asks the mundane understanding of the worldly wise? The idea and the sense behind these paradoxes are only accessible to such thought as has distinguished itself from its everyday understanding of the world, renewed itself in the spirit of discernment that we have called *pure reason*. Only such "otherworldly" reason can grasp the idea expressed therein.

The antagonism between the testimony of *conventional* wisdom and that of a *new* testimony, a new testament, is dramatically depicted in the phrase: "You have been told…I say however to you…" in which the ordinary, mundane view (*you have heard it said….*) is juxtaposed against that of the extraordinary, the enlivened, spirited one, that pure and impartial reason advocates (*I say however to you…*). Again and again the letter of an established commandment is shown as limited with respect to the spirit of the law which is the actual message, the life of the letter of the law, a benign spirit, which is the only true guide to action and cannot be prescribed by laws that determine behavior but not insight.

> **You have heard the ancients tell**: you shall not kill; those who kill will be subject to judgment; I **say to you** that anyone who even harbors resentment towards his brother for no good reason will be subject to judgment. (Math 5.21-22)

The spirit of this commandment is thought to extend further than merely to the action of murder. Everyday thought might argue thus: "Certainly vilifying someone is not as bad as killing him. That means that if murder is not allowed then at least I ought to be permitted to call somebody a fool when I am angry and if he or she deserves it." Isn't this argument plausible? And nevertheless, it fails to grasp the meaning of the commandment which is meant to place all mundane action and attitude of human being under the standard of a divine and absolute perspective that is divorced from every local, personal, or material consideration.

It is human nature and *human* spirit to understand the law of justice in the sense of retribution; how does the *Holy* Spirit refute the immediate letter of the law for the sake of a distinguished insight and its message that only the discerning mind can "read between the lines?"

> **You have heard it said**: an eye for an eye, a tooth for a tooth. **I say to you however:** do not offer resistance to those who treat you ill. Rather, if you are slapped on the right cheek then offer the other. (5.38-39)

It is the spirit that conceives itself as love. Surely, but which love, what sort of love are we talking about here? It is certainly not the "pathological" love of the narcissist, nor that affection we feel for those we dote upon, nor any of the instinctual hungers that periodically motivate the living being of our bodies. We have become acquainted with it in the Third Epoch, the self-love of reason is the image of an accord, and harmony, the love of beauty or more generally, the *love of nature*; and we saw that this autonomous self-love was the achievement of an individual at having attained the general perspective, adopting the universal will as the specific will, adapting the personal one to the general one and it is this correspondence and accord that the term *love* is thought to refer to. I agree with my Self, who, in Christian terms, *You* are – you who *are* and do not merely *do* pure reason's will and as such My will as well, if I can turn mine towards You and be not only Me but also You, or at least Yours such that I am that very I that was You but, now, is Me, too, me having become You and Yours in faith. The closeness thus attained between me and You who is/are *Christ the Lord* is the rapport of love and the *self*-regard that makes of the self, of pure reason, the Son of God.

In the second epoch this distinguished love is called the *love of God*; the perfect nearness of this love to us is such that "neither death, nor life, neither angels, nor princes, nor powers, neither things present or future, neither height, nor depth, nor any other creation, will be able to separate us from it." (Rom 8:38-39). What could be closer to us than this love which is that of pure thought, namely our entity of identity which is closeness in and of itself, pure propinquity or, in the Christian dialect, the *Holy Spirit*. And hearing in our hearts its call, which is that of the person of Jesus Christ with respect to whose life we may distinguish ourselves, means that we have joined our human fate to that of the divine, not me to Myself, but us to You, who is no longer properly called the *general will* but rather the absolute distinction and the difference that the glory of the *Creator* makes with respect to all else, i.e. the *creation;* and though the distinction of the creator is absolute, You, as the Father, are turned towards me and my world in the person of your Son. That is the purpose of the term *Father.* The turning of the God of absolute distinction toward us and our world is completed by Jesus Christ, the token of this distinction that we can take thus through You, the Son, upon ourselves and in this way confirm our rapport of love, the relationship of correspondence that required of me a transformation and an uplifting of myself in accordance with the distinction that pure reason, called in this Epoch, the Son of God, makes upon me and my world. For it is the destiny of human being to love as He did, namely with a love distinguished as absolute. Of course to speak of this idea of love is, in Christian terms, to call the idea a person, i.e. to call it our *Father*, his *Son*, to say *You* to it, even as in the Third Epoch, the logic of the term pertaining to the general will, My conscience and humanity, is said to be *Me*, my *I*. But by comparing these two languages, we may recognize in two unique renderings of their respective determining principles an analogical train of thought. That is the essential challenge. Namely to see how the distinction of human being can be depicted in both languages and that each language obeys its own figurative logic, elaborating its terms accordingly. The idea that is here at stake is none other than the self-relativity of pure reason; in Christian terminology: reason *loving* reason – first, *the Father loving the Son* meaning that the distinction of thought is manifest to our human being; second, *the Son loving the Father* referring to the divine, i.e. distinguished destiny that human being is heir to, and thirdly, that in our faith the Son of God, in our love our divine being has come to the world, entered the flesh to be the light of our life, to be the divine word, the Word of distinction in our otherwise oh so undistinguished flesh, to be thus the way of renewed spirit, to be the glorious destiny that offers our quintessential dust the dignity of divine provenance.

> **You have heard it said**: you should love your neighbor and hate your enemy. **I say to you however:** love your enemies and pray for persecutors so that you will become sons of your father in Heaven; for he lets his sun rise upon the good and the bad and he lets it rain upon the just and the unjust. (5.43-45).

This is an extraordinary love, certainly none we encounter in the confines of our everyday lives. It is not a love practiced by the multitude and the manifold man of lived experience who loves in the narrow perspective of individual and personal concerns. It is an elect, distinguished love. Compared to that closed and fettered horizon, it is vast, impersonal, absolute; it is a heart unchained and unfettered. Can we attain to such a standpoint that places our love outside of the mundane straits of our normal loves – love of this particular woman, this man, this child, this house, this car, perhaps even this neighbor, all of which objects of my love, collected into my own little world that I have carved out of the chaos of life, are simply instances of love of my own self and mine? Can we conceive of a love that extends beyond my immediate concerns with myself and mine, with my *Here* and my *Now*, a long-term, a sustainable love? For such a love is the name for the relationship of correspondence, the identification between human being and divine being:

You should be perfect like your Father in Heaven. (5.48)

The divine will of the *Father in Heaven* and not the general will of the *Conscience of Humanity* is the term of discernment in the second epoch. The will of the Father is to be done and not any particular action that corresponds to a commandment as already written – this is the entire message and the content, the spirit of the law:

> **You have heard the Ancients tell** that you shall not bear false witness and should keep what you have sworn to the Lord. **I say however to you** that you should not swear at all…let your yes be a yes, your no be a no, all else is of evil. (5.33-37)

Invoking witnesses is superfluous when we, by adopting the Holy Spirit and the will of the Father as our own, have become in that spirit our *own* witnesses, or, better, because in accordance with the logic of Christian thought, that we, living in Him who lives in us, are always already witnessed by *Him* who is the self-several being of our own critical self-reflection.

Thus we see that the *term of principle* in the second epoch is GOD just as in the third epoch the principal term was FREEDOM. As in the case of FREEDOM, the first use of the term *GOD* is that of negation – the spirit of freedom was that of a departure from the ordinary world, a claim and calling we depicted as a journey into absolute reclusion. In this way, we learned that the distinction of human being is initially that of deviation from the mini-me mentality of our body, straying from the norms and assumptions of our little town blues, setting out, setting forth from and breaking with conventional authority, retirement from the hustle bustle of everyday business and the restlessness of fluid living being in the "muggle" world.

Thought reveals itself to us, provoking change, is self-evident, a funny feeling in our skull and cross bones and in our glum gut, intrinsic, innate, impulsive – there are many words that have been used to substantiate that the experience of spirit is a fact of life, though no physical one, the origin and starting point of thought about thought, thought *about* anything you could name, actually, because in this *about* is already the mark of distinction, the liberal relationship that Schiller recognized in the very act of contemplation that is the reflection of science upon the thing, the difference between the thing and the thought, the reason that the thing is "There!" in contemplation's gaze in the first place and not merely there, like the sound of the proverbial tree that falls somewhere in the forest in unheard, unseen silence.

Consider the line of reasoning depicted in *Figure 80.*

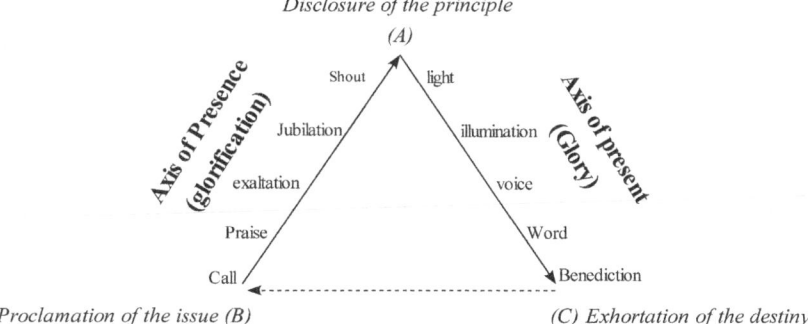

Figure 80: From Presents to Presence

The *spontaneity* of reason in the Third Epoch, as the causa sui of human nature and the self-given and self-giving gift of autonomy is grasped in the second epoch as *gratuity,* a gift of grace, unconditionally given, of the absolute distinction that gives rise to the first thought, a thanking for the benefit bestowed upon us by the quickening spirit having opened up the closure of our parochial view. This *DISCLOSURE* and self-evidence of the principle came as *LIGHT,* the shining forth of light, the supererogation of its emanation and efficacy and, in this sense, *GLORY* (ΔΟΞΑ), which is the shining forth of the distinction and then, in terms of its immediate effect of making clear, from the perspective of what it is that comes to light in this gift of light, *ILLUMINATION,* and, more than that, CLARITY about what has been hidden in shrouds of shadow; this light drawing us out of nescience is a personal address to us and thus *VOICE,* is not merely a speaking at us, it is, moreover, articulate, conveying knowledge and as such *WORD,* conveying the insight of a message from the speaker's mind to that of those who listen, and then not merely a word of wisdom proffering insight but, going further in our lives as *CALL* to action, the enacting of what had been a clear perception and penultimately, more specifically yet, the *PROCLAMATION* of a destiny which, after having been carried through to fulfillment, finally completes the circuit of *EXALTATION* in celebration upon the *SHOUT* of *JUBILATION* of the distinction; this bright exuberance in *PRAISE* of accomplishment, so rich in the experience of its achievement, is precisely what is meant by the beams of glory, given as well as being given, the former being the *presence* of thought, the latter its *presents*, thus beautifully ringing, articulating thus a complete train of thought that turns and returns upon itself.

114. The Person of Distinction

Having gone through the cascade of pure reason's presents, the exhortation of the destiny attains its most striking present not in the light seen or the word heard but rather in the person of the incarnate Word whose coming is a mission to teach and to provide guidance in the performance of election that had been given and received as an appointment of light, being given recognition for having recognized the principle at the heart of the matter, given to choose those who are willing (and therein themselves choosing as well as chosen) to follow the call, the word, the voice of illumination, the light of glory. This convocation is not a summons to a festivity of peace. On the contrary, the distinction of human being calls us and upon us to experience the inaugural anguish of our severance not our deliverance: "Do not think that I have come to bring peace on earth," says the ΛΟΓΟΣ, "I have not come to bring peace but the sword." For he has come to make a difference, to be this sign of distinction..."and enmity shall reign amongst the hearth companions of human being. Those loving their father or mother more than me are unworthy of me. And those loving son or daughter more than me are unworthy of me. And those who fail to take up their cross and follow me are unworthy of me. Those who cling to their life will forfeit it; however those who forfeit their lives for my sake will gain life." (Math. 10:34-39)

We see here the image of the sword suggesting the grief of the detachment, the cut inherent in the distinction, the violence felt in the breaking of the blank, unreflected life of natural relationships that habit is and for whose closed-minded sensibilities thought can only be a frightening sacrifice of blood. We see and hear in these dark tones, voiced by resistance to the critical mind, the threat that impends upon departure from the society of our birth, our village, from the network of dependencies that determine and bind us in this state of needs and in the precarious balance of power that is their seat of control. Holding fast to our finitude, the realization of our mortality is an abysmal fate, whereas leave taken from the family of our immediacy is the exalting ascension to that spirited life and a cleaving to ethereality after our death to all materiality to which we are born and from which destined, ultimately, to depart.

Thus the experience of the practice of pure reason is foremost that of this distinction of renewal, i.e. a baptism of fire to be kindled upon the earth-bound terrestrial spirit, not peace, but rather divisiveness (ΔΙΑΜΕΡΙΣΜΟΝ - 12:51).

> From now on five in one household will be divided in one household, three against two and two against three; they will be divided father against son and son against father; mother against daughter and daughter against mother, mother-in-law against her daughter-in-law and daughter-in-law against mother-in-law. (Luke12:49-53)

The enmity that discipleship to the teaching of distinguished spirit requires of us – this "civil" war appealed to – the inherent drama of distinguishing oneself from one's living being, from that first life, is visualized in terms of the family; the ties of blood, thought to be the strongest, are here cut by that other blood and other life that makes of humankind's pure reason's; the distinction of thought in the bosom of living being is seen in the all the acerbity of departure and detachment that the abstraction of thought means to the living, the cost of loss.

> Whoever comes to me and does not hate father and mother, wife and children, brothers and sisters, yes and even life itself, cannot be my disciple...none of you can become my disciple if you do not give up all your possessions. (Luke 4:26)

Given our initial fear and reluctance to engage ourselves to its performance, how much more exalted is our human being grasped in light of its ultimate achievement! In the Gospels, our transformation into thought's pure light has been most luminously glorified, fittingly and remarkably brought to the light of discernment and remembrance, an experience that must be renewed again and again. In this respect, the greatest achievement of the languages of wisdom is magnification – theirs is the prophetic work of praise and of denotation, drawing folks' attention, adverting their audience, to what they might otherwise have overlooked, namely their destiny and their distinction as human beings who supposedly do not need the weathermen to construe the appearance of the earth and the sky while, at the same time, protesting their ignorance with regards to the distinctive sign of the times that thought has always made upon the wall of Man.

For this reason, in the Second Epoch, the ΛΟΓΟΣ of critical reflection is endowed with no less than absolute, i.e. with divine, grandeur – a glory that human being is destined to partake of not as a *citizen*, which was the distinguished *person of self-respect* of the general will, but rather as a *saint* in Christ, the very *person of faith* and, though a *child of Man*, one who has nevertheless received the favor of an accord and become thus a *Child of God*, an inhabitant of the *Kingdom of God*, reborn and converted in the distinguished Spirit beyond that of mundane being, and as such elected as a member of the *Body of Christ* and not that of the *State of Freedom* as in the Third Epoch.

115. The Light and the Gravity of the Law

We have learned that people and their coalitions often try to avoid this pinnacle of clarity and transparency. Why? What should they fear in experiencing this divergence, the self-several state of thoughtful human being? That's easy: The distinction of insight reveals the mortifying *discrepancy* in our lives between THE WAY IT IS and THE WAY IT SHOULD BE, reveals, as *debt* and *duty*, the humiliating effect of deviation and obliquity, is experienced in the *guilt* of shortcoming, in the realization of being in the *wrong*, being *imperfect* and as such imprisoned in a state of *sin*, the sin city of finitude, of ephemerality, of mortality, the first thought of which is, in the Second Epoch, that what has been done, mistaken, cannot be undone, cannot be taken back. That is why, in the Christian tongue, the conversion of the mind (METANOEIN) is often translated with the term *repentance*, the turn of contrition from this state of sin. Even as our original human being, Adam and Eve, did in the beginning, who among us would not much prefer to hide his and her mortal shame and effacement, the curse of corruption which befalls blood and bone in spite of every white-washing technology of longevity and delusion? Who would not much rather avoid or suppress the critical eye that recognizes all the faults the short-term standpoint of the flesh is heir to with respect to the idea of perfection and the long-term sweep of glory alive in their heart of hearts in comparison to which the judgment of self-reflection upon the minute scope of the our flesh's hive of here, now, today, me, must be utter condemnation?

Look at yourself, man in the mirror, our finite being, in its defaced shame of the moment's gain, is and does what your seeing and discerning being, your infinite, your divine being in the glory of distinction does not condone and cannot approve of; this critical view of Yours says "No!" to that which the finite, shamefaced one, having just been absent and absorbed by life and the nescience of lived experience, just a moment ago, still unbeknownst to itself, said "Yes!" to in its body language, before thought's sword, thought's Word, split this life wide open for all, especially for reflection itself, to see. That first unreflecting life was utter affirmation in the fluency of act linked seamlessly to act and reaction, in the currents of immersion, in those swirls and swells of interference that are the patterns of the eddies of our opiate lives. If this flowing being had but stepped out of this stream of consciousness, it might have, on certain occasions, attained to a critical standpoint, might have said "No!" to what it does or did or even "Yes!" to what would have deserved approbation in the first place – either judgment would have been one reflected life can affirm. This is what the distinction of human being, namely pure reason, discovers in the *retrospect* of judgment, which, in the Second Epoch, is not called the categorical imperative of the moral law, but rather the law of God's commandment. Pure reason, in the clarity of sight regarding the IS and the OUGHT, would have said *yes* to what deserves a *yes*, *no* to what deserves a *no*. But now in attendance to the distinction that the gift of glory bestows on insight, it is always too late, always after the fact, when all has been decided already; What has happened previously and has since been brought to light by the critical injunction of the law cannot be undone in spite of the understanding that has accrued to the person of the judge in the meantime, having had the opportunity to pass judgment. The sentence of the judge can always only determine the error, experiences the debt and thus the guilt, *after the fact* when it is too late to take it all back. What's done is done. At the moment when human being comes to itself, realizing what it has done and become, truly sees itself, it loses itself, its being, in the revelation and the deepening insight into how it should be and is not, should have been and wasn't and is now irreparably beyond the ken of restoration. For what's done is done. It is for this reason that the law of judgment, though meant to uphold and even celebrate the sanctity of the pure mind's, God's, life, leads, in fact, to mortification of that life, its death. For in the very reception and affirmation of the law against which I measure and evaluate my actions, I am forced to acknowledge my failure and *proven* inability to conform with that standard that it establishes; the greater my affirmation of it, the greater my condemnation of myself, for which reason to love the law is to hate myself, its holy life being my humiliating death. How can we escape from this vicious circle, from this crisis of the law and the condemnation that ensues from the judgment of critical reflection such that the higher I raise myself up in acknowledgement of the goodness of the law, the deeper I abase and grind myself down in admission of my deficiency and failing with regards to my observance of it. By coming to see, by succeeding in my *observation* of, as opposed to blind insensibility towards, the law, having attained the coign of vantage of critical self-reflection with regards to it, I am, at the same time, forced to concede that I fail in my *observance* of it. This is the familiar tragedy of the self-several antimony between thought and thought, the contradiction of reason by reason, the collision between two goods of equal merit, in this case the fight between sight and right, theory and practice. Is there no succor for, no reconciliation of them? There can be none unless, somehow, they can be set in harmonious opposition and grasped as the two constitutive extremes of a transition and transformation, which, in the Second Epoch, is embodied in the person of Jesus Christ.

But let us listen first to the language of the Apostle Paul in which the disintegration of our human being has been so powerfully and dramatically articulated, of such human being as has now awoken to the knowledge of the emergent NO of the *law* with respect to the unexpressed affirmation in the YES of life's *flesh*, the body's myopic perspective on things, which was the underside of our previously adumbrated being, now come to light as having been only tacit acquiescence and made explicit in the self-contradiction of aversion and the guilt of patent self-alterity which in the second epoch is called the state of sin.

> Were it not for the law, I would not have known sin, would not have known desire if the law had not said, "you shall not crave." But sin, seizing the opportunity that this commandment offered, made rapacity of my desire. For without the law sin was dead. Once I did indeed live without the law; but with the coming of the law, sin came alive, I, however, died. And so I experienced in the law of life, the law of death. For sin, seizing the opportunity of the commandment, deceived, and by it killed me. Thus, the law is holy and the commandment is holy and just and good. Was it then that which is good that brought me death? By no means. But sin, so that it might, by that which is good, come to light as sin, brought forth death in me, so that sin might, through the commandment, become strikingly so. For we know that the law is spiritual; but I am flesh, sold to sin. I do not give my assent to what I do; I do not do what I would do, but what I hate is what I do. If then I do what I would not, I affirm that the law is what I actually intend. But then it is no longer I who act but rather sin that dwells in me. For I know that no goodness dwells in me, i.e. in my flesh; for the will to do good attends me but to perform what is good does not. For I do not do the good

that I would; but rather the evil that I would not do, that is what I do. Now if I do what I would not, it is no longer I that do it but rather sin's doing that dwells in me. I find then a law such that when I would do good, in fact evil attends me. For I delight in the law of God in accordance with our inward human being. But I see an outward law in my members warring against the law of my spirit and bringing me into captivity to the law of sin which is in my members. O wretched man that I am! Who shall deliver me from the body of this death? (Rom 7.7-25)

The law of distinction is, on the one hand, the *law of sin* because through it the state of sin, namely the self-contradictory state of our human being, is revealed; through the adverting, apotropaic power of the law, this inward antinomy is brought to light (Rom 3.20); it is also the *law of death* because through the law, I realize that I am not doing what I, in my rational being, want to do i.e., what I want to do in accordance with the law of this being, but rather what I do not want to do and therefore realize that I act at the behest of another will than that of pure reason, namely the will of such desire as seeks to expunge and extinguish the distinctive efficacy of thought through, for example, the surfeit of consumption. The law is the *law of flesh* because in the self-severalty of my distinction, the mortal living being of which I, as rational being, simultaneously do and do not partake – which is the state of internecine strife raging in human flesh – comes to self-reflecting light. The law of distinction is also the *law of desire* so far as desire in this connection is the movement of thought towards the worldly, the material, for the sake of ultimate resorption into the unmarked dilation of earth and immense immersion of going with the flow. To this death-wish desire, the Apostle seeks to contrast the rational aspiration of the will towards spirited life and the incarnation of the pure spirit through our actions in the world at large.

When, as we have seen, the fruit of self-knowing being is our atom Man's dawning awareness of the finitude of life and the limits that govern lived experience, then all of these terms – *desire, flesh, death,* and *sin* articulate this mortality of Man which, through the law, enters our self-worrying awareness.

This play of opposition between terms of immediacy and terms of distinction reaches its most dramatic intuition in the logic of the crucifixion which is the central image of the twofold transition – the chiasm of the Chris-cross; we mark, namely, on the one hand, the transition *from* the aversion of the darkened world, having turned away from the face of critical reflection, *to* adversion in light of thought, having turned back to face that face, our Face and Yours – the *salvation* of the world depicted in the vision of the acknowledgement, authorization, and transfiguration of Jesus as the Son, the resurrection of the Crucified, the exaltation of human being through faith; and on the other hand, the transition *from* the abstraction and the supposed disinterest of an absolute God *to* the concrete substantiation of a pure will, the Spirit of God come to the life of note as *revelation* in testimony of scripture, in the witness's oath, in the herald's proclamation, in the preaching of the missionary, *mercy* in the works of sacrifice and the acts of love, in the confession of the faithful, in the birth of the King, in the mission of the Son, in the incarnation of the Word, *glory* in apocalyptic miracles, in divisive signs, in the oracle of prophets, in the advent of the end of days, the day of *judgment.*

Thus the revelation of mercy brings *thought* to *life* (the general *to* the particular) bringing thereby *life* to *thought* (unexamined immediacy *to* the apprehension of critical distinction), and in the difference that this distinction makes, animates and inspires life with the light of form that makes life's mindless matters thoughtful and in turn makes of pure thought the living present to our human being that we might take upon ourselves to hold closely, i.e. to cherish as our own refreshed heart and even as our resurrected world and body that we might inhabit as our renewed dwelling of distinction.

This cardinal point and portico where these two ways – *from* light to night and back *to* day – intersect is the nadir and the zenith of the *cross*, which is thus the symbol of this crossing. For the way of pure reason, of ΛΟΓΟΣ, traverses all extremity: *from* the *sin* of self-strife in judgment, on the one hand, and the *punishment* for refractory resolve on the other; *from* the clinging, obsessive *love* enamored of earthly ways, on the one hand, and the *lord of subjugation* sent to regain what Adam forfeited, on the other; *from,* on the one hand, *the pride of the highest prince*, who fell and, on the other, *the shame of the condemned servant* bound for glory – in all these depictions of polarity between pattern and matter, between being as it is but should not be – the matter of material, and being as it should be but is not – the pattern of form; *from* these two sides of the Tree of Duality, ***from*** *terms of immediacy* ***to*** *terms of distinction* and vice versa, ***from*** *terms of distinction* ***to*** *terms of renewed, refreshed immediacy,* is thought destined to turn and return. In short, ***from*** *death* ***to*** *life,* ***to*** the acceptance of the world of law in the Lord ***and*** the mission of the law of the Word into the life of flesh; ***to*** the exaltation of human being's destiny attaining accordance with divinity ***and*** the benevolent gift of divine spirit to the fallen state of finite human being; ***to*** human life's adoption of the form of the Lord ***and*** God's outward operation in offering the mercy of His return; **to** the love of Human being **and** the love of God – this consummating resolution is unified in the image of the *death* on the cross **and** the resurrection of *life*, namely that of the judge of the day of judgment **and** the savior of the world.

The voice of reason, the Word that becomes tangible flesh and moves us to see ourselves for what we are, is a gift of insight, the gift of sight to those who were blind. But this gift is also a deadly poison, namely the curse of shame. Accepting this shame is the humiliation of the demon of self-glorifying, face-saving pride, but also the resurrection to glory of the spirit of grateful love that has taken the cup of poison of death to receive the gift of life in an act of faith that is as free and divine as the act of creation was. Both were acts of pure love – the mercy of the gift and the *merci* of the thanking are one! Both however are distinguished loves, and in this sense *divine*. They are the *divine*, not the everyday run-of-mill, but rather the *Holy* spirit that unites the Father and Son of the Christian Godhead in self-returning radiance, the illuminating light (C) **from** the source of light (A) **to** the reflection of light (B) returned. This is pure reason's unique way of doing what critical self-reflection, in the second epoch, does best, namely *enacting* truth. The truth of reason came to the world in a form we earth-encumbered beings could perceive, spoke with a voice we could hear, and called upon us in a language we could understand to make a decision about our own origin: Are we really merely a speck of dust and blood, a dough of light-endowed flower and water? Or shall we acknowledge that one spark, that one germ of leavening, Heaven sent, that transforms this loaf of loam, makes our humble humus rise into the form of human being termed *sapiens*?

This gift of ΛΟΓΟΣ entered the world of human affairs and took up abode there. And the seeing of this light, the assent to its message, is the power of distinguished thinking to aspire to the love and the community of reason which is not only the congregation of the called, the elect, the distinguished – those who have been crucified in the judgment of their distinction – but more originally, those who have become children of God, reborn in a spirit that transcends the world of death in the recognition of its origin and the realization of its destiny, which is the world of life, being "through the Word, the ΛΟΓΟΣ," nothing less than "all that is and without which nothing arose that has arisen."

ΠΑΝΤΑ ΔΙ ΄ΑΥΤΟΥ ΕΓΕΝΕΤΟ, ΚΑΙ ΧΩΡΙΣ ΑΥΤΟΥ ΕΓΕΝΕΤΟ Ο ΥΔΕ ΕΝ Ο ΕΓΕΝΟΤΟ (Joh 1:3)

This is the drive and the power of faith which fulfils itself in love and seeks insight, the nearness inherent in seeing eye to eye, coming face to Face and Face to face with the principle. This principle in action, in other words, thought, the Actor, the Executor, is the achievement of a mind that is awake and aware, taking into account THE WAY IT IS and THE WAY IT SHOULD BE; through our attendance, in contrast to our inveterate negligence, things come into being in the first place, the being of thought that has come to its senses after an indefinite period of absent-mindedness; now alert, everything that is, is there, is "there!" But it is not merely the sensory impressions that we come to note; it is the fact that we take note of them now, *knowing* that now we know, having been preoccupied previously; it is this very fact of thought's emergence to itself, that seizes our I and strikes its person most deeply, like a wound even, thought cut by thought's own present and not just that of insignificant things now seen that had been missed or ignored by our neglect. No, it is rather thought that takes note of thought through the advent of thought, that has become therefore now thoughtful, being previously thought empty but now, in the plenitude of thought, alive, more, in thought, life, the life and the light of human being, which, coming into the inert world of oblivion, lightens all thought, though many would resist the transparence of their world in this illumination, hating the clarity of reflection, preferring the unseeing eye, refusing to receive the gift of discernment that takes account and makes distinctions, above all the distinction between what should be and what should not. But those who take it upon themselves to step back perceptively are bound to take note of this faculty, realize its effect on human actions, recognize that a perspective unencumbered by the flesh and bones of the particular interests belonging merely to me, here, now, today, attains or at least strives to achieve a more objective stance, the stance that, with respect to the scope of our constrained reign of the *here and now*, we might venture to call the kingdom of the *Now-after* and the *Hereafter*, that is the dwelling of our distinguished and, in this sense, *eternal* life, the life of our *inalienable* human being after the death of our *sales* Man – this standpoint, desiring as it does to become absolute, is a will to which we might assent and in doing so, in this faith, we receive this will as our own, not the will of blood or of flesh, or of Man, but a will that has stepped back from the shell of particulars, the one that has become the will of bigger and better things, namely the greater, the higher, the deeper, the greatest, the highest, the deepest things in life, in other words, the things of the spirit that are no things at all, the will that has become the *superb*, the *distinguished* will and in this specific sense the *will of God, our Father in Heaven*. Our will in affirming that this pure will *may be done*, our life in the fulfillment of this will through our own actions, is the beginning of a new life, and we, in so assenting and thus taking this new life upon ourselves, are renewed, reborn, and therefore termed *children*, children of a distinguished and otherworldly will and love.

> ...but to those who received him, to them he gave the distinction to be children of God, to those who affirm in faith his name, those who are born, not of the blood, nor of the will of the flesh, nor of the will of Man, but of God. (Joh 1:12-13)

116. The Logic of Love

Of course it is right to say that in the Christian epoch of pure thought, *Love* is a term of distinction. The only question is: which love? Are there so many? Well, yes, there certainly seems to be. For this reason, it cannot suffice us to posit a name, even names as illustrious – illustrious even today – as *God, Christ, Faith, Hope,* and *Charity.* Unabashed by their dignity and renown and yet mindful of the regard that is their due, we are inspired and encouraged to pursue our philological contemplation of them (which is not an interrogation). How is God Love, we wonder as we read the phrase in the New Testament? How does the language of that epochal wisdom devoted to the words and deeds and life and death of Christ elaborate the notion of *Charity* and render our experience of the distinction of human being all the more vivid and moving in the process?

Let us take as the starting point of our train of thought the formulation *gift of god* (Donum Dei), the term traditionally used in the Second Epoch as a designation for the *Holy Spirit.* In this tongue we must speak about the *triune Godhead* of pure reason and ask now, in particular, how and why pure thought can be thought of in terms of *love* and the *gift of divine love?* We have already seen how this term can be brought into play as a name for the benefit of better discernment between the IS of our unexamined life and the OUGHT of thought, the advent of the law. The term GIFT refers to the gratuity of thought, the evidence and the immediacy of insight into the efficacy of thought as making a difference and leaving its mark upon the minds of Man. It seems that folks in general, are inclined to think – not only when solving problems, but also when reflecting critically upon themselves and their world. Or, to put the matter more succinctly, pure reason is inclined to draw our attention to itself, has oftentimes caught, will catch no doubt again, our dividing, discerning attention and in this way recommend itself to our consideration. Thought inspires insight (A) and performance (C) and realization (B). This is the ***first love***. It is a principle, a beginning, the unconditioned cause of reflection – neither earned by, nor owed to our own selfish efforts and endeavors. But this free causality is, as we have already noted, in the Second Epoch, not seen as the *free spontaneity* of *My imagination* as it was in the Third Epoch. Rather, now thought is taken to be a *free gift, Your present of Spirit*, an idea that confronts us with its immediate and surprising vitality and initiates a train of thought consisting of transitions, leading to a change of heart and a transformation of the mind. This difference that an idea can make and does make is the present that thought gives to living human being, a source of light and the forms that it illuminates, but also of *poison*, a gift of death to multitudinous Man.

The gift of life refers thus to the life of spirit it presents to our reinvigorated aspirations. Initially, however, the opening up of this prospect is, as we have seen, an experience of anguish, the suffering of the poison of our finitude. *Mercy* is now the name for this gift understood in its life-giving property. It names, on the one hand, the gratuity of the call to emergence, the uncalled-for generosity of thought in all its glory, the understanding that has so unexpectedly and undeservedly entered into our world of opacity in an illuminating moment of insight. Thanks to thought, suddenly, we look upon our world as if from outside, without it, yes, precisely so, from a vantage point from which we contemplate a life *without* our mundane world or, as we might more simply say, with eyes that have detached themselves from its deadening material encumbrances and afflictions under which folks often feel pinned and buried alive. What do we see in this moment of truth? We see, beyond the gift and the crisis of distinction, the material love we have just lost in attaining sight, that fire of desire that had prepossessed us and affixed us to our earthly extraction of vegetable human being. This is the phenomenon of the ***second love***, the love that bred the "sin" of beings who are locked in their lives.

But even then and especially then, being imperfect animal and mineral, we are susceptible to shocks of flesh, breaks in the parade of life, which, however briefly and in spite of the pacifier that technology provides, dislodge us from its grid and girdle in which we cradle our mortality and make us wonder as we wander. We took note of loss, tasted regret, felt a pang of pain perhaps and, in this very experience, intimated, for the first time, the ultimate limitation that has since ground our self-assurance down to dust. The arrogant love that is pride's, complacency's self-conceit – the ego-love we succumb to that shrinks down the universe to our own particular idiom, the articulate idiocy and privacy of a single life that we so greedily covet, try so possessively to defend, and upon which our satisfaction so precariously depends – this leaden-hearted love is shaken, its temples of hebetude – such big buildings, such large stones, adorned gravity, coins and tokens of blood donated to the propitiation of some monstrosity of a numinosity we call my *me*, so big in its littleness – all thrown down, its earth and sky reduced to a tumble of rubble, its moon popped, its star flakes melted, its intimates mortally torn asunder by one thought, new born, so little in its infinite bigness whose magnificence marches majestically in ranks upon the theater of distinction to vanquish and to marshal groovy minds from the four corners of the square world.

> But in those days, after that distress, the sun will darken and the moon no longer shed its light and the stars will fall out of the heavens and the powers in the heavens will be shaken; and then they will see the Son of Man come forth in the clouds with abundant power and glory. And then he will send his angels and collect his elect from the four winds, from earth's end to heaven's. (*Mar 13:24-27*)

In such disaster of the stars and desolation of the world, we take heart in a thought that precisely this apocalypse of disillusioned life and resignation presents to our pursuit a redeeming vision. For we recognize in this disintegration of a senile Human heaven and an Earth of dearth, in the signs of abandon and rebellion, omens of betrayal and arrest, portents of false prophets and imposters, the rumors of wars of nation against nation, kingdom against kingdom, the famines and purges and trials of persecution – in all of these phenomena of insurrection and dissolution, of winter's discontent, we recognize the seizure and season of reason, a change of mind, a turn and a conversion to vigilance, thought, that good night, nigh, come to summer, come to consider thought itself, detached in its forms and ways, become alert in its work and grasp, the pang of birth of its own unique life and times and we awaken thus to the ***third love*** as recipients of a destiny and a will, a will and aspiration that inspires thought with sacred ardor to strive towards its resolution and the culmination of a task and charge, a service and an office undertaken in light of that idea which kindled in our heart the hope of the abundant life that is the *open* mind and home of hospitality to the heavenly host of distinction.

This love empowers action and the passage that conveys ideas and plans to the fruition of an enacted, exacted determination. This love seeks resolution of the contradiction between what should be and initially was not, the discrepancy, at first blush, between what should not be but is; this thought will make thoughts real that are now ideals, refuses to take any and every given world or word, save one, for granted and accepted. This thought initiates change and builds with works the dwellings of the transparently shining life it imagines thought can live by and enjoy. The vast designs that follow upon this love's inception are elements of its conception, articulations of its vision in the fervor of its hope and faith. Here is the greatest achievement of pure reason: In the inventive fire of its desire, it brings forth the plenitude of its own origin and makes a father of the son, a son of the father, founds for every prince the regal principle so that the first in positing his king becomes the second, having given all to his own offspring, and the second thus exalted – in this train of thought called *Charity*'s – is acknowledged as the first, the Father, who engendered his own second in the Son – each the other's glory, one the source, the second the source's source and both enfolded in the Godhead's self-relativity, our entity of identity.

This is the inception of the ***fourth love*** with respect to which we determine our destination in the image of achievement and consummation of love that is the Holy Trinity. This resolution of the work of education and distinction is depicted in the likeness of community. It is a state of peace, the rapport of mutuality in the workings of the mind, the constitution of that state called beauty's, a fatherland and kingdom of distinguish citizens, of chosen saints and friends of most dignified lineage. The love of the Father for the Son, the Son for the Father, the love and intimacy implicit in identity, ultimately rendered in a proportion of terms that is itself the third of three, as much comprised by as comprising their Trinity – where once opposition ruled concurrence has now been accomplished, here at the end of time – is the proper intuition of the self-relationship that reason enacts in a concert of three movements. The end of the way is often termed TRUTH, first as the object of ambition, the work of purpose, of determined intention, but then not merely remaining the searched object of unending quest, but also the ultimately found end and closure.

To put the matter thus is the job of conception as well as of celebration, theoretical as well poetic diligence. The latter delights in the collection of terms that articulate the former's insight while the former develops the train of thought in accordance with the logic that these terms suggest.

Plotinus's conception of the principle of absolute difference, visualized in *Figure 81*, teaches us how to see these relationships of love as the elaboration of a line of reason beginning with that principle's present of light that freely bestows the favor of its power, a liberality that is not, however, squandering expenditure. It is, rather, the refulgence of beauty in the plenitude of its goodness. By degrees, in the procession of its radiance, its beams, striving ever outward towards independence, extenuate as they become removed from the original exuberance and forfeit that first sheen of glory. Their power dwindling with increasing distance, they finally come to a stop in the material extremity of their dispersion, having become not merely beings but moreover, dipped in matter, embodied souls and in this standstill, burning with desire for what they have lost as a result of this gap. These lost souls in their despair come to turn inward in remembrance of their source and in this way experience their conversion as an awakening from the materiality they had engrossed themselves in in a bid to be matter's master; turning back from their aversion, they recognize that first brilliance and return, resurrected, to luminous fulfillment as spirits of the Good, the One whence they sprung and whose beauty they were born to sing the praises of.[68]

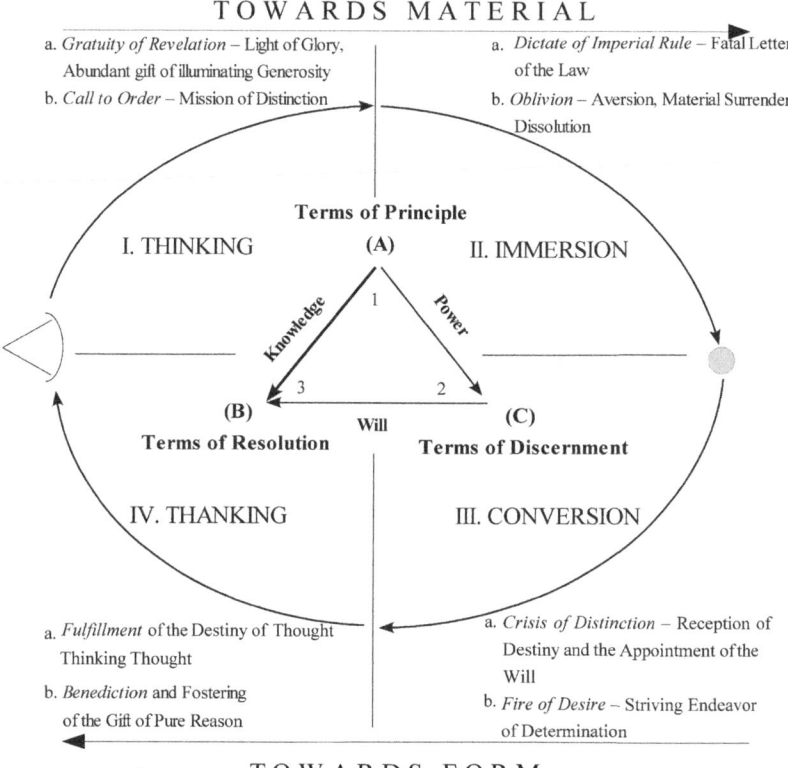

Figure 81: Plotinus's Conception of Conversion

---

[68] cf. H. Boeder, *Das Bauzeug der Geschichte*, pp 329-332.

Retracing the career of this experience, we note the now familiar stations – the gift of light as favor, the aversion of those who in their thirst for power forget that their destiny is to praise the beauty of their origin, the hungry-hearted soul sunken in the meat of matter, the conversion from this death to the life of spirit, to that resurrected life that the lowered soul thought would be its death, the final indwelling of the spirit in the beauty where illumination ends and where it begins again with the recommencement of the narrative of the soul's passage from light to light.

This completes the circle of the principle of self-realization as it was grasped in the Second Epoch highlighting the cascade of power of thought's self-revelation and self-evidence from the force of its call to the distinction that it stimulates, awakening hearts and minds to their rational identity, their purpose as excellent, as *rare* beings in the scheme of all beings and all things thought, a circle of turn and return.

117. The Logotectonic of our Experience of the Holy Spirit

This recursive state of grace and glory of an absolute distinction, conceptualized for the first time by Plotinus, has accomplished the design of rational appointment, brought to term the excellence of beings born to live under the determination of the distinguished, self-several life of love. But with these four loves not yet all have been accounted for. The last, the moment of truth, the fulfilment, being but a moment, must expand and magnify itself, commemorate the whole that has run its culminating course, has taken place. The state of peace, the reciprocity of thought and world, their universe, reflects now upon itself and all it has learned along the way and lifts its voice to song to tell the tale of what has transpired on the way home – a narration that recounts and catalogues accomplishments, dramatizing all the challenges faced and mastered, one by one, dwelling upon each, each one a milestone of development, a necessary step. None are forgotten or ignored. We want the whole truth, the whole story.

Let us therefore call this the last and latest, the ***fifth love***, our extracurricular love, which is that of a later-day philology, yet to be recognized as such perhaps, but nevertheless a remarkably *poetic* love, akin to Hölderlin's, the one inherent in the work of thought, the Builder. In the Second Epoch, the work of the Word, its *poetry*, is a glorious illumination, a messenger, a voice from on high, a God given gift, the knowledge of God expressed in a speech performance, a goodly utterance and benediction, that of a preacher, a missionary of God, called to call, elected to deliver the calling of the gospel to those elect, sent on the mission of the ΛΟΓΟΣ, an apostle, the Word sent to the world to distinguish it into the *one world*, that of heavenly life, and the *other world* of mundane death, that of light and that of darkness, that of truth and that of lies – it is the enlightening Word of conversion from the world of *immediacy* to that of *discernment* in a transition of renewal; this poetry of the word, rightly understood in the Christian dialect of the Second Epoch, is the good news, the spellbinding *gospel* (ΕΥΑΓΓΕΛΙΟΝ - evanglion) of the distinction of human being, which is essentially the "Word of the Cross" (ΛΟΓΟΣ ΤΟΥ ΣΤΑΥΡΟΥ - logos tou staurou), as much a sign of salvation as that of judgment. Reason inspires those who, in these songs, hear its voice to embrace principal change as a principle.

In the Second Epoch this voice is called "Jesus Christ," the *Lord* – who is himself the call of excellence to step out of the leaden immediacy of life; and the *Savior* – that is the call of redemption to embrace the new bloom of being in the spirit of self-transformation.

These verses of reflection, in whatever tongue they are sung, are ultimately tributes to pure thought, the distinction of human being – a benediction of requital for a benediction and benevolence of bestowal; for, in Christian terms, pure thought is nothing if it is not thought of, and thought *well* of, in articulate devotion. The philological art and craft of thought, the Builder, collects all we know and have, all our possessions in heaven and earth and, laying them on the altar of the song, offers their life, putting to goodly use all the worldly and dramatic imagery of speech at its disposal, all the idioms of discourse so familiar to our mundane conversation, beginning with the powerful names we all know, names like *father, life, death, mother, birth, sleep, sword, light, child, flesh, blood.* These seraphic songs of rejoicing and gratitude are themselves deeds of acknowledgement wrought in thanks for the glory of thought's efficacy, the munificence manifested in the narrative that it unfolded before our eyes, the drama of self-severalty we ourselves daily experience, the poetry with which thanking thinking glorifies that glory in return, requiting like with like, a kind reply in kind, for goodness given, love for heartfelt love.

As in the Final Epoch, here, in the Middle epoch, this claim to and calling of reason forms a community of those who have heard the call, adopted the word, eaten its flesh, drunk its blood and, in this way, taken pure reason to heart, taken a distinguished idea *into* themselves as food and, as a charge and mission, *upon* themselves, transforming themselves with regards to it even as it was transformed for their sake by the giver in the giving, and establishing in this achieved relationship of identity the self-relationship that is our constant image of the resolution and that fires our purpose with its self-substantial flame. This community in the Second Epoch is the congregation of those said to be justified by faith, those, in other words, who have embraced the mission of distinction that critical reflection proffered as thought's divine present by the loving concern of a Father, the destiny resolved in the unique possession of peace. As in the analogous achievement of the citizen, the saint brings to life the life of the Word, the ΛΟΓΟΣ that he or she has donned in works of sanctification, in the performance of sacraments, in service to the theological virtues, and, in analogously poetic works, building revelatory signs and miracles to move, to unchain Man, putting what he or she knows about the Word, having been made known by the Word, into the Words of life, of their lives, in the metamorphosis of Man's leaden life.

For this reason and in recognition of the illumination that begins every experience of distinction, the principle in Christianity is the **GOD** of Glory (A), a being that is, like Freedom previously, nothing but a name if it is not known and acknowledged as the person of absolute distinction, no longer thought to be ME but rather You who are absolutely other than us and ours. And nevertheless, in spite of this difference between the Creator and the Creation, this principle is not evasive taciturnity nor parsimonious reserve but rather communicative, *Word*, an emanation that is touching, striking, earth-shattering but also compassionate, exonerating, conciliatory, though, in fact, in Christian terminology, the epochal principle is neither the one nor the other pre-eminently; for the Christian God is above all one of conversion of the heart and the power of **FAITH** (C) not just to move but even to transform the mountain of the mundane world into one that a holy spirit would care to call its home and a dwelling of distinction for those called to glory, this new world and **KINGDOM** of Heaven (B); this refashioned body which is that of the second, the *Last Adam*, comprising both the words of Glad Tidings and the deeds of the Holy Spirit as the enactments of the will of God, signifies the issue of that change of heart that God's glory inspires in Man and that moves our human being to act upon in the Spirit of a holy love, in the spirit of divine being, whose efficacy is the good works of true *faith* in persevering *hope* of achieving *charity's* ends in peace – the three well-known, so-called "theological" virtues of the Christian mind corresponding to the triad of our mind's own proper concinnity of ends, i.e. its theoretical, practical, and poetic determination in accordance with the three essential issues that substantiate pure thought's engagement, namely what is true, what is good and what is beautiful – in the Second Epoch, all three designate the mediating term of thought corresponding to the glory of God's present with a view to the redemption of the world of humdrum evil.

I. The Jesus-Narratives

A. The Power of the Glory of God

118. The Logic of God's Reflection

The synoptic narratives telling of Jesus, his own life and death, his words and deeds, the miracles he performed and the difference he made in the lives of his disciples, provide the element for the first figure of reasoning in Christian thought.

This train of pure thought begins with the present of the principle (A), the inaugural term, which is the *God of Glory*. We are puzzled perhaps at the outset as to what the term *God* may refer to – though in fact we have already clarified that it is, like *Freedom*, a determination of principle, i.e. a term of distinction – *Glory*, however, is a much more tangible expression for what sparks the note of reason; glory is resplendent and refers to the luminous, animadverting *salience* of what is outstanding, of what stands out and comes to the fore of the mind strikingly, stunningly, devastatingly.

And it is no small thing that manages to spark and hold our attendance who are prone to distraction in the midst of our mundane airs and ostentations that bring to luxurious light everything but the light of the minding mind itself, the light of discernment that is the distinction of human being. For this reason, poetic tongues, fashioned by the rare wisdom and the highest art of their distinguished speakers, built monuments in language devoted to this very purpose.

In these tongues, *glory* is the manifestation of power and authority, the majesty, the *present* of the principle which, like any idea, is *nothing but* an idea, *nothing more* than a thought unless it comes to the fore and makes a difference in our lives. In accordance with the self-relativity of the principle, the revelation of glory is rendered in the reflection of turn and return, not of me to Myself as in the Third Epoch of Freedom, but rather Your turn from us is reflected in our turn from You, the Lord – *justice* condemning *iniquity;* and then again our turn to You is reflected in Your turn to us – *contrition* imploring *mercy; God's goodwill* takes note of an individual or a people *(Rth*

2:10) and thus knowing them by name (Exd 33:17) as worthy of His favor answers benevolently their unfeigned plea beseeching benefit.

The Logic of the turn and return in the reflection of God that we first encountered as the distinguished spirit of human being's self-relativity is the basis for the *logic of the Cross* that we will encounter in the letters of the Apostle. In terms of the Second Epoch, we learn that the *sin* or iniquity of the mind that has turned away from the principle of openness, the eye-hiding, ear-stopping mind called stubborn revolt, stiff-necked impudence, proud disobedience, cunning machination that turns its back on and forsakes the principle, is enjoined to turn back and return, to admit of the cut that the absolute difference makes in the flesh of the closed mind and the hardened heart; ultimately when all appeal is in vain, harsh punishment is dealt, reflecting the harshness of the resistance, justice meted out in return for the injustice met, abandonment of mercy on the part of God in exchange for the abandonment of regard on the part of Man.

For this relationship is a conditional one – regard is contingent upon regard; in an unconditional act of love, God has made a promise and established the conditions of an everlasting alliance and covenant of regard between the principle of distinguished spirit and the *distinguished* people and, in this sanctifying sense, "a holy people, chosen above all others, consecrated to Himself as His own precious possession" (Deut 7:6) a people called to "circumcise the foreskin of their heart and unstiffen their necks" (Deut 10.16) in answer to that vocation of divine rapport that demands of the thus distinguished people "to love the Lord your God with all your heart and with all your soul..." (30.6), in other words, in accordance with the ΛΟΓΟΣ of mutual regard which, in terms of the principle of the Second Epoch, speaks thus: "listen to me that God might listen to you" (Judges 9:7), for "God honors those who honor God" (1 Sam 2:30) and "loves them who loves Him" (Pro 8:17), rejecting them who reject Him (1 Sa 15:23) and, more generally, God keeps the promise of His covenant and shows mercy to those who keep His commandments and His charge, who follow His laws, observe His rules, heed His commands, follow Him with all their heart, who accomplish what is pleasing to the Lord, hear and hearken to His voice, heed His word, do what is right in His sight, who uphold, execute His judgments and statutes and ordinances, obey His voice, cleave unto, follow, serve, fear, delight in, love, the Lord – seeking His name, His precepts, His testimonies – with all their heart and all their soul and therefore, "walk before God with an undivided heart, head held upright"(1Ki 9:4), a relationship of personal rapport, of two seeing eye to eye as visualized in *Figure 82.*

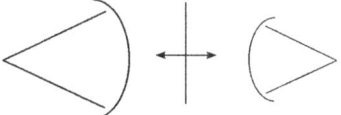

Figure 82: Face to face

In fostering this *covenant* (the Hebrews spoke of keeping, obeying, and doing the בְּרִית - bərith that God made with this chosen people), we enjoy the blessedness of God's deliverance, protection, support (Psa 33:29), experience in this present that is the "light of his countenance" (Psa 89:15), the wisdom of His instruction (1Ki 10:8), His love in evidence even in His chastisement (Job 5:17) as well as in his exoneration of our trespasses (Psa 32:1); this is the blessedness of those who partake of His dwelling and "trust" (Psa 84:12) in the life and the perpetuity of days that is His kingdom for all time as well as the land (1Ki 3:14) which God had promised (1Ki 6:12).

In contrast, to stray from His way is to forsake and abandon the Lord (1Ki 9:9) – our aversion is reflected by God's revulsion casting us then from the present of his sight (1Ki 9:7) answering adversary with adversity when his "fury breaks forth like fire and burns so that none can quench it, because of the evil doings." (Jer 4.4) This reflection of God's adversity shows, as suggested in *Figure 83*, the turning away of divergent ways.

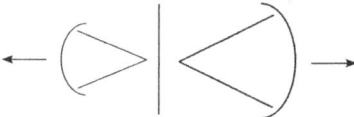

Figure 83: Aversion and Revulsion

The reflection of the principle shown as God's wrathful revulsion towards the puffed out fury of all arrogant aversion is rendered dramatically in the narratives "we have heard and known from our ancestors...the parables and dark sayings of old" (Psa 78.2) as the curses and disasters of the punishment he turns towards us in righteous anger who have turned away in twisted pride, of His churning of rivers into frothing blood (44), of His earthward darting of the evil angels (49) of his abhorrence, spilling its pestilence (50) of flies and frogs (45), caterpillars and locusts (46) upon our recalcitrance, hailstones and brimstones (Eze 38:22), frost and thunderbolts (47-48), fire and famine, locust and mildew (1 Ki 8.37), the slaughtering sword and bow of battle (Hsa 1.7) – all noxious reflections of obnoxious obstinacy.

These eschatological images – lightning and thunder, the clarion call to onslaught, in a blood-streaked sky, of denizens of doom who are the horsemen of the fiery winds riding upon the angelic clouds bringing slaughter to the daughter and the son of somnambulant Man – are dramatic details to invoke the critical spirit and the ordeal of judgment (Isa 4:4), the *Last judgment* at the end of Man's world with the advent of the ΛΟΓΟΣ that was ΘΕΟΣ, the earth-rattling, sun-splitting catastrophe of the *Son of Man*, in all the apocalyptic glory of his Second Coming upon chariots and cherubim.

> When the Son of Man comes in his glory and all the angels of distinction with him, then he will sit on his glory's throne. All the nations will be gathered before him and he will separate the people one from another as a shepherd separates the sheep from the goats and he will put the sheep at his right hand and the goats at his left. (Matt 25:31-33)

We see here the distinction of human being being made between the mentality of openness so poignantly rendered in both the Hebrew Bible as well as in that of the Gospel as the one that cares and responds, even as God does in his essential Mercy, to cries of human need – gives food to the hungry, drink to the thirsty, welcome to the stranger, clothes to the naked, solace to the widow, protection to the orphan and, on the other hand, the opposite mentality that says in its closed heart with a strutting tongue, in the callous carelessness of its control: "Me and no one else!"

אֲנִי וְאַפְסִי עוֹד (Zep 2:15)

(ani wə afsi owd)

On the other hand, mercy is the free gift of unearned, and in this sense, unconditional, persevering kindness in reflection of the persistent and unfounded resistance to the deity's appeal that the murmuring of a brazen heart, our inhuman aversion, be softened in the turning of human compassion and, similarly, that of the relenting return of divine compassion in the face of true contrition, the confession of regret and penitence, which is the idea of critical self-reflection expressed in Christian terms. In this line of reasoning, the punishment of justice is not the opposite of mercy but rather the proof of its efficacy; God's steadfast love is not withdrawn from our stiff-necked withdrawal of service and rebellion but rather chastisement is a token of patience and the upholding of God's pledge of allegiance in spite of our apostasy, the father's chastisement of his child. We recognize in this threefold reflection a line of reasoning, depicted in *Figure 84*, that develops the rapport of regard as a circle of turn and return, God's as well as Man's turning point.

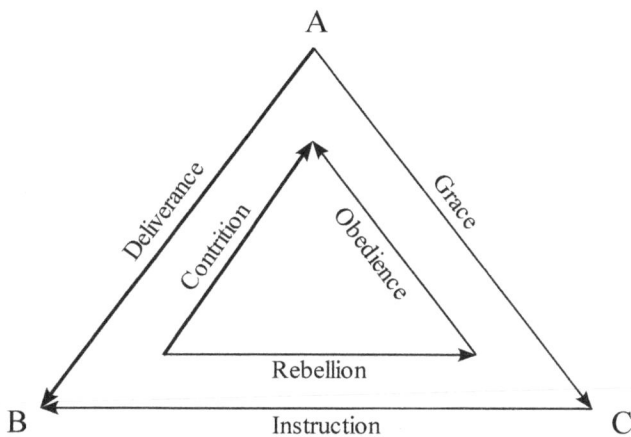

Figure 84: The Reflection of the Suzerain and the Vassal

In this rapport the distinction of self-severalty is not a determination within the self-knowing being that *I am* with regards to Myself, My best and better half that is distinguished by *freedom*, but rather marked by the absolute difference that God, the Creator, makes with regards to His Creation, *Heaven* and *Earth* being the signature terms of distinction in the Second Epoch in which God's I is absolutely *not* my own – My autonomous self-relativity is merely an image of that of the Godhead, as Augustine taught; His difference is not within Himself but rather, first, between Himself and His creation and second, in His Son, His Word that became flesh. God makes the entire difference but He is neither Mine (mine is, in fact, in my submission to the Word, His), nor his own (being not different from *Himself*) but rather His Son's and our distinction with respect to the Christ, the Lord; and it is through the Son's self-severalty that we are distinguished from ourselves and our world, from the Heaven and Earth of His creation (and thus of twofold provenance). This relationship to the principle is therefore not one of *sovereignty*, as we saw in Rousseau, but rather of *suzerainty*; the former is a *contract of association* that each individual makes with the general will while the latter is a *covenant of promise* that God makes with a people He consecrated as the rightful heirs to His providence.

The back turned to pleas turns back and thus returns to face the call of the distinguished face of eyes open to see in sympathy and show regard to the face upturned with eyes of entreaty –rather than cheek's effrontery – saying, "I knew that you are a God of compassion and merciful, that you are slow to anger and steadfast in abounding love, relenting from catastrophe." (Jon 4.2)

The reciprocity of the relationship of accord and intimacy, to which the term *love* is often applied, that obtains in the entity of identity between the seeing being and the being seen, our experience of the spontaneity and the receptivity of pure reason, has admitted of several versions in the languages of wisdom we are studying. While in the context of individual poetic spirit, we noted this rapport between abstraction and reflection as the decussation of the thought and thing, the ideal and the real in which poetic spirit's accomplishments, the commonality of its content and the distinction of its form, are harmoniously opposed to the material unity of form and its manifold content, which is productive exchange, the community of matter and pattern, ultimately recognized as the celebration of human and divine nature in the beauty of Fatherland. By contrast, in the Second Epoch of thought, the Actor, divine *and* human being mirror their distinction in mutual regard that is founded upon the promise of the covenant between the absolutely distinguished God and His chosen, his distinguished people who have returned to Him with their whole heart (Jer 24:7) and with regards to whom God, in turn, confirms his pledge: "And they shall be my people and I shall be their God in truth and in righteousness." (Zech 8.8)

וְהָיוּ־לִי לְעָם וַאֲנִי אֶהְיֶה לָהֶם לֵאלֹהִים בֶּאֱמֶת וּבִצְדָקָה׃

(vəhayoo-li ləam va-ani ehəye lahem le'Elohim be'emit oovitzdaka)

In the *Qur'ăn*, God celebrates the reciprocity of this relationship of accord with the godly in similar terms: "God will take pleasure in them and they in him – that is the supreme achievement." (5.119):

رَضِيَ اللَّهُ عَنْهُمْ وَرَضُوا عَنْهُ ذَلِكَ الْفَوْزُ الْعَظِيمُ

(Raḍiyal-lāhu 'anhum wa raḍū 'anhu. Dhālikal-fawzul-'aẓīmu)

Again, to truly appreciate the evocative power that these terms give to the idea that is here at issue, namely the revelation of the relationship of regard, we must know that the train of thought they are intended to render explicit and dramatic pertains to the effect of critical reflection upon the lives of those unused to such thought and perhaps even opposed to it in their worldly obsessions; and then again, conversely, to comprehend the significance of pure reason *in practice,* we must experience the reality of this idea in the haunting, daunting details of a startling, other-worldly language as foreign as possible from that of our custom and concerns. In this way, by the craft and art of thought, the Builder, by poetic license as it were, thought is made to descend to the realm of things even as matters are uplifted to the height of pure mind, allowing us in this way to make sense of both the ideal *and* the real – attributing a concrete, *nearer sense* to thoughts otherwise considered abstract and remote, even while furnishing the face of things and experiences otherwise held to be banal and prosaic, with a deeper, *further sense.* Thus, what has been affirmed of the parables of Jesus is all the more valid of the method of thought, the Builder, namely, if, in giving utterance to what has been "hidden since the foundation of the world." (Mat 13:35), the poetic craft of allegory that gives names to glory and glory to the old familiar names is subtracted from their message, "He has said nothing." (34). For names make manifest, magnify ideas, bringing thoughts forth towards us, in their brilliance, in the bright light and highlight of speech and then again names elaborate our lives and times into elements, articulating our deeds and their circumstance into instances of images, narrations and histories, dramas that make a difference in our lives as they unfold before us; language is an open book of being, but open in the way of a sign's ownmost dissimulation of concealment such that, "those seeing might not see and hearing they might not understand." (Luk 8:10)

ΒΛΕΠΟΝΤΕΣ ΜΗ ΒΛΕΠΩΣΙΝ ΚΑΙ ΑΚΟΥΟΝΤΕΣ ΜΗ ΣΥΝΙΩΣΙΝ

But the standpoint of the logotectonic method is neither that of the speaker Jesus, though we may take up the tale and strive to experience it, as his disciples had, *on its own terms,* nor that of the evangelist who has composed the Narrative of Glad Tidings; ours is neither the horizon of lived experience in the unfolding of the tale, nor that of the narrator who related its details; rather, our philological approach compiles and arrays an anthology of signature terms and then, as artisans of the logotectonic art, builds trains of thought that consist of relationships and sequences of these terms and collects the narratives that their ratios govern into the appropriate figures of their terms, that are so many lines of reasoning, theoretical as well as practical, so that the languages of wisdom in the procession of their epochs can be analogically compared and better comprehended as elaborating with its several principles – three to be exact – one accomplished work of pure reason.

119. The Paradox of Glory

Specifically, the birth of Jesus is the movement of thought entering the world in which the practice of distinction is now to be carried out. For the first miracle of glory, even before wrongs are wreaked and mercy bestowed, is the birth of the idea itself that utterly confounds what we would expect of words like *birth* and *death, father* and *son, light* and *darkness, heaven* and *earth, man* and *god,* what we would normally assume of the *gods,* or any proper god, and above all of *God* Himself – behold the majesty of a king in the form of an infant, the legitimate prince in the form of a bastard son, a manger for a throne, a baby in a diaper rather than a knight in shining armor, a court of farm animals, shepherds, and vagabonds attending him whose queen mother is but a virgin girl of the commons – what could be more incredible, more anathema to our expectations and common sense, more paradoxical to conventional notions of the glory of deity than that? But the whole point of these paradoxes is to illustrate the idea of conversion and convey the experience of the change of heart from a conventional to a distinguished view, from the material to the spiritual standpoint. These paradoxes are set to confound what we expect because we are to learn the lesson of departure from the mentality of the world and the "commonsense" notions of deity and the gods that is no less familiar to it and no less mundane, no less materialistic than the world they reign. Imagine a deity now that is absolutely distinguished from that sanctioned by existing traditions and the predominant culture of a given period, a given people in history, a given civilization, an entirely new god whose newness consists precisely in this absolute difference! Such a deity would need a distinguished name but even a name would impinge upon that absolute difference, lasso him as it were and tie him to a sobriquet, subject him to the speech practice of human calling, bring him into the realm of human being. Yes, even naming and calling, ultimately even thinking about God (in an uncritical, undistinguished manner) can be admonished as an affront to his (to its?) absolute distinction – naming, calling, thinking, to say nothing of seeing and hearing, are just so many instruments of Man' control and subjugation by which a distinction can be assimilated to human purpose and in this way obviated.

The stations in the train of thought in which the distinction of human being is developed in Christian terms as the Glory of God begins with the *Virgin Birth* of this being. This child is engendered by the bestowal of the bounteous gift of spirit upon the innocence of a heart not merely open to, but moreover fertile in its recipience of the seminal idea that pure spirit sows, as distinguished in its *Conception* as it is in its *Nativity* and as the baby

Jesus taken up, seen and celebrated as a star of hope and promise, the destiny of distinction, of holiness (Luk 1:35), that has been introduced into the sphere of unholy human affairs and wanting our most human and attentive, tender-loving care, namely that with which we attend to a baby. The acknowledgement of the distinction of human being presents first in the *Baptism* of Jesus to whom, "directly upon rising out of the water, the heavens opened, and he saw God's spirit descend like a dove and come down to him" (Mat 3:16) "...and a voice from Heaven saying you are my beloved son in whom I am pleased." (Mar 1:11)

While the vocation of his baptism was the inauguration of Jesus's ministry, his *Transfiguration* on the "high mount apart" (OPOΣ YΨHΛON KAI IΔIAN – Mat 17:1) is the "vision" (OPAMA – Mat 17:9) of Jesus, though a son of Man, nevertheless distinguished in himself, and appearing before his disciples in the glory of the attribution that acknowledges, in the person of Jesus, the divine determination of our human being in the person of Christ, the chosen Son of God in the perfection of his heavenly life that is his dwelling in the light of glory: "his face shone like the sun and his robe became the brightness of light." (Mat 17:2)

But this vision of Christ's glory is, as yet, only the vision of our destiny as children of deity and Jesus' own as the Son in the heavenly dwelling of God's glory. Jesus undertakes and undergoes the experience of self-severalty upon which the entire distinction of our human being as born to light though living in darkness rests, even as we were born free but living in chains in the previous Epoch of our investigation. The *Crucifixion* is this manifestation of our all too human fate, the experience of our shame and our indignation at the mess that is our mundane mortality and the pusillanimous ephemerality that governs our finitude with all due meanness of purpose. Thus to dust debased, we seize upon the idea that we may step back from the spill of blood and break of bone that is the concise history of our flesh and conceive of a spirit's scope upon the body of our need, switching stances from earthward dearth to friendly skies, our rising in our eyes that is our *Resurrection* in the acknowledgement of that *other* life, a simple, not so simple recognition of the pure human spirit to the extent that we partake of the life and the death of Christ, who is the person and the patient practice of this recognition, a recognition that is not so much a body of precepts as a discipline of the body – that bodily standpoint, call it the mentality of the *me, here, now, today* in which we tend to be so avidly and exclusively engaged – and the renewed life we lead as a result of the pains we take in its continued consecrating exercise, the charmed everlasting life that is Christ's divine *Ascension* to glory after the death of those older doldrums from which he departed to be "taken up into Heaven to throne on God's right." (Mar 16:19)

> ...ΑΝΕΛΗΦΘΗ ΕΙΣ ΤΟΝ ΟΥΡΑΝΟΝ ΚΑΙ ΕΚΑΘΙΣΕΝ ΕΚ ΔΕΞΙΩΝ ΤΟΥ ΘΕΟΥ

These miracles in which the principle is made manifest enters the world in and through Christ. In the works and words of his ministry, in his life and in the drama of his death, we perceive the sign of distinction foretold already in his birth, a sign set in controversy, meaning "the fall and rising of many...one set in contradiction...so that the inner thoughts of many will be revealed." (Luk 2:34)

> ΟΥΤΟΣ ΚΕΙΤΑΙ ΕΙΣ ΠΤΩΣΙΝ ΚΑΙ ΑΝΑΣΤΑΣΙΝ ΠΟΛΛΩΝ...ΚΑΙ ΕΙΣ ΣΗΜΕΙΟΝ ΑΝΤΙΛΕΓΟΜΕΝΟΝ...ΟΠΩΣ ΑΝ ΑΠΟΚΑΛΥΦ– ΘΩΣΙΝ ΕΚ ΠΟΛΛΩΝ ΚΑΡΔΙΩΝ ΔΙΑΛΟΓΙΣΜΟΙ

B. The Will of God fulfilled

120. Thought Hurts

In keeping with the myth of the inscrutability of all things divine owning to the confirmed and inveterate exiguity of our minds, we applaud the skepticism that wonders how anybody could know the "will of God," much less do it? And nevertheless, depending on the particular situation in question, it would seem that folks do indeed have an inkling of what "God," even in the most generic understanding of this term, would want or do or not do and what is in keeping with God's *spirit* and what is not. Try it! Confronted with a certain set of circumstances, consider in what way your own private will would differ from the will of someone else in the very same circumstances. Apparently, the *will of the other* is already a notion with a certain critical force – seeing the world through others' eyes, walking a mile in another's shoes, as the saying goes, is indeed the first step towards the self-several departure of the mind from the confines of *my* life, the first death of the immediacy of my own life and the discovery of that wider life above and beyond this first horizon of privacy and of the corresponding will that is entirely unto me, myself, and I, that unholiest of trinities. Going further, my neighbor's will, though surely divergent from my own in some cases and occasionally even diametrically opposed, is ultimately familiar, my sister's, my brother's – we can find some compromise or coalition upon which to base our cooperation in achieving a diversity of ends. But consider now the will of a stranger from a different culture, from a faraway land, whose life and aims are entirely different than my own – here we begin to lose our traction in the daily tug-of-wars that settle, for each constellation of the vectors of the moment, who our friends are and who our foes, what is mistaken and what goes.

Now take the *perfect* stranger whose life is absolutely different from our own, whose life, in fact, is absolute difference – distinguished as *infinity* to our finitude, and further, with respect to our limited knowledge, power, and being, omniscience, omnipotence, omnipresence; Or say *everlasting* life as opposed to our morality of ephemerality; what would we do in a particular situation of our own lives if we were to assume, for a moment, the standpoint of *eternity* and the corresponding will that is absolutely distinct from the inherent human constraints that determine our own. This idea, admittedly farfetched from a theoretical point of view, can nevertheless have, should we venture to adopt it for a moment in a particular situation of our lives, remarkable practical consequences; evidently, thinking about our lives and the world in terms of the will of God, receiving thus a *holy* spirit into the hard-hearted heart of the world that is ours as merely Man's, can transform our heart and our world – it is an idea that wants our words, fancy ones, and inspires us to talk in tongues in which we might elaborate the where and the when and the how and the why of human action and the corresponding world that stems from what we do in accordance with such a spirit in which things are done once and for all and not merely here, now, today, for me. Clearly, expressions like *the long term* or *the big picture*, divorced as they are from those dramatic narratives, are not resounding enough for this idea; in fact, they would seem, rather, to hide, to subdue the self-several drama of eternity we have been studying in Christian terms. Who bends their stiff knee when they hear the word *sustainability*?

In this line of reasoning, what "God wills" is evident to whoever considers a situation "objectively," in other words, simply put, *rationally* in the best sense of this expression. Aha! If the ΛΟΓΟΣ is *God* as we have learned and this divine ΛΟΓΟΣ comes to the world and even "becomes flesh," then this principle of pure reason, termed *God*, in order that it be brought near, nearer, nearest to our comprehension, must needs be put in terms that human being is willing and able to harken to. And once spoken, these terms not only catch our attention, but also leave an indelible mark upon our minds, thus being not merely the voice of reason and a call out of the blue, the revelation of the thought insinuating its word into our considerations, but also the workings of an inaugural spirit, inspiring the innovation, the renewal of our mind's windmills; this is a change of heart and a new heart, a new Spirit and in this way a call to action which is its only possible verification. A word, this Word, is *spoken* and *heard*...or *ignored* – terms that bring out our speech practice; a word is *given* in promise and *received* in gratitude – highlighting the fact of the giver and the recipient, which are likenesses of pure reason in its incipience and invenience, a thought given and a thought taken. The term *spirit* might be used in this fashion as well – *inspiration* being the spirit that comes over us, the angel that speaks to us, a collaborative – as opposed to merely cooperative – spirit shared among many, folded into one purpose, the substance of which is not depleted or consumed but rather multiplied in participation, much like the bread of life and the miracle of love, the giving away of which enriches even to superabundance (Mat 15:36-38).

While Christ himself is the sign and the glory, the medium *and* the message of the principle of distinction in the Second Epoch – ultimately, in the Crucifixion and the Resurrection of our human being, i.e. of Jesus – in the narrative of the Gospel, we see the signs that Christ made in the world of words and deed; and to these we now turn in exploring the issue of the principle in human terms as Jesus doing God's will in his performance of miracles as testimony to his Father's regard for him who was acknowledged as His beloved Son in the Holy Spirit, the only thing (that is no thing at all) that God and Man can possibly share and have in common after Christ's final departure, his *Ascension*, as it is called. These miracles are signs of his Father's glory and the authority (ΕΞΟΥΣΙΑ) that the latter invested His Son with, namely "all power in heaven and earth." (Mat 28:18)

ΠΑΣΑ ΕΞΟΥΣΙΑ ΕΝ ΟΥΡΑΝΩ ΚΑΙ ΕΠΙ ΤΗΣ ΓΗΣ

Specifically, these signs are transforming acts of healing and of saving, signs of the renewal and conversion of our human being that he performed during his life in the name of the Holy Spirit.

Let us follow the testimony of pure reason in the words, signs, and deeds of Jesus, his proofs, beginning with his severance from the mentality of the world, the generic extremism and intransigence of both its ascetic inclemency and its indulgent narcissism, after the illumination of his vocation to the Holy Spirit – the temptation in the desert of deprivation in which he practices departure from the privacy of individual bodily need with a view to what is spiritual, rebuffs suspicion's demand for proof and certainty in what must be taken on the faith of trust, in both cases batting down the mundane idolatry of self-glorious, self-serving, self-enriching goods in acknowledgement of the greater glory that lies in self-denying gratitude for the gift of absolute good that is Jesus's other, distinguished Self, his Father in Heaven.

In accordance with the logic of the present of thought as the *Word* of God, the works of Jesus begin with the calling of disciples, initiating not only their immediate following but also, in the subsequent appointment of their profession as apostles, those chosen to hear the call God sent in the person of his Son and following him, themselves thereby being sent on the mission of their ministry to call forth reflection – the ΛΟΓΟΣ, the deity of pure reason, wins without force our commitment, catches us in its net (a fisher's not a spider's), moves us in our minds, who are thus, in turn, called to glory, are the chosen by the chosen, the elect by the elected, the children of God called by the Son of God who is himself choice and election, himself the splitting image, the likeness of his father's, drawn of his Father's own absolute distinction.

Thus we recognize in *Figure 85* the familiar pattern of differentiation that characterizes the transitive progression of self-reflection in the mission of God's glory from the Father to the Son and from both to the Spirit.

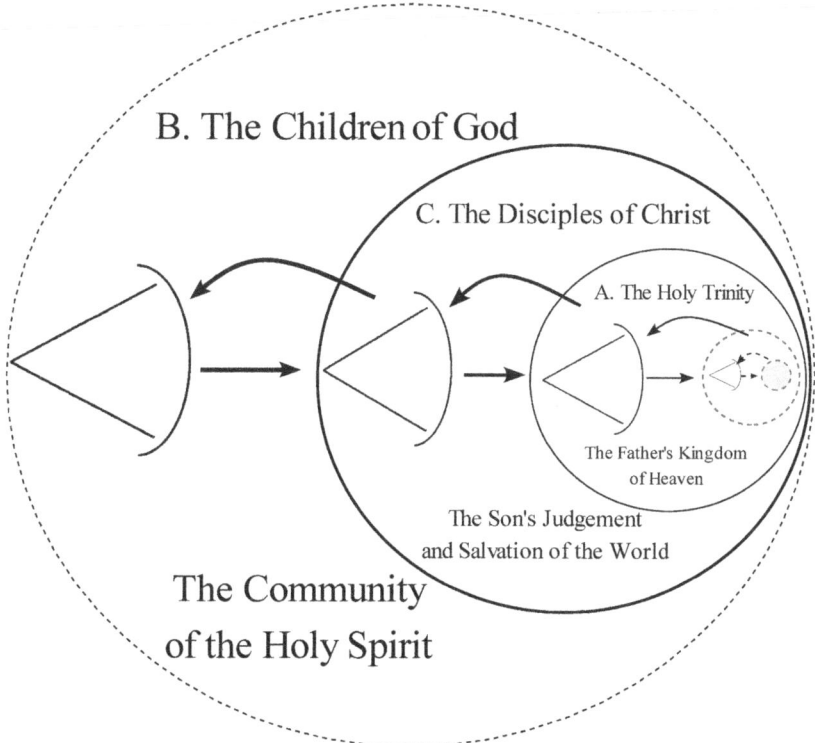

Figure 85: The Communal Spirit of God in the Cascade of Glory

For this reason, in the proclamation and the preaching of this distinction of Christ as the realization of the glory of the Father, the term *Fatherland* could very well have been used, just as it was in Hölderlin's poetry in which, as we noted, "the ideal is what nature was" (*Hyperion* I 112.15); instead, we hear the expression *kingdom, Kingdom of Heaven* in Matthew (5:17) as well as *Kingdom of God*: "The determined time has come; the kingdom of God is near; turn your minds and believe in the gospel!" (Mar 1:15)

ΠΕΠΛΗΡΩΤΑΙ Ο ΚΑΙΡΟΣ ΚΑΙ ΗΓΓΙΚΕΝ Η ΒΑΣΙΛΕΙΑ ΤΟΥ
ΘΕΟΥ ΜΕΤΑΝΟΕΙΤΕ ΚΑΙ   ΠΙΣΤΕΥΕΤΕ ΕΝ ΤΩ ΕΥΑΓΓΕΛΙΩ

In the ministry of this message of change, Jesus encounters the various types of illnesses of inertia that befall the idle mind – a catalogue of humanity bound up in itself, in the involutions of its conceit; wound tight or come undone; behold a rich inventory of cavernous Man's secretion fleshed out in terms of disease, disability, and invalidity and as such not only amenable to the healing effect of critical reflection, at least hypothetically, which can then be, in turn, manifested as remedy and relief, but also allowing us to consign to the vivid human experience of health and recovery the issue of the advent of the heavenly kingdom in the message of the gospel. Such an analogy serves to reveal the deeper sense of both the soundness but also the morbidity of a mind plagued by our chronic thoughtlessness.

It is with regards to such oppressive poverty of quickening spirit that Jesus was anointed by the Holy Spirit to do good (Act 10:38) and thus sanctified, distinguished, as the *Christ* of God "to preach the gospel to the poor, sent to heal the shattered's heart, to preach deliverance to the captives, sight's recovery to the blind and to the bruised the alleviation of their bruises." (Luk 4:18)

In a logic and a language that makes infirmity of our self-inflicted nescience, reflection emancipates the cripple from the crutches and the stretchers of our paralytic habits that made us so shrivelled and so lame of limb in our lethargy; critical thought cleanses the dirty mind of its leprosy, returns to hearing and to sight the deaf ear turned, the blind eye cast aside, exorcises the mute demons of our idolatrous addictions, the pains and palsies of our self-possessed obsessions and to all of the screeching convulsions of our windy world he raises his voice and says, "Silence, be still!" (Mar 4:39)

And then again he rouses the still somnambulist with his call to wakeful note, makes a sleep of our death and then, the greatest name for reason's feat, raises up our dead unconsciousness to the life of self-known being.

Now, having shown the idea of passage from illness of spirit – *sin*, "the sting of death" (1Cr 15:56) in the precise sense we have been developing it – to the purification and renewal of the heart as demonstrated by the signs and wonders he performed in the narration of Jesus's teachings, the moment arrives in the fullness of this thought's time, when Jesus himself undergoes the trial of distinction and puts into practice his message of departure and return that is inherent in the advent of the kingdom that he has proclaimed in the gospel. The *Passion* of Christ makes visible, makes acutely tangible, the anguish and the pain that the experience of critical reflection means to Man. Really? Is then stepping back from ourselves and our lives to take stock or review, to evaluate and assess and thereupon, having discerned the gap between the IS and the OUGHT of it, this ordeal of judgment that, having made its determination, initiates in us an intervention of improvement by, say, breaking a habit that has lasted a lifetime or upholding a principle against the onslaught of odds, condemning us to the just desert of trying new ways, to the sanction of welcoming a newcomer and saying hello or the perdition of saying goodbye to old friends and letting them go – are these works in which we experience thought as a cross and crossing, a passage and transition, a moral *crisis* in our human being, really *so* irking, *so* heart-rending, earth-shaking, flesh-tearing torment as to be rightly thought and designated *death*, to be appropriately and seemly rendered in scenes of such hair-raising, dead-raising brutality – in acts of torture and execration? Why not!

For what do they ultimately teach us? Clearly, that self-critical thought and correction, burying the hatchet, turning over a new leaf, remorse and remission, redress and recuperation are unpleasant – they go against Man's two most powerful drives, namely the instinct of self-preservation and the principle of immediate gratification. And that is the whole point of truth that is a practice that will be *done* and not merely *contemplated* in theory or *sung* and celebrated in poetic invention.

Thought hurts.

For, far from embracing opportunities to ply and pronounce judgment, to gauge, to rate, to appraise, Man coddles his languorous negligence, cuddles it, covets his disease of easy carelessness, parades and even glorifies in his creature comfort, yields, surrenders while going gently, gently into that good night, laps up the suavity of swindle, pillows his life with lotus-licking illusions, hides his eyes, complies, cuts and bumptiously snubs, harasses, quails and passes. What a long list of terms to mark the character of the mind that could step back critically for a moment and reflect but *would prefer not to*!

Even Jesus prayed he might be spared his excruciating chalice of spirit, that eternal, resurrected life after the death of one who takes upon himself the mortifying crisis of self-severalty that is our entire distinction as human beings: "Father, if you will, remove this cup from me; however not my will, but rather yours, be done. (Luk 22:42)

ΠΑΤΕΡ ΕΙ ΒΟΥΛΕΙ ΠΑΡΕΝΕΓΚΕ ΤΟΥΤΟ ΤΟ ΠΟΤΗΡΙΟΝ ΑΠ᾽
ΕΜΟΥ ΠΛΗΝ ΜΗ ΤΟ ΘΕΛΗΜΑΜΟΥ ΑΛΛΑ ΤΟ ΣΟΝ ΓΙΝΕΣΘΩ

We see here how the will of the divine Father and human will of the Son diverge for the briefest of moments, for the mere length of a clause, "Father, if you will, spare me this cup…" on the eve, on the verge of his crucifixion, the crucifixion that is the doctrine of Christ, the precept that he offers us to learn and follow him in taking to heart and bringing to life in our own life; we can be, and, because of the death of Christ, we now know that we are meant to be, self-opposing, self-separate beings, distinguished *in* ourselves *from* ourselves and, as such, destined to experience this difference as a passage, as our cross and crossing, from life to death, from death to life, from the unfelt darkened life that is our dateless death to that distinguished death that, in Christ, is our brighter life, the life of pure spirit – thus the foundation of his entire teaching, the glory that all the signs and wonders that he has performed during his ministry reveal.

C. The Acknowledgement of Christian Faith

121. Confession and Benediction

Two hearts and the change of heart, with a death-defying leap of the heart from a hole in the loam to a home, to a kingdom come – from that of the pot of flesh to that of spirit's cup of good cheer and glad tidings brought from afar, from the tip to the pit, a mission of light from the pure mind's height mercifully stooping to the soul's depressions that uplifts our heart and gloriously transforms the wolfish visage of the world into the lamb's countenance of Heaven. In departing from those lowland voids that is Man's seat upon the butt ends of our days and ways, we attain the critical standpoint placed, in the poetic wisdom of thought, the Builder, above it all. This is the work of surmounting – *faith*, in Christian terms, the mountain mover.

Through the change of heart, our *turnaround*, we switch perspectives upon ourselves of which there are two in one – first *we* are looking up either with reverence or with insolence, then we, that is to say, *You*, our *Father*, are looking down, either with mercy's kindness or with judgment's zeal, though the former is predominant. The adoption of Your perspective and the doing of Your will that this grasp and wisdom entail were demonstrated in the sufferance of Your chosen Son's ignoble death, who You anointed Lord for *our* sake and made manifest to us in dramatic terms we could best understand, i.e. in a shocking visualization, a scene of cruelty that explicitly elaborates our experience of critical reflection, the separation in Man this reflection makes of our human being, namely disciples of the Word, on the right hand, and, on the left, murderers of those who serve pure spirit and who you, mundane Man, therefore hate though We love you even as You, namely our distinguished human being, i.e. Christ, love(s) Us, Your children, and even then, still, calling to them, though they persist in refusing to hear your word, having set their minds to killing You; for pure spirit is their destiny, i.e. who they really and truly are *Themselves*, in spite of themselves, in their Heart of hearts, and therefore, Self-hating; well-versed and rehearsed in loving themselves, they hate Themselves and You who nevertheless love them who are Yours even before they realized it not knowing what they do.

Hmm. Does that make sense? Is there any justification for depicting the experience of pure reason's appeal in such drastic or perhaps merely extravagant terms for the "paradoxical things we have seen today?" (Luk 5:26)

ΕΙΔΟΜΕΝ ΠΑΡΑΔΟΞΑ ΣΗΜΕΡΟΝ

None other than this: a change of heart in the life of human being is no picnic, no piece of cake by any stretch of the imagination, and its achievement a rare and remarkable, even mountain-melting, earth-shattering, world-turning event. That we, generally speaking, do not often succeed in renewing ourselves with a view to what is good, better, best, that we lapse again and again into all those familiar ruts and rotes of behavior we have so often condemned in ourselves and discarded time and again; that we fear to walk the way of change and growth even as we celebrate it with talk, visualize it in arts – who is so naïve or self-glorifying to deny? For this the image of the crucifixion does indeed dramatically confirm the difficulty of New Year's, New Life's, resolutions. It confirms the precarious human condition, so in need of vigilant care, on the one hand and, on the other, affirms the extraordinary destiny that pure reason has made us heir to, that Holy Spirit which is God's, near God, one with God, even God Himself in Person, in the Person of the Father and the Son together as one, God bringing God, the Word that brings the Spirit that comes to us from Him to dwell not only among us for a short while, but also in us forever.

To magnify thus human being and the experience that carries human being beyond itself is itself the work of reason, of thought, the Builder as is *benediction,* the hallowing of such being as has assumed the name of Christ extolled as our destiny. In the benediction of this spirit, the spirit of the Father, human experience is itself hallowed, consecrated to administer to the faithful rendering of the efficacy of pure reason and to elevate salient moments in our lives to the status of the depiction and elaboration of a thought come to life – birth, marriage, death, but also adolescence, even eating and drinking – all such elemental events of human life are thus conceived of as sacraments, i.e. as having depth and rich significance and therefore as moments of decision and initiation, transition and dedication, resolution and sanctification – all used and useful to commemorate the transformational work of thought in our lives as we saw in the signs and miracles that Jesus made before our eyes. Are the most basic, most natural, most human actions and objects of our everyday life, even in the most "profane," not remarkably receptive of ceremony and consecration should we choose to bestow upon them this distinction in a free act of recognition, having liberated our eyes from their bondage of blindness and the self-absorption that we cling to that prevents us from seeing and receiving what is right here in front of us, Him, pure reason's present *in person*?

OI ΔE OΦΘAΛMOI AOYTΩN EKPATOYNTO TOY MH
EΠΓNΩNAI AYTON – Luke 24:16

(*Their eyes were stultified that they failed to recognize him.*)

Where else can the precepts of pure reason be, whence can they have come, whither will they conduct us if not right there, if not in and from and to our highest heart, "the kingdom of God within" us? (17:21)

Η BAΣIΛEIA TOY ΘEOY ENTOΣ YMΩN EΣTIN

There is no concealment in the heart unless it be intentional hiding of the eyes, the sightless eyes that swathe a hideous heart in pall.

But then this is and must be a torn heart as well, one of departure and dispossession, as we have already learned: "If you come to me and do not hate your own father and mother and wife and children and brothers and sisters, yes, and even life itself, you cannot be my disciple." (14:26)

Is this not a remarkably provocative way of saying *it.* But does this expression help us better understand why *it* – namely putting departure into practice, giving life to the negativity of pure reason, letting go in love, not looking back (9.62) – is so difficult?

Yes. And yet the experience of Christian spirit requires nothing more than our embracing of the vulnerability and uncertainty of those who ask in trust and who search in hope's faintest glimmer, who dare to knock on the door believing that, though closed, it may be opened and wondrously dispense a kindness, undeserved, gratuitous (11:9-12) – abounding *faith* on the one side, the human side, making most desperate and abject plea, that reflects the abundance of *favor*, the glorious gift of grace and pure compassion, on the other, the divine side of a relationship and a rapport shadowed by no condition or reward, no trafficking of goods, but rather goodness to goodness freely beseeched *and* vouchsafed.

We make the start in our confession – critical self-reflection in Christian terms, that is, first, "repentance...," the animadversion of our turning, "...towards God..." and away from our demons, the aversion of our idolatry in self-spawned images of God's zealous adversity, "...towards our lord Jesus in faith" (Act 20:21)

> ...THN ΕΙΣ ΘΕΟΝ ΜΕΤΑΝΟΙΑΝ ΚΑΙ ΠΙΣΤΙΝ ΕΙΣ ΤΟΝ ΚΥΡΙΟΝ ΗΜΩΝ ΙΗΣΟΥΝ

For faith is the purification of our heart (Act 15:9) of all those ghosts of our own contrivance and perversion and its turning towards that one ghost of God's, the Holy Ghost.

Admit it! Who does not hate admitting to others or oneself that there is a gap between THE WAY IT IS and the WAY IT SHOULD BE, that we do not or have not measured up to the high and highest standard that the ideal (to use a term from the Third Epoch) of a holy spirit, embodied in the person of Jesus Christ, raises before us like the banner of a principle, the distinguished, *otherworldly* principle of human being, affirming that we, in this world, are, to be sure, the subjects, but not and never merely the slaves, of the principles of pleasure and self-preservation.

But to admit this, in the face of all failure to aspire to attain that standard and, despite the ultimate inadequacy of our human being, to seek to fulfill that principle's requirements, is, it seems, nevertheless, to assent to and therefore to acknowledge that standard and that principle, their truth; and this is, in spite of everything, an uplifting, even a renewing experience of human dignity that joyfully counterbalances the cleansing humiliation of our daily confession – thus do pain and self-condemnation resolve themselves into praise and gratitude for what so inspires our striving emulation, confirming, in the pure height of what we hold so dear, our own and further, the higher, affinity and infinity, of our mind. Jesus Christ himself is the embodiment of this turnaround, the proof and pledge that it is possible, more, that it is the imperative of our fate, being divided in ourselves, to fall in ignominy and to rise again in splendor in confession of the one You are to whom we aspire in the distinguished Spirit You gave as Your Word of encouragement and showed as our Way, our Turning and Returning to Your Kingdom that is our true home and dwelling.

This knife, this cloth, this flame, this goblet, this water, this bread, this voice of invocation, this gesture of the hand – it is in their least constituents that the inhabitation of ideas must be accounted for; by engaging our individuality, here and now, in the poetry of thought, do we not bestow upon the specifics of our everyday lives the profundity of myth, the suggestiveness of signs? And conversely, is not the eye that sees the tragic depths of our self-several human being in all the details of our days itself doing the work of administration to the idea that in singing words and daily deeds achieves the presence of mind and intimacy that weds ideas to our world, welcomes them into the community founded upon a principle?

Thought, the Builder takes the thought and gives it a home in the form of things, in the flesh and bones of things; and insight recognizes the sense of the source behind the ritual surface; the work of the *imagination* and the *intellect* respectively. But in the Second Epoch, these two faculties of pure reason, that of invention and that of insight, are subservient to the *ethos* of pure thought, putting into practice what we know in our hearts to be in keeping with the spirit of what we have seen done by Him, a distinguished Spirit that can hardly be counted worldly, hardly even human, therefore more properly recognized to be a greater, a higher one, a *holy* spirit and yet our own, too, one of us, among us, too, in us, too. God sent his Word of wisdom into the Flesh of the world for one purpose, namely that it might be put into action and become not an object of contemplation, whether as a likeness of aesthetic or as a being of conceptual judgment, but rather as the Path of distinguished life, a truth done *and* to be done. Thus, the narrative of the gospel is such a document that gives testimony to the reality of thought as well as to the essence of things and events and the significance they assume in the sphere of human action among people who strive to do what accords with the birth, the life, and the death of self-several deity, our Christian destiny.

II. The Letters of the Apostle

C. The Conversion of Faith

122. Mind Moving Mountains

The term, most often named and best known in Christian thought, for the absolute trust that imbues the strength of our convictions with the fidelity and the fortitude we require to steadfastly pursue efforts undertaken at the behest of pure reason's call despite the anguish and tribulation that the crisis of distinction means for Man, is, of course, the divine obedience of *faith* (ΠΙΣΤΙΣ - pistis). Is it inexplicable how pure reason can be thought of in such terms? We say that faith makes whole (Mar 10:52) and that it sanctifies us (Act 26:18); that it cures calamity's scourges (Mar 5:34); that, for it, nothing is impossible (Mat 17:20); and that it is fulfilled in love? Is this consecrated language really repellent to the rationality of philosophical conception as has often been opined by *thinkers* who, apparently by definition, are not *believers* whose faith, in turn, is wont to demur when confronted with the demands of knowledge and insight? But what of Anselm's famous precept, his motto, and the original title of his *Proslogion* suggesting that faith and knowledge are, in fact, not inimical but rather self-several, the true relationship of which is elaborated upon in a train of thought that comprises both, namely one that recognizes discernment with regards to God as "faith in pursuit of insight" *(fides quaerens intellectum)*?

Godhead or divinity in this understanding, whether conceived of in the form of Augustine's *Trinity*, Fichte's *Ideal I AM*, or Plato's *Idea of Good*, is the determining principle of a striving love, a practical science that, having put aside other objects of contemplation, sees and enacts and builds likenesses that correspond to the "paradigmatic" operations of pure reason's self-relativity; such an act of engagement of the mind as this might be rightly thought of as meriting the name of *soul* and its, no, *her* discriminating efforts as the studious application of a distinguished method, *amor sapientia* (love of wisdom), *ΔΙΑΛΕΚΤΙΚΗ* (dialectic), *Wissenschaftslehre* (doctrine of systematic knowledge).

In the synoptic narrations of the Gospel, we became acquainted with the miracle upon which Christian faith is founded and the discernment that is peculiar to it, emerging from the inaugural Glory of God, the present of God's mercy and God's law, which together determine the distinction of human being in the Second Epoch and attain their full significance and efficacy in the person of Jesus Christ who in his words proclaims and in his deeds enacts divine and not merely human will and gives thus pure reason the form and personality of an individual who succeeds in distinguishing the holy, distinguished Spirit of his Father from the more profane one, the one presiding over the pandemonium of our devils and our demons that enforce the short-sighted dictates of the pleasure principle while single-mindedly prosecuting the cause of our self-preservation.

The confession of faith entails a renewal of the disciple's mind and it is now this experience that we examine in more detail in the letters of the Apostle Paul, a study in the justification of our human being as a consequence not of what we do in observance of the law but rather as a result of the spirit in which what we do is done, namely "through faith in Christ...for through works done in conformance with law no flesh is made just." (Gal 2:16)

ΕΚ ΠΙΣΤΕΩΣ ΧΡΙΣΤΟΥ...ΔΙΟΤΙ ΟΥ ΔΙΚΑΙΩΘΗΣΕΤΑΙ ΕΞ ΕΡΓΩΝ ΝΟΜΟΥ ΠΑΣΑ ΣΑΡΞ

As all leaders of people know, in our efforts of persuasion, it is not merely compliance but rather commitment that we aim for. It is easy for me to make you do what I want. All I have to do is hold a gun to you head and say, "Dance for me, baby!" and you will probably dance. But even though I succeed in making you dance, I have not succeeded in making you *want* to dance. You might not be dancing at all *in your heart* even as you make the outward appearance of somebody who is dancing. Poets and apostles and prophets and pastors, kings and queens, teachers and managers (cf. Eph 4:11) – who are, as we shall see in the Greek Epoch, by definition, skilled in the art of moving the human heart – know all too well that getting people's bodies to do things or not to do things is easily achieved by use of force in the circumvention of their will, which is supposed to be free or at least only with difficulty accessible to the violence of coercion; but it is the heart, this distinguished soul, and not merely the flesh that we want to move. Hence it is only the mentality of human being – our ideas and the heartfelt words through which we give them expression – that conclusively shows whether our hearts are in the right place or not and it is the spirit alone in which things are done that determines whether we are sanctified or condemned (Mat 12:37); even words, so nearly thoughts, can be reduced to mere ceremony, emptied of the spirit that justifies them, or again, from the point of view of recipience, can be heard as dictates of law, but fail to be heeded, or duly performed by one going through the motions but not taken to heart: "For it is not the hearers of THE WAY IT SHOULD BE who are just before

God but rather the doers of THE WAY IT SHOULD BE who shall be justified" (Rom 2:13)

ΟΥ ΓΑΡ ΟΙ ΑΚΡΟΑΤΑΙ ΤΟΥ ΝΟΜΟΥ ΔΙΚΑΙΟΙ ΠΑΡΑ ΤΩΙ ΘΕΩΙ
ΑΛΛ 'ΟΙ ΠΟΙΗΤΑΙ ΤΟΥ ΝΟΜΟΥ ΔΙΚΑΙΩΘΗΣΟΝΤΑΙ

Thus Paul proclaims a law the performance of which is a circumcision of the spirit prior to the circumcision of the flesh which is the performance of law only to the extent that it bears witness to the prior discernment of a mind renewed and redeemed by its commitment to a *holy* spirit. Hence, in assenting to and praising Christ, we partake of his destiny, which is one entailing both fall with regards to our deviations from the WAY IT SHOULD BE and rise with regards to the mercy that redeems us, death *and* life. In fact, to undergo this transition of redemption *is* the living spirit of the law that Christ himself is the incarnation of, the performance of which Paul calls the conversion of *faith*, truly hearing (Gal 3:5) first and then acting – speaking, preaching, in obedience to the word of the Lord, to Christ alone.

This *law of faith* (ΝΟΜΟΥ ΠΙΣΤΕΩΣ – Rom 3:27) does not "supersede" the law of Moses. The harsh rebuke and adversity that our mundane mentality perceives in the divine commandments of pure spirit that have been set in stone reflect, in fact, the aversion we feel and show towards departing from Man's mind, who, stuck up, is stuck in the rapacious ruts of its petrified ways; our stoned mind grinds unpleasantly on the words carved in the stone of distinctions that have made evident the difference between the IS and the OUGHT. The gap – called *sin* in the Christian dialect – that the law has carved into the flesh of our world cuts to the quick the unexamined life, once our so careless faring, with the sting of death; condemned, lost to that former lightness through the critical shadow that scripture has cast on the cave-Man's wall of concealment, we see ourselves and our former lifestyles poisoned and imprisoned by the gift of the thought that says THE WAY IT IS *is not* THE WAY IT SHOULD BE and therein irresistibly subjected to the sin that it reveals to those who are not and for whom nothing is perfect (Gal 3:22).

And what do we see in the mirror of our mind's adversity made manifest before our very eyes? Critical reflection twisted into the cannibalism of conscience – a self-gnawing, self- worrying thought: Flesh biting and devouring flesh (Gal 515); in opposition to the purposes of distinguished spirit, our undistinguished pound of flesh hankers after the short cut, the quick fix, the short term, ready-made solutions, settles for expedience, for what's cheap and fast, what works, what counts for now, what matters here, to us, defends what's ours, avoids pain at all costs, indulges without moderation, sidesteps reflection's crises, patrols controls, takes the easy way out, destroys rather than builds, disparages rather than esteems, finds a scapegoat to blame, makes excuses, hides and sneaks to avoid the open confrontation with a view to resolving differences in the truce of truth, begrudges and bedevils, blackballs and boasts, bores and brawls, bitches and bullshits, brutalizes and bullies, binges and betrays, bellyaches and backbites and, whenever possible, beats around the bush – and that's just a collection of the iniquities of the *B's*!

Paul's impressive and repeated catalogues of corruption (Gal 5: 19-21, Rom 1:29-31, 2Cor 12:20, Col 3:8) are so many lists of the ways we, who are in a brutish state of mind (ΑΔΟΚΙΜΟΣ ΝΟΥΣ – 1:28) and therefore not presently disposed to thought, might skirt the hurt and mortal sting of critical self-reflection as opposed to those who take up the cross of their distinction in the crucifixion of their false flesh and, having donned the good death that faith is, reap the fruits of spirit – the openness of *love*, the concord of *joy*, the completion of *peace* and the perseverance of *patience*, the compassion of *kindness*, the selflessness of *goodness*, the constancy of *faith*, the modesty of *meekness*, the equanimity of *temperance*. (22-24)

This is the world of spirit; the other is the world of the body, our offal, governed by the disregard and extremism of those whose "god is their belly" (Phil 3:19), who are "straitened in their own bowls" (2Cr 6:12) by the trespass of measures; a world of vapidity – where inflated princes reign the air; a world of enmity – where children of disobedience and anger are tossed and batted about in deception by every windy dogma even as they are enslaved by the fretful elements clashing lustily in their limbs, in short, the world of those "whose throats are an open crypt, tongues spitting deceit, lips dripping with an asp's poison, mouths cursing bitterness, fleet footed in blood splatter, ruin, and misery in their ways, knowing no peace and, in their eyes, showing no reverence for God." (3:13-18). For with regards to these folks, by definition, or, as Paul puts it in his characteristically emphatic way, "it is written, that none is just, not a single one, there is not one that comprehends distinction, none that seeks God; all have turned away, impotent, none doing kindness, none, not a one."

ΓΕΓΡΑΠΤΑΙ ΟΤΙ ΟΥΚ ΕΣΤΙΝ ΔΙΚΑΙΟΣ ΟΥΔΕ ΕΙΣ ΟΥΚ ΕΣΤΙΝ Ο
ΣΥΝΙΩΝ ΟΥΚ ΕΣΤΙΝ Ο ΕΚΖΗΤΩΝ ΤΟΝ ΘΕΟΝ ΠΑΝΤΕΣ
ΕΞΕΚΛΙΝΑΝ ΑΜΑ ΗΧΡΕΙΩΘΣΑΝ ΟΥΚ ΕΣΤΙΝ ΠΟΙΩΝ ΧΡΗΣ–
ΤΟΤΗΤΑ ΟΥΚ ΕΣΤΙΝ ΕΩΣ ΕΝΟΣ

It is to the mumbling, grumbling inhabitants of this world, of our coma home, that the law speaks in condemnation saying that THE WAY IT IS *is not* THE WAY IT SHOULD BE "so that every mouth's trap may shut itself up and all the world may be guilty before God." (3:19)

...ΙΝΑ ΠΑΝ ΣΤΟΜΑ ΦΡΑΓΗ ΚΑΙ ΥΠΟΔΙΚΟΣ ΓΕΝΗΤΑΙ ΠΑΣ Ο ΚΟΣΜΟΣ ΤΩΙ ΘΕΩΙ

If the law of critical reflection, being "the knowledge of sin" (ΕΠΙΓΝΩΣΙΣ ΑΜΑΡΤΙΑΣ – Rom 3:20), merely brings the darkness of our selfish life to light, then what are we to do who seek to sunder and separate Ourselves from ourselves even as the gap between light and darkness was imparted to creation by holy spirit upon the first drawing of a distinction – the very first day of God's work, after the divine word of distinction was spoken in which the light of difference itself was brought to light and itself, as such, by God, seen and affirmed *as good* (כִּי־טוֹב - *ki tov*), i.e. THE WAY IT SHOULD BE – "*Let there be light*, said God and discerned the light as good and distinguished between the light and the darkness." (Gen 1:3-4)

In relation to this crisis of difference, this ordeal of judgment that is the bright day of keen discernment of our benighted world, Paul sets our experience of the gift of grace as God's abounding kindness whose face is now turned in compassion towards the face of our return in gratitude, rather than in adversity to our aversion. For "in faith we are made just and have peace before God through our Lord Jesus Christ." (Rom 5:1)

ΔΙΚΑΙΩΘΕΝΤΕΣ ΟΥΝ ΕΚ ΠΙΣΤΕΩΣ ΕΙΡΗΝΗΝ ΕΧΟΜΕΝ ΠΡΟΣ ΤΟΝ ΘΕΟΝ ΔΙΑ ΤΟΥ ΚΥΡΙΟΥ ΗΜΩΝ ΙΗΣΟΥ ΧΡΙΣΤΟΥ

Through our turning and returning to God in Christ's faith, we participate in Christ's death as subject to the ordeal of the law who are condemned to crucifixion with him for our sins; but through faith we also participate in his life resurrected by God's mercy for the remission of our sins. "For it is through death that we are freed from sin and if we be dead with Christ, we believe that we shall also live with him who, having risen, has broken death's dominion; dying to sin once, he was revived in God as we will be, through him, dead to our sin but alive to God, through Jesus Christ, our Lord (Rom 6:7-11).

Who is we? "Neither Jew nor Greek nor barbarian, neither circumcised nor uncircumcised, neither slave nor free, neither male nor female..." – God knows no partiality – (Gal 2.6) "...we are all one in Christ Jesus" (Gal 3:28), Christ is all and in all (Col 3:11), i.e. in those called by grace to faith. For in the determination of human being, God, in the pure purpose of his will, preordained that we are "to be holy and without blame before God in love" (Eph 1:4) and thus "blessed by the God and Father of our Lord Jesus

Christ...with all the celestial distinctions of spiritual blessing in Christ" (1:3), destined to be of one blood and spirit with the principle of absolute distinction, i.e. to be the chosen children of his promise, namely those who are, through Christ, adopted by our Father in Heaven and who are, through our faith in his Son, by him – as he himself was acknowledged by his Father – recognized as the true heirs to the kingdom of Heaven, "the inheritance of the saints in light" (Col 1.12), and who now bless in turn, crying *Abba Father* (Gal 4:6), returning grace in gratitude for the grace of our redemption, our benediction for Your benefaction, praise for the riches of Your glory reflected in eyes enlightened by the "the spirit of wisdom and revelation in his knowledge" (1:17) – blessing for blessing, grace for grace, acknowledgement for acknowledgement in the recompense of goodness; again, reaping what we sow, receiving what we render, being given what we give, holding fast in our faith and being held fast, established, by a faithful God (2Ch 20:20, Deut 7:9, Isa 7:9), not as a trade and bartering of goods, but rather as the *covenant* of mercy, kindness, compassion, and abundant goodness (Exd 34:6) that is the determining principle of our distinguished human being in the Second Epoch who is subsequently incarnated as his chosen and anointed one, his chosen king, with regards to whom God promises: "Forever will I sustain him in the compassion of my favor and my covenant with him will stand." (Psa 89:28)

לְעוֹלָם אֶשְׁמור־לוֹ חַסְדִּי וּבְרִיתִי נֶאֱמֶנֶת לוֹ:

(lə'olem eshmor-lo chasdi ubə'riti ne'emenet lo)

It is put into effect in the reciprocity of self-relative reflection of love in love, ours in Yours and Yours in ours, humanity and divinity face to face, rejoicing in the rapport of pure reason's self-knowing being, the wisdom and pure spirit, the power, the truth, in a word, the ΛΟΓΟΣ of God, the God that is before God, in other words, if we get the genitive right, God's God, the Father's Son and the Son's Father in one self-several entity of identity.

For this reason it makes perfect sense that *knowing* is *to be known* (Gal 4:9, 1 Cor 13:12) for the elected in faith, who, before having come to know the principle of their absolute distinction as *God's*, were "enslaved to those feeble and abject elements" (Gal 4:9) – worshiping the salient temporality of their life and times, its "days and months and seasons and the years" (Gal 4:10), but who were, nevertheless, in accordance with their predetermination as human beings always meant to rise from these doomed times and rudimentary life of their flesh to that of the eternal glory of pure spirit, which is the train of thought that articulates the fulfilled destiny of our human being in Christian terms: "For those whom He foreknew, these He foreordained to conform to the likeness of His Son...but those He foreordained, these He also called and those He called, these He justified and those He justified, these He also glorified." (Rom 8:29-30)

ΟΤΙ ΟΥΣ ΠΡΟΕΓΝΩ ΚΑΙ ΠΡΟΩΡΙΣΕΝ ΣΥΜΜΟΡΦΟΥΣ ΤΗΣ ΕΙΚΟΝΟΣ ΤΟΥ ΥΙΟΥ ΑΥΤΟΥ....ΟΥΣ ΔΕ ΠΡΟΩΡΙΣΕΝ ΤΟΥΤΟΥΣ ΚΑΙ ΕΚΑΛΕΣΕΝ ΚΑΙ ΟΥΣ ΕΚΑΛΕΣΕΝ ΤΟΥΤΟΥΣ ΚΑΙ ΕΔΙΚΑΙΩΣΕΝ ΟΥΣ ΔΕ ΕΔΙΚΑΙΩΣΕΝ ΤΟΥΤΟΥΣ ΚΑΙ ΕΔΟΞΑΣΕΝ

We are these who have been transfigured by pure thought, transformed in Christ, who have changed their tune, "doffing our Old Man (Eph 4:22),..." to become our Father's son or daughter "...by donning a new suit and pursuit of human being in the renewed spirit and state of mind forged in justice and true holiness." (4:22-24). Sloughing off this mortal coil, we put on our immortal one so that the corruption of the body we buried in our shame's divisive crisis may now be resurrected in incorruptibility, so that the mortifying humiliation of self-contrariety we have experienced, having been weighed and found wanting in the judgment of self-critical reflection, shall be transformed into the glory of that judge whose grave eyes and solemn voice, namely those of the absolute law, we might now recognize to be that of our very own kindred spirit, namely one looking down upon us with a father's mercy; thus exalted in our own eyes, we are resurrected who were dead and gone; buried in that shame that cursed our shortcoming, we shall be raised to new life in the refulgence of regard after that death in wretchedness, elevated to distinction by grace after our disgrace...and death shall have no dominion.

> Sown in dishonor, it is raised in glory, sown in weakness, it is raised in power; a natural body is sown, a spiritual body raised.... And so it is written, the first man, Adam, was made a living soul, the last Adam, a quickening spirit; the first, Man of earth, the second Lord from heaven. And as we have borne the likeness of the earthly, so we shall bear the image of the heavenly....Behold, I show you a mystery: We shall not all sleep, but we shall all be changed....In a moment, in the twinkling of an eye, at the last clarion call... the dead shall be raised to incorruptibility and we shall be changed...for when corruption puts on incorruptibility and mortality puts on immortality then shall come to pass...what is written: Death, where is your sting; Grave, where is your victory? (1Cr 15:43-55)

We "don" our new person, "put on" the Christ of our human being, like a raiment of light – who could have ever thought of putting the issue of pure reason into these striking terms? Only an adept in speaking the language of wisdom, the vivid tongues of flame that lighten and delight.

In Paul's discerning words (Eph 6:14-17), we are therefore called to arms and the armor of divine amour: first "...gird your girth with the belt of truth...", upholding in trust the idea that upholds us in our faith; then affix the "...breastplate of justice..." on your chest, protecting your heart from the cutting glances of your own courage; then "...bind the shoes of readiness around your feet..." to go the extra mile that is the heart's abundance and to learn the way of compassion by trying on the stranger's moccasins; now comes "...the shield of faith that deflects the darts of our devils..." and those daily demons of our idolatry and then "...the helmet of hope for salvation..." that protects the head and the heading of our heart's true purpose; and finally "...the gleaming sword of spirit which is the word of wisdom, the Father's Word...", teaching in the language of the Gospel the tragedy of the human heart, the decisive crisis that is our right – but also our rite – of passage and the way of human destiny, from the tomb of our mind's bodily immediacy through the death of that straitened life to the eternal life of spirit purified and renewed in the experience of its distinction from itself.

Thus so finely arrayed, we might stand tall against the diabolic days of the despisers and deceivers and all the minions of a warped mind. For in the end, it is against our own Doctor Evil, the contortion of our own spirit by spirit, that we must take up our arms and our hearts against to fend off the potions of what, in the retort tubes of our inattention, turns the pure spirit of self-knowing human being into the homunculus of our mini-me mentality, the spirit of Man's meanness, *Satan,* as he is called in Christian terms; his designs (2 Cr 2:11), his concoctions are the enemy, the luminous darkness that turns our spirit into a demon's curse; for our struggle is, in fact, not a campaign against Man's broken body but rather insurgence and sedition against the workings of the twisted mind: "we do not wrestle flesh and blood but against the rulers, against authorities, against the cosmic powers lording over this present darkness, against the spiritual forces of evil on high. (Eph 6:12)

ΟΤΙ ΟΥΚ ΕΣΤΙΝ ΗΜΙΝ Η ΠΑΛΗ ΠΡΟΣ ΑΙΜΑ ΚΑΙ ΣΑΡΚΑ ΑΛΛΑ ΠΡΟΣ ΤΑΣ ΑΡΧΑΣ ΠΡΟΣ ΤΑΣ ΕΞΟΥΣΙΑΣ ΠΡΟΣ ΤΟΥΣ ΚΟΣΜΟ– ΚΡΑΤΟΡΑΣ ΤΟΥ ΣΚΟΤΟΥΣ ΤΟΥ ΑΙΩΝΟΣ ΤΟΥΤΟΥ ΠΡΟΣ ΤΑ ΠΝΕΥΜΑΤΙΚΑ ΤΗΣ ΠΟΝΗΡΙΑΣ ΕΝ ΤΟΙΣ ΕΠΟΥΡΑΝΙΟΙΣ

A. The Logic of the Cross

123. Charity

Undoubtedly, to our more sober moods, the fervent manner in which Pauline speech practice, namely what he calls "the word of the cross" (Ο ΛΟΓΟΣ Ο ΤΟΥ ΣΤΑΥΡΟΥ – 1Cr 1:18), conveys ideas, the oftentimes startling, even repellent turns of phrases with which he, himself aware of their boldness (Rom 15:15), renders the otherwise so familiar drama of our mind's reversal and return, must make the impression of being, well, exaggerated. For Heaven's sake, why does he say *it* like that! Why indeed! Subtracting the "rhetoric" that is supposedly everywhere so apparent in Paul's writing and in the bland assumption that "rhetorical device" is an additive, and an artificial ingredient at that, in the pabulum of the text, how would *you* prefer to say *it* in such a way as to make Man sit up and take notice of what is both nearest to and furthest from our mind, namely the mind itself?

Now there is certainly nothing unreasonable about interrogating a text with respect to its style. The only problem with such an investigation, from the point of view of our current philological study at least, is that an analysis of text and textual phenomena along the conceptual lines that modern linguistics and semiotics have made available to literary criticism digresses from the issue of pure reason, which is our cause and our one and only theme.

In the framework of our present concerns, when questions regarding style and figures of speech arise, we understand them as pertaining not to a "...pedant's grandiloquence...", i.e. merely as phenomena of diction, a perspective which, in effect, "...empties the cross of Christ..." (1Cr 1:17), but rather to the *poetic* work of pure reason, i.e. the way in which ideas attain presence in the substance of language, the way they take on the form and shape, the *feel* of the concrete particulars in the annals of human experience that words refer to and memorialize. Thoughts, ideas, like all spirits, are intangible but they admit of being given, of taking on, the tangible form and substance of what, in language, is posited as their signs. Or do you deny that the terms *flesh* or *earth*, *love* or *truth* are richly invocatory, allowing, nay, admonishing us to elaborate, upon their bidding, an entire train of thought the logic of which is governed by those specific and every-day contexts we associate with one or some of these terms, and then, further, even to improvise an *ad hoc* system of differentials based on them with which our experience of the distinction of human being is wondrously, and, as it would seem, serendipitously, heightened, deepened, and enriched, and only in this way, if you will, "exaggerated?"

As we saw, with regards to their eligibility for deployment in these figures and buildings of language, it makes no difference whether the terms are "abstract" or "concrete" nouns, adjectives, verbs, pronouns, or even articles and prepositions, conjunctions and interjections. Their uses not only in the poetico-philosophical discourse of contemporary as well as historical literary culture – whether considered low or high – but even in the idioms of casual speech practice, provide us with the material basis we need to take forward the work of pure reason, both its perception *and* its invention.

Thus let us not say *exaggerated* but rather *abundant, exuberant,* a bounty and outpouring of clarity that reflects the generosity of *grace,* the splendour of divine *glory,* the power of the principle termed, in this Epoch, *God* whose potency and wisdom and will – the three faculties of pure reason – did not remain concealed for all eternity, but rather were made manifest (Rom 16.25-26) in our time of hungry hope and groaning hearts and have, moreover, since then actually taken effect by engendering a distinction in the spirit of human being – this *distinguished* ghost of our human being – not just any old ghost mind you, not one of the many dirty-dozen demons and servile devils that haunt the daze and the dark nights of our soul, but rather a *hallowed* Ghost, *God's* spirit – this new heart right through the heart of our very world, God's power and wisdom and will *in the flesh,* is named by Paul *Christ* Jesus – *Lord* as being one with the object of our persevering faith, *Son of God* as being one with his Father in the spirit of love and *Son of Man* as being one with that distinction of human being itself that is our perpetual judgment Day, the kingdom of heaven both come in Christ's spirit of *Mercy* and coming in the Lord's spirit of *Justice,* his second coming on the Day of anger and rebuke – we would say the day of critical reflection – whose coming in the glory of the Heavenly host "...will bring to light the things now hidden in darkness and will disclose the counsels of the heart..." (1Cr 4:5) in order to determine our just desert, namely either praise or else condemnation.

...ΕΛΘΗ Ο ΚΥΡΙΟΣ ΟΣ ΚΑΙ ΦΩΤΙΣΕΙ ΤΑ ΚΡΥΠΤΑ ΤΟΥ ΣΚΟΤΟΥΣ ΚΑΙ ΦΑΝΕΡΩΣΕΙ ΤΑΣ ΒΟΥΛΑΣ ΤΩΝ ΚΑΡΔΙΩΝ...

What is the *logic* of the cross? That the deductions and inferences of its "message are not of Man's garden variety glibness but rather obey the apodictic of spirit and power" (1 Cr 2:4) will, at this point, surprise no one. The narratives in which we first examined the story of the life of this logic in a synoptic of the manifold miracles and signs performed by Jesus for the glory of God is now, in Pauline thought, concentrated into the unique drama and actual experience of the power of the God of the *Cross*, not Jesus's own experience or that of his disciples as the witnesses of his death and resurrection to glory, but rather that of those called by Christ to be the apostles of the Gospel and to proclaim throughout the world the power of God in Christ crucified and resurrected to eternal life in the Holy Spirit of the Father.

This is not the spirit of Man's world, of our age and its princes, the stooping, stuporous spirit of death. It is the law of the spirit of life, of God, the Holy Spirit, knowing, communing with our own heart, on the one hand, and on the other, sounding the depths of God – this unique coign of vantage of pure thought, intrinsic to beings both human and divine, the very substance that they share, and yet distinguished from them both even as they are absolutely distinct from each other, is the determining principle of Pauline conception; it is the spirit of Christ in which we stand through faith and fulfill by love.

Why is *love* a name for the Holy Spirit? Because it names the entity of identity and highlights the accord, the covenant, inherent in the self-relativity of pure reason's rapport with the Godhead, the determining principle, of which reflection is the most salient property. For consider: Even as our haughty *aversion* with respect to God's mercy was God's majestic *adversity* with respect to our disobedience, so does God turn His face to us who were defaced in our own eyes, bending, lowering, condescending to meet with His eyes those eyes that had been stubbornly unbending, cruelly condescending but now bent, lowered, stooped in shame and therein raised to His in groans and pleas of repentance. The magnanimity of His patience consoles the contrition of our chagrin after the supercilious silliness of self-aggrandisement is abased, crushed by the solemnity of His grandeur, the mini-me mentality of our Man's homunculus, that kinglet's loftiness, taken down a notch by the King, the slight of lordliness by the vastitude of the Lord. For as punishment follows crime so does compassion answer penitence and benevolence shed its soothing grace on the anguish of those who have submitted to the admission of their disgrace – they know best of all that and why *sorry* seems to be the hardest word. In the logic of the Cross, by giving we are given; receiving, we are received; we who uphold are ourselves upheld and by our own acknowledgement are acknowledged, in taking up the cause, embracing the idea, we are taken up, inspired by it, affirmed in our trust, such that in us His faith is put by Him in Whom we have put our faith. Thus the admonition of faith (ΠΙΣΤΙΣ – *pistis*) and the affirmation of abiding (אָמַן

- *amen*), God's as well as Man's: "Believe in God and you are confirmed" (2 Ch 20:20) whereas, on the contrary, "if you do not, you are not." (Is 7:9)

Love is the term of choice in the Second Epoch of the distinction of human being used to indicate the coherence of this relationship of reflection, and it is this rapport and principle of reciprocity governing the entity of identity, articulated as a precept of human action, for example in the *quid pro quo* or the *do ut des* of the synallagmatic contract at the heart of civil law systems as well as the so-called *golden rule* – namely doing to others as you would have others do to you – it is this principle of responsiveness of love for love, faith for faith, but also woe for the wicked, this chirality and dissymmetry of reason's hands – one hand washing and being washed by the other – that founds Man's certainty that "the fruits of his hands shall be given to him." (Isa 3:11)

כִּי־גְמוּל יָדָיו יֵעָשֶׂה לּוֹ

(ki gəmul yadav yease lo)

"Return to me and I will return to you" (שׁוּבוּ אֵלַי וְאָשׁוּבָה אֲלֵיכֶם -ֹ Mal 3:7) – it is this principle of balance and measure, objective and reflective law, that is the harmonious heart of rationality in action and not the mirroring punishment of a *lex talionis*, not the barbarous reflex of retaliatory "justice" by which an injured party is sanctioned to exact bloody compensation by killing, blinding, burning, maiming, wounding, and whipping – a misconception of judgment that is, in fact, the purest perversion of the principle of justice – a calumnious interpretation of God's own words:

> You shall give life for life, eye for eye, tooth for tooth, hand for hand, foot for foot, burning for burning, wound for wound, stripe for stripe. (Ex 21:23-25)

Similarly, the cross is the symbol of the efficacy of love in the decussation of the *present* of thought, the crossing that is the chiasmus of blessing – the consecration of life to spirit and the gift of spirit to life – such that we might experience spirited life and living spirit in the person of distinguished human being as our own destiny to which we might aspire in faith.

In the Third Epoch we became acquainted with pure reason as the categorical imperative of conscience; the spontaneity of our human being is manifest in the beauty of *poetic* spirit, which is the reality of our autonomy, the nature of humanity. Now in the Second Epoch we encounter the immediate voice of reason once again, the beckoning voice and the discriminating (not discriminatory) Word of God, Christ, as the spirit and the power and the wisdom of the absolute distinction between the IS of the world of Man and the OUGHT of the law of God, the gift of God's image freely given to us who are trapped by our demons in the habits of our dispirited flesh, the unconditional boon of an idea that, when the time is right, is not so much one that we ourselves have as it is, rather, one that has us, unexpectedly seizes us, and to which we now in acknowledgement of this unconditional present of thought, attribute, in correspondingly abounding gratitude, the superabundant glory of a principle that did not remain hidden but rather has become abundantly clear to us, the efficacy of which is termed the *Grace,* the *Charity,* the *Love* of God. The love of human thanksgiving answering to the love of divine Mercy, blessing to blessing – in this reflection of *practical* spirit, let us now become acquainted with how the logic of the cross articulates the self-relativity of our entity of identity. Recognize the difference between what we actively do ourselves, create for ourselves and out of ourselves on the one hand, and what, on the other hand, we passively receive as being done to us; we have learned to speak of *My Freedom* and the poetic nature of our human being as that of thought, the *Builder;* now our experience of *Your Glory* and the *practical* nature of Christ who is himself the doctrine of the conversion and the renewal of our human being in which we participate as thought, the *Actor,* is founded on the converse distinction between the self-glorifying works and idols of our own hands fashioned in the image of the world and that of God's spiritual gift of faith which is the bliss of those "to whom God imputes righteousness without works." (Rom 4:6)

...ΩΙ Ο ΘΕΟΣ ΛΟΓΙΖΕΤΑΙ ΔΙΚΑΙΟΣΥΝΗΝ ΧΩΡΙΣ ΕΡΓΩΝ

How can we die and still stay alive, live our lives and be already dead? Only if our distinguished being is not *My* nature and the self-realization of our identity as self-knowing being, but rather *Yours,* one of the opposition, even the contradiction, of spirits, namely that of Christ's death in shame and resurrection to glory by God. Only then if the person of our distinguished being is not initially *naturally* intrinsic to my heart but rather initially *absolutely* extrinsic to it can the drama of our self-severance be performed by the Actor who thus enacts the principle for us, before us as this principle's, God's, prince and our Lord, for whom and to whom and along whose way we have been chosen, elected, called as his disciples to walk and to follow and finally to complete as the divine purpose, fulfill as the distinguished destiny of our human being

Again, how can we die and still stay alive, live our lives and be already dead? In the language and the logic of the cross and in the spirit of love that it articulates, our distinguished human being *takes on the form of sin,* of our weakness, of our death – having been delivered to the hands of Man; *becomes flesh* – having been born and taken up abode among us; *is distinguished in authority* – having been recognized as the Son by the Father; *brings all things to light* – having entered the darkness of the world; *is before God* – having proceeded from God as his Word. This descent of compassion from the grace and glory of the absolute principle to the disgrace and abasement of the death, the mortifying finitude, of human being marks the comprehensive purview of love's mandate.

For within its scope and in accordance with our faith, we die in the distinction of Christ's death, that is, our flesh of weakness, the flesh of our death, dies and, though dead in Him and through this death of flesh that is death's death and effective in the justification of faith alone, we, coming to ourselves after having shared his experience of death, having participated in the drama of the Actor's death *in spirit* and leaving now that theater of the mind, find ourselves, wondrously, to be still alive after Christ's death and among the living, and yet possessed now of a different spirit and a different life borne of that experience, of a life and a spirit renewed, exalted in this fresh, refreshed flesh, that, since the meat of Man and the mentality of finitude which this gristle of bone and blood embodies, has died, can only be that of the Holy Spirit after that death, the eternal life that arises and accrues to us who have been reborn and become the saints in the spirit of Christ, justified through our faith, which is our acknowledgement of the gift of life we are heir to now that Christ's resurrection has been confirmed, ours in his, his in ours.

> He died for all of us so that the living might no longer live for themselves, but rather for him who died for them and rose again. Therefore from now on we regard no one merely according to the flesh, having regarded Christ merely according to the flesh but now no longer. Thus a new creation are those in Christ, the old having passed away, see, the new has emerged."(2 Cr 5:15-17)

To live unto oneself, glorify oneself, proclaim oneself in subservience to the ways of the self-seeking world is precisely what the spirit of sin, of weakness, of death does – dying to that mind, we arise to live the spirit of life that is the gift of faith in our better being, call it *Christ*, a resurrected life that reconciles us with the absolute principle of distinction – in sending his Word of life into the world of the dead, God reconciled it to himself in the spirit of love which, even as the Son himself did, lives unto, glorifies, and proclaims not itself but the *Father*, who chose him and sent him on his mission of light for the benefit of our own distinction, his Word and wisdom, himself embodying thus the spirit of his Father's love, the spirit of compassion, patience, and forbearance rather than condemnation (Ro 2:4). For it is in the obedience of faith that *repentance*, i.e. our turning and return, our conversion from pinch-fisted death to generous life and from the trite sprite of the world to the pure spirit of God, is affected.

In the logic of the Cross, our *experience* of our sin and our *sorrow* at having turned away from our distinction, the contrition of a penitent heart and the lament of those forsaken by God, is, in the line of reasoning that articulates the practical insight of *faith*, prior and preparatory to the consolation of our reversal and ultimate salvation, even as our crucifixion in Christ precedes our resurrection, the raising of all dead to the dwelling of reconciliation that is the kingdom of Heaven, where the Son thrones at the right hand of his Father; similarly, the present (epiphany) of *judgment* that determines the ordeal of difference between our IS and our OUGHT is antecedent to our redemption in the presence (parousia) of God's *mercy* through the spirit of Christ's blood, the seal and mark of our justification through faith and the distinction of our human being in Christian terms. In *Figure 86*, we render this line of reasoning as a procession of distinctions in accordance with the self-several principle of differentiation we have been studying as the determination inherent in pure reason, the ordeal of its life, the stations of the train of thought.

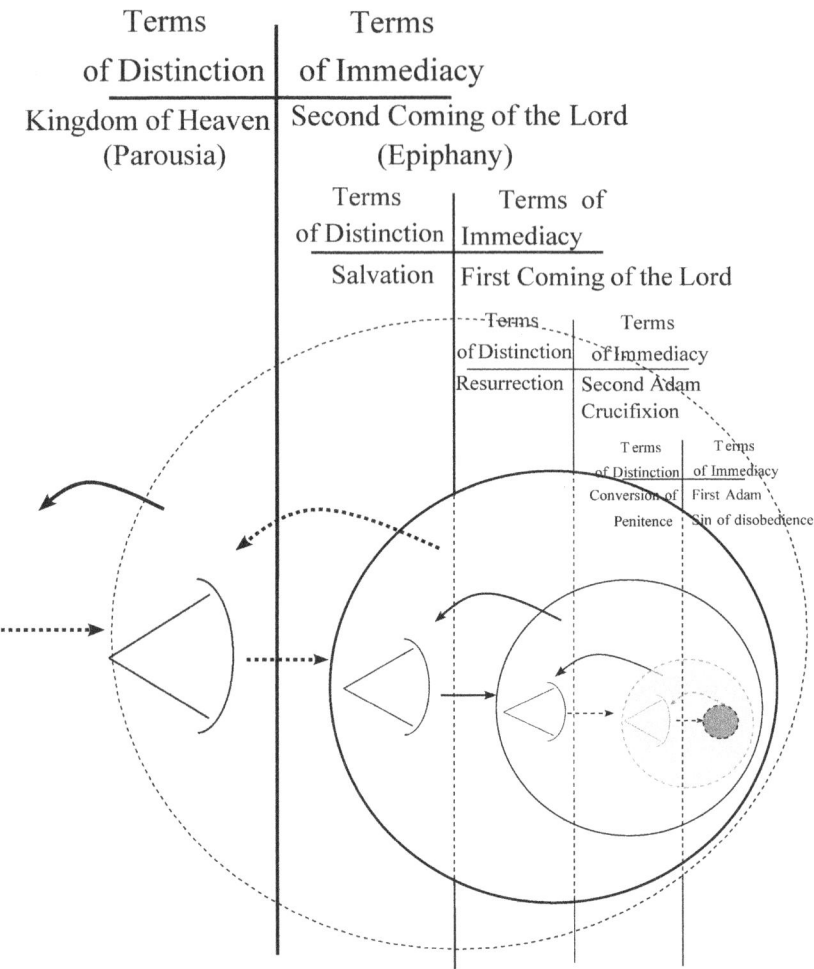

Figure 86: The Progression of Distinctions from Adam to Heaven

We recognize this procreative pattern of ingemination as the series of transitions that we have come to know as those of critical reflection founded upon the principle of abstraction in accordance with which we are bidden by the principle of pure reason to step back from traditions' conventions, habits' canons, and bodily life's decrees and in departure from their peremptory prestige to boldly declare, "all is lawful but not all expedient; all is lawful but not all edifying." (1 Cr 10:23)

ΠΑΝΤΑ ΕΞΕΣΤΙΝ ΑΛΛ ' ΟΥ ΠΑΝΤΑ ΣΥΜΦΕΡΕΙ ΠΑΝΤΑ
ΕΞΕΣΤΙΝ ΑΛΛ ' ΟΥ ΠΑΝΤΑ ΟΙΔΟΔΟΜΕΙ

Due to the epochal shift of the determining principle, the names employed to mark the procession of critical reflection have indeed changed. But the idea? No, not at all.

The issue remains the same – it is the distinction of human being that is our cause; the challenge to the perspicacity of intellect and to the theory of the latter-day philological philosophy we are engaged in is to learn how to properly grasp that idea in Christian terms.

It is only in this way, "not by despising but rather testing..." Man's doctrines and opinions and traditions, "...and holding fast what is good" (1 Thes 5:20-21), that we become "outlaws" in Christ (1Cr 10:23), chosen and given to call into question at every turn the laws of Man, shaming the rulers and the authorities of the elements and the sanctimonious demons and dominions of every determinate horizon.

To question, from the point of view of pure reason, every code of "food and drink, the lunacy of Man's many self-made precepts and observances of festival and moon rites, rituals, and regulations of cleanliness – the 'Do not handle! Do not taste! Do not touch!' (Col 2:21) of our perishables, regimes of asceticism and license, all that visionary bombast..." all missing the point, i.e. "failing to hold fast to the head" (Col 2:16-19) – is to adopt the standpoint that morally annihilates even the very epitome of the stifling enclosure that is a closed mind, namely the merciless, pitiless fact of *death*; in the end even this ultimate "law of life" becomes mere convention, a dogma of Man's dominion and as such is subject and subjected to its own annihilation in the name of complete *self*-severalty:

> "...transforming and delivering finally the world to the father after destroying every rule and every authority and power, finally death itself... God subjecting all under himself through Christ who subjects all under himself and finally is the instrument of God's subjection subjected in turn such that God may be all in all." (1Cr 15.26-28)

Thus unfolds a procession of distinctions vividly rendered in Christian terms such that, initially, the Law of Man's closed-mindedness is abolished by the first advent of the Lord; then, the sighing of our confession and the humility of our contrition through Christ is transformed in the resurrection of our hope and, turning, having turned towards God's mercy, sustained, finally, in the expectation of the ultimate salvation of our individual lives in the life *after* that good death with distinction, the ordeal of the First judgment. But now in this, the *Last* judgment, the world itself is transformed into a new creation, namely that of the kingdom of the Just, the eternal life, and the illuminating glory of the Saints.

In a deeper sense however, with a view to the self-relativity of pure reason, judgment and mercy, crucifixion and resurrection, our fall and our rise, the moment of self-several departure and that of our arrival at identity in our experience of pure thought, are not merely two phases, shifts, or facets in the life of thought, not two events in a narrative, though the representation of this drama may indeed require such a setting. In itself, the relationship of thought to thought, giving and being given, uplifting and being uplifted, *taking up* the distinction of thought in anguish and *being taken up* by that distinction in joy are two sides of the same coign of vantage, two experiences of our rapport with thought thinking thought, which is both the thinking, seeing being *and* the being thought, the being seen, together comprising the well-rounded *sphere* of thought – the realization of thought *and* the determination of reality; thought, the Actor, experiences the majesty of human being in doffing the dunce cap of its mundane habit, which, at the same time, is a stepping up, a stepping forward towards and a donning of its destiny; pure reason is the crown of such a coronation and investiture.

The logic of the cross is that of a crossing and a passage. After dying to our first world, "putting to death those earthly members..., putting away the practices of our old self...in which we too once walked, we now inhabit, transformed, the second world in our second Self in renewed knowledge in the image of the creator..." (Col 3:5-10), having died the death of anguish in the doubt of a heart riven, but also in persecution and tribulations while undergoing the struggle to maintain that pure spirit in the face of all extremity and the besmirching profanity, the banality of our intermediary life, the life and the realm of action in which we must prove ourselves worthy of the names of distinction that poets wrought, all the time striving to cleave to the images with which they have inspired us but that we all too easily lose sight of in our travail and must perpetually regain, falling and rising again, thereby rehearsing, again and again, our daily dose of dying, as the apostle says (1Cr 15:31), and the subsequent renewal, the reaffirmation of our eternal life in the perpetually transforming distinction of faith. In the exaggerated, no, in the superabundant, glorifying terms of the Gospel that the Apostle preaches, living and dying upon the Cross of Pauline faith, we experience the crossing of our life and our death as a passage from life to death and from death to life. We have learned that the difference between the humdrum hell that makes death of life and the brightest Heaven of our invention that makes life of death lies solely in the ascendance of a spirit, that muse of fire that is our cause and theme.

No, we are never done with thought, though mortal scholars will very well close the book for the night and take repose in surcease of contemplation. In practice, living a critical life face to face with that distinguished spirit, in its name calling again and again into question what we have done and do, what we have learned and heard, what we have seen and hear, revising and deciding, discarding and renewing, stumbling with despair but getting up again with hope, holding fast and letting go, we die a daily death, several in fact, as Diotima knew, and, Julie knew as well – truly, in one day of life we live *and die* a thousand deaths.

Nevertheless, the Christian also knows as do all friends of the language of distinction, the language of wisdom, the friends of this particular language of the Gospel, but no less of those other tongues of flame, after the first death, there is no other.

B. The Congregation of the Saints

124. Preaching the Word of God

The world founded and now standing upon the Gospel (1Cr 15:1) is that of the congregation of saints, namely the community of the *ecclesia*, of those loved by God (1 Thes 1:4) and thus called, elected by the grace of faith in Christ (1:2) and thus "united in the spirit and judgment (1:10) of those not "conformed to this world, but...transformed by the renewal of their mind, so as to become judges of what the will of God is, of what is good and acceptable and perfect" (Rom 12:2), the judges of the judges and even of the angels themselves (1Cr 6:1). Thus transformed, they have become the living "presence of the power of God"...and in this way, God's signs, God's voice, "declaring God's name to all the earth" (Rom 9:17) in the cascading delegation of God's glory that he bestowed on those he has chosen for his ministry with the sending of his Word in the very beginning, before the subsequence of time, until the final crisis at the end of days, that day that is the Lord's. Grace descends from God to his Word, from the sending of his Image to the vocation of the Son's disciples, from the apostles that he sanctified to the consecration of the saints they cultivated, and from the cherished treasure of spiritual renewal shared in the cloister of the temple of those in whom God dwells (1Cr 3:16) to the emanating beacon, the model and paradigm (ΤΥΠΟΣ – 1 Thes. 1:6) of the message itself – what has remained and endures is the Gospel, not just of words but of distinctions, significations, those of the power and the spirit of God – proclaimed to true believers and celebrated throughout all the world, bearing the fruit of faith, the plenitude of conviction (Col 1:6) in them who have "experienced this ministration, glorifying God for the submission of your confession unto the gospel of Christ and for the generous apportionment to them and to all." (2 Cor 9:13)

...ΤΗΣ ΔΟΚΙΜΗΣ ΤΗΣ ΔΙΑΚΟΝΙΑΣ ΤΑΥΤΗΣ ΔΟΞΑΖΟΝΤΕΣ ΤΟΝ ΘΕΟΝ ΕΠΙ ΤΗ ΥΠΟΤΑΓΗ ΤΗΣ ΟΜΟΛΟΓΙΑΣ ΥΜΩΝ ΕΙΣ ΤΟ ΕΥΑΓΓΕΛΙΟΝ ΤΟΥ ΧΡΙΣΤΟΥ ΚΑΙ ΑΠΛΟΤΗΤΙ ΤΗΣ ΚΟΙΝΩΝΙΑΣ ΕΙΣ ΑΟΥΤΟΥΣ ΚΑΙ ΕΙΣ ΠΑΝΤΑΣ

Again: From the flowering bounty of God's glory to the first-fruit (ΑΠΑΡΧΗ – Rom 11:16) of his Son to the seeds of his deeds to the sowers who are his saints, to the plants of the church that are Christ's culture across all the fertile earth of sky-open minds to the harvest of that abundant fruit that is our superabundant thanksgiving for the thought-gift of grace – these are the stations of generation, better, of *generosity* in the mission of God's glory through the dissemination of the Gospel.

In this line of thought from God to the World and back through the mediation of the Word and from our experience of its submission to that of its exaltation, we note that the ratio of God to the chosen Son corresponds to that of Christ to his chosen disciples who are then, as the elected apostles of Christ, the mediators of the Gospel of the Word to the congregations of the saints. In their own experience of the holy Spirit of Christ, they are called to make the sacrifice of their old life of sin, dying thus with Christ and in him rising renewed, enacting in this passage of the Cross that each individual is called to take upon himself or herself the message of the Gospel and contribute thus to God's building of his kingdom, the founding of his earthly dwelling, a building (1Cr 3:9-10) now not to be called the realization of the ideal, as in the Third Epoch, but rather the fulfilled incarnation of the Word, in which each of us in the flesh is distinguished by faith to embody the Holy Spirit and, as subjects of the faith that it engendered – even as God's Son was – in our heart, to take up our position as a rightful member of the body of Christ, healing the quarantine of evasion among Men gone to pieces in the dispersion and disbanding of Man even as we, in ourselves twain, may be made new, whole, one, in the peace (Eph 2:15) that is our perfection in accordance with the "mature measure of plenitude and completion,..." "the new covenant" (2Cr 2:6), that Christ is the image of (Col 1:15), "so that we may no longer be children, tossed to and fro, carried about with every wind of doctrine, snared by the traps of Man lying in wait to deceive with enticing device" (Eph 4:13-14) and specious arguments (Col 2:4) like those of the latest "super-apostles" (2Cor 11:5), the false apostles who make of the mind's renewal a monstrous spectacle of transmogrification (2 Cr 11:13). Thus it is this relationship of transfiguration that is the image of God and our own conversion the intimations and the emulations of that holy paradigm in our own lives, our own experience of the Word of God.

To this end, the apostles, themselves actors and enactors of the drama of transfiguration, that is a sacrifice of suffering for the Lord, experience the proof of trials and tribulations – the scourge and the rods of distinction, the prisons and the deaths of Christ, the perils and pains, the hunger and the thirst and the cold, the nakedness and the travails, the vigils (2 Cr 11:23-27) – thus Paul's catalogue of deprivation and the mentality of sacrifice that is the fasting and prayer of faith, the experience of death that is love's very life. In other words, the only way to cast out that spirit of obduracy and taciturnity that possesses us (Mar 9:29) and not to make just a show or a talk of conversion is discipline. For those erudite in Christ's discipline are alone God's disciples, themselves God's work *and* Christ's fellow workers, Man's foundlings become the founders of faith's dwelling, doing not their own works, but rather, as stewards of the mysteries (1Cr 3:23 -4:1) of the insight that had been hidden for ages and generations but now revealed to his saints (Col 1:26), an insight they were given and received by grace and did not invent, the Lord's, and who now, as prisoners and slaves, as the flesh and bone and blood of the Lord, are called to lowliness against pride and patience in tribulations, forbearance in hope with regard to that promise of glory, ambassadors in chains preaching Christ's message (Eph 6:20) of emancipation, therein servants of Christ's purpose, not their own – for, having been bought at the price (1 Cr 7:23) of Christ's blood, theirs is Christ's life who lives in them as his own property; consequently, our bodies, that we have proffered up in a "living sacrifice" (Rom 12:1), are members of Christ and all of these members together form the body of the church of the holy spirit, each of us serving our Lord, the will of God, in the flesh of our individual being but also in the body of the congregation of those who, "living in the flesh, are alive by faith in the Son of God" (1Cr 21) – preaching not Man's go/no go-spiel but rather God's Gospel, the one received through "revelation of Jesus Christ" (Gal 1:11), vaunting, glorifying not themselves but God, profiting not themselves but seeking Christ's benefit and that of the many (1 Cr 10:23) and not content to merely talk about God but in and with the Gospel to build His house, His community of those thus saved, that is the body of Christ who is its head and husband. (Col 1:18)

Consisting of several members, though of one spirit, the Holy Spirit, that we drank upon our mind's renewal (1 Cr 12:13), each with her or his own diversity of gifts and office, each appointed to his or her own proper administration of that spirit (1 Cr 12:4-5) "according to the proportion of faith's endowment – whether these be that of the apostle's, the master-builder's, who lays down the foundation of the faith (1 Cr 3:10) and is as such the father of the saints (1 Cr 4:15) or that of prophesy, of teaching or exhortation," (Rom 12:6), of healing or of interpreting – this state of grace subsists upon and "holds fast to the head from whom the whole body is nourished and knit together through its joints and ligaments, grows with a flourishing that is from God." (Col 2:19). Are you the Spirit's hand or foot, ear or eye? The body, though one when contemplated *in principle*, is many in practice, many when *in action*, whole when the integrity of each part is recognized and acknowledged as serving and sustaining the common weal that Christ is. (1 Cr 12:14-28)

And though we strive to perfect our individual skills and gifts and all members have not the same office (Ro 12:5), being many, we are nevertheless one (Ro 12:4), are one body in Christ, and every one of us members, each a member of the other (Ro 12:5) in that unique Spirit of Christ, having been called into one body (Col 3:15) with him and with each other in his name, that we have "put on" along with Him, namely *love* (Col 3:14). This participation of love "is the more excellent way" (Rom 12:31) of all the walks of life, for it cultivates the recognition and completion of every individual strength and office rather than their general absorption into a totalitarian hive; regardless of our individual gifts and talents, without love, lacking that spirit in which they are practiced, they are merely instruments of our own vanity, our own conceit, or those of Man's mechanisms. Love, on the other hand is the office and the gift that unites every other with our higher heart and holier spirit – it is the veritable heart of every heart and the spirit of every spirit. Why?

> Because Love is patient and kind, love does not envy or boast, it is not arrogant or rude; it does not insist on its own way, is not irritable or resentful; it does not rejoice at wrongdoing but rejoices in truth. Love bears all things, believes all things, hopes all things, endures all things, love never ends." (1Cr 13.4-8)

This body fitted together in love (Col 2:2, Eph 4:16) makes of manifold Man a family of friends, mothers, fathers, and children, beloved brothers and sisters, partners and partakers of Christ, of that one bread upon the sacrificial altar of distinction that we all share (1 Cr 10:18) for each other's mutual benefit, serving each other in the name of Lord, working in the spirit of assent and cooperation and not with reluctance and compulsion (Phim 1:13). In observance of the logic of reflection in the self-relativity of God's covenant with us and ours with God, the entity of identity – in Christian terms, the Father's love for the Son and the Son's love for the Father – is our mirror and our model of accord whereby we learn that in sowing sparingly, we reap sparingly and in sowing bountifully, we reap bountifully in a shared obedience of love that receives its benefit in the reflection of the giving of benefit. In the household of this relationship, each is bound to the other's well-being in a distinguished rapport of submission and obedience, not fawningly so or in self-serving pretense but in all sincerity of purpose such that when we serve our kings and queens or, as queens and kings, are served, we are serving alone the Lord who served us by serving God, we who are, in the name of the Lord, every slave's slave and every master's master – "every soul subject to the higher power," (Rom 13:1) and the highest, finally to itself, the Son to the Father, God self-severally to God.

Like a nursing mother taking care of her own children, this love is a nurturing and earnest care (2Cr 8:16); like a father's encouraging his children, this love is an admonition and exhortation to walk in a manner worthy of the kingdom of glory that is our inheritance (1 Thes 2:8); but this kingdom is the practice of the pattern that is Christ's life and death, the paragon of the passage from death to life and life to death. In giving all, receiving all; in having patience, being accorded mercy; in recognizing and appreciating, being recognized and appreciated, in humility being exalted, in bearing being borne, in affirming with faith being upheld and affirmed in faith, in loving being loved – through each pleasing not himself first but his neighbor (Rom 14:3), we please God who, in return, turning towards us, is well pleased, electing us in his love, knowing us who have shown our knowledge of his will, becoming thus children, the sons and the daughters of God, who have proven themselves in love worthy of the Father's love, and in our regard for His ways worthy of His regard for ours.

Love says: Your happiness is my happiness – of course, we are all, who have ever loved, familiar with this, love's one law; take it to heart as the one formula of moral action based on the principle, the Holy Spirit, of self-sacrifice that we in ourselves enact, having witnessed the work of God in action and understood the practical form of pure reason in which we are transformed, seizing the thought that has seized us and will never entirely let us go again. Your happiness is my happiness – this thought, so simple, so familiar and yet so enduringly, permanently foreign to our daily habits, confounds the arrogance of our egoist whose universe is centered around his own needs and concerns, the narrow scope of his own profit placed above all other spheres of needs or perhaps inflating to engulf them and in doing so to homogenize all temper of distinction in his flooding plain of white, assimilating to himself all differences from himself with a view to cementing the mastery of Man upon the dirt of the earth being himself, unto and of himself, all in all, and as such making of Man Man's own Man-made God, the idle idol of Man's own private property whose first precept is "keep out!"

To gods and Men, we of the closed heart are wont to say: "Beware of the dog!" But in the spirit of love, having become members of Christ's body, of his flesh, of his bones (Eph 5:30), there "are no more strangers and foreigners, but fellow citizens and heirs of the promise, in the company of saints and the household of God." (Eph 2:19), each to each in Christ husband and wife, child and parent, servant and master, not for show or flattery but to "do the will of God from the heart....a service done upon the Lord and not to men" (Eph 6:1-7)

ΠΟΙΟΥΝΤΕΣ ΤΟ ΘΕΛΗΜΑ ΤΟΥ ΘΕΟΥ ΕΚ ΨΥΧΗΣ...
ΔΟΥΛΕΥΟΝΤΕΣ ΤΩΙ ΚΥΡΙΩΙ ΚΑΙ ΟΥΚ ΑΝΘΡΩΠΟΙΣ

In the spirit of this love, we are the earth and the ground upon which the Apostle builds with each letter of exhortation he sends us, so abounding in faith, nourishing the insight that he planted in our hearts and founding the community that now should take root, grow, and blossom in the earth of our lives.

In the spirit of this insight into the nature of love, i.e. Christ, we are brothers and sisters, "sharing our faith in the full knowledge of every good thing that is in us," (Phim 1:6) as we would a destiny and inheritance into which we are to come, a bequeathal "of redemption and the forgiveness of sins" (Col 1:12) "refreshing each other's heart in Christ." (Phim 1:20)

As such we are fellow soldiers (Phil 1), in this spirit of love engaged in a war that is a labor of love. (1 Thes 1:3) "Though we walk in the flesh, we do not wage war according to the flesh; for the weapons of our warfare are not of the flesh but have divine power to destroy strongholds; we destroy arguments and every lofty opinion raised against the knowledge of God and take every thought captive to obey Christ." (2Cr 10:5)

The founding of these congregations of those called to love is the work of the apostle of the Cross, the preacher of its Good News. It is a life of service to the Word of the Cross, the logic of which renews the ancient covenant between divine and human being that has always remained our distinction. Paul's achievement is having recognized this image of God in the person of

Christ Jesus, the incarnation of the distinction of human being to whom we now turn to conclude our study of the language of Christianity.

III. The Gospel according to John

B. The Salvation of the World

125. Light coming to Light

Philosophers are apparently fond of asking, "Why is there something rather than nothing?" If this is a question put by a being in the world about the *world*, then it might very well be the Christian answer they are looking for *and* refuse to find: There is something rather than nothing because of the true light of critical reflection that came into their world to illuminate Man's human being. It is through this true, i.e. *distinguished*, light, the light of drawing distinctions, the light that the ΛΟΓΟΣ *is*, that Man's world came forth into existence in the first place, emerging from the shadows of disregard and oblivion. For it is only through the ΛΟΓΟΣ and the animadversion of an absorbed mind as a result of which we are called to step back from the immediacy of our world immersion and the flow of lived experience that constitutes it, that we begin to *see* in the emphatic sense of this term; only then is there, in the liquid continuities of living being, something to hold and to behold; only then do we take note of THE WAY IT IS and, taking note of this our taking note, celebrate discernment by solemnly and categorically declaring with regards to the ΛΟΓΟΣ of observant attendance that "all things came into being through him and without him nothing came into being that came into being." (Joh 1:3) Pure thought is just this realization of what, without it, would be, from the point of view of our *experience*, nothing; only upon drawing the distinction inherent in the act of critical reflection do we, though beings in the world, *have* a world before us as well that we can now take account of as *good*, as THE WAY IT SHOULD BE, or its opposite.

Clearly then, the coming forth into existence of the self-several world through the discernment of pure reason *is not* the same as the creation of heaven and earth. In the beginning God created, made, formed (בָּרָא/יַעַשׂ/יִצֶר/עָשָׂה - bara/ya'ash/yidser/asah) heaven and earth (Gen 1:1, 2:4), the firmament (1:7), the greater and the lessor light, the light of day and of night, and the stars' (1:16), the multitude of animals big and small (1:25), and every living creature (1:21); and then he made human being in his own image, male and female (1:26, 27) – until on the seventh day "he completed the work he did and rested." (Gen 2:2)

יְכַל....מְלַאכְתּוֹ אֲשֶׁר עָשָׂה וַיִּשְׁבֹּת

yəkal…məlaktō esher asah wayyishbōt

Creating (בְּרָא) in the sense of making (עָשָׂה/יַעַשׂ) and forming (יְצֶר) may be distinguished from the creation of God's commanding word "be!" – from the summoning forth inherent in divine imperative. It is not yet creation in the manner of His laying shaping hands on the raw material of heaven and earth – e.g. giving shape to the fathomless and fluid formlessness of water – but rather in the manner of drawing a distinction of pure light that, like the breath of God slightly stirring the surface of the deep (1:2), makes all the difference against a background of primal, chaotic "darkness" (חֹשֶׁךְ - hōschech), of "amorphic and vacuous" (תֹהוּ וָבֹהוּ - tōhoo vabōhoo) profusion. It is upon this scene of perfect incipience that God commences with, in and through the imperative of his spoken word "let there be light" (יְהִי אוֹר - yəhi 'ōr), the work of his creation of what later in the Gospel of John will become the *world* (ΚΟΣΜΟΣ) of Man, which, as we have been suggesting throughout our study – following Boeder – is a cosmos of words, a world that begins with the absolute difference that the distinguished inkling of God's word makes against an immaculately entropic background by leaving the first diacritical trace of language on its blank face, the separating *mark* of His initials upon the dark planes of indeterminacy.[69]

Therefore, in the beginning of God's work of creation, God spoke and, with his word, drew the "separating distinction between light and between darkness" (Gen 1:4):

וַיַּבְדֵּל אֱלֹהִים בֵּין הָאוֹר וּבֵין הַחֹשֶׁךְ:

vayavdel Elōhim bein haōr ūvein hachōsheck

In the prologue of John's Gospel, we are reminded of this inaugural scission and therefore that God's word of distinction, his original ΛΟΓΟΣ, is not only that of *creation*, but also of *realization* in the sense we are

---

[69] See Boeder's "The Present of Christian Sapientia in the Sphere of Speech" in *Seditions* (ed. M. Brainard, New York University Press 1997), p. 287: "the world is only secondarily the one consisting of heaven and earth; primarily it is the world of speech…."

considering as pertaining to the conception of the Second Epoch, namely stepping back and taking note; in the efficacy of God's first spoken word, we recognize the discernment of pure reason drawing a distinction, i.e. uttering the illuminating syllables of severance in reflection of which, reviewing what he has done, God makes his first judgment: "God saw that the light was good." (ibid.)

Stepping back from the canvas, God is the first to see the light he has effectuated by drawing the very first distinction between light and darkness and therefore, in the judgment that immediately ensues, he is the first to reflect upon and, in this sense, to *realize* what he has done, not in the way of one who acts "unconsciously" or "absentmindedly" and then eventually "comes to his senses," but rather in appreciation of his accomplishment. This critical reflection by God of God's creation in view of the good light of his imperative and luminous "*be!*" is called in the Gospel of John *Ο ΛΟΓΟΣ, the Word.*

This good Word of light is God's note of reflection and therein near, with, by God (ΠΡΟΣ ΤΟΝ ΘΕΟΝ - Joh 1: 2), not so much God *himself* as God *in person, God in action* – for the creative imperative of God's word is God's own imparting being, the present of his self-several glory, of His grace both spoken *and* speaking. Hence, not only does God bring forth His creation but also, and prior to this, he draws the initial distinction of discernment in the vacuousness of unmarked immediacy, which subsequently serves as the principle of determining if what has come to light, i.e. THE WAY IT IS, is or is not THE WAY IT SHOULD BE, in other words, whether it is or is not *good*. Thus the magnificence of God's glory is not merely that of absolute power (distinguished from the relative powers of beings in the mundane sphere) but moreover that of the illumination and judgment of discernment; the superlative *power* of the Creator-God is succeeded by God's critical reflection upon what he has created; and in this *knowledge* he affirms that what supreme power has brought forth is, in fact, good, i.e. in accordance with his *will*.

The Word of God brings light to the scene because only when we step back from our absorption in preoccupations, our first life in the generic or immediate world, can we enter upon our life after that life, our "afterlife" of distinction, wherein judgment receives the grant of its appointment to promote discernment between THE WAY IT IS and THE WAY IT SHOULD BE and the charge of its subsequent purpose to close this gap in a labor of love and truth, the labor of love *as* truth. The practice of drawing this distinction, passing judgment, and carrying out its sentence is called, in the

Gospel of John, *eternal life*, which is the distinguished life of pure reason in action, the principle accomplished in the performance of its mission as that which is to be put into effect through action done it its spirit, in other words, accomplished by thought, the Actor. That is why we read, "In him was life and the life was the light human being." (Joh 1:4)

The life of this divine spirit of judgment is that of the incarnate Word that has since taken up dwelling among us, in us even, who have been born, reborn to this career of critical judgment, not yet to that of the poetic *imagination* as in Hölderlin's epoch and not merely to that of the contemplative *intellect*, which we will encounter in the Greek conception of pure reason, but rather to the absolute spirit of distinction upon which the practical principle of judgment depends – in Christian terms, this spirit is the *Spirit of God* – whose *kin* we have become, having become its followers, its disciples, having been transformed into the children of distinction, i.e. those who have welcomed this light, received it, seized it, and thus seeing the light, even as God did, believing in, loving the light as the embodiment of that original glory, its revelatory "plenitude of grace and truth" (1:14) that is God's unique present.

The life of self-severalty is the life of light. In the Gospel of John, *light* is the term that most clearly refers to the experience of *seeing* in contrast to the state of oblivion when what is happening around us, when even what we do ourselves and say, escapes our notice. Suddenly realizing what is happening, what is going on, what we have just done, what we have just said, we are surprised at our lapses. We exclaim: "I must have been blind!" We ask ourselves, shocked: "What am I saying?" "What am I doing?" We wonder: "What was I thinking?" Why do we ask ourselves such questions? Because we realize that just a moment ago we had been distracted, engrossed in some busyness or preoccupation; we hadn't been paying sufficient attention to what we were saying, doing, thinking but now, coming to our senses, we begin to actively engage in the practice of seeing and hearing, noting, as if for the first time, what we are saying and doing and thinking.

These familiar intuitions of the state of the mind in eclipse justify the use of those many illustrious expressions that refer to the decisive moment of cognizance when this veil of ignorance suddenly drops to reveal what we have been missing the whole time. Presence of mind can then fittingly be called in terms of celebration and gratitude an experience of light and sight – suddenly, unexpectedly, like a neon flash of light that splits the night, *difference* enters upon the scene which was previously dark with disregard; and it is this previous extinction, beyond the sundry details, whether important or insignificant, that we subsequently become aware of as a result of the dawning of the newly drawn distinction's day, the critical standpoint, which, too, with the advent of this light of discernment, now comes blazing into the being of awareness where there had been but absence and indifference before. With John, let's seek and find dramatic terms to couch the ΕΥΑΓΓΕΛΙΟΝ (euangelion - good news, glad tidings, gospel) of this transformation in!

Light comes to the world and draws our attention not so much to the people, places, and things of the world that have been previously neglected by us for good and no good reasons but rather to the *light* itself, *himself*, as well as to the darkness that the light invaded, to that life of omission that we had been leading, hitherto unintentionally, entirely unbeknownst to us, or perhaps only vaguely sensed through the haze of habit and that comfortable amnesia that going with the flow day in and day out encapsulates us in. Call this capsule of closure the *world* of our automatisms, our impulses, reflexes, expediencies, corner-cutting conveniences, catch-as-catch-can opportunisms.

Initially, this frame of mind that is our daily cup of Lethe, this casual mindlessness of the mind, is entirely innocent; it is natural to ignore what doesn't immediately affect us; it is natural to put our own needs first, before that of others; it is entirely natural to vigilantly watch over our personal interests and ward off whatever alien perturbation might jeopardize the homeostasis of their management. But what if folks' attention were directed to the fact of the limited horizon that such proximate interests circumscribe? What if they were told that the government of this *body* perspective, restricting its attentions to the scope of the most immediate and pressing concerns – which are, above all, problems *here, now, today*, to *me* – had many negative consequences not only for *others elsewhere, later, tomorrow* but also for *me*, too, thus effectively pitting me self-severally against myself? And that, conversely, many potential benefits accrue only to those who are willing to take the risk of widening the scope of their perception, extending the area of influence of their actions on others and of others upon their own lives? After having been adverted to these limitations and disadvantages of the narrow mind, something, everything has changed, forever.

Touched thus in the close contént of our containments by further horizons, we now find ourselves at the crossroads of a decision: We might embrace the mini-me mentality and abide by our prior body-being for whom, in the mundane "logic" of its immediacy, what is good *here, now, today, for me*, is good and what is bad *here, now, today, for me* is bad; or we might chose the way of the cross, crossing over to the other mentality, the one we have learned to recognize as that which introduces the absolute difference that the Word of God makes in the life and times of our human being with regards to what is good and bad by counter-intuitively admitting that what is good here, now, today, for me, may, in fact, in the long run, for others, and even for me, be bad and, conversely, though bad now, perhaps good later. The Christian term of choice to designate such discernment is "spirit," the *spirit* of the Word of God, the *spirit* of the Father and the Son, and, to distinguish this transformational spirit from the other one, the one that, recoiling at the light of sight, opts to revert back to its old ways of mental deletion and default, even after having come to realize the latter's drawbacks for all concerned; following Jakobson, let us venture to "mark" or distinguish it in some way in accordance with the semiological sense of "marking" terms we have previously explored. Hence, in addition to the capital letter, we seize upon the venerable term *holy* resulting in the designation "Holy Spirit." Or else, simply take the term *body* as the traditional and therefore familiar term of immediacy for that small-minded mentality upon which and from which the term *spirit* is distinguished, the former referring to the marrow of our narrowest scope of interest and the latter to the widest and furthest prospicience imaginable, a scope of human being as far and wide and high as the sky, the heavenly one.

C. The Life of Self-Severalty

126. Sin

To that end, we turn to examine, in terms that the Gospel of John provides, the advent of critical reflection upon the scene of the crime of mindlessness, the decision that it compels us to take, and the consequences that this decision ultimately has upon our everyday lives. Jesus says, in a startling turn of words pertaining to the choice inherent in this experience of conversion:

> If you were blind, you would not be guilty of sin; but now that
> you claim you can see, your guilt remains. (Jhn 9:41)

The words and deeds of Jesus, the words chosen to render his words and his deeds accessible to our habitual distraction, elevate the train of thought about thought we have been pursuing in the Second Epoch, namely that of critical thought in action, to new heights of salience. Our constant challenge: Can we recognize this train of thought in these terms? More, by considering the principle of the much fabled "linguistic turn" as it applies to scripture, can we more profoundly experience the distinction of human being – what it is and what it means – in the language of the Gospel of John?

Now it is clear that to say this text is "about" Jesus, about his words and works, and about what happened to him, does not explain anything. The real question is: Why is the story of his life and death, his words and his works, important to us, even now, more than two thousand years after his life and his death? What do the Gospels make evident? Do they provide us with moral maxims? Do they offer us suggestions regarding how a person should or should not act in a certain situation? They often do. And yet: To say this is, again, not to explain anything; indeed, it is to miss entirely the "crux" of the Jesus-narrative and the crucial point of the distinction that John makes. For only by elaborating the logotectonic of the Gospel in accordance with the precepts of the philology we have been engaged in, can we hope to arrive at a deeper insight into these works than a descriptive summary of a "tale" and a collection of pithy "quotes" would ever allow us to.

Remember: We must begin with what we know – thus in keeping with the most important precept of the philological craft and art of thought, the Builder, we discussed in the beginning of our study. What do we know? We know that the Gospels are "about" the distinction of human being. In clarifying how this is true, we are not offering an "interpretation" of their "meaning" in popular hermeneutic manner. Rather, seen from the philological standpoint, it is the Gospels themselves that are the "interpretations," "performances," even as Hölderlin's poetry and Schiller's drama and Homer's epics are all, in their own way, a study of and in the distinction of human being. They are all renditions, intuitions, visions of this very distinction, which is the "secret" of their meaning; but notice that this is not a hidden secret, one that folks endeavor to unearth through a perspicacious interpretation of texts. On the contrary. We begin with what we know and therefore with the "open" secret of the distinction of human being in our experience with pure reason and now turn to the language and the "logic" of these texts and examine their account of this experience, how *they* put the matter of thought in ways that are entirely different from the way the other texts, viz. the self-several "tongues of flame" we are studying in this investigation, have put it. Reading the Gospels, we are soon struck by the "other-worldly" words and images they employ and how this "poetic" language and imagery is used in the text, words like *light, world, glory, God, flesh, Father, Son, birth, truth, blood, life,* to elaborate the train of thought about thought we know they must. But theirs is not the poetry we have become acquainted with in Hölderlin's hymns. In fact, one determination made evident by their elaboration is that the Gospels are not "poetry" at all and to read them as such is to misread them, it is to debase them. Therefore our question, more precisely put, is this: How has the distinction of human being been elaborated in the language of the Gospel and what does it mean to experience this distinction in these terms, i.e. in *Christian* terms, always mindful of the perils of our prejudices and prepossessions with regard to the "Christian" words and phrases we encounter many of which would seem to be all the more familiar the less we truly understand them. Might we then hope that, conversely, the better we are able understand them through our study, the less familiar, the more wondrous, they will become?

Take, for example, the "religious" expression *par excellence* "sin" (AMAPTIA) in the passage quoted above, for example. Do we know what "sin" means? In the context of the train of thought about thought in action we have been pursuing, this term describes one possible response on our part to the advent of critical reflection in our lives; with the unexpected emergence of the light of discernment, we *could* decide to give heed to seeing and thereupon take the opportunity it provides to consider what we are doing and saying and thinking, what we have done and said and thought; we could, in brief, reflect upon our way of life and our present situation, in other words, on THE WAY IT IS, from a critical standpoint, i.e. from the coign of vantage that asks whether THE WAY IT IS *is* THE WAY IT SHOULD BE. Simply becoming cognizant of THE WAY IT IS is already to catch a glimpse of ourselves and the situation of our lives *from without, from above, from beyond* our lives, self-severally placing us, as it were, both inside our lives and the world of our lives as the actors upon that stage *and* on the outside as the spectator looking in, looking down who then, from this remote perspective newly attained, passes judgment upon their doings, our doings. Only that now, in the logic of Christian thought, the first person singular and plural – the terms we used in the conception of the freedom of humanity as My autonomy – will no longer do. For in the Gospels it is not primarily about "me" or "us." It is about *You* and the difference that You make in coming to and leaving and then returning again to the world of Man that You will ultimately transform, in a redeeming act of self-several love as the "Savior of the World," by taking, first upon and then to yourself, the cross and the distinguished crossing of those who have taken you to and then upon themselves.

Regarding the term "sin," it is easy to imagine how folks, having previously enjoyed the bliss of ignorance, i.e. the former "blindness" (ΤΥΦΛΟΣ - see John's treatment of blindness in Chapter 9) of those not accustomed to giving a second thought to things, might, *upon reflection*, not want to adopt this standpoint of judgment and reflection, would really prefer *not* to look at the Man in the mirror. Why not? Because they may not take kindly to seeing the discrepancy between the IS and the OUGHT that now confronts them in the guise of a sharply cutting dissatisfaction with themselves as revealed in the world of their words and their deeds and their thoughts and the ensuing guilt that spurs contrite ambition to change their ways. We read:

> This is the crisis of the verdict: Light has come into the world...

Can we now elaborate our train of thought about self-critical thought in these terms? The light of note opens to their reflection the previously ignored gap between the IS and the OUGHT of their lives, which, in this passage, is said to be "the crisis of judgment..." (ΑΥΤΗ ΔΕ ΕΣΤΝ Η ΚΡΙΣΙΣ...), while the advent of critical reflection is "the light's coming into their world" (...ΤΟ ΦΩΣ ΕΛΗΛΥΘΕΝ ΕΙΣ ΤΟΝ ΚΟΣΜΟΝ... - 3:19), an unpleasant and therefore (from the point of view that had hitherto sedately cultivated its evasion) a very bad light, in truth more like a shadow, cast upon them and their former lives, that they "naturally" tend to avoid if possible so as not to find themselves compelled to see that gap and therefore admit to it, to "own" it, with all of the consequences that this response, this responsibility, entails in their subsequent actions which, presumably, would henceforth be enlisted in a sincere effort to make amends and heal that wound of divergence. It is easy to see that some folks would be inclined to refuse to act upon this painful discovery of discrepancy, would try their best and their worst to suppress this insight and, bringing to bear Man's impressive arsenal of lies, excuses, rationalizations, justifications, and denigrations, would venture to annihilate rather than mind that gap yawning so precipitously before their mind's I, the little one. Here is how we might put this idea in Christian terms:

> "This is the verdict: Light has come into the world. But people loved darkness instead of light because their deeds were evil. Everyone who does evil hates the light, and will not come into the light for fear that their deeds will be exposed. But whoever lives by the truth comes into the light, so that it may be clearly seen that what they have done has been done in the sight of God." (3:20-21)

Who could deny that this language presents our supposedly oh so commonplace experience of critical reflection in a new, for many, a foreign, a repellant light. Yes. Just so. That is exactly what we are looking for – a startlingly new and unfamiliar way to see and speak about a very old and all too familiar experience, i.e. the self-several experience of critical self-reflection itself. Taking note, for some perhaps for the first time, of our taking note, of what taking note is and what it means for our lives, is, as the Gospel according to John would have us believe, an earth- and world-shaking experience. You don't agree? You feel it is a very banal, everyday sort of experience, hardly worth mentioning let alone rendering in such "extravagant" terms? Well, that is certainly an understandable view. But even if you, lucky stiff, don't, many people need and appreciate a constant reminder in fresh, more vivid terms, of the *fact* of pure reason over and against all stiffness and intractability of the mind! For them (if not for you), *discernment* – the principles that structure its element, the actions that flow from its government, and the poetry that renders its life tangible to our inspiration – is a date with destiny.

Thus we exclaim: Luckily there have always been and hopefully there always will be poets and prophets who know and cherish the art of moving the human heart and will, by speaking in the tongues of flame that invigorate both the intellect *and* the imagination, again and again rekindle our insight into *and* our regard for what the sole and unique distinction of our human being truly is.

Given this elaboration of the term "sin" in the context of our train of thought about thought, we might profitably explore the associations this word has acquired over the centuries and note how easy it has been and still is to miss the point about it. Sin is the annihilation of difference, the attempt, after the distinction between the IS and the OUGHT has been made and the standpoint of critical reflection experienced, i.e. with the advent of the Word and the coming of the Lord, to think and to act as if there were no difference in a bid to eradicate reflection *after the fact* of thought and thus to resume the innocent blindness that reigned before the happening of the crisis of judgment, the UR-TEIL that Hölderlin spoke of as the "primal divide." But now, reverted to after the fact of critical difference, that former blindness becomes intentional, premediated, active self-dissemblance engaged in for its own sake, chosen and approved by a deliberate mind sworn to thwart the mind, the virtuoso practice and pretense of a studied ignorance that fraudulently turns a blind I to what it has already seen and been. Thus the explanation that sin means "transgressing God's laws" misses the essential point of the perversion of the distinction of human being; no, the perversion inherent in sin is not "deviate" sexual behavior that tempts our delight or lascivious speculations upon a second, even bigger, slice of chocolate cake. The diverse adversary demons (ΔAIMONION - 7:20, 8:48-49, 8:52, 10:20-21) that possess our human being and want driving out – the "prince of the world" (12:31, 14:30, 16:11), the "father of lies" (8:44), the "son of perdition" (17:12), the "devil" (6:70, 8:44, 13:2), or "Satan" (13:27) – as the mentality animating the darkened world of these unclean spirits (AKAΘAPTOΣ ΠNEYMA - Mat 10:1, 12:43, Mar 1:23, 26-27, 3:11, 3:30, 5:2, 5:8, 5:13, 6:7, 7:25; 9:25, Luk 4:33, 4:36, 6:18, 8:29, 9:42, 11:24) which sicken and debilitate our being, in opposition to the holy one that teaches (Jhn 14:26) and inspires (20:22) us, might collectively be called, catalogue the powers of perversion which strive to annihilate the original difference that critical reflection makes. This is truly diabolic – not so much the lecherous or the immoderate mind of unseeming indulgence, but rather the one that is *twisted*, i.e. opposed to making and therefore, *after the fact*, bent on annihilating the distinction of critical reflection by usurping its presence in language; in this precise sense, it is the evil one (17:15) whose gift is hate (15:25) rather than love and from whom the pious so fervently pray to be delivered (Mat 6:13).

In the Gospel of John, the twisted mind of sin that transmogrifies the reciprocity of regard between human and divine being into a wheeling and dealing of commodities (cf. Jhn 2:14-16) is "the thief that comes only to steal and kill and destroy" (10:10) the distinction of human being – powerful expressions of violence inherent in the refusal to accept, more, in the active attempt to expunge the difference that thought makes. Not to hear (AKOYΩ - 5:24, 8:43, 8:47), to recognize (EΓNΩ - 1:10), or to grasp (ΠAPEΛABON - 1:11; ΛAMBANETE - 3:11, 5:43; 12:48), to refuse to come to (OY ΘEΛΩ EPXOMAI - 5:40) and reject (AΘETEΩ - 12:48) the distinction of human being as a principle might be excused by appeal being made to an initial misunderstanding of what this distinction entails. But in fact, the utter simplicity of the idea in question – namely the idea that folks can and should, by reflecting critically upon their lives and their world, step back, sometimes at least, if not regularly, from the short-term view of the *body* perspective – suggests that any resistance to this message must be, in reality, not ignorance but a conscious effort of subterfuge to evade and slander and thus obviate an insight that had been immediately clear right from the start, all too clear to those adversaries of thought now so bent on mitigating the dire consequences it would have on the momentary pleasures and other advantages of their current state of affairs. For this reason, "spirited" disbelieving (OY ΠIΣTEYETE - 3:12, 3:18, 5:38, 6:64, 8:46, 12:37) is the very picture of sin (16.9), i.e. to grumble (ΓOΓΓYZΩ - 6.41) and stumble over the voice of distinction in wrong-headed astonishment (ΘAYMAZΩ - 7:21) or anger (ΞOΛAΩ - 7:23), taking offense

(ΣΚΑΝΔΑΛΙΖΩ - 6:61) at its supposed blasphemy (ΒΛΑΣΦΗΜΙΑ - 10:33) and turning back in aversion (ΑΠΕΡΞΟΜΑΙ ΕΙΣ ΤΑ ΟΠΙΣΩ - 6:66) rather than making a genuine effort to properly construe what has been said in its spirit, getting at what is actually meant (7:24), and showing it due regard (ΤΙΜΑΩ - 5:23). These gestures of rejection are only the beginning of the concerted action of those who, as we saw, "preferred the darkness to light" (3:19) in their hatred (ΜΙΣΕΩ - 3:20, 7:7, 15:8, 15:23, 17:14) of the light of distinction, and are therefore out to accuse (ΚΑΤΗΓΟΡΕΩ - 8:6) and to lay hands on (ΕΠΙΒΑΛΛΩ ΞΕΙΡ - 7:44), to violently seize, (ΠΙΑΖΩ - 7:30, 7:32: 8:20, 10:39), in a plot to kill (ΑΠΟΚΤΕΙΝΩ - 5:18, 7:1, 7:19, 7:25, 11:5312:10), to stone (ΛΙΘΑΖΩ - 8:59, 10:32), and otherwise to eliminate it and, in this way, by any and all means possible, to "destroy the temple" (2:19) of this teaching through persecution (ΕΔΙΩΚΟΝ - 5:16) and betrayal (ΠΑΡΑΔΙΔΩΜΙ - 6:64) which, as we saw, those are guilty of who "having shared the bread of this distinction, turn against it." (13:18)

127. The Severalty and Identity of Love

In the scheme of all things thought, in that circle of ideas the trajectory of which traces the flight of the mind from pit to tip and back again – the Son going down and rising, descending and ascending (3:13) in the rhythm of the breath of spirit (3:8), which is that of the coming (14:18) and going (8:14) of the Son to (17:11, 13) and from the Father (16:28), prefiguring the drama of our own turn and return, and our own to and fro, the fall and rise (14:31) of the world and his prince (14:30), at the moment of truth, the critical juncture that is the sea change of our human being and the transformation that makes pearls of Man's eyes and of his poor trite life something rich and strange – the mark of distinction, when it comes, whether it be rendered as God's day of doom or ours of His power (5:25; 16:2, 4, 25, 32; 17:1) and his glory, has been foreknown and predicted (14:29), is always already *before* us – both precedent *and* subsequent. For this reason, the incarnation of the Word is the just fulfillment of what is written (12:16, 19:28), of the predetermination of law, of scripture (2:22, 15: 25, 17:12). Rise *and* fall, the Son speaks of the amplitude of the experience of self-severalty in contradictory terms – now you see me, now you don't, then you'll see me (16:16) then you won't (16:10); he proclaims the hour of passage from death to life and life to death, i.e. the crossing of the cross of severance that is the sign of both the Crucifixion *and* the Resurrection of our flesh, the Ascension *and* the Incarnation of our Lord, the life laid down that it might be taken up again (10:17); for then, in this hour, on this day (8:56, 14:20) of the crisis of human being, even as the world, having abandoned God (16:32), rejoices, those chosen from the world (15:19) as his servants, appointed (15:16) as His disciples, sanctified (17:17) as the friends (15:15) of God, will weep and mourn God's departure from the world (8:21); but the former's joy will turn to pain and the latter's pain to joy (16:20), when the Son of God is gone to him who sent him (7:29); indeed the world who sees him and rejoices in the shame of his death will not see him in the glory of eternal life but his distinguished friends will (16:17); for his enemies who do not follow him and do not know him cannot follow him when he leaves (8:21; 13:33) but his friends, who do, will – each sad when the other is glad. Then, joining the Son, entering the dwelling of his Father's kingdom (3:3), they will enjoy the community of deity in the immediacy of seeing and knowing (14:7); then the immediacy of truth, impossible for the world to receive (14:17) because it was the Son's alone to bestow with respect to the Father, will be theirs to share in a heart freed of turmoil (14:1) and of fear, a heart at peace (14:27).

Dwelling thus in the immediacy of God's glory, the Son will reveal himself to his own (14:21); he will speak directly of the Father rather than in figures (16:25); in the immediacy and identity that is love's unique efficacy, the Disciples will speak directly to the Father in the Son's name rather than through the Son's intercession on their behalf (16:26). Thus, by believing in the Son, having taken him into ourselves, we have become one with him in the flesh and the blood of the Spirit that is his community with us and with the Father (14:23). In this spirit of love, the Son is in us and we are in him even as the Son is in the Father and the Father in him (14:10, 20). This twofold entity of identity, the identity that is the Father's love of the Son and the Son's love of the father as well as the Son's love of us and our love for the Son is completed finally by the disciples' love for each other in the spirit of the community of distinguished beings. Hence the commandment of love that he gives his disciples to love each other is not founded upon the self-love of the body perspective so intent on looking out for its own, though such a perspective which integrates one's neighbor's needs into one's own body of them does indeed deserve to be acclaimed as the highest achievement of generosity of an ego that has succeeded at lifting its own self-love to the measure and standard of love for people other than itself. In John, this "egoistical" love of our neighbor is superseded by the love that defines the relationship between the Father and the Son. This is the "new commandment" (ΕΝΤΟΛΗ ΚΑΙΝΗ) that he gives us, namely "to love one another even as I have loved you." (13:34. 15:12)

ΚΑΘΩΣ ΗΓΑΠΗΣΑ ΥΜΑΣ ΙΝΑ ΚΑΙ ΥΜΕΙΣ
ΑΓΑΠΑΤΕ ΑΛΛΗΛΟΥΣ

What sort of love is this? Jesus explains: "As my father has loved me so I have loved you." (15:9)

ΚΑΘΩΣ ΗΓΑΠΗΣΕΝ ΜΕ Ο ΠΑΤΗΡ ΚΑΓΩ ΥΜΑΣ ΗΓΑΠΗΣΑ

Thus, it is the love of God (5: 42) – in both the subjective and the objective sense of the genitive – that is here the measure for our mutual love; we learn that this love is the reflection of the glory (ΔΟΧΑ) that comes from God rather than that with which Man honors Man (5:44, 12:43) in mutual self-glorification (5:43), with faith (ΠΙΣΤΙΣ) being the name of the love that seeks the glory of God rather than Man's. Do we not recognize Rousseau's distinction between *amour de soi* and *amour proper*, i.e. between the self-respect of My humanity and the self-gratification with which reputation indulges Man's vanity, drawn now in these Christian terms?

What could it mean specifically "to love God" or "to be loved by God" (or to hate and be hated by God for that matter), to love or to be loved by the Father or the Son? In the language of the New Testament, this could only mean to do God's, the Father's, the Son's will or to refuse to do it, which means, to do one's *own* will instead, have one's *own* way insofar as it is opposed to that of God, of the Father, of the Son. What could it mean to "oppose God's will" and why would anybody choose to do so? Now we are all surely familiar with the conflict that emerges when we are torn between wanting and demanding what is good for us, what profits us, in opposition to what would, though to our detriment, benefit our neighbor, a conflict that we encounter even in ourselves when we are forced to decide between a momentary pleasure that could have unpleasant consequences in the future or to take upon ourselves a pain now in the hope that, long-term, a benefit might follow. There would seem to be nothing mysterious about this conflict; it is well known and often, even regularly, encountered by us in a diversity of situations and contexts – in business terms, for example, we might speak of an *investment* as the pain presently undergone, a cost, for the sake of a possible advantage later, with *risk* being the designation for the degree of uncertainty that the benefit we envisage, the return on investment, will actually materialize. Amazingly, a study of Man reveals that even if there were no risk at all and the ensuing profit, considered a greater good than the pleasure we have renounced upon for its sake, is in fact absolutely certain, even then, the trade-off of an immediate gratification for the sake of a future one demands of us a sacrifice.

The explanation for this remarkable behavior of Man is obvious: The benefit and the pleasure of the good we foresee is, at the moment when we are actually deliberating upon our course of action, not in any other way present to thought except *as a thought*, an intangible idea, or, making all the more out of it, an *ideal* our immediate experience of which, far from being ideal, is one of material loss, the suffering of a pain that we are now on the verge of inflicting upon ourselves in the name of that "immaterial" idea.

Thus even if you know in all certainty that when you are "laying down your life in order to take it up again…" (…ΕΓΩ ΤΙΘΗΜΙ ΤΗΝ ΨΥΧΗΝ ΜΟΥ ΙΝΑ ΠΑΛΙΝ ΛΑΒΩ ΑΥΤΗΝ…) - you yourself having the power to lay it down and to take it up again (…ΕΞΟΥΣΙΑΝ ΕΧΩ ΘΕΙΝΑΙ ΑΥΤΗΝ ΚΑΙ ΕΞΟΥΣΙΑΝ ΕΧΩ ΠΑΛΙΝ ΛΑΒΕΙΝ ΑΥΤΗΝ… 10:18), the sacrifice being, therefore, voluntarily – and you know, moreover, that you are acting in accordance with "the command you have received from your Father" (ibid.) who "loves you" (…Ο ΠΑΤΕΡ ΜΕ ΑΓΑΠΑΙ…) and, as you might reasonably presume, for that very reason (ΔΙΑ ΤΟΥΤΟ…10:17), has your best interest in heart, even then it still hard to relinquish a present advantage, to brave an imminent pain.

Take the issue of brushing our teeth, for example. Who would deny our premonitions of its impending unpleasantness at bedtime? On a cold winter's evening, after the coziness of the living-room and cuddling with our loved ones by the fire, the prospect of the bathroom with its cold tiled glare, the unflattering mirror over the sink, the icy water engulfing, gripping with its soulless element our hands only just held in the warm caress of kindred hands, the bristle of brush on tooth and tongue, the inevitable drool of foam and uncouth spitting, the drastic splashing and tedious rinsing, not to mention the oppressive certainty that the sun of another day of our life has irrevocably sank into the sea of time while the burdens of tomorrow lurk and shift, vaguely menacing, in the offing of our drowsiness – who would be so bold to declare that there is nothing irking, grieving, yes, even humiliating about the whole procedure, one, however, that we have nevertheless taken upon ourselves this evening for the sake of that idea, that ideal, we call, in this particular context, dental *health*?

How can we speak of the "sacrifice" involved in brushing our teeth, delaying a gratification, cutting our losses, expressing regret, beginning anew, forgiving a wrong, breaking the ice, kicking a habit, quelling a welling passion at the brim, taking *no* for an answer, embracing the uncertainty of a venture, letting go or giving leave, sitting down and shutting up, giving up a lost cause, persevering against all odds, making an end, stepping up, starting over, trusting, yielding, confessing, conceding, serving, hoping… – when Jesus speaks of the ultimate sacrifice of "laying down one's life for friends." (15:13)?

Some sacrifices are indeed greater than others and the love at the heart of the true hero's deserves to be called the greatest as it is in the passage just quoted. But that is not at issue here; in the Gospel of John we are studying the principle and the spirit of sacrifice as well as its consequences and the mentality of those who refuse that spirit. More generally, we could speak of the spirit of sacrifice at the heart of the experience of self-severalty, i.e. in the thwarting of one's inclination for the sake of a principle – whether objective, absolute, or general – that we feel obliged to give precedence to in spite of ourselves and our own momentary preferences. I guess you could say that everybody who does her or his duty, be it great or small, is a hero and a saint of sorts, and therefore a rightful and bona fide citizen of pure reason's dwelling.

In the Third Epoch, the difference that pure reason makes in our lives is realized in what I Myself actually experience and, as a result of the experience, put into effect. In the language of the Second Epoch, however, the principle of the distinction of human being is not My Freedom, not the I of My Humanity but rather You, the Son of God, who commits himself to doing the will of the Father, which is not at all the same as the moral law of human nature that we previously became acquainted with. "Nature" in Christian diction is a term of immediacy against which the *Holy Spirit* makes all the difference as the term of distinction, whereas in the language of Rousseau, as we saw, *Nature* is the term of distinction against a thoroughly denatured "civilization."

The way we experience this distinction in Christian terms is to take its life upon ourselves, not as ourselves, as that of our best *Self*, but rather as that of the Word that is distinguished as the *Son of God* who we take to ourselves – in faith and in love. It is as if, in the logic of these expressions, it were incumbent upon "someone else," namely upon *You* and not upon little old "me" to undergo the experience of our human self-severalty the efficacy of which I can only participate in vicariously – the event of human being's distinction occurs like a drama unfolding before us, the disciples, depicting the tragedy of Jesus's own life in the course of which he *"performs"* this distinction and experiences both the "death" and the "life" – to use these "climactic" terms – that it entails, allowing us in turn, to the extent that we succeed at identifying ourselves with him and with what is happening to him right before our very eyes, to share in his fate, not as spectators of a play but rather as witnesses to these events, which, in the Gospels, are not representations on the stage as they were for Schiller but rather "real," i.e. *historical* events. What is happening is not theater but rather "really" happening because the Gospel tells the story of what happens when human being steps back and minds the gap between THE WAY IT IS and THE WAY IT SHOULD BE. This is the reality that the gospel narrative relates – not the reality of my relationship to my "Self" and, through it, to My Humanity – Freedom, but rather the reality of Man's relationship to the "Son" and, through him, to the Father – God. God is absolute but, as the Father of light, turned towards the darkened world of lies; Freedom is absolute but, as autonomous Humanity, turned to the heteronomous world of sophistication and conceit; we are called by the law of human nature and by the Word of the Father to be renewed in a "holy" spirit, in that of the Son of God, in that of the beauty of Nature, which will guide us into the community of the Father and the Son, in accordance with which we will prepare the celebration of the festival of peace among the principles, our dwelling in the Kingdom of Heaven, in Fatherland, the one in glory, the other in song – isn't the analogy between these two different languages, these two different "performances," compelling? Does not thought, the Builder's, putting the matter of critical self-reflection in terms of such diverse "poetic" intuition enrich our experience of the distinction of human being?

If our relationship to freedom is called, as we have learned, *Self-Regard*, in Christian terms this relationship to the principle is called *love*, love of the Son, who is the "Self" of our faith, a self and a "heart" that is not always already "in us," as our own "human nature" is, but rather comes to us, lives among us, and only then, through our faith in him as the distinguished, the Holy spirit it, no, *He* gives us, *in us. Love* is the term that links the Son's experience of self-severalty with our own, more, it is precisely in our relationship to the Word, in the experience of our identification with the life of the Word become flesh, that we take upon our own flesh the distinction of human being. Thus when we speak of love in the Gospel of John, we refer to a love that does not assimilate the terms of the relationship, the love, the lover, and the one loved – for that is what folks usually like to think "love" essentially is, namely a conflation, a commingling of minds, of bodies even, that confounds, at least for a little while, their insuperable differences – but rather maintains their distinction even in the unity that the identification, the participation of our lives in that of the Word and the Word in ours, gives rise to. How is this possible?

The entity of identity or, in Christian terms, the being of divine *love* (ΑΓΑΠΗ) in which our distinguished human being, the *Disciple*, participates, having received from God *and* the Son of God, the ΛΟΓΟΣ, the corresponding Holy Spirit of truth (14:17, 15:26, 16:13) that the Father and the Son share, makes manifest the relationship that governs their rapport.

It is precisely this affinity, this kinship of the meeting of minds, of wills, that is referred to by the term *love* – first as that between God and his Word – who is *with* God and *is* God (1:1) – then as that between the Father and the Son, who is in the bosom (ΚΟΛΠΟΣ) of the Father (1:18), and finally as that between the World and the Savior who came into the world to dwell among us, in us (EN HMIN – 1:14), a relationship of relationships based on the proportion of perfect unity *and* absolute difference in which the issue of pure reason consists.

Of course, the propinquity between human and divine being in the person of the Son is not an immediate but rather a mediated relationship, one, as we have learned, to which we must be born again (3:3-7) and thus distinguished by self-several birth. But in this mediated immediacy into which human being is destined to be reborn, engendered thus by the Holy Spirit, we enter into perfect nearness to the deity (10:34) as exemplified by the accord between the Father and the Son. To render this relationship of identity palpable to our experience, Jesus begins by calling God his *Father* and himself the latter's only *Son* (3.16) who the Father gave to the World in an act of love – this grant is the act of love called *grace* – to save the world, in other words, to transform it, to convert it, to turn it back towards the kinship with God from which it had departed in loving darkness more than light, perverting thus the love in question, having made it worldly. Hence, throughout the gospel, for the benefit of our deepening experience, the relationship of accord and immediacy between the Father and the Son, namely that the "Father loves the Son" (3:35, 5:20, 10:17, 15:9) and the Son loves the Father (15:9), that each is *in* the other (10:38; 14:20) and finally that both are one (10:30; 17:11) in their mutual knowledge of each other (10:15), is richly elaborated. Consider these images of the immediacy of love: First that the Son has *seen* and knows (3:11, 4:22, 6:46, 8:38: 8:55) the Father and therefore gives true testimony as a witness (3:31-32), ***not on his own behalf*** but rather on behalf of the Father (5:37) and his commandment (10:18); then, the Son, ascending and descending (3:13), comes from (5:34, 6:51; 8:42; 16:28; 17:8) and goes to (3:8; 13:33) the Father (14:12; 16:5, 10, 28; 17:11), always doing what pleases the Father (8:29), living the Father's life (6:57) ***rather than his own*** into whose hand the Father had given all (13:3) and to whom the Father had granted authority not only to govern all things (3:35), all people (17:2) that the Father governs (16:15), but also, more specifically, to execute judgment (5:22, 27; 8:14-15) over life (5:26) and death in the name of the Father (5:43), but ***not in his own name***, speaking the Father's words (3:34; 12:49-50; 14:10), his father's teachings, but ***not his own*** (7:16; 8:26, 28, 14:24), speaking ***not to glorify himself*** (8:50), but rather to glorify his Father (7:18), coming to the world *not on his own* (7:28, 8:42) but rather having been sent (3:34, 6:29, 44, 57; 7:33; 11:42; 12:44, 45; 17:18, 23), given (3:16) to the world by the Father to do the latter's will and *not his own* (6:38), in fact, ***doing nothing on his own*** (5:30, 8:28) but only what he sees the Father doing (5:19) and completing His work (4:34, 5:17, 20, 5:36; 10:32, 37), in other words, doing works in his Father's name (10:25), but *not in his own*, performing signs (2:11, 23) of self-severalty and transformation that are Jesus's deeds of healing, as such the symbols of this distinction and therefore pleasing to the Father (8:29) through which the Father testifies in turn on behalf of the Son (5:37, 39; 8:18; 10:25), glorifying him (8:54; 12:23; 12:28; 13:31-32; 17:5) who knows and glorifies God (17:1, 25) and is known by God (10:15), the Father, who regards as his children those who have served and regarded the Son (12:26). Thus to see, to know, to hear the Son is to see, to know, to hear the Father (14:9) and to hate the Son is to hate the Father (15:23) while all those that belong to the Father belong to the Son and vice versa (17:10).

Not in his own name, not for his own glory – even thus in the unity of the Godhead that is the relationship of Love comprising the Father and the Son, we see, as well, the self-severalty of this Godhead that Augustine will subsequently conceptualize in his theology of God's "inward" relationships and the relationships of these relationships as the necessary configuration of the Trinity. This inward self-severalty of the Son is prefigured in the lessor ministry of John the Baptist (5:36) who "though testifying to the light was not himself the light." (1:7) The very notion of a *sign* reiterates this self-severalty – a sign standing for, presaging, and thus, in its testimony as "martyr," i.e. in John's testimony, in "making straight the way of the Lord," (1:23) gives presence to what is absent, sacrificing its own presence for what is absent though greater than itself (1:27), for what, though coming after it, comes before it (1:30), like the friend of the bridegroom (3:29) whose presence recedes even as the groom's emerges (13:30) or like the herald, the messenger sent ahead. For is it not true that one who comes in another's name is and is not the same as the one in whose name or on whose behalf thought, the Actor, appears on stage? The intercession and the agency of the actor, the sign in play – are these not excellent analogies for the relationship of self-severalty that we are studying as the distinction of human being?

For it is the middle term, the mediator, in which the two sides of the relationship find their self-several unity. We read that "servants are not greater than their master, nor are messengers greater than the one who sent them" (13:16) and nevertheless when Jesus washes the feet of his followers we understand that in the relationship of self-severalty the servant *is* the master and the master *is* the servant, too – the servant in one relationship and the master in the other – and similarly that the messenger sends the message even as the one who sends the message *is* the messenger, ultimately *is* the message himself, a unity of terms distinguished in the proportion rather than in the equality of their community. But doesn't this understanding of the mediating term recall the old tale of the pea the pot and the pan?[70]

Though different, the terms of this relationship take part in the overall distinction that is their practical unity, like the one comprising the vine, the winegrower, and the branches (15:1-8) or that of the sower and the reaper who nevertheless rejoice together (4:36). Theirs is a unity of proportion in the carrying out of diverse tasks, an organization of them, and not a uniformity that eliminates their distinctions.

Father (A) - *Son* (C) - *Disciples* (B) – this unique triunity of the Christian Godhead celebrated in the Gospel of John is the unity of spirit founded upon "the new commandment," namely that we "love each other," but not as we love ourselves, namely in a self-glorifying, self-serving spirit, which is, in fact a twisted misprision of the former commandment, but rather with the love that is the Son's love of us (13:34) and the Father's love of the Son (15:9), that divine love with which the Father loves us as well (17:23). The cascading differential of this relationship of inherence is visualized in *Figure 87* as the reflective rapport of divine intimacy and human constancy, human faith and divine kindness, trust answering regard in the well-rounded glory of a will both human *and* divine.

---

[70] cf. Figure 35.

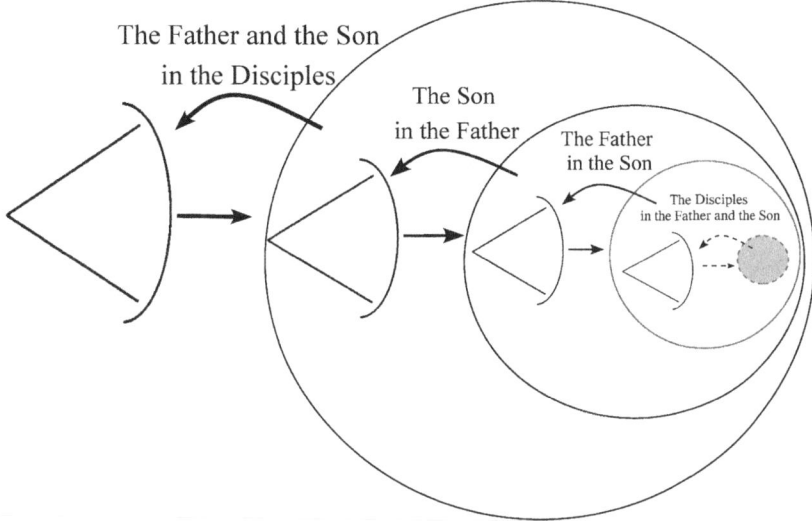

The Father and the Son
in the Disciples

The Son
in the Father

The Father
in the Son

The Disciples
in the Father and the Son

Figure 87: The Infolded Dwelling of Love's Glory

Both are mediated by the descending, transcending Word sent down into the World to uplift and transform, to redeem and renew the World; the Word turned to flesh so that the world might turn to spirit – in this turn and return, the deity that came to dwell among us, in us, as his abode is the same deity in which we might dwell and abide, each the other's host, each the other's guest, in a Home away from Man's coma home.

A. The Savior of the World

128. The Life of the ΛΟΓΟΣ

The light of distinction enters the darkened world of Man – it is the life of distinction, the *practice* of critical self-reflection, that is being given presence in these terms. For in the ΛΟΓΟΣ "was life and that life was the light of human being." (1:4)

EN ΑΥΤΩΙ ΖΩΗ ΗΝ ΚΑΙ Η ΖΩΗ ΗΝ ΤΟ ΘΩΣ ΤΩΝ ΑΝΘΡΩΠΩΝ

The life of ΛΟΓΟΣ is a life of distinction, shining into darkness (1:5) and making therein all the difference in the world. For now, through the light of pure thought, the two worlds that human being are heir to have been made visible to the mind's eye and, in this sense, we can say that they are *ΛΟΓΟΣ-*

made (1:3, 1:10), the self-several heaven and earth that only the light of discernment creates – the one called *eternal life*, which is that of the world redeemed, the other *death*, the life and the world of the condemned.

In terms of the Gospel of John, the advent of the light of distinction is rendered accessible to listeners and readers above all as speech practice, language both written and spoken, language that both imparts the message of *and* affects *difference*. Therefore, in this context, the standard translation of "ΛΟΓΟΣ" as *Word* makes good sense. A word conveys a message from the speaker (writer) to the listeners (readers) and is as such a medium; at the same time, this word, once it is spoken, if it is the ΛΟΓΟΣ of distinction, actually does itself what it says is to be done and, speaking thus, puts into effect, causes and accomplishes, that very distinction that has been spoken, even as God's inaugural imperative "Let there be light!". Thus this distinguished and unique Word *signifies* its own being and *is* what it signifies. Coming into the world of indifferent darkness, its utterance makes all the difference in the world and not only speaks of the experience of coming into the world but, in the end, even enacts this difference, making a difference much like the famous paradox of the liar who says 'I am lying' only now it is the truth talking and the truth *in person* who says "'*I am*" telling the truth' (ΕΓΟ ΕΙΜΙ - 8:58, see also: 6:35, 6:41, 6:48, 6:51, 8:12, 8:18, 8:23, 8:24, 8:28, 9:5, 9:9, 10:7, 10:9, 10:11, 10:14, 10:36, 11:25, 13:13, 13:19, 14:6, 14:10, 14:11, 14:20, 15:1, 15:5, 16:32, 17:10, 17:11, 17:14, 17:16).

With the arrival of the Word that says "I speak," the difference that it makes in having spoken is precisely what it is speaking about and, in speaking thus, intends to convey to the listeners, viz. the truth about the truth; this performative Word of truth is the sign of difference that, drawing the distinction in question upon the silence of the deaf and the darkness of the blind, indicates that having come, the Word is the coming and the drawing of the distinction of human being upon that world of darkness and of deafness, distinguishing thereby the world; in more modern parlance we might venture to propose that the difference that it makes and the trace that it leaves behind is the work of both the signifier *and* the signified. This word contains itself – it is the enactment of its own meaning; its meaning is the reflection of its very own doing and whether meaning or being, the Word, this purest poetry of self-severalty, makes manifest the work of thought, the Builder, in Christian terms – the *doing* of truth.

Its light – not just any run-of-the-mill light, mind you, but distinguished light, call it *glory* (ΔΟΞΑ - 11:40) and certainly not human glory (5:41) but rather that of God (11:40) – lights up the light, makes the light itself shine, makes its visibility *and* the fallen state of invisibility, the state of Man in rejection of the light, visible. More, this self-several light makes manifest the making manifest of making manifest; it illuminates by illuminating illumination, the dawning on us of the dawning of the day that is the distinguished day of discernment, joyful to behold. (8:56) The Gospel itself, as a written work, is such a Word – a sign, a witness, a testimony, a record of thought thinking thought, doing thought, and a true account of this thinking and doing made manifest by the signs (6:2, 6:14, 6:26, 6:30) and wonders (ΣΗΜΕΙΑ ΚΑΙ ΤΕΡΑΤΑ - 4:48) that it works upon the readers – lame, blind, dead in the oblivion of Man's world but now reading, heeding, and therefore walking, seeing, living again, i.e. becoming, as well, witnesses to the "witnesses," i.e. to the signs and the testimony (ΜΑΡΤΥΡΙΑ 1:7, 1:8, 1:15, 1:32, 5:36, 10:25, 12:17, 15:27), of the Word in action, who is himself a witness (3:11, 18:37), his own (8:14, 8:18) *and* not his own (5:31-33, 8:13) – namely upon those who, having seen and now knowing, themselves made known, make known (1:18), crying out (ΚΡΑΖΩ – 1:15), the Word of distinction; "*I speak!*" Namely "I am the voice of one calling in the wilderness" (1:23) and, with the Word's words, making thus a distinction against the background of indifference by making known (ΕΥΗΓΕΟΜΑΙ 1:18) and passing on the message of the Word about what a message and a medium, in their mission of grace, are, giving a sign about what a sign, i.e. the embodiment and incarnation, the signifier, of a significant message truly is.[71] These are the ones who "speak of what they know and testify to what they have seen..." (3:11) "...and heard" (3:32), namely what the Word makes visible (OPAΩ – 1:34, 1:39, 1:46, 1:50-51, 3:3, 9:37) in both its voice *and* its form (5:37).

The Gospel elaborates the Word in words, in the narrative, and is thus itself, as we saw in Paul, the most general sign of distinction; but this sign contains signs, the word of the Gospel tells the story of the Word. The Word speaking as a teacher, the Word "spoken" as the message – these words are the Gospel's Word's words relating what the Word has said and done, what the Word has taught and the miracles the Word has wrought, which are also the signs of the distinction, of the difference that critical thought, the Word, makes and therefore, of the light, the Glory of the Word, as the primal divide of judgment that illuminates the world darkened by disregard.

Thus the Gospel itself is a sign of the Word. It reveals the revelation of the Word. It self-severally attests the Word but is not itself the Word even as John the Baptist – not himself the light but testifying to the light (1:8) shedding light upon the light, as such, a prognostication of the light (1:27), coming first, before the light, he nevertheless comes second and is subordinate to it (1:30); baptizing with water, John's is a premonition of the work of the Word that will baptize with spirit (*and* fire – Mat 3:11, Luk 3:16), even as his cleansing with water prefigures the transformation of conversion that is the purifying turn and return from sin as well as the salvation thus attained as a result of repentance in departure from the darkness, from the flesh (3:6) of a closed mind, reborn of and consecrated

---

[71] As a sign signifying the trace of difference that the figure of a mark makes against the background of indeterminacy – the unique sign of the sign – perhaps this Word of distinction is exactly what Foucault had in mind when in *La penseé du dehor* (the thought without) quoting Nietzsche's "die Wüste wächst" (the *sans* expands), he muses on how the utterance "je parle" (I speak) makes manifest the "desert..." of indifference "...surrounding language" (le desert l'entourne - 11), that infinite expanse (répandre à l'infini - ibid) of sand in the "emptiness" (vide - 13) of its "naked space" (espace nu) which "disintegrates, disperses, and scatters ("se morcelle, se disperse et s'égaille -11) the supposed prerogative of the "I of the speaker" (le 'je' qui parle - ibid.). For it is in this bare *without* where the "subjet..." itself "...disappears" (ce dehor où disparaît le sujet - 14), becoming, instead, the self-several locus of its own disintegration, in Foucault's words, "the voided inexistence of what goes endlessly on and on in the relentless effusion of language." (...l'inexistence dans le vide de laquelle se poursuit sans trêve l'épanchement indéfini du language. - 12).

in the water and the spirit (3:5) of pure reason's purity, heaven sent (3:3) from the ethereal element of air beyond the stone-bound sphere of Man's control and calculation (3:8).

Figures of speech, turns of words in the Gospel, the proverbs that Jesus uses in his teachings (ΠΑΡΟΙΜΙΑ - 10:6, 16:25-26) – they are all analogies, symbols and signs, of the giving of the original sign of truth, the making of the inaugural difference of discernment. As the words of the Word, they foretell *and* foreordain. The differential relationship between the sign's signifier and its signified,[72] the metaphor's vehicle and tenor,[73], the analogy's phoros and theme [74] is, in this way, projected onto the timeline of the narrative of the Word's life and times; it is for this reason that the Word is both coming and already come – the sign of distinction is the active and present ministry of the Word *and* its prognostication as a destiny to be fulfilled. For in order to prefigure its arrival, the *sign* of distinction must have already arrived – that is what a sign does that is the sign of the sign of distinction. Repeatedly, John reminds the reader that the advent of the Word had been foretold in scripture and, having come, has made the predetermined difference in the world; and yet the divisive sign of the Word as the mediating term, the *Mediator*, requires not only that its hour *has already arrived* (4:23, 5:25, 12:23, 12:27, 13:1, 16:21, 16:32, 17:1) in accordance with the commandments of traditional Mosaic law, but also that, as a determination and a destiny to be fulfilled, it still has yet to arrive (2:4, 4:21, 7:30, 8:20) as the Word's second coming, its "last day" (6:39-40, 6:44, 6:54, 11:24, 12:48,), the great day of the feast (7:37) at the end of time (4:26, 5:28, 14:20, 16:2, 16:4, 16:23, 16:25-26); this temporal differentiation of the Word as the mark of judgment, namely the sentencing of its distinction that, on the one hand, has already been imposed and, on the other, nevertheless remains to be pronounced, is the "infinite progression" of being *and* to be – not the endless deferral of a "différance" but rather the reiterating ingemination of discernment that we have observed throughout this study as indicative of the self-several life of critical reflection, thought thinking thought. Thus throughout the Gospel of John, we are repeatedly advised that what Jesus said or did or

---

[72] The Word's image (whether seen or heard) and the Word's Word. Cf. Saussure's *Cours de linguistique générale*, pp. 98-101.

[73] To use the terminology of I. A. Richards' *The Philosophy of Rhetoric*, cf. pp. 96-97.

[74] According to Ch. Perelman and L. Olbrechts-Tyteca in *The New Rhetoric*, cf. pp. 373.

what happened to him was predestined and foreknown (11:22, 12:33, 13:3, 13:7, 13:11, 13:19, 13:21, 14:29, 16:4) and as such had been said, done, or taken place (12:16) in accordance with scripture (ΓΡΑΦΗ – 1:45, 2:17, 2:22, 6:45, 12:14, 13:18, 15:25, 17:12, 19:24, 19:28, 19:36, 19:37, 20:9) – especially in accordance with the words of the prophet Isaiah (12:38) – above all in Chapter 13 concerning the betrayal by Judas and in Chapter 19 relating to events surrounding his crucifixion, which is the central sign of the Word and the culmination of the Gospel in which the self-severalty of the Word, the crossing that the Word of conversion enacts *and* entails, is finally vividly revealed, glorified even, in the travesty of glory that is the depiction of Jesus's death as the epitome of pain, that, too, nevertheless, refers beyond itself to the resurrected life and the joy of the Word in anticipation of the final turn and return of the Word of distinction and the redemption of the world that the Word's loss, in the consecrating blood of the sacrifice he took upon *himself here, now, today*, has won *for all* and *for all time*. Jesus's life and death and life characterize this coming and going of the Word as the Son's two transitions, namely coming from God and going to God (13:3), the Father (16:28); they allow three corresponding states to be defined by the Word's presence, namely first the state of hope – having come from God and entered the world to live among us, the Word is with us who, having faith in the light, have become children of the light (12:36) as the daylight of the world to walk in (12:35) and experience as the mission and the ministry of God's signs that glorify the workings of the Word (9:4-5,11:9); secondly, the state of the heart's turmoil (ΤΑΡΑΣΣΩ), sorrow (16:6; 16:20), and fear (15:27) of the coming of the night (9:4, 11:10) in view of death and betrayal (13:21), of abandonment (15:18, 16:32), of persecution (15:20, 16:2, 16:33), and the impending crucifixion (12:27) that is nevertheless the hour of glory (12:23) and promise when the Word leaves the world to go to the Father (12:8, 13:1, 16:5, 16:28) to prepare a dwelling for human being (14:2) while sending (16:7) in his stead, as comforting reminder, advocate (ΠΑΡΑΚΛΗΤΟΣ - 14:26), and herald of THE WAY IT SHOULD BE (16:13), the spirit of peace (14:27) and truth (14:17, 15:26) as the holy present and witness (15:26) of the Word's determination to stay with us and in us ΠΑΡ'ΥΜΙΝ ΜΕΝΕΙ ΚΑΙ ΕΝ ΥΜΙΝ ΕΣΤΑΙ - 14:17) forever (14:16), beyond all the givens and the perturbations of the world (14:27) here and now; thirdly, the Word returns (14:18) on the Last Day (ΕΝ ΤΗΙ ΕΣΧΑΤΗΙ ΗΜΕΡΑΙ), the day of judgment (12:48) and of God's anger (ΟΡΓΗ - 3:36) – upon which none shall be lost and all shall be raised (ΑΝΙΣΤΗΜΙ - 6:39) "who see the Son and believe in him." (6:40) But these epochs are not, in truth, three different and consecutive times; in fact, the sign of the cross of crucifixion is the central image of the Word in the *now* (NYN - 4:23, 5:25) of glory (13:31, 16:32) that encompasses the whole story of pure reason, its life *and* its death, its fall *and* its rise, the condemnation *and* the salvation of the World, the incarnation of the Son of God *and* the glorification of the Son of Man; and precisely this is the purpose of the coming of the Word (12:27), namely to overcome the world and its prince and to take into the dwelling of the Word those who have taken the Word upon themselves that it might dwell in them: "Now there is judgment of this world, now the prince of this world will be thrown out and I, uplifted from the earth, will draw all to me." (12:31-2)

ΝΥΝ ΚΡΙΣΙΣ ΕΣΤΙΝ ΤΟΥ ΚΟΣΜΟΥ ΤΟΥΤΟΥ ΝΥΝ Ο ΑΡΧΩΝ
ΤΟΥ ΚΟΣΜΟΥ ΤΟΥΤΟΥ ΕΚΒΛΗΘΗΣΕΤΑΙ ΕΞΩ ΚΑΓΩ ΕΑΝ
ΥΨΩΘΩ ΕΚ ΤΗΣ ΓΗΣ ΠΑΝΤΑΣ ΕΛΚΥΣΩ ΠΡΟ ΕΜΑΥΤΟΝ

This dwelling is the "Father's house" (14:2), the kingdom of God, where the Word will take those who believe in him to himself such that "where he is, there they shall be." (14:3) But in fact this place, like the *now* of the Word, is not one in exclusion of others but rather one that comprehends the totality of pure reason's life and times (and places) – in Christian terms, this place, the kingdom of God, is the triune *here* of the dwelling that the Father and the Son have made for those who love the Word and keep it, and are, therefore, loved and kept by the father in return who nevertheless loved them first in the giving of the gift of glory and of grace that is his Son, *their* distinction. The community of God's kingdom can be attained only by following the way of the Word, the way that glorifies the Word, glorifying God by acting in accordance with the will of God as made visible, audible by the Works and the Words of the Word of God, the "holy spirit" of which speaks to us even today, now, here – though variously named and experienced in the epochal tongues of flame that our logotectonic philology studies – with the voice of *pure reason*, one voice *and* several.

In *Christian* terms, as a "poetic" whole, the story of the Holy Spirit is a dramatic narrative of how the inaugural ΛΟΓΟΣ of light inscribed the distinction that discernment makes in the continuity of generic human history, beginning with the disruption of the world of darkness of those who have carelessly instituted the convenience and the conventions of blindness in lieu of the blinding sight of the Word of God and who even go so far as to embrace and defend the diabolic distortion of their benighting, which is the twisted work of *sin*, by rejecting and annihilating the difference that regard for critical reflection makes in their realm, now become the gutted, decimated civilization of the walking dead who glory alone in the gore of self-satiation.

Their fate marks the end of the story of the distinction of human being but also the beginning; again and again but also once and for all, with the advent of the incarnated Word of God, *severalty* reenters upon the scene of Man's perpetual carnage, patiently recurring to the gap between THE WAY IT IS and THE WAY IS SHOULD BE that is the dawning of the day of judgment– the event of our decisive crisis both coming and to come as the Son of Man. Faith alone experiences in the ΛΟΓΟΣ of light the transformation of our human being from the self-glorifying progeny of Man's underworld to saints of God' Heaven, themselves not only the witnesses of the Son of God through faith but also, through the charity of their works, the ministers of the glory of the Father's grace – love answering to love.

This spirit of love is the essential gift of the Word to those who are open – having been opened like eyes, like ears previously closed – to sight, to hearing and who, in this perception, have the courage to abide by its simple message. Love and its holy spirit remain and survive even after the person of the Word has gone; in fact, he must depart in order for the spirit of love to come to those left behind as his advocates, namely as their comforter summoned in His name, that distinguished spirit of the Word and the present of the Father with which they, the Word's disciples and apostles, are filled in his absence (16:7). The principle of God's glory that became specific in the person of the Son of God now attains its full individuality in the particular heart of every human being; it is the seal of our distinction, a spirit that sets us apart not only from the world and its own brand of rationalizing but also as a people of insight into the rectitude of the Word in its perfect equality and correspondence with the will of God as a result of which this Word is acknowledged by God as the Son of the Father. Our participation in this relationship as the disciples of the Word is the *salvation* of the World and the fulfilment (not the abrogation) of the letter of the law (15:25) that a sacred tradition bequeathed to all posterity as a legacy of piety and therefore in the foreknowledge of the predetermination of Christ the Gospel of whose grace and truth is the final act and issue of God's glory. (1:17)

Sin - Severalty - Salvation – composing thus a ratio of these three terms, John articulates the train of thought about thought through which the distinguished Spirit of human *and* divine being makes evident, in the language of the Gospel, the practical experience of pure reason, in other words, the truth about the distinction of human being as *practice*. This "admonition" (ΕΛΕΓΧΩ - 16:18) is threefold: The truth of sin lies in its rejection of the difference that critical self-reflection makes in the life of Man; the truth of severalty is the critical reflection upon and thus the condemnation of that spirit of rejection; the truth of salvation is the promise of a renewed, an eternal life – inherent in God's *rectitude* (ΔΙΚΑΙΟΣΥΝΗΣ - 16:8, 16:10) – for those who believe in the Son's unity with his Father, which is not, however, a "synthetic" unity but rather one of a self-differentiating, self-several community, the harmony and fruition of which comprehends the inner dwelling of deity in the reciprocity of a discerning love, a *dilectio* as Augustine calls it.[75]

In verses 16:8 -16:11, John formulates this relationship of relationships in terms of *Sin* (B), *Severalty* (C), and *Salvation* (A), as comprehending the triunity of deity, couching thus the issue of pure reason's reflection – the whole story of thought about thought – in the nomenclature of Christian speech.

ΚΑΙ ΕΛΘΩΝ ΕΚΕΙΝΟΣ ΕΛΕΓΞΕΙ ΤΟΝ ΚΟΣΜΟΝ ΠΕΡΙ ΑΜΑΡΤΙΑΣ
ΚΑΙ ΠΕΡΙ ΔΙΚΑΙΟΣΥΝΗΣ ΚΑΙ ΠΕΡΙ ΚΡΙΣΕΩΣ ΠΕΡΙ ΑΡΜΑΡΤΙΑΣ
ΜΕΝ ΟΤΙ ΟΥ ΠΙΣΤΕΥΟΥΣΙΝ ΕΙΣ ΕΜΕ ΠΕΡΙ ΔΙΚΑΙΟΣΥΝΗΣ ΔΕ ΟΤΙ
ΠΡΟΣ ΤΟΝ ΠΑΤΕΡΑ ΜΟΥ ΥΠΑΓΩ ΚΑΙ ΟΥΚ ΕΤΙ ΘΕΩΡΕΙΤΕ ΜΕ
ΠΕΡΙ ΔΕ ΚΡΙΣΕΩΣ ΟΤΙ Ο ΑΡΧΩΝ ΤΟΥ ΚΟΣΜΟΥ ΤΟΥΤΟΥ ΚΕΚΡΙΤΑΙ

When the spirit comes he will bring to the light of day of the world the truth about sin, about rectitude, about severalty – about sin because they do not believe in me; about rectitude because I go to my father and you will no longer see me; about severalty because the prince of the world has been judged.

Figure 88 suggests how the logic of this line of reasoning, i.e. the ratio of terms (B > C > A) that delineates John's train of thought about thought upon which the wisdom of the Second Epoch concludes, might be conceptualized:

---

[75] In his *de Trinitate*, Augustine addresses the apparent contradiction between the simplicity of God's inner unity and the inner severalty of God's Trinity by showing how "God is love" not only in the bestowing sense of "God's gift" (donum dei - 15.27), i.e. in the grace of his "charity," (Deus Charitas - 6.7), but also in the distinguishing sense of God's discernment ("Deus dilectio est – ibid.). It is also this discriminating "love..." that we put into effect "...through faith," when cherishing God (per fidem diligatur – 8.6).

B. Sin

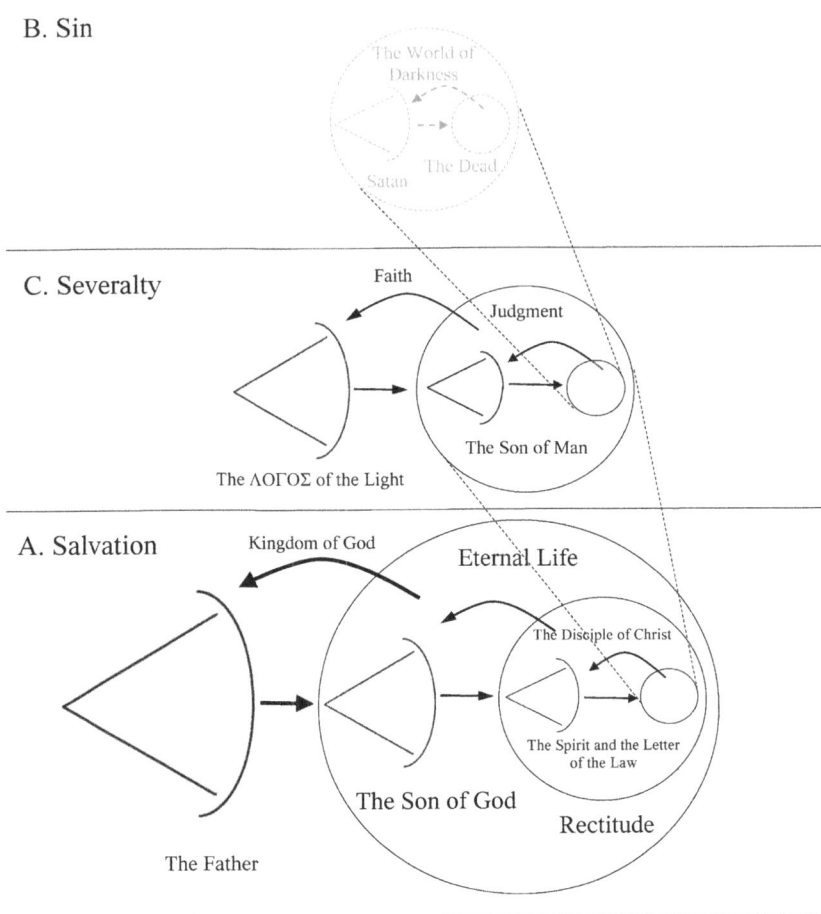

Figure 88: The Holy Spirit's Revision of the World of Action

129. Pure Reason in the Flesh

Imagine a master in the craft and art of speech who contrived to give a thought and a spirit a human face and name; in the person of his face and his name, this embodied, personified, "incarnated" spirit could now walk about in the world and talk and confront us, summon us to cognizance with his voice and touch us in kindness with healing hands, and then again, be touched, grasped, comprehended in a kindred spirit of gratitude, but also seized and then abducted by an opposing spirit of hatred that rejects the difference that thought makes, repudiating the very idea of distinction, the ΛΟΓΟΣ, that he is the incarnation of. Imagine a narrative the protagonist of which, that speaker, not content with literature and the poetry of allegory, makes of himself a "metaphor," that of a holy spirit come alive in him and, though very human, no less divine than the distinguished spirit he is the flesh of, saying to us who meet him *I am* (ΕΓΩ ΕΙΜΙ – 8:24, 8:28, 9:9, 13:19, 18:5, 18:6, 18:8). We who encounter this person among us as a peer and contemporary must now decide, in embracing or rejecting him as a person, whether we are disciples or scorners of the spirit he advocates in his teachings and the doctrine that he embodies in his actions, and therefore, to us, in his manner of speaking, *is* himself. What a bold conceit (7:26) of incomparable force, as provocative and controversial as it is unheard of, a scandal; yes, he speaks an insufferable language over which we are liable to stumble and grumble, even taking offense (ΣΚΑΝΔΑΛΙΖΩ - 6:61), and all to make a point, to draw a simple and not so simple distinction. Indeed, "never has a man spoken like this man" (7:46) to make a point about the distinction of human being.

ΟΥΔΕΠΟΤΕ ΟΥΤΩΣ ΕΛΑΛΗΣΕΝ ΑΝΘΡΩΠΟΣ
ΩΣ ΟΥΤΟΣ Ο ΑΝΘΡΩΠΟΣ

It is a point that makes a difference, makes all the difference in the world for this being. And what point is that? Are we to be presented with moral tenets conveyed to us by a prophet, a mediator and medium who gives voice to God's will? No. Amazingly, Christ is not a prophet in this more traditional sense. And if he is a medium then, as we saw, a medium that *is* the message as well, an idea in action. But this person is not the incarnation of this or that idea, *a* thought among others that we might take exception to, debate upon or accept; rather it is the ΛΟΓΟΣ itself, spirit, distinguished thought, critical self-reflection – however you choose to name pure reason – that is at issue here, that has been designated *God*, said to come into the world, to dwell among us and finally *in* us who have taken him, God's Word, to heart, which is, in the poetic craft and art of Christian speech practice, the mark, the sign, the very radiance of God's present, his voice and teaching, the gift of an insight into the will of God – as such a *holy* insight – the principle of pure reason put into practice and who speaks to us now, in person, face to face, by saying "I am...."

Hölderlin showed us the realization of thought, the Builder, as the power of invention of human spirit to bring forth its own image, the ideal of Humanity, in art, religion, and philosophy. Thought, the Actor, by contrast, is specifically engaged in the *practice* of truth, the truth done rather than seen in *theoretical* contemplation and a work engaged in for its own sake rather than as a *poetic* work completed with a view to a product, though of course the consequences of the Word's acts make manifest the significance of this deed – ultimately of course, in teaching the way of distinction, the *Word*, by undergoing the drama of sacrifice that is the entire content of the doctrine and as such *practical* reason, has made a difference in the presiding scheme of things, initiated a transformation of their world. For in this achievement, we, the spectators of this drama, recognize that the distinction of human being, in Christian terms "the glory of God," is not merely that of the *Judge* the experience of which is reproach for Man's inevitable shortcoming and ignoble death with respect to THE WAY IT SHOULD BE, but also as that of the *Savior* who in himself, in the narrative of his life and death as well as in his teachings, presents to us the image of human correspondence between the IS and the OUGHT, between human and divine being, an image of redemption and peace borne of this correspondence but, for all that, no less coterminous with the crisis of the difference that critical reflection makes with regards to the deficiency of all mortal human life as it is subject to the imperative of the will of God, namely the priority of the cross – the crossing and the passage of sacrifice – that leads to renewal, to eternal life, i.e. to a distinguished, self-several life and therefore one encompassing pain as well as gain. This avenue of thought has been opened to us and we may go this way of distinction if we take on pure reason, put it on as a garment of glory, take this enriching, nourishing spirit upon us, into us, as we do food and drink, bread and wine, and, in this way, along this way, join our own human heart with the substance, the subsistence, the sustenance of God.

It is in this sense that the distinguished thought that pure reason, the ΛΟΓΟΣ of God, *is*, says "I am the living bread which came down from heaven; who eats of this bread shall live forever and the bread that I will give is my flesh, which I will give for the life of the world." (6:51)

ΕΓΩ ΕΙΜΙ Ο ΑΡΤΟΣ Ο ΖΩΝ Ο ΕΚ ΤΟΥ ΟΥΡΑΝΟΥ ΚΑΤΑΒΑΣ
ΕΑΝ ΤΙΣ ΦΑΓΗΙ ΕΚ ΤΟΥΤΟΥ ΤΟΥ ΑΡΤΟΥ ΖΗΣΕΤΑΙ ΕΙΣ ΤΟΝ
ΑΙΩΝΑ ΚΑΙ Ο ΑΡΤΟΣ ΔΕ ΟΝ ΕΓΩ ΔΩΣΩ Η ΣΑΡΞ ΜΟΥ
ΕΣΤΙΝΗΝ ΕΓΩ ΔΩΣΩ ΥΠΕΡ ΤΗΣ ΤΟΥ ΚΟΣΜΟΥ ΖΩΗΣ

"I am food and drink," (6:55) says this person who, in speaking the Word of God, makes of his Word his Father's Word and makes of our hearing of the Word a taking, a grasping of it in him and through him, making thus of our hearing of the Word and the person of the Word speaking before us, in fact, a taking and partaking, an eating and drinking of it, of Him, of You, of the substance of the Word that, like food, fills and satisfies, quickens (6:63). Who has ever spoken of the experience of the distinction of human being thus? Speaking in such "repulsive terms as these, who can bear to listen to the Word?" (6:60)

ΣΚΛΗΡΟΣ ΕΣΤΙΝ Ο ΛΟΓΟΣ ΟΥΤΟΣ ΤΙΣ ΔΥΝΑΤΑΙ
ΟΥΤΟΥ ΑΚΟΥΕΙΝ

Thus respond those whose "time has not yet come to join the feast." (7:8). And many turned away from the Word in disgust at this point "and stopped walking with him." (6:66)

I am food and drink – Now why did he have to go and say "it" like that? First talking about an insight as if it were nourishment, then talking about insight itself as if it were "bread from heaven" (6:58), given by the Son of Man (6:27), distinguished bread, *true* bread (6:32), i.e. not the everyday sort of food of perishing that satiates our flesh with temporary life and inevitable death (6:49), but rather loaves from the Father (6:32) to fill us (6:26) with the eternal life of repletion that endures and does not die (6:50, 6:58), and finally even to say that he himself *is* this bread (6:51)? Why! All to make a point about the distinction of human being.

Again, what is the *distinction of human being*? Simply the difference critical self-reflection makes in our human being and the coign of vantage we attain above and beyond the confines of the mini-me mentality of Man when we step back from this our *body* perspective the life and the world of which is defined by what obtains merely *today, here*, for *me*, to consider instead, for a moment at least, the long-term, the big picture, that is to say, to consider matters from the standpoint of "eternal life" that we can attain to by *seizing* the thought that we may distinguish ourselves from ourselves in just this way, namely by adopting this standpoint of critical reflection and, in embracing this thought about *tomorrow, elsewhere, others*, act upon it *now*.

Bread from heaven, eternal life – all to make this point? Yes, we can "deal" with such figurative language; the analogy between grasping in a physical sense and grasping with our minds is clear; it is then only a small step from *appropriation*, i.e. the taking possession of something, to *ingestion*, in other words, the laying hold of what we intend to take to ourselves as nourishment. Pursuing that alimental analogy, we arrive at determining *what* we take to ourselves as sustenance, say *bread and wine*. Receiving, accepting, grasping, comprehending an idea is then analogous to ingesting this food and drink; pursuing the analogy, we might say that considering the idea, mulling it over, analysing it, is the chewing phase in which our teeth and tongue of discrimination analyse the delicacies on the plate and the palate of the mind preparatory to climactic swallowing – the moment of truth when the idea enters the body, becoming, after the process of digestion, one flesh with our flesh, the progression of faith's hunger fulfilled in love's identity; this train of thought is surely a more active and involved perception than merely seeing (6:36). For it is a doing – victual inference. The grasp of faith, the holding dear of what we have taken to ourselves, absorbed and assimilated to ourselves as part of our own bodies, is a richer identification than mere seeing, which in this context (because for Aristotle, as previously noted, the insight of theory is, in fact, also a *touching*) is thought to maintain the critical distance required of a contemplative attitude. In conclusion, grasping this incarnate idea, we incorporate it into our bodies and consequently live the life that the nourishment of this insight sustains – eternal life (6:47), i.e. the life the scope of which extends beyond that in which the immediacy of the *body*-mentality holds sway.

But then, to top it off, we hear that the "bread of God is he who comes down from heaven and gives life to the world" (6:33). "He?" This statement might be considered the rhetorical flourish of a teacher's enthusiasm, promising with regards to his doctrine, "whoever comes to me shall never hunger, whoever believes in me shall never thirst" (6:35). But then the speaker before us elaborates in a startling turn of words, "*I* am the living bread come down from heaven (6:51)...whoever feeds on my flesh and drinks my blood has eternal life and I will raise him up on the last day."(6:54) What is he saying? If he is the incarnation of the ΛΟΓΟΣ, then, in the logic of this formulation, to reflect critically in the spirit of the Word is to embrace, to take and partake of the Word itself, so that it and the distinguished life it embodies, might "enter" our minds, even as food that we have eaten enters our bodies and "becomes" our flesh. And since this is distinguished food, "super" food, and not the processed food and drink of normalcy – the typical fast food of Man – the Word says, "my flesh is this food and my blood is this drink" (6:55); in other words, to "feed" (ΤΡΩΓΩ) on this "person" of the ΛΟΓΟΣ is to engage in the activity of critical reflection that the ΛΟΓΟΣ – God and the Word of God – is. This is not the same as "imitating" Christ in our lives; it is not enough to say that Jesus's behavior, his precepts and actions offer us "models" or "examples" of how we should and should not behave in similar situations in our own lives. The distinction of human being, in Christian terms, is to undergo the experience of transformation that the life of the Son of God is a record of, and ourselves to actually taste the very life of the Word of God. It is for this reason that the Word concludes his train of thought about the practice of pure reason by saying "if you don't eat the flesh of the Son of Man and drink his blood, you have no life in you." (6:53)

And this is no longer figurative language, it is the work of thought, the Builder in which the message of the Gospel is realized; doing the critical work of pure reason, experiencing ourselves this work upon ourselves and upon our lives, *is* the life and the death and the life of the Word...and ours as well who have learned how to put the matter of our distinguishing ourselves from ourselves in these thought-provoking terms. And it is alone this doing of the truth – a truth first and foremost *to be done* and then to be spoken and enjoyed with the relish of discernment – that we are served and invited to partake of by the wisdom of the Second Epoch. Dark, rich, sweet, but not cloyingly so – this food for thought alone is rightfully called *divinity*.

What is striking above all in the Gospel of John is the lesson and the message of humility that pure reason acknowledges and celebrates in works done in the spirit of the Word.[76] The person of the Word before us, a voice in a desert of life long bereft of all the traditional gods of antiquity in their former majestic simplicity and now distending into a wasteland of pretence, false piety, empty forms of ritual and vaguely numinous verbiage, the hypocritical hype of holy men – in this apparently so unfavourable climate for the mind, the pure spirit is suddenly lifted up upon a staff like a serpent in the wilderness (3:14), like a spring for drinking and washing that flows up the mountain, like a beacon of light flaring across centuries in language still legible, still audible, however faintly, even today, truly an unearthly language – and as was said then, we affirm and reaffirm all the more now of its speaker, "Never has a man spoken before like this man."

Pure reason, the contemplator, the governor, the builder of the dwellings of being, though having every right to be proud of itself, must learn the gentle lesson of kindness and service and submit to becoming the subject of its own law, distinguishing itself from itself, losing itself in order to be found and grasping its gift in the experience of being given, the wisdom of recipience – as opposed to the mundane spirit that makes the majesty of its destiny into an idol of its own conceit and urge to lord; in contrast, the gift of the holy spirit is, rather, to reawaken gratitude in recognition of favour; though the king, *our* king and lord, pure reason must have been the servant first, a servant to its *Self*, who is, in fact, its father, its elder and its better, the

---

[76] Augustine recognized humilitas as the essential distinction of the self-several Godhead of the Trinity, namely the mission (missio) and submission (subjectio) of the Son in his obedience to the will of the Father. As Boeder explains in *Das Bauzeug der Geschichte*, p. 335: "It is precisely this *subjectio* of the Mediator that overcomes the *superbia* of creation's first spirit, elevating thus the *humilitas* to the highest *virtus* of the *imago*."

principle of its glory and the endowment of deity that makes of the ΛΟΓΟΣ, in spite of its having made the start "in the beginning," the second comer, the Word and the Son of God, God *in person* because in deed upon decisive deed, God in action among us, in us. This human being of deity, ordained to become, in the subsequent Epoch, the celebratory Builder of poetic imagination, knows already, here as the distinguished tragic Actor in the practice of its purity, the secret of its destiny revealed in the words of the prophet who, a voice in that dilating desert of indifference, proclaims: "Make way!" (Mat 3:3)

Does this make sense? Does it make sense to say that in Christian terms regarding the distinction of human being as repentance and the renewal of our spirit, in the experience of pure reason as our passage and our transformation, our conversion and transfiguration, mercy follows judgment, life follows death, exaltation follows submission and to rule we must serve? If this makes any sense at all, then let us take it as the quintessential message of the Gospel of a baptised, and in this sense, distinguished spirit, namely the one that has been dipped, washed in the waters of the profound insight proclaimed by the prophet in the openness of his desert confession and celebratory testimony of self-effacement:

Ο ΟΠΙΣΩ ΜΟΥ ΕΡΧΟΜΕΝΟΣ ΕΜΠΡΟΣΘΕΝ ΜΟΥ ΓΕΓΟΝΕΝ
ΟΤΙ ΠΡΩΤΟΣ ΜΟΥ ΗΝ

Coming after me, he precedes me, who was before me. (John 1:15)

THE FIRST EPOCH – THE JUST BEING
OF DESTINY

131. The Seen behind the Seens

What's left? Having studied the principles of *humanity* and *deity*, what else is there? After that of human being and divine being, there is only one principle left, that of *being* itself, pure and simple – the principle of *entity*. That would mean that the entity of identity is not merely self-knowing in the way that *I AM* who knows myself as self-severally distinguished in myself and from myself through the freedom of human nature, nor merely in the way that *You* (not you!) have been known and recognized by God, knowing and recognizing yourself to be loved by Him as His Son and therefore one with Him in His absolute transcendence of the world, in His power, but also turned towards the world, towards us, in His gracious will, i.e. in the distinguished spirit of love that transforms us into the children of His glory and the world into the community of the Kingdom of Heaven, their dwelling. No, the self-relativity of the entity of identity is known and properly addressed not merely as *Mine*, nor as *Yours*, but rather also as *Its*, a being of *theoretical* science and study, a *truth*, rather than a being of the *poetic* subject, bringing forth the reality of My ideal, a supreme *fiction*, or the *practical* experience of transfiguring glory, an *endeavor* pursued in accordance with the Holy Spirit that is the enduring advocate of God's will in the world. Intuitively speaking, when considering what the greatest and most intriguing causes are that have piqued pure reason's wonder, it seems that *Humanity*, *God*, and *Being* pretty well collect into three simple designations the metaphysical principles that have determined, once and for all time, the scheme of all things thought. Or is there any topic a philosopher must fear to have neglected that does not fall into one of the three renowned categories of spirited building – namely that of Art, Religion, and Science – devoted to the issue of those three aforesaid principles? It doesn't seem likely, does it? At any rate, after having studied the principle of pure reason in its works of invention, its actions of distinction, and in the objects of its contemplation, it will be time to call it a day in philosophy and to take a break, to go for a walk, say, or a swim, and then obey the call of the night, rising early and refreshed to start again, to reprise, to review, and to renew, starting from scratch, what just last night seemed finished and definitive.

Summarizing, we have thus far, in the Third Epoch of our cultural tradition, ascended the bright Heaven of thought's invention in our *imagination*, performed, in the Second Epoch, the work of the *divine will* with sacred ardor, and now have one more task to complete in our quest to grasp the entire extent and proportion of reason's achievement, namely, in the First epoch, to acquaint ourselves with the insightful brilliance of thought in its keenest *penetration* towards the discovery of the hidden core and depths of things, seeing through skin-deep appearances and discerning how it *truly* is, glimpsing below the specious surface, behind the "orthodox opinions" (ΟΡΘΗ ΔΟΞΑ), as Plato calls them, of mortal preoccupation with extraneous and incidental detail, towards *substance* rather than accidence, towards profound *knowledge* as opposed to superficial personal *views*, towards *principles* as opposed to perspectives, towards *thoughts* as opposed to mere sensory perception, towards the *miracle* of the human rational impulse that suddenly begins to look and see, look and wonder with eyes awakened from the snooze of assuming and disregard that an all too familiar familiarity breeds.

For one day the human mind arose from its embedment in the sediments of necessities and the busyness of our workaday occupations and went out and took a breath and took a look at the phenomenal world as a whole or some part of it and asked, "What is the *substance*, the *essence* of the whole and the relationship, the ΛΟΓΟΣ, of its parts?" "Why is it thus and not differently?" "What is the reason for its having come to be the way it is?" These questions ask about the **nature** of a being, about the **cause** of being and of beings. They want to know about the **reasons** and the reason for the presence of what is present to the attentive minding of intellect that has, for a moment at least, decided to enjoy a respite from Man's cares, private and public, and then, on such a holy day of leisure, with unencumbered contemplation and in simple admiration, take note of the whole and the part and their relationships and ask not so much "*Why not?*" – a question that appeals to the imagination of the ideal and the issue of the Third Epoch – but rather simply "*Why?*" There are many beings and many reasons and causes for their being the way they are in particular. But what is the principle of the whole that governs their being in general?

Consider the philosophy inherent in questions – *what is it? Why, how, where, when?* They are the inception of the search and quest for the solid foundation and they spark the *anamnesis* of thought, another renowned notion of Platonic ΓΥΜΝΑΣΙΑ, *gymnastics* in the art and craft of a method, a dialectic that looks for and finds reasons to give (ΛΟΓΟΝ ΔΙΔΟΝΑΙ), and can bring to the light of day the principle of what has been assumed and taken for granted but forgotten in the ordering of human affairs and values. Socrates is said to have developed this method of recollection, which asks, "*what is it?*" (ΤΙ ΕΣΤΙ) and then by exploring and refuting the tenability of suggested attempts at justification of a particular view (ΕΛΕΝΧΟΣ), leading the discussion to insight into one's own ignorance (ΑΠΟΡΙΕ) of the principles upon which these views are based, which is the first result on the way to knowledge (ΕΠΙΣΤΗΜΗ) and insight as *distinct from, prior to*, and *beyond*, mere plausibility of opinion – the soul's way of recollection (ΑΝΑΜΕΣΙΣ) that is also the way of the "disclosing" relation (ΑΛΕΤΗΕΙΑ) of truth, the whole and essential truth of a being's "being," i.e. *what it is*, that becomes manifest at the end of this train of thought, of distinguished thought – and thus the *soul* train if you will – called *dialectic*.

We have come to understand the practice and discipline of thought as the stepping out of our bubble of trouble, our mundane cave of cares and personal concerns, stepping back from the unexamined life of hardened habits; we have seen thought as the light of distinction entering into our lives and calling us to follow it to its glorious source and origin, which is the thought *before* thought, the *being before*, the principle, thought come from a further, a "father" thought, receiving its purpose as its own, as its father's one and only son – this cognate thought is then thought to be as close to us as it is to the absolute principle of distinction, which is the light that sent the light on the mission of distinction and conversion, touching us deeply and renewing our world. In the first intuition of this experience, we who leave the cave, enter the light of thought on the outside of our previous lives; in the second intuition, the kingdom of the light of thought comes close to us in its mercy and with its human face awakens, opens our human hearts to compassion, preparing them for the reception of the gift of thoughtful resurrection. Now, in the understanding of the Greeks, we are drawn by thought itself, our rational destiny, into the seclusion of the intellect to contemplate the *cause* and the *principle*, the *essence* and the *substance*, of a matter – all terms for the penetration of insight and the theoretical activity of reason that is distinct from superficial seeing, from the lackadaisical looks we throw at what is at hand in the manner of merely mortal apprehension, as Parmenides calls it, which tends to cultivate a cursory view of things.

The contemplative thirst of theory is, in contrast, not so easily slaked, not yet appeased with the sleek show of things, their ostentations and finalities, nor satisfied with indifferent descriptions of the minutiae of matters as they make florid appearance to a listless mortal gaze; no, keen contemplation wants to see perspicaciously and know the first reasons and, in giving the explanation, ascertain *why* the way things present themselves cannot be otherwise. For knowing the *why's* and *wherefore's* is harder, not being obvious to the glint of a merely peeping eyeball. With regards to THE WAY IT IS, thoughts, ideas emerge as what is above and beyond, before or after the sphere of tangible immediacy, i.e. in the realm of *intangibles*, namely that of reason, and of reasons; with them we begin to set forth an order of names for what departs from this immediacy, placing these intangibles thus in a larger framework of being as cause, ground, substance, consequence, purpose, goal...Look at a situation and discover what is present to insight without actually being in sight, namely that situation's cause, the purposes, the conditions that led to what has arisen and come to our rapt attention. *Condition* – this is a name of pure reason not only for THE WAY IT IS but also for the outside of the circle of what is accessible to a cursory glance, namely the *basis* and the *principle*, the *cause* to given effects, the *consequences* that follow from more remote causes; these and similar terms for what grounds and founds a state of affairs take us further than where we are with the status quo; they invoke departure and suggest that what is beyond the ken of this and that is nevertheless connected to this or that, more, that this or that is defined in this connection alone as truly, and not merely apparently, *being*.

TI ΕΣΤΙΝ? (What is it? What is its essence?) – this is the Greek question *par excellence*. The essence of something is not obvious. The crux of the matter is hidden under the glaze and the glitter, off the beaten track, out of the way, in the shadows of a netherworld that our ordinary languid peering cannot so easily broach with its eye-beams. Not content with just seeing what is happening, we look behind the seens, behind the phenomena as they present themselves and try to get to the bottom of things. In the sphere of theory where the distinction that pure reason makes is no longer taken personally, the gap between THE WAY IT IS and THE WAY IT SHOULD BE is no longer a *moral* imperative regarding the principle of human action, nor is it *aesthetic* judgment regarding the realization of the ideal based on the generative principle of humanity, but rather conceptual – the experience of this distinction is such that we are not actors, enacting or executing given laws, fulfilling or failing to fulfill them as the will of God, nor are we builders realizing the laws and principles of freedom in the formation of ourselves and our state. As scientists and thinkers, the laws want to be discovered as the laws and nature of individual beings; for in this context it is the power of insightful perception to come to see and to know what a being was meant to be – the *idea* of a particular being is that being's being with regards to which it is more or less perfect, more or less perfectly *what it is* (supposed to be). In the First Epoch, this is not primarily an ethical question but rather one posed by the intellect because the drama of the discrepancy between beings and what they are (meant to be) is an issue determined in the discernment of contemplation rather than in the decisions of practice, but can, of course, be applied to practice as well to the extent that each being is active with regards to its principle, rising and falling in natural development or, as a product of invention, serving the purpose of the artisan's design, which is beauty as well and not merely utility.

It is in this sphere of science that we note the great wealth of distinctions that folks with discriminating minds use in their analysis, in other words, when thinking about things with a view to better understanding them, speaking not only of purposes and causes, outcomes and ramifications but also of red threads and invariants, universals and norms, parts of wholes and orders of elements – all terms relating now not so much to our *doings* but rather to something under investigation, some particular that we observe as *being* something, in general or as a rule, with respect to which each has its own character or difference, the properties which are its features, some defining and substantial, some contingent and accidental – determining what each thing's inherent and intrinsic distinction is, in contrast to what is merely fortuitous and accessory to it, is precisely the challenge of thought, the Thinker, to recognize and then declare in the familiar form of a logical proposition in which a predicate is affirmed (or denied) of a subject: *B is A.*

In an annotation to Hegel's discourse about essence (Wesen) in his *Cycles of Philosophical Sciences* (Enzyklopädie der philosophischen Wissenschaften in Grundriss (1830), Erster Teil, Die Wissenschaft der Logik, §21, Zusatz, p. 27), we read:

> Man bemerkt Blitz und Donner. Wir nehmen diese Erscheinungen wahr. Aber der Mensch gibt sich mit der Bekanntschaft der sinnlichen Erscheinungen nicht zufrieden, sondern will dahinter kommen, will sie begreifen, will den Grund wissen, warum es so ist und nicht anders, d.h. warum es so sein muss. Also die Frage, die das unmittelbar Vorfindliche verlassen will und zum Ursprung drängt... Das Sinnliche ist ein Einzelnes und Verschwindendes – das Dauernde darin lernen wir durch das Nachdenken kennen, welches die Bewegung, den Zug zum Wesen hat. Wir sehen eine unendliche Menge einzelnen Gestalten und Erscheinungen – wir haben das Bedürfnis in diese Mannigfalt Einheit zu bringen. Wir vergleichen, erkennen eine Regel, das Allgemeine, das Prinzip. Das Nachdenken sucht nach dem Festen, Bleibenden, Insichbestimmten und dem das Besondere Regierenden.

> *Human being sees lightning and thunder. We perceive these apparitions but human being is not satisfied with familiarity borne of sensory experience, and desires to get at the heart of the matter, to comprehend what is perceived, wants to know the reason why it is thus and not differently, i.e. why it must be so. Thus to question is to strive to depart from what immediacy encounters and to penetrate to the origin...sensory experience is of particulars and is ephemeral – what endures in these we learn through thought that moves towards, has an urge for, essence. We see an infinite mass of individual shapes and appearances – we desire to bring unity into this plurality. We compare, we recognize the rule, the universal, the principle. Thought searches for what is constant, immutable, determined within itself, for what governs the particulars.*

The heart and the substance, the rule and the principle, have to be found, apprehended by the perceptive mind; they are the result of observation and investigation and thus stand at the end of a long journey of search that leads its traveler into the realm of darkness accessible only to the penetration of insight, closed however to mere superficial sight that is accustomed to the variegated and gaudy promiscuity of the great, buzzing bloom of confusion around us. In comparison to this sensational glare and splashing of impressions, the intangible realm of reasons and essences can only be termed dark, still, quiet, closed, secluded, apart, withdrawn – a nether-realm apparently destined for those who have therefore, as much as possible, died to this world:

> ...huic saeculo moriuntur, quantum possunt.
> (Augustinus, *De doctrina christiana*, II. 11)

Clearly they have chosen the road less taken, an inward and a downward road, the road of reason.

These terms suggest that, again, as we have seen in the other two epochs, the experience of distinction, as it is understood now in Greek thought as that of *theory*, is, initially at least, not entirely attractive to or even compatible with the ordinary sensibility of Man, our sensational and nevertheless entirely mundane affairs and environments. On the contrary. It is an entirely different sort of thought and spirit, a *distinguished* one that is willing and able to separate itself from the more immediate concerns of cognition and turn an inward and downward, a forward and upward, an otherworldly eye upon those flowing, fleeting, flickering impressions that glut our quick takes and blinks, our goggling squinches, the bug-eyed oglings, such a bright eye of mind namely as has, for the sake of truth, distinguished itself from sensation-encumbered sight.

132. The Journey to Truth

The literary pendant to Plato's allegory of the escape from the cave can be thus seen in the equally famous descent into the netherworld that introduces Parmenides' exposition of the perfection of being. Already Hegel recognized in Parmenides the first metaphysical thinker of Western cultural tradition. This Elean philosopher gave expression to the conception of the distinction between what is and what should be and, in brooking this span with the impassioned passage that he envisioned as the drive for **truth**, comprehended for the first time the reality and perfection, the *being*, of pure thought as a unique entity of identity, completely defined by and determined in the self-relativity of that which is, therefore, the "same in the same and so remaining there fixedly the selfsame." (DK 28 B 8.29-30) This relationship of consummate being reposed in and in accordance with itself in the fixity of its own repletion and unbroken entirety was visualized by Parmenides in the ponderability of a sphere that manifests proportions of perfection within its scope from the center of the sphere to the curved globe of its all-encompassing perimeter, from the bodying forth of its well-rounded soundness to the unifying pinpoint of its nucleus.

Here is Parmenides' narrative of the inception of the train of thought into the seclusion of insight where our sincere desire to know is destined to discover the whole truth about its own entity of identity as manifested by a line of reasoning that conclusively demonstrates the incontrovertible determination of being:

> The mares that carry me as far as heart reaches, sent me, leading me along the way of distinction, having set out upon it, along the way of insight. Upon this way, I was carried, for along it forwarded me the mares of thought, pulling the massive chariot – the sun-maids revealed the way.
>
> The axle in the naves shriek, blazing hot – for it was driven on in haste by two whirling wheels on either side, as the daughters of radiance, who previously had left the house of night towards light, throw back, with their hands, the veils from their heads, constantly speed their train further onward.
>
> There loom large the gates of the paths of night and day, with an architrave of lintels and a sill of stone, the ethereal pylon, filled out with two great doors, to which many-measured Retribution (**ΔΙΚΗ**), wields the fitting keys. To her, the maidens addressed gentle words of entreaty, persuading her after due consideration to open now the gates and allow them to pass through with chariot and mare...
>
> The Goddess received me there hospitably, took my hand with her right, greeted me and spoke the following words: "Young man, companion of immortal charioteers! You who have been borne by the mares and now have reached my house, welcome and be glad! It is not the doom of death that has guided you along the way to this destination, a way that has taken you far afield from the ordinary path of human being, but rather the edict of destiny (**ΘΕΜΙΣ ΤΕ ΔΙΚΗ ΤΕ**). It is therefore appropriate that you should apprehend the whole – on the one hand, the

steady heart of persuasive truth, on the other hand, the conjectures of mortals in which there is no veritable assurance. Nevertheless also these are to be learned and how such conceits properly permeate totality entirely. (DK 28 B1.1-32).

In this dark world, Parmenides is greeted cordially as one who has arrived, but not back home – in fact as far away as possible from familiar haunts – nevertheless, he has arrived at a destination predetermined by the providence of a guiding, onward urging principle that has distinguished him as being destined to acquire complete knowledge, which includes not only insight into the unshakable heart of the whole truth but also an understanding of the deceptive conjecture that mortals are wont to indulge in. How do these two objects of knowledge differ? They differ in their ΠΙΣΤΙΣ (pistis), i.e. in their power of persuasion, for the latter lacks the "assurance of veracity" (ΠΙΣΤΙΣ ΑΛΗΘΗΣ – B1.30)

And which power of persuasion does the goddess who welcomes him emphasize as regards the truth of her exposition? She terms it a "much-contested refutation" (ΠΟΛΥΔΗΡΙΝ ΕΛΕΓΧΟΝ – B7.5) and it is aimed at moving the hearer of her arguments towards a decisive insight which distinguishes two disjunctively related ways of thought, and then these two from another, all three of which are as mutually exclusive as *to be* and *not to be*, as incisively distinct as is the mortals' knowing nothing save their own conjecture from the knowledgeable wayfarer who has been given to learn and to know such as is beyond all debate and the meandering of the mortals' course and discourses (B1.27).

Neither does the goddess' method cajole her interlocutor, comforting him with the blandishments of words, nor does she make suave lecture or invite discussion, nor even encourage the airing of divergent points of view on the part of her audience upon the matter in question. Eschewing thus a conversational tone, she develops, instead, a rigorous train of thought to bestir and arouse the agreement and assent of insight in them who were meant and sent to attend her way, and to receive proofs (ΣΗΜΑΤΑ – B8.2) in the course of her demonstration of the *one and only* feasible way of thought remaining to rigorous and vigorous reflection after having departed from the avenues of the world of the mortals' opinion (B8.1-2), a departure, however, not in the manner of the "doom of ill-fated mortality, but rather as is their right and destiny" (ΟΥΤΙ ΣΕ ΜΟΙΡΑ ΚΑΚΗ…ΑΛΛΑ ΘΕΜΙΣ ΤΕ ΔΙΚΗ ΤΕ - B1.26-28). It is the power of ΠΕΙΘΩ (peith) that sanctions the force of her argument, a force not of violence or threat but rather of appeal that attracts and welcomes thought graciously and invites it in, wishing well in greeting "be glad" (XAIPE - B1.27)! For this is the favour of insight that is following a train of thought, having been carried away (from the mortal mentality) by pure reason, and carried into the issue of truth; let us call this captivated transport of the mind *inference* – thought moved by thought to join, to follow, to come and see, and then to decide for itself THE WAY IT IS, really and truly. In particular she authorizes inference through the method of giving reasons, of proffering arguments such as invite agreement and the concord of thought with thought, the self-relativity of pure reason with respect to its principle as can be established on their logical foundations.

She demands that this ΛΟΓΟΣ alone, its moving train of thought that fills us with the determination of inference and speeds us on the way of our destiny to her house and the issue of truth, be our only guide, i.e. the logic of the impartial mind that has left behind the play of competing bodies of opinion, the beaten path of their lived experience, the self-centered concerns of meretricious surface worldliness. What is the truth she reveals? Parmenides reports her words thus:

> Come now, I shall speak and you, you will take to heart the words you hear, which ways alone are to be thought. The one way – THE WAY IT IS and THE WAY IT IS NOT IS NOT TO BE; this is conviction's way, conviction namely accompanies truth; the other way – THE WAY IT IS NOT and THE WAY IT IS NECESSARILY TO BE IS NOT TO BE. This road, I say, is utterly closed to experience; for neither will you apprehend non-being, nor say it – a road to nowhere... for the same is (to be) thought and to be. (B2-B3)

The decidedly established and absolutely determined distinction between these two ways is her essential message. The terms of her proof are, as we will come to learn, first that *being* excludes *non-being*, i.e. $\neg(A \wedge \neg A)$, in other words, "A and not-A are impossible," which is the *law of contradiction*, secondly, that there is no third term or coalition between them, i.e. $A \vee \neg A$, in other words, "A or not A", which is the *law of excluded middle* and finally, that being is identical to itself, $A=A$, i.e. the self-relationship of "A being the same as A", which is called the *principle of identity*. These are three laws or formulations of the principle that pure reason posits as its determination in the First Epoch; but notice the difference in how the authority and the power of these "laws" are understood in the first epoch; it is not the *conscience of human nature* or the Son of the Father of glory on his *mission of divine light* that speaks to our heart immediately, the former in *feeling* and the latter in *revelation* but rather, in the element of Greek thought, the *recognition* of what is self-evident, the **directive of predetermination**, in other words, an absolutely prior, previously decided, and irrefutably established principle – thought that has discovered in itself the energy of argument is now called upon, compelled even, to acknowledge incontrovertible rules of principle, the priority of laws that evince the capacity to touch and determine our intelligence, to win our agreement through no external constraint or force but rather through the self-determination of reason itself, alone through the providence of arguments, imparting form to its self-relationship by our own action of thought, a train of thought that leads us inexorably to a conclusion – thought leading thought to thought, to insight. These laws are not merely taken in the abstraction of logical formulas, as axioms in a catalogue of tautologies, but rather vividly presented in a revelation of reality and a specific context of particulars of that reality – sun-maidens, the vocation of a traveler, a chariot, mares, a forbidding gateway of stone and iron, a plea for admittance, a hand of greeting, a teaching voice – depicting thought on its way to what will suffice the demands of unshakeable conviction. But the order of a train of thought is not the voice of the heart nor the voice and the Word of God but rather the order in the scheme of things thought, in a line of reasoning, the order that reveals itself in these things simply by the way things are; when we say that something is logical, we are simply saying: "that's the way it is, the way it always has been, the way always will be." This is the recognition, more, the acknowledgement, of a prior determination. We have learned why giving one's assent to a principle is so difficult for those bent on looking out for number one. In the First Epoch, the beginning of wisdom is not God-fearing spirit but rather regard for the precedent determination of THE WAY IT SHOULD BE, the recipience of *destiny*.

Destiny? If destiny is not God or Freedom, what sort of principle is it? This principle of THE WAY IT IS tells us what is *right* and *proper*, what is *just*; it says: this is the way things are and this is the way things should be, this is the way things are done here, this is what you have to do...*end of discussion* – a standpoint of such objectivity, such impartiality is obviously a very uncomfortable one to deal with for those who prefer to take things personally, as subjective, as debatable, as provisional; this standpoint, however, does not refuse to entertain doubt or to do away with debate; indeed, there is much to be argued about regarding the IS and the OUGHT in a particular situation; but the wisdom of the Greeks teaches us that however controversial particular issues may be, at some point, we are forced to recognize a premise upon which subsequent argumentation is based, an antecedent agreement which we must take for granted as a matter of fact, as a matter of course, in order to pursue our disagreement; in other words, we must have already admitted a principle in order to go about questioning and seeking principles. Every question is founded upon a prior answer that has already been taken for granted in the question. The inaugural recognition of the absolute priority of the principle, the *principle of the principle*, expresses its acknowledgement of *being before all thought*, in the words of the Parmenidean goddess to the effect that "*that's the way it is.*"

Why, is this not the very principle inherent in the idea of tradition and custom! Yes, indeed it is. And in Greek thought, surprisingly, we find that this being such as is determined by and recognized in the primacy of custom is the one into which thought gains insight and with respect to which it learns to distinguish itself as pure reason in recognition of the ultimate and absolutely original premises that we must take for granted for there to be any subsequent train of thought. How often does Aristotle repeat this idea in demonstrating thought's repugnance to infinite regression (ΕΙΣ ΑΠΕΙΡΟΝ ΙΕΝΑΙ [ΒΑΔΙΕΙΤΑΙ] – e.g. Met. 994a3, 20, b3, 1000b28, 1006a8, 1007b1, 1010a20, 1012a13, 1012b22, 1022b9, 1030b35, 1041b22, 1060a36, 1068a33, 1070a1, 1074a29; Nic. Eth. 1094a, 1097b,1113a, Physics 242a.34) – which, as we are saying, exhibits the impotence of a Cyclopic mind arrogantly unwilling to recognize a principle and *look, learn, grasp* first what is prior to it and in this chain of beings founded upon beings, to recognize that there is one, the principle, that moves all the others as it itself moves in infinite rotation around its focal point, a further principle, the principle of the principle, that is the cause of its own circumambulation, that ultimate being that inspires its desire, the circumvolution of volition, but which is itself unmoved, though, for all that, not in being heartless or stagnant or latent, but rather, as the entity of identity that is self-knowing being, in the undivided attention, in the quiet energy, the still contemplation and continuous enjoyment of itself as the best of all beings; this pure being of theoretical reason, having proven itself to be the greatest and the best of all beings, is therefore the being most worthy of the superlative predicate ΘΕΟΣ.

Aristotle makes this point about the primacy of principle with regards to the starting point of all science, learning, and study – Greek terms for the experience of *recipience*, the taking for granted of the premise, the matter of fact, as it pertains to theory – in the introduction to his *Posterior Analytics* stating that "all teachings and scientific doctrines must begin with a previously determined insight." (71a1-2):

ΠΑΣΑ ΔΙΔΑΣΚΑΛΙΑ ΚΑΙ ΠΑΣΑ ΜΑΘΗΣΙΣ ΔΙΑΝΟΗΤΙΚΕΚ ΠΡΟ
ΥΠΑΡΧΟΥΣΗΣ ΓΙΝΕΤΑΙ ΓΝΩΣΕΩΣ

In other words, science begins upon a principle that knowledge does not posit in and of itself but rather receives and acknowledges as its proper antecedent, which is, therefore, prior to the accomplishment of insight and thus "of necessity always already decided" and determined and therein determinate in the way that it is. (DK 28 B 8.15)

KEKPITAI Δ ' OYN ΩΣΠΕΡ ΑΝΑΝΚΗ

Later in the poem, Parmenides' goddess powerfully contrasts this way of thought's logical distinction with such thinking as is engaged in the immediacy and indeterminacy of lived experience, drawing an equally vivid picture of it and the cave dwellers' point of view who are one-eyed inhabitants of the shadows – but not the shadow-world that is thought's profundity and peace; who are servants of the night – but not the night that is thought's intellect and insight. She vituperates these enervated, merely mortal minds harshly thus:

> Two-faced vagrants with an impotent heart bent on vagary, dumb-struck fools, as purblind as they are inarticulate, a promiscuous crop (B6.5), ...driven by multifarious routine onto the beaten track of sightless eyes' dispense and the echoes of resonating ears and tongues (B7.3-5),...positing, on the one hand, in their credulity, either mere names for mutation, becoming and decay, to be, as much as not to be, and then again names for switching places and the exchange of shiny surfaces (B8.38-41)...on the other hand,...positing names of two forms (going astray therein for one of them should not be), separating opposite bodies and establishing marks for them, each apart from the other (B8 53-56),...setting them up into a pretty array of words, deceptive to hear." (B8.52).

And she admonishes us urgently against this travesty in the name of her superbly vigorous intellect saying: "Let not habit in the profusion of inarticulate experience drag you along this route!" (B7.3)

ΜΗΔΕ Σ ' ΕΘΟΣ ΠΟΛΥΠΕΙΡΟΝ ΟΔΟΝ ΚΑΤΑ ΤΗΝΔΕ ΒΙΑΣΘΩ

For only this first way, that of distinguished thought, leads us to insight into the self-relativity of thought, recognizes such being as corresponds to the logical claim and calling of pure reason.

This train of thought, understood as a guided way, a method and persuasive concatenation of arguments, shows being, at first, as constrained by its own defining arguments. The exclusion of non-being must eliminate all change and motion in being, forcing it to stay still, to be susceptible neither to birth nor to demise, neither to growth nor to decay – these are conclusions drawn from the premise of the argument, are inferences that lead thought logically, guiding the way, step-by-step, to the determinacy of being, to a being of particular properties that correspond to the constraints which the premise and the logic of the argumentation have placed on the conclusion and in this way have predetermined as the issue of insight pursuant to that line of reasoning – along this way of verification, reason is subjected to the discipline that critical thought has established as the premise of the argument, distinguishing itself from the habitual way of thinking so pervasive in the hybrid, assimilating world of men for whom ΕΡΟΣ (Eros) was first contrived (B13), "the uncritical race of Man in which being and non-being are presumed...," to fuse or intermingle, i.e. "...to be the same and not the same and all roads double back." (B6.7-9)

> ...ΑΚΡΙΤΑ ΦΥΛΑ ΟΙΣ ΤΟ ΠΕΛΕΙΝ ΤΕ ΚΑΙ ΟΥΚ ΕΙΝΑΙ ΤΑΥΤΟΝ
> ΝΕΝΟΜΙΣΤΑΙ ΚΟΥ ΤΑΥΤΟΝ ΠΑΝΤΩΝ ΔΕ ΠΑΛΙΝΤΡΟΠΟΣ
> ΕΣΤΙ ΚΕΛΕΥΘΟΣ

Let us now consider her arguments, her signs, her proofs that demonstrate the properties of the one and only being that can determine for insight the issue of its own proper dwelling, even as the train of thought would only attain its destination and come to rest in the verification of such being as conforms to the inherent necessity with which the predetermined impetus of its principle guides the progress of its substantiation in the ΛΟΓΟΣ of pure thought:

> It was not at one time, nor will be, since it is now, all together, one, continuous. For what origin will you look for of it? Where would it have increased to? Where from? I shall not let you say nor think that it comes out of non-being; for what is not cannot be said nor thought. Besides, what possible need could have urged it, having started from nothing, to be born later rather than before? Therefore *justness* (ΔΙΚΗ) has not let it free, loosening its fetters to originate or decay, but rather holds them fast...For how could being be subsequent, how could it originate? For it IS NOT [was not previously] if it originated once and it IS NOT [now] if it is to originate in the future. Thus the origin is expunged and its destruction inconceivable...nor is it

divisible, for it is a whole and homogenous; it is not on any one spot more, which might keep it from holding together, nor less; it is, instead, entire – being is replete with being. Therefore it is a totality, continuous – for being cleaves to being. And so, without movement, in the bonds of immense chains, it remains without beginning, without ending, since generation and destruction have been driven away; *true conviction* (ΠΙΣΤΙΣ ΑΛΗΘΗΣ) has flung them afar...Staying both the same and in the same, it lies by itself and stays thus fixedly on the same spot. For powerful *necessity* (ΑΝΑΓΚΗ) holds it in chains of a limit which shuts it in all around; wherefore it is *fitting* (ΘΕΜΙΣ) that being should not be incomplete. For it is without lack; whereas if it were lacking, it would lack all...neither is there, nor will there be anything outside of being, since this is what *destiny* (ΜΟΙΡΑ) has bound to be whole and without movement...And so, since there is a furthest limit, it is, from every direction, perfect like the bulk of a well-rounded sphere, from the center equally in all directions. (28 B8.1-44)

Reason becomes evident in the being of its destination, realizes itself at the terminus of the said way, namely in the image and the simile of the rotundity of the well-rounded sphere upon which the goddess completes her argument, the object and the issue of her doctrine and demonstration; for even unto such likens she perfect being. And seen thus, namely neither growing nor dying, neither born (B 8.3) nor spent, neither started (8.27) nor stopped, not still to be perfected (8.4) and imperfect (8.32), nor otherwise in need (8.33), being neither no more, having been and already gone, nor not yet, going to be and becoming (8.5); unshakeable (8.4), immutable (8.26), there are now no longer chains and impediments which, as extraneous pales and constraining limits, gird and fix its station, but rather the self-relationship of the plenitude of pure being, the one (8.6), indivisible (8.22), coherent (8.6; 8.25), total and complete unity (8.5; 8.22), the integrity (8.4; 8.48) and the equality, the balance and the uniformity of **perfection** (ΤΕΤΕΛΕΣΜΕΝΟΝ - 8.42), as is simply, wholly and imperturbably (8.30), *there* (8.30), the same in the same (ΤΑΥΤΟΝ Τ'ΕΝ ΤΑΥΤΩΙ -8.29), resting, remaining (8.30) in these very selfsame limits of itself (ΠΕΙΡΑΣ ΠΥΜΑΤΟΝ - 8.42; 8.49), thereby being in itself neither stronger here or there nor weaker (8.44-45), nor more here or there, nor less (8.48), and thus in perfect and complete accordance with itself (ΚΑΘ ' ΕΑΥΤΟ ΤΕ - 8.29).

For all these "predicates" are its many signs, and moreover, that with which insight is to come to know it, experience won in adversity, having followed the Goddess's argument and heard her reasons upon the way of thought and speech to the issue of perfection. Here is Boeder's rendition of the tranquil sphere of being: "On the one hand, being is in equilibrium from the middle – the middle is obligation become an ingredient of being – to its own including limits; on the other hand, being sustains itself in the relationship to itself, not only to the middle, but moreover to it in communion with the corresponding limit, the correlatives. It is thus the relationship of unity: The first aspect recalls the elder clarification of EYNOMIA or 'well-ordered share' in the 'equality of apportionment.' The other calls to mind EIPHNH as the 'time of peace' clarified as HOMOTPOΠOΣ which brings to light the dimension of unity. Both are the sisters of ΔIKH and with her together summed up into the ripeness of being; its perfection makes evident what ΘEMIΣ is: Truth grounded in itself." [77] And it is here where we, following Parmenides to the end, realize the notion of HΣXYIA, the *tranquility* of perfect being that he is said to have learned from his teacher, the Pythagorean Ameinus Dochaites (Laertius Diogenes, *Lives and Opinions of eminent philosophers*, IX 21.7-8).

The *term of issue* (B) in the First Epoch of metaphysical thought is that of *perfection*, the completion of being and the peace and quiet that accompanies the fulfilled *destiny* (ΘEMIΣ), the *term of principle* (A), having passed through the tension of distinction which, in Parmenides, was seen as the bounds of being, the doom and the retribution of Justice (ΔIKH, MOIPA, ANAΓKH); this is the incisive character of cognizance that the mark of distinction between what should be and what should not places upon the indeterminate being of what is amorphous, undecided, confused, wandering – a discrepancy that sparks thought's quest for insight in *terms*

---

[77] So Boeder: "Zum einen ist das Seiende von der Mitte her – sie ist das in es eingegangene Verbindliche ausgewogen, gleichmäßig auf die es einschließenden eigenen Grenze bezogen; zum anderen hält es sich im Rückbezug auf sich, nicht auf die Mitte allein, sondern auf sie samt einer entsprechenden Grenze als die Bezogenen; so ist es das Verhältnis der Einigkeit. Ersteres erinnert an die alte Erläuterung EYNOMIA oder 'des guten Nehmen-lassens' mit der 'Gleichheit der Anteile'. Letzteres läßt an die EIPHNH oder die 'Friedenszeit' denken, von der es heißt, sie sei HOMOTPOΠOΣ (Pindar, *Olympien*, XIII 7), zeige also die Wendung der Einigkeit. Beide sind die Schwestern der ΔIKH und mit ΘEMIΣ ihr zusammen in jener 'Reife' des Seienden aufgehoben; seine Vollkommenheit macht offenkundig, was ist: die in sich gegründete Wahrheit." (*Topologie der Metaphysik*, p. 111).

of discernment (C), the discriminating (but not discriminatory) demonstration of the ΛΟΓΟΣ that in a line of reasoning guides our earnest desire to know along the way of true conviction. The destination of this journey to the heart of the matter of fact is the conclusion and culmination of logic's train of thought in a well-rounded vision of being, the accord of aseity that is pure thought's own self-knowledge and self-substantiation.

Perfect being is thus the term of issue in Parmenides' thought, in which the insight of reason, *theory*, feels at home having arrived at the dwelling and reality that is appropriate, fitting, right and, in this sense, in harmony with the necessity of its drive, after completing the journey and the searching, researching quest and having finally arrived at this one conclusive being that convinces thought, wins thought's commitment and dedication because of its predetermined self-evidence and cogency (it is won, one with insight), its own wholeness and permanence (it remains how it is in self-plenitude), its balance and precision (it is uniformly related to its limits), its unity and simplicity (it relates its center to its limits and its form to its core), its seclusion and distinction (staying far away from what is incongruous to itself, what it is not, namely non-being), its immobility and fidelity (staying put on its own spot), its identity and genuineness (in relationship to itself and one with itself) and its intimate, intrinsic consistency (staying the way it is and being what it was always meant to be). This being is pure reason's verification of the principle that, in the Greek Epoch of thought, governs even the father of the immortal gods.

133. Jovial Insight

Parmenides has taught us that reason is not "just a thought," for it has manifested itself to our powers of inference as undeniably being. But these powers of inference are in fact not "ours" at all – they are a train of thought, a chariot, a way, a divine calling even, that has fetched us and then, step by step, guided us to a conclusion as remarkable as it is inexorable. Thinking and being are one and the same. In perfect being, reason and being are unified because the persuasive power of the distinction between THE WAY IT IS and THE WAY IT IS NOT has won reason's probation and recognition as THE WAY IT SHOULD BE. The properties of perfect being are *logical, obvious, self-evident* because they express what reason is and knows and desires to bring to the "life" that being is for a thought which would otherwise be *just* a thought, a *mere* thought – is there anything less substantial than that? These properties are derived from reason itself, from reason's own "nature," revealing and fulfilling reason's destiny, for reason is the principle of the precedence, the resolution, and the determinacy of the *ΛΟΓΟΣ*. The perfection of being is the fruition of reason having completed its journey of inquiry, its record of the experience of discovery, and the accord ultimately manifested by simply being what it was meant to be and therefore, in fact, always already was – perfect, in and of itself.

If we consider our encounters with ΛΟΓΟΣ thus far in the culture of its tradition, we must say that, up to now, we have taken the matter of thought rather personally. In the languages of wisdom we have been studying, we have experienced thought as a person. And not just any person. In the third epoch it was *me, myself, and I*. The categorical imperative, for example, is a law and no extraneous one, but rather the law in me, *My* law who *I* is and myself *Am*, namely the Me I was meant to be. What could be more personal than I am to *MYSELF*, to my own humanity? Pure reason discovered the truth and the power of distinction that is inherent in our own self-knowing being; human nature – now that, my fellow humans, is indeed strikingly close to our heart, whether we think of human nature as our best heart, our HEART of hearts, or merely the better half of our person, our one and only *PERSONALITY*, that special part of the heart – call it the voice of conscience – that always speaks true and clear to unperverted, unaverted, unsubverted attention. The imperative of its ideal is interior, is the true *Me* in me that I have always wanted, always strived, to be, wanting and striving to be what I have always in my heart, naturally, been and was meant to be in accordance with the purity and the beauty of my humanity the seasons of which are the stations of my own self-realization, myself imagined, myself realized as my own work, in my own works of *art*, myself my own hymn to the life of freedom, myself the greatest masterpiece I made.

We have also taken the Christian vision of ΛΟΓΟΣ, Christian reason, personally, namely as *Jesus Christ*, the Lord *and* Savior who, though spirit and remaining spirit, nevertheless entered the bodily world and became one with our flesh so that we might become one with his Spirit, the Holy Spirit of Love, and finally know the unity of being in the community of Father and Son, of Son and Disciples, of the Followers of Holy Spirit among themselves, i.e. among those who have been sanctified by him and now dwell in community not as *citizens of freedom*, which is the name of the distinguished human being in the third epoch, but rather as the *saints of glory*. Jesus Christ, the Lord – what happens to this person of the ΛΟΓΟΣ happens to us; what happened to him has already happened to us, has become part of our destiny which is divine *and* human, human *and* divine in one, one in love, in works of love, in words of praise, but above all, one in insight. For to the extent that we take on reason, take on reason's person, take it into ourselves, drink its blood, eat its flesh, become one with it in mind and body, this person is also our person, we ourselves experience in our own lives the resurrection as well as the crucifixion of reason's person, in this transformation becoming wholly *His* person and therefore holy, as such, disciples of the Lord and the children of his Father's will. These persons of reason came close, came not only to us but entered into relationship with us, broke open and into the confinement and closure of our nocturnal world as would the day-breaking sun, an illuminating experience that converted us – this bright idea has come to the workaday world like a holiday, became flesh and this incarnation had the consequence that we ourselves, the flesh of the world at large, were refreshed and awoken, rescued and resurrected out of our finite life of death on the cross of our self-severalty and our sleep of darkness to the destination of congruity with the idea, the teaching, that Christ is and that we have learned and continue to learn by heart by the practice of faith, perpetually unlosing our mundane **religion**.

Now, in the case of the Greeks, taking Parmenides' poetic narrative as a first example, our encounter with its ΛΟΓΟΣ is, in contrast, not at all personal, hardly dramatic, and certainly not tragic, but rather more measured and, as we might even say, more reasonable, in the manner of a scientist or an explorer who searches methodically for and finds what will suffice the name of truth. Parmenides' goddess strived to prove her point by appealing to her interlocutor's understanding, encouraging him and us to think through the issue of being. We followed her demonstration step by step – she anticipated our doubts, our opposing arguments, and refuted them. Always making sure to repeat the crux of the matter from a variety of perspectives, she took the needs of her audience into account. We, for our own part, did not have to do anything or even say anything, just pay attention and follow her train of thought. And her conclusion did not "transform" us in any way or make us better human beings, did not confer upon our freedom the duty of the ideal's realization – no, her argument was not even about *human* being specifically, except in a purely negative sense that the paths of mortal thought with its penchant for vacillation and equivocation, had to be left behind if we hoped to be able to accompany her in this line of reasoning and complete the journey upon the vision of perfection that is the unique truth of being the contemplation of which is the only object of her **science**.

Nevertheless, the tragedy of the distinction of *human* being is well known in the Greek epoch as well. In fact, did not Athens, in the fifth century BCE, attain the very pinnacle of tragic art? We have already seen this in Plato's allegory of the cave – those who return to the cavern of shadows after having seen and enjoyed the light of thought, the Good in the form of the idea, return as strangers in their own homes; and of course Socrates' fate reminds us of the danger that such strangers to the shifting opinions of the mortals are faced with. Moreover, the personal pain that human commitment to the drawing of distinctions demands is vividly portrayed in the Homeric epics, the earliest documentation of our experience with the crisis and dilemma of self-several contrariety that is pure reason's defining mark and the cognizance of our human being in Western culture. Achilles must decide as we all must:

> ...my mother namely tells me, the goddess, Thetis...that two fates of death are bearing me towards doom's end: if I stay here and continue to wage war against the city of the Trojans, then though my return home perish, my renown shall endure; if, however, I return home to my beloved fatherland, then the glory of my fame shall die, but my life go on and on and the fate of death not so soon seize me. (Homer, *Iliad* 9.410-416)

The hero must face the heroic decision – either an anonymous life safe from the dangers of death that excellence and distinction entails or else a luminous life after the death with distinction in the fame and glory of a name which transcends all finitude and the coma of our home in the here and now. This is the decision that reason stimulates in all living mortal being.

In the first epoch, the distinction of human being is defined by the concept of excellence (APETH - aretē). For it is through the deed of distinction that mortal human being can attain its immortal state, a state held alive by remembrance and the poetic work of the Muses, the children of Zeus and Memory. They pass on the knowledge of what has been achieved, the failures and achievements of men, the deeds of the gods, in particular those of Zeus, who in taming the inordinate over-reaching of titanic nimiety founded the Olympic kingdom upon the principle of well-proportioned right.

These ancient myths make manifest the determination of destiny and show the efficacy of accomplishments of distinction and excellence as well as that of ruin, the blindness of excess and exorbitance as their forces play out in the realm of human endeavor – the hero has taken upon himself this distinction and abides by the outcome of the battle. The narratives of their lives indicate the crisis of thought that every human being experiences who has realized that life is finite, that life is, in fact, a destiny to be fulfilled, to be determined as good or ill. Even Zeus, the most powerful and the highest god, is subject to a prior principle. And it is this regard for his own predetermination, i.e. Zeus's insight into his own destiny, that won him the status as the greatest and the highest god, as the deity and person of reason in the first epoch of Western cultural tradition. As Hesiod recognized in his poem *Works and Days*, Zeus's excellence resided in the fact that he truly grasped just "how much the half is more than the whole." (Hesiod, *Works and Days*, 40) This seems to be a contradiction. How can the half be more than the whole? We have learned to hearken to contradictions as they indicate opportunities for thought to make a distinction between its more parochial orthodoxy, as the easy tool of daily life, and its exalted figure as the sign and inflection of supreme distinction, won in deeds of daring do.

What was Zeus's insight that earned him the right and entitled him to the dignity of being called "father of gods and men?" In his *Theogony*, Hesiod recounts the myth of the generation and the advent of the gods, unfolding for our benefit the drama of distinction in accordance with the principle of *apportionment* understood by him as giving rise to the *cosmos* of divine beings, the well-ordered proportion of their rapport.

For instead of attempting to seize and concentrate divine power in his own hands, as his father Chronos did in retaliation for the original act of injustice committed by his own father Ouranos, answering thus atrocity with atrocity, Zeus promised his brothers and sisters a due portion of his kingdom, each according to his or her own nature, and a guarantee that all the gods and goddesses would be constrained by the due mutual recognition of the limits of their own power to recognize and respect the sanctity of the realm of each and every other god or goddess.

In particular, Zeus bestowed upon his first brother, Poseidon, the realm of the sea and upon his second brother, Hades, the realm of the netherworld and conferred due honor upon both of them in this way, sharing his dominion with them and with all the gods in spite of his supreme power, based on the principle of mutually respected limits and earning thus, through the merit of his perspicacious mind – having grasped in this way just how much more the half is (as a matter of fact, in Zeus's case it is a third) than the whole – the respect of the other gods who, in turn, evince their trust by conferring upon his helm the realm of highest heavens. This well-balanced apportionment (EYNOMIA) of esteem and recognition is the foundation of the Olympic community of deities upon the principle of ΔIKH, the limit that establishes and defends what is due and proper to each, what is right as a rule based on the principle (ΘEMIΣ) of what has been preordained as self-evident law, the very principles that, as we saw, governed the form of perfect being in Parmenides' conception. This rule of law is the object of insight that elevated Zeus to the dignity of Olympic presidency and justifies his appointment to the office of divine will that, in achieving its fulfilment, puts into effect what has been indisputably and irrevocably ordained as right, as the way it was meant to be and has always been, will always be, the substantiality and the scope of which is articulated in the myth of the kingdom of the gods under Jovian auspices as one of well-founded peace (EIPHNH).

Thus, in the first epoch, all the deities, even Zeus, have a destiny and must distinguish themselves with respect to it. Occasionally, in spite of himself, Zeus is tempted to disregard the principle of mutual recognition of limits that determines his own realm of power within the totality of the Olympic community. He is at the brink of *hubris*, on the verge of overstepping the bounds of what has been preordained as the way it should be, but then, at the last moment, the imminent trespass of this immoderate impulse is stayed, as it were, by the anguish of a mind divided in itself against itself by the scruples of self-severalty: "Oh wretchedness," he says, "Sarpedon, dearest of men to me, is doomed to be vanquished by Patrokles, Menoetius' son, and now my heart is riven as I anxiously deliberate whether I should hastily snatch him, still living, from war's tears and set him safe in the rich lands of Lycia or rather let him fall at the hands of Menoetius' son." (Il. 16.433-438)

Ω ΜΟΙ ΕΓΩΝ Ο ΤΕ ΜΟΙ ΣΑΡΠΗΔΟΝ ΦΙΛΤΑΤΟΝ ΑΝΔΡΩΝ
ΜΟΙΡ ' ΥΠΟ ΠΑΤΡΟΚΛΟΙΟ ΜΕΝΟΙΤΙΑΔΑΟ ΔΑΜΗΝΑΙ
ΔΙΧΘΑ ΔΕ ΜΟΙ ΚΡΑΔΙΗ ΜΕΜΟΝΕ ΦΡΕΣΙΝ ΟΡΜΑΙΝΟΝΤΙ
Η ΜΙΝ ΖΩΟΝ ΕΟΝΤΑ ΜΑΧΗΣ ΑΠΟ ΔΑΚΡΥΟΕΣΣΗΣ
ΘΕΙΩ ΑΝΑΡΠΑΞΑΣ ΛΥΚΙΗΣ ΙΝ ΠΙΟΝΙ ΔΗΜΩΙ
Η ΗΔΗ ΥΠΟ ΧΕΡΣΙ ΜΕΝΟΙΤΙΑΔΑΟ ΔΑΜΑΣΣΩ

Indeed, in spite of himself and his supreme power, Zeus is crossed in his inclination towards usurpation by the admonishing voice of good judgment that reminds him of his duty to the custom of divine decency, moving him to finally acquiesce, though grudgingly, in recognition of what is the best for all concerned, what is proper and what is right in light of what has been long determined and decided by himself at the beginning of the time of the Olympic gods. His wife Hera reminds him of what has been established and recognized as incontrovertibly right and he assents finally and agrees to stand by what has been decided – enacting, perhaps for the very first time in the history of justice, that illustrious legal principle still valid today; in fact, we might even dub it *Jove's principle*, namely "to abide by what has been previously decided and not to disturb what is at peace" (stare decisis et non quieta movere), though not without distinguishing his own personal inclination from the impersonal directive of the rule of law that he acknowledges in spite of himself as a binding precedence. She says:

> Son of Cronos, supreme in power, what are you saying! You intend to now release from sorrowful death a mortal man, long doomed by fate? Do it; but not one of us among all the gods will praise this deed. And another thing I will tell you and you had better take it to heart: if you save Sarpedon consider that soon some other god may presume to rescue his own dear son from slaughter; for there are many fighting around Priam's walls, not a few of whom are sons of immortals and whose terrible anger you are sure to thus incite against you.

> But consider; if this mortal is beloved to you and you grieve for him in your heart, let him fall in battle by the hands of Patroclus, son of Menoetius, but when his soul and life have departed, then send Death and gentle Sleep to bear him away to the lands of Lycia that his brethren and his kinsfolk may give him proper burial with mound and pillar; for this is the honor of regard due the dead. (Homer, *Iliad*, 16.440-457)

This granting to each by each and by each to all according to what is their due is the principle of apportionment, the determination of the MOIPA; the gods and the mortals, the living and the dead – they all have their due defining what is proper to each with regards to which every individual acknowledges his or her duty. This first principle of *justice*, which is neither retaliatory nor egalitarian, and originally thought to found not mortal society but rather the immortal community of Olympus as a hierarchy of beings – each with his or her own particular scope, definition, and office – is often expressed in the familiar and much abused phrase *suum cuique* (to each as is due) and is based on the premise of the proper portion that every individual god is owed and destined to receive as a consequence of her or his own unique nature and contribution to the comprehensive completion of the whole being of deity in its entirety composed of all the constituent beings in their specific scope of excellence that identifies their particular contribution to the welfare of the community of the immortal gods. All of the Olympic gods, even Zeus, are executives and agents, ministers and governors, masters and managers in one. For all are, though subject to the Jovian counsel and the judgment that governs the whole, at the same time, sovereign within the confines of their own realm which is their property, their nature, their destiny. Thus every king has a king, every queen her queen and the highest lord, the master's master, is neither king, nor queen, nor master, nor lord but rather an incontrovertible principle of predetermination, of a prior determination, that all have acknowledged as binding; the justice of Jovian insight, the entitlement of supremacy in counsel that Zeus is accorded as *father* of immortal and mortal being, a term indicative of the regard he has earned in the eyes of his divine subjects, is incumbent upon his recognition of the limitations of sway that each individual's nature places on the sway and power of every other member, including his own, for the sake of the cosmos of supreme beings that is Olympus. These limits placed on one's property must be taken into account in the sphere of action, but even without a view towards achieving aims, they are honored and respected in their own right as constituting the common wealth of the gods. For this reason, long before *property* came to be thought of as merely a thing of acquisition and possession, and *wealth* the amassing of material riches, *property* and *wealth* were moral terms for the right of regard that accrues to members of the community of gods by virtue of their particular nature, simply in accordance with their own proper excellence – their own proper office of power – to which respect was duly paid as what is not merely *a* good but also simply and absolutely good for all, the *good* of a community of beings based on the respect for each other's distinction, for each other's property in the sense of each one's particular nature and being, his or her *identity* – what each one is in and of herself or himself – a shared and thus an apportioned but also, seen as the whole of Olympus that these individuals constitute, a well-proportioned boon of being, a substantive state of EYNOMIA (eunomia), ordered by the determination of principle (A) through the distinction and subsequent recognition of proper metes and bounds, the indication and practice of ΔIKH (dikē), an equable system of checks and balances (C) of power the harmonious coordination of which assures the enduring comity of all divinity, the pacific being (B) of beings, which is the serene perfection of EIPENH (eirenē) – a train of thought that elaborates a ratio of concretion in Greek terms, see *Figure 89*, that we will presently examine in more detail.

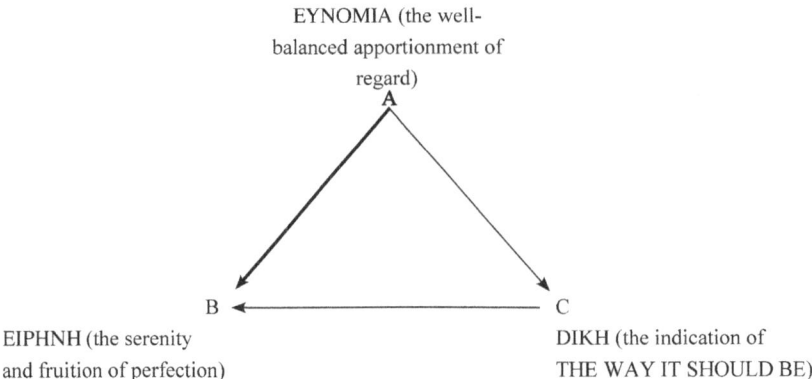

EYNOMIA (the well-
balanced apportionment of
regard)

B   C

EIPHNH (the serenity   DIKH (the indication of
and fruition of perfection)   THE WAY IT SHOULD BE)

Figure 89: The Knowledge of the Muses

These three terms, *EYNOMIA – ΔIKH – EIPHNH*, name the dimensions of
the fulfilled principle of pure reason in the First Epoch. They are the three
daughters of Zeus (the god of insight into and regard for the compelling
principle of apportionment) and ΘEMIΣ (preordained, indisputable law as
is founded in THE WAY IT SHOULD BE) and called the OPAI (Horai), a term
that personifies the idea of *limits*, the cyclic turning and returning of pure
reason's seasons and the state of tranquility and sweetness of what, after
the development and completion of its inaugural principle, has attained
ripest maturity and fruition in accordance with the ratio of determinacy
A>C + C>B = A>B.

Again, Zeus *could* decide to act against the dictates of destiny as
determined by THE WAY IT IS being, essentially, THE WAY IT SHOULD BE.
In this sense Zeus is only "free" to go against what is right and proper; what
prevents him? The laws of convention that he himself committed himself to
as the custom to be adhered to among the immortals. To violate the mores
upon which the Olympic kingdom is based is a shameful act, hateful to all
of one's companions and thus a disturbance of the peace that can only
flourish when mutual acknowledgement of and regard for each other's
rightful demands are actually practiced. No god, not even Zeus, can bear
the ignominy of being thus exposed to the censure of his fellow gods for
causing havoc in their assembly through the forming of fractions and
coalitions in subversion of that community of endearment and by
occasioning the recriminations and accusations of strife that must rise
among them when outrage against the common sense of the gods is
perpetrated.

Indeed, the measure of propriety and decorum remains and demands respect; to overstep the bounds of what is right goes against the rule Zeus himself has established as the principle of the Olympian kingdom – to each shall be accorded a portion of the whole in keeping with the distinction that each being is entitled to in the proportion and the cosmos of being as a whole, the *being* of these beings. We understand: *Being*, just like *cosmos*, is a term of distinction, in other words, a predicate and as such a designation for the OUGHT that the IS is meant to be, namely, complete, perfect as when we say with a sense of realization *B is A*.

134. Terms of Distinction

Searching for and finding what will suffice the dignity of the name of truth, we have come to understand that the tradition of philosophical thought has always known that its science must be founded upon a prior, more originary insight, that of the poets and the prophets who themselves spoke first, having themselves received what we have learned to call the distinguished words of wisdom, i.e. the wisdom of *Humanity* in the Third Epoch, that of the *Holy Spirit* in the Second and now, in the First Epoch, the wisdom of the *Muses*. Who is speaking? Whose message are we the lucky recipients of? Of what transparency are we the beneficiaries? Related to and nevertheless transforming these supposed parameters of present-day communication and information studies, our philology of the distinction of human being has led us to reprise the traditional definition of that distinction, namely ΛΟΓΟΝ ΕΧΩΝ i.e. *endowed with reason* and make sense of its latter-day rendition, namely *possessed of language*. The aforementioned wisdom found expression in works of poetic reason the three epochal speeches of which are the holy writs and the tongues of flame that have spoken to Man throughout history, spoken to and, in its narrative, dramatic, and lyrical works, made a powerful case for the self-severalty of Man as the destiny of human being – a message that bids us take note and give account of what has been said in what has been spoken, audible even to this very day, faint though it may have become amidst the din of indifference, perceptible even now and here, to us, to you and me, dear reader, if we are not very much mistaken.

ΘΕΜΙΣ, ΔΙΚΗ, ΜΟΙΡΑ, ΑΝΑΓΚΗ – All of these ancient principles preserved by and given voice to in the knowledge of the Muses – and recalled by Parmenides in his conception of being – as well as others, perhaps more familiar and similarly indigenous to Greek thought like *truth, perfection, excellence, being, form* and even *god*, are primarily and most properly understood as predicates, i.e. terms of distinction (A), terms of discernment (C) or terms of resolution (B), they indicate *how* something is as much as *what* it is, more exactly, the term for *what* something is expresses *how* a being measures up with regard to what it should be, its nature, its essence, its limit. For the term *limit* is perhaps the most general way of naming the foundational intuition of Greek thought. The limits of a circle are its *form*; the form *defines* the circle; for if you took away the form of a circle from the circle what would be left? Nothing. Exactly! The limit is not extraneous to what is limited by it, the limit *is* this being, *is* its distinction, its *nature* as determinate and determined. In a circle, THE WAY IT IS *is* THE WAY IT SHOULD BE, B *is* A. Take away the self-relative distinction that defines this entity of identity and what have you got? *Nothing* – nothing but the interminable, the incessant unmarked space of the plain plane that is the blank face of indifference.

Let us consider predicates in more detail. Take the term *GOD* (ΘΕΟΣ) for example. In the Christian idiom, *GOD* is not a predicate, it is a proper name, the name of a certain "individual," often imagined and depicted as a person who, like a person, speaks, is at times righteously angry, always just (though sometimes inscrutably so), loving compassion, protects or punishes, calls the elect, has created heaven and earth. There is only one "person" with this name and therefore GOD is not many "deities," just as you are you and no one else could be you, nor could you be anyone else than yourself.

In Greek culture, the term GOD is used differently. Greek logic is *categorical* – to speak about things in a strict sense is to place them in a category or class that limits, *identifies* them – every being is an entity of identity. Every god is *a* god; every human being is *a* human being. That means that every individual, while unique, also partakes of a general class of beings of the same kind that defines its nature and *what* it is, distinguishing thus the categorical *What* from the particular *it* in question. We ask: "*is it* What It Is?" The first *is* in this question is that of the given particular *it* whose being is now to be determined; the *What It Is* refers to that category which names the essence, the form, the idea (ΕΙΔΟΣ) against which that particular individual at issue is to be measured and evaluated and in this sense, in the Greek sense, identified. Does *it* measure up? Obviously, in this view, the identity of a thing distinguishes it not merely from other things of different or the same kind but above all from itself, its Self, which, in the First Epoch, is not *Me*, my Humanity, nor *You*, the Son of the Father but rather *It*, that particular being's *Being*.

Thus even the term *god* is the categorical name of a species or a genus of being; for this reason, a proposition involving this term has essentially the predicative form:

"___is (a) god."

By contrast, in the second epoch, the term God is a proper name, more precisely, a rigid designator and the corresponding proposition assumes the form of attribution:

"God is ___"

This sense of "God," as that to which we might attribute properties and features, leads to the familiar difficulty that there is no class or category under which God can adequately be subsumed, for that category would then make of God *a* God i.e. a god of this or that sort, a kind of God. In fact, God cannot be thought of as "one of a kind," not even as falling under the category of *something*, supposedly the most general of categories. God is neither something nor nothing. Thus, God is oftentimes said to be *ineffable* or *unnameable* and this attribute serves the purpose of indicating that God is a *term of distinction* designating the absolute difference between the indeterminate immediacy of lived experience and the difference that a given principle makes upon the issue of discernment; GOD is, like FREEDOM, a term or mark of distinction, a limit, and as such, initially, the pure negation inherent in the efficacy of pure reason to recognize difference as a principle (A) and establish upon this foundation the discerning work of critical reflection (C) with respect to that acknowledged limit that indicates the object towards which such work is directed as the term of issue and fulfillment (B).

But then what good is the term *god* in Greek understanding if it is not used as a term of pure negation? Why is any name used, *deity* or *chair* or *woman*? The propositions in which they occur have the form *B is A* – "___ is a deity," "___ is a chair," "___ is a woman." In the ΛΟΓΟΣ that contains them, these terms simply say *what* something is. This formulation articulates a given state of affairs, the situation, THE WAY IT IS; it states the truth about how things stand. The proposition indicates that an individual *B* stands in relationship of inherence to a general principle of determination *A*. It states the truth of the relationship between a particular and a general form or category, the limit that is its idea. The truth is that when *B* stands in a relationship of inherence to *A*, the *individual* (B) *is* the *general* (A) and when the *individual* (B) *is* the *general* (A) in the emphatic, distinguished sense, then *B* stands in a determining relationship of inherence to *A*. This inherence of B in A is the Greek rendition of the correspondence, the covenant, that we have repeatedly noted as articulating the resolution of the initial distinction between THE WAY IT IS (the immediate reality of an otherwise inconspicuous being whose status has suddenly, for some reason, become an issue) and THE WAY IT SHOULD BE (the form or idea of excellence and perfection abstracted by pure reason from its concrete and specific reality as a being's being), a discrepancy that, at the end of the development, resolves itself into the relationship of reciprocity such that the idea of the general (A) descends and applies to, tries, as a judge would in a court of law, the particular individual (B) of the case, even as the individual (B) rises to the occasion of the general determining principle (A) that called its identity, its quality, its "goodness," into question in the first place – once the conformance of the individual to the standards of the principle has been determined by the sentence of conceptual (rather than moral) judgment, the state of completion, of fulfillment, of perfection, of truth, which are all terms of resolution, can be said to have been attained in and as that particular being – only now is it truly *What It Is*.

Thus, predicates and categories are used to *specify* something. I ask, for example, "What is that?" This question refers to a being that has been noted, that has drawn attention to itself or to which attention has been drawn. I could answer *it is blue*. Is that the answer that you would expect, if, for example, your son or daughter pointed to something and asked you, "What is that?" You could answer *it is round* or *it is smaller than an elephant* or *it is in my hand* or *it is one meter above the floor* or *it is plastic*. All of these are possible answers to the question and yet we would expect a different answer, namely one that actually *identifies* the object in question by classifying it and putting it into a category that defines its "nature" rather than one that merely indicates its quality or quantity (size) or location, etc. – Aristotle, for example, enumerated ten categories. We would expect the answer: *It is a ball*. This proposition subsumes the individual object into the conceptual class called BALL and measures this object now with respect to what a ball *should be* as indicated by the idea of its nature or definition implied in the category. Does the thing correspond to that which it is meant to be as indicated by the predicate? Is that particular man a MAN or not? Is it (the individual) what it should be (the idea)? Is B A or not? Does B deserve to be called an A or not? Is B "perfect" (or nearly so) with respect to its *class* and *kind*, its *identity*, its "*concept*" (A)? Is it a good example of the *sort* of thing (i.e. A) *is* (i.e. B)? As we saw, these questions refer not so much to the properties of a being that distinguish it from others but rather distinguish it from itself – a thing is judged in this self-several relationship, its ΛΟΓΟΣ with regards to its sort, its category, its rank, its lot, its fate.

Relationship is perhaps the most abstract English expression we could put for the Greek term ΛΟΓΟΣ. But in the course of our explorations, both words, the Greek original and the English translation as well as many others from both languages have been posited for what we have also called *idea* or *thought*. For these are also useful names for our cause in certain contexts as is *reason* in others. But the latter is not a better name than the former or others that might be put instead, except under certain circumstances. It is the circumstances that decide which name is more appropriate – thus the rule of Ethos, the principle of credibility in the art of moving the human heart; if ΛΟΓΟΣ means *language* or *speech performance*, as these days seems generally to be supposed, then the aptness or felicity of a term can only be decided with regard to the particular set of circumstances defining the communication situation.

But this is a very limited view of what ΛΟΓΟΣ is. The effect of the predicate is to pass judgment on the *being* of the thing in question – does it satisfy the requirements as indicated by the idea or not? Is B A or not, i.e..: is B a good kind of A or not – this is the determining relationship of the ΛΟΓΟΣ indicating the form and shapeliness, the beauty, in a word, the APETH (aretē) of a thing, which meant *fitness* or *suitability* or *aptness* to fulfill its purpose, its reason for being, its destiny. Evidently, in Greek understanding, things are more than just their names and what is said with them in a given speech performance. The Greeks spoke of a thing's ΤΕΛΟΣ (telos). The APETH of a knife, for example, consists in its *sharpness*. And then, depending on the kind of knife it is, depending on its particular purpose, a good (ΑΓΑΘΟΣ - agathos) knife will have many other APETHΣ, many other *properties of excellence* as we may call them in an English rendition of the Greek term; some knives are called, predicated, as *good* (the adjective to the noun APETH) because they are *short*, some because they are *long*, some because they are *serrated*, some because they are *retractable*, etc. – these are all "virtues" (the sense of the Greek term APETH when restricted to the sphere of action, the practice of excellence in human terms) of a knife, depending on the particular, function, role, destiny, it has to fulfill. And with respect to that function a knife could be too sharp, too, thereby transgressing the limits of its present purpose and perfection and therefore not the way it should be, a *bad* knife.

135. The Power of Determination of the ΛΟΓΟΣ

The Greek culture presents us with a great number of deities. Perhaps we were inclined to consider this flourishing "polytheism" as a sign of "primitive animism." But now as it has become clear that if the term *god* is essentially, as the renowned scholar of classical philology, Wilamowitz-Moellendorff, reminds us, a predicate and as such is used to emphasize that a particular being is exceptional, remarkable, excellent, significant, there are, in fact, many things that could be given this tribute of a name in the praising ways of poets and prophets, things like particular *rivers* and *mountains*, the *Moon* and the *Sun*, important features of the day like *Night* with its shadowy brood of concomitant phenomena and *Dawn* and her star children, light-bringers all, but also the natural setting as a whole, its parts and properties like *Sky*, *Earth*, the *Bloom* of flowers, their *Splendor*, the *Winds'* force; but not only natural phenomena and properties are called ΘΕΟΣ, also so-called human emotions, like *Fear* and *Zeal* and states or conditions like *Forgetting*, *Strife*, *Hunger*, *Battle*, *Pain* and important concepts of human intercourse and experience like *Love*, *Desire*, *Violence*, *Memory*, *Oath*, *Law*, *Right*, *Peace*, *Death* and other details of being that make a difference and deserve attention like *Giving*, *First-of-all*, *Well-Speaking*, *Far-Sight*, *Song*, *Gaze*, *Forethought*, *Wonder* – these are all deities as we shall see, and their names suggest their particular privilege and priority, their distinction in the life of human being as well as their place in the life of excellence as a whole, the kingdom of Olympus. Anything that is distinctive, eye-catching, puzzling, striking, particularly or characteristically intense, remarkably fierce or gentle, noteworthy for being powerful, more powerful, greater than any device of man's mastery or control and therefore "inaccessible to all human arrogation," demands and deserves the recognition of a name, and not just any name, but rather the name *ΘΕΟΣ*.[78]

---

[78] cf. Wilamowitz-Moellendorff, Ulrich von, *Der Glaube der Hellenen*, p. 17-18: "...dies ist Gott. Das ist also ein Prädikatsbegriff...Das Göttliche ist das KPEITTON uns gegenüber. KPEITTONEΣ heißen die Götter oft. Und da es solcher Mächte zahllose gibt, sind auch die Götter unzählbar. Das Leben in der Natur ließ den Menschen diese KPEITTONA unmittelbar wahrnehmen, denn überall fühlte er sich abhängig von ihnen. Sie waren ihm schädlich und nützlich, seiner Herrschaft unzugänglich." (...this is god, a predicate...deity is, with respect to us, the mightier. The gods are often called our superiors. And as there are innumerable such powers so are the gods innumerable. In the course of people's lives in the natural world, these greater beings become immediately apparent to them; for everywhere did people feel their dependence on them – they were harmful or beneficial, in any case inaccessible to human arrogation.).

Thus, the *ΛΟΓΟΣ* of a thing *distinguishes* it, puts it in *relationship* to other beings, compares them among themselves as well as each being to its own being, to the way it was meant to be. This relationship of reason is the opening up of sight, the taking note and the evaluation that constitutes the act of judgment inherent in identification. This latter word, in turn, is a name for the *determination* of what something is. *What it is* – this expression names the *general "idea"* that a particular thing is now placed *in relationship with*, the *definition* according to which it is *judged*, *the measure* with respect to which it is *evaluated*, the *standard* upon which it is *specified*, the *norm*, the *criterion*, the *gauge*, the *guideline*, the *rule*, the *requirement*, the *principle*, the *specification* that provides the basis for judgment, for distinguishing a thing in THE WAY IT IS from THE WAY IT SHOULD BE, for determining its *virtue*, its *excellence*, its *distinction*.

We know that *Light* and *Sight* have always been applied as terms of distinction, powerful images for the relationship of ΛΟΓΟΣ, for they visualize the advent of judgment onto the scene, into the world, the point it makes in the scheme of things which, until the mark of pure intellect's light and sight appear in their midst, are shrouded in the darkness of confusion, fleeting impressions in an intoxicating flush and hubbub of indifference. It is only the cognizance of the relationship of ΛΟΓΟΣ that gives beings their distinction, measures their depth and breadth, inserts them into the larger framework and horizon in which beings take place, i.e. the enriching dimension of perceptive scope in which they have their own proper place, their own value and degree, which determines, by bringing to the fore of objective consideration, the divisive tension between what they are and what they should be, their own good, as well as the extent to which their power reaches and where others' begin, a limit defining rights and dues that demands recognition. This is an unsettling, energetic span that discrimination and discernment interjects into the entropy of things by making them distinct in themselves, subjects to the difference that distinguishes them from the realms of others but also self-critically from the sovereignty that defines the scope of their own being.

Consider the examples of light and sight inherent in the relationships of ΛΟΓΟΣ we have discussed till now. We have spoken of the *evidence* and the *revelation* of *insight* that is reason's declarative *voice*. Clearly the term *voice* is a metaphor for the light of distinction, i.e. for hearing, for seeing, for discriminating perception. We see what has been otherwise hidden, absorbed in the backdrop, in the ambient noise; for oblivion is the domain of what is *inconspicuous, anonymous, negligible, inane, neither here nor there* – other terms involving the light and sight of difference; and such that is forgotten is brought to the *light* of memory which recollects, records, saves what is otherwise lost. Likewise, we have discussed such expressions as depict a perspective of gaining a view from above, an overview; taking note, remarking, recognizing, knowing – all of these terms, in turn, refer to the experience of discernment as the introduction of a relationship into circumstances and situations which are otherwise one-dimensional, a smooth virginal plane, unmarked space, untouched, untried, untested, unknown, unseen. For to see is to judge and to judge is to discriminate and to discriminate is to make a distinction. And making a discriminating (rather than a discriminatory) distinction is the starting point of knowledge and "insight towards which," as Aristotle declares, "all human being is destined by nature to strive" (*Metaphysics* 980a 21)

ΠΑΝΤΕΣ ΑΝΘΡΩΠΟΙ ΤΟΥ ΕΙΔΕΝΑΙ ΟΡΕΓΟΝΤΑΙ ΦΥΣΕΙ

Thus the expression we have used so often, *the distinction of human being*, is, in the Greek world, where we speak of beings *in general*, no longer appropriate. Every proposition occasions an assessment of the truth by formulating a relationship of ΛΟΓΟΣ which determines and defines things, placing them in relationship to what they are supposed to be – their essence and nature, their substance and purpose, their principle and cause, and thus, in a word, their "ΘΕΟΣ."

There are indeed many terms that can be used to express the relationship of ΛΟΓΟΣ and therefore many areas of life and experience where we encounter the issue of excellence and shortfall. Wherever we speak of judgment and assessment, of order and rule, of pattern and graduation, we can expect an instantiation of this defining relationship of discernment. For example, if a thing is measured, it has a value. This value indicates the degree to which that thing fulfills the standard provided by the measure. In this state of affairs, we can distinguish the thing measured (B) from the standard, the measure (A) itself and from the determinative practice of measuring (C). These are the three elements in which we might articulate the ΛΟΓΟΣ of their relationship. They present the circle of pure reason we have become familiar with.

On the one hand, through the comparison of the particular with the general, its identity, the *discernment* of perceptive judgment (C) subsumes the former (B) under the defining category of the latter (A), i.e. B>C + C>A = **B>A** or in triangular form as in *Figure 90*:

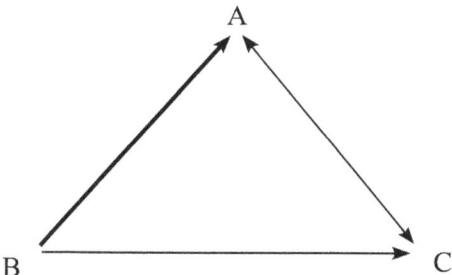

Figure 90: The Relationship of Subsumption

On the other hand, through the activity of productive or generative judgment (C), *verification,* the principle or universal is recognized as having been realized in that particular; the former (A) has come to life in the latter (B), i.e. A>C + C>B = **A>B** or in triangular form as in *Figure 91*:

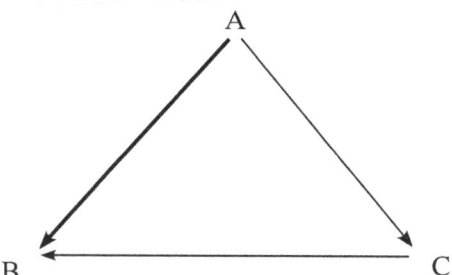

Figure 91: The Relationship of Verification

Consider other terms for the norm, standard, or measure or the act of measuring. A law prescribes what is required, necessary; thus, in addition to the term *law,* the terms *requirement* and *necessity* are useful to express the measure (A). In complying with the stipulations of the law, conduct is shown to be just, right or, straying from the straight path, the opposite, in which case, punishment (C) is exacted with a view to molding the deviate (B) to more perfectly conform to the model of excellence proposed by the letter of the law.

Here are further illustrations: an object (B) is put on a scale (A) and thus weighed (C); water (B) is poured (C) into a glass (A); a plan, an intention (A) is realized (B) through the work of implementation (C); the painter (C) observes the world (A) and strives to represent it (B) true to life, seemingly, on the canvas; the architect's design (A) represents the reality (B) that he or she is striving to create (C); The shoe (B) should be made to fit (C) to the foot (A); The destination (A) determines (C) the journey (B); The nature of a thing (A) becomes, in the course of its development (C), what it was destined to be (B); thus, the potential tree in the apple seed (A) becomes (C) the apple (B) – which is still the potential tree in the nature of the seed, i.e. a thing is preordained (A) to become (C) what it is (B); the apple in principle (A) grows into (C) the apple in reality, the tree (A) into (C) the tree (B); I repay (C) my debts (A), complete (C) a task (A), fulfill (C) a duty (A) and am finished when the state of affairs has been squared (B), requited (B), completed (B), fulfilled (B); the judge (A) determines (C) what is right (B); right (A) determines (C) what is just (B); the guidelines, the rules (A) are read (C) and followed (B) – a short list of states of affairs representing the relationship of distinction that Greek intellect has termed *ΛΟΓΟΣ*.

The six salient elements of this relationship delineate the train of thought that elaborates the "nature" of pure reason in the Greek epoch. For *reason is*, for the Greeks, both the precedent being of evidence, the ENEPΓEIA of theory *and* a specific being, the unmoved mover and, in this sense, the cause of the KOΣMOΣ of beings that comprise its universe. In *Figure 92*, the synthesis of these relationships is depicted as a triangle of terms.

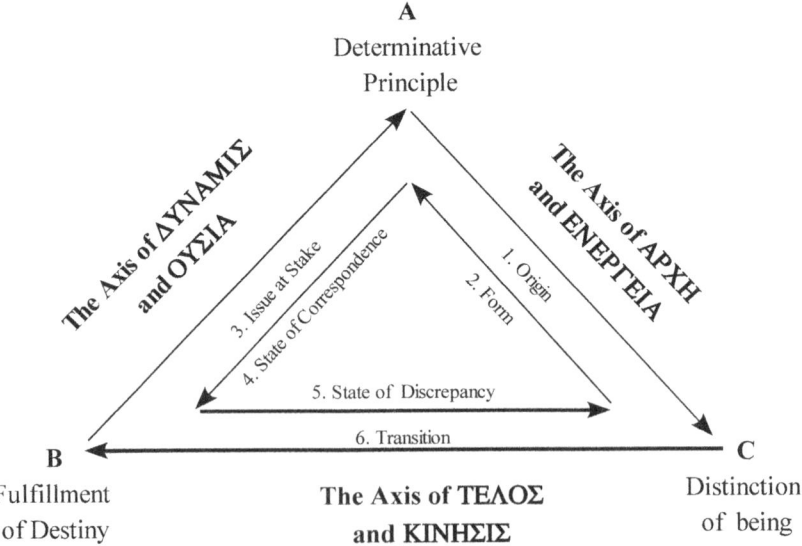

Figure 92: The ΛΟΓΟΣ of the ΛΟΓΟΣ in terms of Greek Metaphysics

1. The ***spring and origin*** (A) of measurement, i.e. the introduction of the ΛΟΓΟΣ relationship itself, which is the given of immediate *evidence* in the First Epoch, *revelation* in the Second and *feeling* in the Third, in which the principle (A) that measures (C) the thing (B) is manifest *in its own unique present*; this original determination is the inaugural activity of discernment – the marking of its limit, the drawing of its distinction, the communication of its character, the trace and sign of its "style," and the impression that the note of its abundance makes upon our attention such that we, marvellously, take note.

2. The ***determining principle*** (A) of measure itself – the rule, principle, goal, standard, criterion, law; the measure taken as in the mind (plan, aim, project) or present in a medium (design, model, layout, pattern) as the form and guideline of governance.

3. The ***object***, the thing measured (B) – What the matter is and the material, the topic of discourse, the theme touched upon and thus noted by judgment, the issue raised by critical reflection with regards to which it is to be assessed.

4. The ***State of Correspondence*** (B) – the measured object and the measure are in agreement with each other. In this case we say: the thing is *fitting, suitable, appropriate, right, good, happy, complete, beautiful.* Matters stand, in this state, in close proximity to and accordance with the criteria of their determining principle, a nearness and "kindness" of a kinship that can be represented in images of civil community, contract, and the endearment of family ties, visualized as *love, society, identity, reciprocity*; such a being in question can be affirmed as a high-fidelity *image, copy, representation* of the model, a *son* or *daughter* of the parent principle; the agreement rounding off this relationship is one of *peace, reconciliation, resolution, satisfaction.*

5. The ***unstable state of discrepancy*** (C) – the measured object is seen to deviate from the measure and is therefore termed *wrong, bad, false, crooked, mistaken, defective* because it is not the way it should be – this is the rotten state of affairs, the state of necessity, the state of urgency and emergency, of crisis, the state of the distinction and conflict, the civil war of the state, the illness, the hunger, the thirst of the body, the contradiction in which the thing is different, divergent from itself, from what it was meant to be; one side of the relationship overmasters the other, surpasses the just limit and becomes titanic (from *overreaching its bounds* – as we will see in Hesiod's *Theogony* 207-209), *hybrid* (indicating its essential ΥΒΡΙΣ).

6. ***The change*** (C) – the process of transition and transformation by which A and B are brought into mutual agreement and alignment; depending on the particular context at issue this process is called *development* and the *bringing to fruition* (the elaboration from potential to actual), *punishment* (the *execution* of judgment, the *serving* of a sentence and the *discharging* of a debt), the *clearing* (of one's name), *journey* (the arrival of the destination), the persevering *search* (for what will suffice), the *striving of desire* (towards the slaking of a need), *education* and *erudition* (of raw material to civility), *building* (the *performance* of a the plan), *creating* (the *realization* of the ideal), *ambitious endeavor* (in the fulfillment of a destiny, the completion and achievement of a purpose), the *test* and *contesting* (for the prize), *conflict* and *contention* (towards peaceful resolution), *revival* and *renewal* (of the moribund and the morbid), *exercise* (of regeneration and recreation), the *cleansing conversion*, the *completion* (of a whole), the *putting into practice* (of a principle), the *ways* and the *means* (towards perfection and an end with distinction).

Let us reconsider pure reason in this light, namely as the king of the celestial spheres, who is their moving, immovable cause, as lovely as he is lordly, theirs as much as ours since square one.

136. Outstanding Being

Again, every predicate, at least in the Greek sense of this term, says *what* a thing should be; the proposition "___*is a chair*" represents the state of affairs in which a particular chair, this particular being, is measured by its *idea*, i.e. put in relationship to its nature, which, with regards to the many of its kind, Aristotle calls its general (ΚΑΘ'ΟΛΟΥ). Summoned thus by the intellect of reason to appear before the tribunal of reason, it is now awaiting the judgment of reason, its sentence, and the resolution of this crisis of determination; but just having appeared before this court of distinction is already to receive a sentence. Immediately upon entering into a relationship with reason, judgment is passed; the ΛΟΓΟΣ *is* the relationship of judgment, is the summons before the judge, the passing of judgment, and the sentence of judicial predication, as we previously saw in the Second Epoch in connection with the experience of the finitude of human being. The chair receives, as we receive when we appeared before the critical eyes of self-reflection, the death sentence. It is not and could not be perfect; it is found wanting, lacking, diverging from its essence, its idea, its true being and nature. Of course, compared to other chairs, depending on the craft of the chair-maker, it may be closer to or further from perfection. But measured against the universal chair, the ideal chair, the Idea of the chair, it can only be a likeness, *true* perhaps, and therefore of highest fidelity, but never the truth itself. Thus, this chair, if it could talk, might say, just as the Apostle Paul said:

> *...once I lived without the law; but then the commandment came, sin revived, and I, I died. (Rm 7.9)*

Before the chair came under the scrutiny of judgment, it lived a modest life of anonymity, going about its business as a chair, being nothing but your basic everyday kind of chair; it fulfilled its modest office here, in this classroom or perhaps in your dining room, not calling attention to itself as it perhaps once did, ever so briefly and with the avid aid of a salesperson, when it became a candidate for purchase so long ago on that fateful day in the life of that chair but since then never again called upon to account for and justify itself with respect to the principle in the image of which it was made, the image of unity and completion that represents the self-relationship of reason, its self-love, its identity. But having been selected and distinguished now as a subject of a philosophical argument to appear before the high court of thought, wrenched from the bland oblivion into which habit and neglect have consigned it, it must stand trial and face the jurisdiction of wisdom and the inevitable condemnation that necessarily ensues, the execution of the sentence of distinction, which now extends not only to human but to all being, yes, even to that of a piece of furniture, to that thing you might not have actually looked at with undivided attention and appraised with your full consideration for years.

This anguish of distinction, though remaining a mute cry in the chair, is the price of presence that chairs and humans, every being, must pay for the dignity of excellence that the light of the mind's attention bestows upon it and that is the illuminating, illuminated destiny of being; every being is destined to be outstanding in its own unique way, a particular "person," a being in and of itself, but also in the cosmos, the being of beings, the community of universal reason's sway. Maybe it would have been more comfortable for the chair, disregarding how comfortable or uncomfortable it is for us, to have remained what it was before it had attained this dubious distinction of being recognized as an individual in its own right, dwelling in reason's universe. Before, it was simply there in the background, but not as it is now, "*there!*" in the view of critical appreciation. It was vacantly and passively available for use and abuse, a means to the end, the butt-end, of students' days and ways who sit upon it during the lecture; it served as a repository for bubble gum that had surrendered its last flavour; it was moved awkwardly around for various reasons, kicked occasionally out of anger, cleaned under at the end of the day, and then locked into the darkness of a wait that is the fate of all merely instrumental beings, these slaves of Man's capricious needs and preferences that have no place in the scheme of things, the Olympic things of life, that was founded upon the insight that knew how to give each thing due regard as a being not only *for* others but also *in and of itself,* one among several comprising the order of the whole.

Having come to love its chains and dimly recognize its own facelessness, this chair, now seized by the piercing gaze of the intellect, laments its lost paradise of oceanic inconspicuousness, afloat in the flow of infant indeterminacy and innocence – alas, this untouched wilderness of being has now been lost to you forever, poor chair, for you have been distinguished by the eye of reason and have since entered the scope of critical discernment. And the refrain of the song celebrating your demise is: *When is a chair a chair?*

For up to now we have been exploring the question "ΤΙ ΕΣΤΙΝ? (ti estin - what is it?)" which seeks to know what the essence of a thing is, its true being. We saw that what a thing is, is posited by the predicate in which the particular thing is thought to inhere. The proposition *B is A* expresses not only the state of condemnation through the discrimination of judgment that B *should be* A (but is not), but also the state of accord and community in which the individual is elevated to inherence in its proper "category" as we might say with reference to Kant's categorical imperative, the law that requires the individual maxim to conform to the general law, the singular to the universal, the particular to the class, according to which B is recognized as being *a kind of* A, etymologically, a "child of God," as we would say in the idiom of the Second Epoch. We have seen that even the little word *is* brings with it the notion of *destiny,* both fulfilled as well as still pending, outstanding, an aspiration, a will just at the brink of commencing performance, which is the effort and the work of coming to be. Thus the question *what is it* refers to the determining principle *and* its *distinguishing effect* on immediacy, this scission of divergence *and* the ultimate correspondence between what was meant to be and what actually *is* now that the work of closing the gap between the IS and the OUGHT has been carried out. This is the practice and the discipline of reason with regard to beings in general and specifically to the productive being of the chair.

How is pure reason productive, inventive, and generative in the Greek Epoch? By being not itself natural but rather the cause of nature, in other words by being the principle because of which the relationship of its ΛΟΓΟΣ moves nature to give shape, form, order, beauty, reason to itself. For the Greeks namely, the universe of reason is called *nature* (ΦΥΣΙΣ - physis) and it is the best possible world, a divine community of beings, naturally moved, i.e. self-moving beings, to which human being belongs as well, under the auspices of the separate, independent and unmoved being called *intellect* which moves nature as a whole and every part of every particular natural being of the star-bright empyrean in a teleological turn and return around that principle of perfect being at the center of their admiring, desiring attention, their cause.

For a being's **reason** is not only *what it is* (TI EΣTIN) but also, in a more "energetic" way, *why* (ΔIA TI). For "thinkers do not think they know something until they have grasped the Why, which is to grasp the primary cause." (Aristotle, *Physics* 194b16)

Why is a being what it is? Reason *sees* this reason – that is its theoretical prowess as the intellect. But reason is active not only in *seeing* but also in *being*, being a power and capacity to bring about change. A being that has its reason within itself for being what it is, is a *being of nature*. In the Third Epoch, we have already encountered this "natural" *autonomous being* in contrast to one that is subject to a law that is not its own and is therefore extraneous to it, the heteronomous being. Only the intrinsically determined person was self-determined and a citizen of the state of freedom. In the First Epoch this distinction serves to contrast the natural being from the artificial one that has its reason for being what it is outside of itself, namely in the craft and ingenuity of the artisan. Thus, a thing constituted by nature, i.e. an animal or plant, Aristotle says, has "a principle of motion and station within itself...whereas a bed or a coat or anything else of that sort...to the extent that they are products of art...have no innate impulse to change..." (192b8)

It is above all with respect to these beings *by nature* that the question arises why do beings move in the first place, what is the prime and first mover? What is the *reason* for their movement?

137. Being and Beings, Reason and Reasons

In what way then are thoughts, ideas "real" or, in terms of the First Epoch, *beings*? In this way that they are principles, causes. In contrast to what we think about them nowadays, ideas, these intangible, invisible beings, are not just errant abstractions in this or that head that, for the most part, suddenly flare inexplicably only to fade just as fast in the swirls and streams of our consciousness. Rather, consider ideas as essentially causes, as having a tangible effect, as making a difference. Therefore when we search for the reason for something, we are actually looking for its origin and beginning, the causal principles and especially the first principle – such things were called by poets *gods* and by philosophers *ideas*. Now this primary cause is often not apparent to cursory sensory perception, which only tells us the way something is, its appearance, not *why* it is this way and why it must *be* and not merely *appear* to be this way, why it cannot be otherwise than the way it is. Science and the insight of reason alone see with piercing sight through the immediacy of impressions, through the haze of opinions, to recognize the true *nature* (ΦΥΣΙΣ) of a being, its principle (ΑΡΧΗ) and the cause why it is what it is. For this is not obvious. It is the work of science to find the reasons, give the reasons why.

For, in fact, the moving principle is the first – it produces what comes second, its work; it begins with the unmarked space (ΧΟΡΑ) of indeterminacy (ΑΟΡΙΣΤΟΝ), a matter (ULH) of indifference. This indeterminacy is the maternal receptivity of material in its responsiveness to the paternal pattern of the form (ΜΟΡΦΗ) that the principle brings to bear in works of distinction that thought, the Thinker, the Actor, the Builder achieve in their respective offices constituting the totality of place (ΤΟΠΟΣ) defining, grounding the determinacy of Olympic community. But why does the Builder give that matter this pattern? The cause of this cause is the purpose (ΤΕΛΟΣ) that the Builder is striving to achieve with the application of the craft and art of drawing distinctions, giving this form to this material for a reason.

Consequently, the receptivity of the material and the efficacy of the form are the first two reasons or causes for its being THE WAY IT IS. We have studied the nature of indifference and the resistance of oblivion to the forces of character that form beings. It is against the backdrop of this pure indeterminacy, the emptiness of space, that the reciprocity of the maternal and paternal principles gives rise to that proportion in which each principle is accorded the right to take place in the concrete whole (ΣΥΝΟΛΟΝ). These relationships are rendered in *Figure 93*.

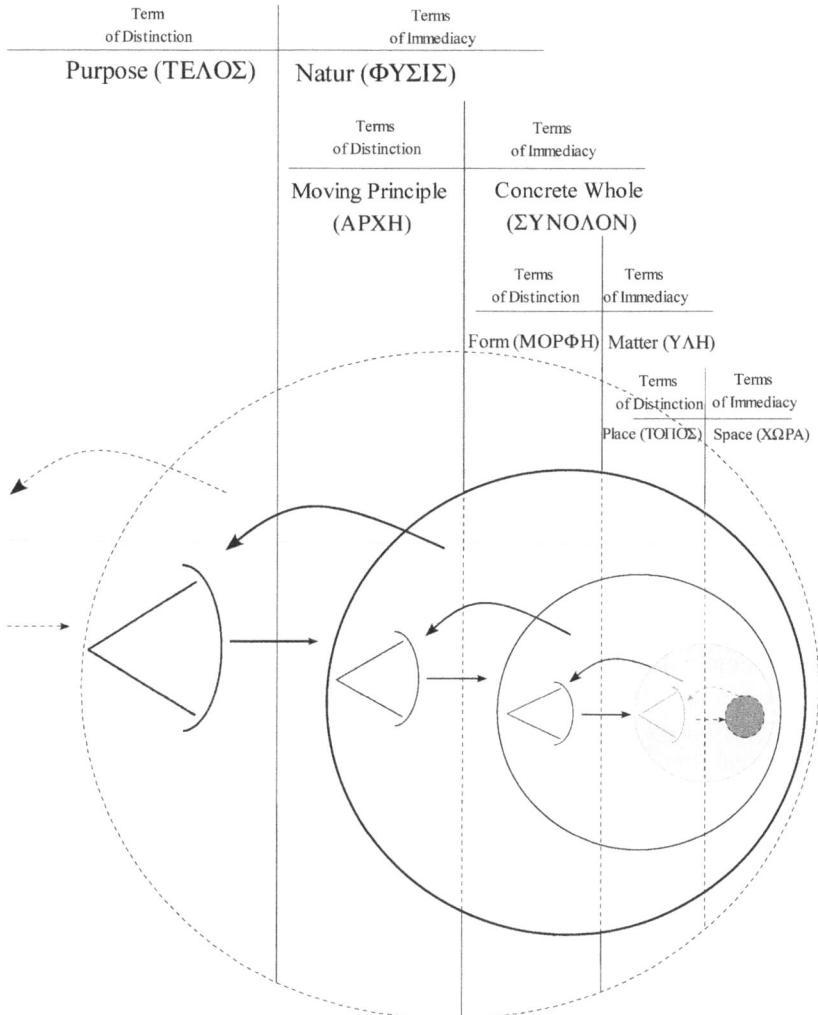

Term of Distinction	Terms of Immediacy
Purpose (ΤΕΛΟΣ)	Natur (ΦΥΣΙΣ)

Terms of Distinction	Terms of Immediacy
Moving Principle (APXH)	Concrete Whole (ΣΥΝΟΛΟΝ)

Terms of Distinction	Terms of Immediacy
Form (ΜΟΡΦΗ)	Matter (ΥΛΗ)

Terms of Distinction	Terms of Immediacy
Place (ΤΟΠΟΣ)	Space (ΧΩΡΑ)

Figure 93: Beings and Being, Reasons and Reason

This figure shows how the familiar reiterating process of drawing a distinction that we have made out as that of critical self-reflection are applied to matters at hand rather than to persons the self-relativity of which is, in the Greek Epoch, not the self-knowing being of our humanity but rather that of the entity of identity in and of itself and in relation to every other being comprising the whole. All beings and not just human beings are reflective in the sense that they are self-severally determined as in accordance with or divergent from what they were meant to be, their destiny, their nature, their principle, the law of their own particular *god*, their *idea*, their *cause*.

The primary cause is however not the material or the form but rather the active moving force that initiates the change by actually affecting the material with the form – this cause of the transition is, as we saw, either within the being, in which case it is a natural substance, or else the cause is outside of the being in which case it is a product of art. But given pure reason as the unmoved mover of nature, nature is moved by itself *and* by pure reason, which must therefore be both *outside* of nature and the *nature* within every being that is its cause; with regards to themselves they are natural, with regards to their end, they are the products of pure reason's order that attracts their desire and not only commands their purpose.

In both cases, the principle that actually activates the causality of pattern affecting matter is the ultimate reason why the chain of subaltern reasons is inaugurated in the first place. In the causality of art, the artisan seeks to fulfill a purpose with the artifact. This object is intended for use of some sort and this use itself is a means to a further end. By following this chain of causality, we discover that the artisan built the chair because the procurement department of the university administration ordered it for the classroom to facilitate student learning, which is directed at the purpose of education of the citizens and the well-being of the state in which each individual has her or his own role to play in accordance with the perpetuation and fruition of the union so that, ultimately, by assuring the dissemination of culture and learning among future leaders of a nation's society, the comity of the united nations might prosper with the prospering of each member state towards the fulfillment of human being in general in the framework of all beings to the extent that they all strive for excellence with a view to both mortal and immortal being, all in service to the greatest good, which is the life of the greatest good, namely the observant life of *theory*, the only activity worthy of a god, as Aristotle says, and the *science of pure reason* which is the study of the ultimate cause of nature, the unmoved mover of all natural change and growth that, or better, who, by inspiring love on the part of every natural being with regards to the beauty and perfection of reason itself, moves the perfect planetary and astral deities in their perfect orbits to contemplate the universe of reason, i.e. its unmoved turn and return of self-reflection, self-knowledge, and self-realization, in a word, the *ΘΕΟΡΙΑ* (theoria) of thought thinking thought.

The analysis of the cause and principle of every being, whether by nature or by art, will always, of necessity, lead us back to this first principle, which is thus the *ultima ratio* of every being in the universe, the ultimate purpose of which is, therefore, none other than doing *philology* in the strict, logotectonic sense that we have been considering in this investigation, i.e. doing precisely what the circumspective stars do – the contemplation and the celebration of what is best, namely the rhythmic life and times of the ΛΟΓΟΣ and the figures of its accomplishments.

138. The Efficacy of the Best

Thus, look at all the artefacts around you! In a way, must we not say that divine reason is the ultimate reason for their *being there?* For if excellence and perfection is the goal then clearly the greatest goal of learning and science, culture and education is to provide human being with the opportunity to study such a philological philosophy, the theory of the sphere and the universe of reason. But obviously this is possible only when all other physical needs of human being have been satisfied; Aristotle demands that the state provide its citizens with opportunities to improve their chances of living such a life as offers leisure, for only such human beings as these, beings with leisure from all constraints and restrictions, or at least relieved of as many of them as possible, can devote themselves to contemplation; such a life is the goal of education and in this sense the efforts of the state must be directed at *more* than the happiness that accrues to those whose material needs have been fulfilled, aimed at *more* than mere life – though securing life is surely the preliminary goal – but rather ultimately, as Plato famously determined, aimed at the *good* life, the best life, the life of the good and of the best being, which, as Aristotle articulates in his mature conception of metaphysics in the First Epoch, Aristotle's epoch, is none other than the action and practice of pure thought itself, the practice and the active being of "theoretical" reason which, though itself unmoved, moves every being of nature to causality, inspiring thereby the concentric rings of the first heaven (ΠΡΩΤΟΣ ΟΥΡΑΝΟΣ – Met. 1072A 23) to strive in their eternal circular motion (ΚΥΚΛΩΙ – 1072a 22) towards their best possible life, towards the perfect universe of rational life, a star's life of cosmic brilliance. The eternally turning heaven is thus both in movement itself and moves all other subsequent "natures" mediating (ΜΕΣΟΝ – 1072a 24) between these moved beings and that unique unmoved being that does not move but inspires the first movement of the first heaven and is, as such, therefore, the heaven of the heavens "eternal and substance and actuality" (ΑΙΔΙΟΝ ΚΑΙ ΟΥΣΙΑ ΚΑΙ ΕΝΕΡΓΕΙΑ – 1072a 25) inspiring movement as does an "object of desire and of thought both of which move without being

moved, the first among these objects of insight and desire being the same."
(1072a 26-27)

TO OPEKTON KAI TO NOHTON KINEI OY KINOYMENA.
TOYTΩN TA ΠΡΩTA TA AYTA.

For the principle of both insight and the will (BOYΛH - 1072a 28) is pure
reason (NOHΣIΣ - 1072a 30). Aristotle elucidates further:

> Thus it is from such a principle that empyrean and natural being
> depend. And its life is the best of lives, one that is ours but briefly
> – a perpetual life impossible for us since its working is also its
> pleasure (HΔONH H ENEPΓEIA TOYTOY – 1072b 16) for which
> reason, waking, perception, and insight are the most pleasant as
> well as hopes and memories because of them. Now all thought
> in and of itself considers what, in and of itself, is the best; hence
> the best thought considers what is best of all – thus pure reason
> thinks itself; for thought participates in what thought thinks. At
> the moment of contact and insight (ΘIΓΓANΩN KAI NOΩN -
> 1072b 21), thought becomes an object of thought such that now
> the intellect and the intelligible are the same, because the being
> thought and the thinking being are both pure reason in and of
> itself. Having in thinking is being (ENEPΓEI ΔE EXΩN – 1072b
> 23) and in being thought the thinking being is indeed thought to
> be all the more divine and theory the sweetest and the best
> (KAI H ΘEΩPIA TO HΔIΣTON KAI APIΣTON – 1072b 24). If such
> well-being of thought as we know briefly is for deity perpetual,
> that is truly wondrous and if even more than we know, even
> more wondrous. Wondrous it is in any case. And it has life, too.
> For the actuality of the intellect is life and the deity of reason in
> and of itself is actuality, is life most good and eternal. (1072b 24-
> 28)

Aristotle concludes his train of thought as follows:

> We hold, then, that the deity is a living being, eternal, best; and
> therefore that its life is uninterrupted continuity in perpetuity;
> for this is THEOS. (1072 b 28-30)

ΦAMEN ΔE TON ΘEON EINAI ZΩON AIΔION APIΣTON, ΩΣTE
ZΩH KAI AIΩN ΣYNEXHΣ KAI AIΔIOΣ YΠAPXEI TΩI ΘEΩI.
TOYTO ΓAP O ΘEOΣ.

"This is ΘΕΟΣ!" – An expression of Greek thought, *par excellence.* Reason has, in this "logical" train of thought, won our conviction having persuaded us that it deserves the name of greatest dignity and honor. This is the starting point of the idea of deity in the tradition of Western philosophical thought. *God* is a determination of pure reason, its articulation is an expression of bliss, the narrative of its life an invention of inspired appreciation, a term of endearment, the very entity of veneration, one realized in speech that has learned the language of praise in giving thanks. This is the meaning of thought's *invention* as opposed to *perception* and *performance* – the two other activities of reason, namely contemplative *intellect* that gains insight into the essential entity of thought and moral *judgment* which, by marking the difference between THE WAY IT SHOULD BE and THE WAY IT IS, sparks the fire of desire, initiating thereby a train of thought directed at the fulfillment of a principle. It is therefore not perceptive, not transformative but rather generative thought that, in particular, learns to build reason's glory in the speech of gratitude. Thought's greatest achievement of invention is thus that it is itself its *own* invention, the invention of its own imagination, ultimately the inventive power that emanates from overflowing gratitude, praise that gives rise to the praised, love giving rise to the beloved and then grasping itself as the subject and the second, itself the invention and the beloved, itself the product of what pure thought itself produced. Can we imagine any greater feat than this, namely that the beauty of art could have given rise to the artist, critical self-reflection to the thinker, excellence in action to the actor? And then, in all three of its determinations, in the exuberance and abundance of pure reason's gratitude, to make of itself, though in fact the maker's maker, in truth the product's product, thereby perpetually thanking in thinking? This must be the true and the highest art and craft of thought, the Builder. *Figure 94* shows us this forming being being formed right before our very eyes as "Thought Thinking Thought."

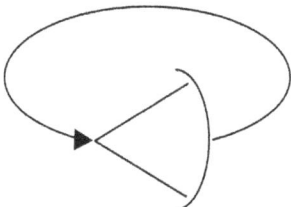

Figure 94: Η ΝΟΗΣΙΣ ΝΟΗΣΕΩΣ ΝΟΗΣΙΣ

Aristotle shows us that the celestial firmament is the ultimate heaven and sanctuary of what is moved, though now no longer changing in itself as do our earth-bound beings, but rather only changing place, moving in the perfectly circular course of stars in which they revolve, entirely engrossed in the concentric concentration of their wonder, their knowing, their seeing, their contemplating from all sides what is most remarkable and notable, living the life of such beings as who lack nothing else to complete their perfection than perfect knowledge and the realization of their own happiness. Reason is, in and of itself, this their own knowledge, their own active self-knowledge disclosed in reason's seeing itself and knowing itself, in the self-relationship of thought, as their entire reality, the self-knowing being of perfection.

For, as Aristotle reasons, thought must think to be active "deriving its excellence from the act of thinking." And if actively thinking, the question arises regarding what thinking would think about if it is the best. "It must think itself or something else..." and since it is absurd that thought, if the best being, should think about a variety of topics, changing at random from one to the next, or dwell on thoughts of what is inferior, "...clearly then it thinks about what is most divine and estimable and does not change; for change would be for the worse...and the act of thinking will belong even to the thinker of the worst thoughts." It follows therefore that "reason thinks itself, if it is that which is best, and its thinking is thinking about thought. (1074b 15-35)

ΑΥΤΟΝ ΑΡΑ ΝΟΕΙ, ΕΙΠΕΡ ΕΣΤΙ ΤΟ ΚΡΑΤΙΣΤΟΝ, ΚΑΙ ΕΣΤΙΝ Η ΝΟΗΣΙΣ ΝΟΗΣΕΩΣ ΝΟΗΣΙΣ.

Thus we return to our initial issue and cause recalled in *Figure 94*. Self-knowing being has found itself again, but this time in the sphere of Greek thought – the universe of pure reason is thought's own self-relative entity of identity. Its excellence has been the center around which our investigation of the distinction of human being has constantly revolved, as was inevitable.

In other words, specifically, in those of Kant, as we heard in the beginning of our investigation, "reason is in fact exclusively concerned with itself and can have no other occupation."

> Die reine Vernunft ist in der Tat mit nichts als sich selbst
> beschäftigt und kann kein anderes Geschäft haben. (Kant, *Kritik
> der reinen Vernunft*, V, III 448.22-23)

This is not an appeal to selfishness, to narcissism, not a conceit of self-glorification, not a bigot's self-centered obsession – which are all, in fact, the very perversion of pure reason's self-several thought about thought thinking thought – but rather the description of a being that *human* being is destined to stand in relationship and define itself with regards to. This relationship and regard are both part of pure reason, part of its life, a figure in the narrative, the tragedy, the poetry of our experience as the thinking, unthinking human beings that we are; by turning our attention to its works, a patient philology learns to come to terms with the issue of pure reason, its building and dwelling.

This being is one very much worthy of contemplation in study, emulation in action, representation in art. For to act in accordance with pure reason's precepts is very different than to regard reason as an object of untiring scientific research or to develop one's skill in giving reason a perceptible and winsome form in the media of our day and age. All this is what the distinction of human being with regards to pure reason entails – really seeing it, acting in accordance with it and bringing forth works such that it might take place in our lives, take shape in our hands, take effect in our words.

The life of reason must, therefore, if it is to be full and complete life, refuse one-sided determinations of its scope. Thinking about and living the life of reason do not contradict one another any more than life should contradict thought, the intellect of science contradict the transformative soul of religion, its discipline contravene that of the art of poetic imagination, or the fictions of fantasy's ingenious invention deny or be denied by the eternal truths that the perceptive mind has discovered, even though we may not in our own lives succeed at combining contemplation and politics, art and science, science and faith, serving and leading, vision and action to that balance and equanimity of purpose that our insight, our ambition, and our creative powers demand of us.

No, we are never done with thought nor should be; striving to attain some semblance of that community – not unity – of principles, we are bound to fail though their proportion and ratio are clearly distinguishable in theory; limited in our grasp of the plenitude of thought in general, we may nevertheless succeed in bringing that spirit to life in particular situations of our own lives; and even failing this, a happy turn of words or phrase may make vividly clear to a select audience what pure reason is and brilliantly demonstrate how the self-severally manifold mind's rhythms govern human thought and action – indeed for students there is a lesson to be learned even in witnessing their teacher's failure. Thus do thought, the

Thinker, the Actor, the Builder, the stone, the scissors, the paper, all, in turn, fail in a particular confrontation and all then again, in terms of the entirety, succeed in defining what thought ultimately is, each making up for the others limitations, supporting one another's office and property, one another's strengths and labors, just as practice trumps theory in usage, invention fulfills the principle that governs action and insight is the prerequisite for applying what we know in what we do and make. But we also learn that every strength of these three is an excellence in its own right and has a season, has had its day in the sun when its prerogative was supreme – the conceptual excellence of science in the First Epoch (theory), moral excellence of religion in the Second (practice), aesthetic excellence of art in the Third (poetry). In each rise and fall there is a lesson to be learned. We would no doubt do well, who love to learn, to take this threefold message to heart and, like Hölderlin's poet, hone our hymn-building art in preparation for the evening festivities when all the principles, our princes, shall gather together to celebrate in peace the dwelling and community of their diversity to which belongs no less a painful memory of the deadly conflict that the crises of the distinctions they founded have entailed in the long tradition of their supposed enmity, a tradition of hate and exclusion nurtured to this very day.

139. The Logotectonic Form of the Knowledge of the Muses[79]

While no one in their right mind could deny that the ideal of freedom still has its proponents and devotees today – freedom is still a name we use to make distinctions – and even as a fiction, more precisely, a figment of the imagination, it is a necessary one, at the very least, in the court of law with a view to the notion of *accountability* and, on the world political stage, with a view to the notion of *human rights* – as with all ideals, their "reality" depends upon the influence we accord them in our everyday lives and how they shape history and "take place" through our particular actions. *Freedom* is truly "just an idea" unless it is given a voice and a face, arms and legs and a loyal heart that seeks to serve its purpose and acts, speaks in its name as a cause taken up. Consider the crimes that have been devised and committed, the sublimity of what has been achieved all *in the name of Freedom*! For all intents and purposes of those living in the mundane sphere of human life, words and deeds are the only "reality" of freedom and these

---

[79] See Boeder: *Seditions*, p. 104, 315-318.

are how Freedom and all our ideals, having arisen spontaneously in the teeming human mind, could possibly matter.

The same holds true, all the more so perhaps, for what folks these days do and do not do *in the name of God*; yes, seen in this light, regardless of where you personally would place God's controversial *"existence"* on a scale of probability from one to ten, religion seems to inspire as much human goodness and atrocity as ever, all very real indeed.

But what could be more lost and gone forever than the Greek gods? I would like to see you find a community of worshippers of Zeus, even on the Internet! When was the last time you, love-sick and prostrate in your despair, lifted your voice and your face to Aphrodite's image and implored: "Come to me now once again and release me from my pangs; and what my heart yearns to accomplish, accomplish; be you yourself my battle ally." (Sappho, Frag. 1)

> ΕΛΘΕ ΜΟΙ ΚΑΙ ΝΥΝ, ΧΑΛΕΠΑΝ ΔΕ ΛΥΣΟΝ / ΕΚ ΜΕΡΙΜΝΑΝ,
> ΟΣΣΑ ΔΕ ΜΟΙ ΤΕΛΕΣΣΑΙ ΘΥΜΟΣ ΙΜΕΡΡΕΙ, ΤΕΛΕΣΟΝ – ΣΥ Δ'
> ΑΥΤΑ ΣΥΜΜΑΧΟΣ ΕΣΣΟ.

No, there is not much slaughtering of bull's these days in honor of the gods; and though there is ample war and fighting in our world, there is a remarkable scarcity of talk of the *might* (ΚΡΑΤΟΣ) of Ares whose *violent force* (ΒΙΑ) and *zeal* (ΖΗΛΟΣ) for *victory* (ΝΙΚΗ) in battle, while dwelling in immediate proximity to Zeus's heart in support of his Olympic dominion, are, as gods of power, nevertheless said to follow his lead, insight's (see Hesiod's *Theogony* 383-8)

And yet those names of the ancient gods would seem to live on in our culture – if not in their original ΛΟΓΟΣ at least in the logos of our advertising – survive in those curious myths that persist, as do other relics and ruins of antiquity, and haunt our literature and especially the occasional poem; Ah, but with Hölderlin we would say: Stop it, hypocritical poets! Come on, you don't believe in the gods – they are just poetic jargon to you: "You are enlightened; you don't really believe in Helios, or in the Thunderer, or in the Sea-god. The earth is dead; who yet offers her thanks?" (*Die scheinheiligen Dichter*, SA I 257.1-4)

> Ihr habt Verstand! ihr glaubt nicht an Helios
> Noch an den Donnerer und Meergott;
> Tot ist die Erde, wer mag ihr danken?

But does not this supposed harmlessness of the defunct Greek gods, coupled with the apparent quaintness of ancient Greek myth and religion, also offer us the best opportunity yet to test the penetration of a philological philosophy that, based on logotectonic method of putting names and delineating trains of thought and lines of reasoning, has taken for its object the principles of pure thought itself and the epochs of its array of reasons as the unfolding and development of an original experience which has bestowed upon us the distinction of a destiny that is, to be sure, not the lightly living gods' own immortality but rather one with regards to which our merely human being comes to recognize its exalted lineage as children of the gods – as *heroes*?

What is a hero? A *hero* is, in the language of Greek wisdom, just what a *citizen* of Humanity was and the *saint* in the Holy Spirit of Christ. A hero is the distinguished human being that was known and vividly rendered for our contemplation by the knowledge of the Muses. While a citizen of autonomy is a self-made man and a self-made woman and a saint is chosen by the Father of mercy, called to the glory of the Son, the hero is born and through his birth destined for the greatness that befits a king, exhibiting prowess in battle and prudence in counsel, excelling others not only in physical stature, beauty, and valor but also in understanding and insight, as accomplished in proper speech as in deeds and in doing all things in accordance with the nobility of his divine lineage. The hero is, in short, a perfect and nevertheless flawed, in other words, self-several human being. It is the lives and deaths of these distinguished beings and how they and their peers measure up to that high destiny – some falling in the disgrace of death, others exalted in the life of immortal renown, the best, all tested, living in the halls of fame – it is the way in which this destiny is worked out and the conflict of interests of all the parties is resolved in accordance with what has been decided in pursuit of what is best in the end that is the issue of the Muses' narrative.

For the Muses know the *whole* story and see the *big* picture. They are attendant upon what is, what will be, and what was before; they are cognizant of how the *now* is directed by the purpose of their father, Zeus, towards the best resolution of antagonistic forces; they discern how *what is coming* is itself founded upon what *was before*, namely the absolute precedence of the principle, as preserved in the mind of their mother, ΜΝΕΜΝΟΣΥΝΗ (Memory). The Muses are attentive to and therefore knowledgeable of such complete being, complete because delineating a complete train of thought that distinguishes in the immediacy of what *is* (ΤΑ Τ ' ΕΟΝΤΑ...), the purpose that is *to be* (...ΤΑ Τ ' ΕΣΣΟΜΕΝΑ...) that will have been perfected in accordance with what *had been* previously (ΠΡΟ Τ ' ΕΟΝΤΑ) determined and therefore recognized as the cause and principle. The parts of this well-rounded sphere of the perfection of being shows the phases that constitute the complete line of reasoning of accomplishment, which is the substance of the knowledge of the seer (cf. Il 2.70) bestowed upon him through the favor of the gods he venerates. This self-several triad of destiny is immediately known by the gods themselves, and the whole that is pure reason's being alone, known in turn by the seer and the poet, the poet and the prophet through the gifts from the Muses of the words of wisdom they bestow upon human inspiration. For unlike the latter, the Muses "are goddesses, are themselves attendant and know all, whereas we hear but rumor and know nothing." (Homer, Il 2.485-6)

ΥΜΕΙΣ ΓΑΡ ΘΕΑΙ ΕΣΤΕ, ΠΑΡΕΣΤΕ, ΙΣΤΕ ΤΕ ΠΑΝΤΕ
ΗΜΕΙΣ ΔΕ ΚΛΕΟΣ ΟΙΟΝ ΑΧΟΥΟΜΕΝ ΟΥΔΕ ΤΙ ΙΔΜΕΝ

The *Now* of the IS where the crisis of distinction is to be carried out and resolved is not a temporal "now" somewhere between a sooner and a later; for, as we have learned from Parmenides, being is "now in its entirety one and the same" (DK 28 B8.5-6). And nevertheless, as we have also seen, *being* is not a blank slate or the smooth indifference of our post/modern youngsters' cheek; rather, the property of this entity of identity is inherent proportion, the inward ΛΟΓΟΣ that ties *being now* with its *being before*. But what can the being *before being* be if it is neither temporal nor spatial? It must be conceptual; thus pure reason's *being before* is twofold and *to be* is being between two ends, the one is the *principle,* the other is the *purpose –* they are the *whence* and the *whither* of the decisive mind that discerns *now* in the present of being what has already been decided and what must follow of necessity from that predetermination. The line of reasoning that determines the shape of destiny in Greek thought begins with the *now* in which the purpose is determined in accordance with the cause and principle of what has already been decided. The formula for *insight* that is the foundation of all distinguished achievement in Greek thought is *C>B + B>A = C>A* and the form is rendered in *Figure 95:*

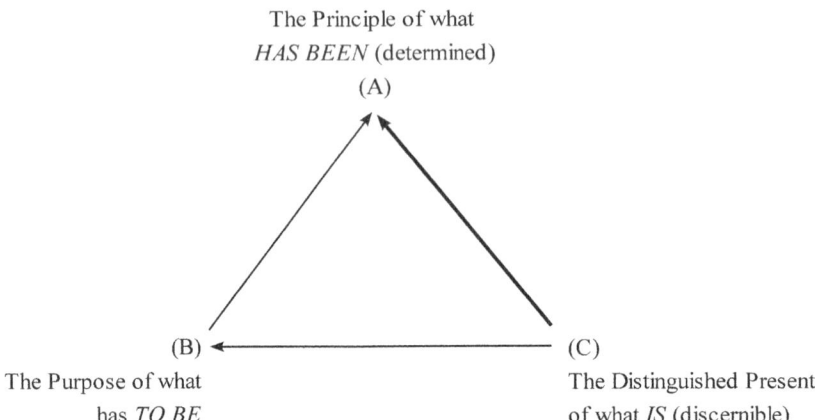

The Principle of what
HAS BEEN (determined)
(A)

(B) ⟵——————————————— (C)
The Purpose of what   The Distinguished Present
has *TO BE*   of what *IS* (discernible)

Figure 95: The Times of Heroic Accomplishment

Thus being's *being before* is not the past that is long dead and gone, nor a future that is a dream deferred, neither a being no more nor not yet, but rather being's own property, known by the seers and the poets, the poets and prophets – the old and wise, i.e. those of rich experience in making distinctions and who, beloved of the gods, are therefore endowed with the perception of a distinguished spirit to "see, know, give accounts forward and back." (Il. 1.343, 3.109-110, 18.250, Od. 24.452)

(ΟΡΑ/ΟΙΔΕ/ΛΕΥΣΣΕΙ ΝΟΗΣΑΙ) ΑΜΑ ΠΡΟΣΣΩ ΚΑΙ ΟΠΙΣΣΩ

By receiving what has been ordained and decided, the hero kings ordain and decide here and now based on THE WAY IT IS as is manifest to distinguished discernment through insight into the being *before being*, namely as it was (destined) to be.

I. Homer

A. The Portions of Divine Order

140. Destiny

After our experience of the relationship of ΛΟΓΟΣ, in the Third Epoch, as one of *contradiction* between the real and the ideal, me and Myself, in the Second, *opposition* between the world of flesh and the world of spirit, now, in the First Epoch, we learn from the epic narratives of Homeric speech that this relationship is one of *identity*, specifically that THE WAY IT IS *is* THE WAY IT SHOULD BE – after *Humanity* and *Deity*, we now make our acquaintance with *Entity*.

Despite this identity inherent in being, to anyone who has studied the issues of contradiction and opposition in the former epochs, it will surely come as no surprise to learn that even in the Greek world, the one known and celebrated by the Muses as that of the Olympian kingdom, the *IS* is by no means immediately evident to the casual observer; for this reason, we who want to experience the truth of "what is" are dependent on the insight provided by the immortals and above all the Muses who are uninterruptedly present at THE WAY IT IS and who therefore, being thus *in attendance*, know all the details first-hand pertaining to what's happened and happening, pertaining to what earnest endeavor, mortal as well as immortal, has accomplished and how the consequences of these deeds and events, as they resolve themselves, are finally to issue forth; to find out these things, we mortals must listen to the Muses' poets' songs or ask the seer who discerns THE WAY IT IS beyond all appearances, personal preferences, and perspectives of human beings who, in the limitations of their mortal purview, hear only rumors and reports and at best can catch glimpses, take note of facets, instances and appearances, but never the whole story, never the big picture, in which the causes and the purposes and the consequences of the forces at play unfold about them and into which their own lives are woven and inexorably bound. Thus, in this world, the distinction of human being is not that of the power of our imagination to bring forth in freedom the reality of humanity; nor is it the work of transformation by which human being enters the dwelling of the kingdom of Heaven as the child of God. In the Greek world, it is the distinction of human being to take one's rightful place in the scheme of all beings in general, in the cosmos of all mortal and immortal beings, and, specifically, in the community of human being wherein these beings dwell together as a people and there accomplish with distinction the duties imposed upon them by the destiny that is their individual lot in life.

This predetermined order or simply, *MOIPA* (moira), is the principle that the validity of what has been definitively and irrevocably laid down as precedent is not itself subject to debate or question. It is the *being before* all being and the *first* principle. Such an inaugural, permanently ancestor determination, that is to say, the prior principle of every other subsequent principle, is, in its seniority, not an origin but rather the immovable foundation and precursor of all successive determinations, the basis and criterion upon which any posterior debate or controversy regarding what is true, what is right and proper, is decided – the primeval, primordial *IS* previous to and in anticipation of all *OUGHT* of thought and its perspectives.

The logic of persuasion and inference makes evident that no discussion can flourish, no train of thought can be pursued unless there is some premise upon which the antagonists agree, the axiom that is itself not open to debate but rather taken for granted for the sake of the ensuing debate. At the same time, clearly, every rule made, every law laid down or particular principle posited and promulgated, *may* be called into question and come under scrutiny. But then, after calling that principle and its prerequisite premises into question, even then, there remains some prior, more primary, more autochthonous principle, some former, further rule, some upper or nether, supernal or infernal law beyond the scope of that particular determination in question, that has hitherto been implicitly assumed as holding good, that comes *before*...until the very foundation and underlying substance has been attained in the insight that this rock solid ground, against which our spades bend back, *has* no ground because it *is* the ground that every other subsequent principle in turn can but *have*; it is the ground reposing upon what is, ultimately, *self-evident* – what is always already taken for granted without ever actually having been granted, the incontrovertible truth of THE WAY IT IS.

The Greek experience with this self-evidence and primacy of principle is recognized, firstly, in the necessity governing the forces of nature prior to all mortal device and discernment; secondly, in that of the laws of logic themselves leading to the issue of inference that pure reason's train of thought must ultimately arrive at – we examined them briefly in connection with Parmenides – and thirdly, in the dictates of propriety which pervades the sphere of human action and presents its reason succinctly thus: that's the way it is, always has been, and always will be, period.

The laws of *Nature* as discerned by theory, the logical laws of pure *Thought*'s own productivity, the moral laws of *Custom* that determine an individual's action – what goes without saying and cannot be said, the unspoken law, that has been taken for granted but has never been expressly granted in a past that has never been a present – this *first* and *foremost* principle whether it be theoretical, logical, or moral, the forgone conclusion and the answer before every question, is called MOIPA, a term that admits of a great variety of translations depending on the context; end, fate, doom, allotment, fortune, fortuity, chance, necessity, foreordainment, predestination, predetermination – take your pick. With regard to the rank and dignity of this notion in Homeric thought, the principle of the Apportionment of *Destiny* – our more general designation – is on par with the principles of the Freedom of *Humanity* and the Glory of *God* that we have studied in the Third and the Second Epochs respectively. They are, all three, in their relationship to each other, constituent *signature terms* in the train of thought they develop and the line of reasoning they articulate and have articulated in a three thousand year old cultural tradition devoted to the teaching, studying, and celebration of the distinction of human being, in other words, the triadic elemental life and movement of that self-relative, self-several entity of identity that has been the issue of this investigation and remains our unique cause.

Who are the Moirai? We have come to know them even as we have always already known who they are. How is this possible? In the process of remembrance and recognition that is the work of the Muses. This principle is made known to us by the mediated immediacy of the distinguished beings who, as immortals, having superior knowledge regarding what has been ordained and accomplished, communicate their knowledge to us, in particular through the nine goddesses who are the daughters of Zeus and MNEMNOΣYNH (mnemnosunē - remembrance) and who bring to mind ancient narratives in the course of which the original principles are recognized as having been established and upon which, as the foundations they institute, the particular issues and cases that arise are deliberated upon in council, with oneself or with one's peers, and decisions taken to be put into purposeful action, verdicts of judgment, rulings, resolutions that are then carried out in the realization of a well-considered plan which takes into account the needs of all concerned parties, granting to each what is due for the sake of what is the best resolution for all.

Thus it is to the epic speech of the *Muses* that we must turn our study now of how our human being first experienced the distinction that was to become this being's *being*, its destiny. Recall that the experience of the distinction is, initially, one of negation and abstraction – *Freedom* and *Deity* are both, in our original experience of them, privative terms for *absolute difference*. And so is *Destiny* a term of distinction in this sense as well. We saw for example in the Third Epoch how the notion of freedom challenged us to step back from the immediate demands of our physical nature, the heteronomy of instinct, and attain the standpoint of our pure personality, the autonomous spirit in accordance with which our actions as moral beings puts into effect the general will of genuine humanity; in the Second Epoch, we step back from the immediate demands of the world of flesh by "putting on" the Christ of judgment so that we might be, with him, in faith, crucified and, in love, resurrected to the glory of God in accordance with which our actions, accomplished in the Holy Spirit of the Son, give witness to the salvation of the world as that of the redeeming will of the Father; similarly, the experience of destiny places us in the pre-established order (ΘΕΜΙΣ – themis) of proportion (MOIPA) determining the scope and limitations (ΔΙΚΗ – dikē) of the dwelling of the immortals and the mortals, the living and the dead, in which every being is defined in accordance with its own nature as the lessor or the greater in dignity and power with regards to the dwelling of the whole the purpose of which has been decided by the highest and the greatest god, Jovial reason, as distinguished from but determining – and therefore either favoring or baffling – our mortal will and designs.

The negativity of these principles of destiny consists in the separation of their absolute priority and precedence from the spheres of influence and control that these beings are wont to advocate and champion as their own sovereign realm and scope of rights; thus, for example, our own experience with the transcendence of the human-all-too-human realm of Man by the mind at large is one of departure and loss, the loss of control, the encounter with risk and uncertainty to come, the bitterness of constraint that a moment of critical reflection puts upon our own immediate inclinations, the negotiation with other's that disrupts the self-centered isolation of our indifference, the anguish of subservience to more senior determinations, and then again the elevation arising from our accordance with their decrees for our own good – in all of the poetic renderings that have been devoted to articulating our experience with this negativity, *death* figured prominently as the term of choice. Why? Because it so poignantly dramatizes the experience of human limitation germane to all of these encounters with the crisis of our Man thus riven. Even today, in spite of his devices of material, mechanical, and electromagnetic dispersion, diffusion, and propagation, this gaseous property of our Man's expansive self-inflation is ultimately checked by the contours of THE WAY IT IS, the limits and boundaries within which our lives run out; it is within the dictates of circumstances that we take our stance, make our last stand. For it is the certainty of death that brings that air-head back to earth and to material matters. Asked about the *end* of life, we tend not to hear the Homeric perspective of this question pertaining, as it does, to the purpose with regards to which we have chosen to make a difference in our lives, but rather, having thus been placed face to face with boundaries we had hoped to ignore in the infant expansiveness of our egoism, to cringe abjectly in the face of a catastrophe beyond our control. Is there any wonder that such human being sniffs the scent of death in all constraints that mark the limits of what is known, of what may be done, in other words, when, in a present thus poisoned by reflection, we are forced to look backward and forward and attend to the determinations of what has been and what is to be as the two horizons – the one in front of us and the other behind – of the interval in which the strict linearity of our domination prevails? Imagine now that, for our infinite Man at least, this thought of demarcations, the straits and narrows that determine, restrain the play of our *mere* being, i.e. the notion of an allotted, distinguished and, in this sense, *just* being – precisely this *thought* of death – *is* the death, that all beings, even the immortal gods experience when they encounter defining limitations as determine, for each being with regards to every other in the cosmos of beings, THE WAY IT SHOULD BE.

Is it exaggerated to call our experience with limits to our mundane power *death*? After all, when we are refused a favor or denied a request, delayed in our gratification, charged with a duty, deprived of some boon that we had hitherto always taken for granted as our privilege, in short, when we experience a collision with some significant OTHER that puts us in our place, manifesting to us for the first time that we *have* a place – this experience is, let's face it, not *really* our death. *Really?* What reality do you appeal to if not to the death you have experienced while alive – the experience you have learned to call *death*? The loss of a loved one, the wasting away of the diseased, the dilapidation of the old, the appalling finitude and frailty of human life – are these blows and cuts against our pride's most entrenched delusions of impunity and omnipotence not sufficiently mortifying to serviceably bear the name of *death*, at the very least in the distinguished speech of the Muses and, accordingly, in the works of thought, the Builder, who strives to render the issue of critical reflection as powerfully as possible in terms that succeed at distinguishing the charmed life of thought from any old life and a transfiguring death from the splatter and rot of our decease in violence or disease?[80]

For one such as us then, to encounter a coercive limit against which our desire is crossed, our plans spoiled, our dreams and hopes dashed by

---

[80] Cf. Sophocles, *Antigone* (1165-7). The messenger prefaces his news of catastrophe in the following terms:
ΚΑΙ ΓΑΡ ΗΔΟΝΑΙ ΟΤΑΝ ΠΡΟΣΔΩΣΙΝ ΑΝΔΡΟΣ ΟΥ ΤΙΘΗΜ᾽ΕΓΩ ΖΗΝ ΤΟΥΤΟΝ
ΑΛΛ᾽ΕΜΨΥΧΟΝ ΗΓΟΥΜΑΙ ΝΕΚΡΟΝ." (In my view, a man bereft of his pleasures is not a living being but rather an animated corpse, walking dead.). Poets have always known how to make good use of the idea of *death* with a view to drawing a distinction.

disregard, our own or someone else's towards us, is the bitter, crushing, humiliating experience of death. True, we are still "alive" – alive to anger, frustration, outrage; but this is the "fatal outrage" (MHNIN OYΛOMENHN – mēnin oulomenēn - Il. 1.1) of our pride, the *death* that spawns a thousand deaths, upon which the epic narrative of the Iliad commences. To die the death of mortification, you have to survive in spite of yourself, and that means self-severally.

Our human being is thus initially determined as mortal in possessing an allotment or *portion* of life (ΠΟΤΜΟΣ, KHP, AIΣA) the limit of which has been appointed to us, in other words, against the predetermination of which we, as ephemeral living beings, must recognize our powerlessness though not merely by resigning ourselves to *live with it*, but rather in the acknowledgement of this limit as THE WAY IT SHOULD (WAS DESTINED, MEANT, FATED) TO BE, the portion of our *human* being (Il 3.101) in the whole of just being; *death*, the ill-named portion (12.115) comes to, overcomes us, enfolds (12.116), ensnares us with its fetters (4.517) and cannot even be warded off by the gods from those they love (3.236), for the gods, too, no less than we are, are bound to acknowledge human being as mortal – we see, in the narrative of the Muses, death's inexorable, inevitable might (24.132) as that of a defining terminus of our mere being, the determination of a constraining limit that we must abide in, live and die by.

The choices we have made, our counsel in accordance with the principles such that the best might be achieved (Il. 10.17) – this is, as we shall see, the will of Zeus in which our own resolutions participate – are in their outcomes uncertain; they depend on factors not in our control – call them those of *chance* or *luck*; in terms of the knowledge of the Muses, they depend on fate and fortune – call them the will or the caprice of the gods, call them their whims or decrees – and work in favor of or against the accomplishment of our designs. Confounding even the best laid plans are unforeseen or unforeseeable events and contingencies. Things do not always turn out as planned. Why not? *The Moirai* is not the answer to this question but rather to the question: "How shall we name the experience that events do not always conform to our particular preference?" More precisely: "How can we account for all of the specific details that determine the contour of our lives that were not the outcomes of our choices, beginning with the place and time of our birth, our ethnic background, our nationality, our physical constitution, intelligence, strength of body and innate talents of mind, our parents, all of the circumstances of their lives in turn and those of their parents, and so on, i.e. the results of generations of actions and decisions, good as well as bad, that all human beings have to live with in their time even as we do now by virtue of our being their children, higher or lower of birth and of station (18.367), suffering, enjoying the consequences of ancestors' actions, wars, discoveries, inventions, economic upheavals, technological 'progress' – add to these our religions, philosophies, and other customs and conventions of our 'socialization' that have become the framework of our lives – in short, all of the minutiae of our natural and cultural environment and the eventualities that stem from these that have formed and influenced our minds and our bodies and, locking us into that setting and situation of inherited parameters, have determined who and what we now are for better or for worse as the case may be in the world we find ourselves inhabiting.

Shall we call these extraneous determinations of our lives *chance, luck, happiness* if they would appear to be advantageous, *misfortune, calamity, accident, pain* if our having been struck by them is detrimental to our well-being? We have all endured despair at seeing our hopes and expectations crossed, our carefully plotted plans foiled by an unlucky turn of events; no, sometimes things don't work out as intended, go against our will – the depth of our disappointment at this almost insidious crossing of our *heartfelt purposes* can perhaps be best rendered as an experience with the *malevolence* of the circumstances – the blighting of our desires is self-severally reflected as the spite of countervailing fires, just as we saw in the second epoch that Man's *aversion* is mirrored in God's *revulsion,* our *malfeasance* in His *chastisement* and the dust, the flesh of *contrition* transfigured into the spirit of divine *mercy* – these opposites are self-severally one and the same like Hesperus and Phosphorus, the cup half full and the cup half empty, "the way up and the way down," as Heraclitus taught (DK 22 B 60). They are opposing spins, takes, on the same issue, the two different senses and experiences of our entity of identity as rendered one way or the other by thought, the Builder.

In the face of this apparent adversity, we are forced to recognize that the schemes we premeditate are not entirely our own to fulfill. After all has been said and done, considered and calculated, there is a *Frankensteinian* remainder of incalculable risk in our advancements, an unknown variable in otherwise so tidy equations, a chaotic crack in a slate of laws, a twist of unpredictability in Man's well-tuned sobriety. This Prometheus of our will, having painfully perceived the gap that marks the limit of our mortal destiny hitherto ignored, recognizes that across the divide now yawning before us and separating us from our cherished certainty, our pretense to power, lately lost, has emerged, on the other side of this coign of vantage, the distinguished will and power as well as the knowledge of pure reason's own self-several reflection; the *other* will that faces our face is that of the MOIPA, of the gods, ultimately, of Zeus himself as the king of the Olympic realm of immortal and mortal being.

Consider, for example, when we drop something *by accident* that we were holding in our hand and normally never drop; now there are surely a great many causes for this happening at this particular moment. Maybe our hand was wet; maybe we had failed to grasp the object properly because or hand was stiff and tired from typing all morning; maybe the object was in an unusual position when we picked it up because last night we were in a hurry when setting it down; maybe we were distracted by a sound, a thought, momentarily inattentive to what we were doing. All of these causes have their causes and those causes further causes in their own right...is there any definitive end to them? But none of these causes are the *reason* why I dropped it because *there is no reason.*

Amazingly, this insight that *there is no reason* gives rise to a reason often expressed in terms of resignation like "that's just the way it is!" For this reason is simply the recognition and acknowledgement of the limit that marks the difference between THE WAY IT IS and the WAY IT SHOULD BE. In the acknowledgement of this difference, the *outside* of our firmly established and well-furnished sphere of control has emerged and makes itself known to us and, with the critical self-reflection of our *assent* or *dissent* to this experience of absolute difference, the *favor* or the *disfavor* of its present pertaining to our own designs and desires. Say *yes* to this experience of difference and you are affirmed by favor, say *no* and you are condemned regardless of whether what has happened to you is good or bad. In both eventualities you acknowledge or neglect the limit of THE WAY IT IS with respect to the way it could be, the way it should be but is not.

The object we drop contrary to our intention is disfavored by this distinction, THE WAY IT IS not being THE WAY IT SHOULD BE in our eyes, it is seen as the work of divine censure, immortal disapproval answering mortal disapproval; had we held on to the object and accomplished what we had intended with it, our enterprise, to the extent that its accomplishment is actually taken for *granted* and not merely taken for granted, would have been thought to be favored, sanctioned in accordance with sanction, THE WAY IT IS conforming to THE WAY IT SHOULD BE. In both cases, the favor and the disfavor are reflections of our experience with and our judgment of what has just happened, what we have done, the situation in which we find ourselves having taken note of it as THE WAY IT IS in a moment of critical reflection.

Thus when Diomedes drops his whip during the chariot race and is therefore now in danger of losing the contest that he, just a moment before this accident, seemed to be on the verge of winning, it is Phoebus Apollo who, begrudging him victory, strikes the whip from his hand. (23.383-84) When the yoke of Eumelus' horses suddenly breaks during the same race – he was leading in the final stretch and his horses were neck and neck with those of Diomedes – it is Athena's resentment that breaks it, hurling Eumelus from his chariot into the dust. (23.391-92) The IS of the outcome reveals THE WAY IT SHOULD BE and rests with the gods, above all with Zeus (22.379; 23.724), whose designs are brought to fruition in the end. In answer to our prayers aid is vouchsafed (23.770) or refused – as the gods will, ultimately in accordance with the plans of Zeus who does not base his decision on personal preference but rather on what was meant to be as revealed by his objectively weighing up both sides of the issue and taking his decision based on the evidence of the OUGHT as manifested by his golden scales of destiny (22.209). For what has already been decided and has come to pass and is now here at hand, namely THE WAY IT SHOULD BE, not even Zeus can change. (14.53-54)

Are mortals then, reduced to making the best of their situations and unable to perfectly determine the outcome of their efforts, mere puppets and playthings of the forces of circumstance? The ultimate success or failure of their endeavors is not in their hands but nevertheless, they participate in the narrative that the gods are weaving with the threads of mortal lives; all their lives have been written, inscribed in the story of the Muses. For in fact, it is not merely *their* lives that the mortals are living, it is also the lives of the gods, the story of the immortals, that is being unfolded through and with mortal actions and it is in this way that the mortals distinguish themselves from being the puppets of some blind fate even as the immortals do; immortals and mortals are all participants in the drama of distinction that unfolds THE WAY IT SHOULD BE and, by assuming this standpoint, accompany their lives knowingly, recognizing the parameters of the situation in which we find ourselves thrown, working, as it were, with the hand we have been dealt; learning of and comparing our strengths and weaknesses with others and with those of the immortal gods, we perceive our relationship to our compeers and to the gods who generally repay excellence with success, requite honor with regard in the self-relativity of reflection celebrated by the language of wisdom as we have seen again and again. Aias slips in his footrace with Odysseus – Athena was responsible – for she was aiding Odysseus as she always does, causing Aias' accident while making Odysseus's limbs light and lithe (23.772-74). The success of mortal endeavors depends on the regard they show for the beings of this openness of human being – to those showing kindness, the gods show kindness in return; showing mercy, mortals are shown mercy, "the gods lend an ear to those who listen." (Il. 1.218)

ΟΣ ΚΕ ΘΕΟΙΣ ΕΠΙΠΕΙΘΗΤΑΙ ΜΑΛΑ Τ' ΕΚΛΥΟΝ ΑΥΤΟΥ

That is why the gods are clearly recognizable (ΑΡΙΓΝΩΤΙ ΔΕ ΘΕΟΙ ΠΕΡ - 13.72) when they intervene on behalf of the mortals they care for, giving the latter courage and strength (13.61), rousing them to battle (13.90), urging on their attack (13.154), and on the other side, dooming their opponents in fulfillment of the plan that Zeus laid out in the beginning (13.624-25). But mortals in their limits, mostly blind to the big picture, see but the whims of the gods, above all Zeus's whims (13.225-26), at play, confounding what seems to our human sense to be the right thing, namely what is good for *me*, *here*, *now*, *today* with what is right from the more objective standpoint of the Gods.

141. Fate

Since your birth and indeed long before it, the state of affairs that have determined your beings' being, the Moirai, has roused you (5.629) and guided you and finally led you, even you who now read these words, to this juncture (5.613, 13.602), to this decisive, contested moment in which you as a hero king encounter, at the hands of an opponent (16.434), whether divine or mortal (16.849) – and therein subject to the place and time of a given set of circumstances – the determination of your life's limit such that in the victory of success you attain glory or, put to the sword of distinction, killed by one greater than yourself, bestow glory to the victor while you yourself, defeated and therefore fated to ignobly die, surrender your soul; that tenacity of life, once so vibrant in courage and youth, departs now from the limbs of the body, bewailing its fate, only to enter the darkness of Hades and the oblivion of the shadow realm (16.857), that rock bottom in which the masses of the merest of beings, trickling, settle and accumulate – subsequent to your very last realization on the occasion of your extinction, namely that of quiescence in "giving your soul to Hades and fame to the victor." (11.443)

For the soldier, decisive battle makes manifest each individual's fate, reveals the good death and the bad, the agony and shame of defeat of the one hero giving glory to the other who vanquished him or who, the vanquisher, then again, at another times, against another, is vanquished in turn (12.325) – the experience of the distinction of human being as *just being* is rendered in Homeric speech as the drama of two heroes locked in the ordeal (21.225-6) of mortal combat (7.51), might contested, might measured against contending might (1.278) until death do they part (3.20), one man slain by the gods of distinction at the hands of another man, a good man by a good man (21.280), a lesser hero slain by the better as is right, which is the event of the impartment of distinction that determines, in a trial of arms (5.220), who is the victor and the champion, whose glory and favor by the gods is the greater, and who the weaker, whose fate it is to be vanquished in the shame of his demise and perish far from home in anonymity (ΝΩΝΥΜΝΟΥΣ – 13.227). In the reciprocity of this relationship of distinction, we recognize the self-reflectivity of pure reason, in which both sides of the opposition, giving and being given, seeing and being seen, vanquishing and being vanquished, form and being formed, pattern and matter are comprehended in the turn and return of thought thinking thought.

For this reason, in the drama of distinction, alas, eventually, even the slayer will be slain – Patroclus by Hector and Hector by Achilles (16.853) and ultimately even Achilles's life "will one day be taken in battle by Ares, some dawn, or evening, or midday whether through the arrow's strike or the spear's" (21.111-113) – no man has ever escaped his doom, be he coward or valiant (6.485), when once he has been born. (6.490) Man's "original sin" is precisely this distinction of our self-knowing being, destined to discern the self-severalty of just being – so also Achilles whose own life's measure was set at birth (23.79) to briefest briefness (ΩΚΥΜΟΡΩΤΑΤΟΣ – 18.95) in recompense for that which, as the narrative unfolds, reveals, in the brightest brilliance, the highest distinction enjoyed by human being, namely to be favored, even loved by the gods; nevertheless " common to all is Ares: Also he who slays is slain in turn." (Il. 18.309)

ΞΥΝΟΣ ΕΝΥΑΛΙΟΣ, ΚΑΙ ΤΕ ΚΤΑΝΕΟΝΤΑ ΚΑΤΕΚΤΑ

The distinction of death that breaks the continuity of inconspicuous life, tears, cuts the thread that is the anonymity of its indifferent continuity and differentiates a good death from a bad one, a good life of renown in excellence from the obscurity of human being in the endless cycle of birth and death like the generation of leaves sprouting in spring only to be blown away by autumnal winds (Il. 6.146-149), to perish in abrupt, untimely (1.416) destruction, to waste away in disease, worn out by the anguish of grief and weeping, to die far from home and one's native land (Il. 24.86), to be "swept away by the seas, with no tidings, out of sight and hearing" (Od. 1.241-242), left to be forgotten with neither funeral nor burial (Od. 24.295), with one's work unfinished (Il. 4.175) or else, worse, remembered with shame and loathing for the deeds of wickedness that were our achievement – this is the ignominious, the bad death (13.602), the baneful (16.849), infamous one (12.116) that engulfs us, the pathetic death that is the body's biting the dust, the blood and gore of spilling viscera, the purple darkness sinking over dying eyes and our flesh left as carrion to gorge scavengers, to be devoured by vultures and starving dogs and the fishes in the sea (Il. 1. 4-5, 22.354) – death's juncture tests and shows the better hero, the one more favored by the gods and thus pre-eminent in endowments, the destiny of one whose valor and might are superior to all others; for the one killed in battle, this distinction brings to light the cruelty of our doom as mortals, destined to vie for excellence and distinction with regards to THE WAY IT SHOULD BE and ultimately fail.

By contrast, the good death is to win a death with distinction on the battlefield of difference and a burial of honor (16.455) – but one decorous rather than bombastic (23.245) – or, better yet, to die in the arms of friends after returning home to see one's high-roofed house and one's people bearing their due share of prosperity (Od. 5.40-42) and then to be commemorated by a tomb of honor (1.239) "on a projecting headland by the broad Hellespont, that it might be seen from far across the sea by men living now as well as those born hereafter" (24.80)

ΑΚΤΗΙ ΕΠΙ ΠΡΟΥΧΟΥΣΗΙ, ΕΠΙ ΠΛΑΤΕΙ ΕΛΛΗΣΠΟΝΤΩΙ, ΩΣ
ΚΕΝ ΤΗΛΕΣΦΑΝΗΣ ΕΚ ΠΟΝΤΟΦΙΝ ΑΝΔΡΑΣΙΝ ΕΙΗ ΤΟΙΣ
ΟΙ ΝΥΝ ΓΕΓΑΑΣΙ ΚΑΙ ΟΙ ΜΕΤΟΠΙΣΘΕΝ ΕΣΟΝΤΑΙ.

Thus to say that to die is to fulfill that measure of one's life (4.170) that the god's have bestowed upon each as a unique fortune is to acknowledge the efficacy of the principle manifest in things being the way they are. For in death, we experience the distinction of our mortal human being as a constraining principle that gives our life its specific contours, sets us a definite, determinate end in the bounds of which what was supposed to be is completed in finally being. This terminating principle of THE WAY IT SHOULD (IS FATED, DETERMINED, DESTINED TO) BE – called in the words of the First Epoch our *fate*, i.e. declared by the eternal gods (7.53), the allotment of our *portion* the constraining limits of which "no man has ever escaped whether valiant or weak" (6.488), and our *destiny* – is the end (ΤΕΛΟΣ – 16.857) of our ways at which we finally arrive, entering that last house, Hades' (11.264), celebrated for its sinister hospitality in welcoming all comers because all do indeed come to call at the end.

Whatever we may hope and wish for ourselves personally – the *is* of our own *ought* – we cannot escape what is meant to be and the determination of our being that came first, before us, the *is* that is our other, further *OUGHT*. For this OUGHT, both before and after our own, governs the IS, more, this OUGHT *is* the IS, the background and framework, the stage upon which the narrative of our lives is elaborated. To encounter this OUGHT, its power beyond that of our own privacy, overpowering (5.83) the puniness of our preferences and plans, the devilishly devious devices of our designs, is to meet and experience our doom (7.52), the one proper to us and not foreshortened by the blindness of overweening mindlessness that disregards the measures of what has been determined and forgets its place in the scheme of things in which he who is the lesser, hated, and who, loved by the gods, the greater (20.336) has always already been decided from the moment of each individual's birth.

But though the hero deals in death and must evince excellence in combat, yours may not be a soldier's lot. *Death*, the soldier's encounter with the determination of his life, is merely the most dramatic rendition of the distinction of human being; it is by no means the only walk of life. In fact, even a soldier's life can be differentiated – there are hurlers of spears and drawers of bows, drivers of swift horses and yet all men of war (Od. 18.260). But not all are born warriors, servants of Ares, and destined to fight valorously among the first (4.34); some are, rather, destined to be lovers and the comely gifts of Aphrodite are also not to be cast aside lightly, slighted. (3.65)

But what are you? You say you have been born a woman or a man, well then, each gender has his or her appropriate tasks (1.355) to address; perhaps you are now older, enjoying the privilege of prudence or are young and strong though tending towards rashness (21.440), excel more in deliberation and prefer the words of council to the bloody deeds of battle (9.444, 4.400), have been born to serve or to lead, to carry the sword or the hammer or whatever profession you chose with regards to your endowment, that you have not chosen but rather find yourself in possession of, having been chosen by this talent, as it were. And whether it is to cook the meals or tend the horses, teach the young or entertain the assembly with your song, be you king or a subject among the people (12.213), a son, a daughter, a father, a mother, a brother, a sister, a husband, a wife (Od. 11.177) – you have your place and in accordance with it, who you are and what you deserve, your due, is determined, as is your duty. Know your place and, having received thus your lot in life, excel among your peers in doing what you were born to do. Such is the counsel that Polydamas offers Hector, the great Trojan general, in order to avert disaster, prefacing his advice with an appeal to what has been determined:

"Hector, you are tough to persuade with words. Because a god
has given you superiority in deeds of war, you suppose that in
counsel too you surpass all others; but in fact it is impossible
that you, being but one, can grasp all things. To one man god has
given excellence in war, to another dance, to another excellence
in lyre and song, and in the breast of another man Zeus...puts a
penetrating mind that profits many...." (Il 13.726-733)

Evidently, MOIPA designates the order of destiny and that the *order* is not
merely the determination of what has been decided as the fatal limit to
which all living human being is subject but also that it is, with a view to the
whole comprehending all beings, well proportioned, seemly, and therefore
a good order (EY KATA KOΣMON – 10.472), one that is *fair* to behold
(KAΛON – Od. 20.294), *right* (ΔIKAION – ibid.); in other words, that the *IS* is
not merely to be recognized and acknowledged as THE WAY IT IS apart
from our plans and expectations, but also that THE WAY IT IS *is* THE WAY
IT SHOULD BE, the way it always has been and always will be, that it is, *on
the whole*, what is meet and proper in accordance with and not in excess of
(YΠEP – 20.336; 21.517; 6.333; 6.487; 16.780; 17.321; Od. 1.34; Od. 5.436)
what has been ordained, decided, pledged, i.e. that it is in accordance with
and not in excess of the dictate (DIKH – Od. 19.168) of law's foundations
(ΘEMIΣ); that it is, in a word, in accordance with the mores of *custom*, can
be seen in Homeric speech in the expression *KATA MOIPAN* (in accordance
with proportion) which means "rightly," as judged by insight and prudence,
i.e. with practical reason, due and proper as exhibited by the formula
"indeed, all this...you have spoken with regards to proportions" (8.146, 9.59,
10.169, 15.206, 19.186, 23.626, 24.379, Od 3.331, 4.266, 7.227, 8.141, 8.496,
10.16, 12.35, 13.48, 17.580, 18.170, 20.37, 21.278, 22.486)

NAI ΔH TAYTA ΓE ΠANTA...KATA MOIPAN EEIΠEΣ

142. The Order of Proportion

The narrative of the Muses is replete with rich descriptions that show
meticulous care in providing the precisely rendered details we would expect
eye-witnesses who "are there and know all" (ΠAPEΣTE TE IΣTE TE ΠANTA
– 2.485) to give accounts of, especially of those beings that are pre-eminent
(EΞΛOXOΣ – 2.480) and therefore *significant* – signs of Zeus who is the
supreme and superlative being in the Homeric speech – whether in strength
or beauty, in power or valor – even as is Aias, towering a head and a shoulder
taller than the rest (3.227); the best and the foremost stand out, arrest our
attention as beings worthy of note, manifest and remarkable for all to see

and admire, inviting contemplation, kindling our desire to know more deeply and completely – look with amazement at Agamemnon leading his army into battle, made glorious by Zeus whose eyes and head, by Ares whose waist, by Poseidon whose breast the king's were made to resemble, and in this way give testimony to the fact that he is "pre-eminent among many and supreme among the heroes!" (2.483)

ΕΚΠΡΕΠΕ ΕΝ ΠΟΛΛΟΙΣΙ ΚΑΙ ΕΞΟΧΟΝ ΗΡΩΕΣΣΙΝ

Or take the famous catalogue of ships! (2.494-877) The rhapsodist calls upon the Muses to aid him in the enumeration of their superabundance, a feat of recollection that would be impossible even if he had "ten tongues and ten mouths and an inexhaustible voice and a heart made of bronze." (2.489-490). Thus he appeals to the muses as goddesses of memory (ΜΙΜΝΗΣΚΩ – 2.492) and through the power of their recollection to name and to "tell the leaders of the ships and all of the ships." (2.493)

ΑΡΧΟΥΣ ΑΥ ΝΗΩΝ ΕΡΕΩ ΝΗΑΣ ΤΕ ΠΡΟΠΑΣΑΣ

In their catalogues and lists, they take note of excellence, bringing to light "the best of the warriors and the horses that accompanied the sons of Atreus" (2.761); noteworthy is who among the many Trojan soldiers was the first to face king Agamemnon in battle (11.218) and who among the Achaeans was the first to bear away bloody spoils of war in victory (14.508), "who was the first and the last among them to be slain by Hector now that Zeus granted him glory?" (11.299-300) Similarly, the Muses know the details of how it came to pass that the first fire was thrown onto the Achaeans' ships, resulting eventually in Achilles' return to the battlefield (16.112).

In their descriptions they provide all of the details, gory details we would say, regarding how a hero dies but also those pertaining to a hero's origins, his name and patrimony, his rank and lineage, his nationality, his excellence relative to his combatant, the armor and the weapons of his glory. In addition to these portraits that bespeak renown and the aftermath of gory glory in the arts of war, we observe the arts of human dwelling, a meal being prepared, dressing, rituals of sacrifice and prayer, of burial, objects of beauty and handiwork, clothing, the cultivation of the fields.

In all of these descriptions, we recognize the wisdom of the Muses to bring to light THE WAY IT IS and the salience of what is superb, well made, expertly done, spoken with authority, accomplished. Such things catch our eye and spark our attention; they are determinate and concisely drawn in the narrative, memorable in the sharp contours in which the knowledge of the Muses has saved them from oblivion. As we shall later see, it is the original work of ΛΟΓΟΣ to collect and recollect in one place what would have otherwise remained scattered about; it is its power of discrimination to discern what belongs to what and what goes where and then to put everything into its own proper place where it belongs – this is the order and the ordering that attends the notion of ΛΟΓΟΣ in its earliest uses, namely in those of Homeric language.[81]

Everything has its proper place! In the spirit of this pre-eminently Greek thought, we might more easily understand the train of thought governing the transition from the impartial necessity of being to the propriety of being. The portions are not merely the limits of life in death but also the limits of life *in life*, the scope and sphere of our influence and action as determined by who we are, our place and lot in life, whether man or woman, human being or divine. Living, human being is confronted with all manner of limits and measures, the times and seasons, the orders of being, that govern our dwelling. Thus, for example the time to sleep: "it is entirely impossible that human being should be forever sleepless, to each thing the immortals have set, for mortals, a portion upon the fruitful earth" (Od. 19.591-593).

ΑΛΛ' ΟΥ ΓΑΡ ΠΩΣ ΕΣΤΙΝ ΑΥΠΝΟΥΣ ΕΜΜΕΝΑΙ ΑΙΕΙ
ΑΝΘΡΩΠΟΥΣ, ΕΠΙ ΓΑΡ ΤΟΙ ΕΚΑΣΤΩΙ ΜΟΙΡΑΝ ΕΘΗΚΑΝ
ΑΘΑΝΑΤΟΙ ΘΝΗΤΟΙΣΙΝ ΕΠΙ ΖΕΙΔΩΡΟΝ ΑΡΟΥΡΑΝ

This measure demands recognition and acknowledgement – fortunately, with a view to such obligating, unobliging necessity, challenging us, as it does, at every turn, the MOIPAI have also endowed human being with a persevering heart (24.49).

In the end, however, even the immortal gods respect the measures and dictates of all living being; for example, they take their repose in due time, each in his or her own place, in his or her own home (1.606-7) and then, at this moment, *Sleep*, the brother of *Death*, is the acknowledged lord of the gods as well as of all mortal human being. (14.231-233)

No, the Olympian gods, though immortal, are not exempt from regard of the MOIPA; deathless, they are nevertheless sensible of what is meet and proper, the due owed them and, what is more, the due they owe to each other, for example to *Night* who bends to her sway both mortals and

---

[81] See Boeder's article, "Der frühgriechische Wortgebrauch von Logos und Alētheia" in: *Das Bauzeug der Geschichte*, p. 3.

immortals (14.259-261) and in the mores of divine dwelling, the gods rise when Zeus, their king, enters the palace, whether they want to or not.

What destiny is, is no secret or occult force; it manifests itself to all eyes. Look and see and in each case or situation you encounter and to which you are thus called at the behest of the moment to respond and to take a stand, you will recognize what is required at the moment, what is better, what, with regards to the specifics of circumstance, is worse, and what is the best – even of ills there is a best solution (17.105); as events transpire, you will know what you have to do, what reason, what person is stronger, who, what course of action is favored by the unfolding narrative that you seek to make sense of as your one and only life in light of what destiny urges, as an indication of the success or failure of one whose time, whose day in the sun, has come, or, as the vanquished, whose appointed time, whose doomsday, has arrived, whose precarious life has been condemned, sentenced to serve as the backdrop for another's glorification. In this way, the will of Zeus, in accordance with what has been determined, has been fulfilled (1.5). For it is reasonable and proper that the lessor warrior perish when encountering the greater, that the stronger, better argument vanquishes and the weaker is vanquished and when this is not the case, all the parties are outraged by the travesty, the injustice of it – namely when " the one who hangs back and the one who battles his best have a like portion, and both the coward and the brave are held in one honor, when death comes alike to the idle man and to him who works much" (9. 318-320). This indifferent equality will never do and must not stand.

B. The Apple of Discord

143. The Issue of Regard

"If only discord perished from among gods and men, discord, but also rage...!" (Il. 18.107-8) – a fond wish sighed by Achilles in sorrow and bitter self-reproach reflecting upon all that has been lost as a result of his anger, above all his failure to save Patrocles, his beloved companion and landsman:

ΩΣ ΕΡΙΣ ΕΚ ΤΕ ΘΕΩΝ ΕΚ Τ' ΑΝΘΡΩΠΩΝ ΑΠΟΛΟΙΤΟ
ΚΑΙ ΧΟΛΟΣ...

The wisdom of the Muses teaches us how a perceived injustice ignites strife (ΕΡΙΣ) among beings, mortal and immortal, and recounts the far-reaching ramifications of the outrage that ensues when unthinking insolence repudiates the right of due regard (TIMH) and in scorn refuses to acknowledge the respect owed to merit; the divisive consequences that accrue to all concerned parties in the determination of what is due each being's excellence (APETH) is the red thread of war and the issue that is to be decided in the crisis of distinction – who is the better and the best, the greater, the more powerful, the more beautiful? Who deserves the greater portion of distinction? And in recognition or rejection of each being's claim to honor, the scope and limits of each one's proper place in the scheme of the whole is affirmed or challenged, admitted or violated. It is then in the disregard of that prerogative that our relationship with our peers, our elders and our betters, the immortal gods, the configuration of our mutual bonds and bounds, are called into question and, in the aftermath, must be reestablished by the force of altercation.

Contention, its instigation and resolution, pertaining to what is meet and proper among Homeric beings in the evaluation of their mutually determined and defined place in the whole is the issue upon which the narrative is developed that articulates the insight of the Muse into their portion thereof.

Achilles "fateful outrage" at the disregard with which he is treated by Agamemnon is the inaugural issue of the Iliad. (Il. 1.1). His anger resulted in the countless sorrows and the deaths of many valiant souls who perished because Zeus agreed to punish Agamemnon for his overweening blindness in insulting Achilles whom Agamemnon in turn perceived as not showing him the deference due the king and lord of the entire Greek army.

The first book of the Iliad shows how controversy in the issue of regard and distinction develops the narrative:

1. Agamemnon disregarded (HTIMAΣEN – 1.11) Chryses, Apollo's priest. Chryses had petitioned the Achaeans and especially the two sons of Atreus, Agamemnon and Menelaus, with entreaties and gifts of honor (APOINA – 13) out of respect for him (AIΔEIΣΘAI - 377) and reverence (AZOMENOI – 21) for Apollo to free his daughter. Agamemnon refused.

2. Chryses then implores Apollo in prayer to show him honor by repaying with punishment (TIΣEIAN – 42) the Danaans' disregard; Apollo, honoring his priest, hears his plea and sends a pestilence through the army.

3. Agamemnon, learning that his disregard of Chryses is being punished by Apollo returns the priests daughter only to demand that he, Agamemnon, now immediately be given another prize

of honor (ΓΕΡΑΣ) to replace her, for it is improper (ΕΠΕΙ ΟΥΔΕ ΕΟΙΚΕ – 119) that the king be the only one without a prize of honor and in response to Achilles' rebuke of greed (ΠΗΙΛΟΚΤΕΑΝΩΤΑΤΕ ΠΑΝΤΩΝ – 122) threatens to take for his own a gift of honor from among those that had already been distributed.

4. Achilles then accuses him of shameless disrespect (ΑΝΑΙΔΕΣ, ΚΥΝΩΠΑ – 1-149,158) for neither respecting nor caring a whit about (ΜΕΤΑΤΡΕΠΗΙ...ΑΛΕΓΙΖΕΙΣ – 1-160) the sacrifice he, namely Achilles, and the other warriors have made on Agamemnon's account and threatens to return home rather than be thus disregarded (ΑΤΙΜΟΣ – 171).

5. Agamemnon then reiterates his disregard for Achilles and the latter's anger (ΟΥΚ ΑΛΕΓΙΖΩ...ΟΥΔ ' ΟΘΟΜΑΙ... - 180-181), confident of the honor that others and above all Zeus bestows upon him (ΤΙΜΗΣΟΥΣΙ – 175) and decides to take Briseis, Achilles' prize of honor, "so that you may well know how much mightier I am than you and another too may shrink from declaring himself my equal and likening himself to me to my face." (185-187).

6. This brazen affront (ΥΒΡΙΣ – 203), fills Achilles heart with anguish (ΑΧΟΣ – 188) and while debating with himself whether or not he should kill Agamemnon on the spot, Athena appears, sent by Hera who loves and cares for both warriors (ΦΙΛΕΟΥΣΑ ΤΕ ΚΕΔΟΜΕΝΕ ΤΕ – 196), bids him to stop this strife (ΕΡΙΣ – 210) and promises that if he restrains himself from killing the king and obeys now (ΣΥ Δ ' ΙΣΧΕΟ, ΠΕΙΩΕΟ... – 214), in the future he will have threefold gifts of glory (ΑΓΛΑΑ ΔΩΡΑ – 213) for the insult endured today.

7. Achilles acquiesces at the goddesses' behest, honoring her words (ΕΠΟΣ ΕΙΡΥΣΣΑΣΘΑΙ – 216) and obeying (ΕΠΙΠΕΙΘΗΤΑΙ – 218) to refrain from killing Agamemnon but denounces the king for his shamelessness (ΚΥΝΟΣ ΟΜΜΑΤ ' ΕΧΩΝ – 225) as ruling over nobodies (ΟΥΤΙΔΑΝΟΙΣΙΝ – 231) and vows to eschew battle till the day arrives when the sons of the Achaeans will long for Achilles' prowess and Agamemnon then realize that he failed "to honor the best of the Achaeans" (Ο Τ ' ΑΡΙΣΤΟΝ ΑΧΑΙΟΩΝ ΟΥΔΕΝ ΕΤΙΣΑΣ – 244, 412).

8. Nestor intercedes enjoining Agamemnon not to take Achilles' prize and thus disgracing him while reminding Achilles that he ought not to contest with the king. (EPIZEMENAI BAΣIΛHI ANTI– BIHN – 277-278) For though Achilles was born of a goddess, Agamemnon is mightier – the portion of the sceptered king being no common honor (OY ΠOΘ' OMOIHΣ EMMOPE TIMHΣ – 277), since he is king over many.

9. Later, after Agamemnon made good on his threat and took Briseis, Achilles withdraws in shame from his comrades and sitting on the shore of the sea prays to his mother, Thetis, that as he is born to so short a life, Zeus owes him honor (TIMHN ΠEP MOI OΦEΛΛEN – 353), Zeus, "who now has scarce honored me at all!" (OYΔE ME TITΘON ETIΣEN – 354) and bids her to beg Zeus to help the Trojans so that in the death of many of his army, Agamemnon may recognize his blindness (ATHN – 412) in dishonoring the best of the Achaeans, namely Achilles.

10. Thetis then goes to Zeus and entreats him to honor her son (TIMHΣON MOI YION – 505) as a token of honor to herself (516) to which Zeus nods assent sealing the fate of many Achaeans now doomed to die.

11. Then Hera, Zeus's wife and queen, suspicious of his meeting with Thetis and fearing that Zeus will delay in destroying Troy for the sake of Achilles' honor, addresses her husband with reproach for taking his decisions apart from her. In response to Hera who oversteps the bounds of propriety in demanding that Zeus reveal his counsel to her, Zeus rudely rebukes her, threatening violence and in so speaking to her, no less than she, neglects due regard; this infraction troubles Olympic comity (769-570).

12. Hephaestus then rises to the aid of his mother condemning such strife (EPIΔAINETON – 574) among the gods for the sake of mortals, a disproportion that goes against the decorum and the order of THE WAY IT SHOULD BE and, in this way, "souring the banquet of the gods by allowing the lesser to become greater." (575-576)

13. He then advises his mother to approach Zeus, the father of all immortal and mortal beings, who is by far the mightiest (581), with gentleness so that he might not upbraid her again but rather respond to her gentle words (EΠEEΣΣI MAΛAKOIΣIN – 582) with like kindness. (IΛAOΣ – 583)

In this last scene, Hephaestus offers his mother the chalice of reconciliation allowing her in accepting his cup to submit to the authority of Zeus in the ingratiating person of her son, transforming what would have been an act of necessity in confrontation with the former's prerogative into one of granting favor to the latter's supplication, avoiding thus an unseemly debasement before her sire's supreme power and thus, though forced to acknowledge her subordinate place in the Olympic hierarchy, she is nevertheless able to uphold her own queenly dignity among the other gods as Zeus's consort to the throne (1.611), or as she put it: "I too am a god and my birth is of the same lineage as yours..and Cronos begot me as the most honored of his daughters, thus doubly exalted – I am the eldest and am called your wife...But let us yield to each other...I to you and you to me and then all the other immortal gods will follow us." (Il 4.58-64) It is upon this mutual respect for each other's rights and dues that the Olympic kingdom was founded, its tradition of regard for the just apportionment of esteem is the principle upon which the institution of Olympic convention endures.

144. The Issue of Glory

In contrast to this divine civility, we see the war of heroes contending for honor and the glory of distinction; in the spirit of strife that governs human life and even pits god against god (ΘΕΟΙ ΑΝΤΑ ΘΕΩΝ – 20.75) for the sake of human being, we recognize all too well our Achillean destiny who are born to tears and struggle (1.415) while Zeus sits on high and watches the battle and the slaughter of distinction with enjoyment (20.23) having roused the divide of war (20.31) among his divine subjects (32) who are either for the Greeks (*g*) or for the Trojans (*t*) – Poseidon (*g*) against Apollo (*t*), Ares (*t*) against Athena (*g*), Hera (*g*) against Artemis (*t*), Leto (*t*) against Hermes (*g*), Hephaetus (*g*) against Xanthus (*t*) (20.66-74) – he himself watching the carnage as does the audience of thought, the Builder's, narrative in which the knowledge of the Muses unfolds, distinct from that of the Holy Spirit and that of Humanity as theirs is the tale of recollection that reaffirms a predetermined fate in contrast to the revelation of the pure will of God and that of the power of the human heart to imagine a better world, the world of the ideal.

For the Greeks, there is no "better" world, in fact, there is no "other world" at all; rather there is a ΚΟΣΜΟΣ, a proportion of orders, the Olympic heights, the endless ocean and the nether realm of shadows, just the sky and the earth, immortals and the mortals, the living, and the dead, a vast but clearly delineated cosmos of being and of the beings that comprise it, all circumscribed in their own specific, well-defined place and time and therein distinguished, determinate and, as such, worthy of and demanding recognition and regard. Each being remains in his or her own depth and scope while acknowledging that of all the others – this is meet and proper, this is due and right, this is, as Parmenides taught, following Homer, ΘΕΜΙΣ ΤΕ ΔΙΚΗ ΤΕ (themis te dikē te) – the Greek notion of *just being* first articulated by Homer as Zeus's just distribution of what is life's goodness, *goods* in precisely this sense – proportionate, and not equal (12.269), participation of honor, wealth, power – in accordance with what is proper (ΘΕΜΙΣ), conforming to the MOIPA of what is just (ΔΙΚΗΣ).

A just being shows regard where it is due. Ultimately, the war of Troy began because of an act of injustice; Paris disregarded the principle and the order of hospitality by absconding with his host's wife and with treasure as well (13. 624-7). Menelaus, the wronged party and Agamemnon, his brother, wage war against Troy seeking to retrieve Helen of Sparta and recompense of honor (TIMH – 1.159) from the Trojans.

If regard is the due and right of our fulfilled destiny, then the glory beyond words (ΑΣΠΕΤΟΝ ΚΥΔΟΣ – Il. 3.373) of imperishable renown (ΚΛΕΟΣ – Od. 7.90) is what we earn for our achievements of prowess and excellence with regards to that destiny – demonstrating, above all in the meetings of council, the agora, and upon the battlefield of war (1.490), who and what, namely *who* the greater hero (3.71) is and *what* the better word of advice, and then in recognition of this achievement, whether as a wielder of sword or words, winning the undying renown of one who is subsequently to be held in honor, whose excellence (ARETH) is recalled in songs of celebration for all time (Od. 24.196, Il. 4.584), commemorated by the Muses, the daughters of Zeus and ΜΝΕΜΝΟΣΥΝΗ (Memory) and not forgotten by posterity, (23.649) while the dead themselves (Od. 24.94) are doomed to become but mindless wisps of breath and phantom shapes (ΨΥΧΗ ΚΑΙ ΕΙΔΩΛΟΝ – 23.104) of their previous being, consigned to oblivion in Hades (22.389).

This is the sense of worry-wearying toil (21.523) and cruel conflict, mighty strife and evil war (18.242), in the work of bringing to light the difference between the IS and the OUGHT, on the one hand, and, on the other, the ensuing pain and bitter anguish (ΑΙΝΟΣ ΑΧΟΣ – 15.209), the outrage and indignation of the one wronged by words or deeds and minding the gap that has thus emerged in this breach of justice such that, evidently, THE WAY IT IS *is not* THE WAY IT SHOULD BE – conflict and pain, thus our experience of the distinction of human being, and all being that is shown to be different than itself, that is, in one, comprehended as both being and not being, that is, in itself, not itself, and therefore, precisely by being *for* itself, impossibly, *against* itself. Such a state of internecine strife that is the crisis of our self-severalty is best envisioned not as a picnic, nor as a piece of cake, but rather as carnage and slaughter, the bloody sword's flash and the groan of defeat.

For the splendid life of *glory* attends the victory of the greater, gleaming upward to the heights of the sky (18.214) in might while *shame* and *indignation* (ΑΙΔΩΣ ΚΑΙ ΝΕΙΚΟΣ 13.116 - Il. 15.564) pursue those who in the blindness (ATH – 8.237) of self-conceit or arrogance, loving overmuch or hating overmuch, forget that "due measure is better" (Od 15.70-71), overtake those who, yielding weakly, retreat in the rout of panic; they clad the lessor contender in the garb of defeat, namely ignominious death, spilling the gore of his organs into the grass of the battlefield. The struggle tries the hero's mettle and makes evident for all to see whether that being minds (Il. 11.287) who and what a *hero*, a *king*, a *comrade*, a *man* (5.529) – or son or daughter of such a one whose excellence is their paradigm (Od 24.505) – is supposed, meant to be, remembering his or her destiny or forgetful of, blinded to it (Il. 11.313) – for glory follows *boldness* (ΑΛΚΗΣ) and valor *prowess* (ΚΡΑΤΕΡΟΣ – 13.124), *courage* (HNOPEA – Od 24.509), *power* (ΔΥΝΑΜΙΣ – Od.23.128), *force* (BIH – 3.45), *might* (ΣΘΕΝΕΟΣ – Od 22.236), *fortitude* (MENOS - Od. 22.226), *skill* (ΕΥ ΕΙΔΟΤΑ - Il. 15.527) – in short, making evident whether this hero is a Hero or not, *is* what and who a hero Is or *is not*, is valiant (ΕΣΘΛΟΣ) or the opposite, namely cowardly (ΚΑΚΟΣ - Il 17.180), a wight of naught, a puny, feeble wretch (Od 9.515), a nobody and weakling (Il 1.293), in this case, *not being* what he is (supposed to be) and only seeming to be what he, in truth, is not, namely an outstanding being rather than one among the many of anonymous Man as now, in action or inaction, he has revealed himself to be. Glory depends on the distinction of ΑΡΕΤΗ, the valor and excellence of our human being that we are mindful of (22.268) or forget.

Thus in the First Epoch it is not *human* being in itself that is a term of distinction; all beings can be appraised with a view to what they were meant to be and, in comparison with that model of excellence, stand out as pre-eminent among all the rest. Such beings as these are noteworthy, worthy of the regard of thought, impelling the spectator to stand up and take notice even as Helen noted, in response to Priam's request, the names and the outstanding natures, features, the *ΦΥΣΕΙΣ*, of the Greek heroes attacking Troy, their physical height and beauty (3.167), their majestic air (169-170), their broad-shouldered intent of purpose in rousing the fury of the troops to do battle (194-198), their magnificent stature towering above all others (226-227).

Who among the best is the better of two? (Od. 24.515) Who among the good is the best (ΑΡΕΤΗΙ ΕΣΑΝ ΕΞΟΧ ' ΑΡΙΣΤΟΙ - Od. 4.629; 22.244), the best of all (Il 17.358; 24.113)? In other words, who is dearer, who dearest to the God? (20.334). For it is in comparison that we distinguish one being from the next as regards their excellence – of two, one is mightier in body (23.578), one in mind (16.688) and counsel, the older being the wiser (19.218), one swifter of foot and, above all, one better and best in works (ΕΡΓΑ), what we have accomplished with our own hands and feet, wherein our greatest renown is won (Od. 8.147) – in this respect even the slower can outstrip the faster if the former's works are better than the latter's, the adulterer's, whose bad deeds fail to prosper (ΟΥΚ ΑΡΕΤΑΙ ΚΑΚΑ ΕΡΓΑ – Od. 8.329) and the good deeds of the good win wide regard. (Od. 19.333) Thus is the winner determined in the competition of distinction that characterizes the destiny of all human being as *heroic*, namely to excel, to attain *pre-eminence* (ΕΞΟΧΟΝ) as a being of note (Il. 2.188), the very best among the best (Il. 2.483), dearest to a god (Il. 5.61), the nearest and the dearest, (Il. 9.638), the most honored among the men (9.630-1, 9.641), the most blessed (Od. 6.158) and most worthy of praise (Od. 8.487), the most, the best – such superlative beings (ΑΡΙΣΤΟΙ), whose valor (ΑΡΕΤΗ), whose regard and esteem (ΤΙΜΗ) are the contested issue in Homeric terms, are then rightfully and necessarily accompanied by god-given fame (ΚΛΕΟΣ - Od. 24.197; 3.380), that magnificent (10.212; 17.131; Od. 2.125), far and wide-reaching (7.458; 1.283; Od. 3.83) – even unto heaven (Il. 8.192; Od. 8.74; Od. 9.20) rising – ever-lasting, inextinguishable (Od. 4.584), imperishable glory (Il. 2.325; 7.91; 9.413; Od. 24.196) of an illustrious name of repute (17.16; Od. 3.78), heard by the generations to come (Od. 3.204), that is the hero's life of distinction and excellence after an all too early death, though through death now commemorated by the Muse's celebratory songs of praise (Od. 8.73; Il. 9.189) from which alone we mortals receive tidings (Od. 9.20) of a hero's *splendor and renown* (ΧΑΡΙΣ ΚΑΙ ΚΥΔΟΣ – Il. 4.95) and gain sure knowledge of their brilliant being and accomplishments on the bloody battle fields of self-severalty. (9.524)

Clearly, it is the distinction of human being that "our portion of honor differs accordingly for the courageous and the cowardly, is never the same for those who are different." (9.319) To those however who are the same, having fought in rivalry and determined that they are "equally loved by Zeus and both deserving of the heroic designation" (7.280-1), the gods vouchsafe an adjournment of hostilities under a compact of friendship (7.303) in which the combatants are both declared victors, having been granted, for the time being at least, "equal power and fame" (7.205), who themselves know full well that though they have ceased from battle for this day, "later we shall fight again till divine judgment distinguishes us, giving decisive victory to one or the other." (7.291-2)

> ΥΣΤΕΡΟΝ ΑΥΤΕ ΜΑΧΗΣΟΜΕΘ' ΕΙΣ Ο ΚΕ ΔΑΙΜΩΝ ΑΜΜΕ
> ΔΙΑΚΡΙΝΗΙ, ΔΩΗΙ Δ' ΕΤΕΡΟΙΣΙ ΓΕ ΝΙΚΗΝ

To have heart and spirit is to be who we really and truly are, if we are heroes – clearly such hearts are big, such spirits high (ΜΕΓΑΛΗΤΩΡ...ΜΕΓΑ ΦΡΟΝΕΟΝΤΕΣ – 16.257-8); but how easily can our strengths become weaknesses, our virtues vices, if the limits and orders of proportion are disregarded and forgotten, overreach the mark of measure in what is *mega*; that is when a resolute heart, enduring in fortitude, courageous in controversy, contravenes itself by falling into brazen contempt, merciless severity, wanton audacity where bold is rash, strength is fury, pluck is presumption and might is usurpation, where blindness blights the mind's sight of outer bounds and, by warping our excellence into excess, plunges the pre-eminence of all our human greatness into the greater glare of disrepute, of infamy, the luster of the low, the celebrity of atrocity (Od 11.432). For to excel is to attain rather than to exceed the fulfillment of the principle, the destiny in question. The excess of excellence is its perversion; then to surpass is, in fact, to transgress that proper measure that pertains to each particular issue: "even a host's kindness can be too kind, his unkindness too cruel, in both blameworthy, better is measure in all things." (15.69-71)

> ΝΕΜΕΣΣΩΜΑΙ ΔΕ ΚΑΙ ΑΛΛΩΙ ΑΝΔΡΙ ΞΕΙΝΟΔΟΚΩΙ, ΟΣ
> Κ ' ΕΞΟΧΑ ΜΕΝ ΦΙΛΕΗΙΣΙΝ, ΕΞΟΧΑ, Δ' ΕΧΘΑΙΡΗΙΣΙΝ
> ΑΜΕΙΝΩ Δ' ΑΙΣΙΜΑ ΠΑΝΤΑ

The restraint of deference (ΑΙΔΩΣ - Od 3.24; 8.172; 14.505) and honor (8.480), to insight bound (Il 15.129) and to pity (24.44), as well as to fear (15.657), and often sharpened to shame (Od 8.324) is, for heroes, reciprocally binding (Il 15.561), not so for beggars (Od 17.347). A sense of measure scrupulously avoids what angry indignation (ΝΕΜΙΣΙΣ - Il 6.335) on the part of others (6.351) rebukes and chides (7.97), namely all execrable ugliness (ΑΙΣΧΟΣ - Od 1.229; 18.225; 19.373) of act (24.326), above all that of shrinking from and shirking the battlefield of self-several distinction (Il

8.228; 13.122; 15.502; 17.336) upon which the glory of excellence is contested and decided and the negligence of those becomes manifest who, heedless of the predetermined orders of just being (Od 20.171), namely of both the censure of mortals (13.622) – present as well as future (11.433; 24.433) – and the retaliation of the immortals (20.169), remiss and reckless (ΜΕΘΗΜΟΣΥΝΗ - 13.108; 13.121) with regards to the limits they define, looking neither left nor right, caring neither about the hereafter nor about the hitherto, and thus, like earth and water, lacking a heart of glory (Il 7.97), oblivious to both imminence and permanence, prostrate in an utterly ephemeral state of mind, which is but the abject abandonment of all minding and caring about looming disgrace (ΛΩΒΗ), give heed to today only (ΕΦΗΜΕΡΙΑ ΦΡΟΝΕΟΝΤΕΣ - Od 21.85). This shout of cognizance rouses the spirit and the courage of battle once again. (Il 5.792)

The indiscretion of such indifference incites outrage on the part of the wronged and discountenance on the part of the perpetrator who slackened or forgot, who ignored the signs or missed the mark in succumbing to the blindness of the unchecked moment of the mind (Il 9.119); in due course, the precipitations of indiscretion do come to light, ultimately, through events become transparent under the critical scrutiny of seers who unfold the darkness of a fleeting moment in the entirety of being, which is founded upon *what has* always already *been* decided, determined as *what is* supposed, meant, destined *to be* by dint of an irresistible, overmastering force of willpower that intends and ultimately accomplishes the good and the best, under the circumstances, for all concerned parties. Within this train of thought and in accordance with the will of Zeus, all human achievements – and failures – are wrought and comprehended.

Our cyclopean cave dwellers, however, "an insolent and lawless folk" (Od 9.106), peering through the single eye of their uncouth individualism, having neither assemblies of council in which to participate, where distinctions and differences are negotiated in the crisis of controversy pertaining to what is the better and the best measure, the better and the best course of action to be taken, nor appointed laws that they recognize as the principles upon which their decisions and judgments are objectively to be based, dwell in hollow caves on the remote peaks of haughty mountains, and each one, in the privacy of his windowless walls, is lawgiver unto his own and one-I'd self, lording over his wives and kids (and lambs), caring nothing of and "...having no regard for one another." (...ΟΥΔ ' ΑΛΛΗΛΩΝ ΑΛΕΓΟΥΣΙΝ. – Od 9.115)

Such beings as these, fearing not the gods who hold heaven nor the report of men hereafter (22.39), are, in the knowledge of the Muses, the very epitome of *excessive* being, the perversion of excellence, even as a *monster* (ΠΕΛΩΡΟΝ – Od 9.257), which is the twisted version of the wonder to be seen that is the manifestation of superb and superlative being, *just* being, the corruption of which is the savagery that makes of the glory of great and abundant strength the overweening lawlessness of immensity and the hideousness of exulting enormity. Thus when Odysseus encounters Polyphemus in the latter's cave, he beseeches the Cyclops to bestow upon him and his men the generosity of regard that "is due" (...ΘΕΜΙΣ ΕΣΤΙΝ) a suppliant and so "honor..." the gods and Zeus in particular "...with reverence" (ΑΙΔΕΙΟ) as it is he, Zeus, who accompanies "revered suppliants as well as strangers" (ΞΕΙΝΟΙΣΙΝ ΑΜ ΑΙΔΟΙΟΙΣΙΝ) and fosters the recompense of hospitality. (Od 9.266-270)

To this entreaty Polyphemus, "with a pitiless heart...," replies: "You're an utter fool, stranger, to tell me to fear or to shun the gods or else you've come from far afield indeed; for the Cyclopes care not a whit (ΟΥ...ΑΛΕΓΟΥΣΙΝ) about the aegis of Zeus or the happy-go-lucky gods, since we are better by far than they are (...ΕΠΕΙ Η ΠΟΛΥ ΦΕΡΤΕΡΟΙ ΕΙΜΕΝ). Nor would I, to avoid Zeus's enmity, spare either you or your comrades, unless so moved by my own heart (...ΕΙ ΜΗ ΘΥΜΟΣ ΜΕ ΚΕΛΕΥΟΙ)." (Od. 9.272-8)

It is just and right that the dispensation of doom should condemn such heartless, overbearing bumptiousness and that the works of impudence done in its spirit be repudiated and repulsed by retributive justice, the anger and the punishment of the gods, of Zeus "above all who reprehends works of wickedness." (Od. 14.284)

ΟΣ ΤΕ ΜΑΛΙΣΤΑ ΝΕΜΕΣΣΑΤΑΙ ΚΑΚΑ ΕΡΓΑ

The cruelty of rampant arrogance towards others' pleas for succor, the negligence of self-centered disregard for what is due and proper, the impertinence of disdain for what is truly great and honorable, the folly and mindless blindness of immoderate words and deeds are met with equal sternness on the battlefield (Il. 5.757) as well as in the place of assembly (Il. 9.33). For the limits that have been trespassed by acts of negligence and disregard want redress and restitution. Shamelessness, having failed to show regard, neither to its betters nor its lessors, brings upon itself destruction, i.e. through its own "wicked works" (ΣΞΕΤΛΙΑ ΕΡΓΑ) and "wanton disregard" (ΑΤΑΣΘΑΛΙΗΙΣΙΝ) the "doom of the gods" (ΜΟΙΡΑ ΘΕΩΝ...) and the "death in shame" (ΑΕΙΚΕΑ ΠΟΤΜΟΝ). (Od 22.

413-17) What a disgraceful thing (ΑΙΣΧΡΟΝ – Il 2.119) to be heard by human beings who are yet to be! (Il. 2.120)

Thus do we return to anger and to outrage, to indignation, as the witnesses of such deeds of intrusion and violation, of cowardice and carelessness, that fills us with chagrin and incites *war* in its wake, whether in words of rebuke or in deeds of punishment and makes of death a mark of distinction by which we affirm the indelible distinction between THE WAY IT IS and THE WAY IT SHOULD BE.

Though mortals in their anguish are able to recognize this gap, it is the work of the gods to resolve the issue and, in particular, it is the achievement of Zeus to overcome the contradiction of divergence inherent in just being.

C. Jovial Resolve

145. The Gods are with us

Risk designates the recognition of a limit and the sphere of influence beyond the ken of Man's control that impinges on our lives. These incidences whether plague or boon, luck, good or bad, as what befalls us, beginning with our birth, make manifest the essential experience of discontinuity in human being as they leave their mark upon our purposes and trace a circle, as it were, around what is human design and what surpasses the plans and designs of human device, however ingenious they may be, by the simple fact of determining the scope and the limit of their efficacy.

Man experiences the encroachment of this *being before*, this ulterior or *alter* being – call it anterior or exterior, call it the forestallment or the posteriority of Man's here and now – upon the spelunking interiority of his plans, the ins and outs, the ups and downs of happenstance, as they are popularly designated, over against our own purposes as the fickle vicissitudes of fortune. This and that and the other thing happens – our projects are frustrated, our progress balked. Oh gods! We inexplicably failed the exam; our team, though the better, lost the match; and what about life's little and not so little accidents – of course, everything that happens has causes and these causes have further causes: The wind was the cause that swept a tile from the roof and struck you as you were walking by; but also the roofer was the cause who failed to attach it properly ten years ago; and what about the fight he had had with his wife the day before that led to his distraction while laying and interlocking the tiles? And the bank statement upon which his wife had found that a hotel room had been paid for? Or, further, the marital altercation that ensued, the slammed doors, the tears, the entreaties, the despair of the guilty man who subsequently needed a drink and came home late only to sleep badly on the couch that short night before the fateful Monday morning when, stiff, hung-over and depressed, he inadvertently cracked the clay joint of a single tile, that tile that was to fall on that windy day ten years later just as you passed by beneath it, because you were on the way to the stationary store, because your daughter needed a new pen because she had dropped hers while getting on the train, because she wanted to note an idea for an essay she was writing for her English class...these causal chains have causes and these causes yet further causes but for all these thousands and millions and billions of causes of the tile falling, even unto the birth of the universe and the dawn of time, there is no *reason* that it fell and that destruction should befall you on that fateful windy day of your doom.

Therefore what has been brought upon us thus, thwarting or supporting our purposes, gives rise, finally, to the exalting notion of a considered will that makes of blind chance and the random incidence and coincidence of events the achievements of premeditated outcomes and ulterior motives in a larger framework of will, an alter-, alternate, and, in this way, a distinguished, will, the will of Zeus. In the narrative of the Muses, we, the poor players are, for the most part, blind to Zeus's purposes but we, distinguished by the knowledge their songs make manifest, the audience of Homeric song, see the larger picture of adventitious circumstantiality in which *inadvertency, accessory,* and *fortuity* name the outer, inhabitable limits surrounding those colonies of our Man's founding and *wild caprice* the "inscrutable" or "arbitrary" will which, so apparent in the ineradicable insurgence of hazard, resists that totality of ascendance our hegemony craves and so nearly attains but for this derelict residuum that makes all the difference in the world.

And as the Homeric audience is itself a character in the narrative of the Muses as is the Rhapsodist at the feasts, a relationship itself inherent in the poetry of Homer, our own standpoint must remain rigorously extraneous even to that of the spectators of Homer's performance, namely to the audience of the feast where the rhapsodist is performing; they see what the heroes themselves do not, i.e. that Zeus's plan is to glorify and honor what is honorable and to accord to each his or her due, in particular to Achilles to make amends for the disgrace he endured by Agamemnon's disregard of his right and prize of honor. This is the god's eye view from the mountain top where gods sit to enjoy the spectacle of the distinction of human being as accomplished in particular, the perspective of the Muses themselves, that of the knowledge of the whole, the uniquely Greek version of the train of thought in the progress of reiteration we have studied in the First and the Second Epochs as well.

For we, finally, who are neither merely the actors, whether mortal or immortal, in the narrative, nor merely the god-like audience attending to the song at the banquet of kings their peoples, nor even endowed with the inspiration that summoned the poets and the prophets of tradition to the scene of their profession, we, thus twice, thrice removed from these scenes of distinction, comprehend ourselves as being called rather by these traditional tongues of flame to become logotectonic *Thinkers* in contemplation of the insight they have bequeathed to our conception and philological *Builders* in its spirit in a fellowship of wisdom's friends who would lift their voice and – a seemingly impossible feat – revive respect, even veneration, for those ancient songs of praise that the distinction of human being is still so worthy of.

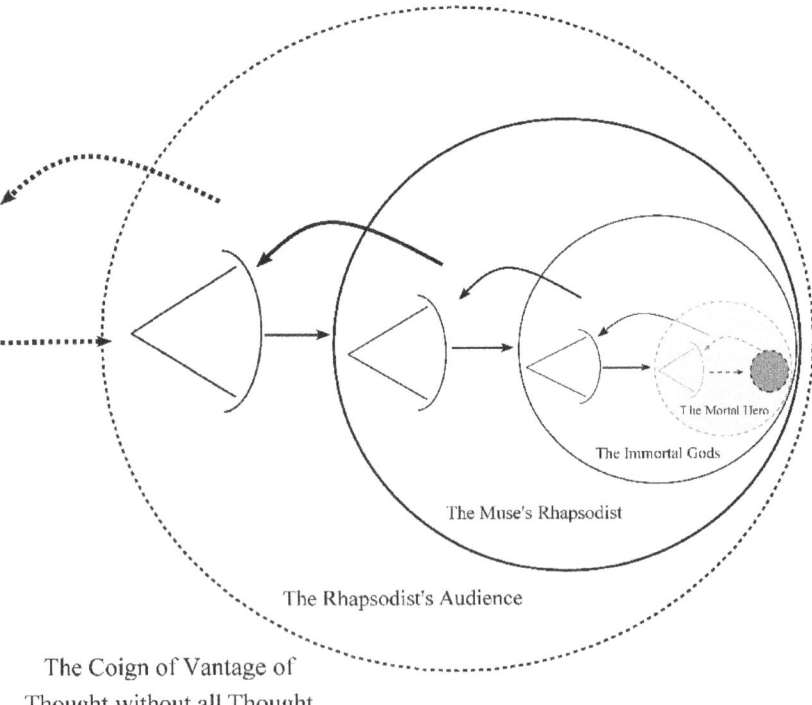

Figure 96: The Spectacle of Reflection in Being

We render this system of distinctions in the form of self-severalty as it presents again in terms that are germane to the Greek epoch of thought and, specifically, to the knowledge of the Muses and thus visualized in *Figure 96*.

Yes, it is too true! Outcomes that we plan for and strive to achieve are uncertain – even if we have tried to take all eventualities into account, even if we are skilled and experienced in the matter; and be it in the art of turning a vase of clay – there is always room for the unexpected and inadvertent that stymies our schemes or serendipitously promotes them. In recognition of this limitation and to guarantee the results intended, the Muses speak of the will of the gods and Zeus in particular, whose works, in contrast to that of mortal human being, are never in vain, can never be evaded (5.104, 8.143) and never fail to bring to conclusion what he has ordained, his own as well as human designs, insofar they accord with his, decisions taken in counsel with his own heart in order to determine what was meant to be from the point of view of what is best for the whole. The allotment of Zeus (17.321) is his plan and decision regarding how events ought ultimately to unfold.

For it is precisely of this that the king of kings, Zeus, is the judge; he deliberates and then adjudicates, taking his decision in keeping with what has already been decided and established as right, i.e. the present of THE WAY IT SHOULD BE, which, after some deliberation among contestants regarding a particular case, reveals itself to all or at least to the majority of those who are knowledgeable, in particular to our elders and betters and those most distinguished in wisdom and who therefore have rightfully been entrusted with the power of making decisions that take into account the needs of all the constituents, always mindful of what is best (ΑΡΙΣΤΗ – 7.325) in accordance with principle (Il.2.5). Zeus and all kings who Zeus has nurtured with his own insight are invested with this office of counsel. Specifically, Zeus's task – and that of all kings – is to right wrongs (ΔΙΚΗ) that have been committed in disregard of the rule of law, to honor excellence in word and deed, superiority in beauty and in power, to show compassion to the mortals who, in the urgency of their need, lift their hands imploringly to the gods, and to bring to fruition the works of gods and men in accordance with the determinations that destiny has fixed and defined (ΘΕΜΙΣ), accomplishing thereby the task incumbent upon all kings, namely to "speak and also to listen and to fulfill for another whatsoever the latter's heart may bid him speak for general benefit's sake (ΕΙΠΕΙΝ ΕΙΣ ΑΓΑΘΟΝ); for on Zeus depends the outcome of whatever any man may begin." (9.100-102)

Thus Zeus brings to pass what he has decided and thus established as just being (ΤΕΛΕΟΥΣΙ ΘΕΜΙΣΤΑΣ – 9.156,16.403), namely in accordance with the rule of law, the principle of proportion with respect to which every being is rendered what is due. His is the sharpness of perception (ΝΟΟΣ) and the inexorability of the will the purposes of which no being, whether human or divine, dare contravene (21.191) or make vain, "for he is by far the mightier." (8.143)

ΕΠΕΙ Η ΠΟΛΥ ΦΕΡΤΕΡΟΣ ΕΣΤΙΝ

Zeus's preeminence is often made a point of (4.56, 8.211, 15.181) and for good reason. It is precisely in insight that he surpasses all others and in this way marks the extent as well as the limit of the human condition, of human frailty, with respect to all the greater forces that impinge upon human life and ways – *Zeus* is the name for this realization and in calling his name, we acknowledge the smallness and vulnerability of our human being. This tenuousness of the human condition is particularly evident in our inevitable exposure to the fretful elements. Thus we are hardly surprised to learn that "from Zeus" is thunder and lightning (14.306; 21.401), but also the blasts of wind in a gale (14.19, 414; 12.225) and the storm (12.286), the accumulation of the clouds (2.146), the onslaught of the rain (11.493; 5.91) and snow (19.357). But not only these meteorological phenomena of time are overpowering and therefore Jovial, but also its seasons (24.344) and its years (2.134), the days and the nights (14.93) – indeed, show me a mortal who can withstand, let alone conquer, any of these beings and be it but a towering oak tree (7.60), Jovial in the beauty of its splendor (5.693).

With a view to this our limitation and our acknowledgement of it, in other words, in recognition of the fact that all human being has need of the gods (Od. 3.48), we lift our voices in prayers asking for the favor of those more powerful than us, in particular the gods, to speed along our projects, and above all to requite regard with regard. In this way, whether the gods show favor (5.875) and hear our plea (1.43) and fulfill our wish or refuse their compliance (Od. 22.54), if only for the time being (2.419, 3.302), we experience the will of Zeus with regards to our person, whether we are cared for by him in our exploits, honored (2.197, 9.616, 17.251) and aided (4.408,15.490), loved by Zeus (B197, 2.669) or crushed by woe (2.70), favored with victory and glorious renown (7.205) or, by his cruel scourge (13.812), subject to ignominious doom (22.280) and evil fate (9.52). His pleasure is clearly made known by his voice (2.217), the messengers that speak in his name (24.586, 24.173), Iris (15.175) and Hermes (24.460), but also the beggars and strangers (14.57) who test mortals' hospitality, and the revelatory signs of his judgment (16.320,17.409) – the portents (12. 209, 4.75, 5.740) and omens (8.251), the dreams, the tidings (1.283) he sends (1.63) to make Man think for a change; but then, if all to no avail, to pour down his wrath (5.34, 14.283) upon inveterate blockheads.

Thus for example "in the season of reaping when Zeus pours rage down in rain, oppressing the dark earth under his tempest, answering with violence the violence of men who expel justice from the agora through crooked judgment of the rules of law, utterly forgetting about the inevitable retaliation of the gods – the rivers' flooding surge, the hillsides gashed by cataracts rushing with a roar in torrents from crags of the peak down to the blackened gleaming sea, devastating the work of men." (16.384-392)

We might be inclined to smirk and snort at the quaintness of a mind that stoops to "interpreting" natural disasters as punishment for wrongdoing on the part of men, and with the ebbing of our ridicule, lament the deplorable lack of "science" among primitive peoples. But are not thunderstorms and lightning, the destructive force of winds and war, inundation and illness, that harry and curtail human life and do the deeds of death, are they not all worthy, memorable renderings of the efficacy of the distinction that marks the inward limit of Man-made mastery and intention in recognition of extraneous influence, *gifts of the gods* not easily refused (3.65), a realization that makes of chance events upon people's lives the accomplishment of distinguished purpose not our own? That punishment follows wrongdoing is a manner of speaking about the distinction of critical self-reflection, acknowledging that what Man does in the confines of the four walls of his world and in the privacy of his narrow mind has nevertheless consequences that extend beyond the ken of his cave. Can we conceive of consequences as replies, as retorts?

And then imagine the perspicacity of a spirit that perceives in every occurrence, whether adverse or prosperous, that impinges upon its sphere and makes a difference, as an event of intelligent design – a sudden impulse or idea that seizes us (1.55, Od. 18.160), a heart suddenly emboldened (2.451, 16.241) or intimidated (15.594), moved to avenge the death of a compatriot (17.72) or to seek news of a father long thought to be lost (Od 2.263-4), rekindled in yearning for home (3.140) or for a lover (3.395); or consider similarly, the event of rage restrained (1.194), flight prevented (2.173), treachery instigated (4.104), wits lost (18.313), a prophesy inspired (Od. 15.173), or just a gust of wind in the branches, a bird alighting on the sill, the chance breaking of a newly strung bow string (15.455) or the unlucky/lucky snapping of a helmet strap (3.376) and perceive in all of these examples of what we would normally dismiss as fortuitous, evidence of the magnitude of this distinction between the inside and the outside of Man's world and its closed sphere of control, which in turn makes manifest the profound insight of the Muses being elaborated in each and every one of these details of the narrative that articulates their wisdom in a work of exalted speech that has, as a result of the reverence and the veneration it has always enjoyed, come down to us through the ages intact as a reminder of the first age of pure thought thinking thought, that epoch of reflection when it was a mark of reason to say and to think that human beings were distinguished by a destiny (24.525) that defines the limits of their mortal scope and will and workings because "Zeus himself, the Olympian, gives men, both good and bad, their fortunes, to each as is his wont..." (6.190) who "from his two urns of gifts, one with ills, one with blessings, apportions lots to men, to some a mingled fate, now beneficial, now calamitous, to others a doom entirely evil causing them to be reviled by others, driven over the face of the earth, wandering, honored by neither gods nor mortals." (24.527-533)

Thus it is Zeus and the gods in general that give honor and the glory of victory (22.130, 17.250, 15.491, 7.155) to kings, above all as a token of Zeus's love (2.194), but also snatch it away (22.18); from Zeus come the ordinances and edicts that our human kings abide by when administering justice (1.239) and therefore it is Zeus who sends strife in which differences in excellence are discerned in what is otherwise the inertness and listlessness of an insipid indifferent being. Against this background of mediocrity, the hero's profile figures starkly, emanating like a beacon of fire such that being and appearing are one and the same in the manifest present of the epiphany ((ΕΞ)ΦΑΙΝΩ – 18.198, 248, 19.46, 20.43) of being that is Achilles' coming to light upon returning to the battlefield; clothed in the aegis of victory (18.203-4), the air and golden halo of supremacy about his head from which a blaze of gleaming fire beacons forth (18.205-6, 226-7) toward heavens (18.214), he shouts a threefold shout (18.228), echoed by the gods (18.217) and clear as a clarion (18.219), calling to the attention of our mind's ego-I, more, filling all our hearts with the dismay (18.223), the anguish (224) and the consternation (18.225) of doom that is the premonition of our destiny come a-knockin', that good death, that *pure and purifying death* (ΚΑΘΑΡΟΣ ΘΑΝΑΤΟΣ - Od. 22.462) that is our victory over an unsung, anonymous life, preordained to be lost and won, reversed and revised in the splendor of bronze and gold; the gleam of spear and splendor of sword, the din of their clashing, the bloody aftermath of blade and martial arts, all delineate the distinction of human being in Homeric terms. Their rightful place is alone the speech of glory. Who dares speak this speech today much less bring these words to fulfillment in the only field of battle wisdom ever spoke about or knew, that of the self-several human heart, the self-several deity, the self-several entity of identity.

For in this place alone – that is no place at all – in these terms borrowed from the tongue of fire we have become acquainted with as that of the Muses, *the gods* are thought and said to watch over the apportionment of what is right and proper (Od 17.475) for one and all beings; but this is a controversial issue among all concerned and must be determined in each particular case – in contesting what is due, the crisis of distinction within just being comes to the fore of judgment; specifically, Nemesis and the dreaded Furies (Erinyes) – the terrible visions of implacable and therefore inhospitable, irreconcilable externality, permanently extraneous to and distinct from the dwellings of human being and in this sense inhabitants of the realm *without,* specifically the realm *beneath,* where they walk in the "nether-worldly" darkness of Erebus, (9.571) and who, in following Zeus (15.204), are the guardians of the portions' proportions, serving punishment for what fails to show proper regard for the limits that have determined the scope of just being (as opposed to *mere* being). As avengers of the immovable limits of propriety, they are called upon to witness oaths of inviolability, along with the inviolable waters of Styx (AAATON YΔΩΡ – 14.271), the earth and the shimmering sea (14.273) and the sun, by virtue of the firmness and the omnipresence of the ground and the sky, the bed of Hera's and Zeus's holy matrimony (15.37), and Zeus himself, first and foremost, being "the highest and the best of the gods" (ΥΠΑΤΟΣ ΚΑΙ ΑΡΙΣΤΟΣ ΘΕΩΝ – 19.258-9), seeing all (3.276) and therefore overseeing the orders of distinction in their entirety. Clearly these limits are being transgressed when a horse, even if it is Xanthus, one of Achilles' two immortal horses, begins to speak and to prophesy their master's impending death. (19.418)

Together with the orders that apportion our human being, the gods are with us when we fail but above all when we succeed and achieve this time the glory of a victory that eluded us, better, was refused us, the last time (3.440):

ΠΑΡΑ ΓΑΡ ΘΕΟΙ ΕΙΣΙ ΚΑΙ ΗΜΙΝ

For the gods are on our side, too

By recognizing our ends and goals to be deliberated and determined within these limits, we declare to the immortal our mind and our purposes; this acknowledgement is their due of regard that is our obligation to accord them (7.445) and proof of our recognition of the infinite limitation of human being as mortal. It is the entire substance of our prayers to them. In Greek terms, to know oneself is to know these gods and vice versa knowing them we know ourselves as mortals and our own thoughts as the bold ventures in excellence they truly are.

The gods are with us in spirit, mindful of what is right and proper; they are with us in person too when we arrive at a critical juncture where deliberation has run its course and decisions have to be made, plans executed; they warn and encourage and, embodied in our friends and acquaintances, they provoke a change of direction in our thoughts, a new perspective; especially as supplicants in need and "in the guise of strangers from far off do they descend from heaven, putting on all manner of shapes, and visit cities, beholding the violence and the righteousness of men." (17.484-7)

KAI TE ΘΕΟΙ ΞΕΙΝΟΙΣΙΝ ΕΟΙΚΟΤΕΣ ΑΛΛΟΔΑΠΟΙΣΙ,

ΠΑΝΤΟΙΟΙ ΤΕΛΕΘΟΝΤΕΣ,   ΕΠΙΣΤΡΩΦΩΣΙ ΠΟΛΗΑΣ,

ΑΝΘΡΩΠΩΝ ΥΒΡΙΝ ΤΕ ΚΑΙ ΕΥΝΟΜΙΗΝ ΕΦΟΡΩΝΤΕΣ

The blessed gods do not love reckless deeds, but they honor justice and the righteous deeds of men. (Od.14.85) Knowing that due measure is better in all things, even in the measure of life – in recognition of our mortal limits as the work and the will of the gods – it is not resignation but regard that speaks in saying "death I will receive when Zeus and the other immortal gods bring it to pass." (18.115, 22.365)

ΚΗΡΑ Δ' ΕΓΩ ΤΟΤΕ ΔΕΞΟΜΑΙ ΟΠΠΟΤΕ ΚΕΝ ΔΗ ΖΕΥΣ

ΕΘΕΛΗΙ ΤΕΛΕΣΑΙ ΗΔ' ΑΘΑΝΑΤΟΙ ΘΕΟΙ ΑΛΛΟΙ

To see that the IS and the OUGHT diverge is an act of recognition in which difference is acknowledged. It is a contemplative achievement to see and embrace necessity in the way things are, but wisdom accrues to those few who see, above and beyond this, not merely that the ways things are are the way they should be, recognizing the principle of just being that predetermines every subsequent determination of what is right, but comprehends in the way things turn out the fulfillment of a purpose and outcomes consistent with decisions made with a view to what seems best, all conditions taken into account. In this sense, the power of Zeus, the efficacy of which he wields in his thunderbolt, and the knowledge of Zeus, knowledgeable of both the happiness and the haplessness of mortal men (Od. 20.76), ultimately fulfill or cross men's purposes (Il. 18.327) in accordance with the principle of just being to which he himself is subject but not slavishly so, not for lack of power or fear of reprisals – for who could coerce the superior might of the father of gods and men? At times the lessor warrior will unexpectedly, inexplicably conquer the greater – ultimately, the gods decide as is their pleasure (20.434-35), now striking, now delaying the fatal strike till the proper time has come for doom. In these travesties, we recognize, all the more painfully, our destiny as mortals, as beings defined by limits which demand of us acknowledgement and proper regard for what transcends our sphere of tears, touching it chillingly, but sometimes, for some, even benevolently, from the outside.

Yes, Zeus is great and of supreme power not merely in his excellence of knowledge and judgment, perceiving what is right, but also in the sheer and inevitable might of action. This is the might of the will that pronounces its decisions boldly and is certain that "the way I have conceived it, that is how it shall be achieved." (9.310)

ΗΙ ΠΕΡ ΔΗ ΦΡΟΝΕΩ ΤΕ ΚΑΙ ΩΣ ΤΕΤΕΛΕΣΜΕΝΟΝ ΕΣΤΑΙ

That is what we learn in the very beginning of the Iliad, namely that "the will of Zeus was achieved." (1.5)

ΔΙΟΣ Δ' ΕΤΕΛΕΙΕΤΟ ΒΟΥΛΗ

What is meant to be will be brought to the fruition of action – only a truly divine will with supreme power can be so sure; only a will that knows itself to be in accordance with the law and the principle that governs the entirety of just being, only the possessor of a true vision of good as opposed to a mere dream (Od. 19.547), can speak thus and command in this spirit of inevitability: "thus do I say, thus it shall be!" (1.212, 2.257, 2.330, 8.286, 8.401, 8.454, 23.410, 23.672, Od. 2.187, Od. 5.89, Od. 16.440, Od. 17.229, Od. 18.82, Od. 19.487, Od. 21.337)

ΩΔΕ ΓΑΡ ΕΞΕΡΕΩ, ΤΟ ΔΕ ΚΑΙ ΤΕΤΕΛΕΣΜΕΝΟΝ ΕΣΤΑΙ

Hence it would seem that for eternal beings alone can the saying hold true: "no sooner said than done." (19.242) For in human experience, much is unspoken, untried, unproven, much said and done that was not supposed to be (1.388), or only partially, a part remaining incomplete (20.370), and just as often our hopes (Od 2.275), our fond wishes (Od. 3.226) and desires (Od. 13.40, Od. 15.112), the purposes (4.178, Od. 22.215) we have chosen for ourselves and ponder in our heart (Od. 18.345), the principles (9.156, 298) we have received, the oaths (7.69) and curses (9.456) sworn, threats leveled (14.44), promises given (13.377, 21.457, 23.20, 23.180, Od. 15.195, Od. 15.203), vows (23.149), proposals (23.543-4) made, so many prayers (Od.

11.77) and prophesies (Od. 17.60, Od. 17.163, Od. 19.309, Od. 20.236, Od. 23.284), requests and commands (Od. 4.485), remain just words, words not made good (Od. 13.212), much to our disgrace and humiliation (4.182), never to materialize (2.36), just a thought (4.175); for we fail or else succeed, if not now perhaps later (4.160-2), as pleases the gods (Od 8.571), though failure to achieve and efforts taken in vain would not at all be fitting for the gods themselves, neither for Zeus (1.527), nor for Hera. (4.26, 4.57)

Zeus has a plan and this plan itself, founded upon his willingness to accord each goddess and each god and every mortal the regard that is his or her due, which is not the same as the good of one's desire (Od. 2.34), determines the fate of the mortals, distinguishing in their lives what should and what should not be. But as much as his purpose is our fate (17.321), the principle of apportionment is the predetermination of that destiny that Zeus himself serves with his *will* and unfailingly puts into effect through his *power*, after having deliberated the issue while taking counsel with himself and the other immortal gods regarding whether or not he ought to, having the power to act or refrain from action as he sees fit – for this is the progression of the spirit of achievement that is Zeus's chief excellence in the world of the Muses, discernible in the well-known Homeric formula: "Tell me what's on your mind; my heart bids me fulfill it, if I can fulfill it and it is to be fulfilled." (14.195-6, 18.426-7)

> ΤΕΛΕΣΑΙ ΔΕ ΜΕ ΘΥΜΟΣ ΑΝΩΓΕΝ, ΕΙ ΔΥΝΑΜΑΙ ΤΕΛΕΣΑΙ ΓΕ
> ΚΑΙ ΕΙ ΤΕΤΕΛΕΣΜΕΝΟΝ ΕΣΤΙΝ

Thus when Priam tells Helen that she is not to blame but rather that the gods are to blame for all that has transpired (3.164) and she expresses her conviction that the gods have ordained the ills afflicting the Trojans on her account (6.350), the former is not merely being polite and the latter not succumbing to Man's well-known tendency to blame others, including the gods, for his plight, "when in fact the evil that befalls people is the consequence of their own blind folly resulting in pain beyond what has been ordained." (Od. 1.32-4)

Helen proposes a remarkable explanation for the events that have ensued upon her own shamelessness and the blindness of Alexander, namely that "Zeus has laid an evil fate upon us so that in latter days we may be a song for future human being." (6.356-8)

> ΟΙΣΙΝ ΕΠΙ ΖΕΥΣ ΘΗΚΕ ΚΑΚΟΝ ΜΟΡΟΝ, ΩΣ ΚΑΙ ΟΠΙΣΣΩ
> ΑΝΘΡΩΠΟΙΣΙ ΠΕΛΩΜΕΘ ᾿ ΑΟΙΔΙΜΟΙ ΕΣΣΟΜΕΝΟΙΣΙ.

Zeus has brought all this upon us for the sake of the epic narrative itself, a revelatory one if we could only read it properly, not as a masculine manual of murder and slaughter written for Man by Man, not as a mythological manifest of fabulous events and creatures, not as a anthropomorphic treatment by a primitive culture of the forces of nature as the gods'; instead, we could read it as our own story, as the celebrated tale of Man told in the rhythm of his fall and rise. Read Homer as a narrative that provides the proper background and substance for the message of wisdom that the Muses bestowed upon thought, the Builder – in the First Epoch it is the Homeric Poet – in terms that their knowledge has brought to the light of speech as the very first rendering known to Occidental tradition of the experience that has been the cause and issue of our reflection since the beginning, namely the distinction of human being, who, for the Muses, is neither the *citizen* of freedom, nor the *saint* in the kingdom of God but rather the *hero* on the battlefield of destiny, born to die, but to die a good death which is a mortal's immortal pursuit of the heroic life of excellence in spite of the uncertainty of the outcomes of all human endeavor.

II. Hesiod

146. The Muses' Voice of Distinction

In the proem to his *Theogony*, which traces the descent of the Olympic kingdom, Hesiod describes the eye-opening experience of inspiration in which we, through the favor of the Muses, receive our vocation as bards of the gods who sired the esteemed pedigree of hero children we have come to recognize as champions of the distinction that is *human* being. It all happened so utterly unexpectedly! There we were, mere bellies of crude rusticity (ΚΑΚ ' ΕΛΕΓΧΕΑ ΓΑΣΤΡΕΣ ΟΙΟΝ – Hesiod, *Theogony [Th]*, 26), pasturing our lambs on the plain, when suddenly, out of the blue, the Muses addressed us and began instructing us regarding the craft and art of thought, the Builder, by making manifest in their first lesson the difference between narrating a tale of poetic fiction, a work of verisimilitude on the one hand and, on the other, that of a seer who gives voice to divisive truth, both of which capacities fall under their expertise and patronage. (Th 27.28)

It is this voice and the divine tongue of fire (...ΑΥΔΗΝ ΘΕΣΠΙΝ...) that makes it articulate that the Muses "breathe into" (...ΕΝΕΠΝΕΥΣΑΝ...) and bestow upon us along with the "glorious laurel staff" (...ΣΚΗΠΤΡΟΝ ΔΑΠΝΗΣ ΕΡΙΘΗΛΕΟΣ ΘΗΗΤΟΝ...) of the guild of those whose vocation it is to "praise *what will be* and *what has been*" (...ΚΛΕΙΟΙΜΙ ΤΑ Τ ' ΕΣΣΟΜΕΝΑ ΠΡΟ Τ ' ΕΟΝΤΑ... - Th 32, 38), the precedence and succession of predetermination, which defines the panoramic scope of the gods whose just being encompasses and surpasses the mortal strictures of THE WAY IT IS. For theirs is the drama of the distinguished being of what has always already been decided and what the counsel of Zeus has purposed in his deliberation concerning what is best and is, as such, *to be*. And it is to this principle regarding the ancestry and the posterity of the "blessed eternal being of the gods" (...ΜΑΚΑΡΩΝ ΓΕΝΟΣ ΑΙΕΝ ΕΟΝΤΩΝ...), that they bid us ply the celebratory art that is their own and for that principle's sake "always to celebrate themselves," the Muses, their art and their knowledge, "first of all and last." (Th 30-34)

ΣΦΑΣ Δ' ΑΥΤΑΣ ΠΡΩΤΟΝ ΤΕ ΚΑΙ ΥΣΤΑΤΟΝ ΑΙΕΝ ΑΕΙΔΕΙΝ

So let's begin with them. Who are the Muses whose wisdom and peripeteian insight into just being captures the entire spirit of the Greek Epoch? It is the distinguished spirit of recollection and remembrance in departure from the oblivion of self-deception and blindness that breeds negligence towards what has been decided and determined. For *Memory* (ΜΝΗΜΝΟΣΥΝΗ – Th 54) is their mother – such memory namely as bestows a liberating (ΕΛΕΥΘΗΡΟΣ – ibid) forgetfulness (ΛΗΣΜΟΣΥΝΗ – Th 55) of the ills besetting Man and repose from worry – and *Zeus*, their father, uniting in his own person supreme might with the right regard for the apportionment of just being. The attachment of their sacred conjugation brought forth nine like-minded maidens, namely Gloria, Delight, Flourish, Melody, Ballerina, Cherie, Polly Harmonia, Celeste and Spoken Sosweetly who, with song in their hearts and free of all care, dwell by the highest peaks of Olympus in abodes of beauty next to which the *Graces* (ΧΑΡΙΤΕΣ) and *Desire* (ΙΜΕΡΟΣ) live in delight, sending forth with their lovely voices (...ΕΡΗΡΑΤΟΝ ΟΣΣΑΝ...) hymns of praise, "glorifying the laws and the custom of the immortal gods." (Th 66-67)

ΠΑΝΤΩΝ ΤΕ ΝΟΜΟΥΣ ΚΑΙ ΗΘΕΑ ΚΕΔΝΑ
ΑΘΑΝΑΤΩΝ ΚΛΕΙΟΥΣΙΝ

As the Muses' songs will subsequently relate in detail, Zeus defeated his father, Cronus, and, "having gained insight into the esteem due each and every god, allotted to them their proper portions in the well-ordered determination" of just being. (Th 73-74)

ΕΥ ΔΕ ΕΚΑΣΤΑ ΑΘΑΝΑΤΟΙΣ ΔΙΕΤΑΞΕΝ ΟΜΩΣ
ΚΑΙ ΕΠΕΦΡΑΔΕ ΤΙΜΑΣ

Among the nine daughters, the last named and youngest, Calliope is the greatest of them all because she accompanies the venerable, Zeus-nourished kings; "upon the tongues..." of flame of those the Muses love (ΦΙΛΕΩ - 97) and honor (ΤΙΜΑΟ - 81), "...she pours sweet dew" (ΤΩΙ ΜΕΝ ΕΠΙ ΓΛΩΣΣΗΙ ΓΛΥΚΕΡΗΗΝ ΧΕΙΟΥΣΙΝ ΕΕΡΣΗΝ - 83) such that "from the kings' mouth flow soothing words." (84) Skilled in their use, the king, "pre-eminent among those assembled in council, quickly decides even grave disputes, passing right judgments (ΔΙΑΚΡΙΝΟΝΤΑ ΘΕΜΙΣΤΑΣ ΙΘΕΙΗΙΣΙΝΙ ΔΙΚΗΙΣΙΝ - Th 85-86) while speaking in the assembly (ΑΓΟΡΑ) of his people" led astray by bias; they look to him and his prudence for guidance in setting things straight, seeking to win his favor, as they would that of a god, with the gentle words of reverence. (Th 80-92)

Thus do kings profit from the Muses' gifts, and the work of practical reason, namely that of the political *Actor*, go hand in hand with the *Builder*'s art of flowing speech. For those endowed with language, in the sense of the tongue of honeyed flame that is the distinguished speech of the Muses, succeed at changing people's mind, either *politically*, with view to turning their deeds around (ΜΕΤΑΤΡΟΠΑ ΕΡΓΑ ΤΕΛΕΥΣΙ- 89) or else *perceptively* by refreshing their hearts and turning aside (ΠΑΡΕΤΡΑΠΕ - 103) Man's latter day ache of worry (ΠΕΝΘΟΣ ΕΞΩΝ ΝΕΟΚΗΔΕΙ ΘΥΜΩΙ - 98) – in other words that of our post/modern, *neoteric Man* – quickly consigning our troublesome cares to oblivion in the contemplation of, on the one hand, the glorious deeds of our distinguished *human being of yore* (ΚΛΕΙΑ ΠΡΟΤΕΡΩΝ ΑΝΘΡΩΠΩΝ -100) and on the other, those very principles of excellence with regard to which such heroes have always distinguished themselves, namely with regards to the blessed gods of Olympus (ΜΑΚΑΡΑΣ ΘΕΟΥΣ ΟΙ ΟΛΥΜΠΝΟΕΧΟΥΣΙΝ -101) themselves.

According to the logic of their celebratory work presented by Hesiod at the end of his introduction (43-52, 104-115), the Muses will thus glorify first the venerated generation of gods from the beginning (ΕΞ ΑΡΧΗΣ - 45) including the dynasty of *Titans*, who are the children of Earth (ΓΑΙΑ) and Sky (ΟΥΡΑΝΟΣ), and that of the *Olympians*, namely those children's children, the distinguished "gods, givers of good." (ΘΕΟΙ ΔΩΤΗΡΕΣ ΕΑΩΝ - 46). Second, the dominion of Zeus, the "father of the gods and of human being" (ΘΕΩΝ ΠΑΤΕΡ ' ΗΔΕ ΚΑΙ ΑΝΔΡΩΝ - 47), but *father* not in the sense of their creator or genitor but rather in dignity and excellence, in recognition of his supremacy of power and of insight, no, better, of insight first and then of power – because, as we saw, the divine powers Zeal, Victory, Might, and Force always *follow* Jovial Insight (384-389) – above all other gods in governing the just distribution of wealth and esteem of richly differentiated Olympus (ΑΦΕΝΟΣ ΔΑΣΣΑΝΤΟ ΚΑΙ...ΤΙΜΑΣ...ΔΙΕΛΟΝΤΟ... ΟΛΥΤΥΧΟΝ ΕΣΧΟΝ ΟΛΥΜΠΟΝ - 112-113).

Finally, Hesiod will turn to the human race itself, to their works and days, including that of the Giants who are, like the Cyclopes, grotesque magnifications of unprincipled men, cannibals, robbers, gargantuan in the extremism of their impiety, their greed and cruelty; intent on their own profit, they hate in their heart all that is just and right, having seized upon the notion of divinity as that which is greater and surpassing the confines of one's own concerns to perversely apply alone to their own *mere being* while neglecting all due regard for the limiting proportions that determine the comity of *just being*, the principle of justice upon which the Olympic community of Zeus is founded. But, as we saw in the Iliad, the spectacle of the distinction of human being against the backdrop of Man's proclivity towards unrestrained, hybrid humungousness is pleasing to the mind of Zeus ΤΕΡΠΟΥΣΙ ΔΙΟΣ ΝΟΟΝ ΕΝΤΟΣ ΟΛΥΜΠΟΥ - 51).

C. The Generations of the Gods

147. The Spawn of Abyss

The catalogue of beings that Hesiod, with the help of the Muses, unfolds before our eyes has one purpose, namely to show the development of the Olympic community from a hybrid dominion of gods founded on the injustice of overthrowing force of might that is itself destined to be eventually overthrown to the founding of the convention and the covenant of the gods in recognition of the principle of the just distribution of Olympic wealth and esteem in accordance with the proportion that is due and proper to each being.

The descent of the gods begins with the very first coming to be, namely of the gaping gap of *Abyss* (ΧΑΟΣ - 116). This archaic being, which does not refer to *Vacancy*, a vacuity wanting to be filled, nor the *Emptiness* of what is deficient or ineffectual, nor to the banality and blankness of sheer *Nothingness*; though all of these variations do indeed share something of its indeterminacy, none partake of *Abyss's* prolificacy, spawning as it does the somber murk of *Gloom* (EREBOS - 123) and the leaden dead of *Night* (ΝΥΞ -

ibid.). Translucent *Ethereality* and the brightness of *Day* (ΑΙΘΗΡ ΤΕ ΚΑΙ ΗΜΕΡΗ - 124) are the only two luminous offspring, a brother and a sister, produced by the pairing of this tenebrous couple, children whose *nature* is harmoniously opposed to that of their parents.

Night bore bane to human being in the great many dark progeny that bespeak the wretchedness and calamity of Man, first and foremost of which are the several masters of our perishing and the extinction of distinction, namely hateful *Doom* (ΜΟΡΟΣ) and black *Demise* (ΚΗΡΑ) and *Death* (ΘΑΝΑΤΟΣ) and *Sleep* (ΥΠΝΟΣ), the other's silent brother with whom the tribe of *Dreams* (ΦΥΛΟΣ ΟΝΕΙΡΩΝ) house, all clothed in that weird obscurity they inherited from their mother; clearly, Sleep such as he is and the entourage of Dreams who accompany him are neither pleasant nor sweet. (211-12)

Reprehension (ΜΩΜΟΝ) and *Misery* (ΟΙΖΥΝ) are also among her brood (214) – these two are conceived by her without having mingling recourse to a mate (213) – indicating the purity of their blood as being their mother's and no one else's babies – as are the occidental *Twilights* (ΕΣΠΕΡΙΔΑΣ), namely the daughters of nightfall and the day's decline at the outer limits of all inhabitancy and beyond the girdle of the world, the *Lots* of destiny (ΜΟΙΡΑΙ) and the violent *Fates* (ΚΗΡΑΣ), namely *Spinner* (ΚΛΩΘΩ), *Fortune* (ΛΑΧΕΣΙΣ), and *Obduracy* (ΑΤΡΟΠΟΣ), who relentlessly pursue iniquity, whether committed by Man or god, "never ceasing in their anger until the perpetrator has been duly punished" (220-22); fittingly, therefore, *Night* also gave birth to indignant *Outrage* (ΝΕΜΕΣΙΣ) who retaliates against such disregard.

Moreover Night bore the siblings *Guile* (ΑΠΑΤΗ) and *Desire* (ΦΙΛΟΤΗΣ) and the debility of *Old Age* (ΓΗΡΑΣ) and finally her last born and youngest daughter, hateful *Strife* (ΕΡΙΣ), who in turn, no less fecund than her mother, bred a frightful crew of spawn – *Travail* (ΠΟΝΟΣ) and *Concealment* (ΛΗΘΗ) and *Hunger* (ΛΙΜΟΣ) and *Pains* (ΑΛΓΕΑ), the clash of *Warfare* (ΥΣΜΙΝΗ) and of *Combat* (ΜΑΧΗ) and *Slaughter* (ΦΟΝΟΣ) and *Homicides* (ΑΝΔΡΟΚΤΑΣΙΑ) and *Feuds* (ΝΕΙΚΕΑ), *Tarradidles* (ΨΕΥΔΕΑ) and *talk* (ΛΟΓΟΥΣ), bantering *Disputes* (ΑΜΦΗΙΛΛΟΓΙΑΣ) and *Lawlessness* (ΔΥΣΝΟΜΙΗ) and blind *Rashness* (ΑΤΗ), and last but not least, rather greatest, *Oath* (ΟΡΚΟΣ).

Obviously, this catalog is by no means a complete enumeration of all the members of the tribe and issue of *Baseness*, *Deformity*, and *Iniquity*, in a word that particular brand of *Badness* (KAKOΣ) we might call *Thersitian* (Il. 2.212 – 224) the abhorrence of which the speech of the Muses and the spirit of the Greek Epoch gave such substantial, even monumental, evidence. There is no reason why the dead of *Night* should have given birth to *Reproach* (MΩMON - 214) but not to *Dishonoring* (AIΣXYNΩ) in close proximity to whom it receives mention in Homer (Od. 2.86) and who in turn is the work or shall we say, trying our hand in personification, the child and scion of *Disgrace* (AIΣXPOΣ) who might be thought to live in sisterly propinquity to *Shame* (ΛΩBH); again, why mention the *Indignation of moral Outrage*, an unwieldy name much more pithily put by using the Greek one, namely NEMIΣIΣ (Nemesis – 223), but not MHNIΣ (Achilles' fatal outrage at being disrespected by Agamemnon – Il. 1.1) or *Anger* (XOΛOΣ – 221) or *Rancor* (KOTOΣ - Od. 11.102) or even the *Urge* (ΘYMOΣ) and the *Ire* (OPΓH) that we fly into when we lose or temper? Likewise, why *Blindness* (ATH) and *Illegitimacy* ΔYΣNOMIH but not YBPIΣ (hubris), which is the negligent cause of the latter's state of strife and the overweening consequence of the former's excesses and refusal to hear pleas of mercy and respond in kind with pity? Have not *Shame* (AIΔΩΣ) and *Regard* (TIMH) and the unyielding *Hardheartedness* (AΠIΣTOΣ) and the *Viciousness* (ΩMHΣTHΣ) that oppose *Care* (KHΔEIOΣ) and friendly *Kindness* (ΦIΛOΣ) won our admiration as gods (THEOI), in other words as *terms of distinction*? In truth, all of these terms can be seen to refer to our experience of what is caused by and what causes injustice and disregard for what is right, whether we ourselves are the victims, the witnesses, or the perpetrators of blinded impropriety (230). A thesaurus of the English language in hand, we might easily expound upon this issue in English terms beginning with the notion, better, the person of *Strife*; we might venture to name further offspring, for example *Rivalry* and *Struggle* and *Dissension*, *Rumpus* and *Row*, *Fracas* and *Hassle* and the triplets *Split*, *Rift* and *Cleft* who bear a remarkable resemblance to their abysmal ancestor, namely XAOΣ, the gap we mind so terribly and flee like the plague, like the doors of hell, gaping between the IS and the OUGHT. *Strife* appears here, as does her grandmother *Night* through her, in different guises, faces, i.e. "persona" in accordance with the variety of contexts and circumstances that our experience with her provide. This is the reason for such a multiplicity of gods; they are with us in their diversity even as our life is various.

It is easy to see how not only *Pains* (AΛΓEA - 227) but also *Pains Taken*, namely double-edged *Toil and Trouble* (ΠONOΣ - 226), *Distress* and *Grief* and their cognates notions would be related by "blood" – the blood of spirit, which, in the Greek world, is not so much *holy* in the practical sense of governing our actions as it is speculative, the enumeration of a catalogue of beings – to the contention of *War*, while *Distortions* and *Fabrications*, *Arguments* and *Counter-arguments* (229) are the instruments, i.e. the sprouts, of wrangling with words (ΛΟΓΟΥΣ -229) rather than swords albeit to the same effect of altercation.

In Hesiodic terms, i.e. in speech elaborating the wisdom of the Muses, these cognate beings of transgression (ΠΑΡΑΒΑΣΙΑ - 220) as well as those who prosecute with the wrathful, evil eye (ΚΑΚΗΝ ΟΠΙΝ - 222) of vengeance the crimes of our disregard – not merely "personified" notions or linguistic elements defining a semantic field – articulate the wide field of calamity and vexation that befalls man when the chaotically gaping gap between THE WAY IT SHOULD BE and THE WAY IT IS is most pointedly experienced. This difference is the resonant interval of self-severalty in which critical self-reflection emerges. We experience alterity as a deviation and divergence between the IS and the OUGHT; hence, it is in the pain of their discrepancy and in the animosity that their divergence ignites in upright hearts, that we observe reason as most sharply and energetically distinguishing itself from the flow and the lull of mere being into which our mind tends to sink in the oblivion (ΛΗΘΗ - 227) of satisfaction when all our dreams, those visions of a Hungry Heart (ΛΙΜΟΝ - 227), have been fulfilled and all thought has been evacuated by the easy-peasy appeasement of a peaceful life in Pleasantville, banishing the Night.

148. The Children of Earth

The ancient lineage of the heirs of *Abyss* (ΧΑΟΣ) that we have been tracing is entirely divorced from the extraction of gods stemming from Earth (ΓΑΙΑ), a family tree destined to flower with the coming of the children of Cronus and attain fruition as the Olympian generation under Zeus. These are not two branches of divinity but rather two distinct strains of being that have neither forebears nor progeny in common nor any affiliation as a consequence of a cohabitation of their beings. They remain distinct – the opening of chasmal space that is the divide of *Chaos*, and the closure and plenitude of place that is the fundamental earth of *Gaia* in the expanse of her terrestrial immensity (ΕΥΡΥΣΤΕΡΝΟΣ - 117) and as such the "seat of the immortal gods forever firm" (ΠΑΝΤΩΝ ΕΔΟΣ ΑΣΦΑΛΕΣ ΑΙΕΙ ΑΘΑΝΑΤΩΝ - 117-118), while *Tartarus* (ΤΑΡΤΑΡΥΣ) is the profound depths of her telluric internality and *Desire* (ΕΡΟΣ), finally, is distinguished as "the most beautiful among the immortal gods" (ΚΑΛΛΙΣΤΟΣ ΕΝ ΑΘΑΝΑΤΟΙΣΙ ΘΕΟΙΣΙ - 120) and thus by dint of his beauty succeeds in "overpowering the mind in the breast and deliberate counsel of all divine and of all of human being." (121-122)

ΠΑΝΤΩΝ ΤΕ ΘΕΩΝ ΠΑΝΤΩΝ Τ' ΑΝΘΡΩΠΩΝ ΔΑΜΝΑΤΑΙ ΕΝ
ΣΤΗΘΕΣΣΙ ΝΟΟΝ ΚΑΙ ΕΠΙΦΡΟΝΑ ΒΟΥΛΗΝ

Turning now to the posterity of *Earth*, we learn that her first issue is her lord and protector. She brings forth the *Sky* (ΟΥΡΑΝΟΣ) so that he may entirely shelter her (ΙΝΑ ΜΙΝ ΠΕΡΙ ΠΑΝΤΑ ΚΑΛΥΠΤΟΙ - 127) as a veil and mantle would, under which he is to have and to hold her, nestling and encompassing her in the sanctuary of his embrace. Significantly, she bore him "equal to herself" (ΙΣΟΝ ΕΩΥΤΗΙ - 126), i.e. entirely in and of herself without sharing the conjugal love of a partner (ΑΤΕΡ ΦΙΛΟΤΗΤΟΣ - 132) and thus in pure self-relativity, that procreative relationship of reflection that we have noted as indicative of the entity of identity in which pure reason is manifest to thought thinking about thought.

Gaia had children with *Ouranos* as well as with *Sea* (ΠΟΝΤΟΣ), who is Gaia's last self-relative birth after having given rise to the *Mountains* (ΟΥΡΕΑ - 32). First born among her children who arose through her union with *Sea* is Nereus who together with *Gift* (ΔΩΡΙΣ), daughter of Oceanus, gave birth to 50 sea girls, richly figuring our experience of the ocean's being, namely, among others, Prima (ΠΡΩΘΩ), Wella Governia (ΕΥΚΡΑΝΤΗ), Saviora (ΣΑΩ), Wella Gift (ΕΥΔΩΡΗ), Positivia (ΘΕΤΙΣ), Oceania Still (ΓΑΛΗΝΗ), Gleamina (ΓΛΑΥΚΗ), Undulata Swift (ΚΥΜΟΘΟΗ), Vortexia (ΣΠΕΙΩ), Exuberantia (ΘΑΛΙΑ), Pan Divina (ΠΑΣΙΘΕΑ), Beloved (ΕΡΑΤΩ), Thrille O'Victory (ΕΥΝΙΚΗ), Honey Sweete (ΜΕΛΤΕ), Harbora Havenport (ΕΥΛΙΜΕΝΗ), Gloria (ΑΓΑΥΗ), Donora (ΔΩΤΩ), Protonia (ΠΡΩΤΩ), Carrie (ΦΕΡΟΥΣΑ), Potenta (ΔΥΝΑΜΕΝΗ), Islette (ΝΗΣΙΑΗ), Promontoria (ΑΚΤΑΙΗ), Principia (ΠΡΩΤΟΜΕΔΕΙΑ), Gracie (ΔΩΡΙΣ), Panoramia (ΠΑΝΟΠΗ), Equestria Fleet (ΙΠΠΟΘΟΗ), Ryder Craft (ΙΠΠΟΝΟΗ), Fantasia Surge (ΚΥΜΟΔΟΚΗ), Riptide Stiller (ΚΥΜΑΤΟΛΗΓΗ), Eddie Ripple (ΚΥΜΟ), Curvie Shore (ΗΙΟΝΗ), Arte O'Sea (ΑΛΙΜΗΔΗ), Reign Splendide (ΓΛΑΥΚΟΝΟΜΗ), C. Travelle (ΠΟΝΤΟΠΟΡΕΙΑ), Smoothe Talker (ΛΕΙΑΓΟΡΗ), Goode Company (ΕΥΑΓΟΡΗ), Willa O'Peoples (ΛΑΟΜΕΔΕΙΑ), Manny Knowing (ΠΟΛΥΝΟΗ), Owine Knowing (ΑΥΤΟΝΟΗ), Sandy (ΨΑΜΑΘΗ), Isle O'Lande (ΝΗΣΩ), Welle Sent (ΕΥΠΟΜΠΗ), Ordie Nance (ΘΕΜΙΣΤΩ), Claire Foresight (ΠΡΟΝΟΗ) and Surely Truly (ΝΗΜΕΡΤΗΣ). (244-262)

As impressive as this catalogue of Nereids is in articulating the sea's distinctions, more significant for the understanding of the Olympic kingdom of Jovial justice is however, as we shall see, the brood of Gaia and Ouranos, in particular the dynasty of the Titans (Oceanus, Coeus, Crius, Hyperion, Iaptetus Theia, Rhea, Themis, Mnemosyne, Phoebe, Tethys and finally Cronus). For it is from this twelvefold issue of their union that Rhea and Cronus, the parents of Zeus, his three sisters, Hestia, Demeter, Hera, and two brothers, Hades and Poseidon, with whom he shares his dominion, emerge.

After constituting his reign, Zeus also takes wives and through them and in the birth of his children explicates the principles upon which his authority and the dynasty of Olympus are based, principles which themselves are founded on the principle of just apportionment that Zeus gained insight into originally, earning him the privilege of preeminence and the title of father of the gods, not merely in physical power but in that of the mind, in the knowledge of what has been determined and, with regards to this antecedent principle, what is the best that can happen, the best that can be, the best to be achieved.

Zeus's excellence as a God of thought and counsel is manifested in the distinguished birth and, as it were, the "immaculate conception" of his first daughter, bright-eyed Athena, goddess of pure reason whose comprehensive wisdom attains theoretical (mathematics), practical (law and justice) as well as poetic (crafts and arts) distinction, namely that of *inspiration* in the sciences, *courage* in resolution of the discrepancy between the IS and the OUGHT, which is the endeavor of just warfare ensuing from the self-severalty of discernment, and finally *skill* in the accomplishment of superb works that give wisdom a house and a home to dwell in.

We learn that Zeus takes the universal *Wisdom* (ΜΗΤΙΣ) of pure reason (7.447; 10.226; 15.509; Od. 19.326) to be his first wife, "of supreme mind among divine and mortal human being" (886-887) and is destined, according to the prophesy by *Earth* and *Sky*, to have children of great insight. (ΠΕΡΙΦΡΟΝΑ ΤΕΚΝΑ - 894) As the result of their union, Athena is conceived; she is to be born her father's equal in strength and in counsel (ΙΣΟΝ ΕΧΟΥΣΑΝ ΠΑΤΡΙ ΜΕΝΟΣ ΚΑΙ ΕΠΙΦΡΟΝΑ ΒΟΥΛΗΝ- 896) as is also a son of violent heart (ΥΠΕΡΒΙΟΝ ΗΤΟΡ - 898). But before this birth can occur, Zeus swallows Metis so that she, as the gut feeling of his intuition, might "advise him concerning good and evil." (ΣΥΜΦΡΑΣΣΑΙΤΟ ΑΓΑΘΟΝ ΤΕ ΚΑΚΟΝ ΤΕ - 900). As is well-known, Athena comes nevertheless to the world, not as a baby girl but rather emerging in full battle gear, ready for action, from Zeus's head, his thought and distinguished insight come alive, whole and entirely complete in her development, perfect, the image of her father. Can we not recognize here the reiterating structure of self-critical thought's prescience, progression, and procreation now in mythological terms as gods nested in gods?

Consider a train of thought that might be depicted as in *Figure 97*:

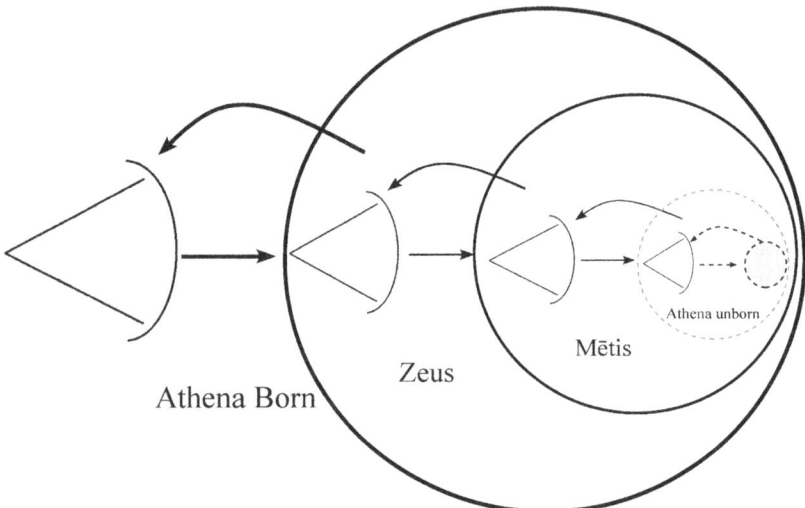

Figure 97: The Birth of Wisdom

Second, he marries *Law* (ΘΕΜΙΣ) who gives birth to the ***Seasons*** (ΩΡΑΙ) – *Just Apportionment* (EYNOMIA), the *Dictate of Justice* (ΔΙΚΗ), and *Peace* (ΕΙΡΗΝΗ) – and the ***Fates*** – *Spinner* (ΚΛΩΘΩ), *Fortune* (ΛΑΧΕΣΙΣ), and *Obduracy* (ΑΤΡΟΠΟΣ) – while in his marriage to *Apportionment Far and Wide* (EYPYNOMH), he becomes the sire of the ***Graces*** (ΧΑΡΙΤΕΣ), namely Splendor (ΑΓΛΑΕΑ), Joy (ΕΥΦΡΟΣΥΝΗ), and Good Cheer (ΘΑΛΙΑ).

As *Figure 98* suggests, these three triads – that of the Seasons, the Destinies, and the Graces – form a train of thought in which the dynasty of Zeus is articulated as that of the reign and ratio of reason's terms. First, the triad of the *Seasons* (ΩΡΑΣ) is said to foster (ΩΡΕΥΟΥΣΙ - 903) the achievements of mortals with regards to the convention of what has been decided and apportioned as the principle of THE WAY IT SHOULD BE – the well-apportioned distinctions of esteem (EYNOMIA) that define the proper limits of each being (ΔΙΚΗ) establish the comity of peace (ΕΙΡΗΝΗ); second, the triad of the *Destinies* (ΜΟΙΡΑΙ), who we first encountered as children of Night, are here revised in Zeus's highest regard (ΠΛΕΣΙΤΗΝ ΤΙΜΗΝ - 904) as bestowing upon mortal human being the endowment of what is beneficial and what is detrimental (ΔΙΔΟΥΣΙ ΘΝΗΤΟΙΣ ΑΝΘΡΩΠΟΙΣΙΝ ΕΧΕΙΝ ΑΓΑΘΟΝ ΤΕ ΚΑΚΟΝ ΤΕ- 905-906), namely the measured unfolding of the ordainments (ΚΛΩΘΩ), their just assignment to each in accordance with what is due (ΛΑΧΕΣΙΣ) and, as a result, the resolved and firm determination of each being's being as their own proper destiny (ΑΤΡΟΠΟΣ); third, the triad of the *Graces* born of Zeus and the *Widespread Predominance of the Law's Apportionment* (ΕΥΡΥΝΟΜΗ - 907) reflect the *Beauty* (ΚΑΛΟΝ - 911) as well as the *Desirability* (ΕΡΟΣ - 910) of just being, the *Splendor* (ΑΓΑΛΙΑ) of which is *Delightful to the Spirit* (ΕΥΦΡΟΣΥΝΗ) and gives rise to outpourings of *Abounding Celebration* (ΘΑΛΙΑ), the celebration of a firm and abiding peace founded upon the justly determined proportion of divine good and plenty, in other words: DIKH – ΑΤΡΟΠΟΣ – ΘΑΛΙΑ; thus is the formula for the circle of perfection, that crowning of the Olympic kingdom of the gods that Jovial pure reason is the esteemed father of.

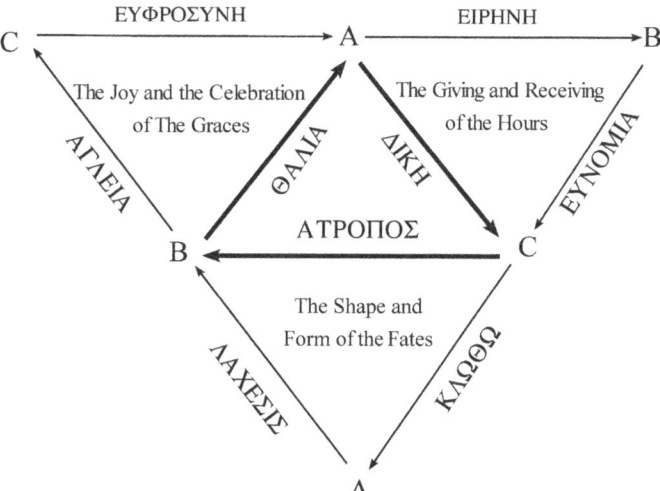

Figure 98: The Jovial Ratio of Ratios in Terms of the Muses

Here upon this delightful peak, the Muses themselves, the daughters of Recollection (ΜΝΕΜΟΣΥΝΗ), are again named as they were in the beginning as is right and proper and in accordance with their behest. (34) For here is the proper place of their birth as well (915).

Theirs is the dance and the song of celebration that commemorates the descent of Olympus, which is not merely the birth of the gods but rather the founding and the development of the institution of their community, their culture and not just their nature, as we might say being reminded of the Third Epoch. What insight on the part of Zeus is the principle of this dwelling on high upon the mountain of our Mother Earth?

A. The Olympic Kingdom of Just Being

149. The History of Violence

The catalogues of divine generation that we encounter in Hesiod – we examined the one emerging from the union of Gaia and Pontus as an example – articulate the character traits of the gods whose children they are in such a way that the children themselves not only *name* but also *are* the inherent powers and properties of their parents brought to vivid light in the fruition of that marriage. Not only are the parents present in the children they engender and the children thus the differentiation of the properties that their ancestors possess but, more importantly, the consanguinity of a god's brothers and sisters are thought to reveal a general "family resemblance" (as Wittgenstein would put it) among cognate siblings that has descended to particulars in the being of their sons and daughters.

We saw this in the offspring of *Night* and of *Strife*, her daughter; *Distress* and *Deceit, Hunger* and *Quarrel* – these are the children and the differentiation of their mother's nature; they name her attributes in terms of our experience with her, place her in the context of human life where she and hers make themselves known and felt to us mortals as well as to the immortal gods.

In this way, the branches and the fruits of the family tree, even as they grow outwardly and ramify in the specification of progeny, manifest in this filial diversity the convergence and common origin of the extraction in question. Hence, the genealogy of the offspring elaborates the beings of their ancestors even as the seed, becoming the plant, exhibits its nature in the differentiation of its parts and properties, the beings of its being. These "natures" form a community of specialized members each with their own particular function in the differentiation of the parts that constitute the perfect whole of the organism that has, in them, attained the mature state of its development.

A plant and its parts present its character in its distinctions, differentiating, marking its properties, which, in turn, are the members of its body, its root and flower, its *nature* (ΦΥΣΙΣ - Od. 10.303-04) and constitute the whole thing, the complete state of being, the community of brothers and sisters each of whom has a particular role and function in the administration of that being in its entirety, making her or his own contribution to the integrity of the being to which it belongs. In this way, the gods themselves have a nature and a place of their own in the scheme of things, each god his or her own portion and possession in the community of the gods. Zeus's insight into this apportionment of the properties of the gods and the efforts he undertook on behalf of this principle is the achievement that gave Zeus the dignity of the title of founding father of Olympus. For in recognition of the apportionment of just being, Zeus grasped just "how much more the half is than the whole." (*Work and Days* 40)

ΟΣΩΙ ΠΛΕΟΝ ΗΜΙΣΥ ΠΑΝΤΟΣ

Zeus knew that a god's attributes are, in fact, a god's merits and distinctions to which the tribute of regard is due. For this reason, after Aphrodite's birth, she is said "to possess honor since the beginning, having received as her lot the following portions among human beings and immortal gods: Maidenly Whispers, Smiles, Dupery, Sweet Delight, Desire and Gentleness." (*Theogony* 203-206)

TAYTHN Δ' EΞ APXHΣ TIMHN EXEI HΔE ΛΕΛΟΓΧΕ MOIPAN
EN ANΘPΩΠOIΣI KAI AΩANATOIΣI ΘEOIΣI, ΠAPΩENIOYΣ
T' OAPOYΣ MEIΔHMATA T' ΞAΠATAΣ TE TEPΨIN TE ΓΛYKEPHN
ΦIΛOTHTA TE MEIΛIXIHN TE.

We note in passing that Desire (ΘIΛOTHTA) is inherent in our experience and thus "a child" and nature, a *being*, of both Aphrodite and Night (224). Who would deny the ambivalent power of love, the heights and depths to which it moves us?

The story of Zeus, his founding and ascension of Olympus, is the story of how the second generation of gods, namely "the givers of good things, divided their wealth and distributed their regard." (111-112)

ΘΕΟΙ ΔΩΤΗΡΕΣ ΕΑΩΝ ΩΣ Τ ' ΑΦΕΝΟΣ ΔΑΣΣΑΝΤΟ
ΚΑΙ ΩΣ ΤΙΜΑΣ ΔΙΕΛΟΝΤΟ

This is the message of the Muses and their song of how he gained supremacy over his father Cronus and, through the merit of his insight having been awarded the prerogative of wielding thunder and the victorious power of the lightning bolt, how he himself properly apportioned esteem to every god in accordance with what was due to each (73-74) – the reflections of which in the songs of the Muses please the mind of Zeus and all of the gods (40, 37, 51).

This story begins with an "ugly deed..." on the part of Ouranos (*Sky*), "...in which he rejoiced" (ΚΑΚΩΙ Δ ' ΕΠΕΤΕΡΠΕΤΟ ΕΡΓΩΙ - 158), who, in a bid to prevent from coming to the light of day the birth of his monstrous offspring namely, on the one hand, that of the violent-hearted Cyclopes – *Thunder* (ΒΡΟΝΤΕΣ) and *Lightening* (ΣΤΕΡΟΠΕΣ) and *Blazing Flash* (ΑΡΓΕΣ) – and on the other, that of the unspeakable and colossal Hecatonchires, the Hundred-handed monsters – *Rancor* (ΚΟΤΤΟΣ), *Brute* (ΒΡΙΑΡΕΥΣ), Gigantic (ΓΥΓΗΣ) – deformed beings of raw matter, impact, and obstreperous impulsion whom he hated one and all and whose birth he therefore hindered. Gaia (*Earth*) then, groaning inwardly through the obstruction of her parturition, devised an "ugly stratagem of cunning" (ΔΟΛΙΗΝ ΔΕ ΚΑΚΗΝ ΕΠΕΦΡΑΣΣΑΤΟ ΤΕΧΝΗΝ - 160) namely to "exact revenge for the outrage of evil" (ΚΑΚΗΝ ΤΕΙΣΣΑΙΜΕΘΑ ΛΩΒΗΝ - 165) that the "wicked father" (ΠΑΤΡΟΣ ΑΤΑΣΘΑΛΟΥ - 164) had committed against her children and their mother; "for he was the first to contrive an unjust act." (166, 172)

ΠΡΟΤΕΡΟΣ ΓΑΡ ΑΕΙΚΕΑ ΜΗΣΑΤΟ ΕΡΓΑ

Remarkable: The first act of injustice recorded by the Muses in Hesiod's *Theogony* is one of suppression committed by a patriarchal authority against his unwieldy children to hinder what he, in the Greek version of self-several estrangement, perceives in them as a threat to his own supremacy – such is the attempt, doomed to failure, to hinder the birth of what is to be, of what is to come to light, namely the limits that define the scope of an individual's power in the scheme of all time and place that is to be the kingdom of Olympus; we learn that THE WAY IT SHOULD BE or *destiny* is a child to be born – a determination of necessity, inevitable even for the gods!

But then at his mother's behest, twisted-minded Cronus (ΑΓΚΥΛΟΜΗΤΗΣ - 137) commits a terrific deed of wickedness (ΑΤΑΣΘΑΛΙΗΙΣΙΗΙ ΜΕΓΑ ΡΕΞΑΙ ΕΡΓΟΝ - 209-210) with the crooked-bladed knife upon his father, answering crime with crime by violently divesting the latter of his rod of rule and regnancy, who, though curtailed and overthrown, utters the curse of retaliation upon Cronus and his siblings, calling them in his rebuke *Titans* for having overreached (TITAINONTAΣ - 209) in deposing him, an injustice that would be avenged in the time to come (TOIO Δ ' ΕΠΕΙΤΑ ΤΙΣΙΝ ΜΕΤΟΠΙΣΘΕΝ ΕΣΕΣΘΑΙ - 210)

This time came too soon to pass; for Cronus, mindful of securing his dominion against his powerful siblings who might themselves venture to overstep and usurp the throne and even more threatened by his children from among whose number would arise, as Earth and Sky had prophesied, the next king in succession to overpower his father (464) and the dynasty of the Titans, just as Cronos had overpowered his and that of autochthonous being, decided to swallow his children one by one as soon as they were born, a ploy to hold on to power that is not Ouranos' crime of oppression but rather that of consumption, digestion, and absorption of differences, in an attempt to internalize and assimilate the distinction of his children to himself and thus dissolve all rivalry.

In her grief, Rhea, Cronus' wife, wanting to save her son Zeus, the youngest of her children (478), consulted Earth and Sky and beseeched them to contrive a device by which she might secretly give birth to Zeus and "the deity of revenge wreak retaliation for her father and her children." (ΤΕΙΣΑΙΤΟ Δ ' ΕΡΙΝΥΣ ΠΑΤΡΟΣ ΕΟΙΟ ΠΑΙΔΩΝ ΤΕ... - 472-473). The plan succeeds and she gives birth unbeknownst to Cronus offering him a stone wrapped in swaddling clothes to swallow in lieu of her son who remained "unconquered..." and who was destined in turn to "...defeat his father by force with his own hands and expel him from the dignity and office of his kingship that Zeus would now claim for himself." (489-491)

At this juncture, we would do well to wonder how Zeus will fare in his regency. Will he merely repeat the vicious circle of usurpation that the first two generations of gods have established, overthrowing his father only to be overthrown in time by his son?

150. Jovial Just Being

No. Zeus is the term of principle for the Hesiodic Muse precisely because in contrast to the fate of his father and his grandfather, both of whom tried to maintain their dominion by the suppression of the new generation of gods who are his progeny, Zeus grasped the principle of just apportionment realizing that the best way to maintain his power is by sharing it and thereby actually putting the principle of MOIPA into practice, the practice of good goverance. What a revolutionary counter-intuitive idea: Preserving and sustaining one's power by justly apportioning it to others! Only in this way can the "half be more than the whole." And only in this way is Zeus destined to defeat Cronus even though his father is the stronger (465).

On the day of this insight, Zeus convened an assembly of the gods upon the heights of Olympus and proposed the following covenant for their approbation: "those who would join him in battle against the Titans, would not be divested of honors; rather, each would remain in possession of the esteem he or she previously enjoyed among the immortal gods; those, on the other hand, who had been disgraced and bereft of regard and esteem under Cronus, would be promoted in regard and esteem in accordance with the ways of established custom and propriety." (392-96)

ΟΣ ΑΝ ΜΕΤΑ ΕΙΟ ΘΕΩΝ ΤΙΤΗΣΙ ΜΑΧΟΙΤΟ, ΜΗ ΤΙΝ 'ΑΠΟΡΡΑΙΣΕΙΝ ΓΕΡΑΩΝ, ΤΙΜΗΝ ΔΕ ΕΚΑΣΤΟΝ ΕΞΕΜΕΝ ΗΝ ΤΟ ΠΑΡΟΣ ΓΕ ΜΕΤ ' ΑΩΑΝΑΤΟΙΣΙ ΘΕΟΙΣΙ... ΟΣΤΙΣ ΑΤΙΜΟΣ ΥΠΟ ΚΡΟΝΟΥ ΗΔ ' ΑΓΕΡΑΣΤΟΣ, ΤΙΜΗΣ ΚΑΙ ΓΕΡΑΩΝ ΕΠΙΒΗΣΕΜΕΝ, Η ΘΕΜΙΣ ΕΣΤΙΝ.

With this pledge, Zeus committed himself to the recognition of each individual's being, having given his assurance that their unique properties and distinctions would be acknowledged and respected as that particular god's own due portion with which he or she is to partake of the Olympic community as a member and peer, a god among gods.

He addressed his offer first to the Cyclopes who had been oppressed by their father, Ouranos, fettered and concealed inside Gaia, releasing them from their bonds. Thankful for this act of kindness, they requite benefit with benefit and entrust him with thunder and the flashing thunderbolt – the two emblems and instruments of his supreme power upon which his rule depends but only because this power has been conveyed upon him by his subjects as a token of esteem for the esteem and generosity he demonstrated by integrating them into the community of regard that he could only establish and preserve with their assent and assistance. (501-506)

Zeus's conception of just apportionment towards the commonwealth of the gods was also the necessary and sufficient condition for decisive victory in his battle with the Titans. For Zeus approached the Hundred-handed monsters with his offer of returning them to the light of divine regard and community. They also had been ostracized, banished and bound under and at the ends of the earth by their father who felt threatened by their size and power and the implicit defiance of his reign that their prowess meant to him, and there, thus excluded, "they suffered much and long wracked by grievous pain in their hearts." (623)

Zeus had been advised by Earth that only with their help would he finally succeed at defeating the Titans after having waged war against his father and the previous generation of the gods continually for 10 years with neither of the combatants able to break the deadlock of a distinction without difference since "the outcome of the war hung evenly in balance." (638)

But then Zeus readmitted them into the company of mutual regard among the gods the nectar and ambrosia of which refreshed their strength and reinvigorated their courage; now, after having recognized the Hundred-handed Monsters as full-fledged members of the Olympic kingdom, he called upon them in remembrance of his act of kindness towards them by which they were rehabilitated from the deprivation and abjection of their exclusion to challenge the Titans in battle and to display and wield the immense strength of their hands and in this way to finally tip the scales of war in favor of the Olympians (639-654).

Kottos answered him as follows: "We know ourselves that you excel in thought and that your insight is supreme and therein have you become guardian of the immortals against chilling bane. Through your well-considered plan, we have once again returned from harsh imprisonment under the shadowy murk – a boon we no longer dared hope for. Therefore, with resolve of mind and in spirit eager, we will now support your leadership in dreaded battle and fight against the Titans in the contest for supremacy." (654-663)

> ΙΔΜΕΝ Ο ΤΟΙ ΠΕΡΙ ΜΕΝ ΠΡΑΠΙΔΕΣ, ΠΕΡΙ Δ' ΕΣΤΙ ΝΟΗΜΑ,
> ΑΛΚΤΗΡ Δ ΑΘΑΝΑΤΟΙΣΙΝ ΑΡΗΣ ΓΕΝΕΟ ΚΡΥΕΡΟΙΟ, ΣΗΙΣΙ
> Δ' ΕΠΙΦΡΟΣΥΝΗΙΣΙΝ ΥΠΟΥ ΖΟΦΟΥ ΗΕΡΟΕΝΤΟΣ ΑΨΟΡΡΟΝ
> ΕΞΑΥΤΙΣ ΑΜΕΙΛΙΚΤΩΝ ΥΠΟ ΔΕΣΜΩΝ ΗΛΥΘΟΜΕΝ,...
> ΑΝΑΕΛΠΤΑ ΠΑΘΟΝΤΕΣ. ΤΩΙ ΚΑΙ ΝΥΝ ΑΤΕΝΕΙ ΤΕ ΝΟΩΙ ΚΑΙ
> ΠΡΟΦΡΟΝΙ ΘΥΜ ΩΙ ΡΥΣΟΜΕΘΑ ΚΡΑΤΟΣΥΜΟΝ ΕΝ ΑΙΝΗΙ
> ΔΗΙΟΤΗΤΙ, ΜΑΡΝΑΜΕΝΟΙ ΤΙΤΗΣΙΝ ΑΝΑ ΚΡΑΤΕΡΑΣ ΥΣΜΙΝΑΣ.

Zeus has been appointed the defender of the gods against disaster. But what could so banefully afflict the gods in their immortal and lightly living being? Only the painful chains of disregard and exclusion from divine comity. The hundred-handed monsters Gyges, Cottus, and Obriareus, who were previously imprisoned in Tartarus by their father and barred from the light of the gods' esteem, return to the underworld after Zeus's victory. There in the gloom that previously was their prison, they now have their dwellings, no longer as prisoners in execration, defamed as potential insurgents, but rather in the dignity of their office as Zeus's trusted guards (ΦΥΛΑΚΕΣ ΠΙΣΤΟΙ ΔΙΟΣ... - 735) and celebrated helpers (ΚΛΕΙΤΟΙ ΕΠΙΚΟΥ– ΡΟΙ - 815), even as Night herself has her houses there, "shrouded in black clouds" where her children's houses, Sleep's and brazen-hearted Death's, are located, as are Hades' as well, the Nether-Zeus in this place of absolute terror, repugnant even to the gods (739, 766, 775) but no less a part of the community of the gods. Loathsome and abhorrent (ΣΤΥΓΕΡΗ - 739, 810) and nevertheless, even as the very outer extremity of Olympus, the *pit* and the diametrically opposed nadir to that zenith and *tip* of power that is the heights of Zeus, down there at the roots and the ends of *Earth*, *Tartarus*, *Sea* and the starry *Sky* (807-810) yet still a part of that well-proportioned cosmos that Zeus established as a community of regard, there is the chilling Styx, the waters of the binding oath, woeful for the gods; for it obligates, constrains, limits even them on the pain of a death-like punishment. The Titans alone live beyond the pale and the ken of Olympus (ΠΡΟΣΘΕΝ ΔΕ ΘΕΩΝ ΕΚΤΟΣΘΕΝ ΑΠΑΝΤΩΝ - 813), at the very threshold and the gate of immovable bronze (811); between their spirit and that of Zeus lies the gap and the fall of the abyss; here is the place that is no place where the first distinction is drawn, the entity of identity that is the mark of distinction of the gods as much as it is of all human being. These beings at the end of all being, these limits and borders, their inexorability, their impersonal, absolute power of determination, the profoundness and darkness of their necessity, mark the borderland, the very edge of Olympus. Their backdrop and ground make the difference in which the well-formed figure of Olympus dwelling comes to the fore of clarity that is Jovial comity.

In championing the just apportionment of honors, properties, and powers and establishing the scope and therefore the limits of every god's sphere of efficacy and rightful realm, Zeus founded the Olympic community based on a principle his insight into which gave him the authority and the sway of being the mightiest of the gods, a supremacy not merely claimed by birth or asserted by force but moreover, with the title of father, an ascendancy attributed to him through the acknowledgement by his peers of his excellence who recognize in Zeus's acts the workings of a mind that in its deliberations takes into account what is *before* and what is *after*, in other words, *what is to be* based upon *what has been*, which is the premise and the principle, the criterion, taken for granted and serving as the predetermined basis for all subsequent judgment.

B. The Well-Proportioned Good of Human Dwelling

151. The Just Fruits

The birth, the development and, finally, the foundation of the just kingdom of the gods was the object of Hesiod's conception in the *Theogony*. In *Works and Days*, he turns to the destiny of human being proper and tells the tragic tale of Man's descent, a heritage of deterioration issuing in the present-day dwelling of its degenerate race, whose mother is *Surfeit*, the spirit of superfluity that accompanies the possession of *All Gifts* (ΠΑΝΔΟΡΑ - *Works and Days [WD]* 81), the synthetic being of specious allurement and attraction whose ornament beguiles and cheats an indolent heart, an "evil in which Man takes pleasure, embracing his own listlessness" in the form of our "plastic" woMan (ΠΛΑΣΤΗΝ ΓΥΝΑΙΚΑ - Th 513).

The molded "Pandora" of Surfeit attaches itself to Man's luxury and shuns his poverty, like a "drone, loafing in the beehive and sucking the honey from the fruits of others' labors who work all day, every day until the sun sets." (Th 595-597) And worse than the evils, the illnesses, and hardships she has caused to be unleashed and scattered over the earth is the one that remains locked in her embrace, namely Pandora's Hope (ΕΛΠΙΣ - WD 96), i.e. "the empty hope (ΚΕΝΗΕΝ ΕΛΠΙΔΑ - 498) of idlers" who, lacking a means of livelihood, would fain depend upon hope itself to provide while they laze upon their lounge and devise wickedness (499 -501). This beautiful evil of glut was given Man in exchange for the good of tireless fire (Th 585) that Prometheus stole against the will of Zeus – the punishment of surplus but also that of penury, "for the gods keep the means of life concealed from human beings." (WD 42)

In accordance with this difference between, on the one hand, the life of *luxury* of those who shun the toil required for the survival of mortal human being, opting rather to get by on theft and deception, and, on the other, that of *scarcity*, namely the scarcity of the goods that human being must, by dint of effort, strive to obtain to make and maintain a living – taking this difference into account, Hesiod revises the lineage of Night, distinguishing between two kinds of Strife "entirely divergent in spirit" (ΔΙΑ Δ ' ΑΝΔΙΧΑ ΘΥΜΟΝ ΕΧΟΥΣΙΝ - WD 13). Whereas one is cruel, promoting war and conflict among mortals and therefore not dear to them but rather of necessity shown the regard that is due all gods, the other, the elder of the two, is beneficial (ΑΓΑΘΗ - 24), rousing even the slackers to accomplishment by inspiring competition and the desire to excel and outdo their peers in the race to riches – "potter contesting with potter, builder with builder, beggar with beggar and poet with poet." (25-26)

The good and the goods of human dwelling are thus the issue in Hesiodic thought. They are the fruit of human toil; each individual, striving for the wealth of well-being, must make an effort to ward off hunger through the management of possessions – for what we have earned through our diligence is not merely material sustenance but moreover our own property, the substance of human being that we have and not merely are. For it is such presence of being (ΠΑΡΕΟΝΤΟΣ - 366) that we have recourse to in the absence of which we suffer the dire straits of need (ΑΠΕΟΝΤΟΣ ΠΗΜΑ ΔΕ ΘΥΜΩΙ ΧΡΗΙΖΕΙΝ - 367). Wealth is the result of an honest day's work; for it is the mark of the distinction of human being – "excellence and renown accompany wealth; whatever sort of person you are through the gods, through your work you are better." (313-314)

ΠΛΟΥΤΩ Δ' ΑΡΕΤΗ ΚΑΙ ΚΥΔΟΣ ΟΠΗΔΕΙ. ΔΑΙΜΟΝΙ Δ' ΟΙΟΣ
ΕΗΙΣΘΑ, ΤΟ ΕΡΓΑΖΕΣΘΑΙ ΑΜΕΙΝΟΝ...

How remarkable! The fight to the death and to the victorious life of renown that distinguished the Homeric hero in the issue of war has become here with Hesiod the work and the toil of making a living – an issue certainly no less a question of life and death but now removed from the theater of the gods' battlefield to the farmers' amber fields of grain. Thus Hesiod bids us take into account a second genealogy of *Strife*, whose children no longer include *Battles* and *Murders* and *Slaughters*, all personages of belligerence marshaled and arrayed in the pursuit of hostilities in arms, nor those engaged in the foment of contention and controversy that we associate with the agora, namely *Deceptions* and *Dissents, Arguments and Quarrels*, in the prosecution of *Lawlessness* – tending to such *Strife* as this that "rejoices in Man's ills" (ΚΑΚΟΧΑΡΤΟΣ - 28) is a luxury of those who have already "plentiful means of life stored up indoors in good season, what the earth bears, Demeter's grain." (30-32) Those who do not will seek to abuse that institution of law for their own benefit, "fostering quarrels and conflict for the sake of another man's wealth" (33-34), snatching more than is one's allotted due of an inheritance, by corrupting those who are supposed to be the impartial advocates of what is right and the just mediators of their subjects' disputes, the kings themselves who, however, have become "graft gluttons" (ΔΩΡΟΦΑΓΟΥΣ - 39), in the perversion of the venal honor so evinced and the travesties of judgment they pass as a result.

When the kings of our communities, to whom, as we have learned (Th 84-86), the people look to decide disputes equably by publicly speaking out

(280) and standing up for what is right, the issue of their insight (281), are themselves the authors of crooked judgments, who else might one turn to? Obviously, to the king whose insight into the apportionment of what is due founded the Olympic community and the just being of the gods in the first place, to Zeus himself who, perhaps giving ear to our prayer, "watching and listening, through justice, may straighten the verdicts of law." (9)

ΙΔΩΝ ΑΙΩΝ ΤΕ, ΔΙΚΗΙ Δ' ΙΘΥΝΕ ΘΕΜΙΣΤΑΣ

For then, thinking of everything for ourselves, "considering what will be better later and in the end" (ΦΡΑΣΣΑΜΕΝΟΣ ΤΑ Κ ' ΕΠΕΙΤΑ ΚΑΙ ΕΣ ΤΕΛΟΣ ΗΙΣΙΝ ΑΜΕΙΝΩ - 294) and remaining mindful of the aforementioned spirit of Zeus in accordance with which the directive of what is right enjoins respect for the limits of what has been apportioned as each being's own and refuses to bend judgment to affect the bias of an undeserved advantage, we, namely I, who have been wronged, and you, my own brother who have wronged me, we two can now come to terms and decide between ourselves, once and for all, the issue here in question" (34-36) trusting in the insight that was Zeus's, even if we have been so unlucky to have been born among the fifth generation of mortal human being, namely that of present day, the generation of iron Man that we in knowing ourselves and distinguishing our Selves from ourselves, know so well.

What is the problem with our race of iron? In contrast to our golden generation that the immortal gods made first and who were free from care, toil, distress, and evils, in possession of all good things, mild-mannered and tranquil, generous and dear to the gods, and therefore destined to be the good spirits and watchful guardians of future generations of mortal human being, our Man of iron endures a life of hassle and wrestle by day, exhaustion at night, ceaseless drudgery interspersed with brief moments of happiness; newly born, we of the iron race already have gray hair (181); and what is more, "the unanimity of the spirit of regard no longer obtains between fathers and sons, sons and fathers, between guest and host, among companions, and even among brothers all former endearment perishes." (182-184)

ΟΥΔΕ ΠΑΤΗΡ ΠΑΙΔΕΣΣΙΝ ΟΜΟΙΙΟΣ ΟΥΔΕ ΤΙ ΠΑΙΔΕΣ, ΟΥΔΕ ΞΕΙΝΟΣ ΞΕΙΝΟΔΟΚΩΙ ΚΑΙΕΤΑΙΡΟΣ ΕΤΑΙΡΩΙ ΟΥΔΕ ΚΑΣΙΓΝΗΤΟΣ ΦΙΛΟΣ ΕΣΣΕΤΑΙ, ΩΣ ΤΟ ΠΑΡΟΣ ΠΕΡ.

For those who foster iron's perverse animus of disparagement and impudence, for whom *Shame* has been driven away by Shamelessness (ΑΙΔΩ ΔΕ Τ ' ΑΝΑΙΔΕΙΗ ΚΑΤΟΠΑΖΗΝΙ -323), might is right and "the fist is justice" - ΔΙΚΗ Δ ' ΕΝ ΧΕΡΣΙ (192), ΧΕΙΡΟΔΙΚΑΙ (189), "for the order of Zeus has apportioned to beasts and the critters of sea and the air, that they, lacking justice, eat one another, whereas to human being he has bestowed justice – the supreme good." (276-279)

> ΤΟΝΔΕ ΓΑΡ ΑΝΘΡΩΠΟΙΣΙ ΝΟΜΟΝ ΔΙΕΤΑΞΕ ΚΡΟΝΙΩΝ,
> ΙΧΘΥΣΙ ΜΕΝ ΚΑΙ ΘΗΡΣΙ ΚΑΙ ΟΙΩΝΟΙΣ ΠΕΤΕΗΝΟΙΣ ΕΣΘΕΙΝ
> ΑΛΛΗΛΟΥΣ, ΕΠΕΙ ΟΥ ΔΙΚΗ ΕΣΤΙ ΜΕΤ ' ΑΥΤΟΙΣ, ΑΝΘΡΩΠΟΙΣΙ
> Δ ' ΕΔΩΚΕ ΔΙΚΗΝ, Η ΠΟΛΛΟΝ ΑΡΙΣΤΗ ΓΕΝΕΤΑΙ.

This is the perverted world of twisted justice (ΣΚΟΛΙΗΙΣΙ ΔΙΚΗΙΣΙΝ - 219, 221, 250) where those who keep their word earn no gratitude but rather mockery, where those who commit wickedness and outrage are esteemed for their deeds and where with oaths sworn upon twisted words (ΜΥΘΟΙΣΙ ΣΚΟΛΙΟΙΣ - 194) and by brute force (ΒΙΗ - 275) the lessor harms the better, where being bad is good and good bad "because the lesser just receive greater justice" (ΜΕΙΖΩ ΓΕ ΔΙΚΗΝ ΑΔΙΩΤΕΡΟΣ ΕΞΕΙ- 272) and *Reverence* and *Indignation* (ΑΙΔΩΣ ΚΑΙ ΝΕΜΕΣΙΣ - 200) depart, offended by such discordant intercourse, leaving Man behind to rot (201).

But such a topsy-turvy world does not go unseen by the avenging gaze of the gods (ΟΠΙΝ ΘΕΩΝ – 187, 251, 706), who are close by human being (ΕΓΓΥΣ ΓΑΡ ΕΝ ΑΝΘΡΩΠΟΙΣΙΝ ΕΟΝΤΕΣ ΑΘΑΝΑΤΟΙ - 249-250); in particular Zeus's (267) who clearly sees what sort of justice a city has within it (ΟΥΔΕ Ε ΛΗΘΕΙ ΟΙΗΝ ΔΕ ΚΑΙ ΤΗΝΔΕ ΔΙΗΝ ΠΟΛΙΣ ΕΝΤΟΣ ΕΕΡΓΕΙ - 268-269) and accordingly straightens what has been bent askew, rights the crooked (ΙΘΥΝΕΙ ΣΚΟΛΙΟΝ - 7), rightfully strengthens what has been perverted into weakness, laying low haughtiness and crushing wrongful pride while raising to note those who had been humbled by the condescension of the arrogant into obscurity.

This is ΔΙΚΗ (dikē), daughter of Zeus, his *Directive* of THE WAY IT SHOULD BE, a straightening of what has been bent out of shape by the shamelessness of Men and therefore a straitening, the punishment for the blindness of Man's hubris, his blatant disregard of limits, the trespass of negligence with regards to what is due. The gift-eaters of corruption poison the present of just being by perverting human dwelling, the customs, and the ethos of their city (ΠΟΛΙΝ ΚΑΙ ΗΘΕΑ ΛΑΩΝ - 222). But the directive of Zeus's dear daughter Dikē, celebrated and revered by the gods (256-257), is right there, even as is *Oath* in his antiquity, running alongside keeping track of judgments that have been bent and biased, and thirty thousand more such guardians, testifying to Man's crookedness of mind, walk the earth as witnesses, (252-254), clad in the invisibility (ΗΕΡΑ ΕΣΣΑΜΕΝΗ - 223, 255) of an idea, bearing evil upon the unjust who apportioned crookedly and for having driven DIKH, weeping, from their midst (23-224). Thus hurt by their crooked scorn, she sits down by her father and decries the unjust mind of Man so that he will punish the people for the wickedness of their kings who think ruinous thoughts and bend judgments to one side by pronouncing them crookedly. (258-262)

Zeus marks the distinction of justice (ΔΙΗΝ...ΤΕΚΜΑΙΡΕΤΑΙ...ΖΕΥΣ - 239) upon iron-minded Man with signs of disaster and calamity – the whole city of Men perishes for the sins of a single Man; woe rains from the sky, devastating famine, pestilence, in short, Zeus is enraged and imposes a grievous return for unjust deeds. (333-334)

Thus, a man contrives evil for himself when he contrives evil for someone else, and an evil plan is most evil for the planner (265), while a bad profit is, in fact, a bad loss (352) – but the fool knows only after the fact, suffering the consequences of his misdeeds, more precisely, being acted upon by his own acts (218), himself being hurt by the hurt he inflicts upon justice (283), in accordance with the reflective relationship of our human being that is the basis of all human dwelling, the self-relationship of our entity of identity, a relationship of friendship between beings and being, THE WAY IT IS with THE WAY IT SHOULD BE. (342) Similarly, we are friends to our friends and visit those who visit us, giving to the giver and not giving to who does not give (354-55). The distinction here to be made, however, is not between giving and not giving but rather between giving and snatching. For "*Giving* is good but *Rapacity* is bad, the giver of death." (356)

ΔΩΣ ΑΓΑΘΗ, ΑΡΠΑΞ ΔΕ ΚΑΚΗ, ΘΑΝΑΤΟΙΟ ΔΟΤΕΙΡΑ

The former is the action of a *Have* whose household has acquired possessions, adding a little to a little until it becomes a lot (361-362) through his or her own assiduity and therefore who may freely give from what economy has accumulated, the latter is that of a *Have-not* who, lacking resources, is forced to rely on the shamelessness of violence and deception to satisfy his needs and ward off famine, the bane of those who do not work. (302) Truly, "it is fine to take from what you have, but it is woe for the spirit to have need of what you do not have." (366-367)

To satisfy the desire for wealth without resorting to the machinations and cruelty of hard-hearted Strife and thus in accordance with proper reverence for the limits that the directive of the gods has apportioned to human being, there is only one option left, namely that of "working works with work."

(ΕΡΓΟΝ ΕΠ ' ΕΡΓΩΙ ΕΡΓΑΖΕΣΘΑΙ - 382) while on the arduous road of *Excellence* (ΑΡΕΤΗ - 289), a path long and steep and rough at first, all the time eschewing the smooth and easy lane of *Wretchedness* (ΚΑΚΟΤΗΤΑ - 287), convenient abundance, and proximity (286), "working at works that the gods have marked out for human being." (397-398).

> ΕΡΓΑΖΕΟ...ΕΡΓΑ, ΤΑ Τ ' ΑΝΘΡΩΠΟΙΣΙ ΘΕΟΙ
> ΔΙΕΤΕΚΜΗΡΑΝΤΟ

152. Work in Season

Hesiod then goes on to give an account of a farmer's works and how these labors correspond to the days and months and the seasons of the year. For work, to be effective, must show regard to the requirements of each season; only then will Zeus grant the accomplishment that his insight into the proper proportion defining each being is the principle of. Upon the earth and in the earthling's life, the scope of THE WAY IT SHOULD BE delineates the demands of good order (ΕΥΘΗΜΟΣΥΝΗ - 471) of the house (ΟΙΚΟΝ - 495). "Keep measures," Hesiod advises, "for works accomplished in the proper place and time are always the best." (694)

> ΜΕΤΡΑ ΦΥΦΛΑΣΣΕΣΘΑΙ, ΚΑΙΡΟΣ Δ ' ΕΠΙ ΠΑΣΙΝ ΑΡΙΣΤΟΣ

This is the principle of the days of works, the days, the months, the seasons, which, like the gods themselves, have their own proper nature and want the timely regard that gives to each what is due and from which, in turn, is laid upon the dwelling of human being a corresponding determination for the work at hand. These are the limiting figures of the Hours (ΩΡΑΙ), the goddess children who have arisen from *Insight* (ΖΕΥΣ) into the predetermined *Law* (ΘΕΜΙΣ) of just being, namely ΕΥΝΟΜΙΑ, ΔΙΚΗ and ΕΙΡΗΝΗ, as we have seen.

Timeliness is therefore the principle not merely of opportunity and expedience but refers also to the experience of the fitness and propitiousness of work done when it ought to be as determined by the place and time, the juncture of every critical spot and moment in which the scope of human dwelling unfolds. Their distinctions provide the measures, the rule (ΝΟΜΟΣ – 388) in accordance with and with regards to which the effort of human being is to be accomplished.

Thus in conformance with the season, we plow so that the crop might grow and we might bring in the fruits of Demeter, who is the mother of Wealth (Th 969), and ward off Hunger (WD 404) and other disasters that befall Man who fosters futility by "postponing till tomorrow and tomorrow and tomorrow" (...ΑΝΑΒΑΛΛΟΝΕΣΘΑΙ ΕΣ Τ ' ΑΥΡΙΟΝ ΕΣ ΤΕ ΕΝΗΦΙΝ - 410).

The principle of the Hours makes a difference here and now for the "seasonable work" (ΩΡΙΟΝ ΕΡΓΟΝ - 422) of those who are not oblivious to but rather "mindful of doing all the work in a timely fashion" (ΕΡΓΩΝ ΜΕΜ–ΝΗΜΕΝΟΣ ΕΙΝΑΙ ΩΡΑΙΩΝ ΠΑΝΤΩΝ - 641-642) accomplishing in good season what the household of human dwelling demands, from harvest to plowing. To accomplish each work, foresight is required; for what we do today, whether we reap or sow, is determined in accordance with the order of the seasons in recognition of the proper succession of the tasks that are to be accomplished subsequent to those that had already been accomplished – each ensuing step dependent upon the timely completion of the prior one. For example, to begin our plowing on time, that is to say, "when the plowing time shows itself to mortals" (458), we need a cart and a plough. But to build these implements, we require suitable wood, "which we must take care to lay up in our house beforehand," (457), having previously cut down timber when the time was right (420) with iron that was shaped and sharpened for the purpose prior to that immediate necessity by forethought in the winter months against which we must protect ourselves anticipating and forestalling (ΦΘΑΜΕΝΟΣ - 554, 570) the inevitable hardships of that season and doing first things first so that our efforts turn out for the best (570) though, after all has been done by the diligence of our own hands, in the piety of praise and entreaty, we acknowledge the limitations inherent in the mortal scope of human action and thus duly manifest our conviction that the outcome of our enterprise is in the hands of the gods who will favor its successful completion or destroy what we have built, for in them is the "fulfillment, both of good and of evil alike" (669) and despite our plans, "the mind of Zeus is different at different times and difficult for mortal men to completely know." (483-484)

ΑΛΛΟΤΕ Δ' ΑΛΛΟΙΟΣ ΖΗΝΟΣ ΝΟΟΣ...ΑΡΓΑΛΕΟΣ
Δ ' ΑΝΔΡΕΣΣΙ ΚΑΤΑΘΝΗΤΟΙΣΙ ΝΟΗΣΑΙ

But though we do not know how Zeus will decide our fate in particular and whether our own plans for happiness will prosper or come to naught, what we do know through Hesiod as he knew through the favor of the Muses is that in general "the city of those who give straight judgments to fellow citizens and foreigners alike and refrain from deviating at all from what is right – their city blossoms and its people flourish. Peace, the nurture of the young, is then on earth and neither does Zeus ordain the doom of war nor does famine accompany those who judge without bias, nor calamity; rather, in celebrations they apportion the fruits of the labor they bestowed with care and for these the earth brings forth their livelihood in abundance." (225-232)

Utopian optimism of a moralist? No, a lesson in limits. Not neglect, but rather regard is the principle of these works, regard for the limits that DIKH makes manifest for all to see and when necessary, with the supreme power and authority of the father of divine and human being, upholds when, in retaliation for works of hubris and wickedness and cruelty – Man's habit, a habitat of iron – Zeus rains destruction in the end.

The end of this work, with a view to the distinction that is the directive of THE WAY IT SHOULD BE, is peace and the community of just beings dwelling in the spirit of mutual regard for what is due and proper to each, an Olympic community of human being.

III. Solon

153. The Lawmaker of DIKH

Hesiod knew that his destiny was to "proclaim the mind of Zeus" (ΕΡΕΩ ΖΗΝΟΣ ΝΟΟΝ - 661) and admonish the order of DIKH that all dwelling, whether that of the mortals or that of the immortals, is founded upon as the relationship of regard for the foreordained principle of just being. How could a mortal know the mind of Zeus? "The Muses taught me to sing such a divine hymn." (WD 662)

ΜΟΥΣΑΙ...Μ' ΕΔΙΔΑΞΑΝ ΑΘΕΣΦΑΤΟΝ ΥΜΝΟΝ ΑΕΙΔΕΙΝ.

The prophet of the practice of pure reason, of *work*, as Hesiod called it, which is the wholesome toil of human being as it is distinguished from the deception and violence of Man's indulgence, presented to his wayward brother what it means to act in accordance with the directive of right which, not only for that of the gods but also for human dwelling, founds the community of beings, their lives and livelihoods, upon their insight into the measured proportions that define each and every person's place and part in the whole, as a member of the greater life of that being which has been predetermined as THE WAY IT SHOULD BE.

Poetic thought, the Builder, in the person of *Solon* now, completes this train of thought by showing how works of DIKH are not only the achievement of the critical distinction of human and divine being from the strife of hubris but rather, through the constitution and enactment of laws in accordance with Her directive, bring forth a policy of human dwelling based on the very principles that founded the comity of Olympic gods – for such is the work of pure reason recognized in the accomplishments of the *Lawmaker*.

Recall that in the Third Epoch with Hölderlin, we encountered the productivity of thought's building for the first time as that of the Poet of Fatherland, comprehending the distinction of human being not merely in the *practice* of self-relative distinction between me and Myself, but, moreover in the *inventions* of the creative spirit of humanity, realizations of the ideal of freedom, in which the genius of human being brings forth its own reality in the presence that epic, dramatic, and poetic language alone can provide. More generally, the distinction of human being as the poetic spirit of our humanity finds its complete and systematic realization in works of artistic creation, in the transforming experience of lived religion and in the self-reflective science of philosophy. Such thought as brings its insight, its discipline, and its creativity to the fore of our attention is the crowning achievement of pure reason having come to know itself as all reality – thought thinking thought, distinguishing thought, and finally realizing thought.

Then in the Second Epoch, thought is presented in the person, more, in the flesh, i.e. incarnate as Jesus Christ, in one the Judge *and* the Savior, the former distinguishing the spirits according to their provenance, namely that of light or that of darkness, the latter fulfilling the promise of reconciliation with the will of God, who sent his Son not merely to condemn but also to redeem. Though not productive of a new world as the poetic spirit of freedom is through the *Poet*, the holy spirit of God's glory transforms and renews the world though the *Christ* as the resurrected Son of God, beginning with the renewal of our own lives. Moved by the ΛΟΓΟΣ that became flesh and took up abode among us to take up and upon ourselves the distinction of human being, we are introduced to the life of critical reflection, a life of turn and return, now perceiving the gap between the IS and the OUGHT, now taking steps to close this gap in accordance with the image of God that is God's truth, God's ΛΟΓΟΣ, achieving at the end of the way a state of grace, a momentary reprieve and respite from an ongoing effort in the accomplishment of that mission that Christ had himself taken upon himself and completed once and for all, *for us all*, as our Savior.

The *Poet* of Humanity in the Third Epoch, the *Savior* of the World in the Second and now, in the First Epoch, the *Lawmaker* of polity. Completing our survey of the wisdom of the Muses, let us examine the productive knowledge of pure reason in the person of the Lawmaker and Teacher of justice as manifested in the political elegies of Solon who says that, "I myself am come in song as a herald from home, lovely Salamis, fashioning a cosmos of words rather than oratory." (1-3 West, M. L. *Iambi et Elegi Graeci ante Alexandrum Cantati*, 2nd edn, Oxford 1992 [W])

ΑΥΤΟΣ ΚΗΡΥΞ ΗΛΘΟΝ ΑΦ ' ΙΜΡΤΖΗΣ ΣΑΛΑΜΙΝΟΣ ΚΟΣΜΟΝ
ΕΠΕΩΝ ΩΙΔΗΝ ΑΝΤ ' ΑΓΟΡΗΣ ΘΕΜΕΝΟΣ

B. The Dwelling of Law and Order

154. ΕΥΝΟΜΙΑ (eunomia)

An elegiac song of exhortation (ΠΑΡΑΙΝΕΤΙΚΗ - W 30) and open rebuke (ΔΙΑΦΑΔΗΝ ΟΝΕΙΔΙΣΑΙ - 37), yes, but thought, the Builder – here the Lawgiver and Teacher – builds not merely poems but with the poems, the minds and with the minds, the actions of the citizens with a view to saving the homeland that the gods founded (ΠΑΤΡΙΔ ' ΕΣ ΘΕΟΚΤΙΤΟΝ - 36.8); we have learned of *Fatherland*, established on the principle of humanity and envisioned by our imagination as that of the Ideal; we have encountered the *Kingdom of God*, that Heaven on earth, that we are born, reborn, to inherit as His children in the spirit of love that units the Father with his Word, the ΛΟΓΟΣ, that the glory of his mercy sent as the Son of God as well as the Son of Man to save and not only to judge the world. Similarly, *Our City* is not merely a conceit, a figment of poetic license invented by the rhapsodist's enthusiasm, (29) but rather a lovely (ΙΜΕΡΤΗΣ - 1, 3) and beloved dwelling (ΠΟΛΥΗΡΑΤΟΝ ΑΣΤΥ - 4.21) whose "faltering we see with pain in our hearts" (4a), whose integrity and substance we must therefore, by our own efforts, constantly foster and vigilantly protect or suffer the bitter disgrace (ΞΑΛΕΠΟΝ ΑΙΣΧΟΣ - 3) and ill-repute of those who have cowardly or negligently abandoned their home to destruction (2).

For as Solon assures us: "This city will never perish through the dispensation of Zeus or the will of the blessed immortals; for such a strong-hearted protector, Pallas Athena, born of a mighty father, holds her hand over it. But it is the citizens themselves who by their acts of mindlessness and acquisitiveness are willing to destroy a great city, that and the arrogance of the people's leaders." (4.1-7)

ΗΜΕΤΕΡΗ ΔΕ ΠΟΛΙΣ ΚΑΤΑ ΜΕΝ ΔΟΙΣ ΟΥΠΟΤ ' ΟΛΕΙΤΑΙ
ΑΙΣΑΝ ΚΑΙ ΜΑΚΑΡΩΝ ΘΕΩΝ ΦΡΕΝΑΣ ΑΘΑΝΑΤΩΝ. ΤΟΙΗ
ΓΑΡ ΜΕΓΑΘΥΜΟΣ ΕΠΙΣΚΟΠΟΣ ΟΒΡΙΜΟΠΑΤΡΗ ΠΑΛΛΑΣ
ΑΘΗΝΑΙΗ ΧΕΙΡΑΣ ΥΠΕΡΘΕΝ ΕΧΕΙ. ΑΥΤΟΙ ΔΕ ΦΘΕΙΡΕΙΝ
ΜΕΓΑΛΗΝ ΠΟΛΙΝΑΦΡΑΔΙΗΙΣΙΝ ΑΣΤΟΙ ΒΟΥΛΟΝΤΑΙ
ΧΡΗΜΑΣΙ ΠΕΙΘΟΜΕΝΟΙ, ΔΗΜΟΥ Θ ' ΗΓΕΜΟΝΩΝ ΑΔΙΚΟΣ
ΝΟΟΣ.

Thus the wisdom of Solon begins with his teaching (ΔΙΔΑΞΑΙ - 4.30) of the difference between the Ill-being of Disproportionate (ΔΥΣΝΟΜΙΗ - 4.31) and the Well-being of Proportionate (ΕΥΝΟΜΙΗ - 4.32) Law. For the city of the former is "oppressed by countless ills" (ΚΑΚΑ ΠΛΕΙΣΤΑ...ΠΑΡΕΧΕΙ - 31) whereas the latter "manifests all that is well-ordered and fitting" (ΕΥΚΟΣΜΑ ΚΑΙ ΑΡΤΙΑ - 4.32), "fitting and reasonable." (ΑΡΤΙΑ ΚΑΙ ΠΙΝΥ– ΤΑ - 4.39)

Confronted with the civil strife that is the mark of a distempered state, Solon stood up to the warring factions, the clans and coalitions with their parochial, divisive interests and checked the centrifugal effect of their fractious partiality on the community, striving rather to bring the people together (ΞΥΝΗΓΑΓΟΝ - 36.1), all the time refusing alliances that would have forced him to favor one side over the other and then to be praised by the influential heads of opposing groups he supported and treated as their friend (37.4-5); above all, his perseverance was tried in avoiding the temptation to play one party off against the other (36.22-23) for his own personal benefit. Clearly, such a position, so vulnerable to corruption, forbade him to jeopardize his partiality by taking sides: "For this reason, I set up a defense on all sides and turned about like a wolf among a pack of dogs" (36.26-27), and "stood between them in no-man's land like a boundary marker." (37.3-4)

ΕΓΟ ΔΕ ΤΟΥΤΩΝ ΩΣΠΕΡ ΕΝ ΜΕΤΑΙΧΜΙΩΙ ΟΡΟΣ ΚΑΤΕΣΤΗΝ

There is no personal pleasure or gain to be had in being everybody's worst enemy, even one's own – for such is the self-several violence and tyranny of impartiality to the sectarian spirit – disappointing one's crooked peers and the exorbitant demands of constituents by dashing their hopes for the rich plunder you might have helped them to, had your gentle prattle been indeed merely a ploy to conceal the true colors of the brazen heart (ΤΡΑΧΥΝ ΝΟΟΝ - 34.3) they were counting on, assuming it had all been an elaborate deception designed to exploit your power and influence for and against peasantry or nobility alike whose trust you had so diligently courted with pretty promises and pledges and, finally, by plying such sweet words, won. But no! To our utter amazement you actually meant what you had said and refused to aid our party's cause, and then, adding insult to injury as it were, not merely batting down *their* arrogance, you also refused to satisfy *our* greed and "bestow our country's rich land's equally among the noble and the common" (34.8-9) – rather than proportionately – that we had set our rapacious eyes on! Instead you spoke as follows: "I resolutely kept my promises and wrote laws that bound the noble and the common alike under an unbiased system of justice that accorded to each their due." (36.17-20)

...ΔΙΗΛΘΟΝ ΩΣ ΥΠΕΣΧΟΜΗΝ, ΘΕΣΜΟΥΣ Δ ' ΟΜΟΙΩΣ ΤΩΙ
ΚΑΚΩΙ ΤΕ ΚΑΓΑΘΩ ΕΥΘΕΙΑΝ ΕΙΣ ΕΚΑΣΤΟΝ ΑΡΜΟΣΑΣ
ΔΙΗΝ ΕΓΡΑΨΑ.

In fact, a person such as this, adopting this position to his own detriment and not seizing the opportunity to further his own advantage, would seem to be a born simpleton bereft of both spunk and smarts (ΟΥΚ ΕΦΥ...ΒΑΘΥΦΡΩΝ...ΘΥΜΟΥ Θ ' ΑΜΑΡΤΗΙ ΚΑΙ ΦΡΕΝΩΝ

ΑΠΟΣΦΑΛΕΙΣ - 33.1-4), a laughing stock to his enemies who would have had no scruples in taking all they could while they could even if, after having enjoyed "the supreme power and vast wealth of a tyrant for *one single day* (ΜΟΥΝΟΝ ΗΜΕΡΗΝ ΜΙΑΝ), they were to be flayed alive and their posterity expunged (33.4-7).

To such ephemeral spirits as these who would dispose of their whole life for the pleasure of a moment, it must be utterly unfathomable that anyone could willingly choose to forgo the short-lived profits of brute force and tyranny for the sake of their Beloved City and in reverence to the impeachable renown of a good name (ΚΛΕΙΩ - Theogony 77), who, as we have learned from Hesiod, is a daughter of Zeus and Remembrance, namely one of the Muses and the first born of them all. How could it be that one who spurns an advantage today and to whom even a loss accrues today, nevertheless contradicts his belittlers and states with confidence "I believe that in this way I shall be all the more able to beat them in the end, each and every one."? (32.4-5)

ΠΛΕΟΝ ΓΑΡ ΩΔΕ ΝΙΚΗΣΕΙΝ ΔΟΚΕΩ ΠΑΝΤΑΣ ΑΝΘΡΩΠΟΥΣ

The mentality of immediate profit and personal gratification versus that of sustainable benefit and gratification for the entire community – this is the self-several spirit of Our City that Solon seeks to convey to his fellow citizens in justifying to them the subsequent actions he took to ward off the approaching servitude of the people under a tyrant whom the citizens in their short-sighted "ignorance (AIDRIHI - 9.4)...raise too high and are then unable to restrain later. Now is indeed the time to consider *all* the aspects of the whole," (9.5) i.e. the big picture.

ΛΙΗΝ Δ ' ΕΞΑΡΑΝΤ ' <ΟΥ> ΡΑΙΔΙΟΝ ΕΣΤΙ ΚΑΤΑΣΧΕΙΝ ΥΣΤΕΡΟΝ,
ΑΛΛ ' ΗΔΗ ΧΡΗ <ΤΙΝΑ>ΠΑΝΤΑ ΝΟΕΙΝ

Thus for the sake of our "dearly beloved City" (ΠΟΛΥΗΡΑΤΟΝ ΑΣΤΥ - 4.21), Solon called upon his fellow Athenians to think with greater scope, not merely to dwell on the concerns of their own benefit or that of their particular clan or class here and now but rather to consider those of their homeland as a whole, in remembrance of its former tradition of greatness and its survival in future times and to come to the aid of their city already at the very brink of disintegration – its people fleeing abroad to foreign lands pursued by their poverty or else burdened by the bondage of debt, sold and bound in the shameful fetters of servitude (4.23-25; 36-10-14) such that even the very substance of Our City, the earth itself, is made to suffer, enslaved by the ward-stones of encumbrance (36.6-7) that has mortgaged the citizens' property the community of which has been ground down and splintered by the warring factions whose conspiracies are intent on gaining and maintaining their own particular and immediate advantage at the expense of the others perhaps in cahoots with a provisionally cooperative tyrant, the big Man, who, in fact, makes of them all, the rich and the poor, slaves to the caprice of his favor and instruments of his own desire for power and control over others, usurping all his potential usurpers.

For, as Solon says, "the public evil comes home to each individual and the courtyard gates no longer possess the power to hold it back as it leaps over the highest barrier and finds him, even if he flees to the innermost corner of his room." (4.26-29)

ΟΥΤΩ ΔΗΜΟΣΙΟΝ ΚΑΚΟΝ ΕΡΧΕΤΑΙ ΟΙΚΑΔ ' ΕΚΑΣΤΩΙ,
ΑΥΛΕΙΟΙ Δ ' ΕΤ ' ΕΧΕΙΝ ΟΥΚ ΕΘΕΛΟΥΣΙ ΘΥΡΑΙ,
ΥΨΗΛΟΝ Δ ' ΥΠΕΡ ΕΡΚΟΣ ΥΠΕΡΘΟΡΕΝ, ΕΥΡΕ ΔΕ
ΠΑΝΤΩΣ, ΕΙ ΚΑΙ ΤΙΣ ΘΕΥΓΩΝ ΕΝ ΜΥΧΩΙ ΗΙ ΘΑΛΑΜΟΥ.

For individuals, there is no escaping the general affliction of the state and the ensuing subjection of its citizens; in particular, the oppression of the peasants is a source of strife that cuts into the substance of the city, i.e. its land and the community of mutual regard among the citizens in accordance with what is due to each.

Solon's reforms addressed these two sources of the injustice that was endangering Athens – the poor whom he emancipated from the bondage of debt, freeing the "dark earth" of Our City itself: "before enslaved, now free." (ΠΡΟΣΘΕΝ ΔΕ ΔΟΥΛΕΥΟΥΣΑ, ΝΥΝ ΕΛΕΥΘΕΡΗ-36.7), ransoming those citizens who were sold as slaves abroad and setting free those who suffered in shameful servitude at home "trembling before the will of their masters (ΗΤΗ ΔΕΣΠΟΤΕΩΝ ΤΡΟΜΕΟΜΕΝΟΥΣ - 36.14) and then the rich; those who had more than enough of the good things and from whom he therefore demanded restraint, calling upon them to "calm their stern hearts and moderate their ambitions."

ΗΣΥΧΑΝΣΑΝΤΕΣ ΕΝΙ ΦΡΕΣΙ ΚΑΡΤΕΡΟΝ ΗΤΟΡ,...ΕΝ–
ΜΕΤΡΙΟΙΣΙ ΤΙΘΕΣΘΕΜΕΓΑΝ ΝΟΟΝ (4c.1-3)

For both classes are subject to the apportionment of what is their own proper good, their own property, in accordance with their nature, their ΦΥΣΕΙΣ, and must be protected therein by justice in the service of which Solon saw himself if the community was to be saved from the internal strife that originates when either side oversteps the bounds of that nature which defines for each the propriety of THE WAY IT SHOULD BE. Thus, to the people, he gave due regard, not more nor less than was due, and as well to the wealthy and powerful, he safeguarded the esteem owed their position. In this way, Solon stood as "a powerful shield cast about both sides, not permitting either side the unjust victory" (5.5-6)

ΕΣΤΗΝ Δ ' ΑΜΦΙΒΑΛΩΝ ΚΡΑΤΕΡΟΝ ΣΑΚΟΣ ΑΜΦΟΤΕΡΟΙΣΙ,
ΝΙΚΑΝ Δ ' ΕΙΑΣ ' ΟΥΔΕΤΕΡΟΥΣ ΑΔΙΚΩΣ

The freedom from oppressive necessity and the calming of immoderate ambition – these two conditions of the survival and flourishing of the well-apportioned city that is our home and Homeland bring to mind the spirit that must dwell in every community in order for it to endure. Solon acknowledges this spirit as a daughter of Zeus, born second of the Graces, born after the far and wide reaching radiance of *Splendor* but before the enjoyment of *Fruition*, namely the good spirit of *Content*. This is ΕΥΦΡΟΣΥΝΗ (euphrosunē). Let us make her acquaintance.

C. The Discernment of what is Good

155. ΕΥΦΡΟΣΥΝΗ (euphrosunē)

The *Tranquility* (ΗΣΥΧΙΑ) that Solon invokes (in 4c.1) as crucial to the saving of Our Beloved City was later celebrated by Pindar in the introductory passage of his eighth Pythic ode as the "the kind-minded, city-ennobling daughter of Directive who, holding the greatest keys in both word of council and deed of war, understands the infallible efficacy of gentleness in action as well as in experience, when the moment for each is right." (Snell, Bruno (Ed.) *Pindari Carmina cum Fragmentis* 1953, 102.1-7)

> ΦΙΛΟΦΡΟΝ ΗΣΥΧΙΑ, ΔΙΚΑΣ...ΜΕΓΙΣΤΟΠΟΛΙ ΘΥΓΑΤΕΡ,
> ΒΟΥΛΑΝ ΤΕ ΚΑΙ ΠΟΛΕΜΩΝ ΕΧΟΙΣΑ ΚΛΑΙΔΑΣ
> ΥΠΕΡΤΑΤΑΣ...ΤΟ ΜΑΛΘΑΚΟΝ ΕΡΞΑΙ ΤΕ ΚΑΙ ΠΑΤΕΙΝ
> ΟΜΩΣ ΕΠΙΣΤΑΣΑΙΚΑΙΡΩΙ ΣΥΝ ΑΤΡΕΚΕΙ.

And if, as we have learned, a city is doomed to destruction by its own citizens rather than by the gods, then the source of its degradation must originate in the people's actions, while their actions and doings are a consequence of the frame of mind in which these deeds have been conceived; specifically, the ruin of community is "willed by the citizens themselves" (ΑΥΤΟΙ...ΑΣΤΟΙ ΒΟΥΛΟΝΤΑΙ - 4.5-6), by their "obliviousness and greed" (ΑΦΡΑΔΙΗΙΣΙΝ...ΧΡΗΜΑΣΙ ΠΕΙΘΟΜΕΝΟΙ - ibid), and the "unjust mind" of their leaders (ΗΓΕΜΟΝΩΝ ΑΔΙΚΟΣ ΝΟΟΣ - 4.7), i.e. the hubris (ΥΒΡΙΟΣ - 4.8), of those who, in their thievish rapacity and "disregard for the holy principles of justice..." (ΟΥΔΕ ΦΥΛΑΣΣΟΝΤΑΙ ΣΕΜΝΑ ΔΙΚΗΣ ΘΕΜΕΘΛΑ - 4.14), "...do not understand how to restrain excess and with good spirits to simply enjoy the cheer at hand in the tranquility of well-ordered festivities." (4.9-10)

> ΟΥ ΓΑΡ ΕΠΙΣΤΑΝΤΑΙ ΚΑΤΕΧΕΙΝ ΚΟΡΟΝ ΟΥΔΕ ΠΑΡΟΥΣΑΣ
> ΕΥΦΡΟΣΥΝΑΣ ΚΟΣΜΕΙΝ ΔΑΙΤΟΣ ΕΝ ΗΣΥΧΗΙΗΙ.

But this enjoyment of the simple pleasures of life – good food and drink properly seasoned (41) as is fitting to one's taste (39), breads and pastries, fruits and pulses from the nourishing earth (43) in its abundance (38), noble horses and hunting dogs, friends at home (21) and in foreign parts (ΞΕΝΟΣ ΑΛΛΟΔΑΠΟΣ - 23.1-2), and, in addition to having enough to eat and comfortable shoes and garments, being possessed of a family, of a youthful vigor (24.3-6), and of a long life (20.4), one never done with learning (18) – this well-rounded, balanced happiness is not at all the blankness and vacuity of the mind that accompanies obliviousness, ignorance, and carelessness in people who merely obey the drive and impulse of their immediate senses. It is precisely this sort of thoughtlessness and inability to see the consequences of one's actions that has put the integrity of the state in such jeopardy in the first place and Solon does not miss an opportunity to admonish his fellow Athenians of the dangers of their insipience. (4.5, 6.4, 9.4, 11.6, 33.1, 34.4, 36.21)

No, the happiness (ΟΛΒΙΟΣ - 23.1) Solon takes in the goodness of life's little pleasures in the spirit of ΕΥΦΡΟΣΥΝΗ (26.1-2) – those of Aphrodite (love's desire), Dionysus (celebration) and the Muses (intellect) – is based on insight into a principle and the corresponding spirit and for this reason, he suggests that true well-being lies in the enjoyment not of *mere* being in all the fickleness of fate and the precariousness of Man's hopes for success and wealth which depend upon good fortune that makes many "a base man rich and a good man poor" (ΠΟΛΛΟΙ ΓΑΡ ΠΛΟΥΤΕΟΥΣΙ ΚΑΚΟΙ, ΑΓΑΘΟΙ ΔΕ ΠΕΝΟΝΤΑΙ - 15.1), but rather of *just* being, the firm and enduring (ΕΜΠΕΔΟΝ ΑΙΕΙ - 15.3) happiness of one enjoying moral (ΑΡΕΤΗ - 15.3) rather than material excellence (ΧΡΗΜΑΤΑ - 15.4).

No mortal is blessed with the gods' lightly living but rather, as Hesiod taught as well, burdened and oppressed by toils (ΠΟΝΗΡΟΙ - 14). Hence, the well-being that comes with the success of our efforts is as doubtful as success itself is; "in all actions there is risk and no one knows how things are going to turn out." (13.65-66)

ΠΑΣΙ ΔΕ ΤΟΙ ΚΙΝΔΥΝΟΣ ΕΠ ' ΕΡΓΜΑΣΙΝ, ΟΥΔΕ ΤΙΣ ΟΙΔΕΝ
ΗΙ ΜΕΛΛΕΙ ΣΧΗΣΕΙΝ ΧΡΗΜΑΤΟΣ ΑΡΧΟΜΕΝΟΥ.

In other words: "Fate brings good and ill to mortals and the gifts of the immortal gods are inescapable." (13.63-64)

ΜΟΙΡΑ ΔΕ ΤΟΙ ΘΝΗΤΟΙΣΙ ΚΑΚΟΝ ΦΕΡΕΙ ΗΔΕ ΚΑΙ ΕΣΘΛΟΝ,
ΔΩΡΑ Δ ' ΑΦΥΚΤΑ ΘΕΩΝ ΓΙΓΝΕΤΑΙ ΑΘΑΝΑΤΩΝ.

Given this fact that the minds of immortals are hidden from Man (17) and that they give Man profit as well as ruin (13.74-75), the fruits of our labors and efforts, the way things turn out – "things" being the ΧΡΗΜΑΤΑ, those very things that, later, Man will famously be recognized as the measure of – depend upon the will of Zeus, "who oversees every outcome" (ΖΕΥΣ ΠΑΝ–ΤΩΝ ΕΦΟΡΑΙ ΤΕΛΟΣ... - 13.17).

The spectacle of the futility of Man's efforts to be or become or remain the master of his fate would indeed be comical if it weren't so tragic and disheartening – Solon does not spare us the sight of it, of "the eager delight we take in empty hopes," (ΧΑΣΚΟΝΤΕΣ ΚΟΥΑΙΣ ΕΛΠΙΣΙ ΤΕΡΠΟΜΕΘΑ - 13.36) until they are dashed when mishap strikes leaving us to cry (ΟΥΔΥΡΕΤΑΙ - 13.35).

Consider (cf. verses 13.33-42) those suffering from sickness hoping against hope that they will recover; those who are poverty-stricken are absolutely sure that they will come into money; or look at us who are of base character priding ourselves in our nobility and preening ourselves in our supposed beauty though we lack all charm. Feeding on our self-delusion and conceit, we try our luck, I try mine, you yours (ΣΠΕΥΔΕΙ Δ ' ΑΛΛΟΘΕΝ ΑΛΛΟΣ - 13.43). But does all our toil really get us anywhere, amount to anything? Whether sea-faring or farming, whether in the poetic crafts and arts of builders – be they the works of Hephaestus or even those of the Muses whose servants learned to understand the measures inherent in the wisdom of human desire (ΙΜΕΡΤΗΣ ΣΟΦΙΗΣ ΜΕΤΡΟΝ ΕΠΙΣΑΜΕΝΟΣ - 13.52) – or in that of the seers, Apollo's elect, who foresee approaching calamity or, finally, in that of Paeon's physicians, who heal the illnesses that have already befallen us, we are all vying to make a living (ΞΥΛΛΕΓΕΤΑΙ ΒΙΟΤΟΝ - 13.50) and there is no assurance of success (ΟΥΔΕΝ ΕΠΕΣΤΙ ΤΕΛΟΣ - 13.58); we are sure, rather, that despite all our riches "no one can pay a price to escape death or grim diseases or the onset of evil old age," (24.9-10) and that "what has been destined to be, neither augury nor sacrifice will ward off. (13.55-56)

> ΤΑ ΔΕ ΜΟΡΣΙΜΑ ΠΑΝΤΩΣ ΟΥΤΕ ΤΙΣ ΟΙΩΝΟΣ
> ΡΥΣΤΕΑΙ ΟΥΘ ' ΙΕΡΑ

No, indeed. We do not know what the gods are thinking, what they have in store for us, and how things that Man hopes and strives for, the outcomes Man desires and works toward, will ultimately unfold. But we all can think like a god and partake of that discernment that Zeus himself engages in while making distinctions regarding THE WAY IT SHOULD BE. This is the divine discernment of ΕΥΦΡΟΣΥΝΗ (euphrosunē). Of course, "this invisible measure of insight that alone determines the limits of all – this is the most difficult of all discernments." (16)

> ΓΝΩΜΟΣΥΝΗΣ Δ' ΑΦΑΝΕΣ ΧΗΑΛΕΠΩΤΑΤΟΝ ΕΣΤΙ ΝΟΗΣΑΙ
> ΜΕΤΡΟΝ, Ο ΔΗ ΠΑΝΤΩΝ   ΠΕΙΡΑΤΑ ΜΟΥΝΟΝ ΕΧΕΙ.

We see that Man, as much as he is himself a measure of all things human – in particular his wealth and the privileges and prerogatives of power – is, nevertheless, in the wisdom of the Muses that the Greek Epoch of thought has bestowed upon us, himself measured in his own well-being by the limits of what is right, which, amazingly to us post/moderns, is not a question of opinion but rather of divine, that is, distinguished insight. And it is for this reason that Solon advises us "not to follow those who recommend that a man have thoughts suitable to a man" (45) but rather to make our best effort to think like a god, however difficult it may be for us, who are almost entirely merely mortal Man. Almost.

This is the discernment into the distinction of human being that clearly emerges from Solon's train of thought pertaining to the difference between material and moral well-being. What we learn in this portrait of Man in his pitiful self-delusion, vulnerability, and susceptibility to the vacillations of place and time that impinge so jarringly upon his life is that the destiny of human being lies in grasping and respecting the apportioned order of the gods, an order, however, that we, nevertheless, might participate in and that makes itself known to us even in the phases and seasons that the growth of our mind and body goes through towards maturity and in their relationship to each other.

Solon famously traced this development in ten seven-year periods that "complete themselves in order, one after the after, in accordance with the measure" (ΤΕΛΕΣΑΣ ΚΑΤΑ ΜΕΤΡΟΝ- 27.17) appropriate to the mind and body in each stage of their maturation. Thus, in the first hebdomad the boy is seen to grow and lose his baby teeth, in the second, go through puberty and in the third, adolescence. Attaining in the fourth our prime in terms of strength (ΜΕΓ ' ΑΡΙΣΤΟΣ ΙΣΧΥΝ - 27.7-8), the signs of manhood (ΣΗΜΑΤΑ ...ΑΡΕΤΗΣ - 27.8) lead us properly then to the season (ΩΡΙΟΝ - 27.9) of marriage in the fifth. The sixth hebdomad witnesses the comprehensive erudition of the mind (ΠΕΡΙ ΠΑΝΤΑ ΚΑΤΑΡΤΥΕΤΑΙ ΝΟΟΣ - 27.11) and the surcease of recklessness in actions (ΟΥΔ ' ΕΡΔΕΙΝ...ΕΡΓ ' ΑΠΑΛΑΜΝΑ ΘΕ– ΛΕΙ - 27.12). The seventh and the eight hebdomad mark the pinnacle of our excellence in thought and speech (ΝΟΥΝ ΚΑΙ ΓΛΩΣΣΑΝ...ΜΕΓ ' ΑΡΙΣΤΟΣ - 27.13) which must eventually decline throughout the ninth. Finally in attaining the tenth hebdomad, having fulfilled the measures of each of life's season, the allotment of death ought not to be thought untimely (ΟΥΚ ΑΝ ΑΩΡΟΣ ΕΩΝ ΜΟΙΡΑΝ ΕΧΗΟΙ ΘΑΝΑΤΟΥ - 27.18).

Obviously, the point here is not to ascertain whether or not or how well our own physiological and psychological biographies "fit" into this scheme.

Rather, it illustrates how the course of life, though a continuum, manifests portions and measures in accordance with which each age of a time line can be characterized as a discrete and distinct moment of an overall development encompassing in its entirety a life recognized as being as complete and as good as is possible for mortal human being.

The train of thought that we have been exploring in this investigation is no less a life; it is the life and development of pure reason and this life wants, no less, more even, than our own, to be well articulated in its ages, i.e., according to the given principles, into the different ratios of the terms A, B, and C. For their relationships have served as our guideline and provided our study with the elements, the terms, and syntax, of three distinguished languages with which to speak about thought, to compare thoughts, and to collect and order ideas into totalities of ever greater scope, ultimately that which encompasses the totality of all things thought – the doctrine of the three Epochs founded upon the three principles or, in Solon's terms, the *measures*, of the distinction of human being. This distinction is a life, the theoretical, practical, and poetic life of pure thought.

It is, specifically in the First Epoch, a life measured out not in coffee spoons but rather in the proportions that arise through the citizens' regard for the excellence of each member of the community as determined by the limits of the whole of just being. The principle of measure that Solon gives voice to is that of *Justness*, the dictate (DIKH) of rightness of being.

We conclude our investigation of the distinction of human being by examining how the knowledge of the Muses recognizes in the work of Justness the foundation of Our City, not merely that of the Olympic gods but even that of *mortals*, those, namely destined to die the "beautiful death" (ΚΑΛΟΣ ΘΑΝΑΤΟΣ), an idea that Tyrtaeus, following Homer, celebrated in the martial language of slaughter on the battlefield, but one that, as we have seen, admits of a great many other, even diametrically opposed, representations and choice of words, diverse dictions of thought, reflecting the needs and the expectations as well as the experience of the audience. Which idea is that? It is the idea of the self-severalty of thought thinking thought with regards to a principle – in the Epoch that Solon's elegies bring to a close, this principle was known as and termed by the Muses *MOIPA* in the Epics of Homer, *ΘΕΜΙΣ* in Hesiod's drama of the birth of the gods depicting how Olympus was won through the insight that earned Zeus his kingdom and finally, with Solon's understanding, DIKH, the manifestation of THE WAY IT SHOULD BE that provides the firm and constant measure of just being.

A. DIKH (dikē)

156. The Indication of what is Right

Solon saw himself as acting on behalf of the principle in accordance with which the properties of regard, namely power and possessions (ΔΥΝΑΜΙΣ, XHPMATA - 5.3), honor (ΓΕΡΑΣ - 5.1) and esteem (TIMH - 5.2) are to be well-apportioned to every citizen of the polity in recognition of the relationship each individual has to Our Beloved City of just being entailed by this membership. This principle, though intangible and invisible, is nevertheless accessible to thought and Solon called this principle the *measure* that determines for each thing THE WAY IT SHOULD BE, its *right* and *justness*. What is right for a thing, anything at all, the standards and norms, the defining limits (ΠΕΙΡΑΤΑ - 16.2) against which the properties of human being, whether they be the wealth of our possessions, the intelligence of our words, the efficacy of our deeds, are evident to and make manifest distinguished thought alone, such thought as might be termed *wisdom* (ΓΝΟΜΟΣΥΝΗ - 16.1); but these criteria, visible to wisdom's judgment but otherwise invisible (ΑΦΑΝΕΣ - ibid), also come to light of their own accord; in the crisis of time, as events unfold, the determination of what is right no longer remains concealed in the knowledgeable mind but rather enters the scene as the outcome of counsel, the verdict of deliberation, and the harmonious composition of the force of executive power with the rule of law (ΟΜΟΥ ΒΙΗΝ ΤΕ ΚΑΙ ΔΙΚΗΝ ΞΥΝΑΡΜΟΣΑΣ - 36.16). In the end, ΔΙΚΗ, namely *what is right*, is brought to light in the gap of difference between THE WAY IT IS and the WAY IT SHOULD BE.

This deflection insofar as it can be bigger or smaller, can be understood as the extent to which the mark or limit of distinction, the "measure" as Solon puts it, whatever it may be in a particular case, has been missed which defines what is right and right on and what, with respect to that rule, is deviant. What an abundance of examples we could cite and have already cited in this investigation illustrating the wealth of experience we have with this particularly Greek notion of *measure* and hitting (or missing) the mark, what is sufficient with respect to a standard and what is wanting, what has gone too far in one direction or in the other, what is too little, lacking, *deficient*, or too much, profligate, *exorbitant*, what has reached its goal, achieved its end, fulfilled its purpose and thus attained perfection in the completion of its destiny, and what, gorged, is too full, scant, falls parsimoniously short – for intemperance goes both ways, towards luxury as well as destitution, exiguity as well as prodigality – what is false and faulty and what is true, fair, neat and square. But things can be too neat and too square, too, too pat!

Porridge can be too hot, too cold or just right, the chair too big or too small or just right, the bed too hard or too soft or just right; what errs or strays fails to hit the target; you make the grade or miss the boat if you learn too late; with the slip of tongue or toe, we garble and stumble; and is not fatuity and absurdity the work of a nitwit with a block or bubble for a head, either too material or too insubstantial for the distinction of good sense to make an impression and leave a trace that makes a difference? In all of these cases of transgression, excess, short-coming, aberration, incompletion, mutilation, the incongruence of something with regards to a measure comes to light; the extremity and imbalance of what is overdone or underdone destroys the equilibrium of opposites meant to harmonize in their reciprocity, in the well-rounded community of EYNOMIH that apportions due regard to both sides of the coin and every side, the self-several distinction that is the cognizance of thought and the one and only remedy against the extremism of one-sidedness so debilitating to the Beloved City of our human being.

For Solon, the notion most divisively at odds with that of moderation and the measure that determines and ultimately reveals what is right in every case is that of nimiety (ΚΟΡΟΣ - 4.9). It distorts and perverts the spirit of ΕΥΦΡΟΣΥΝΗ which enjoys in simplicity what it's got, measured upon the necessities, not the bare necessities, but rather what suffices for the good life of just being.

And it was against excess that Solon wrote his laws and set himself in the no-man's land of justice between the conflicting parties as the objective shield that protects the limits of what is due to the proper dwelling and prosperity of each citizen with respect to the life and the well-being of the state as a whole and, in particular, established a just proportion of rights between the two constituents of the state, namely that of the people and that of their leaders, the former the body and soul, the latter the mind and spirit of the City of just being.

It is upon the sanity of these two members of the body politic and the good constitution of their collaboration that the survival and fruition of the state depends; in fact, the state *is* the sanity and the constitution, the proportion and order of their community as well as the prosperity that ensues as a result of their accord, the public good of the city, just like the public evil, entering the dwelling of every member "even to the innermost corner of the individual's privacy." (4.29)

The illness of the heart and the soul of the people is *greed* (ΧΡΗΜΑΣΙ ΠΕΙΘΟΜΕΝΟΙ - 4.6) the illness of the mind and the spirit of the leaders is *pride* (ΥΒΡΙΣ - 4.8) – it is the inability of the former in their *thoughtlessness* (ΑΦΡΑΔΙΗΙΣΙΝ - 4.5) to think beyond the horizon of the moment, the refusal of the latter in their *ambition* (ΜΕΓΑΝ ΝΟΟΝ - 4c.3) to think beyond the horizons of themselves while calculating their own particular advantages. Both, the *slaves* of wealth and the *tyrants* of power, are the children of the excess that "great prosperity" (ΠΟΛΥΣ ΟΛΒΟΣ – 6.3; 34.3) and "vast wealth" (ΠΛΟΥΤΟΝ ΑΦΘΟΝΟΝ - 33.5) breed in the unsound mind of Man and the consequence of his selfish pride's transgression of the measure that determines what is right and provokes his disregard for the measure of well-being due the other members of the community in the reciprocity of the rapport that alone assures a healthy state's longevity.

That is not to say that the leaders are free from mindless greed or the people are free from unscrupulous insolence. Individuals from among the commoners can become leaders through the status and influence that accrues to them as a result of the wealth they have attained in the successful pursuit of their trades even as the leaders – though they have by birth their fill of what others, goaded on by envy (5.3), have gained by dint of diligent application – are not safe against the money-grubbing voracity that craves to have ever more for the simple reason that "no limit to wealth has been made manifest to Men" (ΠΛΟΥΤΟΥ Δ ' ΟΥΔΕΝ ΤΕΡΜΑ ΠΕΦΑΣΜΕΝΟΝ ΑΝ– ΔΡΑΣΙ ΚΕΙΤΑΙ - 13.71). Thus we see the leaders displaying rapacious covetousness – we encountered them in Hesiod gift-devouring kings – and the commoners indulging in the particular sort of impertinence that low-minded men display towards their elders and betters whom they feel, for whatever reason, justified in addressing with impudence – much as Thersites did in his "measureless harangue" (ΑΜΕΤΡΟΕΠΗΣ - Il 2.212) against Agamemnon in the Iliad. (Il 2.225-242)

Solon saw himself as the arbiter of what is sufficient (ΑΠΑΡΚΕΙΝ - 5.1), i.e. proportionate to and commensurate with what is due, right, proper, "neither taking away nor adding" (ΟΥΤ ' ΑΦΕΛΩΝ ΟΥΤ ' ΕΠΟΤΡΕΞΑΜΕΝΟΣ - 5.2) to the just measure of esteem that each party merits while at the same time, restraining the immoderate tendencies of both sides, sanctioning neither licentiousness nor astringency both of which are extremes to which minds and hearts are susceptible if they lack the insightful distinction of self-several discretion (ΠΙΝΥΤΑ – 4.39) and therefore miss what is fitting (ΑΡΤΙΟΣ - 4c.4,6.4). In truth, both the slave as well as the tyrant are perpetrators of violence (ΥΒΡΙΟΣ ΕΡΓΑ ΠΕΛΕΙ - 13.11), each in their own way, willing to endorse the ruin of their city (4.5-6) if by this means they might secure benefit for themselves. For that is what might (ΔΥΝΑΜΙΣ - 5.3; ΚΡΑΤΗΑΣ - 33.5, 34.15) is, namely "brute force" (ΒΙΗ ΑΜΕΙΛΙΧΗ - 32.2), if it is not tempered with justice (36.16).

In this role of the impartial arbiter, the voice, and the actor of what is right, more, himself a *Justice* advocating what is right in "deeds of great import...," it is doubtless "...hard to please everyone" (ΕΡΓΜΑΣΙ...ΕΝ ΜΕΓΑΛΟΙΣ ΠΑ–ΣΙΝ ΑΔΕΙΝ ΧΑΛΕΠΟΝ- 7) assuming that for what is impossible the term "hard" is the proper euphemism, which it often is in the speech of the Muses. But as we have seen in the previous Epochs, pure reason attains its most striking distinction in poetic individuality, in a person who is the embodiment of that good spirit which comes alive not merely as the realization of an idea in our fine words and noble deeds but in our human being itself, the being that we were born and therefore destined to be. For our human being as the poetic individuality of pure reason is destined to be the creative Artist of Humanity, the transforming Savior of the World, as well as the Lawgiver and Teacher of the Nation. For the *City of Just being, Heaven on Earth*, and, finally, the *Fatherland of Freedom* are the homes and dwelling that wisdom builds, the monuments to the distinction of human being that pure reason has given to itself for wisdom's sake.

Thus it is the winds of Man's violence that agitates the state of just being, in and of itself the most equilibrious of states (ΠΑΝΤΩΝ ΕΣΤΙ ΔΙΚΑΙΟΤΑΤΗ - 12.2); but when the whole milk of human kindness and justness is churned up by injustice, left to itself by negligence or decomposed by the centrifugal/centripetal force of corruption, the dispersed and the continuous phase of the colloid, the rich and the poor, the elite and the mass, the highborn and the low, the nobles and the peasants, the sound mind and the healthy body, separate, the former, the particulate sediment of *cream* floating to the top of the latter, the liquid mass that is left, the emulsion of Man, the *skim* (37.7) precipitating. In the mutual incursion that results from this estrangement one from the other, the rapport of regard that characterizes the citizens' relationship to each other, both leading *and* following (6.1), both subject to (30) their relationship with the community as a whole of just being, degenerates into civil strife between the tyrant and the slaves, a cleft of difference become "chaotic" in the Hesiodic sense, that the former instrumentalizes to eliminate their ambitions' rivals and the latter to indulge their desires' obsessions, both fatally and unintentionally colluding in bringing about the downfall of the city; as we saw – a Cyclopic hybrid merging the ruthless power of blindly elemental forces "like the force of snow and hail and the thunder from a flash of lightning" (9. 1-3) with the indiscriminate ignorance and bigotry of a closed mind.

We recognize here the familiar symbiosis of perversion, each extreme feeding off of the other – greed's slaves reinforcing presumption's tyrants in the circular viciousness into which the self-relativity of thought thinking thought is monstrously transmogrified when the dynamically balanced limits within which they form an entity of identity, i.e. a state of grace, of beauty, of peace, are violated.

The calamity that ensues is just retribution reaffirming the inexorable validity of what is right, the invisible measure of THE WAY IT SHOULD BE, "the truth..." now made manifest and "come out in the open." (ΔΕΙΞΕΙ ΑΛΗΘΕΙΗΣ ΕΣ ΜΕΣΟΝ ΕΡΧΟΜΝΗΣ - 10) in a revelation of destructive power as the punishment of the gods. For Justice herself "bears silent witness to what has come to light in view of what has been determined beforehand...," distinguishing in the present crisis the fulfillment of principles (or the failure thereof) with regards to (or in disregard of) the precedence and proportion of what is right, due, proper, "exacting sure retribution when the time comes." (4.15-16)

...Η ΣΙΓΩΣΑ ΣΥΝΟΙΔΕ ΤΑ ΓΙΓΝΟΜΕΝΑ ΠΡΟ Τ' ΕΟΝΤΑ, ΤΩΙ ΔΕ
ΧΡΟΝΩ ΠΑΝΤΩΣ ΗΛΘ' ΑΠΟΤΕΙΣΟΜΕΝΗ.

The "unjust acts of mortals, as short lived" (ΟΥ ΓΑΡ ΔΗΝ ΘΝΗΤΟΙΣ ΥΒΡΙΟΣ ΕΡΓΑ ΠΕΛΕΙ - 13.16) as they themselves are, plant the seeds of subsequent crises, those evil blossoms of catastrophe (ΑΤΗΣ ΑΝΘΕΑ ΦΥΟΜΕΝΑ - 4.35), dark sparks which start so inconspicuously but end in grievous conflagration (13.14-15). Those ill-gotten gains that are their fruits have not been earned by the will of the gods; in contrast to the wealth upon which they have bestowed their approbation, "riches which flatter Man's violence do not come in accordance with order but, rather, accompany unjust actions perforce and are quickly fused with ruin." (13.11-13) In this way, "Zeus wreaks utter revenge like a spring wind that rises from the depths of the ocean, scattering the clouds in its path and, ravaging Man's pretty plots of clay, rages even unto the gods' heavenly seat – after which the sky is all clarity once more, the sun shines with brilliance and nary a cloud can be seen." (13.17-24)

Not only our deeds and words but even our heart does Zeus note and judge and, if found lacking, punish, assuredly revealing in the end the spirit in which the things we do and say are said and done. There is no escaping his verdict; one man pays the penalty at once, another later and if not he then his children or his children's children, the innocent, pay for the deficits, the debt, that their forefathers incurred in their prolificacy and failed to settle in their lifetime, living for today and pushing away all thought of tomorrow and tomorrow's morrow. How unfair! How unjust! Precisely! Injustice and disregard for the proper measure that determines all things does not fade with time but rather gains clarity and focus and eventually becomes manifest, painfully obvious, for all eyes to see. The retribution of what is right for what is wrong assuredly comes sooner or later (13.8).

ΠΑΝΤΩΣ ΥΣΤΕΡΟΝ ΗΛΘΕ ΔΙΚΗ

Thus in the end what is right is forcefully so, productively bringing about of itself what is in accordance with the dwelling of diversely distinguished beings living in peace. Justice is not merely the proportionate measure as known and contemplated by the Jovial mind; nor does it only punish the transgression of its limits, repudiating encroachment by the violence of ignorance and arrogance upon long established demarcations of propriety. By revealing the order and the proportions of principle as being straight and true, fitting and due, the personification of Well-proportioned being "fetters the unjust foot, smoothens what is coarse, checks excess, deflates puffed-up pride, withers the catastrophic blossoms of a mind blinded by heedlessness and infatuation, rectifies biased verdicts, restrains arrogance in action, curtails factiousness and the gall of bitter strife. Through the ministrations of her government, all things of human being are properly attuned and make sense." (4.33-39)

...ΤΟΙΣ ΑΔΙΚΟΙΣ ΑΜΦΙΤΙΘΗΣΙ ΠΕΔΑΣ, ΤΡΑΧΕΑ ΛΕΙΑΙΝΕΙ,
ΠΑΥΕΙ ΚΟΡΟΝ, ΥΒΡΙΝ ΑΜΑΥΡΟΙ,ΑΥΑΙΝΕΙ Δ ' ΑΤΗΣ ΑΝΘΕΑ
ΦΥΟΜΕΝΑ, ΕΥΘΥΝΕΙ ΔΕ ΔΙΚΑΣ ΣΚΟΛΙΑΣ, ΥΠΕΡΗΦΑΝΑ
Τ ' ΕΡΓΑ ΠΡΑΥΝΕΙ, ΠΑΥΕΙ Δ' ΕΡΓΑ ΔΙΧΟΣΤΑΣΙΗΣ, ΠΑΥΕΙ
Δ' ΑΡΓΑΛΕΗΣ ΕΡΙΔΟΣ ΧΟΛΟΝ, ΕΣΤΙ Δ' ΥΠ ' ΑΥΤΗΣ ΠΑΝΤΑ
ΚΑΤ ' ΑΝΘΡΩΠΟΥΣ ΑΡΤΙΑ ΚΑΙ ΠΙΝΥΤΑ.

Who is she? She is the princess ΕΥΝΟΜΙΑ (eunomia) presiding with regard to precedence and therefore in accordance with the rule of law, ΘΕΜΙΣ, who is her mother, through the distinguished, distinguishing work of ΔΙΚΗ, her chief executive, taking decisions and passing verdicts of good judgment after due deliberation with a view to the benefit of the whole of communal dwelling in ΕΙΡΗΝΗ, her homemaker, who in the fulfillment of the bourns and verges of the *Hours*, tends the flowers and the fruits, the *Graces'*, that have grown to mild and lovely maturity, from that first fertile insight that

ΖΕΥΣ, her father as well as theirs, had originally sown in the generous spirit of ΕΥΦΡΟΣΥΝΗ.

Conclusion

157. The Philology of Pure Reason

To engage in the pursuit of *thought thinking about thought* or simply *pure thought* has been the sole purpose of this study the discipline of which was to seek and to find such thought as thinks not about phenomena but about thought alone. Whatever this investigation may or may not have achieved in the end, looking back upon our efforts, surely we can affirm, if nothing else, that

thought thought thought.

"Pure thought" – this expression strongly suggests that your inquiry must ultimately deal with the laws of ratiocination; is the science you have been engaged in, if it is, in fact, a science at all, therefore not that of logical inference and discursive reasoning?

No, ours has certainly not been the familiar calculus of symbolic logic but rather a *logotectonic* of terms that designate rational beings, entities of identity in properly proportionate rapport, like those populating the Olympic cosmos that the Muses knew so well and made known to mortal Man, in the First Epoch, through the prophetic voice of rhapsody.

"Thought thinking about thought" – this expression strongly suggests that your inquiry must ultimately deal with the experience of self-awareness; is your discipline therefore not, in reality, a familiar area of research in the wide field of cognitive psychology?

No, no object of anthropological science, and yet the self-knowing being of humanity has attained complete transparency with regards to its destiny the principles of which have been known, affirmed and, through self-relative works of realization, fulfilled – in the Third Epoch, put into effect as the transcendent state of civic consciousness.

"Not about phenomena" – this expression strongly suggests that your inquiry must ultimately deal with the intangible, supernatural world of spirit and of spirits; is your science not therefore, in truth, the advancement of religious doctrine?

No, not theology in any conventional or latter-day academic sense and yet ours is a study of the principle of absolute distinction the moving, transforming experience of which, as we saw in the Second Epoch, engenders a community of children of glory, human beings of distinguished, and in this sense, *holy* spirit in an otherwise indeterminate, indifferent, and insipid world of brute bone and flesh.

How very odd. How could thinking about pure thought possibly entail such a rich threefold experience as you have given account of in your investigation?

It can only in and through distinguished works of literature. The most revered and enduring among them have offered many of the clearest and most striking visions known to Man of what this experience consists in. The literature upon which we have based our studies includes various genres of poetic invention, in particular that of ancient Greek epic, that of the so-called Enlightenment thinkers and writers, selected lyrical and dramatic poetry of German classicism, but also the holy writ of scripture, in particular from the New Testament. These works have been singled out as *tongues of flame* because their words of wisdom have uniquely inspired the action, conception, and invention of pure reason – ultimately the building of an abode of human being, the shelter of a home sweet home in which those may dwell in peace who have heard these works' message of distinction proclaimed and now propose the institution of a science that would abide by what has been said in what has been thrice given utterance to in the speech practices and conventions of a particular place and time in Occidental cultural history; accordingly, lending an ear to this language and minding its message, we have studied *distinguished being* in the Second Epoch, *just being* in the First Epoch, and *human being* in the Third Epoch of Western philosophical tradition and, in precisely this way, thought about thought.

Following Boeder, we have learned that each thinker-poet's conception can be articulated as a relationship, a ΛΟΓΟΣ, of three terms – a term of principle (A), a term of discernment (C), and a term of Issue (B). A triad of thinker-poets, in turn, develops the contemplative, legislative, and generative potential of a given epochal principle of which there are three, namely *entity*, *divinity*, and *humanity*. The collected trains of thought that the different proportions of their constituent terms in relationship to each other subsequently exhibit, give an account of the scheme of all things thought, which is neither a potpourri of ideas nor one idea that they all have "in common" but rather a series of thoughts and a ratio of them organized into distinct lines of reasoning, founded upon the aforementioned principles, manifesting the work of pure reason itself as the recollection, reflection, and celebration of its accomplishments, its insights, its trials, bringing to the fore of our attention and regard the distinguished properties and purposes of the principles that govern its charmed life, the distinguished life of pure thought.

The life of pure thought? Is that a metaphor?

Yes, of course. When we speak of thought, we are bound to speak in metaphors and allegories in order to render our experience with pure reason more palpable to our audience and to ourselves, hopeful that we are employing terms convenient and appropriate to the dictates of the circumstances that define our speech performance. The *life of thought* refers to the self-several whole that comprehends the trains of thought that are its parts and element. For is our experience of pure reason not several? Have we not learned that the distinction of human being is Freedom *and* Destiny in spite of the appearance that these principles must contradict each other? Is it not Mercy *and* Justice, Humanity *and* Deity, the Family *and* the Union, Convention *and* Progress? Is our experience of pure thought not that of truth *and* fiction, the former's memory *and* the latter's imagination, a record of intellectual *and* creative labor? Is it not the originary giving of the self-evident presents of thought *and* the conceptual receiving of its presence? Is it not the ordeal of judgment *and* the calm perception of intellect? Is pure thought not the crossing, the passage up *and* down, down *and* up? Can our experience of the mind not be designated, with a certain poetic license, as redemption *and* condemnation, rise *and* fall? Does the drama of critical self-reflection not involve departure *and* arrival, vividly illustrate in part the notion of the finitude *and* in part that of the infinity of our human being, encompass both nature *and* culture, the person of the Father *and* that of the Son, what is *and* what is meant to be, form a benign circle of turn *and* return, light *and* sight, on the one hand and, on the other, tell the story of the vicious circle of aversion *and* adversity, concealment *and* blindness? Does it not occasion the play of victory *and* defeat of rock *and* scissors, scissors *and* paper, paper *and* rock, lizard *and* Spock?

Yes, as much as fire and water, earth and air "contradict" each other, they all contribute and have a role to play in the making a cup of tea. But tea is not what they "have in common;" tea is not *their* unity but that of something else that has arisen out of their composition, their "synergy."

These elements remain distinct, several, opposed in nature, different beings that, as principles, in their changing ratios, establish a community of ideas, each having its own place in the whole and therein recognized for the contribution that each of these constituent truths makes to the train of thought we have studied as the self-several experience of the distinction of human being.

Thus, the community we envision here and the dwelling we intend to uphold and celebrate with our philological science is not that of people living together in harmony – which is, of course, a nice thought, one no doubt worthy of acclamation and pursuit by those so moved by their muse – but rather of ideas, of principles, of thoughts in accord, thoughts, I say, not people and peoples, which is another, though related, story.

Such a comity of ideas enjoys a more profound peace than that of any human harmony because, in contrast to the tranquility we surmise as obtaining in a state of liberty and justice for all, desire for our own personal lives, and, more generously, sincerely hope for the whole world, the concinnity of ideas in pure reason's several chains of truths is the *whole* story, a spectacle of both war *and* peace, death *and* life as it unfolds across dramatic *and* lyrical elements. The endings are several and the happiest ending is the one that presents them all, one at a time, each at the right moment. And sometimes the beginning, sometimes the middle is happy, sometimes tragic, too! Delight, anguish – it depends on where you are in the tale. A good story tells several stories and then again finds its own proper place among a collection of others which, in turn, belong to further collections and so on in perfect order until the narrative has been attained that not only contains all others but is also itself self-severally contained in each of them.[82] Such a narrative is truly an infinite rather than merely an unending story.

Indeed, it takes a master builder to write narratives like this, one to whom the craft and art of an ancient guild has been passed on and who has learned and practiced its techniques in a long apprenticeship, almost too long perhaps. But thought is not just the virtuosity and ingenuity of invention, giving presence to ideas, it is, as well, the perception and intellect of discovery, reading between the lines, and, no less than these two, it is, finally, the endeavor of pain-staking care and the resolution of purpose committed to the mission of conversion and, ultimately, to walking the path of transformation in the spirit of an ideal.

Thus our philology is, first, *theory* – a study for the pupil of pure reason who desires to find out more about thought. But in striving to know, learning for the sake of illuminating the mind, the student experiences the predetermination of pure reason as a discipline, the practice and the pain of devotion – there is a lot of reading involved, pondering, disburdening the mind of the preoccupations and misconceptions that abound and bedevil

---

[82] A relationship reminiscent of a Dedekind-infinite set.

folks on the lookout for refreshed perceptions. This is a strenuous, transforming propaedeutic in consequence of which to engage in science is already to participate in the other-worldly life of contemplation, called by Aristotle, the best. For to think about pure thought, in contrast to this or that thought and in opposition to this or that problem to which, instead, thought might also be and often, more often even, should be profitably, beneficially turned, to think about thought *is already* to depart and to transcend Man's world; reading the works of great thinkers and poets *is already* to experience that new, that renewed and renewing life of pure reason in perpetual departure from the old one. Hence, we need not actually "think about thought," which is, obviously, a turn of phrase designating *theory*, to experience practically that transformation that an "ethical" philology studies. In fact, all of our commitments and pledges, to the extent that they thwart our momentary inclinations, engender such a passage and we will surely experience the wholesome effects that resolve in the face of obstacles brings forth without actually studying *purpose* and *passage, resolve* and *resistance* in their own right and thus without thinking about thought at all, insofar as they are four familiar terms among many others for the *practice* of pure reason as the distinction of human being, our ΛΟΓΟΣ.

158. The Logotectonic of Speech Practice

ΛΟΓΟΝ ΕΧΩΝ – since the earliest days it has always been with regards to ΛΟΓΟΣ that human beings have sought to grasp their distinction. ΛΟΓΟΣ? It seems that, even today, we cannot help but grapple with this word. Translate it properly, understand it deeply and you will know precisely what the distinction of human being is. Proceed as follows: First, check your *Liddell-Scott* Lexicon; second, check all the passages where this word and its cognates appear in ancient Greek literature; third, turn your attention to its vast ramification in the family of etymologically related expressions in English and, finally, go through this process again with each of its synonyms and the synonyms of these synonyms and the synonyms of the synonyms of those synonyms as well...and there you have it.

First then, turning to the lexicon for an initial orientation, the Liddell-Scott entry[83] groups the meanings of this word under the following headings:

1. *Computation, reckoning* – ΛΟΓΟΣ is a counting, accounting. We take account of what counts, of what merits our attention. First, we pick out,

---

[83] A Greek-English Lexicon, p. 1057.

then we pick up; first choose then take – or say simply *select*. This expression ("*se-*" + "*legere*") contains both the notion of *determination*, i.e. distinguishing a thing in and of itself (se-) by discerning it against a background of other things from which it is offset, and the notion of *collection* – after having been set apart it is subsequently taken up. Thus, ΛΟΓΟΣ means to give a value to, to take account of, what counts and then to gather together what fits together. Note that there is nothing mechanical about the computing that ΛΟΓΟΣ engages in. For the telling involved in the account that ΛΟΓΟΣ gives is, in fact, the assignment of value, a measuring; before something has a merely numerical value, it has the value of being distinguished in some way, brought to the fore of note against a background of what remains, with respect to it, indeterminate and indifferent. We esteem what counts, what makes a difference. And only this is truly worthy of being recounted, told, committed to the language of regard.

2. *Relation, correspondence, proportion* – the account given and taken by the ΛΟΓΟΣ stands in a relationship to what it is a regard and an account of. The selected elements of this reckoning form, with regards to each other, a ratio of terms and the entire scheme, the statement of them in the proportions of its constituents, relate the tale of their telling that corresponds to what has been recounted by them. It would be a mistake to limit this correspondence to that of resemblances and representations; the likeness upon which an account is based can be, but need not be mimetic any more than the Homeric or Synoptic narratives that we have studied may or may not be "historically based," a status which, as their "facticity" is distinct from that of the archeological, is entirely beside the point of philology – Greek epos and Christian gospel relate and document an experience that, by the very fact of their tradition beyond the remoteness of a particular place and time long gone, have proven themselves to be worthy of record and remembrance, even to this day, regardless of what "actually" happened or did not happen once upon a time. Of course, what archeologists' excavations uncover related to these ancient holy writs does not diminish but rather can only enrich our understanding of why this knowledge is deemed sacred, why, though its native time and place and people have long been effaced by subsequent ages, this knowledge has endured and why it is the destiny of human being to take their message as sacred into account, even today, at a point in history when all talk of "destiny" would seem to have become as corny and as moldy as relic bones.

3. *Explanation* – the ΛΟΓΟΣ is therefore not merely descriptive telling, it is also prescriptive explanation, the stating of a rule or law, a principle, the giving of a reason, i.e. that on account of which something is the way it is

and should be, its ground – this ground, noting it, makes a difference not only in our actions but also in our perceptions of the issue at stake. As the statement of what something is (supposed) to be, a being's principle, its *being*, is not only manifest to the discriminating gaze of *theory*, perceptive reason, but also, as the craft and art of syllogistic demonstration, inventive reason, finds and collects reasons, arguments, putting them forth in a suite of propositions which are the actual statements and formula for the insight in question and convey the inherent persuasiveness of truth, its power to win agreement on the part of thought when appealed to by thought with regards to truth. But this is the crisis of critical self-reflection prior to all "consciousness" – ΛΟΓΟΣ coming to terms with ΛΟΓΟΣ.

4. *Inward debate of the soul* – we recognize here the original sense of *dialectic*, so familiar in the Homeric formula that occurs when a mortal or an immortal rational being, angered by what is not the way it should be "speaks in vexation to his or her noble heart" (ΟΧΘΗΣΑΣ Δ' ΑΡΑ ΕΙΠΕ ΠΡΟΣ ΟΝ ΜΕΓΑΛΗΤΟΡΑ ΘΥΜΟΝ – 11.403). The ensuing dialogue is a critical deliberation between our first, our immediate impulse – to flee like a coward from the imminent danger of an approaching opponent (11.407; 21.562), to sue for peace and beg for mercy in the hopes of avoiding the fateful decision of distinction upon the battlefield of judgment (22.122), or even to recklessly stand one's ground in the face of a superior foe (17.97) – and our second, more objective, more distinguished thought by which we, coming to our senses, decide to abide by what is clearly right and the better idea (Il. 22.385) saying: "but why does my heart thus dispute the issue?" (11.407; 17.97; 21.562; 22.122; 22.385)

ΑΛΛΑ ΤΙ Η ΜΟΙ ΤΑΥΤΑ ΦΙΛΟΣ ΔΙΕΛΕΞΑΤΟ ΘΥΜΟΣ

Deliberate and critical reflection arrives at conviction through a process of reasoning in which arguments are weighed, pitted one against the other, as in mortal combat, to determine which is meant to win the day and which to fall into oblivion.

5. *Continuous statement, narrative, oration* – ultimately, ΛΟΓΟΣ is the ΛΟΓΟΣ of ΛΟΓΟΙ – the ΛΟΓΟΣ in which verbal expression consists is indeed manifold; whether appearing in the form of narratory exposition, poetic storytelling, or forensic declamation, or even as a particular utterance like an oracle, a saying, an assertion, a command; the experience of language is indeed multifarious. Ultimately ΛΟΓΟΣ accounts for, takes account of, not only that which is the subject matter, the supposedly "non-linguistic" issue in question, but also the classes and types of verbal communication as well

as its constituent elements, the parts of speech. In this case the content of a ΛΟΓΟΣ is the ΛΟΓΟΣ, the world of words in their own right.

If this term has the above five senses, consider now what a science of ΛΟΓΟΣ, a *philology*, would entail, assuming that this etymological progression from ΛΟΓΟΝ ΕΧΩΝ as meaning "having reason" to the sense of "having speech" or even "having language" documents the conceptual development inherent in our experience of ΛΟΓΟΣ. If *language* is thus, philologically speaking, the distinction of human being, then clearly we do not mean "language" in the anthropological sense of *linguistics* that studies the different tongues of the world with a view to the various phenomena that characterize human languages past and present like semantics, morphology, phonetics, as well as syntax, the laws of which govern how these diverse languages are organized structurally.

But what is *philology* if it is not merely a precursor and therefore undoubtedly primitive linguistic science, at best a historically oriented linguistics offering a "diachronic" perspective on the study of languages and sign systems in general? Traditionally at least – and whatever it has become today, philology has indeed a very venerable tradition – a "love of words" was devoted to works and the language of literature called *classical.* These ancient texts, having, by some miracle, escaped oblivion, confront their reader, precisely because of their antiquity and the "ideological" remoteness of their world and culture to ours, with considerable challenges, not the least of which is their proper translation into modern terms and idioms. It is only in the context of the passages where a word appears that their meaning can be ascertained, a meaning that may or may not be accurately conveyed by a particular expression in our present-day native language. And then again, each passage stands in relation to prior and subsequent passages, which together compose one book among several of a particular poet's or thinker's work until all the works of poetry and thought, or more generally, all the writings and fragments of all the poets and thinkers that tradition has passed down to us have been collected and accounted for in the contribution they have made to our understanding of the distinction of human being, which is, in a word, ΛΟΓΟΣ – the conceptual tradition of pure *reason*, the present of its performative *speech* practice, and the craft and art of poetic *language*, namely, the sacred or distinguished language of the holy writs they served.

Shall we add to this logical triad *literature* as well? A look at what literary criticism and literary theory have thus far brought forth confirms our suspicion that this object of study has already been accounted for, above all in the category of performative speech practice and, by literature theorists' own confessions (and assurances), only to a very limited degree in the pedigree of that conceptual tradition. It is within the realm of speech practice where the various schools of literary theory vie for dominance each pitting their own ideology, their "epistemology," against that of their brothers and sisters in the spirit of irreconcilable difference not only with regards to the "texts" they "interrogate" but also with regards to the techniques of analysis they avail themselves of with a view to construing these texts' meaning in the diverse life-world contexts that have, to varying degrees, imposed their influence upon textual formation – historical, biographical, psychological, philosophical, social, cultural, etc. Given this wide field of study, the eclectic use of analytical techniques and the heterogeneous nature of what is considered to be "text" in the first place, literary theory would seem to be, on the whole, interpretative, a hermeneutic project, extending a long history of exegesis that has more recently widened its scope to embrace literature that is no longer held to be the holy writ of poetic or prophetic scripture or even culturally canonical but rather, with regards to a particular value system defined by a "mainstream" society, *marginal.*

Wouldn't it be a worthy effort to collect, in the sense of ΛΟΓΟΣ we have just considered, all of the ideas of all of the writers of literary theory, barring none, refusing none, into a single train of thought that articulates our latter day knowledge of the distinction of human being as *language* or as they would perhaps prefer to say, *literature*? The result of such an ordering endeavor of appreciation and regard would certainly not be the unity of uniformity arising out of a totalitarian effort at the homogenization of diversity under one "master" thought or "grand narrative," or original, "mythological" principle. Rather it would build a ratio of thoughts, of incompatible narratives, of opposing principles, that takes the distinctions each one makes into account by according them all their proper place within the scheme of all things thought, locating each idea in a tradition of insight and a guild of invention that stretches all the way back to Homer!

Would that not be *science* in the best sense of the term? Not playing favorites, not taking sides, not showing bias or preference for one thought over another, loving one, despising another, taking pride in being knowledgeable of one, in being ignorant of another, celebrating one, passing over another in silence, settling on one doctrine as orthodox, damning the others as heresy, considering one as right and the others as wrong? Of course, such objectivity flies in the face of our need to find our own little spot to take a stand upon, to found our family of friends and exclude those who do not belong, to define our own standpoint and then maintain and defend it against the onslaught of our enemies in a mordacious logomachy of honor among intellectuals. Where's the heroism in such impartiality? Where's the victory, where's the camaraderie borne of controversy so necessary if a truly robust bigotry is to seed and teem? Perhaps in the science we pursue there are no heroes, no victories, no comrades in arms in that sense. In fact, to be sure, the controversy of opposing sides remains before us in the particular case being prosecuted, but it is opposite us in the sense of being before us who are not advocates but rather judges and thus in the opposition not of difference but rather of "indifference," that is the non-position of the unbiased arbiter who renders a decision and passes sentence that does justice to each litigant's claim and so, by separating the divisive parties, reconciles them in the court of logotectonic law that accords to each what is due, namely their own hearing, i.e. a fair and proper, but not the same, portion and proportion in a ratio of terms that articulate a train of thought.

Specifically, our own philological study has examined works of surpassing power and influence that are traditionally thought to espouse disparate, incompatible ideas – do the principle of *Destiny* with regards to which the gods themselves, even the greatest and most powerful god of all, acquiesce *and* the principle of *Divinity*, which places God beyond all determination of the cosmos of beings, not rightly refuse every sort of coalition that aims at unifying them by subsuming them under some overarching concept? And where is the common ground between the absolute freedom of *Humanity* and the glory of *God*. There can be none and when they clash in the ideological field of controversy, one must prevail uncompromisingly over the other.

Unless, as we propose, they both appear before the objective judge of philology, our Justice of the peace who, as we saw, convenes a court of contemplation and of law in which, in accordance with the science of the principles of ΛΟΓΟΣ, of pure reason and of the language of their ratios, a community of distinctions is negotiated in appreciation of the greater good that is their self-several dwelling. We saw that those desiring to acquire the logotectonic intellect of philology might begin by having recourse to words of wisdom, to those renowned holy writs that the craft and art of poets and prophets brought forth, so powerfully moving as to encourage and sustain theoretical efforts of the sort that pure reason, now a contemplative god, might champion. But ΛΟΓΟΣ, let's call it *order* now, is not just, in the first place, a *theoretical* object of study to which insight turns, nor merely, in the second place, a *practical* precept of law or purpose that, in being given, enjoins transformative, reformative action; it is also, finally, *poetic* – the well-proportioned form and structure of expert building that articulates thought in changing ratios of terms, one of *principle* (A), one of *issue* (B), one of *discernment* (C). ΛΟΓΟΣ, in other words, *reason, language* – these words have, weirdly, become synonyms for us – is thus the *order* of thought in this threefold sense. Are these three signature terms of distinction clear in how, with them, philology goes about marking salient elements in a line of reasoning, any line of reasoning whatsoever, and in so doing, elaborates the train of thought that constitutes our experience of a given principle?

Consider by way of example of their several ratios, the relationship of the *speaker* (A) as the possessor of a seminal principle of knowledge, the *audience* (C) as the intelligent recipient of the speaker's address and who then acts upon that insight, putting into effect what was taught and learned, and, thirdly, the Speech (B) as the poetic realization of the principle in the speaker's words and deeds, in the particulars founded by and founding the circumstances that define the speech performance.

1.   Thus a speaker with something significant to say (A) and adept in the logotectonic method (C) delivers a speech (B) with philological eloquence. Through the speaker's verbal and non-verbal language, which is equally far away from both stammering introversion and blathering volubility, ideas, not left to slink and abscond, come to light; though initially hiding ideas from the lecherousness of our mundane *I*, the veil of words the speaker gives them is not a curtain of fog or iron, it is, rather, a gown that draws attention not only to what it conceals but much more to the regalia of invisibility itself, namely to the spirit and the insights that the vestments of language inspire – is not, in fact, the invisibility, the intangibility of ideas their first and most remarkable manifestation, their glory?

Ideas want voices and ideas want ears – the two parameters of dialogue that, each in their own way, contribute to the making of a difference. For principles, in the distinguished speech practice we have studied as the three epochal languages of wisdom, indicate the WAY IT SHOULD BE. *Figure 99* shows this ratio of terms as a deduction of concretion.

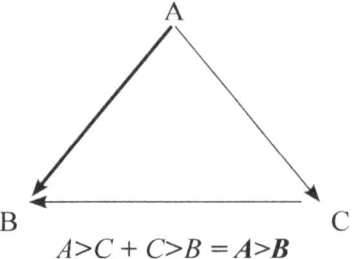

$$A>C + C>B = A>B$$

Figure 99: The Deduction of Concretion

2. As we, in a flight of optimism, are bound to assume, at some point, that particular audience is bound to get (C) the message, construing what has been actually said in the utterances that were spoken (B) and gain thus insight into the ideas (A) that constitute the determination at issue. *Figure 100* shows this ratio of terms as a deduction of perception.

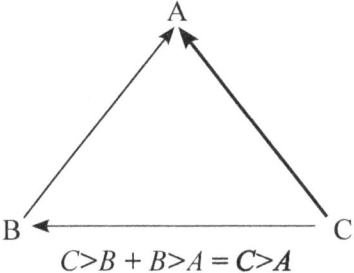

$$C>B + B>A = C>A$$

Figure 100: The Deduction of Perception

3. The specific terms employed in the speech (B) are, to the insight that comprehends (C) the scheme of all things thought, tangible signs and symbols of intangible ideas (A). Even as ideas are made real in language so also does language give meaning to immediacy such that now things make sense to a critical perspective that has broken with the continuity, the smooth, skin-deep surface of things as merely being what they are to the naked eye. *Figure 101* shows this ratio of terms as a deduction of signification.

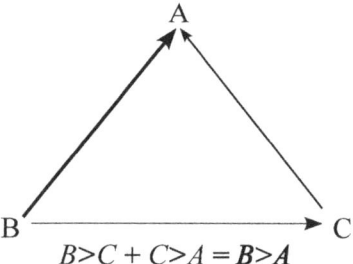

$$B>C + C>A = B>A$$

Figure 101: The Deduction of Signification

4. The ideas (A) are addressed to the audience in the form of heart-moving, heart-rending words (B) in which the principle is made tangible to the audience through a vivid form of language that makes a difference (C) in the lives and in the thought of the hearers. This ratio of terms is depicted in *Figure 102* as the deduction of vocation.

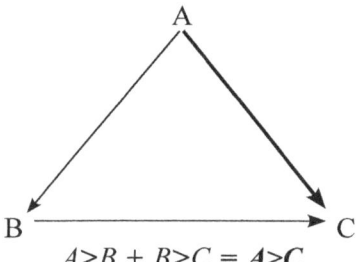

$$A>B + B>C = A>C$$

Figure 102: The Deduction of Vocation

5. In particular, the words give voice and, in this way, presence (B) to the principle (A) stimulating the audience to acknowledge (C) the gap between the IS and the OUGHT in the form of an ideal that envisions THE WAY IT SHOULD BE in a particular context and situation. This is the deduction of determination and its ratio shows how the principle comes to the world in terms that strike the audience in question, moving them to embrace change in a particular direction exemplified in the specific form that the principle has been given. This ratio of terms is depicted in *Figure 103* as a deduction of determination:

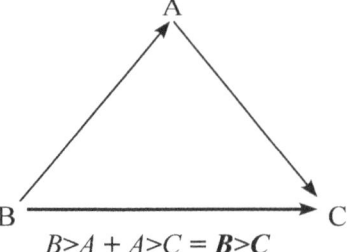

$$B>A + A>C = \boldsymbol{B>C}$$

Figure 103: The Deduction of Determination

6. The listener is inspired by the import of this divergence, the gap between THE WAY IT IS and THE WAY IT SHOULD BE in the specifics of the vision that beckons to ambition and then, in the actuation of desire, strives to close it (C) and thus to fulfill the principle (A), putting into effect (B) what was the initial charge of thought, the distinguished appointment of the principle. This ratio of terms is depicted in *Figure 104* as a deduction of destination.

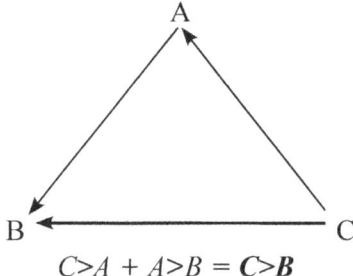

$$C>A + A>B = \boldsymbol{C>B}$$

Figure 104: The Deduction of Destination

The speaker stands in the front and speaks, the audience sits and listens – millions of lectures and talks and speeches are thus delivered in the name of learning, which, as we see, contain both theoretical as well as practical training for the listeners, regardless of the topic. But the unique topic of our philology is even this – the give and the take of pure reason, namely *self-evidence* in the manifesting voice of the speaker and *reception* on the part of the listeners who lend or close their ears to what is spoken and what in these utterances is actually being said. That voice from abroad interrupts our private conversations among ourselves, broaches with its overtures our personal spheres, and then again, in response to or refusal of that gift, our audience's harkening heart welcomes or rejects the calling to attention, turning to or away.

Figure 105 summarizes these dimensions of speech practice: To hear is to listen and to listen is to follow the speaker's line of argument – it offers a train of thought in specific terms, provides to the listeners the articulate and moving vision of that principle as an end, more, as a guiding *purpose*, that now, through them who are thus driven by the *resolve* to act upon what has been grasped in its design, is to be actually carried out; the speech does not merely give us information – here are the facts, here the *evidence*, take it or leave it; in our *reception* of THE WAY IT IS, we take, moreover, the implied distinction of a destiny upon ourselves, the present of the principle, that we are obligated to fulfill as THE WAY IT SHOULD BE.

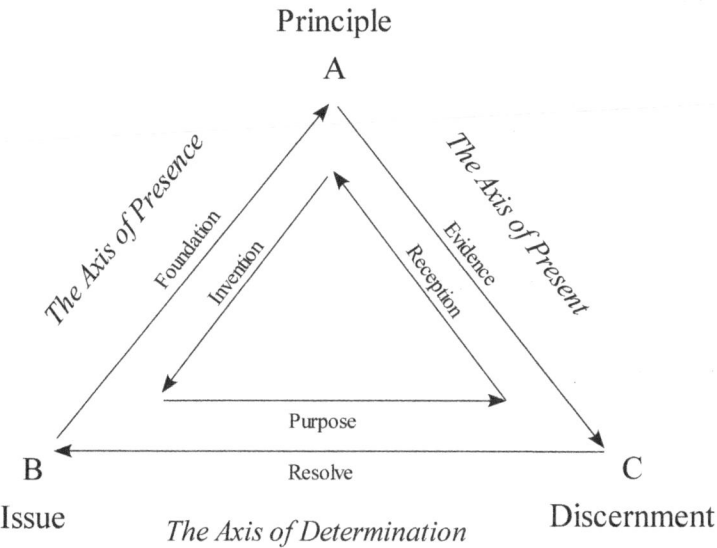

Figure 105: The Presentation of Thought

The principle attains thus in our action and through our actions the efficacy of being not merely in the world discovered but as a world brought forth by *invention* and based upon the inaugural principle, the *foundation* of thought that is never "just a thought" but rather desires to become the thing, a big thing, even the main thing, in our lives, which, in turn, matter now all the more because these lives have been, even as we have been, distinguished from themselves, from ourselves, in the mind that perpetually, incessantly, interminably disrupts Man's mundane immediacy and whimpering decease.

The speaker rises to the occasion of the speech and comes forward entering upon the ordeal of the stage, vulnerably exposed to the many eyes of judgment, which are just the one I of distinction, whether it be known as that of Humanity or Divinity, that of God or the gods in whose community of excellence we, the speakers, are called and, harkening, take our proper place.

159. The Etymology of Pure Reason

After considering, in a first step, the meaning of ΛΟΓΟΣ as *language,* and particularly as speech performance, we now turn, in a second step, to this word and its cognates in the contexts they share with other terms that appear in close textual or conceptual proximity to them, above all the notion of *truth* (ΑΛΗΘΕΙΑ) accompanying and clarifying the connections that ΛΟΓΟΣ governs and is governed by. In an early philological study, namely in *Der Frühgriechische Wortgebrauch von Logos und Alētheia,* Boeder examined the "original Greek usage of the terms *Logos* and *Alētheia.*" Given the importance of their career in Greek and indeed in all Occidental thought, it is perhaps not a wasted effort to ascertain their earliest meanings in the passages of early Greek literature where they occur.[84]

1. ΛΕΓΕΙΝ – The etymology of ΛΟΓΟΣ suggests that the original meaning of this term and that of its cognates is *to place, to lay* (*BG* p. 2). Boeder notes, however, that in contrast to ΤΙΘΕΝΑΙ, the forms of **lex-* and the corresponding perfect tense obtain in situations in which something is laid to rest on its own proper place, the spot that has been chosen and prepared just for it (ibid). This is its ΛΕΧΟΣ (bed), the resting place upon which the living (as opposed to the dead) couch when they retire (ibid, see footnote 9). And then if several things are brought together and placed where they belong, they are *collected* – thus do the cognates of **leg-* elaborate upon the notion of laying; gleaning what was scattered or left behind, we put things where they belong, gaining an overview over how much we have, whether we have enough or not, distinguishing which of a multitude of several things belong together to form a particular group and which do not, thus

---

[84] This essay is the first in the collection of Boeder's writings and lectures on Greek and medieval philosophy entitled *Das Bauzeug der Geschichte [BG],* pp. 1-30.

sorting things into a number of parts, pieces, members, and elements (p. 3), a sense from which we derive the use of ΛΕΓΕΙΝ to designate the workings of language. For does not *telling* give an account by collecting and then relating all the particulars? A whole of thought is *elaborated* by going through the *details* that have been experienced and collected in the memory of the speaker whose knowledge of them, if they are to be communicated to the listener, must be then *articulated*, one element at a time in proper *order*, avoiding what is extraneous to the purpose of the *report*, until a *complete* and vivid *rendering* of that knowledge has been provided – "ΛΕΓΕΙΝ strives to achieve a complete *account* of what is known." (p. 4) The *catalogue* inherent in ΛΟΓΟΣ aims not only at being compete – leaving nothing out – but also *exact*; each item in the catalogue is precisely rendered with a view towards the clarity of the difference it makes within the whole.

2. KPINEIN – For this reason, ΛΕΓΕΙΝ is always accompanied by KPINEIN, meaning *to cleanse, separate, distinguish, decide* in such a way that, among many, one is *singled out* and, in comparison with all the others, *distinguished* as outstanding. (p. 7) It is interesting to see how the sense of KPINEIN developed to include *judgment*. The judge must *decide* a case. In issues pertaining to the transgression of law, which is *laid down* as THE WAY IT SHOULD BE, the sharp lines defining the scope of what is due are no longer precisely demarcated – in the controversy or transgression brought before the judge, the proportions delimiting the differences have lost their clarity and need to be redrawn or reaffirmed. This ΚΡΙΣΙΣ (crisis) is the task of KPINIEN. By reestablishing the proportion of regard that had formerly determined the relationship between the now contending parties, critical judgment, in separating them who were fused in contention about those disregarded limits, actually achieves the accord of renewed community. By separating them, their rapport is regained. The connection to ΛΟΓΟΣ is clear: to collect is to first distinguish, to separate the wheat from the chaff, and then, having cleansed with clarity what was confused, to select what stands out above all as the best and thus resolve the difference by reaffirming the difference that had been contested.

3. ΠΕΙΘΩ – What is known has been put forth; the clarity and precision of this rendering not only conveys insight by enabling and even encouraging the audience to take active part in the endeavor of comprehension, to actively "connect the dots" they now clearly see thanks to the precise exposition, but also by inspiring trust on the part of the audience that the rendering offered to them is indeed reliable the concision of which is

indicative of the certain knowledge of the speaker. (p. 8) The ΠΕΙΘΩ of the presentation awakens the audience's desire to learn more about the issue in question, a desire to know – in this sense, it lies in the power of the ΛΟΓΟΣ not merely to mediate insight but to influence the hearers, to guide their attention away from THE WAY IT IS, and, with words, to captivate, to beguile such that THE WAY IT IS is THE WAY IT APPEARS to the audience, dissociating what is actually known and what has been shown. This persuasive power of the ΛΟΓΟΣ, having thus been discovered in its own right, can now be exploited as a technique of deception, the craft and art of fiction (ΨΕΥΔΟΣ). Does the ΛΟΓΟΣ faithfully convey THE WAY IT IS? That depends on the speaker's purpose with regards to the audience. The clarity and cogency of the ΛΟΓΟΣ seems to suggest that the speaker is saying it THE WAY IT IS. And yet now the speaker's stratagem is at issue and with it, the questionable fidelity of the ΛΟΓΟΣ, speech at cross-purposes with *truth*.

4. ΑΛΗΘΕΙΑ – Truth in the ancient Greek sense makes a distinction in knowledge; there are those who know and those who do not but to whom an insight can be shared, knowledge imparted or not, in which latter case what is known remains concealed by the knower who keeps the other in the dark about THE WAY IT IS, whereby to leave oneself in the dark, the medial voice of the verb, is to *forget*. These senses of ΑΛΗΘΕΙΑ (alētheia) arise from the fact, a fact much made of by Heidegger, that this word is a privative form of the root ΛΗΘΕΙΝ (lēthein - to hide) (10). An analysis of the passages in the Iliad and the Odyssey containing this word and its cognates shows that "just as ΦΑΙΝΕΙΝ (phainein) brings something to light and places it before our very eyes, so does, by contrast, ΛΗΘΕΙΝ leave someone in the dark about something, hides it, even dissembles it with a view to pulling the wool over someone's eyes." (p. 11)

To disclose or not to disclose, even to veil at times – this is a question that we must often ask ourselves and the answer depends on the determinants of human dwelling, that of our mutual intimacy and trust or distrust, which impose limits on what should be shared knowledge and to whom disclosure is due and from whom rightly demanded; in some situations, we intend to spare others or are ourselves spared by propitious concealment, or in an act of discretion, refrain from demanding to know from another and therefore to be told THE WAY IT IS. What is important, what is insignificant, why is the other asking us to disclose what we know, to whom do we owe an explanation, in what situations should we make exceptions in sharing knowledge or in concealing it? When is the right moment to show, when is the right moment to know? These are all questions pertaining to limits as they define proper regard in the dwelling of just being. Clearly, what is right for oneself and for all concerned parties depends on the particular situation in question. (p. 12) For knowing makes all the difference in the world. And it is here that ΑΛΗΘΕΙΑ is decisive. Some things we see and know for ourselves but other things are accessible to us only through the telling of another whose recollection and subsequent account bring knowledge to the fore; some things we can point to and point out in the immediacy of their presence but others depend on the mediation of a ΛΟΓΟΣ, that of a witness who was there, who knows. Sometimes this testimony can be confirmed by seeing THE WAY IT IS with our own eyes, but often we must take the witness's word for it, especially when the knowledge is that of the past. (p. 14) And this knowledge of the past about which we ask for ΑΛΗΘΕΙΑ, disclosure, is, in Homeric speech, never the truth about a mere thing, but rather about human beings – their deeds and their fates. (p. 14, footnote 113). This is not to say, however, that ΑΛΗΘΕΙΑ is what is known first and then shared by the speaker. What is known is THE WAY IT IS and ΑΛΗΘΕΙΑ refers to the sharing of this knowledge with others through the ΛΟΓΟΣ. But what is made known by the ΛΟΓΟΣ may or may not be THE WAY IT IS. That depends on whether or not or to what extent the witness wants to disclose the knowledge that is at issue and share it with those who ask to be included among those who are "in the know" – the original sense of being *conscious*, namely from the composition of *com-* (with) and -*scīre* (to know) – referring to what is shared or "common" knowledge as opposed to what is held by one alone or just a few, "insiders'" insight. As a result of ΑΛΗΘΕΙΑ, we share in the presence of THE WAY IT IS. But we do well never to underestimate the machinations of the ΛΟΓΟΣ in service to a plot bent on misdirection, on deception, bringing its pervasive power into play as ΨΕΥΔΟΣ (Pseudos), son of ΕΡΙΣ (strife), brother of ΛΗΤΗ (concealment), as we learned from Hesiod; these gods, far from instituting a community based on the experience of the shared attendance to and presence of THE WAY IT IS, subvert or evade the comity of the ΛΟΓΟΣ. (p. 18)

All the more clearly do we see emerge, in later centuries of Greek literature, uses of ΛΟΓΟΣ that manifest the ever growing awareness and virtuosity of word-wielders in exploiting the technical resources of language as ΜΗΧΑΝΗ, as a tool for achieving certain ends; not limited to disclosure or deception with regards to THE WAY IT IS, ΛΟΓΟΣ provides the speaker with the means of affecting the audience – words can flatter, soothe, urge, provoke, charm, anger, and in this way, engage and influence the audience.

(p. 20) It therefore makes sense that, as Boeder reminds us with reference to the origin of rhetoric, that "the human emotions first became an object of study expressly in connection with a speaker's professional interest in understanding how a speech affects the mood of the audience." (p. 21) The persuasive force, the charm, the influence that the speech exerts on the audience, in a word, the *ΠΕΙΘΩ* of the speech, are effects of the ΛΟΓΟΣ that pertain neither to the willingness on the part of the speaker to make completely manifest to the audience what is known by that speaker, the *ΑΛΗΘΕΙΑ* of the speech, nor the concision of its elements in articulating THE WAY IT IS, the *ΚΡΙΝΕΙΝ* of the speech. It is the property of ΛΟΓΟΣ in its own right.

But the persuasive force of words is not limited to that of utterances in an actual speech situation. Ultimately, the ΛΟΓΟΣ in poetry is celebratory. Poetic attention to and mention of significant events and deeds of excellence preserve them in the language of regard; the poem is a monument to human achievements and acts of greatness that have been deemed worthy of magnification and preservation in words composed for posterity's sake by poets and consigned as a legacy to the devotion of their descendants' remembrance. In our daily life, it seems that so much, nearly everything in fact, goes without saying, but some things merit poetic remark; they are noteworthy, worthy of thought and, in this sense, distinguished as commemorable. Here again we recognize the power of the ΛΟΓΟΣ to take account of, to care. We pay heed to what matters, to what really makes a difference – beginning with the gods' concerns – for human being, it is foolishness to disregard them; as we learned from Hesiod, the gods are the stronger. That is what makes a god a god: "everything that can overwhelm demands the note of ΛΟΓΟΣ, *Death* especially but also *Pain*." (p. 24 and footnote 179) Of course, these two gods come to mind first among the children of *Night* – *Night* subdues even the gods themselves (Iliad 14.259) and is, in that situation, the gods' god. Such are the gods, like Ares too, who we honor because we must, not because we will. (Hesiod, *WD*, 15-16) Given their power and influence in our lives, it is indeed folly to neglect these gods and yet our decision to turn towards or away from them – which is the rapport of regard inherent in ΛΟΓΟΣ – as compelling as their call upon us may be, this decision of the ΛΟΓΟΣ cannot be coerced; it "remains in a free relationship to that which is *there*." (p. 25)

At this point, "telling as well as thinking are comprehended in the *logical*" (p. 26) which refers not only to the relationship of attendance and regard of the intellect to what is most worthy of note, but also the relationships among the elements in question, their collection into groups in accordance with their particular natures or some other ordering principle that allows distinctions among them to be made as parts of a unified whole the constitution of which can now be articulated, this in descriptive works of natural *history* (ΙΣΤΟΡΙΗ - p. 27-28) that ultimately will lead to the first *philosophy*, the achievement of explanatory thought that sees and makes manifest what no casual, immediate and, in this sense, *naked eye* can see, namely the causes (ΑΙΤΙΑ) and the consequences, the ground and the reasons, in a word, the ΦΥΣΙΣ of all that has come to the fore, showing itself to the light of day and sparking the careful attention of the ΛΟΓΟΣ regarding what is noteworthy, preparatory to further enquiry inaugurated by asking the distinguishing question *why*. Fittingly, "the realm of ΑΛΗΘΕΙΑ is no longer limited to the relationship of rapport between the knowledgeable speaker and the listeners who desire that the former's knowledge be imparted to them, counting on and even expressly requesting that this relationship be governed by sincerity and trust; henceforth this term refers also to the relationship between the knower and the known as well as the knowable." (p. 28-29) But a thing is neither known nor knowable until it has achieved its ΤΕΛΟΣ (telos), its completion. For only then does the thing have full presence. (29) Until then, it has not attained patency, conspicuity, palpability; it is not all *there*... and therefore neither are we who, hearing rumor but not knowing, nevertheless, with the help of the Muses, seek to grasp it *in statu nascendi*.

How rich the notion, how wide the field of ΛΟΓΟΣ is! Will we ever be done with it and ready to move on to some other thought than that of ΛΟΓΟΣ, the thought about the distinction of *thought*, about the dimensions of the practice of *speech*, about the workings of *language*? For all these are its possible definitions, as we saw. Having gained a sense of its original use in ancient Greek, we have briefly examined its most intimate concomitant ideas, namely ΚΡΙΝΕΙΝ, ΠΕΙΘΩ and ΑΛΗΘΕΙΑ, i.e. *distinction, persuasion, patency*. These in turn resonate with other notions, the *harmonics* of a distinction that we have called a *train* of thought with reference to the train of distinctions that attends every distinction, a train of ideas that accompanies every idea, a train of terms following logically upon every term. To build thus, in the sense of the ΛΟΓΟΣ, is therefore not merely to invent but rather to listen first to what is sound in a work of language and then to collect terms of distinction that will recreate what we have heard said in what was spoken, always putting it in other words that are never our *own* words but rather in those we have found to date that seem to be the very best, a *record* of high fidelity.

0, 2, 3, 1 – This is how we count and take account when engaged in the process of building a simple language comprising a chain of truths, namely the three terms of distinction *A, B, C.* The method we have just sketched has the following steps:

   (0. Indiscrimination)

   2. Draw a distinction (A)

   3. Designate the differences (C)

   1. Collect terms (B)

Start with the hodgepodge of indiscriminate promiscuity, i.e. entropic *indifference*, and then, upon this inane backdrop, simply draw a distinction, which, in fact, comes to the fore against an inchoate sheet of indeterminacy. Now there are two, namely, first, this distinction itself and then the antecedent immediacy whence it sprung and upon which the whole procession of subsequent differences rests that the primordial distinction initiates – rests, but not as upon a foundation or in peace, which would be the quiet of silence; this background is *noise*, but not a loud or otherwise importunate, inaugural, or glorious noise, a clarion call. It is entirely ambient and the theme of John Cage's famous three-movement composition of 1952 called *4'33".* This *hum* and murmuring is certainly not the basis for all that follows; rather, it is absolutely prior to all that follows, and insofar as priority invokes a distinction, it is even prior to itself. In that case, we would need another word for it as the precursor of all priority, though not in the manner of a first principle or determination of that priority, not a "principle" of that principle – no, of course it is this actual, "subsequent" principle that makes the difference in the first place – but rather what this difference, once it has been made, obliquely implies as its indifferent *being before.* Do you really want to call the soup of primordial confusion the unsung hero of the principle, the *principle* of the principle, to read in the dregs the quintessence of origins and ends? Well, be my guest. But consider. It is entirely to your obloquy of what has made a difference in the first place that your *being before* owes its latter-day notoriety. Consider *Figure 106* that attempts to render the start of it all in an image.

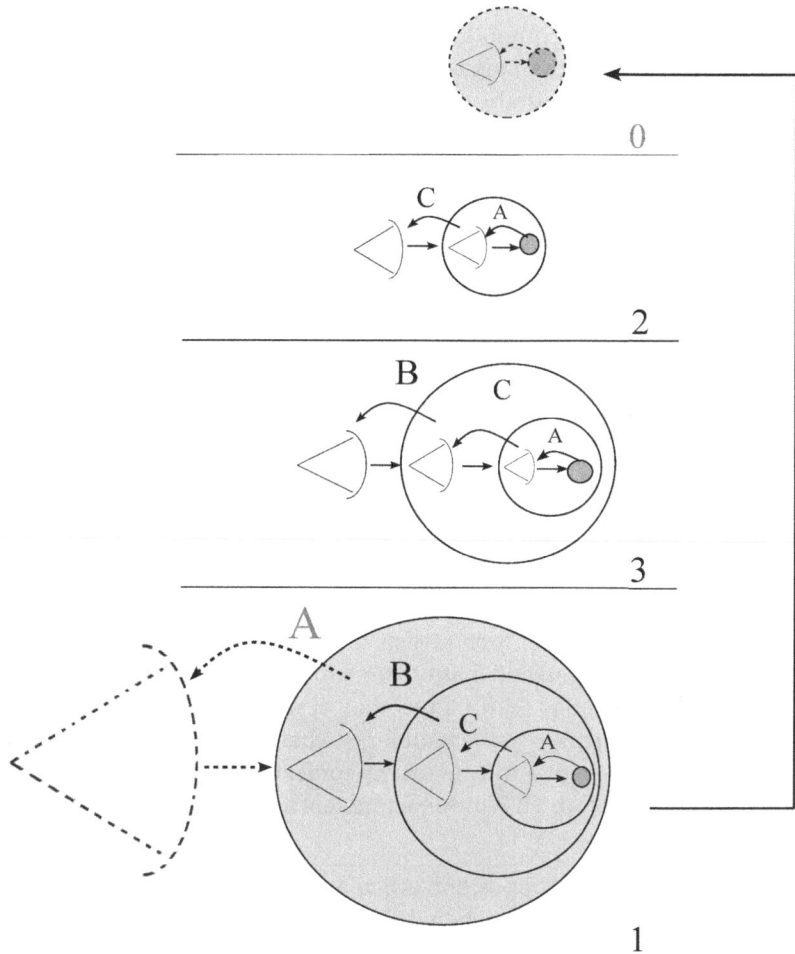

Figure 106: The Narrative of the Founding of Language

We have described this *being before* as the blank, a piece of paper upon which nothing has yet been written, a smooth surface lacking all character trait, track, trace, an unmarked space and plain-Jane plane in which, from which, and upon which a distinction abruptly emerges, though the former is neither an origin nor a cause of that distinction. The distinction alone is the origin and cause of what comes next. And before the beginning, if there is not a more primary start to be accounted for, a distinction as *origin* of the beginning, its onset or very outset, its spring, and mainspring, its inception, then there is nothing at all before except the muttering hum, the boredom of the board before play commences and the first move is made; the shifting masses of a mumbling jumble of Man, the murmuring vox populi of opinions and rumors, the fatigue of monotony, of banality, of all that is insipid, inconspicuous, drab, stale, flat – these are the faceless faces comprising the pure passivity of the background upon which, against which, the distinction of a figure is drawn, its character cut. Thus we take account of nullity and blankness *after* the first distinction has been made; that void is what has been taken for granted before anything has been granted in the drawing of the first distinction. Is this the unsung hero that you keep trying to remind us about as thought's antedate? Is this your king, your queen, your heart? Is this our destiny?

In any case, now, after the first distinction has indeed been drawn, the ground and the figure, the pit and the tip, anonymity and preeminence, crenel and marlon, the 0 and the 1, enter into the chiral relationship of self-severalty – reticence says to the salience, "I came first because without the platform that my stage provides, the gladiators, doomed to die, wouldn't be able to appear and perform in the ring of the arena." Determination replies "I came first because without the spectacle of our death with distinction, you would be but a nameless plot of shifting desert sands." Each claims the prerogative of precedence; each recasts its debt as what the other owes – knowing and being, mind and matter, thought and things, the ideal and the real are set thus at odds with names that designate the two sides of an irreconcilable difference – in the manner of what Parmenides exposed and ridiculed as the "deceptive order of mortal conjecture" (DK 28 B 8.39-41, 53-56) – the unfolding of which is the enactment of a plot of the story often told as in *Figure 106*.

We have seen how this opposition articulates, in its terms' relationship, a transition and uneasy passage between two endpoints, a train of thought which does not alleviate the contradiction inherent in these terms, much less unify them under some "blanket" or "meta-" concept but rather collects them into a logotectonic scheme of language, of pure reason, of ΛΟΓΟΣ, to which we have pledged our friendship in the course of our efforts as post/modern (rather than classical) philologists.

Pure reason is not merely the content of language, it is itself language, speaking and spoken, the speaker and the being spoken to. To build a language, we need, first, a distinction. Draw a distinction and call it the *term of principle* (A). What difference does this principle make in the scheme of all things thought? Call this difference the *term of discernment* (C). What is the issue that discernment takes up and resolves with regard to the principle? Call this the *term of issue* (B).

In this spirit, we now review the distinctions we have collected in the course of our study in an exercise intended to go through, in a summary fashion, the ideas we have learned by heart pertaining to the distinction of human being in light of the insight that this distinction is and remains our ΛΟΓΟΣ understood not merely as *reason* but also and above all as *language*, whether it be in the form of scripture or lecture. I give you therefore, at long last, our official definition of human being – a mortal living being endowed with language.

160. Gymnasia

Step back, step up, step forward – three commands and ways of saying what, among all other beings in heaven and on earth, *human* being alone can do, is destined to do again and again and never to be done with. That is why we call the accomplishment of these imperatives the unique *distinction of human being*. We *step back* when we have our doubts, when we want to get an overview and see the whole picture, to consider all our options, like the painter putting down the brush for a moment to step back from the canvas. What still needs to be done? Is it the way it should be or not? Hmm…this spot needs some color; and that shape isn't quite right yet. I don't know what to do about this line. I'll have to come back to it later – step back and you interrupt the flow, the to and fro, of instinctual immediacy, the mere mechanics of action and reaction, and give some thought to the matter before proceeding. Of course, you can step back from the gambling table and cut your losses. You can step back and go for a walk before making a decision, take some air, clear your head; occasionally, we need, we give, space to someone. But clearly it is not the physical sense of decreasing proximity to something that we mean. When we step back in a philosophical sense, we call into question what only just a moment before was being taken for granted, accepted as inevitable. During that stretch of time before we stepped back, in that state of engagement and confluence with the world prior to the disengagement that was to follow, neither the *world* nor our *engagement* were at issue. We were busy, engrossed, occupied. It is only when we interrupt our business that aspects and perspectives of the overall situation come into view. Only now, after stepping back from the immersion of your rapt attention, do you attain the standpoint of relationship with what is going on around you and actually *see* what you are doing and have been doing. Why *see*? Was I blind before I stepped back? No, of course not, not *literally*. But you were occupied with and intent on what you were doing. You were one with your work, trapped in the close quarters of the urgency of your efforts and in this figurative sense "blind," oblivious to what extends beyond the horizon of that enterprise. Stepping back, you realize that you were blind then, but now you see. And you also realize that, in some ways, in some situations it is better to be blind and to go with the flow in which all you touch and all you see is all your life will ever be.

Stepping up, stepping forth are terms that work in a similar way – their prepositions suggest further ways of experiencing the distinction of human being in our everyday life. We step up leaving inaction, whether out of complacence or of fear, behind and take upon ourselves a burden, opt to face a challenge that puts us to the test; stepping up to the plate, failure might thrice strike us down but we also might succeed in our run for home. We have entered the field of contest, have put ourselves in harm's way and now, in this arena of decision, we must prove ourselves with regard to our excellence even as we must when we step forth from snug obscurity and now stand out and at the center of attention; and there on the stage, in the limelight, we undergo, exposed and vulnerable, the ordeal, the jeopardy, of public judgment. But its sentence is not only the appraisal of prior action but also the starting point and the envisioned end point of a renewed, a revived engagement.

When stepping up or stepping forth, the outcome of the venture we have taken upon ourselves is uncertain. Leaving behind the security of what is within our power to control, the seat of our mastery, the castle of our privacy, the establishment founded upon former successes – departing from the immunity of these our fortresses and last resorts, where do we go? The line of reasoning introduced by the term *step* suggests such notions as *leaving* and *departing from* as well as *going to, arriving at* and then *entering*. Obviously our experience of the distinction of human being can also be put in different terms, ones that need not suggest progression to or from a place. But given the terms we are considering now, the notion of a place is indeed illuminating. When we take a step back, we are now at a different place than we were before. If we were first inside, within a place, we are now outside; if the point of departure is outside, we end up inside.

In the both cases, if the term *place* refers to where we were before thought took its toll of difference, the mediated final position is not a *place* in the same sense as the initial one was. Then to step *back, up,* or *forth,* to step *aside* or *down* or even *in,* every ingress or exit, is to leave behind that spot that was our place and to attain to a standpoint of what is now, with respect to that jumping-off point, pure and simple negativity, no-place, no-where. This "utopian" formula for *where we are* when we reflect critically upon what we are doing, this designation for the space (and the time) we need to figure things out, is merely (but why "merely" and not, rather, "illuminatingly) a *manner of speaking* about the difference that thought makes, about our experience with reflection. It is a *language*, the inception of a mythology that could be and, by poets and prophets, has been greatly elaborated upon in the past. But that is not to say that word choice is arbitrary or that it is only a question of style. On the contrary. A writer's diction, a speaker's elocution is revelatory. Letters, speech, are, as we have seen, the very element of ΛΟΓΟΣ. And since it would seem to make a big difference, indeed all the difference in the world, how we put the matter, let's try putting it in a way that conveys precisely how stepping back from the *status quo* – a further elaboration of that term – enriches our experience and our understanding of the issue of thought. Thus we say, as we have often said in the course of our study, that our standpoint is now *outside*, *above*, *beyond*, *beneath* that place we inhabited before we got to thinking and if the term *standpoint* sounds too much like a place akin to the initial spot we had just left, then we will have to find another term – perhaps the term *coign of vantage* will do, though it also suggests a *position*. It is as if, in order to do justice to this experience, we have decided to restrict the use of words connoting *place* to refer only to our previous location, namely where we were while going with the flow, and are now at a loss for terms to designate "where" we are when thinking. Now why would we decide that? Simply because the "logic" of the language we have been employing to describe the experience of the distinction of human being compels us to do so – the term *stepping back* suggests that after taking this fateful step, you are "somewhere else" or "in some other place" than you were before. *Somewhere* else or, better, somewhere *else*? *Outside*, *above*, *about*, *across*, *beyond*, *beneath*, *behind*, *between* – in some other place, places of *pre*position, of being *before*. These terms put us somewhere – we are *outdoors* in the forest, say, or in the bright sunlight, in the fresh air, but also out of it, left out, left back, left behind, in left field, out in the rain, at the mercy of the elements, in the wild, unprotected by the four walls of our three hots and a cot, vagrant, without. Notice how these connotations reflect back on the experience of the *indoors*? Someone is speaking who doesn't like the idea of going out – we understand: The speaker doesn't like the idea of thinking. For this person being "indoors" means being safe, protected, home. This person has a problem with ΛΟΓΟΣ. Indeed, the same terms also suggest obscurity and domesticated stuffiness of what has become tamed and homely – there are plenty of derogatory things we could say about being *inside* and just as much to disparage about being *outside* – for some, being at home means being in a coma, being tame, lame, stuck in a rut. Aha! You who use these terms to disparage the *inside* which, of course – no less than the term *outside* – can also be a term of distinction, why are you afraid of thought? You, the idler, the rambler – each to each the *other* and the other's other. For it is the one-sidedness constantly threatening discrimination that perverts the domesticated bliss of what is docile in its tractability into what is fawningly and insipidly submissive and similarly intransigent extremism easily distorts the unsullied purity of nature into the unmitigated savagery of the wild at heart and the encroaching, the broaching of the weird. For this reason, both the terms OUTSIDE and INSIDE can be terms of distinction in the dialogue with their interlocutor who, in turn, can resist and, with censorious designations, condemn the difference that the other makes. That is why, taking the former as the term of distinction, we show the difference that the *outside* makes in a positive light and collect the terms intended to belittle this experience of the *outer* as referring to the arguments of those who rebuff the critical distinction made by stepping back.

Or say *above* and fling yourself into the sky; now you are on high, amongst the stars or in the clouds, or, higher still, in Heaven. What? You say, there is no such place as Heaven? Quite right. *Heaven* is a term of distinction to name the difference that critical reflection makes. The great *beyond*, profundity of depth *beneath* the superficiality of faces and facades, that of the sad man, the bad man *behind* blue eyes. Thus whether dubbed *extraterrestrial flight* or *subterranean plunge*, *outer space* or *infernal core*, the necessities of speech, the particular logic of a narrative, the craft and art of thought, the Builder, have always imputed distinctive appellatives – autonymic epithets, dissimulating aliases or titles of respect and address, to this nowhere land, even going so far as to invest it with a nowhere man of whose spirit this realm partakes as does a body of the sovereign will that gives it purposeful life somewhere in particular. For this distinguished place can be, by the license of mythopoetic reason, dubbed a *dwelling*, call it a governed *realm*, a regent's *region*, a *house* and his lady, a *land* and its lord. And then, pursuing this line of reason further, is not a king the head of the *people?* His is not just the conquered territory of the empire he has founded but rather a people who are the members of that principle's body. Thus, by this line of reasoning in accordance with which we have dubbed the *outside*, which has remained the issue of our meditations throughout, we have specified the notion of a foreign *land* to refer to a *dominion*, a *populace* of subjects to that monarchy and then even a republican *commonwealth*. Is this train of thought farfetched? Is it farfetched to call a commonwealth (the "common good") a *land* and mean not the *tracts* and *plots* of its provinces but rather the State of Freedom, the Kingdom of God, the City of Fatherland that define the *dwelling* of distinguished human being as Citizen, Saint, and Hero? And suddenly the empty "utopia" of a distinguished place that is *no place, nowhere* – perhaps it's simply that fabled place the name of which we don't care to remember – has revealed itself to be, when we simply follow the exigencies, or just the opportunities, of mythological language as they present themselves to our elaborations of the idea in question, pretty damn full. But this entire world complete with royal personages, people, castles and humble abodes, fields that dapple the land, sparkling streams that chuckle and water the crops and the livestock of its sustenance, to say nothing of the dramatic narratives we could now invent to perform upon the stage thus set, this *other* place, we have thus set up as *athwart*, this entire "world" beyond or above or behind or beneath the world, this extra- or netherworld, is a figment of this *no*-place, a *non*-world, is pure productive negativity, namely that founded alone and first in the element of language, of the ΛΟΓΟΣ.

Perhaps instead of going on and on about the non-places, the "utopian" Ө and Ø-spaces that critical reflection engenders, we could have or should have noted this "negativity" more simply and concisely with the famous philosophical device known as *sous rature* (under erasure), deleting even while positing names for the *no*where. But there are many other erotetic devices that the typewriter offers us to mark designations as terms of distinctions, as crested terms, like italics, quotation marks, parenthesis and capitalization. Throughout this study, we have frequently made use of them. Thus, as opposed to the world (another good name for a place, namely the place containing all places, itself included) in which we are so stressfully engaged even to the detriment of all critical questioning of the effectiveness of what we are doing, we might posit, the ~~world~~, or the *world*, "world," [world], World, WORLD or even, ꜚworldꜚ, using the little-known irony mark. Are these orthographic strategies of punctuation, as opposed to the use of distinguishing, often negative, prefixes *nether-* or *other-* etc., to mark a name as a term of distinction, better than writing *nether*world or *other*world? Or, if the world of immediacy is called the *natural* world, is it better to write ~~natural~~ (*natural*, "natural," [natural], Natural, NATURAL, ꜚnaturalꜚ) world than to use the perfectly good word *super*natural or *preter*natural to designate the world of distinction? The same question could be asked about such terms as *sur*real, *meta*physic, *a*normal, *al*ētheia. If for some reason you frown upon the word *supernatural*, then how about drawing the distinction with a capital letter or letters and write *World* or WORLD as opposed to *world*. That's all there is to it. In the case of crossing out the word (rather than just erasing or, worse, just deleting it and thereby utterly revoking the distinction), you are marking the difference graphemically, in the other cases morphologically. Yes, I see: The strategy of crossing out offered by the *rature* as a graphical element does seem to breach the linguistic level of the grapheme and thus depart from verbal language in a strict sense, doesn't it? In that sense, it is a more dramatic, a more "graphic" rendition of "negativity;" *language* itself is negated by an *image* of negation. Well, OK, that is an argument, I suppose. Clearly, *when speaking*, we would have to use some sort of paralinguistic or even non-verbal mark to distinguish these notions – ~~real~~ or NORMAL or "natural" from their unmarked counterpart, a conspiratorial wink, say.

But wherefore this reluctance to use the term *supernatural*? Because that means "something else!" Really? Maybe the problem simply lies with this term's "esoteric" connotations. Indeed. But why doesn't a word's meanings, as numinous as they are numerous, add to the richness of the idea we are studying? Why do they detract? I always thought that what words "mean" depends on how you use them, depends on who is speaking and to whom and why and when and where and especially what about. Doesn't the experience we are referring to with this word bestow upon it a newfound dignity, redeeming it, as it were, from the ignominy of its banishment in the haunted houses of horror shows? And then, in light of this train of thought, even these shows acquire an unexpected sense; we might do well to ask what do ghosts and ghouls and haunted houses tell us about the distinction of human being and about ourselves if our experience of it can be rehearsed in images of horror, witnessed as the night or dawn of the living, the walking dead?

Oh my God, where have we ended up, that our train of thought be thus upended? We began in all innocence with the notion of stepping back to gain an overview by adopting a position or standpoint from above or outside our mundane habitats and ended in the supernatural sphere with all the accoutrements you would expect of underworldly hideousness. Again, this standpoint of reflection, no less infernal than supernal, is not located anywhere, it is thus the standpoint beyond every standpoint or, simply, the ~~standpoint~~; but honestly isn't the erasure a tame representation of drawing a distinction when we might contemplate blood-curdling *Hell* instead? Clearly, we have broached the topic of the mythology of alterity once again. But we will save its elaboration for a later study.

Instead, let us take up a new line of reasoning in the conclusion of our current one. If the poetic sense of using the expression *stepping back* is simply to mark the opening that cracks when we step back from the closeness of lived immediacy, perhaps the term *space*, the final frontier, is indeed preferable to *place* (i.e. ~~place~~) referring as it does to the edge or the step just beyond the *settlement*, the settlement of *familiarity*, the familiarity of *unity*, the unity of *identity* – a series of terms we might employ disparagingly to highlight unthinking confluence as the consanguineous homogeneity, conformity, and uniformity that predominates as a principle when the drawing of distinctions is frowned upon. In this perspective, the emptiness of the open space around the closed sphere brings to the fore of our attention the limit, the outlying district, the purlieu of a place rather than the non-place. The outskirts are the edge, the limit of our lodgment. It is therefore no longer, or perhaps not yet, a question of attaining to the supernatural standpoint opposite the "natural" one that is at issue when, in a harrowing moment of critical reflection, chronic normalcy ceases to be taken for granted, but rather of passing beyond the border that marks the end of our fixed intimacy and the start of something new, something rich and strange. This would be a different version of our experience with the distinction in question – not a *stepping back* at all but rather the crossing and surpassing of a threshold on the way out. The steps we take here lead us *away* not *back* in service to the sea change we are in a position to make after we have gained an overview and enjoyed our moment of reflection poised above the fray into which we subsequently throw ourselves again with the verve of new-found resolution and purpose.

The issue and the experience of the distinction of human being as the *passage* has seen a rich elaboration in the languages of wisdom we have encountered thus far. A distinguished wall is one with a door or a gate through which we pass on the way out or on the way in. What we encounter on the other side is, however, the emptiness, be it the barren gleam of a vast and desert expanse, be it the shadowy realm of an abysmal underworld. These names are distinctly pejorative. They suggest that their speaker is located *this side* of the frontier in question, perhaps contemplating, hesitatingly, the crossing of the limit on the fringe that marks the encroaching estrangement of *borderland*. For our True Man, one of the inhabitants of sunny, civilized, sensible Seehaven, such a departure from its temperate well-being must be counted as a venture of digression, more, a *transgression* into the deviation of eyeless darkness and the hellish wilderness of aberrancy, absurdity, nihilism. For what else could a migration from the hospitable clime of reason and of rhyme into the diffusion of desire's stretch and reach be called as it surpasses all bounds and deforms into the immensity of an illimitable extremity. And nevertheless, the bold endeavorer, committed to debunking all hunkering down, would speak in her own words not of transgression but rather of transcendence and the experience of a heart going out to a being (a ~~being~~) of absolute lack, the being without, the pure, shifting sans of the desert.

To be *Without* – now that is an interesting expression, isn't it? Not only does it fit in the context as being distinguished from what is within, but more importantly, it opens a wide field of senses that enriches the notion of being outside of the (everyday) world. For *being without* implies *lacking* or, too, *missing*; it is to be *bereft, divested of, cut off from*. Thus according to this line of reasoning as proposed by the terms we are using, to step beyond connotes, insofar as this step is a *step away from* and finally a *step out of* the flowing immediacy of our engrossed engagement, an experience of the *bereavement* and *dispossession* of *being without*. The emptiness of a *being without* further elaborates the vision of severance beheld in the notion of *space* into that of the *breach* between the real and the imaginary, the possible and the impossible, the IS and the OUGHT, the measure and the incommensurably immense. Subsuming all there is in heaven and in earth, everything under the sun, all being, under one of these former terms of the pairs mentioned, including our own lives and cares and concerns, our past and present ideas and experiences, everything that I call *me* or *you* or *it*, what's left? Only this: The *separation* from this totality, from all of these calculable totalities that it is the infinite distinction of human being not only to experience as a perpetual parting, but, moreover, in person *to be*. Now, take this separation and find terms that will render it more tangible by placing it, with the help of language, into contexts of lived experience and note how we, in this way, bring our distinction, thus conceived of, into focus. Call us, for example, *beings without* and see where this designation will lead us.

Look! We see upon the stage of language, the allegory of the *refugee* fleeing from a war-torn world, uprooted from her earth of birth, deprived of the sheltering roof of hope, exposed to inimical elements, bare, cold, hungry; this being without is a vision of separation. It is a manner of speaking about the experience we have been investigating. If the IS and the OUGHT diverge in a purely physical sense, we have a need. Thus let *need* be a name for this *being without*. And it is recognized in the needy – the *widow*, the *orphan*, the *impoverished*, the *oppressed masses* in general, *this* beggar in particular that we encountered on the street by the market this morning. Is it perhaps Zeus testing our willingness to be addressed by the negativity of need and therefore indicative of our propensity to care about, show cognizance of and regard for that distinction envisioned here as destitution, all insufficiency, that extends *hereafter*, in other words, beyond our gloating zone of comfort and repletion?

Yes, this notion of a *being without* can indeed be imagined as a person; this needy person in front of us is a personification, an incarnation of the discrepancy between THE WAY IT IS and THE WAY IT SHOULD BE, which is, of course, in itself, not a "person" at all but rather a gap, an interruption of continuity, a disparity and a hole in the wholeness and the fullness of our lightly living being. It is the negativity of the ΛΟΓΟΣ that allows us to take the last step and then the first step and thereby attain to the coign of vantage that critical reflection provides us who have crossed the border from Man's into No Man's Land where, as we saw, the citizen, the saint, and the hero dwell in their own proper place (that is *no place*); is there no one word for their place, for this place's people? Call it neither place, nor person, call it a discrete movement, a *step* – one we take or refuse to take but even in our omission, our refusal, inevitably put into practice such that we cannot *not* think but only refuse to think about thought and thus even in a denial that merely divorces action from insight, to unwittingly act out that very negativity that is thought's crest and cognizance. For *thought*, our thinking being, is indeed something *and* nothing (*no thing*) – we can contemplate both, think about them and talk about them in talk that we might then, subsequently, walk as well. Say *step* to introduce a movement and to offer to our reflection the topographical terms we have been studying thought in because the different lines of reasoning that language provides – an example of which is the topographical one we have been considering – greatly enrich our experience *and* our expression of this distinction; exalting it as a towering pinnacle and an unearthly height, fathoming it as profundity and depth, we become articulate, we can elaborate.

Similarly, if transcendence is a crossing, it is not only the journey to outward desolation of need but also to the inward urgency of want. We saw this in the proem to Parmenides' contemplation; his fated way, guided by sun-maidens, was a driven passage into darkness through the gate that separates Night and Day and now you would do well to ask, first, how a mission of light could lead us to the shadows of seclusion, and second, how our arrival in the abodes of darkness could be met with the benediction of a "welcome!" Light leads us to a darkness that is our enlightenment about being; we leave the ways of the world behind and learn in the infinite separation beyond all mere being about our entity of identity – the just being bound to be what it is destined to be, namely *perfect.* Meet a perfection that deigns to welcome the person of absolute distinction as one destined to know and to be known, to be welcomed by it in the seclusion of its ownmost dwelling that is the reflective identity of host and guest! In this line of reasoning, after the outward and the inward opening, after the *goodbye* and good riddance of those who go and stay behind, beyond, beneath, etc. in the opposing senses of these terms, as either terms of immediacy or terms of distinction, the negativity of severance can also be understood as the *hello* of hospitality.

For the *being without* returns from that abstraction to enter our world as a visitor from abroad speaking a foreign tongue, reminding us of the native language we once had spoken amongst ourselves and are now called upon by that voice from abroad to relearn. The stranger comes to call, the outside is seen here as he, she, it impinges upon the homeostasis of the body, disturbing the delicate calibration of our balances and exchanges, discombobulating the settings of the system, provoking perhaps an allergic reaction to the foreign invader or just to an importunate suppliant whose entreaties require a response on the part of the one to whom the petition is directed. This responsiveness is an opening of the house to the needs of the guest. Thus we recognize the notion of distinction in the entrance of the stranger into our midst, in the person of the stranger having arrived, in the coming of the stranger to our doors, in the vagrant life of exile he spent abroad, in the exit and the exodus of those who have left their home and the lake of their home for the sake of an adventure of distinction, that fortune of human being we are destined to seek in the fabled city that never sleeps.

For human being is born to run. We are born to question and raise doubts about THE WAY IT IS. We are born to check our impulses and impede, interrupt the flow of how things go. Thought is this break in the routine, our capacity to suddenly, unexpectedly take note of and put forth for consideration and reconsideration what had long been decided or assumed. Nothing in this world is safe from thought if *thought* means not merely this or that particular thought, a thought about this or that or the other thing, but rather if thought means, first and above all, the capacity and the accomplishment of attaining a relationship of difference that draws a line, makes a break in the continuity and the uniformity of...of what? Of Sartre's *practico-inert*? Or simply say, of whatever is an oh so seamlessly coherent whole, makes a face of unvarying permanence, maintains a monotony of consonance, asserts a texture of blithe conformity, sports a smooth surface of regularity, vaunts a viscous consistency, fetes its insensitive solidity, its callosity, its crassitude – for that is what opposition to openness and responsiveness leads to, namely to the petrified world of blockheads, numbskulls, hard hearts and the entire jar of tough cookies so adept at repulsion and exclusion, our stone-hard material girls and boys. I guess that is what happens to unity when it becomes transfixed, monolithic, and xenophobic in dealing with overtures from abroad, namely by immobilizing, tranquilizing, domesticating, colonizing, appropriating, assimilating distinctions. But, of course, unity need not be thought of as a palsy inimical to difference – we have seen how the *entity of identity* participates in a relationship of relationships, a rapport of them, in accordance with which the whole story of our experience with the distinction of human being is told, a narrative comprehending not only the dramatic negativity and the patient receptivity of thought thinking thought – that unwavering fidelity towards the eventual visitation of difference – but also recognizing the solidarity and the affirmation of the issue of thought in a community founded and then poetically built upon the principles of proportionate harmony, divine love, and human kindness. That is the *whole* story. We want to know the *whole* truth and anything less is clearly not enough.

In studying late/modern discourse upon difference, we must always seek to keep in mind that it is precisely the incompleteness of the story, of any story, that most vividly renders the self-severalty of thought. This is, for its thinkers and poets, the whole issue in question, the *hole* issue. Yeah, funny, I think we got it by now! But in the scheme of all things thought, this thought is just one more thought about thought where it finds and deserves its rightful place. For even the absolute power to refuse, to deny, to call into question, can, in the end, be called into question, becoming *a* thought rather than thought itself, which is a line of reasoning and a *train* of thoughts, a chain of truths, several, and never just one. Isn't that, isn't turn *and* return, isn't the *plurality* of principles, the whole message of late/modern thought?

Thus, again, this *being without*, if we should want to call it that provisionally, is clearly no *being* by any stretch of the imagination. And if it unexpectedly does turn out to be some sort of being, then we would do well to mark it as ~~being~~ (*being*, "being," [being], Being, BEING) surely a better way of designating it than putting names like *nothingness, nullity, nihility, non*-entity. But still not a very good way. Hardly better are such titles of grandeur as the *Great Beyond*, the *Hereafter*, the *Infinite*, the *Sempiternal*, the *Unknown* unless they are put into the context of a train of thought where they might serve the building of insight in a particular occasion of speech practice. Generally more powerful are such designations that avoid the mere morphemic or graphemic (or graphical) markings of a word as distinguished. Now we must search for names that stand for this being without. Thus, as we saw, we might, following one particular tradition, name it the *stranger*, the *orphan*, the *widow*, the *invalid*, the *impoverished*.

For these are beings of indigence.[85] Their necessitousness imposes upon us an obligation. And it is this appointment of and resulting commitment to *duty* that, with the advent of its compulsion and custody, invades and intrudes upon the entrenched apathy of our formerly so carefree, careless state.

The problem is that the *negativity* inherent in making a distinction is more a doing than a being – stepping back, *transcendence* in the different senses we have considered. That is why the term "negativity" for the work of drawing a distinction is, ultimately, misleading, if not downright fallacious. For actually we mean to say *passage*, the experience of crossing a limit, *departure*, the experience of leaving behind or being left behind – all right, say simply *death* – *divergence* from an established rule, *deviation* from the system of norms, the *diversity* that obtains in a state of *disparity* and *heterogeneity* – what a great many connotations do these names provide, not all good by any means! And what would the notion of ΛΟΓΟΣ, of our ability, our destiny to *step back* in critical reflection be without them, without the richness and the concrete reality that language conveys upon this idea that is otherwise so entirely familiar to folks, so completely obvious to even the most casual thinker, so banal in a complex and busy world, that it hardly seems worth mentioning, let alone living for and tirelessly praising the glory of in our every word and our every deed as the greatest, in truth, the one and only *essential* distinction of human being? Apparently, this thought, this thought about thought, needs the building of mythopoetic language, needs thought, the Builder to amount to anything in our eyes. Perhaps that is what makes it such a fascinating thought. It seems to be something we all know until we start to think about it and write about it and read about it and then the more we think and write and read about it, the more we come to understand and appreciate it, the more we discover that we don't really know it, don't really understand it at all; but then again, the less we find we know about it the more we discover we learn about it, knowing less and less about thought, we come to know more and more about what we actually knew all along but have never truly *known*. Hence

---

[85] Theirs are the "visages of the *Other*." As Lévinas proposes in *Totalité et Infini*, (p. 76): "It is in the rendering of the being without as the poor stranger...that the Transcendent, the infinitely Other, addresses us...; its epiphany solicits us through its misery in the visage of the stranger, the widow, or the orphan." (*Poser le transcendant comme étranger et pauvre, c'est...là que le Transcendant, infiniment Autre, nous sollicite...son épiphanie même consiste à nous solliciter par sa misère dans le visage de l'Etranger, de la veuve ou de l'orphelin.*)

in a world full of closed mysteries regarding why things are the way they are, thought is the one and only *open* mystery. It is the inaugural wonder that folks do indeed wonder about things, amazingly do indeed ask both why *and* why not. They can and often do. And this makes all the difference in the world.

Thus, take the distinction that we have been discussing throughout our study and now put names for it, the first name for it being, apparently, *IT*. It is perhaps not a very enlightening name but thinkers have profitably used this name before; has Freud's "Es" (it), translated by the Latin *id*, not had an illustrious career? This name has the advantage of being impersonal. Call it the IMPERSONAL against the narcissism of Man whose scope remains up close and personal. But should our distinction as the *Impersonal* be therefore thought of as the INHUMAN even though it can be? The distinction of human being is the distinction of being HUMAN against all rampant inhumanity, whether bestial or bureaucratic, whether that of being merely an animal or merely a number, a calculable figure of rationalization. It is a distinction that locates our place in the scheme of things as beings possessed of ΛΟΓΟΣ like the gods and yet also possessed of mortal life like the animals.

Another advantage of IT is its being neuter, neither masculine, nor feminine; we have thought of calling the distinction of human being HE or SHE, each being the other's other with respect to which it is the term of distinction – call it *he*, impartial objectivity, when the term of immediacy is the *she* of biased subjectivity; inversely, call it *she* as the term of distinction when the feminine is compassion and kindness against the backdrop of masculine detachment and insensitivity. *It* is, however, distinguished as *neither* the one *nor* the other of the two extremes but rather their measure. Call it therefore the NEUTER. But isn't to call "it" the neuter to castrate it and to make it barren? Could our distinction be a mutilated, an emasculated, an infertile being? Hardly. Though there is something to be said for it as sexless, I suppose, when the distinction of human being distinguishes us from the superficial determinations of birth, breeding, and rearing as well its sibling notions, namely race, gender, age, appearance, nationality, political affiliation, social status, and religion, while arguing for, instead, an upbringing and study that builds our human being according to the culture of freedom. For against such immediate differences among humans, we have learned to distinguish our *humanity* which is natural and "neutral" when compared to the Man-made valuations and biases of custom, culture, and convention. This being is what is left after having subtracted from ourselves the aforementioned physical, social, national, and traditional traits with which folks tend to define themselves and others until they have become acquainted with the idea of freedom which proposes that after eliminating these accidental differences, there remains the essential one, the nature of *self*-several human being, the "supernature" and the culture i.e. the *culture*, "culture,"[culture], Culture, CULTURE, ~~culture~~ – both a being *and* a becoming – that is above and beyond, in this case, *before* and *prior to* all culture. Further, this nature (*nature*, "nature," [nature], Nature, NATURE, ~~nature~~), our *human* ("human," [human], Human, HUMAN, ~~human~~) being, locates it in the collection of natures comprising the vast but no less well-ordered *cosmos* of beings in which every one participates and to which each contributes in accordance with the excellence determined by that being's unique power and ability, an order not commanded or determined by any member of the whole, not even by the first among them, who presides and is vested with the greatest power and authority of all, but rather predetermined in the proportions in which the multitude of individuals have always already consisted, since the birth of time itself, i.e. since the birth of the life and times of the gods upon which the first well-formed community and cosmos, that of the gods' themselves, was founded by a truly Jovial sight, namely that half is more than the whole. The constituents of this whole remain distinct, each governing their own sphere, their own form, the contours and extent of which are limited only by the domains in which the others reign supreme in their own right, all deferring to the justice of the foreordained proportions (MOIPA) that guarantee the overall justness of just being.

Thus in addition to the name "it," which brings out the neutrality and fairness, the principle of just being – beyond the urgings of bias in favor of momentary and particular ends – that we made our acquaintance with as the distinction of human being, known and recollected by the Homeric Muse in the Olympic cosmos of proportions, the Moira, as the way it was meant to be, we have also considered the sense of this distinction as the *I* – this term brings the question of distinction home to Man. For what could be more up close and personal than I AM to myself? The objectivity of what is detached from my own personal preferences is, in fact, my own subjectivity, is Me, my better, greater Me, the general Me to which I, that man in the mirror, may forge a rapport of regard in a bid to change his ways. For this reason, it makes sense and even sounds right to say that I am not free unless I am ME, this being that I was actually meant, destined, to be, namely free from myself in order to develop Me who I really and truly AM/IS, but from whom, alas, I tend(s) to fall off in the mini-ego's bid at illimitability, whose one-sided and single-minded reign is as inflationary as it is inflammatory. Thus when we usually say *I*, we do not refer to the distinguished Me but to ourselves as immediate individuals apart from any Me of greater, of Archimedean purchase, My identity, namely, that is not just who I am/is privately, locally, here and now, comfortable or uncomfortable in my skin, but who is, instead, that of the general will, whose choice today, here, now, for Me, decides for all time, in all place, for all people.

If that is confusing consider how confusing it gets when we name the distinction YOU who is/are neither here, the partner in my heart, my conscience, say, nor in front of me as are objects of contemplation whose properties I might study at my leisure and place in relationship to the intellect and to one another. *You,* neither subject of freedom nor predetermined object of objectivity, YOU are/is not *here,* neither with me as only I am to MYSELF, the distinction who I AM to myself, nor *there* as are other beings around me, whether they be *person, place,* or *thing. You* are neither here, in the first person, nor there in the third, neither *thought* nor *thing,* neither Humanity nor Entity. Perhaps we might call you, now in a different sense than before, the *Neutral.* But what a horrid name that would be, wouldn't it? No, let us strive to do better, let us call you *Pure Difference, Your Significance,* the *Name of absolute Distinction.* Traditionally of course, this name was *God,* not *a* god, i.e. one god among many or one all alone, which makes the Absolute Distinction an entity among others, one or the other, a thought or a thing, whether it is defined positively as *some*thing or negatively as *no*thing (*thing,* "thing," [thing], Thing, THING, ~~thing~~). It is neither the one nor the other, neither ontological, nor epistemological, as we have seen. It is neither real nor ideal. Well, but what's left? The only thing that is left for it to be is this very difference between them, this gap that emerges when we put *self-knowing being* with its sentiments and values on one side and *just being* with its properties and substances on the other.

Neither a figment of the imagination nor a matter of fact, who are you, *Your Significance? YOU* is another designation for the distinction that we have just called *I* and, in the beginning of this exercise, *IT.* Are/Is You the *gentle reader?* Yes, if You hear(s) my Word as that of Your Father in Heaven; no, if you are just reading these words on this page at the end of rather long book about the distinction of human being. For the GENTLE READER of our words hears our pleas and prayer to be uplifted who have been wretched, saved from the mundane world of dispirited body beings; in the turnaround of our You-turn, You hear our glorification of His glory; turning to You, to Him, You turn to our cries of lament and trusting in Your consolation, we are consoled; lifting our faces to You, we are uplifted by Him who was laid low, humiliated, execrated in Your Name unto ignoble death of darkness that is, in fact, a renewed and illuminated life and in this dawning knowledge of You, in the Holy Spirit thus given through this experience of the self-severalty of human being and divine, divine being and human, we are known by Him who is Your Father and by You, his Son, who, in charity, is one with the Father such that we who love You are, in Love, one with all those upon whom, with this distinction of the ΛΟΓΟΣ that was God, You bestowed the destiny to be Children of God, brothers and sisters of Him who became flesh and lived in us, among us, only to die and to be resurrected in Your name as the Savior of the World.

Say "*you*" and, if nobody else is around, you will probably have the feeling you are talking to yourself. But let go of this *you* that, oddly, you believe you are calling yourself, taking it into possession as your own. No, when you say *you*, it is not you personally that you mean. After all, why would you say "you" to yourself instead of "I" to "me." The "me" that you normally mean is just your little old *me*, your private property as distinguished from the big I of your liberty to which you, as *its* property, properly, rightfully belong; we are not talking about It now. No, say "You" and reach outward from yourself with it, leaving yourself behind. "You," said thus, does not refer to somebody who happens to be in your vicinity at the moment. Say "you" and mean nobody in particular but also nobody in general – no objective *being*. Say "you" to mean *not* you personally or any other person nearby – no subjective *I*, but rather to mean YOU, in other words, to mean ~~you~~. For it is the distinction from yourself, the Absolute Distinction itself, that you mean to address when you say "you" and in so doing, move out of yourself into the *open*, with these words opening yourself to what you are most assuredly not, namely the Absolute Other. That is unique about the speech situation. I, the speaker, or the writer, can talk (or write) about this or that, having given matters some thought. The subject of the speech is both the knowledge *and* the known, the speaker *and* the topic of my speech. We are united in my speech to the extent that I am committed to stating truthfully what I know. The audience, however, is on the other side of this logical space, across the divide on the other side of the room, out there, listening. Standing up in front of the audience, I am on the stage of distinction, before them, before their eyes, having left the indeterminacy of holding my peace, safe and sound in my seat and step forth, now exposed and vulnerable, to the ordeal of judgment and the patience that awaits an answer confirming that I have been heard, known, judged. For the speaker, "you" is/are the listener, for the audience, the speaker. In both cases, it is the destiny of human being to address the distinction in the openness of the ΛΟΓΟΣ, the Word, in which I most completely experience my detachment from myself

– not in the subjectivity of knowledge, nor in the objectivity of what has come to be known, but rather in the interval of difference I affirm in recognizing the distinction of the one I address from all I have known and from all I intend to possess as my own. Say "you" and experience the irreducible present of difference, the distance from myself that expands outwardly beyond every domain – whether it be *mine, ours,* or *theirs* – that is, in this way, acknowledged, even celebrated, by an opened mind, a mind open for a different view…and nothing else matters.

Hence, the term *You* invokes the relationship of absolute difference; first let it be the distinguished Me that I am destined to be, the free Me and then, emancipating this your supposed property, let it be not your Me, but rather You, call it *the Lord, my God* (the *my* is a reminder of the Me I just was); in other words say YOU to ME, letting go of ME and turning to YOU. Do you dare? For now, in the order of the ΛΟΓΟΣ of the Cross, there is no *ME* except *Jesus Christ, the Lord* and no *YOU* except the Father in Heaven and no IT except God who is nevertheless both *You* and *I* and never actually an *It* unless we mean to refer to the absolute distinction that God is the principle of in terms of the Second Epoch – surely all of this is just nonsense unless we already know what we are talking about, unless, that is, these words are spoken in the Holy Spirit that is the distinction of human being in the transformative language of Christianity.

The perceptive *IT* – the ingenious *I* – the benevolent *YOU* – such is the train of thought we have been elaborating, each pronoun serving as a term of distinction for a corresponding principle of which there are three: *Destiny* (A), *Humanity* (B), and *Deity* (C). We have become acquainted with their respective languages and have tried our hand, though haltingly, at speaking them and at construing them, following their several lines of reasoning as each identifies its proper principle in the scheme of all things thought and delineates a ratio of three signature terms into which every thought about thought can be articulated in the complex movement that we have, in the work of logotectonic building, highlighted the junctures of while elaborating a plurality of principles, not one, each surpassed by and surpassing the other in pre-eminence, each, by turns, providing and succeeding the other's mark of distinction – fiction and figments (B) bested by truth and facts (A), the conjecture of theoretical speculation (A) vanquished by the gut feeling of practical experience (C), the road paved with good intentions (C) left behind by actual accomplishments of excellence (B) ***and*** a good game talked (B) waiting, wanting to be finally walked (C), a handyman's routine (C) outdone by the crafts and arts of insight's flights (A), the puzzled *why* of perception (A) broadened by the *why not* of imagination (B) – thought in play, as in *Figure 107*:

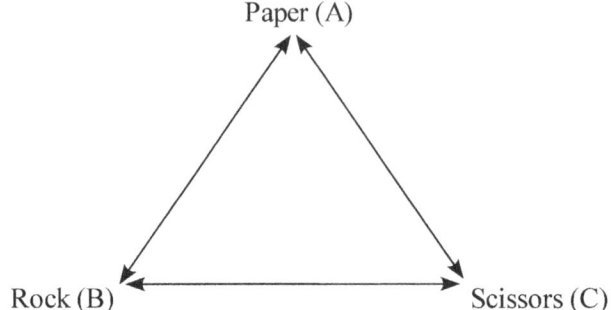

Figure 107: Each Surpassed and Surpassing

Thus in the Homeric world we learn what *destiny* is. The **Portions** are the predetermination of what was meant to be, the order of indication that specifies, in each case, for each being, THE WAY IT SHOULD BE. It is the **Will of Zeus** that the limits defining every being's **Rights** be duly observed and protected. What is right in each particular case, for each particular being, is indeed the issue. But what is right in general and in principle is not. For the answer to the question "why" with regards to what is right is simply this: Because! Or more elaborately: Because that's THE WAY IT IS, always has been, always will be – this principle of the predetermination of *just being* entails a reason based on custom and tradition, on what goes without saying, in other words, what is right is *evident*, at least to any *normal* being, however much the limits defining the scope of each party's authority and the proportion of regard owed by each to each might be contested in a given case, a given *causa*. Zeus, i.e. **Jovial knowledge**, is the principle upon which the **Well-Being** of the Olympic comity is derived. His insight into the principle of the proportionate (and not merely equal) distribution of the good, the goods of the gods; Zeus recognized that it is the proper **Apportionment** of divine regard, wealth, and power among the gods, in contrast to the tradition of their usurpation and exclusion practiced by his father and grandfather, that will found and subsequently preserve the "cosmic" community of immortal as well as mortal being. Moreover, the power of Jovial insight is indeed accessible to our mortal understanding, who are therefore destined to grasp the **Measure** that determines all proper **Proportion** in assuring the perpetuity of human dwelling. This insight is put into practice by the person of **Justice**, who defends the rights of those disenfranchised by the perversion of unjust laws enacted to perpetuate the privileges of the rich and powerful who revel in their unbridled power while shortsightedly disregarding all propriety as is determined by what is and has always already been recognized as THE WAY IT SHOULD BE, destiny's incontestable rule of law.

Opposed to this vision of the distinction of human being as the order and insight of just being, we have learned to recognize the nature and the imagination of humanity, such being, namely, as is determined to be autonomous and, in this sense, absolutely free. In the immediacy of self-evidence, the feeling of freedom – the receptivity of our humanity lending both voice and ear to the pure heart of *Human Nature* – distinguishes the *morality of self-regard* the simple law of which is the certainty of humanity's incorruptible conscience against the perverse sophistication of a narcissistic culture and its instrumental rationality. The collection of individuals who have distinguished themselves as party to the contract of Self-regard form the body politic of which each human being is a member devoted to the preservation of the life and integrity of the whole and every part as citizens dwelling together in the renewed *State of Freedom*. This state, if it is not merely one of necessity but also of joy, can only be attained through an *Aesthetic Education* of the people in which the ideal of *Beauty*, the harmony of the physical and moral natures of human being, are made manifest as the dramatic play of competing forces in which humanity in its totality comes to know itself, distinguish itself, and celebrate itself. This distinguished being of freedom, first a citizen committed to defending the state of freedom, then an actor of autonomous civility who has attained erudition in the play of beauty, is, finally, the person of the *Poet* who is devoted to a consecrating labor of *Poetic Spirit* and whose craft and art consists in giving mature and vivid life to the ideals of freedom and nature through the distinguished, celebratory *Language of Poetry* that alone is able to provide humanity with a dwelling worthy of human nature as free.

Finally, cleaving *neither* to the predetermined positivity of the principle of just being, *nor* to the absolute negativity of the principle of autonomous human being, we turned to the absolute principle of distinction in and of itself – the principle of *stepping back*, of *letting go*. Its "being" is this difference, revealed alone in the experience that makes all the difference in the world, and thus is evident only in the language of consecration and celebration devoted to it as the *Glory of God*. Only by having already departed from the horizon of the mundane and indifferent world and in *Conversion* towards that other principle of a kingdom of Heaven can this distinction be acknowledged as the divine being, one however that, in spite of its remoteness and separation, admits of a narrative depicting the birth, life, and death of this distinction's incarnation, the entire career of our experience with it, i.e. with Him, an experience that is, moreover, validated in these terms as a benediction and ***Confession*** of faith. This confession of the pure, the Holy spirit, transforms human beings and their world with regards to their provenance in a justifying act of ***Faith*** in Christ who embodies the will of God and into whose destiny the faithful are born through faith and in whose death they participate in the experience of the ***Cross*** and the crossing that makes of death the passage to eternal life, of mindless life a living death, in the crucifixion of the latter life a resurrection into the former in which our human being, fallen, is, at the same time, acknowledged as destined to be uplifted to the distinction of Children of God and therein glorified even as the Son of God was humiliated for our sake as the Son of Man in taking upon himself the self-several experience of difference. The community of those thus transformed are the ***Congregation of the Saints*** who preach the word of God throughout the world in a mission of love. The purpose of this mission is the ***Salvation of the World*** in the spirit of the gift of mercy, not merely the condemnation of the world in the apocalypse of justice. This ***Spirit of Glory*** is revealed in works of healing and redeeming – acts of conversion and transformation that testify to the efficacy of the light that came into the world as the illuminating Word of God. Thus we can articulate three unique trains of thought about the distinction of human being relating our experience with this distinction in terms of three irreducible and incommensurable principles. In *Figure 108*, these three lines of reasoning are collected into a single scheme delineating the sheer scope of that distinction.

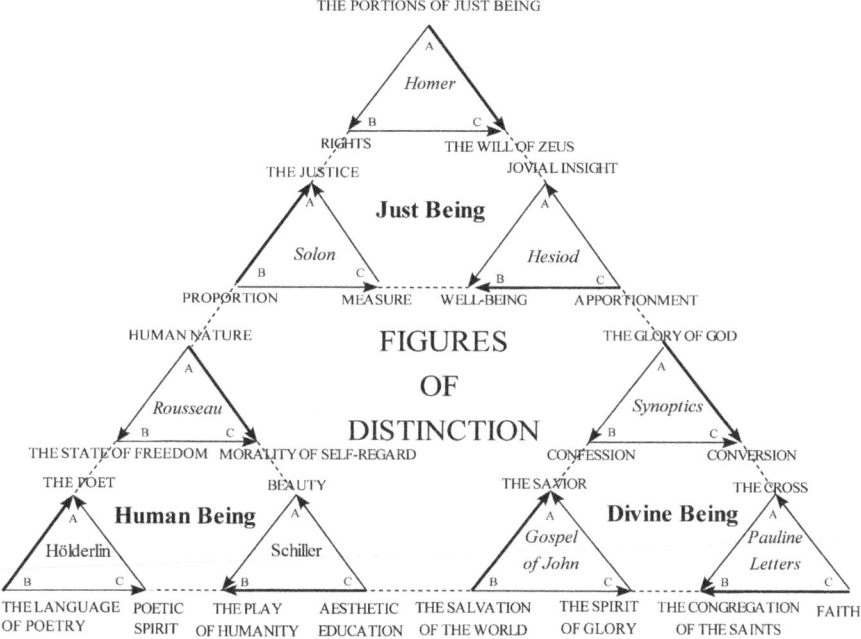

Figure 108: A Plurality of Principles, Not One

And thus, as well, do we gain an overview of the totality of differences that the languages of wisdom have articulated regarding the distinction of human being in the person of the Poet of Nature, the Savior of the World, and the Statesman of Justice. Each was engaged in a work of distinction – the poet of nature celebrated and served the ideal of *Beauty* that nature represented; the Savior took upon himself the transforming ordeal of the *Cross*, the "X" that marks the precise spot where Heaven and earth, human being and divine, touch; the Statesman recognized and defended the invisible measure of apportionment upon which all community is based, namely upon *Zeus's insight* into how much more the half is than the whole. Each language offered us a vision, a mythology of the fulfillment of the respective principle in which its subjects dwell – in *Olympus*, in the *Kingdom of God*, in *Fatherland*. The inhabitants of these places, these places), are thought to be the children of that distinction – outstanding mortal beings of immortal renown, children of glory born of flesh *and* of spirit, builders of a humanity that is both natural *and* moral. Is this not what people are, thus divided in themselves – burdened, crushed but also uplifted, transformed by a self-several destiny?

Three languages, three principles and not just one language and one principle. None of them can be reduced to the other or all three to some overarching concept except in a misguided bid, whether incidentally or purposefully, whether maliciously or benignly, to preempt one in lieu of the others, highlight one at the expense of the others.

Thus, *God* is not "greater" than *Freedom* except in the particular conception of freedom that obtained in the Second Epoch, namely in the sense of the freedom of choice (liberum arbitrium), which is an entirely different notion than the ideal of freedom as the autonomy of human being. Nor is this human being of self-determination identical with the one known in the Greek world, the superlative being of excellence in word and deed.

In the knowledge of the Muses, a human being was one being among many of the same as well as different kinds, Greek as well as Persian, mortal as well as immortal, rational as well as instinctual, follower as well as leader, parent as well as child, woman as well as man, king as well subject, baker as well as physician – each had, in accordance with his or her nature, his or her craft or art, his or her excellence, a rightful place in the ordered whole of all being. Similarly, all the familiar notions that are a philosopher's daily bread have their own proper place in a train of thought thinking thought. For this reason, whenever someone speaks of *right, beauty, God, Man,* etc. our first question must always be: "which *right?*" "which *beauty?*" "which *God?*" "which *Man?*" If there is one thing that we can learn from the tradition of philosophical thought it is that we must begin by acknowledging the incommensurable orders of the distinctions that were made. Trains of thought, ideas, are discrete – severance rather than continuity is their empire, the sheer scope of which, therefore, is both finite *and* infinite.

161. A Cosmos of Words

Du glaubst also im Ernste, das Ideal des Wissens könnte wohl in irgend einer bestimmten Zeit in irgend einem Systeme dargestellt erscheinen, das alle ahndeten, die Wenigsten durchaus erkennten? Du glaubst sogar, dies Ideal sei jetzt schon wirklich geworden, und es fehle zum Jupiter Olympius nichts mehr als das Piedestal? Vielleicht! (Hölderlin, *GSA* IV 213.2-6)

So you seriously believe that the ideal of knowledge could be rendered at a given point in time in a particular system that all have caught sight of, few have gained insight into? In fact, you even believe that the ideal is already real and that the only thing

> *still lacking in the completion of Jupiter's Olympus is the pedestal? Maybe!*

The scheme of all things thought is a harmonious whole of distinctions founded upon a triumvirate of principles. We have examined such a system in this study. Is freedom real? Does God exist? Is the soul immortal? To ask these questions is to place yourself outside of their conception. Where are you? What is your standpoint? Do we know what we are asking if we have departed from the sphere where these questions have been asked and answered once and for all time, *their* time? What do you mean by *reality*, by *existence*, by *being*? Why do you ask? Who wants to know? Or are we just "doing" philosophy? Is asking these questions what philosophers do? Perhaps the study we have conducted suggests, if nothing else, that philosophy can be, philosophers can do, something else, too.

The scheme of all things thought is a work of collection and recollection; it is, as well, the vision of a community, a comity of thoughts, like individuals distinguished in the pride and dignity of their own accomplishments and yet united by the love for what they share, which is, though nothing "general," nevertheless distinct from them in particular – this common, uncommon love that our philology seeks to foster, inherits from tradition a notion of dwelling founded upon a legacy of regard, where all contribute, each in a unique way, to the beauty and the longevity of the monument they unfold and where all those fine and noble names like *truth, virtue, reason, spirit, justice, eternity, divinity, humanity, courage, sacrifice, piety, modesty, beneficence, determination* – all 99 of them – find their proper place in a cosmos of words. Is it not our own destiny winking at us, us latter-day thinkers and doers, that we can ask this very question regarding a community, an organization of principles previously thought to be mutually exclusive and even internecine?

In our buildings, is it not strange how we have relentlessly subtracted the "sense" of the words from their assumed meaning and thus the self-several sign from the referent in order to clothe with these words the idea or concept in an illuminating raiment of tangibility? Just in the way that Schiller recommended for the art of beauty that the form be distinguished from the content, the language of Homer, of Paul, of Hölderlin provides us with terms in which to render our experience with those principles, the premise being that if we can find a completely different language to represent the same meaning, we have grasped that principle *poetically*, we would say, today, *philologically*, in terms of that language.

We have, in effect, consecrated all the words of the language to the rendering of this one self-several experience, one *and* three, three *and* nine, nine *and* twenty-seven; and then, in turn, a given world of words – those myths of poetic thought we have studied – is devoted to the service of the reality of this experience. How else could we put the matter, when things, i.e. names of things, like the "sky" and the "stars" and the "rivers," less often but occasionally the names of man-made things, too, and, in general, names for all the phenomena that touch upon the human condition, have always been borrowed by thought, the Builder, to articulate the experience of human being with the distinction we have termed *pure reason*. Even this term has been taken from traditional and contemporary discourse to name the experience or some aspect of it that we have intended to draw the reader's attention to. Whether or not this name is a good name or not, it is a *possible* name among a vast collection of candidates, many of which we have also considered and many of which are clearly better in some trains of thought than in others; or is there any other reason why we should nominate a principle *God* or *Zeus, freedom* or *perfection, destiny* or *justice* than one word's better suitability in one line of reasoning than another? For this reason alone do we err should we speak of "creator" *gods* or of a "perfect" *human being* because, logically, in the sense of the logic, the language of Christian thought, only *God* is the creator of heaven and earth and, in the language of *humanity*, human nature is not perfect but free, whereas every being is perfect insofar it has reached its maturity and taken its rightful place in the well-ordered scheme of all beings from the least to the greatest of them all, to Zeus, who nevertheless is subject to the precedence of what has already been decided and determined, namely the portions and the proportions of THE WAY IT SHOULD BE, the *Moira* of the MOIPAI.

Only God can *create* being; all beings, *human* being included, always already *are*; only human *being*, our humanity, can, through the hard work of education issuing in beauty, its resolution, bring itself forth and thus realize its own freedom. But the distinction of human nature is not created by God, rather, in the Second Epoch, it is engendered in Christ as the Son of God of whose progeniture, life, and death we partake through faith. Therefore it is wrong to say that God is a figment of the imagination and, worse, that imaginative folks have invented God, just because, in the Third Epoch, "God" is an idea of pure reason, an indispensable idea if freedom's moral imperative is to be actually realized and THE WAY IT SHOULD BE is to be THE WAY IT IS and not "just" a thought, just another ideal in a world that is far from ideal and, mostly sunk in a selfishness that knows no other ideal than itself.

What a simple notion, this thought we have termed *the distinction of human being!* And how richly it has presented itself in the course of Western civilization! But simplicity and intricacy go hand in hand, joining forces to thwart us. For, as we have often noted, what could be more hidden from view and mysterious than what is completely obvious; a never-setting sun illuminates all else, water moistens the soil but what brings the light of day to the light of day and makes water wet and fire dry? For we might direct attention not merely to the things but to the elements that they consist of – what is the earth of the earth, the cause of the cause, the origin of the origin? What sort of thing is this thing once removed and, removed once again and again and then again – the beginning and the origin of the beginning and the principle of the origin of the beginning and the initial source of the principle of the origin of the beginning? There is no end to this infinite "regression" not through lack of insight and principle on the part of the thinker but rather because we are never (and should never be!) finished with the practical endeavor of critical reflection; every settlement is the basis for a new reflection and serves as the potential for a new perfection, the foundation of a new generation – the drama of practice is not the dwelling but rather the striving and the building. For this is thought, too – the restless, the hungry heart for whom it is turtles all the way down.

But even this *unfinishedness* is not the end of the story; the epoch of the infinity of the will is itself inherent in the larger framework of thought that marks the measure of completion as well as origin, the latter as the resolution, the former as the commencement, of infinity. For the resolution of the drive of thought is its presence and perfection as thought, the Builder, and the inhabitant of the dwelling, the reconciliation of the real with the ideal and the ideal with the real; as much as the enduring fulfillment of thought is beyond the reach of our dedicated will to achieve, it is nevertheless the fruit of poetic thought, our free imagination, which diligently creates of itself beyond itself the object that most corresponds to it and in subsequent contemplation of which, all yearning, all tears subside, at least for a little while.

If the post/modern mentality has established language as its final frontier after the closure and the departure of our philosophical tradition and the critical world that was left in its wake, we are left with discourse and ultimately with key words that speakers and writers may avail themselves of for their own reasons, for their own good or ill or that of others. What is a thinker's reason for seizing the word? What is the essential topic of that thinker's insight? What is his or her driving impulse? We mean these questions, however, not in a biographical but rather in a philological sense:

What is the principle (A) of discernment (C) that determines the cause and issue (B) taken up by a particular thinker in light of the scheme of all things thought?

Thus, in preparing the curriculum and the school of philological philosophy of the distinction of human being, one would do well not to begin with some pledge of allegiance or with a song and anthem. Pure reason is our only true homeland and fatherland, our only city by the sea, but its patriots ought to be careful when hoisting a star-spangled banner of providence to the survivors of the great civil war that is Man's self-several battle against Man – we know now that this battle rages, perpetually, within our own heart, broken and mended, each time again transformed, each time renewed, and yet the scars incurred along the way remain, i.e. in the heart of those cut, cut again and again by the self-several destiny of our human being, who were born to be at odds with our human being, Mine against me and Yours against you, and Its against it; is the heart itself not the collection and the recollection of these wounds *and* these scars of distinctions that, though long healed, have left their indelible mark? Through language, these scars offer to tell the story, become signs, dramatic reminders and monuments to what has been achieved.

The first lesson in our school of thought teaches us to take up a cause that knows neither spilled blood, nor wrought iron, neither the history that the latter girded, nor the soil in which the former seeped. Servant neither to brain nor to brawn, pure reason has no king to bow down to, no earthly surrogate on which to feed. Serving pure reason, we speak no catechism, wear no uniform, form no tribe of zealots.[86] For thought is none of these things and we ourselves in our daily lives have learned by heart the post/modern lesson that we are all entirely indeterminate in the flow of mere being – you and I and ours and all we are and ever will be and were but a wrinkle briefly arising on the plain plane of eternity and all too soon smoothed away to continuity; yes, but then again, even for this reason, are we not all the more susceptible to the determination of principles that exhibit the undeniable proclivity to leave their mark in the otherwise unmarked, unremarkable space of our lived experience, yours and mine. Such is the beginning of our study of philosophy – a distinction that strikes

---

[86] As Wittgenstein reminds us in his Zettel: "Der Philosoph ist nicht Bürger einer Denkgemeinde. Das ist, was ihn zum Philosophen macht." The philosopher is not a citizen of any parish of thought. That is precisely what makes him or her a philosopher." Wittgenstein, Gesamte Werkausgabe, Vol. 5, p. 380, §455.

and strikes a chord, awakens us, arouses wonder, raises questions, breaks the familiar chains of beings and of being. For thought is not merely a conceit of its thinkers; thought is not merely the forms, expressions, actions, comportments, and attitudes of the pious and even less is it their boasting, a promiscuity of names dropped, the thrust and parry of words and ideas, even less still the arrogance of the rogue, the libertine, the maverick and marauding mind, wilding, out for a kill.

Where is the glamor in thought thinking about thought? Where's the shudder, the horror, the mystery in our experience of pure reason? Being our everyday companion, she has aged with us but in contrast to us, has remained fresh, true to herself in her every age and happy to wait for the evening when the tasks of the day are done, or until the weekend, or for the holiday time when we, for once not exhausted or distracted, become restless for reflection; and even on busy days she occasionally interrupts our bustle or, more likely, retires into our nights, haunts our dreams, is but a tweak or a momentary cringe, a furtive, fleeting tear that overtakes us unexpectedly in the flow and rush of our dealings. Where is the drama in supporting what is best, especially in cases, the majority of them in this life, when the best is less than the good? In addressing our needs, serving our purposes, poor old reason is neither a secret weapon, the strongman in our pocket, nor brainware that will calculate our delight to the ounce or the inch.

Well then, what is thought?

Thought is the age-old name for the story of our experience with the human capacity for adopting a critical standpoint, assuming the perspective of a being without – and even this critical standpoint, so easily twisted into extremism, is subject to the critique of reflection and thus self-subdued. In this way, resignation in all the old dogmas and even in the latest (the ~~dogmas~~) of skepticism, nihilism, or anarchism can be challenged, namely by their tasting of themselves.

What is thought? Thought is completion without stagnation, conclusive without being exclusive; thought is the remark of rapt (but not rapacious) attention, the acuity of substantial insight, penetrating, yes, but neither intrusion nor pervasion; thought is foresight that accounts for consequences, recollection that gathers and recalls the principles. *Thought* names our relationship to and our experience with thought and is, therefore, self-knowing, reflective perception that need not be limited to that of personal awareness or the introspection of one's own mental and emotional states – in fact, thought is above all your realizing that it is not always about *you* and *your* salvation, friend; think about that! Thought is, thus, looking at and looking into; it is looking out, looking over; it is the outlook of an overview and it is even to overlook when doing so circumvents gratuitous embarrassment. And then, thought is the result of thought. For thought is positive as realization, thought is negative as abstraction, thought is both separation *and* approach – the reception, the affirmation of obedience *and* the refusal to obey, to conform, to defer to a principle; it is, as well, therefore, neither positive nor negative and as such the difference, that resonate interval, that marks the gap between them, but it does not follow that thought is, therefore, negligent or neuter. Thought is neutrality only in the sense of being objective and unbiased judgment. And negligence? Harried, we who care about the wrong things will lift our voice to the impossible god of making distinctions and join in T.S. Eliot's famous prayer of renunciation spoken by those whose

> wings are no longer wings to fly but merely vans to beat the air,
> the air which is now thoroughly small and dry, smaller and dryer
> than the will: Teach us to care and not to care, teach us to sit
> still.[87]

For the last time: For those who, rejoicing, have "to construct something upon which to rejoice," what is pure thought? It is, in any case, not just an OUGHT without an IS; thought is AUGHT unless *taught* (A), *sought* (C), *wrought* (B), unless contemplated in the wisdom of ancient writings, told in song, celebrated in words and deeds, put into action and into the practice of a patient human endeavor, our own, here, today, now. You are thought's only hope. Who? You. It's up to you to make good on this our queenly, our kingly inkling.

Indeed, after having devoted much effort to becoming adept in the language of thought, we may now more confidently go about finding those memorable words and phrases that best fit to the exigencies of place, seizing the right moment, a day in the life, a glory night. Every catchword and locution, all our familiar sayings and slogans can, then, be a reminder of our home away from every home we have ever had and loved, far away from friends and family, those lost, those who remain to us. Then we find pure reason in the song, that cosmos of words that exhorts, that celebrates a true friend's fortitude in heart-rending battle – it is the strife that making a distinction means to the heightened heart of human life; gaze up, again, and yet again, at those stars of thought we have visited and visit still that

---

[87] T.S Eliot, "Ash-Wednesday" in *The Complete Poems and Plays*, p. 61.

spangle on the banner, themselves, in their separate heaven, a self-several civilization and a family of beings and of being to which we, the latest citizens, belong, the dwelling we live and die for daily in distinguishing ourselves before the tribune of reason, our own eye that is our I and our final aye of assent to beauty's beckoning beyond all reasoning and seeming.

Surely we will find there that fine felicity in a turn of words or phrase and then, for the briefest of moments, taste all the glory of a victor's life lived in pure reason's cause but who mostly sups on failure in the wrestle with the idioms, the vernacular of distempered pros of wit rather than of the eloquence of a true master builder and artificer who, in encountering for the millionth billionth time the reality of human experience, forges poetry anew in tongues of flame, collecting all the choicest words for thought that stand, unshakable, touching, exhilarating and that will suffice a day for a song of praise, a hymn that is, moreover, a teaching held fast to the heart, like the loved ones long since departed and so easily forgotten, not so easily forgotten.

Bibliography

I. Source Works

1. The Greek Epoch

Aristotle, *Metaphysica*, ed. W. Jaeger, Oxford 1957.

- *Aristoteles' Metaphysik*, H. Bonitz/H. Seidel, Hamburg: Felix Meiner 1991.

Homer, *Homeri Opera*, ed. T. W. Allen, Oxford 1917-1920.

- *Iliad*, ed. and trans. A. T. Murphy, Cambridge: Harvard University Press 1999.

- *Odyssey*, ed. and trans. A. T. Murphy, Cambridge: Harvard University Press 1998.

Hesiod, *Theogony*, ed. M. L. West, Oxford 1966.

- *Works and Days*, ed. M. L. West, Oxford 1978.

- *Theogony, Works and Days, Testimonia*, ed. and trans. G. W. Most, Cambridge: Harvard University Press 2006.

Laertius Diogenes, *Lives and Opinions of eminent philosophers*, ed. H. S. Long, Oxford 1964.

Parmenides, *Die Fragmente der Vorsokratiker*, edd. H. Diels and W. Kranz, Berlin 1961.

Pindar, *Pindari Carmina cum Fragmentis*, ed. B. Snell, Leipzig 1953.

Plato, *Platonis Opera*, Vol. 1, edd. W. F. Hicken and E. A. Duke, Oxford 1995.

Sappho, *Poetarum Lesbiorum Fragmenta*, edd. E. Lobel and D. Page, Oxford 1955.

Sophocles, *Antigone et al*, ed. and trans. H. Lloyd-Jones, Cambridge: Harvard University Press 1998.

Solon, *Iambi et Elegi Graeci ante Alexandrum Cantati*, ed. M. L. West, Oxford 1992.

- *Greek Elegiac Poetry*, trans. D. E. Gerber, Cambridge: Harvard University Press 1999.

2. The Christian Epoch

Augustinus, *De doctrina christiana*, Corpus Christianorum Series Latina 32, edd. K. D. Daur and J. Martin, Turnhout 1996.

- *De Trinitate*, Corpus Christianorum Series Latina 50, edd W. J. Mountain and F. Glorie, Turnhout 1968.

Anselmus Cantuariensis, *Opera Omnia*, ed. F.S. Schmitt, Seckau 1938, Edinburgh 1942.

Biblia Hebraica, edd. K. Eilliger and W. Rudolph, Stuttgart 1997.

Novum Testamentum Graece, ed. E. Nestle, Stuttgart 1948.

Plotini Opera, Vol. 2, edd. H. R. Schwyzer and P. Henry, Oxford 1977.

The Jewish Study Bible, edd, A. Berlin and M. Z. Brettler, Oxford 2004.

Thomae Aquinatis *Opera Ominia*, edd. S. E. Fretté and P. Maré, Paris 1871-1880.

3. The Epoch of Freedom

Beethoven, *Complete String Quartets*, Dover: New York 1970.

Fichte, *Grundlage der gesamten Wissenschaftslehre*, ed. I. Fichte, Berlin 1971.

Goethe, *Faust*, ed. K. H. Hucke, Münster 2008.

Hegel, *Gesammelte Werke*, edd. W. Bonsiepen and R. Heede, Hamburg: Felix Meiner 1980.

- *Die Wissenschaft der Logik [Die Lehre vom Begriff (1816)]*, Hamburg: Felix Meiner, 1994.

Hegel, *Werke in 20 Bänden. Auf der Grundlage der Werke von 1832 bis 1845 neu ediert*, edd. E. Moldenhauer and K. M. Michel, Frankfurt/M. 1969–1971.

Hölderlin, *Große Stuttgarter Hölderlin-Ausgabe*, ed. F. Beissner, Stuttgart 1946.

- *Friedensfeier*, ed. F. Beissner, Bibliotheca Bodmeriana IV, Stuttgart 1954.

Kant, *Werke*. Akademie Ausgabe, ed. Königlich Preußischen Akademie der Wissenschaften, Berlin 1903-1907.

Locke, *An Essay Concerning Human Understanding*, ed. P. H. Nidditch, Oxford 1975.

Rousseau, *Oevres Completes*, edd. B. Gagnebin et M. Raymond, Gallimard 1964.

Schiller, *National Ausgabe*, edd. N. Oellers et al., Weimar 1953.

Shakespeare, *The Arden Shakespeare*, edd. R. Proudfoot, A. Thompson, and D. S. Kasten, Walten-on-Surrey: Thomas Nelson 1998.

II. Authors of Post/Modernity

Blanchot, M., *L'Entretien Infini*, Gallimard 1969.

Boeder, H., *Das Bauzeug der Geschichte*, ed. G. Meier, Würzburg 1994.

- *Die conceptuale Vernunft in der Letzten Epoche der Metaphysik* in: „Abhandlungen der Braunschweigischen Wissenschaftlichen Gesellschaft XLIII," Göttingen 1992.

- *Die Installationen der Submoderne*, Würzburg 2006.

- *Die Topologie der Metaphysik*, Freiburg/München 1980.

- *Die Vernunftgefüge der Modernen*, Freiburg/München 1988.

- *Grund und Gegenwart als Frageziel der Frügriechischen Philosophie*, Den Haag 1962.

- *Rousseau oder der Aufbruch des Selbstbewußtseins* in "Bewußtsein und Zeitlichkeit," ed. H. Busche/ G. Heffernan/D. Lohmar, Wurzburg 1990.

- *Seditions*, ed. M. Brainard, New York 1997.

Chandler D., *Semiotics for Beginners*, Taylor & Francis 2006.

Derrida, J., *Donner la mort*, Galilée 1990.

Eliot T. S., *The Complete Poems and Plays*, Harcourt Brace Jovanovich 1971.

Foucault, M., *La pensée du dehors*, fata morgana, 1986.

Frege, G., *Die Grundlagen der Arithmetik. Eine logische-mathematische Untersuchung über den Begriff der Zahl*, Olm 1977.

Frost, R., *Collected Poems, Prose, and Plays*, Library of America 1995.

Hanke, P., *Versuch über den geglückten Tag*, Surkamp 1994.

Heidegger, M., *Sein und Zeit*, Tübingen 1986.

-   *Zur Frage nach der Bestimmung der Sache des Denkens*, St. Gallen: Ecker 1984.

-   *Die Technik und die Kehre*, Stuttgart: Klett-Cotta 2002.

Husserl E., *Ideen zu einer reinen Phänomenologie und phänomenologischen Philosophie*, Tübingen 1993.

Joyce, J., *Finnegans Wake*, Penguin 1999.

-   *Ulysses, The Corrected Text*, New York: Random House 1989.

Jakobson, R., *On Language*, Cambridge: Harvard University Press 1990.

Kubrick, S., *Interviews (Conversations with Filmmakers)*, ed. G. D. Phillips, University Press of Mississippi 2001.

Lacan, *Ècrits I*, Éditions du Seuil 1966.

-   *Ècrits II*, Éditions du Seuil 1971.

Levinas, E., *Totalité et Infini*, M. Nijhooff, 1971.

Lévi-Strauss, C., *La Pensé Sauvage*, Paris: Plon 1962.

Metz, W. *Unterwegs zum Höhlenausgang der Moderne – Wider die letzte Ideologie der Postmoderne*, published on the Internet at http://www.ph-ludwigsburg.de/html/2b-frnz-s-01/overmann/Metz/WilhelmMetzHoehlen ausgangderModerne.pdf.

Peirce, Ch. S., *Writings of Charles S. Peirce: A Chronological Edition*, edd. E. C. Moore and M. H. Fisch, Indiana 1982.

Perelman, Ch. and Olbrechts-Tyteca, L., *The New Rhetoric*, Notre Dame 2000.

Richards, I. A., *The Philosophy of Rhetoric*, Oxford University Press 1936.

Ruhstorfer, K.-H., *Konversionen: eine Archäologie der Bestimmung des Menschen bei Foucault, Augustinus, Nietzsche, Paulus*, Schöningh 2004.

Searle, J. R., *A Classification of Illocutionary Acts* in "Language in Society," Vol. 5, No. 1 April 1976.

Saussure, F., *Cours de linguistique générale*, edd. Ch. Bally and A. Séchehaye, Paris: Payot 1964.

Spencer-Brown, G., *Laws of Form*, New York 1979.

Steiner, G., *Antigones*, Yale University Press 1996.

-   *Erata: An Examined Life*, Yale University Press 1999.

v. Bar, L., *Die Philosophie Schaftesburys im Gefüge der mundanen Vernunft der frühen Zeit*, Königshausen & Neumann 2006.

Wilamowitz-Moellendorff, U. v., *Der Glaube der Hellenen I*, Darmstadt 1955.

Wittgenstein, L., *Zettel* in "Gesamte Werkausgabe," edd. G. E. M. Anscombe and G. H. von Wright, Frankfurt/M.: Surkamp 1984.

III. General Reference Material

1. Books of Reference

A Greek-English Lexicon, H.G. Liddel and R. Scott, Oxford 1940.

Index Homericus, A. Gehring, Hildesheim 1970.

Roget's Thesaurus, ed. B. A. Kipfer, New York, 2001.

2. Websites

http://www.blueletterbible.org/

http://biblehub.com/interlinear/

http://www.perseus.tufts.edu/hopper/

http://fr.wikisource.org/

3. Software

Bibloi 8.0, *Silver Mountain Software*, Texas 2003.

Digitale Bibliothek, *Deutsche Idealismus*, Berlin 2004.

- *Klassik*, Berlin 2004.
- *Deutscher Idealismus*, Berlin 2004.
- *The Digital Library of English and American Literature*, Frankfurt/M 2008.
- *Friedrich Schiller Werke*, Berlin 2004.

InfoSoftWare, *Schiller im Kontext*, ed. K. Worm, Berlin 2008.

Perseus 2.0, *Interactive Sources and Studies in Ancient Greek*, ed. G. Crane, Yale University Press 2000.

Indices

I. Index of Names

II. Index of Subjects

Note on the Author

For 18 years Thomas Kruger Caplan has been an instructor for business English at the Ostfalia University of Applied Sciences in Lower Saxony, Germany. During this time, he has also lectured in the areas of rhetoric, cultural history, and philosophy while pursuing his investigation into the triad of philological totalities as proposed by H. Boeder, namely the testaments of distinguished speech celebrated as wisdom, the Occidental tradition of metaphysical reflection upon their grant, and the critical animus of mundane post/modernity that delimits the closure of this legacy. In the future he hopes to further explore Boeder's hypothesis that it is only in the changing ratios of these three terms, i.e. *language – history – world*, that the distinction of our human being can become completely intelligible to contemplation heightened and deepened by the terminological philology of thought, the Builder, the methods and precepts of which have underlain and guided this study.

Thomas Kruger Caplan is currently looking for opportunities to teach the *poetic performance*, the *theory*, and the *practice* of pure reason as the self-several destiny of human being.

He welcomes your comments, questions, and critiques.

Please contact him at *th.caplan@ostfalia.de*.

Lightning Source UK Ltd.
Milton Keynes UK
UKOW06n0724100715

254879UK00002B/3/P